D0253696

New Zealand

Bay of Islands & Northland (p121)

Auckland (p60)

Waikato & Coromandel Peninsula (p163)

Rotorua & the Bay of Plenty (p273)

Taupo & the Central Plateau (p246)

Taranaki & Whanganui (p213)

The East Coast (p314)

Marlborough & Nelson (p378)

✪ **Wellington Region** (p346)

The West Coast (p423)

Christchurch & Canterbury (p456)

Queenstown & Wanaka (p542)

Dunedin & Otago (p509)

Fiordland & Southland (p579)

THIS EDITION WRITTEN AND RESEARCHED BY

Charles Rawlings-Way,
Brett Atkinson, Sarah Bennett, Peter Dragicevich, Lee Slater

Contents

PLAN YOUR TRIP

Welcome to New Zealand . 4
New Zealand Map 6
New Zealand's Top 20 8
Need to Know 20
What's New 22
If You Like.... 23
Month by Month 27
Itineraries 31
Hiking in New Zealand . . 36
Skiing & Snowboarding
in New Zealand 44
Extreme New Zealand . . 49
Regions at a Glance 55

KIERAN SCOTT/GETTY IMAGES ©

COROMANDEL PENINSULA
P192

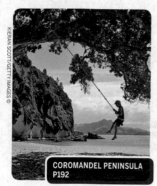

VLADIMIR PISKUNOV/GETTY IMAGES ©

MT TARANAKI P223

ON THE ROAD

AUCKLAND 60
Auckland 62
Waiheke Island 98
Great Barrier Island 106
Piha 112
Matakana & Around 118

BAY OF ISLANDS &
NORTHLAND 121
Mangawhai 124
Whangarei 126
Tutukaka Coast & the
Poor Knights Islands 131
Bay of Islands 134
Russell 138
Paihia & Waitangi 141
Kerikeri. 145
Doubtless Bay. 150
Cape Reinga &
Ninety Mile Beach 152
Ahipara. 154
Opononi & Omapere 158
Kauri Coast 159

WAIKATO &
COROMANDEL
PENINSULA. 163
Hamilton 167
Raglan 173
Te Awamutu. 177
Cambridge. 179
Waitomo Caves. 185
Thames 194
Coromandel Town 197
Whitianga. 202
Waihi & Around. 209

TARANAKI &
WHANGANUI. 213
New Plymouth 216
Mt Taranaki (Egmont
National Park). 223

Surf Highway 45. 227
Whanganui. 229
Whanganui
National Park 235
Palmerston North 240

TAUPO &
THE CENTRAL
PLATEAU 246
Taupo 248
Turangi & Around 259
Tongariro National Park. . . 262
Whakapapa Village. 266
National Park Village 267
Ohakune. 269

ROTORUA & THE
BAY OF PLENTY . . . 273
Rotorua 275
Tauranga 292
Mt Maunganui. 298
Whakatane 305
Opotiki 311

THE EAST COAST. . . 314
Pacific Coast Hwy 315
Gisborne 321
Te Urewera
National Park 328
Napier. 331
Hastings, Havelock
North & Around 339
Cape Kidnappers 343

WELLINGTON
REGION 346
Wellington 348
Paekakariki 370
Waikanae & Around 371
Martinborough 373
Greytown 375
Masterton & Around 376

Contents

MARLBOROUGH & NELSON.......... 378

Picton..................380
Queen Charlotte Track...386
Kenepuru &
Pelorus Sounds 388
Blenheim 390
Kaikoura...............394
Nelson 400
Motueka...............408
Abel Tasman
National Park 412
Golden Bay 416
Kahurangi
National Park 420
Nelson Lakes
National Park 421

THE WEST COAST ..423

Murchison &
Buller Gorge 425
Reefton................426
Westport & Around 428
Karamea & Around 431
Punakaiki & Paparoa
National Park 434
Greymouth 436
Hokitika 440
**Westland Tai Poutini
National Park 445**
Franz Josef Glacier......446
Fox Glacier............450
Haast 454

CHRISTCHURCH & CANTERBURY 456

Christchurch 457
Banks Peninsula........478
Hanmer Springs........485
Waipara Valley.........489
Selwyn District 490
Methven...............492

Peel Forest............494
Geraldine 495
Timaru 496
Lake Tekapo 500
Aoraki/Mt Cook
National Park 502
Twizel 507

DUNEDIN & OTAGO 509

Omarama............. 511
Waitaki Valley 512
Oamaru 513
Dunedin 520
Otago Peninsula........531
Naseby...............535
Lauder, Omakau
& Ophir................536
Alexandra.............537
Clyde 538
Cromwell & Around 539

QUEENSTOWN & WANAKA 542

Queenstown.........543
Glenorchy & Around 561
Arrowtown.............565
Wanaka..............569
Cardrona 577
Makarora 578

FIORDLAND & SOUTHLAND...... 579

Te Anau 581
Milford Sound/
Piopiotahi 590
Manapouri 591
Doubtful Sound 592
Invercargill............595
The Catlins 599
Stewart Island/Rakiura ..603

UNDERSTAND

New Zealand
Today 612
History.............. 614
Environment 624
Maori Culture 631
The Kiwi Psyche 638
Arts & Music.........643

SURVIVAL GUIDE

Directory A–Z 650
Transport............ 662
Language............ 670
Index................. 676
Map Legend.......... 686

SPECIAL FEATURES

Hiking in
New Zealand........ 36
Skiing &
Snowboarding
in New Zealand 44
Extreme
New Zealand........ 49
Maori Culture.......631

Welcome to New Zealand

There aren't many places on this lonely planet where travellers are so well catered for – in terms of both man-made enticements and splendours of the natural realm.

Walk on the Wild Side

There are just 4.5 million New Zealanders, scattered across 270,534 sq km: bigger than the UK with one-fourteenth the population. Filling in the gaps are the sublime forests, mountains, lakes, beaches and fiords that have made NZ one of the best hiking (locals call it 'tramping') destinations on Earth. Tackle one of nine epic 'Great Walks' – you've probably heard of the Heaphy and Milford Tracks – or just spend a few dreamy hours wandering through some easily accessible wilderness.

The New 'Big Easy'

Forget New Orleans... NZ can rightly claim the 'Big Easy' crown for the sheer ease of travel here. This isn't a place where you encounter many on-the-road frustrations: buses and trains run on time; roads are in good nick; ATMs proliferate; pickpockets, scam merchants and bedbug-ridden hostels are few and far between; and the food is unlikely to send you running for the nearest public toilets (usually clean and stocked with the requisite paper). And there are no snakes, and only one poisonous spider – the rare katipo – sightings of which are considered lucky. This decent nation is a place where you can relax and enjoy (rather than endure) your holiday.

Maori Culture

If you're even remotely interested in rugby, you'll have heard of NZ's all-conquering All Blacks, who would never have become world-beaters without their formidable Maori players. But this is just one example of how Maori culture impresses itself on contemporary Kiwi life: across NZ you can hear Maori language, watch Maori TV, see main-street *marae* (meeting houses), join in a *hangi* (Maori feast) or catch a cultural performance with traditional Maori song, dance and usually a blood-curdling *haka* (war dance). You might draw the line at contemplating *ta moko*, traditional Maori tattooing (often applied to the face).

Food, Wine & Beer

Kiwi food was once a bland echo of a British Sunday dinner, but these days NZ chefs find inspiration in new-world culinary oceans, especially the Pacific with its abundant seafood and encircling cuisines. And don't go home without trying some Maori faves: paua (abalone), kina (sea urchin) and kumara (sweet potato) make regular menu appearances. Thirsty? NZ's cool-climate wineries have been collecting wine-award trophies for decades now, and the country's craft-beer scene is booming. Contemporary coffee culture is also firmly entrenched.

Why I Love New Zealand

By Charles Rawlings-Way, Coordinating Author

As an English-born Australian raised in Tasmania, every trip to New Zealand presents a mix of landscapes and cultures that's at once familiar and quirkily different. The rolling hills and hedgerows of Devonshire collude with the irreverent, easy-going locals (somehow less cynical than Australians: could it be the sweetly mangled vowels?) to disarm, distract and delight. Maori culture is potent, the surf is world class and the beer is awesome! The best of old and new worlds synching-in with social and environmental sensibility: a template for a new world order? I love NZ!

For more about our authors, see page 688

Above: Lake Tekapo (p500)

New Zealand

Bay of Islands
Gorgeous bay studded with 150-odd islands (p134)

Hauraki Gulf
Islands, yachts, dolphins... Aquatic splendour! (p97)

Rotorua
Geysers, mud pools and sulphurous gases (p275)

Auckland
Restaurants, bars and Pacific Island culture (p62)

Waitomo Caves
Glowworms and subterranean cave adventures (p185)

Tongariro Alpine Crossing
The country's best wilderness day walk (p264)

SOUTH PACIFIC OCEAN

TASMAN SEA

Cape Reinga
North Cape
Great Exhibition Bay
Kaitaia
Kerikeri
Kaikohe
Paihia
Russell
Bay of Islands
Opononi
Northland
Whangarei
Dargaville
Kaipara Harbour
Wellsford
Hen & Chicken Islands
Helensville
Auckland
Drury
Pukekohe
Great Barrier Island
Hauraki Gulf
Whitianga
Coromandel Peninsula
Thames
Huntly
Ngaruawahia
Hamilton
Cambridge
Raglan
Waikato
Te Uku
Kawhia
Otorohanga
Waitomo Caves
Te Kuiti
Mt Maunganui
Tauranga
Rotorua
Bay of Plenty
Te Kaha
Whakatane
Opotiki
Te Araroa
Hicks Bay
Ruatoria
Tokomaru Bay
Tolaga Bay
Gisborne
Lake Taupo
Taupo
Tongariro National Park
Mt Ngauruhoe
Mt Ruapehu (2797m)
New Plymouth
Mt Taranaki (Mt Egmont) (2518m)
Opunake
Hawera
Stratford
Ohakune
Whanganui National Park
Whanganui
Wairoa
Hawke Bay
Napier
Hastings
Waipawa
Waipukurau
Dannevirke
Palmerston

Oops on Jenny
Ohakune Mountain
Stay by Mountain
Togariro
Lake Taupo
Raglan
Auckland

200 km
100 miles

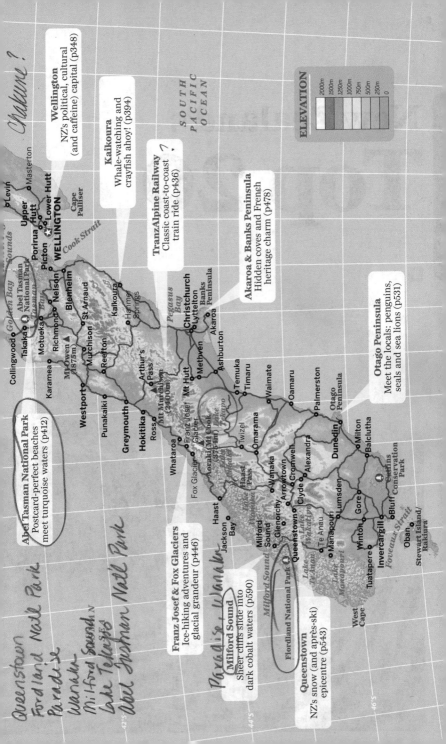

New Zealand's
Top 20

1

Auckland Harbour & Hauraki Gulf

1 A yachty's paradise, the island-studded Hauraki Gulf (p97) is Auckland's aquatic playground, sheltering its harbour and east-coast bays and providing ample excuse for the City of Sails' pleasure fleet to breeze into action. Despite the busy maritime traffic, the gulf has its own resident pods of whales and dolphins. Rangitoto Island is an icon of the city, its near-perfect volcanic cone providing the backdrop for many a tourist snapshot. Yet it's Waiheke, with its beautiful beaches, acclaimed wineries and upmarket eateries, that is Auckland's most popular island escape. Below left: Man O' War Vineyards (p99), Waiheke Island

Urban Auckland

2 Held in the embrace of two harbours and built on the remnants of long-extinct volcanoes, Auckland (p62) isn't your average metropolis. It's regularly rated one of the world's most liveable cities, and while it's never going to challenge NYC or London in the excitement stakes, it's blessed with good beaches, is flanked by wine regions and has a large enough population to support a thriving dining, drinking and live-music scene. Cultural festivals are celebrated with gusto in this ethnically diverse city, which has the distinction of having the world's largest Pacific Islander population. Below right: View of Auckland from Mt Eden (p65)

OLIVER STREWE/GETTY IMAGES ©

AMOS CHAPPLE/GETTY IMAGES ©

Wellington

3 Named the 'coolest little capital in the world' in Lonely Planet's *Best in Travel,* windy Wellington (p348) lives up to the mantle by keeping things fresh and dynamic. It's long famed for a vibrant arts-and-music scene, fuelled by excellent espresso and more restaurants per head than New York, and now a host of craft-beer bars have elbowed in on the action. Edgy yet sociable, colourful yet often dressed in black, Wellington is big on the unexpected and unconventional. Erratic weather only adds to the excitement. Below: Havana Coffee Works (p362)

Bay of Islands

4 Turquoise waters lapping in pretty bays, dolphins frolicking at the bows of boats, pods of orcas gliding gracefully by: chances are these are the kinds of images that drew you to NZ in the first place, and these are exactly the kinds of experiences that the Bay of Islands (p134) delivers so well. Whether you're a hardened sea dog or a confirmed landlubber, there are myriad options to tempt you out on the water to explore the 150-odd islands that dot this beautiful bay.

Kaikoura

5 First settled by Maori with their keen nose for seafood, Kaikoura (p394; meaning 'to eat crayfish') is now NZ's best spot for both consuming and communing with marine life. When it comes to 'sea food and eat it', crayfish is still king, but on fishing tours you can hook into other edible wonders of the unique Kaikoura deep. Whales are definitely off the menu, but you're almost guaranteed a good gander at Moby's mates on a whale-watching tour. There's also the option of swimming with seals and dolphins, or spotting some of the many birds – including albatross – that soar around the shore. Left: Sperm whale near Kaikoura

Franz Josef & Fox Glaciers

6 Franz Josef (p446) and Fox (p450) Glaciers are remarkable for many reasons, including their rates of accumulation and descent, and their proximity to the loftiest peaks of the Southern Alps and the Tasman Sea around 10km away. Several short walks meander towards the glaciers' fractured faces (close enough for you to feel insignificant!), or you can take a hike on the ice with Franz Josef Glacier Guides or Fox Glacier Guiding. The ultimate encounter is on a scenic flight, which often also provides grandstand views of Aoraki/Mt Cook, Westland forest and a seemingly endless ocean. Top left: Franz Josef Glacier

Geothermal Rotorua

7 The first thing you'll notice about Rotorua (p275) is the sulphur smell – this geothermal hot spot whiffs like old socks. But as the locals point out, volcanic by-products are what everyone is here to see: gushing geysers, bubbling mud, steaming cracks in the ground, boiling pools of mineral-rich water... Rotorua is unique: a fact exploited by some fairly commercial local businesses. But you don't have to spend a fortune – there are plenty of affordable (and free) volcanic encounters to be had in parks, Maori villages or just along the roadside. Bottom left: Champagne Pool (p292), Wai-O-Tapu Thermal Wonderland

Waitomo Caves

8 Waitomo (p185) is a must-see: an astonishing maze of subterranean caves, canyons and rivers perforating the northern King Country limestone. Black-water rafting is the big lure here (like whitewater rafting but through a dark cave), plus glowworm grottoes, underground abseiling and more stalactites and stalagmites than you'll ever see in one place again. Above ground, Waitomo township is a quaint collaboration of businesses: a craft brewery, a cafe, a holiday park and some decent B&Bs. But don't linger in the sunlight – it's party time downstairs!

9

10

GARETH MCCORMACK/GETTY IMAGES ©

Tongariro Alpine Crossing

9 At the centre of the North Island, Tongariro National Park presents an alien landscape of alpine desert punctuated by three smoking and smouldering volcanoes. This track (p264) offers the perfect taste of what the park has to offer, skirting the base of two of the mountains and providing views of craters, brightly coloured lakes and the vast Central Plateau stretching out beyond. It's for these reasons that it's often rated as one of the world's best single-day wilderness walks. Top left: Emerald Lake

Rugby

10 Rugby Union is NZ's national game and governing preoccupation. If your timing's good you might catch the revered national team (and reigning world champions), the All Blacks, in action. The 'ABs' are resident gods: mention Richie McCaw or Dan Carter in any conversation and you'll win friends for life. Visit the New Zealand Rugby Museum (p240) in Palmerston North, watch some kids running around a suburban field on a Saturday morning, or yell along with the locals in a small-town pub as the big men collide on the big screen.

Abel Tasman National Park

11 Here's nature at its most seductive: lush green hills fringed with golden sandy coves, slipping gently into warm shallows before meeting a crystal-clear cerulean sea. Abel Tasman National Park (p412) is the quintessential postcard paradise, where you can put yourself in the picture assuming an endless number of poses: tramping, kayaking, swimming or sunbathing. This sweet-as corner of NZ raises the bar and keeps it there. Top right: Abel Tasman Coast Track (p412)

Maori Culture

12 NZ's indigenous Maori culture is accessible and engaging: join in a *haka* (war dance); chow down at a traditional *hangi* (Maori feast cooked in the ground); carve a pendant from bone or *pounamu* (jade); learn some Maori language; or check out an authentic cultural performance with song, dance, legends, arts and crafts. Big-city and regional museums around NZ are crammed with Maori artefacts and historical items, but this is also a living culture: vibrant, potent and contemporary. See p631 for more. Right: Maori warriors

TIM GRAHAM/GETTY IMAGES ©

Otago Peninsula

13 The Otago Peninsula (p531) is proof there's more to the South Island's outdoor thrills than heart-stopping alpine and lake scenery. Amid a backdrop of coastal vistas combining rugged, hidden beaches with an expansive South Pacific horizon, it's very easy to come face to face with penguins, seals and sea lions. Beyond the rare yellow-eyed penguin (hoiho), other fascinating avian residents include the royal albatross. Otago Peninsula's Taiaroa Head is the world's only mainland royal albatross colony: visit in January or February for the best views of these magnificent ocean-spanning birds.

Heaphy Track

14 Beloved of NZ trampers, and now mountain bikers in winter, the four- to six-day Heaphy Track (p420) is the jewel of Kahurangi National Park, the great wilderness spanning the South Island's northwest corner. Highlights include the mystical Gouland Downs and surreal nikau palm coast, while the townships at either end – at Golden Bay and Karamea – will bring you back down to earth with the most laid-back of landings.

DAVID WALL/GETTY IMAGES ©

Central Otago

15 Here's your chance to balance virtue and vice, with some of NZ's most starkly beautiful landscapes (p533) in the background. Take to two wheels to negotiate the easygoing Otago Central Rail Trail, cycling into heritage South Island towns such as Clyde and Naseby. Tuck into well-earned beers in laid-back country pubs, or linger for a classy lunch in the vineyard restaurants of Bannockburn. Other foodie diversions include Cromwell's weekly farmers market and the summer stone-fruit harvest of the country's best orchards. Top: Otago Central Rail Trail (p534)

Skiing & Snowboarding

16 New Zealand is studded with massive mountains, and you're guaranteed of finding decent snow right through the winter season (June to October). Most of the famous slopes are on the South Island: hip Queenstown and hippie Wanaka, with iconic ski runs like Coronet Peak, the Remarkables and Treble Cone close at hand. There are also dedicated snowboarding and cross-country (Nordic) snow parks here. And on the North Island, Mt Ruapehu offers the chance to ski down a volcano. See p44 for more. Above: Coronet Peak (p46)

Milford Sound

17 Fingers crossed you'll be lucky enough to see Milford Sound (p590) on a clear, sunny day. That's definitely when the world-beating collage of waterfalls, verdant cliffs and peaks, and dark cobalt waters is at its best. More likely though is the classic Fiordland combination of mist and drizzle, with the iconic profile of Mitre Peak revealed slowly through shimmering sheets of precipitation. Either way, keep your eyes peeled for seals and dolphins, especially if you're exploring NZ's most famous fiord by kayak.

Queenstown

18 Queenstown (p543) may be renowned as the birthplace of bungy jumping, but there's more to NZ's adventure hub than leaping off a bridge attached to a giant rubber band. Against the scenic backdrop of the Remarkables mountain range, travellers can spend days skiing, hiking or mountain biking, before dining in cosmopolitan restaurants or partying in some of NZ's best bars. Next-day options include hang gliding, kayaking or river rafting, or sleepier detours to Arrowtown or Glenorchy. Right: View of Lake Wakatipu (p544) from the Remarkables

17

DAVID WALL/GETTY IMAGES ©

DAVID WALL/GETTY IMAGES ©

TranzAlpine Railway

19 One of the world's most scenic train journeys, the TranzAlpine (p436) cuts clear across the country from the Pacific Ocean to the Tasman Sea in less than five hours. Yes, there's a dirty great mountain range in the way – that's where the scenic part comes in. Leaving the Canterbury Plains, a cavalcade of tunnels and viaducts takes you up through the Southern Alps to Arthur's Pass, where the 8.5km Otira tunnel burrows right through the bedrock of NZ's alpine spine. Then it's all downhill (but only literally) to sleepy Greymouth.

Akaroa & Banks Peninsula

20 Infused with Gallic ambience, French-themed Akaroa (p478) bends languidly around one of the prettiest harbours on Banks Peninsula. Sleek dolphins and plump penguins inhabit clear waters perfect for sailing and exploring. Elsewhere on the peninsula, the spidery Summit Rd prescribes the rim of an ancient volcano while winding roads descend to hidden bays and coves. Spend your days tramping and kayaking amid the improbable landscape and seascape, while relaxing at night in chic bistros or cosy B&B accommodation. Above right: Swimming with Hector's dolphin near Akaroa

Need to Know

For more information, see Survival Guide (p649)

Currency
New Zealand dollars ($)

Language
English, Maori and New Zealand Sign Language

Visas
Citizens of Australia, the UK and 56 other countries don't need visas for NZ (length-of-stay allowances vary). See www.immigration.govt.nz.

Money
ATMs are widely available in cities and larger towns. Credit cards accepted in most hotels and restaurants.

Mobile Phones
European phones will work on NZ's network, but most American or Japanese phones will not. Use global roaming or a local SIM card and prepaid account.

Time
NZ time is GMT/UCT plus 12 hours (two hours ahead of Australian Eastern Standard Time).

When to Go

Auckland
GO Feb–Apr

Rotorua
GO Oct–Dec

Wellington
GO Dec–Feb

Christchurch
GO Jan–Mar

Queenstown
GO Jun–Aug

High Season
(Dec–Feb)

➡ Summer: busy beaches, outdoor explorations, festivals and sporting events.

➡ Big-city accommodation prices rise.

➡ High season in the ski towns is winter (Jun–Aug).

Shoulder Season
(Mar–Apr)

➡ Prime travelling time: fine weather, short queues, kids in school and warm(ish) ocean.

➡ Long evenings supping Kiwi wines and craft beers.

➡ Spring (Sep–Nov) is shoulder season too.

Low Season
(May–Aug)

➡ Head for the slopes of the Southern Alps for some brilliant southern-hemisphere skiing.

➡ No crowds, good accommodation deals and a seat in any restaurant.

➡ Warm-weather beach towns might be half asleep.

Useful Websites

100% Pure New Zealand
(www.newzealand.com) Official tourism site.

Department of Conservation
(www.doc.govt.nz) DOC parks and camping info.

Lonely Planet (www.lonelyplanet.com/new-zealand) Destination information, hotel bookings, traveller forum and more.

Destination New Zealand
(www.destination-nz.com) Resourceful tourism site.

DineOut (www.dineout.co.nz) Restaurant reviews.

Te Ara (www.teara.govt.nz) Online encyclopedia of NZ.

Important Numbers

Regular NZ phone numbers have a two-digit area code followed by a seven-digit number. When dialling within a region, the area code is still required. Drop the initial 🕿0 if dialling from abroad.

NZ country code	🕿64
International access code from NZ	🕿00
Emergency (ambulance, fire, police)	🕿111
Directory assistance	🕿018
International directory	🕿0172

Exchange Rates

Australia	A$1	NZ$1.06
Canada	C$1	NZ$1.06
China	Y10	NZ$1.89
Euro zone	€1	NZ$1.63
Japan	¥100	NZ$1.15
Singapore	S$1	NZ$0.92
UK	UK£1	NZ$1.94
US	US$1	NZ$1.17

For current exchange rates see www.xe.com.

Daily Costs

Budget:
Less than $130

➡ Dorm beds or campsites: $25–$35 per night

➡ Main course in a budget eatery: less than $15

➡ Explore NZ with a Naked Bus or InterCity bus pass: five trips from $151

Midrange:
$130–$250

➡ Double room in a midrange hotel/motel: $100–$200

➡ Main course in a midrange restaurant: $15–$32

➡ Hire a car and explore further: starting at $30 per day

Top End:
More than $250

➡ Double room in a top-end hotel: from $200

➡ Three-course meal in a classy restaurant: $80

➡ Domestic flight Auckland to Christchurch: from $100

Opening Hours

Opening hours vary seasonally (eg Dunedin is quiet during winter!), but use the following as a general guide:

Banks 9.30am–4.30pm Monday to Friday, some also 9am–noon Saturday

Cafes 7am–4pm

Pubs & Bars noon–late

Restaurants noon–2.30pm and 6.30–9pm

Shops 9am–5.30pm Monday to Friday and 9am to noon or 5pm Saturday

Supermarkets 8am–7pm, often 9pm or later in cities

Arriving in New Zealand

Auckland International Airport (p662) Airbus Express buses run into the city every 10 to 30 minutes, 24 hours. Door-to-door shuttle buses run 24 hours. A taxi into the city costs around $70 (45 minutes).

Wellington Airport (p367) Airport Flyer buses run into the city every 10 to 20 minutes from 6.30am to 9.30pm. Door-to-door shuttle buses run 24 hours. A taxi into the city costs around $30 (20 minutes).

Christchurch Airport (p476) Christchurch Metro Red Bus Numbers 3 and 29 run into the city regularly from 6.30am to 11pm. Door-to-door shuttle buses run 24 hours. A taxi into the city costs around $50 (20 minutes).

Getting Around

New Zealand is long and skinny, and many roads are two-lane country byways: getting from A to B requires some thought.

Car Travel at your own tempo, explore remote areas and visit regions with no public transport. Hire cars in major towns. Drive on the left; the steering wheel is on the right (...in case you can't find it).

Bus Reliable, frequent services around the country (usually cheaper than flying).

Plane Fast-track your holiday with affordable, frequent, fast internal flights. Carbon offset your flights if you're feeling guilty.

Train Reliable, regular services (if not fast or cheap) along specific routes on both islands.

For much more on **getting around**, see p663

What's New

Gap Filler, Christchurch

Thanks to this eccentric project, new things are constantly springing up on Christchurch's flattened blocks – and many of them are delightfully oddball. Check the website to see what's new. (p461)

Rotorua Canopy Tours

A new network of flying foxes, zip lines and rope bridges, 22m high in a canopy of native New Zealand forest outside Rotorua. (p278)

Nga Toi/Arts Te Papa, Wellington

This new and improved multigallery space within the national museum shows frequently changing art exhibitions from its own collection and beyond. (p354)

Transitional Cathedral, Christchurch

Called the Cardboard Cathedral by practically everyone, Christchurch's pop-up architectural showcase is endeavouring to fill the big shoes left by its wounded stone sister. (p462)

Quake City, Christchurch

The tragic story of Christchurch's earthquakes is succinctly told in this affecting new museum in the heart of the devastated city centre. (p461)

West Coast Wilderness Trail

Crossing a spectacular landscape at the foot of the Southern Alps, this 120km cycle trail offers easy day rides through to a four-day journey from Greymouth to Hokitika. (p439)

MTG Hawke's Bay, Napier

Napier's sparkling new waterfront Museum Theatre Gallery complex is a sure-fire winner, the many millions spent on renovations rewarding visitors with accessible film, theatre, museum and art experiences. (p333)

Silo Park Markets, Auckland

From December to March, Auckland's Wynyard Quarter hosts weekly markets with local arts and crafts and a selection of food trucks serving tasty food. On Friday nights, classic movies are shown outdoors. (p79)

Good George Brewing, Hamilton

Make the short trek from central Hamilton to this excellent craft brewery in a renovated church. Acoustic music sessions in the garden bar make for a perfect Sunday afternoon. (p171)

Whakatane District Museum

On the Whakatane waterfront, this beaut new regional museum and gallery delivers the historic low-down on NZ's sunniest town. (p305)

Coaltown Museum, Westport

Doing justice to its pioneer settlers, the rehomed and reinvented Coaltown Museum retells the old yarns of hard times in a truly modern fashion. (p428)

Hairy Feet, Piopio

The newest addition to NZ's array of Hobbit-themed movie locations is in the rugged Mangaotaki Valley in the King Country. Here's your chance to visit Trollshaw Forest. (p190)

For more recommendations and reviews, see **lonelyplanet.com/ new-zealand**

If You Like...

Cities

Auckland Sydney for beginners? We prefer 'Seattle minus the rain', infused with vibrant Pacific Islander culture. (p62)

Wellington All the lures you'd expect in a capital city, packed into what is really just a very big town. A treat for walkers. (p348)

Christchurch Reemerging from recent earthquakes with energy and verve, largely due to the determination and resilience of proud locals. (p457)

Dunedin Exuding artsy, boozy ambience (so many students!) and close to superb wildlife-viewing opportunities on the Otago Peninsula. (p520)

Hamilton New Zealand's fourth-largest town doesn't raise much of a blip on the tourist radar, but the bar scene, restaurants, museum and Waikato River deserve a second look. (p167)

Extreme Activities

Queenstown bungy Strap yourself into the astonishing Shotover Canyon Swing or Nevis Bungy and propel yourself into the void. (p546)

Skydive Abel Tasman Worth it for the views over Motueka alone. (p409)

Waitomo black-water rafting Don a wetsuit, a life vest and a helmet with a torch attached and rampage along an underground river – wild times! (p187)

Extreme Auckland Check out SkyWalk and SkyJump at the Sky Tower, and EcoZip Adventures – adventurous thrills with ocean and Waiheke Island views. (p73)

Canyonz Negotiate cliffs, water-falls and streams as you climb and abseil through pristine NZ bush near Thames. (p196)

Rafting the Buller River Widely regarded as NZ's classic rafting experience. There are two excellent operators based in Murchison. (p425)

History

Waitangi Treaty Grounds In the Bay of Islands, where the contentious Treaty of Waitangi was first signed by Maori chiefs and the British Crown. (p142)

Arrowtown Step back into the gold-rush era in this cute town, crammed with heritage buildings and the remains of one of NZ's earliest Chinese settlements. (p565)

Oamaru Victorian Precinct Beautifully restored white-stone buildings and warehouses, now housing eclectic galleries, restaurants and artisan workshops. (p515)

Denniston Plateau Explore the ghostly former coal-mining town of Denniston near Westport, once home to 1500 sooty locals. (p428)

Te Papa Wellington's vibrant treasure-trove museum, where history – both Maori and Pakeha (European New Zealanders) – speaks, sparkles, shakes...and is even shaped like a squid. (p354)

Dunedin Railway Station More than 100 years old, trimmed with mosaic tiles and stained-glass windows; one of NZ's most photographed buildings. (p521)

Shantytown South of Grey-mouth on the West Coast is this authentic re-creation of an 1860s gold-mining town. (p436)

Maori Culture

Rotorua Catch a cultural performance at one of several venues: experience a *haka* (war dance) and a *hangi* (Maori feast), with traditional song, dance, folklore and storytelling. (p275)

Footprints Waipoua Explore the staggeringly beautiful Waipoua Kauri Forest on Northland's west coast with a Maori guide. (p158)

Te Ana Maori Rock Art Centre Learn about traditional Maori rock art in Timaru before exploring remote sites around South Canterbury. (p497)

Hokitika The primary source of NZ *pounamu* (greenstone) and home to numerous master carvers of stone, bone and paua in traditional Maori designs. (p440)

Sandtrails Hokianga Explore the upper North Island's less-visited but rugged and spectacular west coast with this Maori-owned company. (p156)

Off-the-Beaten-Track Experiences

Stewart Island/Rakiura The end of the line! Catch the ferry to Oban and get lost for a few days. (p603)

Northern West Coast Some of the best spectacles on the coast are in the northwest, including the eye-popping Oparara Basin. (p432)

East Cape Take a few days to detour around this very untouristy corner of NZ. (p315)

Whanganui River Road Drive alongside the slow-curling Whanganui River past Maori towns and stands of deciduous trees, remnants of failed Pakeha farms. (p235)

Forgotten World Highway A lonesome, forested 155km between Taumaranui and Stratford (or the other way around). (p226)

Tramping

Milford Track A justifiably famous 'Great Walk', Milford features 53.5km of gorgeous fiords, sounds, peaks and raindrops. (p586)

Routeburn Track Those with plenty of 'Great Walk' kilometres in their boots rate the Routeburn as the best of the bunch. (p562)

Top: Stewart Island/Rakiura (p603)
Bottom: Sea kayaks at Cathedral Cove (p205)

Banks Peninsula Track The peninsula's rolling hills and picturesque bays might not look like the eroded remains of twin volcanoes. Geology lesson, anyone? (p481)

Mt Taranaki short walks You can loop around the mountain or bag the summit, but a couple of hours spent strolling on its photogenic flanks is equally rewarding. (p224)

Lake Angelus Track Yes, the zigzag up Pinchgut Track is a bit of a rude awakening, but the views along Mt Robert Ridge last all day. (p422)

Whanganui Journey This 'Great Walk' is actually a 145km paddle down NZ's longest navigable river, through the depths of Whanganui National Park. (p236)

Queen Charlotte Track The joys of camping (sea breezes, lapping waves, starry nights) or luxurious lodges. Either way, you win. (p386)

Kaikoura Coast Track Twitchers delight! Riflemen, bellbirds, grey warblers, long-tailed cuckoos, hawks... Look seaward for dolphins, seals and soaring seabirds. (p398)

Pubs, Bars & Beer

Wellington craft beer Malthouse and Hashigo Zake, just two of around 20 craft-beer bars in the capital (something to do with thirsty politicians?). (p364)

Queenstown The only place in NZ where you can head out for a big night on a Monday or Tuesday and not be the only one there. (p559)

Auckland The country's biggest city is developing as a hoppy hub: head to Galbraith's Alehouse, Hallertau or Brothers Beer for microbrewed goodness. (p90)

Nelson craft beer Home of NZ hops, Nelson boasts its own craft-beer trail featuring a host of breweries and legendary inns. (p405)

Invercargill Brewery This workhorse not only produces its own range but also brews on behalf of some of NZ's best small producers. (p595)

Dunedin There are plenty of great bars to keep you off the streets in NZ's best university town. (p528)

Mike's Organic Brewery Taranaki's finest craft brews are wobbling distance from New Plymouth. (p219)

Foodie Experiences

Eating in Auckland New restaurants, ethnic culinary enclaves and a growing food-truck scene all make Auckland New Zealand's eating capital. (p82)

Central Otago vineyard restaurants Eye-popping scenery combined with the best of NZ food and wine. (p533)

Bay of Plenty kiwifruit Pick up a dozen fuzzy, ripe and delicious kiwifruit from roadside stalls for as little as $1 per dozen. (p304)

Hokitika Wildfoods Festival You're a big baby, Bear Grylls – eating insects can be lots of fun! (p442)

West Coast whitebait Have a patty and a pint at a country pub, or buy some from an old-timer's back door. (p425)

Stewart Island/Rakiura Good cod! Is everyone on this island a fisher? (Answer: yes. Bring lemons). (p609)

Wine Regions

Marlborough The country's biggest and best wine region just keeps on turning out superb sauvignon blanc (and other varieties): drink some. (p392)

Martinborough A small-but-sweet wine region a day trip from Wellington: easy cycling and easy-drinking pinot noir. (p373)

Waiheke Island Auckland's favourite weekend playground has a hot, dry microclimate: perfect for Bordeaux-style reds and rosés. (p99)

Central Otago Stretching from the Cromwell Basin in the north to Alexandra in the south and west to Gibbston, Central Otago is responsible for much of the country's best pinot noir and reisling. (p533)

Waipara Valley A short hop north of Christchurch are some spectacular vineyards producing equally spectacular riesling. (p489)

Markets

Dunedin Farmers Market Organic fruit and veg, Dunedin's own Green Man beer, robust coffee and homemade pies; stock up for life on the road. (p526)

Nelson Market A big, busy weekly market featuring everything from Doris' traditional bratwursts to new-age clothing. (p401)

River Traders Market Whanganui's riverside market is a Saturday-morning fixture: up to 100 stalls, with a particularly good farmers market section. (p234)

Harbourside Market The ulterior motive for visiting this weekly fruit-and-veg market in

Marlborough wine region (p392)

Wellington is the multiethnic food stalls and adjacent artisan City Market. (p361)

Otara Market A taste of the South Pacific in Auckland. (p94)

Rotorua Night Market Thursday-night hoedown in downtown Rotorua. Food, drink, buskers...it's all good. (p287)

Beaches

Karekare Classic black-sand beach west of Auckland, with wild surf (Eddie Vedder nearly drowned here). Look, but don't touch. (p111)

Hahei Iconic Kiwi beach experience on the Coromandel Peninsula, with mandatory side trip to Cathedral Cove. (p205)

Wainui On the North Island's East Coast: surfing, sandcas-tles, sunshine... The quintessential beach-bum beach. (p324)

Wharariki Beach No car park, no ice-cream van, no swim-suits... This isolated stretch near Farewell Spit is for wanderers and ponderers. (p419)

Hillary Trail For sheer ocean drama you can't beat a wild West Coast beach. Unless you tag on another, and another, and another... (p111)

Manu Bay NZ's most famous surf break (seen *Endless Summer*?) peels ashore south of Raglan. There's not much sand, but the point break is what you're here for. (p176)

Abel Tasman Coast Track No need to Photoshop this postcard paradise. These golden beaches, blue bays and verdant hills are for real. (p412)

Skiing

Treble Cone Everything from challenging downhill terrain to snowboard half-pipes and cross-country skiing at the nearby Cadrona Snow Farm, 26km from Wanaka. (p47)

Whakapapa and Turoa The North Island's best ski fields wind down Mt Ruapehu in Tongariro National Park, easily accessible from Taupo. (p265)

Canterbury From Mt Hutt and Methven's après-ski buzz, to smaller fields like Ohau, Round Hill, Porters and Broken River. (p47)

Coronet Peak The Queenstown area's oldest ski field, just 18km from town; night skiing on Friday and Saturday. (p47)

Cardrona More skiing in the Wanaka area, with slopes to suit all levels of experience. (p577)

Month by Month

TOP EVENTS
....

Fringe NZ, February

Wellington Sevens, February

World of Wearable-Art Award Show, September

Marlborough Wine & Food Festival, February

World Buskers Festival, January

January

New Zealand gets set for another year. Great weather, cricket season in full swing and happy holidays for the locals.

☆ Festival of Lights

New Plymouth's Pukekura Park is regularly plastered with adjectives like 'jewel' and 'gem', but the gardens really sparkle during this festival (www.festivalof-lights.co.nz). It's a magical scene: pathways glow and trees are impressively lit with thousands of lights. Live music, dance and kids' performances too.

☆ World Buskers Festival

Christchurch hosts a gaggle of jugglers, musos, tricksters, puppeteers, mime artists and dancers, performing throughout this 10-day summertime festival (www.worldbuskersfestival. com). Shoulder into the crowd, see who's making a scene in the middle and maybe leave a few dollars. Avoid if you're scared of audience participation.

February

The sun is shining, the kids are back at school, and the sav blanc is chillin': this is prime party time across NZ. Book your festival tickets (and beds) in advance.

☆ Waitangi Day

On 6 February 1840 the Treaty of Waitangi (www. nzhistory.net.nz) was first signed between Maori and the British Crown. The day remains a public holiday across NZ, but in Waitangi itself (the Bay of Islands) there's a lot happening: guided tours, concerts, market stalls and family entertainment.

☆ Marlborough Wine & Food Festival

NZ's biggest and best wine festival (www.wine-marlborough-festival.co.nz) features tastings from around 50 Marlborough wineries (also NZ's biggest and best), plus fine food and entertainment. The mandatory over-indulgence usually happens on a Saturday early in the month. Keep quiet if you don't like sauvignon blanc...

☆ New Zealand Festival

Feeling artsy? This month-long spectacular (www.fest-ival.co.nz) happens in Wellington in February–March every even-numbered year, and is sure to spark your imagination. NZ's cultural capital exudes artistic enthusiasm with theatre, dance, music, writing and visual arts. International acts aplenty.

☆ Fringe NZ

Music, theatre, comedy, dance, visual arts...but not the mainstream stuff that makes it into the New Zealand Festival. These are the fringe-dwelling, unusual, emerging, controversial, low-budget and/or downright weird acts that don't seem to fit in anywhere else (www. fringe.co.nz). Great stuff!

☆ Art Deco Weekend

In the third week of February, Napier, levelled by an earthquake in 1931 and

igh art-deco
...ates its archi-
...itage with this
...n' fiesta (www.
.....per.com), featur-
ing music, food, wine, vintage cars and costumery.

🎎 Splore

Explore Splore (www.
splore.net), a cutting-
edge, three-day outdoor
summer fest in Tapapa-
kanga Regional Park on
the Coromandel Peninsula.
Contemporary live music,
performance, visual arts,
safe swimming, pohutu-
kawa trees... If we were
feeling parental, we'd tell
you to take sunscreen, a hat
and a water bottle.

☆ Wellington Sevens

Yeah, we know, it's not
rugby season, but Febru-
ary sees the world's top
seven-a-side rugby teams
crack heads in Wellington
(www.sevens.co.nz) as part
of the HSBC Sevens World
Series: everyone from stal-
warts like Australia, NZ
and South Africa to min-
nows like the Cook Islands,
Kenya and Canada. A great
excuse for a party.

March

March brings a hint of
autumn, harvest time in
the vineyards and orchards
(great if you need work),
long dusky evenings and
plenty of festivals plumping
out the calendar. Locals
unwind post-tourist season.

🎎 Te Matatini National Kapa Haka Festival

This Maori *haka* (war
dance) competition (www.

tematatini.co.nz) happens
in early March in odd-
numbered years: much ges-
ticulation, eye-bulging and
tongue extension. Venues
vary: 2015 will be Christchurch. And it's not just the
haka: expect traditional
song, dance, storytelling
and other performing arts.

🚴 BikeFest Lake Taupo

Feeling fit? Try racing a
bicycle 160km around Lake
Taupo and then talk to us...
In the week prior to the
big race, BikeFest (www.
bikefest.co.nz) celebrates
all things bicycular: BMX,
mountain bike, unicycle,
tandem – whatever your
preferred conveyance, you'll
find someone who's into it.

🍴 Wildfoods Festival

Eat worms, hare testicles or
crabs at Hokitika's comfort-
zone-challenging food fest
(www.wildfoods.co.nz). Not
for the mild-mannered or
weak-stomached... But even
if you are, it's still fun to
watch! There are usually
plenty of quality NZ brews
available, too, which help
subdue any difficult tastes.

🎎 WOMAD

Local and international
music, arts and dance
performances fill New
Plymouth's Bowl of Brook-
lands to overflowing (www.
womad.co.nz). An evolution
of the original world-music
festival dreamed up by
Peter Gabriel, who launched
the inaugural UK concert
in 1990. Perfect for families
(usually not too loud).

🎎 Pasifika Festival

With upwards of 140,000
Maori and notable commu-
nities of Tongans, Samoans,

Cook Islanders, Niueans,
Fijians and other South
Pacific Islanders, Auckland
has the largest Polynesian
community in the world.
These vibrant island cul-
tures come together at
this annual fiesta (www.
aucklandcouncil.govt.nz) in
Western Springs Park.

April

April is when canny
travellers hit NZ: the ocean
is still swimmable and the
weather still mild, with
nary a tourist or queue in
sight (...other than during
Easter, when there's
pricey accommodation
everywhere).

☆ National Jazz Festival

Every Easter, Tauranga
hosts the longest-running
jazz fest (www.jazz.org.nz)
in the southern hemisphere.
The line-up is invariably
impressive (Kurt Elling,
Keb Mo), and there's plenty
of fine NZ food and wine to
accompany the finger-snap-
pin' za-bah-de-dah sonics.

May

The nostalgia of autumn
runs deep: party nights
are long gone and another
chilly Kiwi winter beckons.
Thank goodness for
the Comedy Festival!
Last chance to explore
Fiordland and Southland
in reasonable weather.
Farmers markets overflow.

🍴 Bluff Oyster & Food Festival

Bluff and oysters go together like, well, like a bivalve.

Truck down to the deep south for some slippery, salty specimens (www.bluffoysterfest.co.nz). It's chilly down here in May, but the live music and oyster eating/opening competitions warm everybody up.

☆ New Zealand International Comedy Festival

Three-week laugh-fest (www.comedyfestival.co.nz) with venues across Auckland, Wellington and various regional centres: Whangarei to Invercargill with all the mid-sized cities in between. International gag-merchants (Arj Barker, Danny Bhoy) line up next to home-grown talent (anyone seen that Jermaine Clement guy lately?).

June

Time to head south: it's ski season! Queenstown and Wanaka hit their stride. For everyone else, head north: the Bay of Plenty is always sunny, and is it just us, or is Northland underrated?

✈ Matariki

Maori New Year is heralded by the rise of Matariki (aka Pleiades star cluster) in May and the sighting of the new moon in June. Three days of remembrance, education, music, film, community days and tree planting take place, mainly around Auckland and Northland (www.teara.govt.nz/en/matariki-maori-new-year).

☆ New Zealand Gold Guitar Awards

We like both kinds of music: country and western! These awards (www.goldguitars.co.nz) in chilly Gore cap off a week of ever-lovin' country twang and boot-scootin' good times, with plenty of concerts and buskers.

July

Wellington's good citizens clutch collars, shiver and hang out in bookshops: Auckland doesn't seem so bad now, eh? Ski season slides on: hit Mt Ruapehu on the North Island if Queenstown is overcrowded.

✈ Queenstown Winter Festival

This southern snow-fest (www.winterfestival.co.nz) has been running since 1975, and now attracts around 45,000 snow bunnies. It's a 10-day party, studded with fireworks, jazz, street parades, comedy, a Mardi Gras, a masquerade ball and lots of snow-centric activities on the mountain slopes.

☆ New Zealand International Film Festival

After separate film festivals (www.nzff.co.nz) in Wellington, Auckland, Dunedin and Christchurch, a selection of flicks hits the road for screenings in regional towns from July to November (film buffs in Gore and Masterton get positively orgasmic at the prospect).

🏃 Russell Birdman

Birdman rallies are just so '80s...but they sure are funny! This one in Russell (www.russellbirdman.co.nz) features the usual cast of costumed contenders propelling themselves off a jetty in pursuit of weightlessness. Bonus points if your name is Russell.

August

Land a good deal on accommodation pretty much anywhere except the ski towns. Winter is almost spent, but there's not much happening outside: music and art are your saviours... or watch some rugby!

✈ Taranaki International Arts Festival

Beneath the snowy slopes of Mt Taranaki, August used to be a time of quiet repose and reconstitution. Not anymore: this whizz-bang arts festival (www.taft.co.nz/artsfest) now shakes the winter from the city (New Plymouth) with music, theatre, dance, visual arts and parades.

☆ Bay of Islands Jazz & Blues Festival

You might think that the Bay of Islands is all about sunning yourself on a yacht while dolphins splash saltwater on your stomach. And you'd be right. But in the depths of winter, this jazzy little festival (www.jazz-blues.co.nz) will give you something else to do.

September

Spring is sprung. The amazing and surprising World of WearableArt Award Show is always a hit. And will someone please beat Canterbury in the annual ITM rugby cup final?

⚜ World of WearableArt Award Show

A bizarre (in the best possible way) two-week Wellington event (www.worldofwearableart.com) featuring amazing hand-crafted garments. Entries from the show are displayed at the World of WearableArt & Classic Cars Museum in Nelson after the event (Cadillacs and corsetry?). Sometimes spills over into October.

⚜ Wanganui Festival of Glass

Whanganui has earned its artistic stripes as a centre for gorgeous glass, myriad local artists and workshops gearing up for this classy glassy fest in September (www.wanganuiglass. co.nz). Expect lots of 'how-to' demonstrations, exhibitions and open studios.

🏃 Auckland Boat Show

Auckland harbour blooms with sails and churns with outboard motors (www. auckland-boatshow.com). It doesn't command the instant nautical recognition of Sydney or San Diego, but Auckland really is one of the world's great sailing cities. And here's proof.

October

Post-rugby and pre-cricket, sports fans twiddle their thumbs: a trip to Kaikoura, perhaps? Around the rest of NZ October is 'shoulder season' – reasonable accommodation rates, minimal crowds and no competition for the good campsites.

⚜ Nelson Arts Festival

Sure, Nelson is distractingly sunny, but that doesn't mean the artsy good stuff isn't happening inside and out. Get a taste of the local output over two weeks in October (www.nelsonfestivals.co.nz).

🍴 Kaikoura Seafest

Kaikoura is a town built on crayfish. Well, not literally, but there sure are plenty of crustaceans in the sea here, many of which find themselves on plates during Seafest (www.seafest.co.nz). Also a great excuse to drink a lot and dance around.

November

Across Northland, the Coromandel Peninsula, the Bay of Plenty and the East Coast, NZ's iconic pohutukawa trees erupt with brilliant crimson blooms. The weather is picking up, and a few tourists are starting to arrive.

🍷 Toast Martinborough

Bound for a day of boozy indulgence, wine-swilling Wellingtonians head over Rimutaka Hill and into upmarket Martinborough (www.toastmartinborough. co.nz). The Wairarapa region produces some seriously good pinot noir: don't go home without trying some (...as if you'd be so silly).

⚜ Oamaru Victorian Heritage Celebrations

Ahhh, the good old days... When Queen Vic sat dourly on the throne, when hems were low, collars were high, and civic decency was a matter of course. Old Oamaru thoroughly enjoys this tongue-in-cheek historic homage in November (www.historicoamaru. co.nz): dress-ups, penny-farthing races, choirs, guided tours etc.

⚜ Pohutukawa Festival

A week of markets, picnics, live music, kite-flying, cruises, snorkelling and poetry on the Coromandel Peninsula. It's all very clean-living and above-board, but not everything has to be about drinking, dancing and decadence. And just look at those pohutukawa trees (www. pohutukawafestival.co.nz). Sometimes strays into early December.

December

Summertime! The crack of leather on willow resounds across the nation's cricket pitches, and office workers surge towards the finish line. Everyone gears up for Christmas: avoid shopping centres like the plague.

⚜ Rhythm & Vines

Wine, music and song (all the good things) in sunny east-coast Gisborne on New Year's Eve (www. rhythmandvines.co.nz). Top DJs, hip-hop acts, bands and singer-songwriters compete for your attention. Or maybe you'd rather just drink some chardonnay and kiss someone on the beach.

Itineraries

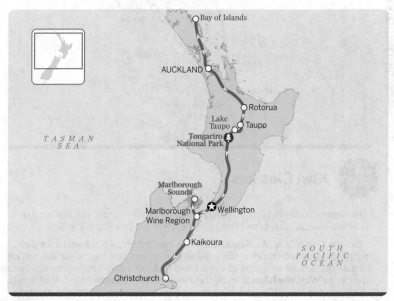

2 WEEKS North & South

From the top of the north to halfway down the south: a taste of New Zealand's best.

Kick things off in **Auckland**: it's NZ's biggest city, with awesome restaurants and bars, galleries and boutiques, beaches and bays. Not an urbanite? Head north to the salt-licked **Bay of Islands** for a couple of days R&R.

Tracking south, **Rotorua** is a unique geothermal hot spot: geysers, mud pools, volcanic vents and Maori culture make for an engaging experience. Further south, progressive **Taupo** has the staggeringly beautiful **Lake Taupo** and **Tongariro National Park** nearby. Try some tramping, mountain biking or skydiving, then hoof it down to **Wellington**, a hip little city with an irrepressible arts scene.

Across Cook Strait, see what all the fuss is about in the **Marlborough Wine Region**. The hypnotically hushed inlets, ranges and waterways of the **Marlborough Sounds** are nearby. Swinging south, spend a day whale-watching in **Kaikoura**, then cruise into **Christchurch** for some southern culture and hospitality.

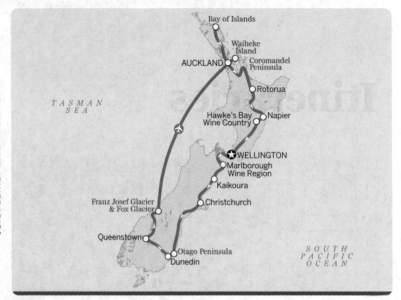

 ## Kiwi Classics

Classy cities, geothermal eruptions, fantastic wine, Maori culture, glaciers, extreme activities, isolated beaches and forests: just a few of our favourite NZ things.

Aka the 'City of Sails', **Auckland** is a South Pacific melting pot. Spend a few days shopping, eating and drinking: this is NZ at its most cosmopolitan. Make sure you get out onto the harbour on a ferry or a yacht, and find half a day to explore the beaches and wineries on **Waiheke Island**. Truck north to the **Bay of Islands** for a dose of aquatic adventure (dolphins, sailing, sunning yourself on deck), then scoot back southeast to check out the forests and beaches on the **Coromandel Peninsula**. Further south in **Rotorua**, get a nose full of egg gas, confront a 30ft geyser, giggle at volcanic mud bubbles and experience a Maori cultural performance (work your *haka* into shape).

Cruise down to **Napier** on the East Coast, NZ's archetypal art-deco sun city. While you're here, don't miss the bottled offerings of the **Hawke's Bay Wine Country** (...*ohh*, the chardonnay). Down in **Wellington**, the coffee's hot, the beer's cold and wind from the politicians generates its own low-pressure system. This is NZ's arts capital: catch a live band, some buskers, a gallery opening or some theatre.

Swan over to the South Island for a few days to experience the best the south has to offer. Start with a tour through the sauvignon blanc heartland of the **Marlborough Wine Region**, then jump on a boat/plane/helicopter for a close encounter with a massive marine mammal in **Kaikoura**. Next stop is **Christchurch** – the southern capital is finding its feet again after the earthquakes – followed by the coast road south to the wildlife-rich **Otago Peninsula**, jutting abstractly away from the Victorian facades of Scottish-flavoured and student-filled **Dunedin**. Catch some live music while you're in town.

Head inland via SH8 to bungy-obsessed **Queenstown**. If you have time, detour over to the West Coast for an unforgettable encounter with **Franz Josef Glacier** and **Fox Glacier**. From here you can keep driving back north, or play airport hopscotch from Hokitika to Christchurch then back to Auckland.

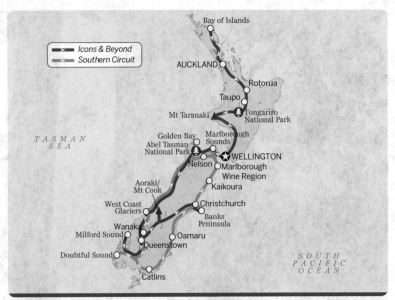

Icons & Beyond
Southern Circuit

Bay of Islands

AUCKLAND

Rotorua

Taupo

Mt Taranaki   Tongariro
               National Park

TASMAN
SEA

Golden Bay   Marlborough
Abel Tasman   Sounds
National Park
              WELLINGTON
Nelson   Marlborough
              Wine Region
Aoraki/   Kaikoura
Mt Cook
West Coast   Christchurch
Glaciers
              Banks
Wanaka   Peninsula
Milford Sound   Oamaru
         Queenstown

Doubtful Sound   SOUTH
                                  PACIFIC
                                  OCEAN
         Catlins

Icons & Beyond

5 WEEKS

Virgin visitors to NZ will want to check out NZ's tourist icons, plus a few active wilderness experiences.

Cruise sail-dappled **Auckland** harbour, then take SH1 north to the winterless **Bay of Islands**: surfboards, sailing, kayaks, scuba gear... Heading south, hold your nose in sulphurous **Rotorua**, then hook into idyllic **Taupo** for some volcanic tramping in nearby **Tongariro National Park**. Take SH43 west to photogenic **Mt Taranaki**, then stay up late in **Wellington**.

Across Cook Strait, disappear into the **Marlborough Sounds** or launch into some sea-kayaking in **Abel Tasman National Park**. Track down the rainy West Coast with its iconic **glaciers**, then experience adrenaline-addicted **Queenstown**. Mix and match highways to Te Anau for the side road to **Milford Sound**, then backtrack to SH6 and head north for cloud-piercing **Aoraki/Mt Cook**. Veer east back to **Christchurch**, a city on the mend. Don't miss exploring the **Banks Peninsula**, southeast of town.

Southern Circuit

3 WEEKS

Take a long loop through the best of the South Island. Winging into **Christchurch** to launch this three-week escapade, you'll find a vibrant city rebuilding post-earthquakes. Grab a coffee at a cafe (try Addington Coffee Co-op), then visit the excellent Canterbury Museum. Check out the Avon River, cutting lazily through the Botanic Gardens.

City saturated? Visit the geologically and culturally eccentric **Banks Peninsula**, then head north for whale-watching in **Kaikoura**. Continue through the famous **Marlborough Wine Region**, and lose a day on the **Marlborough Sounds** waterways.

Detour west past artsy **Nelson** to eco-friendly **Golden Bay** (more paintbrushes than people). Southbound, dawdle down the dramatic West Coast with its **glaciers** and wilderness, and continue through to hip/hippie **Wanaka** and ski central **Queenstown**. Desolate **Doubtful Sound** is mesmerising, while the overgrown **Catlins** are perfectly chilled out.

Back up the east coast, wheel through Dunedin to surprisingly hip **Oamaru**, before rolling back into Christchurch.

MATT MUNRO/LONELY PLANET ©

Top: Waitakere Ranges Regional Park (p111)

Bottom: Mt Ngauru-hoe, Tongariro National Park (p262)

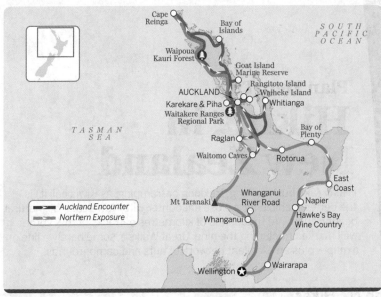

Legend:
- Auckland Encounter
- Northern Exposure

2 WEEKS Auckland Encounter

Is there another 1.4-million-strong city with access to *two* oceans and vibrant Polynesian culture? **Auckland** also offers stellar bars and restaurants, museums, islands and beaches.

Check out the Maori and South Pacific Islander exhibits at Auckland Museum, then wander across the Domain to K Rd for lunch. Pay a visit to the grand Auckland Art Gallery and the iconic Sky Tower, then Ponsonby for dinner and drinks.

Ferry over to **Rangitoto Island**, then chug into Devonport for a meal. Have a look at the tall timber in **Waitakere Ranges Regional Park**, or check out the wild surf at **Karekare** and **Piha**, then hit the Kingsland restaurants. Have breakfast in Mt Eden, climb Maungawhau, then ferry-hop to **Waiheke Island** for wineries and beaches.

Activities within easy reach of the big smoke: snorkelling at **Goat Island Marine Reserve**, sailing the **Bay of Islands**, ocean-gazing at **Cape Reinga**, ogling giant trees at **Waipoua Kauri Forest**, delving into **Waitomo Caves**, surfing at **Raglan** or beaching yourself at **Whitianga**.

3 WEEKS Northern Exposure

Three-quarters of New Zealanders live on the North Island – find out why!

Begin in **Auckland**, NZ's biggest city. Eat streets abound: try Ponsonby Rd in Ponsonby, K Rd in Newton, and New North Rd in Kingsland. Hike up One Tree Hill (Maungakiekie) to burn off resultant calories, and don't miss Auckland Art Gallery and Auckland Museum.

Heading north, the amazing **Waipoua Kauri Forest** is home to some seriously tall timber. The rugged tip of the far north is **Cape Reinga**, rich in Maori lore.

Venture back south through geothermal **Rotorua** then the **Bay of Plenty** to the sunny **East Coast**. Art-deco **Napier** is surrounded by the chardonnay vines of **Hawke's Bay Wine Country**. Follow SH2 south into the sheepy/winey **Wairarapa** then continue down to hip **Wellington**.

Heading northwest, there's crafty glass in **Whanganui**, the joyously scenic **Whanagnui River Road** and epic **Mt Taranaki**. Go underground at **Waitomo Caves**, surf the point breaks near **Raglan**, then hit Auckland again.

Plan Your Trip
Hiking in New Zealand

Hiking (aka bushwalking, trekking or tramping, as Kiwis call it) is the perfect vehicle for a close encounter with New Zealand's natural beauty. There are thousands of kilometres of tracks here – some well marked (including the nine 'Great Walks'), some barely a line on a map – plus an excellent network of huts and campgrounds.

Top NZ Hikes

Top Five Short Tramps
Tongariro Alpine Crossing, Tongariro National Park

Avalanche Peak, Canterbury

Kohi Point Walkway, Whakatane

Mangawhai Cliff Top Walkway, Northland

Pinnacles Walk, Coromandel Peninsula

Top Five Wildlife Encounters
Birdlife St Arnaud Range Track, Nelson

Seals Cape Foulwind Walkway, West Coast

Gannets Cape Kidnappers Walkway, East Coast

Tuatara and birdlife Tiritiri Matangi Island, Hauraki Gulf

Kiwi Rakiura Track, Stewart Island

Best for Beginners or with Kids
Queen Charlotte Track, Marlborough Sounds

Huka Falls Walkway, Taupo

Coast to Coast Walkway, Auckland

Mauao Summit Track, Mt Maunganui

Coromandel Coastal Walkway, Coromandel Peninsula

Planning

When to Go

Mid-December–late January Tramping high season is during the school summer holidays, starting a couple of weeks before Christmas – avoid it if you can.

January–March The summer weather lingers into March: wait until February if you can, when tracks are (marginally) less crowded. Most non-alpine tracks can be walked enjoyably at any time from about October through to April.

June–August Winter is not the time to be out in the wild, especially at altitude – some paths close in winter because of avalanche danger and reduced facilities and services.

What to Bring

Primary considerations: your feet and your shoulders. Make sure your footwear is tough and well worn-in, and your pack isn't too heavy. Wet-weather gear is essential, especially on the South Island's waterlogged West Coast. If you're camping or staying in huts without stoves, bring a camping stove. Also bring insect repellent to keep sandflies away, and don't forget your scroggin – a mixture of dried fruit and nuts (and sometimes chocolate) for munching en route.

Books & Resources

Before plodding off into the forest, get up-to-date information from the appropriate authority – usually the **DOC** (Department of Conservation; www.doc.govt.nz) or regional i-SITE visitor information centres. As well as current track condition and weather info, DOC supplies detailed books on the flora, fauna, geology and history of NZ's national parks, plus leaflets (mostly $2 or less) detailing hundreds of NZ walking tracks.

➡ Lonely Planet's *Hiking & Tramping in New Zealand* describes around 50 walks of various lengths and degrees of difficulty.

➡ *101 Great Tramps* by Mark Pickering and Rodney Smith has suggestions for two- to six-day tramps around the country. The companion guide, *202 Great Walks: The Best Day Walks in New Zealand,* by Mark Pickering, is handy for shorter, family-friendly excursions.

➡ *Accessible Walks,* by Anna and Andrew Jameson, is an excellent guide for elderly, disabled and family trampers, with detailed access information on more than 100 South Island walks.

➡ *New Zealand Tramper's Handbook* by Sarah Bennett and Lee Slater is all about being safe and happy on the track, perfect for new trampers.

➡ *Shelter from the Storm* by Shaun Barnett, Rob Brown and Geoff Spearpoint is a meticulously researched history of NZ's backcountry huts (you'll no doubt stay in a few if you're planning on doing any serious hiking).

➡ Bird's Eye Tramping Guides from Craig Potton Publishing have fab topographical maps, and there are countless books covering tramps and short urban walks around NZ – scan the bookshops.

Maps

The topographical maps produced by **Land Information New Zealand** (LINZ; www.linz.govt.nz) are a safe bet. Bookshops don't often have a good selection of these, but LINZ has map-sales offices in major cities and towns, and DOC offices often sell LINZ maps for local tracks. Outdoor stores also stock them. LINZ map series includes 1:250,000 'Topo250' regional maps and more detailed 'Topo50' maps (you may need two or three of these per track).

Websites

www.trampingtracks.co.nz Descriptions, maps and photos of long and short tramps all over NZ.

www.tramper.co.nz Articles, photos, forums and excellent track and hut information.

www.trampingnz.com Region-by-region track info with readable trip reports.

www.topomap.co.nz Online topographic map of the whole country.

www.mountainsafety.org.nz Safety tips, gear advice and courses.

www.peakbagging.org.nz Find a summit and get up on top of it.

Track Classifications

Tracks in NZ are classified according to various features, including level of difficulty. We loosely refer to the level of difficulty as easy, medium, hard or difficult. The widely used track classification system is as follows:

Short Walk Well formed; possibly allows for wheelchair access or is constructed to 'shoe'

TRACK SAFETY

Thousands of people tramp across NZ without incident, but every year a few folks meet their maker in the mountains. Some trails are only for the experienced, fit and well equipped – don't attempt these if you don't fit the bill. Ensure you are healthy and feel comfortable walking for sustained periods.

NZ's climatic changeability subjects high-altitude walks to snow and ice, even in summer: always check weather and track conditions before setting off, and be ready for them to change rapidly. Resources include:

www.doc.govt.nz Weather and track info.

www.adventuresmart.org.nz Log your walk intentions online (and tell a friend!).

www.mountainsafety.org.nz Tramping safety tips.

www.metservice.co.nz Weather updates.

standard (ie walking boots not required). Suitable for people of all ages and fitness levels.

Walking Track Easy and well-formed longer walks; constructed to 'shoe' standard. Suitable for people of most ages and fitness levels.

Easy Tramping Track or **Great Walk** Well formed; major water crossings have bridges and track junctions have signs. Light walking boots required.

Tramping Track Requires skill and experience; constructed to 'boot' standard. Suitable for people of average physical fitness. Water crossings may not have bridges.

Route Requires a high degree of skill, experience and navigation skills. Well-equipped trampers only.

Great Walks

NZ's nine official 'Great Walks' (one of which is actually a canoe trip down a river!) are the country's most popular tracks. Natural beauty abounds, but prepare yourself for crowds, especially over summer.

All nine Great Walks are described in Lonely Planet's *Hiking & Tramping in New Zealand*, and are detailed in pamphlets provided by DOC visitor centres and online at www.greatwalks.co.nz.

Tickets & Bookings

To tramp these tracks you'll need to buy **Great Walk Tickets** before setting out. These track-specific tickets cover you for

NZ'S NINE 'GREAT WALKS'

WALK	DISTANCE	DURATION	DIFFICULTY	DESCRIPTION
Abel Tasman Coast Track *	54km	3-5 days	Easy to medium	NZ's most popular walk (or sea kayak); beaches and bays in Abel Tasman National Park (South Island)
Heaphy Track *	78km	4-6 days	Medium to hard	Forests, beaches and karst landscapes in Kahurangi National Park (South Island)
Kepler Track **	60km	3-4 days	Easy to medium	Lakes, rivers, gorges, glacial valleys and beech forest in Fiordland National Park (South Island)
Lake Waikaremoana Track *	46km	3-4 days	Easy to medium	Lake views, bush-clad slopes and swimming in Te Urewera National Park (North Island)
Milford Track **	53.5km	4 days	Easy	Rainforest, crystal-clear streams and 630m-high Sutherland Falls in Fiordland National Park (South Island)
Rakiura Track *	39km	3 days	Medium	Bird life (kiwi!), beaches and lush bush on remote Stewart Island (Rakiura; off the South Island)
Routeburn Track **	32km	2-4 days	Medium	Eye-popping alpine scenery around Mt Aspiring and Fiordland National Parks (South Island)
Tongariro Northern Circuit **	43km	3-4 days	Medium to hard	Through the active volcanic landscape of Tongariro National Park (North Island); see also Tongariro Alpine Crossing
Whanganui Journey **	145km	5 days	Easy	Canoe or kayak down the Whanganui River in Whanganui National Park (North Island)

* Bookings required year-round
** Bookings required peak season only (Oct-Apr)

Great Walks

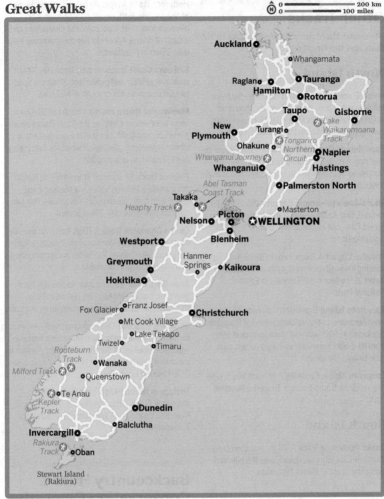

hut accommodation (from $22 to $54 per adult per night, depending on the track) and/or camping ($6 to $18 per adult per night). You can camp only at designated camping grounds; note there's no camping on the Milford Track. In the off-peak season (May to September) you can use Backcountry Hut Passes or pay-as-you-go Hut Tickets instead of Great Walk Tickets on all Great Walks except for the Lake Waikaremoana Track, Heaphy Track, Abel Tasman Coast Track and Rakiura Track (Great Walk Tickets required year-round).

Kids under 17 stay in huts and camp for free on all Great Walks. (Note: we hear whispers of hut tickets being phased out over coming years: Backcounty Hut Passes are the way of the future).

For bookings see www.greatwalks.co.nz, email greatwalksbookings@doc.govt.nz, phone ☎0800 694 732, or visit DOC offices close to the tracks. Trampers must book and pay for their chosen accommodation in advance and specify dates. Book as far in advance as possible, especially if you're planning on walking during summer.

Other Tracks

Of course, there are a lot more walks in NZ than just the Great ones!

North Island

Aotea Track This 25km, two- to three-day track follows routes laid down by loggers who came to Great Barrier Island in a quest for kauri trees, leaving historic relics in their wake.

Cape Reinga Coastal Walkway A 53km, three- to four-day, easy beach tramp (camping only) in Northland. A 132km six- to eight-day route is also possible.

Mt Holdsworth–Jumbo Circuit A 25km, medium-to-hard, two- to three-day tramp in Holdsworth Forest Park, out of Masterton, scaling alpine Mt Holdsworth.

Pouakai Circuit A 25km, two- to three-day loop passing lowland rainforest, cliffs and subalpine forest at the foot of Mt Taranaki in Egmont National Park.

Rangitoto Island Summit It's an easy day trip from Auckland to the volcanic island of Rangitoto, blanketed in 600-year-old black lava, best seen from its crater summit (two hours return, plus time to ogle the view).

Tongariro Alpine Crossing A brilliant 18km, one-day, medium tramp through Tongariro National Park.

South Island

Banks Peninsula Track A 35km, two-day (medium) or four-day (easy) walk over the hills and along the coast of Banks Peninsula.

TE ARAROA

Epic! **Te Araroa** (The Long Pathway; www.teararoa.org.nz) is a 3000km tramping trail from Cape Reinga in NZ's north to Bluff in the south (or the other way around). The route links existing tracks with new sections. Built over a decade, mostly by volunteers, it's one of the longest hikes in the world: check the website for maps and track notes, plus blogs and videos from hardy types who have completed the end-to-end epic.

Hollyford Track A typically hair-brained scheme of the era, the settlement of Jamestown was always a long shot. Cue: colourful characters and a dash of drama. A four- to five-day tramping track over 56km in Fiordland.

Kaikoura Coast Track An easy three-day, 40km walk over private and public land along the spectacular coastline 43km south of Kaikoura.

Mueller Hut Route Yes, it's a hardcore 1040m, eight-hour return climb on the Sealy Range near Aoraki/Mount Cook, but this is a quintessential alpine experience: geological wonders, fascinating plant life and an amazing hut.

Pelorus Track So scenic it starred in *The Hobbit*, the gorgeous Pelorus Valley – a boulder-lined gorge with deep green pools – is followed for two days on this three-day, 28km tramp.

Queen Charlotte Track A 71km, three- to five-day medium walk in the Marlborough Sounds, affording great water views. Top-notch accommodation and water transport available.

Rees-Dart Track A 70km, four- to five-day hard tramping track in Mt Aspiring National Park, through river valleys and traversing an alpine pass.

St James Walkway This tramping track passes through a significant conservation area, home to some 430 species of flora from lowland grasses to mountain beech and alpine herbs. Five days over 66km around Lewis Pass.

Tuatapere Hump Ridge Track An excellent three-day, 53km circuit beginning and ending at Bluecliffs Beach on Te Waewae Bay, 20km from Tuatapere.

Backcountry Huts & Conservation Campsites

Backcounty Huts

In addition to Great Walk huts, DOC maintains more than 950 Backcountry Huts in NZ's national and forest parks. Hut categories are as follows:

Basic Huts Just a shed; free.

Standard Huts No cooking equipment and sometimes no heating, but mattresses, water supply and toilets. Fees are $5 per adult per night.

Serviced Huts Mattress-equipped bunks or sleeping platforms, water supply, heating, toilets

RESPONSIBLE TRAMPING

If you went straight from the cradle into a pair of hiking boots, some of these tramping tips will seem ridiculously obvious; others you mightn't have considered. Online, www.lnt.org is a great resource for low-impact hiking, and the DOC site www.camping.org.nz has plenty more responsible camping tips. When in doubt, ask DOC or i-SITE staff.

The ridiculously obvious:

➡ Time your tramp to avoid peak season: less people = less stress on the environment and fewer snorers in the huts.

➡ Carry out *all* your rubbish. Burying rubbish disturbs soil and vegetation, encourages erosion, and animals will probably dig it up anyway.

➡ Don't use detergents, shampoo or toothpaste in or near watercourses (even if they're biodegradable).

➡ Use lightweight kerosene, alcohol or Shellite (white gas) stoves for cooking; avoid disposable butane gas canisters.

➡ Where there's a toilet, use it. Where there isn't one, dig a hole and bury your by-product (at least 15cm deep, 100m from any watercourse).

➡ If a track passes through a muddy patch, just plough straight on through – skirting around the outside increases the size of the bog.

You mightn't have considered:

➡ Wash your dishes 50m from watercourses; use a scourer, sand or snow instead of detergent.

➡ If you *really* need to scrub your bod, use biodegradable soap and a bucket, at least 50m from any watercourse. Spread the waste water around widely to help the soil filter it.

➡ If open fires are allowed, use only dead, fallen wood in existing fireplaces. Leave any extra wood for the next happy camper.

➡ Keep food-storage bags out of reach of scavengers by tying them to rafters or trees.

➡ Feeding wildlife can lead to unbalanced populations, diseases and animals becoming dependent on handouts. Keep your dried apricots to yourself.

and sometimes cooking facilities. Fees are $15 per adult per night.

Note that bookings are required for some huts (see the website for listings): book online at https://booking.doc.govt.nz or at DOC visitor centres. Prices for kids aged 11 to 17 are half those listed here; kids 10 and under stay free. For comprehensive hut details see www.doc.govt.nz/parks-and-recreation/places-to-stay.

If you do a lot of tramping, a six-month **Backcountry Hut Pass** ($92 per adult) might be a good idea; otherwise use pay-as-you-go **Hut Tickets** ($5: you'll need to use three of these for a Serviced Hut). Date your tickets and put them in the boxes provided at huts. Accommodation is on a first-come, first-served basis. In the low season (May to September), Backcountry Hut Tickets and Passes can also be used to procure a bunk or campsite on some Great Walks.

Backcountry Campsites are often nearby the huts, and usually have toilets and fresh water; possibly picnic tables, fire places and/or cooking shelters. Prices vary from free to $8 per person per night.

Conservation Campsites

Aside from Great Walk campsites, DOC also manages 250-plus 'Conservation Campsites' (often vehicle-accessible) with categories as follows:

Basic Campsites Basic toilets and fresh water; free on a first-come, first-served basis.

Top: Aoraki/Mt Cook
(p502)

Bottom: Milford Track
(p586)

COLIN MONTEATH/GETTY IMAGES ©

Standard Campsites Toilets and water supply, and perhaps barbecues and picnic tables; $6 on a first-come, first-served basis.

Scenic Campsites High-use coastal sites with toilets and tap water, and sometimes barbecues, fireplaces, cooking shelters, showers, picnic tables and rubbish bins. Fees are $10 per night.

Serviced Campsites Full facilities: flush toilets, tap water, showers and picnic tables. They may also have barbecues, a kitchen and a laundry; $15 per night.

Note that bookings are necessary for all Serviced Campsites, plus some Scenic and Standard Campsites in peak season (October to April). Book online – https://booking.doc.govt.nz – or at DOC visitor centres. Kids' prices are half those listed here.

DOC publishes free brochures with detailed descriptions and instructions to find every campsite (even GPS coordinates). Pick up copies from DOC offices before you hit the road, or visit the website.

Guided Walks

If you're new to tramping or just want a more comfortable experience than the DIY alternative, several companies can escort you through the wilds, usually staying in comfortable huts (showers!), with meals cooked and equipment carried for you.

Places on the North Island where you can sign up for a guided walk include Mt Taranaki, Lake Waikaremoana and Tongariro National Park. On the South Island try Kaikoura, the Banks Peninsula, Milford Track, Queen Charlotte Track, Heaphy Track or Hollyford Track. Prices for a five-day/four-night guided walk start at around $1800, and rise towards $2200 for deluxe guided experiences.

Getting To & From Trailheads

Getting to and from trailheads can be problematic, except for popular trails serviced by public and dedicated trampers' transport. Having a vehicle only helps with getting to one end of the track (you still have to collect your car afterwards). If the track starts or ends down a dead-end road, hitching will be difficult.

Of course, tracks accessible by public transport or shuttle bus services (eg Abel Tasman Coast Track) are also the most crowded. An alternative is to arrange private transport, either with a friend or by chartering a vehicle to drop you at one end then pick you up at the other. If you intend to leave a vehicle at a trailhead, don't leave anything valuable inside – theft from cars in isolated areas is a significant problem.

Plan Your Trip
Skiing & Snowboarding in New Zealand

New Zealand is an essential southern-hemisphere destination for snow bunnies, with downhill skiing, cross-country (Nordic) skiing and snowboarding all passionately pursued. The NZ ski season is generally June to October, though it varies considerably from one ski area to another, and can run as late as November.

Best Skiing & Snowboarding

Best for Beginners or with Kids
Coronet Peak, Queenstown

Mt Hutt, Central Canterbury

Mt Dobson, South Canterbury

Roundhill, South Canterbury

Best Snowboarding
Treble Cone, Wanaka

Cardrona, Wanaka

Ohau, South Canterbury

Whakapapa & Turoa, Tongariro National Park

Best Après-Ski Watering Holes
Cardrona Hotel, Cardrona

Blue Pub, Methven

Ballarat Trading Company, Queenstown

Barluga, Wanaka

Planning

Where to Go

The variety of locations and conditions makes it difficult to rate NZ's ski fields in any particular order. Some people like to be near Queenstown's party scene or Mt Ruapehu's volcanic landscapes; others prefer the quality high-altitude runs on Mt Hutt, uncrowded Rainbow or less-stressed club skiing areas. Club areas are publicly accessible and usually less crowded and cheaper than commercial fields, even though nonmembers pay a higher fee.

Practicalities

NZ's commercial ski areas aren't generally set up as 'resorts' with chalets, lodges or hotels. Rather, accommodation and après-ski carousing are often in surrounding towns, connected with the slopes via daily shuttles. Many club areas have lodges where you can stay, subject to availability.

Visitor information centres in NZ, and Tourism New Zealand (www.newzealand. com) internationally, have info on the various ski areas and can make bookings and organise packages. **Lift passes** usually

Ski Areas

cost between $50 and $100 per adult per day (half-price for kids). Lesson-and-lift packages are available at most areas. Ski and snowboard equipment rental starts at around $50 a day (cheaper for multi-day hire). Private/group **lessons** start at around $130/60 per hour.

Websites

www.brownbearski.co.nz Brilliant reference detailing all of NZ's ski areas.

www.snow.co.nz Reports, cams and ski info across the country.

www.nzski.com Reports, employment, passes and webcams for Mt Hutt, Coronet Peak and the Remarkables.

www.chillout.co.nz Info on Mt Lyford, Awakino, Hanmer Springs, Cheeseman, Roundhill, Rainbow, Temple Basin, Treble Cone, Fox Peak, Mt Dobson, Mt Olympus, Porters, Craigieburn Valley and Broken River ski areas.

www.nzsnowboard.com Snowboarding info around NZ.

North Island

Tongariro National Park

Whakapapa & Turoa (p265) On either side of Mt Ruapehu, these well-run twin resorts comprise NZ's largest ski area. Whakapapa has 30 intermediate groomed runs, plus snowboarding, cross-country, downhill, a terrain park and the highest lift access in NZ (and highest cafe!). Drive from Whakapapa Village (6km; free parking) or shuttle-bus in from National Park Village, Taupo, Turangi or Whakapapa Village. Smaller Turoa has a beginners lift, plus snowboarding, downhill

WILL SALTER / GETTY IMAGES ©

Top: Ski jumper at Treble Cone

Bottom: Snowboarder at Coronet Peak

and cross-country skiing. There's free parking or shuttle-bus transport from Ohakune, 17km away, which has the North Island's liveliest après-ski scene.

Tukino (p266) Club-operated Tukino is on Mt Ruapehu's east, 46km from Turangi. It's quite remote, 14km down a gravel road from the sealed Desert Rd (SH1), and you need a 4WD vehicle to get in. It's uncrowded, with mostly beginner and intermediate runs.

Taranaki

Manganui (p224) Offers volcano-slope, club-run skiing on the eastern slopes of spectacular Mt Taranaki in Egmont National Park, 22km from Stratford (and a 20-minute walk from the car park). Ski off the summit when conditions permit: it's a sweaty two-hour climb to the crater, but the exhilarating 1300m descent compensates.

South Island

Queenstown & Wanaka

Coronet Peak (Map p544; ☎03-450 1970, snow-phone 03-442 4620; www.nzski.com; daily lift pass adult/child $97/54) At the Queenstown region's oldest ski field, snow-making systems and treeless slopes provide excellent skiing and snowboarding for all levels. There's night skiing Friday and Saturday from July to September. Shuttles run from Queenstown, 18km away.

The Remarkables (☎03-450 1970, snow-phone 03-442 4615; www.nzski.com; daily lift pass adult/child $97/54) Visually remarkable, this ski field is also near Queenstown (28km away) – shuttle buses run during ski season. It has a good smattering of intermediate, advanced and beginner runs (kids under 10 ski free). Look for the sweeping 'Homeward Bound' run.

Treble Cone (☎03-443 7443, snow-phone 03-443 7444; www.treblecone.com; daily lift pass adult/child $97/49) The highest and largest of the southern lakes ski areas is in a spectacular location 26km from Wanaka, with steep slopes suitable for intermediate to advanced skiers (a rather professional vibe). There are also half-pipes and a terrain park for boarders.

Cardrona (p577) Around 34km from Wanaka, with several high-capacity chairlifts, beginners tows and extreme snowboard terrain (including the 'Heavy Metal' snowboard park). Buses run

HELISKIING

NZ's remote heights are tailor-made for heliskiing, with operators covering a wide off-piste area along the Southern Alps. Costs range from around $825 to $1450 for three to eight runs. HeliPark New Zealand (p48) at Mt Potts is a dedicated heliski park. Resort-run heliskiing is also available at Coronet Peak, Treble Cone, Cardrona, Mt Hutt, Mt Lyford, Ohau and Hanmer Springs. Alternatively, independent operators include the following:

Alpine Heli-Ski (☎03-441 2300; www.alpineheliski.com; Queenstown)

Harris Mountains Heli-ski (☎03-442 6722; www.heliski.co.nz; Queenstown, Wanaka & Aoraki/Mt Cook)

Methven Heliskiing (☎03-302 8108; www.methvenheli.co.nz; Methven)

Over The Top (☎0800 123 359, 03-442 2233; www.flynz.co.nz; Queenstown)

Southern Lakes Heliski (☎03-442 6222; www.heliskinz.com; Queenstown & Wanaka)

Wilderness Heliski (☎03-435 1834; www.wildernessheli.co.nz; Aoraki/Mt Cook)

from Wanaka and Queenstown during ski season. A friendly scene with good services for skiers with disabilities, plus an on-field crèche.

Snow Farm New Zealand (p577) NZ's only commercial Nordic (cross-country) ski area is 35km from Wanaka on the Pisa Range, high above Lake Wanaka. There are 50km of groomed trails, huts with facilities, and thousands of hectares of open snow. Plus full-moon fondue!

South Canterbury

Ohau (☎03-438 9885; www.ohau.co.nz; daily lift pass adult/child $79/32) This commercial ski area is on Mt Sutton, 42km from Twizel. There are plenty of intermediate and advanced runs, excellent snowboarding/cross-country terrain, and a ski lodge.

Mt Dobson (☎03-685 8039; www.dobson.co.nz; daily lift pass adult/child $75/44) The 3km-wide basin here, 26km from Fairlie, caters for learners and intermediates, and has a terrain park and famously dry powder. On a clear day you can see Aoraki/Mt Cook and the Pacific Ocean from the summit.

Fox Peak (☎03-685 8539, snow-phone 03-688 0044; www.foxpeak.co.nz; daily lift pass adult/child $50/10) An affordable club ski area 40km from Fairlie in the Two Thumb Range. Expect rope tows, good cross-country skiing and dorm-style accommodation.

Roundhill (☎021 680 694, snow-phone 03-680 6977; www.roundhill.co.nz; daily lift pass adult/child $75/46) A small field with wide, gentle slopes, perfect for beginners and intermediates. It's 32km from Lake Tekapo village. 'Ski Tekapo!'.

Central Canterbury

Mt Hutt (☎03-302 8811; www.nzski.com; adult/child $95/53; ☺9am-4pm) One of the highest ski areas in the southern hemisphere, as well as one of NZ's best. It's close to Methven; Christchurch is 118km to the west – ski shuttles service both towns. Road access is steep – be extremely cautious in lousy weather. Plenty of beginner, intermediate and advanced slopes, with chairlifts, heliskiing and wide-open faces that are good for learning to snowboard.

HeliPark New Zealand (☎03-303 9060; www.snow.co.nz/helipark; access incl 1st run $325, per subsequent run $75) One of NZ's snow-white gems, sitting on Mt Potts above the headwaters of the Rangitata River, 75km from Methven. It offers a helicopter-accessed skiing experience. Accommodation and meals are available at a lodge 8km from the ski area.

Porters (☎03-318 4002, snow-phone 03-379 9931; www.skiporters.co.nz; daily lift pass adult/child $84/44) The closest commercial ski area to Christchurch (96km away on the Arthur's Pass road). 'Big Mama', at 620m, is one of the steepest runs in NZ, but there are wider, gentler slopes, too. There's a half-pipe for snowboarders, good cross-country runs along the ridge, and lodge accommodation.

Temple Basin (☎03-377 7788; www.temple-basin.co.nz; daily lift pass adult/child $68/37) A club field 4km from the Arthur's Pass township. It's a 40-minute walk uphill from the car park to the ski-area lodges. There's floodlit skiing at night and excellent backcountry runs for snowboarders.

Craigieburn Valley (☎03-318 8711; www.craigieburn.co.nz; daily lift pass adult/child $72/35) Centred on Hamilton Peak, Craigieburn Valley is 40km from Arthur's Pass. It's one of NZ's most challenging club areas, with intermediate and advanced runs (no beginners). Accommmodation in please-do-a-chore lodges.

Broken River (☎03-318 8713; www.broken-river.co.nz; daily lift pass adult/child $70/35) Not far from Craigieburn Valley is another club field, with a 15- to 20-minute walk from the car park and a real sense of isolation. Reliable snow; laid-back vibe. Catered or self-catered lodge accommodation available.

Cheeseman (☎03-344 3247, snow-phone 03-318 8794; www.mtcheeseman.co.nz; daily lift pass adult/child $79/39) Another cool club area in the Craigieburn Range, this family-friendly operation is 99km from Christchurch (the closest club to the city). Based on Mt Cockayne, it's a wide, sheltered basin with drive-to-the-snow road access. Lodge accommodation available.

Mt Olympus (☎03-318 5840; www.mtolympus.co.nz; daily lift pass adult/child $70/35) Difficult to find (but worth the search), 2096m Mt Olympus is 58km from Methven and 12km from Lake Ida. This club area has intermediate and advanced runs, and there are solid cross-country trails to other areas. Access is sometimes 4WD-only, depending on conditions. Lodge accommodation available.

Northern South Island

Hanmer Springs (p486) A commercial field based on Mt St Patrick, 17km from Hanmer Springs township, with mostly intermediate and advanced runs. There are pipe-rides for snowboarders, a new beginners tow and family lodge accommodation.

Mt Lyford (p487) Around 60km from both Hanmer Springs and Kaikoura, and 4km from Mt Lyford village, this is more of a 'resort' than most NZ ski fields, with accommodation and eating options. There's a good mix of runs and a terrain park.

Rainbow (☎03-521 1861, snow-phone 0832 226 05; www.skirainbow.co.nz; daily lift pass adult/child $70/35) Borders Nelson Lakes National Park (100km from Nelson, a similar distance from Blenheim), with varied terrain, minimal crowds and good cross-country skiing. Chains are often required. St Arnaud is the closest town (32km).

Otago

Awakino (☎021 890 584; www.skiawakino.com; daily lift pass adult/child $50/25) A small player in North Otago, but worth a visit for intermediate skiers. Oamaru is 45km away; Omarama is 66km inland. Weekend lodge-and-ski packages available.

Plan Your Trip

Extreme New Zealand

New Zealand's astounding natural assets tempt even the laziest lounge lizards outside to get active. 'Extreme' sports are abundant and supremely well organised here. Mountaineering is part of the national psyche; skydiving, mountain biking, jetboating and rock climbing are well established; and pant-wetting, illogical activities like bungy jumping are everyday pursuits.

On the Land

Bungy Jumping

Bungy jumping was made famous by Kiwi AJ Hackett's 1986 plunge from the Eiffel Tower, after which he teamed up with champion NZ skier Henry van Asch to turn the endeavour into a profitable enterprise. And now you can get crazy too!

Queenstown is a spiderweb of bungy cords, including AJ Hackett's triad: the 134m Nevis Bungy (the highest); the 43m Kawarau Bungy (the original); and the Ledge Bungy (at the highest altitude – diving off a platform 400m above Queenstown). Other South Island bungy jumps include above the Waiau River near Hanmer Springs, and Mt Hutt ski field. On the North Island, head to Taihape, Rotorua, Auckland and Taupo (arguably the prettiest place in NZ to have a near-death experience). Varying the theme, try the 109m-high Shotover Canyon Swing or Nevis Swing in Queenstown, both seriously high rope swings: *swooosh...*

Caving

Caving (aka spelunking) opportunities abound in NZ's honeycombed karst (limestone) regions. You'll find local clubs and

Top Extreme NZ

Best Anti-Gravity Action

Bungy Jumping There are plenty of places in NZ where you can hurl yourself into oblivion attached to a giant rubber band, but why mess around: head straight to Queenstown for the biggest and the best.

Top Five White-Water Rafting Trips

Buller Gorge, Murchison

Tongariro River, Taupo

Kawarau River, Queenstown

Kaituna River, Rotorua

Shotover Canyon, Queenstown

Top Five Mountain-Biking Tracks

Nga Haerenga, New Zealand Cycle Trail, 22 trails nationwide

Redwoods Whakarewarewa Forest, Rotorua

Queenstown Bike Park, Queenstown

Ohakune Old Coach Road, Central Plateau

Hanmer Springs, Canterbury

organised tours around Auckland, Waitomo, Whangarei, Westport and Karamea. Golden Bay also has some mammoth caves. Waitomo is home to 'black-water rafting': like white-water rafting but inside a pitch-black cave! Useful resources:

Wellington Caving Group (www.caving.org.nz)

Auckland Speleo Group (www.asg.org.nz)

New Zealand Speleological Society (www.caves.org.nz)

Hang Gliding & Paragliding

Suspend yourself below an enormous fake wing – either rigid (hang gliding) or frameless (paragliding) – and set sail from a hillside or clifftop. Check out those views! Tandem flights happen in Queenstown, Wanaka, Nelson and Te Mata Peak in Hawke's Bay, or after a half-day of instruction you should be able to do limited solo flights. The **New Zealand Hang Gliding & Paragliding Association** (www.nzhgpa.org.nz) rules the roost.

Horse Trekking

Unlike some other parts of the world where beginners get led by the nose around a paddock, horse trekking in NZ lets you really get out into the countryside, on a farm, in the forest or along a beach. Rides range from one-hour jaunts (from around $60) to week-long, fully catered treks.

On the North Island, Taupo, the Coromandel Peninsula, Waitomo, Pakiri, Ninety Mile Beach, Rotorua, the Bay of Plenty and East Cape are top places for an equine encounter.

On the South Island, all-day horseback adventures happen around Kaikoura, Nelson, Mt Cook, Lake Tekapo, Hanmer Springs, Queenstown, Glenorchy, Methven, Mt Hutt, Cardrona, Te Anau and Dunedin. Treks are also offered alongside Paparoa National Park on the West Coast. For info and operator listings, check out the following:

100% Pure New Zealand (www.newzealand.com)

True NZ Horse Trekking (www.truenz.co.nz/horsetrekking)

Mountain Biking

Aside from the New Zealand Cycle Trail, NZ is laced with quality mountain-biking opportunities. Mountain bikes can be hired in major towns or adventure-sports centres like Queenstown, Wanaka, Nelson, Picton, Taupo and Rotorua, which also have repair shops (as do most NZ towns of any size).

Rotorua's Redwoods Whakarewarewa Forest offers famously good mountain biking, as does the 42 Traverse near National Park Village (close to Tongariro National Park), the Alexandra goldfield trails in Central Otago, the Queenstown Bike Park, and Twizel near Mt Cook. Other North Island hot spots include Woodhill Forest, Waihi, Te Aroha, Te Mata Peak in Hawke's Bay and Makara Peak in Wellington; down south try Waitati Valley and Hayward Point near Dunedin, Canaan Downs near Abel Tasman National Park, Mt Hutt, Methven and the Banks Peninsula.

Not feeling so energetic? Various companies will take you up to the tops of mountains and volcanoes (eg Mt Ruapehu, Christchurch's Port Hills, Cardrona and the Remarkables) so you can hurtle down without the grunt-work of getting to the top first.

Some traditional tramping tracks are open to mountain bikes, but the **DOC** (Department of Conservation; www.doc.govt.nz) has restricted access in many cases due

---

NGA HAERENGA, NEW ZEALAND CYCLE TRAIL

The **Nga Haerenga, New Zealand Cycle Trail** (www.nzcycletrail.com) is a major nationwide project that has been in motion since 2009, expanding and improving NZ's extant network of bike trails. Funded to the tune of around NZ$50 million, the project currently has 22 'Great Rides' up and running across both islands (10 up north, 12 down south), all of which are either fully open to cyclists or have sections open in some capacity. The network is proving to be extremely popular: the West Coast Wilderness Trail and Hauraki Rail Trail are two easy trails winning plenty of fans, as is the Great Taste Trail in Nelson.

See the website for detailed info, maps and updates, including grade and duration info, photos, videos and links to weather and accommodation sites.

to track damage and the inconvenience to walkers, especially at busy times. Never cycle on walking tracks in national parks unless it's permissible (check with DOC), or risk heavy fines and the unfathomable ire of hikers. The Queen Charlotte Track is a good one to bike, but part of it is closed in summer. Resources include the following:

➡ *Classic New Zealand Mountain Bike Rides* (see www.kennett.co.nz) Details short and long rides all over NZ.

➡ *New Zealand Mountain Biker* (www.nzmtbr. co.nz) A mag that comes out every two months.

Cycle Touring

OK, so cruising around the country on a bicycle isn't necessarily 'extreme', but it is super-popular in NZ, especially during summer. Most towns offer bike hire, at either backpacker hostels or specialist bike shops, with bike repair shops in bigger towns.

If you're not after altitude, the Otago Central Rail Trail between Middlemarch and Clyde is a winner. The Little River Rail Trail in Canterbury (en route to Banks Peninsula) is also fabulous. For an off-the-beaten-highway option, try the Southern Scenic Route from Invercargill round Tuatapere to Te Anau. For more detailed touring info, see Lonely Planet's *Cycling New Zealand*.

Online resources:

Independent Cycle Tours (www.cyclehire.co.nz)

Paradise Press (www.paradise-press.co.nz) *Pedallers' Paradise* booklets by Nigel Rushton.

Mountaineering

NZ has a proud mountaineering history – this was, after all, the home of Sir Edmund Hillary (1919–2008), who, along with Tenzing Norgay, was the first to reach the summit of Mt Everest. When he came back down, Sir Ed famously uttered to friend George Lowe, 'Well, George, we knocked the bastard off!'

The Southern Alps are studded with impressive peaks and challenging climbs. The Aoraki/Mt Cook region is outstanding; other mountaineering areas extend along the spine of the South Island from Tapuaenuku (in the Kaikoura Ranges) and the Nelson Lakes peaks in the north to the rugged southern mountains of Fiordland. Another area with climbs for all levels is

Mt Aspiring National Park. To the south in the Forbes Mountains is Mt Earnslaw, flanked by the Rees and Dart Rivers.

The Christchurch-based **New Zealand Alpine Club** (www.alpineclub.org.nz) proffers professional information and produces the annual *NZAC Alpine Journal* and the quarterly *The Climber* magazine. Professional outfits for training, guiding and advice can be found at Wanaka, Aoraki/Mt Cook, Lake Tekapo, and Fox and Franz Josef Glaciers.

Rock Climbing

Time to chalk-up your fingers and don some natty little rubber shoes. On the North Island, popular rock-climbing areas include Auckland's Mt Eden Quarry; Whanganui Bay, Kinloch, Kawakawa Bay and Motuoapa near Lake Taupo; Mangatepopo Valley and Whakapapa Gorge on the Central Plateau; Humphries Castle and Warwick Castle on Mt Taranaki; and Piarere and Wharepapa South in the Waikato.

On the South Island, try the Port Hills area above Christchurch or Castle Hill on the road to Arthur's Pass. West of Nelson, the marble and limestone mountains of Golden Bay and Takaka Hill provide prime climbing. Other options are Long Beach (north of Dunedin), and Mihiwaka and Lovers Leap on the Otago Peninsula.

Raining? You'll find indoor climbing walls all around the country, including at Rotorua, Whangarei, Auckland, Tauranga, Taupo, Wellington, Christchurch and Hamilton.

Climb New Zealand (www.climb.co.nz) has the low-down on the gnarliest overhangs around NZ, plus access and instruction info.

Skydiving

For most first-time skydivers, a tandem skydive will help you make the leap, even if common sense starts to get the better of you. Tandem jumps involve training with a qualified instructor, then experiencing up to 45 seconds of free fall before your chute opens. The thrill is worth every dollar (around $250/300/350 for an 8000/10,000/12,000ft jump; extra for a DVD/photograph). The **New Zealand Parachute Federation** (www.nzpf.org) is the governing body. Ask your operator if it has Civil Aviation Authority (CAA) accreditation before you take the plunge.

On the Water

Jetboating

Hold onto your breakfast: passenger-drenching 360-degree spins ahoy! On the South Island, the Shotover and Kawarau Rivers (Queenstown) and the Buller River (Westport) have fab jetboating. The Dart River (Queenstown) is less travelled but also good, while the Waiatoto River (Haast) and Wilkin River (Mt Aspiring National Park) are superb wilderness experiences. Try also the Kawarau River (Cromwell), Waiau River (Te Anau), Wairaurahiri River (Tuatapere) and the Waiau River at Hanmer Springs.

On the North Island, the Whanganui, Motu, Rangitaiki and Waikato Rivers (Huka Falls) are excellent for jetboating, and there are sprint jets at the Agrodome near Rotorua. Jetboating around the Bay of Islands in Northland is also de rigueur.

Parasailing & Kiteboarding

Parasailing (dangling from a modified parachute that glides over the water while being pulled along by a speedboat or jet

SURFING IN NZ

As a surfer I feel particularly guilty in letting the reader in on a local secret – NZ has a sensational mix of quality waves perfect for beginners and experienced surfers. As long as you're willing to travel off the beaten track, you can score some great, uncrowded waves. The islands of NZ are hit with swells from all points of the compass throughout the year. So, with a little weather knowledge and a little effort, numerous options present themselves. Point breaks, reefs, rocky shelves and hollow sandy beach breaks can all be found – take your pick!

Surfing has become increasingly popular in NZ and today there are surf schools up and running at most premier surf beaches. It's worth doing a bit of research before you arrive: **Surfing New Zealand** (www.surfingnz.co.nz) recommends a number of surf schools on its website. If you're on a surf holiday in NZ, consider purchasing a copy of the *New Zealand Surfing Guide* by Mike Bhana.

Surf.co.nz provides information on many great surf spots, but most NZ beaches hold good rideable breaks. Some of the ones I particularly enjoy:

Waikato Raglan, NZ's most famous surf break and usually the first stop for overseas surfies

Coromandel Whangamata

Bay of Plenty Mt Maunganui, now with a 250m artificial reef that creates huge waves, and Matakana Island

Taranaki Fitzroy Beach, Stent Rd and Greenmeadows Point all lie along the 'Surf Highway'

East Coast Hicks Bay, Gisborne city beaches and Mahia Peninsula

Wellington Region Beaches such as Lyall Bay, Castlepoint and Tora

Marlborough & Nelson Kaikoura Peninsula, Mangamaunu and Meatworks

Canterbury Taylors Mistake and Sumner Bar

Otago Dunedin is a good base for surfing on the South Island, with access to a number of superb breaks, such as St Clair Beach

West Coast Punakaiki and Tauranga Bay

Southland Porridge and Centre Island

NZ water temperatures and climate vary from north to south. For comfort while surfing, wear a wetsuit. In summer on the North Island you can get away with a spring suit and boardies; on the South Island, a 2mm–3mm steamer. In winter on the North Island use a 2mm–3mm steamer, and on the South Island a 3mm–5mm with all the extras.

Josh Kronfeld, surfer and former All Black

Top: Jetboating down Shotover River (p547)

Bottom: Surfer at Manu Bay (p176)

PAUL KENNEDY/GETTY IMAGES ©

ski) is perhaps the easiest way for humans to achieve assisted flight. There are operators in the Bay of Islands, Bay of Plenty, Taupo, Wanaka and Queenstown.

Kiteboarding (aka kitesurfing), where a mini parachute drags you across the ocean on a mini surfboard, can be attempted at Paihia, Tauranga, Mt Maunganui, Raglan, Wellington and Nelson. You can tee up lessons at most of these places, too. Karikari Peninsula near Cape Reinga on NZ's northern tip is a kiteboarding mecca.

Scuba Diving

NZ is prime scuba territory, with warm waters in the north, brilliant sea life and plenty of interesting sites.

Up north, get wet at the Bay of Islands Maritime and Historic Park, Hauraki Gulf Maritime Park, the Bay of Plenty, Great Barrier Island, Goat Island Marine Reserve, the Alderman Islands, Te Tapuwae o Rongokako Marine Reserve near Gisborne, and Sugar Loaf Islands Marine Park near New Plymouth. The Poor Knights Islands near Whangarei are reputed to have the best diving in NZ (with the diveable wreck of the Greenpeace flagship *Rainbow Warrior* nearby). Stay tuned to see whether the MV *Rena,* grounded off Tauranga in 2011, will become a dive site.

Down south, the Marlborough Sounds Maritime Park hosts the *Mikhail Lermontov,* the largest diveable cruise-ship wreck in the world. In Fiordland head for Dusky Sound, Milford Sound and Doubtful Sound, which offer amazingly clear pseudo-deep-water conditions not far below the surface. Invercargill, with its Antarctic waters, also has a diving club.

Expect to pay anywhere from $180 for a short, introductory, pool-based scuba course, and around $600 for a four-day, PADI-approved, ocean dive course. One-off organised boat- and land-based dives start at around $170. Resources include:

New Zealand Underwater Association (www. nzu.org.nz)

Dive New Zealand (www.divenewzealand.com)

Sea Kayaking

Sea kayaking is a fantastic way to see the coast, and get close to wildlife.

Highly rated sea-kayaking areas in NZ's north include the Hauraki Gulf (particular-

ly off Waiheke and Great Barrier Islands), the Bay of Islands and Coromandel Peninsula; in the south, try the Marlborough Sounds (Picton) and along the coast of Abel Tasman National Park. Fiordland is also a hot spot, with a heap of tour operators in Te Anau, Milford, Doubtful Sound and Manapouri. Also try the Otago Peninsula, Stewart Island and Kaikoura down south; or Waitemata Harbour, Hahei, Raglan and East Cape up north. Useful resources:

Kiwi Association of Sea Kayakers (www.kask. org.nz)

Sea Kayak Operators Association of New Zealand (www.skoanz.org.nz)

White-Water Rafting, Kayaking & Canoeing

There are almost as many white-water rafting and kayaking possibilities as there are rivers in NZ, and there's no shortage of companies to get you into the rapids Rivers are graded from I to VI, with VI meaning 'unraftable'. On the rougher stretches there's usually a minimum age of 12 or 13 years.

Popular South Island rafting rivers include the Shotover and Kawarau Rivers (Queenstown), Rangitata River (Christchurch), Buller River (Murchison) and the Arnold and Waiho Rivers on the West Coast. The grading of the Shotover Canyon varies from III to V+, depending on the time of year. The Kawarau River is rated IV; the Rangitata River has everything from I to V.

On the North Island try the Rangitaiki, Wairoa, Motu, Mokau, Mohaka, Waitomo, Tongariro and Rangitikei Rivers. There's also the Kaituna Cascades near Rotorua, with a 7m drop at Okere Falls.

Canoeing is so popular on the North Island's Whanganui River that it's been designated one of NZ's 'Great Walks'! You can also dip your paddle into northern lakes like Lake Taupo and Lake Rotorua, as well as freshwater lakes on the South Island. Many backpacker hostels close to canoe-friendly waters have Canadian canoes and kayaks for hire (or for free), and loads of commercial operators run guided trips.

Resources include:

New Zealand Rafting Association (www.nz-rafting.co.nz)

Whitewater NZ (www.rivers.org.nz)

New Zealand Kayak (see www.kayaknz.co.nz)

Regions at a Glance

Auckland

Eating & Drinking
Geology
Coastline

Restaurants, Bars & Cafes
As well as having the lion's share of the nation's best restaurants, Auckland has excellent markets, a plethora of cheap Asian eateries, a lively cafe and bar scene, and wine regions on three of its flanks. And coffee culture is booming (don't tell anyone from Wellington...).

Volcanic Viewpoints
Auckland is a global hot spot: over 50 separate volcanoes have formed this unique topography – and the next one could pop up at any time. Take a hike up one of the dormant cones dotting the landscape for a high, wide and handsome city panorama.

Beaches
From the calm, child-friendly bays facing the Hauraki Gulf to the black-sand surf beaches of the west coast, to the breathtaking coastline of the offshore islands, beach-lovers are spoilt for choice here.

p60

Bay of Islands & Northland

Coastline
Wilderness
History

Beaches & Bays
Bay after beautiful bay lines Northland's east coast, making it a favourite destination for families, surfers and fishing enthusiasts. To the west, windswept beaches stretch for kilometres, in places forming towering sand dunes.

Ancient Forests
Kauri forests once blanketed the entire north, and where the giants remain, particularly in the Waipoua Forest, they're an imposing sight.

Kerikeri & Waitangi
New Zealand was settled top down by both Maori and Europeans, with missionaries erecting the country's oldest surviving buildings in Kerikeri. In nearby Waitangi, the treaty that founded the modern nation was first signed.

p121

Waikato & the Coromandel Peninsula

Coastline
Towns
Caves

Beaches & Surf
Around Raglan you'll find safe swimming and world-class surf at legendary Manu Bay. Beaches on the Coromandel are extremely popular in summer, but splendid isolation can still be found.

That Small-town Vibe
Te Aroha, Cambridge, Matamata and Raglan have great pubs, cafes, restaurants and friendly locals, while Thames and Coromandel Town display their historic gold-rush roots.

Waitomo Caves
Don't miss blackwater rafting (along underground rivers) at Waitomo Caves, NZ's most staggering cave site. Or just float lazily through amazing grottoes of glowworms.

p163

Taranaki & Whanganui

Wilderness
Cities
Coastline

National Parks

Steeped in Maori lore, Whanganui National Park is one of NZ's most isolated and interesting parks. Lording over New Plymouth, Mt Taranaki (Egmont National Park) is picture-perfect peak fabulous tramping.

Underrated Hubs

New Plymouth, Whanganui and Palmerston North are mid-sized cities usually overlooked by travellers. But stay a day: you'll find fantastic restaurants, hip bars, great coffee, wonderful museums and friendly folk.

Surf & Sand

Hit Surf Hwy 45 for black-sand beaches and gnarly breaks. Whanganui offers remote, storm-buffered beaches, while the Horowhenua District has acres of empty brown sand.

p213

Taupo & the Central Plateau

Wilderness
Scenery
Outdoor
Activities

Lakes & Rivers

NZ's mightiest river (the Waikato) is born from NZ's greatest lake (Taupo): aquatic pursuits in picturesque settings abound (kayaking, sailing, fishing). The water is famously chilly, but hot springs bubble up on the lakeside and riverbank.

Epic Landscapes

The three steaming, smoking, occasionally erupting volcanoes at the heart of the North Island are an imposing sight, the focus of skiing in winter and tramping the rest of the year.

Extreme Taupo

Skydiving, bungy jumping, whitewater rafting, jetboating, mountain biking, wakeboarding, parasailing, skiing – you want thrills, you got 'em.

p246

Rotorua & the Bay of Plenty

Geothermal
Activity
Indigenous
Culture
Activities

Volcanic Hubbub

The Rotorua landscape is littered with geysers, geothermal vents, hot mineral springs and boiling mud pools. NZ's only active volcano, Whakaari (White Island), is 48km off the coast of Whakatane.

Maori Cultural Experiences

Engage with Maori culture in Rotorua: cultural experiences for travellers include traditional dance and musical performances, *haka* (war dances) and *hangi* (Maori feasts).

Outdoor Sports

Try paragliding, surfing, skydiving, zorbing, jetboating, blokarting, white-water rafting, mountain biking, kayaking...or just have a swim at the beach.

p273

The East Coast

Coastline
Wine
Architecture

Coastal Scenery

Follow in the footsteps (or rather wake) of early Maori and James Cook along this stretch of coastline, home to the East Cape Lighthouse and Cape Kidnappers' gaggling gannet colony.

Gisborne & Hawke's Bay Wine Regions

Sip your way through Gisborne's bright chardonnays then head to Hawke's Bay for seriously good Bordeaux-style reds and some excellent winery dining.

Art Deco Napier

Napier's art-deco town centre is a magnet for architecture lovers, the keenest of whom time their visit for the annual Art Deco Weekend, an extravaganza of music, wine, cars and costume.

p314

Wellington Region

Arts
Eating & Drinking
Nightlife

Museums & Galleries

Crow-barred into the city centre is a significant collation of quality display spaces, including the highly interactive Te Papa museum and internationally flavoured City Gallery.

Cafe Culture

With more than a dozen roasters and scores of hip cafes, Wellington remains the coffee capital of NZ. Get a hit from one of the best: Havana Coffee Works or Fidel's.

Bars

Between the boho bars around Cuba St and Courtenay Pl's glitzy drinking dens, you should find enough to keep you entertained until sun-up.

p346

Marlborough & Nelson

Wilderness
Wine
Wildlife

National Parks

Not satisfied with just one national park, the Nelson region has three: Nelson Lakes, Kahurangi and Abel Tasman. You could tramp in all three over a week.

Marlborough Wine Region

Bobbing in Marlborough's sea of sauvignon blanc, riesling, pinot noir and bubbly are barrel-loads of quality cellar-door experiences and some fine regional food.

Kaikoura

The top of the South Island is home to myriad creatures, both in the water and on the wing. Kaikoura is a great one-stop shop: spot a whale or swim with dolphins and seals.

p378

The West Coast

Wilderness
Outdoor Activities
History

Natural Wonders

With around 90% of its territory lying within the conservation estate, the West Coast is flush with natural wonders. Don't miss Oparara's famous arch and Punakaiki's Pancake Rocks.

Tramping

The West Coast offers tracks from an easy hour through to hard-core epics. Old mining and milling routes like Charming Creek Walkway and Mahinapua Walkway entice beginners and history buffs.

Pioneering Heritage

The West Coast's pioneering heritage comes vividly to life at places like Denniston, Shantytown, Reefton and Jackson's Bay.

p423

Christchurch & Canterbury

History
Outdoor Activities
Scenery

Christchurch & Akaroa

Earthquakes have damaged Christchurch's heritage, but the Canterbury Museum, Botanic Gardens and New Brighton St showcase the city's history. Akaroa proudly celebrates its French heritage.

Tramping & Kayaking

Explore alpine valleys around Arthur's Pass, kayak with dolphins on Akaroa Harbour, or visit Aoraki/Mt Cook National Park for tramping and kayaking.

Banks Peninsula & the Southern Alps

Descend from Banks Peninsula's Summit Rd to explore hidden bays and coves, and experience nature's grand scale: the river valleys, soaring peaks and glaciers of the Southern Alps.

p456

Dunedin & Otago

Wildlife
Wine
History

Birds, Seals & Sea Lions

Otago Peninsula's wild menagerie – seals, sea lions and penguins – patrol the rugged coastline; while rocky Taiaroa Head is the planet's only mainland breeding location for the magnificent royal albatross.

Bannockburn & Waitaki Valley

Barrel into the craggy valleys of Bannockburn for excellent vineyard restaurants and the world's best pinot noir, or delve into the up-and-coming Waitaki Valley wine scene for riesling and pinot gris.

Victoriana

Explore the arty and storied streets of Dunedin, or escape by foot or penny-farthing bicycle into the heritage ambience of Oamaru's Victorian Precinct.

p509

Queenstown & Wanaka

Outdoor Activities
Scenery
Wine

Extreme Queenstown

Nowhere else on earth offers so many adventurous activities: bungy jumping, river rafting and mountain biking only scratch Queenstown's adrenaline-fuelled surface.

Mountains & Lakes

Queenstown's photogenic combination of Lake Wakatipu and the soaring Remarkables is a real jaw-dropper. Or venture into prime NZ wilderness around Glenorchy and Mt Aspiring National Park.

Southern Wineries

Start with lunch at Amisfield Winery's excellent restaurant, then explore the Gibbston subregion and finish with a riesling tasting at Rippon, overlooking gorgeous Lake Wanaka.

p542

Fiordland & Southland

Scenery
Wilderness
Outdoor Activities

Epic Landscapes

The star of the show is remarkable Milford Sound, but take time to explore the rugged Catlins coast or experience the remote, end-of-the-world appeal of Stewart Island.

National Parks

Fiordland National Park comprises much of NZ's precious Southwest New Zealand (Te Wahipounamu) World Heritage Area. Further south, Rakiura National Park showcases Stewart Island's beauty.

Tramping & Sea Kayaking

Test yourself by tramping the Milford or Tuatapere Hump Ridge Tracks, or negotiate a sea kayak around glorious Doubtful Sound.

p579

On the Road

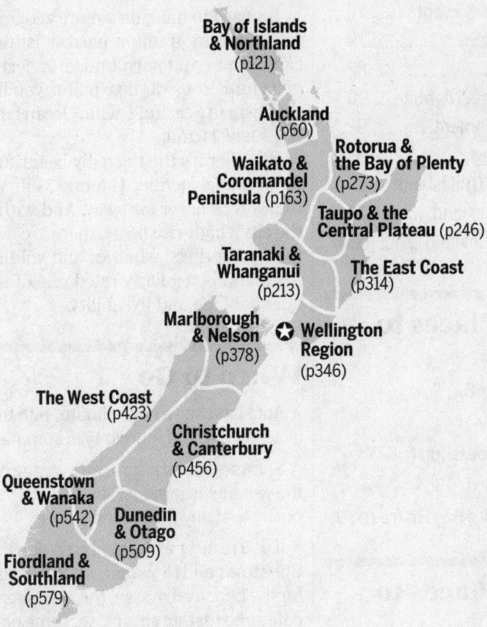

Bay of Islands & Northland
(p121)

Auckland
(p60)

Rotorua & the Bay of Plenty
(p273)

Waikato & Coromandel Peninsula (p163)

Taupo & the Central Plateau (p246)

Taranaki & Whanganui
(p213)

The East Coast
(p314)

Marlborough & Nelson
(p378)

✪ **Wellington Region**
(p346)

The West Coast
(p423)

Christchurch & Canterbury
(p456)

Queenstown & Wanaka
(p542)

Dunedin & Otago
(p509)

Fiordland & Southland
(p579)

Auckland

09 / POP 1.42 MILLION

Includes ➡

Sights 62
Activities...................... 72
Tours 74
Festivals & Events 76
Sleeping....................... 79
Eating 82
Drinking & Nightlife 90
Entertainment.............. 92
Shopping 93
Hauraki Gulf Islands.... 97
West Auckland............110
North Auckland 115

Best Places to Eat

➡ Depot (p83)

➡ Ima (p84)

➡ Blue Breeze Inn (p87)

➡ Little Bird (p85)

➡ St Heliers Bay Bistro (p89)

Best Places to Stay

➡ Hotel de Brett (p79)

➡ Auckland Takapuna Oaks (p82)

➡ Verandahs (p80)

➡ 23 Hepburn (p80)

Why Go?

Paris may be the city of love, but Auckland is the city of many lovers, according to its Maori name, Tamaki Makaurau. Those lovers so desired this place that they fought over it for centuries.

It's hard to imagine a more geographically blessed city. Its two harbours frame a narrow isthmus punctuated by volcanic cones and surrounded by fertile farmland. From any of its numerous vantage points you'll be surprised how close the Tasman Sea and Pacific Ocean come to kissing and forming a new island.

Whether it's the ruggedly beautiful west-coast surf beaches, or the glistening Hauraki Gulf with its myriad islands, the water's never far away. And within an hour's drive from the city's high-rise heart, there are dense tracts of rainforest, thermal springs, wineries and wildlife reserves. No wonder Auckland is regularly rated one of the world's top cities for quality of life and liveability.

When to Go

➡ Auckland has a mild climate, with the occasional chilly frost in winter and high humidity in summer.

➡ Summer months have an average of eight days of rain, but the weather is famously fickle, with 'four seasons in one day' possible at any time of the year.

➡ If you're after a big-city buzz, don't come between Christmas and New Year, when Aucklanders desert the city for the beach en masse; the sights remain open but many cafes and restaurants close, some not surfacing again until well into January.

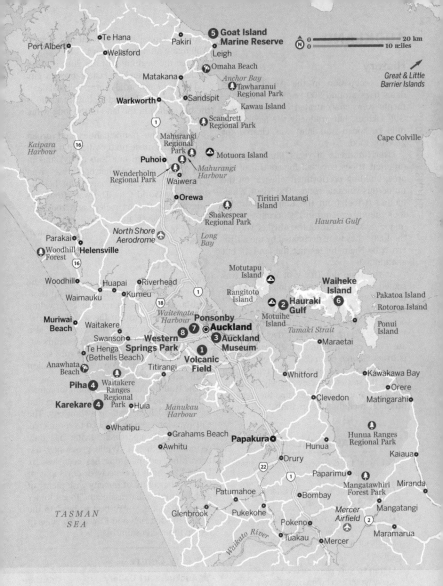

Auckland Highlights

1 Going with the flows, exploring Auckland's fascinating **volcanic field** (p73)

2 Getting back to nature on the island sanctuaries of the beautiful **Hauraki Gulf** (p97)

3 Being awed by the Maori *taonga* (treasures) of the **Auckland Museum** (p68).

4 Going west to the mystical and treacherous black sands of **Karekare** (p111) and **Piha** (p112)

5 Swimming with the fishes at **Goat Island Marine Reserve** (p120)

6 Schlepping around world-class wineries and beaches on **Waiheke Island** (p98)

7 Buzzing around the cafes, restaurants and bars of **Ponsonby** (p85)

8 Soaking up the Polynesian vibe at the **Pasifika Festival** (p77), held in March at Western Springs Park

AUCKLAND

History

Maori occupation in the Auckland area dates back around 800 years. Initial settlements were concentrated on the Hauraki Gulf islands, but gradually the fertile isthmus beckoned and land was cleared for growing food.

Over hundreds of years Tamaki's many different tribes wrestled for control of the area, building *pa* (fortified villages) on the numerous volcanic cones. The Ngati Whatua *iwi* (tribe) from the Kaipara Harbour took the upper hand in 1741, occupying the major *pa* sites. During the Musket Wars of the 1820s they were decimated by the northern tribe Ngapuhi, leaving the land all but abandoned.

At the time the Treaty of Waitangi was signed in 1840, Governor Hobson had his base in the Bay of Islands. When Ngati Whatua chief Te Kawau offered 3000 acres of land for sale on the northern edge of the Waitemata Harbour, Hobson decided to create a new capital, naming it after one of his patrons, George Eden (Earl of Auckland).

Beginning with just a few tents on a beach, the settlement grew quickly, and soon the port was busy exporting the region's produce, including kauri timber. However,

---

ESSENTIAL AUCKLAND

Eat Amid the diverse and cosmopolitan scene of Ponsonby Central

Drink West Auckland craft beers at Hallertau in Riverhead

Read *Under the Mountain* (1979) – Maurice Gee's teenage tale of slimy things lurking under Auckland's volcanoes

Listen to *Pure Heroine* (2013) – savvy lyrics and beats from Devonport's very own Lorde

Watch *Matariki* (2010) – five interwoven multicultural stories set in South Auckland

Festival Pasifika

Online www.aucklandnz.com; www.lonelyplanet.com/new-zealand/auckland

Area code ✆09

---

it lost its capital status to centrally located Wellington after just 25 years.

Since the beginning of the 20th century Auckland has been NZ's fastest-growing city and its main industrial centre. Political deals may be done in Wellington, but Auckland is the big smoke in the land of the long white cloud.

In 2010 the municipalities and urban districts that made up the Auckland Region were merged into one 'super city', and in 2011 the newly minted metropolis was given a buff and shine to prepare it for hosting the Rugby World Cup. The waterfront was redeveloped, the art gallery and zoo were given a makeover, and a swag of new restaurants and bars popped up – leaving a more vibrant city in the cup's wake.

◉ Sights

Auckland is a city of volcanoes, with the ridges of lava flows forming its main thoroughfares and its many cones providing islands of green within the sea of suburbs. As well as being by far the largest, it's also the most multicultural of New Zealand's cities. A sizeable Asian community rubs shoulders with the biggest Polynesian population of any city in the world.

The traditional Kiwi aspiration for a freestanding house on a quarter-acre section has resulted in a vast, sprawling city. The CBD was long ago abandoned to commerce, and inner-city apartment living has only recently caught on. While geography has been kind, city planning has been less so. Unbridled and ill-conceived development has left the centre of the city with plenty of architectural embarrassments. To get under Auckland's skin, you're best to head to the streets of Victorian and Edwardian villas in its hip inner-city suburbs.

◉ City Centre

★ **Auckland Art Gallery**   GALLERY
(Map p66; www.aucklandartgallery.com; cnr Kitchener & Wellesley Sts; admission varies for special exhibitions; ☉10am-5pm) **FREE** Following a significant 2011 refurbishment, Auckland's premier art repository now has a stunning glass-and-wood atrium grafted onto its 1887 French-chateau frame. Along with important works by Pieter Bruegel the Younger, Guido Reni, Picasso, Cézanne, Gauguin and Matisse, it also showcases the best of NZ art. Highlights include the intimate 19th-

AUCKLAND IN...

Two Days

Start by acquainting yourself with the inner city. Take our **walking tour** (p75) from Karangahape Rd (K Rd) to the Wynyard Quarter, stopping along the way to have at least a quick whiz around the NZ section of the **Auckland Art Gallery**. Catch a ferry to **Devonport**, head up North Head and cool down at **Cheltenham Beach** (weather and tide permitting), before ferrying back to the city for dinner.

On day two, head up **One Tree Hill**, wander around **Cornwall Park** and then visit the **Auckland Museum** and **Domain**. Take a trip along **Tamaki Drive**, stopping at **Bastion** or **Achilles Point** to enjoy the harbour views. Spend the evening dining and bar hopping in **Ponsonby**.

Four Days

On the third day, get out on the **Hauraki Gulf**. Catch the ferry to **Waiheke Island** and divide your time between the beaches and the wineries.

For your final day, head west. Grab breakfast in **Titirangi** before exploring the **Waitakere Ranges Regional Park**, **Karekare** and **Piha**. Freshen up for a night on the town on **K Rd** or **Britomart**.

---

century portraits of tattooed Maori subjects by Charles Goldie, and the starkly dramatic text-scrawled canvasses of Colin McCahon. Free tours depart from the main entrance daily at 11.30am and 1.30pm.

Albert Park
PARK

(Map p66) On the city's eastern flank, Albert Park is a Victorian formal garden bordering **Auckland University**'s campus, and incorporates a row of stately Victorian merchant houses (Princes St) and Old **Government House** (Map p66; Waterloo Quadrant). The latter was the colony's seat of power from 1856 until 1865, when Wellington became the capital. The stately **University Clock Tower** (1926) has influences from art nouveau (the incorporation of NZ flora and fauna into the decoration), and the Chicago School.

At the centre of the campus is a wall of the Albert Barracks (1847), a fortification that enclosed 9 hectares, including Albert Park, during the New Zealand Wars.

Sky Tower
LANDMARK

(Map p66; www.skycityauckland.co.nz; cnr Federal & Victoria Sts; adult/child \$28/11; ⊙8.30am-10.30pm) 🖋 The impossible-to-miss Sky Tower looks like a giant hypodermic giving a fix to the heavens. Spectacular lighting renders it space-age at night and the colours change for special events. At 328m it is the southern hemisphere's tallest structure. A lift takes you up to the observation decks in 40 stomach-lurching seconds; look down through the glass floor panels if you're after an extra kick. Visit at sunset and have a drink in the Sky Lounge Cafe & Bar.

The Sky Tower is also home to the Sky-Walk (p73) and SkyJump (p73).

Civic Theatre
ARCHITECTURE

(Map p66; www.civictheatre.co.nz; cnr Queen & Wellesley Sts) The 'mighty Civic' (1929) is one of seven 'atmospheric theatres' remaining in the world and a fine survivor from cinema's Golden Age. The auditorium has lavish Moorish decoration, and the starlit southern-hemisphere sky in the ceiling (complete with cloud projections) gives the illusion of being under a night sky. It's mainly used for touring musicals, international concerts and film-festival screenings.

Even if nothing is scheduled, try and sneak a peek at the foyer, an Indian indulgence with elephants and monkeys hanging from every conceivable fixture. Buddhas were planned to decorate the street frontage but were considered too risqué at the time – they chose neoclassical naked boys instead!

St Patrick's Cathedral
CHURCH

(Map p66; www.stpatricks.org.nz; 43 Wyndham St; ⊙7am-7pm) Auckland's Catholic cathedral (1907) is one of the city's loveliest buildings. Polished wood and Belgian stained glass lend warmth to the interior of the majestic Gothic Revival church. There's a historical display in the old confessional on the left-hand side.

Auckland

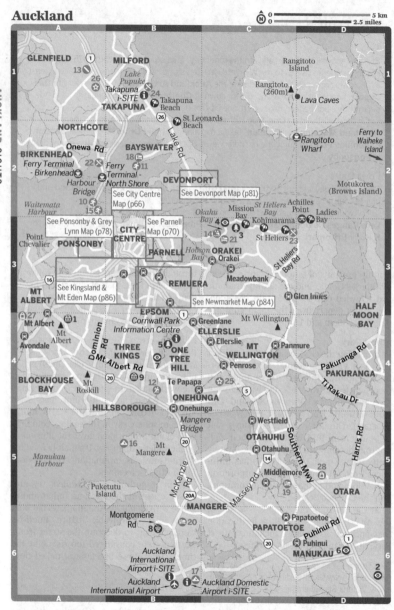

◉ Britomart, Viaduct
Harbour & Wynyard Quarter

Stretching for only a small grid of blocks above the train station, Britomart is a compact enclave of historic buildings and new developments that has been transformed into one of the city's best eating, drinking and shopping precincts. Most of Auckland's top fashion designers have recently decamped to the Britomart area from further uptown in High St.

Auckland

◉ Sights
1 Alberton A4
2 Auckland Botanic Gardens................D6
3 Bastion Point.....................................C3
4 Kelly Tarlton's Sealife
   Aquarium..C3
5 One Tree Hill......................................B4
6 Rainbow's End...................................D6
7 Stardome Observatory.......................B4
8 Villa Maria Estate...............................B6
9 Wallace Arts Centre...........................B4

◉ Activities, Courses & Tours
10 Auckland Bridge Climb &
   Bungy...A2
11 CharterLink......................................B2
12 Coast to Coast Walkway....................B4
13 Dive Centre......................................A1
14 Fergs Kayaks....................................C3
15 Gulfwind...A2
   Penny Whiting Sailing School ....(see 15)

◉ Sleeping
16 Ambury Regional Park.......................B5
17 Auckland Airport Campervan
   Park...B6
18 Auckland Takapuna Oaks...................B2
19 Grange Lodge....................................C5
20 Jet Park...B6
21 Nautical Nook...................................C3

◉ Eating
22 Engine Room.....................................A2
23 St Heliers Bay Bistro..........................C3
   Takapuna Beach Cafe...............(see 24)
24 The Commons....................................B1

◉ Entertainment
25 Mt Smart Stadium.............................C4
26 North Shore Events Centre................A1

◉ Shopping
27 Avondale Sunday Market....................A4
28 Otara Market.....................................D5

Once a busy commercial port, the Viaduct Harbour was given a major makeover for the 1999/2000 and 2003 America's Cup yachting events. It's now a fancy dining and boozing precinct, and guaranteed to have at least a slight buzz any night of the week. Historical plaques, public sculpture and the chance to gawk at millionaires' yachts make it a diverting place for a stroll.

Connected to the Viaduct by a raiseable bridge, Wynyard Quarter opened in advance of another sporting tournament, 2011's Rugby World Cup. With its public plazas, waterfront cafes, events centre, fish market and children's playground, it has quickly become Auckland's favourite new place to promenade. At the adjacent Silo Park (p79) area, free outdoor Friday night movies and weekend markets have become summertime institutions, and new restaurants have further boosted the precinct's culinary buzz.

Voyager – New Zealand
Maritime Museum   MUSEUM
(Map p66; ☑09-373 0800; www.maritimemuseum.co.nz; 149-159 Quay St; admission adult/child $17/8.50, with harbour cruise $29/14.50; ⊙9am-5pm, free guided tours at 10.30am & 1pm) This museum traces NZ's seafaring history, from Maori voyaging canoes to the America's Cup. Recreations include a tilting 19th-century steerage-class cabin and a 1950s beach store and bach (holiday home). *Blue Water Black Magic* is a tribute to Sir Peter Blake, the Whitbread-Round-the-World and America's Cup–winning yachtsman who was murdered in 2001 on an environmental monitoring trip in the Amazon. There are also optional one-hour harbour cruises on the *Ted Ashby,* a ketch-rigged sailing scow.

Auckland Fish Market   MARKET
(Map p66; www.aucklandfishmarket.co.nz; 22-32 Jellicoe St; ⊙6am-7pm) Early-morning auctions combine with fish shops, cafes and restaurants, and a seafood-cooking school.

◉ Mt Eden

Mt Eden   VOLCANO
(Maungawhau; Map p86; ⊙road access 7am-11pm) From the top of Auckland's highest volcanic cone (196m) the entire isthmus and both harbours are laid bare. The symmetrical crater (50m deep) is known as Te Ipu Kai a Mataaho (the Food Bowl of Mataaho, the god of things hidden in the ground) and is highly *tapu* (sacred). Do not enter it, but feel free to explore the remainder of the mountain. The remains of *pa* terraces and food storage pits are clearly visible.

Drive to the top or join the fitness freaks jogging or trudging up. Tour buses are banned from the summit, but shuttles will transport infirm passengers to the top from the car park on the lower slopes.

Eden Garden   GARDENS
(Map p84; www.edengarden.co.nz; 24 Omana Ave; adult/child $8/6; ⊙9am-4pm) On Mt Eden's eastern slopes, and noted for its camellias, rhododendrons and azaleas.

City Centre

0.25 miles
500 m

Waitemata Harbour

Bledisloe Wharf
Bledisloe Terminal

Captain Cook Wharf
Marsden Wharf
Queens Wharf

Princes Wharf
Hobson Wharf
Viaduct Harbour

Wynyard Wharf
Ferry to Great Barrier Island
Wynyard Quarter

Viaduct Events Centre
Karanga Plaza Kiosk

DOC Auckland Information Centre
i-SITE

Ferry Building
Fullers Cruise
Pier 2

Queen Elizabeth Sq
Britomart

Victoria Park
Victoria Park Market

Sky City Coach Terminal
SkyCity
i-SITE

Jellicoe St
Daldy St
Madden St
Gaunt St
Beaumont St
Halsey St
Fanshawe St
Customs St W
Market Pl
Sturdee St
Hobson St
Nelson St
Wyndham St
Victoria St
Wellesley St
Sale St
Franklin Rd

Quay St
Tyler St
Galway St
Gore St
Commerce St
Customs St
Fort St
Shortland St
Chancery St
High St
Victoria St
Elliot St
Albert St
Federal St
Queen St
Swanson St
Wolfe St
Mills La
Vulcan La
Durham St
Kingston St
Wellesley St
Emily Pl
Beach Rd
Bankside St
Kitchener St
Bowen Ave
Bowen La
Princes St
Waterloo Qd
Parliament St
Anzac Ave
Eden Cres
Short St
Te Taoa Cres
Mathuhu Cres
Tangihua St
Albert Park

9 14 13 11 8 10 15 53 62 65 40 48 81 87 63 68 34 26 55 85 84 82 22 46 42 41 61 44 56 50 21 86 12 38 47 16 6 17 78 54 43 39 36 59 33 3 80 29 23 28 27 5 45

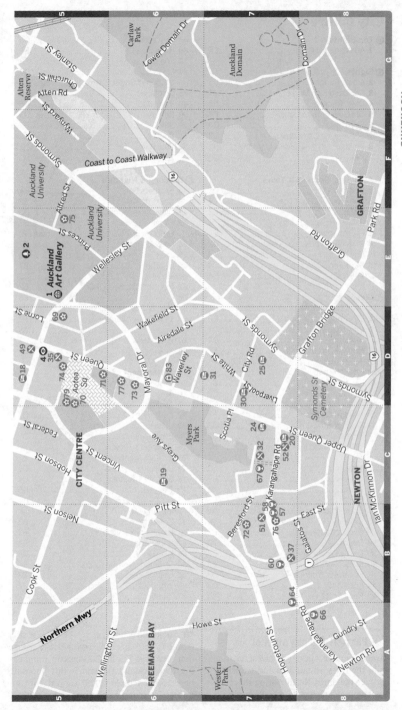

CITY CENTRE

FREEMANS BAY

NEWTON

GRAFTON

Northern Mwy

Cook St

Nelson St

Hobson St

Federal St

Vincent St

Greys Ave

Pitt St

Wellington St

Howe St

Hopetoun St

Karangahape Rd

Gundry St

Newton Rd

Ian McKinnon Dr

Galatos St

East St

Karangahape Rd

Beresford St

Scotia Pl

Myers Park

Western Park

Mayoral Dr

Queen St

Aotea Sq

Lorne St

Wakefield St

Airedale St

Waverley St

White St

City Rd

Liverpool St

Symonds St

Upper Queen St

Symonds St

Symonds St Cemetery

Grafton Bridge

Grafton Rd

Park Rd

Domain Dr

Auckland Domain

Lower Domain Dr

Carlaw Park

Coast to Coast Walkway

Wynyard St

Alten Rd

Churchill St

Stanley St

Alten Reserve

Symonds St

Princes St

Alfred St

Wellesley St

Auckland University

Auckland University

Auckland Art Gallery

1 Auckland Art Gallery

2

City Centre

◎ **Top Sights**
1 Auckland Art Gallery E5

◎ **Sights**
2 Albert Park...E5
3 Auckland Fish Market...........................B1
4 Civic Theatre D5
5 Old Government House F4
6 Sky Tower D4
7 St Patrick's Cathedral D3
8 Voyager – New Zealand Maritime
   Museum D2

🎫 **Activities, Courses & Tours**
9 360 Discovery D2
10 Auckland Jet Boat Tours C1
11 Fullers..E2
12 G-MAX Reverse Bungy.........................D4
13 GreatSights..E2
14 Riverhead Ferry...................................D2
15 Sail NZ D2
16 SkyJump C4
17 SkyWalk C4

🛏 **Sleeping**
18 Attic Backpackers D5
19 City Lodge C6
20 City Travellers C7
21 CityLife D4
22 Hotel de Brett......................................E3
23 Jucy Hotel..F3
24 Kiwi International Hotel........................C7
25 Langham...D7
26 Nomads Auckland E3
27 Quadrant..F4
28 Waldorf Celestion F3
29 Waldorf Stadium..................................G3
30 YHA Auckland City...............................D7
31 YHA Auckland International.................D7

🍴 **Eating**
32 Alleluya C7
33 Baduzzi...B1
34 Box of Bird E3
35 Burgerfuel D5
36 Clooney A4
37 Coco's Cantina B7
38 Depot..D4
39 Dida's Freemans Bay B4
40 Ebisu...F2
41 Federal & Wolfe....................................D3
42 Food Alley D3
43 Food Truck Garage...............................C4

44 Grove..D3
45 Hansan E4
46 Ima...E3
47 Masu...D4
   O'Connell Street Bistro................(see 22)
48 Ortolana...E2
49 Remedy...D5
50 Revive...D3
51 Satya..B7
52 Scullery...C7
53 Soul Bar..D2
   Zap 4 ....(see 34)

🍷 **Drinking & Nightlife**
54 Brothers Beer B4
55 Cassette Nine E3
56 Ding Dong Lounge................................D3
57 Family...B7
   Hotel de Brett...............................(see 22)
58 Ink & Coherent.....................................B7
59 Jack Tar B1
60 Legend B7
61 Mo's..D3
62 Northern Steamship Co. E2
63 Orleans...E3
64 Thirsty Dog..B7
65 Tyler Street Garage.............................F2
66 Urge..A8
67 Wine Cellar & Whammy Bar................C7
68 Xuxu E2

🎭 **Entertainment**
69 Academy Cinemas.................................D5
70 Aotea Centre..D5
71 Auckland Town Hall D5
72 Centurian B7
73 Classic Comedy Club............................D6
74 Event Cinemas.....................................D5
75 Maidment Theatre...............................E5
76 NZ Film Archives B7
77 Q Theatre..D6
78 SkyCity Theatre....................................C4
79 Ticketek D5

🛍 **Shopping**
80 Countdown..G3
81 Karen Walker..E2
82 Pauanesia...E4
83 Real Groovy..D6
84 Strangely Normal E4
85 Unity Books E3
86 Whitcoulls...D4
87 Zambesi...F2

⊙ Parnell & Newmarket

Parnell is one of Auckland's oldest areas, and amid the cafes, restaurants and retailers are heritage buildings. Neighbouring Newmarket is a shopping precinct with boutiques.

★ **Auckland Museum**   MUSEUM
(Map p70; ☎ 09-309 0443; www.aucklandmuseum.
com; adult/child $25/10; ⊙ 10am-5pm) Dominating the Auckland Domain is this imposing neoclassical temple (1929) capped with an impressive copper-and-glass dome (2007).

The displays of Pacific Island and Maori artefacts on the ground floor are essential viewing. Highlights include a 25m war canoe and an extant carved meeting house (remove your shoes before entering). There's also a fascinating display on Auckland's volcanic field, including an eruption simulation, and the upper floors showcase military displays, fulfilling the building's dual role as a war memorial.

Hour-long museum highlights tours (included with admission) depart at 10.45am, 12.45pm and 2.15pm. Admission options incorporating Maori culture and performances are also available.

Auckland's main Anzac commemorations take place at dawn on 25th of April at the cenotaph in the museum's forecourt.

Auckland Domain   PARK

(Map p70) Covering about 80 hectares, this green swathe contains sports fields, interesting sculpture, formal gardens, wild corners and the Wintergarden (Map p70; www.wintergardenpavilion.co.nz; ⊘9am-5.30pm Mon-Sat, 9am-7.30pm Sun Nov-Mar, 9am-4.30pm Apr-Oct) FREE, with its fernery, tropical house, cool house, cute cat statue, coffee kiosk and neighbouring cafe. The mound in the centre of the park is all that remains of Pukekaroa, one of Auckland's volcanoes. At its humble peak, a totara surrounded by a palisade honours the first Maori king.

Holy Trinity Cathedral   CHURCH

(Map p70; www.holy-trinity.org.nz; Parnell Rd; ⊘10am-3pm) Auckland's Anglican cathedral is a hodgepodge of architectural styles, especially compared to St Mary's (1886) next door, a wooden Gothic Revival church with a burnished interior and interesting stained-glass windows. Holy Trinity's windows are also notable, especially the rose window by English artist Carl Edwards, which is particularly striking above the simple kauri altar.

Parnell Rose Gardens   GARDENS

(Map p70; 85-87 Gladstone Rd; ⊘7am-7pm) These formal gardens are blooming excellent from November to March. A stroll through the park leads to peaceful Judges Bay and tiny St Stephen's Chapel (Map p70; Judge St), built for the signing of the constitution of NZ's Anglican Church (1857).

Highwic   HISTORIC BUILDING

(Map p84; www.historic.org.nz; 40 Gillies Ave; adult/child $9/free; ⊘10.30am-4.30pm Wed-Sun) A marvellous Carpenter Gothic house (1862), sitting amid lush, landscaped grounds.

Kinder House   HISTORIC BUILDING

(Map p70; www.kinder.org.nz; 2 Ayr St; entry by donation; ⊘noon-3pm Wed-Sun; 🎈) Built of volcanic stone, this 1857 home displays the watercolours and memorabilia of Reverend Dr John Kinder (1819–1903), headmaster of the Church of England Grammar School.

Ewelme Cottage   HISTORIC BUILDING

(Map p70; www.historic.org.nz; 14 Ayr St; adult/child $8.50/free; ⊘10.30am-4.30pm Sun) Built in 1864 for a clergyman, this storybook cottage is in exceptionally good condition.

◎ Tamaki Drive

This scenic, pohutukawa-lined road heads east from the city, hugging the waterfront. In summer it's a jogging/cycling/rollerblading blur.

A succession of child-friendly, peaceful swimming beaches starts at Okahu Bay. Around the headland is Mission Bay, a popular beach with an iconic art-deco fountain, historic mission house, restaurants and bars. Safe swimming beaches Kohimarama and St Heliers follow. Further east along Cliff Rd, the Achilles Point lookout offers panoramic views. At its base is Ladies Bay, popular with nudists.

Buses 745 to 769 from Britomart follow this route.

Kelly Tarlton's Sealife Aquarium   AQUARIUM

(Map p64; ☑09-531 5065; www.kellytarltons.co.nz; 23 Tamaki Dr; adult/child $36/20; ⊘9.30am-5pm) 🐟 Sharks and stingrays swim over and around you in transparent tunnels that were once stormwater tanks. You can also enter the tanks in a shark cage with snorkel ($95), or dive into the tanks ($165). Other attractions include the Penguin Discovery tour (daily 10am, $199 per person) where just four visitors per day can get up close with Antarctic penguins. For all experiences, book online for a 10% to 20% discount and to check times.

A free shark-shaped shuttle bus departs from 172 Quay St (opposite the ferry terminal) on the half-hour from 9.30am to 3.30pm.

Bastion Point   PARK

(Map p64; Hapimana St) Politics, harbour views and lush lawns combine on this pretty headland with a chequered history. An elaborate cliff-top garden mausoleum honours Michael Joseph Savage (1872–1940), the country's first Labour prime minister, whose socialist reforms left him adored by the populace. Follow the lawn to a WWII gun embankment – one of many that line the harbour.

Parnell

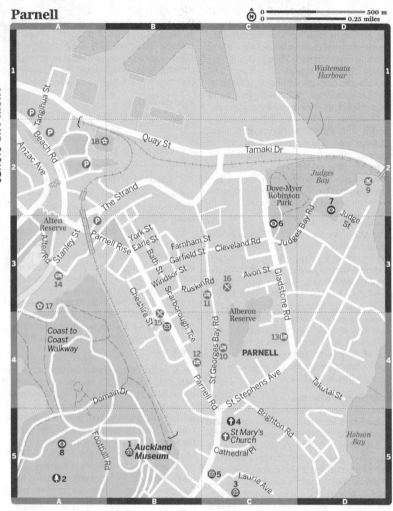

Devonport

With well-preserved Victorian and Edwardian buildings and loads of cafes, Devonport is a short ferry trip from the city. There are also two volcanic cones to climb and easy access to the first of the North Shore's beaches.

For a self-guided tour of historic buildings, pick up the *Old Devonport Walk* pamphlet from the i-SITE. Bikes can be hired from the ferry terminal.

Ferries to Devonport (adult/child return $11/5.80, 12 minutes) depart from the Auckland Ferry Building every 30 minutes (hour-ly after 8pm) from 6.15am to 11.15pm (until 1am Friday and Saturday), and from 7.15am to 10pm on Sundays and public holidays. Some Waiheke Island and Rangitoto ferries also stop here.

Mt Victoria & North Head VOLCANO
Mt Victoria (Takarunga; Map p81; Victoria Rd) and **North Head** (Maungauika; Map p81; Takarunga Rd; ⏱6am-10pm) were Maori *pa* and they remain fortresses of sorts, with the navy maintaining a presence. Both have gun embankments and North Head is riddled with tunnels, dug at the end of the 19th cen-

Parnell

⊙ **Top Sights**
1 Auckland Museum.................................B5

⊙ **Sights**
2 Auckland Domain.................................A5
3 Ewelme Cottage.................................C5
4 Holy Trinity Cathedral.........................C5
5 Kinder House....................................C5
6 Parnell Rose Gardens..........................C3
7 St Stephen's Chapel...........................D2
8 Wintergarden....................................A5

⊙ **Activities, Courses & Tours**
9 Parnell Baths....................................D2

⊙ **Sleeping**
10 City Garden Lodge..............................C4
11 Lantana Lodge...................................C3
12 Parnell Inn.......................................B4
13 Quality Hotel Parnell..........................C4
14 Quest Carlaw Park..............................A3

⊗ **Eating**
15 Burgerfuel..B4
16 La Cigale...C3

⊙ **Entertainment**
17 ASB Tennis Centre.............................A3
   Ticketmaster..............................(see 18)
18 Vector Arena....................................A2

tury in response to the Russian threat, and extended during WWI and WWII. The gates are locked at night, but that's never stopped teenagers from jumping the fence for scary subterranean explorations.

Between the two, Cambria Reserve stands on the remains of a third volcanic cone that was largely quarried away.

Navy Museum   MUSEUM
(Map p81; www.navymuseum.mil.nz; Torpedo Bay; ⊙10am-5pm) FREE The navy has been in Devonport since the earliest days of the colony. Its history is on display at this well-presented and often moving museum, focusing on the stories of the sailors themselves.

⊙ Western Springs

Auckland Zoo   ZOO
(Map p86; www.aucklandzoo.co.nz; Motions Rd; adult/child $25/10; ⊙9.30am-5pm, last entry 4.15pm) 🖉 At this modern, spacious zoo, the big foreigners tend to steal the attention from the timid natives, but if you can wrestle the kids away from the tigers and orang-utans, there's a well-presented NZ section. Called *Te Wao Nui*, it's divided into six ecological zones: Coast (seals, penguins), Islands (mainly lizards, including NZ's pint-sized dinosaur, the tuatara), Wetlands (ducks, herons, eels), Night (kiwi, naturally, along with frogs, native owls and weta), Forest (birds) and High Country (cheekier birds and lizards).

Frequent buses (adult/child $3.40/2) run from the Britomart Transport Centre to bus stop 8124 on Great North Rd, from where it is a 700m walk to the zoo's entrance. See www.at.govt.nz.

Western Springs   PARK
(Map p86; Great North Rd) Parents bring their children to this picturesque park for the popular adventure playground. It's a picnic spot and a good place to get acquainted with playful pukeko (swamp hens), easygoing ducks and pushy, bread-fattened geese. Formed by a confluence of lava flows, more than 4 million litres bubble up into the central lake daily. From the city, catch any bus heading west via Great North Rd (adult/child $3.40/2). By car, take the Western Springs exit from the North Western Motorway. Until 1902 this was Auckland's main water supply.

MOTAT   MUSEUM
(Museum of Transport & Technology; Map p86; www.motat.org.nz; 805 Great North Rd; adult/child $16/8; ⊙10am-5pm) This technology boffin's paradise is spread over two sites and 19 hectares. In **MOTAT Great North Rd** look out for former Prime Minister Helen Clark's Honda 50 motorbike and the pioneer village. **MOTAT Meola Rd** features the Aviation Display Hall with rare military and commercial planes. The two sites are linked by a vintage tram (free with admission, $2 otherwise), which passes the park and zoo. It's a fun kids' ride whether you visit MOTAT or not.

⊙ Other Suburbs

One Tree Hill   PARK
(Maungakiekie; Map p64; www.cornwallpark.co.nz) This volcanic cone was the isthmus' key *pa* and the greatest fortress in the country, and from the top (182m) there are 360-degree views. At the summit is the grave of John Logan Campbell, who gifted the land to the city in 1901 and requested that a memorial be built to the Maori people on the summit. Nearby is

the stump of the last 'one tree'. Allow time to explore surrounding Cornwall Park with its mature trees and Acacia Cottage (1841).

The information centre has fascinating interactive displays illustrating what the *pa* would have looked like when 5000 people lived here. Near the excellent children's playground, the **Stardome Observatory** (Map p64; ☑09-624 1246; www.stardome.org.nz; 670 Manukau Rd; admission to exhibits free, shows adult/child $10/8; ⊙10am-3pm Mon, 9.30am-4.30pm & 6.30-9.30pm Wed-Fri) **FREE** offers regular stargazing and planetarium shows that aren't dependent on Auckland's fickle weather (usually 8pm Wednesday to Sunday; phone ahead or check the website).

To get to One Tree Hill from the city take a train to Greenlane and walk 1km along Green Lane West. By car, take the Greenlane exit of the Southern Motorway and turn right into Green Lane West.

Wallace Arts Centre
GALLERY

(Map p64; www.tsbbankwallaceartscentre.org.nz; Pah Homestead, 72 Hillsborough Rd, Hillsborough; ⊙10am-3pm Tue-Fri, 10am-5pm Sat & Sun) **FREE** Housed in a gorgeous 1879 mansion with views to One Tree Hill and the Manakau Harbour, the Wallace Arts Centre is endowed with contemporary New Zealand art from an extensive private collection, which is changed every four to six weeks. Have lunch on the verandah and wander amongst the magnificent trees in the surrounding

---

ONE TREE TO RULE THEM ALL

Looking at One Tree Hill, your first thought will probably be 'Where's the bloody tree?' Good question. Up until 2000 a Monterey pine stood at the top of the hill. This was a replacement for a sacred totara that was chopped down by British settlers in 1852. Maori activists first attacked the foreign usurper in 1994, finishing the job in 2000. It's unlikely that another tree will be planted until local land claims have moved closer to resolution, but you can bet your boots that when it does happen, the tree will be a native.

Auckland's most beloved landmark achieved international recognition in 1987 when U2 released the song 'One Tree Hill' on their acclaimed *The Joshua Tree* album. It was only released as a single in NZ, where it went to number one.

---

park. The art is also very accessible, ranging from a life-size skeletal rugby ruck to a vibrant Ziggy Stardust painted on glass.

Bus 299 (Lynfield) departs every 15 minutes from Wellesley St in the city (near the Civic Theatre) and heads to Hillsborough Rd ($4.50, about 40 minutes).

Auckland Botanic Gardens
GARDENS

(Map p64; www.aucklandbotanicgardens.co.nz; 102 Hill Rd, Manurewa; ⊙8am-6pm mid-Mar–mid-Oct, 8am-8pm mid-Oct–mid-Mar) **FREE** This 64-hectare park has over 10,000 plants (including threatened species), dozens of gardens and an infestation of wedding parties. By car, take the Southern Motorway, exit at Manurewa and follow the signs. Otherwise take the train to Manurewa ($6.80, 40 minutes) and then walk along Hill Rd (1.5km).

Alberton
HISTORIC BUILDING

(Map p64; www.historic.org.nz; 100 Mt Albert Rd; adult/child $9/free; ⊙10.30am-4.30pm Wed-Sun) A classic colonial mansion (1863), Alberton featured as a backdrop for some scenes in *The Piano*. It's a 1km walk from Mt Albert train station.

Rainbow's End
AMUSEMENT PARK

(Map p64; www.rainbowsend.co.nz; 2 Clist Cres; Superpass unlimited rides adult/child $52/42; ⊙10am-5pm) 🌱 It's a bit dull by international standards but Rainbow's End has enough rides (including a corkscrew rollercoaster) to keep the kids happy all day.

🏃 Activities

Nothing gets you closer to the heart and soul of Auckland than sailing on the Hauraki Gulf. If you can't afford a yacht cruise, catch a ferry instead.

Visitors centres and public libraries stock the city council's *Auckland City's Walkways* pamphlet, which has a good selection of urban walks, including information on the Coast to Coast Walkway (p74).

Trading on the country's action-packed reputation, Auckland has sprouted its own set of thrill-inducing activities. Look around for backpacker reductions or special offers before booking anything.

Sailing

Sail NZ
SAILING

(Map p66; ☑0800 397 567; www.explorenz.co.nz; Viaduct Harbour) 🌱 Shoot the breeze on a genuine America's Cup yacht (adult/child $160/115) or head out on a 'Whale & Dolphin Safari' (adult/child $160/105); dolphins

AUCKLAND VOLCANIC FIELD

Some cities think they're tough just by living in the shadow of a volcano. Auckland's built on 50 of them and, no, they're not all extinct. The last one to erupt was Rangitoto about 600 years ago and no one can predict when the next eruption will occur. Auckland's quite literally a hot spot – with a reservoir of magma 100km below, waiting to bubble to the surface. But relax: this has only happened 19 times in the last 20,000 years.

Some of Auckland's volcanoes are cones, some are filled with water and some have been completely quarried away. Moves are afoot to register the field as a World Heritage Site and protect what remains. Most of the surviving cones show evidence of terracing from when they formed a formidable series of Maori *pa*. The most interesting to explore are Mt Eden (p65), One Tree Hill (p71) and Rangitoto, but Mt Wellington (Maungarei), Mt Albert (Owairaka), Mt Roskill (Puketapapa), Lake Pupuke, Mt Mangere and Mt Hobson (Remuwera) are all worth a visit.

are spotted 90% of the time and whales 75%. The *Pride of Auckland* fleet of glamorous large yachts offers 90-minute Harbour Sailing Cruises (adult/child $75/55), 2½-hour Dinner Cruises ($120/85) and full-day Sailing Adventures (adult/child $165/125).

CharterLink SAILING
(Map p64; ☑ 09-445 7114; www.charterlink.co.nz; Bayswater Marina; per day $395-1126) Well-maintained older yachts, luxury yachts and catamarans.

Gulfwind SAILING
(Map p64; ☑ 09-521 1564; www.gulfwind.co.nz; Westhaven Marina) Charters (half-/full day $445/895) and small-group sailing courses (two days $595).

Penny Whiting Sailing School SAILING
(Map p64; ☑ 09-376 1322; www.pennywhiting.com; Westhaven Marina; course $750) Runs 15-hour learners' courses either as five afternoon lessons or over two weekends.

Extreme Sports

SkyWalk EXTREME SPORTS
(Map p66; ☑ 0800 759 925; www.skywalk.co.nz; Sky Tower, cnr Federal & Victoria Sts; adult/child $145/115; ⊙ 10am-4.30pm) SkyWalk involves circling the 192m-high, 1.2m-wide outside halo of the Sky Tower without rails or a balcony. Don't worry, they're not completely crazy – there is a safety harness.

SkyJump EXTREME SPORTS
(Map p66; ☑ 0800 759 586; www.skyjump.co.nz; Sky Tower, cnr Federal & Victoria Sts; adult/child $225/175; ⊙ 10am-5pm) This thrilling 11-second, 85km/h base wire leap from the observation deck of the Sky Tower is more like a parachute jump than a bungy. Combine it with the SkyWalk in the Look & Leap package ($290).

Auckland Bridge Climb & Bungy BUNGY
(Map p64; ☑ 09-360 7748; www.bungy.co.nz; Curran St, Herne Bay; climb adult/child $120/80, bungy $150/120) Climb up or jump off the Auckland Harbour Bridge.

NZ Skydive SKYDIVING
(☑ 09-373 5778; www.nzskydive.co.nz; 12,000ft $330) Tandem skydives from Mercer airfield, 55km south of Auckland. A free shuttle for overseas visitors is available from Auckland.

G-MAX Reverse Bungy BUNGY
(Map p66; ☑ 09-377 1328; cnr Albert & Victoria Sts; ride $40; ⊙ 9am-10pm Sun-Thu, 10am-2am Fri & Sat) Imagine a giant slingshot with yourself as the projectile as you're reverse-bungyed 60m into the air.

Diving

Dive Centre DIVING
(Map p64; ☑ 09-444 7698; www.divecentre.co.nz; 97 Wairau Rd, Takapuna; PADI Open Water $599) PADI courses and diving charters.

Kayaking

Fergs Kayaks KAYAKING
(Map p64; ☑ 09-529 2230; www.fergskayaks.co.nz; 12 Tamaki Dr, Okahu Bay; ⊙ 9am-6pm) Hires kayaks and paddleboards (per hour/day from $20/50), bikes (per hour/day $20/120) and inline skates (per hour/day $15/30). Day and night guided kayak trips are available to Devonport (8km, three hours, $95) or Rangitoto Island (13km, six hours, $120).

Auckland Sea Kayaks KAYAKING
(☑ 0800 999 089; www.aucklandseakayaks.co.nz) Guided trips (including lunch) to Rangitoto ($175, 10 hours) and Motukorea (Browns Island; $135, six hours). Multiday excursions also available.

DON'T MISS

NORTH SHORE BEACHES

Fine swimming beaches stretch from North Head to Long Bay. The gulf islands shelter them from strong surf, making them safe for supervised children. Aim for high tide unless you fancy a lengthy walk to waist-deep water. **Cheltenham Beach** is a short walk from Devonport. **Takapuna Beach**, closest to the Harbour Bridge, is Auckland's answer to Bondi and the most built up. Nearby **St Leonards Beach**, popular with gay men, requires clambering over rocks at high tide.

Other Water Activities

Auckland Jet Boat Tours   JETBOATING
(Map p66; ☑ 050 825 5382; www.aucklandjetboattours.co.nz; floating pavilion, 220 Quay St; adult/child incl museum $85/45) Take a 35-minute blast around the harbour.

New Zealand Surf'n'Snow Tours   SURFING
(☑ 09-828 0426; www.newzealandsurftours.com; 5-/12-day tour $799/1699) Day-long surfing courses including transport, gear and two two-hour lessons ($120). Day tours usually head to Piha (year-round; with/without own gear $50/99), while five- and 12-day tours include accommodation in Ahipara (October to May only).

Parnell Baths   SWIMMING
(Map p70; www.parnellbaths.co.nz; Judges Bay Rd, Parnell; adult/child $6.30/free; ⊙ 6am-8pm Mon-Fri, 8am-8pm Sat & Sun) Outdoor saltwater pools with an awesome 1950s mural.

Olympic Pools & Fitness Centre   SWIMMING
(Map p84; www.theolympic.co.nz; 77 Broadway, Newmarket; adult/child $8/5; ⊙ 5.30am-9.30pm Mon-Fri, 7am-8pm Sat & Sun) Pools, gym, sauna, steam room and crèche.

Ballooning

Balloon Expeditions   BALLOONING
(☑ 09-416 8590; www.balloonexpeditions.co.nz; flight $340) Hour-long flights in a hot-air balloon at sunrise, including breakfast and bubbles.

Tramping

Coast to Coast Walkway   WALKING
(Map p64; www.aucklandcity.govt.nz) Right across the country from the Tasman to the Pacific (actually, only 16km), this walk encompasses One Tree Hill, Mt Eden, the Domain and the University, keeping mainly to reserves rather than city streets. Do it in either direction: starting from the Viaduct Basin and heading south, it's marked by yellow markers and milestones; heading north from Onehunga there are blue markers. Our recommendation? Catch the train to Onehunga and finish up at the Viaduct's bars.

From Onehunga Station, take Onehunga Mall up to Princes St, turn left and pick up the track at the inauspicious park by the motorway.

☞ Tours

Cultural Tours

Potiki Adventures   CULTURAL TOUR
(☑ 021 422 773; www.potikiadventures.co.nz; adult/child from $150/80) Tours to Waiheke Island and explorations of Auckland from a Maori cultural perspective.

Tamaki Hikoi   CULTURAL TOUR
(☑ 0800 282 552; www.tamakihikoi.co.nz; 1-/3hr $40/95) Guides from the Ngati Whatua *iwi* (tribe) lead various Maori cultural tours, often including walking and a cultural performance.

TIME Unlimited   CULTURAL TOUR
(☑ 09-446 6677; www.newzealandtours.travel) 🖉 Cultural, walking and sightseeing tours from a Maori perspective.

Food & Wine

NZ Winepro   WINE TASTING
(☑ 09-575 1958; www.nzwinepro.co.nz; tours $85-275) Explores Auckland's wine regions, combining tastings with sightseeing.

Wine Trail Tours   WINE TASTING
(☑ 09-630 1540; www.winetrailtours.co.nz) Small-group tours around West Auckland wineries and the Waitakere Ranges (half-/full day $115/245); further afield to Matakana ($255), or a combo of the two ($255).

Fine Wine Tours   WINE TASTING
(☑ 0800 023 111; www.insidertouring.co.nz) Tours of Kumeu, Matakana and Waiheke wineries, including four-hour Kumeu tour ($199), with cheese ($229) and a six-hour tour including Muriwai Beach ($245).

The Big Foody Food Tour   GUIDED TOUR
(☑ 021 481 177, 0800 366 386 877; www.thebigfoody.com; per person $65-165) Small-group city tours including market visits, visits to artisan producers, and lots of tastings.

City Walk
City Centre Ramble

START ST KEVIN'S ARCADE,
KARANGAHAPE RD
FINISH WYNYARD QUARTER
LENGTH 4.5KM; AROUND THREE HOURS

Start among the secondhand boutiques of
1 St Kevin's Arcade and take the stairs
down to Myers Park. Look out for the reproduction of **2 Michelangelo's Moses** at the
bottom of the stairs. Continue through the
park, taking the stairs on the right just before
the overpass to head up to street level.

Heading down Queen St, you'll pass the
3 Auckland Town Hall and **4 Aotea Sq**,
the civic heart of the city. On the next corner
is the wonderful **5 Civic Theatre** (p63).
Turn right on Wellesley St and then left
onto Lorne St. Immediately to your right is
6 Khartoum Pl, with tiling that celebrates
NZ women as the first in the world to win the
vote.. Head up the stairs to the **7 Auckland
Art Gallery** (p62).

Behind the gallery is **8 Albert Park** (p63).
Cross through it and turn left into Princes St,
where a row of **9 Victorian merchant's**
houses faces the **10 University Clock Tower**.
Cut around behind the clock tower to **11 Old
Government House** and then follow the di-
agonal path back to Princes St. The attractive
building on the corner of Princes St and Bowen
Ave was once the city's main **12 synagogue**.

Head down Bowen Ave and cut through
the park past the **13 Chancery precinct** to
14 High St with its good cafes and shopping.
Take a left onto **15 Vulcan Lane**, lined with
historic pubs. Turn right onto Queen St and
follow it down to the **16 Britomart Train Station**, housed in the former central post office.
You're now standing on reclaimed land – the
original shoreline was at Fort St. Detour to
the nearby **17 Britomart precinct** for good
bars, restaurants, and fashion boutiques.

From the Britomart Train Station, turn left
on Quay St and head to **18 Viaduct Harbour**, bustling with bars and cafes, and then
continue over the bridge to the rejuvenated
19 Wynyard Quarter.

Walking

Waitakere Tours
TRAMPING

(📞0800 492 482; www.waitakeretours.co.nz; per day $150) Lifelong Westies (West Aucklanders) offer guided tours of the west-coast beaches, and guided walks in the Waitakeres.

Bush & Beach
TRAMPING, WINE TASTING

(📞09-837 4130; www.bushandbeach.co.nz) 🌿 Guided walks in the Waitakere Ranges and along west-coast beaches (half-/full day $140/225, including transfers); three-hour city minibus tours ($75); and food, wine and art tours in either Matakana or Kumeu (half-/full day $219/310).

Auckland Ghost Tours
WALKING TOUR

(📞09-630 5721; www.aucklandghosttours.com; adult/child $50/25) Stories of Auckland's scary side on a two-hour walking tour of the central city.

Hiking NZ
TRAMPING

(📞0800 697 232; www.hikingnewzealand.com) Runs 'hiking safaris' leaving from Auckland, including Far North ($1280, six days), and Volcanoes & Rainforest ($2480, 10 days).

Bus Tours

Explorer Bus
BUS TOUR

(📞0800 439 756; www.explorerbus.co.nz; adult/child $40/20) 🌿 This hop-on, hop-off service departs from the Ferry Building every hour from 10am to 3pm (more frequently in summer), heading to 14 tourist sites around the central city.

Gray Line
BUS TOUR

(📞0800 698 687; www.graylinetours.co.nz; adult/child $59/29.50; ☺departs 9.30am) 🌿 Three-hour bus tour of Auckland's highlights.

GreatSights
BUS TOUR

(Map p66; 📞0800 744 487; www.greatsights.co.nz; adult/child $59/29; ☺departs 9.45am) 🌿 The city highlights on a three-hour bus tour.

AUCKLAND FOR CHILDREN

All of the east coast beaches (St Heliers, Kohimarama, Mission Bay, Okahu Bay, Cheltenham, Narrow Neck, Takapuna, Milford, Long Bay) are safe for supervised kids, while sights such as Rainbow's End, Kelly Tarlton's, Auckland Museum and Auckland Zoo are all firm favourites. Parnell Baths has a children's pool, but on wintry days, head to the thermal pools at Parakai or Waiwera.

Toru Tours
SIGHTSEEING

(📞027 457 0011; www.torutours.com; $69) The three-hour Express Tour will depart with just one booking – ideal for solo travellers.

Cruises

Riverhead Ferry
CRUISE

(Map p66; 📞09-376 0819; www.riverheadferry.co.nz; Pier 3, Ferry Building; tour $35) Harbour and gulf cruises including a 90-minute jaunt up the inner harbour to Riverhead, returning after two hours' pub time.

Fullers
CRUISE

(Map p66; 📞09-367 9111; www.fullers.co.nz; Ferry Building, 99 Quay St; adult/child $40/20; ☺10.30am & 1.30pm) Daily 1½-hour harbour cruises including Rangitoto and a free return ticket to Devonport.

Other Tours

Auckland Seaplanes
SCENIC FLIGHTS

(📞09-390 1121; www.aucklandseaplanes.com; from $150 per person) Flights in a cool 1960s floatplane that explore Auckland's harbour and islands.

Red Carpet Tours
FILM LOCATIONS

(📞09-410 6561; www.redcarpet-tours.com) Day trips to Hobbiton/Matamata ($255), or all around Middle Earth across 14 days ($6650).

★ Festivals & Events

Also see www.aucklandnz.com.

Auckland Anniversary Day Regatta
SPORTS

(www.regatta.org.nz) The 'City of Sails' lives up to its name; Monday of last weekend in January.

Laneway Festival
MUSIC

(www.lanewayfestival.com.au) International indie bands in a one-day festival on Anniversary Day.

Music In Parks
MUSIC

(www.musicinparks.co.nz) Free gigs from January until March.

Movies In Parks
FILM

(www.moviesinparks.co.nz) Free movies in February and March.

Lantern Festival
CULTURAL

(www.asianz.org.nz) Three days of Asian food and culture in Albert Park to welcome the Lunar New Year (usually held in early February).

Auckland Pride Festival
GAY & LESBIAN

(www.aucklandpridefestival.org.nz) Two-week festival of music, arts, sport and culture in February celebrating the LGBT community. Highlights include the Auckland Pride Parade and the **Big Gay Out** (www.biggayout.co.nz).

Devonport Food & Wine Festival FOOD & WINE
(www.devonportwinefestival.co.nz; admission $30) Across two days in mid-February.

Splore MUSIC
(www.splore.net; Tapapakanga Regional Park) Three days of camping and music (generally of the dancy and soulful variety), held by the beach in mid-February. Headliners include big-name international acts.

Auckland Cup Week SPORTS
(www.ellerslie.co.nz; Ellerslie Racecourse) The year's biggest horse race; early March.

Auckland Arts Festival ARTS
(www.aucklandfestival.co.nz) Held over three weeks in March in odd-numbered years, this is Auckland's biggest celebration of the arts.

Pasifika Festival CULTURAL
(www.aucklandnz.com/pasifika) Western Springs Park hosts this giant Polynesian party with cultural performances, food and craft stalls; held early to mid-March.

Polyfest CULTURAL
(www.asbpolyfest.co.nz; Sports Bowl, Manukau) Massive Auckland secondary schools' Maori and Pacific Islands cultural festival held in mid-March.

**Auckland International
Cultural Festival** CULTURAL
(www.facebook.com/Culturalfestival; May Rd, War Memorial Park, Mt Roskill) One-day festival with ethnic food stalls and cultural displays and performances; late March.

Royal Easter Show AGRICULTURAL
(www.royaleastershow.co.nz; ASB Showgrounds, 217 Green Lane West) It's supposedly agricultural but most people attend for the funfair rides.

NZ International Comedy Festival COMEDY
(www.comedyfestival.co.nz) Three-week laugh-fest with local and international comedians; late April to early May.

Out Takes FILM, GAY & LESBIAN
(www.outtakes.org.nz; Rialto Cinemas) Gay and lesbian film festival; late May to early June.

NZ International Film Festival FILM
(www.nzff.co.nz) Art-house films from mid-July.

MAORI NEW ZEALAND: AUCKLAND

Evidence of Maori occupation is literally carved into Auckland's volcanic cones. The dominant *iwi* of the isthmus was Ngati Whatua, but these days there are Maori from almost all of NZ's *iwi* living here.

For an initial taste of Maori culture, start at Auckland Museum (p68), where there's a wonderful Maori collection and a culture show. For a more personalised experience, take a tour with TIME Unlimited (p74), Potiki Adventures (p74) or Ngati Whatua's Tamaki Hikoi (p74), or visit the *marae* and recreated village at Te Hana (p117).

Auckland Art Fair ARTS
(www.artfair.co.nz; The Cloud, Queens Wharf, Quay St) Lots of art for sale in August in odd-numbered years.

NZ Fashion Week FASHION
(www.nzfashionweek.com) In early September.

Auckland International Boat Show SPORTS
(www.auckland-boatshow.com) Boat show held in September.

Heritage Festival CULTURAL
(www.aucklandcouncil.govt.nz) Two weeks of (mainly free) tours of Auckland's neighbourhoods and historic buildings; mid-September.

Diwali Festival of Lights CULTURAL
(www.asianz.org.nz) Music, dance and food from Auckland's Indian community; mid-October.

Grey Lynn Park Festival CULTURAL
(www.greylynnparkfestival.org) Free festival of arts and crafts, food stalls, and live music in one of Auckland's more interesting inner suburbs; third Saturday in November.

Santa Parade PARADE
(www.santaparade.co.nz) Along Queen St before partying in Aotea Sq; last Sunday of November.

Christmas in the Park FAMILY
(www.christmasinthepark.co.nz) Mid-December Christmas concert and party in Auckland Domain.

Ponsonby & Grey Lynn

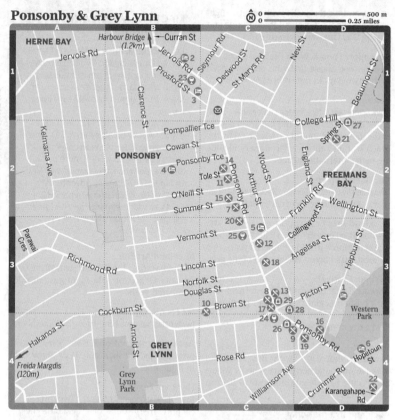

Ponsonby & Grey Lynn

Sleeping
1	23 Hepburn	D3
2	Abaco on Jervois	B1
3	Brown Kiwi	B1
4	Great Ponsonby Arthotel	B2
5	Ponsonby Backpackers	C3
6	Verandahs	D4

Eating
7	Bird on a Wire	C2
8	Blue Breeze Inn	C3
9	Burgerfuel	C4
10	Cocoro	C3
11	Dizengoff	C2
12	Fred's	C3
13	Il Buco	C3
14	Landreth & Co	C2
15	Little Bird	C2
	Mekong Baby	(see 11)
16	MooChowChow	D4

17	Ponsonby Central	C3
18	Ponsonby Road Bistro	C3
19	Ponsonby Village International Food Court	D4
20	Prego	C3
21	Queenie's	D2
22	Satya	D4

Drinking & Nightlife
23	Dida's Wine Lounge & Tapas Bar	B1
24	Golden Dawn	C4
25	Poof	C3

Shopping
26	Karen Walker	C4
27	New World	D2
28	Texan Art Schools	C3
29	Women's Bookshop	C3
	Zambesi	(see 18)

Silo Park Markets   FILM
(www.silopark.co.nz; Wynyard Quarter) Classic
movies screened outdoors on a Friday night,
and markets with food trucks, DJs and craft
stalls on Friday nights and Saturday afternoons; December to Easter.

🛏 Sleeping

🏨 City Centre

Auckland has plenty of luxury hotels, with
several international chains taking up inner-
city real estate. At the other extreme, any
backpackers who leave with a bad impression of Auckland have invariably stayed in
crummy, noisy digs in the city centre. Not
all of the cheap city accommodation is bad,
but you'll find much better hostels in inner
suburbs like Ponsonby, Parnell, Freemans
Bay and Mt Eden, and central Auckland is
still easily reached by bus.

Attic Backpackers   HOSTEL $
(Map p66; ☑ 09-973 5887; www.atticbackpack-
ers.co.nz; 31 Wellesley St W; dm $26-33, s/tw/d
$50/78/78; @ 🛜) Centrally located Attic Back-
packers features contemporary and colourful
decor, spotless and modern facilities, and a
cool rooftop area for meeting other travellers.

Kiwi International Hotel   HOTEL $
(Map p66; ☑ 09-379 6487; www.kiwihotel.co.nz; 411
Queen St; r $59-109, apt $169; ℗ 🛜) Rooms –
most with en suite bathrooms – definitely
are compact, but they're clean and well kept,
and the location bordering Queen St and Karangahape Rd is very convenient.

Jucy Hotel   HOTEL $
(Map p66; ☑ 09-379 6633; www.jucyhotel.com; 62
Emily Pl; hostel s/d $54/79, hotel r $109; ℗ @ 🛜)
This zippy budget hotel is from the Jucy car-
rental company. Rooms in the main section
have en suites, and there's a hostel wing with
bunks and shared bathrooms.

YHA Auckland International   HOSTEL $
(Map p66; ☑ 0800 278 299, 09-302 8200; www.
yha.co.nz; 5 Turner St; dm $32, r $90-105; ℗ 🛜)
Clean and brightly painted, this 170-bed
YHA has a friendly vibe, good security, a
games room and lots of lockers.

YHA Auckland City   HOSTEL $
(Map p66; ☑ 0800 278 299, 09-309 2802; www.yha.
co.nz; 18 Liverpool St; dm/s/d $27/60/85; 🛜) 🖉
Struggle up one of the city's steepest streets

to this big, impersonal tower block near the
K Rd party strip. The rooms are clean and
well kept, some with views and terraces.

Nomads Auckland   HOSTEL $
(Map p66; ☑ 09-300 9999; www.nomadsauckland.
com; 16 Fort St; dm $25-37, r $96-116; @ 🛜) This
bustling backpackers has a cafe, bar, travel
agency, female-only floor and a roof deck
with sauna and spa. The private rooms have
TVs but not all have windows.

Waldorf Celestion   APARTMENT $$
(Map p66; ☑ 09-280 2200; www.celestion-waldorf.
co.nz; 19-23 Anzac Ave; apt $170-277) 🖉 A rash
of Waldorfs have opened in recent years, all
presenting similar symptoms: affordable,
modern apartments in city-fringe locations.
We prefer this one for its stylish red, black
and grey colour palette.

CityLife   HOTEL $$
(Map p66; ☑ 09-379 9222; www.heritagehotels.
co.nz/citylife-auckland; Durham St; apt $179-339;
℗ @ 🛜🏊) 🖉 A worthy tower-block hotel offering numerous apartments over dozens of
floors, ranging from studios to three-bedroom
suites. Facilities include a heated lap pool,
gym, valet parking and a babysitting service.

Waldorf Stadium   APARTMENT $$
(Map p66; ☑ 09-337 5300; www.stadium-apart-
ments-hotel.co.nz; 40 Beach Rd; apt $150-330)
🖉 This large newish block has spacious (if
generic) family-friendly apartments with
double-glazing to keep out the road noise.

City Lodge   HOTEL $$
(Map p66; ☑ 09-379 6183; www.citylodge.co.nz;
150 Vincent St; s $79, d $103-119; @ 🛜) 🖉
YMCA-run and purpose-built tower for the
budget market. The tiny rooms and stamp-
sized bathrooms make for clean and secure
accommodation. There's an industrial-style
kitchen and comfy lounge.

★ Hotel de Brett   BOUTIQUE HOTEL $$$
(Map p66; ☑ 09-925 9000; www.hoteldebrett.
com; 2 High St; r $300-600; @ 🛜) This hip, re-
furbished historic hotel has been zhooshed
up with stripy carpets and clever designer
touches in every nook of the extremely com-
fortable rooms. Prices include breakfast, free
broadband and a pre-dinner drink.

Quadrant   HOTEL $$$
(Map p66; ☑ 09-984 6000; www.thequadrant.com;
10 Waterloo Quadrant; apt $250-380; 🛜) 🖉 Slick,
central and full of all the whiz-bang gadgets,

this apartment-style complex is an excellent option. The only catch is that the units are tiny and the bathrooms beyond small.

Freemans Bay

Verandahs HOSTEL $
(Map p78; ☑ 09-360 4180; www.verandahs.co.nz; 6 Hopetoun St; dm $28-32, s $56, d $74-94, tr $96; P@☎) Ponsonby Rd, K Rd and the city are an easy walk from this grand hostel, housed in two neighbouring villas overlooking the mature trees of Western Park. Definitely one of Auckland's best backpackers.

23 Hepburn B&B $$$
(Map p78; ☑ 09-376 0622; www.23hepburn.co.nz; 23 Hepburn St; r $210-250; P☎) The three boutique rooms are a symphony in muted whites and creams. Continental breakfast is left in your fridge the previous evening to enjoy at your leisure.

Ponsonby & Grey Lynn

Ponsonby Backpackers HOSTEL $
(Map p78; ☑ 09-360 1311; www.ponsonby backpackers.co.nz; 2 Franklin Rd; dm $26-28, s/d $45/62; P@☎) This elegant two-storied turreted villa has a friendly vibe, sunny rooms, and a nice garden area. Central Auckland is a pleasant 20-minute walk away, and the buzz of Ponsonby Rd is right on your doorstep.

Brown Kiwi HOSTEL $
(Map p78; ☑ 09-378 0191; www.brownkiwi.co.nz; 7 Prosford St; dm $28-31, s/d $52/72; @☎) This low-key hostel is tucked away in a busy-by-day commercial strip, a stone's throw from Ponsonby's good shopping and grazing opportunities. The garden courtyard is made for mooching.

Abaco on Jervois MOTEL $$
(Map p78; ☑ 09-360 6850; www.abaco.co.nz; 57 Jervois Rd; r $135-155, ste $194-215; P) A contemporary, neutral-toned motel including stainless-steel kitchenettes (with dish drawers and ovens) and fluffy white towels for use in the spa. The darker rooms downstairs are priced accordingly.

Great Ponsonby Arthotel B&B $$$
(Map p78; ☑ 09-376 5989; www.greatpons.co.nz; 30 Ponsonby Tce; r $265-400; P@) In a quiet cul-de-sac near Ponsonby Rd, this deceptively spacious Victorian villa has gregarious hosts, impressive sustainability practices

and great breakfasts. Studio apartments open onto an attractive rear courtyard.

Newton

City Travellers HOSTEL $
(Map p66; ☑ 09-377 6027; www.kroadcitytravellers.co.nz; 146 Karangahape Rd; dm $29-33, s/tw/d $61/76/76; @☎) Smaller hostel well located on bustling and bohemian Karangahape Rd.

Langham HOTEL $$$
(Map p66; ☑ 09-379 5132; www.auckland.langhamhotels.co.nz; 83 Symonds St; r $220-390, ste $510-2430; P@☎) The Langham's service is typically faultless, the beds are heavenly, and its day spa is one of Auckland's best.

Mt Eden

Bamber House HOSTEL $
(Map p86; ☑ 09-623 4267; www.bamberhouse.co.nz; 22 View Rd; dm $26-28, s $57, d $72-90; P@☎) The original house here is a mansion of sorts, with some nicely maintained period trimmings and large grounds. The new prefab cabins have less character but come with en suites.

Pentlands HOSTEL $
(Map p86; ☑ 09-638 7031; www.pentlands.co.nz; 22 Pentland Ave; dm $25-28, s/d $46/68; P@☎) Set down a peaceful tree-lined cul-de-sac, this powder-blue villa has stylish rooms, a sunny deck with a barbecue, and quiet tables on the lawn.

Oaklands Lodge HOSTEL $
(Map p86; ☑ 09-638 6545; www.oaklands.co.nz; 5a Oaklands Rd; dm $25-27, s $43-50, d $62-68; P@☎) In a leafy cul-de-sac, this bright, well-kept hostel is close to Mt Eden village and city buses.

Bavaria GUESTHOUSE $$
(Map p86; ☑ 09-638 9641; www.bavariabandbhotel.co.nz; 83 Valley Rd; s $95-130, d $150-180; P@☎) This spacious villa offers large, airy rooms and a buffet breakfast. The communal TV lounge, dining room and deck all encourage mixing and mingling.

Eden Park B&B B&B $$$
(Map p86; ☑ 09-630 5721; www.bedandbreakfastnz.com; 20 Bellwood Ave; s $135-150, d $235-250; ☎) The hallowed turf of Auckland's legendary Eden Park rugby ground is only a block away and, while the rooms aren't overly large, they mirror the Edwardian elegance of this fine wooden villa.

Devonport

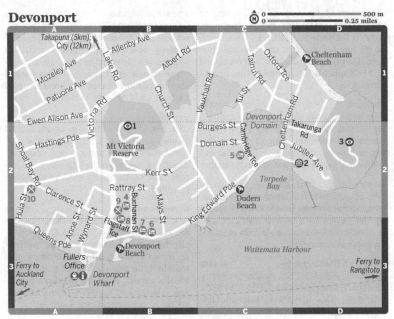

Takapuna (5km);
City (12km)

Cheltenham
Beach

Mozeley Ave
Patuone Ave
Allenby Ave
Albert Rd
Lake Rd
Oxford Tce
Tainui Rd
Tui St
Cheltenham Rd
Takarunga
Rd

Ewen Alison Ave
Victoria Rd
Church St
Vauxhall Rd

Hastings Pde
Mt Victoria
Reserve
⊙1
Burgess St
Cambridge Tce
Devonport
Domain
Jubilee Ave
3⊙

Kerr St
Domain St
5🍴
🏛2

Shoal Bay Rd
Clarence St
Rattray St
Huia St
⊗10
9⊗4
8⊗
Buchanan St
Mays St
King Edward Pde
Torpedo
Bay
Duders
Beach

Anne St
Wynard St
Queens Pde
Flagstaff
Tce
7 6
Devonport
Beach

Waitemata Harbour

Ferry to
Auckland
City
Fullers
Office
🅿ℹ
Devonport
Wharf

Ferry to
Rangitoto

Parnell & Newmarket

City Garden Lodge HOSTEL $
(Map p70; ☎09-302 0880; www.citygardenlodge.
co.nz; 25 St Georges Bay Rd; dm $28-30, s/d
$56/72; 🅿@🛜) Occupying a character-
filled, two-storey house, this well-run
backpackers has a lovely garden and high-
ceilinged rooms.

Lantana Lodge HOSTEL $
(Map p70; ☎09-373 4546; www.lantanalodge.
co.nz; 60 St Georges Bay Rd; dm $27-31, s $58,
d $70-74; 🅿🛜) There are only eight rooms
available in this cosy villa on a quiet street.
It's not flash, but it's clean enough to be
homely.

Quest Carlaw Park APARTMENT $$
(Map p70; ☎09-304 0521; www.questcarlawpark.
co.nz; 15 Nicholls Lane; apt $170-335; 🅿@🛜)
🔖 It's in an odd spot but this set of smart,
modern apartments is handy for Parnell, the
city and the Domain, and if you've got a car
you're practically on the motorway.

Parnell Inn MOTEL $$
(Map p70; ☎09-358 0642; www.parnellinn.co.nz;
320 Parnell Rd; r $105-130; 🅿@🛜) You'll get a
chipper welcome from the friendly folks at
this good-looking, revamped motel. Rooms

Devonport

⊙ Sights
1 Mt Victoria	B2
2 Navy Museum	D2
3 North Head	D2

🛏 Sleeping
4 Devonport Motel	B2
5 Devonport Sea Cottage	C2
6 Hampton Beach House	B3
7 Parituhu	B3
8 Peace & Plenty Inn	B3

⊗ Eating
9 Bette's Bar & Eatery	B2
10 Calliope Road Cafe	A2

3 and 4 have great harbour views and some
rooms have kitchenettes.

Quality Hotel Parnell HOTEL $$
(Map p70; ☎09-303 3789; www.theparnell.co.nz;
20 Gladstone Rd; r $150-310; 🅿🛜) More than
100 motel rooms and units are available in
this recently renovated complex. The newer
north wing has great harbour views.

Devonport

Devonport has beautiful Edwardian B&Bs
within a relaxing ferry ride of the city.

Devonport Motel
MOTEL **$$**

(Map p81; ☑ 09-445 1010; www.devonportmotel. co.nz; 11 Buchanan St; r $150; 🖨) This minimotel has two units in the tidy back garden. They're modern, clean, self-contained and in a quiet location close to Devonport's attractions.

Parituhu
B&B **$$**

(Map p81; ☑ 09-445 6559; www.parituhu.co.nz; 3 King Edward Pde; r $125-155; 🖨) There's only one double bedroom (with its own adjoining bathroom) available in this relaxing and welcoming Edwardian waterfront bungalow.

Devonport Sea Cottage
COTTAGE **$$**

(Map p81; ☑ 09-445 7117; www.devonportseacottagenz.com; 3a Cambridge Tce; d $130-150; 🖨) Head up the garden path to your own cute and cosy self-contained cottage. Weekly rates are available in summer.

Hampton Beach House
B&B **$$$**

(Map p81; ☑ 09-445 1358; www.hamptonbeachhouse.co.nz; 4 King Edward Pde; s $185-225, r $225-325; @🖨) This upmarket, waterside Edwardian B&B has tasteful rooms that open onto a rear garden. Expect quality linen and gourmet breakfasts.

Peace & Plenty Inn
B&B **$$$**

(Map p81; ☑ 09-445 2925; www.peaceandplenty. co.nz; 6 Flagstaff Tce; s $195-265, d $265-465; P🖨) 🕭 Stocked with antiques, this perfectly located, five-star Victorian house has romantic and luxurious en suite rooms with TVs, flowers, free sherry/port and local chocolates.

Other Areas

Auckland Airport

Campervan Park
CARAVAN PARK **$**

(Map p64; ☑ 09-256 8527; www.aucklandairport. co.nz; Jimmy Ward Crescent, Mangere; sites from $29; 🖨) Caravan park with powered spaces, toilets and showers, all within 1km of the terminals. It's a great option for those wanting to rest up after arriving on a long flight.

Ambury Regional Park
CAMPSITE **$**

(Map p64; ☑ 09-366 2000; www.arc.govt.nz; Ambury Rd, Mangere; sites per adult/child $6/3) A slice of country in suburbia, this regional park is also a working farm. Facilities are limited (a vault toilet, warm showers and not much shade) but it's handy to the airport, right on the water and dirt cheap.

Auckland Takapuna Oaks
HOTEL **$$**

(Map p64; ☑ 09-445 7100; www.aucklandtakapunaoaks.co.nz; 1 Beresford St, Bayswater; apt $160-300; P@🖨) Spacious apartments (with full kitchens and laundry facilities) on a peaceful peninsula that's close to beaches and a short ferry ride from the city. Breakfast, plus harbour and city views, is included.

Jet Park
HOTEL **$$**

(Map p64; ☑ 09-275 4100; www.jetpark.co.nz; 63 Westney Rd, Mangere; r $120-150; @🖨🛪) 🕭 Comfortable rooms and a decent vibe; with departure screens in the lobby and free airport shuttles, there's no excuse for missing your flight.

Grange Lodge
MOTEL **$$**

(Map p64; ☑ 09-277 8280; www.manukauaccommodation.co.nz; cnr Grange & Great South Rds, Papatoetoe; units $125-190; 🖨) 🕭 If you've driven up from the south, consider staying at this friendly little suburban motel that's handy for the airport. From the Southern Motorway, take the East Tamaki Rd exit, turn right and right again onto Great South Rd.

Nautical Nook
B&B **$$**

(Map p64; ☑ 09-521 2544; www.nauticalnook.com; 23b Watene Cres, Orakei; s/d $108/162; 🖨) If you're a sailing buff you'll find a kindred spirit in Keith, who runs this cosy homestay with his wife Trish. The lounge and terrace have views over the harbour, and the beach is close.

🍴 Eating

Because of its size and ethnic diversity, Auckland tops the country when it comes to dining options and quality. Lively eateries have sprung up to cater to the many Asian students, and offer inexpensive Japanese, Chinese and Korean staples. If you're on a budget, you'll fall in love with the city's food halls.

Aucklanders demand good coffee, so you never have to walk too far to find a decent cafe, especially in suburbs like Ponsonby, Mt Eden and Kingsland. Some double as wine bars or have gourmet aspirations, while others are content to fill their counters with fresh, reasonably priced snacks.

The hippest new foodie enclaves are Britomart (the blocks above the train station) and Federal St (under the Sky Tower), and recent openings have also resurrected and reinforced the culinary reputation of Ponsonby. The Wynyard Quarter west of Viaduct Harbour and the new City Works Depot on Wellesley St are also up-and-coming areas.

You'll find large supermarkets in most neighbourhoods: there's a particularly handy Countdown (Map p66; 76 Quay St; ⊙24hr) at the bottom of town and a New World (Map p78; 2 College Hill, Freemans Bay; ⊙7am-midnight) by Victoria Park. Self-caterers should consider the Otara Market (p94) and Avondale Sunday Market (p94) for cheap, fresh vegetables and La Cigale (p89) for fancier fare and local artisan produce.

City Centre

Food Truck Garage
CAFE $

(Map p66; www.foodtruckgarage.co.nz; 90 Wellesley St, City Works Depot; mains $10-14; ⊙11am-10pm, limited menu 3-5pm; ⊘) ⬤ In the funky new City Works Depot, the Food Truck Garage serves up healthy versions of fast food classics like burgers, tacos and wraps. Across the menu there's definitely no trade-off of taste for wellbeing.

Food Alley
FOOD HALL $

(Map p66; 9 Albert St; mains $7-13; ⊙10.30am-10pm) There's Chinese, Indonesian, Indian, Thai, Vietnamese, Turkish, Malaysian, Korean and Japanese all on offer at this no-frills food hall.

Hansan
VIETNAMESE $

(Map p66; www.hansan.co.nz; 22-24 Kitchener St; mains $10-16; ⊙11am-10pm) Great value Vietnamese food, just a short walk from Queen St. There's another branch (Map p84; 55 Nuffield St; ⊙11am-10pm) in Newmarket.

Remedy
CAFE $

(Map p66; 1 Wellesley St; snacks & mains $8-16; ⊙6.30am-6pm Mon-Fri, 9am-3pm Sat) Quirky inner-city spot with excellent coffee, and the old-school thrills of a book exchange.

Revive
VEGETARIAN $

(Map p66; www.revive.co.nz; 24 Wyndham St; mains $11-13; ⊙11am-8pm Mon-Thu, 11am-3pm Fri; ⊘) Vegetarian heaven with an enticing salad bar and economical daily meal deals.

Zap 4
THAI $

(Map p66; www.zap.getcellgroup.cpm; 10 Commerce St; mains $12-17; ⊙11am-9pm) All your Thai favourites with a side order of bustling ambience.

★ Depot
MODERN NZ $$

(Map p66; www.eatatdepot.co.nz; 86 Federal St; dishes $17-32; ⊙7am-late) TV chef Al Brown's first Auckland eatery offers first-rate Kiwi comfort food in informal surrounds

---

AUCKLAND'S MULTICULTURAL MENU

Around 30% of New Zealanders live in Auckland, and the country's biggest city is also the most ethnically diverse. With immigration – especially from Asia – has come a more cosmopolitan restaurant scene, and savvy Auckland foodies (and a few of the city's top chefs) keenly explore central fringe neighbourhoods for authentic tastes of the city's multicultural present and future.

Head to Dominion Rd in Balmoral – catch bus 258 ($3.40) from stop 7058 near the intersection of Queen St and Wellesley St – and get off at stop 8418 to be in the centre of Auckland's best Chinese food. Our favourites are Barilla Dumplings (571 Dominion Rd, Balmoral; snacks & mains $8-20; ⊙11.30am-midnight) and Shaolin Kung Fu Noodle (636 Dominion Rd, Balmoral; ⊙11.30am-11.30pm Fri-Wed, 5-11.30pm Thu), and Spicy Joint (533 Dominion Rd; mains $10-20; ⊙noon-late Wed-Mon, 5pm-late Tue) does excellent Sichuan food.

A few blocks west – catch bus 233 ($3.40) from stop 7022 in Victoria St East to stop 8316 on Sandringham Rd – for the best of the city's Indian and Sri Lankan restaurants. Jai Jalaram Khaman (570 Sandringham Rd, Sandringham; snacks & mains $7-15; ⊙11.30am-10pm; ⊘) does excellent vegetarian Gujarati food, and, a few doors away, 7 Siri's (580 Sandringham Rd, Sandringham; mains $10-15; ⊙11.30am-10pm Wed-Sun, 5-10pm Tue; ⊘) Sri Lankan highlight is the 'lump rice', a prosaically named but very tasty array of curries and sambal.

At the city's bustling night markets (www.aucklandnightmarket.co.nz) – held at a variety of suburban locations from Thursday to Saturday – around 80 ethnic food stalls offer cuisine from Argentina and Samoa, to Hungary and Turkey. Most convenient for travellers is the Onehunga market on a Thursday night. Catch a train ($4.50) from Britomart to Onehunga and walk around 650m to the Dress-Smart Outlet Shopping Centre.

If you're in town in late-March, the Auckland International Cultural Festival (p77) offers a very tasty peek into the city's ethnically diverse future, and, online, Cheap Eats (www.cheapeats.co.nz) scours Auckland for the city's best ethnic food for under $20.

Newmarket

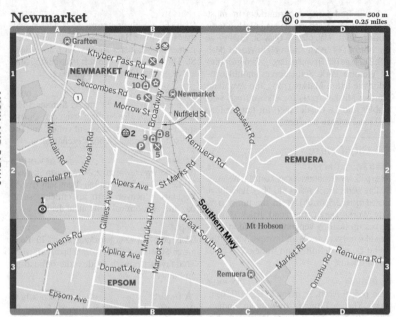

Newmarket

◎ Sights
1 Eden Garden...A2
2 Highwic...B2

◷ Activities, Courses & Tours
3 Olympic Pools & Fitness Centre.........B1

⊗ Eating
4 Basque Kitchen Bar.............................B1
5 Hansan...B2
6 Teed St Larder B1

◷ Entertainment
7 Rialto..B1

⌂ Shopping
8 Karen Walker.......................................B2
9 Texan Art Schools Newmarket..........B2
10 Zambesi Newmarket..........................B1

(communal tables, butcher tiles and a constant buzz). Dishes are designed to be shared, and a pair of clever shuckers serve up the city's freshest clams and oysters.

Ima — MIDDLE EASTERN **$$**
(Map p66; ☏09-300 7252; www.imacuisine.co.nz; 57 Fort St; breakfast $11-20, lunch $16-24, dinner shared dishes $18-30; ⊙7am-2.30pm Mon-Fri, 5.30-10.30pm Tue-Sat) Named after the Hebrew word for mother, the menu blends Israeli, Palestinian, Yemeni and Lebanese dishes. Try the *shakshuka* (baked eggs in a spicy tomato sauce) for breakfast or lunch, or rustle up a group for Ima's excellent shared dinners.

Federal & Wolfe — CAFE **$$**
(Map p66; 10 Federal St; mains $12-21; ⊙7am-3pm Mon-Sat; 🛜) 🍴 Packing crates and mismatched chairs lend an air of recycled chic to this corner cafe. Look forward to first-rate coffee and delicious food, much of it organic and free range.

Grove — MODERN NZ **$$$**
(Map p66; ☏09-368 4129; www.thegroverestaurant.co.nz; St Patrick's Sq, Wyndham St; mains $45, tasting menu with/without wine pairing $240/145; ⊙noon-3pm Thu-Fri, 6pm-late Mon-Sat) Romantic fine dining at its best: the room is cosy and moodily lit, the menu encourages sensual experimentation and the service is effortless. If you can't find anything to break the ice from the extensive wine list, give it up mate – it's never going to happen.

O'Connell Street Bistro — FRENCH **$$$**
(Map p66; ☏09-377 1884; www.oconnellstbistro.com; 3 O'Connell St; two-course lunch $60, din-

ner $28-45; ⊘lunch Mon-Fri, dinner Mon-Sat) O'Connell St is a grown-up treat, with elegant decor and wonderful food and wine, satisfying lunchtime powerbrokers and dinnertime daters alike. If you're dining before 7.30pm, a fixed-price menu is available (two/three courses $37/43).

Masu
JAPANESE $$$

(Map p66; www.skycityauckland.co.nz; 90 Federal St, SKYCITY Grand Hotel; mains $30-45, tasting menu $88; ⊘noon-3pm & 5.30pm-late) Superb Japanese food – especially from the sushi bar and the robata grill – and the added attraction of refreshing cocktails made from *shochu* (Japanese liquor).

Britomart, Viaduct Harbour & Wynyard Quarter

Baduzzi
ITALIAN $$

(Map p66; ✆09-309 9339; www.baduzzi.co.nz; cnr Jellicoe St & Fish Lane; small plates $10-20, mains $22-32; ⊘11.30am-late) This smart and sassy eatery does sophisticated spins on meatballs – try the crayfish (lobster) ones – and other robust but elegant Italian dishes. Cosy up in the intimate booths, grab a seat at the bar, or soak up some Auckland sunshine outside.

Ortolana
MEDITERRANEAN $$

(Map p66; www.britomart.org/ortolana; 31 Tyler St; small plates & mains $15-32; ⊘7am-11pm) Mediterranean and regional Italian flavours feature at this stylish restaurant with a spacious al fresco area. Much of the produce comes from the owners' small farm in rural West Auckland. There's a no-bookings policy, so try and dine between the busy lunch and dinner services.

Ebisu
JAPANESE $$$

(Map p66; www.ebisu.co.nz; 116-118 Quay St; large plates $30-36; ⊘noon-late Mon-Fri, 5pm-late Sat & Sun) Ebisu specialises in *izakaya*, a style of drinking and eating that eschews Japanese formality, yet doesn't involve food being flung around the room or chugging along on a conveyor belt. This large bar gets it exactly right, serving exquisite plates designed to be shared.

Soul Bar
MODERN NZ $$$

(Map p66; ✆09-356 7249; www.soulbar.co.nz; Viaduct Harbour; mains $22-42; ⊘11am-late) Eating seafood by the water is a must in Auckland; this modernist gastrodome boasts an unbeatable see-and-be-seen location.

Freemans Bay

Queenie's
CAFE $$

(Map p78; ✆09-378 8977; www.queenies.co.nz; 24a Spring St; breakfast & lunch $11-25, dinner $28-29; ⊘8am-10pm Wed-Sat, 8am-3pm Sun-Tue) Kiwiana reigns supreme at this eccentric corner cafe with one wall devoted to a 1950s paint-by-numbers Maori maiden mural. The food is a step up from standard cafe fare, with an adventurous menu justifying the prices. Bistro-style dinners kick in from Wednesday to Saturday.

Clooney
MODERN NZ $$$

(Map p66; ✆09-358 1702; www.clooney.co.nz; 33 Sale St; mains $40-46, seven-course tasting menu with/without wine pairings $235/140; ⊘6pm-late Tue-Sun, noon-3pm Fri) Like the Hollywood actor of the same name, Clooney is suave, stylish and extremely sophisticated, suited up in basic black. While the taste combinations are complex, the results are faultless – which, coupled with impeccable service, puts Clooney firmly in the pricey-but-worth-it category.

Ponsonby & Grey Lynn

Auckland's busiest restaurant-cafe-bar strip is so damn cool it has its own website (www.iloveponsonby.co.nz).

★Little Bird
CAFE $

(Map p78; www.littlebirdorganics.co.nz; 1a Summer St; mains $9-16; ⊘7am-4pm; ✆) ✆ Welcome to an 'unbakery', where virtually everything on the menu is prepared uncooked, but still very tasty and healthy. Tuck into dishes studded with açaí berries, quinoa and organic fruit, and there are even bagels, pad thai and tacos. Also great are the juices, smoothies and cakes.

Il Buco
PIZZA $

(Map p78; www.ilbuco.co.nz; 113 Ponsonby Rd; pizza per slice $6; ⊘8am-9pm Mon-Fri, to 8pm Sat & Sun; ✆) Delicious pizza by the slice – including vegetarian options – and tasty Italian nibbles like stuffed mushrooms and potato croquettes. Arrive before lunchtime for the best selection.

Dizengoff
CAFE $

(Map p78; 256 Ponsonby Rd; mains $7-19; ⊘6.30am-5pm) This stylish shoebox crams in a mixed crowd of corporate and fashion types, gay guys, Ponsonby denizens and travellers. Mouth-watering scrambled eggs, tempting counter food, heart-starting coffee, plus a great stack of reading material.

AUCKLAND

Kingsland & Mt Eden

500 m
0.25 miles

GRAFTON

Grafton Rd

Khyber Pass Rd

Nugent Rd

Symonds St

Boston Rd

NEWTON

France St

20

24 18

Mt Eden Rd

Normanby Rd

Enfield St

Edwin St

EDEN
TERRACE

Mt Eden

Clive Rd

P

3

Mt Eden Rd

Esplanade Rd

Bellevue Rd

MT EDEN

Oaklands Rd

15 8

Stokes Rd

Sherbourne St

5

Pentland Ave

6

Woodford Rd

Valley Rd

Spicy Joint (660m);
Shaolin Kung Fu Noodle (780m);
Barilla Dumplings (830m);

Prospect Tce

Horoeka Ave

Wynyard St

View Rd

Bellevue Rd

Valley Rd

19

11

Dominion Rd

Newton Rd

Ian McKinnon Dr

New North Rd

ARCH
HILL

16

Bond St

Onslow Rd

Walters Rd

Bellwood Ave

7

Eden
Park

23

King Edward Pde

14

SANDRINGHAM

Reimers Ave

Sandringham Rd

Jai Jalaram Khaman (1.2km);
7 Siri (1.3km)

Central Rd

Kingsland

KINGSLAND

10

13

16

22

21

25

Great North Rd

Cummer Rd

GREY
LYNN

Surrey Cres

North Western Mwy

Kingsland Ave

School Rd

17

New North Rd

Morningside

MORNINGSIDE

Morningside Dr

Sainsbury Rd

Bullock Track

Old Mill Rd

WESTERN
SPRINGS

Western Springs Rd

St Lukes Rd

Great North Rd

2

4

1

MT
ALBERT

Linwood Ave

Asquith Ave

Baldwin Ave

K

Kingsland & Mt Eden

◎ Sights
1 Auckland Zoo A1
2 MOTAT B2
3 Mt Eden G4
4 Western Springs A2

⊜ Sleeping
5 Bamber House F3
6 Bavaria F3
7 Eden Park B&B E4
8 Oaklands Lodge G4
9 Pentlands F4

⊗ Eating
10 Atomic Roastery D3
11 Burgerfuel E3
12 French Cafe G1
13 Fridge D3
14 Merediths E4
15 Molten G4
16 Petra Shawarma D3
17 Sake Bar 601 .... C3

◎ Drinking & Nightlife
18 Galbraith's Alehouse G1
19 Ginger Minx E3
20 Kings Arms Tavern F1
   Liquid Molten .... (see 15)
21 Neighbourhood D3
22 Portland Public House D3

◎ Entertainment
23 Eden Park D3
24 Power Station G1

◎ Shopping
25 Royal Jewellery Studio D3

Fred's CAFE $
(Map p78; 181 Ponsonby Rd; snacks & mains $7-16) This funky little spot features home-style baking, good coffee, and interesting fare like coconut porridge, *menemen* (Turkish baked eggs), and breakfast bruschetta. Scour the stacks of cool magazines inside or chill in the compact garden.

Bird on a Wire SANDWICHES, CAFE $
(Map p78; www.birdonawire.co.nz; 234 Ponsonby Rd; sandwiches & burgers $8-14, salads $11-21; ⊙11am-9.30pm) Tasty sandwiches and healthy burgers, seasonal salads, and rotisserie chickens to take away. Select your baste of choice – like Jamaican jerk or salsa verde – and you're sorted. There's another smaller **Box of Bird** (Map p66; 12 Commerce St; ⊙10am-7pm Mon-Fri) branch in the central city.

Ponsonby Village International Food Court FOOD HALL $
(Map p78; www.ponsonbyfoodcourt.co.nz; 106 Ponsonby Rd; mains $8-20; ⊙10am-10pm; 🖉) Italian, Japanese, Malaysian, Chinese, Turkish, Thai, Lao and Indian flavours all on offer, and excellent Vietnamese and Indonesian.

Burgerfuel BURGERS $
(Map p78; www.burgerfuel.com; 114 Ponsonby Rd; burgers $6-13; 🖉) 🍴 Gourmet burgers. Also has branches in the **city** (Map p66; 291 Queen St; ⊙10am-11pm), **Parnell** (Map p70; 187 Parnell Rd; ⊙11am-10pm) and **Mt Eden** (Map p86; 214 Dominion Rd; ⊙11am-10pm).

⭐**Blue Breeze Inn** CHINESE $$
(Map p78; 🖉09-360 0303; www.thebluebreezeinn. co.nz; 146 Ponsonby Rd, Ponsonby Central; small plates $10-18, larger plates $26-38; ⊙5pm-late) Regional Chinese flavours combine with a funky retro Pacific ambience. The waitstaff are sassy, the rum cocktails are deliciously strong, and menu standouts include steamed buns with Peking pork belly and pickled cucumber, and cumin-spiced lamb.

Ponsonby Central CAFES, RESTAURANTS $$
(Map p78; www.ponsonbycentral.co.nz; 136-138 Ponsonby Rd; mains $15-35; ⊙11.30am-10.30pm Sun-Wed, 11.30am-midnight Thu-Sat) From Auckland's best pizza to Argentinean, Thai and Japanese, loads of flavour-filled restaurants and cafes fill this upmarket laneway collection of eateries and gourmet food shops.

MooChowChow THAI $$
(Map p78; 🖉09-360 6262; www.moochowchow. co.nz; 23 Ponsonby Rd; dishes $16-30; ⊙noon-3pm Tue-Fri, 5.30pm-late Mon-Sat) It's Thai, Nahm Jim, but not as we know it. Bangkok's street food has been channelled into this supremely Ponsonby mooching spot without missing a piquant note. Killer Asian-inspired cocktails, too. Be ready to share a table with other diners.

Mekong Baby ASIAN $$
(Map p78; www.mekongbaby.com; 262 Ponsonby Rd; mains $24-32; ⊙noon-late Tue-Sun) Stylish and buzzing restaurant and bar offering excellent Southeast Asian flavours, mainly from Vietnam, Cambodia and Laos. Try the goat curry.

Satya INDIAN $$
(Map p78; 🖉09-361 3612; www.satya.co.nz; 17 Great North Rd; mains $11-26; ⊙11.30am-2.30pm Mon-Sat, 5.30-10pm daily; 🖉) Hugely popular, this humble-looking and humbly priced eatery

has the best *dahi puri* (chickpea, potato and yoghurt on a pappadam) in town. Also on **K Rd** (Map p66; ☑ 09-377 0007; 271 Karanahape Rd; ⏱ 11.30am-2.30pm Mon-Sat, 5.30-10pm daily).

Ponsonby Road Bistro
INTERNATIONAL **$$**

(Map p78; ☑ 09-360 1611; www.ponsonbyroadbistro.co.nz; 165 Ponsonby Rd; mains $25-36; ⏱ noon-3pm Mon-Fri, 5.30pm-late Mon-Sat) Portions are large at this modern, upmarket restaurant with an Italian/French sensibility and first-rate service. Imported cheese and wine are a highlight, and the crispy-based pizzas make a delicious shared snack.

Prego
ITALIAN **$$**

(Map p78; ☑ 09-376 3095; www.prego.co.nz; 226 Ponsonby Rd; mains $23-40; ⏱ noon-midnight) This friendly and stylish Italian restaurant covers all the bases, with a fireplace in winter and a courtyard in summer.

Landreth & Co
CAFE **$$**

(Map p78; www.landrethandco.co.nz; 272 Ponsonby Rd; mains $11-25; ⏱ 6.30am-4pm; 🛜) A popular brunch spot with a sunny rear courtyard and free wi-fi. It's fully licensed, just in case you feel the urge for a beer with your truffled eggs.

Cocoro
JAPANESE **$$$**

(Map p78; ☑ 09-360 0927; www.cocoro.co.nz; 56a Brown St; dishes $7-28, degustation $85; ⏱ noon-2pm & 5.30-10pm Tue-Sat) Japanese elegance infuses everything about this excellent restaurant, from the soft lighting and chic decor, to the delicate flavours of the artistically arranged food. Dishes are designed to be shared.

✹ Newton

K Rd is known for its late-night clubs, but cafes and plenty of inexpensive ethnic restaurants are mixed in with the vintage clothing stores, secondhand boutiques, tattooists and adult shops.

Alleluya
CAFE **$**

(Map p66; St Kevin's Arcade, Karangahape Rd; mains $10-19; ⏱ 9am-5.30pm Mon-Sat, to 3pm Sun; 🛜☑) To the bohemian denizens of K Rd, Alleluya means good coffee, moreish cakes and lots of vegetarian options. It's situated at the end of the city's hippest arcade, with windows offering a wonderful snapshot of the city skyline.

Scullery
CAFE **$$**

(Map p66; 166 Karangahape Rd; mains $12-20; ⏱ 7am-6.30pm Sun-Wed, to 9pm Thu-Sat; ☑) 🍃 Healthy breakfast options include mush-

room ragu with halloumi cheese, and the Korean-tinged beef tacos are great for lunch. From Thursday to Saturday dinner is served with a small selection of local wine and craft beer, and a zingy quartet of cocktails.

Coco's Cantina
ITALIAN **$$**

(Map p66; www.cocoscantina.co.nz; 376 Karangahape Rd; mains $25-32; ⏱ 5pm-late Tue-Sat) Rub shoulders with Auckland's hipsters and foodsters at this bustling cantina where the wait for a table is part of the experience. Propping up the bar is hardly a hardship: the ambience and drinks list see to that. The rustic menu is narrowly focused, seasonal and invariably delicious.

French Cafe
FRENCH **$$$**

(Map p86; ☑ 09-377 1911; www.thefrenchcafe.co.nz; 210 Symonds St; mains $46, tasting menu with/without wine pairings $220/140; ⏱ noon-3pm Fri, 6pm-late Tue-Sat) The legendary French Cafe has been rated as one of Auckland's top restaurants for more than 20 years now and it still continues to excel. The cuisine is nominally French-influenced, but chef Simon Wright sneaks in lots of tasty Asian and Pacific Rim touches.

✹ Kingsland

Petra Shawarma
MIDDLE EASTERN **$**

(Map p86; 482 New North Rd; mains $10-15; ⏱ 11am-late) Owned by a friendly Jordanian family, Petra serves up lighter, healthier kebabs, and the dips and salads are also worth the short train ride to Kingsland.

Atomic Roastery
CAFE **$**

(Map p86; www.atomiccoffee.co.nz; 420c New North Rd; snacks $9-10; ⏱ 8am-3pm Mon-Sat, 9am-2pm Sun) Java hounds should follow their noses to this, one of the country's best-known coffee roasters. Tasty accompaniments include pies served in mini-frypans, bagels, salads and cakes.

Fridge
CAFE **$$**

(Map p86; 7.30am-4pm; 507 New North Rd; mains $9-22; ⏱ breakfast & lunch) Gourmet pies, healthy salads and wraps, and drool-inducing cakes.

Sake Bar 601
JAPANESE **$$**

(Map p86; ☑ 09-849 7268; www.601newnorthroad.co.nz; 601 New North Rd; mains $20-35; ⏱ 11.30am-1.30pm & 6-9.30pm Tue-Sat) Order a frosty Sapporo beer and watch the friendly Japanese surf-crazy owners prepare some of the best sushi and sashimi in town. Other standouts are the tempura prawns and terikayi chicken. The compact restaurant is very popular, so book ahead.

✕ Mt Eden

Merediths   MODERN NZ **$$$**
(Map p86; 📞 09-623 3140; www.merediths.co.nz; 365 Dominion Rd; 6-9 course degustation $90-140; ⊘noon-3pm Fri, 6pm-late Tue-Sat) Dining at Merediths is the culinary equivalent of blackwater rafting – tastes surprise you at every turn, you never know what's coming next and you're left with a sense of breathless exhilaration.

Molten   MODERN NZ **$$$**
(Map p86; 📞 09-638 7236; www.molten.co.nz; 422 Mt Eden Rd; mains $29-37; ⊘noon-3pm Wed-Fri, 6pm-late Mon-Sat) Under the volcano's shadow, Molten oozes neighbourhood charm and erupts with flavour. The consistently excellent menu takes advantage of seasonal produce to create innovative meals.

✕ Parnell & Newmarket

Teed St Larder   CAFE **$**
(Map p84; www.teedstreetlarder.co.nz; 7 Teed St; ⊘8am-4pm) Polished concrete floors, beer crate tables and colourful oversized lampshades set the scene at Newmarket's best cafe. There are plenty of enticing cooked items on the menu but it's hard to go past the delicious sandwiches and tarts.

Basque Kitchen Bar   TAPAS **$**
(Map p84; 📞 09-523 1057; www.basquekitchenbar. co.nz; 61 Davies Cres; tapas $7-15; ⊘4.30pm-late Mon-Thu & Sat, noon-late Fri) This dark little bar serves delectable tapas accompanied by Spanish wine, beers and sherry. The braised octopus and the chorizo and prawns are both excellent; leave room for dessert of *churros* (Spanish doughnuts).

La Cigale   FRENCH **$$**
(Map p70; 📞 09-366 9361; www.lacigale.co.nz; 69 St Georges Bay Rd; cafe mains $8-18, bistro mains $34; ⊘cafe 9am-4pm Mon-Fri, bistro dinner Wed-Fri from 6pm, market 9am-1.30pm Sat & Sun) Catering to Francophile foodies, this warehouse stocks French imports and has a patisserie-laden cafe. During the weekend farmers markets, this *cigale* (cicada) really chirps, with stalls laden with local artisan produce. From Wednesday to Friday the space is converted into a quirky evening bistro. Booking ahead is recommended.

✕ Devonport

Calliope Road Cafe   CAFE **$**
(Map p81; 33 Calliope Rd; mains $9-18; ⊘8am-3pm Wed-Mon) Devonport's best cafe is a little back from the main tourist strip, and serves a tasty mix of cafe classics and Southeast Asian dishes to locals in the know.

Bette's Bar & Eatery   CAFE, BAR **$$**
(Map p81; www.facebook.com/bettesdevonport; 8 Victoria Rd; tapas $15-18; ⊘11am-late) Decent wine, cocktails and beer, and good tapas and bar snacks make for a top spot to chill out after exploring Devonport.

✕ Other Areas

★ St Heliers Bay Bistro   MODERN NZ **$$**
(Map p64; www.stheliersbaybistro.co.nz; 387 Tamaki Dr; mains $14-26; ⊘7am-11pm) Catch the bus along pretty Tamaki Dr to this classy eatery with harbour views. No bookings are taken, but the switched-on crew soon find space for diners. Look forward to dishes infused with mainly Mediterranean and Middle Eastern flavours.

Takapuna Beach Cafe   CAFE **$$**
(Map p64; www.takapunabeachcafe.co.nz; 22 The Promenade; mains $15-27; ⊘7am-late; ⚑) Sophisticated cafe fare, combined with excellent views of Takapuna Beach, sees this cafe constantly buzz If you can't snaffle a table, grab an award-winning ice cream – our favourite is the salted caramel – and take a lazy stroll along the beach.

Engine Room   MODERN NZ **$$$**
(Map p64; 📞 09-480 9502; www.engineroom.net. nz; 115 Queen St, Northcote; mains $34-36; ⊘6pm-late Tue-Sat, noon-2.30pm Fri) One of Auckland's best restaurants, this informal eatery serves up lighter-than-air goats cheese soufflés, inventive mains and oh-my-God chocolate truffles. It's worth booking ahead and catching the ferry to Northcote wharf; the restaurant is a further 1km walk away.

The Commons   MODERN NZ **$$$**
(Map p64; 📞 09-929 2791; www.thecommons. co.nz; 21 Hurstmere Rd, Takapuna; bar snacks $9-16, mains $36; ⊘11.30am-late) Part of a culinary makeover of a former department store – other adjacent eateries include good Mexican and Italian flavours – The Commons is a spacious and sophisticated combination of elegant restaurant and buzzy bar.

♟ Drinking & Nightlife

Auckland's nightlife is quiet during the week – for some vital signs, head to Ponsonby Rd, Britomart or the Viaduct. K Rd wakes up late on Friday and Saturday; don't even bother staggering this way before 11pm.

♟ City Centre

Brothers Beer   BEER HALL

(Map p66; www.brothersbeer.co.nz; 90 Wellesley St, City Works Depot; ⊙noon-10pm Wed-Sat, noon-8pm Tue & Sun, closed Mon) Our favourite Auckland bar combines industrial decor with 18 taps crammed with Brothers' own brews and guest beers from NZ and further afield. Hundreds more bottled beers await chilling in the fridges, and bar food includes top-notch pizza. Check the website for occasional tap takeovers.

Mo's   BAR

(Map p66; www.mosbar.co.nz; cnr Wolfe & Federal Sts; ⊙4pm-3am Mon-Fri, 6pm-3am Sat) There's something about this tiny corner bar that makes you want to invent problems just so the barperson can solve them with soothing words and an expertly poured martini.

Hotel de Brett   BAR

(Map p66; www.hoteldebrett.com; 2 High St; ⊙noon-late) Grab a beer in the corner bar, a cocktail in the chic art-deco house bar, or nab a spot by the fire in the atrium, which is an interesting covered space fashioned from the alleyway between the old buildings.

Cassette Nine   CLUB

(Map p66; www.cassettenine.com; 9 Vulcan Lane; ⊙noon-late Tue-Sat) Hipsters gravitate to this eccentric bar/club for music ranging from live indie to international DJ sets.

Ding Dong Lounge   CLUB

(Map p66; www.facebook.com/dingdongloungenz; 26 Wyndham St; admission varies; ⊙8pm-4am Wed-Sat) Rock, indie and alternative sounds from live bands and DJs.

♟ Britomart, Viaduct Harbour & Wynyard Quarter

Tyler Street Garage   BAR

(Map p66; www.tylerstreetgarage.co.nz; 120 Quay St; ⊙11.30am-late) Just in case you were in any doubt that this was actually a garage, they've left the parking lines painted on the concrete floor. A compact roof terrace looks over the wharves.

Jack Tar   PUB

(Map p66; www.jacktar.co.nz; 34-37 Jellicoe St, North Wharf; ⊙10am-late Mon-Thu, 8am-late Fri-Sun) A top spot for a late-afternoon/early-

---

GAY & LESBIAN AUCKLAND

The Queen City (as it's known for completely coincidental reasons) has by far the country's biggest gay population, with the bright lights attracting gays and lesbians from all over the country. However, the even brighter lights of Sydney eventually steal many of the 30- to 40-somethings, leaving a gap in the demographic. There are a handful of gay venues, but they only really kick off on the weekends.

For the latest, see the fortnightly newspaper *Express* (available from gay venues) or www.gaynz.com. The year's big events are the Auckland Pride Festival (p76) and the Out Takes (p77) film festival.

Venues change with alarming regularity, but these ones were the stayers at the time of research:

Family (Map p66; www.familybar.co.nz; 270 Karangahape Rd, Newton) Trashy, brash and young, this bar can be a lot of fun, with dancing into the wee hours.

Urge (Map p66; www.urgebar.co.nz; 490 Karangahape Rd, Newton; ⊙9pm-late Thu-Sat, 3-7pm Sun) Older and hairier, this black-painted pocket-sized venue has DJs on Friday and Saturday nights.

Poof (Map p78; www.facebook.com/PoofonPonsonby; 212 Ponsonby Rd, Ponsonby; ⊙5pm-late Tue-Sat) Cocktail bar with a colourful pop-culture vibe.

Legend (Map p66; www.facebook.com/legend.co.nz; 373 Karangahape Rd, 1st fl; ⊙10pm-4am Thu-Sun) Friendly, clubby vibe, drag shows and excellent views of the city.

Centurian (Map p66; www.centuriansauna.co.nz; 18 Beresford St, Newton; admission before/after 3pm $23/28; ⊙11am-2am Sun-Thu, 11am-6am Fri & Sat) Gay men's sauna.

evening beer or wine amid the relaxed vibe of the waterfront Wynyard Quarter. Try the prawn and sweet chilli pizza or the salt-and-pepper-squid salad.

Xuxu
COCKTAIL BAR

(Map p66; cnr Galway & Commerce Sts; ⊗ 3pm-late Mon-Sat) A winning combination of Asian-tinged cocktails and bar snacks inspired by Vietnamese street food. DJs kick in around weekends.

Orleans
BAR, LIVE MUSIC

(Map p66; www.orleans.co.nz; 48 Customs St; ⊗11.30am-midnight Sun-Thu, to 4am Fri & Sat) This South Pacific gumbo spin on a southern US jazz bar has wicked cocktails, and live jazz and blues every night. Bar snacks include po'boy sandwiches.

Northern Steamship Co.
PUB

(Map p66; www.northernsteamship.co.nz; 122 Quay St; ⊗11am-late) Standard lamps hang upside down from the ceiling while the mural behind the bar dreams of NZ summer holidays in this good-looking large pub near the train station.

Ponsonby & Grey Lynn

Along Ponsonby Rd, the line between cafe, restaurant, bar and club gets blurred. A lot of eateries also have live music or become clubs later on.

Golden Dawn
BAR

(Map p78; www.goldendawn.co.nz; 134b Ponsonby Rd, cnr Ponsonby Rd & Richmond Rd; ⊗4pm-late Tue-Thu, from 3pm Fri-Sun) Occupying an old shopfront and an inviting stables yard, this hip late-night drinking den regularly hosts happenings including DJs and live bands. There's also excellent food on offer ($12 to $16), including pulled-pork rolls, and prawn buns with Japanese mayo and chilli. Entrance is via the unmarked door just around the corner on Richmond Rd.

Freida Margolis
BAR

(www.facebook.com/FreidaMargolis; 440 Richmond Rd, West Lynn; ⊗4pm-late) Formerly a butchers – look out for the West Lynn Organic Meats sign – this corner location is now a great little neighbourhood bar with a backstreets-of-Bogotá ambience. Loyal locals sit outside with their well-behaved dogs, supping on sangria, wine and craft beer, snacking on sliders and platters, and enjoying eclectic sounds from the owner's big vinyl collection.

Dida's Wine Lounge & Tapas Bar
WINE BAR

(Map p78; www.glengarrywines.co.nz; 54 Jervois Rd; ⊗11.30am-midnight) Great food and an even better wine list attract a grown-up crowd. There's an associated wine store, providore and cafe next door, and another, more food-focused branch in Freemans Bay (Map p66; cnr Sale & Wellesley Sts; tapas $7-12; ⊗8am-6pm Sun & Mon, 7am-8pm Tue-Sat).

Newton

Wine Cellar & Whammy Bar
BAR, LIVE MUSIC

(Map p66; www.facebook.com/thewhammybar; St Kevin's Arcade, Karangahape Rd; ⊗5pm-midnight Mon-Thu, 5.30pm-2am Fri & Sat) Secreted downstairs in an arcade, this bar is dark, grungy and very cool, with regular live music in the neighbouring Whammy Bar from Thursday to Saturday.

Galbraith's Alehouse
BREWERY, PUB

(Map p86; www.alehouse.co.nz; 2 Mt Eden Rd; ⊗noon-11pm) Brewing real ales and lagers on site, this cosy English-style pub offers bliss on tap. There are always more craft beers on the guest taps, and the food's also very good.

Kings Arms Tavern
LIVE MUSIC, PUB

(Map p86; www.kingsarms.co.nz; 59 France St; ⊗varies by event) Auckland's leading small venue for local and up-and-coming international bands.

Ink & Coherent
CLUB

(Map p66; www.inkcoherent.co.nz; 262 & 268 Karangahape Rd) Neighbouring venues for serious dance aficionados, sometimes hosting big-name DJs.

Thirsty Dog
LIVE MUSIC, PUB

(Map p66; www.thirstydog.co.nz; 469 Karangahape Rd) Pub with comedy, folk, reggae and poetry slams.

 Mt Eden

Liquid Molten
WINE BAR, TAPAS

(Map p86; www.molten.co.nz; 42 Mt Eden Rd; ⊙4pm-late Mon-Sat) Grab a spot in the cosy leather banquettes or venture out the back to the al fresco garden. Either way enjoy a grown up but relaxed ambience, a great wine and beer list, and innovative bar food.

Ginger Minx
BAR

(Map p86; www.facebook.com/GingerMinxNZ; 117 Valley Rd; ⊙4pm-3am Wed-Sun) Quirky decor, retro furniture, and a serious attitude to cocktails feature at this hipsterish neighbourhood bar.

 Kingsland

Neighbourhood
BAR

(Map p86; www.neighbourhood.co.nz; 498 New North Rd; ⊙11am-late;) With picture windows overlooking Eden Park and a front terrace that's pick-up central after dark, this upmarket pub is the place to be either side of rugby fixtures. DJs play on weekends.

Portland Public House
BAR, LIVE MUSIC

(Map p86; 463 New North Rd; ⊙noon-late Tue-Sun) With mismatched furniture, cartoon-themed art, and lots of hidden nooks and crannies, the Portland Public House is like spending a few lazy hours at a good mate's place. It's also an excellent location for live music.

★ Entertainment

For listings, check the *NZ Herald's Time Out* magazine on Thursday and again in its Saturday edition. Visit www.kroad.co.nz for Karangahape Rd bars and clubs.

Tickets for most major events can be bought from the following:

Ticketek
TICKETING AGENCY

(Map p66; ☑0800 842 538; www.ticketek.co.nz) Outlets include Real Groovy (p93) and SkyCity Theatre (Map p66; ☑09-363 6000; www.skycity.co.nz; cnr Victoria & Federal Sts).

Ticketmaster
TICKETING AGENCY

(Map p70; ☑09-970 9700; www.ticketmaster.co.nz) Outlets at Real Groovy (p93), Vector Arena (p92), Aotea Centre (p93).

Live Music

Power Station
LIVE MUSIC

(Map p86; www.powerstation.net.nz; 33 Mt Eden Rd; admission varies) Midrange venue popular with up-and-coming overseas acts and established Kiwi bands.

Vector Arena
STADIUM

(Map p70; ☑09-358 1250; www.vectorarena.co.nz; Mahuhu Cres; admission varies; ⊙9am-2pm) Auckland's top indoor venue for major touring acts.

Cinema

Most cinemas offer cheaper rates on weekdays before 5pm; Tuesday is usually bargain day.

Rialto
CINEMA

(Map p84; ☑09-369 2417; www.rialto.co.nz; 167 Broadway, Newmarket; adult/child $16.50/10) Mainly art-house and international films, plus better mainstream fare and regular specialist film festivals.

Academy Cinemas
CINEMA

(Map p66; ☑09-373 2761; www.academycinemas.co.nz; 44 Lorne St, City; adult/child $15.50/10) Foreign and art-house films in the basement of the Central Library.

Event Cinemas
CINEMA

(Map p66; ☑09-369 2400; www.eventcinemas.co.nz; Level 3, 297 Queen St, City; adult/child $17/12) Blockbusters, bowling alley and food court.

NZ Film Archives
CINEMA

(Map p66; ☑09-379 0688; www.filmarchive.org.nz; 300 Karangahape Rd, Newton; ⊙11am-5pm Mon-Fri) Around 2000 Kiwi feature films, documentaries and TV shows, which you can watch for free on a computer monitor.

Theatre, Classical Music & Comedy

Auckland's main arts and entertainment complex is grouped around Aotea Sq. Branded The Edge (☑09-357 3355; www.theedge.co.nz), it comprises the Town Hall, Civic Theatre (p63) and Aotea Centre.

Auckland Town Hall
CLASSICAL MUSIC

(Map p66; 305 Queen St) This elegant Edwardian venue (1911) hosts the NZ Symphony Orchestra (www.nzso.co.nz) and Auckland Philharmonia (www.apo.co.nz). Also used by international rock bands.

Aotea Centre THEATRE
(Map p66; 50 Mayoral Dr; ⊙ 9am-5.30pm Mon-Fri, Sat & Sun 10am-4pm) Theatre, dance, ballet and opera. **NZ Opera** (www.nzopera.com) regularly performs here.

Q Theatre THEATRE
(Map p66; ☑ 09-309 9771; www.qtheatre.co.nz; 305 Queen St) Theatre by various companies and intimate live music. **Silo Theatre** (www.silotheatre.co.nz) often performs here.

Classic Comedy Club COMEDY
(Map p66; ☑ 09-373 4321; www.comedy.co.nz; 321 Queen St; tickets $5-27) Performances on Mondays and from Wednesday to Saturday.

Maidment Theatre THEATRE
(Map p66; ☑ 09-308 2383; www.maidment.auckland.ac.nz; 8 Alfred St) The University's theatre often stages **Auckland Theatre Company** (www.atc.co.nz) productions.

Sport

Eden Park RUGBY, CRICKET
(Map p86; www.edenpark.co.nz; Reimers Ave, Kingsland) This stadium for top rugby (winter) and cricket (summer) tests by the **All Blacks** (www.allblacks.com) and the **Black Caps** (www.blackcaps.co.nz), respectively. Also home ground for **Auckland Rugby** (www.aucklandrugby.co.nz), the **Blues** (www.theblues.co.nz) Super Rugby team, and **Auckland Cricket** (www.aucklandcricket.co.nz). Catch the train from Britomart to Kingsland and follow the crowds.

Mt Smart Stadium RUGBY, FOOTBALL
(Map p64; www.mtsmartstadium.co.nz; Maurice Rd, Penrose) Home ground for the **Warriors** (www.warriors.co.nz) rugby league team, **Auckland Football Federation** (www.aucklandfootball.org.nz) and **Athletics Auckland** (www.athleticsauckland.co.nz). Also *really* big concerts.

North Shore Events Centre BASKETBALL
(Map p64; ☑ 09-443 8199; www.nseventscentre.co.nz; Argus Pl, Wairau Valley) Along with Vector Arena, this is one of the two home courts of the **NZ Breakers** (www.nzbreakers.co.nz) basketball team and an occasional concert venue.

ASB Tennis Centre TENNIS
(Map p70; www.aucklandtennis.co.nz; 1 Tennis Lane, Parnell) In January the women's **ASB Classic** (www.asbclassic.co.nz) is held here, followed by the men's **Heineken Open** (www.heinekenopen.co.nz).

🛍 Shopping

Followers of fashion should head to the Britomart Precinct, Newmarket's Teed and Nuffield Sts, and Ponsonby Rd. For vintage clothing and secondhand boutiques try K Rd or Ponsonby Rd.

🛍 City Centre

Real Groovy MUSIC
(Map p66; www.realgroovy.co.nz; 438 Queen St; ⊙ 9am-7pm Sat-Wed, 9am-9pm Thu & Fri) Masses of new, secondhand and rare releases in vinyl and CD format, as well as concert tickets, giant posters, DVDs, books, magazines and clothes.

Pauanesia GIFTS
(Map p66; www.pauanesia.co.nz; 35 High St; ⊙ 9.30am-6.30pm Mon-Fri, 10am-4.30pm Sat & Sun) Homewares and gifts with a Polynesian and Kiwiana influence.

Unity Books BOOKS
(Map p66; www.unitybooks.co.nz; 19 High St; ⊙ 8.30am-7pm Mon-Thu, 8.30am-8pm Fri, 9am-6pm Sat, 11am-6pm Sun) Independent bookshop.

Strangely Normal CLOTHING
(Map p66; www.strangelynormal.com; 19 O'Connell St; ⊙ 10am-5pm Mon-Sat, 11am-4pm Sun) Quality, NZ-made, men's tailored shirts straight out of *Blue Hawaii* sit alongside hipster hats, sharp shoes and cufflinks.

Karen Walker CLOTHING
(Map p66; www.karenwalker.com; 18 Te Ara Tahuhu, The Pavilions, Britomart Precinct; ⊙ 10am-6pm) Join Madonna and Kirsten Dunst in wearing Walker's cool (but pricey) threads. Also

---

AUCKLAND, THE BIG TARO

There are nearly 180,000 Pacific Islanders (PI) living in Auckland, making it the world's principal Polynesian city. Samoans are by far the largest group, followed by Cook Islanders, Tongans, Niueans, Fijians, Tokelauans and Tuvaluans. The biggest PI communities can be found in South Auckland and pockets of West and Central Auckland.

Like the Maori renaissance of recent decades, Pasifika has become a hot commodity for Auckland hipsters. You'll find PI motifs everywhere: in art, architecture, fashion, homewares, movies and especially in music.

in **Ponsonby** (Map p78; 128a Ponsonby Rd) and **Newmarket** (Map p84; 6 Balm St).

Zambesi CLOTHING
(Map p66; www.zambesi.co.nz; 56 Tyler St; ☺10am-6pm) Iconic NZ label much sought after by local and international celebs. Also in **Ponsonby** (Map p78; 169 Ponsonby Rd) and **Newmarket** (Map p84; 38 Osborne St).

Whitcoulls BOOKS
(Map p66; www.whitcoulls.co.nz; 210 Queen St; ☺8am-6pm) Main branch of the biggest local chain.

🔒 Ponsonby & Grey Lynn

Women's Bookshop BOOKS
(Map p78; www.womensbookshop.co.nz; 105 Ponsonby Rd; ☺10am-6pm) Excellent independent bookshop.

Texan Art Schools ART & CRAFTS
(Map p78; www.texanartschools.co.nz; 95 Ponsonby Rd; ☺9.30am-5.30pm) A collective of 200 local artists sell their wares here. Also in **Newmarket** (Map p84; 366 Broadway).

🔒 Kingsland

Royal Jewellery Studio JEWELLERY
(Map p86; www.royaljewellerystudio.com; 486 New North Rd; ☺10am-5pm) Work by local artisans, including beautiful Maori designs and authentic *pounamu* (greenstone) jewellery.

🔒 Other Areas

Otara Market MARKET
(Map p64; Newbury St; ☺6am-noon Sat) Held in the car park between the Manukau Polytech and the Otara town centre, this market has a palpable Polynesian atmosphere and is good for South Pacific food, music and fashions. Take bus 497 from Britomart ($6.80, 50 minutes).

Avondale Sunday Market MARKET
(Map p64; www.avondalesundaymarkets.co.nz; Avondale Racecourse, Ash St; ☺6am-noon Sun) Strong Asian and Polynesian atmosphere and good for fresh produce. Take the train from Britomart station to Avondale.

ℹ️ Information

INTERNET ACCESS
Auckland Council offers free wi-fi in parts of the city centre, Newton, Ponsonby, Kingsland, Mt Eden and Parnell. All public libraries offer free wi-fi, and internet cafes catering to gaming junkies are scattered about the inner city.

MEDIA
Metro Glossy monthly magazine covering Auckland issues in depth.
New Zealand Herald (www.nzherald.co.nz) The country's biggest daily newspaper.
The Denizen (www.thedenizen.co.nz) The newest cafes, bars and restaurants in town.

MEDICAL SERVICES
Auckland City Hospital (☎09-367 0000; www.adhb.govt.nz; Park Rd, Grafton; ☺24hr) The city's main hospital has a dedicated accident and emergency (A&E) service.
Auckland Metro Doctors & Travelcare (☎09-373 4621; www.aucklandmetrodoctors.co.nz; 17 Emily Pl; ☺9am-5.30pm Mon-Fri, 10am-2pm Sat) Health care for travellers, including vaccinations and travel consultations.
Starship Children's Hospital (☎09-367 0000; www.adhb.govt.nz; Park Rd, Grafton; ☺24hr) Has its own A&E department.

TOURIST INFORMATION
For more information about i-SITE centres, see www.aucklandnz.com.
Auckland Domestic Airport i-SITE (Map p64; ☎09-256 8480; ☺7am-9pm) In the Air New Zealand terminal.
Auckland International Airport i-SITE (Map p64; ☎09-275 6467; ☺24hr) On your left as you exit the customs hall.
Cornwall Park Information Centre (Map p64; ☎09-630 8485; www.cornwallpark.co.nz; Huia Lodge; ☺10am-4pm)
Devonport i-SITE (Map p81; ☎09-446 0677; www.northshorenz.com; Devonport Wharf; ☺8.30am-5pm; 🖥️)
DOC Auckland Information Centre (Department of Conservation; Map p66; ☎09-379 6476; www.doc.govt.nz; 137 Quay St, Princes Wharf; ☺9am-5pm Mon-Sat)
Karanga Plaza Kiosk (Map p66; www.waterfrontauckland.co.nz; Wynyard Quarter; ☺10am-5.30pm)
Princes Wharf i-SITE (Map p66; ☎09-307 0612; 137 Quay St; ☺9am-5.30pm)
SkyCity i-SITE (Map p66; ☎09-363 7182; SkyCity Atrium, cnr Victoria & Federal Sts; ☺8am-8pm)
Takapuna i-SITE (Map p64; ☎09-486 8670; 34-36 Hurstmere Rd; ☺8.30am-5pm Mon-Fri, 10am-3pm Sat & Sun)

ℹ️ Getting There & Away

AIR
Auckland is the main international gateway to NZ, and a hub for domestic flights. **Auckland International Airport** (AKL; Map p64; ☎09-275

0789; www.aucklandairport.co.nz; Ray Emery Dr, Mangere) is 21km south of the city centre. It has separate international and domestic terminals, each with a tourist information centre. A free shuttle service operates every 15 minutes (5am to 10.30pm) between the terminals and there's also a signposted footpath (about a 10-minute walk). Both terminals have left-luggage facilities, ATMs and car-rental desks, although you may get better rates from companies in town.

For flights to Great Barrier Island, see p109.

Air New Zealand (☑09-357 3000; www.airnewzealand.co.nz) Flies to Kaitaia, Kerikeri, Whangarei, Hamilton, Tauranga, Whakatane, Gisborne, Rotorua, Taupo, New Plymouth, Napier, Whanganui, Palmerston North, Masterton, Wellington, Nelson, Blenheim, Christchurch, Queenstown and Dunedin.

Jetstar (☑0800 800 995; www.jetstar.com) To Wellington, Christchurch, Queenstown and Dunedin.

Sunair (☑0800 786 847; www.sunair.co.nz) To Whitianga (one way $160).

BUS

Coaches depart from 172 Quay St, opposite the Ferry Building, except for InterCity services, which depart from **SkyCity Coach Terminal** (Map p66; ☑09-913 6220; 102 Hobson St). Many southbound services also stop at the airport.

Go Kiwi (☑07-866 0336; www.go-kiwi.co.nz) Daily Auckland City–International Airport–Thames–Tairua–Whitianga shuttles.

InterCity (www.intercity.co.nz)

Naked Bus (☑0900 62533; www.nakedbus.com) Naked Buses travel along SH1 as far north as Kerikeri (four hours) and as far south as Wellington (12 hours), as well as heading to Tauranga (3½ hours) and Napier (12 hours). The cost of calling their helpline is $1.99 per minute.

CAR, CARAVAN & CAMPERVAN
Hire

Auckland has many hire agencies around Beach Rd and Stanley St close to the city centre.

A2B (☑0800 545 000; www.a2b-car-rental.co.nz; 167 Beach Rd; ⊘8am-5pm) Cheap older cars with no visible hire-car branding.

Apex Car Rentals (☑09-307 1063; www.apex-rentals.co.nz; 156 Beach Rd; ⊘8am-5pm)

Budget (☑09-976 2270; www.budget.co.nz; 163 Beach Rd; ⊘7am-6pm Mon-Fri, 8am-5pm Sat & Sun)

Escape (☑0800 216 171; www.escaperentals.co.nz; 39 Beach Rd; ⊘8am-5pm) Eccentrically painted campervans.

Kea, Maui & Britz (☑09-255 3910; www.maui.co.nz; 36 Richard Pearse Dr, Mangere; ⊘8am-6pm)

Gateway 2 NZ (☑050 822 5587; www.gateway2nz.co.nz; 50 Ascot Rd, Mangere; ⊘8am-6pm)

Gateway Motor Home Hire (☑09-296 1652; www.motorhomehire.co.nz; 33 Spartan Rd, Takanini)

Go Rentals (☑09-257 5142; www.gorentals.co.nz; George Bolt Memorial Drive, Bay 2-10, Cargo Central; ⊘6am-10pm)

Hertz (☑09-367 6350; www.hertz.co.nz; 154 Victoria St; ⊘7.30am-5.30pm)

Jucy (☑0800 399 736; www.jucy.co.nz; 2-16 The Strand; ⊘8am-5pm)

Kea Campers (☑09-448 8800; www.keacampers.com; 36 Richard Pearse Drive, Mangere; ⊘8am-4.30pm)

NZ Frontiers (☑09-299 6705; www.newzealandfrontiers.com)

Omega (☑09-377 5573; www.omegarentals.com; 75 Beach Rd; ⊘8am-5pm)

Quality Rentals (☑0800 680 123; www.qualityrental.co.nz; 8 Andrew Baxter Dr, Mangere; ⊘8am-4pm)

Thrifty (☑09-309 0111; www.thrifty.co.nz; 150 Khyber Pass Rd; ⊘8am-5pm)

Wilderness Motorhomes (☑09-255 5300; www.wilderness.co.nz; 21 Rennie Drive, Mangere; ⊘8am-5pm)

Purchase

Mechanical inspection services are on hand at secondhand car fairs, where sellers pay to display their cars.

Auckland Car Fair (☑09-529 2233; www.carfair.co.nz; Ellerslie Racecourse, Green Lane

---

PLANE DELAYED? TIME FOR A TIPPLE!

Clearly the roar of jets doesn't bother grapes, as NZ's most awarded winery is just 4km from the airport. The park-like grounds of **Villa Maria Estate** (Map p64; www.villamaria.co.nz; 118 Montgomerie Rd; platters $40-50, lunch $28-35; ⊘9am-6pm Mon-Fri, 9am-4pm Sat & Sun) are a green oasis in the encircling industrial zone. A series of concerts is held here every January and February featuring big international artists popular with the 40- to 50-something wine-swilling demographic.

Short tours ($5) take place at 11am and 3pm. There's a charge for tastings ($5), but lingering over wine and cheese on the terrace sure beats hanging around the departure lounge.

East; display fee $35; ☉9am-noon Sun) Auckland's largest car fair.

City Car Fair (☑09-837 7817; www.aucklandcitycarfair.co.nz; 155 Fanshawe St; display fee $25; ☉8am-1pm Sat)

MOTORCYCLE

NZ Motorcycle Rentals (☑09-486 2472; www.nzbike.com; 72 Barrys Point Rd, Takapuna; per day $145-360) Guided tours of NZ also available.

TRAIN

Northern Explorer (☑0800 872 467; www.kiwirailscenic.co.nz) trains leave from **Britomart station** (Queen St) at 7.50am on Monday, Thursday and Saturday and arriving in Wellington at 6.25pm. Stops include Hamilton (2½ hours), Otorohanga, (three hours), Tongariro National Park (5½ hours), Ohakune (6½ hours), Palmerston North (9½ hours) and Paraparaumu (11 hours). Standard fares to Wellington range from $119 to $186, but some discounted seats are available at $99 (first in, first served).

ⓘ Getting Around

TO & FROM THE AIRPORT

A taxi between the airport and the city usually costs between $65 and $85, more if you strike traffic snarls.

Airbus Express (☑09-366 6400; www.airbus.co.nz; one way/return adult $16/28, child $6/12) Runs between the terminals and the city, every 10–15 minutes from 7am to 7pm and at least hourly through the night. Stops include Mt Eden Rd or Dominion Rd (on request), Symonds St, Queen St and the Ferry Building. Reservations are not required; buy a ticket from the driver or online. The trip usually takes less than an hour (longer during peak times).

Super Shuttle (☑0800 748 885; www.supershuttle.co.nz) This convenient door-to-door shuttle charges $29 for one person heading between the airport and a city hotel; the price increases for outlying suburbs. Save money by sharing a shuttle.

BICYCLE

Auckland Transport (☑09-366 6400; www.at.govt.nz) publishes free cycle maps, available from public buildings such as stations, libraries and i-SITEs. Bikes can be taken on ferries and trains for free (dependent on available space), but only folding bikes are allowed on buses.

Adventure Cycles (☑09-940 2453; www.adventure-auckland.co.nz/adventurecycles; 9 Premier Ave, Western Springs; per day $30-40, per week $120-160, per month $260-350; ☉7.30am-7pm Thu-Mon) Hires road, mountain and touring bikes, runs a buy-back scheme, and does repairs.

CAR & MOTORCYCLE

Auckland's motorways jam badly at peak times, particularly the Northern and Southern Motorways. It's best to avoid them between 7am and 9am, and from 4pm to 7pm. Things also get tight around 3pm during term time, which is the end of the school day.

Expect to pay for parking in central Auckland from 8am to 6pm from Monday to Saturday. Most parking meters are pay-and-display; display tickets inside your windscreen. You usually don't have to pay between 6pm and 8am or on Sunday, but check the meters and parking signs carefully.

Prices can be steep at parking buildings. Better value are the council-run open-air parks near the old train station at 126 Beach Rd ($8 per day) and on Ngaoho Pl, off The Strand ($6 per day).

PUBLIC TRANSPORT

Auckland's public transport system is run by a hodgepodge of different operators, but there is now an integrated AT HOP smartcard (www.athop.co.nz), which provides discounts of around 10% on most buses, trains and ferries. AT HOP cards cost $10 (nonrefundable), so are really only worthwhile if you're planning on an extended stay in Auckland.

The **Auckland Transport** (☑09-366 6400; www.at.govt.nz) information service covers buses, trains and ferries and has an excellent trip-planning feature. A Discovery Pass provides a day's transport on most trains and buses and on North Shore ferries ($16); buy it on the bus or train or at Fullers offices.

Bus

Bus routes spread their tentacles throughout the city and you can purchase a ticket from the driver. Many services terminate around Britomart station. Some bus stops have electronic displays giving an estimate of waiting times, but be warned, they are often inaccurate.

Single-ride fares in the inner city are $1 for an adult and $0.60 for a child. If you're travelling further afield there are fare stages from $1.90/1.10 (adult/child) to $10.30/6.10.

The most useful services are the environmentally friendly Link Buses that loop in both directions around three routes (taking in many of the major sights) from 7am to 11pm:

City Link (adult/child $0.50/0.30, free for AT HOP cardholders, every seven to 10 minutes) Britomart, Queen St, Karangahape Rd, with some buses connecting to Wynyard Quarter.

Inner Link ($1.90, every 10 to 15 minutes) Queen St, SkyCity, Victoria Park, Ponsonby Rd, Karangahape Rd, Museum, Newmarket, Parnell and Britomart.

Outer Link (maximum $3.40, every 15 minutes) Art Gallery, Ponsonby, Herne Bay, Westmere, MOTAT 2, Pt Chevalier, Mt Albert, St Lukes Mall, Mt Eden, Newmarket, Museum, Parnell, University.

Ferry

Auckland's Edwardian baroque **Ferry Building** (Map p66; Quay St) sits at the end of Queen St. **360 Discovery** (Map p66; ✆ 0800 360 3472; www.360discovery.co.nz; Pier 4, 139 Quay St; cruise adult/child $27/17, three-day pass $35/21; ⏰10am, noon & 2.30pm) Ferries to Coromandel, Gulf Harbour, Motuihe, Rotoroa and Tiritiri Matangi.

Fullers (Map p66; ✆ 09-367 9111; www.fullers. co.nz; Ferry Building, 99 Quay St) Ferries to Bayswater, Birkenhead, Devonport, Great Barrier Island, Half Moon Bay, Northcote, Motutapu, Rangitoto and Waiheke leave directly behind the Ferry Building

Sealink (✆ 09-300 5900; www.sealink.co.nz) Ferries to Great Barrier Island leave from Wynyard Wharf, along with some car ferries to Waiheke, but most of the ferries to Waiheke leave from Half Moon Bay in East Auckland.

Train

Auckland's train services are limited and infrequent but the trains are generally clean, cheap and on time – although any hiccup on the lines can bring down the entire network. For timetables and trip planning see www.at.govt.nz.

Impressive Britomart station (p96) has food retailers, foreign-exchange facilities and a ticket office. Downstairs are left-luggage lockers.

There are just four train routes: west to Waitakere, south to Onehunga, and two run south to Pukekohe. Services are at least hourly from around 6am to 8pm (later on the weekends). Buy a ticket from machines or ticket offices at train stations. All trains have wheelchair ramps.

TAXI

Auckland's many taxis usually operate from ranks, but they also cruise popular areas. **Auckland Co-op Taxis** (✆ 09-300 3000; www.3003000.co.nz) is one of the biggest companies; has a surcharge for transport to and from the airport and ships, and for phone orders.

HAURAKI GULF ISLANDS

The Hauraki Gulf, stretching between Auckland and the Coromandel Peninsula, is dotted with *motu* (islands) and gives the Bay of Islands stiff competition in the beauty stakes. Some islands are only minutes from the city and make excellent day trips. Winesoaked Waiheke and volcanic Rangitoto really shouldn't be missed. Great Barrier re-

quires more effort (and cash) to get to, but provides an idyllic escape from modern life.

There are 47 islands in the Hauraki Gulf Maritime Park, administered by DOC. Some are good-sized islands, others are no more than rocks jutting out of the sea. They're loosely put into two categories: recreation and conservation. The recreation islands can easily be visited and their harbours are dotted with yachts in summer. The conservation islands, however, have restricted access. Permits are required to visit some, while others are closed refuges for the preservation of rare plants and animals, especially birds.

The gulf is a busy highway for marine mammals. Sei, minke and Bryde's whales are regularly seen in its outer reaches, along with orcas and bottlenose dolphins. You might even spy a passing humpback.

Rangitoto & Motutapu Islands

POP 75

Sloping elegantly from the waters of the gulf, 259m Rangitoto (www.rangitoto.org), the largest and youngest of Auckland's volcanic cones, provides a picturesque backdrop to all of the city's activities. As recently as 600 years ago it erupted from the sea and was probably active for several years before settling down. Maori living on Motutapu (Sacred Island; www.motutapu.org.nz), to which Rangitoto is now joined by a causeway, certainly witnessed the eruptions, as footprints have been found embedded in ash, and oral history details several generations living here before the eruption.

Rangitoto makes for a great day trip. Its harsh scoria slopes hold a surprising amount of flora (including the world's largest pohutukawa forest) and there are excellent walks, but you'll need sturdy shoes and plenty of water. Although it looks steep, up close it's shaped more like an egg sizzling in a pan. The walk to the summit only takes an hour and is rewarded with sublime views. At the top a loop walk goes around the crater's rim. A walk to lava caves branches off the summit walk and takes 30 minutes return. There's an information board with walk maps at the wharf.

Motutapu, in contrast to Rangitoto, is mainly covered in grassland, which is grazed by sheep and cattle. Archaeologically, this is a very significant island, with the traces of centuries of continuous human habitation etched into its landscape.

At Home Bay on Motutapu there's a DOC campsite (www.doc.govt.nz; adult/child $6/3) with only basic facilities (running water and a flush toilet). Bring cooking equipment, as open fires are forbidden, and book online. It's a three-hour walk from Rangitoto wharf (Map p64); Fullers run a weekend-only service to Home Bay in the summer months.

In 2011 both islands were officially declared predator-free after an extensive eradication programme. Endangered birds such as takahe and tieke (saddleback) have been released and others such as kakariki and bellbirds have returned of their own volition.

ⓘ Getting There & Around

Fullers (☏09-367 9111; www.fullers.co.nz; Ferry Building, 99 Quay St; adult/child return Auckland or Devonport $29/14.50) Has ferry services to Rangitoto from Auckland's Ferry Building (20 minutes, three daily on weekdays, four on weekends) and Devonport (two daily). It also offers the Volcanic Explorer (adult/child incl ferry $60/30; ⊙ departs 9.15am & 12.15pm), a guided tour around the island in a canopied 'road train'.

Motuihe Island

Between Rangitoto and Waiheke Islands, 176-hectare Motuihe has a lovely white-sand beach and a fascinating history. There are three *pa* sites, last occupied by the Ngati Paoa tribe. The island was sold in 1840 (for a heifer, blankets, frocks, garden tools, pots and pans) and from 1872 to 1941 served as a quarantine station. During WWI the dashing swashbuckler Count von Luckner launched a daring escape from the island (where he was interned with other German and Austrian nationals), making it 1000km to the Kermadec Islands before being recaptured.

Motuihe has been rendered pest-free and is now subject to a vigorous reforestation project by enthusiastic volunteers. As a result, endangered birds have returned, including the loquacious tieke.

Apart from the trust's headquarters, the only accommodation on the island is a basic DOC campsite (www.doc.govt.nz; adult/child $6/3); only toilets and water are provided, and booking ahead online is essential. There are no permanent residents or shops, except for a lunchtime kiosk during January.

ⓘ Getting There & Away

360 Discovery (☏0800 360 3472; www.360discovery.co.nz; adult/child return $28/17.50) A ferry taking one hour departs from Auckland daily at 8.45am, returning at 3.30pm.

Waiheke Island

POP 8300

Waiheke is 93 sq km of island bliss just a 35-minute ferry ride from the CBD. Once they could hardly give land away here; nowadays multimillionaires rub shoulders with the old-time hippies and bohemian artists who gave the island its green repute. Auckland office workers fantasise about swapping the daily motorway crawl for a watery commute and a warm, dry microclimate.

On Waiheke's city side, emerald waters lap at rocky bays, while its ocean flank has some of the region's best sandy beaches. While beaches are the big drawcard, wine is a close second. There are 19 boutique wineries to visit, many with swanky restaurants and breathtaking city views. The island also boasts galleries and craft stores.

Waiheke has been inhabited since at least the 14th century, most recently by Ngati Paoa, and there are more than 40 *pa* sites scattered around the island. Europeans arrived with the missionary Samuel Marsden in the early 1800s and the island was soon stripped of its kauri forest.

There are petrol stations in Oneroa, Ostend and Onetangi, ATMs in Oneroa and Ostend, and a supermarket in Ostend.

◎ Sights & Activities

Beaches

Waiheke's two best beaches are Onetangi, a long stretch of white sand at the centre of the island, and Palm Beach, a pretty little horseshoe bay between Oneroa and Onetangi. Both have nudist sections; head west just past some rocks in both cases. Oneroa and neighbouring Little Oneroa are also excellent, but you'll be sharing the waters with moored yachts in summer. Reached by an unsealed road through farmland, Man O' War Bay is a compact beach that's excellent for swimming.

Wineries

Goldie Vineyard WINERY
(www.goldiewines.co.nz; 18 Causeway Rd; tastings $10, refundable with purchase; ⊙ tasting room noon-4pm daily, cafe noon-4pm Sat & Sun & daily late Dec–mid-Jan) Founded as Goldwater

Estate in 1978, this is Waiheke's pioneering vineyard. The tasting room sells well-stocked baskets for a picnic amongst the vines ($60 for two people).

Passage Rock   WINERY
(☑ 09-372 7257; www.passagerockwines.co.nz; 438 Orapiu Rd; ⊙ noon-4pm Sat & Sun Aug-Dec, daily Jan, Wed-Sun Feb-Apr) Excellent pizza among the vines.

Man O' War Vineyards   WINERY
(www.manowarvineyards.co.nz; Man O' War Bay; ⊙ 11am-6pm summer, to 4.30pm winter) Settle in with a tapas platter and a glass of Man O' War's Valhalla chardonnay at our favourite Waiheke winery. If the weather is good, go for a swim in beautiful Man O' War Bay.

Stonyridge   WINERY
(☑ 09-372 8822; www.stonyridge.com; 80 Onetangi Rd; tastings per wine $3-15; ⊙ 11.30am-5pm) ✐ Famous organic reds, an atmospheric cafe, tours ($10, 35 minutes, 11.30am Saturday and Sunday) and the occasional dance party.

Wild On Waiheke   WINERY, BREWERY
(☑ 09-372 3434; www.wildonwaiheke.co.nz; 82 Onetangi Rd; tastings per beer or wine $2; ⊙ 11am-4pm Thu-Sun, daily in summer) This winery and microbrewery offers tastings, archery, laser clay shooting, pétanque, a sandpit and a giant chess board.

Art & Culture
The *Waiheke Art Map* brochure, free from the i-SITE, lists galleries and craft stores.

Artworks Complex   ARTS CENTRE
(2 Korora Rd; 🛜) The Artworks complex houses a community theatre (☑ 09-372 2941; www.artworkstheatre.org.nz), an art-house cinema (☑ 09-372 4240; www.waihekecinema.net; adult/child $14/7), an attention-grabbing art gallery (☑ 09-372 9907; www.waihekeartgallery. org.nz; ⊙ 10am-4pm) FREE and Whittaker's Musical Museum (☑ 09-372 5573; www.musical-museum.org; ⊙ 1-4pm, live shows 1.30pm Sat) FREE, a collection of antique concert instruments. This is also the place for free internet access, either on a terminal at the library (⊙ 9am-5.30pm Mon-Fri, 10am-4pm Sat; 🛜) or on their wi-fi network.

Stony Batter Historic Reserve   HISTORIC SITE
(www.fortstonybatter.org; Stony Batter Rd; adult/child $8/5; ⊙ 9am-5pm) At the eastern end of the island, Stony Batter has WWII tunnels and gun emplacements that were built in 1941 to defend Auckland's harbour. The 20-minute walk from the carpark leads through private farmland and derives its name from the boulder-strewn fields. Bring a torch and cash.

Waiheke Museum
& Historic Village   MUSEUM
(www.waihekemuseum.org.nz; 165 Onetangi Rd; admission by donation; ⊙ noon-4pm Wed, Sat & Sun) Displays Islander artefacts in six restored buildings.

Dead Dog Bay   GARDENS
(www.deaddogbay.co.nz; Margaret Reeve Lane; adult/child $10/free; ⊙ 10am-5pm) Wander steep pathways through rainforest, wetlands and gardens scattered with sculpture.

Connells Bay   GARDENS
(☑ 09-372 8957; www.connellsbay.co.nz; Cowes Bay Rd; adult/child $30/15; ⊙ by appointment, late Oct-late Mar) A pricey but excellent private sculpture park featuring a stellar roster of NZ artists. Admission is by way of a two-hour guided tour; book ahead.

LOCAL KNOWLEDGE

WAIHEKE ISLAND

Thirty years ago, Waiheke Island was home to an eclectic mix of outlaws who could not (or chose not to) live in 'normal' society: hippies and hermits, alternative healers and writers, potters and pot growers, and everything in between. Sometime in the late '80s, Waiheke was 'discovered', and it's quite a different place now. But even with all the changes – fine dining, vineyards and luxury holiday homes – Waiheke Island's identity and spirit are still undeniable. The beautiful weather remains the same, as do the phenomenal vistas, the lush bush and native birds, the chooks in your neighbours' backyards, the feeling that everything deserves to move a little slower (we call it 'Waiheke time'), the smell of honeysuckle, the crystal waters, the best fish and chips ever, the house I was born in and, probably, still a few pot growers. Waiheke was, and remains, like nowhere else on the planet.

Zoë Bell, Stuntwoman & Actor

Waiheke Island

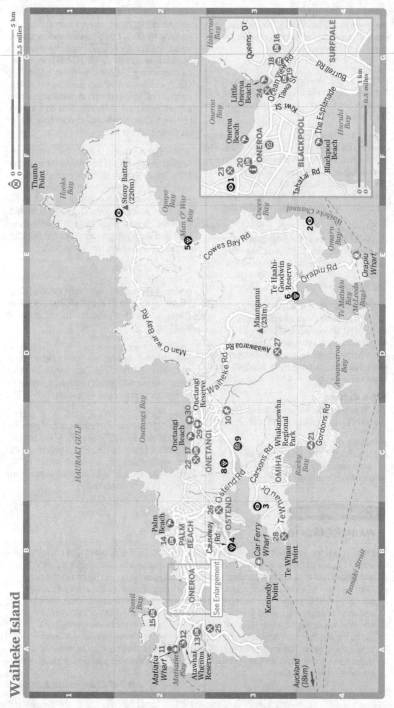

HAURAKI GULF

Thumb Point

Hooks Bay

Stony Batter (220m) 7

Opopo Bay

Man O' War Bay

5

Cowes Bay Rd

Cowes Bay

2

Waiheke Channel

Omaru Bay

Orapiu Rd

Te Haahi-Goodwin Reserve 6

Maunganui (231m)

Te Matuku Bay

McLeods Bay

Orapiu Wharf

Awaawaroa Rd

27

Man O' War Bay Rd

Onetangi Bay

Onetangi Reserve

Waiheke Rd

30

Onetangi Beach

29

22 17 10

ONETANGI

9

8

Carsons Rd

OMIHA

Whakanewha Regional Park

Rocky Bay

21

Gordons Rd

Awaawaroa Bay

Palm Beach

14

PALM BEACH

Causeway Rd

26

OSTEND

Ostend Rd

3

Te Whau Dr

28

Te Whau Point

4

Car Ferry Wharf

Fossil Bay

15

ONEROA

See Enlargement

Kennedy Point

Matiatia Wharf 11

8

12

Matiatia Bay

13

Atawhai Whenua Reserve

25

Auckland (18km)

Tamaki Strait

5 km
2.5 miles

Enlargement

Hekerua Bay

Queens Dr

SURFDALE

24

18

16

Ocean View Rd

Tawa St 19

Burrell Rd

Oneroa Bay

Little Oneroa Beach

Kiwi St

Oneroa Beach

23

20

ONEROA

1

BLACKPOOL

The Esplanade

Huruhi Bay

Blackpool Beach

Tahatai Rd

1 km
0.5 miles

Waiheke Island

◎ Sights
Art Gallery	(see 1)
1	Artworks Complex	F3
2	Connells Bay	E4
3	Dead Dog Bay	B3
4	Goldie Vineyard	B3
5	Man O' War Vineyards	E2
6	Passage Rock	E3
7	Stony Batter Historic Reserve	E2
8	Stonyridge	C3
9	Waiheke Museum & Historic Village	C3
Whittaker's Musical Museum	(see 1)
Wild On Waiheke	(see 8)

◎ Activities, Courses & Tours
10	EcoZip Adventures	C3
11	Fullers	A2
12	Ross Adventures	A2

◎ Sleeping
13	Cable Bay Views	A2
14	Enclosure Bay	B2
15	Fossil Bay Lodge	A2
16	Hekerua Lodge	G3
17	Kina	C2
18	Punga Lodge	G3
19	Tawa Lodge	G3
20	The Oyster Inn	F3
21	Whakanewha Regional Park Campsite	C4

◎ Eating
Cable Bay	(see 13)
22	Casita Miro	C2
23	Delight	F3
24	Dragonfired	G3
25	Mudbrick	A3
26	Ostend Market	B3
27	Poderi Crisci	D3
Solar Eating House	(see 23)
28	Te Whau	B3
The Oyster Inn	(see 20)
Wai Kitchen	(see 20)

◎ Drinking & Nightlife
29	4th Avenue Eatery & Bar	C2
30	Charlie Farley's	C2

◎ Entertainment
Art-House Cinema	(see 1)
Community Theatre	(see 1)

Walks

Ask at the i-SITE about the island's beautiful coastal walks (ranging from one to three hours) and the 3km Cross Island Walkway (from Onetangi to Rocky Bay). Other tracks traverse **Whakanewha Regional Park**, a haven for rare coastal birds and geckos, and the Royal Forest & Bird Protection Society's three reserves: **Onetangi** (Waiheke Rd), **Te Haahi-Goodwin** (Orapiu Rd) and **Atawhai Whenua** (Ocean View Rd).

Other Activities

Hike Bike Ako WALKING, CYCLING
(☑021 465 373; www.hikebikeako.co.nz; hiking adult/child $99/79, biking & combination $139) Explore the island on a guided wallking (three hours) or biking (five hours) tour, or a combination (five hours) of both. Tours all include pick up from the ferry, lunch at a cafe or vineyard, and Maori legends, history and culture. There's a minimum age of seven for walking and 16 for biking.

Ross Adventures KAYAKING
(☑09-372 5550; www.kayakwaiheke.co.nz; Matiatia Beach; half-/full-day trips $85/145, per hr hire from $25) It's the fervently held opinion of Ross that Waiheke offers kayaking every bit as good as the legendary Abel Tasman National Park. He should know – he's been offering guided kayak trips for over 20 years. Experienced sea kayakers can comfortably circumnavigate the island in four days, exploring hidden coves and sand spits inaccessible by land.

EcoZip Adventures ZIPLINE
(☑0800 246 947; www.ecozipadventures.co.nz; Trig Hill Rd; adult/child $99/69) With vineyard, native bush and ocean views, three separate 200m stretches make for an exciting ride, and there's a gentle 1.5km walk back up through the bush after the thrills. Costs include free transfers from Matiatia Wharf or Oneroa if you don't have your own transport.

◎ Tours

Ananda Tours FOOD & WINE
(☑09-372 7530; www.ananda.co.nz) Gourmet wine and food tours ($120), and a wine connoisseurs' tour ($230). Small-group, informal tours can be customised, including visits to artists' studios.

Fullers FOOD & WINE
(☑09-367 9111; www.fullers.co.nz) Runs a 'Wine on Waiheke' tour (adult $119, 4½ hours, departs Auckland 1pm) visiting three of the island's top wineries, and includes a platter of nibbles; 'Taste of Waiheke" (adult $129, 5½ hours, departs Auckland 11am) includes three wineries plus an olive grove and light

lunch. There's also a 1½-hour Explorer Tour (adult/child $52/26, departs Auckland 10am, 11am and noon). All prices include the ferry and an all-day local bus pass.

Sunshine Tours
FOOD & WINE

(☑ 09-372 6127; www.waihekeislandadventures.com) Scenic tours ($45) and vineyard tours ($45).

Waiheke Executive Transport
WINE, CULTURAL

(☑ 0800 372 200; www.waiheketransport.co.nz) Options include island highlights tours ($26) and wine tours ($110 to $115).

⚜ Festivals & Events

Sculpture on the Gulf
ARTS

(www.sculptureonthegulf.co.nz) A 2.5km cliff-top sculpture walk, held for three weeks from late January in odd-numbered years.

Waiheke Island of
Wine Vintage Festival
WINE, FOOD, MUSIC

(www.waihekevintagefestival.co.nz; ☉ late Mar-early Apr) Held for the first time in 2014, featuring a week of jazz and classical concerts in the vines, plus art exhibitions, a farmers market, and food and wine matching. Seventeen different vineyards are involved, and shuttle buses travel between the different locations.

Waiheke Island International
Jazz Festival
MUSIC

(www.waihekejazzfestival.co.nz; prices vary by event) Local and international acts across the island from Friday to Sunday during Easter.

🛏 Sleeping

Waiheke is so popular in the summer holidays that many locals rent out their houses and bugger off elsewhere. You'll need to book ahead and even then there are very few bargains. Prices drop considerably in winter, especially midweek. For midrange accommodation, a good option is to book a holiday home through www.bookabach.co.nz or www.holidayhouses.co.nz, but you'll need transport to get around.

Fossil Bay Lodge
CABIN $

(☑ 09-372 8371; www.fossilbay.webs.com; 58 Korora Rd; s $49, d $80-125, tents $80-105; ☎) Three cute cabins open onto a courtyard facing the main building, which houses the toilets, a communal kitchen and living area, and a compact upstairs apartment. Recently added are two cosy bell tents for 'glamping' accommodation, and apart from the occasional squawking duck – or toddler from the adjacent Steiner kindergarten – it's a peaceful place.

Hekerua Lodge
HOSTEL $

(☑ 09-372 8990; www.hekerualodge.co.nz; 11 Hekerua Rd; sites from $18, dm $30-36, s $55, d $90-120; @ 🖥 🏊) This secluded hostel is surrounded by native bush and has a barbecue, stone-tiled pool, sunny deck, casual lounge area and its own walking track. It's far from luxurious, but it has a laid-back and social feel, no doubt assisted by the cool, neutral decor and the serene images of Buddha scattered about.

Kina
HOSTEL $

(☑ 09-372 8971; www.kinabackpackers.co.nz; 421 Seaview Rd; dm $28-34, s/tw $55/72, d $72-90; @ 🖥) This old-style, well-positioned hostel has a large garden and lawn overlooking Onetangi Beach. Relatively compact dorms and private rooms are shared between an older building and a newer wing, and it's run efficiently by a Kiwi couple with young children and a friendly Border Collie.

Whakanewha Regional
Park Campsite
CAMPSITE $

(☑ 09-366 2000; www.arc.govt.nz; Gordons Rd; sites per adult/child $13/6) A pretty but basic campsite with toilets, gas barbecues and drinking water. Self-contained campervans can stay in the adjacent Poukaraka Flats campground.

Tawa Lodge
GUESTHOUSE $$

(☑ 09-372 9434; www.pungalodge.co.nz; 15 Tawa St; r $120, apt $175-240; 🖥) Between the self-contained cottage at the front and the apartment at the rear are three reasonably priced loft rooms sharing a small kitchen and bathroom. Look forward to excellent ocean views from the shared deck.

Punga Lodge
B&B $$

(☑ 09-372 6675; www.pungalodge.co.nz; 223 Ocean View Rd; r $145-150, units $140-200; @ 🖥) Both the colourful en suite rooms in the house and the self-contained garden units have access to decks looking onto a lush tropical garden. There's a spa, and prices include homemade breakfast, afternoon tea and wharf transfers.

The Oyster Inn
BOUTIQUE HOTEL $$$

(☑ 09-372 2222; www.theoysterinn.co.nz; 124 Ocean View Rd; r $285-335) With a breezy and cool ambience inspired by classic American Cape Cod style, The Oyster Inn has just three luxury rooms in the heart of Oneroa. Guests are picked up from the ferry at Matiatia wharf in a retro VW combi van, and this attention to luxurious detail is further enhanced with chic decor, stellar bathroom products and personalised service.

Enclosure Bay
B&B $$$

(☏ 09-372 8882; www.enclosurebay.co.nz; 9 Great Barrier Rd; r $450-499) If you're going to shell out for a luxury B&B you're going to want something a little special, and that's certainly what's offered here. Each of the three guest rooms have sumptuous views and balconies, and the owners subscribe to the nothing's-too-much-trouble school of Kiwi hospitality.

Cable Bay Views
APARTMENTS $$$

(☏ 09-372 2901; www.cablebayviews.co.nz; 103 Church Bay Rd; d $250; ☎) These three modern, self-contained studio apartments have stellar vineyard views and are handily close to a couple of Waiheke's best vineyard restaurants. Check the website for good midweek and off-peak discounts.

✗ Eating

Waiheke has some excellent eateries and, if you're lucky, the views will be enough to distract from the hole being bored into your hip pocket.

Dragonfired
PIZZERIA $

(Little Oneroa Beach; mains $8-16; ⊙10.30am-8.30pm; ⊠) Specialising in 'artisan wood-fired food', this caravan by the beach serves the three Ps: pizza, polenta plates and pocket bread. It's easily Waiheke's best place for cheap eats.

Ostend Market
MARKET $

(www.ostendmarketwaiheke.co.nz; War Memorial Hall, Belgium St; ⊙7.30am-1pm Sat) Fresh local produce, and local craft and secondhand knick-knacks.

Wai Kitchen
CAFE $$

(www.waikitchen.co.nz; 1/149 Ocean View Rd, Oneroa; mains $17-23; ⊙9am-4pm, extended summer) Why? Well firstly there's the lively menu that abounds with Mediterranean and Asian flavours. Then there's the charming service and the breezy ambience of this glassed-in wedge, facing the *wai* (water).

Casita Miro
SPANISH $$

(☏ 09-372 7854; www.mirovineyard.co.nz; 3 Brown St, Onetangi; dishes $19-40; ⊙noon-3pm daily, 6-10pm Thu-Sat Jan-Feb, reduced hours in winter) A wrought iron and glass pavilion backed with a Gaudí-esque mosaic garden is the stage for a very entertaining troupe of servers who will guide you through the menu of delectable *ración tapas* – dishes bigger than regular tapas, designed to be shared.

The Oyster Inn
SEAFOOD, MODERN NZ $$

(☏ 09-372 2222; www.theoysterinn.co.nz; 124 Ocean View Rd; mains $23-36; ⊙11am-late) The Oyster Inn is a popular destination for Auckland's smart set. It has an excellent seafood-skewed bistro menu, oysters and champagne, and a buzzy but relaxed vibe that's part bar and part restaurant. Brunch from 11am on the verandah is a great way to ease into another Waiheke day.

Delight
CAFE, TURKISH $$

(☏ 09-372 9035; www.delightcafe.co.nz; 29 Waikare Rd, Oneroa; mains $14-23, mezze $10-19; ⊙8am-3pm) If you're bored with eggs Benedict, try one of the piquant breakfast tagines at this stylish cafe/mezze bar. Paninis, wraps and salads are served along with more traditional mezze, and the views are just as delicious.

Solar Eating House
CAFE, BAR $$

(139 Oceanview Rd; mains $15-24; ⊙8am-9.30pm) 🖋 With a spacious outdoor area and ocean views, Solar is our relaxed choice for the first coffee – or beer or glass of wine – of the day. Lots of local organic and sustainable produce underpins the menu.

Poderi Crisci
ITALIAN $$

(☏ 09-372 2148; www.podericrisci.co.nz; 205 Awaawaroa Rd; mains $24-33; ⊙noon-3pm Thu-Mon, extended hrs in summer) Poderi Crisci has quickly gained a sterling reputation for its food, particularly its legendary four-hour long lunches on Sundays ($65 per person). Italian varietals and olives have been planted alongside the existing vines. Definitely worth the drive into the restaurant's isolated valley.

Te Whau
WINERY $$$

(☏ 09-372 7191; www.tewhau.com; 218 Te Whau Dr; mains $37-42; ⊙11am-5pm Wed-Mon, 6.30pm-late Sat Nov-Easter, reduced hrs in winter) 🖋 Perched on the end of Te Whau peninsula, this winery restaurant has exceptional views, food and service, and one of the finest wine lists you'll see in the country. Try its own impressive Bordeaux blends, merlot, chardonnay and rosé for $3 per taste (11am to 5pm).

Cable Bay
WINERY $$$

(☏ 09-372 5889; www.cablebayvineyards.co.nz; 12 Nick Johnstone Dr; two/three courses $72/90; ⊙noon-3pm & 6pm-late daily) 🖋 Impressive ubermodern architecture, sculpture and beautiful views set the scene for this acclaimed restaurant. The food is sublime, but if the budget won't stretch to a meal, stop in for a wine tasting (from $8), or snacks from the small-plates menu ($10 to $15) on the terrace from 11am.

Mudbrick
WINERY $$$

(☑09-372 9050; www.mudbrick.co.nz; 126 Church Bay Rd; mains $42-49, tasting menu with/without wine $190/110; ⏰11.30am-3.30pm & 6pm-10.30pm) Auckland and the gulf are at their glistening best when viewed from Mudbrick's picturesque verandah. The winery also offers tours and tastings (from $10, 10am to 5pm).

 ## Drinking & Nightlife

You'll find bars in Oneroa and pubs in Surfdale and Ostend.

Charlie Farley's
BAR

(www.charliefarleys.co.nz; 21 The Strand, Onetangi; ⏰8.30am-late) It's easy to see why the locals love this place when you're supping on a Waiheke wine or beer under the pohutukawa on the beach-gazing deck.

4th Avenue Eatery & Bar
PUB, CAFE

(www.fourthavenue.co.nz; 1 Fourth Ave, Onetangi) Part bar and part bistro, all served up with cool and classy decor and Onetangi Beach views from the sunny deck. There's a good selection of tap beers and decent shared plates and platters ($20 to $49).

❶ Information

Waiheke Island i-SITE (☑09-372 1234; www.waihekenz.com; 118 Ocean View Rd; ⏰9am-5pm) As well as the very helpful main office, there's a (usually unstaffed) counter in the ferry terminal at Matiatia Wharf.

❶ Getting There & Away

360 Discovery (☑0800 360 3472; www.360discovery.co.nz) You can pick up the 360 Discovery tourist ferry at Orapiu on its journey between Auckland and Coromandel Town. However, note that Orapiu is quite remote and not served by buses.

Fullers (☑09-367 9111; www.fullers.co.nz; return adult/child $36/18; ⏰5.20am-11.45pm Mon-Fri, 6.25am-11.45pm Sat, 7am-9.30pm Sun) Frequent passenger ferries from Auckland's Ferry Building to Matiatia Wharf (on the hour from 9am to 5pm), some via Devonport.

Sealink (☑09-300 5900; www.sealink.co.nz; adult/child/car/motorcycle return $36.50/20/152/58; ⏰4.30am-6.30pm Mon-Thu, 4.30am-8pm Fri, 6am-6.30pm Sat & Sun) Runs car ferries to Kennedy Point, mainly from Half Moon Bay (east Auckland) but some leave from Wynyard Wharf in the city. The ferry runs

at least every two hours and takes 45 minutes (booking essential).

❶ Getting Around

BIKE

Various bicycle routes are outlined in the *Bike Waiheke!* brochure, available from the wharf and the i-SITE; be prepared for a few hills.

Waiheke Bike Hire (☑09-372 7937; www.waihekebikehire.co.nz; Matiatia Wharf) Hires mountain bikes (half-/full day $25/35) from their base near the wharf and at the Oneroa i-SITE.

Waiheke E Bikes (☑027 467 883, 022 050 2233; www.waihekeebikes.co.nz; per day $50) Parts of Waiheke are quite hilly, so ease the load with these hybrid machines combining pedalling with electric motors. If you order two bikes, they'll pick you up and return you to the ferry for free.

BUS

The island has regular bus services, starting from **Matiatia Wharf** and heading through Oneroa (adult/child $1.60/0.80, five minutes) on their way to all the main settlements, as far west as Onetangi (adult/child $4.40/2.40, 30 minutes); see **Auckland Transport** (☑09-366 6400; www.at.govt.nz) for timetables. A day pass (adult/child $9/5.50) is available from the Fullers counter at Matiatia Wharf.

Waiheke Vineyard Hopper (☑09-367 9111; www.waihekevineyardhopper.co.nz; per person $20; ⏰Dec 26-early Feb) Handy option with dedicated shuttles travelling around eight different Waiheke vineyards every 40 minutes during summer. A $54 pass also includes ferry tickets and local Waiheke buses.

CAR, MOTORBIKE & SCOOTER

Fun Rentals (☑09-372 8001; www.funrentals.co.nz; 14a Belgium St, Ostend; per day car/scooter/4WD from $59/49/59)

Rent Me Waiheke (☑09-372 3339; www.rentmewaiheke.co.nz; 14 Ocean View Rd, Matiatia; per day cars/scooters $59/49)

Waiheke Auto Rentals (☑09-372 8998; www.waihekerentals.co.nz; Matiatia Wharf; per day car/scooter from $69/79)

Waiheke Rental Cars (☑09-372 8635; www.waihekerentalcars.co.nz; Matiatia Wharf; per day car/4WD from $59/79)

TAXI

Island Taxis (☑0800 372 4111; www.island-taxis.co.nz)

Waiheke Express Taxis (☑0800 700 789; www.waihekeexpresstaxis.co.nz)

Waiheke Independent Taxis (☑0800 300 372)

Rotoroa Island

From 1911 to 2005 the only people to have access to this blissful little island on the far side of Waiheke were the alcoholics and drug addicts who came (or were sentenced) here to dry out, and the Salvation Army staff who cared for them. In 2011, after 100 years, 82-hectare **Rotoroa** ([☎]0800 76 86 76; www.rotoroa.org.nz; access fee $5) opened to the public, giving visitors access to three sandy swimming beaches and the social history and art displays in the restored buildings of the former treatment centre. There are also three well-appointed, wildly retro holiday homes for rent ($375 to $650), and excellent hostel accommodation in dorms (per person $35) in the former Superintendent's House.

ℹ Getting There & Away

360 Discovery ([☎]0800 360 3472; www.360discovery.co.nz; adult/child from Auckland $49/29, from Orapiu $21/13) From Auckland the ferry takes 75 minutes, stopping at Orapiu on Waiheke Island en route. There are four boats per week from Labour Day in October to Easter (daily in January) and two boats per week over the cooler months.

Tiritiri Matangi Island

This magical, 220-hectare, predator-free **island** (www.tiritirimatangi.org.nz) is home to the tuatara (a prehistoric lizard) and lots of endangered native birds, including the very rare and colourful takahe. Other birds that can be seen here include the bellbird, stitchbird, saddleback, whitehead, kakariki, kokako, little spotted kiwi, brown teal, NZ robin, fernbird and penguins; 78 different species have been sighted in total. The saddleback was once close to extinction, with just 150 left, but now there are more than 600 on Tiritiri alone. To experience the dawn chorus in full flight, stay overnight at the **DOC bunkhouse** ([☎]09-425 7812; www.doc.govt.nz; adult/child $30/20); book well ahead and ensure there's room on the ferry.

The island was sold to the Crown in 1841, deforested, and farmed until the 1970s. Since 1984 hundreds of volunteers have planted 250,000 native trees and the forest cover has regenerated. An 1864 lighthouse stands on the eastern end of the island.

ℹ Getting There & Away

360 Discovery ([☎]0800 360 3472; www.360discovery.co.nz; return Auckland/ Gulf Harbour $69/37; [☉]Wed-Sun) Book a guided walk ($5) with your ferry ticket; the guides know where all the really cool birds hang out.

Motuora Island

Halfway between Tiritiri Matangi and Kawau, Motuora has 80 predator-free hectares and is used as a kiwi 'crèche'. There's a wharf on the west coast of the island, but you'll need your own boat to get here. The **DOC campsite** ([☎]027-492 8586; www.doc.govt.nz; adult/child $6/3) requires bookings and provides toilets, cold showers and water. There's also a cottage that sleeps five ($52); bring your own linen and food.

Kawau Island

POP 300

Kawau Island lies 50km north of Auckland off the Mahurangi Peninsula. There are few proper roads through the island, the residents relying mainly on boats. The main attraction is **Mansion House** (adult/child $4/2; [☉]noon-2pm), an impressive wooden manor extended from an 1845 structure by Governor George Grey, who purchased the island in 1862. It houses a fine collection of Victoriana, including some of Grey's effects, and is surrounded by the original exotic gardens. A set of short walks (10 minutes to two hours) are signposted from Mansion House, leading to beaches, the old copper mine, and a lookout; download DOC's *Kawau Island Historic Reserve* map (www.doc.govt.nz).

🛏 Sleeping & Eating

Kawau Lodge　　　　　　　B&B $$$
([☎]09-422 8831; www.kawaulodge.co.nz; North Cove; s $160, d $210-245) [✆] This ecoconscious boutique hotel has its own jetty, wraparound decks and views. Meals ($10 to $75) can be arranged, as can excursions.

Mansion House Cafe Restaurant　　CAFE $$
([☎]09-422 8903; lunch $12-18, dinner $18-28; [☉]hours vary) If you haven't packed a picnic, this idyllically situated eatery serves all-day breakfasts, sandwiches and hearty evening meals.

ℹ️ Getting There & Away

Kawau Water Taxis (☎0800 111 616; www.
kawaucruises.co.nz) Daily ferries from Sandspit
to Kawau (adult/child return $55/31) and a
water-taxi service (minimum charge $142.50).
The Super Cruise (adult/child $68/30, barbe-
cue lunch $27/15) departs Sandspit at 10.30am
and circles the island, delivering the post to 75
different wharves.

Great Barrier Island

POP 860

Named Aotea (meaning cloud) by the Maori,
and Great Barrier (due to its position at the
edge of the Hauraki Gulf) by Captain James
Cook, this rugged and exceptionally beautiful place falls in behind South, North and
Stewart as NZ's fourth-largest island (285
sq km). It closely resembles the Coromandel
Peninsula to which it was once joined, and
like the Coromandel it was once a mining,
logging and whaling centre. Those industries have long gone and today two-thirds of
the island is publicly owned and managed
by DOC.

Great Barrier has unspoilt beaches, hot
springs, old kauri dams, a forest sanctuary
and a network of tramping tracks. Because
there are no possums on the island, the native bush is lush.

Although only 88km from Auckland,
Great Barrier seems a world – and a good
many years – away. The island has no supermarket, no electricity supply (only private
solar, wind and diesel generators) and no
main drainage (only septic tanks). Many
roads are unsealed and petrol costs are high.
Mobile-phone reception is very limited and
there are no banks, ATMs or street lights.

From around mid-December to mid-
January is the peak season, so make sure
you book transport, accommodation and
activities well in advance.

Tryphena is the main settlement, 4km
from the ferry wharf at Shoal Bay. Strung
out along several kilometres of coastal road,
it consists of a few dozen houses and a handful of shops and accommodation places.
From the wharf it's 3km to Mulberry Grove,
and then another 1km over the headland to
Pa Beach and the Stonewall Store (p109).

The airport is at Claris, 12km north of
Tryphena, a small settlement with a general
store, bottle shop, laundrette, garage, pharmacy and cafe.

Whangaparapara is an old timber town
and the site of the island's 19th-century

whaling activities. Port Fitzroy is the other
main harbour on the west coast, a one-hour
drive from Tryphena. These four main settlements have fuel available.

🏃 Activities

Water Sports

The beaches on the west coast are safe, but
care needs to be taken on the surf-pounded
eastern beaches. Medlands Beach, with its
wide sweep of white sand, is one of the most
beautiful and accessible beaches on the
island. Remote Whangapoua, in the northeast, requires more effort to get to, while
Kaitoke, Awana Bay and Harataonga on
the east coast are also worth a visit.

Okiwi Bar has an excellent right-hand
break, while Awana has both left- and right-
hand breaks. Pohutukawa trees shelter the
pretty bays around Tryphena.

Diving is excellent, with shipwrecks, pinnacles, lots of fish and more than 33m vis-
ibility at some times of the year.

Hooked on Barrier   DIVING, FISHING
(☎09-429 0740; www.hookedonbarrier.co.nz;
89 Hector Sanderson Rd; half-/full-day charter
$700/1200) Hires out diving, snorkelling,
fishing, surfing and kayaking gear, and runs
fishing, diving and sightseeing charters.

Mountain Biking

With rugged scenery and relatively little traffic on the roads, mountain biking is a popular activity. There's a designated 25km ride
beginning on Blind Bay Rd, Okupu, winding
beneath the Ahumata cliffs before crossing
Whangaparapara Rd and beginning the
15km Forest Rd ride through beautiful forest
to Port Fitzroy. Cycling on other DOC walking tracks is prohibited.

Tramping

The island's very popular walking tracks are
outlined in DOC's free *Great Barrier Island
(Aotea Island)* booklet. Before setting out,
make sure you're properly equipped with
water and food, and be prepared for both
sunny and wet weather.

The most popular easy walk is the
45-minute Kaitoke Hot Springs Track,
starting from Whangaparapara Rd and leading to natural hot springs in a bush stream.
Check the temperature before getting in and
don't put your head under the water.

Windy Canyon, which is only a 15-minute
walk from Aotea Rd, has spectacular rock
outcrops and affords great views of the

island. From Windy Canyon, an excellent trail continues for another two to three hours through scrubby forest to Hirakimata (Mt Hobson, 621m), the highest point on the island, with views across the Hauraki Gulf and Coromandel. Near the top of the mountain are lush forests and a few mature kauri trees that survived the logging days. From Hirakimata it is 40 minutes south to Mt Heale Hut or two hours west through forest and past a kauri driving dam to Kaiaraara Hut, where it's another 45 minutes on to Port Fitzroy.

A more challenging tramp is the hilly **Tramline Track** (five hours), which starts on Aotea Rd and follows old logging tramlines to Whangaparapara Harbour. The initial stages of this track are not maintained and in some parts the clay becomes slippery after rain.

Of a similar length, but flatter and easier walking, is the 11km **Harataonga Coastal Walk** (five hours) which heads from Harataonga Bay to Whangapoua.

Many other trails traverse the forest, taking between 30 minutes and five hours. The **Aotea Track** combines bits of other paths into a three-day walk, overnighting in each of the huts.

See p110 for details of shuttle buses to and from the trailheads.

🛏 Sleeping

Unless you're camping, Great Barrier isn't a cheap place to stay. At pretty much every price point you'll pay more than you would for a similar place elsewhere. In the off-seaon, however, rates drop considerably. **Island Accommodation** (☎09-429 0995; www.islandaccommodation.co.nz) offers a booking service, which is handy for finding self-contained houses for longer stays. Check accommodation and island information websites for packages including flights and car rental. Note that accommodation rates soar for around two weeks following Christmas and the island also gets very busy during this time.

Medlands Beach Backpackers   HOSTEL **$**
(☎09-429 0320; www.medlandsbeach.com; 9 Mason Rd; dm $35, d/units from $70/120) Chill out in the garden of this house on the hill, overlooking beautiful Medlands Beach. The backpackers' area is simple, with a little double cabin for romantic budgeteers at a slight remove from the rest. The self-contained houses sleep up to six.

Crossroads Lodge   HOSTEL **$**
(☎09-429 0889; www.xroadslodge.com; 1 Blind Bay Rd; dm/s/d $30/50/75; @🛜) This low-key backpackers is 2km from the airfield and close to forest walks and hot springs. Mountain bikes can be hired, and golf clubs can be borrowed to play on the nearby nine-hole golf course.

Kaiaraara & Mt Heale Huts   HUT **$**
(www.doc.govt.nz; dm per adult/child $15/7.50) These DOC huts in the Great Barrier Forest have bunk beds, cold running water, chemical toilets and a kitchen/dining area. Bring your own sleeping bag and cooking/eating equipment and book online. Mt Heale Hut sleeps 20 people and has a gas cooker, but Kaiaraara Hut (which sleeps 24) doesn't. Both must be booked in advance.

DOC Campsites   CAMPSITE **$**
(☎09-379 6476; www.doc.govt.nz; site per adult/child $10/5) There are campsites at Harataonga Bay, Medlands Beach, Akapoua Bay, Whangapoua, The Green (Whangaparapara) and Awana Bay. All have basic facilities, including water, cold showers (except for at The Green), toilets and a food-preparation shelter. You need to bring your own gas cooking stove as open fires are prohibited. Book in advance online.

Aotea Lodge   APARTMENT **$$**
(☎09-429 0628; www.aotealodge.com; 41 Medland Rd; units $100-150; 🛜) A well-tended, sunny garden surrounds these reasonably priced units, perched on the hill just above Tryphena. They range from a two-bedroom house to an unusual mezzanine unit loaded with bunks, and each has its own cooking facilities.

Shoal Bay Lodge   APARTMENT **$$**
(☎09-429 0890; www.shoalbaylodge.co.nz; 145 Shoal Bay Rd; apt $160-290) Hidden among the trees these comfy self-contained apartments offer sea views, bird song and solar power. Best is the three-bedroom lodge with its sunset-guzzling deck.

Tipi & Bob's Waterfront Lodge   MOTEL **$$$**
(☎09-429 0550; www.waterfrontlodge.co.nz; 38 Puriri Bay Rd; units $195-250) West of Tryphena, these smart motel-style units have some wonderful sea views and very helpful owners. The complex includes a restaurant and bar, and there's also a compact double room available for $135.

Great Barrier Island

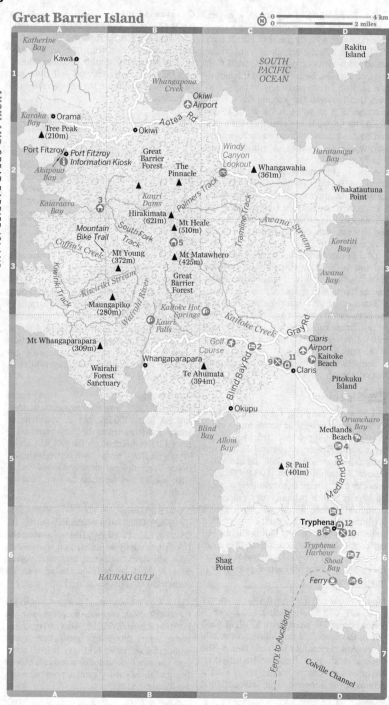

0 _____ 4 km
0 _____ 2 miles

SOUTH PACIFIC OCEAN

Rakitu Island

Katherine Bay

Kawa

Whangapoua Creek

Okiwi Airport

Karaka Bay

Orama

Tree Peak (210m)

Okiwi

Aotea Rd

Windy Canyon Lookout

Whangawahia (361m)

Harataonga Bay

Port Fitzroy

Port Fitzroy Information Kiosk

Great Barrier Forest

The Pinnacle

Akapoua Bay

Whakatautuna Point

Kaiaraara Bay

Kauri Dams

Hirakimata (621m)

Mt Heale (510m)

Palmers Track

Tramline Track

Awana Stream

Korotiti Bay

Mountain Bike Trail

South Fork Track

Mt Matawhero (425m)

Coffin's Creek

Mt Young (372m)

Great Barrier Forest

Awana Bay

Kiwiriki Track

Kiwiriki Stream

Wairahi River

Maungapiko (280m)

Kaitoke Hot Springs

Kauri Falls

Kaitoke Creek

Gray Rd

Mt Whangaparapara (309m)

Golf Course

Claris Airport

Kaitoke Beach

Whangaparapara

Te Ahumata (394m)

Blind Bay Rd

Claris

Pitokuku Island

Wairahi Forest Sanctuary

Okupu

Blind Bay

Allom Bay

St Paul (401m)

Medlands Beach

Oruawharo Bay

Medland Rd

HAURAKI GULF

Shag Point

Tryphena

Tryphena Harbour

Shoal Bay

Ferry

Ferry to Auckland

Colville Channel

Great Barrier Island

🕑 Activities, Courses & Tours
Hooked on Barrier .... (see 11)

🛏 Sleeping
1 Aotea Lodge D6
2 Crossroads Lodge C4
3 Kaiaraara Hut A2
4 Medlands Beach Backpackers............D5
5 Mt Heale Hut...B3
6 Shoal Bay Lodge D6
7 Sunset Waterfront Lodge D6
8 Tipi & Bob's Waterfront Lodge D6

🍽 Eating
9 Claris Texas C4
Currach Irish Pub...................... (see 10)
Tipi & Bob's.................................. (see 8)
10 Wild Rose D6

🛍 Shopping
11 Aotea Community Art Gallery............ C4
12 Stonewall Store................................... D6

Sunset Waterfront Lodge MOTEL $$$
(☎ 09-429 0051; www.sunsetlodge.co.nz; Mulberry Grove; apt $195-245) Gaze across the lawn to the sea from the attractive studio units, or fight over who's going to get the pointy room in the two-bedroom A-frame villas. There's a small shop and cafe next door.

✗ Eating & Drinking

In summer, most places are open daily but for the rest of the year the hours can be sporadic. A monthly guide to opening hours is on www.thebarrier.co.nz, but it pays to call ahead for an evening meal.

Self-caterers will find small stores in Tryphena, Claris, Whangaparapara and Port Fitzroy. The **Stonewall Store** (82 Blackwell Dr; ⊙ 8.30am-6pm) in Tryphena has a good selection of wine, beer and locally grown produce, and also operates a small al fresco market from 10am on Saturday mornings.

Wild Rose CAFE $
(☎ 09-429 0905; Blackwell Dr; mains $11-21; ⊙ 10am-3pm Wed-Sun; 📷) 🍴 Wild Rose does the best impersonation of an Auckland cafe on the island, albeit with the addition of local crowd-pleasers such as toasted sandwiches and legendary burgers. It uses free-range, organic and sustainable local produce whenever possible.

Claris Texas CAFE $
(129 Hector Sanderson Rd; mains $7-18; ⊙ 8am-4pm; 📶) While it doesn't live up to the promise of its quirky name, this is the best gap-filler in the centre of the island, serving cooked breakfasts, nachos, salads and pies.

Currach Irish Pub PUB $$
(☎ 09-429 0211; www.currachirishpub.co.nz; Blackwell Dr; mains $19-30; ⊙ from 4pm) This lively, child-friendly pub has a changing menu of seafood, steak and burgers, and is the island's main social centre. Rub shoulders with local musos on jam nights.

Tipi & Bob's RESTAURANT $$$
(☎ 09-429 0550; www.waterfrontlodge.co.nz; 38 Puriri Bay Rd; breakfast $16-20, dinner $34-40; ⊙ 8.30-10am & 5.30-10pm) Serving simple but satisfying meals in large portions, this popular haunt has an inviting deck overlooking the harbour. There's a cheaper pub menu in the bar.

🛍 Shopping

Aotea Community Art Gallery ARTS & CRAFTS
(80 Hector Sanderson Rd; ⊙ 10.30am-3.30pm) This eclectic showcase for the island's artsy fraternity sells everything from paintings and sculpture to handmade soap and local honey.

ℹ Information

There's an information kiosk at the GBI Rent-A-Car office (p110) in Claris. Claris Texas cafe has internet access.

Great Barrier Island i-SITE (www.greatbarriernz.com; Claris Airport; ⊙ 11am-noon Mon, Wed & Fri, 8am-2.30pm Sat, extended in summer) Brochures including their own *Great Barrier Island* pamphlet with useful information and a handy map.

Port Fitzroy Information Kiosk (☎ 09-429 0848; www.thebarrier.co.nz; ⊙ 9.30am-3pm Mon-Sat) Privately run kiosk that publishes the *Great Barrier Island Visitor Information Guide*.

ℹ Getting There & Away

AIR

FlyMySky (☎ 09-256 7025, 0800 222 123; www.flymysky.co.nz) Flies at least three times a day to Claris from Auckland. Cheaper flights are available if you travel to the island on a Sunday or leave on a Friday ($89), and there's a special return fare for flying one way and ferrying the other (adult/child $187/138).

AUCKLAND GREAT BARRIER ISLAND

Great Barrier Airlines (☑09-275 9120, 0800 900 600; www.greatbarrierairlines.co.nz) Departs from Auckland Domestic Airport (at least twice daily) and North Shore Aerodrome (at least daily) for the 30-minute flight to Claris. In summer it also flies from Whangarei.

Sunair (☑0800 786 847; www.sunair. co.nz; one way $150-190) Flies to Claris from Whitianga and Tauranga daily.

BOAT

Fullers (☑09-367 9111; www.fullers.co.nz; Ferry Building, 99 Quay St) Runs the fastest services (2½ hours) from Auckland's Ferry Building to Shoal Bay and Port Fitzroy from mid-December to the end of January, as well as around Labour Weekend in late October and on the Easter long weekend. Passengers only.

SeaLink (☑09-300 5900, 0800 732 546; www.sealink.co.nz) Runs car ferries from three to five days a week from Wynyard Wharf in Auckland to Tryphena's Shoal Bay (six hours).

ⓘ Getting Around

Most roads are narrow and windy but even small hire cars can handle the unsealed sections. Many of the accommodation places will pick you up from the airport or wharf if notified in advance.

Aotea Car Rentals (☑0800 426 832; www. aoteacarrentals.co.nz; Mulberry Grove) Rents cars (from $60), 4WDs (from $80) and vans (from $99). Rental clients can use Great Barrier Travel trampers shuttles for free.

GBI Rent-A-Car (☑09-429 0062; www.great-barrierisland.co.nz; 67 Hector Sanderson Rd) Has a somewhat battered fleet of cars starting at $40 and 4WDs from $70. They also operate shuttle services from Claris to Tryphena ($20), Medlands ($15), Whangaparapara ($20) and Port Fitzroy ($30, minimum four passengers), as well as trampers shuttles. There's a $5 flagfall for solo passengers; call ahead to book.

Great Barrier Travel (☑09-429 0474, 0800 426 832; www.greatbarriertravel.co.nz) Runs shuttles between Tryphena and Claris (timed to meet all the planes and boats), a daily shuttle from Claris to Port Fitzroy, and transfers to and from the walking tracks. Call ahead to confirm times and to book.

WEST AUCKLAND

West Auckland epitomises rugged: wild black-sand beaches, bush-shrouded ranges, and mullet-haired, black-T-shirt-wearing 'Westies'. The latter is just one of several stereotypes of the area's denizens. Others include the back-to-nature hippie, the eccentric bohemian artist and the dope-smoking surfer dude, all attracted to a simple life at the edge of the bush.

Add to the mix Croatian immigrants, earning the fertile fields at the base of the Waitakere Ranges the nickname 'Dallie Valley' after the Dalmatian coast where many hailed from. These pioneering families planted grapes and made wine, founding one of NZ's major industries.

Titirangi

POP 3200

This little village marks the end of Auckland's suburban sprawl and is a good place to spot all of the stereotypes mentioned above over a coffee, wine or cold beer. Once home to NZ's greatest modern painter, Colin McCahon, there remains an artsy feel to the place. Titirangi means 'Fringe of Heaven' – an apt name for the gateway to the Waitakere Ranges. This is the last stop for petrol and ATMs on your way west.

⊙ Sights

McCahon House MUSEUM
(www.mccahonhouse.org.nz; 67 Otitori Bay Rd; admission $5; ⊙10am-3pm Wed, Sat & Sun) It's a mark of the esteem in which Colin McCahon is held that the house he lived and painted in during the 1950s has been opened to the public as a mini-museum. The swish pad next door is home to the artist lucky enough to win the McCahon Arts Residency. Look for the signposts pointing down Park Rd, just before you reach Titirangi village.

Lopdell House Gallery GALLERY
(www.lopdell.org.nz; 418 Titirangi Rd; ⊙10am-4.30pm) FREE An excellent modern art gallery housed in the former Hotel Titirangi (1930), on the edge of the village. A significant restoration from 2012–2014 has further restored the building's heritage glory.

🛏 Sleeping & Eating

Fringe of Heaven B&B $$$
(☑09-817 8682; www.fringeofheaven.com; 4 Otitori Bay Rd; r $230) Surrounded by native bush, this Frank Lloyd Wright–inspired house offers glorious views over Manukau Harbour, an outdoor bath, glowworms in the garden and a songbird choir – all within 20 minutes of the city centre.

Hardware Cafe
CAFE **$$**

(www.hardwarecafe.org.nz; 404 Titirangi Rd; brunch $10-18, dinner $18-28; ⊙6am-4.30pm Sun-Tue, 6am-late Wed-Sat) This popular licensed cafe serves delicious, reasonably priced cooked breakfasts and lunches along with tempting counter food. More substantial evening meals start from $18.

Waitakere Ranges

This 160-sq-km wilderness was covered in kauri until the mid-19th century, when logging claimed most of the giant trees. A few stands of ancient kauri and other mature natives survive amid the dense bush of the regenerating rainforest, which is now protected inside the Waitakere Ranges Regional Park. Bordered to the west by wildly beautiful beaches on the Tasman Sea, the park's rugged terrain makes an excellent day trip from Auckland.

⊙ Sights & Activities

Arataki
VISITORS CENTRE

(☑09-817 0077; www.arc.govt.nz; Scenic Dr; ⊙9am-5pm) ⌀ As well as providing information on the 250km of trails within the park, this impressive centre also features Maori carvings and spectacular views. The carvings at the entrance depict the ancestors of the Kawerau *iwi*. You can also book here for several basic campsites (adult/child $6/4) within the park. A 1.6km nature trail opposite the centre leads visitors past labelled native species, including mature kauri.

Hillary Trail & Other Tracks
TRAMPING

(www.arc.govt.nz/hillarytrail) Arataki Vistor Centre is the starting point for this challenging 70km trail honouring Everest-conquerer Sir Edmund Hillary. It can be tackled in stages or in its four-day entirety, staying at campsites along the way. Walkers head to the coast at Huia, then continue past Whatipu, Karekare, Piha and Anawhata. From here continue up the coast to Te Henga and Muriwai, or head through bush to the Cascades Kauri to end at Swanson train station.

Other noted walks in the park include the Kitekite Track (1.8km, 30 minutes one way), the Fairy Falls Track (5.6km, 2½-hour loop) and the Auckland City Walk (1.5km, one-hour loop).

Rain Forest Express
RAILWAY

(☑09-302 8028; www.watercare.co.nz; 280 Scenic Dr; 2½hr trip adult/child $25/12) Departs from Jacobsons' Depot and follows an old logging track through several tunnels deep into the bush. You'll need to book well ahead; check the website for the schedule. Less regular are the 3½-hour twilight trips (adult/child $28/14), offering glimpses of glowworms and cave weta.

Waitakere Tramline Society
RAILWAY

(☑09-818 4946; www.waitakeretramline.org.nz; adult/child $15/5) Runs four scenic trips every Sunday that pass through a glowworm tunnel en route to the Waitakere Falls and Dam. Trips start from the end of Christian Rd, which runs south of Swanson station. Closed temporarily at the time of writing; check the website for the latest.

AWOL Canyoning Adventures
CANYONING

(☑09-834 0501; www.awoladventures.co.nz; ⊙half-/full day $160/195) Offers plenty of slippery, slidey, wet fun in Piha Canyon and the Blue Canyon, including glowworm-illuminated night trips ($185); transfers from Auckland are included.

Karekare

Few stretches of sand have more personality than Karekare. Those prone to metaphysical musings inevitably settle on descriptions such as 'spiritual' and 'brooding'. Perhaps

---

LOCAL KNOWLEDGE

HILLARY TRAIL

My family grew up loving Auckland's wild west coast, where the Tasman Sea pounds the black-sand beaches and black-back gulls ride the westerlies. Our family has walked and explored and lived out here for nearly a century and this is also where we came to grieve after my mother and sister were killed in 1975, where the invigorating salty air and the marvellous wild vistas to the Tasman Sea worked like a balm for our broken hearts. My father would come here to dream up and then prepare for new expeditionary challenges. It seemed the right sort of environment for someone like him: not a passive coastline, but active and exciting, with huge cliffs, crashing waves, thick bush and a tantalising far-away horizon.

Peter Hillary,
Mountaineer & Explorer

history has left its imprint: in 1825 it was the site of a ruthless massacre of the local Kawerau *iwi* by Ngapuhi invaders. Wild and gorgeously undeveloped, this famous beach has been the setting for onscreen moments both high- and lowbrow, from Oscar-winner *The Piano*, to *Xena, Warrior Princess*.

From the car park the quickest route to the black-sand beach involves wading through a stream. Karekare rates as one of the most dangerous beaches in the country, with strong surf and ever-present rips, so don't even think about swimming unless the beach is being patrolled by lifeguards (usually only in summer). In 1995 Pearl Jam singer Eddie Vedder nearly drowned here while visiting Neil Finn's Karekare pad.

Follow the road over the bridge and up along Lone Kauri Rd for 100m, where a short track leads to the pretty **Karekare Falls**. This leafy picnic spot is the start of several walking tracks.

Karekare has no shops of any description and no public transport. To get here take Scenic Dr and Piha Rd until you reach the well-signposted turn-off to Karekare Rd.

Piha

If you notice an Auckland surfer dude with a faraway look, chances are they're daydreaming about Piha... or just stoned. This beautifully rugged, iron-sand beach has long been a favourite for refugees from the city's stresses – whether for day trips, weekend teenage parties or family holidays.

Although Piha is popular, it's also incredibly dangerous, with wild surf and strong undercurrents; so much so that it's spawned its own popular reality TV show, *Piha Rescue*. If you don't want to inadvertently star in it, always swim between the flags, where lifeguards can provide help if you get into trouble.

Piha may be bigger and more populated than Karekare, but there's no supermarket, liquor shop, bank or petrol station, although there is a small general store that doubles as a cafe, takeaway shop and post office.

◉ Sights & Activities

The view of the coast as you drive down Piha Rd is spectacular. Perched on its haunches near the centre of the beach is **Lion Rock** (101m), whose 'mane' glows golden in the evening light. It's actually the eroded core of an ancient volcano and a Maori *pa* site. A path at the south end of the beach takes you

to some great lookouts. At low tide you can walk south along the beach and watch the surf shooting through a ravine in another large rock known as the **Camel**. A little further along, the waves crash through the **Gap** and form a safe swimming hole. A small colony of blue penguins nests at the beach's north end.

For surfboard hire, refer to the Piha Store and Piha Surf Shop listings.

🛏 Sleeping & Eating

Piha Beachstay – Jandal Palace HOSTEL $
(☑ 09-812 8381; www.pihabeachstay.co.nz; 38 Glenesk Rd; dm $33, r $80-120; @ 🛜) Attractive and ecofriendly, this wood-and-glass lodge has extremely smart facilities. It's 1km from the beach but there's a little stream at the bottom of the property and bushwalks nearby. In winter an open fire warms the large communal lounge.

Piha Domain Motor Camp CAMPSITE $
(☑ 09-812 8815; www.pihabeach.co.nz; 21 Seaview Rd; sites from $15, s/d cabin $50/60; 🛜) Smackbang on the beach, this well-kept campsite is great for those seeking an old-fashioned, cheap-as-chips, no-frills, family holiday. To keep unruly teens at bay, under 20s must be accompanied by parents. The cabins are tiny.

Piha Surf Accommodation CABIN $
(☑ 09-812 8723; www.pihasurf.co.nz; 122 Seaview Rd; caravans & cabins $60-90) Each basic but charmingly tatty caravan has its own linen, TV, fridge, cooker and long-drop toilet, and they share a very simple shower. The private cabins have the same rudimentary bathroom arrangement but are a more comfortable option.

Black Sands Lodge APARTMENT $$
(☑ 021 969 924; www.pihabeach.co.nz/Black-Sands-Lodge.htm; Beach Valley Rd; cabin $130, apt $180-220; 🛜) These two modern conjoined apartments with private decks match their prime location with attractive touches such as stereos and DVD players. The cabin is kitted out in a 1950s Kiwiana bach style and shares a bathroom with the main house. Bikes and wi-fi are free for guests, and in-room massage and lavish dinners can be arranged on request.

Piha Store BAKERY $
(Seaview Rd; snacks $2-10; ⊙ 7.30am-5.30pm) Call in for pies and other baked goods, groceries and ice creams. The attached Lion Rock Surf Shop rents surfboards (two

hours/half-day/day $20/30/40) and body boards ($10/20/30).

Piha Cafe   CAFE $$
(20 Seaview Rd; mains $14-23; ⊗8.30am-4pm Mon-Thu, 8.30am-7pm Fri-Sun) 🏄 Big-city standards mesh seamlessly with sand-between-toes informality at this attractive ecofriendly cafe. Cooked breakfasts and crispy pizzas provide sustenance for a hard day's surfing. After the waves, head back for a cold beverage on the deck.

🛍 Shopping

West Coast Gallery   ARTS & CRAFTS
(www.westcoastgallery.co.nz; Seaview Rd; ⊗10am-5pm Wed-Sun) The work of more than 180 local artists is sold from this small not-for-profit gallery next to the Piha fire station.

Piha Surf Shop   OUTDOOR EQUIPMENT
(www.pihasurf.co.nz; 122 Seaview Rd; ⊗8am-5pm) A family-run venture, with well-known surfboard designer Mike Jolly selling his wares and wife Pam selling a small range of crafts. Surfboards (per three hours/day $25/35), wet suits ($8/15) and body boards ($15/25) can be hired, and private surfing lessons can be arranged.

❶ Getting There & Away

There's no public transport to Piha, but **NZ Surf'n'Snow Tours** (☑09-828 0426; www.newzealandsurftours.com; one way $25, return trip incl surfing gear $99) provides shuttles when the surf's up. **Go Hitch** (☑0800 467 442; www.gohitch.co.nz; per person $40; ⊗departs 8.30am & 10.30am Sat & Sun) also operates a Piha shuttle from downtown Auckland and Ponsonby on weekends.

Te Henga (Bethells Beach)

Breathtaking Bethells Beach is reached by taking Te Henga Rd at the northern end of Scenic Dr. It's another raw, black-sand beach with surf, windswept dunes and walks, such as the popular one over giant sand dunes to Lake Wainamu (starting near the bridge on the approach to the beach).

Kumeu & Around

West Auckland's main wine-producing area still has some vineyards owned by the original Croatian families who kick-started NZ's wine industry. The fancy eateries that have mushroomed in recent years have done lit-

tle to dint the relaxed farmland feel to the region, but everything to encourage an afternoon's indulgence on the way back from the beach or the hot pools. Most cellars offer free tastings.

🍴 Eating & Drinking

Tasting Shed   TAPAS $$
(☑09-412 6454; www.thetastingshed.co.nz; 609 SH16; dishes $5-24; ⊗4-10pm Wed & Thu, noon-11pm Fri-Sun) Complementing its rural aspect with rustic chic decor, this slick eatery conjures up delicious dishes designed to be shared. It's not strictly tapas, as the menu strays from Spain, and appropriates flavours from Asia, the Middle East, Croatia, Serbia, Italy and France.

Hallertau   BREWERY
(☑09-412 5555; www.hallertau.co.nz; 1171 Coatesville-Riverhead Hwy, Riverhead; shared plates $11-15, mains $24-31; ⊗11am-midnight) Hallertau offers tasting paddles ($14) of its craft beers served on a vine-covered terrace edging the restaurant. Regular guest beers, good food, and occasional weekend DJs and live music make it very popular with Auckland's hopheads.

Soljans Estate   WINERY
(www.soljans.co.nz; 366 SH16; mains $19-33; ⊗tastings 9am-5.30pm, cafe 9.30am-3pm) One of the pioneering Croat-Kiwi family vineyards, Soljans has a wonderful cafe offering brunch, Dalmatian-style squid and Vintner's platters crammed with Mediterranean treats.

Riverhead   PUB
(www.theriverhead.co.nz; cnr Queen & York Sts, Riverhead; mains $20-31; ⊗11am-late Mon-Fri, 10am-late Sat & Sun) A blissful terrace, shaded by oak trees and overlooking the river, makes this 1857 hotel a memorable drink stop, even if the menu doesn't quite live up to its gastropub ambitions. Make a day of it, with a boat cruise (p76) from the city to the pub's own jetty.

Kumeu River   WINERY
(www.kumeuriver.co.nz; 550 SH16; ⊗9am-5pm Mon-Fri, 11am-5pm Sat) Owned by the Brajkovich family, this winery produces one of NZ's best chardonnays, among other varietals.

Coopers Creek   WINERY
(www.cooperscreek.co.nz; 601 SH16, Huapai; ⊗10.30am-5.30pm) Buy a bottle, spread out

a picnic in the attractive gardens and, from January to Easter, enjoy Sunday afternoon jazz sessions.

❶ Getting There & Away

From central Auckland, Kumeu is 25km up the Northwestern Motorway (SH16). Helensville-bound buses head here from Lower Albert St (adult/child $7.90/4.50, 50 minutes), but you'll really need a car or bike to get around.

Muriwai Beach

Yet another rugged black-sand surf beach, stretching 60km, Muriwai Beach's main claim to fame is the Takapu Refuge gannet colony, spread over the southern headland and outlying rock stacks. Viewing platforms get you close enough to watch (and smell) these fascinating seabirds. Every August hundreds of adult birds return to this spot to hook up with their regular partners and get busy – expect lots of outrageously cute neck-rubbing, bill-touching and general snuggling. The net result is a single chick per season; December and January are the best times to see the little fellas testing their wings before embarking on an impressive odyssey.

Nearby, a couple of short tracks will take you through beautiful native bush to a lookout that offers views along the length of the beach. Wild surf and treacherous rips mean that swimming is safe only when the beach is patrolled (swim between the flags). Apart from surfing, Muriwai Beach is a popular spot for hang gliding, parapunting, kiteboarding and horse riding. There are also

---

THE GREAT GANNET OE

After honing their flying skills, young gannets get the ultimate chance to test them – a 2000km journey to Australia. They usually hang out there for several years before returning home, never to attempt the journey again. Once back in the homeland they spend a few years waiting for a piece of waterfront property to become available in the colony, before settling down with a regular partner to nest – returning to the same patch of dirt every year. In other words, they're your typical New Zealander on their OE (Overseas Experience). Why are they called Kiwis again?

---

tennis courts, a golf course and a cafe that doubles as a takeaway chippie.

Helensville

POP 2600

A smattering of heritage buildings, antique shops and cafes makes village-like Helensville a good whistle-stop for those taking SH16 north.

🏃 Activities

Parakai Springs   THERMAL POOLS

(www.parakaisprings.co.nz; 150 Parkhurst Rd; adult/child $20/10; ⊙10am-9pm) Aucklanders bring their bored children to Parakai, 2km northwest of Helensville, on wet wintry days as a cheaper alternative to Waiwera. It has large thermally heated swimming pools, private spas ($8 per hour) and a couple of hydroslides.

Woodhill Mountain
Bike Park   MOUNTAIN BIKING

(☑027 278 0949; www.bikepark.co.nz; Restall Rd, Woodhill; adult/child $7/2, bike hire per hr $30; ⊙9am-5pm Thu-Tue, 10am-10pm Wed) Maintains many challenging tracks (including jumps and beams) within Woodhill Forest, 14km south of Helensville.

Tree Adventures   OUTDOORS

(☑0800 827 926; www.treeadventures.co.nz; Restall Rd, Woodhill; courses $16-40; ⊙9.30am-5.30pm) A set of high-ropes courses within Woodhill Forest, consisting of swinging logs, nets, balance beams, Tarzan swings and a flying fox.

4 Track Adventures   QUAD BIKES

(☑09-420 8104; www.4trackadventures.co.nz; Restall Rd, Woodhill; 1½/2½/3½hr tours $155/255/295) Rattle through Woodhill Forest (and along Muriwai Beach on the longer tours) on a quad bike. Pick up from Auckland is available at $50 per person.

❶ Information

Helensville Library (Commercial Rd; 🛜)

Visitor Information Centre (☑09-420 8060; www.helensville.co.nz; 87 Commercial Rd; ⊙10am-4pm Mon-Sat) Pick up free brochures detailing the Helensville Heritage Trail and Helensville Riverside Walkway.

❶ Getting There & Away

Bus 60 heads from Lower Albert St in Auckland (near Britomart) to Helensville ($10.30, 1½ hours).

NORTH AUCKLAND

The Auckland supercity sprawls 90km north of the CBD to just past the point where SH16 and SH1 converge at Wellsford. Beaches, regional parks, tramping trails, quaint villages, wine, kayaking and snorkelling are the main drawcards.

Long Bay Regional Park

The northernmost of Auckland's east coast bays, Long Bay is a popular family picnic and swimming spot, attracting over a million visitors a year. A three-hour-return coastal walk heads north from the sandy beach to the Okura River, taking in secluded Grannys Bay and Pohutukawa Bay (which attracts nude bathers).

Regular buses head to Long Bay from Albert St in the city (adult/child $6.80/4, one hour). If you're driving, leave the Northern Motorway at the Oteha Valley Rd exit, head towards Browns Bay and follow the signs.

Shakespear Regional Park

Shooting out eastward just before Orewa, the Whangaparaoa Peninsula is a heavily developed spit of land with a sizable South African expat community. At its tip is this gorgeous 376-hectare regional park, its native wildlife protected by a 1.7km pest-proof fence.

Sheep, cows, peacocks and pukeko ramble over the grassy headland, while pohutukawa-lined **Te Haruhi Bay** provides great views of the gulf islands and the city. Walking tracks take between 40 minutes and two hours, exploring native forest, WWII gun embankments, Maori sites and lookouts. If you can't bear to leave, there's an idyllic beachfront **campsite** (☑09-301 0101; www.arc.govt.nz; adult/child $13/6) with flush toilets and cold showers.

It's possible to get here via a torturous two-hour bus trip from Albert St. The one-way fare is $10.30, so it's best to buy a $16 Discovery day pass. An alternative is to take the **360 Discovery** (☑0800 360 3472; www.360discovery.co.nz; adult/child $14/8.30) ferry service to **Gulf Harbour**, a Noddy-town development of matching townhouses, a marina, country club and golf course. Enquire at the ferry office about picking up a bus or taxi from here. Alternatively, walk or cycle the remaining 3km to the park. The ferry is a good option for cyclists wanting to

skip the boring road trip out of Auckland; carry-on bikes are free.

Orewa

POP 7400

Locals have fears that Orewa is turning into NZ's equivalent of Queensland's Gold Coast, but until they start exporting retirees and replacing them with bikini-clad parking wardens that's unlikely to happen. It is, however, very built-up and high-rise apartment towers have begun to sprout.

◉ Sights & Activities

Orewa Beach   BEACH
Orewa's 3km-long stretch of sand is its main drawcard. Being in the gulf, it's sheltered from the surf but it's still patrolled by lifeguards in the peak season.

Alice Eaves Scenic Reserve   FOREST
(Old North Rd) Ten hectares of native bush with labelled trees, a *pa* site, a lookout and easy short walks.

Millennium Walkway   WALKING
Starting from South Bridge this 8km route loops through various parks before returning along the beach; follow the blue route markers.

Snowplanet   SNOW SPORTS
(www.snowplanet.co.nz; 91 Small Rd, Silverdale; day pass adult/child $66/47; ⊙10am-10pm Sat-Thu, 10am-midnight Fri) Snowplanet offers indoor skiing, tobogganing and snowboarding throughout the year. It's just off SH1, 8km south of Orewa.

⊨ Sleeping

Orewa Beach Top 10   HOLIDAY PARK $
(☑09-426 5832; www.orewaholidaypark.co.nz; 265 Hibiscus Coast Hwy; sites $40, units $60-115; @)
🍃 Taking up a large chunk of the beach's south end, this well-kept park has excellent facilities but road noise can be a problem.

Orewa Motor Lodge   MOTEL $$
(☑09-426 4027; www.orewamotorlodge.co.nz; 290 Hibicus Coast Hwy; units $170-190; 🐾) One of the motels lining Orewa's main road, this complex has scrupulously clean wooden units prettied up with hanging flower baskets. There's also a spa pool.

Waves   APARTMENT $$$
(☑09-427 0888; www.waves.co.nz; cnr Hibiscus Coast Hwy & Kohu St; units $175-299; 🐾) Like a

---

ⓘ WHICH HIGHWAY?

From Auckland, the multilane Northern Motorway (SH1) bypasses Orewa and Waiwera on a **tolled section** (☑0800 40 20 20; www.tollroad.govt.nz; per car & motorbike $2.20). It will save you about 10 minutes, provided you pay online or by phone (in advance or within five days of your journey) rather than stopping to queue at the toll booths.

Between Christmas and New Year SH1 can be terribly gridlocked heading north between the toll road and Wellsford; SH16 through Kumeu and Helensville is a sensible alternative. The same is true if heading south in the first few days of the New Year.

---

motel only much flasher, this complex offers spacious, self-contained apartments, and the downstairs units have gardens and spa baths. It's only a few metres from the beach.

✗ Eating

Asahi   JAPANESE $
(6 Bakehouse Lane; mains $11-20; ☺9am-3pm Mon, 9am-9pm Tue-Sat) Excellent for a sushi fix, with good bento boxes ($21.50).

Casablanca   TURKISH, CAFE $$
(www.casablancacafenz.co.nz; 336 Hibiscus Coast Hwy; mains $13-30; ☺10am-late Mon-Fri, 9am-late Sat & Sun) Turkish, North African and Mediterranean flavours feature at this buzzy cafe. Try the hearty baked Moorish eggs and you'll be set for the next chapter of your Kiwi road trip.

ⓘ Information

Orewa Information Centre (☑09-426 5338; www.orewabeach.co.nz; 40-46 Orewa Sq; ☺9am-3.30pm Mon-Fri, 10am-noon Sat) Part of the local Citizens Advice Bureau.

ⓘ Getting There & Away

Direct buses run between Orewa and Albert St in the city (adult/child $10.30/6.10, 1¼ hours), as well as Shakespear Regional Park (adult/child $1.90/1.10, 50 minutes) and Waiwera (adult/child $1.90/1.10, 10 minutes).

Waiwera

This pleasant river-mouth village has a great beach, but it's the *wai wera* (hot waters) that people come here for. Warm mineral water bubbles up from 1500m below the surface to fill the 19 pools of the **Waiwera Thermal Resort** (☑09-427 8800; www.waiwera.co.nz; 21 Main Rd; adult/child $26/15; ☺9am-9pm). There's a movie pool, 10 big slides, barbecues, private tubs ($40) and a health spa. Luxury modern houses have also been built nearby (doubles $180); enquire about indulgence packages.

Squeezed between the Waiwera and Puhoi Rivers, the exquisite 134-hectare **Wenderholm Regional Park** (☑09-366 2000; www. arc.govt.nz; sites per adult/child $13/6, houses $120-145) has a diverse ecology, abundant bird life, beaches and walks (30 minutes to 2½ hours). **Couldrey House** (www.historicouldreyhouse.co.nz; adult/child $5/free; ☺1-4pm Sat & Sun, daily Jan), the original homestead dating from the 1860s, is now a museum. The campsite provides only tap water and long-drop toilets, and the council also rents two comfortable self-contained houses.

Bus 895 from Auckland's Albert St heads to Waiwera (adult/child $10.30/6.10, one hour) via Orewa.

Puhoi

POP 450

Forget dingy cafes and earnest poets – this quaint village is a slice of the real Bohemia. In 1863 around 200 German-speaking immigrants from the present-day Czech Republic settled in what was then dense bush.

◉ Sights & Activities

Church of Sts Peter & Paul   CHURCH
(www.holyname.org.nz; Puhoi Rd) The village's pretty Catholic church dates from 1881 and has an interesting tabernacle painting (a copy of one in Bohemia), stained glass and statues.

Bohemian Museum   MUSEUM
(www.puhoihistoricalsociety.org.nz; Puhoi Rd; adult/child $3/free; ☺1-4pm Sat & Sun, daily Christmas-Easter) Tells the story of the hardship and perseverance of the original Bohemian pioneers.

Puhoi River Canoe Hire   CANOEING
(☑09-422 0891; www.puhoirivercanoes.co.nz; 84 Puhoi Rd) ✈ Hires kayaks and Canadian canoes, either by the hour (kayak/canoe $25/50) or for an excellent 8km downstream journey from the village to Wenderholm Regional Park (single/double kayak $50/100, including return transport). Bookings are essential.

✕ Eating & Drinking

Puhoi Valley   CAFE $$
(www.puhoivalley.co.nz; 275 Ahuroa Rd; mains $13-22; ⊙10am-4pm) Renowned across NZ, Puhoi Valley cheese features heavily on the menu of this upmarket cheese shop and cafe, set blissfully alongside a lake, fountain and children's playground. In the summer there's music on the lawn, perfect with a gourmet ice cream.

Puhoi Hotel   PUB
(www.puhoipub.co.nz; cnr Saleyards & Puhoi Rds; ⊙10am-10pm) There's character and then some in this 1879 pub, with walls completely covered in old photos, animal heads and vintage household goods.

Puhoi Cottage   TEAHOUSE
(www.puhoicottage.co.nz; 50 Ahuroa Rd; ⊙10am-4pm Fri-Sun) Drop in for a Devonshire cream tea ($11).

❶ Getting There & Away

Puhoi is 1km west of SH1. The turn-off is 2km past the Johnstone Hills tunnel.

Mahurangi & Scandrett Regional Parks

Straddling the head of Mahurangi Harbour, **Mahurangi Regional Park** (☎09-366 2000; www.arc.govt.nz; sites from $6, baches $120-145) has three distinct fingers: Mahurangi West, accessed from a turn-off 3km north of Puhoi; Scott Point on the eastern side, with road access 16km southeast of Warkworth; and isolated Mahurangi East, which can only be reached by boat. This boater's paradise incorporates areas of coastal forest, *pa* sites and a historic homestead and cemetery. Its sheltered beaches offer prime sandy spots for a dip or picnic and there are loop walks ranging from 1½ to 2½ hours. Accommodation is available in four basic campsites and four baches sleeping six to eight. Campervans can also park for $6 per person.

On the way to Mahurangi West you'll pass **Zealandia Sculpture Garden** (☎09-422 0099; www.zealandiasculpturegarden.co.nz; 138 Mahurangi West Rd; admission $10; ⊙by appointment Nov-Mar), where the work of Terry Stringer is showcased within impressive architecture and grounds.

On the ocean side of the Mahurangi Peninsula, **Scandrett Regional Park** (☎09-366 2000; www.arc.govt.nz; bach $145) has a sandy beach, walking tracks, patches of regenerating forest, another historic homestead, more *pa* sites and great views towards Kawau Island. Three baches (sleeping six to eight) are available for rent and there's room for campervans ($6 per person).

Warkworth

POP 3300
River-hugging Warkworth makes a pleasant pit stop, its dinky main street retaining a village atmosphere.

◎ Sights

Dome Forest   FOREST
(SH1) Two kilometres north of Warkworth, a track leads through this regenerating forest to the Dome summit (336m). On a fine day you can see the Sky Tower from a lookout near the top. The summit walk takes about 1½ hours return, or you can continue for a gruelling seven-hour one-way tramp through the Totora Peak Scenic Reserve, exiting on Govan Wilson Rd.

WORTH A TRIP

TE HANA TE AO MARAMA

You'll see the terraces of a lot of historic *pa* (fortified village) sites etched into hillsides all around NZ, but if you want to get an idea of how these fortified villages actually looked, take a guided tour of the re-created *pa* at **Te Hana Te Ao Marama** (www.tehana.co.nz; 307-308 SH1, Te Hana). Tours leave on the hour from 10am to 3pm daily (adult/child $25/13). The daytime tours can be combined with a *powhiri* (formal welcome) on to the very real *marae* next door, with some packages including a meal and a cultural concert.

For the most atmospheric experience, take one of the Friday night *Starlight Tours* (adult/child $100/50, bus from Auckland $25 extra), where you'll be on the receiving end of a *powhiri*, have a meal within the *marae* complex and then proceed into the dramatically lit village for a guided tour and concert.

Sheepworld
FARM

(www.sheepworldfarm.co.nz; SH1; adult/child $15/8, incl show $28/10; ⊗9am-5pm) This agricultural attraction offers farm experiences for little city slickers (pony rides, lamb feeding) and the ubiquitous sheep and dog show, including a shearing demonstration (showtimes 11am and 2pm).

Warkworth & District Museum
MUSEUM

(www.wwmuseum.orcon.net.nz; Tudor Collins Dr; adult/child $8/2; ⊗9am-3pm) Pioneer-era detritus is displayed at this small local museum. Of more interest is the surrounding **Parry Kauri Park**, which harbours a couple of giant kauri trees, including the 800-year-old McKinney kauri (girth 7.6m).

✕ Eating & Drinking

Chocolate Brown
CAFE, SWEETS $$

(www.chocolatebrown.co.nz; 6 Mill Lane; mains $10-20; ⊗8.30am-4pm) Decked out with quirky NZ-themed art – mostly for sale – this cafe turns out excellent coffee, robust eggy breakfasts and delicious homestyle baking. Definitely leave room for a few cacao-infused goodies from the chocolate shop next door; there are also plenty of gift packs for the folks back home.

Ransom Wines
WINERY

(www.ransomwines.co.nz; Valerie Close; tasting with purchase free, otherwise donation to Tawharanui Open Sanctuary $5; ⊗10am-5pm Tue-Sun) Well signposted from SH1, about 3km south of Warkworth, Ransom produces great food wines and showcases them with good-value tasting platters (per person $20), crammed with smoked meats and local cheeses. A tasting flight of five wines is $12.

Tahi Bar
CRAFT BEER

(www.tahibar.com; 1 Neville St; ⊗noon-late Wed-Sun) Tucked down a quiet laneway, Tahi features eight ever-changing taps of New Zealand craft beer. It's an exceptionally friendly spot with decent platters and pub grub and a rustic and sunny deck.

🔒 Shopping

Honey Centre
FOOD

(www.honeycentre.co.nz; cnr SH1 & Perry Rd; ⊗8.30am-5pm) About 5km south of Warkworth, the Honey Centre makes a diverting pit stop, with its cafe, free honey tasting and glass-fronted hives. The shop sells all sorts of bee-related products, from candles to mead.

ℹ️ Information

Warkworth i-SITE (☑09-425 9081; www.warkworthnz.com; 1 Baxter St; ⊗8.30am-5pm Mon-Fri, 9am-3pm Sat & Sun)

ℹ️ Getting There & Away

InterCity (☑09-583 5780; www.intercity.co.nz) and **Naked Bus** (www.nakedbus.com) services both pass through town, en route between Auckland and the Bay of Islands.

Matakana & Around

Around 15 years ago, Matakana was a nondescript rural village with a handful of heritage buildings and an old-fashioned country pub. Now the locals watch bemused as Auckland's chattering classes idle away the hours in stylish wine bars and cafes. The striking **Matakana Cinemas** (☑09-422 9833; www.matakanacinemas.co.nz; 2 Matakana Valley Rd) complex has a domed roof reminiscent of an Ottoman bathhouse, and an excellent **farmers market** (www.matakanavillage.co.nz; ⊗8am-1pm Sat) is held in its shadow.

The reason for this growth is the area's boutique wineries, which are developing a name for pinot gris, merlot, syrah and a host of obscure varietals. Local vineyards are detailed in the free *Matakana Coast Wine Country* (www.matakanacoast.com) and *Matakana Wine Trail* (www.matakanawine.com) brochures. Both are available from the Matakana Information Centre in the foyer of the cinema.

◉ Sights & Activities

⭐ Tawharanui Regional Park
BEACH

(☑09-366 2000; www.arc.govt.nz; Takatu Rd) A partly unsealed road leads to this 588-hectare reserve at the end of a peninsula. This special place is an open sanctuary for native birds, protected by a pest-proof fence, while the northern coast is a marine park (bring a snorkel). There are plenty of walking tracks (1½ to four hours) but the main attraction is **Anchor Bay**, one of the region's finest white-sand beaches. Camping is allowed at two basic sites near the beach (adult/child $13/6) and there's a six-person bach for hire ($145).

Blue Adventures
WATER SPORTS

(☑022 630 5705; www.blueadventures.co.nz; lessons per hour $60-75) Based in Matakana, but offering kitesurfing, paddle boarding and wakeboarding lessons, and tours from Auckland to Mangawhai. Also jetboat tours (per person $75 to $300) along the Matakana coast.

Matakana Cycle Hire　　　BICYCLE RENTAL
(☑09-423 0076; www.matakanabicyclerental.co.nz; 951 Matakana Rd; half-/full-day hire $30/40, tours from $60) Bike hire to explore local vineyards and beaches.

Omaha Beach　　　BEACH
The nearest swimming beach to Matakana, Omaha has a long stretch of white sand, good surf and ritzy holiday homes.

Brick Bay Sculpture Trail　　　PARK
(www.brickbaysculpture.co.nz; Arabella Lane, Snells Beach; adult/child $12/8; ⊙10am-5pm) After taking an hour-long artistic ramble through the beautiful grounds of Brick Bay Wines, recuperate with a wine tasting at the architecturally impressive cafe.

Morris & James　　　ARTS & CRAFTS
(www.morrisandjames.co.nz; 48 Tongue Farm Rd; ⊙9am-5pm) **FREE** Watch the potters at work during the free daily tour (11.30am) or just call in to check out the colourful finished products and the courtyard cafe.

🛏 Sleeping

Sandspit Holiday Park　　　HOLIDAY PARK $
(☑09-425 8610; www.sandspitholidaypark.co.nz; 1334 Sandspit Rd; sites from $17, units $70-120; @🛜) A camping ground masquerading as a pioneer village, this place incorporates historic buildings and faux shopfronts into its facilities. It's right by the water at Sandspit.

Matakana Country Lodge　　　B&B $$$
(☑09-422 3553; www.matakanacountry.co.nz; 149 Anderson Rd; r $275-375; 🛜🐾) It's only five minutes from Matakana by way of an unsealed road and a long driveway, but this lodge offers tranquillity in bucketloads and expansive views over the countryside. The three guest rooms have the run of the entire villa, including the kitchen, pool and spa.

🍴 Eating & Drinking

Charlie's Gelato Garden　　　ICE CREAM $
(www.charliesgelato.co.nz; 17 Sharp Rd; ice cream $4-6, pizza from $5; ⊙9am-5pm, reduced hours in winter) Superb sorbet and gelato made from fresh fruit and interesting ingredients – try the liquorice or ginger beer flavours – and excellent wood-fired pizzas during summer from Friday to Sunday.

Mahurangi River Winery & Restaurant　　　WINERY $$$
(☑09-425 0306; www.mahurangiriver.co.nz; 162 Hamilton Rd; mains $24-36, platters $25-45; ⊙11am-4pm Thu-Mon Feb-Dec, 11am-4pm daily Jan) Expansive vineyard views partner with a relaxed ambience and savvy food at this rural spot off Sandspit Rd.

The Matakana　　　PUB $$
(www.matakana.co.nz; 11 Matakana Valley Rd; mains $17-25; ⊙noon-late) Following a trendy makeover, Matakana's heritage pub now features quirky decor, Matakana wines and craft beers, and decent bistro food including local Mahurangi oysters. Occasional DJs and live acts enliven the cool outdoor space.

Plume　　　WINERY $$
(☑09-422 7915; www.plumerestaurant.co.nz; 49a Sharp Rd; mains $29-40; ⊙11am-3pm Wed-Sun, 6pm-late Fri & Sat) Plume has rural views from its terrace and an adventurous menu that jumps from China to Spain by way of Thailand and India.

Vintry　　　WINE BAR
(☑09-423 0251; www.thevintry.co.nz; 2 Matakana Valley Rd; tastings from $5; ⊙10am-10pm) In the Matakana Cinemas complex, this wine bar serves as a one-stop cellar door for all the local producers.

ℹ Information

Matakana Information Centre (☑09-422 7433; www.matakanainfo.org.nz; 2 Matakana Valley Rd; ⊙10am-1pm) In the foyer of the cinema complex.

ℹ Getting There & Away

Matakana village is a 10km drive northeast of Warkworth along Matakana Rd; there's no public transport. Ferries for Kawau Island leave from Sandspit, 8km east of Warkworth along Sandspit Rd.

Leigh

POP 390

Appealing little Leigh (www.leighbythesea.co.nz) has a picturesque harbour dotted with fishing boats, and a decent swimming beach at Matheson Bay. Long-standing Goat Island Dive & Snorkel (☑0800 348 369; www.goatislanddive.co.nz; 142a Pakiri Rd; mask, snorkel & fin hire $22, dive trips incl equipment $110-250, PADI Open Water $499) offers PADI courses and boat dive trips in the Hauraki Gulf throughout the year.

Apart from its proximity to Goat Island, the town's other claim to fame is the legendary **Leigh Sawmill** (☑ 09-422 6019; www.sawmillcafe.co.nz; 142 Pakiri Rd; mains $14-35; ☺ 10am-late daily Jan–mid-Feb, 10am-3pm Mon-Wed & 10am-late Thu-Sun mid-Feb–Mar, 10am-late Thu-Sun Apr-Nov), a spunky little pub and beer garden that's a regular stop on the summer rock circuit, sometimes attracting surprisingly big names. If you imbibe too much at the on-site **microbrewery** (☺ 1.30-5pm Fri & Sat), there's accommodation inside the old sawmill shed, including basic backpacker rooms (from $25) and massive doubles with en suites (from $125). Alternatively, you can rent the Cosy Sawmill Family Cottage (from $300, sleeps 10).

Goat Island Marine Reserve

Only 3km from Leigh, this 547-hectare aquatic area was established in 1975 as the country's first marine reserve. In less than 40 years the sea has reverted to a giant aquarium, giving an impression of what the NZ coast must have been like before humans arrived. You only need step knee deep into the water to see snapper (the big fish with blue dots and fins), blue maomao and stripy parore swimming around. There are dive areas all round Goat Island, which sits just offshore, or you can snorkel or dive directly from the beach.

Excellent interpretive panels explain the area's Maori significance (it was the landing place of one of the ancestral canoes) and provide pictures of the species you're likely to encounter. Colourful sponges, forests of seaweed, boarfish, crayfish and stingrays are common sights, and if you're very lucky you may see orcas and bottle-nosed dolphins. Visibility is claimed to be at least 10m, 75% of the time.

A **glass-bottomed boat** (☑ 09-422 6334; www.glassbottomboat.co.nz; adult/child $28/15) provides an opportunity to see the underwa-ter life while staying dry. Trips last 45 minutes and run from the beach all year round, weather permitting; ring to check conditions and to book.

Staffed by marine experts and graduate students from the University of Auckland, the recently opened **Goat Island Marine Discovery Centre** (☑ 09-923 3645; www.goatislandmarine.co.nz; Goat Island Rd, Leigh; adult/child/family $10/5/20; ☺ 10am-4pm daily mid-Dec–March) is packed with interesting exhibitions on the ecosystem of the marine reserve, and is definitely worth visiting before venturing into Goat Island's waters. The interactive displays and the tide pool full of marine creatures is great for children. Phone ahead for opening hours outside of mid-December to March.

You can usually rent kayaks and snorkelling gear right from the beach. Snorkelling gear (from $9) and wetsuits (from $12) can also be hired at **Seafriends** (☑ 09-422 6212; www.seafriends.org.nz; 7 Goat Island Rd; ☺ 9am-7pm), further up the road, which also has saltwater aquariums and a cafe.

Pakiri

Blissful Pakiri Beach, 12km past Goat Island (4km of the road is unsealed), is an unspoilt expanse of white sand and rolling surf – a large chunk of which is protected as a regional park.

Right by the water, **Pakiri Beach Holiday Park** (☑ 09-422 6199; www.pakiriholidaypark.co.nz; 261 Pakiri River Rd; sites from $50, units $80-400) has a shop and tidy units of varying degrees of luxury in a secure setting under the shade of pohutukawa.

Just 6km on from Pakiri is **Pakiri Horse Riding** (☑ 09-422 6275; www.horseride-nz.co.nz; Rahuikiri Rd), which has more than 80 horses available for superb bush-and-beach rides, ranging from one hour ($65) to multiday 'safaris'. Accommodation is provided in basic but spectacularly situated beachside **cabins** (dm/cabin $35/155) or in a comfortable four-bedroom **house** ($500), secluded among the dunes.

Bay of Islands & Northland

🎯 09

Includes ➡

Mangawhai.................124
Waipu & Bream Bay....125
Whangarei..................126
Tutukaka Coast & the
Poor Knights Islands ..131
Russell Road 133
Bay of Islands 134
Russell........................138
Paihia & Waitangi........141
Kerikeri.......................145
Cape Reinga &
Ninety Mile Beach.......152
Hokianga.....................156
Kauri Coast 159

Best Places to Eat

➡ à Deco (p130)

➡ Havana Cabana (p133)

➡ Bennetts (p125)

➡ Food at Wharepuke (p148)

Best Places to Stay

➡ Endless Summer Lodge (p155)

➡ Relax a Lodge (p146)

➡ Tree House (p156)

➡ Kahoe Farms Hostel (p150)

Why Go?

For many New Zealanders, the phrase 'up north' conjures up sepia-toned images of family fun in the sun, pohutukawa in bloom and dolphins frolicking in pretty bays. From school playgrounds to work cafeterias, owning a bach (holiday house) 'up north' is a passport to popularity.

Beaches are the main drawcard and they're here in profusion. Visitors from more crowded countries are flummoxed to wander onto beaches without a scrap of development or another human being in sight. The west coast shelters the most spectacular remnants of the ancient kauri forests that once blanketed the top of the country; the remaining giant trees are an awe-inspiring sight and one of the nation's treasures.

It's not just natural attractions that are on offer: history hangs heavily here. The site of the earliest settlements of both Maori and Europeans, Northland is unquestionably the birthplace of the nation.

When to Go

➡ Northland's beaches go crazy at New Year and remain busy throughout the January school holidays, with the long, lazy days of summer usually continuing into February and March.

➡ The 'winterless north' boasts a subtropical climate, most noticeable from Kerikeri upwards, which averages seven rainy days per month in summer but 16 in winter.

➡ In winter the average highs hover around 16°C and the average lows around 7°C.

➡ Temperatures are often a degree or two warmer than Auckland, especially on the east coast.

Bay of Islands & Northland Highlights

1 Splashing about, body surfing, sunbathing and strolling at **Matauri Bay** (p148)

2 Watching oceans collide while souls depart at **Cape Reinga** (p152)

3 Paying homage to the ancient kauri giants of the **Waipoua Forest** (p159)

4 Diving at one of the world's top spots, the **Poor Knights Islands** (p131)

5 Frolicking with dolphins and claiming your own island paradise among the many in the **Bay of Islands** (p134)

6 Surfing the sand dunes at **Ninety Mile Beach** (p152) or Hokianga's **North Head** (p156)

7 Delving into history and culture at the **Waitangi Treaty Grounds** (p142)

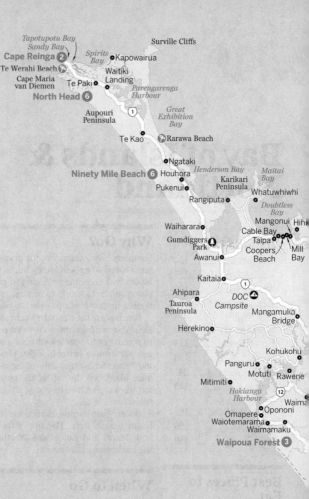

Surville Cliffs

Tapotupotu Bay
Sandy Bay
Cape Reinga **2**
Te Werahi Beach
Cape Maria
van Diemen
Te Paki
North Head **6**

Spirits
Bay
Kapowairua

Waitiki
Landing

Parengarenga
Harbour

Aupouri
Peninsula

Great
Exhibition
Bay

Te Kao

Rarawa Beach **7**

Ngataki

Ninety Mile Beach **6**
Houhora

Pukenui

Henderson Bay
Karikari
Peninsula

Maitai
Bay

Whatuwhiwhi

Rangiputa

Doubtless
Bay

Waiharara

Mangonui   Hihi
Cable Bay
Taipa
Mill
Bay

Gumdiggers
Park

Coopers
Beach

Awanui

Kaitaia

Ahipara
Tauroa
Peninsula

DOC
Campsite

Mangamuka
Bridge

Herekino

Kohukohu

Panguru
Motuti
Rawene

Mitimiti

Hokianga
Harbour

12

Waima

Omapere
Waiotemarama
Oponomi
Waimamaku

Waipoua Forest **3**

TASMAN
SEA

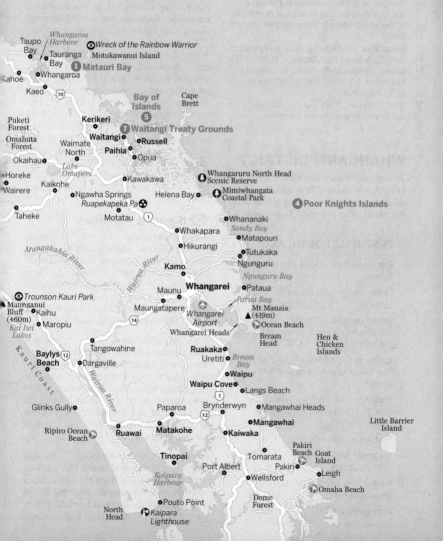

SOUTH PACIFIC OCEAN

0   50 km
0   25 miles

Taupo Bay
Whangaroa Harbour
Tauranga Bay
Whangaroa
Kahoe
Kaeo
(10)

① Wreck of the Rainbow Warrior
Motukawanui Island
① Matauri Bay

Bay of Islands
Cape Brett
⑤

Puketi Forest
Omahuta Forest
Waimate North
Okaihau
Horeke
Wairere
Taheke
Kaikohe

Kerikeri
⑦ Waitangi Treaty Grounds
Waitangi
Paihia
Russell
Opua
Lake Omapere
Kawakawa
Ngawha Springs
Ruapekapeka Pa
Motatau
(1)

Whangaruru North Head Scenic Reserve
Mimiwhangata Coastal Park
Helena Bay

④ Poor Knights Islands

Mangakahia River
Whakapara
Hikurangi
Kamo
Whananaki
Sandy Bay
Matapouri
Tutukaka
Ngunguru
Ngunguru Bay

Wairua River

Maunu
Whangarei
Maungatapere
Whangarei Airport
Whangarei Heads
Pataua
Parua Bay
Mt Manaia (419m)
Ocean Beach

⊙ Trounson Kauri Park
Maunganui Bluff (460m)
Kaihu
Maropiu
Kai Iwi Lakes
(14)
Tangowahine

Baylys Beach (12)
Dargaville

Bream Head
Hen & Chicken Islands

Ruakaka
Uretiti
Bream Bay
Waipu
Waipu Cove
Langs Beach

Wairoa River

(1)
Paparoa
Brynderwyn
Mangawhai Heads

Glinks Gully
(12)

Little Barrier Island

Ripiro Ocean Beach
Ruawai
Matakohe
Kaiwaka
Mangawhai

Tinopai
Tomarata
Pakiri Beach
Goat Island

Kaipara Harbour
Port Albert
Pakiri
Leigh
Wellsford

Pouto Point
North Head
⊙ Kaipara Lighthouse
Dome Forest
⊙ Omaha Beach

ℹ Getting There & Around

AIR

Air New Zealand (☏ 0800 737 000; www.air-newzealand.co.nz) Daily flights from Auckland to Whangarei, Kerikeri and Kaitaia, and from Wellington to Whangarei.

Great Barrier Airlines (☏ 0800 900 600, 09-275 9120; www.greatbarrierairlines.co.nz) Friday and Sunday flights from November to March that link Whangarei to Great Barrier Island.

BUS

InterCity (☏ 09-583 5780; www.intercity.co.nz) InterCity and associated Northliner services head from Auckland to Kerikeri via Waipu, Whangarei and Paihia; and from Paihia to Kaitaia via Kerikeri, Mangonui and Coopers Beach.

Naked Bus (☏ 09-006 2533; www.nakedbus.com) Daily buses from Auckland to Paihia (3¾ hours), via Warkworth, Waipu, Whangarei and Kawakawa. Note that calls to this number cost $1.99 per minute.

West Coaster (☏ 021 380 187) Weekday shuttles linking Whangarei and Dargaville.

WHANGAREI DISTRICT

To truly experience this area you'll need to get wet, and scores of beaches offer opportunities for swimming, surfing or just splashing about. The hot spots heave with Kiwi

---

ESSENTIAL NORTHLAND

Eat Kumara, Dargaville's knobbly claim to fame

Drink Orange juice, Kerikeri's signature squeeze

Read *The House of Strife* (1993), Maurice Shadbolt's riveting novel set during the Northland War

Listen to *Cape Reinga Way* (2011) by The Nukes, ukeleles heading to the afterlife

Watch *Land of the Long White Cloud* (2009) – fishing philosophers on Ninety Mile Beach

Festival Waitangi Day

Go green Sing to the trees with Footprints Waipoua

Online www.northlandnz.com; www.kauricoast.com

Area code ☏ 09

---

holidaymakers at peak times, but even then it's possible to find isolated stretches of sand where your footprints are the only ones.

North of Whangarei, the Tutukaka Coast is one of the planet's top three coastlines, according to *National Geographic Traveler* magazine, and the late Jacques Cousteau rated the neighbouring Poor Knights Islands as one of the world's best dive sites.

Online, see www.whangareinz.com.

Mangawhai

POP 2400

Mangawhai Village sits at the base of a horseshoe harbour, but it's Mangawhai Heads, 5km further on, that's really special.

Various Maori tribes inhabited the area before the 1660s, when Ngati Whatua became dominant. In 1807, Ngati Whatua defeated Ngapuhi from the north in a major battle, letting the survivors escape. One of them was Hongi Hika, who in 1825 returned, armed with muskets obtained from Europeans. The ensuing bloodbath all but annihilated Ngati Whatua and the district became *tapu* (sacred, taboo). British squatters moved in and were rewarded with land titles by the government in the 1850s. Ceremonies were only performed to lift the *tapu* in the 1990s.

◉ Sights & Activities

Mangawhai Heads   BEACH
A narrow spit of sand stretches for kilometres to form the harbour's south head, sheltering a seabird sanctuary. Across the water sits the holiday town with a surf beach at its northern tip. Lifesavers patrol on weekends in summer and daily during school holidays, but it's not especially dangerous.

Mangawhai Museum   MUSEUM
(www.mangawhai-museum.org.nz; Molesworth Dr; admission by donation; ⊗10.30am-1pm Thu-Sun) Scheduled to open by the time you read this, the Mangawhai Historical Society's new museum occupies a spectacular building on the main road that links Mangawhai Village to Mangawhai Heads; check out the roof shaped like a stingray.

Mangawhai Cliff Top Walkway   TRAMPING
Starting at Mangawhai Heads, this track affords extensive views of sea and land. It takes two to three hours, provided you time it with a return down the beach at low tide. This is part of Te Araroa, the national walking track.

🛏 Sleeping

Coastal Cow Backpackers   HOSTEL **$**
(☑09-431 5246; www.mangawhaibackpackers.
com; 299 Molesworth Dr, Mangawhai Heads; dm
$28, s $55-88, d & tw $66-95) This homely
hostel has simple rooms decorated with
a quirky bovine theme. There's also a self-
contained unit ($95).

Milestone Cottages   APARTMENTS **$$**
(☑09-431 4018; www.milestonecottages.co.nz; 27
Moir Pt Rd, Mangawhai Heads; apt $125-170; ✸) A
Pasifika paradise, with lush tropical gardens
and self-contained apartments. A walking
track leads to a compact beach that's great
for swimming and kayaking.

Mangawhai Lodge   B&B **$$$**
(☑09-431 5311; www.seaviewlodge.co.nz; 4
Heather St, Mangawhai Heads; s/d $185/190, unit
$175-220; @🖥) 🖋 Smartly furnished rooms
have access to a picture-perfect wraparound
verandah at this boutique B&B, which also
features great views.

🍴 Eating & Drinking

Mangawhai Market   MARKET **$**
(Moir St; ⊙9am-1pm Sat) Held in the library
hall in Mangawhai Village, this is a good
place to stock up on organic produce (including wine and olive oil) and peruse local craft. Another market is held on Sunday
mornings in the Mangawhai Heads Domain
from mid-October to Easter.

Bennetts   CAFE **$$**
(☑09-431 5072; www.bennettsofmangawhai.com;
52 Moir St, Mangawhai Village; mains $13-23;
⊙shop 9.30am-4.30pm, cafe 9am-4pm Mon-Fri,
from 8.30am Sat & Sun) Rural Europe comes
to Mangawhai at this atmospheric *chocola-
terie*, *gelateria* and cafe, where you can sit
by the fountain while dining on French and
Italian flavours and sipping a glass of wine.

Sail Rock Cafe   CAFE **$$**
(12a Wood St, Mangawhai Heads; mains $13-32;
⊙9.30am-late, closed Wed outside of summer)
The standout here is the salt-and-pepper
squid, plus there are Kiwi craft brews on
tap and dairy-free and gluten-free menu options. Good pizzas ($13 to $25) are also available for take away.

Frog & Kiwi   CAFE **$$**
(www.facebook.com/FrogAndKiwiRestaurant; The
Hub, 6 Molesworth Dr, Mangawhai Village; break-
fast & lunch $9-21, dinner $32-38; ⊙9am-2.30am
& 6-10pm) This French-Kiwi cafe and bistro
does great counter food, good-value $12
lunch specials – also available to take away –
and more refined French classics at night.

Mangawhai Tavern   PUB, LIVE MUSIC
(www.mangawhaitavern.co.nz; Moir St; ⊙11am-
late) One of the country's oldest pubs – built
in 1865 – the tavern's harbourside location
is a top spot for an afternoon beer. There's
live music most Saturday nights and Sunday
afternoons, and across the Christmas-New
Year period some of NZ's top bands rock the
garden bar.

ℹ Information

Visitor Information Centre (☑09-431 5090;
www.mangawhai.co.nz) Staffed sporadically
(mainly on weekends and in summer), but there
are information boards outside.

Waipu & Bream Bay
POP 1854

The original 934 British settlers came to
Waipu from Scotland via Nova Scotia (Can-
ada) between 1853 and 1860. These dour
Scots had the good sense to eschew frigid
Otago, where so many of their kindred set-
tled, for sunnier northern climes. The story
comes to life through holograms, a short
film and interactive displays at the Waipu
Museum (www.waipumuseum.co.nz; 36 The Cen-
tre; adult/child $8/3; ⊙10am-4pm).

Only 10% of current residents are direct
descendants of the original Scots, but there's
a big get-together on 1 January every year,
when the Highland Games (www.waipugames.
co.nz; adult/child $15/5), established in 1871,
take place in Caledonian Park. Just south of
Waipu township, there's good swimming at
Waipu Cove and Langs Beach.

There are also excellent walks in the area,
including the Waipu Coastal Trail, which
heads south from Waipu Cove – around to
Langs Beach, passing the Pancake Rocks
on the way. The 2km Waipu Caves Walk-
ing Track starts at Ormiston Rd and passes
through farmland and a scenic reserve en
route to a large cave containing glowworms
and limestone formations; bring a torch, a
compass and sturdy footwear to delve the
depths.

Bream Bay has miles of blissfully deserted
beach, blighted only slightly by a giant oil re-
finery at the north end. At Uretiti, a stretch
of beach south of a DOC campsite (www.doc.
govt.nz; SH1; sites per adult/child $10/5) is unof-
ficially considered 'clothing optional'. Over

New Year the crowd is evenly split between Kiwi families, serious European nudists and gay guys.

🛏 Sleeping

Waipu Wanderers Backpackers HOSTEL $
(☏09-432 0532; www.waipu-hostel.co.nz; 25 St Marys Rd; dm/s/d $30/45/66; 🛜) There are only three rooms at this friendly backpackers in Waipu township. Look forward to free fruit in season.

Ruakaka Reserve Motor Camp HOLIDAY PARK $
(☏09-432 7590; www.motorcamp.co.nz; 21 Ruakaka Beach Rd; sites from $30, cabins $50-90; 🛜) Priced and positioned somewhere between a DOC campsite and a holiday park, this ginormous motor camp offers simple facilities on a grassy area fronting the beach and rivermouth at Ruakaka.

Stonehouse GUESTHOUSE $$
(☏09-432 0432; www.stonehousewaipu.co.nz; 641 Cove Rd; apt $80-160; 🛜) Nestled between the road to Waipu Cove and a saltwater lagoon, this Cornish style house built of stone slabs offers three brightly decorated, self-contained units. They range from the budget-orientated 'cutesy' (with a double sofa bed and six bunks), to more comfortable rooms which can be rented individually or as a three-room apartment.

🍴 Eating

Cafe Deli CAFE $
(29 The Centre; mains $10-22; ⊙9am-4pm) Enticing salads, pasta, muffins and organic, fairtrade coffee are served at this attractive little cafe on Waipu's main drag.

Pizza Barn ITALIAN $$
(2 Cove Rd; mains $19-30; ⊙11.30am-late Wed-Sun Apr-Nov, daily Dec-Mar) Popular platters, light fare and great pizzas ($12 to 26) go well with cold beer when this cool place morphs into a bar.

Two Fish Cafe CAFE $$
(www.twofishcafe.co.nz; 910 Cove Rd; mains $18-30; ⊙9am-8pm Thu-Sun Apr-Jun & Aug-Dec, 9am-late daily Jan-Mar, closed Jul) Grab a spot on the deck of this heritage cottage near Waipu Cove and devour excellent home baking, good pizzas and quite possibly Northland's best gourmet fish burger.

ℹ Information

Tourist brochures and internet access are available at the museum.

ℹ Getting There & Away

Waipu Cove can be reached by a particularly scenic route that heads from Mangawhai Heads through Langs Beach. Otherwise turn off SH1 38km south of Whangarei.

InterCity and Naked Bus both operate bus services.

Whangarei

POP 52,900

Northland's only city is surrounded by natural beauty, and its compact town centre offers plenty of rainy-day diversions. There's a thriving artistic community, some good walks, and interesting cafes and bars.

◎ Sights

◎ Town Basin

This attractive riverside marina is home to vintage car and clock museums, cafes, shops, public art and an information centre. It's a great place for a stroll, with a marked Art

---

MAORI NZ: NORTHLAND

Known to Maori as Te Tai Tokerau, this region has a long and proud Maori history and today has one of the country's highest percentages of Maori people. Along with East Cape, it's a place where you might hear Maori being spoken. In mythology the region is known as the tail of the fish of Maui.

Maori sites of particular significance include Cape Reinga, the Waitangi Treaty Grounds, Ruapekapeka Pa Historic Reserve and, in the Waipoua Forest, Tane Mahuta.

Maori cultural experiences are offered by many local operators, including Footprints Waipoua, Sandtrails Hokianga, Motuti Marae, Ahikaa Adventures, Sand Safaris, Terenga Paraoa, Native Nature Tours, Taiamai Tours, Rewa's Village and Culture North. Many businesses catering to travellers are owned or run by Maori individuals or *hapu* (subtribal) groups. **Tai Tokerau Tourism** (www.taitokerau.co.nz) lists many of them on its website.

Walk and Heritage Trail. An artisans market is held on Saturdays from October to April under the shade of the pedestrian bridge.

★**Whangarei Art Museum** GALLERY
(www.whangareiartmuseum.co.nz; The Hub, Town Basin; admission by donation; ⊙10am-4pm) Accessed through the Hub information centre (p131), Whangarei's public gallery has an interesting permanent collection, the star of which is a 1904 Maori portrait by Goldie. Also planned is a new **Hundertwasser Art Centre**, based on architectural plans by the late Austrian artist, Friedensreich Hundertwasser. See www.hundertwasser.co.nz for details of the campaign to raise support and funding of the project. A model of the proposed building is in the information centre.

★**Clapham's Clocks** MUSEUM
(www.claphamsclocks.com; Town Basin; adult/child $8/4; ⊙9am-5pm) This very interesting collection of 1400 ticking, gonging and cuckooing timepieces constitutes the National Clock Museum.

◉ City Centre

Old Library Arts Centre GALLERY
(www.oldlibrary.org.nz; 7 Rust Ave; ⊙10am-4pm Tue-Thu) FREE The work of local artists is exhibited in this wonderful art-deco building. Check the website for occasional concerts. Set between the old and new libraries is **Pou**, an intriguing sculpture consisting of 10 large poles carved with Maori, Polynesian, Celtic, Croatian and Korean motifs. Grab an interpretive pamphlet from the library.

Botanica & Cafler Park GARDENS
(First Ave & Water St; ⊙10am-4pm) FREE Native ferns, tropical plants and cacti are displayed in this little council-run fernery, set on the edge of cute Cafler Park. The park encloses the Waiarohia Stream and includes a rose garden and a scented garden.

◉ Surrounds

Abbey Caves CAVE
(Abbey Caves Rd) FREE Abbey Caves is an undeveloped network of three caverns full of glowworms and limestone formations, 6km east of town. Grab a torch, strong shoes, a mate for safety, and prepare to get wet. The surrounding reserve is a forest of crazily shaped rock extrusions. If you're staying at neighbouring Little Earth Lodge, you can borrow helmets and hire head torches.

Kiwi North MUSEUM, WILDLIFE
(www.kiwinorth.co.nz; 500 SH14, Maunu; adult/child $15/5; ⊙10am-4pm) Five kilometres west of Whangarei, this complex includes 19th-century buildings and a museum displaying Maori and colonial artefacts. A gecko and kiwi house offers a rare chance to see the country's feathery fave in a darkened nocturnal house.

Native Bird Recovery Centre WILDLIFE CENTRE
(www.nbr.org.nz; 500 SH14, Maunu; ⊙10am-4.30pm Tue-Thu, 1-4.30pm Mon & Fri) FREE This avian hospital nurses sick and injured birds back to health. Say hi to the talking tuis.

Whangarei Falls WATERFALL
(Otuihau; Ngunguru Rd) Short walks around these 26m-high falls provide views of the water cascading over the edge of an old basalt lava flow. The falls can be reached on the Tikipunga bus ($3, no service on Sundays), leaving from Rose St in the city.

AH Reed Memorial Kauri Park FOREST
(Whareora Rd) A grove of immense 500-year-old kauri trees has been preserved in this lush tract of native bush, where a cleverly designed boardwalk leads you effortlessly up into the canopy. To get here, head north on Bank St and turn right into Whareora Rd.

Quarry Gardens GARDENS
(www.whangareiquarrygardens.org.nz; Russell Rd; admission by donation; ⊙8am-5pm) Green-fingered volunteers have transformed this old quarry into a blissful park with a lake, waterfalls, pungent floral aromas, wild bits, orderly bits and lots of positive energy. To get here, take Rust Ave, turn right into Western Hills Dr and then left into Russell Rd.

Quarry Arts Centre ARTS CENTRE
(www.quarryarts.org; 21 Selwyn Ave; ⊙9.30am-4.30pm) FREE An eccentric village of artists' studios and co-operative galleries where you can often pick up well-priced art and craft.

Kingdom of Zion ZOO
(☑09-435 0110; www.kingdomofzion.co.nz; Gray Rd, Kamo; adult/child/family from $60/25/150; ⊙9am-5pm) An essential destination if you're a fan of big cats, with more than 30 lions, tigers, cheetahs and leopards. A variety of tours is available – most popular is the Feed Tour (adult/child $80/30) – and there are also behind-the-scenes opportunities to meet the cats. Kingdom of Zion is around

Whangarei

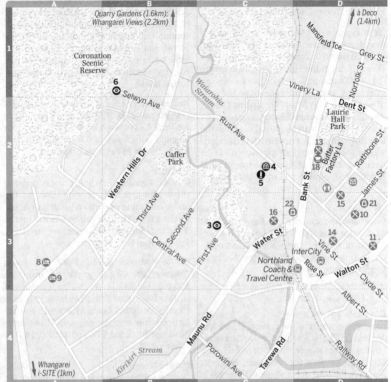

9km northwest of Whangarei. A return shuttle bus ($25) leaves from the Town Basin daily at 1.15pm.

🏃 Activities

The free *Whangarei Walks* brochure, available from the i-SITE (p131), has maps and detailed descriptions of some excellent local tracks. The **Hatea River Walk** follows the river from the Town Basin to the falls (three hours return). Longer tracks head through **Parihaka Reserve**, which is just east of the Hatea River and encompasses the remnants of a volcanic cone (241m) and a major *pa* (fortified village) site. The city is spread out for inspection from the lookout at the top, which is accessible by car. Other tracks head through **Coronation Scenic Reserve**, an expanse of bush immediately west of the centre that includes two *pa* sites and abandoned quarries.

Skydive Ballistic Blondes　　　SKYDIVING
(☎0800 695 867; www.skydiveballisticblondes. co.nz; 12,000ft tandem $320) Not only is this the oddest-named skydiving outfit in the country, it's also the only one licensed to land on the beach (Ocean Beach or Paihia).

Pacific Coast Kayaks　　　KAYAKING
(☎09-436 1947; www.nzseakayaking.co.nz; hire 4/8hr $60/80, tours $40-130) Hires kayaks and offers guided paddles to various Whangarei region locations.

👉 Tours

Pupurangi Hire & Tour　　　CULTURAL TOUR
(☎09-438 8117; www.hirentour.co.nz; Jetty 1, Riverside Dr; ⊙9.30am-5.30pm Oct-Apr, weekends only May-Sep) Various hour-long tours of Whangarei, all with a Maori flavour, including *waka* (canoe) trips on the river ($35). Also hires kayaks (per hour $17), *waka* ($25), aquacycles ($17) and bikes ($15).

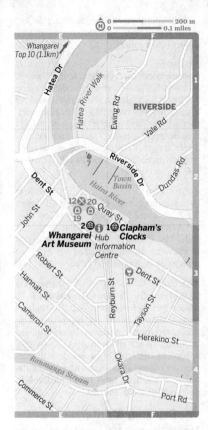

Whangarei

⊚ Top Sights
1 Clapham's Clocks F3
2 Whangarei Art Museum E3

⊚ Sights
3 Botanica & Cafler Park C3
4 Old Library Arts Centre C2
5 Pou C2
6 Quarry Arts Centre B1

⊕ Activities, Courses & Tours
7 Pupurangi Hire & Tour E2

⊟ Sleeping
8 BK's Pohutukawa Lodge A3
9 Lodge Bordeaux A3

⊗ Eating
10 Fresh D3
11 La Familia D3
12 Mokaba E2
13 Nectar D2
14 Nomad D3
15 Pimarn Thai D3
16 Whangarei Growers' Market C3

⊙ Drinking & Nightlife
17 Brauhaus Frings F3
18 The Old Stone Butter Factory D2

⊟ Shopping
19 Bach E2
20 Burning Issues E2
21 Kathmandu D3
22 Tuatara C3

Terenga Paraoa CULTURAL TOUR
(☑ 09-430 3083; departs Town Basin; adult/child morning $55/30, afternoon $32/20; ⊙ 9.30am & 1pm) Guided Maori cultural tours taking in Whangarei Harbour, Mt Manaia (131), the Kauri Park and, in the mornings, Parihaka *pa*.

🛏 Sleeping

Little Earth Lodge HOSTEL $
(☑ 09-430 6562; www.littleearthlodge.co.nz; 85 Abbey Caves Rd; dm/s/d/tr $31/68/72/93; @ ⛭) Set on a farm 6km from town and right next to Abbey Caves, Little Earth makes most other hostels look downright shabby. Forget dorm rooms crammed with nasty, spongy bunks: settle down in a proper cosy bed with nice linen and a maximum of two room-mates. Resident critters include miniature horses Tom and Jerry, and the lovable pooch Muttley.

Whangarei Falls Holiday Park & Backpackers HOSTEL $
(☑ 09-437 0609; www.whangareifalls.co.nz; 12 Ngunguru Rd, Glenbervie; dm $26-28, s $42-52, d & tw $56-66; ⛭⛭) Located 5km from Whangarei CBD but a short walk from Whangarei Falls, with good-value cabins and dorms, some with small kitchenettes. There's also room for tents and campervans.

Whangarei Top 10 HOLIDAY PARK $
(☑ 09-437 6856; www.whangareitop10.co.nz; 24 Mair St; sites from $21, units $75-130; @ ⛭) ⏻ This centrally located riverside holiday park has friendly owners, a better-than-average set of units, and supershiny stainless-steel surfaces. Mair St is off Hatea Dr, north of the city centre.

Whangarei Views B&B $$
(☑ 09-437 6238; www.whangareiviews.co.nz; 5 Kensington Heights Rise; s/d/apt $109/139/149; @ ⛭)

Modern and peaceful, with a self-contained two-bedroom flat downstairs and a B&B room in the main part of the house. To get here, follow the directions to Quarry Gardens (p127). Kensington Heights Rise is off Russell Rd, and yes, the views are excellent.

BK's Pohutukawa Lodge　　　MOTEL $$
(☑ 09-430 8634; www.pohutukawalodge.co.nz; 362 Western Hills Dr; units $125-150; @ 🛜) Just west of town, this nicely furnished motel has 14 units with well-kept facilities and ample parking.

Lodge Bordeaux　　　MOTEL $$$
(☑ 09-438 0404; www.lodgebordeaux.co.nz; 361 Western Hills Dr; apt $195-230; @ 🛜) Lodge Bordeaux has tasteful units with stellar kitchens and bathrooms (most with spa baths), private balconies and access to excellent wine. To get here, take Rust Ave and turn left into Western Hills Dr.

✕ Eating

Nectar　　　CAFE $
(www.nectarcafe.co.nz; 88 Bank St; mains $12-20; ⏱ 7am-3pm Mon-Fri, 8am-2pm Sat) 🍴 Nectar offers the winning combination of friendly staff, fairtrade coffee, and generous servings from a menu full of Northland produce. Check out the urban views from the back windows, and settle in for a lazy brunch of Israeli baked eggs with organic quinoa.

Fresh　　　CAFE $
(12 James St; mains $10-22; ⏱ 7.30am-4pm Sat-Wed, 7.30am-7pm Thu & Fri) Fresh as a daisy, and with supersized-flower photography on the walls, this chic cafe serves up great coffee and interesting breakfasts. It's open later for after-work drinks on Thursday and Friday.

La Familia　　　CAFE $
(www.lafamila.co.nz; 84 Cameron St; mains $10-15, pizzas $12-19; ⏱ 7am-4pm Tue-Sat, 9am-2.30pm Sun) Versatility rules at this cosy corner location. Good pastries, counter food and coffee segue to robust Italian-themed mains and pizzas for lunch. At the time of writing, the owners were also planning on opening for dinner on Friday and Saturday nights.

Whangarei Growers' Market　　　MARKET
(Water St; ⏱ 6.30-11am Sat) Stock up on local produce at this farmers market.

Mokaba　　　CAFE $$
(www.mokabacafe.co.nz; Town Basin; mains $9-21; ⏱ 8am-5pm) The best of the Town Basin's cafes has outdoor tables overlooking the forest of yacht masts, and indoor seating that segues into a gallery.

Nomad　　　MOROCCAN $$
(www.nomadcafe.co.nz; Quality St Mall, 71 Cameron St; mains $24-28; ⏱ 5pm-late Tue-Sat) 'Dining & Vibe' is the claim on the window, and it's a good description of this chic Moroccan-themed bar and eatery. Menu standouts include spicy prawns, kofta and tagines. There are other dining options in the same pedestrian mall including Israeli, Japanese and Italian cuisine.

Pimarn Thai　　　THAI $$
(www.pimarnthai.co.nz; 12 Rathbone St; mains $16-23; ⏱ 11am-2.30pm Mon-Sat, from 5pm daily; 🍴) As gaudy as every good Thai restaurant should be, Pimarn features all of Thailand's blockbuster dishes, including an excellent *yum talay* (spicy seafood salad).

★ à Deco　　　MODERN NZ $$$
(☑ 09-459 4957; 70 Kamo Rd; mains $37-42; ⏱ noon-3pm Fri, 6pm-late Tue-Sat) Northland's best restaurant offers an inventive menu that prominently features local produce, including plenty of seafood. Art-deco fans will adore the setting – a wonderfully curvaceous marine-style villa with original fixtures. To get here, head north on Bank St and veer left into Kamo Rd.

🍸 Drinking & Entertainment

The Old Stone Butter Factory　　　CAFE, BAR
(www.facebook.com/OldStoneButterFactory; 84 Bank St; ⏱ 10am-late Mon-Sun) Occupying a converted bank building, this tapas and cocktail bar hosts live musicians on Fridays. As the hours dissolve, DJs kick in. It's also a popular spot for touring Kiwi bands and musos, and has interesting beers and wine. The sunny courtyard is also a good spot for a coffee.

Brauhaus Frings　　　BREWERY
(www.frings.co.nz; 104 Dent St; ⏱ 10am-10pm) This popular microbrewery has good beers, a terrace, wood-fired pizzas, and live music on Wednesday (jam night) and every second Sunday from 4pm. It's usually closed by 10pm on weekdays, but can push on to 3am on weekends.

🛍 Shopping

See also Quarry Arts Centre (p127).

Tuatara ART & CRAFTS
(www.tuataradesignstore.co.nz; 29 Bank St; 9.30am-5pm Mon-Fri, 8am-2pm Sat) Maori and Pasifika design, art and craft.

Bach ART & CRAFTS
(www.thebach.org.nz; Town Basin; 9.30am-4.30pm) Co-op store representing over 100 Northland artisans.

Burning Issues ART & CRAFTS
(www.burningissuesgallery.co.nz; Town Basin; 10am-5pm) Glassware, ceramics and jewellery.

Kathmandu OUTDOOR EQUIPMENT
(www.kathmandu.co.nz; 22 James St; 9am-5.30pm Mon-Fri, 9am-4pm Sat, 10am-3pm Sun) Outdoor gear and travel clothing.

ⓘ Information

DOC Office (📞 09-470 3300; www.doc.govt.nz; 2 South End Ave, Raumanga; 8.30am-4pm Mon-Fri) Located on South End Ave; turn right off SH1 around 2km south of central Whangarei.

Hub Information Centre (📞 09-430 1188; Town Basin; 8.30am-5pm Mon-Fri, 9am-4pm Sat & Sun; 🖥) More central branch of the i-SITE, in the foyer of the Art Museum.

Whangarei i-SITE (📞 09-438 1079; www.whangareinz.com; 92 Otaika Rd/SH1; 8.30am-5pm Mon-Fri, 9am-4pm Sat & Sun; 🖥) Information, cafe, toilets and internet access.

ⓘ Getting There & Around

AIR

Whangarei Airport (WRE; 📞 09-436 0047; www.whangareiairport.co.nz; Handforth St) Whangarei Airport is at Onerahi, 6km southeast of the centre. Air New Zealand and Great Barrier Airlines flights both service Whangarei. Taxis into town cost around $30. A city bus stops 400m away on Church St ($3, 18 buses on weekdays, seven on Saturdays).

BUS

Bus services to Whangarei are run by InterCity, whose buses stop outside the **Northland Coach & Travel Centre** (📞 09-438 3206; 3 Bank St; 8am-5pm Mon-Fri, 8.30am-2.30pm Sat & Sun), and Naked Buses, whose buses stop at the Hub (p131), in the Town Basin. West Coaster shuttles also service Whangarei.

TAXI

A1 Cabs (📞 0800 438 3377)

Whangarei Heads

Whangarei Heads Rd winds 35km along the northern reaches of the harbour to the Heads' entrance, passing mangroves and picturesque pohutukawa-lined bays. Holiday homes, B&Bs and galleries are dotted around the water-hugging small settlements. There are great views from the top of Mt Manaia (419m), a sheer rock outcrop above McLeod Bay, but prepare for a lung- and leg-busting 1½-hour climb.

Bream Head caps off the craggy finger of land. A five-hour one-way walking track from Urquharts Bay to Ocean Beach passes through the Bream Head Scenic Reserve and lovely Smugglers Bay and Peach Cove.

Magnificent Ocean Beach stretches for miles on the other side of the headland. There's decent surfing to be had and lifeguards patrol the beach in summer. A detour from Parua Bay takes you to glorious Pataua, a small settlement that lies on a shallow inlet linked to a surf beach by a footbridge.

🛏 Sleeping & Eating

Kauri Villas B&B $$
(📞 09-436 1797; www.kaurivillas.com; 73 Owhiwa Rd, Parua Bay; d $130-175; 🖥🎿) Perched on a hill with views back over the harbour to Whangarei, this pretty blue-trimmed villa has an old-world feel, due in part to some very chintzy wallpaper. The decor's more restrained in the self-contained lodge and annex rooms.

Parua Bay Tavern PUB $$
(www.paruabaytavern.co.nz; 1034 Whangarei Heads Rd; meals $15-31; 11.30am-late) A magical spot on a summer's day, this friendly pub is set on a thumb-shaped peninsula, with a sole pohutukawa blazing red against the green water. Grab a seat on the deck, a cold beverage and a decent pub meal.

Tutukaka Coast & the Poor Knights Islands

If Goat Island Marine Reserve whetted your appetite, diving at the Poor Knights is the feast followed by a wafer-thin mint that might cause your stomach to explode. Apart from the natural underwater scenery, two decommissioned navy ships have been sunk nearby for divers to explore.

Following the road northeast of Whangarei for 26km, you'll first come to the sweet village of Ngunguru near the mouth of a broad river. Tutukaka is 1km further on, its marina bustling with yachts, dive crews and game-fishing boats.

From Tutukaka the road heads slightly inland, popping out 10km later at the golden sands of Matapouri. A blissful 20-minute coastal walk leads from here to Whale Bay, fringed with giant pohutukawa trees.

Continuing north from Matapouri, the wide expanse of Sandy Bay, one of Northland's premier surf beaches, comes into view. Long-boarding competitions are held here in summer. The road then loops back to join SH1 at Hikurangi. A branch leading off from this road doubles back north to the coast at Whananaki, where there are more glorious beaches and the Otamure Bay DOC campsite (☑ 09-433 8402; www.doc.govt. nz; sites per adult/child $10/5).

🏃 Activities

Dive trips leave from Tutukaka and cater for both first-timers and experts. There are some excellent walks along the coast. Pick up a copy of the *Tutukaka Coast Tracks & Walks* brochure from the Whangarei i-SITE (p131).

Dive! Tutukaka DIVING
(☑ 0800 288 882; www.diving.co.nz; Marina Rd; 2 dives incl gear $249) 🖉 Dive courses and excursions, including a five-day PADI openwater course ($799). For nondivers, the Perfect Day Ocean Cruise ($149) includes lunch and snacks, snorkelling in the marine reserve, kayaking through caves and arches,

paddle boarding, and sightings of dolphins (usually) and whales (occasionally). Cruises run from November to April, departing at 11am and returning at 4.15pm. In off months, snorkellers can tag along on the dive boats. Dive! Tutukaka has twice-daily shuttles from Whangarei for its customers ($20).

Yukon Dive DIVING
(☑ 09-434 4506; www.yukon.co.nz; 2 dives incl full gear $245) An owner-operator offering dive trips for a maximum of 12 people at a time.

Tutukaka Surf Experience SURFING
(☑ 09-434 4135; www.tutukakasurf.co.nz; Marina Rd; 2hr lesson $75) Runs surf lessons at 9.30am most days in summer and on the weekends otherwise, operating from whichever beach has the best beginner breaks that day. Also hires surfboards (per day $45) and stand-up paddle boards (per day $20).

🛏 Sleeping

Lupton Lodge B&B $$
(☑ 09-437 2989; www.luptonlodge.co.nz; 555 Ngunguru Rd; s $125-155, d $170-245; @ 🛜 🏊) The rooms are spacious, luxurious and full of character in this historic homestead (1896), peacefully positioned in farmland halfway between Whangarei and Ngunguru. Wander the orchard, splash around the pool or shoot some snooker in the guest lounge.

Pacific Rendezvous MOTEL $$
(☑ 09-434 3847; www.pacificrendezvous.co.nz; Motel Rd; apt $199-250) Perfectly situated for spectacular views on the south head of Tutukaka harbour, this is a great choice for families and small groups. Most of the units are 1960s duplexes with multiple bedrooms, but they're all individually owned and decorated.

MARINE RICHES AT THE POOR KNIGHTS

Established in 1981, the Poor Knights marine reserve is rated as one of the world's top-10 diving spots. The islands are bathed in a subtropical current from the Coral Sea, so varieties of tropical and subtropical fish not seen in other NZ waters can be observed here. The waters are clear, with no sediment or pollution problems. The 40m to 60m underwater cliffs drop steeply to the sandy bottom and are a labyrinth of archways, caves, tunnels and fissures that attract a wide variety of sponges and colourful underwater vegetation. Schooling fish, eels and rays are common (including manta rays in season).

The two main volcanic islands, Tawhiti Rahi and Aorangi, were home to the Ngai Wai tribe, but since a raiding-party massacre of 1825 the islands have been *tapu* (forbidden). Even today the public is barred from the islands, in order to protect their pristine environment. Not only do tuatara and Butler's shearwater breed here, but there are unique species of flora, such as the Poor Knights lily.

✖ Eating & Drinking

★ Havana Cabana   SOUTH AMERICAN $
(www.havanacabana.co.nz; 23 McAuslin Rd, Sandy
Bay; snacks & meals $5-16; ⊙11am-8pm daily Box-
ing Day to early Feb, Sat & Sun only early Feb-Easter)
Nestled away near the beach at Sandy Bay,
around 20 minutes' drive north of Tutukaka,
this colourful caravan turns out excellent
Cuban and South American food. Tuck into
empanadas, tacos, great roast pork Cuban
sandwiches, or Caribbean jerk pulled pork,
all washed down with Cuban coffee or frozen pina coladas.

Schnappa Rock   CAFE, BAR $$
(www.schnapparock.co.nz; cnr Marina Rd & Mar-
lin Pl; breakfast/lunch $10-27, dinner $26-35, bar
snacks $8-19; ⊙8am-late, closed Sun night Jun-
Oct) 🍴 Filled with expectant divers in the
morning and those capping off their Perfect
Days in the evening, this cafe-restaurant-bar
is often buzzing. Top NZ bands sometimes
play on summer weekends.

Marina Pizzeria   PIZZERIA $$
(www.marinapizzeria.co.nz; Tutukaka Marina;
pizzas $15-30; ⊙4pm-late Fri, 10am-late Sat &
Sun) Everything is homemade at this excellent takeaway and restaurant – the bread,
the pasta, the pizza and the ice cream.
Hearty breakfasts are served from 10am on
weekends.

Russell Road

The quickest route to Russell takes SH1 to
Opua and then crosses by ferry. The old Russell Rd is a snaking scenic route that adds
about half an hour to the trip.

The turn-off is easy to miss, located 6km
north of Hikurangi at Whakapara (look
for the sign to Oakura). Stop after 13km
at the Gallery & Cafe (www.galleryhelena-
bay.co.nz; 1392 Old Russell Rd, Helena Bay; mains
$14-18; ⊙10am-5pm) high above Helena Bay
for fairtrade coffee, scrummy cake, amazing views and interesting Kiwiana art and
craft.

At Helena Bay an unsealed detour leads
8km to Mimiwhangata Coastal Park,
which features sand dunes, pohutukawa
trees, jutting headlands and picturesque
beaches. DOC-managed accommodation
includes a simple but comfortable cottage,
and a beach house ($613 per week), both
of which sleep seven to eight people. Basic

camping (per adult/child $10/5) is available
at secluded Waikahoa Bay.

Back on Russell Rd, you'll find the Farm
(☑09-433 6894; www.thefarm.co.nz; 3632 Russell Rd; sites from $13, dm/s/d $20/30/80), a
rough-and-ready backpackers that rambles
through various buildings, including an
old woolshed fitted out with a mirror ball.
The rooms are basic, and the Farm is popular with trail bikers during the summer
holidays; off season it's a chilled-out rustic
escape. On offer are horse treks (1½ hours,
$50) or motorbike rides (one hour $60)
through the 1000-acre working farm.

At an intersection shortly after the Farm,
Russell Rd branches off to the left for an
unsealed, winding section traversing the
Ngaiotonga Scenic Reserve. Unless you're
planning to explore the forest (there are two
short walks: the 20-minute Kauri Grove
Nature Walk and the 10-minute Twin Bole
Kauri Walk), you're better off veering right
onto the sealed Rawhiti Rd.

After 2.6km, a side road leads to the
Whangaruru North Head Scenic Reserve, which has beaches, walking tracks
and fine scenery. A loop route from DOC's
Puriri Bay Campsite (☑09-433 6160; www.
doc.govt.nz; sites per adult/child $10/5) leads
up to a ridge, offering a remarkable coastal
panorama.

If you want to head directly to Russell,
continue along Rawhiti Rd for another 7km
before veering left onto Manawaora Rd,
which skirts a succession of tiny idyllic bays
before reconnecting with Russell Rd.

Otherwise take a detour to isolated
Rawhiti, a small Ngapuhi settlement where
life still revolves around the *marae* (meeting house). Rawhiti is the starting point
for the tramp to Cape Brett, a tiring eight-
hour, 16.3km walk to the top of the peninsula, where overnight stays are possible in
DOC's Cape Brett Hut (dm $15). The hut
must be booked in advance. An access fee
is charged for crossing private land (adult/
child $30/15), which you can pay at the
Paihia i-SITE (p145). Another option is to
take a water taxi to Cape Brett lighthouse
from Russell or Paihia and walk back.

A shorter one-hour walk leads through
Maori land and the Whangamumu Scenic
Reserve to Whangamumu Harbour. There
are more than 40 ancient Maori sites on the
peninsula and the remains of an unusual
whaling station.

BAY OF ISLANDS

The Bay of Islands ranks as one of NZ's top tourist drawcards, and the turquoise waters of the bay are punctuated by around 150 undeveloped islands. In particular, Paihia has excellent budget accommodation, and boat trips and water sports are very popular.

The Bay of Islands is also a place of enormous historical significance. Maori knew it as Pewhairangi and settled here early in their migrations. As the site of NZ's first permanent British settlement (at Russell), it is the birthplace of European colonisation in the country. It was in this region that the Treaty of Waitangi was drawn up and first signed in 1840; the treaty remains the linchpin of race relations in NZ today.

Activities

The Bay of Islands offers some fine subtropical diving, made even better by the sinking of the 113m navy frigate HMNZS *Canterbury* in Deep Water Cove near Cape Brett. Local operators also head to the wreck of the *Rainbow Warrior* off the Cavalli Islands, about an hour north of Paihia by boat. Both offer a colourful feast of pink anemones, yellow sponges and abundant fish life.

There are opportunities for kayaking or sailing around the bay, either on a guided tour or by renting and going it alone. Cruises and dolphin swimming are also available.

Dive North   DIVING
(☑09-402 5369; www.divenorth.co.nz; reef & wreck $225) Based in Kerikeri but offering free pick-ups from Paihia.

Paihia Dive   DIVING
(☑09-402 7551; www.divenz.com; Williams Rd, Paihia; reef & wreck $229) Combined reef and wreck trips to either the *Canterbury* or the *Rainbow Warrior*.

Dive Ops   DIVING
(☑0800 387 892, 09-402 5454; www.diveops. co.nz; 2 dives incl equipment $230-280) Family-run diving operators, based out of Paihia.

**Island Kayaks & Bay
Beach Hire**   KAYAKING, BOATING
(☑09-402 6078; www.baybeachhire.co.nz; Marsden Rd, Paihia; half-day kayaking tour $69; ◷ 9am-5.30pm) Hires kayaks (from $15 per hour), sailing catamarans ($50 first hour, $40 per additional), motor boats ($85 first hour, $25 per additional), mountain bikes ($35 per day), boogie boards ($25 per day), fishing rods ($10 per day), wet suits and snorkelling gear (both $20 per day).

Coastal Kayakers   KAYAKING
(☑0800 334 661; www.coastalkayakers.co.nz; Te Karuwha Pde, Paihia) Runs guided tours (half-/full day $85/115, minimum two people) and multiday adventures. Kayaks (per hour/half-/full day $15/40/50) can also be rented for independent exploration.

Flying Kiwi Parasail   PARASAILING
(☑0800 359 691; www.parasail-nz.co.nz; solo $99, tandem each $89, child $69) Departs from both Paihia and Russell wharves for NZ's highest parasail (1200ft).

**Tango Jet Ski &
Island Boat Tours**   BOAT TOUR, JET-SKIING
(☑0800 253 8752; www.tangojetskitours.co.nz; boat tours/jet-ski hire from $65/100) Zip around the bay in a speedy inflatable boat or skipper your own jet ski. Jet skis can take two people.

Great Escape Yacht Charters   SAILING
(☑09-402 7143; www.greatescape.co.nz) Offers introductory sailing lessons (two-day course $445) and longer options.

POU HERENGA TAI TWIN COAST CYCLE TRAIL

Planned to be completed by late 2014, this cycle route stretches from the Bay of Islands clear across the country to the Hokianga Harbour. OK, so that's only 84km, but as far as we're concerned that still gives you boasting rights when you get home. The complete route will travel from Opua via Kawakawa, Ngawha Springs, Kaikohe and finish up in Horeke.

At the time of research, around half of the total distance had been completed, and most popular was a 20km section from Kaikohe to Okaihau, starting west of Kaikohe and passing through an abandoned rail tunnel before skirting Lake Omapere. For maps, tips and updates on the progress of the trail, see www.nzcycletrail.com. Visit www.toptrail.co.nz for details of bike hire and shuttle transport, including from Paihia if you're staying in the Bay of Islands.

Bay of Islands

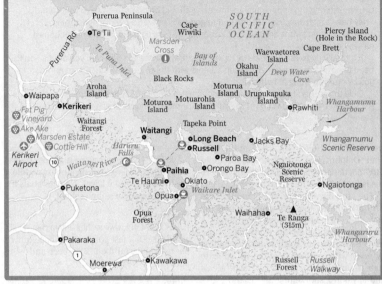

Northland Paddleboarding PADDLE BOARDING
(☑027 777 1035; www.northlandpaddleboarding.
co.nz; beginner lessons per hr $50) Lessons and
guided cruises.

Horse Trek'n HORSE RIDING
(☑027 233 3490; www.horsetrekn.co.nz; 2hr ride
$120) Through the Waitangi Forest.

☞ Tours

Where do you start? First by praying for
good weather, as torrential rain or choppy
seas could exclude some options. The Paihia
i-SITE (p145) and accommodation operators
can book tours.

Boat

Options include sailing boats, jetboats and
large launches. Boats leave from either
Paihia or Russell, calling into the other town
as their first stop.

One of the bay's most striking islands
is **Piercy Island (Motukokako)** off Cape
Brett, at the bay's eastern edge. This steep-
walled rock fortress features a vast natural
arch – the famous **Hole in the Rock**. Provided the conditions are right, most boat
tours will pass right through the heart of the
island. En route it's likely you'll encounter
bottlenose and common dolphins, and you
may see orcas, other whales and penguins.

The best way to explore the bay is under
sail. Either help crew the boat (no experience required), or just spend the afternoon
island-hopping, sunbathing, swimming,
snorkelling, kayaking and fishing.

Explore NZ CRUISE, SAILING
(☑09-402 8234; www.explorenz.co.nz; cnr
Marsden & Williams Rds, Paihia) ⏷ The four-
hour Swim with the Dolphins Cruise (adult/
child $89/45, additional $15 to swim) departs at 8am and 12.30pm. The four-hour
Discover the Bay Cruise (adult/child $99/49)
departs at 9am and 1.30pm, heading to the
Hole in the Rock and stopping at Urupukapuka Island. There are also combo options
available including a bus trip along Ninety
Mile Beach.

Another option (December to March
only) is a day sail on *Lion NZ* (adult/child
$110/70), the 80ft maxi yacht used by the
late Sir Peter Blake in racing around the
world and from Sydney to Hobart.

Fullers Great Sights CRUISES
(☑0800 653 339; www.dolphincruises.co.nz; Paihia
Wharf) ⏷ The four-hour Dolphin Cruise
(adult/child $95/50) departs at 9am
and 1.30pm, actively seeking out dolphins en
route to the Hole in the Rock, and stopping
at Urupukapuka Island on the way back. You

ℹ SWIMMING WITH DOLPHINS

Cruises offering the opportunity to interact with wild dolphins operate all year round. They have a high success rate and you're generally offered a free trip if dolphins aren't sighted. Dolphin swims are subject to weather and sea conditions, with restrictions if calves are present.

It's totally up to the dolphins as to whether they choose to swim with you or not. You'll need to be a strong swimmer to keep abreast with them – even when they're humouring you by cruising along at half-speed.

Only three operators are licensed for dolphin swimming: Explore NZ (p135), Fullers (p135) and the yacht Carino (p136). All pay a portion of the cost towards marine research, via DOC.

won't visit the Hole in the Rock on the four-hour Dolphin Eco Experience (adult/child $109/55, departs 8am and 12.30pm); the focus is finding dolphins to swim with.

The full-day Cream Trip (adult/child $119/60) follows the mail route around the bay and includes dolphin swimming. A glamorous option for an overnight cruise from September to April is on the launch *Ipipiri*, with accommodation in en-suite state rooms from $299 per person. Meals and kayaking, snorkelling and island walks are included.

R Tucker Thompson   SAILING
(☎ 09-402 8430; www.tucker.co.nz) Run by a charitable trust with an education focus, the *Tucker* is a majestic tall ship offering day sails (adult/child $145/73, including a barbecue lunch) and late-afternoon cruises (adult/child $59/30).

Rock   CRUISE
(☎ 0800 762 527; www.rocktheboat.co.nz; dm/s/d from $158/346/376) A former vehicle ferry that's now a floating hostel, the *Rock* has dorms, private rooms and a bar. The cruise departs at 5pm and includes a barbecue and seafood dinner with live music, then time spent island-hopping, fishing, kayaking, snorkelling and swimming the following day. Day cruises only are $98 per person.

Carino   SAILING, DOLPHIN SWIMMING
(☎ 09-402 8040; www.sailingdolphins.co.nz; adult/child $114/69) This 50ft catamaran is the only yacht licensed for swimming with dolphins. A barbecue lunch is available for $6.

Ecocruz   SAILING
(☎ 0800 432 627; www.ecocruz.co.nz; dm/d $650/1500) Three-day/two-night sailing cruise aboard the 72ft ocean-going yacht *Manawanui*. Prices include accommodation, food, fishing, kayaking and snorkelling.

She's a Lady   SAILING
(☎ 0800 724 584; www.bay-of-islands.com; day sail $97) On day sails go snorkelling or paddle a see-through-bottom kayak. Charter boats for longer trips and a sailing school.

Phantom   SAILING
(☎ 0800 224 421; www.yachtphantom.com; adult/child $110/60) A fast 50ft racing sloop, known for its wonderful food. BYO beer and wine allowed.

Gungha II   SAILING
(☎ 0800 478 900; www.bayofislandssailing.co.nz; day sail $95) A 65ft ocean yacht with a friendly crew; lunch included.

Mack Attack   JETBOATING
(☎ 0800 622 528; www.mackattack.co.nz; 9 Williams Rd, Paihia; adult/child $95/40) An exhilarating, high-speed 1½-hour jetboat trip to the Hole in the Rock.

Bus

It's cheaper and quicker to take trips to Cape Reinga from Ahipara, Kaitaia or Doubtless Bay, but if you're short on time, several long day trips (10 to 12 hours) leave from the Bay of Islands. They all drive one way along Ninety Mile Beach, stopping for sandboarding on the dunes.

Fullers (p135) runs regular bus tours and backpacker-oriented versions, both stopping at Puketi Forest. The standard, child-friendly version (adult/child $135/68) includes an optional lunch at Pukenui. It also runs **Awesome NZ** (☎ 0800 653 339; www.awesomenz.com; tours $119) tours, with louder music, more time sandboarding, and stops to chuck a frisbee around at Tapotupotu Bay and devour fish and chips at Mangonui.

Dune Rider by Explore NZ (p135; adult/child $149/110) also samples Mangonui's feted fish and chips and includes a stop at Gumdiggers Park.

Transport options to the Hokianga and Waipoua Forest are limited, so a day trip makes sense if you don't have your own car or if you're time starved. Discover Hokianga by Fullers (p135; adult/child $112/65) takes in Tane Mahuta and Wairere Boulders in an eight-hour tour with local Maori guides.

Cultural

Native Nature Tours　　CULTURAL TOUR, TRAMPING
(☑ 0800 668 873; www.nativenaturetours.co.nz; 581 Tipene Rd, Motatau; day treks $145-235, overnight $375) A local Maori couple formally welcome you to their *marae* and lead treks on their ancestral lands, including visits to sacred sites and an introduction to Maori food and medicine. Other options include tree planting, and overnight stays include a traditional *hangi* (earth-cooked meal) and glowworm-spotting.

Taiamai Tours
Heritage Journeys　　CULTURAL TOURS, CANOEING
(☑ 09-405 9990; www.taiamaitours.co.nz; 2½hr tour $135; ⊙ 10am & 1pm Oct-Apr) 🍃 Paddle a traditional 50ft carved *waka* (canoe) from the Waitangi bridge to the Haruru Falls. The Ngapuhi hosts wear traditional garb, and perform the proper *karakia* (incantations) and share stories.

Other Tours

Salt Air　　SCENIC FLIGHTS
(☑ 09-402 8338; www.saltair.co.nz; Marsden Rd, Paihia) Scenic flights include a five-hour light-aircraft and 4WD tour to Cape Reinga and Ninety Mile Beach ($425), and helicopter flights out to the Hole in the Rock ($230).

A new tour even lands on the famed island (from $379).

Total Tours　　FOOD & WINE
(☑ 0800 264 868; www.totaltours.co.nz) Explore around Kerikeri on a half-day Food, Wine and Craft tour ($65) or half-day wine tour ($75).

🎉 Festivals & Events

Tall Ship Race　　SPORTS
Held in Russell on the first Saturday after New Year's Day.

Waitangi Day　　CULTURE
Various ceremonial events at Waitangi on 6 February.

Country Rock Festival　　MUSIC
(www.country-rock.co.nz; festival pass $50) Second weekend in May.

Russell Birdman　　LUNACY
(www.russellbirdman.co.nz) Lunatics with various flying contraptions jump off wharf in frigid (July) waters.

Jazz & Blues Festival　　MUSIC
(www.jazz-blues.co.nz; festival pass $50) Second weekend in August.

Weekend Coastal Classic　　SPORTS
(www.coastalclassic.co.nz) NZ's largest yacht race, from Auckland to the Bay of Islands, held on Labour Weekend in October.

**Bay of Islands Food
& Wine Festival**　　FOOD, WINE
(www.paihianz.co.nz/it_festival; adult/child $45/15; ⊙ 11am-6pm) Food, wine and local music in Paihia on the last Saturday of October.

> **WORTH A TRIP**
>
> ### HOLD ON UNTIL KAWAKAWA
>
> Kawakawa is just an ordinary Kiwi town, located on SH1 south of Paihia, but the public toilets (60 Gillies St) are anything but. They were designed by Austrian-born artist and eco-architect Friedensreich Hundertwasser, who lived near Kawakawa in an isolated house without electricity from 1973 until his death in 2000. The most photographed toilets in NZ are typical Hundertwasser – lots of organic wavy lines decorated with ceramic mosaics and brightly coloured bottles, and with grass and plants on the roof. Other examples of his work can be seen in Vienna and Osaka.
>
> Kawakawa also has a railway line running down the main street. Take a 45-minute spin pulled by **Gabriel the Steam Engine** (☑ 021 171 2697; www.bayofislandsvintagerailway.org.nz; adult/child $20/5; ⊙ 10.45am, noon, 1.15pm, 2.30pm Fri-Sun, daily school holidays).
>
> South of town, a signpost from SH1 points to **Kawiti Glowworm Caves** (☑ 09-404 0583; www.kawiticaves.co.nz/; 49 Waiomio Rd; adult/child $15/7.50; ⊙ 8.30am-4.30pm). Explore the insect-illuminated caverns with a 30-minute subterranean tour. Guided tours only.
>
> Minibus tours from Paihia to Kawakawa and the caves are offered by Russell Mini Tours (p139).

Russell

POP 720

Although it was once known as 'the hellhole of the Pacific', those coming to Russell for debauchery will be sadly disappointed: they've missed the orgies on the beach by 170 years. Instead they'll find a historic town with gift shops and B&Bs, and, in summer, you can rent kayaks and dinghies along the Strand.

Before it was known as a hellhole, or even as Russell, it was Kororareka (Sweet Penguin), a fortified Ngapuhi village. In the early 19th century the tribe permitted it to become Aotearoa's first European settlement. It quickly became a magnet for rough elements such as fleeing convicts, whalers and drunken sailors. By the 1830s dozens of whaling ships at a time were anchored in the harbour. Charles Darwin described it in 1835 as full of 'the refuse of society'.

In 1830 the settlement was the scene of the so-called Girls' War, when two pairs of Maori women were vying for the attention of a whaling captain called Brind. A chance meeting between the rivals on the beach led to verbal abuse and fighting. This minor conflict quickly escalated as family members rallied around to avenge the insult and harm done to their respective relatives. Hundreds were killed and injured over a two-week period before missionaries managed to broker a peace agreement.

After the signing of the Treaty of Waitangi in 1840, Okiato (where the car ferry now leaves from) was the residence of the governor and the temporary capital. The capital was officially moved to Auckland in 1841 and Okiato, which was by then known as Russell, was eventually abandoned. The name Russell ultimately replaced Kororareka.

◉ Sights

Pompallier Mission HISTORIC BUILDING
(www.pompallier.co.nz; The Strand; tours adult/child $10/free; ⊙10am-4pm) Built in 1842 to house the Catholic mission's printing press, this rammed-earth building is the mission's last remaining building in the western Pacific. A staggering 40,000 books were printed here in Maori. In the 1870s it was converted into a private home, but it is now restored to its original state, complete with tannery and printing workshop.

Christ Church CHURCH
(Church St) English naturalist Charles Darwin made a donation towards the cost of

Russell

◉ Sights
1 Christ Church A2
2 Haratu A2
3 Pompallier Mission A3
4 Russell Museum A2

◉ Activities, Courses & Tours
5 Russell Mini Tours A2

◉ Sleeping
6 Arcadia Lodge B3
7 Commodore's Lodge A2
8 Duke of Marlborough A2
9 Hananui Lodge & Apartments A2
10 Pukeko Cottage B3
11 Russell Motel B3
12 Russell Top 10 .... B1

◉ Eating
Duke of Marlborough .... (see 8)
13 Gables A2
14 Hone's A2
15 Newport Chocolates A2
The Wharf .... (see 5)
16 Tuk Tuk A2

◉ Drinking & Nightlife
17 Pub 'round the Corner A2

◉ Shopping
18 Just Imagine A1

Russell

HONE HEKE & THE NORTHLAND WAR

Just five years after he had been the first signatory to the Treaty of Waitangi, Ngapuhi chief Hone Heke was so disaffected that he planned to chop down Kororareka's flagstaff, a symbol of British authority, for the fourth time. Governor FitzRoy was determined not to let that happen and garrisoned the town with soldiers and marines.

On 11 March 1845 the Ngapuhi staged a diversionary siege of the town. It was a great tactical success, with Chief Kawiti attacking from the south and another party attacking from Long Beach. While the troops rushed off to protect the township, Hone Heke felled the Union Jack on Maiki (Flagstaff Hill) for the fourth and final time. The British were forced to evacuate to ships lying at anchor. The captain of the HMS *Hazard* was wounded severely in the battle and his replacement ordered the ships' cannons to be fired on the town; most of the buildings were razed. The first of the New Zealand Wars had begun.

In the months that followed, British troops (united with Hokianga-based Ngapuhi) fought Heke and Kawiti in several battles. During this time the modern *pa* (fortified village) was born, effectively the world's first sophisticated system of trench warfare. It's worth stopping at **Ruapekapeka Pa Historic Reserve** (Ruapekapeka Rd), off SH1 south of Kawakawa, to see how impressive these fortifications were. Here you can wander the site of the last battle of the Northland War, brought to life through detailed information boards. Eventually Heke, Kawiti and George Grey (the new governor) made their peace, with no side the clear winner.

building the country's oldest church (1836). The graveyard's biggest memorial commemorates Tamati Waka Nene, a powerful Ngapuhi chief from the Hokianga who sided against Hone Heke in the Northland War. The church's exterior has musket and cannonball holes dating from the 1845 battle.

Maiki   HILL
(Flagstaff Rd) Overlooking Russell, this is the hill where Hone Heke chopped down the flagpole four times. You can drive up but the view justifies a climb. Take the track west from the boat ramp along the beach at low tide, or head up Wellington St.

Tapeka Point   LOOKOUT, BEACH
North of Russell, on the other side of Maiki hill, Tapeka Rd heads down to a sandy beach in the shadow of a craggy headland. A *pa* once stood at the top of the hill. Follow the pathway for views stretching to the far northern reaches of the Bay of Islands.

Long Beach   BEACH
(Long Beach Rd) About 1.5km behind Russell (an easy walk or cycle) is this placid, child-friendly beach. Turn left (facing the sea) to visit Donkey Bay, a small cove that is an unofficial nudist beach.

Russell Museum   MUSEUM
(www.russellmuseum.org.nz; 2 York St; adult/child $7.50/2; ☺10am-4pm) This small, modern museum has a well-presented Maori section, a large 1:5-scale model of Captain Cook's *Endeavour*, and a 10-minute video on the town's history.

Haratu   CULTURAL BUILDING
(www.kororarekanz.com; cnr The Strand & Pitt St; ☺gallery 11am-3pm, walking tours 11am & 2pm) Run by the local *marae* society, Haratu has Maori art and craft, mostly available for purchase. There are also audiovisual displays and information boards. One-hour guided walks featuring Maori stories are available in summer and by arrangement other times. It's volunteer-run, so opening times can vary.

☞ Tours

Russell Mini Tours   MINIBUS
(☎0800 646 486; www.russellminitours.com; cnr The Strand & Cass St; adult/child $29/15; ☺tours 10am, 11am, 1pm, 2pm, 3pm & 4pm) Minibus tour around historic Russell with commentary. Tours departing Paihia (adult/child $40/20) visiting Kawakawa and the Kawiti Glowworm Caves are also available.

🛏 Sleeping

Russell has a few decent midrange options. There are several small budget lodges, but you'll need to book ahead at busy times. If budget is not a consideration, Russell does luxury B&Bs very well.

Wainui
HOSTEL $

(☑09-403 8278; www.pelnet.org/wainui; 92d Te Wahapu Rd; dm/r $28/66; 🛜) Hard to find but worth the effort, this modern bush retreat with direct beach access has only two rooms that share a pleasant communal space. It's 5km from Russell on the way to the car ferry. Take Te Wahapu Rd and then turn right into Waiaruhe Way.

Ferry Landing Backpackers
HOSTEL $

(☑09-403 7985; www.ferrylandingrussell.co.nz; 395 Aucks Rd, Okiato Pt; dm/s/d $30/50/60; @🛜) More like a homestay than a hostel, with only two rooms on offer within the owners' house. It sits on the hill directly above the ferry landing in Okiato – you'll need a car to get here.

Russell-Orongo Bay Holiday Park
HOLIDAY PARK $

(☑09-403 7704; www.russellaccommodation.co.nz; 5960 Russell Rd; unpowered/powered site $40/44, teepee $80-90, cabins & units $80-165; @🛜⛲) ✿ Surrounded by 14 acres studded with native forest and birdlife, this relaxed holiday park is around 3km from Russell after departing the ferry from Opua to Okiato. The wide range of accommodation includes a quirky teepee and comfortable self-contained units.

Russell Top 10
HOLIDAY PARK $

(☑09-403 7826; www.russelltop10.co.nz; 1 James St; sites/cabins/units from $41/80/140; @🛜) ✿ This leafy park has a small store, good facilities, wonderful hydrangeas, tidy cabins and nice units. Showers are clean, but metered.

Pukeko Cottage
HOSTEL $

(☑09-403 8498; www.pukekocottagebackpackers.co.nz; 14 Brind Rd; per person $30; 🛜) More like staying at a mate's place than a hostel, this homely house has just two bedrooms for rent and a caravan in the back garden. It's certainly not dirty, but the cleanliness is bloke-standard. Barry, the artist owner, is always up for a chat.

Lesley's B&B Homestay
B&B $$

(☑09-403 7099; www.lesleys.co.nz; 1 Pomare Rd; s $110-150, d $140-180; 🛜) Rooms are bright and colourful at this welcoming B&B owned by a well-travelled local artist. Breakfasts are legendary – the owner Lesley is also a trained chef – and the guests can fire up the barbecue. Gardens and palms surround the property, and the attractions and cafes of Russell are a 10-minute walk away.

Russell Motel
MOTEL $$

(☑09-403 7854; www.motelrussell.co.nz; 16 Matauwhi Rd; units $130-165; 🛜⛲) Sitting amid well-tended gardens, this old-fashioned motel offers a good range of units and a kidney-shaped pool that the kids will love. The studios are a little dark but you really can't quibble for this price in central Russell.

Duke of Marlborough
HISTORIC HOTEL $$

(☑09-403 7829; www.theduke.co.nz; 35 The Strand; r $165-360; 🛜) Holding NZ's oldest pub licence, the Duke boasts about 'serving rascals and reprobates since 1827', although the building has burnt down twice since then. The upstairs accommodation ranges from small, bright rooms in a 1930s extension to snazzy, spacious doubles facing the water.

Arcadia Lodge
B&B $$$

(☑09-403 7756; www.arcadialodge.co.nz; 10 Florance Ave; d $200-270; 🛜) ✿ The characterful rooms of this 1890 hillside house are decked out with interesting antiques and fine linen, while the breakfast is probably the best you'll eat in town – organic, delicious and complemented with spectacular views from the deck.

Commodore's Lodge
MOTEL $$$

(☑09-403 7899; www.commodoreslodgemotel.co.nz; 28 The Strand; units $200-310; 🛜⛲) Being the envy of every passer-by makes up for the lack of privacy in the front apartments that face the waterfront promenade. Spacious, nicely presented units are the order of the day here, along with a small pool and free kayaks, dinghies and bikes.

Orongo Bay Homestead
LODGE $$$

(☑09-403 7527; www.thehomestead.co.nz; Aucks Rd; r $585; 🛜) ✿ This wooden homestead (c 1860) was NZ's first American consulate, located a discreet 4km from Russell's rabble. Accommodation is by way of three stylishly plush rooms in the converted barn facing a chocolate-box lake. Breakfast is memorable and dinners are by arrangement.

Hananui Lodge & Apartments
MOTEL $$$

(☑09-403 7875; www.hananui.co.nz; 4 York St; units $185-320; 🛜) Choose between sparkling motel-style units in the trim waterside lodge or apartments in the newer block across the road. Pick of the bunch are the upstairs waterfront units with views straight over the beach.

✕ Eating & Drinking

For a country so hooked on cafe culture and a town so touristy, it's disappointing that Russell doesn't have more on offer.

Newport Chocolates CAFE, SWEETS $
(www.newportchocolates.co.nz; 3 Cass St; chocolates around $3; ⊙10am-5pm) Delicious artisan chocolates – handmade on site – with flavours including raspberry, lime and chilli, and, our favourite, caramel and sea salt. Also a top spot for rich hot chocolate and refreshing frappes.

Gables MODERN NZ $$
(☑09-403 7670; www.thegablesrestaurant.co.nz; 19 The Strand; lunch $19-25, dinner $25-32; ⊙noon-3pm Fri-Mon, from 6pm Thu-Mon) Serving an imaginative take on Kiwi classics (lamb, beef and lots of seafood), the Gables occupies an 1847 building on the waterfront, built using whale vertebrae for foundations. Ask for a table by the windows for watery views and look forward to local produce including oysters, cheese and Kerikeri citrus fruits.

Duke of Marlborough PUB $$
(www.theduke.co.nz; 35 The Strand; lunch $12-32, dinner $24-37; ⊙11am-late) There's no better spot in Russell to while away a few hours, glass in hand, than the Duke's sunny deck. Thankfully the upmarket pub grub matches the views, plus there's an excellent wine list and a great selection of NZ craft beers.

Tuk Tuk THAI $$
(www.tuktukrestaurant.co.nz; 19 York St; mains $18-24; ⊙10.30am-11pm; 🖋) Thai fabrics adorn the tables and Thai favourites fill the menu. In clement weather grab a table out front and watch Russell's little world go by.

The Wharf CAFE $$
(www.thewharfrussell.co.nz; 29 The Strand; breakfast $12-18, dinner $25-35; ⊙11am-3pm & 5pm-late Wed-Sun) Cosy, nautical-themed nook with a focus on well-prepared seafood, meaty stonegrill dishes and lighter tapas-style plates. Good-value breakfasts will set you up for the day's exploring.

Hone's PIZZERIA, BAR $$
(York St; pizza $19-27; ⊙noon-late summer only) Head out to the pebbled courtyard behind the Gables restaurant for wood-fired pizza, cold beer and a good vibe.

Pub 'round the Corner PUB
(19 York St; ⊙noon-late) A cool, cosy tavern with pool tables and a local's vibe.

🔒 Shopping

Just Imagine... ARTS & CRAFTS
(www.justimagine.co.nz; 25 York St; ⊙10am-5pm) Glassware, paintings and gifts.

❶ Information

Russell Booking & Information Centre (☑09-403 8020; www.russellinfo.co.nz; Russell Pier; ⊙8am-5pm, later in summer)

❶ Getting There & Away

The quickest way to reach Russell by car is via the car ferry (car/motorcycle/passenger $11/5.50/1), which runs every 10 minutes from Opua (5km from Paihia) to Okiato (8km from Russell), between 6.40am and 10pm. Buy your tickets on board. If you're travelling from the south, a scenic alternative is Russell Rd.

On foot, the easiest way to reach Russell is on a passenger ferry from Paihia (adult/child one way $7/3, return $12/6). They run from 7am to 7pm (until 10pm October to May), generally every 20 minutes but hourly in the evenings. Buy your tickets on board or at the i-SITE (p145) in Paihia.

Paihia & Waitangi

POP 1800

The birthplace of NZ (as opposed to Aotearoa), Waitangi inhabits a special, somewhat complex place in the national psyche – aptly demonstrated by the mixture of celebration, commemoration, protest and apathy that accompanies the nation's birthday (Waitangi Day, 6 February).

It was here that the long-neglected and much-contested Treaty of Waitangi was first signed between Maori chiefs and the British Crown, establishing British sovereignty or something a bit like it, depending on whether you're reading the English or Maori version of the document. If you're interested in coming to grips with NZ's history and race relations, this is the place to start.

Joined to Waitangi by a bridge, Paihia would be a fairly nondescript coastal town if it wasn't the main entry point to the Bay of Islands. If you're not on a tight budget, catch a ferry to Russell, which is far nicer.

Paihia

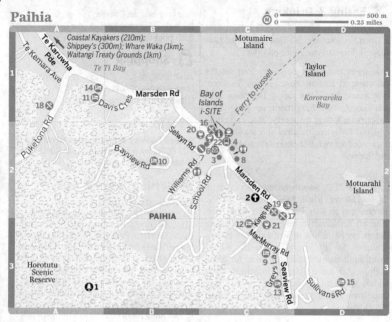

Paihia

⊙ Sights
1 Opua Forest	A3
2 St Paul's Church	C2

⊕ Activities, Courses & Tours
3 Explore NZ	C2
4 Fullers Great Sights	C2
5 Island Kayaks & Bay Beach Hire	C2
6 Mack Attack	C2
7 Paihia Dive	C2
8 Salt Air	C2

⊜ Sleeping
9 Admiral's View Lodge	C3
10 Allegra House	B2
11 Cap'n Bob's Beachhouse	A1
12 Peppertree Lodge	C3
13 Pickled Parrot	C3
14 Seabeds	A1
15 Tarlton's Lodge	D3

⊗ Eating
16 35 Degrees South	C2
17 Alfresco's	C2
18 Countdown	A1
19 El Cafe	C2
Paihia Farmers Market	(see 3)

⊚ Drinking & Nightlife
20 Bay of Islands Swordfish Club	C2
21 Pipi Patch Bar	C3
22 Sauce	C2

There are some good walks in the area, including an easy 5km track that follows the coast from Opua to Paihia.

⊙ Sights & Activities

★ **Waitangi Treaty Grounds**　HISTORIC SITE
(☏09-402 7437; www.waitangi.net.nz; 1 Tau Henare Dr; adult/child \$25/free; ⊙9am-5pm Mar-Dec, to 7pm Jan-Feb) 🌿 Occupying a headland draped in lawns and bush, this is NZ's most significant historic site. Here, on 6 February 1840, the first 43 Maori chiefs, after much discussion, signed the Treaty of Waitangi with the British Crown; eventually, over 500 chiefs would sign it.

The Treaty House was built in 1832 as the four-room home of British resident James Busby. It's now preserved as a memorial and museum containing displays, including a copy of the treaty. Just across the lawn, the magnificently detailed *whare runanga* (meeting house) was completed in 1940 to mark the centenary of the treaty. The fine carvings represent the major Maori tribes.

Near the cove is the 35m *waka taua* (war canoe), also built for the centenary. A photographic exhibit details how it was fashioned from gigantic kauri logs.

The importance of the treaty is well understood by a NZ audience, but visitors might find it surprising that there's not more information displayed here about the role it has played in the nation's history: the long litany of breaches by the Crown, the wars and land confiscations that followed, and the protest movement that led to the current process of redress for historic injustices.

International visitors will get more out of what is already quite a pricey admission fee if they pay extra for a guided tour ($10) or cultural performance ($15). The 30-minute performance (11am and 1pm) demonstrates traditional Maori song and dance, including the *haka* (war dance). The Ultimate Combo (adult/child $40/free) is a combined ticket including tour and performance. Other options include a Maori Cultural Workshop (adult/child $60/35), and a *hangi* and concert (adult/child $105/50, Wednesday and Saturday December to March) at the Treaty Ground's Whare Waka (p144) cafe.

Entry is free to NZ citizens upon presentation of a passport or drivers licence.

Haruru Falls WATERFALL

(Haruru Falls Rd) A walking track (1½ hours one way, 5km) leads from the Treaty Grounds along the Waitangi River to these attractive horseshoe falls. Part of the path follows a boardwalk through the mangroves. Otherwise you can drive here, turning right off Puketona Rd onto Haruru Falls Rd.

St Paul's Church CHURCH

(Marsden Rd) The characterful St Paul's was constructed of Kawakawa stone in 1925, and stands on the site of NZ's first church, a simple *raupo* (bulrush) hut erected in 1823. Look for the native birds in the stained glass above the altar – the kotare (kingfisher) represents Jesus (the king plus 'fisher of men'), while the tui (parson bird) and kereru (wood pigeon) portray the personalities of the Williams brothers (one scholarly, one forceful), who set up the mission station here.

Opua Forest FOREST

Just behind Paihia, this regenerating forest has walking trails ranging from 10 minutes to five hours. A few large trees have escaped axe and fire, including some big kauri. Walk up from School Rd for about 30 minutes to good lookouts. Information on Opua Forest walks

is available from the i-SITE. Drive into the forest by taking Oromahoe Rd west from Opua.

🛏 Sleeping

If your budget is more flexible, Russell has more atmosphere, but Paihia is more convenient and has motels, apartments and B&Bs on the waterfront and around the surrounding hills. Paihia has an excellent range of hostels, and Kings Rd is the main 'backpackers' row'.

Seabeds HOSTEL $

(📱09-402 5567; www.seabeds.co.nz; 46 Davis Cres; dm/s/d/apt $28/68/85/95; @ 🛜) Offering comfortable, friendly, stylish budget digs in a converted motel, Seabeds is one of Paihia's best hostels. Little design touches give it a stylish ambience, and it's in a quieter location than most of Paihia's more social hostels along Kings Rd.

Peppertree Lodge HOSTEL $

(📱09-402 6122; www.peppertree.co.nz; 15 Kings Rd; dm $25-28, r $72-110; @ 🛜) Simple, clean rooms with high ceilings and good linen, plus bikes, racquets, kayaks and two barbecues for guests' use, making this a sociable choice.

Pickled Parrot HOSTEL $

(📱09-402 6222; www.pickledparrot.co.nz; Greys Lane; sites per person $19, dm $26, r $66-84; @ 🛜) Surrounded by tropical plants, this friendly, well-maintained backpackers' stalwart has cute cabins, free bikes and a good vibe.

Cap'n Bob's Beachhouse HOSTEL $

(📱09-402 8668; www.capnbobs.co.nz; 44 Davis Cres; dm/s/tw/d $25/49/64/86; @🛜) This small backpackers is a homely place, with sea views from the verandah, and more than a touch of easygoing charm.

Beachside Holiday Park HOLIDAY PARK $

(📱09-402 7678; www.beachsideholiday.co.nz; 1290 SH11; sites/units from $18/65; @ 🛜) 🏄 Wake up at the water's edge at this sheltered camping ground, south of the township. The angular lemon cabins have 1970s charm, and there are kayaks for hire.

Bay of Islands Holiday Park HOLIDAY PARK $

(📱09-402 7646; www.bayofislandsholidaypark. co.nz; 678 Puketona Rd; site/unit from $38/70; @ 🛜 ✳) Under tall trees by a set of shallow rapids on the Waitangi River, 7km down Puketona Rd, this wonderful holiday park has excellent units and shady campsites.

Tarlton's Lodge
B&B $$

(✆09-402 6711; www.tarltonslodge.co.nz; 11 Sullivans Rd; r $175-220; ⟨icons⟩) Striking architecture combines with modern decor in this hilltop B&B with expansive bay views. All three suites have their own outdoor spa, perfect for a romantic stay. Look forward to excellent breakfasts.

Baystay B&B
B&B $$

(✆09-402 7511; www.baystay.co.nz; 93a Yorke Rd, Haruru Falls; r $140-175; ⟨icons⟩) Enjoy valley views from the spa pool of this slick, gay-friendly establishment. Yorke Rd is off Puketona Rd, just before the falls. Minimum stay of two nights; no children under 12.

Cook's Lookout
MOTEL $$

(✆09-402 7409; www.cookslookout.co.nz; Causeway Rd; r $145-175, apt $255; ⟨icons⟩) Cook's Lookout is an old-fashioned motel with friendly owners, breathtaking views and a solar-heated swimming pool. Take Puketona Rd towards Haruru Falls, turn right into Yorke Rd and then take the second right.

Admiral's View Lodge
MOTEL $$

(✆09-402 6236; www.admiralsviewlodge.co.nz; 2 MacMurray Rd; apt $120-195; ⟨icon⟩) This hillside lodge offers natty units with balconies just begging for a relaxed sunset gin and tonic. Some have spa baths and bay views.

Allegra House
B&B $$$

(✆09-402 7932; www.allegra.co.nz; 39 Bayview Rd; r $220-245, apt $275; ⟨icons⟩) Offering quite astonishing views of the bay from an eyrie high above the township, Allegra has three handsome B&B rooms and a spacious self-contained apartment.

✗ Eating

El Cafe
CAFE, SOUTH AMERICAN $

(2 Kings Rd; snacks $5-10; ⊙8am-5pm) Excellent Chilean-owned cafe with the best coffee in town and good breakfast burritos, tacos, empanadas and Latin American sweet treats. The smoothies are also great on on a warm Bay of Islands day. Say *hola* to owner Javier for us.

Shippey's
FISH & CHIPS $

(www.shippeys.com; Waitangi Bridge; mains $7-16; ⊙11am-late) Tuck into fresh fish and chips served as the good Lord intended them – in newspaper with a cold beverage in hand – onboard a permanently moored 19th-century tall ship. The views over the inlet and bay are magical, particularly at sunset.

Paihia Farmers Market
MARKET $

(www.bayofislandsfarmersmarket.org.nz; Village Green; ⊙2-5.30pm Thu) Stock up on local fruit, vegetables, pickles, preserves, honey, fish, smallgoods, eggs, cheese, bread, wine and oil, straight from the producer.

Countdown
SUPERMARKET $

(6 Puketona Rd; ⊙7am-9pm) The main place to stock up on provisions.

Whare Waka
CAFE $$

(Waitangi Treaty Grounds; mains $15-24; ⊙9am-5pm) Located beside a pond studded with ducks, backed by bush and overlooking the Treaty Grounds, the Whare Waka cafe is a top spot for good cafe fare during the day, and to return to for a *hangi* dinner on Wednesday and Saturday evenings from December to March.

Alfresco's
PUB $$

(✆09-402 6797; www.alfrescosrestaurantpaihia.com; 6 Marsden Rd; breakfast & lunch $12-20, dinner $18-33; ⊙8am-late) Locals flock to this casual restaurant-cafe-bar for great food – including lots of local seafood and reasonable prices. Settle in for live music from 3pm to 6pm every Sunday afternoon. There's Happy Hour bar prices from 3pm to 6pm every day too.

35 Degrees South
MODERN NZ, SEAFOOD $$

(www.35south.co.nz; 69 Marsden Rd; shared plates $10-15, mains $25-30) Service was a bit disorganised when we visited, but you can't beat the over-the-water location in central Paihia. The menu is at its best with local oysters and fish and the shared small plates. Try the tempura fish tortillas, and maybe share a dessert of Dutch raisin doughnuts.

☐ Drinking

God bless backpackers: they certainly keep the bars buzzing. There are plenty of places along Kings Rd and in the town centre to explore, so don't feel hemmed in by our list.

Pipi Patch Bar
BAR

(18 Kings Rd; ⊙5pm-late) The party hostel has the party bar: a popular spot with large video screens and a decent terrace. You'll be shuffled inside at midnight to keep the neighbours happy – although most of them are backpackers who'll be here anyway.

Sauce
BEER

(Marsden Rd; pizza $12-22; ⊙11am-late Tue-Sun) Design-your-own pizzas plus the added attraction of excellent craft beer on tap from Hamilton's Good George Brewery.

Bay of Islands Swordfish Club BAR
(Swordy; www.swordfish.co.nz; upstairs, 96 Marsden Rd; ☉4pm-late) Great views, cold beer and tall tales abound at this brightly lit club-bar where creatures from the deep protrude from every available surface. Decent burgers, steaks and seafood ($12 to $28) are also served.

ⓘ Information

Bay of Islands i-SITE (☑09-402 7345; www.northlandnz.com; Marsden Rd; ☉8am-5pm Mar–mid-Dec, to 7pm mid-Dec–Feb) Information and bookings.

ⓘ Getting There & Around

All buses serving Paihia, such as InterCity and Naked Bus, stop at the Maritime Building by the wharf.

Ferries depart regularly for Russell.

For bikes, visit Bay Beach Hire (p134).

Urupukapuka Island

The largest of the bay's islands, Urupukapuka is a tranquil place criss-crossed with walking trails and surrounded by aquamarine waters. Native birds are plentiful thanks to a conservation initiative that has rendered this and all of the neighbouring islands predator free; check that there aren't any rats, mice or ants stowing away on your boat or in your gear before leaving the mainland.

Most of the regular boat tours moor at Otehei Bay for a little island time; if you want to stay over, you can usually arrange to split the trip up and return at a later date. There are DOC campsites (www.doc.govt.nz; sites per adult/child $10/5) at Cable, Sunset and Urupukapuka Bays, which have water supplies, cold showers (except Sunset Bay) and composting toilets; bring food, a stove and fuel.

The Waterfront Bar & Cafe (www.oteheibay.co.nz; Otehei Bay; mains $15-25; ☉11am-8pm) serves light meals and snacks to boat-tour passengers, and at the height of summer also offers evening meals. Kayaks can be rented on the island from Bay of Islands Kayaking (☑021 272 3353; www.bayofislandskayaking.co.nz; hire from $10, island transfer & guided paddle $160).

Kerikeri

POP 6500

Kerikeri means 'dig dig', which is apt, as lots of digging goes on around the area's fertile farmland. Famous for its oranges, Kerikeri also produces kiwifruit, vegetables and wine. If you're looking for some backbreaking, poorly paid work that the locals aren't keen to do, your working holiday starts here.

A snapshot of early Maori and Pakeha (European New Zealander) interaction is offered by a cluster of historic sites centred on the picturesque river basin. In 1819 the powerful Ngapuhi chief Hongi Hika allowed Rev Samuel Marsden to start a mission under the shadow of his Kororipo Pa. There's an ongoing campaign to have the area recognised as a Unesco World Heritage Site.

⊙ Sights & Activities

★ **Stone Store**
& Mission House HISTORIC BUILDINGS
(www.historic.org.nz; 246 Kerikeri Rd; ☉10am-4pm) Dating from 1836, the Stone Store is NZ's oldest stone building. It sells interesting Kiwiana gifts as well as the type of goods that used to be sold in the store. Tours ($10) of the wooden Mission House, NZ's oldest building (1822), depart from here and include entry to *The Soul Trade* exhibition on the 1st floor of the store.

Just up the hill is a marked historical walk, which leads to the site of Kororipo Pa. Huge war parties led by Hika once departed from here, terrorising much of the North Island and slaughtering thousands during the Musket Wars. The role of missionaries in arming Ngapuhi remains controversial. The walk emerges near the cute wooden St James Anglican Church (1878).

Rewa's Village MUSEUM
(Landing Rd; adult/child $5/1; ☉9.30am-4.30pm) If you had a hard time imagining Kororipo Pa in its original state, take the footbridge across the river to this fascinating mock-up of a traditional Maori fishing village.

Aroha Island WILDLIFE RESERVE
(☑09-407 5243; www.arohaisland.co.nz; 177 Rangitane Rd; ☉9.30am-5.30pm) ⚑**FREE** Reached via a permanent causeway through the mangroves, this 5-hectare island provides a haven for the North Island brown kiwi and other native birds, as well as a pleasant

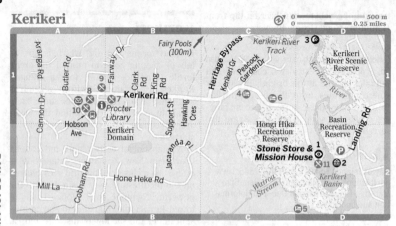

Kerikeri

⊙ Top Sights
1 Stone Store & Mission House D2

⊙ Sights
2 Rewa's Village...D2
3 Wharepuke Falls D1

🛏 Sleeping
4 Bed of Roses...C1
5 Pagoda Lodge...D2
6 Wharepuke Subtropical
   Accommodation C1

⊗ Eating
7 Cafe Jerusalem B1
8 Cafe Zest..A1
9 Fishbone...A1
   Food at Wharepuke ....(see 6)
10 Kerikeri Farmers Market......................A1
11 Pear Tree...D2
   The Village Cafe ....(see 7)

picnic spot for their nonfeathered admirers. It has a visitor centre, kayaks for rent, and after-dark walks to spy kiwi in the wild (per person $35) can also be arranged. You've got around a 50% chance of seeing a kiwi, and booking ahead is essential.

Kerikeri River Track   WALKING
Starting from Kerikeri Basin, this 4km-long track leads past **Wharepuke Falls** and the **Fairy Pools** to the **Rainbow Falls**, where the sheet of water encloses a moss-covered cavern. Alternatively, you can reach the Rainbow Falls from Rainbow Falls Rd, in which case it's only a 10-minute walk.

🛏 Sleeping

Relax a Lodge   HOMESTAY $
(☎09-407 6989; www.relaxalodge.co.nz; 1574 Springbank Rd/SH10; s $55, d & tw $70-90, cottages $110-135; @🛜⊠) Less a farm, more an orange grove, this quiet rural house 4km out of town sleeps just 12 people and is a cosy and welcoming place. Some newly refurbished cottages dotted around the property are also very good value.

Aroha Island   CAMPSITE $
(☎09-407 5243; www.arohaisland.co.nz; 177 Rangitane Rd; sites/units from $18/119) 🍃 Kip among the kiwi on the eco island of *aroha* (love). There's a wide range of reasonably priced options, from the peaceful campsites with basic facilities by the shelly beach to a whole house. The entire island, indoors and out, is nonsmoking.

Pagoda Lodge   LODGE, CAMPSITE $$
(☎09-407 8617; www.pagoda.co.nz; 81 Pa Rd; sites/safari tent/caravan from $40/120/130, apt $120-350; 🛜) Built in the 1930s by an oddball Scotsman with an Asian fetish, this lodge features pagoda-shaped roofs grafted onto wooden cottages. The property descends to the river and is dotted with Buddhas, gypsy caravans, and safari tents with proper beds, or you can pitch your own. To get here, take Cobham Rd, turn left into Kerikeri Inlet Rd and then left into Pa Rd.

Kauri Park   MOTEL $$
(☎09-407 7629; www.kauripark.co.nz; 512 Kerikeri Rd; units $130-170; @🛜⊠) Hidden behind tall trees on the approach to Kerikeri, this well-priced motel has a mixture of units of vary-

ing layouts – some quite stylishly furnished and others a little more old fashioned.

Wharepuke Subtropical Accommodation
CABINS $$

(☏09-407 8933; www.accommodation-bay-of-islands.co.nz; 190 Kerikeri Rd; cabins $150; ☏) Best known for its food and lush gardens, Wharepuke also rents five self-contained one-bedroom cottages hidden among the palms. They have the prefabricated look of holiday-park cabins but are a step up in terms of fixtures and space.

Bed of Roses
B&B $$$

(☏09-407 4666; www.bedofroses.co.nz; 165 Kerikeri Rd; r $295-475; @) It's all petals and no thorns at this stylish B&B, furnished with French antiques, luxe linens and comfy beds. The house has an art-deco ambience and awesome views.

✖ Eating & Drinking

Cafe Jerusalem
MIDDLE EASTERN $

(www.cafejerusalem.co.nz; Village Mall, 85 Kerikeri Rd; snacks & mains $9-18; ⊗10am-late Mon-Sat, 5pm-late Sun in summer) Northland's best felafels and lamb kebabs, all served with a smile and a social vibe. Good salads, and wine and beer are also available. Try the *shakshuka* (baked eggs in a spicy tomato sauce) for a hearty brunch.

Fishbone
CAFE, BAR $

(www.fishbonecafe.co.nz; 88 Kerikeri Rd; mains $10-18; ⊗8am-4pm Mon-Wed, to 8pm Thu-Fri, 8.30am-3pm Sat & Sun) Kerikeri's best brekkie spot serves excellent coffee and food. Dr Seuss fans should try the green (pesto) eggs and ham. From 4pm to 7pm on Thursdays and Fridays, Fishbone morphs into a wine bar.

The Village Cafe
CAFE $

(Village Mall, 85 Kerikeri Rd; mains $10-17; ⊗8am-4pm Mon-Fri, to 2pm Sat & Sun) This chic and cosmopolitan spot is popular with locals for good coffee, freshly prepared counter food, and a relaxed menu of brunch and lunch dishes. Grab a table outside in the Northland sunshine, and order the hearty potato hash.

Cafe Zest
CAFE, BAR $

(73 Kerikeri Rd; mains $10-19; ⊗7.30am-4pm Mon-Wed, to 8.30pm Thu-Sat, to 2pm Sun) Cute Zest serves cafe fare during the day and tapas in the evening, but the main reason to drop by is to sample wines from all of the local producers.

KERIKERI COTTAGE INDUSTRIES

You'd be forgiven for thinking that everyone in Kerikeri is involved in some small-scale artisanal enterprise, as the bombardment of craft shops on the way into town attests.

While Northland isn't known for its wine, a handful of vineyards are doing their best to change that. The little-known red grape chambourcin has proved particularly suited to the region's subtropical humidity, along with pinotage and syrah.

Look out for the *Art & Craft Trail* and *Wine Trail* brochures. Here are our tasty recommendations.

Kerikeri Farmers Market (www.boifm.org.nz; Hobson Ave; ⊗8.30am-noon Sun) From gourmet sausages to *limoncello*.

Get Fudged & Keriblue (www.getfudged.co.nz; 560 Kerikeri Rd; ⊗9am-5pm) An unusual pairing of ceramics and big, decadent slabs of fudge.

Makana Confections (www.makana.co.nz; 504 Kerikeri Rd; ⊗9am-5.30pm) Artisan chocolate factory with lots of sampling.

Marsden Estate (www.marsdenestate.co.nz; 56 Wiroa Rd; mains $19-32, platters $35; ⊗10am-5pm) Excellent wine and lunch on the deck.

Ake Ake (☏09-407 8230; www.akeakevineyard.co.nz; 165 Waimate North Rd; tastings $5, tour $5, mains $27-34, lunch platters $25-48; ⊗cellar door 10am-4.30pm Wed-Sun, restaurant noon-late Wed-Sun winter, daily summer) Vineyard tours (11.30am) and tastings, both free with lunch or purchase of wine. The swanky restaurant is open for lunch and dinner on the days the cellar door is open.

Cottle Hill (www.cottlehill.co.nz; Cottle Hill Dr; tastings $5, free with purchase.; ⊗10am-5.30pm Nov-Mar, 10am-5pm Wed-Sun Apr-Oct) Wine and port.

Fat Pig Vineyard (www.fatpig.co.nz; 177 Puketotara Rd; ⊗3-7pm Fri, 11am-7pm Sat & Sun) Wine and port.

WORTH A TRIP

PUKETI & OMAHUTA FORESTS

Inland from Kerikeri, the Puketi and Omahuta Forests form a continuous expanse of native rainforest. Logging in Puketi was stopped in 1951 to protect not only the remaining kauri but also the endangered kokako bird. Keep an eye out for this rare charmer (grey with a blue wattle) on your wanders.

The forests are reached by several entrances and contain a network of walking tracks varying in length from 15 minutes (the wheelchair-accessible Manginangina Kauri Walk) to two days (the challenging Waipapa River Track); see the DOC website for other walks.

You'll find a DOC campsite (☑09-407 0300; www.doc.govt.nz; Waiare Rd; sites per adult/child 6/3), two three-person cabins ($21) and a 18-bunk hut (exclusive use $62) at the Puketi Recreation Area on the forests' eastern fringe. The hut has hot showers, a kitchen and a flush toilet, while the cabins and campsite make do with cold showers.

Adventure Puketi (www.forestwalks.com; tours $75-155) leads guided ecowalks through the forest, including night-time tours to seek out the nocturnal wildlife.

Just next door the owners have opened a funky space serving freshly made waffles.

Food at Wharepuke CAFE $$
(☑09-407 8936; www.foodatwharepuke.co.nz; 190 Kerikeri Rd; breakfast $14-22, lunch $24-38, dinner $30-40; ⊙10am-10pm Tue-Sat, 9am-3pm Sun) 🍴
With one foot in Europe, the other in Thailand and its head in the lush vegetation of Wharepuke Subtropical Gardens, this is Kerikeri's most unusual and inspired eatery. On Friday nights it serves popular Thai banquets (three courses $47.50), while on Sunday afternoons it screens live jazz. Adjacent is the interesting Wharepuke Print Studio & Gallery.

Pear Tree RESTAURANT, BAR $$
(☑09-407 8479; www.thepeartree.co.nz; 215 Kerikeri Rd; lunch $15-20, dinner $25-32; ⊙10am-2pm daily, 6pm-late Wed-Mon) Kerikeri's best-located and most upmarket restaurant occupies an old homestead right on the basin (book ahead for a table on the verandah). Mains run the gamut of bistro favourites, along with the occasional Asian dish.

ℹ Information

Procter Library (Cobham Rd; ⊙8am-5pm Mon-Fri, 9am-2pm Sat, 9am-1pm Sun; 🛜) Tourist information and free internet access.

ℹ Getting There & Away

AIR

Bay of Islands (Kerikeri) Airport (☑09-407 7147; www.bayofislandsairport.co.nz; 218 Wiroa Rd) is 8km southwest of town. Air New Zealand flies from Auckland to Kerikeri. **Super Shuttle** (☑0800 748 885; www.supershuttle.co.nz; $25) operates a shuttle service from the airport to Kerikeri, Paihia, Opua and Kawakawa.

BUS

InterCity (p124) and partner buses leave from a stop at 9 Cobham Rd, opposite the library.

THE FAR NORTH

Here's your chance to get off the beaten track, even if that does mean onto unsealed roads. The far-flung Far North always play second fiddle to the Bay of Islands for attention and funding, yet the subtropical tip of the North Island has more breathtaking coastline per square kilometre than anywhere but the offshore islands. While the 'winterless north' may be a popular misnomer, summers here are long and leisurely. Note that parts of the Far North are noticeably economically depressed and in places could best be described as gritty. Online see www.topofnz.co.nz.

Matauri & Tauranga Bays

It's a short detour from SH10, but the exceptionally scenic loop route leading inland to these awesome beaches is a world away from the glitzy face presented for tourists in the Bay of Islands.

Matauri Bay is a long, sandy surf beach, 18km off SH10, with the 17 Cavalli Islands scattered offshore. Matauri Bay Holiday Park (☑09-405 0525; www.matauribayholiday-park.co.nz; sites from $20, units $130-140) takes up the north end of the beach and has a shop selling groceries, booze and petrol. On top of the headland above the park is a monument to the *Rainbow Warrior;* the Greenpeace ship's underwater resting place among the Cavalli Islands is a popular dive site.

DOC maintains a 12-person hut (☏09-407 0300; www.doc.govt.nz; adult/child $15/10) on Motukawanui Island, but you'll need a boat or kayak to reach it and you'll need to book ahead. Only water, mattresses and a composting toilet are provided; bring everything else.

Back on the main road, the route heads west, passing through pleasant Te Ngaere village and a succession of little bays before the turn-off to Tauranga Bay, a smaller beach where the sand is a peachy pink colour. Tauranga Bay Holiday Park (☏09-405 0436; www.taurangabay.co.nz; sites from $20, cabins $97-170; @🛜) has campsites and log cabins on the beachfront, but it lacks trees and bears the brunt of the weather. A minimum $59 charge per night for campsites and a seven-night minimum stay applies in January.

Down a private road leading from Tauranga Bay, Northland Sea Kayaking (☏09-405 0381; www.northlandseakayaking.co.nz; half-/full-day tours $75/95) leads kayak explorations of this magical coastline of coves, sea caves and islands. Accommodation is available in conjunction with tours for $25 extra per person.

There's no public transport to these parts or to neighbouring Whangaroa.

Whangaroa Harbour

Just around the headland from Tauranga Bay is the narrow entrance to Whangaroa Harbour. The small fishing village of Whangaroa is 6km from SH10 and calls itself the 'Marlin Capital of NZ'.

There are plenty of charter boats for game-fishing (December to April); prices start at around $1200 a day. If you're planning to hook a monster, insist on it being released once caught – striped marlin and swordfish are among NZ's least-sustainable fishing options.

An excellent 20-minute hike starts from the car park at the end of Old Hospital Rd and goes up St Paul's Rock (213m), which dominates the village. At the top you have to use a wire cable to pull yourself up, but the views make it worth the effort.

The Wairakau Stream Track, heading north to Pekapeka Bay, begins near the

---

THE BOMBING OF THE RAINBOW WARRIOR

On the morning of 10 July 1985, New Zealanders awoke to news reporting that a terrorist attack had killed a man in Auckland Harbour. The Greenpeace flagship *Rainbow Warrior* had been sunk at its anchorage at Marsden Wharf, where it was preparing to sail to Moruroa Atoll near Tahiti to protest against French nuclear testing.

A tip-off from a Neighbourhood Watch group eventually led to the arrest of two French foreign intelligence service (DGSE) agents, posing as tourists. The agents had detonated two mines on the boat in staggered explosions – the first designed to cause the crew to evacuate and the second to sink her. However, after the initial evacuation, some of the crew returned to the vessel to investigate and document the attack. Greenpeace photographer Fernando Pereira was drowned below decks following the second explosion.

The arrested agents pleaded guilty to manslaughter and were sentenced to 10 years' imprisonment. In response, the French government threatened to embargo NZ goods from entering the European Economic Community – which would have crippled NZ's economy. A deal was struck whereby France paid $13 million to NZ and apologised, in return for the agents being delivered into French custody on a South Pacific atoll for three years. France eventually paid over $8 million to Greenpeace in reparation – and the bombers were quietly freed before their sentence was served.

Initially French President François Mitterrand denied any government involvement in the attack, but following an inquiry he eventually sacked his defence minister and the head of the DGSE, Admiral Pierre Lacoste. On the 20th anniversary of the attack, *Le Monde* newspaper published a report from Lacoste dating from 1986, declaring that the president had personally authorised the operation.

The bombing left a lasting impact on NZ, and French nuclear testing at Moruroa ceased for good in 1996. The wreck of the *Rainbow Warrior* was resunk near Northland's Cavalli Islands, where, today, it can be explored by divers. The masts were bought by the Dargaville Museum and overlook the town. The memory of Fernando Pereira endures in a peaceful bird hide in Thames, while a memorial to the boat sits atop a Maori *pa* (fortified village) site at Matauri Bay, north of the Bay of Islands.

church hall on Campbell Rd in Totara North on the other side of the bay. It's an extremely beautiful, undeveloped stretch and you can cool off in swimming holes along the way. The two-hour hike passes through forest, an abandoned farm and around a steep-walled estuary before arriving at DOC's Lane Cove Hut (☑09-407 0300; www.doc.govt.nz; sole occupancy $164), which has 16 beds, plus composting toilets. Bring everything else and reserve well ahead; it's usually booked out by Kiwi families over summer.

Duke's Nose Track (1¼ hours return) starts behind the cottage and leads up Kairara Rocks; look for the Duke of Wellington's aquiline profile in the rock face. You'll need to haul yourself up a chain for the last 10m but the views are worth it. If you don't fancy walking back – or if you don't fancy walking at all – Bushmansfriend (☑09-405 1844; www.bushmansfriend.co.nz) arranges water taxis from Lane Cove ($20) and one-hour boat tours ($45).

On the other side of the harbour's north head is Taupo Bay, a surf beach that attracts a loyal Kiwi contingent in summer. On easterly swells, there are quality righthanders to surf at the southern end of the bay, by the rivermouth. It's reached by an 11km sealed road signposted from SH10.

⨠ Sleeping & Eating

★Kahoe Farms Hostel HOSTEL $
(☑09-405 1804; www.kahoefarms.co.nz; dm $30, r $76-96) On SH10, 10km north of the turn-off to Whangaroa, this hostel has a deservedly great reputation – for its comfortable accommodation, for its bucolic setting, for its home-cooked Italian food, but mostly for its welcoming owners. The backpackers cottage is great, but slightly up the hill there's an even more impressive villa with excellent-value en suite rooms.

Sunseeker Lodge HOSTEL $
(☑09-405 0496; www.sunseekerlodge.co.nz; Old Hospital Rd; dm/s/d/tr $25/50/66/90, units $120-150; @🐾) Up the hill in Whangaroa, this friendly lodge has a spa with a jaw-dropping view, hires out kayaks and motor boats, and will pick you up from Kaeo on SH10.

Marlin PUB $$
(Whangaroa Rd; mains $15-20; ☺lunch & dinner) A friendly local pub with good honest tucker served from the attached cafe.

ⓘ Information

Boyd Gallery (☑09-405 0230; Whangaroa Rd; ☺8am-7pm) General store and tourist information office.

Doubtless Bay
POP 6030

The bay gets its unusual name from an entry in Cook's logbook, where he wrote that the body of water was 'doubtless a bay'. No kidding, Cap'n. It's a bloody big bay at that, with a string of pretty swimming beaches heading towards the Karikari Peninsula.

The main centre, Mangonui (meaning 'Big Shark'), retains a fishing-port feel, despite cafes and gift shops now infesting its well-labelled line of historical waterfront buildings. They were constructed in the days when Mangonui was a centre of the whaling industry (1792–1850) and exported flax, kauri wood and gum.

The popular holiday settlements of Coopers Beach, Cable Bay and Taipa are restful pockets of beachside gentrification.

⊙ Sights & Activities

Grab the free *Heritage Trail* brochure from the information centre for a 3km self-guided walk that takes in 22 historic sites. Other walks lead to attractive Mill Bay, west of Mangonui, and Rangikapiti Pa Historic Reserve, which has ancient Maori terracing and a spectacular view of Doubtless Bay – particularly at sunrise and sunset. A walkway runs from Mill Bay to the *pa,* but you can also drive nearly to the top.

Butler Point Whaling Museum MUSEUM
(www.butlerpoint.co.nz; Marant Rd, Hihi; adult/child $12/2; ☺by appointment) At Hihi, 15km northeast of Mangonui, this small private museum and Victorian homestead (1843) is set in lovely gardens. Its first owner, Captain Butler, left Dorset when he was 14 and at 24 was captain of a whaling ship. He settled here in 1839, had 13 children and became a trader, farmer, magistrate and Member of Parliament.

⨠ Sleeping

There's plenty of accommodation, but most is overpriced in summer. Outside the peak months things settle down considerably.

Puketiti Lodge
HOSTEL $

(☑09-406 0369; www.puketitilodge.co.nz; 10 Puketiti Dr; dm/s/d $40/100/150; @ 🛜) If this is what they mean by flashpacking, bring it on. For $40 you get a comfy bunk in a spacious six-person dorm that opens on to a large deck with awesome views, a locker big enough for the burliest backpack and, perhaps most surprisingly, breakfast. Turn inland at Midgley Rd, 6km south of Mangonui village, just after the Hihi turn-off.

Old Oak
BOUTIQUE HOTEL $$

(☑09-406 1250; www.theoldoak.co.nz; 66 Waterfront Dr, Mangonui; d $175-275, ste $295-325; 🛜) This atmospheric 1861 kauri inn is now an elegant boutique hotel with contemporary design and top-notch furnishings. It oozes character, not least because the building is reputedly haunted.

Mangonui Waterfront Apartments Motel
APARTMENTS $$

(☑09-406 0347; www.mangonuiwaterfront.co.nz; 88 Waterfront Dr, Mangonui; apt $120-225; @🛜) Sleeping two to eight people, these historic apartments on the Mangonui waterfront have loads of character, each one different but all with balconies, a sense of space and their own barbecue. Try to book 100-year-old Tahi.

✗ Eating

There are also cafes, takeaways and stores around the other beaches.

Mangonui Fish Shop
FISH & CHIPS $

(137 Waterfront Dr, Mangonui; fish & chips $10; ⊙10am-8pm; 🛜) Eat outdoors over the water at this chippie, which also sells smoked fish and seafood salads. Grab a crayfish salad and a beer and you'll be sorted. The other fish-and-chip shop across the road is also good.

Waterfront Cafe & Bar
CAFE $$

(Waterfront Dr, Mangonui; brunch $11-18, dinner $14-29; ⊙8.30am-late) Waterfront has water views and old-world charm. A pizza menu kicks in at lunch and extends into dinner, when it supplements bistro dishes.

Thai Chef
THAI $$

(☑09-406 1220; www.thaichef.co.nz; 80 Waterfront Dr, Mangonui; mains $18-26; ⊙5-11pm Tue-Sun) Northland's best Thai restaurant serves piquant dishes with intriguing names like The 3 Alcoholics, Spice Girls and Bangkok Showtime.

🛍 Shopping

Flax Bush
ARTS & CRAFTS

(www.flaxbush.co.nz; 50 Waterfront Dr, Mangonui; ⊙10am-5pm) Seashells, Pasifika and Maori crafts.

Exhibit A
ARTS & CRAFTS

(Old Courthouse, Waterfront Dr; ⊙10am-4.30pm) This co-op gallery showcases Far North artists.

ℹ Information

Doubtless Bay Visitor Information Centre (☑09-406 2046; www.doubtlessbay.co.nz; 118 Waterfront Dr, Mangonui; ⊙10am-4pm Mon-Sat)

ℹ Getting There & Away

InterCity buses depart near the Watefront Cafe in Mangonui, outside the wholesalers in Coopers Beach, opposite the shop in Cable Bay and outside the Shell station in Taipa. **Busabout Kaitaia** (☑09-408 1092; www.cbec.co.nz) has services to Kaitaia ($5, one hour).

Karikari Peninsula

The oddly shaped Karikari Peninsula bends into a near-perfect right angle. The result is beaches facing north, south, east and west in close proximity, so if the wind's annoying you or you want to catch some surf, a sunrise or a sunset, just swap beaches. Despite its natural assets, the sun-baked peninsula is blissfully undeveloped, with farmers well outnumbering tourist operators. There's no public transport and you won't find a lot of shops or eateries either.

◉ Sights & Activities

Tokerau Beach is the long, sandy stretch forming the western edge of Doubtless Bay. Neighbouring **Whatuwhiwhi** is smaller and more built-up, facing back across the bay. **Maitai Bay**, with its tiny twin coves, is the loveliest of them all, at the lonely end of the peninsula down an unsealed road. It's a great spot for swimming – the waters sheltered enough for the kids but with enough swell to body surf.

Rangiputa faces west at the elbow of the peninsula; the pure white sand and crystal-clear sheltered waters come straight from a Pacific Island daydream. A turn-off on the road to Rangiputa takes you to remote

Puheke Beach, a long, windswept stretch of snow-white sand dunes forming Karikari's northern edge.

Various local watersports operators can be contacted under the umbrella of Watersports Paradise (☑ 050 872 7234; www.watersportsparadise.co.nz).

Karikari Estate   WINERY
(www.karikariestate.co.nz; Maitai Bay Rd; tastings $12; ⊙11am-4pm Nov-Apr) A sign of creeping gentrification is this luxury golf club and winery on the way to Maitai Bay. Impressive Karikari Estate produces acclaimed red wines and has a cafe attached – and while the wine tastings are shamelessly overpriced, at least the sublime views are free.

Airzone Kitesurfing School   KITESURFING
(☑ 021 202 7949; www.kitesurfnz.com; 1-/2-/3-day course $195/350/485) The unique set-up of Karikari Peninsula makes it one of the world's premium spots for kitesurfing. Learners get to hone their skills on flat water before heading to the surf, while the more experienced can chase the wind around the peninsula.

A to Z Diving   DIVING
(☑09-408 3336; www.atozdiving.co.nz; 13-15 Whatuwhiwhi Rd; 2 dives incl equipment $160-230) Offers PADI courses and dive trips in Doubtless Bay and to the *Rainbow Warrior*.

🛌 Sleeping

Whatuwhiwhi Top
10 Holiday Park   HOLIDAY PARK $
(☑09-408 7202; www.whatuwhiwhitop10.co.nz; 17 Whatuwhiwhi Rd; sites from $62, units $82-385) 🏊 Sheltered by hills and overlooking the beach, this friendly complex has a great location, good facilities, free barbecues and kayaks for hire. It also offers dive fills and PADI diving instruction.

Maitai Bay DOC Campsite   CAMPSITE $
(www.doc.govt.nz; Maitai Bay Rd; sites per adult/child $10/5) 🏊 A large first-in, first-served (no bookings) camping ground at the peninsula's most beautiful beach, with chemical toilets, drinking water and cold showers.

Pepper's Carrington Resort   RESORT $$$
(☑09-408 7222; www.peppers.co.nz; r from $245; @⚊) 🏊 There's something very Australian-looking about this hilltop lodge with its wide verandahs and gum trees, tempered by Maori and Pacific design in the spacious rooms and villas. The view over the golf course to the dazzling white beach is exquisite.

Cape Reinga & Ninety Mile Beach

Maori consider Cape Reinga (Te Rerenga-Wairua) the jumping-off point for souls as they depart on the journey to their spiritual homeland. That makes the Aupouri Peninsula a giant diving board, and it even resembles one – long and thin, it reaches 108km to form NZ's northern extremity. On its west coast Ninety Mile Beach (Ninety Kilometre Beach would be more accurate) is a continuous stretch lined with high sand dunes, flanked by the Aupouri Forest.

🎯 Sights & Activities

Cape Reinga   LANDMARK
Standing at windswept Cape Reinga Lighthouse (a rolling 1km walk from the car park) and looking out over the ocean engenders a real end-of-the-world feeling. This is where the waters of the Tasman Sea and Pacific Ocean meet, breaking together into waves up to 10m high in stormy weather. Little tufts of cloud often cling to the ridges, giving sudden spooky chills even on hot days.

Visible on a promontory slightly to the east is a spiritually significant 800-year-old pohutukawa tree; souls are believed to slide down its roots. Out of respect to the most sacred site in Maoridom, don't go near the tree and refrain from eating or drinking anywhere in the area.

Cape Reinga Coastal Walkway   TRAMPING
Contrary to expectation, Cape Reinga isn't actually the northernmost point of the country; that honour belongs to Surville Cliffs further to the east. A walk along Te Werahi Beach to Cape Maria van Diemen (a five-hour loop) takes you to the westernmost point of the north island. This is one of many sections of the three- to four-day, 53km Cape Reinga Coastal Walkway (from Kapowairua to Te Paki Stream) that can be tackled individually. Beautiful Tapotupotu Bay is a two-hour walk east of Cape Reinga, via Sandy Bay and the cliffs. From Tapotupotu Bay it's an eight-hour walk to Spirits Bay, one of NZ's most beautiful beaches. Both bays are also accessible by road.

Te Paki Recreation Reserve   NATURE RESERVE
A large chunk of the land around Cape Reinga is part of the Te Paki Recreation Reserve managed by DOC. It's public land with free access; leave the gates as you found them and don't

disturb the animals. There are 7 sq km of giant sand dunes on either side of the mouth of Te Paki Stream. Clamber up to take flying leaps off the dunes or to toboggan down them. During summer, Ahikaa Adventures (p153) are on hand to rent sandboards ($15).

Great Exhibition Bay   BEACH

On the east coast, Great Exhibition Bay has dazzling snow-white silica dunes. There's no public road access, but some tours pay a *koha* (donation) to cross Maori farmland or approach the sand by kayak from Parengarenga Harbour.

Nga-Tapuwae-o-te-Mangai   TEMPLE

(6576 Far North Rd) With its two domed towers (Arepa and Omeka, alpha and omega) and the Ratana emblem of the star and crescent moon, you could be forgiven for mistaking this temple for a mosque. Ratana is a Maori Christian sect with more than 50,000 adherents, formed in 1925 by Tahupotiki Wiremu Ratana, who was known as 'the mouthpiece of God'. The temple is built on land where Ratana once stood, and the name translates as 'the sacred steps of the mouthpiece'. You'll pass it at Te Kao, 46km south of Cape Reinga.

Gumdiggers Park   MUSEUM

(www.gumdiggerspark.co.nz; 171 Heath Rd, Waiharara; adult/child $14/7; ☉9am-5pm) Kauri forests covered this area for 100,000 years, leaving ancient logs and the much-prized gum (used for making varnish and linoleum) buried beneath. Digging it out was the region's main industry from the 1870s to the 1920s. In 1900 around 7000 gumdiggers were digging holes all over Northland, including at this site. Start with the 15-minute video, and then walk on the bush tracks, leading past gumdiggers' huts, ancient kauri stumps, huge preserved logs, and holes left by the diggers.

Ancient Kauri Kingdom   WOODTURNERS

(www.ancientkauri.co.nz; 229 Far North Rd, Awanui; ☉8.30am-5pm; ☎) Here, 50,000-year-old kauri stumps dragged out of swamps are fashioned into furniture, woodcraft products and a fair bit of tourist tat. The large complex includes a cafe, gift shop and workshop. A huge kauri log has been transformed into an impressive spiral staircase.

☞ Tours

Bus tours go to Cape Reinga from Kaitaia, Ahipara, Doubtless Bay and the Bay of Islands, but there's no scheduled public transport up here.

Cape Reinga Adventures   4WD TOURS

(☎09-409 8445; www.capereingaadventures.co.nz; half-/full-day 4WD trips $75/135) Runs 4WD tours (including sunset visits to the cape after the crowds have gone), plus fishing, kayaking and sandboarding as day activities or as part of overnight camping trips.

Far North Outback Adventures   4WD TOURS

(☎09-408 0927; www.farnorthtours.co.nz; price on application) Flexible, day-long tours from Kaitaia/Ahipara, including morning tea and lunch. Options include visits to remote areas such as Great Exhibition Bay.

Harrisons Cape Runner   ADVENTURE TOUR

(☎0800 227 373; www.harrisonscapereingatours.co.nz; adult/child $50/25) Day trips from Kaitaia along Ninety Mile Beach that include sandboarding and a picnic lunch.

Sand Safaris   ADVENTURE TOUR

(☎09-408 1778, 0800 869 090; www.sandsafaris.co.nz; adult/child $50/30) Coach trips from Ahipara and Kaitaia including sandboarding and a picnic lunch.

Ahikaa Adventures   CULTURAL TOUR

(☎09-409 8228; www.ahikaa-adventures.co.nz; tours $70-190) Maori culture permeates these tours, which can include sand-surfing, kayaking, fishing and pigging out on traditional *kai* (food).

🛏 Sleeping & Eating

Unless you're a happy camper you won't find much decent accommodation up here. Pukenui – literally 'Big Stomach' – is the best place to fill yours; there's a cafe, takeaways and grocery store. Another option is the friendly fishing club at Houhora.

North Wind Lodge Backpackers   HOSTEL $

(☎09-409 8515; www.northwind.co.nz; 88 Otaipango Rd, Henderson Bay; dm/s/tw/d $30/60/80/80) Six kilometres down an unsealed road on

SEED FOR THE FUTURE

The local Ngati Kuri, guardians of the sacred spaces around the Cape, have come up with a unique way of funding reforestation. For $20 you can assuage your carbon guilt by planting a native tree or bush of your choice – or, if you don't want to break a nail, letting the staff plant it for you; contact **Natives** (☎09-409 8482; www.natives.co.nz).

the Aupouri peninsula's east side, this unusual turreted house offers a homely environment and plenty of quiet spots on the lawn to sit with a beer and a book.

DOC Campsites　　CAMPSITES $
(www.doc.govt.nz; sites per adult/child $10/5) There are spectacularly positioned sites at Kapowairua, Tapotupotu Bay and Rarawa Beach. Only water, composting toilets and cold showers are provided. Bring a cooker, as fires are not allowed, and plenty of repellent to ward off mosquitoes and sandflies. 'Freedom/Leave No Trace' camping is allowed along the Cape Reinga Coastal Walkway.

❶ Getting There & Around

Apart from numerous tours, there's no public transport past Pukenui, which is linked to Kaitaia ($5, 45 minutes) by **Busabout Kaitaia** (☑ 09-408 1092; www.cbec.co.nz).

As well as Far North Rd (SH1), rugged vehicles can travel along Ninety Mile Beach itself. However, cars have been known to hit soft sand and be swallowed by the tides – look out for unfortunate vehicles poking through the sands. Check tide times before setting out; avoid it 2½ hours either side of high tide. Watch out for 'quicksand' at Te Paki Stream – keep moving. Many car-rental companies prohibit driving on the sands; if you get stuck, your insurance won't cover you.

Fill up with petrol before hitting the Aupouri Peninsula.

Kaitaia

POP 4900

Nobody comes to the Far North to hang out in this provincial town, but it's a handy stop if you're after a supermarket, a post office or an ATM. It's also a jumping-off point for tours to Cape Reinga and Ninety Mile Beach.

◉ Sights

Te Ahu Centre　　ARTS CENTRE
(www.teahu.org.nz; Matthews Ave; ☎) This civic and community centre features a cinema, the eclectic local-history **Te Ahu Heritage** (www.teahuheritage.co.nz; ☺10am-4pm Mon-Fri, to 2pm Sat) FREE exhibits of the Far North Regional Museum, and the local i-SITE information centre. There's also a cafe and free wi-fi at the library.

Okahu Estate Winery　　WINERY
(www.okahuestate.co.nz; 520 Okahu Rd; ☺noon-5pm Thu-Sat, also open holiday weekends) Just south of town, off the road to Ahipara, Kaitaia's only winery offers free tastings and sells local produce, including the famous Kaitaia Fire chilli sauce. Enquire about tours ($5).

⊨ Sleeping & Eating

Mainstreet Lodge　　HOSTEL $
(☑ 09-408 1275; www.mainstreetlodge.co.nz; 235 Commerce St; dm $27-30, s $55-70, d & tw $64-78; @ ☎) Maori carvings abound at this groovy old cottage, which has a modern purpose-built wing facing the rear courtyard. The friendly owners know the area inside-out.

Loredo Motel　　MOTEL $$
(☑ 09-408 3200; www.loredomotel.co.nz; 25 North Rd; units $130-160; ☎☒) Opting for a breezy Spanish style, this tidy motel has well-kept units set among palm trees and lawns, with a swimming pool.

Beachcomber　　RESTAURANT $$
(www.beachcomber.net.nz; 222 Commerce St; lunch $19-33, dinner $24-36; ☺11am-3pm Mon-Fri, 5pm-late Mon-Sat) Easily the best place to eat in town, with a wide range of seafood and meaty fare and a well-stocked salad bar.

❶ Information

Far North i-SITE (☑ 03-408 9450; www.northlandnz.com; Te Ahu Centre, cnr Matthews Ave & South Rd; ☺8.30am-5pm)

❶ Getting There & Away

Kaitaia Airport (www.bayofislandsairport.co.nz; Quarry Rd) is 6km north of town. **Busabout Kaitaia** (☑ 09-408 1092; www.cbec.co.nz) has services to Doubtless Bay ($5, one hour), Pukenui ($5, 45 minutes) and Ahipara ($3.50, 15 minutes). Both Air New Zealand (p124) and InterCity (p124) operate services to Kaitaia.

Ahipara

POP 1130

All good things must come to an end, and Ninety Mile Beach does at this spunky beach town. A few holiday mansions have snuck in, but mostly it's just the locals keeping it real, rubbing shoulders with visiting surfers.

The area is known for its huge sand dunes and massive gum field, where 2000 people once worked. Sandboarding and quad-bike rides are popular activities on the dunes above Ahipara and further around the Tauroa Peninsula.

◉ Sights

Shipwreck Bay BEACH
(Wreck Bay Rd) The best surfing is at this small cove at Ahipara's western edge, so named for shipwrecks still visible at low tide.

Ahipara Viewpoint LOOKOUT
(Gumfields Rd) This lookout on the bluff behind Ahipara is reached by an extremely rough road leading off the unsealed Gumfields Rd, which starts at the western end of Foreshore Dr.

🏃 Activities

Ahipara Adventure Centre ADVENTURE SPORTS
(⌨ 09-409 2055; www.ahiparaadventure.co.nz; 15 Takahe St) Hires sand toboggans ($10 per half day), surfboards ($30 per half day), mountain bikes ($50 per day), kayaks ($25 per hour), blokarts for sand yachting ($65 per hour) and quad bikes ($95 per hour).

Tua Tua Tours QUAD BIKES
(⌨ 0800 494 288; www.ahipara.co.nz/tuatuatours; 250 Ahipara Rd; s/d rides from $100/110) Reef- and dune-rider tours, plus the Gumfields Safari (per one/two people $175/185), three hours that includes sand tobogganing.

NZ Surf Bros SURFING
(⌨ 09-945 7276; www.nzsurfbros.com; 27 Kaka St; surf lessons $60, paddle boarding $60-100) Based in a cool house with amazing views of the surf, NZ Surf Bros offer surfing and paddleboarding lessons, plus day excursions and multiday trips that take in beaches on both the west and east coasts of Northland.

Ahipara Treks HORSE RIDING
(⌨ 09-409 4122; www.ahiparahorsetreks.moonfruit.com; 1/2/3 hours $50/70/110) Offers beach canters, including some farm and ocean riding (when the surf permits).

🛏 Sleeping

★ Endless Summer Lodge HOSTEL $
(⌨ 09-409 4181; www.endlesssummer.co.nz; 245 Foreshore Rd; dm $30, d $70-85; @) Across from the beach, this superb kauri villa (1880) has been beautifully restored and converted into an exceptional hostel. There's no TV, which encourages bonding around the long table and wood-fired pizza oven on the vine-covered back terrace. Body boards and sandboards can be borrowed and surfboards can be hired.

90 Mile Beach
Ahipara Holiday Park HOLIDAY PARK $
(⌨ 0800 888 988; www.ahiparaholidaypark.co.nz; 168 Takahe St; sites from $40, dm/r $28/95, units $75-125; @ 🛜) There's a large range of accommodation on offer at this holiday park, including cabins, motel units and a worn but perfectly presentable YHA-affiliated backpackers' lodge. The communal hall has an open fire and colourful murals.

Beachfront APARTMENTS $$
(⌨ 09-409 4007; www.beachfront.net.nz; 14 Kotare St; apt $175-310; 🛜) Who cares if it's a bit bourgeois for Ahipara? These two upmarket, self-contained apartments have watery views and there's direct access to the beach.

NGATI TARARA

As you're travelling around the north you might notice the preponderance of road names ending in '-ich'. The sign leading into Kaitaia proclaims, 'haere mai, dobro došli and welcome', denoting one of the more peculiar ethnic conjunctions in the country.

From the end of the 19th century, men from the Dalmatian coast of what is now Croatia started arriving in NZ looking for work. Many ended up in Northland's gum fields. Pakeha (white) society wasn't particularly welcoming to the new immigrants, particularly during WWI, as they were on Austrian passports. Not so the small Maori communities of the north. Here the immigrants found an echo of Dalmatian village life, with its emphasis on extended family and hospitality, not to mention a shared history of injustice at the hands of colonial powers.

The Maori jokingly named them Tarara, as their rapid conversation in their native tongue sounded like 'ta-ra-ra-ra-ra' to Maori ears. Many Croatian men married local wahine (women), founding clans that have left several of today's famous Maori with Croatian surnames, like singer Margaret Urlich and former All Black Frano Botica. You'll find large Tarara communities in the Far North, Dargaville and West Auckland.

✖ Eating

Bidz Takeaways FISH & CHIPS $
(Takahe St; meals $6-12; ⊙9am-8pm; 🛜) Fresh
fish for sale, and the best fish, chips and burgers in town (plus free wi-fi with purchase).
There's also a small grocery store attached.

Gumdiggers Cafe CAFE $$
(3 Ahipara Rd; mains $6-26; ⊙7am-2pm & 5-10pm)
Good coffee and huge portions are the
hallmarks of this friendly little cafe, serving cooked breakfasts, nachos, burgers and
huge platters. Dinners are on offer from 5pm
most nights.

❶ Getting There & Around

Busabout Kaitaia (☑09-408 1092; www.cbec.
co.nz) runs services from Kaitaia ($3.50, 15
minutes).

HOKIANGA

The Hokianga Harbour stretches out its skinny tentacles to become the fourth-biggest in
the country. Its ruggedly beautiful landscape
is painted in every shade of green and brown.
The water itself is rendered the colour of ginger ale by the bush streams that feed it.

Of all the remote parts of Northland, this
is the pocket that feels the most removed
from the mainstream. Pretension has no
place here. Isolated, predominantly Maori
communities nestle around the harbour's
many inlets, as they have done for centuries.
Discovered by legendary explorer Kupe, it's
been settled by Ngapuhi since the 14th century. Hippies arrived in the late 1960s and
their legacy is a thriving little artistic scene.

Many of the roads remain unsealed,
and, while tourism dollars are channelled
eastward to the Bay of Islands, this truly
fascinating corner of the country remains
remarkably undeveloped, just how many of
the locals like it.

See www.hokiangatourism.org.nz.

Mitimiti

The tiny community at Mitimiti, which
consists of only 30 families and not even a
shop, has the unspoilt 20km stretch of coast
between the Hokianga and Whangape Harbours all to itself. The 40km drive from Kohukohu via Panguru (14km of it unsealed) is
quite an experience: prepare to dodge cows,
sheep, potholes and kids.

Sandtrails Hokianga (☑09-409 5035; www.
sandtrailshokianga.co.nz; 32 Paparangi Dr) offers
an inside perspective on Mitimiti's tight-knit
Maori community, with two-hour Sandscapes
dune-buggy tours, which head 12km along
the beach to the giant dunes that form the
harbour's north head ($155), or personally tailored tours on which you can stay overnight in
the guide's house ($640 for two people).

Motuti

It's worth taking a short detour from the
road to Mitimiti to visit **St Mary's Church**
(Hata Maria; www.hokiangapompallier.org.nz; Motuti Rd), where NZ's first Catholic bishop is
buried beneath the altar. Jean Baptiste Pompallier arrived in the Hokianga in 1838, celebrating NZ's first Mass at Totara Point. He
was interred here in 2002 after an emotional
14-week pilgrimage full of Maori ceremony
brought his remains back from France.

The nearby **Motuti Marae** (☑09-409 5545;
www.motuti.co.nz; 318 Motuti Rd; tours 90min/
day $36/60, stay $214) offers *marae* tours and
stays, including a traditional Maori welcome
and, on the longer tours, the opportunity to
take part in flax-weaving, carving and stick
games.

Kohukohu

POP 190

Quick, someone slap a preservation order
on Kohukohu before it's too late. There can
be few places in NZ where a Victorian village full of interesting kauri buildings has
been so completely preserved with hardly a
modern monstrosity to be seen. During the
height of the kauri industry it was a busy
town with a sawmill, shipyard, two newspapers and banks. These days it's a very quiet
backwater on the north side of Hokianga
Harbour, 4km from the Rawene car ferry
(p158). There's good eating at the local pub
and on the cosy deck of the **KB Cafaway** (cnr
Beach Rd & Kohukohu Rd; mains $12-14; ⊙noon-
8pm Wed-Sun). **Village Arts** (www.villagearts.
co.nz; 1376 Kohukohu Rd; ⊙10am-4pm, to 3pm
winter) is an excellent little art gallery.

Tree House (☑09-405 5855; www.treehouse.
co.nz; 168 West Coast Rd; sites/dm $19/32, s $60-
70, tw & d $86; 🛜) 🌿 is the best place to stay
in the Hokianga, with helpful hosts and
brightly painted little cottages set among exotic fruit and nut trees. This quiet retreat is

HOKIANGA

I love the north of the north island, the beaten, bloody and beautiful landscape and *wairua*. The small towns up north, where I grew up, reach out all along the moody west coast. As kids, my brother and I would sneak in to Ngawha Springs and have our mud baths in the morning – smelling of rotten eggs for the rest of the day. In Opononi we'd go crab hunting on the rocks with Uncle Rata, then take the car ferry from Rawene home. At Pawarenga – a dusty old Maori town – we'd go horse riding with the cuzzies, learn Maori with my Grandpa, eat *karahu* and oysters, and, as we grew up, drink with the aunties and uncles. We'd drive to Kaitaia to buy all our food for the next week, and hang at the local pubs. Then further north for the Mangonui fish 'n' chip shop, the best *kai* in Aotearoa. When we were tired, we'd drive to Ahipara and sleep on the beach.

Anika Moa, singer/songwriter

2km from the ferry terminus (turn sharp left as you come off the ferry).

Horeke & Around

Tiny Horeke was NZ's second European settlement after Russell. A Wesleyan mission operated here from 1828 to 1855, while, in 1840, 3000 Ngapuhi gathered here for what was the single biggest signing of the Treaty of Waitangi. The rustic **Horeke Tavern** (www.horeketavern.co.nz; 2118 Horeke Rd; ⊙1pm-late Wed-Sun, bistro Thu-Sun 5.30-8pm) is reputedly New Zealand's oldest pub – the first cold one was poured back in 1826 – and the garden bar rocks with live music on occasional weekends during summer.

Horeke is also the western end point of the Pou Herenga Tai Twin Coast Cycle Trail (p134).

◉ Sights & Activities

Mangungu Mission House HISTORIC BUILDING
(www.historic.org.nz; Motukiore Rd; adult/child $10/free; ⊙noon-4pm Sat & Sun) Completed in 1839, this sweet wooden cottage contains relics of the missionaries who once inhabited it, and of Horeke's shipbuilding past. In the grounds there's a large stone cross and a simple wooden church. Mangungu is 1km down the unsealed road leading along the harbour from Horeke village.

Wairere Boulders Nature Park NATURE PARK
(www.waireboulders.co.nz; McDonnell Rd; adult/child/family $15/5/35; ⊙to 5pm/7pm winter/summer) 🐾 At Wairere, massive basalt rock formations have been eroded into odd fluted shapes by the acidity of ancient kauri forests. Allow an hour for the main loop track, but wear sensible shoes and expect a few dips and climbs. An additional track leads through rainforest to a platform at the end

of the boulder valley (allow 1½ hours). The park is signposted from SH1 and Horeke; the last 3km are unsealed.

Without your own transport, get here on a Discover Hokianga tour by Fullers (p135), which departs from Paihia.

Wairere Adventure Park QUAD BIKES, KAYAKING
(☑09-401 9544; www.waireadventurepark.co.nz; 34 McDonnell Rd; quad-bike tours $65-135, kayak hire $15) Offers quad-bike tours with harbour, bush and boulders scenery, and kayak hire to explore a scenic tidal estuary. Booking ahead for kayaks is recommended to catch the best tidal conditions.

Rawene

POP 440

Founded shortly after Horeke, Rawene was NZ's third European settlement. A surprising number of historic buildings (including six churches!) remain from a time when the harbour was considerably busier than it is now. Information boards outline a heritage trail of the main sights.

There's an ATM in the Four Square grocery store, and you can get petrol here.

◉ Sights

Clendon House HISTORIC BUILDING
(www.historic.org.nz; Clendon Esplanade; adult/child $10/free; ⊙10am-4pm Sat & Sun Nov-Apr, Sun May-Oct) Clendon House was built in the bustling 1860s by James Clendon, a trader, shipowner and magistrate. After his death, his 34-year-old half-Maori widow Jane was left with a brood of kids and a whopping £5000 debt. She managed to clear the debt and her descendants remained in the house until 1972, when it passed to the Historic Places Trust.

🛏 Sleeping & Eating

Rawene Holiday Park HOLIDAY PARK $
(☑09-405 7720; www.raweneholidaypark.co.nz;
1 Marmon St; dm $20, sites/units from $32/65;
@ 🛜 🏊) Tent sites shelter in the bush at this
nicely managed park. The cabins are simple,
with one converted into a bunkroom for
backpackers (linen costs extra).

Boatshed Cafe CAFE $
(☑09-405 7728; 8 Clendon Esplanade; mains $10-
20; ⊗8.30am-4pm) Eat overlooking the water
at this cafe, a cute place with excellent food
and a gift shop that sells local art and crafts.
The cafe sometimes opens for dinner at the
weekend.

ℹ Getting There & Away

There are no regular bus services to Rawene. A
car ferry (☑09-405 2602; car/campervan/mo-
torcycle $20/40/5, passenger $2; ⊗7.30am-
8pm) heads to the northern side of the Hokianga, docking 4km south of Kohukohu at least
hourly. You can buy your ticket for this 15-minute
ride on board. It usually leaves Rawene on the
half-hour and the north Kohukohu side on the
hour.

Opononi & Omapere

POP 480

These tranquil settlements near the south
head of Hokianga Harbour run into one
another. The water's much clearer here
and good for swimming, and views are
dominated by the mountainous sand dunes
across the water at North Head. If you're
approaching Omapere from the south, the
view of the harbour is nothing short of
spectacular.

🏃 Activities

Hokianga Express SANDBOARDING
(☑021 405 872; www.hokiangaexpress.webs.com;
adult/child $25/15; ⊗from 10am) A boat departs
from Opononi Jetty and takes you across
the harbour to the large golden sand dunes,
where you can sandboard down a 30m slope
and skim over the water. Boats leave on the
hour. Bookings essential.

Jim Taranaki's
Bone Carving Studio BONE CARVING
(☑09-405 8061; hokiangabonecarvingstudio@
gmail.com; 15 Akiha St, Omapere; $60) Create
your own Maori-inspired bone carving in a
studio with ocean views.

Arai te Uru Heritage Walk WALKING
Starting at the car park at the end of Signal
Station Rd, this short walk (30 minutes return) follows the cliffs and passes through a
tall stand of manuka before opening out to
the grassy southern headland of the Hokianga and the remains of an old signal station.
Built to assist ships making the treacherous
passage through the harbour mouth, the station was closed in 1951 due to the decline in
shipping in the harbour.

Six Foot Track TRAMPING
The Six Foot Track at the end of Mountain
Rd gives access to many Waima Forest
walks.

👉 Tours

Footprints Waipoua CULTURAL TOUR
(☑09-405 8207; www.footprintswaipoua.co.nz;
adult/child $95/35) 🍃 Led by Maori guides,
this four-hour twilight tour into Waipoua
Forest is a fantastic introduction to both the
culture and the forest giants. Tribal history
and stories are shared, and mesmerising
karakia (prayer, incantation) recited before
the gargantuan trees.

Sandtrails Hokianga DUNE BUGGY
(☑09-409 5035; www.sandtrailshokianga.co.nz)
Jump off the Hokianga Express (p158) boat
and into a dune buggy for a sandy ride to
Mitimiti ($185, three hours), or a 70-minute
Sandsecrets tour ($95).

🛏 Sleeping & Eating

Each of these neighbouring villages has its
own grocery store and takeaway, and there
is a good bistro and bar at the Opononi
Hotel.

GlobeTrekkers Lodge HOSTEL $
(☑09-405 8183; www.globetrekkerslodge.com;
SH12, Omapere; dm/s/d $29/53/67; @) Unwind
in casual style at this home-style hostel with
harbour views and bright dorms. Private
rooms have plenty of thoughtful touches,
such as writing desks, mirrors, art and fluffy
towels. There's a stereo but no TV, encouraging plenty of schmoozing in the grapevine-
draped BBQ area.

Hokianga Haven B&B $$
(☑09-405 8285; www.hokiangahaven.co.nz;
226 SH12, Omapere; r $140-200) This modern
house with original Kiwi art on the walls
offers spacious accommodation on the har-
bour's edge and glorious views of the sand

dunes. Alternative healing therapies can be arranged.

Copthorne Hotel & Resort HOTEL **$$**
(☎09-405 8737; www.milleniumhotels.co.nz; 336 SH12, Omapere; r $140-200; ☎☒) ☞ Despite the original grand Victorian villa having been violated by aluminium joinery, this waterside complex remains an attractive spot for a summer's drink or bistro meal ($19 to $36). The more expensive rooms in the newer accommodation block have terraces and water views.

Opononi Hotel HOTEL **$$**
(☎09-405 8858; www.oponohotel.com; 19 SH12; r $110-130) The rooms at the old Opononi pub aren't huge but the white-paint and blond-wood makeover has left them quietly stylish. Try to grab one of the front two – they're a bit bigger and have the best views. Otherwise aim for those facing away from the pub for a quieter stay.

Kokohuia Lodge B&B **$$$**
(☎021 779 927; www.kokohuialodge.co.nz; d incl breakfast $295; ☎) ☞ Luxury and sustainable and ecofriendly practices combine at this new B&B, nestled in regenerating native bush high above the silvery dune-fringed expanse of the Hokianga harbour. Solar energy and organic and free-range produce all feature, but there's no trade-off for luxury in the modern and stylish accommodation.

ⓘ Information

Opononi i-SITE (☎09-405 8869; 29 SH12; ☺8.30am-5pm) Includes the Hokianga Art Gallery.

ⓘ Getting There & Away

There's no regular public transport to these parts, so you'll need to rent a car from Kerikeri or Paihia for independent exploration. Another option is a Discover Hokianga day trip (adult/child $112/56) from Paihia with Fullers (p135), taking in Opononi, Omapere and the Waiere Boulders.

Waiotemarama & Waimamaku

These neighbouring villages, nestled between the Hokianga Harbour and the Waipoua Forest, are the first of many tiny rural communities scattered along this underpopulated stretch of SH12.

🏃 Activities

Labyrinth Woodworks MAZE
(www.nzanity.co.nz; 647 Waiotemarama Gorge Rd; maze $4; ☺9am-5pm) Crack the code in the outdoor maze by collecting letters to form a word. The puzzle museum and lots of retro board games are also interesting. Nearby walks lead to a waterfall and magnificent kauri trees.

🍴 Eating

Morrell's Cafe CAFE **$$**
(7235 SH12, Waimamaku; mains $10-24; ☺9am-4pm) This cafe and craft shop occupies a former cheese factory. It's the last good eatery before Baylys Beach, so drop in for coffee or an eggy breakfast.

KAURI COAST

Apart from the odd bluff and river, this coast is basically unbroken and undeveloped for the 110km between the Hokianga and Kaipara Harbours. The main reason for coming here is to marvel at the kauri forests, one of the great natural highlights of NZ. You'd need 8m arms to get them around some of the big boys here.

There are few stores or eateries and no ATMs north of Dargaville, so stock up beforehand. Trampers should check DOC's website for walks in the area (www.doc.govt.nz).

For visitor information see www.kauri-coast.com.

Waipoua Forest

The highlight of Northland's west coast, this superb forest sanctuary – proclaimed in 1952 after much public pressure – is the largest remnant of the once-extensive kauri forests of northern NZ. The forest road (SH12) stretches for 18km and passes some huge trees – a kauri can reach 60m in height and have a trunk more than 5m in diameter.

Control of the forest has been returned to Te Roroa, the local *iwi* (tribe), as part of a settlement for Crown breaches of the Treaty of Waitangi. Te Roroa runs the **Waipoua Forest visitor centre** (☎09-439 6445; www.waipouakauriforest.co.nz; 1 Waipoua River Rd; ☺9am-6.30pm summer, to 4pm winter), near the south end of the park.

Another option to visit the forest is on a twilight tour, departing from Omapere with Footprints Waipoua (p158).

◉ Sights & Activities

Tane Mahuta   TREE
Near the north end of the park, not far from the road, stands mighty Tane Mahuta, named for the Maori forest god. At 51.5m, with a 13.8m girth and wood mass of 244.5 cu metres, he's the largest kauri alive, and has been holding court here for somewhere between 1200 and 2000 years.

Te Matua Ngahere, Four Sisters & Yakas   TREE
From the Kauri Walks car park, a 20-minute (each way) walk leads past the Four Sisters, a graceful stand of four tall trees fused together at the base, to Te Matua Ngahere (the Father of the Forest). At 30m, he's shorter than Tane Mahuta, but still has a significant presence. Reinforced by a substantial girth – he's the fattest living kauri (16.4m) – the tree presides over a clearing surrounded by mature trees resembling mere matchsticks in comparison.

A 30-minute (one way) path leads from near the Four Sisters to Yakas, the seventh-largest kauri.

Lookout   LOOKOUT
For a bird's-eye view over the canopy, head to the forest lookout, near the very south end of the park. You can either drive to it (the road is well signposted but not suitable for campervans) or take the 2.5km Lookout Track from the visitor centre.

Waipoua Visitor Centre   ARTS & CRAFTS
(www.waipouakauriforest.co.nz; 1 Waipoua River Rd; ◷ 9am-6.30pm summer, to 4pm winter) Interesting exhibition on the kauri forests, guided tours ($25), flax-weaving lessons ($5) and a good cafe. You can also plant your own kauri tree – complete with GPS coordinates – for $180.

⌂ Sleeping & Eating

Waipoua Forest Campground   CAMPSITE $
(☑ 09-439 6445; www.waipouakauriforest.co.nz; 1 Waipoua River Rd; site/unit/house from $15/20/175) Situated next to the Waipoua River and the visitor centre, this peaceful camping ground offers hot showers, flush toilets and a kitchen. The cabins are extremely spartan, with unmade squab beds

(bring your own linen or hire it). There are also whole houses for rent, sleeping 10.

Waipoua Lodge   B&B $$$
(☑ 09-439 0422; www.waipoualodge.co.nz; SH12; r $585) This fine old villa at the southern edge of the forest has four luxurious, spacious suites, which were originally the stables, the woolshed and the calf-rearing pen. Decadent dinners ($75) are available.

Trounson Kauri Park

The 450-hectare Trounson Kauri Park has an easy half-hour loop walk that leads from the picnic area by the road. It passes through beautiful forest with streams, some fine kauri stands, a couple of fallen trees and another Four Sisters – two pairs of trees with conjoined trunks. DOC operates a campsite (www.doc.govt.nz; sites per adult/child $10/5) at the edge of the park with a communal kitchen and hot showers.

Just 2km from SH12, Kauri Coast Top 10 Holiday Park (☑ 09-439 0621; www.kauricoasttop10.co.nz; Trounson Park Rd; site/unit from $42/95; @) ⌀ is an attractive riverside camping ground with good facilities and a small shop. It also organises night-time nature walks (adult/child $25/15), which explain the flora and nocturnal wildlife that thrives here. This is a rare chance to see a kiwi in the wild. Trounson has a predator-eradication program and has become a mainland refuge for threatened native bird species, so you should at least hear a morepork (a native owl) or a brown kiwi.

If you're approaching from the north, it's easier to take the second turn-off to the park, near Kaihu, which avoids a rough unsealed road.

Kai Iwi Lakes

These three trout-filled freshwater lakes nestle together near the coast, 12km off SH12. The largest, Taharoa, has blue water fringed with sandy patches. Lake Waikere is popular with water-skiers, while Lake Kai Iwi is relatively untouched. A half-hour walk leads from the lakes to the coast and it's another two hours to reach the base of volcanic Maunganui Bluff (460m); the hike up and down it takes five hours.

Camping (☑ 09-439 0986; lakes@kaipara.govt.nz; adult/child $10/5) is permitted at the side of Lake Taharoa; cold showers, drinking water and flush toilets are provided.

Baylys Beach

A village of brightly coloured baches and a few new holiday mansions, Baylys Beach is 12km from Dargaville, off SH12. It lies on 100km-long Ripiro Ocean Beach, a surf-pounded stretch of coast that has been the site of many shipwrecks. The beach is a gazetted highway: you can drive along its hard sand at low tide, although it is primarily for 4WDs. Despite being NZ's longest drivable beach, it's less well known and hence less travelled than Ninety Mile Beach. Ask locals about conditions and check your hire-car agreement before venturing onto the sand. Quad bikes (single/double $75/95) can be hired at the holiday park. Ask there also about an equine outing with **Baylys Beach Horse Treks** (☑ 0800 229 597; www.baylysbeachhorsetreks.webs.com; 24 Seaview Rd; 1/2/3 hours $50/70/90; ⊘ late Oct-Easter).

🛏 Sleeping

Baylys Beach Holiday Park   HOLIDAY PARK $
(☑ 09-439 6349; www.baylysbeach.co.nz; 24 Seaview Rd; site/unit from $16/65; @ ☎) Circled by pohutukawa trees, this midsized camping ground has tidy facilities and attractive cream and green units, some with funky Kiwiana decor. Options range from basic cabins to a cottage sleeping six.

Sunset View Lodge   B&B $$
(☑ 09-439 4342; www.sunsetviewlodge.co.nz; 7 Alcemene Lane; r $175-190; @ ☎) If gin-in-hand sunset-gazing is your thing, this large, modern B&B fits the bill. The upstairs rooms have terrific sea views and there's a self-service bar with an honesty box in the guest lounge.

🍴 Eating

Funky Fish   CAFE, BAR $$
(☑ 09-439 8883; www.thefunkyfish.co.nz; 34 Seaview Rd; lunch $14-22, dinner $22-32; ⊘ 11am-late Tue-Sun, reduced hours in winter) Brightly decorated with murals and mosaics, this highly popular cafe, restaurant and bar has a wonderful back garden and a wide-ranging menu, including lots of seafood. Bookings are advisable in summer. Check its Facebook page for occasional live music.

Dargaville

POP 4500

When a town proclaims itself the 'kumara capital of NZ' (it produces two-thirds of the country's sweet potatoes), you should know not to expect too much. Founded in 1872 by timber merchant Joseph Dargaville, this once-important river port thrived on the export of kauri timber and gum. As the forests were decimated, it declined, and today is a quiet backwater servicing the agricultural Northern Wairoa area.

◉ Sights & Activities

Dargaville Museum   MUSEUM
(www.dargavillemuseum.co.nz; adult/child $15/2; ⊘ 9am-4pm) The hilltop Dargaville Museum is more interesting than most regional museums. There's a large gumdigging display, plus maritime, Maori and musical-instrument sections and a neat model railway. Outside, the masts of the *Rainbow Warrior* are mounted at a lookout near a *pa* site, and there's a re-creation of a gumdiggers' camp.

Kumara Box   FARM
(☑ 09-439 7018; www.kumarabox.co.nz; 503 Pouto Rd; tours $20) To learn all about kumara, book ahead for Kumara Ernie's show. It's surprisingly entertaining, usually involving a journey by home-built tractor-train through the fields to 'NZ's smallest church'.

🛏 Sleeping & Eating

Campervans can stay at the Dargaville Museum car park for $15 per night.

Greenhouse Backpackers   HOSTEL $
(☑ 09-439 6342; greenhousebackpackers@ihug.co.nz; 15 Gordon St; dm/s/d $28/45/70; @ ☎) This converted 1921 schoolhouse has classrooms partitioned into a large dorm and a communal lounge, both painted with colourful murals. Better still are the cosy units in the back garden.

The Hangi Hut   MAORI $
(☑ 09-439 4264; www.facebook.com/thehangihut; 1 Murdoch St; hangi $12; ⊘ 11am-6pm Tue-Sat) Opposite the information centre, The Hangi Hut does heaped plates of meat and vegies – including, of course, local kumara. Choose from lamb, pork or chicken, all served with delicious stuffing, and steamed slowly on hot volcanic rocks. Raw fish and

coconut ($5) and traditional Maori *paraoa parae* (fried bread, 50c) are also available.

Riverside Produce Market   MARKET $
(Kapia St; ☉2.30-5.30pm Thu) Local produce and crafts.

Blah, Blah, Blah...   CAFE, BAR $$
(101 Victoria St; breakfast $12-25, lunch $13-18, dinner $22-34; ☉9am-late Tue-Sat, to 4pm Sun-Mon) The number-one eatery in Dargaville has a garden area, hip music, deli-style snacks, a global menu including *dukkah*, pizza and steak, and beer, wine and cocktails.

ⓘ Information

DOC Kauri Coast Area Office (☏09-439 3450; www.doc.govt.nz; 150 Colville Rd; ☉8am-4.30pm Mon-Fri)

Visitor Information Centre (☏09-439 4975; www.kauriinfocentre.co.nz; 4 Murdoch St; ☉9am-5.30pm; ☎) Operates out of the Woodturners Kauri Gallery & Studio. Books accommodation and tours.

ⓘ Getting There & Away

Weekday shuttle buses run by West Coaster (p124) link Dargaville with Whangarei.

Pouto Point

A narrow spit descends south of Dargaville, bordered by the Tasman Sea and Wairoa River, and comes to an abrupt halt at the entrance of NZ's biggest harbour, the Kaipara. It's an incredibly remote headland, punctuated by dozens of petite dune lakes and the lonely Kaipara Lighthouse (built from kauri in 1884). Less than 10km separates Kaipara Harbour's north and south heads, but if you were to drive between the two you'd cover 267km.

A 4WD can be put to its proper use on the ocean-hugging 71km stretch of beach from Dargaville. DOC's *Pouto Hidden Treasures* is a helpful guide for motorists, with tips for protecting both your car and the fragile ecosystem. It can be downloaded at www.doc.govt.nz.

To explore the huge expanse of sand dunes on an organised tour, contact Jock at **Poutu Sand Safaris** (☏09-439 6678; www.poutu.co.nz; per person from $35).

Matakohe

POP 400

Apart from the rural charms of this village, the key reason for visiting is the superb **Kauri Museum** (www.kaurimuseum.com; 5 Church Rd; adult/child $25/8; ☉9am-5pm). The giant cross sections of trees are astounding, but the entire industry is brought to life through video kiosks, artefacts, fabulous furniture and marquetry, and reproductions of a pioneer sawmill, boarding house, gumdigger's hut and Victorian home. The Gum Room holds a weird and wonderful collection of kauri gum, the amber substance that can be carved, sculpted and polished to a jewel-like quality. The museum shop stocks mementoes crafted from kauri wood and gum.

Facing the museum is the tiny kauri-built **Matakohe Pioneer Church** (1867), which served both Methodists and Anglicans, and acted as the community's hall and school. Nearby, you can wander through a historic **school house** (1878) and **post office/telephone exchange** (1909).

🛏 Sleeping & Eating

Matakohe Holiday Park   HOLIDAY PARK $
(☏09-431 6431; www.matakoheholidaypark.co.nz; 66 Church Rd; site/unit from $38/65; @☎🐾) This little park has modern amenities, plenty of space and good views of Kaipara Harbour.

Petite Provence   B&B $$
(☏09-431 7552; www.petiteprovence.co.nz; 703c Tinopai Rd; s/d $120/160) 🌿 This attractive, French-influenced B&B is a popular weekender for Aucklanders, so it pays to book ahead. Excellent dinners can be arranged for $45 per person.

Matakohe House   B&B $$
(☏09-431 7091; www.matakohehouse.co.nz; 24 Church Rd; d $160; @☎) This B&B occupies a pretty villa with a cafe attached. The simply furnished rooms open out onto a verandah and offer winning touches like complimentary port and chocolates.

ⓘ Getting There & Away

No scheduled buses run to Matakohe, but return day trips from Auckland to the Kauri Museum are $149. See www.kauri-museum.com for tour bookings.

Waikato & Coromandel Peninsula

Includes ➡

Waikato......................165
Hamilton....................167
Raglan.......................173
Cambridge.................179
Matamata..................180
Te Aroha.....................181
Waitomo Caves..........185
Thames.....................194
Coromandel Town......197
Whitianga 202
Hahei 205
Waihi & Around..........209

Best Beaches & Outdoors

➡ New Chum's Beach (p201)

➡ Cathedral Cove (p205)

➡ Otama Beach (p201)

➡ Surfing at Manu Bay (p176)

➡ Black-water rafting at Waitomo Caves (p185)

Best Places to Stay

➡ Wairua Lodge (p202)

➡ Driving Creek Villas (p199)

➡ Purangi Garden Accommodation (p206)

➡ Solscape (p176)

Why Go?

Verdant rolling hills line New Zealand's mighty Waikato River, and adrenaline junkies can surf at Raglan, or undertake extreme underground pursuits in the extraordinary Waitomo Caves.

But this is also Tainui country. In the 1850s this powerful Maori tribal coalition elected a king to resist the loss of land and sovereignty. The fertile Waikato was forcibly taken from them, but they retained control of the rugged King Country to within a whisper of the 20th century.

To the northeast, the Coromandel Peninsula juts into the Pacific, forming the Hauraki Gulf's eastern boundary. The peninsula's east coast has some of the North Island's best white-sand beaches, and the muddy wetlands and picturesque stony bays of the west coast have long been a refuge for alternative lifestylers. Down the middle, the mountains are criss-crossed with walking tracks, allowing trampers to explore large tracts of isolated bush studded with kauri trees.

When to Go

➡ Beachy accommodation in Waihi, Whitianga, Whangamata and Raglan peaks across the summer holidays from Christmas until the end of January. New Year's Eve in particular can be very busy.

➡ Balmy February and March are much quieter around the Coromandel Peninsula with settled weather and smaller crowds. Rainfall peaks in the mountainous Coromandel region from May to September.

➡ The Waikato region can see summer droughts, but the southern area around Taumarunui is often wetter and colder.

➡ If you avoid the height of summer school holidays (Christmas to January), accommodation is plentiful in the Waikato region.

➡ Raglan's surf breaks are popular year-round.

Waikato & Coromandel Peninsula Highlights

1 Travelling remote gravel roads under a crimson canopy of ancient pohutukawa trees in **Far North Coromandel** (p200)

2 Kayaking around the hidden islands, caves and bays of **Te Whanganui-A-Hei Marine Reserve** (p206)

3 Pigging out on smoked mussels in **Coromandel Town** (p197)

4 Penetrating the mystical depths of the dense bush of **Coromandel Forest Park** (p198) and **Karangahake Gorge** (p211)

5 Watching the offshore islands glow in the dying haze of a summer sunset from **Hahei Beach** (p205)

6 Seeking subterranean stimulation in the **Waitomo Caves** (p185) – this is your chance to try blackwater rafting

7 Hitting the surf (and then the pub) in unhurried **Raglan** (p173)

8 Tramping through an inland island paradise at **Sanctuary Mountain Maungatautari** (p178)

ℹ️ Getting There & Around

Hamilton is the region's transport hub, with its airport servicing extensive domestic routes. Buses link the city to everywhere in the North Island. Most inland towns are also well connected on bus routes, but the remote coastal communities (apart from Mokau on SH3) are less well served. See p172 for more information on transport options to Hamilton.

Options on the Coromandel Peninsula are more limited, and the beaches and coastline of the area are most rewarding with independent transport.

AIR

Sunair (☑0800 786 247; www.sunair.co.nz) Regional North Island airline linking Auckland, Whitianga, Hamilton, Gisborne, Napier, Tauranga, Great Barrier Island and New Plymouth.

BOAT

360 Discovery (☑0800 360 3472; www.360discovery.co.nz) Operates ferries to/from Auckland (one-way/return $57/92, two hours) via Orapiu on Waiheke Island (one-way/return $37/62, 70 minutes), five times per week (daily in summer). The boats dock at Hannafords Wharf, Te Kouma, where free buses shuttle passengers the 10km into Coromandel Town. It makes a great day trip from Auckland (same-day return $69), and there's a day-tour option that includes a hop-on, hop-off bus (adult/child $94).

BUS

Go Kiwi (☑07-866 0336; www.go-kiwi.co.nz) Has daily Auckland City–International Airport–Thames–Tairua–Whitianga shuttles year-round, with a connection to Opoutere and Whangamata. From mid-December to Easter it also runs Rotorua–Tauranga–Waihi–Whangamata–Whitianga and Coromandel Town–Whitianga shuttles.

InterCity (www.intercity.co.nz) Has two routes to/from the Coromandel peninsula: Auckland–Thames–Paeroa–Waihi–Tauranga and Hamilton–Te Aroha–Paeroa–Thames–Coromandel Town. Local routes include Thames–Coromandel Town–Whitianga and Whitianga–Tairua–Thames.

Naked Bus (www.nakedbus.com) Buses on the Auckland–Tauranga–Mt Maunganui–Rotorua–Gisborne route stop at Ngatea, where local associate Tairua Bus Company continues on to Whitianga.

Tairua Bus Company (TBC; ☑07-808 0748; www.tairuabus.co.nz) Local buses on the Thames–Tairua–Hahei–Whitianga–Coromandel Town route and a Hamilton–Cambridge–Te Aroha–Thames–Tairua service.

CAR

Car is the only option for accessing some of the more remote areas, but be careful to check hire agreements as there are plenty of gravel roads and a few streams to ford. Most of them are in good condition and even a small car can cope unless the weather's been particularly wet.

WAIKATO

History

By the time Europeans started to arrive, this region – stretching as far north as Auckland's Manukau Harbour – had long been the homeland of the Waikato tribes, descended from the Tainui migration. In settling this land, the Waikato tribes displaced or absorbed tribes from earlier migrations.

Initially European contact was on Maori terms and to the advantage of the local people. Their fertile land, which was already cultivated with kumara and other crops, was well suited to the introduction of new fruits and vegetables. By the 1840s the Waikato economy was booming, with bulk quantities

---

ESSENTIAL WAIKATO & COROMANDEL PENINSULA

Eat Coromandel bivalves – mussels, oysters and scallops are local specialities

Drink Local craft beer from Hamilton's Good George (p171)

Read *The Penguin History of New Zealand* (2003) by the late Michael King, an Opoutere resident

Listen to The Waikato-influenced sounds of Kimbra, the Topp Twins and the Datsuns

Watch The birds at Miranda the Firth of Thames

Festival The Coromandel Peninsula–wide Pohutukawa Festival (www.pohutukawafestival.co.nz)

Go green Off-the-grid tepees at Solscape (p176)

Online www.thecoromandel.com, www.hamiltonwaikato.com, www.kingcountry.co.nz

Area code ☑07

Waikato & King Country

of produce exported to the settlers in Auckland and beyond.

Relations between the two cultures soured during the 1850s, largely due to the colonists' pressure to purchase Maori land. In response, a confederation of tribes united to elect a king to safeguard their interests, forming what became known as the Kingitanga (King Movement).

In July 1863 Governor Grey sent a huge force to invade the Waikato and exert colonial control. After almost a year of fighting, known as the Waikato War, the Kingites retreated south to what became branded the King Country.

The war resulted in the confiscation of 3600 sq km of land, much of which was given to colonial soldiers to farm and defend. In 1995 the Waikato tribes received a full Crown apology for the wrongful invasion and confiscation of their lands, as well as a $170 million package, including the return of land that the Crown still held.

Rangiriri

Following SH1 south from Auckland you're retracing the route of the colonial army in the spectacular land grab that was the

Waikato War. On 20 November 1863, around 1500 British troops backed by gunboats and artillery, attacked the substantial fortifications erected by the Maori king's warriors at Rangiriri. They were repulsed a number of times and lost 49 men, but overnight many of the 500 Maori defenders retreated; the remaining 183 were taken prisoner the next day after the British gained entry to the *pa* (fortified village) by conveniently misunderstanding a flag of truce.

The Rangiriri Heritage Centre (☑07-826 3663; www.nzmuseums.co.nz; 12 Rangiriri Rd; admission $3, film $5; ◷8am-4pm) screens a short documentary about the battle, and across the road the Maori War & Early Settlers Cemetery (Rangiriri Rd; ◷24hr) FREE houses the soldiers' graves and a mound covering the mass grave of 36 Maori warriors.

Next to the heritage centre is the historic Rangiriri Hotel (☑07-826 3467; 8 Talbot St; lunch mains $11-20, dinner $17-30; ◷11am-11pm), a cheery spot for lunch or a beer.

Ngaruawahia & Around

POP 4940

The headquarters of the Maori King movement, Ngaruawahia is 19km north of Hamilton on SH1. The impressive fences of Turangawaewae Marae (☑07-824 5189; 29 River Rd) maintain the privacy of this important place, but twice a year visitors are welcomed. Regatta Day is held in mid-March, with *waka* (canoe) races and all manner of Maori cultural activities. For a week from 15 August the *marae* (meeting house) is open to celebrate Koroniehana, the anniversary of the coronation of the current king, Tuheitia.

Hamilton

POP 206,400

Landlocked cities in an island nation are never going to have the glamorous appeal of their coastal cousins. Rotorua compensates with boiling mud and Taupo has its lake, but Hamilton, despite the majestic Waikato River, is more prosaic.

However, the city definitely has appeal. The main street has vibrant bars around Hood St and Victoria St, and excellent restaurants and cafes mean you're guaranteed to eat really well in the city after visiting highlights like the Hamilton Gardens.

Oddly, the great grey-green greasy Waikato River rolls right through town, but the city's layout largely ignores its presence: unless you're driving across a bridge you'll hardly know it's there.

◉ Sights

★Hamilton Gardens　　　　　　　GARDENS
(www.hamiltongardens.co.nz; Cobham Dr; ◷enclosed sector 7.30am-5pm, info centre 9am-5pm) FREE Hamilton Gardens, spread over 50

MAORI NZ: WAIKATO & COROMANDEL PENINSULA

The Waikato and King Country region remains one of the strongest pockets of Maori influence in NZ. This is the heartland of the Tainui tribes, descended from those who disembarked from the *Tainui waka* (canoe) in Kawhia in the 14th century. Split into four main tribal divisions (Waikato, Hauraki, Ngati Maniapoto and Ngati Raukawa), Tainui are inextricably linked with the Kingitanga (King Movement), which has its base in Ngaruawahia.

The best opportunities to interact with Maori culture are the Kawhia Kai Festival (p183), and Ngaruawahia's Regatta Day and Koroneihana celebrations (p167). Interesting *taonga* (treasures) are displayed at museums in Hamilton and Te Awamutu.

Reminders of the Waikato Land War can be found at Rangiriri, Rangiaowhia and Orakau. See www.waikatowar.co.nz to download maps, audio files and and a smartphone app covering various locations of the fighting from 1863 to 1864.

Dozens of *marae* (meeting-house) complexes are dotted around the countryside – including at Awakino, and at Kawhia, where the *Tainui waka* is buried. You won't be able to visit these without permission but you can get decent views from the gates. Some regional tours include an element of Maori culture, including Ruakuri Cave (p186) and Kawhia Harbour Cruises (p183).

Although it has a long and rich Maori history, the nearby Coromandel Peninsula doesn't offer many opportunities to engage with the culture. Historic *pa* (fortified village) sites are dotted around, with the most accessible being Paaku (p207). There are others at Opito Beach, Hahei and Hot Water Beach.

Hamilton

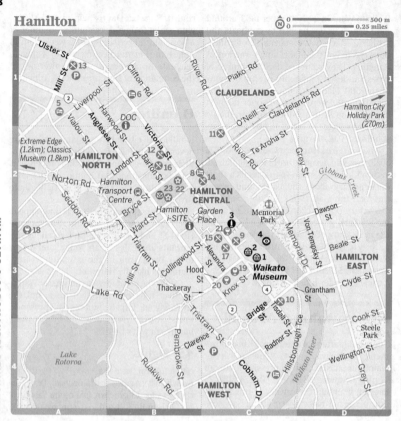

Hamilton

◎ Top Sights
1 Waikato Museum C3

◎ Sights
2 ArtsPost C3
3 Riff Raff C3
4 Waikato River C3

🛏 Sleeping
5 Anglesea Motel A1
6 Backpackers Central B1
7 City Centre B&B C4
8 Ibis Hotel B2

⊗ Eating
9 Banh Mi Caphe C3
10 Chim Choo Ree C3

11 Hamilton Farmers Market C2
12 Hazel Hayes B2
13 Pak 'n Save A1
14 Palate C2
15 River Kitchen C3
16 Rocket Coffee B2
17 Scott's Epicurean C3

◎ Drinking & Nightlife
18 Good George A3
19 Gothenburg C3
20 House on Hood C3
21 Wonderhorse C3

◎ Entertainment
22 Lido Cinema B2
23 Metro by Hoyts B2

hectares, incorporates a large park, cafe, restaurant and extravagant themed enclosed gardens. There are separate Italian Renaissance, Chinese, Japanese, English, American and Indian gardens complete with colonnades, pagodas and a mini Taj Mahal. Equally interesting are the sustainable Productive Garden Collection, a fragrant herb garden and the precolonisation Maori Te Parapara garden. Look for the impressive *Nga Uri O Hinetuparimaunga* (Earth Blanket) sculpture at the main gates. The gardens are southeast of Hamilton city centre.

★ Waikato Museum   MUSEUM
(www.waikatomuseum.co.nz; 1 Grantham St; free-$6.50; ⊘10am-4.30pm) The excellent Waikato Museum has five main areas: an art gallery; interactive science galleries; Tainui galleries housing Maori treasures, including the magnificently carved *waka taua* (war canoe), *Te Winikawaka*; a Hamilton history exhibition entitled 'Never a Dull Moment'; and a Waikato River exhibition. The museum also runs a rigorous program of public events. Admission is charged for some exhibits.

Waikato River   RIVER, PARK
Bush-covered riverside walkways run along both sides of the river and provide the city's green belt. Jogging paths continue to the boardwalk circling Lake Rotoroa, west of the centre. Memorial Park is closer to town, and has the remains of *PS Rangiriri* – an iron-clad, steam-powered gunboat from the Waikato War – embedded in the riverbank.

Riff Raff   MONUMENT
(www.riffraffstatue.org; Victoria St; 🛜) One of Hamilton's more unusual public artworks is a life-size statue of *Rocky Horror Picture Show* writer Richard O'Brien, aka Riff Raff, the time-warping alien from the planet Transsexual. It looks over a small park on the site of the former Embassy Theatre where O'Brien worked as a hairdresser, though it's hard to imagine 1960s Hamilton inspired the tale of bisexual alien decadence. Free wi-fi emanates from Riff Raff's three-pronged stun gun.

ArtsPost   GALLERY
(www.artspost.co.nz; 120 Victoria St; ⊘10am-4.30pm) FREE This contemporary gallery and gift shop is housed in a grand former post office. It focuses on the best of local art: paintings, glass, prints, textiles and photography.

Hamilton Zoo   ZOO
(☏07-838 6720; www.hamiltonzoo.co.nz; 183 Brymer Rd; adult/child/family $19/9/56; tours extra; ⊘9am-5pm, last entry 3.30pm) Hamilton Zoo houses 500-plus species including wily and curious chimpanzees. Guided-tour options include Eye2Eye and Face2Face opportunities to go behind the scenes to meet various animals, plus daily 'Meet the Keeper'

talks from the critters' caregivers. The zoo is 8km northwest of Hamilton city centre.

Classics Museum   MUSEUM
(www.classicsmuseum.co.nz; 11 Railside Pl, Frankton; adult/child $20/8; ⊘9am-4pm) Travel in time amid this collection of over 100 classic cars from the first half of the 20th century. Even if you're not a motorhead, you'll still be dazzled by the crazy Amphicar and the cool Maserati and Corvette sports cars. The museum is just off SH1 northwest of central Hamilton.

🏃 Activities

Extreme Edge   ROCK CLIMBING
(☏07-847 5858; www.extremeedge.co.nz; 90 Greenwood St; day pass incl harness adult/child $18.50/14; ⊘noon-9.30pm Mon-Fri, 9am-7pm Sat & Sun) Near the Frankton train station, with hyper-coloured climbing walls, 14m of which is overhanging. There's a kids' climbing zone, and free safety lessons.

Waikato River Explorer   CRUISE
(☏0800 139 756; www.waikatoexplorer.co.nz; Hamilton Gardens jetty; adult/child $26/13; ⊘Thu-Sun) Scenic 90-minute cruises along the Waikato River depart from the Hamilton Gardens jetty. On Sunday afternoons, three-hour wine-tasting cruises (adult/child $55/24) operate.

Kiwi Balloon Company   BALLOONING
(☏021 912 679, 07-843 8538; www.kiwiballooncompany.co.nz; per person $350) Floating above lush Waikato countryside, the whole experience takes about four hours and includes a champagne breakfast and an hour's flying time.

🎉 Festivals & Events

Hamilton Gardens Arts Festival   PERFORMING ARTS
(www.hamiltongardensartsfestival.co.nz; Hamilton Gardens) Music, comedy, theatre, dance and movies, all served up alfresco in the Hamilton Gardens during the last two weeks of February.

Balloons Over Waikato   SPORTS
(www.balloonsoverwaikato.co.nz) A colourful hot-air-balloon fest held in March.

🛏 Sleeping

The road into town from Auckland (Ulster St) is lined with dozens of unremarkable, traffic-noisy motels: passable for short stays.

J's Backpackers
HOSTEL $

(☑ 07-856 8934; www.jsbackpackers.co.nz; 8 Grey St; dm/s/d/tr $28/55/66/84; @ 🛜) A homely hostel occupying a characterful house near Hamilton Gardens, friendly J's offers good security, a cosy kitchen, free bikes and bright, tidy rooms. There's a barbecue out the back and a Mongolian yurt lounge-space on the front lawn.

Backpackers Central
HOSTEL $

(☑ 07-839 1928; www.backpackerscentral.co.nz; 846 Victoria St; dm $25, s $50-60, r $75-140; @ 🛜) Well-run hostel with dorms, singles, doubles and family rooms, some with en suite bathrooms and all with access to a shared kitchen and lounge. Worth considering as an alternative to a motel room if you're travelling as a couple or in a group.

Hamilton City Holiday Park
HOLIDAY PARK $

(☑ 07-855 8255; www.hamiltoncityholidaypark. co.nz; 14 Ruakura Rd; campsites/cabins/units from $37/47/75; @ 🛜) Simple cabins and leafy sites are the rule at this shady park. It's reasonably close to town (2km east of the centre) and very affordable.

City Centre B&B
B&B $$

(☑ 07-838 1671; www.citycentrebnb.co.nz; 3 Anglesea St; r $90-165; @ 🛜 🏊) At the quiet riverside end of a central city street (five minutes' walk to the Victoria/Hood St action), this sparkling self-contained apartment opens on to a swimming pool. There's also a bedroom available in a wing of the main house. Self-catering breakfast is provided.

Anglesea Motel
MOTEL $$

(☑ 0800 426 453, 07-834 0010; www.angleseamotel.co.nz; 36 Liverpool St; units $140-300; @ 🛜 🏊) Getting great feedback from travellers and a preferred option to anything on Ulster St's 'motel row', the Anglesea has plenty of space, friendly managers, a pool and squash and tennis courts, and not unstylish decor.

Ibis Hotel
HOTEL $$

(☑ 07-859 9200; www.ibis.com/hamilton; 18 Alma St; r $100-130; 🛜) The rooms are compact, but they're clean and well designed, and the riverfront Ibis is a good option if you're looking for quiet, centrally located digs just a short walk from the best of Hamilton's bars and restaurants. The shared public areas – complete with a restaurant for a good-value breakfast buffet ($20) – are spacious and colourful.

✖ Eating

Rocket Coffee
CAFE $

(www.rocketcoffee.co.nz; 302 Barton St; coffee from $4; ◷ 8am-4pm Mon-Fri) Duck down a lane off Barton St for what some locals reckon is Hamilton's hippest cafe. Rocket Coffee is a warehouselike bean barn, roasting on site and enticing caffeine fiends to the communal table strewn with newspapers. Staff spin old-school vinyl (and take requests) in between playing barista and packaging up sacks of beans for shipment.

Scott's Epicurean
INTERNATIONAL $

(☑ 07-839 6680; www.scottsepicurean.co.nz; 181 Victoria St; mains $11-20; ◷ 7am-3pm Mon-Fri, 8.30am-4pm Sat & Sun) This gorgeous joint features swanky leather banquettes, pressed-tin ceilings, great coffee and an interesting and affordable menu: try the *pytti panna* (Swedish bubble-and-squeak) or the ever-popular *spaghetti aglio e olio*. Friendly service and fully licensed.

Banh Mi Caphe
VIETNAMESE $

(www.facebook.com/banhmicaphe; 198/2 Victoria St; snacks & mains $7-14; ◷ 11am-4pm Tue, Wed, Sat & Sun, to late Thu & Fri) Fresh spring rolls, Vietnamese *banh mi* sandwiches and steaming bowls of *pho* (noodle soup) all feature at this hip spot channelling the backstreets of Hanoi. In the immediate vicinity there are plenty more tasty opportunities for ethnic dining, with Indian, Thai, Chinese, Mexican and Japanese restaurants also lining Victoria St and nearby Hood St.

Hamilton Farmers Market
MARKET $

(www.waikatofarmersmarkets.co.nz; River Rd Carpark, 204 River Rd; ◷ 8am-noon Sun) Take a stroll across the Claudelands Rd bridge to this farmers market with local cheeses, baked goods and produce. A coffee from the Rocket caravan and a flash hot dog from Bangin Bangaz is our recommended breakfast combo.

Pak 'n Save
SUPERMARKET $

(Mill St; ◷ 7am-10pm) North of downtown Hamilton.

Hazel Hayes
CAFE $$

(www.hazelhayes.co.nz; 587 Victoria St; mains $10-20; ◷ 7am-4pm Mon-Fri, 8am-3pm Sat) This mash-up of country-kitchen decor showcases inventive cafe fare. Free range this and organic that punctuate the short, focused menu, and both the service and coffee are very good. A concise wine and beer list also focuses on quality fare, and next door the Hazel's Counter deli is also worth visiting.

River Kitchen
CAFE $$

(www.theriverkitchen.co.nz; 237 Victoria St; mains $10-18; ⊙ 7am-4pm Mon-Fri, 8am-4pm Sat & Sun; ♪) River Kitchen does things with simple style: cakes, gourmet breakfasts and fresh seasonal lunches (angle for the salmon hash), and a barista who knows his beans. It's the kind of place you visit for breakfast, come back to for lunch, then consider for breakfast the next day.

★ Chim Choo Ree
MODERN NZ $$$

(☏ 07-839 4329; www.chimchooree.co.nz; 14 Bridge St; mains $30-34; ⊙ 11.30am-2pm & 5pm-late Mon-Sat) In an airy heritage building beside the river, Chim Choo Ree focuses on shared plates like tuna tartare, smoked potato ravioli and Sichuan pork belly, and larger, equally inventive mains using duck, lamb, venison and snapper. Local foodies wash it all down with a great wine list and flavourful New Zealand craft beers.

Palate
MODERN NZ, FUSION $$$

(☏ 07-834 2921; www.palaterestaurant.co.nz; 20 Alma St; mains $34-38; ⊙ 11.30am-2pm Wed-Fri, 5.30pm-late Mon-Sat) Simple, sophisticated Palate has a well-deserved reputation for lifting the culinary bar across regional NZ. The innovative menu features highlights like red roasted duck with yams, scallops, shiitake and a chilli broth. The wine selection is Hamilton's finest.

🍷 Drinking & Nightlife

The blocks around Victoria and Hood Sts make for a boozy bar-hop, with weekend live music and DJs. Friday is the big night of the week.

Wonderhorse
COCKTAIL BAR

(www.facebook.com/wonderhorsebar; 232 Victoria St; ⊙ 5pm-3am Wed-Sat) Look for the subtle spraypainted Wonderhorse logo on the footpath and follow the white arrow to this cool cocktail bar that also regularly features craft beers from tiny local brewers like Shunters Yard, Brewaucracy and 666. Vintage vinyl is often spinning on the turntable, and $5 cheeseburger sliders and killer cocktails complete the picture at Hamilton's best bar.

Good George
BREWERY

(☏ 07-847 3223; www.goodgeorge.co.nz; 32a Somerset St, Frankton; tours incl beer & food $15;

TAUPIRI

About 26km north of Hamilton on SH1 is Taupiri (287m), the **sacred mountain** of the Tainui people. You'll recognise it by the cemetery on its slopes and the honking of passing car horns – locals saying hi to their loved ones as they pass by. In August 2006 thousands gathered here as the much-loved Maori queen, Dame Te Atairangikaahu, was transported upriver by *waka* (canoe) to her final resting place, an unmarked grave on the summit.

⊙ 11am-late, tours from 5.30pm Mon-Thu) Channelling a cool industrial vibe, the former Church of St George is now a shrine to craft beer. Order a tasting flight of six beers ($19), and partner the hoppy heaven with wood-fired pizzas ($20 to $23), platters ($12 to $16), and larger main meals ($20 to $34). Our favourites are the zesty White Ale and the zingy Drop Hop cider. Tours must be booked ahead.

Gothenburg
BAR

(www.gothenburg.co.nz; 15 Hood St; ⊙ 10.30am-late) This cosy hybrid of bar and restaurant takes a serious approach to beer and wine, with local craft brewers joined by a very impressive range of Belgian brews. Foodwise the menu steers from tapas to mains – try the Vietnamese-style pork belly or the gin-soaked salmon – and the service is a cut-above other nearby places along sometimes-rambunctious Hood St.

House on Hood
BAR

(www.houseonhood.co.nz; 27 Hood St; ⊙ 11am-late) House on Hood is a 1915 barn with lots of drops to slake your thirst. Beer specials, tasting sessions and meal deals abound, plus Saturday-night bands and Sunday-afternoon DJs.

☆ Entertainment

Lido Cinema
CINEMA

(www.lidocinema.co.nz; Level 1, Centre Place, 501 Victoria St; adult/child $15.50/9.50; ⊙ 10am-late) Art-house movies with $10 Tuesday tickets.

Metro by Hoyts
CINEMA

(www.hoyts.co.nz; Centre Place Shopping Centre, 12 Ward St; adult/child $14/10) Blockbuster flicks with $10 Tuesday tickets.

Information

Anglesea Clinic (☑07-858 0800; www.angleseamedical.co.nz; cnr Anglesea & Thackeray Sts; ⊙24hr) For accidents and urgent medical assistance.

DOC (Department of Conservation; ☑07-858 1000; www.doc.govt.nz; Level 5, 73 Rostrevor St; ⊙8am-4.30pm Mon-Fri)

Hamilton i-SITE (☑0800 242 645, 07-958 5960; www.visithamilton.co.nz; cnr Caro & Alexandra Sts; ⊙9am-5pm Mon-Fri, 9.30am-3.30pm Sat & Sun; ⊛) Accommodation, activities and transport bookings, plus free wi-fi right across Garden Pl.

Waikato Hospital (☑07-839 8899; www.waikatodhb.govt.nz; Pembroke St; ⊙24hr)

Getting There & Away

AIR

Air New Zealand (☑0800 737 000; www.airnewzealand.co.nz) Regular direct flights from Hamilton to Auckland, Christchurch, Palmerston North and Wellington.

Sunair (☑0800 786 247; www.sunair.co.nz) Direct flights to Gisborne, Napier and New Plymouth.

BUS

All buses arrive and depart from the **Hamilton Transport Centre** (☑07-834 3457; www.hamilton.co.nz; cnr Anglesea & Bryce Sts; ⊛).

Waikato Regional Council's **Busit!** (☑0800 4287 5463; www.busit.co.nz) coaches serve the region, including Ngaruawahia ($3.20, 25 minutes), Cambridge ($6.70, 40 minutes), Te Awamutu ($6.70, 50 minutes) and Raglan ($8.50, one hour).

InterCity (☑09-583 5780; www.intercity.co.nz) services numerous destinations including the following:

DESTINATION	PRICE ($)	DURATION	FREQUENCY (DAILY)
Auckland	12-35	2hr	11
Cambridge	10-20	25min	9
Matamata	10-25	50min	4
Ngaruawahia	10-21	20min	9
Rotorua	14-35	1½hr	5
Te Aroha	10	1hr	2
Te Awamutu	10-22	35min	3
Wellington	27-70	5hr	3

Naked Bus (☑0900 625 33; www.nakedbus.com) services run to the following destinations (among many others):

DESTINATION	PRICE ($)	DURATION	FREQUENCY (DAILY)
Auckland	17-19	2hr	5
Cambridge	15	30min	5-7
Matamata	20	1hr	1
Ngaruawahia	15	30min	5
Rotorua	10	1½hr	4-5
Wellington	20-30	9½hr	1-2

SHUTTLE BUSES

Minibus Express (☑0800 646 428, 07-856 3191; www.minibus.co.nz) Shuttles between Hamilton and Auckland airport (one way $75).

Raglan Scenic Tours (☑021 0274 7014, 07-825 0507; www.raglanscenictours.co.nz) Shuttle linking Hamilton with Raglan (one way $35). Auckland airport service also available.

TRAIN

Hamilton is on the **Northern Explorer** (☑0800 872 467; www.kiwiscenic.co.nz) route between Auckland ($48, 2½ hours) and Wellington ($186, 9½ hours) via Otorohanga ($48, 45 minutes). Trains depart Auckland on Monday, Thursday and Saturday and stop at Hamilton's **Frankton train station** (Fraser St), 1km west of the city centre; there are no ticket sales here – see the website for ticketing details.

ⓘ Getting Around

TO/FROM THE AIRPORT

Hamilton International Airport (HIA; ☑07-848 9027; www.hamiltonairport.co.nz; Airport Rd) is 12km south of the city. The **Super Shuttle** (☑0800 748 885, 07-843 7778; www.supershuttle.co.nz; one way $26) offers a door-to-door service into the city. A taxi costs around $50.

BUS

Hamilton's **Busit!** (☑0800 4287 5463; www.busit.co.nz; city routes adult/child $3.30/2.20) network services the city centre and suburbs daily from around 7am to 7.30pm (later on Friday). All buses pass through Hamilton Transport Centre. Busit! also runs a free Onboard CBD shuttle looping around Victoria, Liverpool, Anglesea and Bridge Sts every 10 minutes (7am to 6pm weekdays, 9am to 1pm Saturday).

CAR

Rent-a-Dent (☑07-839 1049; www.rentadent.co.nz; 383 Anglesea St; ⊙7.30am-5pm Mon-Fri, 8am-noon Sat) Car hire.

TAXI

Hamilton Taxis (☑0800 477 477, 07-8477 477; www.hamiltontaxis.co.nz)

Raglan

POP 2740

Laid-back Raglan may well be NZ's perfect surfing town. It's small enough to have escaped mass development, but it's big enough to exhibit signs of life including good eateries and a bar that attracts big-name bands in summer. Along with the famous surf spots to the south, the harbour just begs to be kayaked upon. There's also an excellent arts scene, with several galleries and shops worthy of perusal.

◉ Sights & Activities

Old School Arts Centre ARTS CENTRE, GALLERY
(www.raglanartscentre.co.nz; Stewart St; ⊙10am-2pm Mon & Wed, exhibition hours vary) FREE A community hub, the Old School Arts Centre has changing exhibitions and workshops, including weaving, carving, yoga and storytelling. Movies screen here regularly through summer ($11): grab a curry and a beer to complete the experience. The hippie/artsy **Raglan Creative Market** happens out the front on the second Sunday of the month (9am to 2pm).

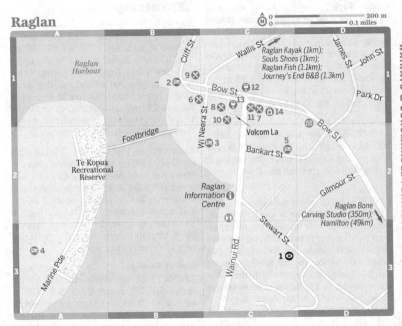

Raglan

◉ **Sights**
1 Old School Arts Centre C3

◆ **Activities, Courses & Tours**
Raglan Scenic Tours .... (see 5)

◎ **Sleeping**
2 Bow St Studios B1
3 Raglan Backpackers C2
4 Raglan Kopua Holiday Park A3
5 Raglan Sunset Motel C2

✕ **Eating**
6 Aloha Market Place B1

7 Banteay Srey C1
8 Juantanameras C1
9 Orca B1
10 Raglan Roast C1
11 The Shack C1

◉ **Drinking & Nightlife**
12 Harbour View Hotel C1
13 Yot Club C1

⌂ **Shopping**
14 Jet Collective C1

WAIKATO & COROMANDEL PENINSULA RAGLAN

Raglan Surf School
SURFING

(☑ 07-825 7873; www.raglansurfingschool.co.nz; 5b Whaanga Rd; 3hr lesson incl transport from Raglan $89) Raglan Surf School prides itself on getting 95% of first-timers standing during their first lesson. Rental gear includes surfboards (from $20 per hour), body boards ($5 per hour) and wet suits ($5 per hour). It's based at Karioi Lodge in Whale Bay. It also operates **Surfdames** (www.surfdames.co.nz), offering women-only surfing experiences incorporating lessons with yoga, massage and beauty treatments.

Raglan Rock
ROCK CLIMBING, CAVING

(☑ 0800 724 7625; www.raglanrock.com; climbing half-/full day $89/119, caving $89-99, minimum 2 people) Full instruction and all equipment for climbing on the limestone cliffs of nearby Stone Valley, or the exciting 'Stupid Fat Hobbit' climb and abseil above Raglan harbour. Caving options include Stone Valley and the more challenging 'Rattlesnake'.

Solscape
SURFING

(☑ 07-825 8268; www.solscape.co.nz; 611 Wainui Rd) Supersustainable Solscape offers 2½-hour surfing lessons ($85), as well as board and wetsuit hire (per half-day $35).

Raglan Kayak
KAYAKING

(☑ 07-825 8862; www.raglanco.co.nz; Raglan Wharf) Raglan Harbour is great for kayaking. This outfit runs three-hour guided harbour paddles (per person $75) and rents out single/double kayaks (per half-day $40/60). Learn the basics on the gentle Opotoru River, or paddle out to investigate the nooks and crannies of the pancake rocks on the harbour's northern edge. Stand up paddleboards are also available (one hour/half-day $20/40).

Raglan Bone Carving Studio
BONE CARVING

(☑ 021 0223 7233; raglanbonecarvingstudio@ hotmail.com; workshops $69) Carve your own bone pendant with Rangi Wills, a reformed 'troubled teenager' who found out he was actually really good at carving things. Workshops run for four hours and Rangi can provide transport from Raglan township to his studio. Bookings essential.

☞ Tours

Raglan Scenic Tours
GUIDED TOUR

(☑ 07-825 0507; www.raglanscenictours.co.nz; 5a Bankart St) Sightseeing tours, including 2½ hours around the Raglan area (adult/child $55/20) and four hours around Mount Ka-

rioi including Bridal Veil Falls and Te Toto Gorge ($90/40). Various treks and paddleboarding instruction can be arranged, and kayaks, mountain bikes and paddle boards can be hired.

Cruise Raglan
CRUISE

(☑ 07-825 7873; www.raglanboatcharters.co.nz; adult/child $40/29) Two-hour sunset cruises around Raglan Harbour on the *Wahine Moe*, with fish and chips and a few drinks. Ninety-minute morning harbour cruises ($30/15 per adult/child) are also available.

🛌 Sleeping

Raglan Backpackers
HOSTEL $

(☑ 07-825 0515; www.raglanbackpackers.co.nz; 6 Wi Neera St; dm $27-29, s $58, tw & d $72-82; @) This laid-back hostel is right on the water, with sea views from some rooms. Other rooms are arranged around a garden courtyard or in a separate building. There are free bikes and kayaks, and surfboards for hire, or take a yoga class; strum a guitar or drip in the sauna. No wi-fi – it 'ruins the vibe'.

Raglan Kopua Holiday Park
HOLIDAY PARK $

(☑ 07-825 8283; www.raglanholidaypark.co.nz; Marine Pde; campsites from $34, dm/cabins/units from $56/85/100; @🖱) A neatly maintained outfit with lots of sleeping options, on the spit across the inlet from town (there's a footbridge, or drive the long way around). No shade, but there's beach swimming and plenty of room to run amok.

Bow St Studios
APARTMENTS $$

(☑ 07-825 0551; www.bowstreet.co.nz; 1 Bow St; studios $145-225, cottage $205; 🖱) With a waterfront location right in town, Bow St has self-contained studios and a historic cottage. The property is surrounded by a subtropical garden and shaded by well-established pohutukawa trees, and the cool and chic decor is stylish and relaxing.

Journey's End B&B
B&B, APARTMENTS $$

(☑ 07-825 6727; www.raglanaccommodation.co.nz; 49 Lily St; s/d $100/140, exclusive use $200; 🖱) These two attractive en suite rooms share a central modern lounge with a kitchenette and a lovely deck overlooking the wharf and harbour. You can book out the whole place, or just one of the rooms. Fifteen minutes' walk from town.

Raglan Sunset Motel
MOTEL $$

(☑ 07-825 0050; www.raglansunsetmotel.co.nz; 7 Bankart St; d from $150; 🖱) A block from Bow

St's shops and restaurants with spacious and modern units. The owners also have self-contained apartments (doubles from $160) and beach houses (four people $300) available. Bike and kayak hire is available (per half-day $30 and $45 respectively).

✗ Eating

Juantanameras SOUTH AMERICAN $
(Electric Ave, off 5 Wainui Rd; snacks $3-7; ⊘9am-5pm) Hunt down this summer-only food caravan for tasty Venezuelan *arepas* (corn cakes) or Mexican quesadillas and tacos. Get there early for *churros* (Mexican doughnuts), perfect for a local Raglan coffee just next door. It's only open Friday to Sunday in winter, and even then it can be subject to surf conditions. Welcome to laid-back Raglan.

Aloha Market Place JAPANESE $
(5 Bow St; sushi $1.20-2.20, mains $10-13; ⊘9am-5pm; ✐) Rolled-to-order sushi, udon noodles and *donburi* rice bowls, all with a touch of hip Hawaiian-Japanese surfer style. Reduced opening hours in winter.

Raglan Roast CAFE $
(www.raglanroast.co.nz; Volcom Lane; coffee $4; ⊘7am-5pm) Hole-in-the-wall coffee roaster with the best brew in town. Stop by for a cup, a cookie and a conversation. Reduced winter hours.

Raglan Fish FISH & CHIPS $
(www.facebook.com/RaglanFishShop;RaglanWharf, 92 Wallis St; fish & chips $6-10; ⊘9am-8pm) Super-fresh fish and chips and funky decor at this locals' favourite right on Raglan's recently restored wharf. Fresh oysters, mussels and seafood salads are also available.

The Shack CAFE, INTERNATIONAL $$
(www.theshackraglan.com; 19 Bow St; tapas $6-14, mains $12-27; ⊘8am-5pm Sun-Thu, to late Fri & Sat; ☎✐) Brunch classics – try the chickpea-and-corn fritters – and interesting shared-plate mains like tempura squid and star-anise chicken feature at the best cafe in town. A longboard strapped to the wall, wobbly old floorboards, up-tempo tunes and international staff serving Kiwi wines and craft beers complete the picture.

Banteay Srey CAMBODIAN $$
(☎07-825 0952; www.raglancambodian.weebly.net; 23 Bow St; mains $18-24; ⊘8.30am-9pm) The menu also strays into Western flavours, but the authentic Cambodian dishes are the ones to go for. Our pick is the Char Kreoung

chicken or beef with lemongrass and lime, or the delicate Amok steamed and curried fish. On Tuesdays from 6.30pm, the restaurant hosts a buffet (per person $28). Booking ahead is recommended.

Orca CAFE, MODERN NZ $$
(☎07-825 6543; www.orcarestaurant.co.nz; 2 Wallis St; breakfast $11-21, mains $19-30; ⊘10am-late Mon-Fri, 9am-late Sat & Sun) A day started at an Orca window seat, looking over the water, with some eggs Benedict and coffee, is a day well launched. Come back in the evening for salmon risotto, shared platters and live music.

🍷 Drinking & Nightlife

Yot Club BAR, LIVE MUSIC
(www.mukuna.co.nz/waikato/raglan/yot-club.htm; 9 Bow St; admission free-$25; ⊘9pm-late) Raucous, nocturnal bar with DJs and touring bands.

Harbour View Hotel PUB
(14 Bow St) Classic old pub with main-street drinks on the shaded verandah. Decent pizza too and occasional live music on weekends and during summer.

🛍 Shopping

Jet Collective ARTS & CRAFTS
(www.jetcollective.co.nz; 19a Bow St; ⊘10am-4pm Wed-Mon) Funky gallery-shop showcasing 100% Raglan artists with everything from music CDs and mixed-media pieces through to retro Kiwiana-inspired work. It's also a good spot to drop in and chat with the friendly team about Raglan's growing and diverse arts scene.

Soul Shoes SHOES, ACCESSORIES
(www.soulshoes.co.nz; Raglan Wharf, Wallis St; ⊘10am-5pm) World famous in Raglan since 1973, and in a new century, Soul Shoes' range of handmade leather footwear has been joined by equally cool satchels, backpacks and bags.

ℹ Information

Raglan Information Centre (☎07-825 0556; www.raglan.org.nz; 13 Wainui Rd; ⊘9.30am-5pm Mon-Fri, 10am-5pm Sat, 10am-4pm Sun) Department of Conservation (DOC) brochures plus information about accommodation and activities including kitesurfing and paddle boarding. Check out also the attached museum, especially the exhibition on the history of Raglan's surfing scene.

WAIKATO & COROMANDEL PENINSULA RAGLAN

West Coast Health Centre (☎07-825 0114; wchc@wave.co.nz; 12 Wallis St; ⊙9am-5pm Mon-Fri) General medical assistance.

❶ Getting There & Around

From Hamilton, Raglan is 48km west along SH23. Unsealed back roads connect Raglan to Kawhia, 50km south; they're slow, winding and prone to rockslides, but scenic and certainly off the beaten track. Head back towards Hamilton for 7km and take the Te Mata/Kawhia turn-off and follow the signs; allow at least an hour.

Waikato Regional Council's **Busit!** (☎0800 4287 5463; www.busit.co.nz; adult/child $8.50/5.50) heads between Hamilton and Raglan (one hour) three times daily on weekdays and twice daily on weekends.

Raglan Scenic Tours (p174) runs a Raglan–Hamilton shuttle bus (one way $35) and direct transfers to/from Auckland International Airport.

For a cab call **Raglan Taxi** (☎07-825 0506).

South of Raglan

The surf spots near Raglan – Indicators, Whale Bay and Manu Bay – are internationally famous for their point breaks. Bruce Brown's classic 1964 wave-chaser film *The Endless Summer* features Manu Bay.

Ocean Beach

Ocean Beach sits at the mouth of the harbour, 4km southwest of Raglan down Riria Kereopa Memorial Dr. It's popular for windsurfing and kitesurfing, but strong currents make it extremely treacherous for swimmers.

Ngarunui Beach

Less than 1km south of Ocean Beach, Ngarunui Beach is a great for grommets learning to surf. On the clifftop is a club-

---

WORTH A TRIP

RUAPEKE BEACH

Whale Bay marks the end of the sealed road, but a gravel road continues to the wild spans of Ruapuke Beach, 22km from Raglan. It's dangerous for swimmers here, but popular with surfcasting fisherfolk. The gravel road continues to Mt Karioi and rejoins the inland road at Te Mata.

house for the volunteer lifeguards who patrol part of the black-sand beach from late October until April. This is the only beach with lifeguards, and is the best ocean beach for swimming.

Manu Bay

A 2.5km journey from Ngarunui Beach will bring you to Manu Bay, a legendary surf spot said to have the longest left-hand break in the world. The elongated uniform waves are created by the angle at which the Tasman Sea swell meets the coastline (it works best in a southwesterly swell).

🛏 Sleeping

★Solscape   HOSTEL, CABINS $
(☎07-825 8268; www.solscape.co.nz; 611 Wainui Rd; campsites from $17, caboose dm/d $30/72, teepees per person $36, cottages d $82-189; @ 🖘)
🍃 With a hilltop location fringed by native bush, Solscape's ecofriendly accommodation includes teepees, rammed-earth domes, railway carriages and stylish eco baches. There's room for tents and campervans, and simpler cottages are also available. Environmental impact is minimised with solar energy, and organic produce from the permaculture garden is used for guests' meals in the Conscious Kitchen cafe.

Yoga, massage and surfing lessons are all available, and Solscape is also YHA-affiliated.

Whale Bay

Whale Bay is a renowned surf spot 1km west of Manu Bay. It's usually less crowded than Manu Bay, but from the bottom of Calvert Rd you have to clamber 600m over the rocks to get to the break.

🛏 Sleeping

Karioi Lodge   HOSTEL $
(☎07-825 7873; www.karioilodge.co.nz; 5b Whaanga Rd; dm/d $30/75; @ 🖘) 🍃 Deep in native bush, Karioi Lodge offers a sauna, a flying fox, mountain bikes, bush and beach walks, sustainable gardening, tree planting and the Raglan Surf School. There are no en suites but the rooms are clean and cosy. These friendly folks also run Sleeping Lady Lodges (☎07-825 7873; www.sleepinglady.co.nz; 5b Whaanga Rd; lodges $175-260), a collection of six luxury self-contained houses nearby, all with ocean views.

Mt Karioi

In legend, Mt Karioi (756m), the Sleeping Lady (check out that profile), is the sister to Mt Pirongia. At its base (8km south of Whale Bay), Te Toto Gorge is a steep cleft in the mountainside, with a vertigo-inducing lookout perched high over the chasm.

Starting from Te Toto Gorge car park, a strenuous but scenic track goes up the western slope. It takes 2½ hours to reach a lookout point, followed by an easier hour up to the summit. From the east side, the Wairake Track is a steeper 2½-hour climb to the summit, where it meets the Te Toto Track.

Waireinga (Bridal Veil Falls)

Just past Te Mata (a short drive south of the main Raglan–Hamilton road) is the turn-off to the 55m Waireinga (Bridal Veil Falls), 4km from the main road. From the car park, it's an easy 10-minute walk through mossy native bush to the top of the falls (not suitable for swimming). A further 10-minute walk leads down to the bottom. Lock your car: theft is a problem here.

Magic Mountain Horse Treks (☑07-825 6892; www.magicmountain.co.nz; 334 Houtchen Rd, Te Mata; 1/2hr rides $50/80) runs horse treks around the hills, plus a ride to Waireinga (Bridal Veil Falls, $100).

Pirongia Forest Park

The main attraction of this 170-sq-km forest park is Mt Pirongia (www.mtpirongia.org.nz), its 959m summit clearly visible from much of the Waikato. The mountain is usually climbed from Corcoran Rd (three to five hours, one way) with tracks to other lookout points. Interestingly, NZ's tallest-known kahikatea tree (66.5m) grows on the mountainside. There's a six-bunk DOC hut near the summit if you need to spend the night; maps and information are available from Hamilton DOC (p172).

Te Awamutu

POP 9800

Deep into dairy-farming country, Te Awamutu (which means 'The River Cut Short'; the Waikato beyond this point was unsuitable for large canoes) is a pleasant rural service centre. With a blossom-treed main street and a good museum, TA (aka Rose Town) makes a decent overnighter.

TE AWAMUTU'S SACRED SOUND

In the opening lines of Crowded House's first single *Mean to Me*, Neil Finn single-handedly raised his sleepy home town, Te Awamutu, to international attention. It wasn't the first time it had provided inspiration – Split Enz songs *Haul Away* and *Kia Kaha*, with Neil's big bro Tim, include similar references.

Despite NZ's brilliant songwriting brothers being far from the height of their fame, Finn devotees continue to make the pilgrimage to Te Awamutu. Ask at the i-SITE about Finn postage stamps and the interesting scrapbook focused on the brothers' achievements.

⊙ Sights

★ Te Awamutu Museum   MUSEUM
(www.tamuseum.org.nz; 135 Roche St; admission by donation; ⊙10am-4pm Mon-Fri, 10am-1pm Sat, 1-4pm Sun) Te Awamutu Museum, 'where history never repeats', has a *True Colours*–painted shrine to local heroes Tim and Neil Finn. There are gold records, original lyrics, Finn memorabilia and oddities such as Neil's form-two exercise book. There's also a fine collection of Maori *taonga* (treasures), and an excellent display on the Waikato War. A great little museum.

Rose Garden   GARDENS
(cnr Gorst Ave & Arawata St; ⊙24hr) FREE The Rose Garden is next to the i-SITE and has 2500 bushes and 51 varieties with fabulously fruity names like Lady Gay and Sexy Rexy. The roses usually bloom from November to May.

🛏 Sleeping

Rosetown Motel   MOTEL $$
(☑07-871 5779, 0800 767 386; www.rosetownmotel.co.nz; 844 Kihikihi Rd; d $120-145; ☎☀) The older-style units at Rosetown have kitchens, new linen and TVs, and share a spa. A solid choice for a straight-up small-town sleep.

✗ Eating

Walton St Coffee   CAFE $
(www.facebook.com/WaltonStreetCollective; 3 Walton St; snacks $5-10; ⊙6.30am-2pm Mon-Fri) 🌀 In a rustic building with exposed beams and retro furniture, this combo of cafe, gallery

and performance space is Te Awamutu's top spot for a coffee. There's a strong focus on organic and gluten free with the food.

Sugoi Sushi SUSHI $
(343 Alexandra St; sushi $8-10; ⊙7.30am-6pm) Quite probably Waikato's best sushi, with a huge selection and exemplary service.

Red Kitchen CAFE $$
(www.redkitchen.co.nz; 51 Mahoe St; mains $14-20; ⊙7am-5.30pm Mon-Fri, 7.30am-2.30pm Sat) Excellent coffee, counter food and cosmopolitan brunches and lunches – try the macadamia and cranberry muesli – all feature at this sunny spot also incorporating a food store and a cookery school. Drop in for one of its gourmet TV dinners – actually really good – and fire up the motel microwave for your evening meal.

Redoubt Bar & Eatery PUB $$
(www.redoubtbarandeateryta.co.nz; cnr Rewi & Alexandra Sts; mains $16-34; ⊙10am-late) A relaxed place to eat or drink, with cheap-but-potent cocktails, classic old photos of Te Awamutu sports teams on the walls, and a decent menu stretching from pasta to curry.

☆ Entertainment

Regent Theatre CINEMA
(www.facebook.com/RegentTeawamutu; 235 Alexandra St; adult/child $15.50/9.50; ⊙10am-late) Art-deco cinema with movie memorabilia.

ℹ Information

Te Awamutu i-SITE (☑07-871 3259; www.teawamutuinfo.com; 1 Gorst Ave; ⊙9am-5pm Mon-Fri, 10am-4pm Sat & Sun) Local information and bookings.

ℹ Getting There & Away

Te Awamutu is on SH3, halfway between Hamilton and Otorohanga (29km either way). The regional bus service **Busit!** (☑0800 4287 5463; www.busit.co.nz) is the cheapest option for Hamilton (adult/child $6.70/4.50, 50 minutes, eight daily weekdays, three daily weekends).

Three daily **InterCity** (☑09-583 5780; www.intercity.co.nz) services connect Te Awamutu with Auckland ($14 to $45, 2½ hours) and Hamilton ($21, 35 minutes).

Rangiaowhia

Before the Waikato invasion, Rangiaowhia (5km east of Te Awamutu on Rangiaowhia Rd; ask at the i-SITE for directions) was a thriving Maori farming town, exporting wheat, maize, potatoes and fruit to as far afield as Australia. It was home to thousands of inhabitants, two churches, a flour mill and a racecourse, and was the perfect model of what NZ under the Maori version of the Treaty of Waitangi had outlined for NZ – two sovereign peoples interacting to mutual advantage.

In February 1864 the settlement was left undefended while King Tawhiao's warriors held fortified positions further north. In a key tactical move, General Cameron outflanked them and took the town, killing women, children and the elderly. This was a turning point in the campaign, demoralising the Maori and drawing the warriors out of their near-impregnable *pa* fortifications.

Sadly, all that remains of the town is the cute 1854 Anglican **St Paul's Church** (☑07-871 5568; Rangiaowhia Rd; ⊙services 9am 1st &

> WORTH A TRIP
> ### SANCTUARY MOUNTAIN MAUNGATAUTARI
> Can a landlocked volcano become an island paradise? Inspired by the success of pest eradication and native-species reintroduction in the Hauraki Gulf, a community trust has erected 47km of pest-proof fencing around the triple peaks of Maungatautari (797m) to create the impressive **Sanctuary Mountain Maungatautari** (www.sanctuarymountain.co.nz; adult/child $15/6). This atoll of rainforest dominates the skyline between Te Awamutu and Karapiro and is now home to its first kiwi chicks in 100 years. The main entrance is at the visitor centre on the sanctuary's southern side.
>
> **Out in the Styx** (☑07-872 4505; www.styx.co.nz; 2117 Arapuni Rd, Pukeatua; dm/s/d $95/130/260) is near the south end of the Maungatautari guided day- and night-walk options. The three stylishly furnished themed rooms (Polynesian, African or Maori) are especially nice, plus there are bunk rooms and a spa for soothing weary legs. Prices include a four-course dinner and breakfast. It also provides a pick-up service if you wish to walk across the mountain from south to north (around six hours).

3rd Sun of month) and the Catholic mission's cemetery, standing in the midst of rich farming land – confiscated from the Maori and distributed to colonial soldiers.

The war ended further south at Orakau, where a roadside obelisk marks the site where 300 Maori, led by Rewi Maniapoto, repulsed three days of attacks against an unfinished *pa* by 1500 troops, before breaking out and retreating to what is now known as the King Country (losing 70 warriors).

Wharepapa South

A surreal landscape of craggy limestone provides some of the best rock climbing in the North Island. It's an area best suited to travellers with at least basic climbing skills.

Bryce's Rockclimbing (☑ 07-872 2533; www.rockclimb.co.nz; 1424 Owairaka Valley Rd; 1-day instruction for 1-2 people $440) is suited to the serious climber. On site is NZ's largest retail climbing store, selling and hiring out a full range of gear. It also has an indoor bouldering cave, free to those staying out back in the shipshape accommodation (dorm/double $30/76). There's a licensed cafe (light meals $6 to $16, open 8am to 5pm Friday to Monday), and accommodation is also open to nonclimbers.

Cambridge

POP 15,200

The name says it all. Despite the rambunctious Waikato River looking nothing like the Cam, the good people of Cambridge have done all they can to assume an air of English gentility with village greens and tree-lined avenues.

Cambridge is famous for the breeding and training of thoroughbred horses. Equine references are rife in public sculpture, and plaques boast of past Melbourne Cup winners.

◎ Sights & Activities

Cambridge Museum   MUSEUM
(www.cambridgemuseum.org.nz; 24 Victoria St; admission by donation; ⊙10am-4pm Mon-Fri, to 2pm Sun) In a former courthouse, the quirky Cambridge Museum has plenty of pioneer relics, a military-history room and a small display on the local Te Totara Pa before it was wiped out.

Jubilee Gardens   GARDENS, MONUMENT
(Victoria St; ⊙24hr) Apart from its Spanish Mission town clock, Jubilee Gardens is a wholehearted tribute to the 'mother country'. A British lion guards the cenotaph, with a plaque that reads, 'Tell Britain ye who mark this monument faithful to her we fell and rest content'.

Lake Karapiro   LAKE
(☑ 07-827 4178; www.waipadc.govt.nz; Maungatautari Rd) Eight kilometres southeast of Cambridge, Karapiro is the furthest downstream of a chain of eight hydroelectric power stations on the Waikato River. It's an impressive sight, especially when driving across the top of the 1947 dam. The 21km-long lake is also a world-class rowing venue.

Boatshed Kayaks   KAYAKING
(☑ 07-827 8286; www.theboatshed.net.nz; 21 Amber Lane; single/double kayak for 3hr $25/50, paddle board $20; ⊙9am-5pm Wed-Sun) Located at the Boatshed Cafe with basic kayaks and paddle boards for hire. You can paddle to a couple of waterfalls in around an hour. There are also guided kayak trips at twilight (adult/child $110/40) to see a glowworm canyon up the nearby Pokewhaenua stream. Bookings are essential for these trips.

Waikato River Trails   CYCLING, TRAMPING
(www.waikatorivertrails.com) Winding east from Cambridge, the 100km Waikato River Trails track is part of the Nga Haerenga, New Zealand Cycle Trail (www.nzcycletrail.com) project. You can either walk or cycle the five combined trails (or parts thereof), with lots of history and local landscapes en route.

Heritage & Tree Trail   WALKING TOUR
This Cambridge walking tour includes the Waikato River, the 1881 St Andrew's Anglican Church (look for the Gallipoli window) and leafy Lake Ko Utu. Grab a map at the i-SITE,

Camjet   JETBOATING
(☑ 0800 226 538; www.camjet.co.nz; adult/child $75/50) Exciting 35-minute spins to Karapiro dam on a jetboat. A 15-minute ride costs $45. Minimum two people.

⊨ Sleeping

Cambridge Motor Park   HOLIDAY PARK $
(☑ 07-827 5649; www.cambridgemotorpark. co.nz; 32 Scott St; campsites from $17, cabins s/d from $47/57, units d $110; ☞) A quiet,

well-maintained camping ground with lots of green, green grass. The emphasis is on tents and vans here, but the cabins and units are fine. Drive over the skinny Victoria Bridge from Cambridge town centre.

Cambridge Coach House B&B, CABIN **$$**
(☑ 07-823 7922; www.cambridgecoachhouse.co.nz; 3796 Cambridge Rd, Leamington; d/cottage $150/160; ☎❄) This farmhouse accommodation is slightly chintzy, but it's still a beaut spot to relax amid Waikato's rural splendour. There are two separate doubles and a self-contained cottage. It's a couple of kilometres south of town en route to Te Awamutu.

Cambridge Mews MOTEL **$$**
(☑ 07-827 7166; www.cambridgemews.co.nz; 20 Hamilton Rd; d $160-200; ☎) All the spacious units in this chalet-style motel have double spa baths, decent kitchens and are immaculately maintained. It's a 10-minute walk to town.

✖ Eating

Boatshed Cafe CAFE **$**
(www.theboatshedkarapiro.co.nz; 21 Amber Lane, off Gorton Rd; mains $10-19; ⊙ 10am-3pm Thu-Sun) This stylish cafe on the edge of Lake Karapiro (heading south from Cambridge on SH1, turn right into Gorton Rd) is a top place for a leisurely brunch or lunch. Order the eggs Benedict, and grab an outside table for lake views and Waikato birdsong.

Red Cherry CAFE **$$**
(www.redcherrycoffee.co.nz; cnr SH1 & Forrest Rd; meals $16-20; ⊙ 7.30am-4.30pm; ☑) With a cherry-red espresso machine working overtime, barnlike Red Cherry offers coffee roasted on site, delicious counter food and impressive cooked breakfasts. For lunch, the gourmet beef burger is hard to beat. Cambridge's best cafe is 4km from town en route to Hamilton.

Onyx CAFE, RESTAURANT **$$**
(☑ 07-827 7740; www.onyxcambridge.co.nz; 70 Alpha St; mains $17-30; ⊙ 9am-late) All-day Onyx occupies a lofty space, with onyx black furnishings and warm-toned timber floors. Wood-fired pizzas ($20 to $24) are the mainstay, plus salads, tortillas, sandwiches, steaks, cakes, organic coffee and NZ wines and beer.

❶ Information

Cambridge i-SITE (☑ 07-823 3456; www.cambridge.co.nz; cnr Victoria & Queen Sts;

⊙ 9am-5pm Mon-Fri, 10am-4pm Sat & Sun; ☎) Free Heritage & Tree Trail and town maps, and internet access.

❶ Getting There & Away

Being on SH1, 22km southeast of Hamilton, Cambridge is well connected by bus. Waikato Regional Council's **Busit!** (☑ 0800 4287 5463; www.busit.co.nz) heads to Hamilton ($6.70, 40 minutes, seven daily weekdays, three daily weekends).

InterCity (☑ 09-583 5780; www.intercity.co.nz) services numerous destinations including the following:

DESTINATION	PRICE ($)	DURATION	FREQUENCY (DAILY)
Auckland	27-45	2½hr	12
Hamilton	10-25	30min	8
Matamata	10-22	30min	2
Rotorua	17-35	1¼hr	5
Wellington	28-68	8½hr	3

Naked Bus (☑ 0900 625 33; www.nakedbus.com) services to the same destinations are as follows:

DESTINATION	PRICE ($)	DURATION	FREQUENCY (DAILY)
Auckland	13-17	2½hr	6
Hamilton	20	30min	5
Matamata	24-25	2¼hr	1
Rotorua	10	1¼hr	4
Wellington	28	9½hr	1

Matamata

POP 7800

Matamata was just one of those pleasant, horsey country towns you drove through until Peter Jackson's epic film trilogy *Lord of the Rings* put it on the map. During filming 300 locals got work as extras (hairy feet weren't a prerequisite).

Following the subsequent filming of *The Hobbit*, the town has now ardently embraced its Middle Earth credentials, including a spooky statue of Gollum, and given the local information centre an appropriate extreme makeover.

Most tourists who come to Matamata are dedicated hobbit-botherers: for everyone else there's a great cafe, avenues of mature trees and undulating green hills.

☉ Sights & Activities

Hobbiton Movie Set Tours FILM LOCATION
(☎0508 446 224 866, 07-888 1505; www.hobbi-tontours.com; 501 Buckland Rd, Hinuera; adult/child $75/37.50; ⊙tours 10am-4.30pm) Due to copyright, all the intricate movie sets around the country were dismantled after filming of *Lord of the Rings*, but Hobbiton's owners negotiated to keep their hobbit holes, which were then rebuilt for the filming of *The Hobbit*. Tours include a drink at the wonderful Green Dragon Inn. Free transfers leave from the Matamata i-SITE; check timings on the Hobbiton website. Booking ahead is strongly recommended.

With your own transport, head towards Cambridge from Matamata, turn right into Puketutu Rd and then left into Buckland Rd, stopping at the Shire's Rest Cafe.

Wairere Falls WATERFALL
About 15km northeast of Matamata are the spectacular 153m-high Wairere Falls (the highest on the North Island). From the car park it's a 45-minute walk through native bush to the lookout or a steep 90-minute climb to the summit.

Firth Tower MUSEUM, HISTORIC BUILDING
(www.firthtower.co.nz; Tower Rd; grounds free, tours adult/child $5/1; ⊙grounds 10am-4pm daily, buildings 10am-4pm Thu-Mon) Firth Tower was built by Auckland businessman Josiah Firth in 1882. The 18m concrete tower was a fashionable status symbol, and is now filled with Maori and pioneer artefacts. Around it are 10 other historic buildings, including a schoolroom, church and jail. It's 3km east of town.

Opal Hot Springs SWIMMING
(www.opalhotsprings.co.nz; 257 Okauia Springs Rd; adult/child $8/4, 30min private spas $10/5; ⊙9am-9pm) Opal Hot Springs isn't nearly as glamorous as it sounds but it does have three large thermal pools. Turn off just north of Firth Tower and follow the road for 2km. There's a holiday park here too.

🛏 Sleeping

Broadway Motel & Miro Court Villas MOTEL $$
(☎07-888 8482; www.broadwaymatamata.co.nz; 128 Broadway; s $89-145, d $99-165, 2-bedroom villa $265; @⊛) This sprawling family-run motel complex has spread from a well-maintained older-style block to progressively newer and flasher blocks set back from the street. The nicest are the chic apartment-style Miro Court villas.

✘ Eating & Drinking

Workman's Cafe Bar CAFE $$
(www.matamata-info.co.nz/workmans; 52 Broadway; brunch $12-18, tapas $11, dinner $20-33; ⊙9am-10pm Wed-Sun, 3-10pm Tue-Sun) Truly eccentric (old transistor radios dangling from the ceiling; a wall-full of art-deco mirrors; Johnny Cash on the stereo), this funky eatery has built itself a reputation that extends beyond Matamata. It's also a decent bar later at night.

Redoubt Bar & Eatery PUB
(www.redoubtbarandeatery.co.nz; 48 Broadway; lunch $11-20, dinner $21-34; ⊙11am-late Mon-Fri, 10am-late Sat & Sun) Look forward to thin-crust pizzas named after LOTR, chowder, steaks, a winning hash stack and live music every Friday. It's also a minishrine to all things sporty and Matamata-related.

ⓘ Information

Matamata i-SITE (☎07-888 7260; www.matamatanz.co.nz; 45 Broadway; ⊙9am-5pm Mon-Fri, to 3pm Sat & Sun) Housed in a wonderful Hobbit gatehouse. Hobbiton tours also leave from here.

ⓘ Getting There & Away

Matamata is on SH27, 20km north of Tirau.

InterCity (☎09-583 5780; www.intercity.co.nz) Runs to Cambridge ($22, 40 minutes, two daily), Hamilton ($27, one hour, three daily), Rotorua ($25, one hour, one daily) and Tauranga ($26, one hour, two daily).

Naked Bus (☎0900 625 33; www.nakedbus.com) Runs to Auckland ($13, 3½ hours, two daily), Cambridge ($20, two hours, one daily), Hamilton ($20, 3½ hours, two daily) and Tauranga ($14, one hour, one daily).

Te Aroha
POP 3800

Te Aroha has a great vibe. You could even say that it's got 'the love', which is the literal meaning of the name. Tucked under the elbow of the bush-clad Mt Te Aroha (952m), it's a good base for tramping or 'taking the waters' in the town's therapeutic thermal springs. It's also the southern trailhead on the Hauraki Rail Trail (p194).

◎ Sights & Activities

Te Aroha Museum
MUSEUM
(www.tearoha-museum.com; Te Aroha Domain; adult/child $4/2; ⊙11am-4pm Nov-Mar, noon-3pm Apr-Oct) In the town's ornate former thermal sanatorium (aka the 'Treasure of Te Aroha'). Displays include quirky ceramics, old spa-water bottles, historic photos and an old printing press.

Te Aroha Mineral Spas
SPA
(☑07-884 8717; www.tearohamineralspas.co.nz; Boundary St, Te Aroha Domain; 30min session adult/child $18/11; ⊙10.30am-9pm Mon-Fri, to 10pm Sat & Sun) In the Edwardian Hot Springs Domain, this spa offers private tubs, massage, beauty therapies and aromatherapy. Also here is the temperamental Mokena Geyser – the world's only known soda geyser – which blows its top around every 40 minutes, shooting water 3m into the air (the most ardent eruptions are between noon and 2pm). Book ahead for spas and treatments.

Te Aroha Leisure Pools
SWIMMING, BATHHOUSE
(☑07-884 4498; www.tearohaleisurepools.co.nz; Boundary St, Te Aroha Domain; adult/child $7/5; ⊙10am-5.45pm Mon-Fri, to 6.45pm Sat & Sun) Outdoor heated freshwater pools, a thermal bath house and a toddlers' pool.

Mt Te Aroha
TRAMPING, MOUNTAIN BIKING
Trails up Mt Te Aroha start at the top of the domain. It's a 45-minute climb to Bald Spur/ Whakapipi Lookout (350m), then another 2.7km (two hours) to the summit. Ask at the i-SITE about mountain-bike trails.

🛏 Sleeping

Te Aroha Holiday Park
HOLIDAY PARK $
(☑07-884 9567; www.tearohaholidaypark.co.nz; 217 Stanley Rd; campsites from $15, on-site vans s/d $30/40, cabins & units $53-90; @ 🛜 🛋) Wake up to a bird orchestra among the oaks at this site equipped with a grass tennis court, gym and hot pool, 2km southwest of town.

★ Aroha Mountain Lodge
LODGE, B&B $$
(☑07-884 8134; www.arohamountainlodge.co.nz; 5 Boundary St; s/d/ste/cottage $115/135/155/295) Spread over two *aroha*-ly Edwardian villas on the hillside above town, the plush Mountain Lodge offers affordable luxury (*sooo* much nicer than a regulation motel) and optional breakfast ($20 per person). The self-contained Gold Miner's Cottage sleeps six.

Te Aroha Motel
MOTEL $$
(☑07-884 9417; www.tearohamotel.co.nz; 108 Whitaker St; units $115-145; 🛜) Old-fashioned but reasonably priced and tidy units with kitchenettes, right in the centre of town.

✖ Eating

Ironique
CAFE $$
(www.ironique.co.nz; 159 Whitaker St; mains $10-35; ⊙8am-late Mon-Fri, 4pm-late Sat & Sun) Come for a coffee and a restorative breakfast of eggs Benedict after tackling the Hauraki Rail Trail, or grilled salmon or confit duck for dinner. Don't overlook venturing to the quiet courtyard out the back for a few drinks.

Berlusconi on Whitaker
ITALIAN, TAPAS $$
(☑07-884 9307; www.tearoha-info.co.nz/berlusconi; 149 Whitaker St; lunch $14-20, pizza $27, dinner $33-24; ⊙11.30am-3.30pm Tue-Sun, plus 6pm-late Wed-Sun) We know the defunct Italian PM has his fingers in a lot of pies, but surely they don't extend to this suave upmarket wine, tapas and pizza bar in Te Aroha.

❶ Information

Te Aroha i-SITE (☑07-884 8052; www.tearohanz.co.nz; 102 Whitaker St; ⊙9.30am-5pm Mon-Fri, to 4pm Sat & Sun)

❶ Getting There & Away

Te Aroha is on SH26, 21km south of Paeroa and 55km northeast of Hamilton. Waikato Regional Council's **Busit!** (☑0800 4287 5463; www.busit.co.nz) runs to/from Hamilton (adult/child $8/4, one hour, two daily Monday to Friday). **Naked Bus** (☑0900 625 33; www.nakedbus.com) runs to Hamilton ($20, one hour, one daily) and Cambridge ($20, 1½ hours, one daily).

THE KING COUNTRY

Holding good claim to the title of NZ's rural heartland, this is a no-nonsense place that raises cattle and All Blacks. A bastion of independent Maoridom, it was never conquered in the war against the King Movement. The story goes that King Tawhiao placed his hat on a large map of NZ and declared that all the land it covered would remain under his *mana* (authority), and the region was effectively off limits to Europeans until 1883.

The Waitomo Caves are the area's major drawcard. An incredible natural phenomenon in themselves, they also feature lots of adrenaline-inducing activities.

Kawhia

POP 670

Along with resisting cultural annihilation, low-key Kawhia (think mafia with a K) has avoided large-scale development, retaining its sleepy fishing-village vibe. There's not much here except for the general store, a couple of takeaways and a petrol station. Even Captain Cook blinked and missed the narrow entrance to the large harbour when he sailed past in 1770.

◉ Sights & Activities

Kayaks can be hired from Kawhia Beachside S-Cape and Kawhia Motel.

Ocean Beach   BEACH, SPRING
(Te Puia Rd) Four kilometres west of Kawhia is Ocean Beach and its high, black-sand dunes. Swimming can be dangerous, but one to two hours either side of low tide you can find the Te Puia Hot Springs in the sand – dig a hole for your own natural hot pool.

**Kawhia Regional
Museum & Gallery**   MUSEUM, GALLERY
(www.kawhiaharbour.co.nz; Omimiti Reserve, Kawhia Wharf; admission by gold coin donation; ⊙ noon-3pm Wed-Sun) Kawhia's modest waterside museum has local history, nautical and Maori artefacts, and regular art exhibitions. It doubles as the visitor information centre.

Maketu Marae   MARAE
(www.kawhia.maori.nz; Kaora St) From the wharf, a track extends along the coast to Maketu Marae, which has an impressively carved meeting house, Auaukiterangi. Two stones here – Hani and Puna – mark the burial place of the *Tainui waka*. You can't see a lot from the road, but the *marae* is private property – don't enter without permission from the Maketu Marae Committee (info@kawhia.maori.nz).

Kawhia Harbour Cruises   CRUISE
(☑ 021 966 754; www.kawhiaharbourcruises.co.nz; cruises per adult $35) There are some gorgeous beaches and kooky rock formations to check out around isolated Kawhia Harbour: bring your swimming gear! Minimum six adults.

Dove Charters   FISHING
(☑ 07-871 5854; www.westcoastfishing.co.nz; full day $110) Full-day fishing trips.

✷ Festivals & Events

Kawhia Traditional Maori Kai Festival FOOD
(www.kawhiakaifestival.co.nz; adult/child $10/2) During the annual Kai Festival in early February, over 10,000 people descend to enjoy traditional Maori *kai* (food) and catch up with *whanau* (relations). Once you've filled up on seafood, *rewana* bread and rotten corn, settle in to watch the bands and rousing *kapa haka* (traditional Maori group singing and dancing) performances.

⌂ Sleeping & Eating

Kawhia Beachside S-Cape   HOLIDAY PARK $
(☑ 07-871 0727; www.kawhiabeachsidescape.co.nz; 225 Pouewe St; campsites from $30, cabins dm/s/d from $30/40/58, cottages $165-185) This water's edge camping ground looks shabby from the road but has comfortable cottages, and cabins and camping with shared bathrooms. Two-hour kayak hire is $12 per person.

Kawhia Motel   MOTEL, RENTAL HOUSE $$
(☑ 07-871 0865; www.kawhiamotel.co.nz; cnr Jervois & Tainui Sts; d $129-169; 🖥) These six perkily

---

KINGITANGA

The concept of a Maori people is a relatively new one. Until the mid-19th century, NZ was effectively comprised of many independent tribal nations, operating in tandem with the British from 1840.

In 1856, faced with a flood of Brits, the Kingitanga (King Movement) formed to unite the tribes to better resist further loss of land and culture. A gathering of leaders elected Waikato chief Potatau Te Wherowhero as the first Maori king, hoping that his increased *mana* (prestige) could achieve the cohesion that the British had under their queen.

Despite the huge losses of the Waikato War and the eventual opening up of the King Country, the Kingitanga survived – although it has no formal constitutional role. A measure of the strength of the movement was the huge outpouring of grief when Te Arikinui Dame Te Atairangikaahu, Potatau's great-great-great-granddaughter, died in 2006 after 40 years at the helm. Although it's not a hereditary monarchy (leaders of various tribes vote on a successor), Potatau's line continues to the present day with King Tuheitia Paki.

KAWHIA'S CANOE

The *Tainui waka* – a 14th-century ancestral canoe – made its final landing at Kawhia. The expedition leaders – Hoturoa, the chief/captain, and Rakataura, the *tohunga* (priest) – searched the west coast until they recognised their prophesised landing place. Pulling into shore, they tied the *waka* to a pohutukawa tree, naming it Tangi te Korowhiti. This unlabelled tree still stands on the shoreline between the wharf and Maketu Marae. The *waka* was then dragged up onto a hill and buried: sacred stones were placed at either end to mark its resting place, now part of the *marae*.

painted, well-kept, old-school motel units are right next to the shops. Kayak/bike hire costs $20/15 per hour.

Annie's Cafe & Restaurant   CAFE, RESTAURANT $
(146 Jervois St; meals $10-22; ⊙ 7am-3pm Easter-Oct, 7am-late Nov–Easter) An old-fashioned licensed eatery in the main street, serving espresso, sandwiches and local specialities such as flounder and whitebait with kumara chips.

ℹ Getting There & Away

Kawhia doesn't have a bus service. Take SH31 from Otorohanga (58km) or explore the scenic but rough road to Raglan (50km, 22km unsealed).

Otorohanga

POP 2700

Otorohanga's main street is festooned with images of cherished Kiwiana icons: sheep, gumboots, jandals, No 8 wire, All Blacks, pavlova, and the beloved Buzzy Bee children's toy. The town's Kiwi House is well worth a visit.

◉ Sights

Otorohanga Kiwi House & Native Bird Park   ZOO
(www.kiwihouse.org.nz; 20 Alex Telfer Dr; adult/child $22/7; ⊙ 9am-4.30pm Sep-May, to 4pm Jun-Aug) This bird barn has a nocturnal enclosure where you can see active kiwi energetically digging with their long beaks, searching for food. This is the only place in NZ where you

can see a great spotted kiwi, the biggest of the three kiwi species. The kiwi get fed at 1.30pm daily. Other native birds, such as kaka, kea, morepork and weka, are also on show.

Ed Hillary Walkway   MEMORIAL
(⊙ 24hr) FREE As well as the Kiwiana decorating the main street, the Ed Hillary Walkway (running off Maniapoto St) has information panels on the All Blacks, Marmite and, of course, Sir Ed.

⌁ Sleeping

Otorohanga Holiday Park   HOLIDAY PARK $
(☑ 07-873 7253; www.kiwiholidaypark.co.nz; 20 Huiputea Dr; campsites from $30, cabins & units $89-120; @ ��) It's not the most attractive locale, but this friendly park's tidy facilities include a fitness centre and sauna. And if you can't find a bed in Waitomo (it happens), Otorohanga is only 16km away.

✖ Eating & Drinking

Origin Coffee Station   CAFE $
(www.origincoffee.co.nz; 7 Wahanui Cres; coffee $4-5; ⊙ 8.30am-4.30pm Mon-Fri) The folks at Origin are dead serious about coffee – sourcing, importing and roasting it themselves.

Countdown   SUPERMARKET $
(www.countdown.co.nz; 123 Maniapoto St; ⊙ 7am-10pm) There's no supermarket at Waitomo Caves, so stock up en route to the caves in Otorohonga.

Thirsty Weta   PUB
(www.theweta.co.nz; 57 Maniapoto St; meals $10-37; ⊙ 10am-1am) Hearty meals including pizza, steak, burgers and quesadillas; later on a pub–meets–wine bar ambience kicks off as the local musos plug in.

ℹ Information

Otorohanga i-SITE (☑ 07-873 8951; www.otorohanga.co.nz; 27 Turongo St; ⊙ 9am-5pm Mon-Fri, 10am-2pm Sat & Sun; ⊜) Free wi-fi and local information.

ℹ Getting There & Away

BUS

InterCity (☑ 09-583 5780; www.intercity.co.nz) Buses run from Otorohanga to Auckland ($47, 3¼ hours, four daily), Te Awamutu ($21, 30 minutes, three daily), Te Kuiti ($20, one hour, three daily) and Rotorua ($53, 2½ hours, two daily).

Naked Bus (✆0900 625 33; www.nakedbus. com) Runs one bus daily to Waitomo Caves ($20, 30 minutes), Hamilton ($25, one hour) and New Plymouth ($30, 3¼ hours).

Waitomo Shuttle (✆0800 808 279, 07-873 8279; one-way adult/child $12/7) Heads to the Waitomo Caves five times daily, coordinating with bus and train arrivals. Bookings recommended.

TRAIN

Otorohanga is on the **Northern Explorer** (✆0800 872 467; www.kiwiscenic.co.nz) train route between Auckland (from $48, 3¼ hours) and Wellington (from $99, nine hours) via Hamilton ($48, 50 minutes).

Waitomo Caves

Even if damp, dark tunnels are your idea of hell, head to Waitomo anyway. The limestone caves and glowing bugs here are one of the North Island's premier attractions.

The name Waitomo comes from *wai* (water) and *tomo* (hole or shaft): dotted across this region are numerous shafts dropping into underground cave systems and streams. There are 300-plus mapped caves in the area: the three main caves – Glowworm, Ruakuri and Aranui – have been bewitching visitors for over 100 years.

Your Waitomo experience needn't be claustrophobic: the electrically lit, cathedral-like Glowworm Cave is far from squeezy. But if it's tight, gut-wrenching, soaking-wet, pitch-black excitement you're after, Waitomo can oblige.

⊙ Sights

Waitomo Caves Visitor Centre VISITOR CENTRE (✆0800 456 922; www.waitomo.com; Waitomo Caves Rd; ⊙9am-5pm) The big-three Waitomo Caves are all operated by the same company, based at the flash Waitomo

WAIKATO & COROMANDEL PENINSULA WAITOMO CAVES

Waitomo Caves

Waitomo Caves

⊙ Top Sights
1 Glowworm Cave A2

⊙ Sights
2 Opapake Pa D1
3 Waitomo Caves Discovery Centre B1
4 Waitomo Caves Visitor Centre A1

⊙ Activities, Courses & Tours
5 CaveWorld B1
6 Legendary Black Water Rafting
   Company D2
   Spellbound .... (see 13)
7 Waitomo Adventures C2

⊙ Sleeping
8 Abseil Inn C2
9 Kiwi Paka B2
10 Waitomo Caves Guest Lodge B1
11 Waitomo Top 10 Holiday Park B1
12 YHA Juno Hall Waitomo D2

⊗ Eating
13 Florence's Kitchen B1
14 Huhu B1
   Morepork Cafe .... (see 9)

⊙ Drinking & Nightlife
   King Country Brewing Company ..(see 13)

GLOWWORM MAGIC

Glowworms are the larvae of the fungus gnat. The larva glowworm has luminescent organs that produce a soft, greenish light. Living in a sort of hammock suspended from an overhang, it weaves sticky threads that trail down and catch unwary insects attracted by its light. When an insect flies towards the light it gets stuck in the threads – the glowworm just has to reel it in for a feed.

The larval stage lasts from six to nine months, depending on how much food the glowworm gets. When it has grown to about the size of a matchstick, it goes into a pupa stage, much like a cocoon. The adult fungus gnat emerges about two weeks later.

The adult insect doesn't live very long because it doesn't have a mouth. It emerges, mates, lays eggs and dies, all within about two or three days. The sticky eggs, laid in groups of 40 or 50, hatch in about three weeks to become larval glowworms.

Glowworms thrive in moist, dark caves but they can survive anywhere if they have the requisites of moisture, an overhang to suspend from and insects to eat. Waitomo is famous for its glowworms but you can see them in many other places around NZ, both in caves and outdoors.

When you come upon glowworms, don't touch their hammocks or hanging threads, try not to make loud noises and don't shine a light right on them. All of these things will cause them to dim their lights. It takes them a few hours to become bright again, during which time the grub will go hungry. The glowworms that shine most brightly are the hungriest.

Caves Visitor Centre (behind the Glowworm Cave), which incorporates a cafe and theatre. Various combo deals are available, including a Triple Cave Combo (adult/child $91/40). Try to avoid the large tour groups, most of which arrive between 10.30am and 2.30pm.

★ **Glowworm Cave**   CAVE
(adult/child $48/21; ⊘45min tours every 30min 9am-5pm) The guided tour of the Glowworm Cave, which is behind the visitor centre, leads past impressive stalactites and stalagmites into a large cavern known as the Cathedral. The highlight comes at the tour's end when you board a boat and swing off onto the river. As your eyes grow accustomed to the dark you'll see a Milky Way of little lights surrounding you – these are the glowworms. Book your tour at the visitor centre.

The acoustics are so good that Dame Kiri Te Kanawa and the Vienna Boys Choir have given concerts here.

Aranui Cave   CAVE
(adult/child $48/21; ⊘1hr tours 9.30am, 11am, 1pm, 2.30pm & 4pm) Three kilometres west from the Glowworm Cave is Aranui Cave. This cave is dry (hence no glowworms) but compensates with an incredible array of limestone formations. Thousands of tiny 'straw' stalactites hang from the ceiling. Book tours at the visitor centre, from where there is also transport to the cave entrance. A 15-minute bush walk is also included.

Ruakuri Cave   CAVE
(✆0800 782 587, 07-878 6219; adult/child $67/26; ⊘2hr tours 9am, 10am, 11.30am, 12.30pm, 1.30pm, 2.30pm & 3pm) Ruakuri Cave has an impressive 15m-high spiral staircase, bypassing a Maori burial site at the cave entrance. Tours lead through 1.6km of the 7.5km system, taking in caverns with glowworms, subterranean streams and waterfalls, and intricate limestone structures. Visitors have described it as spiritual – some claim it's haunted – and it's customary to wash your hands when leaving to remove the *tapu* (taboo). Book tours at the visitor centre, or at the departure point, the Legendary Black Water Rafting Company.

Waitomo Caves Discovery Centre   MUSEUM
(✆07-878 7640, 0800 474 839; www.waitomo-caves.com; 21 Waitomo Caves Rd; adult/child $5/ free; ⊘9am-5.30pm) Adjoining the i-SITE, the Waitomo Caves Discovery Centre has excellent exhibits explaining how caves are formed, the flora and fauna that thrive in them and the history of Waitomo's caves and cave exploration.

🏃 Activities

Underground

Legendary Black Water Rafting Company
CAVING, ADVENTURE TOUR

(📞 0800 782 5874; www.waitomo.com; 585 Waitomo Caves Rd; ⊙ Black Labyrinth tour 9am, 10.30am, noon, 1.30pm & 3pm, Black Abyss tour 9am & 2pm, Black Odyssey tour 10am & 2.30pm) The Black Labyrinth tour (three hours, $125) involves floating in a wetsuit on an inner tube down a river that flows through Ruakuri Cave. The highlight is leaping off a small waterfall and then floating through a long, glowworm-covered passage. The trip ends with showers, soup and bagels in the cafe. The more adventurous Black Abyss tour (five hours, $225) includes a 35m abseil into Ruakuri Cave, a flying fox and more glowworms and tubing.

Recently launched, the Black Odyssey tour (four hours, $175) is a challenging dry caving adventure including flying foxes and negotiating high wires. Minimum ages apply for all tours, and there are 10% discounts if you prebook online.

Spellbound
CAVING, GUIDED TOUR

(📞 0800 773 552, 07-878 7622; www.glowworm.co.nz; 10 Waitomo Caves Rd; adult/child $73/26; ⊙ 3hr tours 10am, 11am, 2pm & 3pm, closed Jun) Spellbound is a good option if you don't want to get wet, are more interested in glowworms than an 'action' experience, and want to avoid the big groups in the main caves. Small-group tours access parts of the heavily glowworm-dappled Mangawhitiakau cave system, 12km south of Waitomo (...and you still get to ride in a raft!).

Waitomo Adventures
CAVING, ADVENTURE TOUR

(📞 07-878 7788, 0800 924 866; www.waitomo.co.nz; 654 Waitomo Caves Rd) Waitomo Adventures offers various cave adventures, with discounts for combos and advance bookings. The Lost World trip ($340/490, four/seven hours) combines a 100m abseil with walking, rock climbing, wading and swimming. Haggas Honking Holes ($260, four hours) includes three waterfall abseils, rock climbing and a subterranean river. TumuTumu Toobing ($180, four hours) is a walking, climbing, swimming and tubing trip. St Benedict's Cavern ($180, three hours) includes abseiling and a subterranean flying fox.

Green Glow Eco-Adventures
CAVING, ADVENTURE TOUR

(📞 0800 476 459; www.greenglow.co.nz; 1117 Oparure Rd, Te Kuiti; 6hr tours per person $220) Green Glow Eco-Adventures runs customised, small-group Waitomo tours, putting a caving, rock-climbing, abseiling, photographic or glowworm spin on your day. It's based in Te Kuiti, 20 minutes from Waitomo.

CaveWorld
CAVING, ADVENTURE TOURS

(📞 0800 228 338, 07-878 6577; www.caveworld.co.nz; cnr Waitomo Caves Rd & Hotel Access Rd) CaveWorld runs the Tube It ($139, two hours) black-water rafting trip through glowworm-filled Te Anaroa. Also available are a glowworm-illuminated night abseil down a 45m crevice called the Glowworm Canyon ($199, two hours), or the Footwhistle Glowworm Cave Tour ($55, one hour).

Kiwi Cave Rafting
CAVING, ADVENTURE TOUR

(📞 07-873 9149, 0800 228 372; www.caveraft.com; 95 Waitomo Caves Rd) These small-group expeditions (five hours, $225) start with abseil training, followed by a 27m descent into a natural cave, and then a float along a subterranean river on an inner tube with plenty of glowworms. After some caving, a belayed rock climb up a 20m cliff brings you to the surface. A three-hour dry tour ($125) without the inner-tube adventure is also available.

WAIKATO & COROMANDEL PENINSULA WAITOMO CAVES

LOCAL KNOWLEDGE

WAITOMO CAVES

The best way to experience the Waitomo glowworm caves is via black-water rafting. It's an exhilarating experience and involves getting dressed up in a wetsuit (laughing at how funny everyone looks is half the fun), choosing an inflatable inner tube to sit in (another hilarious experience) and travelling through the limestone caves with two guides, your wits, and the glowworms. It is a real hands-on experience and requires some agility and the guts to jump backwards down some small waterfalls as you make your way through the tunnels. You finish off the trip quietly drifting through the caves in your tube, looking at the glowworms with your head lamp turned off.

Dr Farah Rangikoepa Palmer,
former captain of the Black Ferns (NZ's women's rugby team)

Tramping

The Waitomo i-SITE has free pamphlets on walks in the area. The walk from **Aranui Cave** to **Ruakuri Cave** is an excellent short path. From the Waitomo Caves Visitor Centre, the 5km, three-hour-return **Waitomo Walkway** takes off through farmland, following Waitomo Stream to the **Ruakuri Scenic Reserve**, where a 30-minute return walk passes by a natural limestone tunnel. There are glowworms here at night – drive to the car park and bring a torch to find your way. Near Waitomo Adventures a steep 20-minute walk leads through bush then along farmland to the abandoned **Opapake Pa**, where terraces and kumara pits are visible.

Dundle Hill Walk
TRAMPING
(📞0800 924 866, 07-878 7788; www.dundlehillwalk.com; adult/child $75/35) The self-guided privately run Dundle Hill Walk is a 27km, two-day/one-night loop walk through Waitomo's bush and farmland, including overnight bunkhouse accommodation high up in the bush.

🛏 Sleeping

Waitomo Top 10 Holiday Park
HOLIDAY PARK $
(📞0508 498 666, 07-878 7639; www.waitomopark.co.nz; 12 Waitomo Caves Rd; campsites from $23, cabins $70-130, units $150-180; @ 🛜 🏊) This lovely holiday park in the heart of the village has spotless facilities, modern cabins and plenty of outdoor distractions to keep the kids busy.

Kiwi Paka
HOSTEL $
(📞07-878 3395; www.waitomokiwipaka.co.nz; Hotel Access Rd; dm/s/d $32/65/70, chalets s/d/tw/q $95/100/110/160; @ 🛜) This purpose-built, alpine-style hostel has four-bed dorms in the main lodge, plus separate peak-roofed chalets, Morepork Cafe on site and super-tidy facilities. Popular with big groups.

YHA Juno Hall Waitomo
HOSTEL $
(📞07-878 7649; www.junowaitomo.co.nz; 600 Waitomo Caves Rd; campsites from $17, dm $30, d with/without bathroom $84/74; @ 🛜 🏊) A slick purpose-built hostel 1km from the village with a warm welcome, a warmer wood fire in the woody lounge area, and an outdoor pool and tennis court.

Abseil Inn
B&B $$
(📞07-878 7815; www.abseilinn.co.nz; 709 Waitomo Caves Rd; d from $150; 🛜) A *veeery* steep driveway takes you to this delightful B&B with four themed rooms, great breakfasts and witty hosts. The biggest room has a double bath and valley views.

Waitomo Caves Guest Lodge
B&B $$
(📞0800 465 762, 07-878 7641; www.waitomo-cavesguestlodge.co.nz; 7 Te Anga Rd; s $90, d incl breakfast $110-130; 🛜) Bag your own cosy little hillside en suite cabin at this central operation with a sweet garden setting. The top cabins have valley views. Large continental breakfast and friendly resident dog included.

🍴 Eating & Drinking

The general store in Waitomo sells the basics, but it's cheaper to stock up in Otorohanga or Te Kuiti before you visit.

⭐ Huhu
CAFE, MODERN NZ $$
(📞07-878 6674; www.huhucafe.co.nz; 10 Waitomo Caves Rd; small plates $11-17, mains $19-33; ⏰noon-late; 🛜) Slick and modern Huhu has great views from the terrace and sublime contemporary NZ food. Sip a strong coffee or Kiwi craft beer, or graze through a seasonal tapas-style menu of delights like slow-cooked lamb, teriyaki salmon and organic Scotch fillet steak.

Florence's Kitchen
CAFE $$
(www.facebook.com/WaitomoGeneralStore; Waitomo General Store, 15 Waitomo Caves Rd; snacks & mains $12-20; ⏰7.30am-10pm) In the Waitomo general store with a wide range of pre- and postcaving sustenance.

Morepork Cafe
CAFE, PIZZERIA $$
(Kiwi Paka, Hotel Access Rd; breakfast & lunch $10-18, dinner $15-27; ⏰8am-10.30pm; 🛜) At the Kiwi Paka backpackers is this cheery joint, a jack-of-all-trades eatery serving breakfast, lunch and dinner either inside or out on the deck. The 'Caveman' pizza is a definite winner.

King Country Brewing Company
BREWERY
(www.facebook.com/kingcountrybrewingcompany; Waitomo General Store, 15 Waitomo Caves Rd) This craft brewery does four top drops – an IPA, a pale ale, a wheat beer and a cider – and features occasional guest beers from other smaller Kiwi breweries. Grab a tasting rack of all four for $16.

ℹ Information

There's no petrol in town, but there's an ATM at Kiwi Paka.

Waitomo i-SITE (📞07-878 7640, 0800 474 839; www.waitomocaves.com; 21 Waitomo Caves Rd; ⏰9am-5.30pm) Internet access, post office and booking agent.

ℹ Getting There & Away

Naked Bus (☑0900 625 33; www.nakedbus. com) Runs once daily to Otorohanga ($20, 20 minutes), Hamilton ($25, 1¼ hours) and New Plymouth ($30, three hours).

Waitomo Shuttle (☑0800 808 279, 07-873 8279; waikiwi@ihug.co.nz; one-way adult/child $12/7) Heads to the caves five times daily from Otorohanga (15 minutes away), coordinating with bus and train arrivals.

Waitomo Wanderer (☑03-477 9083, 0800 000 4321; www.travelheadfirst.com) Operates a daily return services from Rotorua or Taupo, with optional caving, glowworm and tubing add-ons (packages from $133). Shuttle-only services are $99 return.

Waitomo to Awakino

This obscure route, heading west of Waitomo on Te Anga Rd, is a slow but fascinating alternative to SH3 if Taranaki's your goal. Only 12km of the 111km route remains unsealed, but it's nearly all winding and narrow. Allow around two hours (not including stops) and fill up with petrol.

Walks in the **Tawarau Forest**, 20km west of the Waitomo Caves, are outlined in DOC's *Waitomo & King Country Tracks* booklet ($1, available from DOC in Hamilton or Te Kuiti), including a one-hour track to the Tawarau Falls from the end of Appletree Rd.

The **Mangapohue Natural Bridge Scenic Reserve**, 26km west of Waitomo, is a 5.5-hectare reserve with a giant natural limestone arch. It's a five-minute walk to the arch on a wheelchair-accessible pathway. On the far side, big rocks full of 35-million-year-old oyster fossils jut up from the grass, and at night you'll see glowworms.

About 4km further west is **Piripiri Caves Scenic Reserve**, where a five-minute walk leads to a large cave containing fossils of giant oysters. Bring a torch and be prepared to get muddy after heavy rain. Steps wind down into the gloom...

The impressively tiered, 30m **Marokopa Falls** are 32km west of Waitomo. A short track (15 minutes return) from the road leads to the bottom of the falls.

Just past Te Anga you can turn north to Kawhia, 59km away, or continue southwest to **Marokopa** (population 1560), a small black-sand village on the coast with some scarily big new mansions starting to appear. The whole Te Anga/Marokopa area is riddled with caves.

Marokopa Campground (☑07-876 7444; marokopacampground@xtra.co.nz; campsites from $24, dm/van d $18/45) ain't flash but it's in a nice spot, close to the coast. There's a small shop for grocery basics.

The road heads south to **Kiritehere**, through idyllic farmland to **Moeatoa** then turns right (south) into Mangatoa Rd. Now you're in serious backcountry, heading into the dense **Whareorino Forest**. For trampers, the 16-bunk DOC-run **Leitch's Hut** (☑07-878 1050; www.doc.govt.nz; per adult $5) has a toilet, water and a wood stove.

At **Waikawau** take the 5km detour along the unsealed road to the coast near **Ngarupupu Point**, where a 100m walk through a dank tunnel opens out on an exquisitely isolated stretch of black-sand beach. Think twice about swimming here as there are often dangerous rips in the surf.

The road then continues through another twisty 28km, passing lush forest and the occasional farm before joining SH3 east of Awakino (p190).

Te Kuiti

POP 4380

Cute Te Kuiti sits in a valley between picturesque hills. Welcome to the shearing capital of the world, especially if you visit for the annual Great New Zealand Muster.

◉ Sights

Big Shearer LANDMARK
(Rora St) This 7m, 7½-tonne Big Shearer statue is at the southern end of town.

Te Kuititanga-O-Nga-Whakaaro MONUMENT
(Rora St) Te Kuititanga-O-Nga-Whakaaro (The Gathering of Thoughts and Ideas) is a beautiful pavilion of etched-glass, *tukutuku* (woven flax panels) and wooden carvings that celebrates the town's history.

✯ Festivals & Events

Great New Zealand Muster CULTURE, FOOD
(www.waitomo.govt.nz/events/the-great-nz-muster) The highlight of the Great New Zealand Muster is the legendary **Running of the Sheep**: when 2000 woolly demons stampede down Te Kuiti's main street. The festival in late March/early April includes sheep-shearing championships, a parade, Maori cultural performances, live music, barbecues, *hangi* and market stalls.

🛏 Sleeping & Eating

Waitomo Lodge Motel MOTEL **$$**
(📞07-878 0003; www.waitomo-lodge.co.nz; 62 Te Kumi Rd; units $125-140; 🛜) At the Waitomo end of Te Kuiti, this motel's modern rooms feature contemporary art, flat-screen TVs and little decks overlooking Mangaokewa Stream in the units at the back.

Simply the Best B&B B&B **$$**
(📞07-878 8191; www.simplythebestbnb.co.nz; 129 Gadsby Rd; s/d incl breakfast $70/110) It's hard to argue with the immodest name when the prices are this reasonable, the breakfast this generous, and the hosts this charming.

New World SUPERMARKET **$**
(www.newworld.co.nz; Te Kumi Rd; ⊙8am-8pm) Waitomo-bound self-caterers should stock up.

Bosco Cafe CAFE **$**
(theteam@boscocafe.co.nz; 57 Te Kumi Rd; mains $10-20; ⊙8am-5pm; 🛜🍴) This excellent industrial-chic cafe offers great coffee and tempting food (try the bacon-wrapped meatloaf with greens). Free wi-fi with purchase.

ℹ Information

DOC (Department of Conservation; 📞07-878 1050; www.doc.govt.nz; 78 Taupiri St; ⊙8am-4.30pm Mon-Fri)

Te Kuiti i-SITE (📞07-878 8077; www.waitomo.govt.nz; Rora St; ⊙9am-5pm Mon-Fri, 10am-2pm Sat) Internet access and visitor information.

ℹ Getting There & Away

BUS

InterCity (📞09-583 5780; www.intercity.co.nz) buses run daily to the following destinations (among others):

DESTINATION	PRICE ($)	DURATION (HR)	FREQUENCY (DAILY)
Auckland	28-58	3½	3
Mokau	30	1	2
New Plymouth	30	2½	2
Otorohanga	20	¾	3
Taumarunui	34	1¼	1

Naked Bus (📞0900 625 33; www.nakedbus.com) runs once daily to Auckland ($35, four hours), Hamilton ($25, 1½ hours), New Plymouth ($30, 2¼ hours) and Otorohanga ($20, 30 minutes).

Te Kuiti to Mokau

From Te Kuiti, SH3 runs southwest to the coast before following the rugged shoreline to New Plymouth. Detour at Pio Pio northwest to the Mangaotaki valley and **Hairy Feet Waitomo** (📞07-877 8003; www.hairyfeetwaitomo.co.nz; 1411 Mangaotaki Rd, Pio Pio; adult/child $50/25; ⊙10am & 1pm), one of NZ's newest Middle Earth–themed film-location attractions. Scenes from *The Hobbit* were filmed here with a background of towering limestone cliffs.

Along this scenic route the sheep stations sprout peculiar limestone formations before giving way to lush native bush as the highway winds along the course of the Awakino River.

The Awakino River spills into the Tasman at **Awakino** (population 60), a small settlement where boats shelter in the estuary while locals find refuge at the rustic **Awakino Hotel** (📞06-752 9815; www.awakinohotel.co.nz; SH3; meals $11-20; ⊙7am-11pm).

A little further south the impressive **Maniaroa Marae** dominates the cliff above the highway. This important complex houses the anchor stone of the *Tainui waka* which brought this region's original people from their Polynesian homeland. You can get a good view of the intimidatingly carved meeting house, Te Kohaarua, from outside the fence – don't cross into the *marae* unless someone invites you.

Five kilometres further south, as Mt Taranaki starts to emerge on the horizon, is the village of **Mokau** (population 400). It offers a fine black-sand beach and good surfing and fishing. From August to November the Mokau River (the second longest on the North Island) spawns whitebait and subsequent swarms of territorial whitebaiters. The town's interesting **Tainui Historical Society Museum** (📞06-752 9072; mokaumuseum@vodafone.co.nz; SH3; admission by donation; ⊙10am-4pm) has old photographs and artefacts from when this once-isolated outpost was a coal and lumber shipping port for settlements along the river. **Mokau River Cruises** (📞0800 665 2874; www.mokaurivercruises.co.nz; adult/child $50/15) operates a three-hour river cruise with commentary onboard the historic MV *Cygnet*. Twilight cruises are also avialable.

Just north of Mokau, **Seaview Holiday Park** (📞0800 478 786; seaviewhp@xtra.co.nz; SH3; campsites from $14, d cabins/units from $65/90) is rustic, but it's right on an expansive beach. Above the village the **Mokau Motel** (✆06-752 9725; www.mokaumotels.co.nz; SH3; s/d/ste from $95/110/125; 🖰) offers fishing advice, self-contained units and three luxury suites.

Taumarunui

POP 5140

Taumarunui on a cold day can feel a bit miserable, but this town in the heart of the King Country has potential. The main reason to stay here is to kayak on the Whanganui River or as a cheaper base for skiing in Tongariro National Park, and there are some beaut walks and cycling tracks around town.

For details on the Forgotten World Highway between Taumarunui and Stratford, see Taranaki (p226). For details on canoeing and kayaking on the Whanganui River, see Whanganui National Park (p237).

◉ Sights & Activities

The 3km **Riverbank Walk** along the Whanganui River runs from Cherry Grove Domain, 1km south of town, to Taumarunui Holiday Park. **Te Peka Lookout**, across the Ongarue River on the western edge of town, is a good vantage point.

Hakiaha Street   STREET

At the street's eastern end is **Hauaroa Whare**, a beautifully carved house. At the western end **Te Rohe Potae** memorialises King Tawhiao's assertion of his *mana* (authority) over the King Country in a sculpture of a top hat on a large rock.

Raurimu Spiral   RAILWAY

The Raurimu Spiral, 30km south of town, is a unique feat of railway engineering that was completed in 1908 after 10 years' work. Rail buffs can experience the spiral by catching the *Northern Explorer* train linking Auckland and Wellington to National Park township (around $96 return from Otorohonga). Unfortunately this train ceased stopping in Taumarunui in 2012.

Forgotten World Adventures   TOUR

(✆0800 7245 2278; www.forgottenworldadventures.co.nz; 1 Hakiaha St; 1/2 days $285/495; ⊙booking office 9am-2pm) Ride the rails on quirky converted former golf carts on the railway line linking Taumarunui to the tiny hamlet of Whangamomona in the Taranaki region. The spectacular trip takes in 20 tunnels, and other options include a rail and jetboat combo, and longer two-day excursions covering the full 140km from Taumarunui to Stratford (including an overnight stay in

---

PUREORA FOREST PARK & THE TIMBER TRAIL

Fringing the western edge of Lake Taupo, the 78,000-hectare Pureora Forest is home to NZ's tallest totara tree. Logging was stopped in the 1980s after a long campaign by conservationists, and the subsequent regeneration is impressive. Hiking routes through the park include tracks to the summits of **Mt Pureora** (1165m) and the rock pinnacle of **Mt Titiraupenga** (1042m). A 12m-high tower, a short walk from the Bismarck Rd car park, provides a canopy-level view of the forest for birdwatchers.

To stay overnight in one of three standard **DOC huts** (adult/child $5/2.50) you'll need to buy hut tickets in advance, unless you have a Backcountry Hut Pass. The three **campsites** (adult/child $6/3) have self-registration boxes. Hut tickets, maps and information are available from DOC.

Awhina Wilderness Experience (www.awhinatours.co.nz; per person $90) offers five-hour walking tours with local Maori guides through virgin bush to the summit of Titiraupenga, their sacred mountain. Farmstay accommodation is also available.

Another option is to ride the spectacular **Timber Trail** from Pureora village in the north of the forest southwest for 85km to Ongarue. Accommodation and shuttle transport is available at **Pa Harakeke** (✆07-929 8708; www.paharekeke.co.nz; 138 Maraeroa Rd; d $150), an interesting Maori-operated initiative near Pureora village, and **Black Fern Lodge** (✆07-894 7677; www.blackfernlodge.co.nz; Ongarue Stream Rd, Waimiha; per person from $58) at Waimiha gets rave reviews for its home cooking.

See www.thetimbertrail.com for maps, shuttle and bike-hire information and route planning.

Whangamomona). For more information, see p226.

Taumarunui Jet Tours   JETBOATING
(☑0800 853 886, 07-896 6055; www.taumarunui-jettours.co.nz; Cherry Grove Domain; 30/60min tour from $60/100) High-octane jetboat trips on the Whanganui River.

🛏 Sleeping & Eating

Taumarunui Holiday Park   HOLIDAY PARK $
(☑07-895 9345; www.taumarunuiholidaypark.co.nz; SH4; campsites from $16, d cabin & cottage $65-85; @🕯) On the banks of the Whanganui River, 4km east of town, this shady camping ground offers safe river swimming and clean facilities. The friendly owners have lots of ideas on what to see and do.

Twin Rivers Motel   MOTEL $$
(☑07-895 8063; www.twinrivers.co.nz; 23 Marae St; units $90-215; 🕯) The 12 units at Twin Rivers are spick and span, and bigger units sleep up to seven.

Jasmine's Cafe &
Thai Restaurant   CAFE, THAI $$
(43 Hakiaha St; mains $10-16; ☺7am-9pm) Robust all-day breakfasts, decent coffee and stonking toasted sandwiches, before morphing tastily into a Thai restaurant. Lunch specials ($10 to $13) are good value.

ℹ Information

Taumarunui i-SITE (☑07-895 7494; www.visitruapehu.com; 116 Hakiaha St; ☺9am-5pm) Visitor information and internet access.

ℹ Getting There & Away

Taumarunui is on SH4, 81km south of Te Kuiti and 41km north of National Park township.

InterCity (☑0508 353 947; www.intercity.co.nz) buses head to Auckland ($29 to $61, 4½ hours, one daily) via Te Kuiti ($14 to $30, one hour), and to Palmerston North ($29 to $61, 4¾ hours, one daily) via National Park ($21, 30 minutes).

Owhango

POP 210

A pint-sized village where all the street names start with 'O', Owhango makes a cosy base for walkers, mountain bikers (the 42 Traverse ends here) and skiers who can't afford to stay closer to the slopes in Tongariro National Park. Take Omaki Rd for a two-hour loop walk through virgin forest in Ohinetonga Scenic Reserve.

🛏 Sleeping & Eating

Forest Lodge   LODGE $
(☑07-895 4854; www.owhangohotel.co.nz/forest-lodge; 12 Omaki Rd; dm/d $25/60, motel d $80; @🕯) A snug backpackers with comfortable, clean rooms and good communal spaces. For privacy junkies there's a separate self-contained motel next door. Mountain-bike rental and bike-shuttle services for the 42 Traverse are also available.

Blue Duck Station   LODGE, HOSTEL $$
(☑07-895 6276; www.blueduckstation.co.nz; RD2, Whakahoro; dm/d $45/195) 🌿 Overlooking the Retaruke River 36km southwest of Owhango (take the Kaitieke turn-off 1km south of town), this eco-savvy place is actually various lodges, offering accommodation from dorms in an old shearers' quarters to a self-contained family cottage sleeping eight. The owners are mad-keen conservationists, restoring native-bird habitats and historic buildings.

Cafe 39 South   CAFE $
(☑07-895 4800; www.facebook.com/cafe39south; SH4; meals $9-20; ☺8am-3pm Mon-Thu, to 4pm Sat & Sun) The food is delicious – try the sweet-corn fritters – the coffee is excellent, and the electric fire and daily soup specials will make you want to linger on cold days. The 39° South latitude marker is just across the road.

ℹ Getting There & Away

Owhango is 14km south of Taumarunui on SH4. All the **InterCity** (☑0508 353 947; www.intercity.co.nz) buses that stop in Taumarunui also stop here.

COROMANDEL

History

This whole area, including the peninsula, the islands and both sides of the gulf, was known to the Maori as Hauraki. Various *iwi* (tribes) held claim to pockets of it, including the Pare Hauraki branch of the Tainui tribes and others descended from Te Arawa and earlier migrations. Polynesian artefacts and evidence of moa hunting have been found, pointing to around 1000 years of continuous occupation.

The Hauraki *iwi* were some of the first to be exposed to European traders. The region's proximity to Auckland, safe anchorages and ready supply of valuable timber initially led to a booming economy. Kauri logging was big business on the peninsula. Allied to the

Coromandel Peninsula

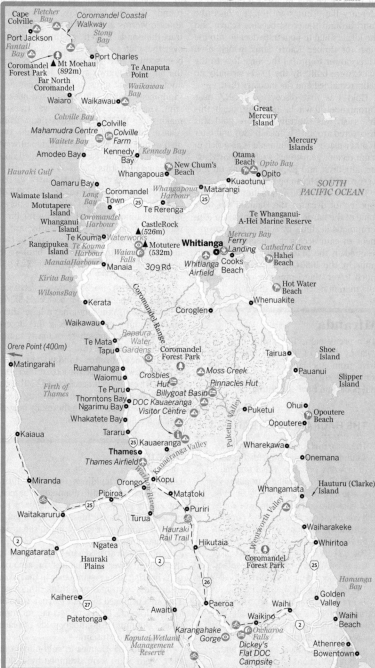

0 ——— 20 km
0 ——— 10 miles

Cape Colville
Fletcher Bay
Coromandel Coastal Walkway
Stony Bay
Port Jackson
Fantail Bay
Port Charles
Coromandel Forest Park
Mt Moehau (892m)
Te Anaputa Point
Far North Coromandel
Waikawau Bay
Waiaro
Waikawau
Colville Bay
Colville
Mahamudra Centre
Colville Farm
Waitete Bay
Kennedy Bay
Great Mercury Island
Amodeo Bay
Haeraki Gulf
Whangapoua
New Chum's Beach
Kennedy Bay
Otama Beach
Opito Bay
Opito
Mercury Islands
Kuaotunu
SOUTH PACIFIC OCEAN
Oamaru Bay
Long Bay
Coromandel Town
Whangapoua Harbour
Matarangi
Waimate Island
Motutapere Island
Te Rerenga
Whanganui Island
Coromandel Harbour
Te Kouma
CastleRock (526m)
Te Whanganui-A-Hei Marine Reserve
Mercury Bay
Rangipukea Island
Te Kouma Harbour
Waterworks
Motutere (532m)
Whitianga
Ferry Landing
Cathedral Cove
ManaiaHarbour
Waiau Falls
Manaia
309 Rd
Whitianga Airfield
Cooks Beach
Hahei Beach
Kirita Bay
WilsonsBay
Hot Water Beach
Kerata
Whenuakite
Waikawau
Coroglen
Orere Point (400m)
Te Mata
Rapaura Water Gardens
Coromandel Range
Tapu
Coromandel Forest Park
Tairua
Shoe Island
Matingarahi
Ruamahunga
Crosbies Hut
Moss Creek
Pauanui
Slipper Island
Waiomu
Te Puru
Billygoat Basin
Pinnacles Hut
Firth of Thames
Thorntons Bay
Ngarimu Bay
DOC Kauaeranga Visitor Centre
Puketui
Ohui
Opoutere Beach
Whakatete Bay
Opoutere
Taruru
Kaiaua
Kauaeranga
Wharekawa
Thames
Kauaeranga Valley
Thames Airfield
Puketui Valley
Onemana
Miranda
Orongo
Kopu
Whangamata
Hauturu (Clarke) Island
Pipiroa
Matatoki
Waitakaruru
Turua
Puriri
Wentworth Valley
Waiharakeke
Ngatea
Hauraki Rail Trail
Hikutaia
Whiritoa
Mangatarata
Hauraki Plains
Coromandel Forest Park
Kaihere
Awaiti
Paeroa
Waihi
Homunga Bay
Golden Valley
Patetonga
Karangahake Gorge
Waikino
Owharoa Falls
Waihi Beach
Kaputai Wetland Management Reserve
Dickey's Flat DOC Campsite
Athenree
Bowentown

timber trade was shipbuilding, which took off in 1832 when a mill was established at Mercury Bay. Things got tougher once the kauri around the coast became scarce and the loggers had to penetrate deeper into the bush for timber. Kauri dams, which used water power to propel the huge logs to the coast, were built. By the 1930s virtually no kauri remained and the industry died.

Gold was first discovered in NZ near Coromandel Town in 1852. Although this first rush was short-lived, more gold was discovered around Thames in 1867 and later in other places. The peninsula is also rich in semiprecious gemstones, such as quartz, agate, amethyst and jasper. A fossick on any west-coast beach can be rewarding.

Despite successful interactions with Europeans for decades, the Hauraki *iwi* were some of the hardest hit by colonisation. Unscrupulous dealings by settlers and government to gain access to valuable resources resulted in the Maori losing most of their lands by the 1880s. Even today there is a much lower Maori presence on the peninsula than in neighbouring districts.

Miranda

It's a pretty name for a settlement on the swampy Firth of Thames, just an hour's drive from Auckland. The two reasons to come here are splashing around in the thermal pools and bird-watching.

THE HAURAKI RAIL TRAIL

The cycle trail running from Thames south to Paeroa, and then further south to Te Aroha, or east to Waihi, the Hauraki Rail Trail, is growing in popularity due to its proximity to the bigger cities of Auckland and Hamilton. Two- and three-day itineraries are most popular, but shorter sections of the trail can be very rewarding too. The spur from Paeroa east through the Karangahake Gorge via Waikino to Waihi is spectacular as it skirts a picturesque river valley. The key centres of Thames, Paeroa, Te Aroha and Waihi have an expanding range of related services including bike hire, shuttles and accommodation. See www.haurakirailtrail.co.nz for detailed information including trail maps and recommendations for day rides.

This is one of the most accessible spots for studying waders or shorebirds all year round. The vast mudflat is teeming with aquatic worms and crustaceans, which attract thousands of Arctic-nesting shorebirds over the winter – 43 species of wader have been spotted here. The two main species are the bar-tailed godwit and the lesser or red knot, but it isn't unusual to see turnstones, sandpipers and the odd vagrant red-necked stint. One godwit tagged here was tracked making an 11,570km nonstop flight from Alaska. Short-haul travellers include the pied oystercatcher and the threatened wrybill from the South Island, and banded dotterels and pied stilts.

The **Miranda Shorebird Centre** (09-232 2781; www.miranda-shorebird.org.nz; 283 East Coast Rd; 9am-5pm) has bird-life displays, hires out binoculars and sells useful bird-watching pamphlets ($2). Nearby are a **hide** and several **walks** (30 minutes to two hours). The centre offers clean bunk-style accommodation (dorm beds/rooms $25/95) with a kitchen.

Miranda Hot Springs (www.mirandahot-springs.co.nz; Front Miranda Rd; adult/child $13/6; 9am-9.30pm), 5km south, has a large thermal swimming pool (reputedly the largest in the southern hemisphere), a toasty sauna pool and private spas ($10 extra).

Next door is **Miranda Holiday Park** (07-867 3205; www.mirandaholidaypark.co.nz; 595 Front Miranda Rd; campsites per adult/child $23/11, units $89-189;), with sparkling-clean units and facilities, its own thermally heated pool and a floodlit tennis court.

Thames

POP 6800

Dinky wooden buildings from the 19th-century gold rush still dominate Thames, but grizzly prospectors have long been replaced by alternative lifestylers. It's a good base for tramping or canyoning in the nearby Kauaeranga Valley.

Captain Cook arrived here in 1769, naming the Waihou River the 'Thames' 'on account of its bearing some resemblance to that river in England'; you may well think otherwise. This area belonged to Ngati Maru, a tribe of Tainui descent. Their spectacular meeting house, Hotunui (1878), holds pride of place in the Auckland Museum.

After opening Thames to gold-miners in 1867, Ngati Maru were swamped by 10,000

Thames

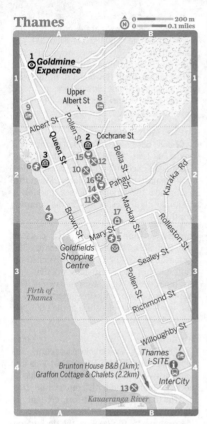

Thames

◎ Top Sights
1 Goldmine Experience A1

◎ Sights
2 Historical Museum A2
3 School of Mines &
   Mineralogical Museum....................A2

✿ Activities, Courses & Tours
4 Karaka Bird Hide................................A2
5 Paki Paki Bike Shop B3
6 Thames Small Gauge Railway.............A2

🛏 Sleeping
7 Gateway Backpackers B4
8 Ocean View on Thames A1
9 Sunkist Backpackers...........................A1

✕ Eating
10 Cafe Melbourne.................................A2
11 Coco Espresso A2
12 Nakontong A2
    Organic Co-op ....(see 12)
13 The Wharf Coffee House & Bar..........B4

◖ Drinking & Nightlife
14 Junction Hotel...................................A2
15 Rick's Wine & Brew............................A2

✪ Entertainment
16 Multiplex Cinemas A2

⊞ Shopping
17 Grahamstown Market B2

European settlers within a year. When the initial boom turned to bust, a dubious system of government advances resulted in Maori debt and forced land sales.

◉ Sights

★ Goldmine Experience
MINE

(www.goldmine-experience.co.nz; cnr Moanataiari Rd & Pollen St; adult/child $15/5; ☉10am-4pm daily Jan-Mar, to 1pm Apr, May & Sep-Dec) Walk through a mine tunnel, watch a stamper battery crush rock, learn about the history of the Cornish miners and try your hand at panning for gold ($2 extra).

School of Mines &
Mineralogical Museum
MUSEUM

(www.historicplaces.org.nz; 101 Cochrane St; adult/child $5/free; ☉11am-3pm Wed-Sun Mar-Dec, daily Jan-Feb) The Historic Places Trust runs tours of these buildings, which house an extensive collection of NZ rocks, minerals and

fossils. The oldest section (1868) was part of a Methodist Sunday school, situated on a Maori burial ground. The Trust has a free self-tour pamphlet taking in Thames' significant buildings.

Butterfly & Orchid Garden
GARDENS

(www.butterfly.co.nz; Victoria St; adult/child $12/6; ☉9.30am-4.30pm) Around 3km north of town within the Dickson Holiday Park is this enclosed jungle full of hundreds of exotic flappers.

Historical Museum
MUSEUM

(cnr Cochrane & Pollen Sts; adult/child $5/2; ☉1-4pm) Pioneer relics, rocks and old photographs of the town.

🏃 Activities

Karaka Bird Hide
BIRDWATCHING

🎟 **FREE** Built with compensation funds from the *Rainbow Warrior* bombing, this hide can be reached by a boardwalk through the mangroves just off Brown St.

Thames Small Gauge Railway
NARROW-GAUGE RAILWAY

(Brown St; tickets $2; ☺11am-3pm Sun) Young 'uns will enjoy the 900m loop ride on this cute-as-a-button train.

Canyonz
CANYONING

(☏0800 422 696; www.canyonz.co.nz; trips $360) 🏄 All-day canyoning trips to the Sleeping God Canyon in the Kauaeranga Valley. Expect a vertical descent of over 300m, requiring abseiling, water-sliding and jumping. Trips leave from Thames at 8.30am, and 7am pick-ups from Hamilton are also available. Note that Thames is only 90 minutes' drive from central Auckland, so with your own transport a day trip from Auckland is possible.

Eyez Open
CYCLING

(☏07-868 9018; www.eyezopen.co.nz) Rents out bikes ($30 per day) and organises small-group cycling tours of the Coromandel Peninsula (one- to three-day tours from $150 to $660).

Paki Paki Bike Shop
BICYCLE RENTAL

(☏07-867 9026; 535 Pollen St; 9am-5pm Mon-Fri, to 1pm Sat) Rents out bikes ($25 per day) and performs repairs.

🛏 Sleeping

Sunkist Backpackers
HOSTEL $

(☏07-868 8808; www.sunkistbackpackers.com; 506 Brown St; dm $26-29, s/d $55/70; @ 🛜) This hostel in a character-filled 1860s heritage building has spacious dorms and a sunny garden. It also offers 4WD and car hire and shuttles to the Kauaeranga Valley ($35 return). Bikes can also be hired and shuttle transport arranged if you're keen on exploring the Hauraki Rail Trail.

Gateway Backpackers
HOSTEL $

(☏07-868 6339; overend@xtra.co.nz; 209 Mackay St; dm $25-27, s $53, d $62-72; @) Generations of Kiwis grew up in state houses just like this, giving this relaxed, friendly hostel a homely feel. Bathrooms are in short supply but there are pleasant rooms, a nice garden and free laundry facilities.

Cotswold Cottage
B&B $$

(☏07-868 6306; www.cotswoldcottage.co.nz; 46 Maramarahi Rd; r $180-210; 🛜) 🏄 Looking over the river and racecourse, 3km southeast of town, this pretty villa features luxuriant linen and an outdoor spa pool. The comfy rooms all open onto a deck.

Ocean View on Thames
B&B $$

(☏07-868 3588; www.retreat4u.co.nz; 509 Upper Albert St; ste $160-180, apt $180-200; 🛜) Aside from the expansive views, it's the little touches that make this place so special – such as fresh flowers and, in the two-bedroom apartment downstairs, a fridge stocked with cost-price beverages offered on an honesty system.

Coastal Motor Lodge
MOTEL $$

(☏07-868 6843; www.stayatcoastal.co.nz; 608 Tararu Rd; units $150-179; 🛜) Motel and chalet-style accommodation is provided at this smart, welcoming place, 2km north of Thames. It overlooks the sea, making it a popular choice, especially in the summer months.

Grafton Cottage & Chalets
CHALET $$

(☏07-868 9971; www.graftoncottage.co.nz; 304 Grafton Rd; units $140-220; @ 🛜 🏊) Perched on a hill, most of these attractive wooden chalets have decks with awesome views. The hospitable hosts provide free internet access and breakfast, as well as use of the pool, spa and barbecue areas.

Brunton House B&B
B&B $$

(☏07-868 5160; www.bruntonhouse.co.nz; 210 Parawai Rd; r $160-180, tr $195; @ 🛜 🏊) This impressive two-storey kauri villa (1875) has a modern kitchen and bathrooms, while staying true to the building's historic credentials (there are no en suites). Guests can relax in the grounds, by the pool, in the designated lounge or on the upstairs terrace.

🍴 Eating

Cafe Melbourne
CAFE $

(www.facebook.com/CafeMelbourneGrahamsTown; 715 Pollen St; mains $12-19; ☺8am-5pm Mon-Thu, 8am-9pm Fri, 9am-4pm Sat & Sun) Stylish and spacious, this cafe definitely channels the cosmopolitan vibe of a certain Australian city. Chic industrial furniture and shared tables promote a convivial ambience, and the menu travels from brunchy ricotta pancakes to beef sliders and fish curry for lunch.

The Wharf Coffee House & Bar
CAFE, BAR $

(www.facebook.com/TheWharfCoffeehouseandbar; Shortland Wharf, Queen St; snacks & mains $10-18; ☺9am-3pm Mon, to 8pm Tue, Wed & Sun, to 9pm Thu-Sat) Perched beside the water, this rustic wood-lined pavilion does great fish and chips. Grab a table outside with a beer or a wine to understand why the Wharf is a firm local favourite.

Coco Espresso
CAFE $
(661 Pollen St; snacks from $4.50; ☉8am-2.30pm Tue-Fri, to noon Sat) Occupying a corner of an old villa, this chic little cafe serves excellent coffee and enticing pastries and cakes.

Organic Co-op
SELF-CATERING $
(736 Pollen St; ☉9am-5pm Mon-Fri, to noon Sat; 🖉) 🍴 A good source of planet-friendly vegetables, nuts, bread, eggs and meat.

Nakontong
THAI $$
(🖉07-868 6821; www.nakontong.com; 728 Pollen St; mains $16-21; ☉11am-2.30pm Mon-Fri, 5-10pm daily; 🖉) This is the most popular restaurant in Thames by a country mile. Although the bright lighting may not induce romance, the tangy Thai dishes will provide a warm glow.

🍷 Drinking & Entertainment

Rick's Wine & Brew
WINE BAR
(746 Pollen St; ☉4pm-late Wed-Sun) With art-deco chandeliers, zany wallpaper and regular live music, Rick's is the sort of place where a solo traveller of any gender can chill out over a glass of wine.

Junction Hotel
PUB
(www.thejunction.net.nz; 700 Pollen St; pizza $16-22, mains $15-30; ☉10am-late) Serving thirsty gold-diggers since 1869, the Junction is the archetypal slightly rough-around-the-edges, historic, small-town pub. Live music attracts a younger crowd on the weekends, while families head to the corner-facing Grahamstown Bar & Diner for hearty pub grub.

Multiplex Cinemas
CINEMA
(www.cinemathames.co.nz; 708 Pollen St; adult/child $15/10) Recent blockbusters with cheaper $11 tickets on Wednesdays.

🔒 Shopping

Pollen St has stores selling local art and craft.

Grahamstown Market
MARKET
(Pollen St; ☉8am-noon Sat) 🍴 On Saturday mornings the Grahamstown Market fills the street with organic produce and handicrafts.

🛈 Information

Thames i-SITE (🖉07-868 7284; www.thames-info.co.nz; 206 Pollen St; ☉9am-5pm)

🛈 Getting There & Around

InterCity (🖉09-583 5780; www.intercity.co.nz), **Tairua Bus Company** (🖉07-808 0748; www.tairuabus.co.nz) and **Go Kiwi** (🖉0800 446 549; www.go-kiwi.co.nz) all run bus services to Thames.

Thames to Coromandel Town

Narrow SH25 snakes along the coast past pretty little bays and rocky beaches. Sea birds are plentiful, and you can fish, dig for shellfish and fossick for quartz, jasper and even gold-bearing rocks. The landscape turns crimson when the pohutukawa (often referred to as the 'New Zealand Christmas tree') blooms in December.

A handful of stores, motels, B&Bs and camping grounds are scattered around the picturesque bays. For backpackers, **Wolfie's Lair** (🖉07-868 2777; 11 Firth View Rd, Te Puru; d & tw $54), a tidy house in **Te Puru**, has three rooms to rent. Just north of Te Puru, stop at the colourful **Waiomu Beach Cafe** (62 Thames Coast Rd, Waiomu Bay; mains $10-23; ☉7am-6pm) for gourmet pizza, freshly squeezed juices and healthy salads.

At **Tapu** turn inland for a mainly sealed 6km drive to the **Rapaura Water Gardens** (🖉07-868 4821; www.rapaurawatergardens.co.nz; 586 Tapu-Coroglen Rd; adult/child $15/6; ☉9am-5pm), combining water, greenery and sculpture. There's accommodation (cottage/lodge $165/275) and a cafe (mains $14 to $29).

From **Wilsons Bay** the road heads away from the coast and climbs over several hills and valleys before dropping down to Coromandel Town, 55km from Thames. The view looking towards the island-studded Coromandel Harbour is exquisite.

Coromandel Town

POP 1480
Crammed with heritage buildings, Coromandel Town is a thoroughly quaint little place. Its natty cafes, interesting art stores, excellent sleeping options and delicious smoked mussels could keep you here longer than you expected.

Gold was discovered at Driving Creek in 1852. Initially the local Patukirikiri *iwi* kept control of the land and received money from digging licences. After initial financial success the same fate befell them as the Ngati Maru in Thames. By 1871, debt had forced them to sell all but 778 mountainous acres of their land. Today, fewer than 100 people remain who identify as part of this *iwi*.

COROMANDEL FOREST PARK

More than 30 walks criss-cross the Coromandel Forest Park, spread over several major blocks throughout the centre of the Coromandel Peninsula. The most popular hike is the challenging six- to eight-hour return journey up to the **Pinnacles** (759m) in the Kauaeranga Valley behind Thames. Other outstanding tramps include the **Coromandel Coastal Walkway** in Far North Coromandel, from Fletcher Bay to Stony Bay, and the **Puketui Valley** walk to abandoned gold mines.

The **DOC Kauaeranga Visitor Centre** (Department of Conservation; ☑ 07-867 9080; www.doc.govt.nz; Kauaeranga Valley Rd; ⊙ 8.30am-4pm) has maps, information and interesting displays about the kauri forest and its history. The centre is 14km off SH25; it's a further 9km along a gravel road to the start of the trails. Ask at Thames hostels about shuttles.

The DOC **Pinnacles Hut** (adult/child $15/7) has 80 beds, gas cookers, heating, toilets and cold showers. The 10-bunk **Crosbies Hut** (adult/child $15/7.50) is a four- to six-hour tramp from Thames or the Kauaeranga Valley, and booking in advance is required. There are also four basic **backcountry campsites** (adult/child $6/3) in this part of the park: one near each hut and others at Moss Creek and Billygoat Basin; expect only a toilet. A further eight **conservation campsites** (adult/child $10/5) are accessible from Kauaeranga Valley Rd. Bookings must be made online for the huts and some of the campsites.

Note that Coromandel Town is just one part of the entire Coromandel Peninsula, and its location on the peninsula's west coast means means it is not a good base for visiting Cathedral Cove and Hot Water Beach on the peninsula's east coast.

◉ Sights

Many historic sites are featured in the Historic Places Trust's *Coromandel Town* pamphlet.

**Coromandel Goldfield
Centre & Stamper Battery** HISTORIC BUILDING
(☑ 021 0232 8262; www.coromandelstamperbattery.weebly.com; 360 Buffalo Rd; adult/child $10/5; ⊙ 10am-4pm, tours hourly 10am-3pm) The rock-crushing machine clatters into life during the informative tours of this 1899 plant. You can also try panning for gold ($5). Outside of tours stop to see NZ's largest working waterwheel.

**Coromandel Mining
& Historic Museum** MUSEUM
(841 Rings Rd; adult/child $5/free; ⊙ 10am-4pm daily mid-Dec–Jan, to 1pm Sat & Sun Feb–mid-Dec) Small museum with glimpses of pioneer life.

🏃 Activities

★ **Driving Creek
Railway & Potteries** NARROW-GAUGE RAILWAY
(☑ 07-866 8703; www.drivingcreekrailway.co.nz; 380 Driving Creek Rd; adult/child $25/10; ⊙ 10.15am & 2pm) 🥾 A lifelong labour of love

for its conservationist owner, this unique train runs up steep grades, across four trestle bridges, along two spirals and a double switchback, and through two tunnels, finishing at the 'Eye-full Tower'. The hour-long trip passes artworks and regenerating native forest – more than 17,000 natives have been planted, including 9000 kauri. It's worth lingering for the video about the extraordinary guy behind it all, well-known potter Barry Brickell. Booking ahead is recommended in summer.

Coromandel Kayak Adventures KAYAKING
(☑ 07-866 7466; www.kayakadventures.co.nz) Paddle-powered tours including half-day ecotours (from $150) and fishing trips (half-/full day $200/340).

Mussel Barge Snapper Safaris FISHING
(☑ 07-866 7667; www.musselbargesafaris.co.nz; adult/child $50/25) Fishing trips with a local flavour and lots of laughs.

🖙 Tours

Tri Sail Charters SAILING
(☑ 0800 024 874; www.trisailcharters.co.nz; half-/full day $55/110) Cruise the Coromandel Harbour with your mates (minimum of four) on an 11.2m trimaran.

Coromandel Adventures DRIVING TOUR
(☑ 07-866 7014; www.coromandeladventures.co.nz; adult/child $25/15) Various trips including a hop-on, hop-off service around Coromandel Town and transfers to Whangapoua Beach.

🛏 Sleeping

Anchor Lodge
MOTEL, HOSTEL **$**

(☑07-866 7992; www.anchorlodgecoromandel.co.nz; 448 Wharf Rd; dm $26, r $55-75, units $165-350; @ 🖘 ⚊) This upmarket backpacker-motel combo has its own gold mine, glow-worm cave, heated swimming pool and spa. The 2nd-floor units have harbour views.

Lion's Den
HOSTEL **$**

(☑07-866 8157; www.lionsdenhostel.co.nz; 126 Te Tiki St; dm/r $27/62; 🖘) Chill out to the hippy boho vibe in this magical place. A tranquil garden with fish pond, fairy lights and wisteria, an on-site massage therapist, and a relaxed collection of comfy rooms make for a soothing stay.

Coromandel Motel & Holiday Park
HOLIDAY PARK **$**

(☑07-866 8830; www.coromandelholidaypark.co.nz; 636 Rings Rd; campsites from $44, units $65-210; @ 🖘 ⚊) Well-kept and welcoming, with nicely painted cabins and manicured lawns, this large park includes the semi-separate Coromandel Town Backpackers. It gets busy in summer, so book ahead. Also hires bikes ($20 per day).

Tui Lodge
HOSTEL **$**

(☑07-866 8237; www.coromandeltuilodge.co.nz; 60 Whangapoua Rd; campsites from $15, dm $28-31, r $70-90; @ 🖘) Pleasantly rural, this cheery backpackers has plenty of trees, free bikes, fruit (in season) and straight-up rooms. The pricier ones have en suites.

Hush Boutique Accommodation
STUDIOS **$$**

(☑07-866 7771; www.hushaccommodation.co.nz; 425 Driving Creek Rd; campervans $35, cabins & studios $120-199) Rustic but stylish studios are scattered throughout a stand of native bush at this easygoing spot. Lots of honey-coloured natural wood creates a warm ambience, and the shared Hush Alfresco area with kitchen facilities and a barbecue is a top spot to catch up with fellow travellers.

Jacaranda Lodge
B&B **$$**

(☑07-866 8002; www.jacarandalodge.co.nz; 3195 Tiki Rd; s $85, d $140-170; 🖘) 🍃 Located among 6 hectares of farmland and rose gardens, this two-storey cottage is a relaxing retreat. Look forward to excellent breakfasts from the friendly owner, often using produce – plums, almonds, macadamia nuts and citrus fruit – from the property's spray-free orchard. Some rooms share bathrooms.

Little Farm
APARTMENTS **$$**

(☑07-866 8427; www.thelittlefarmcoromandel.co.nz; 750 Tiki Rd; r $115-130; 🖘) Overlooking a private wetland reserve at the rear of a fair-dinkum farm, these three comfortable units offer plenty of peace and quiet. The largest has a full kitchen and superb sunset views.

Green House
B&B **$$**

(☑07-866 7303; www.greenhousebandb.co.nz; 505 Tiki Rd; r $160-170; @ 🖘) Good old-fashioned hospitality and smartly furnished rooms are on offer here. The downstairs room opens onto the host's lounge, so it's worth paying $15 more for an upstairs room with a view.

Coromandel Accommodation Solutions
ACCOMMODATION SERVICE **$$**

(☑07-866 8803; www.accommodationcoromandel.co.nz; 265 Kapanga Rd; unit & apt $120-250) Booking service for cottages and rental houses around the Coromandel region; an excellent opportunity for coastal scenery. It also has two stylish apartments centrally located in Coromandel Town.

★ Driving Creek Villas
COTTAGES **$$$**

(☑07-866 7755; www.drivingcreekvillas.com; 21a Colville Rd; villa $325; 🖘) This is the posh, grown-up's choice – three spacious, self-contained, modern, wooden villas with plenty of privacy. The Polynesian-influenced interior design is slick and the bush setting, complete with bubbling creek, sublime.

🍴 Eating & Drinking

Driving Creek Cafe
VEGETARIAN **$**

(180 Driving Creek Rd; mains $9-16; ⊙9.30am-5pm; 🖘 🍽) 🍃 Vegetarian, vegan, gluten-free, organic and fair-trade delights awaits at this funky mudbrick cafe. The food is beautifully presented, fresh and healthy. Once sated, the kids can play in the sandpit while the adults check their email.

> ### ⓘ SENSIBLE CYCLISTS' LEAPFROG
>
> There's no charge for carrying your bike on a 360 Discovery (p165) ferry. Touring cyclists can avoid Auckland's traffic fumes and treacherous roads completely by catching the ferry at Gulf Harbour (north of Auckland) to Auckland's ferry terminal, and then leapfrogging directly to Coromandel Town.

The Chai Tea House
CAFE $

(www.facebook.com/ChaiTeaHouse; 24 Wharf Rd; snacks $6-12; ⊙10am-5pm Tue-Sun; 🚲) 🍃 Welcoming cafe with a bohemian New Age bent serving up lots of organic, vegan and vegetarian goodies. The outdoor garden is a very relaxing space, and is also used for occasional live-music gigs.

Mussel Kitchen
SEAFOOD $$

(www.musselkitchen.co.nz; cnr SH25 & 309 Rd; mains $9-18; ⊙9am-3.30pm & 6-10pm Jan & Feb) This cool cafe-bar sits among fields 3km south of town. Mussels are served either with Thai- and Mediterranean-tinged sauces, or grilled on the half-shell. In summer the garden bar is perfect for a mussel-fritter burger and a frosty beer. Smoked and chilli mussels are available for take away.

Pepper Tree
MODERN NZ $$

(☑07-866 8211; www.peppertreerestaurant.co.nz; 31 Kapanga Rd; lunch $18-26, dinner $26-36; ⊙10am-9pm; 🐾) Coromandel Town's most upmarket option dishes up generously proportioned meals with an emphasis on local seafood. On a summer's evening, the courtyard tables under the shady tree are the place to be.

Umu
CAFE $$

(www.facebook.com/umucafe; 22 Wharf Rd; breakfast $11-18, lunch $12-25, dinner $14-32; ⊙9am-9pm; 🐾) Classy cafe fare, including pizza, counter food (tarts and quiches around $7), superb coffee and tummy-taming breakfasts.

Coromandel Smoking Co
SEAFOOD

(www.corosmoke.co.nz; 70 Tiki Rd; fish $5-15; ⊙9am-5pm) Smoked fish and seafood for cooking and snacking.

Coromandel Oyster Company
SEAFOOD

(1611 Tiki Rd; fish $5-25; ⊙9am-5pm) Briny-fresh mussels, scallops, oysters and cooked crayfish.

Star & Garter Hotel
PUB

(www.starandgarter.co.nz; 5 Kapanga Rd; ⊙11am-late) Making the most of the simple kauri interior of an 1873 building, this smart pub has pool tables, decent sounds and a roster of live music and DJs on the weekends. The beer garden is smartly clad in corrugated iron.

🛍 Shopping

The Source
ARTS & CRAFTS

(31 Kapanaga Rd; ⊙10am-4pm) Creative showcase of more than 30 local artists.

ℹ Information

Coromandel Town Information Centre (☑07-866 8598; www.coromandeltown.co.nz; 85 Kapanga Rd; ⊙10am-4pm)

ℹ Getting There & Away

The best way to Coromandel Town from Auckland is on a 360 Discovery (p165) ferry. The town is also serviced by **InterCity** (☑09-583 5780; www.intercity.co.nz), **Tairua Bus Company** (☑07-808 0748; www.tairuabus.co.nz; advance fares from $1) and **Go Kiwi** (☑0800 446 549; www.go-kiwi.co.nz) buses.

Far North Coromandel

Supremely isolated and gobsmackingly beautiful, the rugged tip of the Coromandel Peninsula is well worth the effort required to reach it. The best time to visit is summer, when the gravel roads are dry, the pohutukawa trees are in their crimson glory and camping's an option (there isn't much accommodation up here).

The 1260-hectare **Colville Farm** (☑07-866 6820; www.colvillefarmholidays.co.nz; 2140 Colville Rd; campsites/units from $12/75, dm/s/d $25/38/76; @📶) has accommodation including bare-basics bush lodges and self-contained houses. Guests can try their hands at farm work (including milking) or go on horse treks ($40 to $150, one to five hours).

The nearby **Mahamudra Centre** (☑07-866 6851; www.mahamudra.org.nz; campsite/dm/s/tw $15/28/45/70) is a serene Tibetan Buddhist retreat with a stupa, a meditation hall and regular meditation courses. The simple accommodation is in a parklike setting.

Another kilometre on is the tiny settlement of **Colville** (25km north of Coromandel Town). It's a remote rural community by a muddy bay and a magnet for alternative lifestylers. There's not much here except for the **Green Snapper Cafe** (☑07-866 6697; www.greensnapper.co.nz; 2312 Colville Rd; mains $13-22; ⊙8am-3pm daily, 6-10pm Fri), which does great wood-fired pizza on Friday nights, and the quaint **Colville General Store** (☑07-866 6805; Colville Rd; ⊙8.30am-5pm), selling everything from organic food to petrol (warning: this is your last option for either).

Three kilometres north of Colville the sealed road turns to gravel and splits to straddle each side of the peninsula. Following the west coast, ancient pohutukawa spread overhead as you pass turquoise waters and stony beaches. The small DOC-run Fantail Bay campsite (adult/child $9.20/2), 23km north of Colville, has running water and a couple of long-drop toilets under the shade of puriri trees. Another 7km brings you to the Port Jackson campsite (adult/child $9.20/2), a larger DOC site right on the beach.

There's a spectacular lookout about 4km further on, where a metal dish identifies the various islands on the horizon. Great Barrier Island is only 20km away, looking every part the extension of the Coromandel Peninsula that it once was.

The road stops at Fletcher Bay – a magical land's end. Although it's only 37km from Colville, allow an hour for the drive. There's another DOC campsite (adult/child $10/5) here, as well as Fletcher Bay Backpackers (07-866 6685; www.doc.govt.nz; dm $26) – a simple affair with four rooms with four bunks in each. Bring sheets and food.

The Coromandel Coastal Walkway is a scenic, 3½-hour one-way hike between Fletcher Bay and Stony Bay. It's a relatively easy walk with great coastal views and an ambling section across farmland. If you're not keen on walking all the way back, Coromandel Discovery (07-866 8175; www.coromandeldiscovery.co.nz; adult/child $125/70) will drive you from Coromandel Town up to Fletcher Bay and pick you up from Stony Bay four hours later.

At Stony Bay, where the east-coast road terminates, there's another DOC campsite (adult/child $10/5) and a small DOC-run bach (holiday home) that sleeps five ($77). Heading south there are a couple of nice beaches peppered with baches on the way to the slightly larger settlement of Port Charles. Tangiaro Kiwi Retreat (07-866 6614; www.kiwiretreat.co.nz; 1299 Port Charles Rd; units $220-350;) offers eight very comfortable one- or two-bedroom self-contained wooden cottages. There's a bush-fringed spa, an in-house masseuse ($70 per hour) and, in summer, a cafe and licensed restaurant.

Another 8km brings you to the turn-off leading back to Colville, or you can continue south to Waikawau Bay, where there's a large DOC campsite (07-866 1106; adult/child $10/5) which has a summer-only store. The road then winds its way south past Kennedy Bay before cutting back to come out near the Driving Creek Railway.

Book DOC campsites at www.doc.govt.nz.

Coromandel Town to Whitianga

There are two routes from Coromandel Town southeast to Whitianga. The main road is the slightly longer but quicker SH25, which enjoys sea views and has short detours to pristine sandy beaches. The other is the less-travelled but legendary 309 Rd, an unsealed, untamed route through deep bush.

State Highway 25

SH25 starts by climbing sharply to an incredible lookout before heading steeply down. The turn-off at Te Rerenga follows the harbour to Whangapoua. There's not much at this beach except for holiday homes, but you can walk along the rocky foreshore to the remote, beautiful and often-deserted and undeveloped New Chum's Beach (30 minutes), regarded as one of the most beautiful in the country. Back in Te Rerenga on SH25, the Castle Rock Cafe (www.castlerock-cafe.co.nz; 1242 Whangapoua Rd, Te Rerenga; mains $15-32; 9am-3pm Sun-Thu, to 8.30pm Fri & Sat) offers cafe dining, good takeaway pizzas and gourmet burgers, and its own range of jams, dressings and sauces.

Continuing east on SH25 you soon reach Kuaotunu, a more interesting holiday village on a beautiful stretch of white-sand beach, with a cafe-gallery, a store and an ancient petrol pump. Black Jack Lodge (07-866 2988; www.black-jack.co.nz; 201 SH25; dm $35, s/tw/d from $55/80/90;) has a prime position directly across from the beach. It's a lovely little hostel with smart facilities and bikes and kayaks for hire. In Kuaotunu village, Luke's Kitchen (www.lukeskitchen.co.nz; 20 Blackjack Rd, Kuaotunu; pizza $12-28; 9am-late daily) has a rustic surf-shack ambience, cold beer and wood-fired pizzas. Occasional live music, local seafood and creamy fruit smoothies make Luke's an essential stop, though hours are reduced outside of summer. For more luxury, head along the beach to Kuaotunu Bay Lodge (07-866 4396; www.kuaotunu-bay.co.nz; SH25; s/d $270/295;), an elegant B&B set among manicured gardens, offering a small set of spacious sea-gazing rooms.

Heading off the highway at Kuaotunu takes you (via an unsealed road) to one of Coromandel's best-kept secrets. First the long stretch of Otama Beach comes into view – deserted but for a few houses and farms. There's extremely basic camping (think long-drop toilet in a corrugated shack) in a farmer's field at Otama Beach Camp (☑ 07-866 2362; www.otamabeachcamp. co.nz; 400 Blackjack Rd; campsites per adult/child $10/5, cottages $220-260). Down by the beach they've also built a couple of self-contained, ecofriendly cottages (sleeping four to six), with solar power, a composting waste-water system and ocean views.

Continue along the narrowing road, the sealed road finally starts again and you reach Opito, a hidden-away enclave of 250 flash properties (too smart to be called baches), of which only 16 have permanent residents. From this magical beach, you can walk to the Ngati Hei *pa* (fortified village) site at the far end.

At Opito, Leighton Lodge (☑ 07-866 0756; www.leightonlodge.co.nz; 17 Stewart Pl; s $135-145, d $175-195; @) is a smart B&B with friendly owners, a self-contained flat downstairs, and an upstairs room with a view-hungry balcony.

309 Road

Starting 3km south of Coromandel Town, the 309 cuts through the Coromandel Range for 21km (most of which is unsealed but well maintained), rejoining SH25 7km south of Whitianga. The wonderfully bizarre Waterworks (www.thewaterworks.co.nz; 471 309 Rd; adult/child $20/15; ☉10am-6pm Nov-Apr, to 4pm May-Oct) 🐾, 5km from SH25, is filled with whimsical water-powered amusements made from old kitchen knives, washing machines, bikes and toilets.

Two kilometres on there's a two-minute walk through bush to the 10m-high Waiau Falls. A further 500m on, an easy 10-minute bush walk leads to an amazing kauri grove. This stand of 600-year-old giants escaped the carnage of the 19th century, giving a majestic reminder of what the peninsula once looked like. The biggest tree has a 6m circumference.

If you enjoy the remoteness and decide to linger, Wairua Lodge (☑ 07-866 0304; www. wairualodge.co.nz; 251 Old Coach Rd; r $150-235) is a peaceful B&B with charming hosts, nestled in the bush towards the Whitianga end of the 309. There's a riverside swimming hole on the property, a barbecue, a spa and a romantic outdoor bathtub.

Whitianga

POP 3800

Whitianga's big attractions are the sandy beaches of Mercury Bay and the diving, boating and kayaking opportunities afforded by the craggy coast and nearby Te Whanganui-A-Hei Marine Reserve. The pretty harbour is a renowned base for game-fishing (especially marlin and tuna, particularly between January and March). Fishing charters start at around $500 and head into the thousands. If you snag an overfished species, consider releasing your catch.

The legendary Polynesian explorer and seafarer Kupe is believed to have landed near here sometime around AD 950. The name Whitianga is a contraction of Te Whitianga a Kupe (the Crossing Place of Kupe).

◉ Sights & Activities

Buffalo Beach stretches along Mercury Bay, north of Whitianga Harbour. A five-minute ferry ride (p205) will take you across the harbour to Ferry Landing. From here you can walk to local sights like Whitianga Rock Scenic & Historical Reserve, a park with great views over the ocean, and the Shakespeare Cliff Lookout. Further afield are Hahei Beach (13km), Cathedral Cove (15km) and Hot Water Beach (18km, one hour by bike). Look forward to relatively flat terrain – with a few hills – if you're keen on riding from Ferry Landing to these other destinations.

Mercury Bay Museum   MUSEUM
(www.mercurybaymuseum.co.nz; 11a The Esplanade; adult/child $5/50c; ☉10am-4pm) A small but interesting museum focusing on local history – especially Whitianga's most famous visitors, Kupe and Cook.

Lost Spring   SPA
(www.thelostspring.co.nz; 121a Cook Dr; per hr/day $35/60; ☉11am-6pm Sun-Fri, to 8pm Sat) This expensive but intriguing Disney-meets-Rotorua thermal complex comprises a series of hot pools in a lush junglelike setting, complete with an erupting volcano. Children under 14 aren't permitted, leaving the grown-ups to marinate themselves in tropical tranquility, cocktail in hand. There's also a day spa and cafe.

Dive Zone   DIVING
(☑ 07-867 1580; www.divethecoromandel.co.nz; 7 Blacksmith Lane; trips $150-225) Shore, kayak and boat dives.

Twin Oaks Riding Ranch HORSE RIDING
(📞07-866 5388; www.twinoaksridingranch.co.nz;
927 Kuaotunu-Wharekaho Rd; 2hr trek $60) Trek
over farmland and through bush on horseback, 9km north of Whitianga.

Highzone ROPES COURSE
(📞07-866 2113; www.highzone.co.nz; 49 Kaimara-
ma Rd; activities $10-70) Hit the ropes for high
adventure, including a trapeze leap, high
swing and flying fox. It's located 7km south
of Whitianga, just off the main road. Call for
opening hours.

The Bike Man BICYCLE RENTAL
(📞07-866 0745; thebikeman@xtra.co.nz; 16 Coghill
St; per day $25; ⊙9am-5pm Mon-Fri, to 1pm Sat)
Rent a bike to take across on the ferry and
journey to Hahei and Hot Water Beach.

Windborne SAILING
(📞027 475 2411; www.windborne.co.nz; day sail
$95) Day sails in a 19m 1928 schooner from
December to April, and also departures to
the Mercury Islands ($150) in February and
March.

👉 **Tours**

There are a baffling number of tours to Te
Whanganui-A-Hei Marine Reserve, where
you'll see interesting rock formations and, if
you're lucky, dolphins, fur seals, penguins and
orcas. Some are straight-out cruises while
others offer optional swims and snorkels.

Banana Boat CRUISE
(📞07-866 5617; www.whitianga.co.nz/bananaboat;
rides $10-35; ⊙Dec 26-Jan 31) Monkey around
in Mercury Bay on the bright-yellow motor-
ised Banana Boat – or split to Cathedral Cove.

Cave Cruzer CRUISE
(📞07-866 0611; www.cavecruzer.co.nz) A rigid-
hull inflatable offering a one-hour (adult/
child $50/30) or two-hour (adult/child
$75/40) tour.

Ocean Leopard BOAT TOUR
(📞0800 843 8687; www.oceanleopardtours.co.nz;
adult/child $70/40; ⊙tours 8am, 10.30am, 1.30pm
& 4pm) Two-hour trips around coastal scenery, naturally including Cathedral Cove. The
boat has a handy canopy for sun protection,
and a one-hour 'Whirlwind Tour' (adult/
child $50/30) is also on offer.

Glass Bottom Boat CRUISE
(📞07-867 1962; www.glassbottomboatwhitianga.
co.nz; adult/child $95/50) Two-hour bottom-
gazing tours.

Whitianga Adventures CRUISE
(📞0800 806 060; www.whitianga-adventures.
co.nz; adult/child $65/40) A two-hour Sea Cave
Adventure in an inflatable.

Whitianga

◉ **Sights**
1 Mercury Bay Museum..........................B2

✦ **Activities, Courses & Tours**
2 Dive Zone..A2
3 Lost Spring..A1
4 The Bike Man..A2

🛏 **Sleeping**
5 Beachside Resort..................................A1
6 Cat's Pyjamas.......................................A2
7 Mercury Bay Holiday Park...................A3

✖ **Eating**
8 Cafe Nina..A2
9 Coghill House..A2
10 Monk St Market...................................B2
11 Motu Kitchen.......................................A2
12 Squids...B2

🍷 **Drinking & Nightlife**
13 Bay Brewery Bistro.............................A2
14 Blacksmith Bar....................................B2

🎭 **Entertainment**
15 Mercury Twin Cinemas.......................A2

✨ Festivals & Events

Coromandel Gold Festival　　　MUSIC
(www.coromandelgold.co.nz; Ohuka Farm, Buffalo Beach Rd; 2-day pass $169) Top NZ and international bands feature at this two-day festival culminating in the early hours of New Year's Day. The festival didn't take place in 2013, but was planned to return for New Year's Eve 2014. Check the website.

Scallop Festival　　　FOOD
(www.scallopfestival.co.nz) In early September, the Scallop Festival provides a week of food and entertainment.

🛏 Sleeping

On the Beach Backpackers Lodge　HOSTEL $
(☑07-866 5380; www.coromandelbackpackers. com; 46 Buffalo Beach Rd; dm/s/d $26/41/80; @) Brightly painted and beachside, this large YHA-affiliate has a wide range of rooms, including some with sea views and en suites. It provides free kayaks, boogie boards and spades (for Hot Water Beach). Camping ($15) and bikes ($20) are also available.

Cat's Pyjamas　　　HOSTEL $
(☑07-866 4663; www.cats-pyjamas.co.nz; 12 Albert St; dm $25, d $60-70; @🌐) Perfectly positioned between the pubs and the beach, this converted house offers bunk-filled dorms as well as private rooms, some with their own bathroom.

Mercury Bay Holiday Park　HOLIDAY PARK $
(☑07-866 5579; www.mercurybayholidaypark. co.nz; 121 Albert St; campsites from $18, units $75-160; @🌐🏊) 🍴 Strangely planted in a suburban neighbourhood, this small holiday park is comfortable and clean, with playgrounds, trampoline, swimming pool and pool table.

Pipi Dune B&B　　　B&B $$
(☑07-869 5375; www.pipidune.co.nz; 5 Pipi Dune; r $160; 🌐) This attractive B&B in a quiet cul-de-sac has guest lounges, kitchenettes, laundries and free wi-fi. To get here, head north on Cook Dr, turn left onto Surf St and then take the first right.

Beachside Resort　　　MOTEL $$
(☑07-867 1356; www.beachsideresort.co.nz; 20 Eyre St; units $175-225; 🌐🏊) Attached to the sprawling Oceans Resort, this modern motel has tidy units with kitchenettes and, on the upper level, balconies. Despite the name, it's set back from the beach but it does have a heated pool.

Within the Bays　　　B&B $$$
(☑07-866 2848; www.withinthebays.co.nz; 49 Tarapatiki Dr; r $295; @) It's the combination of charming hosts and incredible views that make this B&B set on a hill overlooking Mercury Bay worth considering. It's extremely well set up for guests with restricted mobility – there's even a wheelchair-accessible bush track on the property.

🍴 Eating

Coghill House　　　CAFE $
(www.thecog.co.nz; 10 Coghill St; mains $8-17; ☉8am-3pm) Get an early start on the sunny terrace of this side-street cafe, where good counter food is partnered by huge corn-fritter stacks and plump tortilla wraps.

Cafe Nina　　　CAFE $
(20 Victoria St; mains $8-20; ☉8am-3pm) Barbecue for breakfast? Why the hell not. Too cool to be constricted to four walls, the kitchen grills bacon and eggs on an outdoor hotplate while the punters spill out onto tables in the park. Other dishes include robust Greek salads and tasty quesadillas.

Monk St Market　　　DELI $
(1 Monk St; ☉10am-6pm Mon-Sat) 🍴 Self-catering foodies should head here for deli goods, imported chocolate and organic produce.

Squids　　　SEAFOOD $$
(☑07-867 1710; www.squids.co.nz; 15/1 Blacksmith Lane; mains $15-29; ☉11am-2.30pm & 5.30pm-late) On a corner facing the harbour, this informal restaurant offers good-value seafood meals in a prime location. Steamed mussels, smoked seafood platters, and chowder combine with occasional Asian touches, and the steaks are also good.

Motu Kitchen　　　MODERN NZ $$$
(www.motukitchen.co.nz; 2 Mill Rd; small plates $10-15, mains $26-37; ☉4pm-late Tue-Sat) This Mediterranean-style villa – complete with a garden shaded by palm trees – is the most stylish eatery in town. Menu highlights include locally sourced scallops, Coromandel oysters and interesting spins on beef, lamb and duck. Smaller shared plates include mushroom arancini and felafel, and from 4pm to 6pm, craft beers from the Hot Water Brewing Co are just $5. Dinner available from 6pm.

♀ Drinking & Entertainment

Bay Brewery Bistro   PUB
(www.baybrew.co.nz; 25 Coghill St; ⊙5pm-late
Sun-Fri, from noon Sat) Good English-style
beers – brewed up by Toby, an entertainingly
friendly ex-journalist – and decent pub food
($21 to $24) including top-notch fish and
chips and burgers. Plan your next Coromandel detour in the attached garden bar.

Blacksmith Bar   PUB
(www.blacksmithbar.co.nz; 1 Blacksmith Lane;
⊙10.30am-late) On the weekends, live bands
keep the punters pumping until the wee
hours (well, 1am). It's the kind of small-town
pub and beer garden that attracts all ages,
styles and dancing abilities.

Mercury Twin Cinemas   CINEMA
(☑07-867 1001; www.flicks.co.nz; Lee St; adult/
child $15/10) Latest-release films.

ⓘ Information

Whitianga i-SITE (☑07-866 5555; www.
whitianga.co.nz; 66 Albert St; ⊙9am-5pm
Mon-Fri, to 4pm Sat & Sun) Information and internet access. Hours are extended in summer.

ⓘ Getting There & Around

Sunair (☑0800 786 247; www.sunair.co.nz)
operates flights linking Whitianga to Auckland,
Great Barrier Island and Tauranga. Bus services
are offered by InterCity (p165), **Tairua Bus Company** (☑07-864 7770; www.tairuabus.co.nz)
and Go Kiwi (p165).

The **passenger ferry** (☑07-866 5472; www.
whitiangaferry.co.nz; adult/child/bicycle
$3/1.50/1.50; ⊙7.30am-6.30pm Easter-late
Oct, to 10.30pm late Oct-Easter) links Buffalo
Beach with Ferry Landing.

Coroglen & Whenuakite

The blink-and-you'll-miss-them villages of
Coroglen and Whenuakite are on SH25, south
of Whitianga and west of Hot Water Beach.
The legendary **Coroglen Tavern** (www.coro-
glentavern.com; 1937 SH25) is the archetypal
middle-of-nowhere country pub that attracts
big-name Kiwi bands in summer.

Running from Labour Day (late October)
to Queen's Birthday (early June), **Coroglen
Farmers Market** (SH25; ⊙9am-1pm Sun) sells
a bit of everything local from vegetables
to compost. Nearby, the folks at **Rangihau
Ranch** (☑07-866 3875; www.rangihauranch.
co.nz; Rangihau Rd, Coroglen; rides per hr $40) will

lead you on horseback up a historic pack-
horse track, through beautiful bush to spectacular views.

Located at the friendly **Seabreeze Holiday Park** (☑07-866 3050; www.seabreezeholi-
daypark.co.nz; 1043 SH25, Whenuakite; campsites
from $36, dm $30, units $75-195; 🛜), **Hot Water
Brewing Co** (www.hotwaterbrewingco.com; 1043
SH25, Whenuakite; 11am-late) is a modern craft
brewery with lots of outdoor seating. Standout brews include the hoppy Kauri Falls Pale
Ale and the robust Walkers Porter. Platters
and pizzas ($18 to $35) all make it easy to
order another beer. Better than your average highway stop, **Colenso** (www.colensocafe.
co.nz; SH25, Whenuakite; mains $7-14; ⊙10am-
5pm) has excellent fair-trade coffee, scones,
cakes and light snacks, as well as a shop selling homewares and gifts.

Hahei

POP 270 (7000 IN SUMMER)
A legendary Kiwi beach town, little Hahei
balloons to bursting in summer but is nearly
abandoned otherwise – apart from the bus-
loads of tourists doing the obligatory stop
off at Cathedral Cove. It's a charming spot
and a great place to unwind for a few days,
especially in the quieter months. It takes its
name from Hei, the eponymous ancestor
of the Ngati Hei people, who arrived in the
14th century on the Te Arawa canoe.

◉ Sights

Cathedral Cove   BEACH
Beautiful Cathedral Cove, with its famous
gigantic stone arch and natural waterfall
shower, is best enjoyed early or late in the
day – avoiding the worst of the hordes.

From the car park, a kilometre north
of Hahei, it's a rolling walk of around 30
to 40 minutes. On the way there's rocky
Gemstone Bay (which has a snorkelling
trail where you're likely to see big snapper,
crayfish and stingrays) and sandy **Stingray
Bay**. The walk from Hahei Beach to Cathedral Cove takes about 70 minutes. Another
option is a 10-minute ride in a water taxi
(p206).

Hahei Beach   BEACH
Long, lovely Hahei Beach is made more
magical by the view to the craggy islands
in the distance. From the southern end of
Hahei Beach, it's a 15-minute walk up to Te
Pare, a *pa* site with splendid coastal views.

🏃 Activities

Cathedral Cove Sea Kayaking
KAYAKING

(☑07-866 3877; www.seakayaktours.co.nz; 88 Hahei Beach Rd; half-/full day $95/160; ◷9am & 2pm) This outfit runs guided kayaking trips around the rock arches, caves and islands in the Cathedral Cove and Mercury Bay area. The Remote Coast Tour heads the other way when conditions permit, visiting caves, blowholes and a long tunnel.

Cathedral Cove Dive & Snorkel
DIVING

(☑07-866 3955; www.hahei.co.nz/diving; 48 Hahei Beach Rd; dives from $85) Takes daily dive trips and rents out scuba gear, snorkelling gear ($20), bikes ($20) and boogie boards ($20). A Discover Scuba half-day beginners' course costs $195 including all the gear.

Hahei Explorer
BOAT TOUR

(☑07-866 3910; www.haheiexplorer.co.nz; adult/child $70/40) Hour-long jetboat rides touring the coast.

🛏 Sleeping

Tatahi Lodge
HOSTEL, MOTEL $

(☑07-866 3992; www.tatahilodge.co.nz; Grange Rd; dm $30, r $88-123, units $150-275; @🛜) A wonderful place where backpackers are treated with at least as much care and respect as the lush, bromeliad-filled garden. The dorm rooms and excellent communal facilities are just as attractive as the pricier motel units.

★Purangi Garden Accommodation
COTTAGES $$

(☑07-866 4038; www.purangigarden.co.nz; Lees Rd; d $170-190) On a quiet cove on the Purangi River, this relaxing spot has accommodation ranging from comfortable chalets through to larger houses and a spacious, self-contained yurt. Well-established gardens and rolling lawns lead to the water – perfect for swimming and kayaking – and don't be surprised if the friendly owners drop off some organic fruit or freshly baked bread.

Hahei and Hot Water Beach are both a short drive away.

Church
COTTAGE $$

(☑07-866 3533; www.thechurchhahei.co.nz; 87 Hahei Beach Rd; cottages $130-250; @🛜) 🍴 Set within a subtropical garden, these beautifully kitted-out, rustic timber cottages have plenty of character. The ultracharming wooden church at the top of the drive is Hahei's swankiest eatery with excellent Mediterranean- and Asian-inspired dishes

made to be shared, and a stellar, if pricey, selection of Kiwi craft beers.

🍴 Eating & Drinking

Hahei really does have a 'gone fishing' feel in the off-season. The local store remains open and the eateries take it in turns so that there's usually one option open every evening.

Mercury Bay Estate
WINERY $$

(www.mercurybayestate.co.nz; 761a Purangi Rd, Cooks Beach; platters $18-35, wine tasting $8-12) Repurposed timber and corrugated iron feature at this rustic but chic vineyard en route from Ferry Landing to Cooks Beach. Local artwork is for sale, and seafood, cheese and charcuterie platters team well with wines like the excellent Lonely Bay chardonnay.

The Pour House
PUB

(www.coromandelbrewingcompany.co.nz; 7 Grange Rd; ◷11am-11pm) Home base for the Coromandel Brewing Company, this pub and bistro features its five beers alongside regular guest taps from other Kiwi craft breweries. Platters of meat, cheese and local seafood combine with decent pizzas in the beer garden, and our favourite brew is the Cloud 9 Belgian-style wheat beer. Reduced hours outside of summer.

ℹ Getting There & Around

Tairua Bus Company (p165) has bus connections to Hahei. In the height of summer the council runs a bus service from the Cooks Beach side of the ferry landing to Hot Water Beach, stopping at Hahei (adult/child $3/2). Another option on the same route is the **Cathedral Cove Shuttle** (☑027 422 5899; www.cathedralcoveshuttles. co.nz; up to 5 passengers $30).

Cathedral Cove Water Taxi (☑027 919 0563; www.cathedralcovewatertaxi.co.nz; return/one way adult $25/15, child $15/10, every 30 min) Has water taxis from Hahei to Cathedral Cove.

Hot Water Beach

Justifiably famous, Hot Water Beach is quite extraordinary. For two hours either side of low tide, you can access an area of sand in front of a rocky outcrop at the middle of the beach where hot water oozes up from beneath the surface. Bring a spade, dig a hole and voila, you've got a personal spa pool. Surfers stop off before the main beach to access some decent breaks. The headland between the two beaches still has traces of a Ngati Hei *pa*.

Spades ($5) can be hired from the **Hot Water Beach Store** (Pye Pl; ⊙9am-5pm), which also has Hottie's Cafe attached.

Near the beach, **Moko** (www.moko.co.nz; 24 Pye Pl; ⊙10am-5pm) has art, sculpture and jewellery with a modern Pasifika/Maori bent.

🛏 Sleeping & Eating

Hot Water Beach Top 10 Holiday Park HOLIDAY PARK $
(☑07-866 3116; www.hotwaterbeachholidaypark. com; 790 Hot Water Beach Rd; campsites from $18, dm $30, units $70-200; @🤶) 🐾 Bordered by tall bamboo and gum trees, this is a very well-run holiday park with everything from grassy campsites, through to a brand-new and spotless backpackers lodge, and stylish villas with arched ceilings crafted from New Zealand timber.

Hot Water Beach B&B B&B $$$
(☑07-866 3991; www.hotwaterbedandbreakfast. co.nz; 48 Pye Pl; r $260) This hillside pad has priceless views, a spa bath on the deck, and attractive living quarters.

Hot Waves CAFE $
(8 Pye Pl; mains $12-26; ⊙8.30am-4pm, to 8.30pm Fri & Sat Dec-Feb) In summer everyone wants a garden table at this excellent cafe. It also hires spades for the beach ($5). Ask about occasional Sunday-afternoon music sessions from 1pm.

ℹ Getting There & Away

The Hahei bus services Tairua Bus Company (p165) and Cathedral Cove Shuttle (p206) stop here, but usually only on prebooked requests.

Tairua

POP 1270

Tairua and its twin town Pauanui sit either side of a river estuary that's perfect for wind-surfing or for little kids to splash about in. Both have excellent surf beaches (Pauanui's is probably a shade better), but that's where the similarity stops. Where Tairua is a functioning residential town (with shops, ATMs and a choice of eateries), Pauanui is an upmarket refuge for wealthy Aucklanders. Friendly Tairua knows how to keep it real. Both are ridiculously popular in the summertime.

 SAFETY

Hot Water Beach has dangerous rips, especially directly in front of the main thermal section. It's one of the five most dangerous beaches in NZ in terms of drowning numbers, although this may be skewed by the huge number of tourists that flock here. Regardless, swimming here is *not* safe if the lifeguards aren't on patrol.

◉ Sights & Activities

Various operators offer fishing charters and sightseeing trips, including **Pauanui Charters** (☑07-864 9262; www.pauanuicharters.co.nz) and **Epic Adventures** (☑021-227 4354; www. epicadventures.co.nz).

Paaku MOUNTAIN
Around seven million years ago Paaku was a volcanic island but now it forms the north head of Tairua's harbour. Ngati Hei had a *pa* here before being invaded by Ngati Maru in the 17th century. It's a steep 15-minute walk to the summit from the top of Paku Dr, with the pay-off being amazing views over Tairua, Pauanui and the Alderman Islands. Plaques along the way detail Tairua's colonial history, with only one rather dismissive one devoted to its long Maori occupation.

Tairua Dive & Marine DIVING
(☑07-864 8800; www.tairuadiveandmarine.co.nz; 7 The Esplanade; boat dives from $200, PADI Discovery $25; ⊙7.30am-5pm) A solid operator with reliable service. Also hires snorkelling gear, kayaks and paddle-boards ($25 to $40 per hour).

🛏 Sleeping

Tairua Beach Villa Backpackers HOSTEL $
(☑07-864 8345; www.tairuabackpackers.co.nz; 200 Main Rd; dm $25-28, s $60-73, d $70-86; @🤶) Rooms are homely and casual at this estuary-edge hostel in a converted house, and the dorm scores great views. Guests can help themselves to fishing rods, kayaks, sailboards and bikes.

Pacific Harbour Lodge HOTEL $$
(☑07-864 8581; www.pacificharbour.co.nz; 223 Main Rd; chalets $144-233; @🤶) This 'island-style' resort in the town centre has spacious self-contained chalets, with natural wood and Gauguin decor inside and a South Seas

WAIKATO & COROMANDEL PENINSULA TAIRUA

garden outside. Discount packages are usually available online.

Eating

Old Mill Cafe CAFE $
(www.theoldmillcafe.co.nz; 1 The Esplanade; mains $12-33; ⊙8am-4pm daily, from 5.30pm Fri & Sat) Zooshed up with bright-pink feature walls and elegant verandah furniture, Old Mill Cafe serves interesting cafe fare as well as dinner on Friday and Saturday. There's sometimes live music on Friday nights too.

Manaia Kitchen & Bar CAFE $$
(☑07-864 9050; 228 Main Rd; breakfast $11-17, lunch $17-24, dinner $24-33; ⊙8.30am-late) With courtyard seating for lazy summer brunches and a burnished-copper bar to prop yourself up on later in the night, Manaia is the most cosmopolitan spot on the Tairua strip. New owners have revitalised the place, and interesting menu options now include a scallop tortilla and prawn naan pizza.

ⓘ Information

Tairua Information Centre (☑07-864 7575; www.tairua.info; 223 Main Rd; ⊙9am-5pm)

ⓘ Getting There & Around

InterCity, Tairua Bus Company and Go Kiwi all run bus services to Tairua.

Tairua and Pauanui are connected by a **passenger ferry** (☑027-497 0316; one-way/return $3/5; ⊙daily Dec-Jan), which departs every two hours from 9am to 5pm (until 11pm in January). In other months the ferry offers a water-taxi service.

Puketui Valley

Located 12km south of Tairua is the turn-off to Puketui Valley and the historic Broken Hills gold-mine workings, which are 8km from the main road along a mainly gravel road. There are short walks up to the sites of stamper batteries, but the best hike is through the 500m-long Collins Drive mine tunnel. After the tunnel, keep an eye out for the short 'lookout' side trail which affords panoramic views. It takes about three hours return; remember to take a torch and a jacket with you.

There's a basic DOC campsite (www.doc.govt.nz; adult/child $10/5) located in a pretty spot by the river. This is a wilderness area so take care and be properly prepared. Water from the river should be boiled before drinking.

Opoutere

File this one under Coromandel's best-kept secrets. Apart from a cluster of houses there's nothing for miles around. Swimming can be dangerous, especially near Hikinui Islet, which is close to the beach. On the sand spit is the Wharekawa Wildlife Refuge, a breeding ground for the endangered New Zealand dotterel.

🛏 Sleeping

YHA Opoutere HOSTEL $
(☑0800 278 299, 07-865 9072; www.yha.co.nz; 389 Opoutere Rd; dm $30-33, r $80-110) 🍃 Housed partly in the historic Opoutere Native School, this wonderful get-away-from-it-all hostel resounds with birdsong. Kayaks, hot-water bottles, alarm clocks, stilts and hula hoops can all be borrowed.

Copsefield B&B $$
(☑07-865 9555; www.copsefield.co.nz; 1055 SH25; r $100-200) On SH25 but closer to Opoutere than it is to Whangamata, Copsefield is a peaceful country-style villa set in attractive, lush gardens with a spa and a riverside swimming hole. The house has three attractive B&B rooms, while cheaper accommodation is offered in a separate bach-style cottage.

ⓘ Getting There & Away

The **Go Kiwi** (☑0800 446 549; www.go-kiwi.co.nz) seasonal Auckland–Whitianga shuttle stops in Opoutere on request.

Whangamata

POP 3560

When Auckland's socially ambitious flock to Pauanui, the city's young and horny head to Whangamata to surf, get stoned and hook up. It can be a raucous spot over New Year, when the population swells to more than 40,000. It's a true summer-holiday town, but in the off-season there may as well be tumbleweeds rolling down the main street.

Activities

Besides fishing (game-fishing runs from January to April), snorkelling near Hauturu (Clarke) Island, surfing, kayaking, orienteering and mountain biking, there are excellent walks. A popular destination for kayaking and paddle boarding is Whenuakura (Donut Island), around 1km from the beach. Note that in an effort to boost the islands' status as wildlife sanctuaries, it's not permitted to land on them. Boating around the islands is allowed.

The Wentworth Falls walk takes 2½ hours (return); it starts 3km south of the town and 4km down the unsealed Wentworth Valley Rd. A further 3km south of Wentworth Valley Rd is Parakiwai Quarry Rd, at the end of which is the Wharekirauponga walk, a sometimes muddy 10km return track (allow 3½ to four hours) to a mining camp, battery and waterfall that passes unusual hexagonal lava columns and loquacious bird life.

SurfSup
BICYCLE RENTAL, PADDLE BOARDING
(☑ 07-865 8096; www.pedalandpaddelnz.com; 703 Port Rd) Bike hire (half-/full day $15/30), kayak hire (half-/full day from $30/50) and paddle-board hire (one/two hours $20/30). Paddle boarding lessons ($99) and kayaking and paddle-boarding tours are also available.

Kiwi Dundee Adventures
HIKING
(☑ 07-865 8809; www.kiwidundee.co.nz) Styling himself as a local version of Crocodile Dundee, Doug Johansen offers informative one- to 16-day wilderness walks and guided tours in the Coromandel Peninsula and countrywide.

🛏 Sleeping

Wentworth Valley Campsite
CAMPSITE $
(☑ 07-865 7032; www.doc.govt.nz; 474 Wentworth Valley Rd; adult/child $10/5) More upmarket than most DOC camping grounds, this campsite is accessed from the Wentworth Falls walk and has toilets, showers and gas barbecues.

Southpacific Accommodation
MOTEL $$
(☑ 07-865 9580; www.thesouthpacific.co.nz; 249 Port Rd; units $130-216; @ 🕿) This hard-to-miss corner-hogging complex consists of a cafe and warmly decorated, self-contained motel units. Facilities are clean and modern; bikes and kayaks are available for hire.

Breakers
MOTEL $$
(☑ 07-865 8464; www.breakersmotel.co.nz; 324 Hetherington Rd; units $175-230; 🕿🏊) Facing the marina on the Tairua approach to Whangamata, this newish motel compensates for saggy beds with an enticing swimming pool and spa pools on the decks of the upstairs units.

✗ Eating

Lazy Lizard
CAFE $
(427 Port Rd; mains $10-20; ⊘ 7.30am-3.30pm Tue-Sun) Winning points for bizarre hand-shaped stools, this funky lizard does delicious counter food, cooked breakfasts, bagels and salads. We're big fans of the 'It's a Wrap' breakfast tortilla.

Soul Burger
BURGERS $
(www.soulburger.co.nz; 441 Port Rd; burgers $10-15; ⊘ 5-9pm Thu, 8am-9pm Fri-Sun Easter–late Oct, 5pm-late Wed-Sun late Oct–Easter) Serving audacious burgers with names like Soul Blues Brother and Vegan Vibe, this hip corner joint is also licensed so you can have an ice-cold beer with your burger.

The Lincoln
CAFE, PUB $$
(www.thelincolnbar.co.nz; 501 Port Rd; mains $17-34) Part bar, part bistro, part cafe and all-round good times feature at this versatile spot on Whangamata's main drag. DJs kick in on summer weekends.

ℹ Information

Whangamata i-SITE (☑ 07-865 8340; www.whangamatainfo.co.nz; 616 Port Rd; ⊘ 9am-5pm Mon-Fri, 9.30am-3.30pm Sat & Sun)

ℹ Getting There & Away

Go Kiwi (☑ 0800 446 549; www.go-kiwi.co.nz) has a shuttle service to Whangamata.

Waihi & Around
POP 4500 & 1800

Gold and silver have been dragged out of Waihi's Martha Mine, NZ's richest, since 1878. The town formed quickly thereafter and blinged itself up with grand buildings and a show-offy avenue of phoenix palms, now magnificently mature.

After closing down in 1952, open-cast mining restarted in 1988, and current proposals to harness the potential of other nearby mines forecast mining to continue to around 2020. Another more low-key bonanza is also taking place with Waihi an integral part of the excellent Hauraki Rail Trail (p194).

While Waihi is interesting for a brief visit, it's Waihi Beach where you'll want to linger. The two places are as dissimilar as surfing is from mining, separated by 11km of farmland. The long sandy beach stretches 9km to Bowentown, on the northern limits of Tauranga Harbour, where you'll find sheltered harbour beaches such as beautiful Anzac Bay. There's a very popular 45-minute walk north through bush to pristine Orokawa Bay, which has no road access.

◉ Sights

Waihi's main drag, Seddon St, has interesting sculptures, information panels about Waihi's golden past and roundabouts that look like squashed daleks. Opposite the visitor centre, the skeleton of a derelict **Cornish Pumphouse** (1904) is the town's main landmark, atmospherically lit at night. From here the **Pit Rim Walkway** has fascinating views into the 250m-deep Martha Mine. If you want to get down into it, the mining company runs 1½-hour **Waihi Gold Mine Tours** (www.waihigoldminetours.co.nz; adult/child $28/14; ☉10am & 12.30pm Mon-Sat), departing from the Waihi Visitor Centre.

The *Historic Hauraki Gold Towns* pamphlet (free from the visitor centre) outlines walking tours of both Waihi and Paeroa.

Athenree Hot Springs   THERMAL POOLS
(www.athenreehotsprings.co.nz; 1 Athenree Rd, Athenree; adult/child $7/4.50; ☉10am-7.30pm) 🖉 In cooler months, retreat to these two small but blissful outdoor hot pools, hidden within a holiday park.

Waihi Arts Centre & Museum   MUSEUM
(www.waihimuseum.co.nz; 54 Kenny St, Waihi; adult/child $5/3; ☉10am-3pm Thu & Fri, noon-3pm Sat-Mon) The Waihi Arts Centre & Museum has an art gallery and displays focusing on the region's gold-mining history. Prepare to squirm before the collection of miners' chopped-off thumbs preserved in glass jars.

🏃 Activities

Goldfields Railway   RAILWAY
(☑07-863 8251; www.waihirail.co.nz; 30 Wrigley St, Waihi; adult/child return $18/10, bikes extra $2; ☉ daily Sep-Mar, Fri-Mon Apr-Aug) Vintage trains depart Waihi for a 7km, 30-minute scenic journey to Waikino. It's possible to take bikes on the train so they can be used to further explore the Karangahake Gorge section of the Hauraki Rail Trail. The timetable varies seasonally so check the website.

Dirtboard Waihi   DIRTBOARDING
(☑021 244 1646; www.dirtboard.co.nz; off Orchard Rd, Waihi; per hr $30) Hit the slopes on a mutant snowboard-skateboard.

Waihi Bicycle Hire   BICYCLE RENTAL
(☑07-863 8418; www.waihibicyclehire.co.nz; 25 Seddon St, Waihi; bike hire half-/full day from $25/40; ☉8am-5pm) Bike hire and loads of information on the Waihi end of the Hauraki Rail Trail.

Bularangi Motorbikes   MOTORBIKE TOURS
(☑07-863 6069; www.motorbikesnz.co.nz) Based in Waihi, Bularangi Motorbikes offers Harley Davidson rentals and one- to 21-day guided tours throughout the country.

🛏 Sleeping

Bowentown Beach
Holiday Park   HOLIDAY PARK $
(☑07-863 5381; www.bowentown.co.nz; 510 Seaforth Rd, Waihi Beach; campsites from $44, units $72-195; ◉☞) Having nabbed a stunning stretch of sand, this impressively maintained holiday park makes the most of it with first-rate motel units and campers' facilities.

Athenree Hot Springs
& Holiday Park   HOLIDAY PARK $
(☑07-863 5600; www.athenreehotsprings.co.nz; 1 Athenree Rd, Athenree; campsites from $44, units $70-175; ◉☞🏊) 🖉 Harbour-hugging Athenree has smart accommodation and friendly owners. Entry to the thermal pools is free for guests, making this a top choice for the winter months.

Waihi Beach Top 10
Holiday Resort   HOLIDAY PARK $
(☑0800 924 448; www.waihibeachtop10.co.nz; 15 Beach Rd, Waihi Beach; campsites from $27, units $110-220; ◉☞🏊) This massive, resort-style holiday park is pretty darn flash, with a pool, gym, spa, beautiful kitchen and a smorgasbord of sleeping options.

Westwind B&B   B&B $
(☑07-863 7208; westwindgarden@xtra.co.nz; 58 Adams St, Waihi; s/d $50/90) Run by a charming couple who are inverate travellers themselves, this old-fashioned homestay B&B has two comfortable rooms with a shared bathroom.

Beachfront B&B   B&B $$
(☑07-863 5393; www.beachfrontbandb.co.nz; 3 Shaw Rd, Waihi Beach; r $140) True to its name with absolute beachfront and spectacular sea views, this comfortable downstairs flat has a TV, fridge and direct access to the surf.

Manawa Ridge   LODGE $$$
(☑07-863 9400; www.manawaridge.co.nz; 267 Ngatitangata Rd, Waihi; r $850) 🖉 The views from this castlelike eco-retreat, perched on a 310m ridge 6km northeast of Waihi, take in the entire Bay of Plenty. Made of recycled railway timber, mudbrick and lime-plastered straw walls, the rooms marry earthiness with sheer luxury.

✖ Eating

Ti-Tree Cafe & Wine Bar CAFE **$**
(14 Haszard St, Waihi; mains $12-20; ⊙9am-4pm; 🛜) Housed in a cute little wooden building with punga-shaded outdoor seating, Ti-Tree serves fair-trade organic coffee, cooked breakfasts and delicious fruit sorbets and ice cream during summer. Occasional live music on Sunday afternoons.

Porch CAFE, BAR **$$**
(23 Wilson Rd, Waihi Beach; brunch $14-20, dinner $29-36; ⊙9am-3pm Mon & Tue, to 1am Wed-Sun) Waihi Beach's coolest chow-down spot, serving sophisticated, substantial mains.

Waitete CAFE, ICE CREAM **$$**
(☑07-863 8980; www.waitete.co.nz; 31 Orchard Rd; mains $10-34; ⊙11am-3pm & 6pm-late daily, 8.30am-11am Sat & Sun) Delicious ice cream – try the licorice or fig and honey – and a wide menu with a few tasty German and European touches feature at this eatery just off SH2 west of Waihi.

Flatwhite CAFE **$$**
(www.flatwhitecafe.co.nz; 21 Shaw Rd, Waihi Beach; brunch $14-24, dinner $20-33; ⊙8am-late; 🛜) Funky, licensed and right by Waihi Beach, Flatwhite has a lively brunch menu and also serves decent pizzas and flash burgers.

🔒 Shopping

Artmarket ARTS & CRAFTS
(www.artmarket.co.nz; 65 Seddon St, Waihi; ⊙10am-5pm) Local arts and crafts.

ℹ Information

Waihi Visitor Centre (☑07-863 6715; www.waihi.org.nz; 126 Seddon St, Waihi; ⊙9am-5pm) Local information and the interesting Waihi Gold Discovery Centre, a modern and interactive showcase of the gold-flecked past, present and future of the Waihi region.

ℹ Getting There & Away

Waihi is serviced by **InterCity** (www.intercity.co.nz) buses and seasonal **Go Kiwi** (☑0800 446 549; www.go-kiwi.co.nz) shuttles.

Karangahake Gorge

The road between Waihi and Paeroa, through the bush-lined ramparts of the Karangahake Gorge, is one of the best short drives in the country. Walking and biking tracks take in old Maori trails, historic mining and rail detritus, and spookily dense bush. In Maori legend the area is said to be protected by a *taniwha*, a supernatural creature. The local *iwi* managed to keep this area closed to miners until 1875, aligning themselves with the militant Te Kooti.

The very worthwhile 4.5km **Karangahake Gorge Historic Walkway** takes 1½ hours (each way) and starts from the car park 14km west of Waihi. It follows the disused railway line and the Ohinemuri River Waikino station, where you can pick up the vintage train to Waihi, stopping in at **Waikino Station Cafe** (SH2; mains $10-18; ⊙9.30am-3pm) while you wait. The eastern spur of the Hauraki Rail Trail also passes through, and it's possible to combine a ride on the train from Waihi with a spin on the trail through the most spectacular stage of the gorge. Bikes can also be rented from the Waikino Station Cafe (per day $45). Across the river from the cafe, the **Victoria Battery Tramway & Museum** (www.vbts.org.nz; ⊙10am-3pm Wed & Sun) is the former site of the biggest quartz-ore processing plant in Australasia. There's a dinky tram ride and guided tours of the underground kilns.

A few kilometres further west, Waitawheta Rd leads across the river from SH2 to **Owharoa Falls**. Opposite the falls the **Bistro at The Falls Retreat** (www.fallsretreat.co.nz; 25 Waitawheta Rd; pizza $20, mains $20-36; ⊙10am-10pm) is located in a wooden cottage under a shaded canopy of trees. Gourmet pizzas and rustic meat dishes emerge from the wood-fired oven on a regular basis, and there's a great little playground for the kids.

There are a range of shorter walks and loop tracks leading from the main car park at Karangahake Gorge; bring a torch as some pass through tunnels. A two-hour tramp will bring you to **Dickey's Flat**, where there's a free **DOC campsite** (Dickey's Flat Rd) and a decent swimming hole. River water will need to be boiled for drinking. You'll find DOC information boards about the walks and the area's history at both the station and the main car park.

Across from the car park, **Golden Owl Lodge** (☑07-862 7994; www.goldenowl.co.nz; 3 Moresby St; dm $29, r $62-100; @🛜) is a homely, handy tramping base, sleeping only 12. Allow $5 extra for linen in the dorm rooms.

Further up the same road, **Ohinemuri Estate Winery** (☑07-862 8874; www.ohinemuri.co.nz; Moresby St; mains $19-32; ⊙10am-4pm Wed-Sun, daily Dec-Feb) has Latvian-influenced architecture and serves excellent lunches. You'd be right if you thought it was an unusual site for growing grapes – the fruit is imported from other regions. Tastings are $5, refundable with purchase. If you imbibe too much, snaffle the chalet-style hut ($135 per night) and revel in the charming atmosphere of this secluded place.

Paeroa

POP 3980

Paeroa is the birthplace of Lemon & Paeroa (L&P), an icon of Kiwiana that markets itself as 'world famous in NZ'. Ironically, the fizzy drink is now owned by global monster Coca-Cola Amatil and produced in Auckland. Still,

generations of Kiwi kids have pestered their parents to take this route just to catch a glimpse of the giant L&P bottles.

The small museum (37 Belmont Rd; adult/child $2/1; ⊙ noon-3pm Mon-Fri) has a grand selection of Royal Albert porcelain and other pioneer and Maori artefacts. Paeroa is also known for its antique stores.

At the L&P Cafe & Bar (www.lpcafe.co.nz; SH2; mains $7-20; ⊙ 8.30am-3pm Mon-Wed, to 8pm Thu-Sun) you can order L&P fish and chips or an L&P brekkie, washed down with the lemony lolly water itself. The cafe shares the space with the information centre (☑ 07-862 8636; www.paeroa.org.nz; ⊙ 9am-4pm), where you can also rent bikes ($45 per day) to take on the Hauraki Rail Trail (p194).

Taranaki & Whanganui

Includes ➡

New Plymouth............216

Mt Taranaki (Egmont
National Park)...........223

Surf Highway 45........227

Whanganui 229

Whanganui
National Park............235

Palmerston North 240

Manawatu Gorge
& Around 244

Best Outdoors

➡ New Plymouth's Coastal Walkway (p219)

➡ Surfing along Surf Highway 45 (p227)

➡ Walking on Mt Taranaki (p223)

➡ Canoeing the Whanganui River (p235)

➡ Tramping in Whanganui National Park (p235)

Best Places to Stay

➡ Fitzroy Beach Motel (p221)

➡ Ahu Ahu Beach Villas (p227)

➡ Anndion Lodge (p232)

➡ Plum Trees Lodge (p242)

Why Go?

Halfway between Auckland and Wellington, Taranaki (aka 'the 'Naki') is the Texas of New Zealand: oil and gas stream in from offshore rigs, plumping the region with enviable affluence. New Plymouth is the regional hub, home to an excellent art gallery and provincial museum, and enough decent espresso joints to keep you humming.

Behind the city, the moody volcanic cone of Mt Taranaki demands to be visited. Taranaki also has a glut of black-sand beaches: surfers and holidaymakers swell summer numbers.

Further east the history-rich Whanganui River curls its way through Whanganui National Park down to Whanganui city, a 19th-century river port that's ageing with artistic grace.

Palmerston North, the Manawatu's main city, is a town of two peoples: tough-talkin' country fast-foodies in hotted-up cars and caffeinated Massey University literati. Beyond the city the region blends rural grace with yesterday's pace: you might even find time for a little laziness!

When to Go

➡ Mt Taranaki is one of NZ's wettest spots, and frequently cops snowfalls, even in summer: weather on the mountain can be extremely changeable. Ironically, New Plymouth frequently tops the North Island's most-sunshine-hours list. Expect warm summers and cool winters.

➡ Over in Whanganui the winters are milder, but they're chillier on the Palmerston North plains. Sunshine is abundant hereabouts too – around 2000 hours per year!

Taranaki & Whanganui Highlights

① Walking up or around the massive cone of **Mt Taranaki** (p223)

② Riding the big breaks along **Surf Highway 45** (p227)

③ Getting experimental at New Plymouth's **Govett-Brewster Art Gallery** (p216)

④ Bouncing from bean to bean in **New Plymouth's cafes** (p221)

⑤ Watching a glass-blowing demonstration at one of **Whanganui's glass studios** (p230)

⑥ Redefining serenity on a canoe or kayak trip on the **Whanganui River** (p236)

⑦ Traversing the rainy **Whanganui River Road** (p235) by car or bike – it's all about the journey, not how fast you get there

⑧ Flexing your All Blacks spirit at Palmerston North's **New Zealand Rugby Museum** (p240)

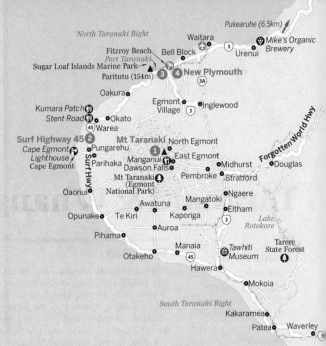

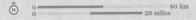

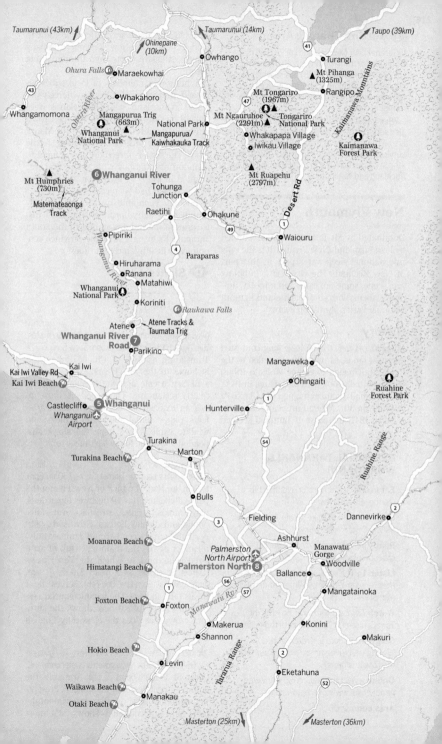

ℹ️ Getting There & Around

In Taranaki, Air New Zealand (p223) has domestic flights to/from New Plymouth. Naked Bus (p223) and InterCity (p223) bus services also service New Plymouth. Shuttle services run between Mt Taranaki, New Plymouth and surrounding towns.

Whanganui and Palmerston North airports are also serviced by Air New Zealand, and both cities are on the radar for InterCity and Naked Bus services. KiwiRail Scenic Journeys (p244) trains stop in Palmerston North too, travelling between Auckland and Wellington.

New Plymouth

POP 53,400

Dominated by Mt Taranaki and surrounded by lush farmland, New Plymouth is the only international deep-water port in this part of New Zealand. The city has a bubbling arts scene, some fab cafes and a rootsy, outdoorsy focus, with surf beaches and Egmont National Park a short hop away.

History

Local Maori *iwi* (tribes) have long contested Taranaki lands. In the 1820s they fled to the Cook Strait region to escape Waikato tribes, who eventually took hold of the area in 1832. Only a small group remained, at Okoki Pa (New Plymouth). When European settlers arrived in 1841, the coast of Taranaki seemed deserted and there was little opposition to land claims. The New Zealand Company bought extensive tracts from the remaining Maori.

When other members of local tribes returned after years of exile, they fiercely objected to the land sale. Their claims were upheld by Governor Fitzroy, but the Crown gradually acquired more land from Maori, and European settlers sought these fertile lands. The settlers forced the government to abandon negotiations with Maori, and war erupted in 1860. By 1870 over 500 hectares of Maori land had been confiscated.

Ensuing economic growth was largely founded on dairy farming. The 1959 discoveries of natural gas and oil in the South Taranaki Bight have kept the province economically healthy in recent times.

◎ Sights

◎ In Town

★Puke Ariki   MUSEUM
(www.pukeariki.com; 1 Ariki St; ◎9am-6pm Mon, Tue, Thu & Fri, to 9pm Wed, to 5pm Sat & Sun) FREE Translating as 'Hill of Chiefs', Puke Ariki is home to the i-SITE (p223), a museum, a library, a cafe and the fabulous Arborio (p221) restaurant. The excellent museum has an extensive collection of Maori artefacts, plus colonial, mountain geology and wildlife exhibits (we hope the shark suspended above the lobby isn't life-size).

★Pukekura Park   GARDENS
(www.pukekura.org.nz; Liardet St; ◎7.30am-6pm, to 8pm Nov-Mar) The pick of New Plymouth's parks, Pukekura has 49 hectares of gardens, playgrounds, trails, streams, waterfalls, ponds and display houses. Rowboats ($10 per half-hour, December and January only) meander across the main lake (full of arm-sized eels), next to which the Tea House (Liardet St; snacks $4-9, mains $10-12; ◎9am-4pm Mar-Nov, 9am-late Dec-Feb) serves light meals (and fudge!). The technicoloured Festival of Lights (p220) here draws the summer crowds, as does the classically English cricket oval.

★Govett-Brewster Art Gallery   GALLERY
(☎06-759 6060; www.govettbrewster.com; 42 Queen St; ◎10am-5pm) FREE Arguably the country's best regional art gallery. Presenting contemporary – often experimental – local and international shows, it's most

---

ESSENTIAL TARANAKI & WHANGANUI

Eat In one of Palmerston North's hip George St eateries

Drink A bottle of Mike's Pale Ale from Mike's Organic Brewery

Read The *Wanganui Chronicle*, NZ's oldest newspaper

Listen to The rockin' album *Back to the Burning Wreck* by Whanganui riff-monsters The Have

Watch *The Last Samurai*, co-starring Tom Cruise (Mt Taranaki gets top billing)

Go green Paddle a stretch of the Whanganui River, an awe-inspiring slice of NZ wilderness

Online www.taranaki.co.nz; www.wanganui.com; www.ourregion.co.nz

Area code ☎06

MAORI NZ: TARANAKI & WHANGANUI

Ever since Mt Taranaki fled here to escape romantic difficulties, the Taranaki region has had a turbulent history. Conflicts between local *iwi* (tribes) and invaders from the Waikato were followed by two wars with the government – first in 1860–61, and then again in 1865–69. Following the wars there were massive land confiscations and an extraordinary passive-resistance campaign at Parihaka.

Further east, a drive up the Whanganui River Rd takes you into traditional Maori territory, passing the Maori villages of Atene, Koriniti, Ranana and Hiruharama along the way. In Whanganui itself, run your eyes over amazing indigenous exhibits at the Whanganui Regional Museum (p230), and check out the superb Maori carvings in Putiki Church (p231).

Over in Palmerston North, Te Manawa (p240) museum has a strong Maori focus, while the New Zealand Rugby Museum (p240) pays homage to Maori All Blacks, without whom the team would never have become a world force.

famous for its connection with famous NZ sculptor, filmmaker and artist Len Lye (1901–80). There's a cool cafe here too. It was closed temporarily for earthquake proofing when we visited: call or check the website for updates.

Puke Ariki Landing   SCULPTURE PARK
(St Aubyn St) Along the city waterfront is Puke Ariki Landing, a historic area studded with sculptures, including Len Lye's wonderfully eccentric **Wind Wand** (www.windwand.co.nz), a kooky kinetic sculpture.

Paritutu   HILL
(Centennial Dr) Just west of town is Paritutu, a steep-sided, craggy hill (154m) whose name translates appropriately as 'Rising Precipice'. From the summit you can see for miles around: out to the Sugar Loaves, down to the town and to the mountain beyond. It's a 20-minute scramble to the top.

Sugar Loaf Islands Marine Park   ISLAND
(www.doc.govt.nz) A refuge for sea birds and over 400 NZ fur seals 1km offshore, these rugged islets (Nga Motu in Maori) are eroded volcanic remnants. Most seals come here from June to October but some stay all year round. Learn more about the marine park at the tiny interpretation booth on the Breakwater Bay waterfront, or take a tour (p220).

Real Tart Gallery   GALLERY
(www.tact.org.nz; 19 Egmont St; ☉10am-5pm Mon-Fri, 10am-3pm Sat & Sun, closed Mon Jun-Aug) FREE
To see what local artists have to offer, visit this 100-year-old reconstructed warehouse. Exhibitions change regularly and most works are for sale. Don't miss the old graffiti preserved under perspex!

Brooklands Park   PARK
(www.newplymouthnz.com; Brooklands Park Dr; ☉daylight hr) Adjoining Pukekura, Brooklands Park is home to the **Bowl of Brooklands** (www.bowl.co.nz; Brooklands Park Dr), a world-class outdoor sound-shell, hosting festivals such as WOMAD (p220) and old-school rockers like Fleetwood Mac. Park highlights include a 2000-year-old puriri tree, a 300-variety rhododendron dell and the farmy **Brooklands Zoo** (www.newplymouthnz.com; Brooklands Park Dr; ☉9am-5pm) FREE.

Taranaki Cathedral   CHURCH
(www.taranakicathedral.org.nz; 37 Vivian St; ☉services daily) The austere Church of St Mary (1846) is NZ's oldest stone church and its newest cathedral! Its graveyard has the headstones of early settlers and soldiers who died during the Taranaki Land Wars, as well as those of several Maori chiefs. Check out the fabulous vaulted timber ceiling inside.

New Plymouth Observatory   OBSERVATORY
(☎021 751 524; www.sites.google.com/site/astronomynp; Marsland Hill, Robe St; adult/child/family $5/3/10; ☉7.30-9.30pm Tue Mar-Oct, 8.30-10pm Tue Nov-Feb) Atop Marsland Hill (great views!) is this wee observatory. Also on the hill is the cacophonous 37-bell **Kibby Carillon**, a huge automated glockenspiel-like device that tolls out across the New Plymouth rooftops.

☉ South of Town

Pukeiti   GARDENS
(www.pukeiti.org.nz; 2290 Carrington Rd; ☉9am-5pm) FREE This 4-sq-km garden, 20km south of New Plymouth, is home to masses of rhododendrons and azaleas. The flowers

New Plymouth

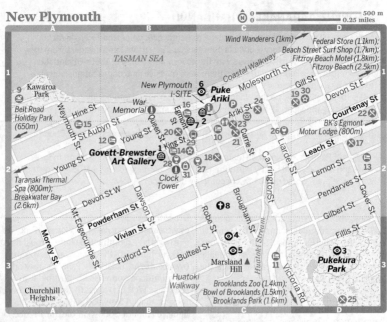

N 0 _____ 500 m
0 _____ 0.25 miles

New Plymouth

◎ Top Sights
1 Govett-Brewster Art Gallery	B2
2 Puke Ariki	C1
3 Pukekura Park	D3

◎ Sights
4 Kibby Carillon	C3
5 New Plymouth Observatory	C3
6 Puke Ariki Landing	C1
7 Real Tart Gallery	B2
8 Taranaki Cathedral	C2
Wind Wand	(see 6)

➕ Activities, Courses & Tours
9 Todd Energy Aquatic Centre	A1

🛌 Sleeping
10 Ariki Backpackers	C2
11 Carrington Motel	C3
12 Dawson Motel	B2
13 Ducks & Drakes	D2
14 King & Queen Hotel Suites	B2
15 Seaspray House	A2
16 Waterfront	B1

✖ Eating
17 Andre's Pies & Patisserie	D2
Arborio	(see 2)
18 Chaos	C2
19 Elixir	D1
20 Frederic's	B2
21 Laughing Buddha	C2
22 Pak 'n Save	D1
23 Petit Paris	C2
24 Portofino	C1
25 Tea House	D3

🍷 Drinking & Nightlife
26 Hour Glass	C2
27 Mayfair	C2
28 Snug Lounge	B2

★ Entertainment
29 Basement	B2
30 Event Cinemas	D1

🛍 Shopping
31 Kina	B2

bloom between September and November, but it's worth a visit any time. The drive here passes between the Pouakai and Kaitake Ranges, both part of Egmont National Park. There's a cafe here too.

Tupare   HISTORIC BUILDING, GARDENS
(www.tupare.info; 487 Mangorei Rd; ⊙9am-5pm Apr-Oct, to 8pm Nov-Mar, tours 11am Fri-Mon Oct-Mar) **FREE** Tupare is a Tudor-style house designed by the renowned architect James

Chapman-Taylor. It's as pretty as a picture, but the highlight of this 7km trip south of New Plymouth will likely be the rambling 3.6 hectare garden surrounding it. Bluebells and birdsong under the boughs...picnic paradise.

Hurworth Cottage HISTORIC BUILDING
(www.historic.org.nz; 906 Carrington Rd; adult/child/family $5/2/10; ⊙11am-3pm Sat & Sun) This 1856 cottage, 8km south of New Plymouth, was built by four-time NZ prime minister Harry Atkinson. The cottage is the sole survivor of a settlement abandoned at the start of the Taranaki Land Wars: a rare window into the lives of early settlers.

Taranaki Aviation, Transport & Technology Museum MUSEUM
(TATATM; http://tatatm.tripod.com/museum; cnr SH3 & Kent Rd; adult/child/family $7/2/16; ⊙10.30am-4.30pm Sat & Sun) Around 9.5km south of New Plymouth is this roadside museum, with ramshackle displays of old planes, trains, automobiles and general household miscellany. Ask to see the stuff made by the amazing bee guy (hexagons ahoy!).

⊙ North via SH3

Heading north from New Plymouth along SH3 are various seaward turn-offs to high sand dunes and surf beaches. **Urenui**, 16km past Waitara, is a summer hot spot.

About 5km past Urenui is arguably the highlight of North Taranaki: **Mike's Organic Brewery** (☑06-752 3676; www.organicbeer.co.nz; 487 Mokau Rd; tastings/tours $15/25; ⊙10am-6pm), which offers tours (book ahead), takeaways, tastings of the legendary Mike's Pale Ale (the pilsener and lager are ace, too), and an Oktoberfest party every (you guessed it) October. A little further on is the turn-off to **Pukearuhe** and **White Cliffs**, huge precipices resembling their Dover namesakes. From Pukearuhe boat ramp you can tackle the **White Cliffs Walkway**, a three-hour loop walk with mesmerising views of the coast and mountains (Taranaki and Ruapehu). The tide can make things dicey along the beach: walk between two hours either side of low tide.

Continuing north towards **Mokau**, stop at the **Three Sisters** rock formation signposted just south of the Tongaporutu Bridge – you can traverse the shore at low tide. Two sisters stand somewhat forlornly off the coast: their other sister collapsed in a heap

10 years ago, but check the progress of a new sis emerging from the eroding cliffs.

🏃 Activities

Surfing

Taranaki's black, volcanic-sand beaches are terrific for surfing. Close to the eastern edge of town are **Fitzroy Beach** and **East End Beach** (allegedly the cleanest beach in Oceania). There's also decent surf at **Back Beach**, near Paritutu, at the western end of the city. Otherwise, head for Surf Hwy 45 (p227).

Beach Street Surf Shop SURFING
(☑06-758 0400; beachstreet@xtra.co.nz; 39 Beach St; 90min lesson $75; ⊙10am-5pm Mon-Thu, to 6pm Fri, to 3pm Sat & Sun) Close to Fitzroy Beach, this surf shop offers lessons, gear hire (surfboard/wetsuit per hour $10/5) and surf tours.

Tarawave Surf School SURFING
(☑021 119 6218; www.tarawavesurfschool.com; 90min lesson $75) Based 15km south of town at Oakura, on Surf Hwy 45.

Tramping

The i-SITE stocks the *Taranaki: A Walker's Guide* booklet, including coastal, local reserve and park walks. The excellent **Coastal Walkway** (11km) from Bell Block to Port Taranaki gives you a surf-side perspective on New Plymouth and crosses the sexily engineered **Te Rewa Rewa Bridge**. **Huatoki Walkway** (5km), following Huatoki Stream, is a rambling walk into the city centre. Alternatively, the **New Plymouth Heritage Trail** brochure, taking in historic hot spots, is a real blast from the past.

Other Activities

Taranaki Thermal Spa SPA, MASSAGE
(☑06-759 1666; www.windwand.co.nz/mineral-pools; 8 Bonithon Ave; treatments $13-245; ⊙10am-5pm Mon & Tue, 10am-9pm Wed-Fri, 3-9pm Sat & Sun) The warm mineral water filling the tanks at Taranaki Thermal Spa was discovered during the search for oil around 1910. The private baths are filled on arrival, and there's a suite of massage and beauty therapies available. An absolute tonic.

Todd Energy Aquatic Centre SWIMMING
(☑06-759 6060; www.newplymouthnz.com; Tisch Ave, Kawaroa Park; adult/child $4.50/3.50, waterslide $3.50; ⊙6am-8.15pm Mon-Fri, 7am-6.45pm Sat & Sun) Just west of town in grassy Kawaroa Park is the Todd Energy Aquatic

Centre, which has a waterslide, outdoor pool and indoor pool.

Wind Wanderers
BICYCLE RENTAL

(📞 027 358 1182; www.windwanderer.co.nz; Nobs Line car park, East End Reserve; bike hire single/tandem per hr $10/15; ⊘ 9am-5pm) Bike hire on New Plymouth's excellent Coastal Walkway. Quirky side-by-side two-seaters also available.

👉 Tours

Chaddy's Charters
BOAT TOUR

(📞 06-758 9133; www.chaddyscharters.co.nz; Ocean View Pde; adult/child $35/10) Take a trip out to visit the Sugar Loaf Islands with Chaddy: expect at least four laughs a minute on a one-hour bob around on the chop. Departs daily from Breakwater Bay, tide and weather permitting. You can also hire kayaks (single/double per hour $15/30) and bikes ($10 per hour) here.

Canoe & Kayak Taranaki
KAYAKING

(📞 06-769 5506; www.canoeandkayak.co.nz; half-day incl hire $95) Paddle out to the Sugar Loaf Islands or over the gentle Waitara River rapids.

🎊 Festivals & Events

Festival of Lights
CULTURAL

(www.festivaloflights.co.nz) Complete with live music and costumed characters roaming the undergrowth, this colourful display lights up Pukekura Park from late December to late January.

WOMAD
MUSIC, CULTURAL

(World of Music Arts & Dance; www.womad.co.nz) A diverse array of local and international artists perform at the Bowl of Brooklands each March. Hugely popular, with music fans trucking in from across NZ.

Taranaki International Arts Festival
ARTS

(www.taft.co.nz/artsfest) The regional big-ticket arts fest happens in August: theatre, dance, music, visual arts, parades and plenty of food and wine.

Taranaki Garden Spectacular
HORTICULTURAL

(www.taft.co.nz/gardenfestnz) A long-running NZ flower fest, held in early November each year: more rhododendrons than you'll ever see in one place again.

🛏 Sleeping

Seaspray House
HOSTEL $

(📞 06-759 8934; www.seasprayhouse.co.nz; 13 Weymouth St; dm/s/d $31/54/74; ⊘ closed Jun-Aug; @ 🛜) A big 100-year-old house with gloriously high ceilings, Seaspray has had a recent makeover inside but remains relaxed, spacey and affordable, with well-chosen retro and antique furniture. Fresh and arty, it's a rare bunk-free backpackers with no TV (conversation encouraged).

Ariki Backpackers
HOSTEL $

(📞 06-769 5020; www.arikibackpackers.com; cnr Ariki & Brougham Sts; dm $27-30, d $70-90; @ 🛜) Upstairs at the old Royal Hotel (Queen Liz stayed here once!), welcoming Ariki offers downtown hostelling with funky carpets, a roomy lounge area with retro couches, and a fantastic roof terrace looking across the park to Puke Ariki. Most rooms have their own shower and toilet. Bikes and surfboards for hire.

Ducks & Drakes
HOSTEL, HOTEL $

(📞 06-758 0404; www.ducksanddrakes.co.nz; 48 Lemon St; hostel dm/s/d $30/63/84, hotel r from $125; @ 🛜) The hostel here occupies a labyrinthine 1920s heritage building with stripy wallpaper and fancy timberwork, brimming with character. The upstairs rooms are the pick: secluded, quiet and catching the morning sun. Next door is a pricier (newer) hotel wing with snazzy studios and one-bedroom suites.

Belt Road Holiday Park
HOLIDAY PARK $

(📞 06-758 0228, 0800 804 204; www.beltroad.co.nz; 2 Belt Rd; campsites from $20, cabins $70-140; @ 🛜) 🐾 This environmentally attuned, pohutukawa-covered holiday park sits atop a bluff overlooking the increasingly interesting Breakwater Bay area, about a 10-minute walk from town. The half-dozen best cabins have million-dollar views. 'Recycle – that's what Kiwis do!', says the manager.

Egmont Eco Lodge
HOSTEL $

(📞 06-753 5720; www.yha.co.nz; 12 Clawton St; dm/d from $29/75; @ 🛜) An immaculate YHA in a glade with chirping birds and a chuckling creek (with eels!). Mixed dorms in the main lodge; smaller pinewood cabins down below (sleeping four). It's a hike uphill from town, but the prospect of free nightly Egmont cake will put a spring in your step.

New Plymouth Top 10 Holiday Park
HOLIDAY PARK $

(📞 06-758 2566, 0800 758 256; www.nptop10.co.nz; 29 Princes St; campsites/cabins from $20/80, units $95-180; @ 🛜 🏊) Sequestered in Fitzroy, 3.5km east of town and a seven-minute walk to the beach, this quaint, family-run Top 10 feels a bit like a school camp, with a dinky little row of units, life-sized chess set, trampoline, laundry and spacious kitchen.

★ Fitzroy Beach Motel   MOTEL $$
(☑06-757 2925; www.fitzroybeachmotel.co.nz; 25 Beach St; 1-/2-bedroom units from $155/190; ☎) This quiet, old-time motel (just 160m from Fitzroy Beach) has been thoroughly re-deemed with a major overhaul and extension. Highlights include quality carpets, double glazing, lovely bathrooms, LCD TVs and an absence of poky studio-style units (all one- or two-bedroom). Free bikes too. Winner!

Dawson Motel   MOTEL $$
(☑06-758 1177; www.thedawsonmotel.co.nz; 16 Dawson St; d from $150, 1-/2-bedroom units from $180/210; ☎) Just a couple of years old, the corporate Dawson is a sharp-looking, two-storey number – all white, red and black inside – with sea and mountain views from the top-floor rooms. The location is primo: a five-minute walk into town and 50m to the Coastal Walkway.

BK's Egmont Motor Lodge   MOTEL $$
(☑0800 115 033, 06-758 5216; www.egmontmotor-lodge.co.nz; 115 Coronation Ave; d $130-200; P☎) Opposite the racecourse, low-slung BK's has ground-floor units and oceans of parking. Rooms are smart, comfortable and clean, and the managers (travellers too) read-ily share a laugh with the cleaners (a good sign). Free wi-fi and DVDs.

Carrington Motel   MOTEL $$
(☑0800 779 431, 06-757 9431; www.carringtonmotel.co.nz; 61 Carrington St; s/d/f from $89/98/155; ☎) Sixteen old but tidy units close to Puke-kura Park and a 10-minute walk to town. It's very family friendly and great value (espe-cially in winter), but noisy when the hoons careen up Carrington St. Wildly eclectic fur-nishings and tsunami-like showers.

★ King & Queen Hotel Suites   BOUTIQUE HOTEL $$$
(☑06-757 2999; www.kingandqueen.co.nz; cnr King & Queen Sts; ste $200-400) The new kid on the New Plymouth accommodation block is this regal boutique hotel on the corner of King and Queen Sts (get it?). Run by unerringly professional staff, it's an interesting 17-room affair over two levels. Each suite features an-tique Moroccan and Euro furnishings, plush carpets, lustrous black tiles, hip art, retro leather couches and *real* flowers. Cafe-bean roastery on site. Nice one!

Waterfront   HOTEL $$$
(☑06-769 5301; www.waterfront.co.nz; 1 Egmont St; r $190-550; @☎) Sleek and snazzy, Water-front is the place to stay if the boss is pay-ing. The minimalist studios are pretty flash, while the penthouses steal the show with big TVs and little balconies. It's got terrific views from some – but not all – rooms, but certain-ly from the curvy-fronted bar and restaurant.

✗ Eating

Chaos   CAFE $
(36 Brougham St; meals $8-16; ◷7.30am-3.30pm Mon-Fri, 8.30am-3pm Sat, 9am-2pm Sun; ☑) Not so much chaotic as endearingly boho, Chaos is a dependable spot for a coffee and a zingy breakfast. Beans with bacon, avocado and sour cream, background jazz, smiley staff and arty interior design – hard to beat! Plen-ty of vegetarian and gluten-free options, too. Love the graffiti-covered side wall.

Petit Paris   BAKERY $
(www.petitparis.co.nz; 34 Currie St; lunches $8-15; ◷7.30am-4.30pm Mon-Fri, to 2.30pm Sat & Sun) *Ooh-la-la!* Lashings of buttery treats! Fly-ing the tricolour with pride, Petit Paris is a boulangerie and patisserie turning out crispy baguettes and *tart au citron* (lemon tart), or an omelette or *croque-monsieur* for lunch.

Andre's Pies & Patisserie   BAKERY $
(44 Leach St; pies $4-8; ◷6am-3.30pm Mon-Fri) Expanding waistlines since 1972, this is an easy pull-over off the main road through town. Hefty pies, buns, sandwiches and calo-rific slabs of cake.

Pak 'n Save   SUPERMARKET $
(www.paknsave.co.nz; 53 Leach St; ◷8am-11pm) Just east of downtown NP.

★ Federal Store   CAFE $$
(440 Devon St E; mains $10-20; ◷7am-5pm Mon-Fri, 9am-5pm Sat & Sun; ☑) Super-popular and crammed with retro furniture, Federal con-jures up a 1950s corner-store vibe. Switched-on staff in dinky head scarves take your coffee order as you queue to order at the counter, keeping you buoyant until your hot cakes, New Yorker sandwich or spicy beans arrive. Terrific cakes, tarts and pre-made counter food (love the vegie frittata), and very kid-friendly, too.

Arborio   MEDITERRANEAN $$
(☑06-759 1241; www.arborio.co.nz; Puke Ariki, 1 Ariki St; mains $13-34; ◷9am-late) Despite

looking like a cheese grater, Arborio, in the Puke Ariki building, is the star of New Plymouth's food show. It's airy, arty and modern, with sea views and faultless service. The Med-influenced menu ranges from an awesome tandoori chicken pizza to pastas, risottos and spicy calamari with garlic and coriander. Cocktails and NZ wines available.

Elixir
CAFE **$$**

(www.elixircafe.co.nz; 117 Devon St E; brunch $8-18, dinner $18-31; ☺7am-4.30pm Mon, 7am-late Tue-Sat, 8am-4pm Sun) Behind a weird louvered wall facing onto Devon St, Elixir fosters an American-diner vibe, serving up everything from coffee, cake, bagels and eggs on toast, through to more innovative evening fare. Below a wall of rock posters, sexy staff give the coffee machine a serious work-out.

Bach on Breakwater
CAFE, RESTAURANT **$$**

(☑06-769 6967; www.bachonbreakwater.co.nz; Ocean View Pde; brunch $11-24, dinner $27-38; ☺9.30am-10pm Wed-Sun; ☑) Constructed from weighty recycled timbers, this cool cafe-bistro in the emerging Breakwater Bay precinct looks like an old sea chest washed up after a storm. Expect plenty of seafood and steak, sunny outdoor tables and killer coffee. The seafood chowder is a real winter warmer. Lots of gluten-free and vegetarian options.

Frederic's
TAPAS **$$**

(www.frederics.co.nz; 34 Egmont St; plates $12-19, mains $18-25; ☺11am-late) Freddy's is a fab gastro-bar with quirky interior design (rusty medieval chandeliers, peacock-feather wallpaper, religious icon paintings), serving generous share plates. Order some lemon-crusted calamari, or green-lipped mussels with coconut cream, chilli and coriander to go with your Monteith's pale ale.

Portofino
ITALIAN **$$**

(☑06-757 8686; www.portofino.co.nz; 14 Gill St; mains $20-49; ☺5pm-late Tue-Sun) This discreet little family-run eatery has been here for years, serving old-fashioned Italian pasta and pizza just like nonna used to make. The rigatoni Portofino is a knockout (spinach, feta, garlic and sun-dried tomatoes).

Laughing Buddha
CHINESE **$$**

(☑06-759 2065; www.facebook.com/laughingbuddha2009; cnr Devon St E & Currie St; mains $12-19; ☺dinner Tue-Sat) Red-glowing windows and a rather menacing-looking Buddha sign

suggest 'nightclub'...but a wander upstairs delivers you instead to New Plymouth's best Chinese restaurant. Load up on entree plates ($4 to $8; try the pork buns), or order a steaming main course (the sliced beef with cumin and chilli is magic). Great for groups.

Drinking & Nightlife

Hour Glass
BAR

(www.facebook.com/thehourglass49; 49 Liardet St; ☺4pm-12.30am Tue-Sat) On an unremarkable rise of Liardet St is this new late-night tapas bar, with richly brocaded crimson drapes, straight-backed wooden chairs and interesting timber paneling. Upwards of 30 craft beers, killer cocktails and zingy tapas: New Plymouth can't get enough!

Snug Lounge
COCKTAIL BAR

(www.snuglounge.co.nz; cnr Devon St W & Queen St; ☺4pm-late Tue-Thu & Sat, noon-late Fri) This savvy new speakeasy on the downtown fringe is the classiest place in town for a drink. Dress to the nines, order a Lychee Long Time (sake, vodka, apple juice and rosewater) and act like you own this town. A few excellent Japanese share plates will ensure you stay vertical.

Mayfair
BAR, LIVE MUSIC

(www.themayfair.co.nz; 69 Devon St W; ☺11am-late) This old theatre has expanded into the adjoining shopfronts to become the Mayfair, a fairly mainstream but always busy bar/restaurant/live-music space. Everyone from rock bands to jazz trios, stand-up comedy acts, DJs and chamber orchestras play the main room out the back; the front bar offers pizzas, shared platters and a decent wine list.

☆ Entertainment

Basement
LIVE MUSIC, COMEDY

(www.facebook.com/thebasementnightclub; cnr Devon St W & Egmont St) Underneath a regulation Irish pub, the grungy Basement is the best place in town to catch up-and-coming live bands, broadly sheltering under a rock, metal and punk umbrella. Opening hours vary with gigs.

Event Cinemas
CINEMA

(www.eventcinemas.co.nz; 119 Devon St E; adult/child $14/9; ☺10am-late) Mainstream, mainstreet megaplex, the carpet a sea of popcorn. All tickets $8.50 on Tuesdays.

🛍 Shopping

Kina JEWELLERY, DESIGN
(www.kina.co.nz; 101 Devon St W; ⊘9am-5.30pm Mon-Fri, 9.30am-4pm Sat, 11am-4pm Sun) Fabulous Kiwi crafts, jewellery, art and design in a lovely shopfront on the main drag, plus regular gallery exhibitions. The perfect spot to pick up an authentic NZ souvenir.

ℹ Information

DOC (Department of Conservation; ☑06-759 0350; www.doc.govt.nz; 55a Rimu St; ⊘8am-4.30pm Mon-Fri)

New Plymouth i-SITE (☑06-759 6060; www.taranaki.co.nz; Puke Ariki, 1 Ariki St; ⊘9am-6pm Mon-Tue & Thu-Fri, to 9pm Wed, to 5pm Sat & Sun) Situated in the Puke Ariki building, with a fantastic interactive tourist-info database.

Phoenix Urgent Doctors (☑06-759 4295; www.phoenixdoctors.co.nz; 95 Vivian St; ⊘8.30am-8pm) Doctors by appointment and urgent medical help.

Post Office (21 Currie St; ⊘8.30am-5pm Mon-Fri, 9am-1pm Sat) Foreign exchange is available at the local post office.

Taranaki Base Hospital (☑06-753 6139; www.tdhb.org.nz; David St; ⊘24hr) Accident and emergency.

ℹ Getting There & Away

AIR

New Plymouth Airport (www.newplymouthairport.com; Airport Dr) is 11km east of the centre off SH3. **Air New Zealand** (☑06-757 3300; www.airnewzealand.co.nz; 12-14 Devon St E; ⊘9am-5pm Mon-Fri) Daily direct flights to/from Auckland, Wellington and Christchurch, with onward connections.

BUS

Services run from the **bus centre** (cnr Egmont & Ariki Sts).

InterCity (www.intercity.co.nz) services include the following:

DESTINATION	PRICE ($)	DURATION (HR)	FREQUENCY (DAILY)
Auckland	73	6	2
Hamilton	49	4	2
Palmerston North	35	4	1
Wellington	45	7	1
Whanganui	29	2½	1

Naked Bus (www.nakedbus.com) services ply similar routes:

DESTINATION	PRICE ($)	DURATION (HR)	FREQUENCY (DAILY)
Auckland	30	6	1
Hamilton	30	4	1
Palmerston North	23	3½	1
Wellington	20	6¼	1
Whanganui	18	2½	1

ℹ Getting Around

Citylink (www.taranakibus.info; adult/child $3.50/2.10) Services run Monday to Friday around town, as well as north to Waitara and south to Oakura. Buses depart from the bus centre.

Chaddy's Charters (☑06-758 9133; www.windwand.co.nz/chaddiescharters; Ocean View Pde; per 30min $10) Bicycle rental.

Cycle Inn (☑06-758 7418; www.cycleinn.co.nz; 133 Devon St E; per 2hr/day $10/20; ⊘8.30am-5pm Mon-Fri, 9am-4pm Sat, 10am-2pm Sun) Bike rental.

Energy City Cabs (☑06-757 5580)

Rent-a-Dent (☑06-757 5362, 0800 736 823; www.rentadent.co.nz; 592 Devon St E; ⊘8am-5pm Mon-Fri, to noon Sat) Cheap car hire.

Scott's Airport Shuttle (☑0800 373 001, 06-769 5974; www.npairportshuttle.co.nz; adult from $25) Operates a door-to-door shuttle to/from the airport.

Mt Taranaki (Egmont National Park)

A classic 2518m volcanic cone dominating the landscape, Mt Taranaki is a magnet to all who catch his eye. Geologically, Taranaki is the youngest of three large volcanoes – Kaitake and Pouakai are the others – which stand along the same fault line. With the last eruption over 350 years ago, experts say that the mountain is overdue for another go. But don't let that put you off – this mountain is an absolute beauty and the highlight of any visit to the region.

Access points for the mountain are North Egmont, Dawson Falls and East Egmont. There are DOC info centres at North Egmont and Dawson Falls; for accommodation and supplies head to Stratford and Inglewood.

History

According to Maori legend, Taranaki belonged to a tribe of volcanoes in the middle of the North Island. However, he was forced to depart rather hurriedly when he was caught with Pihanga, the beautiful volcano near Lake Taupo and the lover of Mt Tongariro. As he fled south (some say in disgrace; others say to keep the peace), Taranaki gouged out a wide scar in the earth (now the Whanganui River) and finally settled in the west in his current position. He remains here in majestic isolation, hiding his face behind a cloud of tears.

🏃 Activities

Tramping

Due to its accessibility, Mt Taranaki ranks as the 'most climbed' mountain in NZ. Nevertheless, tramping on this mountain is dangerous and should not be undertaken lightly. It's *crucial* to get advice before departing and to leave your intentions with a Department of Conservation (DOC) visitor centre or i-SITE.

Most walks are accessible from North Egmont, Dawson Falls or East Egmont. Check out DOC's collection of detailed walk pamphlets ($1 each) or the free *Taranaki: A Walker*'s Guide booklet for more info.

From North Egmont, the main walk is the scenic Pouakai Circuit, a two- to three-day, 25km loop through alpine, swamp and tussock areas with awesome mountain views. Short, easy walks from here include the Ngatoro Loop Track (one hour), Veronica Loop (two hours) and Nature Walk (15-minute loop). The Summit Track also starts from North Egmont. It's a 14km poled route taking eight to 10 hours return, and

---

ⓘ DECEPTIVE MOUNTAIN

Mt Taranaki might look like an easy peak to bag, but this cute cone has claimed more than 60 lives. The mountain microclimate changes fast: from summery to white-out conditions almost in an instant. There are also precipitous bluffs and steep icy slopes.

There are plenty of short walks here, safe for much of the year, but for adventurous trampers January to March is the best time to go. Take a detailed topographic map (the Topo50 1:50,000 *Mt Taranaki or Mt Egmont* map is good) and consult a DOC officer for current conditions. You *must* also register your tramping intentions with the DOC visitor centre (p225), i-SITE (p226) or online via www.adventuresmart.org.nz.

---

should not be attempted by inexperienced people, especially in icy conditions and snow.

East Egmont has the Potaema Track (wheelchair accessible; 30 minutes return) and East Egmont Lookout (10 minutes return); a longer walk is the steep Enchanted Track (two to three hours return).

At Dawson Falls you can do several short walks including Wilkies Pools Loop (1¼ hours return) or the excellent but challenging Fanthams Peak Return (five hours return), which is snowed-in during winter. The Kapuni Loop Track (one hour) runs to the impressive 18m Dawson Falls themselves. You can also see the falls from the visitor centre via a 10-minute walk to a viewpoint.

The difficult 55km Around-the-Mountain Circuit takes three to five days and is for experienced trampers only. There are a number of huts en route, tickets for which should be purchased in advance.

The York Loop Track (three hours), accessible from York Rd north of Stratford, is a fascinating walk following part of a disused railway line.

You can tramp without a guide from February to March when snowfalls are low, but at other times inexperienced climbers can check with DOC for details of local clubs and guides. It costs around $300 per day to hire a guide. Reliable operators include Mt Taranaki Guided Tours, and the following:

Adventure Dynamics   MOUNTAINEERING
(☑ 06-751 3589; www.adventuredynamics.co.nz)

Top Guides   MOUNTAINEERING
(☑ 021 838 513, 0800 448 433; www.topguides.co.nz)

Skiing

Manganui Ski Area   SKIING
(☑ ski lodge 06-765 5493, snow phone 06-759 1119; www.skitaranaki.co.nz; daily lift pass adult/child $40/25) From Stratford take Pembroke Rd up to Stratford Plateau, from where it's a 1.5km (20 minute) walk to the small Manganui Ski Area. The Stratford i-SITE (p226) has daily weather and snow reports; otherwise ring the snow phone or check the webcam online.

👉 Tours

Mt Taranaki Guided Tours   GUIDED HIKE
(☑ 027 441 7042; www.mttaranakiguidedtours.co.nz) Guided hikes on the mountain from one to three days, with the appropriately named Ian McAlpine. Price on application.

Taranaki Tours GUIDED TOUR
(☑ 0800 886 877, 06-757 9888; www.taranakitours.com; per person from $130) Runs an around-the-mountain day tour, strong on Maori culture and natural history.

Heliview SCENIC FLIGHTS
(☑ 0800 767 886, 06-753 0123; www.heliview.co.nz; flights from $149) A 25-minute 'Port to Peak' summit flight costs $249 per passenger.

🛏 Sleeping & Eating

Several DOC huts are scattered about the mountain, accessible by tramping tracks. Most cost $15 per night (Syme and Kahui cost $5); purchase hut tickets in advance from DOC. BYO cooking, eating and sleeping gear, and bookings are not accepted – it's first come, first served. There are also sleeping options in nearby Stratford and Inglewood.

Camphouse HOSTEL $
(☑ 06-278 6523; www.mttaranaki.co.nz; Egmont Rd, North Egmont; dm/d/f $38/90/225) Bunkhouse-style accommodation behind the North Egmont visitor centre in a historic 1850 corrugated-iron building, complete with gun slots in the walls (through which settlers fired at local Maori during the Taranaki Land Wars). Horizon views from the porch. Day use $20 per walker (hot showers).

EcoInn HOSTEL $
(☑ 06-752 2765; www.ecoinnovation.co.nz; 671 Kent Rd; s/tw/d $35/70/70; @ 🛜) 🍴 About 6.5km up the road from the turn-off at the Aviation, Transport & Technology Museum, this ecofriendly place is made from recycled timber and runs on solar, wind and hydropower. There's a spa and pool table, too. Good group rates.

Konini Lodge LODGE $
(☑ 06-756 0990; www.doc.govt.nz; Manaia Rd, Dawson Falls; dm $25) Basic bunkhouse accommodation 100m downhill from the Dawson Falls visitor centre. Six dorm rooms feed off a huge communal space and kitchen.

Mountain House LODGE $$
(☑ 06-765 6100; www.stratfordmountainhouse.co.nz; 998 Pembroke Rd; d $155, extra person $20) This upbeat lodge, on the Stratford side of the mountain (15km from the SH3 turn-off and 3km to the Manganui Ski Area), has recently renovated motel-style rooms and a mod Euro-style restaurant-cafe (brunch $13-38, dinner $34-42; ⊙ 9am-late Wed-Sun). Dinner plus B&B packages available (from $295).

Mountain Cafe CAFE $
(www.mttaranaki.co.nz; Egmont Rd; meals $10-18; ⊙ 9am-3pm Dec-Feb, 10am-3pm Mar-Nov) Inside the North Egmont Visitor Centre.

ℹ Information

Dawson Falls Visitor Centre (☑ 027 443 0248; www.doc.govt.nz; Manaia Rd; ⊙ 9am-4pm Thu-Sun, daily school holidays) On the southeastern side of the mountain, fronted by an awesome totem pole.
MetPhone (☑ 0900 999 06) Mountain weather updates.
North Egmont Visitor Centre (☑ 06-756 0990; www.doc.govt.nz; Egmont Rd; ⊙ 8am-4.30pm) Current and comprehensive national park info.

ℹ Getting There & Away

There are three main entrance roads to Egmont National Park, all of which are well signposted and either pass by or end at a DOC visitor centre. Closest to New Plymouth is North Egmont: turn off SH3 at Egmont Village, 12km south of New Plymouth, and follow Egmont Rd for 14km. From Stratford, turn off at Pembroke Rd and continue for 15km to East Egmont and the Manganui Ski Area. From the southeast, Manaia Rd leads up to Dawson Falls, 23km from Stratford.

There are no public buses to the national park but numerous shuttle-bus/tour operators will gladly take you there for around $40/55 one-way/return (usually cheaper for groups).
Cruise NZ Tours (☑ 0800 688 687) Mountain shuttle bus departing New Plymouth 7.30am for North Egmont; returns 4.30pm. Other pick-ups/drop-offs by arrangement. Tours also available.
Eastern Taranaki Experience (☑ 06-765 7482; www.eastern-taranaki.co.nz) Shuttle services as well as tours and accommodation in Stratford.
Outdoor Gurus (☑ 027 270 2932, 06-758 4152; www.outdoorgurus.co.nz) Pick-up points (New Plymouth) and times to suit; gear hire available.
Taranaki Tours (☑ 06-757 9888, 0800 886 877) Offers New Plymouth to North Egmont return.

Around Mt Taranaki

Inglewood
POP 3250

Handy to the mountain on SH3, the little main-street town of Inglewood is an adequate stop for supermarket supplies and a noteworthy stop for a steak-and-egg pie at

Nelsons Bakery (☑ 06-756 7123; 45 Rata St; pies $3-4; ☺ 6am-4.30pm Mon-Fri, 7am-4pm Sat). Inglewood's other shining light is the cute Fun Ho! National Toy Museum (☑ 06-756 7030; www.funhotoys.co.nz; 25 Rata St; adult/child $6/3; ☺ 10am-4pm), exhibiting (and selling) old-fashioned sand-cast toys. It doubles as the local visitor information centre; online, www.inglewood.co.nz is a good source of information.

On the road into town from New Plymouth, White Eagle Motel (☑ 06-756 8252; www.whiteeaglemotel.co.nz; 87b Rata St; s/d from $90/105, extra person $20; ☎) is an old-school motel but tidy and quiet with blooming flower boxes. The two-bedroom units feel bigger than they are.

Inside a fire-engine-red 1878 heritage building, Caffe Windsor (☑ 06-756 6665; www.caffewindsor.co.nz; 1 Kelly St; brunch $9-23, dinner $23-30; ☺ 8.30am-5pm Mon-Wed, to late Thu-Sat, to 3pm Sun) sells super-sized custard squares and coffee during the day and Thai chicken curry at night (among other things). Nearby, Funkfish Grill (☑ 06-756 7287; www. funkfishgrill.co.nz; 32 Matai St; takeaways $5-10, mains $23-36; ☺ 4pm-late) is a hip pizzeria and fish-and-chippery doing eat-in and takeaway meals, and doubles as a bar at night. Try the tempura scallops.

Stratford

POP 5470

Forty kilometres southeast of New Plymouth on SH3, Stratford plays up its namesake of Stratford-upon-Avon, Shakespeare's birthplace, by naming its streets after bardic characters. Stratford also claims NZ's first glockenspiel. Four times daily (10am, 1pm, 3pm and 7pm) this clock doth chime out Shakespeare's greatest hits with some fairly wooden performances.

Stratford i-SITE (☑ 06-765 6708, 0800 765 6708; www.stratford.govt.nz; Prospero Pl, Broadway S; ☺ 8.30am-5pm Mon-Fri, 10am-3pm Sat & Sun) also houses the Percy Thomson Gallery (☑ 06-765 0917; www.percythomsongal lery.org.nz; Prospero Pl; ☺ 10.30am-4pm Mon-Fri, to 3pm Sat & Sun) FREE, a community gallery (named after the former mayor) displaying eclectic local and touring art shows.

One kilometre south of Stratford on SH3, the Taranaki Pioneer Village (☑ 06-765 5399; www.pioneervillage.co.nz; adult/child $12/5; ☺ 10am-4pm) is a 4-hectare outdoor museum housing 40 historic buildings. It's very bygone-era (and more than a little bit spooky).

Seemingly embalmed in calamine lotion, the old-fashioned Stratford Top Town Holiday Park (☑ 0508 478 728, 06-765 6440; www.stratfordtoptownholidaypark.co.nz; 10 Page St; campsites/dm/cabins/units from $16/20/40/98; @☎) is a trim caravan park offering one-room cabins, motel-style units and backpackers' bunks.

All stone-clad columns, jaunty roof angles, timber louvres and muted cave-colours, the newish Amity Court Motel (☑ 06-765 4496; www.amitycourtmotel.co.nz; 35 Broadway N; d & apt $130-200; ☎) has upped the town's accommodation standings 100%.

OFF THE BEATEN TRACK

FORGOTTEN WORLD HIGHWAY

The 155km road between Stratford and Taumarunui (SH43) has become known as the Forgotten World Hwy. The drive winds through hilly bush country with just a short section (around 11km) of unsealed road, passing Maori pa (fortified villages), abandoned coal mines and memorials to those long gone. Allow four hours and plenty of stops, and fill up with petrol at either end (there's no petrol along the route itself). Pick up a pamphlet from i-SITEs or DOC visitor centres in the area.

The town of Whangamomona (population 30) is a highlight. This quirky village declared itself an independent republic in 1989 after disagreements with local councils. The town celebrates Republic Day in January every odd-numbered year, with a military-themed extravaganza. In the middle of town is the unmissable grand old Whangamomona Hotel (☑ 06-762 5823; www.whangamomonahotel.co.nz; 6018 Forgotten World Hwy; accommodation per person incl breakfast $75, mains $16-35; ☺ 11am-late), a pub offering simple accommodation and big country meals.

If you're not driving, Eastern Taranaki Experience (☑ 06-765 7482, 027 471 7136; www.eastern-taranaki.co.nz; day trips per person from $60) runs tours through the area. See also Forgotten World Adventures (p191).

PARIHAKA

From the mid-1860s Parihaka, a small Maori settlement east of SH45 near Pungarehu, became the centre of a peaceful resistance movement, one which involved not only other Taranaki tribes, but Maori from around the country. Its leaders, Te Whiti-o-Rongomai and Tohu Kakahi, were of both Taranaki and Ati-Awa descent.

After the Land Wars, confiscation of tribal lands was the central problem faced by Taranaki Maori, and under Te Whiti's leadership a new approach to this issue was developed: resisting European settlement through nonviolent methods.

When the government started surveying confiscated land on the Waimate plain in 1879, unarmed followers of Te Whiti, wearing the movement's iconic white feather in their hair and in good humour, obstructed development by ploughing troughs across roads, erecting random fences and pulling survey pegs. Many were arrested and held without trial on the South Island, but the protests continued and intensified. Finally, in November 1881 the government sent a force of over 1500 troops to Parihaka. Its inhabitants were arrested or driven away, and the village was later demolished. Te Whiti and Tohu were arrested and imprisoned until 1883. In their absence Parihaka was rebuilt and the ploughing campaigns continued into the 1890s.

In 2006 the NZ government issued a formal apology and financial compensation to the tribes affected by the invasion and confiscation of Parihaka lands.

Te Whiti's spirit lives on at Parihaka, with annual meetings of his descendants and a public music-and-arts **Parihaka International Peace Festival** held early each year. For more info see www.parihaka.com.

Surf Highway 45

Sweeping south from New Plymouth to Hawera, the 105km-long SH45 is known as Surf Highway 45. There are plenty of black-sand beaches dotted along the route, but don't expect to see waves crashing ashore the whole way. The drive generally just undulates through farmland – be ready to swerve for random tractors and cows. Pick up the *Surf Highway 45* brochure at visitor centres.

Oakura

POP 1380

From New Plymouth, the first cab off the rank is laid-back Oakura, 15km southwest on SH45. Its broad sweep of beach is hailed by waxheads for its right-hander breaks, but it's also great for families (take sandals – that black sand gets scorching hot). A surf shop on the main road, **Vertigo** (☑06-752 7363; www.vertigosurf.com; lessons from $80; ☺9am-5pm Mon-Fri, 10am-4pm Sat), runs surfing and stand-up paddle-boarding lessons. See also Tarawave Surf School (p219).

🛏 Sleeping

Wave Haven　　　　　　　　　　HOSTEL $
(☑06-752 7800; www.thewavehaven.co.nz; cnr Lower Ahu Ahu Rd & SH45; dm/s/d from $25/50/60; @ �》) A surfie backpackers close to the big breaks, this colonial charmer has a coffee machine, a large deck to chill out on, surfboards, a couple of affable Newfoundland dogs and empty wine bottles strewn about the place.

Oakura Beach Holiday Park　　HOLIDAY PARK $
(☑06-752 7861; www.oakurabeach.com; 2 Jans Tce; campsites from $20, cabins $70-140; @ ☞) Squeezed between the cliffs and the sea, this classic beachside park caters best to caravans but has simple cabins and well-placed spots to pitch a tent (absolute beachfront!).

Oakura Beach Motel　　　　　　MOTEL $$
(☑06-752 7680; www.oakurabeachmotel.co.nz; 53 Wairau Rd; d from $115, extra person $20; ☞) A very quiet, seven-unit motel set back from the main road, just three minutes' walk to the beach. It's a '70s number, but the Scottish owners keep things shipshape, and there are 300 DVDs to choose from.

★ Ahu Ahu Beach Villas　　BOUTIQUE HOTEL $$$
(☑06-752 7370; www.ahu.co.nz; 321 Lower Ahu Ahu Rd; d from $270; ☞) Pricey, but pretty amazing. Set on a knoll overlooking the big wide ocean, these luxury, architect-designed villas are superbly eccentric, with huge recycled timbers, bottles cast into walls, lichen-covered French tile roofs and polished-concrete floors with inlaid paua. A new lodge addition sleeps four. Rock stars stay here!

Eating

Carriage Café   CAFE $
(☑06-752 7226; 1143 SH45; meals $10-20; ☺8.30am-3pm) Housed in a very slow-moving 1914 railway carriage set back from the main street, this is an unusual stop for good-value breakfast stacks, bacon-and-egg pies and cheese scones. Good coffee, too.

Cafe Mantra   INDIAN $$
(☑06-752 7303; www.cafemantra.co.nz; 1131 SH45; mains $14-23; ☺7.30am-2pm & 4.30-10pm) 'Let the good times roll' is the mantra at this roadside Indian cafe, which treads cross-cultural lines between curries, burgers, wood-fired pizzas, sandwiches, muffins, cakes and coffee. Closed Monday in winter.

Oakura to Opunake

From Oakura, SH45 veers inland, with detours to sundry beaches along the way. On the highway near Okato the buttermilk-coloured, 130-year-old **Stony River Hotel** (☑06-752 4253; www.stonyriverhotel.co.nz; 2502 SH45; tw/d/tr incl breakfast $95/120/150, mains $10-28; ☺lunch 10am-2pm Wed-Sun; ☎) has simple country-style en-suite rooms and a straight-up public bar.

Just after Warea is **Stent Rd**, a legendary shallow reef break suitable for experienced surfers (look for the painted-boulder sign: the street sign kept being stolen). Another famous spot is **Kumara Patch**, down Komene Rd west of Okato, which is a fast 150m left-hander.

A coastward turn-off at **Pungarehu** leads 3km to **Cape Egmont Lighthouse**, a photogenic cast-iron lighthouse moved here from Mana Island near Wellington in 1881. Abel Tasman sighted this cape in 1642 and called it 'Nieuw Zeeland'. There's a replica lighthouse off Bayly Rd a bit further west around the coast, built to house the original Cape Egmont Lighthouse light after it was automated in 1986.

The road to Parihaka (p227) leads inland from this stretch of SH45.

Opunake

POP 1335

A summer town and the surfie epicentre of the 'Naki, Opunake has a sheltered family beach and plenty of challenging waves further out. **Dreamtime Surf Shop** (☑06-761 7570; www.opunakesurf.co.nz; cnr Tasman & Havelock Sts; surfboards/bodyboards/wetsuits per half-day $30/20/10; ☺9am-5pm, closed Sun Jun-Aug) has internet access and surf-gear hire.

Sleeping

Opunake Beach Holiday Park   HOLIDAY PARK $
(☑0800 758 009, 06-761 7525; www.opunake-beachnz.co.nz; Beach Rd; campsites/cabins/cottages $38/70/105; @☎) Opunake Beach Holiday Park is a mellow spot behind the surf beach. Sites are grassy, the camp kitchen is big, the amenities block is cavernous and the waves are just a few metres away.

**Opunake Motel
& Backpackers**   MOTEL, HOSTEL $
(☑06-761 8330; www.opunakemotel.co.nz; 36 Heaphy Rd; dm/s/d/f from $30/95/110/130; ☎) On the edge of some sleepy fields, Opunake Motel & Backpackers is a low-key, back-steet operation, with old-style motel rooms and a funky dorm lodge (a triumph in genuine retro).

Headlands   HOTEL $$
(☑06-761 8358; www.headlands.co.nz; 4 Havelock St; d $120-250) Just 100m back from the beach, Headlands is a new(ish) operation encompassing a mod, airy bistro (mains $10 to $35; open 8.30am to late) and an upmarket, three-storey accommodation tower. The best rooms snare brilliant sunsets. B&B and DB&B packages available.

Eating

★ **Sugar Juice Café**   CAFE $$
(42 Tasman St; snacks $4-10, mains $10-34; ☺9am-late Tue-Sat, to 4pm Sun; ☑) Sugar Juice Café has the best food on SH45. It's buzzy and brimming with delicious, homemade, filling things (try the crayfish-and-prawn ravioli or cranberry lamb shanks). Terrific coffee, salads, wraps, tarts, cakes and big brekkies too – don't pass it by. Also open Mondays in summer.

SNELLY!

Opunake isn't just about the surf – it's also the birthplace of iconic middle-distance runner Peter Snell (b 1938), who showed his rivals a clean set of heels at the 1960 Rome and 1964 Tokyo Olympics. Old Snelly won the 800m gold in Italy, then followed up with 800m and 1500m golds in Japan. Legend! Check out his funky running statue outside the library.

ℹ️ Information

Opunake Library (📞 0800 111 323; opunakel@
stdc.govt.nz; Tasman St; ⏰ 9am-5pm Mon-Fri,
9.30am-1pm Sat; 📶) Doubles as the local visitor information centre, with a couple of internet
terminals and free 24-hour wi-fi in the forecourt.

Hawera

POP 11,100

Don't expect much urban virtue from agricultural Hawera, the largest town in South
Taranaki. Still, it's a good pit stop for supplies, to stretch your legs, or to bed down for
a night. And don't miss Elvis!

◉ Sights & Activities

★ KD's Elvis Presley Museum   MUSEUM
(📞 06-278 7624; www.elvismuseum.co.nz; 51 Argyle
St; admission by donation) Elvis lives! At least
he does at Kevin D Wasley's astonishing
museum, which houses over 10,000 of the
King's records and a mind-blowing collection of Elvis memorabilia collected over 50
years. 'Passion is an understatement', says
KD. Just don't ask him about the chubby
Vegas-era Elvis: his focus is squarely on the
rock 'n' roll King from the '50s and '60s. Admission is by appointment, phone ahead.

Hawera Water Tower   TOWER, LOOKOUT
(www.southtaranaki.com; 55 High St; adult/child/
family $2.50/1/6; ⏰ 10am-2pm) The austere,
54.21m Hawera Water Tower beside the
i-SITE is one of the coolest things in Hawera. Grab the key from the i-SITE, ascend the
215 steps, then scan the horizon for signs of
life (you can see the coast and Mt Taranaki
on a clear day).

Tawhiti Museum   MUSEUM
(www.tawhitimuseum.co.nz; 401 Ohangai Rd; adult/
child $12/6; ⏰ 10am-4pm Fri-Mon Feb-May & Sep-
Dec, Sun only Jun-Aug, daily Jan) The excellent
Tawhiti Museum houses a collection of exhibits, dioramas and creepily lifelike human
figures modelled on people from the region.
A large collection of tractors pays homage
to rural heritage; there's also a bush railway
and a 'Traders & Whalers' boat ride here (extra charges for both). It's near the corner of
Tawhiti Rd, 4km north of town.

🛏️ Sleeping

Wheatly Downs Farmstay   FARMSTAY $
(📞 06-278 6523; www.mttaranaki.co.nz; 484 Ararata Rd; campsites from $20, dm/s/tw $30/75/75,
d with/without bathroom $130/75; 📶) Set in a

rural idyll, this heritage building is a classic, with its clunky wooden floors and
no-nonsense fittings. Host Gary is an affable bloke, and might show you his special
pigs. To get there, head past the turn-off to
Tawhiti Museum and continue on Ararata
Rd for 5.5km. Pick-ups by arrangement.

Hawera Central Motor Lodge   MOTEL $$
(📞 06-278 8831; www.haweracentralmotorlodge.
co.nz; 53 Princes St; d $140-175; 📶) The pick of
the town's motels (better than any of those
along South Rd), the shiny Hawera Central
does things with style: grey-and-eucalypt
colour scheme, frameless-glass showers, big
flat-screen TVs, good security, DVD players,
free movie library and free wi-fi.

🍴 Eating

Indian Zaika   INDIAN $$
(📞 06-278 3198; www.indianzaika.co.nz; 91 Princes
St; mains $17-20; ⏰ 11am-2pm Tue-Sat, 5pm-late
daily; 🖊️) For a fine lunch or dinner, try this
spicy-smelling, black-and-white diner, serving decent curries in upbeat surrounds. The
$10 takeaway lunches are a steal.

ℹ️ Information

South Taranaki i-SITE (📞 06-278 8599; www.
southtaranaki.com; 55 High St; ⏰ 8.30am-5pm
Mon-Fri, 9.30am-4pm Sat & Sun) The South
Taranaki low-down. Reduced winter weekend
hours.

Whanganui

POP 42,150

With rafts of casual Huck Finn sensibility,
Whanganui is a raggedy historic town on
the banks of the wide Whanganui River.
The local arts community is thriving: old
port buildings are being turned into glass-
art studios, and the town centre has been
rejuvenated – there are few more appealing
places to while away a sunny afternoon than
beneath Victoria Ave's leafy canopy.

History

Maori settlement at Whanganui dates from
around 1100. The first European on the river
was Andrew Powers in 1831, but Whanganui's
European settlement didn't take off until 1840
when the New Zealand Company could no
longer satisfy Wellington's land demands –
settlers moved here instead.

When the Maori understood that the gifts
the Pakeha settlers had given them were in

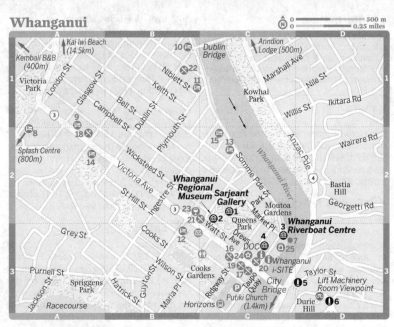

Whanganui

⊙ Top Sights
1 Sarjeant Gallery	C2
2 Whanganui Regional Museum	C2
3 Whanganui Riverboat Centre	C3

⊙ Sights
4 Chronicle Glass Studio	C3
5 Durie Hill Elevator	D3
6 War Memorial Tower	D3

⊕ Activities, Courses & Tours
| 7 Waimarie Paddle-Steamer Tours | C3 |

⬚ Sleeping
8 151 on London Motel	A2
9 Aotea Motor Lodge	A1
10 Astral Motel	B1
11 Braemar House YHA	B1
12 Grand Hotel	B3
13 Riverview Motel	C2
14 Siena Motor Lodge	A2
15 Tamara Backpackers Lodge	C2

⊗ Eating
Big Orange	(see 16)
16 Ceramic Lounge	C3
17 Jolt Coffee House	C3
18 New World	A2
19 Spice Guru	C3
20 Stellar	C3
21 WA Japanese Kitchen	C2
22 Yellow House Café	B1

⊙ Drinking & Nightlife
| Grand Irish Pub | (see 12) |
| 23 Spirit'd | B2 |

⊕ Entertainment
| 24 Embassy 3 Cinemas | C3 |

⊕ Shopping
| 25 River Traders Market | C3 |

permanent exchange for their land, they were understandably irate, and seven years of conflict ensued. Thousands of government troops occupied the Rutland Stockade in Queens Park. Ultimately, the struggle was settled by arbitration; during the Taranaki Land Wars the Whanganui Maoris assisted the Pakeha.

⊙ Sights & Activities

★**Whanganui Regional Museum**   MUSEUM
(www.wrm.org.nz; Watt St, Queens Park; ⊙10am-4.30pm) FREE The Whanganui Regional Museum is one of NZ's better natural-history museums. Maori exhibits include the carved

Te Mata o Hoturoa war canoe and some vicious-looking *mere* (greenstone clubs). The colonial and wildlife installations are first rate, and there's plenty of button-pushing and drawer-opening to keep the kids engaged.

★ **Sarjeant Gallery** GALLERY
(📋 06-349 0506; www.sarjeant.org.nz; Queens Park; ⊙ 10.30am-4.30pm) **FREE** About to temporarily relocate for earthquake-proofing when we visited, the elegant neoclassical Sarjeant Gallery covers the bases from historic to contemporary with its extensive permanent art exhibition and frequent special exhibits (including glass from the annual Wanganui Festival of Glass). Call or check the website to find out if the renovations are complete: if not, you can see selected works in gallery spaces above the i-SITE and nearby at 38 Taupo Quay.

★ **Whanganui Riverboat Centre** MUSEUM
(www.riverboats.co.nz; 1a Taupo Quay; ⊙ 10am-4pm) **FREE** The historical displays are interesting, but everyone's here for the *Waimarie*, the last of the Whanganui River paddle steamers. In 1900 she was shipped from England and paddled the Whanganui until she sank ingloriously at her mooring in 1952. Submerged for 41 years, she was finally raised, restored, then relaunched on the first day of the 21st century. She now offers two-hour tours along the Whanganui.

Chronicle Glass Studio GALLERY
(www.chronicleglass.co.nz; 2 Rutland St; ⊙ 9am-5pm Mon-Fri, 10am-3pm Sat & Sun) **FREE** The pick of Whanganui's many glass studios is the Chronicle Glass Studio where you can watch glass-blowers working, check out the gallery, take a weekend glass-blowing course ($390) or a one-hour 'Make a Paperweight' lesson ($100), or just hang out and warm up on a chilly afternoon.

Durie Hill Elevator TOWER
(www.wanganui.govt.nz; Anzac Pde; adult/child one-way $2/1; ⊙ 8am-6pm Mon-Fri, 10am-5pm Sat & Sun) Across City Bridge from downtown Whanganui, this elevator was built with grand visions for Durie Hill's residential future. A tunnel burrows 213m into the hillside, from where a 1919 elevator rattles 65.8m to the top. At the summit you can climb the 176 steps of the War Memorial Tower and scan the horizon for Mt Taranaki and Mt Ruapehu.

Putiki Church CHURCH
(20 Anaua St; per person $2, plus deposit $20; ⊙ services 9am Sun) Across the City Bridge from town and 1km towards the sea is the Putiki Church (aka St Paul's Memorial Church). It's unremarkable externally but, just like the faithful pew-fillers, it's what's inside that counts: the interior is magnificent, completely covered in Maori carvings and *tukutuku* (woven panels). Show up for Sunday service, or borrow a key from the i-SITE.

Kai Iwi Beach BEACH
Kai Iwi Beach is a wild ocean frontier, strewn with black sand and masses of broken driftwood. To get here follow Great North Rd 4km north of town, then turn left onto Rapanui Rd and head seawards for 10km.

Splash Centre SWIMMING
(www.splashcentre.co.nz; Springvale Park, London St; adult/child $4.50/3, waterslide $3; ⊙ 6am-8pm Mon-Fri, 8am-6pm Sat & Sun) If the sea is angry, try the Splash Centre for a safe swim.

🌀 Tours

Whanganui National Park has canoe, kayak and jetboat tours on the Whanganui River.

Waimarie Paddle-Steamer Tours BOAT TOUR
(📋 06-347 1863, 0800 783 2637; www.riverboats.co.nz; 1a Taupo Quay; adult/child/family $39/15/89; ⊙ tours 10am Oct-Mar; 📷) Take a two-hour trip up ol' man Whanganui on the historic PS *Waimarie*, the last of the river paddle steamers.

Wanganui City Guided Walking Tours WALKING TOUR
(📋 06-349 3258; per person $10; ⊙ 10am & 2pm Sat) Sign up for one of two 90-minute guided tours through old Whanganui, giving your feet a workout as you pass historic sights. Tours depart the i-SITE (book tickets inside).

🎉 Festivals & Events

Vintage Weekend CULTURAL
(www.vintageweekend.co.nz) Time-travelling cars, clothes, music and architecture, and good times over three January days by the Whanganui River.

Wanganui Festival of Glass ARTS
(www.wanganuiglass.co.nz) Classy glass fest in September. Plenty of open studios, demonstrations and workshops.

WHANGANUI OR WANGANUI?

Yeah, we know, it's confusing. Is there a 'h' or isn't there? Either way, the pronunciation is identical: 'wan-ga', not (as in the rest of the country) 'fan-ga'.

Everything was originally spelled Wanganui, because in the local dialect *whanga* (harbour) is pronounced 'wan-ga'. However, in 1991 the New Zealand Geographic Board officially adopted the correct Maori spelling (with a 'h') for the Whanganui River and Whanganui National Park. This was a culturally deferential decision: the Pakeha-dominated town and region retained the old spelling, while the river area – Maori territory – adopted the new.

In 2009 the Board assented that the town and region should also adopt the 'h'. This caused much community consternation, opinions on the decision split almost evenly (outspoken mayor Michael Laws was particularly anti-'h'). Ultimately, NZ Minister for Land Information Maurice Williamson decreed that either spelling was acceptable, and that adopting the querulous 'h' is up to individual businesses or entities. A good old Kiwi compromise! Whanderful...

Whanganui Literary Festival　CULTURAL
(www.facebook.com/whanganuiliteraryfestival) Thoughts, words, and thoughts about words. Every second September (odd-numbered years).

Cemetery Circuit Motorcycle Race　SPORTS
(www.cemeterycircuit.co.nz) Pandemonic motorcycle race around Whanganui's city streets on Boxing Day. The southern hemisphere's version of the Isle of Man TT?

🛏 Sleeping

Anndion Lodge　HOSTEL $
(☑06-343 3593, 0800 343 056; www.anndionlodge.co.nz; 143 Anzac Pde; s/d/f/ste from $75/88/105/135; @🛱🛍) Hell-bent on constantly improving and expanding their fabulous hyper-hostel, hosts Ann and Dion (Anndion, get it?) go to enormous lengths to make things homey: stereo systems, big TVs, spa, swimming pool, barbecue area, restaurant, bar, courtesy van etc. 'No is not in our vocabulary', says super-helpful Ann.

Tamara Backpackers Lodge　HOSTEL $
(☑06-347 6300; www.tamaralodge.com; 24 Somme Pde; dm/s from $28/53, d & tw with/without bathroom $84/70; @🛱) Tamara is a photogenic, maze-like, two-storey heritage house with a wide balcony, lofty ceilings (people weren't taller in 1904 were they?), kitchen, TV lounge, free bikes and a leafy, hammock-hung back garden. Ask for one of the beaut doubles overlooking the river.

Braemar House YHA　HOSTEL $
(☑06-348 2301; www.braemarhouse.co.nz; 2 Plymouth St; dm/s/d/tw $30/50/75/75, f $96-130, guesthouse incl breakfast s/d $95/130; @🛱) Riverside Braemar brings together an 1895 Victorian B&B guesthouse and a reliable YHA backpackers. Centrally heated guesthouse rooms are floral and fancy; airy dorms conjure up a bit more fun out the back. Chooks patrol the back yard.

Whanganui River

Top 10 Holiday Park　HOLIDAY PARK $
(☑06-343 8402, 0800 272 664; www.wrivertop10.co.nz; 460 Somme Pde; campsites/cabins/units from $21/72/135; @🛱🛍) This tidy Top 10 park sits on the Whanganui's west bank 6km north of Dublin Bridge. Facilities (including pool, games room and jumping pillow) are prodigious. Kayak hire also available: the owners shuttle you upriver then you paddle back to camp. The budget cabins by the river have big-dollar views. Self-catering or dining in town is your best bet foodwise. Horizons (p235) buses go past here.

Aotea Motor Lodge　MOTEL $$
(☑06-345 0303; www.aoteamotorlodge.co.nz; 390 Victoria Ave; d from $150, 1-bedroom ste from $190; 🛱) It gladdens the heart to see a job done well, and the owners of one of Whanganui's newest motels have done just that. On the upper reaches of Victoria Ave, this flashy, two-storey motel features roomy suites, lavish linen, leather chairs, dark timbers and plenty of marble and stone – classy stuff.

Kembali B&B　B&B $$
(☑06-347 1727; www.bnb.co.nz/kembali.html; 26 Taranaki St, St Johns Hill; s/d incl breakfast from $110/125) Up on leafy St Johns Hill on the way to Taranaki, this home-spun B&B has two private upstairs guest rooms sleeping four, available on an exclusive-use basis. It's a sedate

place overlooking some wetlands, all achirp with tuis, pukekos and native whistling frogs.

151 on London Motel
MOTEL **$$**

(📞 0800 151 566, 06-345 8668; www.151onlondon.co.nz; 151 London St; d $115-160, apt $200-280; 🛜) This five-year-old, snappy-looking spaceship of a motel wins plenty of fans with its architectural angles, quality carpets and linen, natty lime/silver/black colour scheme and big TVs. At the top of the price tree are some excellent upstairs/downstairs apartment-style units sleeping six: about as ritzy as Whanganui accommodation gets.

Siena Motor Lodge
MOTEL **$$**

(📞 06-345 9009, 0800 888 802; www.siena.co.nz; 335 Victoria Ave; d $130-160; 🛜) Aiming for Tuscany but hitting Taranaki, the compact rooms here are four-star and spotless. Business travellers enjoy double glazing, a DVD library, gym passes, heated towel rails, coffee plungers and real coffee.

Riverview Motel
MOTEL **$$**

(📞 06-345 2888, 0800 102 001; www.wanganuimotels.co.nz; 14 Somme Pde; d $98-150; 🛜) Take your pick from one of 10 older-but-updated kitchenette units in the main block, or the five spa suites out the back. Super-clean, affordable and central, with a charming Irish host.

Grand Hotel
HOTEL **$$**

(📞 0800 843 472, 06-345 0955; www.thegrand-hotel.co.nz; cnr St Hill & Guyton Sts; s/d/ste from $79/99/130; 🛜) If you can't face another soulless motel room, rooms at this stately old-school Whanganui survivor (built 1927) have a bit more personality (and all have bathrooms). Singles and doubles are basic but good value; suites are spacious. The Grand Irish Pub and a restaurant are downstairs.

Astral Motel
MOTEL **$$**

(📞 06-347 9063, 0800 509 063; www.astralmotel.co.nz; 46 Somme Pde; s/d/f from $85/95/110; 🛜🖥) Astrally aligned with the very terrestrial Dublin Bridge nearby, rooms here are a bit dated and a tad noisy but are well serviced and good bang for your buck. There's also a pool and 24-hour check-in if you're rolling in off the midnight highway.

✖️ Eating

Jolt Coffee House
CAFE **$**

(19 Victoria Ave; items $3-8; ⊙7am-4.30pm Mon-Fri, 7.30am-1pm Sat, 8am-1pm Sun) Give your morning a jolt at this hip coffee house inside a 105-year-old former pharmacy. There's not much on the menu (muffins, caramel slice, chocolate croissants): the focus is squarely on fair-trade caffeine. Pretend you're Bob Dylan at acoustic music nights on the second Friday of each month.

WA Japanese Kitchen
JAPANESE **$**

(📞 06-345 1143; www.facebook.com/wa.wanganui; Victoria Court, Victoria Ave; sushi $2-3; mains $7-14; ⊙10am-5pm Mon & Tue, 10am-8pm Wed-Fri, 11am-8pm Sat) Duck into the quiet Victoria Court mini-mall on the main street and discover this sweet little Japanese restaurant, serving great-value sushi, bento boxes and donburi rice bowls.

Yellow House Café
CAFE **$**

(cnr Pitt & Dublin Sts; meals $10-18; ⊙8am-4pm daily; 🖊) Take a walk away from the main drag for funky tunes, buttermilk pancakes, local art and courtyard tables beneath a chunky-trunk cherry blossom tree. Ooh look! Marmalade and almond tart! Actually, it's more of a taupe colour...

Big Orange
CAFE **$**

(www.facebook.com/bigorangecafe; 51 Victoria Ave; meals $9-22; ⊙7.30am-5pm Mon-Fri, 9am-late Sat, 9am-5pm Sun; 🛜) Inside a gorgeous old Whanganui red-brick building, Big Orange is a babbling espresso bar serving gourmet burgers, big breakfasts, muffins, cakes and sandwiches (try the BLT). The outdoor tables go berserk during summer.

New World
SUPERMARKET **$**

(www.newworld.co.nz; 374 Victoria Ave; ⊙7am-9pm) Self-catering option.

Spice Guru
INDIAN **$$**

(📞 06-348 4851; www.spiceguru.co.nz; 23a Victoria Ave; mains $17-25; ⊙11am-2pm Tue-Sat, 5pm-late daily; 🖊) There are a few Indian joints in the River City (an affinity with the Ganges, perhaps?), but the Guru takes the cake for its charismatic black-and-chocolate-coloured interior, attentive service and flavoursome dishes (the chicken tikka masala is great). Plenty of vego options.

Ceramic Lounge
CAFE, LOUNGE **$$**

(www.facebook.com/ceramicloungebar; 51 Victoria Ave; mains $9-33; ⊙4pm-late Tue-Sat; 🛜) In a split-business arrangement with adjacent Orange, Ceramic takes over for the dinner shift, serving upmarket cafe food (killer quesadillas) in a low-lit, rust-coloured interior. Occasional DJs ooze tunes across the tables to cocktail-sipping seducers.

Stellar
CAFE, BAR $$

(www.stellarwanganui.co.nz; 2 Victoria Ave; mains $15-33; ⊘11am-late Mon-Fri, 9am-late Sat & Sun; 🛜) Stellar is a buzzy bar-cum-restaurant in a stellar location on the corner of the main street and Taupo Quay. Inside, try to ignore the gaming machines and tuck into pizzas, steaks, big salads and cold beers.

🍸 Drinking & Nightlife

Check out Stellar and Ceramic Lounge, too.

Grand Irish Pub
IRISH PUB

(www.thegrandhotel.co.nz; cnr St Hill & Guyton Sts; ⊘11am-late) Siphoning into NZ's insatiable (and, it has to be said, annoying) passion for Irish pubs, the Grand Hotel's version is as good a spot as any to elbow down a few pints of Guinness on a misty river afternoon. Good pub meals too.

Spirit'd
BAR

(75 Guyton St; ⊘10am-late) Pool tables, happy hours, Jack Daniels, Metallica on the jukebox and local young bucks trying to out-strut each other – just like 1989 minus the cigarettes.

☆ Entertainment

Embassy 3 Cinemas
CINEMA

(📞06-345 7958; www.embassy3.co.nz; 34 Victoria Ave; adult/child from $12.50/9, Tue from $9; ⊘11am-midnight) Nightly new-release blockbusters selling out faster than you can say 'bored Whanganui teenagers'.

🛍 Shopping

River Traders Market
FARMERS MARKET

(www.therivertraders.co.nz; Moutoa Quay; ⊘9am-1pm Sat) The Saturday-morning River Traders Market, next to the Riverboat Centre, is crammed with local crafts and organic produce.

ℹ Information

DOC (Department of Conservation; 📞06-349 2100; www.doc.govt.nz; 34-36 Taupo Quay; ⊘8.30am-4.30pm Mon-Fri)

Post Office (115 Victoria Ave; ⊘8.30am-5pm Mon-Fri, 9am-1pm Sat)

Whanganui Hospital (📞06-348 1234; www.wdhb.org.nz; 100 Heads Rd; ⊘24hr) Accident and emergency.

Whanganui i-SITE (📞06-349 0508; www.whanganuinz.com; 31 Taupo Quay; ⊘8.30am-5pm Mon-Fri, 9am-3pm Sat & Sun; 🛜) Tourist and DOC information (if the DOC office across

the street is closed) in an impressive renovated riverside building (check out the old floorboards!). Internet access available.

ℹ Getting There & Away

AIR

Whanganui Airport (www.wanganuiairport.co.nz; Airport Rd) is 4km south of town, across the river towards the sea.

Air New Zealand (📞06-348 3500; www.airnewzealand.co.nz; 133 Victoria Ave; ⊘9am-5pm Mon-Fri) Daily direct flights to/from Auckland and Wellington, with onward connections.

BUS

InterCity (www.intercity.co.nz) buses operate from the **Whanganui Travel Centre** (📞06-345 7100; 160 Ridgeway St; ⊘8.15am-5.15pm Mon-Fri). Some destinations:

DESTINATION	PRICE ($)	DURATION (HR)	FREQUENCY (DAILY)
Auckland	65	8	1
Hamilton	58	5½	1
New Plymouth	29	2½	1
Palmerston North	48	2¾	3
Wellington	39	4	3

Naked Bus (www.nakedbus.com) departs from Whanganui i-SITE to most North Island centres, including the following:

DESTINATION	PRICE ($)	DURATION (HR)	FREQUENCY (DAILY)
Auckland	39	9	1
Hamilton	32	7	1
New Plymouth	18	2½	1
Palmerston North	25	1½	1
Wellington	20	4	1

ℹ Getting Around

BICYCLE

Bike Shed (📞06-345 5500; www.bikeshed.co.nz; cnr Ridgway & St Hill Sts; ⊘8am-5.30pm Mon-Fri, 9am-2pm Sat) Hires out bikes from $35 per day, including helmet and lock. Also a good spot for info on the Mountains to Sea (p238) bike trail from Mt Ruapehu to Whanganui, which is part of the **Nga Haerenga, New Zealand Cycle Trail** (www.nzcycletrail.com).

Horizons (www.horizons.govt.nz; tickets adult/child $2.50/1.50) Operates four looped council-run bus routes departing Trafalgar Square shopping centre on Taupo Quay, including orange and purple routes past the Whanganui River Top 10 Holiday Park in Aramoho.

TAXI

Rivercity Cabs (☑06-345 3333, 0800 345 3333; www.wanganui.bluebubbletaxi.co.nz)

Whanganui National Park

The Whanganui River – the lifeblood of Whanganui National Park – curls 290km from its source on Mt Tongariro to the Tasman Sea. It's the longest navigable river in NZ, and today conveys canoes, kayaks and jetboats, its waters shifting from deep mirror greens in summer to turbulent winter browns.

The native bush here is thick podocarp broad-leaved forest interspersed with ferns. Occasionally you'll see poplar and other introduced trees along the river, remnants of long-vanished settlements. Traces of Maori settlements also appear, with old *pa* (fortified village) and *kainga* (village) sites, and Hauhau *niu* (war and peace) poles at the convergence of the Whanganui and Ohura Rivers at Maraekowhai.

The impossibly scenic Whanganui River Rd, a partially unsealed river-hugging road from Whanganui to Pipiriki, makes a fabulous alternative to the faster but less magical SH4.

History

In Maori legend the Whanganui River was formed when Mt Taranaki, after brawling with Mt Tongariro over the lovely Mt Pihanga, fled the central North Island for the sea, leaving a long gouge behind him. He turned west at the coast, finally stopping at his current address. Mt Tongariro sent cool water to heal the gouge – thus the Whanganui River was born.

Kupe, the great Polynesian explorer, is believed to have travelled 20km up the Whanganui around AD 800; Maori lived here by 1100. By the time Europeans put down roots in the late 1830s, Maori settlements lined the river valley. Missionaries sailed upstream and their settlements – at Hiruharama, Ranana, Koriniti and Atene – have survived to this day.

Paddle steamers first tackled the river in the mid-1860s. In 1886 a Whanganui company established the first commercial steamer transport service. Others soon followed, utilising the river between Whanganui and Taumarunui.

NZ's contemporary tourism leviathan was seeded here. Internationally advertised trips on the 'Rhine of Maoriland' became so popular that by 1905, 12,000 tourists a year were making the trip upriver from Whanganui to Pipiriki or downriver from Taumarunui. The engineering feats and skippering ability required on the river became legendary.

From 1918 land upstream of Pipiriki was granted to returning WWI soldiers. Farming here was a major challenge, with many families struggling for years to make the rugged land productive. Only a few endured into the early 1940s.

The completion of the railway from Auckland to Wellington and the improving roads ultimately signed river transport's death warrant; 1959 saw the last commercial riverboat voyage. Today, just one old-fleet vessel cruises the river – the PS *Waimarie* (p231).

◉ Sights

The scenery along the Whanganui River Road en route to Pipiriki is camera conducive – stark, wet mountain slopes plunge into lazy jade stretches of the Whanganui River.

From Aramoana Hill near the southern end of the road there's a terrific view: peaks, paddocks, poplars and the curling river. The Maori villages of Atene, Koriniti, Ranana and Hiruharama crop up as you travel upstream – ask a local before you go sniffing around. You can wander around Koriniti Marae (☑06-342 8198; www.koriniti.com; Koriniti Pa Rd), between the road and the river (look for the signs), unless there's a *marae* function happening.

A French Catholic mission led by Suzanne Aubert established the Daughters of Our Lady of Compassion in Jerusalem in 1892. Around a corner in the road, the picture-perfect spire of St Joseph's Church stands tall on a spur of land above a deep river bend. Other sights along the road include the restored 1854 Kawana Flour Mill (www.historic.org.nz; ☉dawn-dusk) FREE near Matahiwi, Operiki Pa and other *pa* sites.

Pipiriki is beside the river at the north end of Whanganui River Rd. It's a rainy river town without much going on (no shops or petrol), but was once a humming

Whanganui National Park Area

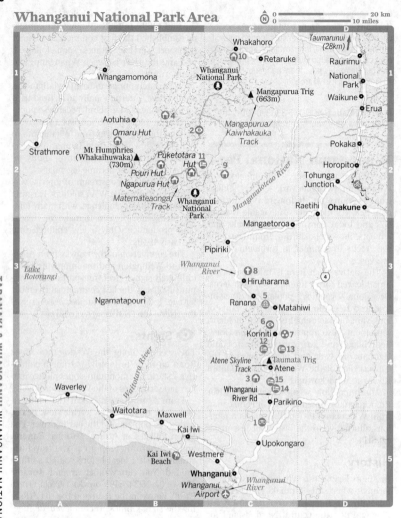

holiday hot spot serviced by river steamers and paddleboats. Seemingly cursed, the old Pipiriki Hotel, formerly a glamorous resort full of international tourists, burned to the ground twice. Recent attempts to rebuild it have stalled due to funding issues; it's been vandalised and stripped of anything of value, leaving a hollow brick husk riddled with potential. Pipiriki is the end point for canoe trips coming down the river and the launching pad for jetboat rides.

Standing in mute testimony to the optimism of the early settlers is the Bridge to Nowhere, built in 1936. The lonesome bridge – once part of a long-lost 4.5m-wide roadway from Raetihi to the river – is on the Mangapurua Track (p239), or it's a 40-minute walk from Mangapurua Landing upstream from Pipiriki, accessible by jetboat.

Activities

Canoeing & Kayaking

The most popular stretch of river for canoeing and kayaking is the 145km downstream run from Taumarunui to Pipiriki. This has been added to the NZ Great Walks system as the Whanganui Journey. It's a Grade II river – easy enough for the inexperienced,

Whanganui National Park Area

◎ **Sights**
1 Aramoana Hill...C5
2 Bridge to Nowhere.............................B2
3 Downes Hut C4
4 John Coull Hut.....................................B1
5 Kawana Flour Mill..............................C3
6 Koriniti Marae......................................C4
7 Operiki Pa...C4
8 St Joseph's Church C3
9 Tieke Kainga..C2
10 Whakahoro Bunkroom.....................C1

🛏 **Sleeping**
11 Bridge to Nowhere Lodge..................B2
12 Flying Fox..C4
13 Kohu Cottage C4
14 Rivertime Lodge.................................C4
   St Joseph's Church ....(see 8)
15 Te Punga Homestead........................C4

with enough moiling rapids to keep things interesting. If you need a Great Walks Ticket you must arrange one before you start paddling; see p238).

Taumarunui to Pipiriki is a five-day/four-night trip; Ohinepane to Pipiriki is a four-day/three-night trip; and Whakahoro to Pipiriki is a three-day/two-night trip. Taumarunui to Whakahoro is a popular overnight trip, especially for weekenders, or you can do a one-day trip from Taumarunui to Ohinepane or Ohinepane to Whakahoro. From Whakahoro to Pipiriki, 87km downstream, there's no road access so you're wed to the river for a few days. Most canoeists stop at Pipiriki.

The season for canoe trips is usually from September to Easter. Up to 5000 people make the river trip each year, mostly between Christmas and the end of January. During winter the river is almost deserted – cold currents run swift and deep as wet weather and short days deter potential paddlers.

To hire a two-person Canadian canoe for one/three/five days costs around $80/200/250 per person not including transport (around $50 per person). A single-person kayak costs about $60 per day. Operators provide you with everything you need, including life jackets and waterproof drums (essential if you go bottom-up).

You can also take guided canoe or kayak trips – prices start at around $350/850 per person for a two-/five-day guided trip.

Operators include the following:

Awa Tours CANOEING, KAYAKING
(☑ 027 698 5135; www.awatours.co.nz; Raetihi)

Blazing Paddles CANOEING, KAYAKING
(☑ 07-895 5261, 0800 252 946; www.blazingpaddles.co.nz; Taumarunui)

Canoe Safaris CANOEING, KAYAKING
(☑ 0800 272 335, 06-385 9237; www.canoesafaris.co.nz; Ohakune)

Taumarunui Canoe Hire CANOEING, KAYAKING
(☑ 07-895 7483, 0800 226 6348; www.taumarunuicanoehire.co.nz; Taumarunui)

Unique Whanganui River Experience CANOEING, KAYAKING
(☑ 06-323 9842, 027 245 2567; www.uniquewhanganuiriver.co.nz; Feilding)

Whanganui River Canoes CANOEING, KAYAKING
(☑ 06-385 4176, 0800 408 888; www.whanganui-rivercanoes.co.nz; Raetihi)

Wades Landing Outdoors CANOEING, KAYAKING
(☑ 027 678 6461, 07-895 4854; www.whanganui.co.nz; Raurimu)

Yeti Tours CANOEING, KAYAKING
(☑ 06-385 8197; www.canoe.co.nz; Ohakune)

Jetboating

Hold onto your hats – jetboat trips give you the chance to see parts of the river that would otherwise take you days to paddle through. Jetboats depart from Pipiriki and Whanganui; four-hour tours start at around $125 per person. The following operators can also provide transport to the river ends of the Matemateaonga and Mangapurua Tracks.

Bridge to Nowhere Tours JETBOATING, CANOEING
(☑ 06-385 4622, 0800 480 308; www.bridgetonowhere.co.nz) Canoe trips also available.

Whanganui River Adventures JETBOATING, CANOEING
(☑ 0800 862 743; www.whanganuiriveradventures.co.nz; Pipiriki) Canoe trips and camping at Pipiriki also available.

Whanganui Scenic Experience Jet JETBOATING, CANOEING
(☑ 06-342 5599, 0800 945 335; www.whanganui-scenicjet.com) Canoe trips also available.

Tramping

Bridge to Nowhere Track TRAMPING
The most popular track in Whanganui National Park is the 40-minute walk from Mangapurua Landing to the Bridge to Nowhere

(p236), 30km upstream from Pipiriki by jetboat. Contact jetboat operators for transport (around $100 per person one-way).

Atene Viewpoint Walk & Atene Skyline Track
TRAMPING

At Atene, on the Whanganui River Rd about 22km north of the SH4 junction, you can tackle the short Atene Viewpoint Walk, about a one-hour ascent. The track travels through native bush and farmland along a 1959 roadway built by the former Ministry of Works and Development during investigations for a Whanganui River hydroelectric scheme (a dam was proposed at Atene that would have flooded the river valley almost as far as Taumarunui). Expect great views across the national park.

From the Viewpoint Walk you can continue along the circular 18km Atene Skyline Track. The track takes six to eight hours, showcasing native forest, sandstone bluffs and the Taumata Trig (523m), with its broad views as far as Mt Ruapehu, Mt Taranaki and the Tasman Sea. The track ends back on the Whanganui River Rd, 2km downstream from the starting point.

Matemateaonga Track
TRAMPING

Three to four days from end to end, the 42km Matemateaonga Track gets kudos as one of NZ's best walks. Probably due to its remoteness, it doesn't attract the hordes of trampers that amass on NZ's more famous tracks. Penetrating deep into wild bush and hill country, it follows the crest of the Matemateaonga Range along the route of the Whakaihuwaka Rd, started in 1911 to create a more direct link from Stratford to the railway at Raetihi. WWI interrupted planning and the road was never finished.

On a clear day, a 1½-hour side trip to the top of Mt Humphries (730m) rewards you with sigh-inducing views all the way to Mt Taranaki and the volcanoes of Tongariro. There's a steep section between the Whanganui River (75m above sea level) and the Puketotara Hut (427m above sea level), but mostly it's easy walking. There are four DOC backcountry huts along the way: Omaru (eight bunks), Pouri (12 bunks), Ngapurua (10 bunks) and Puketotara (12 bunks); hut tickets cost $15 per person per night. There's road access at the track's western end.

Mangapurua/Kaiwhakauka Track
TRAMPING

The Mangapurua/Kaiwhakauka Track is a 40km trail between Whakahoro and the Mangapurua Landing, both on the Whanganui River. The track runs along the Mangapurua and Kaiwhakauka Streams (both Whanganui River tributaries). Between these valleys a side track leads to the 663m Mangapurua Trig, the area's highest point, from which cloudless views extend to the Tongariro and Egmont National Park volcanoes. The route also passes the Bridge to Nowhere (p236). Walking the track takes 20 hours (three to four days). The Whakahoro Bunkroom at the Whakahoro end of the track is the only hut ($10), but there's plenty of good camping (free to $10). There's road access to the track both at the Whakahoro end and from a side track from the end of the Ruatiti Valley–Ohura Rd (from Raetihi).

Mountain Biking

The Whanganui River Rd and Mangapurua/Kaiwhakauka Track have been incorporated into the 317km Mountains to Sea (www.mountainstosea.co.nz) Mt Ruapehu–Whanganui bike track, part of the Nga Haerenga, New Zealand Cycle Trail (www.nzcycletrail.com) project. As part of the experience, from Mangapurua Landing on the Whanganui River near the Bridge to Nowhere, you catch a (prebooked) jetboat downstream to Pipiriki, then continue riding down the Whanganui River Rd. For bike hire and track info try Bike Shed in Whanganui.

Tours

See also Activities (p236) for info on canoe and jetboat tours on the Whanganui River.

---

❶ CAMPING & HUT PASSES

Great Walk Tickets are required in Whanganui National Park from 1 October to 30 April for the use of huts (adult/child $32/free) and campsites (adult/child $14/free) between Taumarunui and Pipiriki. Outside the main season you'll only need a Backcountry Hut Pass (adult/child 1 year $122/61, 6 months $92/46), or you can pay on a night-by-night basis (adult/child $5/free). Passes and tickets can be purchased online (www.greatwalks.co.nz), via email (greatwalks@doc.govt.nz) or by phone (☑0800 694 732); or at DOC offices in Whakapapa, Taumarunui, Ohakune or Whanganui.

Whanganui Tours GUIDED TOUR
(☑06-345 3475; www.whanganuitours.co.nz) Join the mailman on the Whanganui River Rd to Pipiriki ($63; departs 7am) with lots of social and historical commentary. Returns mid-afternoon. Ask about transport/cycling options from Jerusalem back down the road to Whanganui.

Whanganui River Road Tours GUIDED TOUR
(☑0800 201 234; www.whanganuiriverroad.com; per person $80) Take a five-hour minibus ride up the River Rd with lots of stops and commentary. Or, you can take a truncated tour up to Pipiriki then cycle back to Whanganui ($100 per person; bikes supplied). Minimum four people on both tours.

🛏 Sleeping

🛏 Whanganui National Park

The park has a sprinkling of huts, a lodge and numerous camping grounds. Along the Taumarunui–Pipiriki section are three huts classified as Great Walks Huts during summer and Backcountry Huts in the off-season: **Whakahoro Bunkroom**, **John Coull Hut** and **Tieke Kainga Hut**, which has been revived as a *marae* (you can stay here, but full *marae* protocol must be observed). On the lower part of the river, **Downes Hut** is on the west bank, opposite Atene. See the boxed text for booking info.

Bridge to Nowhere Lodge LODGE $
(☑0800 480 308; www.bridgetonowhere.co.nz; dm/d $50/100) Across the river from the Tieke Kainga *marae*, this remote lodge lies deep in the national park, 21km upriver from Pipiriki near the Matemateaonga Track. The only way to get here is by jetboat from Pipiriki or on foot. It has a licensed bar, and meals are quality home-cooked affairs. The lodge also runs jetboat, canoe and mountain-bike trips. Transport/accommodation/meals packages available.

🛏 Whanganui River Road

There's a free informal campsite with toilets and cold water at Pipiriki, and another one (even less formal) just north of Atene. There's also a campsite at Pipiriki run by Whanganui River Adventures (p237) – call for info.

From south to north, non-camping accommodation (book in advance) includes the following:

Rivertime Lodge LODGE $$
(☑06-342 5599; www.rivertimelodge.co.nz; 1569 Whanganui River Rd; d $160, extra person $35) A rural idyll: grassy hills folding down towards the river and the intermittent bleating of sheep. Rivertime is a simple riverside farmhouse with two bedrooms, a laundry, a wood heater, a lovely deck and no TV! Sleeps five; meals available.

Te Punga Homestead LODGE $$
(☑06-342 8239; www.tepunga.co.nz; 2929 Whanganui River Rd; campsites $25, d $150, extra person $25; 🐕) A basic self-contained cottage next to the owner's house, just south of Atene. You can also park your campervan or pitch a tent in the adjacent paddock. Sleeps five.

Flying Fox LODGE, B&B $$
(☑06-342 8160; www.theflyingfox.co.nz; Whanganui River Rd; campsites $20, d $100-200; 🐕) 🍃 This eco-attuned getaway is on the riverbank across from Koriniti. You can self-cater in the Brewers Cottage, James K or Glory Cart (self-contained cottages), opt for B&B ($120 per person) or pitch a tent in a bush clearing. Access is by jetboat; otherwise you can park across the river from the accommodation then soar over the river on the flying fox.

Kohu Cottage RENTAL HOUSE $
(☑06-342 8178; kohu.cottage@xtra.co.nz; 3154 Whanganui River Rd; d from $70) A snug little cream-coloured weatherboard cottage (100 years old) above the road in Koriniti, sleeping three bods. There's a basic kitchen and a wood fire for chilly riverside nights.

St Joseph's Church HOSTEL $
(☑06-342 8190; www.compassion.org.nz; Whanganui River Rd; dm adult/child $25/15, linen $10) Taking in bedraggled travellers and offering

20 dorm-style beds and a simple kitchen, the sisters at St Joe's await to issue your deliverance – book ahead for the privilege. Moutoa Island, site of a historic 1864 battle, is just downriver.

ℹ️ Information

For national park information, try the affable Whanganui (p234) or Taumarunui (p192) i-SITEs, or check out www.doc.govt.nz or www.whanganuiriver.co.nz. Otherwise, a more tangible resource is the NZ Recreational Canoeing Association's *Guide to the Whanganui River* ($10). The **Wanganui Tramping Club** (📞 06-346 5597; www.wanganuitrampingclub.org.nz) puts out the quarterly *Wanganui Tramper* magazine.

There's no mobile-phone coverage along the River Rd, and no petrol or shops. There are a couple of takeaway food vans in Pipiriki open during summer, plus the casual cafe **Matahiwi Gallery** (📞 06-342 8112; www.matahiwigallery.com; 3925 Whanganui River Rd; snacks $3-5; ⊙ 9am-3.30pm Thu-Sun) in Matahiwi (call ahead to ensure it's open).

ℹ️ Getting There & Away

From the north, there's road access to the Whanganui River at Taumarunui, Ohinepane and Whakahoro, though the latter is a long, remote drive on mostly unsealed roads. Roads to Whakahoro lead off from Owhango and Raurimu, both on SH4. There isn't any further road access to the river until Pipiriki.

From the south, the Whanganui River Rd veers off SH4 14km north of Whanganui, rejoining it at Raetihi, 91km north of Whanganui. It takes about two hours to drive the 79km between Whanganui and Pipiriki. The full circle from Whanganui through Pipiriki and Raetihi and back along SH4 takes four hours minimum (longer if you want to stop and look at some things). Alternatively, take a River Rd tour from Whanganui.

Note that the River Rd is unsealed between Ranana and 4km south of Pipiriki, although road crews are making steady progress in sealing the entire route.

Palmerston North

POP 83,800

The rich sheep- and dairy-farming Manawatu region embraces the districts of Rangitikei to the north and Horowhenua to the south. The hub of it all, on the banks of the Manawatu River, is Palmerston North, with its moderate high-rise attempts reaching up from the plains. Massey University, NZ's largest, informs the town's cultural and social structures. As a result 'Palmy' has an open-minded, rurally bookish vibe.

None of this impressed a visiting John Cleese who scoffed, 'If you ever do want to kill yourself, but lack the courage, I think a visit to Palmerston North will do the trick.' The city exacted revenge by naming a rubbish dump after him.

👁 Sights

⭐ **New Zealand Rugby Museum**   MUSEUM
(www.rugbymuseum.co.nz; Te Manawa Complex, 326 Main St; adult/child/family $12.50/5/30; ⊙ 10am-5pm) Fans of the oval ball holler about the New Zealand Rugby Museum, an amazing space overflowing with rugby paraphernalia, from a 1905 All Blacks jumper to a scrum machine and the actual whistle used to start the first game of every Rugby World Cup. Of course, NZ won the 2011 Rugby World Cup: quiz the staff about the All Blacks' 2015 prospects.

⭐ **Te Manawa**   MUSEUM
(www.temanawa.co.nz; 326 Main St; ⊙ 10am-5pm) `FREE` Te Manawa merges a museum and art gallery into one experience. Vast collections join the dots between 'life, art and mind'. The museum has a strong Maori focus, while the gallery's exhibits change frequently. Kids will get a kick out of the hands-on exhibits and interactive play area. The New Zealand Rugby Museum is in the same complex.

The Square   LANDMARK
(The Square) Taking the English village green concept to a whole new level, the Square is Palmy's heart and soul. Seven spacey hectares, with a clock tower, duck pond, giant chess, Maori carvings, statues and trees of all seasonal dispositions. Locals eat lunch on the manicured lawns in the sunshine.

🏃 Activities

Swing into the i-SITE and pick up the *Discover City Walkways* booklet and the *Cycling the Country Road Manawatu* brochure.

Lido Aquatic Centre   SWIMMING
(www.lidoaquaticcentre.co.nz; 50 Park Rd; adult/child $4/3, hydroslide $5; ⊙ 6am-8pm Mon-Thu, 6am-9pm Fri, 8am-8pm Sat & Sun) When the summer plains bake, dive into the Lido Aquatic Centre. It's a long way from Lido Beach in Venice, but it has a 50m pool, waterslides, a cafe and a gym.

Palmerston North

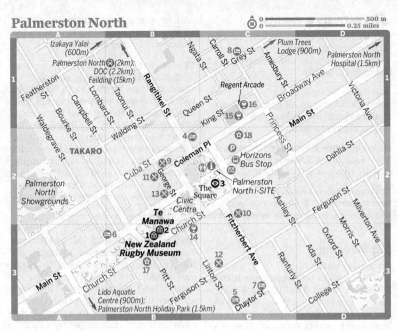

Palmerston North

◎ Top Sights
1 New Zealand Rugby
   Museum B3
2 Te Manawa B3

◎ Sights
3 Square C2

🛏 Sleeping
4 @ the Hub B2
5 Bentleys Motor Inn C3
6 Café de Paris B3
7 Fitzherbert Castle Motel C3
8 Peppertree Hostel C1

✕ Eating
9 Café Cuba B2
10 Halikarnas C2
11 Indian2nite B2
12 Pak 'n Save C3
13 Tomato Cafe B2

🍷 Drinking & Nightlife
14 Brewer's Apprentice B3
15 Celtic Inn C1
16 Fish C1

🎭 Entertainment
17 Centrepoint Theatre B3
18 CinemaGold C2
   Downtown Cinemas .... (see 18)

Manawatu Gorge Experience Jet JETBOATING
(☏ 06-342 5599, 0800 945 335; www.manawatugorgejet.com; 25min tours per person from $75) Jetboat rides through gorgeous Manawatu Gorge, about 25 minutes from Palmy.

🧭 Tours

Feilding Saleyard Tours CULTURAL TOUR
(☏ 06-323 3318; www.feilding.co.nz; Feilding; tours $10; ⊙ 11am Fri) Local farmers instruct you in the gentle art of selling livestock at this small town north of the city centre. Farmers market from 9am to 2pm every Friday.

Tui Brewery Tours GUIDED TOUR
(☏ 06-376 0815.; www.tuibrewery.co.nz; SH2, Mangatainoka; 35min tours per person $20; ⊙ 11am & 2pm) Even if you're more of a craft-beer fan than a drinker of ubiquitous Tui, this boozy tour is a worthwhile outing. Check out the interesting brewery and museum and taste a Tui or three. About 30 minutes east of Palmerston North; bookings essential.

✲ Festivals & Events

Festival of Cultures CULTURAL, FOOD & WINE
(www.foc.co.nz) Massive arts/culture/lifestyle
festival in late March, with a food-and-craft
market in the Square.

International Jazz & Blues Festival MUSIC
(www.jazzandblues.co.nz) All things jazzy, blue-
sy and swingin' in late May/early June, including plenty of workshops.

Manawatu Wine & Food Festival FOOD & WINE
(www.mwff.co.nz) Mid-June weekend fiesta of
culinary creations and the best local drops.

Manawatu Harvest Festival FOOD, CULTURE
(www.maifarm.org.nz) ✐ Showcases local harvest delights and sustainable living practices
in October.

🛏 Sleeping

Peppertree Hostel HOSTEL $
(☑06-355 4054; www.peppertreehostel.co.nz;
121 Grey St; dm/s/d $30/53/72; @🤶) Inex-
plicably strewn with green-painted boots,
this endearing 100-year-old house is the
best budget option in town. Mattresses
are thick, the kitchen will never run out of
spatulas, and the piano and wood fire make
things feel downright homey. Doubles off
the kitchen are a bit noisy – angle for one
at the back.

@ the Hub HOTEL, HOSTEL $
(☑06-356 8880; www.atthehub.co.nz; 10 King St; r
per night/week from $85/350; 🤶) There are lots
of students in Palmy, and lots of them stay
here during the term. But plenty of rooms
are usually available for travellers too. Book
a serviced en-suite double unit with kitchenette, or a simple student shoebox (also with
en suite). Great location, great value.

**Palmerston North
Holiday Park** HOLIDAY PARK $
(☑06-358 0349; www.palmerstonnorthholiday-
park.co.nz; 133 Dittmer Dr; campsites/cabins from
$35/45, d unit $80; 🤶) About 2km from the
Square, off Ruha St, this shady park with
daisy-speckled lawns has a bit of a boot-
camp feel to it, but it's quiet, affordable and
right beside Victoria Esplanade gardens.
Great for kids.

Café de Paris HOTEL $
(☑06-355 2130; www.cafedeparisinn.co.nz; 267
Main St; s/d $60/80; Ⓟ) It ain't Montmartre,
but this friendly, 1893 boozer three minutes'
walk from the Square has a warren of sur-

prisingly decent pub rooms upstairs, all with
TV, en suite and rather kooky furnishings.
Good value! Limited off-street parking.

★**Plum Trees Lodge** LODGE $$
(☑06-358 7813; www.plumtreeslodge.co.nz; 97
Russell St; s/d incl breakfast from $150/185; 🤶)
In a flat-grid town with more motels than
seems plausible, this secluded lodge comes
as sweet relief. It's brilliantly designed us-
ing recycled timbers from demolition sites,
with raked timber ceilings punctuated with
skylights, and a balcony set among swaying
boughs. Romantic nights slide lazily into
breakfast – a sumptuous hamper of fresh
fruit, croissants, jams, eggs, cheese, coffee
and juice.

Fitzherbert Castle Motel MOTEL $$
(☑06-358 3888, 0800 115 262; www.fitzcastle-
motel.co.nz; 124 Fitzherbert Ave; d $110-195; 🤶)
It looks unapologetically like a Tudor castle
from outside, but inside it's more like an
intimate hotel. Fourteen immaculate rooms
with cork-tiled bathroom floors and quality
carpets, plenty of trees, friendly staff and
small kitchens in some units. Free wi-fi and
laundry.

Bentleys Motor Inn MOTEL, APARTMENT $$
(☑06-358 7074, 0800 2368 5397; www.bentleys-
motorinn.co.nz; cnr Linton & Chaytor Sts; ste $155-
320) Putting a corporate spin on the motel
theme, Bentleys' five-star apartments are
worth the investment. Inside are new ap-
pliances, DVD player, spa, stereo, contem-
porary furnishings and Sky TV; outside are
a full-blown gym, squash court and sauna.
You could stay here for weeks...

✕ Eating

Pak 'n Save SUPERMARKET $
(www.paknsave.co.nz; 335 Ferguson St; ◷8am-
10pm) Cheap and cheerful.

★**Tomato Cafe** CAFE, BISTRO $$
(☑06-357 6663; www.tomatocafe.co.nz; 72 George
St; brunch $7-30, dinner $16-30; ◷7am-4pm Sun-
Wed, to 9pm Thu-Sat) This brilliant new cafe is
a buzzy yellow box plastered with 'Kiwiana':
retro NZ album covers, photos, prints and
canvases. Infused with entrepreneurial spirit, the boss gets up at 5am to make the daily
dough. His enthusiasm is infectious: happy
staff deliver beaut salads, pizzas, croissant
BLTs and excellent eggs Benedict. Friday-
evening happy hour; occasional live jazz.
Winner!

Izakaya Yatai
JAPANESE $$

(📞06-356 1316; www.yatai.co.nz; 316 Featherston St; mains $16-30; ⊙noon-2pm Tue-Fri, 6-9pm Tue-Sat) Simple, fresh, authentic Japanese food cooked by Atsushi Taniyama in an unpretentious suburban house with empty sake bottles lining the window sills. Front-of-house host Barbara comes with a big personality. Set menus available.

Indian2nite
INDIAN $$

(📞06-353 7400; www.indian2nite.com; 22 George St; mains $10-19; ⊙10.30am-3pm & 5pm-late daily; 🅿) With just the right touch of Bollywood schmaltz, this reasonably upmarket place smells enticing and certainly won't break the bank. Behind George St picture windows and tucked under a curved wall-cum-ceiling, northern Indian curries are served by super-polite waiting staff. Try the *dahl makhani*.

Café Cuba
CAFE $$

(www.cafecuba.co.nz; cnr George & Cuba Sts; brunch $9-26, dinner $26-31; ⊙7am-10pm Sun-Tue, to late Wed-Sat; 🅿) Need a sugar shot? Proceed to day-turns-to-night Café Cuba – the cakes here are for professional chocoholics only. Supreme coffees and cafe fare (risottos, salads, curries, corn fritters) also draw the crowds. The kumara cakes with avocado, sweet chilli and cream are magic. Live music Friday nights.

Halikarnas
TURKISH $$

(📞06-357 5777; www.halikarnas.co.nz; 15 Fitzherbert Ave; mains $18-25; ⊙noon-2pm Tue-Fri, 5pm-late daily) Angling for an Ali-Baba-and-the-Forty-Thieves vibe, with magic carpets, brass hookahs and funky trans-Bosphorus beats, Halikarnas plates up generous Turkish delights, from lamb shish kebabs to felafels and kick-arse Turkish coffee. Takeaway kebabs next door.

🍸 Drinking & Nightlife

Fish
COCKTAIL BAR

(Regent Arcade; ⊙4-11pm Wed, to 1am Thu, to 3am Fri & Sat) A progressive, stylish, Pacifically hewn cocktail bar, the Fish has got its finger firmly on the Palmy pulse. DJs smooth over your problems on Thursday and Friday nights as a sexy, urbane crew sips Manhattans and Tamarillo Mules (yes, they kick).

Brewer's Apprentice
PUB

(www.brewersapprentice.co.nz; 334 Church St; ⊙4pm-late Mon-Wed, from 11am Thu-Sun) What was once a grungy student pub is now a slick Monteith's-sponsored bar. Business crowds flock for meals (brunch and lunch $8 to $18, dinner $23 to $29), and drinkers over 25 fill the beer terrace after dark. Live music Friday nights. You have been warned: 'No untidy shoes.'

Celtic Inn
IRISH PUB

(www.celticinn.co.nz; Regent Arcade; ⊙11am-late Mon-Sat, 4pm-11am Sun) The Celtic expertly offsets the Fish bar nearby with good old-fashioned pub stuff, labourers, travellers and students bending elbows with a few tasty pints of the black stuff. Friendly staff, live music, red velvet chairs, kids darting around parents' legs – it's all here.

☆ Entertainment

CinemaGold
CINEMA

(www.cinemagold.co.nz; Downtown Shopping Arcade, Broadway Ave; adult/child $17/12; ⊙10am-midnight) In the same complex as the more mainstream **Downtown Cinemas** (www.dtcinemas.co.nz; adult/child $16/10; ⊙10am-midnight), CinemaGold ups the ante with plush seats and a booze licence to enhance art-house classics and limited-release screenings.

Centrepoint Theatre
THEATRE

(www.centrepoint.co.nz; 280 Church St; ⊙box office 9am-5pm Mon-Fri) A mainstay of the simmering Palmerston North theatre scene, Centrepoint serves up big-name professional shows, theatre sports and seasonal plays.

ℹ Information

DOC (Department of Conservation; 📞06-350 9700; www.doc.govt.nz; 717 Tremaine Ave; ⊙8am-4.30pm Mon-Fri) DOC information 3km north of the Square.

Palmerston North Hospital (📞06-356 9169; www.midcentraldhb.govt.nz; 50 Ruahine St; ⊙24hr) Accident and emergency assistance.

Palmerston North i-SITE (📞06-350 1922; www.manawatunz.co.nz; The Square; ⊙9am-5pm Mon-Fri, 10am-2pm Sat & Sun; 🛜) A super-helpful source of tourist information; free wi-fi throughout the Square.

Post Office (cnr Main St & The Square; ⊙8am-5.30pm Mon-Fri, 9am-5.30pm Sat)

Radius Medical, The Palms (📞06-354 7737; www.radiusmedical.co.nz; 445 Ferguson St; ⊙8am-7pm Mon-Fri, 9am-6pm Sat & Sun) Urgent medical help, plus doctors by appointment and a pharmacy.

❶ Getting There & Away

AIR

Palmerston North Airport (www.pnairport.co.nz; Airport Dr) is 4km north of the town centre. Air New Zealand runs daily direct flights to Auckland, Christchurch and Wellington.

BUS

InterCity (www.intercity.co.nz) buses operate from the **Palmerston North Travel Centre** (✆ 06-355 4955; cnr Main & Pitt Sts; ◷ 8.45am-5pm Mon-Thu, 8.45am-7.45pm Fri, 9am-2.45pm & 3.45-5pm Sat, 9am-2.45pm & 3.45-7.15pm Sun). Destinations include the following:

DESTINATION	PRICE ($)	DURATION (HR)	FREQUENCY (DAILY)
Auckland	72	9	2
Napier	29	3½	2
Taupo	35	4	2
Wellington	35	2¼	7
Whanganui	25	1½	3

Naked Bus (www.nakedbus.com) services depart from the i-SITE and outside the courthouse in Main St. Destinations include the following:

DESTINATION	PRICE ($)	DURATION (HR)	FREQUENCY (DAILY)
Auckland	25	9	2
Napier	18	3	1
Taupo	24	4¼	2
Wellington	15	2¼	4
Whanganui	13	1¼	1

TRAIN

KiwiRail Scenic Journeys (✆ 04-495 0775, 0800 872 467; www.kiwirailscenic.co.nz) runs long-distance trains between Wellington and Auckland, stopping at the retro-derelict **Palmerston North Train Station** (Mathews Ave), off Tremaine Ave about 2.5km north of the Square. From Palmy to Wellington, take the *Northern Explorer* ($48, 2½ hours) departing at 4.20pm Monday, Thursday and Saturday; or the *Capital Connection* ($30.50, two hours) departing Palmy at 6.15am Monday to Friday. To Auckland, the *Northern Explorer* ($198, nine hours) departs at 10am on Tuesday, Friday and Sunday. Buy tickets from KiwiRail Scenic Journeys directly, or on the train for the *Capital Connection* (no ticket sales at the station).

❶ Getting Around

TO/FROM THE AIRPORT

There's no public transport between the city and airport, but taxis abound or **Super Shuttle** (✆ 09-522 5100, 0800 748 885; www.super-shuttle.co.nz; tickets $16) can whiz you into town in a minivan (prebooking required). A city-to-airport taxi costs around $20.

BICYCLE

Crank It Cycles (✆ 06-358 9810; www.crankitcycles.co.nz; 244 Cuba St; ◷ 8am-5.30pm Mon-Fri, 10am-3pm Sat, 10am-2pm Sun) Hires out city bikes from $20/30 per half/full day, including helmet and lock (deposit $50).

BUS

Horizons (www.horizons.govt.nz; tickets adult/child $2.50/1.50) Runs daytime buses departing from the Main St bus stop on the east side of the Square. Bus 12 goes to Massey University; none go to the airport.

TAXI

Gold & Black Taxis (✆ 0800 351 2345, 06-351 2345; www.facebook.com/taxisgoldblack) Family-run local outfit.

Around Palmerston North

Just south of 'Student City' in the underrated Horowhenua district, Shannon (population 1250) and Foxton (population 2650) are sedentary country towns en route to Wellington.

Our fine feathered friends at Owlcatraz (✆ 06-362 7872; www.owlcatraz.co.nz; SH57, Shannon; adult/child incl 2hr tour $25/10; ◷ 9am-5pm) have obligingly adopted oh-so-droll names like Owlvis Presley and Owl Capone. It's a 30-minute drive south from Palmerston North.

Foxton Beach is one of a string of broad, shallow Tasman Sea beaches along this stretch of coast – brown sand, driftwood and holiday houses proliferate. Other worthy beaches include Himatangi, Hokio and Waikawa.

The town of Levin (population 19,550) is more sizeable, but suffers from being too close to both Wellington and Palmerston North to warrant the through-traffic making a stop.

Manawatu Gorge & Around

About 15km northeast of Palmerston North, SH2 dips into Manawatu Gorge. Maori named the gorge Te Apiti (the Narrow Passage), believing the big reddish rock near the centre of the gorge was its guardian spirit. The rock's colour is said to change intensity when a prominent Rangitane tribe member dies or sheds blood. It takes around four hours to walk through the gorge from either end, or you can see it via jetboat (p241).

On the southwestern edge of the gorge, about 40 minutes' drive from Palmerston North, is the Tararua Wind Farm (www. trustpower.co.nz), allegedly the largest wind farm in the southern hemisphere. From Hall Block Rd there are awesome views of the turbines. Spinning similarly, north of the gorge is Te Apiti Wind Farm (www.meridianenergy. co.nz). There are great views from Saddle Rd – ask the Palmerston North i-SITE (☏06-350 1922, 0800 626 292; www.manawatunz.co.nz; The Square; ☺9am-5pm Mon-Fri, 10am-2pm Sat & Sun; ☏) for directions to both farms.

Alternatively, flee the city with a visit to Timeless Horse Treks (☏06-376 6157; www. timelesshorsetreks.co.nz; Gorge Rd, Ballance; 1-/2-hr rides from $45/75). Gentle trail rides take in the Manawatu River and surrounding hills, or saddle up for an overnight summertime trek ($225). Palmerston North pick-up/drop-off available.

Taupo & the Central Plateau

Includes ➡

Lake Taupo Region....248
Taupo..........................248
Turangi & Around......259
The Central Plateau ..262
Tongariro
National Park.............262
Whakapapa Village....266
National Park Village ..267
Ohakune.....................269
Waiouru......................272
Taihape & Around......272

Best Places to Eat

➡ Lakeland House (p261)

➡ L'Arté (p257)

➡ Station (p268)

➡ Piccolo (p257)

➡ Bearing Point (p271)

Best Places to Stay

➡ Station Lodge (p271)

➡ Powderhorn Chateau (p271)

➡ Creel Lodge (p261)

➡ Reef Resort (p256)

➡ Lake Taupo Top 10 Holiday Resort (p256)

Why Go?

From river deep to mountain high, New Zealand's geology takes centre stage in this diverse region – and boy, does it shoot for the moon. Much of the drama happens along the Taupo Volcanic Zone – a line of geothermal activity that stretches via Rotorua to Whakaari (White Island) in the Bay of Plenty. It's the commotion below the surface that has gifted the region with some of the North Island's star attractions, including the country's largest lake and the three hot-headed peaks of Tongariro National Park.

And the thrills don't stop there: this area rivals Queenstown for outdoor escapades. How about hooning on a jet-boat up to a waterfall, bouncing on a bungy over a river, skydiving or skiing fresh powder? Or maybe you'd rather take it easy, soaking in thermal baths or frittering away a day or two with some fly-fishing. If so, mark Taupo and the Central Plateau as a must-do on your North Island itinerary.

When to Go

➡ Equally popular in winter and summer; there's not really a bad time to visit the centre of NZ.

➡ The ski season runs roughly from July to October, but storms and freezing temperatures can occur at any time on the mountains, and above 2500m there is a small permanent cap of snow.

➡ Due to its altitude, the Central Plateau has a generally cool climate, with average high temperatures ranging from around 3°C in winter to around 24°C in summer.

➡ Lake Taupo is swamped with Kiwi holidaymakers from Christmas to late January, so it pays to book ahead for accommodation during this time.

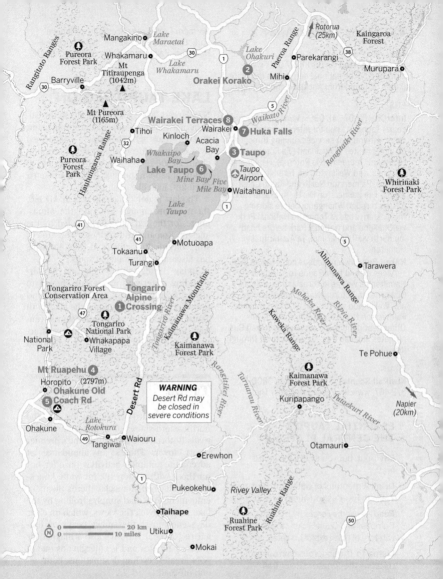

Taupo & the Central Plateau Highlights

1 Exploring fascinating volcanic terrain while tramping the **Tongariro Alpine Crossing** (p264)

2 Rediscovering the 'lost valley' of **Orakei Korako** (p253)

3 Hurtling to earth strapped to a complete stranger above the world's skydiving capital, **Taupo** (p248)

4 Carving fresh powder on **Mt Ruapehu** (p262)

5 Mountain biking over the 284m Hapuawhenua Viaduct on the **Ohakune Old Coach Road** (p270)

6 Paddling Lake Taupo to check out the modern **Maori carvings** (p249)

7 Rocketing up the Waikato River to the base of **Huka Falls** (p249) in a jetboat

8 Soaking in the healing geothermal waters of the **Wairakei Terraces** (p251) hot pools

ⓘ Getting There & Away

AIR

Air New Zealand (☎0800 737 000; www.airnz.co.nz) The national carrier has daily direct flights to Taupo from Auckland and Wellington.

BUS

InterCity (☎07-348 0366; www.intercitycoach.co.nz) Taupo is a hub for Intercity coach services, with regular services running through on direct routes to Auckland (via Rotorua and Hamilton), Tauranga (via Rotorua), Napier and Hastings, and Wellington via Turangi, Waiouru, Taihape, Palmerston North and Kapiti Coast towns. The Palmerston North–Auckland service passes through Whanganui before skirting the western edge of Tongariro National Park via Ohakune and National Park before heading north via Taumaranui, Te Awamutu and Hamilton.

Naked Bus (www.nakedbus.com) Naked Bus services extend from Taupo to Auckland via Hamilton as well as Rotorua and Tauranga, Gisborne via Rotorua, Napier and Hastings, and Wellington via Turangi, Waiouru, Taihape, Palmerston North and Kapiti Coast towns. Other destinations are serviced by Naked Bus affiliates and can therefore be booked through its website.

TRAIN

KiwiRail Scenic (☎04-495 0775, 0800 872 467; www.kiwirailscenic.co.nz) The

---

ESSENTIAL TAUPO & THE CENTRAL PLATEAU

Eat Trout; but you'll have to catch it first!

Drink A mouthful of water from the Waikato River as you bungy over it

Read *Awesome Forces* by Hamish Campbell and Geoff Hicks – the geological story of NZ in explosive detail

Listen to The sonorous chirruping of tui along the Tongariro River Trail

Watch *The Lord of the Rings* and *The Hobbit* movies, and spot Tongariro's movie-star mountains

Pedal Lake Taupo Cycle Challenge

Explore Tongariro National Park's alpine flora and geological oddities

Online www.greatlaketaupo.com; www.visitruapehu.com; www.nationalpark.co.nz; www.visitohakune.co.nz

Area code ☎07

Northern Explorer services stop at National Park, Ohakune and Taihape on the Auckland–Hamilton–Palmerston North–Wellington route.

LAKE TAUPO REGION

NZ's largest lake, Lake Taupo, sits in the caldera of a volcano that began erupting about 300,000 years ago. The caldera was formed by a collapse during the Oruanui eruption about 26,500 years ago, which threw out 750 cu km of ash and pumice, making Krakatoa (8 cu km) look like a pimple.

The last major cataclysm was in AD 180, shooting up enough ash into the atmosphere for the red skies to be noted by the ancient Romans and Chinese. The area is still volcanically active and, like Rotorua, has fascinating thermal hot spots.

Today the 622-sq-km lake and its surrounding waterways are serene enough to attract fishing enthusiasts from all around the world. Well positioned by the lake, both Taupo and Turangi are popular tourist centres. Taupo, in particular, has plenty of activities and facilities catering to families and independent travellers alike.

Taupo

POP 26,100

With a postcard-perfect setting on the northeastern shores of the lake, Taupo now rivals Rotorua as the North Island's premier resort town. There's an abundance of adrenaline-pumping activities on offer but for those with no appetite for white knuckles and churned stomachs, there's plenty of enjoyment to be had simply strolling by the lake and enjoying the views, which on clear days encompass the snowy peaks of Tongariro National Park. It's also a magnet for outdoor athletes and is emerging as one of NZ's greatest cycling destinations, both on- and off-road.

NZ's longest river, the Waikato, originates from Lake Taupo at the township, before crashing its way through the Huka Falls and Aratiatia Rapids and then settling down for a sedate ramble to the west coast, just south of Auckland.

History

When Maori chief Tamatea-arikinui first visited this area, his footsteps reverberated, making him think the ground was hollow;

MAORI NZ: THE CENTRAL PLATEAU

The North Island's central region is home to a group of mountains that feature in several Maori legends of lust and betrayal, which end with a few mountains fleeing to other parts of the island (refer to Mt Taranaki's sad tale).

Long after all that action was over, the *tohunga* (priest) Ngatoro-i-rangi, fresh off the boat from Hawaiki, explored this region and named the mountains that remained. The most sacred was Tongariro, consisting of at least 12 volcanic cones, seen as the leader of all the other mountains.

The major *iwi* (tribe) of the region is **Ngati Tuwharetoa** (www.tuwharetoa.co.nz), one of the few *iwi* in NZ that has retained an undisputed *ariki* (high chief). The current *ariki* is Sir Tumu Te Heuheu Tukino VIII, whose great-great-grandfather, Te Heuheu Tukino IV (a descendent of Ngatoro-i-rangi), gifted the mountains of Tongariro to NZ in 1887.

To discover the stories of local Maori and their ancestors, visit Taupo Museum (p249), the carved cliff faces at Mine Bay (p249), or Wairakei Terraces (p251).

---

he therefore dubbed the area Tapuaeharuru (Resounding Footsteps). The modern name, however, originates from the story of Tia. After Tia discovered the lake and slept beside it draped in his cloak, the area became known as Taupo Nui a Tia (The Great Cloak of Tia).

Europeans settled here in force during the East Coast Land War (1868–72), when it was a strategic military base. A redoubt was built in 1869 and a garrison of mounted police remained until the defeat of Te Kooti later that year.

In the 20th century the mass ownership of the motorcar saw Taupo grow from a lakeside village of about 750 people to a large resort town, easily accessible from most points on the North Island. Today the population increases considerably at peak holiday times, when New Zealanders and international visitors alike flock to the 'Great Lake'.

⊙ Sights

Many of Taupo's attractions are outside the town, with a high concentration around Wairakei Park to the north.

★Taupo Museum   MUSEUM
(Map p252; www.taupo.govt.nz/museum; Story Pl; adult/child $5/free; ⊙10am-4.30pm) With an excellent Maori gallery and quirky displays, which include a 1960s caravan set up as if the occupants have just popped down to the lake, this little museum makes an interesting rainy-day diversion. The centrepiece is an elaborately carved Maori meeting house, Te Aroha o Rongoheikume. Set up in a courtyard, the 'Ora Garden of Wellbeing' is a re-creation of NZ's gold-medal-winning entry into the 2004 Chelsea Flower Show. Historical displays cover local industries, a

mock-up of a 19th-century shop and a moa skeleton, and there's also a gallery devoted to local and visiting exhibitions. Don't miss the rose garden alongside.

Maori Rock Carvings   CARVINGS
Accessible only by boat, these 10m-high carvings were etched into the cliffs near Mine Bay by carver Matahi Whakataka-Brightwell in the late 1970s. They depict Ngatoro-i-rangi, the visionary Maori navigator who guided the Tuwharetoa and Te Arawa tribes to the Taupo area a thousand years ago. See the Watersports section (p253) and Tours section (p255) for companies that arrange trips.

★Huka Falls   WATERFALL
(Map p250; Huka Falls Rd) **FREE** Clearly signposted and with a car park and kiosk alongside, these falls mark the spot where NZ's longest river, the Waikato is slammed into a narrow chasm, making a dramatic 10m drop into a surging pool. As you cross the footbridge, you can see the full force of this torrent that the Maori called Hukanui (Great Body of Spray). On sunny days the water is crystal clear and you can take great photographs from the lookout on the other side of the footbridge. You can also take a few short walks around the area or pick up the Huka Falls Walkway (p252) back to town, or the Aratiatia Rapids Walking/Cycling Track to the rapids.

Aratiatia Rapids   WATERFALL
(Map p250) **FREE** Two kilometres off SH5, this was a spectacular part of the Waikato River until the government plonked a hydroelectric dam across the waterway, shutting off the flow. But the spectacle hasn't disappeared completely, with the floodgates opening from October to March at 10am,

Taupo & Wairakei

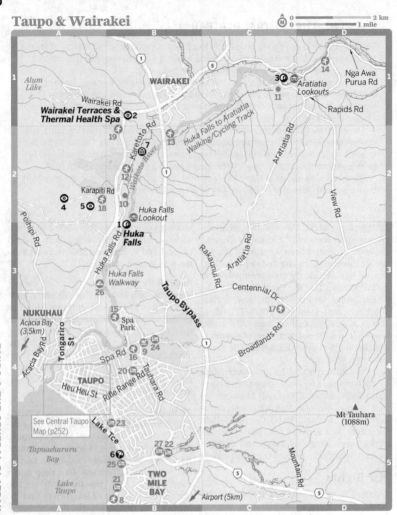

noon, 2pm and 4pm, and from April to September at 10am, noon and 2pm. You can see the water surge through the dam from two good vantage points. Drive here or take a leisurely four-hour return (30km) bike ride along the river from town.

Geothermal Area

Volcanic Activity Centre   MUSEUM
(Map p250; www.volcanoes.co.nz; Karetoto Rd; adult/child $10/6; ⊙9am-5pm Mon-Fri, 10am-4pm Sat & Sun) What's with all the geothermal activity around Taupo? This centre has the an-

swers, with excellent, if text-heavy, displays on the region's geothermal and volcanic activity, including a live seismograph keeping a watch on what's currently going on. A favourite exhibit with kids is the Earthquake Simulator, a little booth complete with teeth-chattering shudders and jarring wobbles. You can also configure your own tornado then watch it wreak havoc, or see a simulated geyser above and below ground. A small theatre screens footage of local eruptions and a 10-minute film of the 2011 Christchurch earthquake.

Taupo & Wairakei

◉ Top Sights
1 Huka Falls..B3
2 Wairakei Terraces & Thermal
   Health Spa B1

◉ Sights
3 Aratiatia Rapids...C1
4 Craters of the Moon A2
5 Craters of the Moon MTB Park.............A2
6 Hot Water Beach.......................................B5
7 Volcanic Activity Centre B2

⊕ Activities, Courses & Tours
8 2 Mile Bay Sailing & Watersports
   Centre B5
9 AC Baths B4
10 Heli Adventure Flights...........................B2
11 Huka Falls River Cruise C1
12 Huka Honey Hive B2
13 Huka Prawn Park B2
   Hukafalls Jet...................................(see 13)

Rapid Sensations & Kayaking
   Kiwi ....(see 10)
14 Rapids Jet...D1
   Rock'n Ropes ....(see 12)
15 Spa Park Hot Spring B3
16 Taupo Bungy...B4
   Taupo DeBretts Hot Springs ....(see 27)
17 Taupo Gliding Club...................................C3
18 Taupo Horse Treks....................................A2
19 Wairakei Golf & Sanctuary....................B2

☐ Sleeping
20 All Seasons Kiwi Holiday Park B4
21 Cottage Mews...B5
22 Hilton Lake Taupo B5
23 Lake..B5
24 Lake Taupo Top 10 Holiday
   Resort...B4
25 Reef Resort..B5
26 Reid's Farm Recreation
   Reserve..A3
27 Taupo DeBretts Spa Resort...................B5

Craters of the Moon   THERMAL AREA
(Map p250; www.cratersofthemoon.co.nz; Karapiti Rd; adult/child $8/4; ☺8.30am-5.30pm) This lesser-known geothermal area sprang to life as a result of the hydroelectric tinkering that created the power station. When underground water levels fell and pressure shifted, new steam vents and bubbling mud pools sprang up. The perimeter loop walk takes about 45 minutes and affords great views down to the lake and mountains beyond. There's a kiosk at the entrance, staffed by kindly volunteers who keep an eye on the car park. It's signposted from SH1, about 5km north of Taupo.

★**Wairakei Terraces &
Thermal Health Spa**   HOT POOLS
(Map p250; ☑07-378 0913; www.wairakeiterraces. co.nz; Wairakei Rd; thermal walk adult/child $18/9, pools $25, massage from $80; ☺8.30am-7pm) 🌿 At our pick of the region's hot pools, mineral-laden waters from the nearby Wairakei geothermal steamfield cascade over silica terraces into pools (open to those 14 years and over) nestled in serene native gardens. Take a therapeutic soak and a self-guided tour on the **Terraces Walkway**. On this you'll find a re-created Maori village, carvings depicting the history of NZ, Maori and local *iwi* Ngati Tuwahretoa, and artificially made geysers and silica terraces, that re-create, on a smaller scale, the famous Pink and White Terraces, which were destroyed by the Tarawera eruption in 1886.

The nighttime **Maori Cultural Experience** (adult/child $98/49) – which includes a traditional challenge, welcome, concert, tour and *hangi* meal – gives an insight into Maori life in the geothermal areas.

🏃 Activities

Tramping & Cycling
Obtain trail maps and hire bikes from **Pack & Pedal** (Map p252; ☑07-377 4346; taupo@ packandpedal.co.nz; 5 Tamamutu St; full day $35) or **Cornershop Cycles** (Map p252; ☑07-378 7381; craig@cornershop.co.nz; cnr Horomatangi & Ruapehu Sts; half/full day $35/50).

Great Lake Walkway   WALKING, CYCLING
This pleasant path follows the Taupo lakefront south to Five Mile Bay (10km). It's flat, easy walking or cycling along public-access beaches.

Great Lake Trail   TRAMPING, CYCLING
(www.greatlaketrail.com) A purpose-built 71km track from Whakaipo Bay to Waihaha in the remote northwestern reaches of the lake. The **W2K** section between Whakaipo and Kinloch has splendid views across the lake to Tongariro National Park. If you are looking for more challenging off-road riding, look up **Craters of the Moon MTB Park** (Map p250; www.biketaupo.org.nz; Craters Rd).

Central Taupo

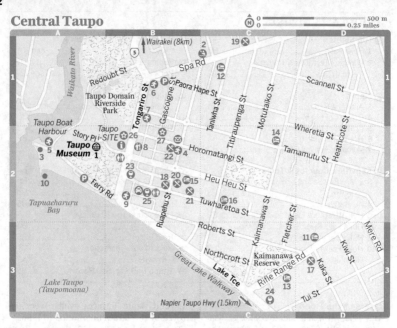

Central Taupo

◎ Top Sights
1 Taupo Museum A2

✪ Activities, Courses & Tours
Big Sky Parasail ....(see 5)
Boating Lake Taupo ....(see 3)
2 Canoe & Kayak.................................. C1
3 Chris Jolly Outdoors.......................... A2
4 Cornershop Cycles............................ B2
Ernest Kemp Cruises ....(see 5)
5 Fish Cruise Taupo............................. A2
6 Greenstone Fishing B1
7 Pack & Pedal..................................... B1
8 Pointons.. B2
Sail Barbary ....(see 5)
9 Taupo Rod & Tackle B2
10 Taupo's Floatplane A2

🛌 Sleeping
11 Beechtree Suites D3
12 Blackcurrant Backpackers................ C1

13 Catelli's of Taupo.............................. C3
14 Silver Fern Lodge............................. C2
15 Taupo Urban Retreat........................ B2
16 Tiki Lodge... C2

✕ Eating
17 Brantry... D3
18 Indian Affair..................................... B2
19 Merchant C1
20 Piccolo B2
21 Plateau B2
22 Saluté... B2

○ Drinking & Nightlife
23 Finn MacCuhal's.............................. B2
24 Jolly Good Fellows............................ C3
25 Vine Eatery & Bar B2

✪ Entertainment
26 Great Lake Centre............................ B2
27 Starlight Cinema Centre................... B2

Huka Falls Walkway WALKING, CYCLING

Starting from the Spa Park car park at the end of County Ave (off Spa Rd), this scenic, easy walk takes just over an hour to reach the falls, following the east bank of the Waikato River. Continuing on from the falls is the 7km **Huka Falls to Aratiatia Rapids Walking Track** (another two-plus hours). The Taupo–Huka Falls–Aratiatia loop bike ride will take around four hours in total.

Hot Springs

Combine a soak in the hot pools with a walk around a fascinating thermal area at Wairakei Terraces (p251).

Spa Park Hot Spring
HOT POOLS

(Map p250; Spa Park) FREE The hot thermal waters of the Otumuheke Stream meet the bracing Waikato River at this pleasant and well-worn spot under a bridge, creating a free natural spa bath. Take care: people have been known to drown while trying to cool off in the fast-moving river. It's near the beginning of the Huka Falls Walkway, about 20 minutes from the centre of town.

Taupo DeBretts Hot Springs
HOT POOLS

(Map p250; ☑ 07-377 6502; www.taupodebretts. com; 76 Napier Taupo Hwy; adult/child $20/10; ☺8.30am-9.30pm) 🏊 A variety of mineral-rich indoor and outdoor thermal pools are on offer. The kids will love the giant dragon waterslide, while the adults can enjoy a wide choice of treatments, such as massage and body scrubs.

Water Sports

Lake Taupo is famously chilly, but in several places, such as **Hot Water Beach** (Map p250), immediately south of the centre, there are thermal springs just below the surface. You can swim right in front of the township, but **Acacia Bay**, 5km west, is a particularly pleasant spot. Even better and quieter is **Whakaipo Bay**, another 7km further on, an undeveloped waterfront reserve perfect for a lazy day.

Canoe & Kayak
CANOEING, KAYAKING

(Map p252; ☑ 07-378 1003, 0800 529 256; www. kayaktoursnz.co.nz; 54 Spa Rd; ☺9am-5pm Mon-Sat) Instruction and boat hire, as well as guided tours, including a two-hour trip on the Waikato River ($49) or a half-day to the Maori carvings (p249) for $95.

Rapid Sensations & Kayaking Kiwi
KAYAKING, RAFTING

(Map p250; ☑ 07-374 8117, 0800 35 34 35; www.rapids.co.nz; 413 Huka Falls Rd) Offers kayak trips to the Maori carvings (four hours, $98), a gentle paddle along the Waikato (two hours, $48), white-water rafting on the Tongariro River ($88 to $115), guided mountain-bike rides ($90) and bike hire (half/full day $45/60).

Taupo Kayaking Adventures
KAYAKING

(☑ 07-376 8981, 0274 801 231; www.tka.co.nz; Acacia Bay) Runs guided kayaking trips from its base in Acacia Bay to the Maori carvings, with the return trip taking around four hours ($100; includes refreshments). Longer trips and walk/bike combos also available.

2 Mile Bay Sailing & Watersports Centre
SAILING, KAYAKING

(Map p250; ☑ 0274 967 350, 0275 886 588; www. sailingcentre.co.nz; Lake Tce; ☺9am-10pm) Has a lakeside cafe-bar and hires out paddle boards ($30), kayaks (from $30), canoes (from $30), windsurfers (from $55), sailboats ($75) and catamarans (from $65); rates are per hour.

AC Baths
SWIMMING, CLIMBING

(Map p250; www.taupodc.govt.nz; 26 AC Baths Ave; adult/child $7/3, slides $5, climbing wall adult/child $14/10; ☺6am-9pm, climbing wall hours vary) At the Taupo Events Centre, about 2km east of town, this complex has three heated pools, two waterslides, private mineral pools and a sauna. There's also a climbing wall and gym.

Adventure & Adrenaline

More than 30,000 jumps a year are made over Taupo, which makes it the skydiving capital of the world. It's certainly a terrific

---

WORTH A TRIP

ORAKEI KORAKO

A bit off the beaten track, **Orakei Korako** (www.orakeikorako.co.nz; 494 Orakeikorako Rd; adult/child $36/15) gets fewer visitors than other thermal areas. Yet, since the destruction of the Pink and White Terraces, it is arguably the best thermal area left in NZ, even though two-thirds of the original site now lies beneath a dammed section of the Waikato River.

A walking track follows stairs and boardwalks around the colourful **silica terraces** for which the park is famous, and passes **geysers** and **Ruatapu Cave** (allow 1½ hours). This impressive natural cave has a jade-green pool, thought to have been used as a mirror by Maori women preparing for rituals (Orakei Korako means 'The Place of Adorning'). Entry includes the boat ride across the lake from the pleasant visitor centre and cafe.

It's about 30 minutes to Orakei Korako from Taupo. Take SH1 towards Hamilton for 23km, and then travel for 14km from the signposted turn-off. From Rotorua the turn-off is on SH5, via Mihi. You can also arrive via the NZ River Jet (p254).

spot to do it with the deep blue lake and snowcapped volcanic peaks of Tongariro National Park providing epic, dizzying views. Just remember to keep your eyes open. Taupo Airport is 8km south of town (free pick-ups available).

Taupo Tandem Skydiving
SKYDIVING

(☑ 07-377 0428, 0800 826 336; www.taupotandemskydiving.com; Anzac Memorial Dr; 12,000/15,000ft $249/339) Various packages that include DVDs, photos, T-shirts etc ($388 to $679); bungy combo available.

Skydive Taupo
SKYDIVING

(☑ 07-378 4662, 0800 586 766; www.skydivetaupo.co.nz; Anzac Memorial Dr; 12,000ft/15,000ft $249/339) Packages available (from $439) including a reduced-price second jump for altitude junkies.

Taupo Bungy
BUNGY JUMPING

(Map p250; ☑ 07-377 1135, 0800 888 408; www.taupobungy.co.nz; 202 Spa Rd; solo/tandem $169 /338; ☺ 9am-5pm, extended hrs in summer) On a cliff high above the Waikato River, this picturesque bungy site is the North Island's most popular, with plenty of vantage points for the chickens. The courageous will be led onto a platform jutting 20m out over the cliff, where they can throw themselves off the edge for a heart-stopping 47m plunge. Tandem leaps are available, as they are for the Cliffhanger giant swing (solo/tandem $119/238).

Hukafalls Jet
JETBOATING

(Map p250; ☑ 07-374 8572, 0800 485 253; www.hukafallsjet.com; 200 Karetoto Rd; adult/child $109/65) ✏ This 30-minute thrill ride takes you up the river to the spray-filled foot of the Huka Falls and down to the Aratiatia Dam, all the while dodging daringly and doing acrobatic 360-degree turns. Trips run all day (prices include shuttle transport from Taupo).

Rapids Jet
JETBOATING

(Map p250; ☑ 07-374 8066, 0800 727 437; www.rapidsjet.com; Nga Awa Purua Rd; adult/child $110/65) This sensational 35-minute ride shoots along the lower part of the Aratiatia Rapids – rivalling the Huka Falls trip for thrills. The boat departs from the end of the access road to the Aratiatia lookouts. Go down Rapids Rd and then turn into Nga Awa Purua Rd.

NZ River Jet
JETBOATING

(☑ 07-333 7111, 0800 748 375; www.riverjet.co.nz; Mihi Bridge, SH5; 1½hr ride incl entry to Orakei Korako adult/child $159/79) NZ River Jet will zip you to Orakei Korako (p253) in thrilling fashion along the Waikato River and through the 50m-high Tutukau Gorge. It also offers the Squeeze jetboat ride, where you disembark in warm water and edge your way through a crevice to a concealed natural thermal waterfall surrounded by native bush (adult/child $145/79), and a 1¼-hour Scenic Safari ($125/79).

Taupo Horse Treks
HORSE RIDING

(Map p250; ☑ 0274 786 104, 0800 244 398; www.taupohorsetreks.co.nz; Karapiti Rd; per hr $70, pony ride $30) Leads treks through mature forest offering views over the Craters of the Moon, Waikato River and beyond.

Big Sky Parasail
PARASAILING

(Map p252; ☑ 0800 724 4759; www.bigskyparasail.co.nz; Taupo Boat Harbour, Redoubt St; trips $95; ☺ 9am-6pm Dec-Apr) Lofty parasailing flights from the lakefront; bookings essential. Early-bird special $85.

Rock'n Ropes
ROPES COURSE

(Map p250; ☑ 07-374 8111, 0800 244 508; www.rocknropes.co.nz; 65 Karetoto Rd; giant swing $20, adrenaline combo $40, half-day $65) A vertiginous and challenging high-ropes course that includes balancing in teetering 'treetops', negotiating a tricky two-wire bridge and scaling ropes. The combo includes the swing, high beam and trapeze.

Taupo Gliding Club
GLIDING

(Map p250; ☑ 07-378 5627; www.taupoglidingclub.co.nz; Centennial Dr; flights $160-205) Flights daily by appointment (weather permitting).

Pointons
SKIING, WATERSPORTS

(Map p252; ☑ 07-377 0087; www.pointons.co.nz; 57 Tongariro St; ski/snowboard hire $35/45; ☺ 7am-7pm Jun-Sep, 9am-5pm Oct-May) Pointons hires ski gear in winter, and water-sports equipment such as wetsuits come summertime.

Fishing

Fish Cruise Taupo
FISHING

(Launch Office; Map p252; ☑ 07-378 3444; www.fishcruisetaupo.co.nz; Taupo Boat Harbour, Redoubt St; ☺ 9am-5pm Oct-Mar, 9.30am-3pm Apr-Sep) Representing a collective of 13 local boats, this booking office can hook you up with private charters whether you're looking for fishing on a small runabout or a leisurely cruise on a yacht.

Boating Lake Taupo
KAYAKING, SAILING

(Map p252; ☑ 0800 262 833; www.boatinglaketaupo.co.nz; Marina) Located five minutes' walk from the town centre at the marina, this out-fit hires out single/double kayaks ($20/30), paddle boards ($25), and self-drive motor boats ($90 to $95), and can take you out for waterskiiing and wakeboarding ($180 to $220); all prices are per hour.

Greenstone Fishing
FISHING

(Map p252; ☑07-378 3714; www.greenstonefish-ingtaupo.co.nz; 147 Tongariro St; fishing rod hire from $20; ☺8am-5pm Mon-Sat, 9am-3pm Sun) Central fishing shop that sells licences, hires gear and arranges guided trips (half-day trips from $250).

Taupo Rod & Tackle
FISHING

(Map p252; ☑07-378 5337; www.tauporodandtack-le.co.nz; 7 Tongariro St; gear hire $20-35; ☺8am-6pm, to 8pm Fri) Rental gear, fishing guides and boat charters.

Other Activities

Huka Prawn Park
AQUARIUM

(Map p250; www.hukaprawnpark.co.nz; Karetoto Rd; adult/child $26/15; ☺9.30am-4pm) One of the world's only geothermally heated fresh-water prawn farms, this place offers a surprising cocktail of activities, including prawn 'fishing', Killer Prawn Golf and an interactive walk around the prawn ponds. And, of course, there's a restaurant.

Huka Honey Hive
FOOD

(Map p250; www.hukahoneyhive.com; 65 Karetoto Rd; ☺10am-5pm) This sweet spot has a glass-enclosed viewing hive, honey tastings and a cafe, and sells all manner of bee products – edible, medicinal and cosmetic – and mead.

Wairakei Golf & Sanctuary
GOLF

(Map p250; ☑07-374 8152; www.wairakeigolf-course.co.nz; SH1; 18 holes $160) ✐ Surrounded by a 2m-high, 5km-long pest-proof fence, this challenging, beautiful golf course doubles as a native bird sanctuary.

☞ Tours

Huka Falls River Cruise
BOAT TOUR

(Map p250; ☑0800 278 336; www.hukafalls-cruise.co.nz; Aratiatia Dam; adult/child $37/15; ☺10.30am, 12.30pm & 2.30pm year-round, plus 4.30pm Dec-Feb) ✐ For a photo-friendly ride, this boat offers a relaxed jaunt (80 minutes) from Aratiatia Dam to Huka Falls.

Sail Barbary
BOAT TOUR

(Map p252; ☑07-378 5879; www.sailbarbary.com; Taupo Boat Harbour, Redoubt St; adult/child $44/16; ☺10.30am & 2pm year-round, plus 5pm Dec-Feb) ✐ A classic 1926 yacht offering 2½-hour cruises to the Maori rock carvings every day. Enquire about the popular movie and music charter cruises in summer.

Chris Jolly Outdoors
BOAT TOUR, FISHING

(Map p252; ☑07-378 0623, 0800 252 628; www.chrisjolly.co.nz; Taupo Boat Harbour, Ferry Rd) Operates the Cruise Cat, a large, modern launch that offers fishing trips and daily cruises to the Maori carvings (adult/child $44/16; 10.30am, 1.30pm and 5pm). Sunday brunch trips (adult/child $62/34) are also worthwhile. Charter, and guided hiking and mountain-biking trips also available.

Ernest Kemp Cruises
BOAT TOUR

(Map p252; ☑07-378 3444; www.ernestkemp.co.nz; Taupo Boat Harbour, Redoubt St; adult/chid $40/10; ☺10.30am, 2pm, 5.30pm Dec-Feb) Board the Ernest Kemp replica steamboat for a two-hour cruise to view the Maori carvings, Hot Water Beach, lakefront and Acacia Bay. Lively commentary and complimentary tea and coffee. Book at Fish Cruise Taupo).

Helipro
HELICOPTER

(☑07-377 8805, 0800 435 4776; www.helipro.co.nz; Anzac Memorial Dr; flights $99-1250) Specialises in heli-tours, which include alpine and landings, as well as shorter scenic flights over the town, lake and volcanoes.

Heli Adventure Flights
HELICOPTER

(Map p250; ☑07-374 8680, 0508 435 474; www.helicoptertours.co.nz; 415 Huka Falls Rd; flights $99-740) Offers a variety of scenic helicopter flights, from 10 minutes to 1½ hours. Combine a flight with the Hukafalls Jet in the Helijet combo ($189). Helibiking and hunting adventures also available.

Taupo's Floatplane
SCENIC FLIGHTS

(Map p252; ☑07-378 7500; www.tauposfloatplane.co.nz; Taupo Boat Harbour, Ferry Rd; flights $105-790) Located near the marina, the floatplane offers a variety of trips, including quick flights over the lake and longer forays over Mt Ruapehu or White Island. Their three-hour 'Taupo Trifecta' ($505) combines a scenic flight, visit to Orakei Korako and jetboat ride.

Paradise Tours
BUS TOUR

(☑07-378 9955; www.paradisetours.co.nz; adult/child $99/45) Three-hour tours to the Aratiatia Rapids, Craters of the Moon and Huka Falls. Also offers day tours to Tongariro National Park, Orakei Korako, Rotorua, Hawke's Bay and Waitomo Caves.

✦ Festivals & Events

Heralding itself as the events capital of NZ, Taupo plays host to numerous shindigs throughout the year, many of them of a sporting nature – and plenty you can participate in. See www.greatlaketaupo.com and www.eventpromotions.co.nz for more details.

Ironman New Zealand SPORTS
(www.ironman.co.nz) Bring a magnet, as buns of steel are plentiful during this pimped-up triathlon. Held in early March, it attracts some of the world's finest athletes.

Erupt Festival ARTS
(www.erupt.co.nz) Biennial arts festival, which is held over 11 days in May on even-numbered years.

Winterfest FAMILY
Billed as a festival of old-fashioned family fun, held around town over three days in August.

Lake Taupo Cycle Challenge SPORTS
(www.cyclechallenge.com) One of NZ's biggest annual cycling events, the 160km Lake Taupo Cycle Challenge, sees around 10,000 people pedalling around the lake on the last Saturday in November.

🛏 Sleeping

Taupo has plenty of accommodation, all of which is in hot demand during late December and January and during major sporting events. Book ahead during these times. Self-contained campervan travellers can camp for free at 'Freedom Camp' between 5pm and 10am in a car park along Ferry Rd; non-self-contained vans have the option of **Reid's Farm Recreation Reserve** (Map p250; Huka Falls Rd), a scruffy spot beside the Waikato River.

⭐**Lake Taupo Top 10**
Holiday Resort HOLIDAY PARK $
(Map p250; ☑07-378 6860, 0800 332 121; www.taupotop10.co.nz; 41 Centennial Dr; campsites from $48, units $97-306; ☎🖈) 🖋 This slick 8-hectare park about 2.5km from the i-SITE has all mod cons, including heated swimming pool, tennis courts and an on-site shop. Manicured grounds, swish new accommodation options and spotless facilities help make it a contender for camp of the year.

Blackcurrant Backpackers HOSTEL $
(Map p252; ☑07-378 9292; www.blackcurrantbp.co.nz; 20 Taniwha St; dm/s/d $27/60/78; ☎)

Fashioned from an ageing motel, our favourite Taupo hostel has private rooms with en suites and super-comfy beds. The staff rival the cartoon blackcurrants in the Ribena ads for chirpiness.

Taupo Urban Retreat HOSTEL $
(Map p252; ☑07-378 6124, 0800 872 261; www.tur.co.nz; 65 Heu Heu St; dm $25-29, d $75; ☎) A younger crowd gravitates to this hostel, attracted by its pub-like hub (with retractable roof) and carefree style. It's refreshingly modern in design with a beach-house feel, despite being on a busy road.

Silver Fern Lodge HOSTEL $
(Map p252; ☑07-377 4929; www.silverfernlodge.co.nz; cnr Tamamutu & Kaimanawa Sts; dm $28-30, d $85-99; ☎) Rooms range from five-bed dorms to studio en-suite units in this large, custom-built complex, trimmed in shiny corrugated steel yet still strangely lifeless, decor-wise. There's a large communal kitchen and lounge.

Tiki Lodge HOSTEL $
(Map p252; ☑07-377 4545, 0800 845 456; www.tikilodge.co.nz; 104 Tuwharetoa St; dm $27, d $76-80; ☎) This hostel has lake and mountain views from the balcony, a spacious kitchen, comfy lounges, Maori artwork and a spa pool out back. Scooters and bikes for hire.

All Seasons Kiwi Holiday Park HOLIDAY PARK $
(Map p250; ☑07-378 4272, 0800 777 272; www.taupoallseasons.co.nz; 16 Rangatira St; campsites from $25, dm $47, units $75-160; ☎) 🖋 A pleasant holiday park, with lovely staff; well-established trees and hedgerows between sites; a playground; games room; thermal pool; bike hire; and good kitchen facilities. Lots of accommodation options from lodge rooms and cabins to self-contained motels. It's a 20-minute walk downhill to town.

Taupo DeBretts Spa Resort HOLIDAY PARK $
(Map p250; ☑07-378 8559; www.taupodebretts.com; 76 Napier Taupo Hwy; campsites from $22, units $95-285; ☎) 🖋 More a trim holiday park than a flashy resort, DeBretts offers everything from hedged tent sites to motel units. The five-minute drive from downtown is well worth the hop for the indulgent thermal pools on site (half-price entry for guests).

⭐**Reef Resort** APARTMENTS $$
(Map p250; ☑0800 733 378, 07-378 5115; www.accommodationtaupo.com; 219 Lake Tce; d $150-250; ☎🖈) This smart complex stands out amongst Taupo's waterfront apartment

complexes for its classy, well-priced one- to three-bedroom apartments, centred upon an appealing pool patio.

Lake
MOTEL $$

(Map p250; ☑ 07-378 4222; www.thelakeonline. co.nz; 63 Mere Rd; d $130-200; ☻) A reminder that 1960s and '70s design wasn't all Austin Powers–style groovaliciousness, this distinctive boutique motel is crammed with furniture from the era's signature designers. The four one-bedroom units all have kitchenettes and dining-living areas, and everyone has use of the pleasant garden out back.

Waitahanui Lodge
MOTEL $$

(☑ 07-378 7183, 0800 104 321; www.waitahanuilodge.co.nz; 116 SH1, Waitahanui; d $119-179; ☻) Ten kilometres south of Taupo, this enclave of genuine retro bach-style units are ideally positioned for swimming, fishing and superb sunsets. Pick of the bunch are the two absolute-lakefront units, but all have lake access, sociable communal areas plus free rowboat and kayaks.

Cottage Mews
MOTEL $$

(Map p250; ☑ 07-378 3004, 0800 555 586; www. cottagemews.co.nz; 311 Lake Tce, Two Mile Bay; d $115-130, q $150; ☻) Few motels muster much charm, but this cute gable-roofed block, festooned with hanging flowers, manages to seem almost rustic. Some units have lake views, most have spa baths and all have a small private garden. Bikes and kayaks for hire.

Catelli's of Taupo
MOTEL $$

(Map p252; ☑ 07-378 4477, 0800 884 477; www. catellis.co.nz; 23-27 Rifle Range Rd; d $135-165, q $230; ☻) ✐ The exterior is all hobbitish '80s curves, sloping roofs and nipple-pink trim, but these orderly motel units have a fresh feel inside. In summer it's worth paying extra for a garden studio.

Beechtree Suites
MOTEL $$

(Map p252; ☑ 0800 233 248, 07-377 0181; www. beechtreemotel.co.nz; 56 Rifle Range Rd; apt $145-380; ☻) The Beechtree offers classy rooms, fresh and modern in design with neutral-toned decor, large windows, ground-floor patios and upstairs balconies.

Acacia Cliffs Lodge
B&B $$$

(☑ 07-378 1551; www.acaciacliffslodge.co.nz; 133 Mapara Rd, Acacia Bay; d $700; ☻) ✐ This luxurious B&B, high above Acacia Bay, offers four comtemporarily and artfully designed suites, three with grand lake views and one that compensates for the lack of them with a curvy bath and a private garden ($595). The chef-owner dishes up high-quality fare, with dinner available. Tariff includes breakfast, pre-dinner drinks, canapes and Taupo airport transfer.

Hilton Lake Taupo
HOTEL $$$

(Map p250; ☑ 07-378 7080; www.hilton.com/laketaupo; 80-100 Napier Rd; from $220; ☻☱) Occupying the historic Terraces Hotel (1889) and a modern extension, this large complex offers the expected Hilton standard of luxury including swish suites, an outdoor heated pool, and Bistro Lago, the decent in-house restaurant. It's a little out of town but is handy for the DeBretts thermal complex.

✘ Eating

★ L'Arté
CAFE $

(www.larte.co.nz; 255 Mapara Rd, Acacia Bay; snacks $4-9, mains $10-19; ☻9am-4pm Wed-Sun, daily Jan) Lots of mouth-watering treats are made from scratch at this fantastically artful cafe on the hill that backs Acacia Bay. Brunch in the sunshine, then check out the sculpture garden and gallery.

Merchant
DELI $

(Map p252; www.themerchant.co.nz; 114 Spa Rd; ☻9am-7pm Mon-Sat, 10am-5pm Sun) Championing NZ artisan producers and importing specialities from abroad, this grocery on the town fringe is a fruitful stop for those looking to stock up on supplies ranging from cheese to chocolate to craft beer.

★ Piccolo
CAFE $$

(Map p252; www.taupocafe.co.nz; 41 Ruapehu St; mains $12-24; ☻7am-4pm; ☻✐) This sharp, modern cafe is well tuned, offering a cabinet-load of pastries, sandwiches and salads, with great value wines by the glass should you feel inclined. Excellent coffee, and sublime home-baked sweets.

Saluté
CAFE, DELI $$

(Map p252; www.salutedelicatessen.co.nz; 47 Horomatangi St; snacks $3-9, mains $10-20; ☻8am-5pm Mon-Fri, 9am-5pm Sat, 9am-4pm Sun; ✐) Bellissimo deli-cafe with operatic soundtrack, Taupo's best espresso and what everyone needs: a walk-in cheese fridge. The Mediterranean-flavoured menu includes pizzas, fresh homemade pasta and aromatic pork *carzuela,* plus a counterful of quality nibbly treats like bagels, slices, cakes and naughty-but-nice cronuts. Picnic supplies aplenty.

Indian Affair   INDIAN $$

(Map p252; ☑ 07-378 2295; www.indianaffair.co.nz;
cnr Ruapehu & Tuwharetoa Sts; mains $16-29;
☺ lunch Mon-Fri, dinner daily; ☑) Eschewing the
staid, traditional curry-house vibe in favour
of bold, floral feature walls and high-back
leather chairs, this thoroughly modern Indian restaurant serves up spicy classics (try
the tikka lamb chops and chicken *jalfrezi*)
with warm service. Alfresco tables bask in
late sun; good whiskies.

Plateau   PUB $$

(Map p252; www.plateautaupo.co.nz; 64 Tuwharetoa
St; mains $20-35; ☺ 11.30am-late; ☎) An ambi-
ent place for a handle or two of the Monteith's range, popular Plateau delivers in the
food department, too. Its menu of modern
pub classics features the likes of smoked
salmon salad with corn cakes, and an artful
steak sandwich.

Brantry   MODERN NZ $$$

(Map p252; ☑ 07-378 0484; www.thebrantry.co.nz;
45 Rifle Range Rd; mains $30, 2-/3-course set menu
$45/55; ☺ dinner) Operating out of an unob-
trusive 1950s house, the Brantry continues
its reign as one of the best in the region for
its well-executed, good-value offerings centred on meaty mains turned out in classical
style. Book-ending with entrée and dessert is
highly recommended.

🍸 Drinking & Nightlife

Things get lively in the height of summer
when the town swells. The rest of the year it
might pay to take a newspaper to read over
your pint.

Vine Eatery & Bar   TAPAS, WINE BAR

(Map p252; www.vineeatery.co.nz; 37 Tuwharetoa St;
tapas $9-20; ☺ 9am-late) The clue's in the name
at this wine bar sharing its barn-like home
with the Scenic Cellars wine store. Share
traditional tapas alongside larger divisible
dishes, accompanied by your choice of an
expansive array of wines at keen prices. This
is Taupo's best bet for a sophisticated nibble
and natter amongst the town's well-heeled.

Jolly Good Fellows   PUB

(Map p252; www.jollygoodfellows.co.nz; 80 Lake
Tce; ☺ 11am-late) Corr 'blimey, Guvnor! You
ain't seen a rubber-dub-dub like this since
Old Blighty, with lashings of colonial cliches
and the likes of London Pride on tap, plus
a couple of NZ craft beers. Solid service,
square meals, outside seating, lake views –
she's pukka!

Finn MacCuhal's   IRISH PUB

(Map p252; www.finns.co.nz; cnr Tongariro & Tuwharetoa Sts; ☺ 11am-late) With Irish ephemera nailed to the walls and a backpackers
next door, you can be sure that there will be
plenty of craic here. A host of locals get in on
the action, likely to involve bands, DJs and
dancing, and a bonanza of well-managed
bacchanalia.

☆ Entertainment

Great Lake Centre   CONCERT VENUE

(Map p252; www.taupovenues.co.nz; Tongariro St)
Hosts performances, exhibitions and con-
ventions. Ask at the i-SITE for the current
program.

Starlight Cinema Centre   CINEMA

(Map p252; www.starlightcinema.co.nz; Starlight
Arcade, off Horomatangi St; adult/child $14.50/10)
Screens the latest Hollywood blockbusters.

ℹ Information

Taupo i-SITE (Map p252; ☑ 07-376 0027, 0800
525 382; www.greatlaketaupo.com; Tongariro
St; ☺ 8.30am-5pm) Handles bookings for accommodation, transport and activities; dis-
penses cheerful advice; and stocks Department
of Conservation (DOC) maps and town maps.

ℹ Getting There & Away

Taupo Airport (☑ 07-378 7771; www.taupoair-
port.co.nz; Anzac Memorial Dr) is 8km south
of town. InterCity and Naked Bus services (see
p248) stop outside the i-SITE, where bookings
can be made.

ℹ Getting Around

Local buses are run by **Busit!** (☑ 0800 4287
5463; www.busit.co.nz), including the Taupo
North service running as far as Huka Falls and
Wairakei, twice daily Monday to Friday.

Hotbus (☑ 0508 468 287; www.alpinehotbus.
co.nz) is a hop-on, hop-off minibus service
around the town's key attractions. **Great Lake
Shuttles** (☑ 021 656 424; www.greatlakeshut-
tles.co.nz) offers charter services around the
area, and can hook you up with bike hire.

Taxi companies include **Taupo Taxi** (☑ 07-378
5100; www.taupotaxi.co.nz) and **Top Cabs** (Map
p252; ☑ 07-378 9250; 23 Tuwharetoa St). Expect to pay about $25 for a cab from the airport
to the centre of town.

There are plenty of shuttle services operating
year-round to Turangi and Tongariro National
Park. Ask at the i-SITE who will best suit your
needs as services vary according to season (ski
or hike).

Turangi & Around

POP 3000

Once a service town for the nearby hydroelectric power station, sleepy Turangi's claim to fame nowadays is as the 'Trout Fishing Capital of the World' and as one of the country's premier white-water-rafting destinations. Set on the Tongariro River, the town is a shortish hop for snow bunnies from the ski fields and walking tracks of Tongariro National Park.

◉ Sights & Activities

The Tongariro River Trail offers enjoyable walks from the centre of town. Further afield, good leg-stretchers include **Hinemihi's Track**, near the top of Te Ponanga Saddle, 8km west of Turangi on SH47 (15 minutes return); **Maunganamu Track**, 4km west of Turangi on SH41 (40 minutes return); and **Tauranga–Taupo River Walk** (30 minutes), which starts at Te Rangiita, 12km north of Turangi on SH1.

The Tongariro River has some superb Grade III rapids for **river rafting**, as well as Grade I stretches suitable for beginners in the lower reaches during summer.

It's also a likely spot for **trout fishing**, as evident by anglers stationed on every bend of the river.

Turangi

Tongariro National Trout Centre AQUARIUM
(www.troutcentre.com; SH1; adult/child $10/free; ☺10am-3pm) The DOC-managed trout hatchery has polished educational displays, a collection of rods and reels dating back to the 1880s and freshwater aquariums displaying river life, both nasty and nice. A gentle stroll along the landscaped walkway leads to the hatchery, keeping ponds, an underwater viewing chamber, the Tongariro River and a picnic area.

★**Tongariro River Trail** WALKING, CYCLING
(www.tongarirorivertrail.co.nz) Should you have at least half a day to spare around Turangi, the must-do is the picturesque Tongariro River Trail, a 16km dual-use walking and cycling loop track starting from town and heading upriver to the Red Hut suspension bridge, taking in the National Trout Centre along the way. It takes around four hours to walk the entire loop, and around two hours to cycle on easy terrain; hire bikes from Tongariro River Rafting who offer a $35 bike-hire and trout centre entry package. Shorten your outing by crossing at Major Jones Bridge – a circuit known as the **Tongariro River Lookout Track** which is a 1½-hour riverside amble passing lookout points to Mt Pihanga.

Tongariro River Rafting RAFTING
(☑07-386 6409, 0800 101 024; www.trr.co.nz; Atirau Rd) ✎ Test the white waters with a Gentle Family Float (adult/child $75/65), splash straight into the Grade III rapids (adult/child $115/105), or try a more physical kayaking trip ($129). Raft fishing available in summer (price on enquiry). Turangi's original rafting company also hires out mountain bikes and

Turangi

◉ Activities, Courses & Tours
Creel Tackle House & Cafe..........(see 6)
1 Greig's Sporting World.......................A1
2 Rafting NZ...B1
3 Sporting Life.......................................A2
4 Tongariro River Rafting.....................A3
5 Tongariro River Trail..........................B3

⛏ Sleeping
6 Creel Lodge B2
7 Extreme Backpackers.........................B1
8 Judges Pool Motel B2
9 Riverstone Backpackers.....................B1
10 Sportmans Lodge................................B1
11 Turangi Kiwi Holiday Park..................A2

⊗ Eating
12 Grand Central Fry B1

runs guided trips around local rides including the 42 Traverse, Tongariro River Trail, Tree Trunk Gorge and Fishers Track. Ask about multi-activity combos.

Rafting NZ RAFTING
(☑07-386 0352, 0800 865 226; www.rafting-newzealand.com; 41 Ngawaka Pl) The main trips offered by this slick outfit are a four-hour, Grade III trip on the Tongariro River with an optional waterfall jump (adult/child $129/119) and a family fun run over more relaxed rapids (Grade II, three hours, adult/

child $85/75). Groups of four or more can tackle a two-day trip overnighting at a riverside camp (Grade III-plus, $350 per person).

Motuoapa Hire Boats BOATING
(☑0275 303 333; Motuoapa Esplanade; kayak hire per hr $20-25) Hires kayaks, paddle boards and small motorboats from its launchpad 10km northeast of Turangi.

Tokaanu Thermal Pools HOT POOLS
(www.tokaanuthermalpools.co.nz; Mangaroa St, Tokaanu; adult/child $6/4, private pools per 20min $10/6; ⊙10am-9pm) Soak in thermally heated

---

ABOUT TROUT

Early European settlers, wishing to improve NZ's farming, hunting and fishing opportunities, were responsible for the introduction of such ghastly wreckers as possums and rabbits. One of their more benign introductions was that of trout – brown and rainbow – released into NZ rivers in the second half of the 19th century.

Today they are much prized by sports anglers, whom you may stumble across flicking their flies, thigh-deep in limpid rivers or on the edge of deep green pools. While this pastime, nay obsession, remains a mystery to the authors of this book, it is apparent that it brings much unbridled joy and satisfaction to the lives of its patrons. To quote NZ author and poet Kevin Ireland in his illuminating book *How to Catch a Fish*, 'It has as much to do with simple stubbornness and personal compulsion as it does with any complex notions of happiness and mystical fulfilment. The last thing to which it has any reasonable relationship is success.'

The Tongariro River is the largest and most important spawning river in the Taupo district, and well known all over the world for its fish. Tall tales boast of Taupo trout weighing more than a sack of spuds and measuring the length of a surfboard. Truth be told, more than 28,000 legal trout are bagged annually, by both domestic and international fishing enthusiasts.

Trout fishing is highly regulated, with plenty of rules regarding where and how, and licences most certainly required. Read more at Fish & Game New Zealand (www.fishandgame.org.nz), but our best advice is to seek out a guide. Most offer flexible trips, with $250 for a half-day a rough ballpark. Local experts include the following:

Creel Tackle House & Cafe (☑07-386 7929; www.creeltackle.com; 183 Taupahi Rd) Fishing equipment, tips, guiding and coffee.

Bryce Curle Fly Fishing (☑07-386 6813; www.brycecurleflyfishing.com) Turangi-based guide.

Fish Tongariro (☑07-386 7775) Turangi-based guide, Peter Canziani.

Flyfishtaupo (☑07-377 8054; www.flyfishtaupo.com) Guide Brent Pirie offers a range of fishing excursions, including seniors-focused 'Old Farts & Tarts' trips.

Greig's Sporting World (☑07-386 6911; www.greigsports.co.nz; 59 Town Centre) Hires and sells gear and handles bookings for guides and charters.

Sporting Life (www.sportinglife-turangi.co.nz; Town Centre) Sports store laden with fishing paraphernalia. Its website details the latest fishing conditions.

AJ Charters (☑07-386 7992; www.ajtaupocharters.com) Turangi-based fishing trips plus scenic lake cruises on a 38ft catamaran.

Ian & Andrew Jenkins (☑07-386 0840; www.tui-lodge.co.nz) Father and son fly-fishing guides.

Central Plateau Fishing (☑07-378 8192, 027 681 4134; www.cpf.net.nz) Turangi-based guide, Brett Cameron.

water at this unpretentious, family-orientated facility, 5km northwest of Turangi. A 10-minute stroll along the boardwalk (wheelchair accessible) showcases boiling mud pools, thermal springs and a trout-filled stream.

🛏 Sleeping

Extreme Backpackers   HOSTEL $

(☑ 07-386 8949; www.extremebackpackers.co.nz; 22 Ngawaka Pl; dm $25-27, s $46-56, d $62-72; 🛜) Crafted from native timber and corrugated iron, this modern backpackers has the bonus of a climbing wall and cafe, a lounge with an open fire and a sunny courtyard with hammocks. Dorms range from four to eight beds and the pricier private rooms have en suites. Staff will happily help with arrangements for the Alpine Crossing and other activites.

Turangi Kiwi Holiday Park   HOLIDAY PARK $

(☑ 07-386 8754, 0800 386 875; www.turangiholidaypark.com; 13 Te Reiti Tamara Grove; campsites per person from $18, d $50-120; 🛜) Roomy, suburban holiday park with established leafy grounds, five minutes' walk from the town centre. Facilities and cabins are old, but clean and continuingly being upgraded by friendly, hard-working owners. Sweet alcoves for campervans and tents.

Riverstone Backpackers   HOSTEL $

(☑ 07-386 7004; www.riverstonebackpackers.com; 222 Tautahanga Rd; dm $26-28, r $64-85; 🛜) This homely backpackers resides in a refitted house close to the town centre. Along with an enviable kitchen and comfortable lounge, it sports a stylish landscaped yard with a pizza oven.

Sportmans Lodge   LODGE $

(☑ 07-386 8150, 0800 366 208; www.sportmanslodge.co.nz; 15 Taupahi Rd; r $80, cottage $115; 🛜) Backing on to the river, this lodge is a hidden bargain for trout-fishing folk unbothered by punctuation. Tidy, compact rooms share a lounge with open fire and a well-equipped kitchen. The self-contained cottage sleeps four.

★Creel Lodge   LODGE $$

(☑ 07-386 8081, 0800 273 355; www.creel.co.nz; 183 Taupahi Rd; units $130-150; 🛜) ⌀ Set in green and peaceful grounds, this heavenly hideaway backs onto a fine stretch of the Tongariro River. Spacious units have separate lounges, kitchens, soothing patios for sundowners and free use of barbecues. Creel Tackle House & Cafe on site.

Judges Pool Motel   MOTEL $$

(☑ 07-386 7892, 0800 583 439; www.judgespoolmotel.co.nz; 92 Taupahi Rd; d $110; 🛜) This older motel has tidy, spacious rooms with kitchenettes. All one-bedroom units have outdoor decks for relaxing beers, although the barbecue area is the best place to talk about the one that got away. Free-range eggs from the owners' chooks sold cheep.

Oreti Village   APARTMENTS $$$

(☑ 07-386 7070; www.oretivillage.com; Mission House Dr, Pukawa; apt $220-280; 🛜) This enclave of smart self-contained apartments sits high over the lake surrounded by bird-filled native bush and landscaped with colourful rhododendrons. Gaze at blissful lake views from the balcony, undertaking a spot of tennis or taking a dip in the indoor pool. Take SH41 for 15km, heading northwest of Turangi, and turn right into Pukawa Rd.

🍴 Eating

Grand Central Fry   FAST FOOD $

(8 Ohuanga Rd; meals $3-8; ⊙11am-8.30pm) A local mainstay serving top fish and chips, plus burgers and anything else fryable. Erratic opening hours.

Licorice   CAFE $

(57 SH1, Motuoapa; mains $9-17; ⊙8am-4pm Mon-Sat, 9am-3pm Sun) Look for the giant licorice allsort on the roof of this roadside cafe, 8km north of Turangi. It's better than any of the cafes in the town itself, with fine coffee and baking.

★Lakeland House   INTERNATIONAL $$

(☑ 07-386 6442; 88 Waihi Rd, Waihi; brunch $16-25, dinner $23-42; ⊙10am-3pm & 6pm-late) Destination dining at the southern end of Lake Taupo, with generous pastas, salads and chowder dominating the daytime menu. Come evening, meat lovers can salivate over a rack of lamb with tamarillo and plum compote, rounded off with a toothsome passionfruit meringue gateau. Six kilometres from Turangi, just off SH41.

ℹ Information

Turangi i-SITE (☑ 07-386 8999, 0800 288 726; www.greatlaketaupo.com; Ngawaka Pl; ⊙8.30am-5pm; 🛜) A good stop for information on Tongariro National Park, Kaimanawa Forest Park, trout fishing, and snow and road conditions. It issues DOC hut tickets, ski passes and fishing licences, and makes bookings for transport, accommodation and activities.

ⓘ Getting There & Away

Both InterCity and Naked Bus (p248) coaches stop outside the i-SITE.

THE CENTRAL PLATEAU

Tongariro National Park

Tongariro National Park (797 sq km) lies in the heart of the North Island. Its major landmarks are three active volcanoes – Ruapehu, Ngauruhoe and Tongariro. These form the southern end of a chain that extends northwest through the heart of the North Island, past Taupo and Rotorua, to finally reach Whakaari (White Island). The volcanic nature of the region is responsible for Tongariro's hot springs, boiling mud pools, fumaroles and craters.

Geologically speaking, the Tongariro volcanoes are relatively young. Both Ruapehu and Tongariro are less than 300,000 years old. They were shaped by a mixture of eruptions and glacial action, especially in the last ice age. At one time, glaciers extended down Ruapehu to below 1300m, leaving polished rock far below their present snouts.

Mt Ruapehu (www.mtruapehu.com), at 2797m, is the highest mountain on the North Island. It is also one of the world's most active volcanoes. One eruption began in March 1945 and continued for almost a year, spreading lava over Crater Lake and sending huge dark clouds of ash as far away as Wellington. No wonder, then, that the mountain's name translates as 'pit of sound'.

Ruapehu rumbled in 1969 and 1973, but its worst disaster was on Christmas Eve 1953, when a crater lake lip collapsed. An enormous lahar swept down the mountainside, taking everything in its path, including a railway bridge. Moments later a crowded train plunged into the river, killing 151 people; it was one of NZ's worst tragedies.

Ruapehu hasn't let up, with significant eruptions occurring with suspicious frequency. In 2007 a primary-school teacher had a lucky shave when a rock was propelled through the roof of a trampers' shelter, crushing his leg.

Ongoing rumbles are reminders that these volcanoes in the area are very much in the land of the living. The last major event was in 2012 when Mt Tongariro – the northernmost and lowest peak in the park

(1967m) – gave a couple of good blasts from its northern craters, causing a nine-month partial closure of the famous Alpine Crossing track. (To see video of recent eruptions, visit www.doc.govt.nz/eruption.)

Northeast of Ruapehu is Mt Ngauruhoe, at 2287m, the youngest of the three volcanoes. Its first eruptions are thought to have occurred 2500 years ago. Until 1975 Ngauruhoe had erupted at least every nine years, including a 1954 eruption that lasted 11 months and disgorged 6 million cu metres of lava. In contrast to the others, which have multiple vents, Ngauruhoe is a conical, single-vent volcano with perfectly symmetrical slopes – the reason that it was chosen to star as Mt Doom in Peter Jackson's Lord of the Rings.

Tongariro was NZ's first national park, established in 1887. The previous year, in the aftermath of the New Zealand Wars (Land Wars), the Native Land Court met to determine the ownership of the land around Tongariro. Ngati Tuwharetoa chief Horonuku Te Heuheu Tukino IV pleaded passionately for the area to be left intact, mindful of Pakeha eyeing it up for grazing. 'If our mountains of Tongariro are included in the blocks passed through the court in the ordinary way,' said the chief, 'what will become of them? They will be cut up and sold, a piece going to one Pakeha and a piece to another.'

In 1887 chief Horonuku ensured the land's everlasting preservation when he presented the area to the Crown for the purpose of a national park, the first in NZ and only the fourth in the world. With incredible vision for a man of his time, the chief realised that Tongariro's value lay in its priceless beauty and heritage, not as another sheep paddock.

Development of the national park was slow, and it was only after the main trunk railroad reached the region in 1909 that visitors arrived in significant numbers. Development mushroomed in the 1950s and 1960s as roads were sealed, tracks cut and more huts built.

Today the park is the most popular in NZ, receiving around one million visitors per annum. Many visitors come to ski – Ruapehu's snowfields being the only legitimate ski area north of Wellington – but more people arrive each summer to tramp up, down and around the mountains. The park can get busy, most noticeably on the popular day walks, but most visitors consider this a small price to pay for the chance to experience its magic.

The most popular tramps in the park are the Alpine Crossing and Northern Circuit, but there are plenty more besides. These range from short ambles to excellent day walks such as the Whakapapa Valley and Tama Lakes tracks, both of which begin from the National Park Visitor Centre at Whakapapa. There are also various challenging routes that should only be attempted by the fit, experienced and well equipped. One of these is the Round the Mountain Track, a remote, 71km, four- to six-day tramp circuiting Mt Ruapehu.

🏃 Activities

Tramping

The DOC and i-SITE visitor centres at Whakapapa (p267), Ohakune (p272) and Turangi (p261) have maps and information on walks in the park, as well as current track and weather conditions. Each January, DOC offers an excellent guided-walks program in and around the park; ask at DOC centres for information or book online.

The safest and most popular time to tramp in the national park is December to March, when the tracks are normally clear of snow and the weather is more settled. In winter many of the tracks become full alpine adventures, requiring mountaineering experience, an ice axe and crampons.

Scattered around the park's tramping tracks are 10 huts, most of which are rated Standard ($5). However, as the Tongariro Northern Circuit is a Great Walk, Mangatepopo, Oturere and Waihohonu huts are designated Great Walk huts ($32) during the Great Walk season (mid-October to 30 April). Each hut has gas cookers, heating, cold running water and good old long-drop toilets, along with communal bunk rooms with mattresses. Campsites are located next to the huts; the $15 fee allows campers use of the hut facilities.

Great Walk hut tickets must be obtained in advance, either from the Tongariro National Park Visitor Centre (p267), **Great Walks Bookings** (✆0800 694 732; www.greatwalks.co.nz), or DOC visitor centres nationwide. It will pay to book early during the Great Walk season. In the off-season, the huts become Standard huts ($5), the gas cookers are removed, and fees can be paid with Backcountry Hut Passes and tickets.

Tongariro Northern Circuit   TRAMPING
Circumnavigating Ngauruhoe, this four-day, 50km track is a Great Walk for a number of good reasons. The route can be easily walked in four days from Whakapapa Village, Mangatepopo Rd or Ketetahi Rd, all regularly serviced by shuttle services. Although there is some moderate climbing, the track is well marked and well maintained, putting it within the ability of people of medium fitness and tramping experience.

The Northern Circuit passes plenty of the spectacular and colourful volcanic features that have earned the park its Unesco World Heritage Area status. Highlights include craters, including the South Crater, Central Crater and Red Crater; brilliantly colourful lakes, including the Emerald Lakes, Blue Lake and the Upper and Lower Tama Lakes; the cold Soda Springs; and various other formations, including cones, lava flows and glacial valleys. Optional side trips include the summits of Ngauruhoe and Tongariro, both of which lie along the Tongariro Alpine Crossing, part of which makes up a leg of this circuit.

The traditional place to start and finish the tramp is Whakapapa Village, the site of the park's visitor information centre. However, many trampers begin at Mangatepopo Rd to ensure they have good weather for the tramp's most dramatic day. This reduces it to a three-day tramp, with stays at Oturere and Waihohonu Huts, ending at Whakapapa Village.

ROUTE	ESTIMATED SUMMER WALK TIME (HR)
Whakapapa Village to Mangatepopo Hut	3-5
Mangatepopo Hut to Oturere Hut	5-6
Oturere Hut to Waihohonu Hut	3
Waihohonu Hut to Whakapapa Village	5-6

ℹ️ MOUNTAIN SAFETY

Many visitors to NZ come unstuck in the mountains. The weather can change more quickly than you expect, and rescues (and fatalities) are not uncommon. When heading out on remote tracks, you must be properly equipped and take safety precautions, including leaving your itinerary with a responsible person. Appropriate clothing is paramount. Think wool, and several layers of it, topped with a waterproof jacket. Gloves and a hat are good too, even in summer. And don't even think about wearing anything other than sturdy boots. Take plenty of water and sunscreen, especially on hot days.

Tongariro National Park & Around

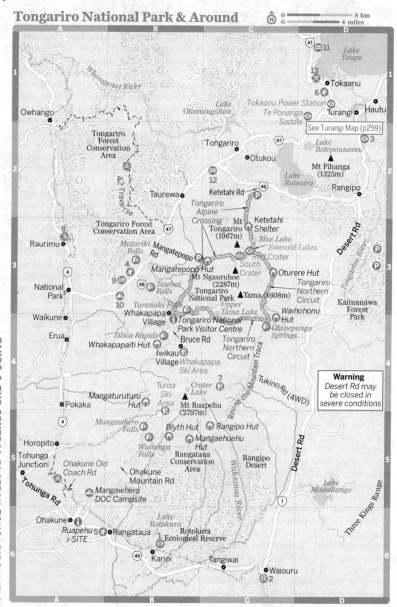

★ **Tongariro Alpine Crossing**   HIKING

This legendary crossing is often lauded as NZ's finest one-day walk. It's certainly the most popular, with 60,000 to 70,000 trampers completing it every year. It's no wonder. Very few day walks offer such thrilling scenery. Among its highlights are steaming vents and springs, crazy rock formations and peculiar moonscape basins, impossible scree slopes and vast views in

Tongariro National Park & Around

◎ Sights
1 Lake Rotokura...B6
2 National Army Museum...........................C6
3 Tongariro National Trout Centre...........D2

◎ Activities, Courses & Tours
4 Mountain Air...B3
5 Ruapehu Homestead A6
6 Tokaanu Thermal Pools...........................D1
7 Tukino Ski Area...C4

8 Wades Landing Outdoors.......................A3

◎ Sleeping
9 Discovery Lodge..B3
10 Mangahuia DOC Campsite.....................B3
11 Oreti Village..D1
12 Tongariro Family Holiday Park..............C2

◎ Eating
13 Lakeland House...D1

---

almost every direction. Along the way it passes diverse vegetation zones from alpine scrub and tussock to higher zones with no plant life at all.

This is a fair-weather tramp. In poor conditions it is little more than an arduous up-and-down, with only orange-tipped poles to mark the passing of the day. Should strong winds be blowing on top, you'll be practically crawling along the ridge of Red Crater, the high point of the trek.

This is an alpine crossing, and it needs to be treated with respect. You need not only a reasonable level of fitness, you should be prepared for all types of weather. Shockingly ill-equipped trampers are legendary on this route – stupid shoes, no rain jackets, blue jeans soaked to the skin – we've seen it all. As well as proper gear, you'll need plenty of water, as there is none available between Mangatepopo and Ketetahi.

The most crowded times on the track are the first nice days after Christmas and Easter, when there can easily be more than 1000 people strung out between the two road ends. The upside of this popularity is excellent shuttle connections, with plenty of operators offering round-trip transport. Be sure to book your ride in advance, and keep an eye on your progress so you don't miss your ride.

The Crossing starts at Mangatepopo Rd car park, off SH47, and finishes at Ketetahi Rd, off SH46. It takes takes seven to eight hours to make the 19.4km journey, although this will vary significantly if you decide to take side-trips up to the summits of Ngauruhoe or Tongariro – both very worthwhile and taking around two and three hours respectively. A word of warning: if you summit Ngauruhoe, keep an eagle-eye out for dislodged boulders careening down the slopes. Injuries do occur.

ROUTE	ESTIMATED SUMMER WALK TIME (HR)
Mangatepopo Rd end to Mangatepopo Hut	¼
Mangatepopo Hut to South Crater	1½-2
South Crater to Mt Ngauruhoe summit (side trip)	2-3 (return)
Red Crater to Tongariro summit (side trip)	1½ (return)
South Crater to Emerald Lakes	1-1½
Emerald Lakes to Ketetahi Shelter	1½
Ketetahi Shelter to road end	1½

Crater Lake HIKING
The unmarked rugged route up to Ruapehu's Crater Lake (seven hours return) is a good one, allowing you to see the acidic lake up close. This moderate-to-difficult walk begins at Iwikau Village at the top of the Bruce Rd. You can cut three hours off it by catching the **chairlift** (adult/child $30/17; ◷9am-3.30pm mid-Dec–April) from Whakapapa Ski Area. **Guided walks** (☏0508 782 734; www.mtruapehu.com; adult/child incl lift pass $145/95) to Crater Lake are hosted by Safety & Mountaineering Guides along with local Ngati Hikairo cultural guides, and run from mid-December to May, weather dependent. Like most of the walks in Tongariro, check conditions before heading out and don't attempt it in winter unless you're a mountaineer.

Other Activities
Whakapapa & Turoa
Ski Areas SKIING, SNOWBOARDING
(☏Turoa 06-385 8456, Whakapapa 07-892 4000; www.mtruapehu.com; day pass adult/child $97/58)

These linked resorts straddle either side of Mt Ruapehu and are NZ's two largest ski areas. Each offers similar skiing at an analogous altitude (around 2300m), with areas to suit each level of experience – from beginners' slopes to black-diamond runs for the pros. The same lift passes cover both ski areas.

The only accommodation at the Whakapapa ski field is in private lodges (mainly owned by ski clubs), so most visitors stay at Whakapaka or National Park Villages. Turoa is only 16km from Ohakune, which has the best après-ski scene.

Tukino Ski Area   SKIING, SNOWBOARDING
(☑ 06-387 6294, 0800 885 466; www.tukino.co.nz; day pass adult/child $50/30) Club-operated Tukino is on Mt Ruapehu's east, 46km from Turangi. It's quite remote, 14km down a gravel road from the sealed Desert Rd (SH1), and you need a 4WD vehicle to get in. It offers uncrowded, backcountry runs, mostly beginner and intermediate.

Mountain Air   SCENIC FLIGHTS
(☑ 0800 922 812; www.mountainair.co.nz; junction SH47 & SH48; 15/25/35min $120/185/225) Offers scenic flights from its base halfway between Whakapapa and National Park Villages. Turangi and Taupo departures also available.

Whakapapa Village

POP 100 (SUMMER), 300 (WINTER)

Located within the bounds of Tongariro National Park on the lower slopes of Mt Ruapehu, Whakapapa Village (pronounced 'fa-ka-pa-pa'; altitude 1140m) is the gateway to the park, home of the park's visitor centre, and the starting point for numerous walking tracks.

🏃 Activities

Whakapapa Nature Walk   WALKING
Suitable for wheelchairs, this 15-minute loop track begins about 250m above the visitor centre and gardens typical of the park's vegetation zones.

Ridge Track   HIKING
A 30-minute return walk from the village that climbs through beech forest to alpine-shrub areas for views of Ruapehu and Ngauruhoe.

Taranaki Falls Track   HIKING
A two-hour, 6km loop track heads from the village to Taranaki Falls, which plunge 20m over an old lava flow into a boulder-ringed pool.

Silica Rapids Track   HIKING
From Whakapapa Village this 2½-hour, 7km loop track leads to the Silica Rapids, named for the silica mineral deposits formed there by rapids on the Waikare Stream.

Tama Lakes Track   HIKING
Part of the Tongariro Northern Circuit, starting at Whakapapa Village, this 17km return track leads to the Tama Lakes, on the Tama Saddle between Ruapehu and Ngauruhoe (five to six hours return). The upper lake affords fine views of Ngauruhoe and Tongariro.

Edge to Edge   EQUIPMENT HIRE
(☑ 0800 800 754; www.edgetoedge.co.nz; Skotel Alpine Resort; 1-day full ski gear $35-65, 1-day snowboard gear $43-71) Stocks an extensive range of skiing, climbing and alpine gear for hire.

🛏 Sleeping & Eating

Whakapapa Village has limited accommodation, and during ski season prices hit their peak. A greater range of options can be found in National Park Village and Ohakune, with the latter offering the most in the way of eating and shopping.

Whakapapa Holiday Park   HOLIDAY PARK $
(☑ 07-892 3897; www.whakapapa.net.nz; campsites from $19, dm $25, units $69-149; 🛜) This popular DOC-associated park beside Whakapapanui Stream has a wide range of accommodation options, including campervan sites perched on the edge of beautiful beech forest, a 32-bed backpackers lodge (linen required), cabins (linen required) and a self-contained unit. The camp store stocks basic groceries.

Mangahuia DOC Campsite   CAMPING GROUND $
(www.doc.govt.nz; sites per adult/child $6/3) 🅿 Situated between National Park Village and the SH48 turn-off heading to Whakapapa, this basic roadside DOC campsite has bushy nooks, cold water and pit toilets for self-contained campers only.

Skotel Alpine Resort   HOSTEL $
(☑ 07-892 3719, 0800 756 835; www.skotel.co.nz; Ngauruhoe Pl; s/tw/tr without bathroom $40/55/75, r with bathroom $110-185, cabins $185; 🛜) If you think of it more as a hostel than a hotel, you'll excuse the odd bit of stained carpet or cheap lino, and enjoy the timber-lined alpine ambience and decidedly non-

hostel-like facilities: free sauna, spa pool and gym, and ski hire, restaurant and bar.

Tongariro Family Holiday Park   HOLIDAY PARK $

(☑ 07-386 8062; www.thp.co.nz; SH47; campsites per person unpowered $18/20, cabins $60-90, units from $130; ☎) Conveniently situated for Alpine Crossing trampers, halfway along the highway between the start and finish points, this wee gem is in the middle of nowhere and everywhere at the same time. It's a welcoming camp – simple, sunny and surrounded by forest, with plenty of grass, trees and a playground. Communal facilities, cabins and self-contained units are unflashy but well tended. It's 24km to both Whakapapa Village and Turangi.

Bayview Chateau Tongariro   HOTEL $$$

(☑ 07-892 3809, 0800 242 832; www.chateau. co.nz; Whakapapa Village; d $155-355; ☎ ▩) With its sublime setting and manor house grandeur, this iconic hotel promises as much as it did when it opened its doors in 1929. Step inside, however, and you will see that its many charms are somewhat faded. But the Chateau remains one of NZ's most romantic hotels, complete with high tea in the library, aperitifs in the elegant foyer bar, and evening dining in the grand **Ruapehu Room** (mains $32-38; ☺ dinner). Other facilities include two cafes, indoor pool, cinema and nine-hole golf course. Choose from rooms in either the historic hotel (with greater charm) or the adjacent modern wing.

Tussock   PUB $

(Whakapapa Village; meals $5-18; ☺ 3pm-late; ☎) An agreeable hybrid of the back-blocks Kiwi pub and ski club rooms, Tussock is a warm and comfortable place to eat a basic meal (bacon and egg muffins, pizza, burgers), play pool, watch the big game, or admire the view from the large windows.

ℹ Information

Further national park information is available from the i-SITEs in Ohakune (p272), Turangi (p261) and Taupo (p258).
Tongariro National Park Visitor Centre
(☑ 07-892 3729; www.doc.govt.nz; Whakapapa Village; ☺ 8am-5pm) Has maps and info on all corners of the park, including walks, huts and current skiing, track and weather conditions. Its exhibits on the geological and human history of the area should keep you busy for a couple of hours on a rainy day. The *Walks in and around Tongariro National Park* brochure

provides a helpful overview of 30 walks and tramps in the park ($3).

ℹ Getting There & Around

BUS

Tongariro National Park is well serviced by shuttle operators, which service Whakapapa Village, National Park Village, Ohakune, Taupo and Turangi, as well as popular trailheads. In summer, tramping trips are their focus, but in winter most offer ski-field shuttles. Book your bus in advance to avoid unexpected strandings.

Many shuttle-bus operators are offshoots or affiliates of accommodation providers so ask about transport when you book your stay. Otherwise, try Taupo-based **Tongariro Expeditions** (☑ 0800 828 763; www.tongariroexpeditions. com), Turangi-based **Turangi Alpine Shuttles** (☑ 0272 322 135, 07-386 8226; www.turangi-rentals.co.nz) and Whakapapa Village-based **Roam** (☑ 021 588 734, 0800 762 612; www. roam.net.nz).

National Park Village

POP 200

This small sprawl of a town lies at the junction of SH4 and SH47 at 825m above sea level, 15km from the hub of Whakapapa Village. In ski season the township is packed, but in summer it's sleepy despite being a handy base for activities in and around the park.

As you'll discover, it's railway country around here. About 20km south on SH4 at **Horopito** is a monument to the Last Spike, the spike that marked the completion of the Main Trunk Railway Line between Auckland and Wellington in 1908 (although Horopito is better known for Smash Palace, NZ's most famous car graveyard). Five kilometres north from National Park, at **Raurimu**, is evidence of the engineering masterpiece that is the 'spiral'. Trainspotters will marvel, while non-trainspotters will probably wonder what the hell they're looking at it (there's not much to see).

🏃 Activities

There's little to do in the village itself, its major enticement being its proximity to national-park tramps, mountain-bike trails (p270), canoe trips on the Whanganui River, and winter skiing. Most accommodation in town offers packages for lift passes and ski hire, sparing you the steeper prices further up the mountain. Ski gear can be hired from **Eivins** (☑ 07-892 2843; www.eivins.co.nz; Carroll

St), **Snow Zone** (☎ 07-892 2757; www.snowzone. co.nz; 25-27 Buddo St) and **Ski Biz** (☎ 07-892 2717; www.skibiz.co.nz; 10 Carroll St).

Daily shuttles leave from here to the Tongariro Alpine Crossing and Whakapapa Village in summer, and the ski area in winter.

Adrift Guided
Outdoor Adventures   CANOEING, HIKING
(☎ 07-892 2751, 0800 462 374; www.adriftnz.co.nz; 3 Waimarino-Tokaanu Road) Runs guided canoe trips on the Whanganui River (one to six days, $245 to $999), as well as freedom canoe hire (three to five days, $185 to $205) and all necessary transfers. It also offers guided tramps in Tongariro National Park (two hours to three days, $95 to $850).

Wades Landing Outdoors   CANOEING, KAYAKING
(☎ 07-895 4854; www.whanganui.co.nz; 11 Kaitieke Rd, Raurimu) Offers freedom kayak and canoe hire for one- to five-day Whanganui River expeditions, including jetboat/road transfers to trailheads ($150 to $190). Also mountain-biking shuttles, Alpine Crossing transport ($35), *Lord of the Rings* tours and a 'prehistoric driftwood sculpture park'.

Kiwi Mountain Bikes   MOUNTAIN BIKING
(☎ 0800 562 4537; www.kiwimountainbikes.co.nz; 54 Carroll St) Affable Rick rents mountain bikes (half/full day from $40/65) and provides bike transport to the 17km (mostly) downhill Fishers Track and 42 Traverse ($35), as well as information and transport for other trails in the area.

Climbing Wall   CLIMBING
(www.npbp.co.nz; 4 Findlay St; adult/child $15/10; ◷ 9am-8pm) For rainy days there's an 8m-high indoor climbing wall at National Park Backpackers. Outdoor climbers with their own gear can find spots near Manataupo Valley and Whakapapa Gorge.

⌁ Sleeping

National Park is a town of budget and midrange accommodation. This makes sense, as you'll probably spend most of your time in the great outdoors.

The following listings give summer prices; be warned that when the ski season is in full swing, accommodation is tight and bookings are essential.

Plateau   LODGE, HOSTEL $
(☎ 07-892 2993; www.plateaulodge.co.nz; 17 Carroll St; dm $30, d $70-110, apt from $160; ☜) Family-friendly Plateau has cosy rooms, some with

en suite and TV, as well as an attractive communal lounge, kitchen and hot tub. The dorms don't get bigger than two sets of bunks and there are two-bedroom apartments sleeping up to six. Local shuttle services available.

National Park Backpackers   HOSTEL $
(☎ 07-892 2870; www.npbp.co.nz; 4 Findlay St; dm $26-29, d $62-86; ☜) This big, old board and batten YHA hostel has a large garden for lounging, a well-equipped kitchen and standard rooms. It's a good one-stop shop for booking activities in the area, and is home to the Climbing Wall for when the weather turns to custard. Small shop on site.

Tongariro Crossing Lodge   LODGE $$
(☎ 07-892 2688; www.tongarirocrossinglodge. com; 27 Carroll St; s $115-125, d $155-165; ☜) As pretty as a picture, this white weatherboard cottage is decorated with a baby-blue trim and rambling blooms in summer. Cosy accommodation ranges from standard doubles to larger self-contained apartments, and is dotted with period furniture. Breakfast is optional ($17 to $26) but wi-fi and use of the barbecue and sunny patio are free.

Adventure Lodge & Motel   LODGE, MOTEL $$
(☎ 07-892 2991; www.adventurenationalpark.co.nz; 21 Carroll St; d/tw $50/70, units from $110; ☜) This place caters particularly to Tongariro Alpine Crossing trampers, offering accommodation and transfers, with all-inclusive packages available (two nights' accommodation, breakfasts, lunch, dinner, T-shirt and transport for $170 to $265). Chill out post-walk in the relaxing lounge, spa pool or barbecue area. The motel units are clean but unspectacular.

Discovery Lodge   LODGE $$
(☎ 07-892 2744; www.discovery.net.nz; SH47; cabins per person $30, units d $145-225) Midway between the village and the Whakapapa turnoff, this complex has a range of rooms from basic cabins and beige motel room, to upmarket chalets sleeping four people. An onsite restaurant has views of Ruapehu, plus there's a large deck, bar and comfy lounge. The zealous owner is keen to help you discover his world; shuttles available.

✖ Eating & Drinking

★ Station   CAFE $$
(☎ 07-892 2881; www.stationcafe.co.nz; cnr Findlay St & Station Rd; lunch $9-18, dinner $29-38; ◷ 9am-

late Wed-Mon, to 3pm Tue) Count your blessings ye who find this little railway station along the line, a lovely old dear, restored with care and now serving eggy brunches, sandwiches, coffee and yummy cakes, plus an impressive à la carte evening menu. Sunday roasts ($35) and Curry Thursdays ($16) are dinnertime highlights.

Four Square Supermarket   SELF-CATERING $
(cnr SH4 & Waimarino-Takaanu Rd; ⊙7am-7pm) This shop-cum-service-station stocks groceries, tramping food and a cornucopia of other useful wares.

Schnapps   PUB
(www.schnappsbarruapehu.com; Findlay St; meals $14-28; ⊙noon-late) This popular pub has a meat-fest menu, open fire, big screen, pool table and a handy ATM. Things crank up on wintry weekends.

ℹ Information

There's no i-SITE in the village, so visit www.nationalpark.co.nz and www.visitruapehu.com for info.

ℹ Getting There & Away

Passing through are buses run by **InterCity** (☑06-835 4326; www.intercity.co.nz) and **Naked Bus** (www.nakedbus.com), as well as *The Northerner* train run by KiwiRail Scenic (p248).

Ohakune

POP 1000
Expect to see carrots crop up all over Ohakune, for this is indisputably the country's carrot capital. Carrots were first grown in the area during the 1920s by Chinese settlers, who cleared the land by hand and explosives. Today, the venerable vegetable is celebrated during the annual **Carrot Carnival** (www.carrotcarnival.org.nz), and immortalised in a roadside tribute – the impossible-to-miss **Big Carrot** (Rangataua Rd), erected in 1984.

But locals needn't mention liver cleansing and eyesight improvement to win us over to the charms of this little town. A pretty retreat in the summer offering outdoor adventure galore, Ohakune springs to life in winter when the snow drifts down on Turoa Ski Area and the snow bunnies invade.

There are two distinct parts to the town: the commercial hub is strung along the highway, but in winter the northern end around the train station, known as the Junc-

tion, is the epicentre of the action. The two are linked by the **Mangawhero River Walkway**, a leafy amble taking around 25 minutes on foot.

☂ Activities

There are several scenic walks near the town, many starting from the Ohakune Mountain Rd, which stretches 17km from Ohakune to the Turoa Ski Area (p265) on Mt Ruapehu. The handy DOC brochure *Walks in and Around Tongariro National Park* ($3), available from the i-SITE, is a good starting point.

The Tongariro Alpine Crossing is readily accessible via regular shuttle services from Ohakune, while the **Round the Mountain** (www.doc.govt.nz) track can be accessed by continuing on the Waitonga Falls track.

Mangawhero Forest Walk   WALKING
An easy stroll starting near the beginning of Ohakune Mountain Rd (one-hour loop, 3km), taking in native forest and the Mangawhero River. It is well graded and suitable for wheelchairs and pushchairs.

Waitonga Falls &
Lake Surprise Tracks   HIKING
The path to Waitonga Falls (1½ hours return, 4km), Tongariro's highest waterfall (39m), offers magnificent views of Mt Ruapehu. A more challenging walk climbs to shallow Lake Surprise (five hours return, 9km). Both tracks start from Ohakune Mountain Rd.

Mountain Bike Station   MOUNTAIN BIKING
(☑06-385 8797; www.mountainbikestation.co.nz; 60 Thames St) Rents mountain bikes (half/full day from $35/50) and provides transfers to local mountain-biking routes, including the Ohakune Old Coach Road (p270) for $20; bike and transport packages are available. Its subsidiary, Ski & Board Station, rents ski and snowboard gear (from $25).

TCB   EQUIPMENT HIRE
(☑06-385 8433; www.tcbskiandboard.co.nz; 29 Ayr St) A good source of information about local mountain-biking routes, TCB publishes a free bike trail map and rents mountain bikes (half/full day $35/50) and skiing/boading gear (from $35/40).

Ski Shed   EQUIPMENT HIRE
(☑06-385 9173; www.skished.com; 71 Clyde St) Hires skiing/boarding gear (from $35/43), and snow-appropriate clothing.

MOUNTAIN BIKING THE OLD COACH ROAD

The **Ohakune Old Coach Road** (www.ohakunecoachroad.co.nz) is a fantastic adventure for moderately fit cyclists, with local operators offering all the gear and transport to make things easy.

An excellent example of restoration for recreation, the dual-use (walking and cycling) track follows the original 15km coach track from Ohakune to Horopito. Dating from 1886, it was built largely by hand by workers who lived in canvas tents and endured harsh winter conditions. The track was gradually upgraded to carry passengers and goods, and used until 1909 when SH49 opened. Largely forgotten and overgrown, the Old Coach Road was resurrected by the locals and restored to glory.

And glorious it is. One of the most enjoyable half-day (three to four hours) cycle rides in NZ, the gently graded route passes a number of unique engineering features, including the historic Hapuawhenua and Toanui viaducts – the only two remaining curved viaducts in the southern hemisphere. It also passes through ancient forest of giant rimu and totara that survived the Taupo blast of AD 180, being in the lea of Ruapehu. Views extend over the odd-shaped hillocks and mesa around the foot of the volcano.

Cyclists are best to start at Horopito (where you can check out the car graveyard known as 'Smash Palace'), as this gives you more downhill, overall. The odd push uphill may well be required, but you'll get sufficient in-the-saddle time to justify the effort – especially on some of the sweeping downhills underlaid with historic cobblestones. This is wobbly, freewheeling fun for the whole family.

And this is just the tip of the Central Plateau's mountain-biking iceberg. The Old Coach Road is the start of the **Mountains to Sea Trail** (Nga Ara Tuhono; www.mountains-tosea.co.nz), a 317km route from Mt Ruapehu to Whanganui. This epic also encompasses the improving Mangapurua and Kaiwhakauka Tracks, easily accessible from Ohakune and National Park and set to challenge the long-established **42 Traverse** and **Fishers Track** as the must-do day-rides in the area.

For bike hire and shuttles, visit TCB (p269) and Mountain Bike Station (p269) in Ohakune, and Kiwi Mountain Bikes (p268) in National Park.

SLR   EQUIPMENT HIRE, CLIMBING
(☑ 06-385 9018; www.slr.co.nz; Goldfinch St) As well as ski/board hire (from $25), SLR runs **Vertigo Climbing Centre** (www.vertigoclimbing.co.nz), a climbing wall behind the shop ($15).

Powderhorn Snow Centre   EQUIPMENT HIRE
(☑ 06-385 9100; www.snowcentre.co.nz; 194 Mangawhero Tce) Sells and hires snow gear and mountain bikes (half/full day $35/55).

Ruapehu Homestead   HORSE RIDING
(☑ 027-267 7057; www.ruapehuhomestead.co.nz; cnr Piwara St & SH49, Rangataua; 30min-3hr adult $30-120, child $15-90) Located 4km east of Ohakune (near Rangataua), Ruapehu Homestead offers guided treks around its paddocks, as well as longer rides along the river and on backcountry trails with views of the mountain.

Canoe Safaris   CANOEING, RAFTING
(☑ 06-385 9237, 0800 272 3353; www.canoesafaris.co.nz; 6 Tay St) Offers guided canoeing trips on the Whanganui River (one to five days, $175 to $995) and Rangitikei River (one to four days, $175 to $875), plus guided rafting trips on the Mohaka River (two to four days, $425 to $950). Canoe and kayak hire (two to five days $170 to $205).

Yeti Tours   CANOEING, KAYAKING
(☑ 06-385 8197, 0800 322 388; www.yetitours.co.nz; 61 Clyde St; guided tours 2-6 days $365-895, 2-6 day hire $175-210) Leads guided canoeing safaris on the Whanganui and Mokau Rivers, and hires canoes and kayaks.

Heliview   HELICOPTER
(☑ 0800 435 426; www.heliview.co.nz; Ohakune Airfield, SH49; flights 35/45mins $329/439) Offers scenic helicopter flights including the 35-minute 'Carrot to Crater' flight over the summit of Ruapehu, or the 45-minute 'Three Peaks' over the park's mountain trio.

🛏 Sleeping

The prices listed are for summer; expect to pay up to twice as much in winter and book ahead. Savings can be made on winter rates by booking midweek.

★ Station Lodge
HOSTEL $

(☑06-385 8797; www.stationlodge.co.nz; 60 Thames St; dm $27, r $54, unit $100-200; ☏) ⌘ Housed in a lovely old villa with wooden floors and high ceilings, this excellent YHA hostel has a well-equipped kitchen, comfortable lounge, spa pool, and tidy garden with a pizza oven. If you're after privacy, separate chalets and apartments are available. The clued-up owners also run Mountain Bike Station and Ski & Board Station.

Ohakune Top 10
HOLIDAY PARK $

(☑06-385 8561, 0800 825 825; www.ohakune.net. nz; 5 Moore St; campsites $42, units $68-135; ☏) ⌘ A bubbling stream borders this holiday park, which has a wide range of accommodation including tidy motel units. Extras include a playground, barbecue area and private spa bath.

Mountain View
MOTEL $

(☑06-385 8675; www.mountain-viewmotel.co.nz; 2 Moore St; units $75-100; ☏) In this old, vaguely Tudor-styled motel, rooms are basic but clean, quiet and good value. Most have kitchen facilities and there's also a spa pool.

Snowhaven
APARTMENTS, B&B $$

(☑06-385 9498; www.snowhaven.co.nz; 92 Clyde St; apt $95-125, r $195, townhouse from $195; ☏) A tasty trio is on offer here: modern studio apartments in a slate-fronted block on the main drag; three self-contained, three-bedroom townhouses by the Junction; or luxury B&B rooms somewhere between the other two. All are top, well-priced options.

Peaks Motor Inn
MOTEL $$

(☑06-385 9144, 0508 843 732; www.thepeaks. co.nz; cnr Mangawhero Tce & Shannon St; units $99-124; ☏) This well-kept motel offers spacious rooms with good bathrooms and full kitchens. Communal facilities include grassy lawns, a basic gym, large outdoor spa, and sauna.

★ Powderhorn Chateau
HOTEL $$$

(☑06-385 8888; www.powderhorn.co.nz; cnr Thames St & Mangawhero Tce; r from $215; ☏⛉) Enjoying a long-standing reputation as the hub of activity during the ski season, the Powderhorn has a Swiss-chalet feel with woody interiors, slate floors and exposed rafters. The spa-temperature indoor pool is a relaxing way to recover from the slopes before enjoying revelry in the popular in-house establishments.

✖ Eating & Drinking

The Junction is the après-ski place to be, but in summer most of the action drifts to the other end of town. Many hotels sprout restaurants during the ski season.

New World
SUPERMARKET $

(12 Goldfinch St; ⊙7am-7pm) Self-caterers should head for New World, your best bet for stocking up before heading to National Park or Whakapapa.

★ Bearing Point
INTERNATIONAL $$

(☑06-385 9006; www.thebearingpointrestaurant. co.nz; Clyde St; mains $26-36; ⊙6pm-late Tue-Sat) Hearty, accomplished fare is offered at this surprisingly chic establishment. Warm your cockles with a venison hot pot, maple-glazed salmon, aged steaks or spicy Thai curry.

OCR
CAFE $$

(☑06-385 8322; www.ocrcafe.co.nz; 2 Tyne St; mains $10-29; ⊙9am-late Fri & Sat, 9am-3pm Sun) Housed in a spacious old bungalow, this groovy cafe has limited opening hours but remains a favourite among locals and visitors alike. Burgers, sandwiches, salads and hearty breakfasts are made with care as are the home-baked cakes and slices. A rootsy soundtrack and wood burner lend a rustic vibe.

Powderkeg & Matterhorn
BAR, RESTAURANT $$

(☑06-385 8888; www.powderhorn.co.nz; cnr Thames St & Mangawhero Tce; bar menu $11-22, à la carte menu $22-36; ⊙4pm-late) The Powderkeg is the party bar of the Powderhorn Chateau, with DJs in winter, regular dancing on the tables and a notable craft beer selection. Upstairs is the swankier Matterhorn,

---

> **WORTH A TRIP**
>
> ## LAKE ROTOKURA
>
> **Rotokura Ecological Reserve** (www.doc.govt.nz) is 14km southeast of Ohakune, at Karioi, just off SH49 (*karioi* means 'places to linger'). There are two lakes here: the first is Dry Lake, actually quite wet and perfect for picnicking; the furthest is Rotokura, *tapu* (sacred) to Maori, so eating, fishing and swimming are prohibited. The round-trip walk will take you 45 minutes; longer if you linger to admire the ancient beech trees and waterfowl such as dabchicks and paradise ducks.

serving cocktails and an à la carte menu of meaty mains and decadent desserts. In summer the Matterhorn closes and its menu descends to the Powderkeg.

Cyprus Tree
ITALIAN $$

(19a Goldfinch St; mains $23-32; ⊙9am-late) Open all year round, this restaurant and bar serves up a tasty mix of Italian and Kiwi-influenced dishes: think pasta, risotto and sumac lamb. The high-season chaos is tempered by a friendly team, cocktails, and quality wines and beer.

Mountain Rocks
BAR, CAFE

(www.themountainrocks.co.nz; cnr Clyde & Goldfinch Sts; mains $14-33; ⊙8am-late) A log-cabin-like space with a nod to the all-American diner. Join the locals for cheap beers and a no-surprises selection of big-portion burgers, lamb shanks, steaks, and fish and chips. Buzzy garden bar with a big screen for the big games.

ⓘ Information

Ohakune Public Library (☑06 385 8364, 37 Ayr St; ⊙8am-5pm Mon-Fri; 🖱) Offers free internet access.

Ruapehu i-SITE (☑06-385 8427; www.visitruapehu.com; 54 Clyde St; ⊙9am-5pm) Can make bookings for activities, transport and accommodation; DOC officers are usually on hand from 10am to 4.30pm most days.

Visit Ohakune (www.visitohakune.co.nz) Useful website for 'The Mountain Town' and around.

ⓘ Getting There & Around

Passing through are buses run by **InterCity** (www.intercity.co.nz) and **Naked Bus** (www.nakedbus.com), as well as *The Northerner* train run by KiwiRail Scenic (p248).

Matai Shuttles (☑06-385 8724; www.mataishuttles.co.nz) is based in Ohakune, offering services around the Central Plateau.

Waiouru

POP 740

At the junction of SH1 and SH49, 27km east of Ohakune, Waiouru (altitude 792m) is primarily an army base and a refuelling stop for the 56km-long Desert Rd leading to Turangi. A barren landscape of reddish sand with small clumps of tussock, **Rangipo Desert** isn't actually a desert. This unique landscape is in fact the result of two million years of volcanic eruptions – especially the Taupo eruption about 2000 years ago which coated the land with thick deposits of pumice and destroyed all vegetation. In winter, the road occasionally closes due to snow.

Housed in a large, concrete bunker at the south end of the township, the **National Army Museum** (www.armymuseum.co.nz; adult/child $15/5; ⊙9am-4.30pm) 🖉 preserves the history of the NZ army and its various campaigns, from colonial times to the present. Moving stories are told through displays of arms, uniforms, medals and memorabilia.

Taihape & Around

POP 1500

Taihape, 20km south of Waiouru, enjoys the dubious distinction of being the Gumboot Capital of the World, celebrated with – you guessed it a giant corrugated gumboot on the main road. It is also the access point for **Mokai Gravity Canyon** (☑06-388 9109, 0800 802 864; www.gravitycanyon.co.nz; 332 Mokai Rd; ⊙9am-5pm), 20km southeast, where adrenaline-junkies can take a 1km, 170m-high flying-fox ride at speeds of up to 160km/h ($155); dive from the North Island's highest bridge bungy (80m, $179); or freefall for 50m on a tandem swing ($159). Multi-thrill packages are available.

Taihape is also the nearest town to **River Valley** (☑06-388 1444; www.rivervalley.co.nz), an adventure centre and lodge 32km to the northeast (follow the signs from Taihape's Gretna Hotel). Their popular half-day white-water rafting trip takes in the thrilling Grade V rapids of the Rangitikei River ($175). Free-style horse treks are also offered, which take in views of Mt Ruapehu, the Ruahine Range and the Rangitikei River (two hours $109, half-day $175). Lodge accommodation (from $31) is also offered, as are meals in the on-site restaurant, featuring fresh ingredients from the lodge's gardens.

For more information, visit www.taihape.co.nz.

Rotorua & the Bay of Plenty

Includes ➡

Rotorua...................... 275

Tauranga................... 292

Mt Maunganui 298

Katikati 303

Te Puke 304

Whakatane 305

Whakaari
(White Island)............309

Ohope 310

Opotiki 311

Best Outdoors

➡ Rotorua Canopy Tours (p278)

➡ Surfing at Mt Maunganui (p298)

➡ Redwoods Whakarewarewa Forest (p289)

➡ Waikite Valley Thermal Pools (p292)

Best Places to Stay

➡ Regent of Rotorua (p285)

➡ Warm Earth Cottage (p304)

➡ Captain's Cabin (p308)

➡ Opotiki Beach House (p312)

Why Go?

Captain Cook christened the Bay of Plenty when he cruised past in 1769, and plentiful it remains. Blessed with sunshine and sand, the bay stretches from Waihi Beach in the west to Opotiki in the east, with the holiday hubs of Tauranga, Mt Maunganui and Whakatane in between.

Offshore from Whakatane is New Zealand's most active volcano, Whakaari (White Island). Volcanic activity defines this region, and nowhere is this subterranean sexiness more obvious than in Rotorua. Here the daily business of life goes on among steaming hot springs, explosive geysers, bubbling mud pools and the billows of sulphurous gas responsible for the town's 'unique' eggy smell.

Rotorua and the Bay of Plenty are also strongholds of Maori tradition, presenting many opportunities to engage with NZ's rich indigenous culture: check out a power-packed concert performance, chow down at a *hangi* (Maori feast) or skill-up with some Maori arts-and-crafts techniques.

When to Go

➡ The Bay of Plenty is one of NZ's sunniest regions: Whakatane records a brilliant 2350 average hours of sunshine per year! In summer (December to February) maximums hover between 20°C and 27°C. Everyone else is here too, but the holiday vibe is heady.

➡ Visit Rotorua any time: the geothermal activity never sleeps, and there are enough beds in any season.

➡ The mercury can slide below 5°C overnight here in winter, although it's usually warmer on the coast (and you'll have the beach all to yourself).

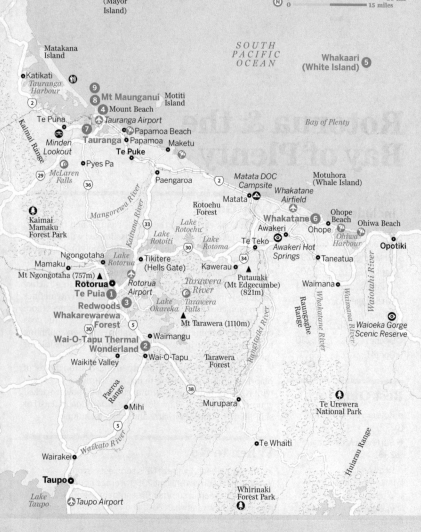

Rotorua & the Bay of Plenty Highlights

① Watching Rotorua's geysers blow their tops at **Te Puia** (p275) or **Whakarewarewa Thermal Village** (p276).

② Ogling kaleidoscopic colours and bubbling mud pools at **Wai-O-Tapu Thermal Wonderland** (p292).

③ Mountain biking in the **Redwoods Whakarewarewa Forest** (p289).

④ Carving up the surf over NZ's first artificial reef at **Mt Maunganui** (p298)

⑤ Flying or boating out to NZ's only active marine volcano, **Whakaari** (p309)

⑥ Kicking back for a few days in **Whakatane** (p305) – NZ's most underrated seaside town?

⑦ Swimming with dolphins at **Tauranga** (p292)

⑧ Drinking in **Mt Maunganui** (p302) after a beach afternoon

⑨ Climbing the pohutukawa-studded flanks of **Mauao** (Mt Maunganui; p300)

ℹ️ Getting There & Around

Air New Zealand (www.airnewzealand.co.nz) has direct flights from Tauranga and Rotorua to Auckland, Wellington and Christchurch, plus Rotorua to Sydney (every Tuesday and Saturday) and Whakatane to Auckland.

InterCity (www.intercity.co.nz) and **Naked Bus** (www.nakedbus.com) services connect Tauranga, Rotorua and Whakatane with most other main cities in NZ. **Bay Hopper** (☑ 0800 422 928; www.baybus.co.nz) bus services run between Tauranga, Whakatane and Opotiki. **Twin City Express** (☑ 0800 422 928; www.baybus.co.nz) buses link Tauranga and Rotorua.

ROTORUA

POP 65,280

Catch a whiff of Rotorua's sulphur-rich, asthmatic airs and you've already got a taste of NZ's most dynamic thermal area, home to spurting geysers, steaming hot springs and exploding mud pools. The Maori revered this place, naming one of the most spectacular springs Wai-O-Tapu (Sacred Waters). Today 35% of the population is Maori, with their cultural performances and traditional *hangi* as big an attraction as the landscape itself.

Despite the pervasive eggy odour, 'Sulphur City' is one of the most touristed spots on the North Island, with nearly three million visitors annually. Some locals say this steady trade has seduced the town into resting on its laurels, and that socially Rotorua lags behind more progressive towns such as Tauranga and Taupo. And with more motels than nights in November, the urban fabric of 'RotoVegas' isn't particularly appealing... but still, where else can you see a 30m geothermal geyser!

History

The Rotorua area was first settled in the 14th century when the canoe *Te Arawa,* captained by Tamatekapua, arrived from Hawaiki at Maketu in the central Bay of Plenty. Settlers took the tribal name Te Arawa to commemorate the vessel that had brought them here.

In the next few hundred years, subtribes spread and divided through the area, with conflicts breaking out over limited territory. A flashpoint occurred in 1823 when the Arawa lands were invaded by tribes from the Northland in the so-called Musket Wars. After heavy losses on both sides, the Northlanders eventually withdrew.

During the Waikato Land War (1863–64) Te Arawa threw in its lot with the government against its traditional Waikato enemies, gaining troop support and preventing East Coast reinforcements getting through to support the Kingitanga movement.

With peace in the early 1870s, word spread of scenic wonders, miraculous landscapes and watery cures for all manner of diseases. Rotorua boomed. Its main attraction was the fabulous Pink and White Terraces, formed by volcanic silica deposits. Touted at the time as the eighth natural wonder of the world, they were destroyed in the 1886 Mt Tarawera eruption.

⦿ Sights

Te Puia GEYSER, CULTURAL TOUR
(Map p290; ☑ 07-348 9047, 0800 837 842; www.tepuia.com; Hemo Rd; tours adult/child $48.50/24.50, daytime tour & performance combo $60.50/30.50, evening tour, performance & hangi combo $150/75; ⊙ 8am-6pm Nov-Apr, to 5pm May-Oct) Rotorua's main drawcard is Te Whakarewarewa (pronounced 'fa-ka-re-wa-re-wa'), a thermal reserve 3km south of the city centre. There are more than 500 springs here, the most famous of which is **Pohutu** ('Big Splash' or 'Explosion'), a geyser which erupts up to 20 times a day, spurting hot water up to 30m skyward. You'll

ROTORUA & THE BAY OF PLENTY ROTORUA

ESSENTIAL ROTORUA & THE BAY OF PLENTY

Eat A buttery corn cob in Rotorua, cooked in a thermal *hangi* at Whakarewarewa Thermal Village (p276)

Drink Croucher Brewing Co's pale ale, brewed in Rotorua

Read *How to Watch a Bird,* an exposition on the joys of avian observation, written by Mt Maunganui schoolboy Steve Braunias

Listen to *Kora,* the eponymous rootsy album from Whakatane's soulful sons

Watch Maori TV and Te Reo, NZ's two Maori TV stations

Go green See www.sustainablenz.com for tips on how to make your Rotorua visit more ecofriendly

Online www.rotoruanz.com; www.bayofplenty.co.nz

Area code ☑ 07

Rotorua

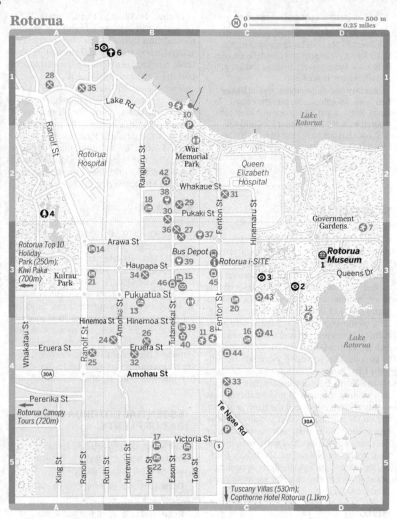

N 0 — 500 m
0.25 miles

know when it's about to blow because the adjacent **Prince of Wales' Feathers** geyser will start up shortly before. Both these geysers form part of Te Puia, the most polished of NZ's Maori cultural attractions. Also here is the National Carving School and the National Weaving School, where you can discover the work and methods of traditional Maori woodcarvers and weavers, plus a carved meeting house, a cafe, galleries, a kiwi reserve and a gift shop.

Tours take 1½ hours and depart hourly from 9am (the last tour an hour before closing). Daytime 45-minute cultural performances start at 10.15am, 12.15pm and 3.15pm; nightly three-hour Te Po indigenous concerts and *hangi* feasts start at 6pm (following on from a 4.30pm tour in a combo package).

Whakarewarewa

Thermal Village   THERMAL RESERVE, CULTURAL TOUR
(Map p290; ☑ 07-349 3463; www.whakarewarewa.com; 17 Tryon St; tour & cultural performance adult/child $35/15; ⏰ 8.30am-5pm) Whakarewarewa Thermal Village is a living village where *tangata whenua* (the locals) still reside, as they have for centuries. The villagers show

Rotorua

◉ **Top Sights**
1 Rotorua Museum D3

◉ **Sights**
2 Blue Baths D3
3 Government Gardens C3
4 Kuirau Park A2
5 Ohinemutu A1
6 St Faith's Anglican Church B1

◉ **Activities, Courses & Tours**
7 Ballbusters D3
8 Bike Barn C4
9 Kawarau Jet B1
   Lakeland Queen .... (see 10)
10 Mana Adventures B1
   Mokoia Island Wai Ora
   Experiences .... (see 9)
11 O'Keefe's Fishing Specialists C4
12 Polynesian Spa D3
   The Wall .... (see 19)
   Volcanic Air Safaris .... (see 10)

◉ **Sleeping**
13 Astray B3
14 Base Rotorua A3
15 Blarney's Rock B3
16 Crash Palace C4
17 Funky Green Voyager B5
   Millennium Hotel .... (see 41)
18 Regent of Rotorua B2
19 Rock Solid Backpackers B4
20 Rotorua Central
   Backpackers C3

21 Rotorua YHA A3
22 Six on Union B5
23 Victoria Lodge B5

◉ **Eating**
24 Abracadabra Cafe Bar B4
25 Bistro 1284 .... A4
26 Capers Epicurean B4
27 Fat Dog Cafe & Bar B3
28 Fish & Chip Shop A1
29 Indian Star B2
30 Leonardo's B2
31 Lime Caffeteria C2
32 Mistress of Cakes B4
33 Pak 'n Save C4
34 Sabroso B3
35 Third Place Cafe A1
36 Weilin's Noodle House B3

◉ **Drinking & Nightlife**
37 Belgian Bar C3
38 Brew B2
39 Pig & Whistle B3

◉ **Entertainment**
40 Basement Cinema B4
41 Millennium Hotel Rotorua C4
42 Novotel Rotorua B2
43 Tamaki Maori Village C3

◉ **Shopping**
44 Mountain Jade C4
45 Out of New Zealand C3
46 Rotorua Night Market B3

ROTORUA & THE BAY OF PLENTY ROTORUA

you around and tell you the stories of their way of life and the significance of the steamy bubbling pools, the silica terraces and the geysers that, although inaccessible from the village, are easily viewed from vantage points (the view of Pohutu is just as good from here as it is from Te Puia, and considerably cheaper).

The village shops sell authentic arts and crafts, and you can learn more about Maori traditions such as flax weaving, carving, and *ta moko* (tattooing). Nearby you can eat tasty, buttery sweetcorn ($2) pulled straight out of the hot mineral pool – the only genuine geothermal *hangi* in town. There are cultural performances at 11.15am and 2pm, and guided tours at 9am, 10am, 11am, noon, 1pm, 3pm and 4pm.

★ **Rotorua Museum**   MUSEUM, GALLERY
(Map p276; ☏ 07-351 8055; www.rotoruamuseum. co.nz; Queens Dr, Government Gardens; adult/child $20/8; ☺ 9am-5pm, to 6pm Dec-Feb, tours hourly 10am-4pm plus 5pm Dec-Feb) This outstanding museum occupies a grand Tudor-style edifice. It was originally an elegant spa retreat called the Bath House (1908): displays in the former shower rooms give a fascinating insight into some of the eccentric therapies once administered here, including 'electric baths' and the Bergonie Chair.

A gripping 20-minute film on the history of Rotorua, including the Tarawera eruption, runs every 20 minutes from 9am (not for small kids – the eruption noises are authentic!). The fabulous **Don Stafford Wing** houses eight object-rich galleries dedicated to Rotorua's Te Arawa people, featuring woodcarving, flax weaving, jade, interactive audiovisual displays and the stories of the revered WWII 28 Maori Battalion. Also here are two **art galleries** (with air swabbed clean of hydrogen sulphide) and a cool cafe with garden views (although the best view in town can be had from the **viewing platform** on the roof).

MAORI NZ: ROTORUA & THE BAY OF PLENTY

The Bay of Plenty's traditional name, Te Rohe o Mataatua, recalls the ancestral *Mataatua* canoe, which arrived here from Hawaiki to make an eventful landfall at Whakatane. The region's history stretches back further than that, though, with the Polynesian settler Toi setting up what's claimed to be Aotearoa's first settlement in about AD 800.

Major tribal groups in the region are the **Ngati Awa** (www.ngatiawa.iwi.nz) of the Whakatane area, **Whakatohea** (www.whakatohea.co.nz) of Opotiki, **Ngai Te Rangi** (www.ngaiterangi.org.nz) of Tauranga, and **Te Arawa** (www.tearawa.iwi.nz) of Rotorua. Tribes in this region were involved on both sides of the Land Wars of the late 19th century, with those fighting against the government suffering considerable land confiscations that have caused legal problems right up to the present day.

There's a significant Maori population around the region, and many ways for travellers to engage with Maori culture. Opotiki has Hiona St Stephen's Church (p311) – the death here of government spy Reverend Carl Volkner in 1865 inspired the charming eyeball-eating scene in *Utu*. Whakatane has a visitor-friendly main-street *marae* (p305) (meeting house complex) and Toi's Pa, perhaps NZ's oldest *pa* (fortified village) site. Rotorua has traditional Maori villages, *hangi* and cultural performances aplenty.

Lake Rotorua
LAKE

FREE Lake Rotorua is the largest of the district's 16 lakes and is – underneath all that water – a spent volcano. Sitting in the lake is Mokoia Island, which has for centuries been occupied by various subtribes of the area. The lake can be explored by boat, with several operators situated at the lakefront.

Kuirau Park
PARK

(Map p276; cnr Ranolf & Pukuatua Sts) **FREE** Want some affordable geothermal thrills? Just west of central Rotorua is Kuirau Park, a volcanic area you can explore for free. In 2003 an eruption covered much of the park (including the trees) in mud, drawing crowds of spectators. It has a crater lake, pools of boiling mud and plenty of huffing steam. Take care – the pools here are boiling, and accidents have happened.

Government Gardens
GARDENS

(Map p276; Hinemaru St) **FREE** The manicured English-style Government Gardens surrounding the Rotorua Museum are pretty as a picture, with roses aplenty, steaming thermal pools dotted about and civilised amenities such as croquet lawns and bowling greens. Also here is the upmarket Polynesian Spa and Ballbusters golf.

Blue Baths
BATHHOUSE

(Map p276; ☎07-350 2119; www.bluebaths.co.nz; Government Gardens; adult/child/family $11/6/30; ☾noon-6pm Apr-Oct, 10am-6pm Nov-Mar) The gorgeous Spanish Mission–style Blue Baths opened in 1933 (and, amazingly, were closed from 1982 to 1999). If you feel like taking a

dip, the **heated pool** awaits. Ask about occasional **dinner-and-cabaret shows** (from $80 per person).

Ohinemutu
MAORI VILLAGE

(Map p276) **FREE** Ohinemutu is a ramshackle lakeside Maori village (access via Kiharoa, Haukotuku or Korokai Sts off Lake St, north of Rotorua Hospital) that traces the fusing of European and Maori cultures. Highlights include the sacred 1905 **Tama-te-kapua Meeting House** (not open to visitors), plenty of steaming volcanic vents, and the historic timber **St Faith's Anglican Church** (Map p276; ☎07-348 2393; cnr Mataiawhea & Korokai Sts; admission by donation; ☾8am-6pm, services 9am Sun & 10am Wed), which features intricate Maori carvings, *tukutuku* (woven panels) and a stained-glass window of Christ wearing a Maori cloak as he walks on the waters of Lake Rotorua.

Be respectful if you're visiting the village: this is private land, and locals don't appreciate loud, nosy tourists wandering around taking photos.

🏃 Activities

Extreme Sports

Rotorua Canopy Tours   EXTREME SPORTS

(Map p290; ☎07-343 1001, 0800 226 679; www.canopytours.co.nz; 173 Old Taupo Rd; 3hr tours per adult/child/family $129/85/399; ☾8am-8pm Oct-Apr, 8am-6pm May-Sep) Explore a 1.2km web of bridges, flying foxes, ziplines and platforms, 22m high in a lush native forest canopy 10 minutes out of town (...they say that rimu tree is 1000 years old!). Plenty of native birds to keep you company. Free pick-ups available.

Agroventures
EXTREME SPORTS

(Map p290; ☏ 07-357 4747, 0800 949 888; www.agroventures.co.nz; Western Rd, off Paradise Valley Rd, Ngongotaha; 1/2/4/8 rides $49/75/99/179; ⊗9am-5pm) Agroventures is a hive of action, 9km north of Rotorua on SH5 (shuttles available). Start off with the 43m bungy and the Swoop, a 130km/h swing that can be enjoyed alone or with friends. If that's not enough, try Freefall Xtreme, which simulates skydiving by blasting you 3m into the air on a column of wind. Also here is the Shweeb, a monorail velodrome from which you hang in a clear capsule and pedal yourself along recumbently at speeds of up to 60km/h. Alongside is the Agrojet, allegedly NZ's fastest jetboat, splashing around a 1km course.

Zorb
EXTREME SPORTS

(Map p290; ☏ 07-357 5100, 0800 227 474; www.zorb.com; cnr Western Rd & SH5, Ngongotaha; 1/2/3 rides $45/70/90; ⊗9am-5pm, to 7pm Dec-Mar) The Zorb is 9km north of Rotorua on SH5 – look for the grassy hillside with large, clear, people-filled spheres rolling down it. Your eyes do not deceive you! There are three courses: 150m straight, 180m zigzag or 250m 'Drop'. Do your zorb strapped in and dry, or freestyle with water thrown in.

Ogo
EXTREME SPORTS

(Map p290; ☏ 07-343 7676, 0800 646 768; www.ogo.co.nz; 525 Ngongotaha Rd; rides from $45; ⊗9am-5pm, to 6.30pm Dec-Feb) Similar to the Zorb, the Ogo (about 5km north of town) involves careening down a grassy hillside in a big bubble, with water or without. Silly? Fun? Terrifying? All of the above...

The Wall
ROCK CLIMBING

(Map p276; ☏ 07-350 1400; www.thewall.co.nz; 1140 Hinemoa St; adult/child incl harness $16/12, shoe hire $5; ⊗noon-10pm Mon-Fri, 10am-10pm Sat & Sun) Get limbered up at the Wall, a three-storey indoor climbing wall with overhangs aplenty.

Skyline Rotorua
EXTREME SPORTS

(Map p290; ☏ 07-347 0027; www.skyline.co.nz; Fairy Springs Rd; adult/child gondola $25/12.50, luge 3 rides $42/32, sky swing $63/53; ⊗9am-11pm) This gondola cruises up Mt Ngongotaha, about 3km northwest of town, from where you can take in panoramic lake views or ride a speedy luge back down on three different tracks. For even speedier antics, try the Sky Swing, a screaming swoosh through the air at speeds of up to 160km/h. Also at the top are a restaurant, a cafe and walking tracks.

Kawarau Jet
JETBOATING

(Map p276; ☏ 07-343 7600, 0800 538 7746; www.kjetrotorua.co.nz; Lakefront; 30min adult/child $74/54; ⊗9am-6pm) Speed things up on a

HINEMOA & TUTANEKAI

Hinemoa was a young woman of a *hapu* (subtribe) that lived on the western shore of Lake Rotorua, while Tutanekai was a young man of a Mokoia Island *hapu*. The pair met and fell in love during a regular tribal meeting. While both were of high birth, Tutanekai was illegitimate, so marriage between the two was forbidden.

Home on Mokoia, the lovesick Tutanekai played his flute for his love, the wind carrying the melody across the water. Hinemoa heard his declaration, but her people took to tying up the canoes at night to ensure she wouldn't go to him.

Finally, Tutanekai's music won her over. Hinemoa undressed and swam the long distance from the shore to the island. When she arrived on Mokoia, Hinemoa found herself in a quandary. Shedding her clothing in order to swim, she could hardly walk into the island's settlement naked. She hopped into a hot pool to think about her next move.

Eventually a man came to fetch water from a cold spring beside the hot pool. In a deep man's voice, Hinemoa called out, 'Who is it?' The man replied that he was Tutanekai's slave on a water run. Hinemoa grabbed the slave's calabash and smashed it to pieces. More slaves came, but she smashed their calabashes too, until finally Tutanekai came to the pool and demanded that the interloper identify himself – imagine his surprise when it turned out to be Hinemoa. He secreted her into his hut.

Next morning, after a suspiciously long lie-in, a slave reported that someone was in Tutanekai's bed. The two lovers were rumbled, and when Hinemoa's superhuman efforts to reach Tutanekai had been revealed, their union was celebrated.

Descendants of Hinemoa and Tutanekai still live around Rotorua today.

ROTORUA IN...

Two Days

Order breakfast at **Third Place Cafe** after which stroll back into town via steamy **Kuirau Park**. Next stop is the fabulous **Rotorua Museum**, followed by a soak at the **Blue Baths**. In the evening, catch a *hangi* and concert at **Tamaki Maori Village** or **Mitai Maori Village**.

Start the second day with a tour of **Whakarewarewa Thermal Village** and watch Pohutu geyser blow its top. From here, it's a quick hop to the **Redwoods Whakarewarewa Forest** for a couple of hours' mountain biking. More forest action awaits in the afternoon courtesy of **Rotorua Canopy Tours**, or pay a visit to the swooping falcons at the **Wingspan National Bird of Prey Centre**.

Four Days

Too much geothermal excitement is barely enough! Explore the hot spots to the south: **Waimangu Volcanic Valley** and **Wai-O-Tapu Thermal Wonderland**. The nearby **Waikite Valley Thermal Pools** are perfect for an end-of-day plunge.

On your last day, head southeast and visit the **Buried Village**, swim in **Lake Tarawera**, or take a long walk on one of the tracks at nearby **Lake Okataina**. Back in town, cruise the restaurants and bars on **Tutanekai St** (aka 'Eat Street') and toast your efforts with a few cold beers at **Brew**.

---

jetboat ride with Kawarau Jet, which tears around the lake. Parasailing (30 minutes tandem/solo $80/115) and fishing trips (from $170 per hour) also available.

Mountain Biking

On the edge of town is the Redwoods Whakarewarewa Forest (p289), home to some of the best mountain-bike trails in the country. There are close to 100km of tracks to keep bikers of all skill levels happy for days on end. Note that not all tracks in the forest are designated for bikers, so adhere to the signposts. Pick up a trail map at the forest visitor centre.

Also here is the Te Ara Ahi ride, one of the New Zealand Cycle Trail (www.nzcycletrail.com) 'Great Rides'. It's an intermediate, two-day, 66km ride heading south of town to Wai-O-Tapu Thermal Wonderland and beyond.

For more information, the Rotorua i-SITE stocks the *Get on Your Bike* Rotorua cycle map. Online, see the Cycling/Mountain Biking info at www.rotoruanz.com/visit/to-do.

Mountain Bike Rotorua　BICYCLE RENTAL
(Map p290; ☑0800 682 768; www.mtbrotorua.co.nz; Waipa State Mill Rd; mountain bikes per 2hr/day from $35/45, guided half-/full-day rides from $130/275; ⊙9am-5pm) This outfit hires out bikes at the Waipa Mill car park entrance to the Redwoods Whakarewarewa Forest, the starting point for the bike trails. There's

also a satellite bike depot across the forest at the visitor centre, so you can ride through the trees one-way then catch a shuttle back.

Planet Bike　BICYCLE RENTAL
(Map p290; ☑027 280 2817; www.planetbike.co.nz; Waipa Bypass Rd; mountain bikes per 2hr/day $35/60) Bike hire and guided rides (two hours/half-day from $75/115) in the Redwoods Whakarewarewa Forest.

Bike Barn　BICYCLE RENTAL
(Map p276; ☑07-347 1151; www.bikebarn.co.nz; 1275 Fenton St; mountain bikes per half-/full day from $45/60; ⊙8.30am-5.30pm Mon-Fri, 9am-4.30pm Sat, 10am-4.30pm Sun) Bike hire and repairs in downtown Rotorua.

White-Water Rafting, Sledging & Kayaking

There's plenty of kayaking and white-water action around Rotorua with the chance to take on the Grade V Kaituna River, complete with a startling 7m drop at Okere Falls. Most of these trips take a day. Some companies head further out to the Rangitaiki River (Grade III–VI) and Wairoa River (Grade V), raftable only when the dam is opened every second Sunday. Sledging (in case you didn't know) is zooming downriver on a body board. Most operators can arrange transport.

River Rats　RAFTING, KAYAKING
(☑07-345 6543, 0800 333 900; www.riverrats.co.nz) Takes on the Wairoa ($129), Kaituna

($105) and Rangitaiki ($139), and runs a scenic trip on the lower Rangitaiki (Grade II) that is good for youngsters (adult/child $139/110). Kayaking options include freedom hire ($40/60 per half-/full day) and guided four-hour Lake Rotoiti trips ($110).

Wet 'n' Wild RAFTING
(☑ 07-348 3191, 0800 462 7238; www.wetnwildrafting.co.nz) Runs trips on the Kaituna ($99), Wairoa ($110) and Mokau ($160), as well as easy-going Rangitaiki trips (adult/child $130/110) and longer trips to remote parts of the Motu and Mohaka (two to five days, $650 to $1095).

Raftabout RAFTING, SLEDGING
(☑ 07-343 9500, 0800 723 822) Rafting trips on the Kaituna ($105), Rangitaiki ($139) and Wairoa ($129), plus sledging on the Kaituna ($119).

Kaituna Cascades RAFTING, KAYAKING
(☑ 07-345 4199, 0800 524 8862; www.kaitunacascades.co.nz) Rafting on the Kaituna ($84), Rangitaiki ($118) and Wairoa ($108), plus kayaking options and combos.

Go Wild Adventures KAYAKING
(☑ 07-533 2926; www.adventurekayaking.co.nz) Takes trips on Lakes Rotorua, Rotoiti, Tarawera and Okataina (per two hours/half-day/full day from $80/95/130). Also offers freedom hire (from $50 per day).

Kaitiaki Adventures RAFTING, SLEDGING
(☑ 07-357 2236, 0800 338 736; www.kaitiaki.co.nz) Offers white-water rafting trips on the Kaituna ($95), Wairoa ($99) and Rangitaiki ($125), plus sledging on the Wairoa ($299) and a Grade III section of the Kaituna ($109).

Kaituna Kayaks KAYAKING
(☑ 07-362 4486; www.kaitunakayaks.co.nz; half-day trips from $199, lessons per half-/full day from $199/299) Guided tandem trips and kayaking lessons (cheaper for groups) on the Kaituna River.

Thermal Pools & Massage
Spa/pool complexes in the area include Hells Gate & Wai Ora Spa (p289), 16km northeast of Rotorua, and Waikite Valley Thermal Pools (p292), around 35km south.

Polynesian Spa SPA, MASSAGE
(Map p276; ☑ 07-348 1328; www.polynesianspa. co.nz; 1000 Hinemoa St; adults-only pools $25, private pools per 30min adult/child from $18/6.50, family pool adult/child/family $14.50/6.50/36, spa therapies from $85; ☺ 8am-11pm, spa therapies 10am-7pm) A bathhouse opened at these Government Gardens springs in 1882, and people have been swearing by the waters ever since. There is mineral bathing (36°C to 42°C) in several picturesque pools at the lake's edge, marble-lined terraced pools and a larger, main pool. Also here are luxury therapies (massage, mud and beauty treatments) and a cafe.

Tramping
There are plenty of opportunities to stretch your legs around Rotorua, with day walks a speciality. The booklet *Walks in the Rotorua Lakes Area* ($2.50), available from the i-SITE, showcases town walks, including the popular lakefront stroll (20 minutes). See also www.doc.govt.nz.

The **Eastern Okataina Walkway** (three hours one way) goes along the eastern shoreline of Lake Okataina to Lake Tarawera and passes the Soundshell, a natural amphitheatre that has *pa* (fortified village) remains and several swimming spots. The **Western Okataina Walkway** (five hours one way) mimics this route on the western side of the lake.

The **Northern Tarawera Track** (three hours one way) connects to the Eastern Okataina Walkway, creating a two-day walk from either Ruato or Lake Okataina to Lake Tarawera with an overnight camp at either Humphries Bay (sites free) or Tarawera Outlet (sites per adult/child $6/3). From Tarawera Outlet you can walk on to the 65m **Tarawera Falls** (four hours return). There's a forestry road into Tarawera Outlet from Kawerau, a grim timber town in the shadow of Putauaki (Mt Edgecumbe), off the road to Whakatane; access costs $5, with permits available from the **Kawerau visitor centre** (☑ 07-323 6300; www.kawerauonline.com; Plunkett St bus terminal; ☺ 8am-6pm Dec-Mar, 8am-4pm Apr-Nov).

The **Okere Falls** are about 21km northeast of Rotorua on SH33, with an easy track (30 minutes return) past the 7m falls (popular for rafting), through native podocarp (conifer) forest and along the Kaituna River. Along the way is a lookout over the river at Hinemoa's Steps.

Just north of Wai-O-Tapu on SH5, the **Rainbow Mountain Track** (1½ hours one way) is a strenuous walk up the peak known to Maori as Maungakakaramea (Mountain of Coloured Earth). There are spectacular views from the top towards Lake Taupo and Tongariro National Park.

For a short stroll try **Hamurana Springs** (Map p290) on the northern edge of Lake Rotorua – a sacred place for Ngati Rangiwewehi Maori – where there's a 1.5km loop walk alongside gin-clear springs through a redwood grove.

There are also a couple of good walks at Mt Ngongotaha, 10km northwest of Rotorua: the easy 3.2km **Nature Walk** loop through native forest, and the steep 5km return **Jubilee Track** to the (viewless) summit. See www.ngongotaha.org.

Fishing

There's always good trout fishing to be had somewhere around Rotorua. Hire a guide or go solo: either way a licence (per day/half-season/full season $23/73/121) is essential, available from **O'Keefe's Fishing Specialists** (Map p276; ☑07-346 0178; www.okeefesfishing.co.nz; 1113 Eruera St; ⊙8.30am-5pm Mon-Fri, 9am-2pm Sat, 9am-1pm Sun). You can fish Rotorua's lakefront with a licence, though not all lakes can be fished year-round; check with O'Keefe's or the i-SITE.

Trout Man   FISHING
(☑07-357 5255, 0800 876 881; www.waiteti.com; 2hr/day trips from $40/140) Learn to fish with experienced angler Harvey Clark, from a couple of hours to multiday trips.

Clark Gregor   FISHING
(☑07-347 1123; www.troutnz.co.nz; per hr $105) Fly- and boat fishing.

Gordon Randle   FISHING
(☑07-349 2555; www.rotoruatrout.co.nz; half-/full-day charters $370/750) Reasonable hourly rates also available.

Horse Riding

Farmhouse   HORSE RIDING
(Map p290; ☑07-332 3771; www.thefarmhouse.co.nz; 55 Sunnex Rd, off Central Rd; 30/60/120min $26/42/74) North of Lake Rotorua at the Farmhouse you can saddle up for a short horse-riding trip for beginners, or a longer trek for experienced riders.

Golf

Ballbusters   GOLF
(Map p276; ☑07-348 9126; www.ballbusters.co.nz; Queens Dr, Government Gardens; ⊙7.30am-8pm) Ballbusters has a nine-hole course (adult/child $18/12), minigolf ($11/8) and driving range (80 balls $11). A $40 golf package includes clubs, green fees, balls and tees. There's also a baseball batting cage (bucket of balls $10).

Tours

Happy Ewe Tours   CYCLING
(☑022 622 9252; www.happyewetours.com; per person $35; ⊙10am & 2pm) Saddle up for a three-hour, small-group bike tour of Rotorua, wheeling past 20 sights around the city. It's all flat and slow-paced, so you don't need to be at your physical peak (you're on holiday after all).

Foris Eco Tours   RAFTING, TRAMPING
(☑0800 367 471; www.foris.co.nz; adult/child $169 /99) 🌿 Check out some ancient rainforest on a one-hour walk in Whirinaki Forest Park then raft along the easy-going Rangitaiki River on this full-day trip. Full-day walks also available. Includes lunch, pick-up/drop-off and lots of wildlife-spotting.

Rotorua Paddle Tours   PADDLE BOARDING
(☑0800 787 768; www.rotoruapaddletours.co.nz; tours from $90; ⊙10am & 3pm) Keen to try stand-up paddle boarding without any waves to contend with? This outfit runs three-hour trips on Lake Rotoiti, Blue Lake and Lake Tarawera, with boundless beautiful scenery. No experience required.

Geyser Link Shuttle   SIGHTSEEING
(☑03-477 9083, 0800 304 333; www.travelheadfirst.com/local-legends/geyser-link-shuttle) Tours of some of the major sights, including Wai-O-Tapu (half-day adult/child $70/35) or Waimangu (half-day adult/child $70/35), or both (full day $120/60). Transport-only options available too.

Rotorua Duck Tours   SIGHTSEEING
(☑07-345 6522; adult/child/family $68/38/175; ⊙tours 11am, 1pm & 3.30pm Oct-Apr, 11am & 2.15pm May-Sep) Ninety-minute trips in an amphibious biofuelled vehicle taking in the major sites around town and heading out onto three lakes (Rotorua, Okareka and Tikitapu/Blue). Longer Lake Tarawera trips also available.

Elite Adventures   SIGHTSEEING
(☑07-347 8282; www.eliteadventures.co.nz; tours adult/child half-day $145/100, full day $240/170) Small-group tours covering a selection of Rotorua's major cultural and natural highlights.

Thermal Land Shuttle   SIGHTSEEING
(☑0800 894 287; www.thermalshuttle.co.nz; tours adult/child from $33/65) Daily scheduled morning, afternoon and night tours around a selection of key sights, including Waimangu, Wai-O-Tapu, Te Puia and Rainbow Mountain. Transport-only options also available.

Mana Adventures
CRUISE, KAYAKING

(Map p276; ☑ 07-348 4186, 0800 333 660; www.manaadventures.co.nz; Lakefront; ☺ 9am-5pm) Down at the lake, Mana Adventures offers (weather permitting) rental pedal boats ($9/6 per adult/child per 20 minutes) and kayaks ($50/75 per hour/half-day). It also runs low-key, one-hour lake cruises ($55/39 per adult/child), trout-fishing charters and three-hour tours to Manupirua Hot Pools on nearby Lake Rotoiti ($95/75 per adult/child).

Volcanic Air Safaris
SCENIC FLIGHTS

(Map p276; ☑ 0800 800 848, 07-348 9984; www.volcanicair.co.nz; Lakefront; trips $95-915) A variety of floatplane and helicopter flights taking in Mt Tarawera and surrounding geothermal sites including Hell's Gate, the Buried Village and Waimangu Volcanic Valley. A 3¼-hour Whakaari (White Island)/Mt Tarawera trip tops the price list.

Helipro
SCENIC FLIGHTS

(Map p290; ☑ 0800 435 477, 07-357 2515; www.helipro.co.nz; Hemo Rd; flights $99-940) Helipro plies the skies over Rotorua in nippy little red choppers (eight-minute city sightseeing flights $99), also extending to Mt Tarawera and as far as Whakaari (White Island). Landings in various places cost extra.

Lakeland Queen
CRUISE

(Map p276; ☑ 07-348 0265, 0800 572 784; www.lakelandqueen.com; Lakefront) The *Lakeland Queen* paddle steamer offers sedate one-hour Lake Rotorua breakfast cruises (adult/child $38/22.50), lunch cruises ($55/22.50) and Saturday-night summer dinners for big groups ($59/30).

Mokoia Island
Wai Ora Experiences
CRUISE, CULTURAL TOUR

(Map p276; ☑ 07-349 0976; www.mokoiaisland.co.nz; Lakefront; tours adult/child $75/38; ☺ 9.30am & 2pm) Visit Mokoia Island in the middle of Lake Rotorua on a 2½-hour Ultimate Island Experience tour, with wildlife-spotting, tales of the island, and a dip in the hot pool of Hinemoa. Minimum numbers may apply.

🛌 Sleeping

Rotorua has plenty of holiday parks and an ever-changing backpacker scene. Generic motels crowd Fenton St: better and more interesting rooms are away from the main drag.

★ Funky Green Voyager
HOSTEL $

(Map p276; ☑ 07-346 1754; www.funkygreenvoyager.co.nz; 4 Union St; dm from $25, d with/without bathroom $68/59; @ 🤖) 🍃 Green on the outside and the inside – due to several cans of paint and a dedicated environmental policy – the shoe-free Funky GV features laid-back tunes and plenty of sociable chat among a spunky bunch of guests and worldly-wise owners, who know what you want when you travel. The best doubles have bathrooms; dorms are roomy with quality mattresses and solid timber beds.

Rotorua Central Backpackers
HOSTEL $

(Map p276; ☑ 07-349 3285; www.rotoruacentralbackpackers.co.nz; 1076 Pukuatua St; dm from $25, tw & d $62; @ 🤖) This heritage hostel was built in 1936 and retains historic features including dark-wood skirting boards and door frames, deep bath-tubs and geothermally powered radiators. Dorms have no more than six beds (and no bunks), plus there's a spa pool and barbecue. Perfect if you're not looking to party.

Waiteti Trout
Stream Holiday Park
HOLIDAY PARK $

(Map p290; ☑ 0800 876 881, 07-357 5255; www.waiteti.com; 14 Okona Cres, Ngongotaha; campsites $36, dm from $25, d cabin/motel from $58/110; @ 🤖) This well-maintained park is a great option if you don't mind the 8km drive into town. Set in two tidy garden acres abutting a trout-filled stream, it's a cute classic with character-filled motel units, compact cabins, a tidy backpackers lodge and beaut campsites by the stream. Free kayaks and dinghies; fly-fishing lessons from $30. And no sulphur smell!

Blarney's Rock
HOSTEL $

(Map p276; ☑ 07-343 7904; www.blarneysrock.com; 1210 Tutanekai St; dm $20-27, d $50-60; @ 🤖) You might expect a backpackers above an Irish pub to be effervescing with drunken antics. Sorry to disappoint: this one's quiet, clean and comfy, with live-in managers who ensure the party stays downstairs. It's a small, homey affair, with a little sunny deck, free wi-fi, free apple pie twice weekly and hot water bottles in your bed on chilly nights.

Rotorua YHA
HOSTEL $

(Map p276; ☑ 07-349 4088; www.yha.co.nz; 1278 Haupapa St; dm $26-35 d with/without bathroom $90/70; @ 🤖) Bright and sparkling clean, this classy, purpose-built hostel is great for those wanting to get outdoors, with staff eager to assist with trip bookings, and storage for bikes and kayaks. Pricier rooms come with bathroom, and there's a barbecue area and deck for hanging out on (though this ain't a party pad). Off-street parking a bonus.

Crash Palace
HOSTEL $

(Map p276; ☑0800 892 727, 07-348 8842; www.crashpalace.co.nz; 1271 Hinemaru St; dm/s/d/f from $22/45/65/95; @ 🛜) Crash occupies a big, mustard-coloured 1930s hotel near Government Gardens. The atmosphere strikes a balance between party and pristine, without too much of either. The nicest rooms have floorboards, and there's lots of art on the walls, a pool table and DJ console in the lobby, and a beaut terrace out the back. Limited off-steet parking.

Astray
MOTEL, HOSTEL $

(Map p276; ☑0800 481 200, 07-348 1200; www.astray.co.nz; 1202 Pukuatua St; dm/s/d from $24/40/60, f $95-150; @ 🛜) Even if you are 6'3", Astray – a 'micro motel' that would probably be more at home in Tokyo than Rotorua – is a decent bet. Clean, tidy, quiet, friendly and central: just don't expect acres of space. Free wi-fi a bonus.

Rotorua Thermal Holiday Park
HOLIDAY PARK $

(Map p290; ☑07-346 3140; www.rotoruathermal.co.nz; 463 Old Taupo Rd; sites from $32, d cabins/units from $51/98; @ 🛜 ≋) This super-friendly holiday park on the edge of town sits deep in the leisure groove, with barbecues, a playground, campsites galore, a shop and a cafe. There's plenty of room and lots of trees and open grassy areas, plus hot mineral pools to soak the day away. Bike hire available.

Rock Solid Backpackers
HOSTEL $

(Map p276; ☑07-282 2053; www.rocksolidrotorua.co.nz; 1140 Hinemoa St; dm $19-25, d & tw $58; @ 🛜) Cavernous, locally owned Rock Solid occupies a former shopping mall: you might be bunking down in a florist or a delicatessen. Dorms over the street are sunny, and there's a big, bright kitchen. Downstairs is the Wall rock-climbing facility and the art-house Basement Cinema. Free wi-fi and pool table.

Rotorua Top 10 Holiday Park
HOLIDAY PARK $

(Map p290; ☑0800 223 267, 07-348 1886; www.rotoruatop10.co.nz; 1495 Pukuatua St; campsites from $38, d cabin/motel from $80/125; @ 🛜 ≋) A small but perfectly formed holiday park with a continual improvement policy that has seen a new playground, shower/toilet blocks and mineral hot pools installed. Cabins are in good nick and have small fridges and microwaves. Shrubberies and picnic tables aplenty.

Kiwi Paka
HOSTEL $

(Map p290; ☑07-347 0931; www.kiwipaka.co.nz; 60 Tarewa Rd; campsites from $15, dm/s/d

$29/60/64, chalets with bathroom d/tr/q $87/107/147; @ 🛜 ≋) This rambling complex is a 10-minute walk through Kuirau Park to town. The vibe is a bit 'school camp', with acceptable amenities and a range of accommodation from campsites to plain dorms, lodge rooms, three kitchens and two-storey pine-clad chalets. There's a cafe and bar on site.

Base Rotorua
HOSTEL $

(Map p276; ☑0800 227 369, 07-348 8636; www.stayatbase.co.nz; 1286 Arawa St; dm/s/d from $25/70/70; @ 🛜 ≋) A link in the Base chain, this huge hostel is ever-popular with partying backpackers who love the trashy Lava Bar (cheap meals, toga parties, wet T-shirt comps etc). Dorms can be tight (up to 12 beds), but extras such as girls-only rooms, en suites in most rooms, a thermally heated pool and campervan parking ($9 per person) compensate.

Tuscany Villas
MOTEL $$

(Map p290; ☑0800 802 050, 07-348 3500; www.tuscanyvillasrotorua.co.nz; 280 Fenton St; d from $145; 🛜) With its Italian-inspired architecture and pointy conifers, this family-owned eye-catcher is the pick of the Fenton St motels. It pitches itself at both corporate and leisure travellers, all of who appreciate the plush furnishings, multiple TVs, DVD players and deep spa baths. Free wi-fi.

Six on Union
MOTEL $$

(Map p276; ☑0800 100 062, 07-347 8062; www.sixonunion.co.nz; 6 Union St; d/f from $105/145; 🛜 ≋) Hanging baskets ahoy! This modest place is an affordable bonanza with pool and spa, and small kitchenettes in all units. Rooms are functional, and the new owners (from Yorkshire) keep the swimming-pool area in good nick. It's away from traffic noise, but still an easy walk into town.

Sandi's Bed & Breakfast
B&B $$

(Map p290; ☑07-348 0884, 0800 726 3422; www.sandisbedandbreakfast.co.nz; 103 Fairy Springs Rd; s/d/f incl breakfast $85/130/160; 🛜 ≋) A friendly, family B&B run by the well-humoured Sandi who offers local advice with a ready smile. It's on a busy road a couple of kilometres north of town, so the best bets are the two bohemian chalets out the back with TV and plenty of room to move.

Victoria Lodge
MOTEL $$

(Map p276; ☑0800 100 039, 07-348 4039; www.victorialodge.co.nz; 10 Victoria St; d/apt from $115/160; 🛜) The friendly Vic has seen a lot of competitors come and go, maintaining its foothold in the market with individual-feeling apartments and studios with thermally heated plunge pools. Fully equipped, freshly painted apartments can squeeze in seven, though four would be comfortable.

Ann's Volcanic Motel
MOTEL $$
(Map p290; ✆ 0800 768 683, 07-347 1007; www.rotoruamotel.co.nz; 107 Malfroy Rd; d/1-bedroom/2-bedroom from $95/129/209; ☏) Ann's is an affordable motel with an ever-friendly host offering loads of local advice. Larger rooms feature courtyard spas and facilities for travellers with disabilities, with a house next door available for big groups (sleeps nine). Rooms close to the street can be a tad noisy.

★ Regent of Rotorua
BOUTIQUE HOTEL $$$
(Map p276; ✆ 0508 734 368, 07-348 4079; www.regentrotorua.co.nz; 1191 Pukaki St; d/ste from $169/239; ☏☀) Wow! It's about time Rotorua showed some slumbering style, and the Regent (a renovated 1960s motel) delivers. 'The '60s were a glamorous time to travel', say the owners: the decor follows suit, with hip black-and-white tones, funky mirrors, retro wallpaper and colourful splashes. There's a pool and restaurant, the Tutanekai St eateries are an amble away, and there's a whole new wing of rooms next door. Terrific value.

Millennium Hotel
HOTEL $$$
(Map p276; ✆ 07-347 1234; www.millenniumrotorua.co.nz; cnr Eruera & Hinemaru Sts; d from $200; @☏☀) The slick Maori-inspired lobby sets the scene for this elegant five-storey motel. Lakefront rooms afford excellent views as does the club lounge, popular with the suits and internationalists swanning about. The poolside *hangi* is fab, as is the in-house restaurant Nikau. Advance booking rates slip into midrange territory.

✗ Eating

The lake end of Tutanekai St – known as Eat Street – has a strip of eateries beneath a new roof, but there are plenty of other options around town.

Mistress of Cakes
BAKERY $
(Map p276; www.mistressofcakes.co.nz; 1224 Eruera St; items $4-8; ☺7.30am-2.30pm Mon-Fri) 'Food that your grandmother made' is the slogan here, but we bet your Grandma couldn't bake a lemon passionfruit meringue like the ones the Mistress makes! Fab muffins, slices, biscuits, scones and quiches too, all homemade with local ingredients.

Fish & Chip Shop
FISH & CHIPS $
(Map p276; ✆ 07-343 7400; 47 Lake Rd; meals $5-15; ☺11am-8pm Mon-Thu, 11am-8.30pm Fri-Sun) What you see is what you get: top-notch takeaway fish and chips from this little sky-blue shopfront out near Ohinemutu.

Weilin's Noodle House
NOODLES, CHINESE $
(Map p276; ✆ 07-343 9998; 1148 Tutanekai St; mains $9-25; ☺noon-3pm & 5-9pm Wed-Mon) A neat and tidy shop serving traditional (and refreshingly un-fatty/salty/stodgy) Chinese dumplings and oodles of noodles in soups and stir-fries. Eat in or take away. Try the noodles with spicy pork and peanuts.

Pak 'n Save
SUPERMARKET $
(Map p276; www.paknsave.co.nz; cnr Fenton & Amohau Sts; ☺7.30am-10pm) On the downtown fringe.

★ Third Place Cafe
CAFE $$
(Map p276; ✆ 07-349 4852; www.thirdplacecafe.co.nz; 36 Lake Rd; mains $12-18; ☺8am-4pm Mon-Fri, 8am-3pm Sat) A really interesting cafe away from the hubbub, Third Place has leapfrogged into first by our reckoning. All-day breakfast/brunch sidesteps neatly between chicken jambalaya, fish and chips, and an awesome 'mumble jumble' of crushed kumara (sweet potato), green tomatoes and spicy chorizo topped with bacon, poached egg and hollandaise sauce. Hangover? What hangover? Slide into a red-leather couch or score a window seat overlooking Ohinemutu.

Abracadabra Cafe Bar
MIDDLE EASTERN, CAFE $$
(Map p276; ✆ 07-348 3883; www.abracadabracafe.com; 1363 Amohia St; mains $19-30; ☺8.30am-11pm Tue-Fri, 9am-11pm Sat, 9am-3pm Sun) Wedged somewhere between Mexico and Morocco, Abracadabra is a magical cave of spicy delights, from beef-and-apricot tagine to king-prawn fajitas and Tijuana pork chilli. Conjure up your own 'Day of the Dead' (tomorrow) with a tour though the dedicated tequila menu. Beaut beer terrace out the back.

Sabroso
LATIN AMERICAN $$
(Map p276; ✆ 07-349 0591; www.sabroso.co.nz; 1184 Haupapa St; mains $18-29; ☺5-9pm Thu-Mon) What a surprise! This modest Latin American cantina – adorned with sombreros, guitars, hessian tablecloths and salt-and-pepper shakers made from Corona bottles – serves adventurous south-of-the-border fare to spice up bland Kiwi palates. The black-bean chilli is a knockout (as are the margaritas).

Lime Caffeteria
CAFE **$$**

(Map p276; ☑ 07-350 2033; cnr Fenton & Whakaue Sts; mains $13-24; ⊙ 7.30am-4.30pm; ☑) Occupying a quiet corner near the lake, this zesty cafe offers alfresco breakfasts and dishes with a welcome twist: try the chicken-and-chorizo salad or prawn-and-salmon risotto in lime sauce. Classy counter snacks and excellent coffee, too. 'This is the best lunch I've had in ages', says one happy punter.

Indian Star
INDIAN **$$**

(Map p276; ☑ 07-343 6222; www.indianstar.co.nz; 1118 Tutanekai St; mains $14-22; ⊙ 11am-2pm & 5pm-late; ☑) This is one of several Indian eateries around town, elevating itself above the competition with immaculate service and marvellous renditions of subcontinental classics. It has sizeable portions and good vegetarian selections (try the chickpea masala). Book for dinner.

Leonardo's
ITALIAN **$$**

(Map p276; ☑ 07-347 7084; www.leonardospureitalian.nznic.biz; 1176 Pukaki St; mains $22-32.50; ⊙ 5-10pm Mon Thu, 11.30am-2pm & 5-10pm Fri-Sun) Not far from the lake in an unpretentious shopfront, Leonardo's goes heavy on the hokey 'just like mama used to make' marketing, but what comes out of the kitchen is far from kitsch. Try the simple but perfect gnocchi with tomato, mozzarella and pesto, or the angel-hair pasta with mussels and anchovies.

Capers Epicurean
CAFE, DELICATESSEN **$$**

(Map p276; ☑ 07-348 8818; www.capers.co.nz; 1181 Eruera St; mains breakfast & lunch $7-23, dinner $27-32; ⊙ 7.30am-9pm; ☑) This slick, barn-like cafe is perennially busy, with diners perusing cabinets full of delicious gourmet sandwiches, pastries, salads and cakes, and the excellent blackboard menu of breakfasts and other tasty hot foods (try the pork belly with pumpkin dumplings). The deli section is stocked with olive oils, marinades, relishes, jams and chocolates.

Urbano Bistro
MODERN NZ, CAFE **$$**

(Map p290; ☑ 07-349 3770; www.urbanobistro. co.nz; cnr Fenton & Grey Sts; mains breakfast & lunch $14-21, dinner $24-43; ⊙ 9am-11pm Mon-Sat, to 3pm Sun) This hip suburban diner, with mega-checkerboard carpet and curvy wallpaper, is a bold move by reputable local restaurateurs. Try the beef, pineapple and kumara curry – rich in flavour and well executed. Fine wines and five-star service to boot.

Fat Dog Cafe & Bar
CAFE **$$**

(Map p276; ☑ 07-347 7586; 1161 Arawa St; mains breakfast & lunch $12-23, dinner $28-30; ⊙ 7am-9pm; ☑) With paw prints and silly poems painted on the walls, this is the town's friskiest and most child-friendly cafe. During the day it dishes up burgers (try the Dogs Bollox version), nachos, salads and sandwiches; in the evening it's candlelit lamb and venison. Takeaway caffeine in the shopfront next door.

Bistro 1284
MODERN NZ **$$$**

(Map p276; ☑ 07-346 1284; www.bistro1284.co.nz; 1284 Eruera St; mains $35-39; ⊙ 5pm-late) A fine-dining hot spot on an unremarkable stretch of Eruera St, this intimate place (all chocolate and mushroom colours) serves stylish NZ cuisine with an Asian influence. The lamb is always good, but be sure to leave room for the delectable desserts.

🍷 Drinking & Entertainment

Brew
BAR, CRAFT BEER

(Map p276; www.brewpub.co.nz; 1103 Tutanekai St; ⊙ 4pm-late Mon-Thu, noon late Fri, 11am-late Sat & Sun) Run by the lads from Croucher Brewing Co, Rotorua's best microbrewers, Brew sits in a sunny spot on Rotorua's main eat-street. Sip down a pint of fruity pale ale, aromatic drunken hop bitter or malty pilsener and wonder how you'll manage a sleep-in tomorrow morning. Good coffee and pizzas, plus Friday DJs and Tuesday open-mike nights.

Pig & Whistle
PUB, BREWERY

(Map p276; www.pigandwhistle.co.nz; cnr Haupapa & Tutanekai Sts; ⊙ 11am-late) Inside a former police station, this busy microbrewery-pub serves up Swine lager, big-screen TVs, a beer garden and live music Thursday to Saturday, plus solid grub (mains $19 to $32). The menu runs the gamut from crispy pork-belly salad to burgers and vegetarian nachos.

Belgian Bar
BAR, LIVE MUSIC

(Map p276; www.facebook.com/pages/belgian-bar/137762819598058; 1151 Arawa St; ⊙ 4pm-late Tue-Fri, 2pm-late Sat & Sun) The best bar in town for lovers of gigs and good beer. Half a dozen Euro-beers on tap and 42 in the bottle accompany regular blues and acoustic acts ('Clapton is God' is spraypainted behind the stage). Garden bar out the back.

Basement Cinema
CINEMA

(Map p276; ☑ 07-350 1400; www.basementcinema. co.nz; 1140 Hinemoa St; tickets $14.50; ⊙ noon-

DON'T MISS

MAORI CONCERTS & HANGI

Maori culture is a big-ticket item in Rotorua and, although it is commercialised, it's a great opportunity to learn about the indigenous culture of NZ. The two big activities are concerts and *hangi* feasts, often packaged together in an evening's entertainment featuring the famous *hongi* (Maori greeting; the pressing of foreheads and noses, and sharing of life breath) and *haka* and *poi* dances.

An established favourite, **Tamaki Maori Village** (Map p276; ☑ 07-349 2999; www.maoriculture.co.nz; booking office 1220 Hinemaru St; adult/child/family $110/20-60/250; ☺ tours depart 5pm, 6.15pm & 7.30pm Nov-Apr, 6.15pm May-Oct) does an excellent twilight tour to a *marae* (meeting house) and Maori village 15km south of Rotorua. Buses collect from the Hinemaru St booking office and local accommodation. The experience is very hands-on, taking you on an interactive journey through Maori history, arts, traditions and customs from pre-European times to the present day. The concert is followed by an impressive *hangi*.

The family-run **Mitai Maori Village** (Map p290; ☑ 07-343 9132; www.mitai.co.nz; 196 Fairy Springs Rd; adult/child/family $111/21.50-55/290; ☺ 6.30pm) offers a popular three-hour evening event with a concert, *hangi* and glowworm bushwalk. The experience can be combined with a tour (adult/child $150/75) of Hells Gate thermal reserve (p289) , or a tour ($126/67) of Ohinemutu (p278) Maori village. Pick-ups available.

Te Puia (p275) and Whakarewarewa Thermal Village (p276) also put on shows, and many of the big hotels offer mainstream Maori concerts and *hangi,* including the following:

Copthorne Hotel Rotorua (Map p290; ☑ 07-348 0199; www.millenniumhotels.co.nz; 328 Fenton St; concert adult/child $25/15, incl hangi $55/25.25)

Holiday Inn Rotorua (Map p290; ☑ 0800 476 488, 07-348 1189; www.holidayinnrotorua.co.nz/cultural-show.php; cnr Froude & Tryon Sts; concerts & hangi adult/child $69/34.50)

Millennium Hotel Rotorua (Map p276; ☑ 07-347 1234; www.millenniumrotorua.co.nz; cnr Eruera & Hinemaru Sts; concerts adult/child $30/15, incl hangi $70/35)

Novotel Rotorua (Map p276; ☑ 07-346 3888; www.novotelrotorua.co.nz; 11 Tutanekai St; concerts adult/child $39/18, incl hangi $69/19)

10pm Mon-Fri, 10am-10pm Sat & Sun) Part of the same complex as the Wall rock-climbing gym, the Basement screens offbeat, foreign-language and art-house flicks.

🔒 Shopping

South of town, Te Puia and Whakarewarewa Thermal Village have excellent selections of genuine Maori-made arts.

Rotorua Night Market MARKET
(Map p276; www.rotoruanightmarket.co.nz; Tutanekai St; ☺ 5pm-late Thu) Tutanekai St is closed off on Thursday nights between Haupapa and Pukuatua Sts to allow the Rotorua Night Market to spread its wings. Expect local arts and crafts, souvenirs, cheesy buskers, coffee, wine and plenty of deli-style food stalls for dinner.

Mountain Jade ARTS & CRAFTS, JEWELLERY
(Map p276; www.mountainjade.co.nz; 1288 Fenton St; ☺ 9am-6pm) High-end hand-crafted greenstone jewellery and carvings. You can watch the carvers at work through the streetside window.

Out of New Zealand ARTS & CRAFTS, JEWELLERY
(Map p276; 1189 Fenton St; ☺ 10am-6pm, to 9pm Dec-Mar) Stocks NZ-made craft and gifts including carvings, ceramics and jewellery: affordable, packable souvenirs.

ℹ️ Information

There are plenty of ATMs around town. Most banks offer currency exchange.

Lakes Care Medical (☑ 07-348 1000; 1165 Tutanekai St; ☺ 8am-10pm) Urgent medical care.

Police (☑ 111, non-emergency 07-349 9400; 1190 Fenton St; ☺ 24hr)

Post Office (Map p276; cnr Tutanekai & Pukuatua Sts; ☺ 8am-5.30pm Mon-Fri, 9am-1pm Sat)

Rotorua Hospital (☑ 07-348 1199; www.lakesdhb.govt.nz; Arawa St; ☺ 24hr) Round-the-clock medical care.

Rotorua i-SITE (Map p276; ☑ 0800 768 678, 07-348 5179; www.rotoruanz.com; 1167 Fenton

St; ☉7.30am-7pm Sep-May, reduced hours Jun-Aug) The hub for travel information and bookings, including Department of Conservation (DOC) walks. Also has an exchange bureau, a cafe, showers and lockers.

❶ Getting There & Away

AIR

Rotorua Airport (Map p290; ☏07-345 8800; www.rotorua-airport.co.nz; SH30; ☎) is 10km northeast of town. **Air New Zealand** (☏07-343 1100; www.airnewzealand.co.nz; 1267 Tutanekai St; ☉9am-5pm Mon-Fri) has direct flights between Rotorua and Auckland, Wellington and Christchurch, plus Sydney (every Tuesday and Saturday).

BUS

All the major bus companies stop outside the Rotorua i-SITE, from where you can arrange bookings.

InterCity destinations include the following:

DESTINATION	PRICE ($)	DURATION (HR)	FREQUENCY (DAILY)
Auckland	55	3½	7
Gisborne	64	4½	1
Hamilton	40	1½	5
Napier	60	4	1
Taupo	32	1	4
Tauranga	25	1½	2
Wellington	65	7	5
Whakatane	35	1½	1

Naked Bus services include the following:

DESTINATION	PRICE ($)	DURATION (HR)	FREQUENCY (DAILY)
Auckland	15	4	3
Gisborne	19	4¾	1
Hamilton	10	1½	3
Napier	18	3	3
Taupo	10	1	3
Tauranga	10	1½	3
Wellington	19	8	1
Whakatane	14	1½	1

Twin City Express buses run twice daily Monday to Friday between Rotorua and Tauranga/Mt Maunganui via Te Puke ($11.60, 1½ hours).

White Island Shuttle (☏0800 733 529, 07-308 9588; www.whiteisland.co.nz; one way/return $35/60), run by White Island Tours in Whakatane, operates return shuttles to Whakatane from Rotorua. It's ostensibly for tour customers, but you can use the service without taking the tour.

❶ Getting Around

TO/FROM THE AIRPORT

Super Shuttle (☏0800 748 885, 09-522 5100; www.supershuttle.co.nz) offers a door-to-door airport service for $21 for the first person then $5 per additional passenger. **Baybus** (☏0800 422 928; www.baybus.co.nz) runs a daily airport bus service ($2.50). A taxi to/from the city centre costs about $25.

BUS

Many local attractions offer free pick-up/drop-off shuttle services. Shuttle services are also available to/from outlying attractions – see p282.

Baybus operates local bus services around town, and also to Ngongotaha (route 1, $2.50) and the airport (route 10, $2.50).

CAR

The big-name car-hire companies vie for your attention at Rotorua Airport. Otherwise, try **Rent a Dent** (☏07-349 3993; 39 Fairy Springs Rd; ☉8am-5pm Mon-Fri, 8am-noon Sat).

TAXI

Rotorua Taxis (☏07-348 1111; www.rotorua-taxis.co.nz)

AROUND ROTORUA

North of Rotorua

◉ Sights & Activities

Rainbow Springs   WILDLIFE RESERVE
(Map p290; ☏0800 724 626; www.rainbowsprings.co.nz; 192 Fairy Springs Rd; 24hr pass adult/child/family $40/20/99; ☉8.30am-late) About 3km north of central Rotorua, Rainbow Springs is a family-friendly winner. The natural springs here are home to wild trout and eels, which you can peer at through an underwater viewer. There are interpretive walkways, a new 'Big Splash' water ride, and plenty of animals, including tuatara (a native lizard) and native birds (kea, kaka and pukeko).

A highlight is the **Kiwi Encounter**, which offers a rare peek into the lives of these endangered birds: excellent 30-minute tours (an extra $10 per person) have you tiptoeing through incubator and hatchery areas.

Wingspan National
Bird of Prey Centre   WILDLIFE CENTRE
(Map p290; ☑ 07-357 4469; www.wingspan.co.nz; 1164 Paradise Valley Rd, Ngongotaha; adult/child $25/8; ☺ 9am-3pm) Wingspan is dedicated to conserving three threatened NZ birds: the falcon, the hawk and the owl. Learn about the birds in the museum display, then take a sneaky peek into the incubation area before walking through the all-weather aviary. Don't miss the 2pm flying display.

Paradise Valley Springs   WILDLIFE RESERVE
(☑ 07-348 9667; www.paradisevalleysprings.co.nz; 467 Paradise Valley Rd; adult/child $30/15; ☺ 8am-dusk) In Paradise Valley at the foot of Mt Ngongotaha, 8km from Rotorua, is Paradise Valley Springs, a 6-hectare park with trout springs, big slippery eels and various land-dwelling animals such as deer, alpacas, possums and a pride of lions (fed at 2.30pm). There's also a coffee shop and an elevated treetop walkway.

Agrodome   AGRICULTURAL
(Map p290; ☑ 07-357 1050; www.agrodome.co.nz; 141 Western Rd, Ngongotaha; 1hr tour adult/child/family $41/20/84.50, 1hr show $31/15.50/79.50, tour & show $51/25.50/118.50; ☺ 8.30am-5pm, shows 9.30am, 11am & 2.30pm, tours 10.40am, 12.10pm, 1.30pm & 3.40pm) Learn everything you need to know about sheep at the educational Agrodome. Shows include a parade of champion rams, a livestock auction, and shearing and doggy displays. The tour lets you check out farm animals including, among others, sheep. Other agro-attractions include a shearing-shed museum and cafe.

aMAZEme   MAZE
(Map p290; ☑ 07-357 5759; www.amazeme.co.nz; 1335 Paradise Valley Rd, Ngongotaha; adult/child/family $16/9/45; ☺ 9am-5pm) This amazing 1.4km maze is constructed from immaculately pruned, head-high escallonia hedge. Lose yourself (or the kids) in the endless spirals.

Northeast of Rotorua
◉ Sights & Activities
Hells Gate & Wai Ora Spa   VOLCANIC AREA, SPA
(Map p290; ☑ 07-345 3151; www.hellsgate.co.nz; SH30, Tikitere; admission adult/child/family $35/17.50/85, mud bath & spa $75/35/185, massage per 30/60min $85/130; ☺ 8.30am-8.30pm) Known as Tikitere to the Maori, Hells Gate is an impressive geothermal reserve 16km

northeast of Rotorua on the Whakatane road (SH30). Tikitere is an abbreviation of *Taku tiki i tere nei* (My youngest daughter has floated away), remembering the tragedy of a young girl jumping into a thermal pool. The English name originates from a 1934 visit by George Bernard Shaw. The reserve covers 10 hectares, with a 2.5km walking track to the various attractions, including a hot thermal waterfall. You can also see a master woodcarver at work, and learn about flax weaving and other Maori traditions.

Long regarded by Maori as a place of healing, Tikitere also houses the Wai Ora Spa, where you can get muddy with a variety of treatments. A courtesy shuttle to/from Rotorua is available.

Southeast of Rotorua
◉ Sights & Activities
Redwoods Whakarewarewa Forest   FOREST
(Map p290; www.redwoods.co.nz; Long Mile Rd, off Tarawera Rd; ☺ 5.30am-8.30pm) **FREE** This magical forest park is 3km southeast of town

---

WORTH A TRIP

WHIRINAKI FOREST PARK

This lush podocarp (conifer) forest park is 90km southeast of Rotorua off SH38, en route to Te Urewera National Park (take the turn-off at Te Whaiti to Minginui). Also here are canyons, waterfalls, lookouts and streams, plus the Oriuwaka Ecological Area and Arahaki Lagoon.

Walking tracks here vary in length and difficulty: the DOC booklet *Walks in Whirinaki Forest* ($2.50) details walking and camping options. Pick one up at DOC's Murupara visitor centre (☑ 07-366 1080; www.doc.govt.nz; SH38, Murupara; ☺ 9am-5pm Mon-Fri).

A good short walk is the Whirinaki Waterfalls Track (four hours return), which follows the Whirinaki River. Longer walks include the Whirinaki Track (two days), which can be combined with Te Hoe Track (four days). There's also a rampaging 16km mountain bike track here.

There are several accessible camping areas and 10 backcountry huts (free to $15) in the park; pay at the DOC office.

Around Rotorua

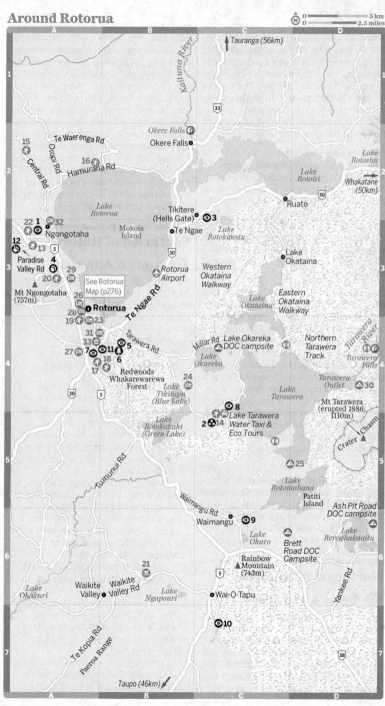

Around Rotorua

⦿ **Sights**
  1 Agrodome A3
  2 Buried Village C5
  3 Hells Gate & Wai Ora Spa C2
  4 Rainbow Springs A3
  5 Redwoods Gift Shop & Visitor
    Centre B4
  6 Redwoods Whakarewarewa Forest B4
  7 Te Puia A4
  8 The Landing C4
  9 Waimangu Volcanic Valley C6
 10 Wai-O-Tapu Thermal Wonderland C7
 11 Whakarewarewa Thermal Village B4
 12 Wingspan National Bird of Prey
    Centre A3

⊕ **Activities, Courses & Tours**
    Agroventures .... (see 13)
 13 aMAZEme A3
 14 Clearwater Cruises C5
 15 Farmhouse A2
 16 Hamurana Springs A2
    Helipro .... (see 7)
 17 Mountain Bike Rotorua A4
    Ogo .... (see 20)
 18 Planet Bike B4

 19 Rotorua Canopy Tours A4
 20 Skyline Rotorua A3
 21 Waikite Valley Thermal Pools B6
 22 Zorb A3

⊜ **Sleeping**
 23 Ann's Volcanic Motel A4
 24 Blue Lake Top 10 Holiday Park B4
 25 Hot Water Beach Campsite D5
 26 Kiwi Paka A3
 27 Rotorua Thermal Holiday Park A4
 28 Rotorua Top 10 Holiday Park A3
 29 Sandi's Bed & Breakfast A3
 30 Tarawera Outlet Campsite D4
 31 Tuscany Villas A4
 32 Waiteti Trout Stream Holiday
    Park A3

⊗ **Eating**
    Urbano Bistro .... (see 31)

⊕ **Entertainment**
 33 Copthorne Hotel Rotorua A4
    Holiday Inn Rotorua .... (see 33)
    Mitai Maori Village .... (see 20)

on Tarawera Rd. It was originally home to over 170 tree species (a few less now), planted from 1899 to see which could be grown successfully for timber. Radiata pine proved a hit (as evident throughout NZ), but it's the mighty Californian redwoods that give the park its grandeur today.

Clearly signposted walking tracks range from a half-hour wander through the Redwood Grove to an enjoyable whole-day route to the Blue and Green Lakes. Most walks start from the **Redwoods Gift Shop & Visitor Centre** (Map p290; ☎ 07-350 0110; www.redwoods.co.nz; ⊘ 8.30am-5.30pm Mon-Fri, 10am-5pm Sat & Sun Oct-Mar, 8.30am-4.30pm Mon-Fri, 10am-4pm Sat & Sun Apr-Sep), where you can get maps and view displays about the forest. Aside from walking, the park is great for picnics and acclaimed for its accessible **mountain biking**. Mountain Bike Rotorua (p280) and Planet Bike (p280) offer bike hire, across the park off Waipa State Mill Rd.

Buried Village   ARCHAEOLOGICAL SITE, MUSEUM
(Map p290; ☎ 07-362 8287; www.buriedvillage. co.nz; 1180 Tarawera Rd; adult/child/family $35/10/66; ⊘ 9am-5pm Nov-Mar, to 4.30pm Apr-Oct) Fifteen kilometres from Rotorua on Tarawera Rd, beyond the pretty Blue and Green Lakes, is the buried village of Te Wairoa, interred by the eruption of Mt Tarawera in 1886. Te Wairoa was the staging post for travellers coming to see the Pink and White Terraces. Today a museum houses objects dug from the ruins, and guides in period costume escort groups through the excavated sites. There's also a walk to the 30m **Te Wairoa Falls** and a teahouse if you're feeling more sedate.

Lake Tarawera   LAKE
(www.doc.govt.nz; Tarawera Rd) Tarawera means 'Burnt Spear', named by a visiting hunter who left his bird spears in a hut and on returning the following season found both the spears and hut had been burnt. The lake is picturesque and good for swimming, fishing, cruises and walks.

A good place to access the lake is at the **Landing** (Map p290), about 2km past the Buried Village. Here you'll find **Clearwater Cruises** (Map p290; ☎ 027 362 8590, 07-345 6688; www.clearwater.co.nz; per hr cruise vessel/self-drive runabout $550/140), which runs scenic cruises and self-drive boat options aboard a variety of vessels. Also here is the **Landing Café** (www.thelandinglaketarawera.co.nz; mains $15-30; ⊘ 10am-late), serving hearty mains like lamb rump and seafood chowder with beaut lake views. Also at the Landing is Lake Tarawera Water Taxi & Eco Tours (Map p290; ☑ 07-362 8080; www. ecotoursrotorua.co.nz; 1375 Tarawera Rd; from $55), which can take you anywhere on the lake, at any time: a trip to Hot Water Beach is $55.

There's a privately run camping ground (boat access only; bookings required) at Hot Water Beach (Map p290; ☑ 07-349 3463; www. whakarewarewa.com/tarawera; adult/child $10/5), and a DOC-managed site at Tarawera Outlet (Map p290; ☑ 07-323 6300; www.doc.govt.nz; adult/child $6/3). The Blue Lake Top 10 Holiday Park (Map p290; ☑ 0800 808 292, 07-362 8120; www.bluelaketop10.co.nz; 723 Tarawera Rd; campsites from $21, cabins $73-120, units $125-180; @ ⚥) offers camping next to the Blue Lake (good for swimming and kayaking), 6km before you get to Lake Tarawera; well run, it has spotless facilities and a handy range of cabins.

South of Rotorua

◎ Sights & Activities

Waimangu
Volcanic Valley
VOLCANIC AREA, SPRING

(Map p290; ☑ 07-366 6137; www.waimangu. com; 587 Waimangu Rd; adult/child walking tour $34.50/11, boat cruise $42.50/11; ☑ 8.30am-5pm daily, to 6pm Jan, last admission 3.30pm, 4.30pm Jan) This interesting thermal area was created during the eruption of Mt Tarawera in 1886 – geologically young! Waimangu (Black Water) refers to the dark, muddy colour of much of the water here.

The easy downhill stroll through the valley passes spectacular thermal and volcanic features, including Inferno Crater Lake, where overflowing water can reach 80°C, and Frying Pan Lake, the largest hot spring in the world. The walk continues down to Lake Rotomahana (meaning 'Warm Lake'), from where you can either get a shuttle ride back up to where you started or take a 45-minute boat trip on the lake, past steaming cliffs and the former site of the Pink and White Terraces.

Waimangu is 20 minutes south of Rotorua, 14km along SH5 (towards Taupo) and then 6km from the marked turn-off.

Wai-O-Tapu Thermal
Wonderland
VOLCANIC AREA, GEYSER

(Map p290; ☑ 07-366 6333; www.waiotapu.co.nz; 201 Waiotapu Loop Rd, off SH5; adult/child/family $32.50/11/80; ☑ 8.30am-5pm, last admission 3.45pm) Wai-O-Tapu (Sacred Waters) is a fairly commercial operation with a lot of interesting geothermal features packed into a small area, including the boiling, multi-hued Champagne Pool, bubbling mud pool, stunning mineral terraces and Lady Knox Geyser, which spouts off (with a little prompting from an organic soap) punctually at 10.15am and gushes up to 20m for about an hour (be here by 9.45am to see it).

Wai-O-Tapu is 27km south of Rotorua along SH5 (towards Taupo), and a further 2km from the marked turn-off.

Waikite Valley Thermal Pools
SWIMMING

(Map p290; ☑ 07-333 1861; www.hotpools.co.nz; 648 Waikite Valley Rd; public pools adult/child/family $15/8/38, private pools 40min $18; ☑ 10am-9pm) Around 35km south of Rotorua are these excellent open-air pools, formalised in the 1970s but utilised for centuries before then. There are four main pools, two more relaxing, smaller pools, and four private spas, all ranging from 35°C to 40°C. There's also a cafe and camping (adult/child unpowered sites $20/10, powered sites $22/12; pools free for campers).

To get here, turn right off SH5 opposite the Wai-O-Tapu turn-off, and continue 6km (worth the drive if only for the gorgeous valley view as you come over the hill).

BAY OF PLENTY

The Bay of Plenty stretches along the pohutukawa-studded coast from Waihi Beach to Opotiki and inland as far as the Kaimai Range. This is where New Zealanders have come on holiday for generations, lapping up salt-licked activities and lashings of sunshine.

Tauranga

POP 114,800

Tauranga (pronounced 'toe-rung-ah') has been booming since the 1990s and remains one of NZ's fastest-growing cities. It's also NZ's busiest port – with petrol refineries and mountains of coal and lumber – but it's beach-seeking holidaymakers who have seen the old workhorse reborn as a show pony. Restaurants and bars line the vamped-up waterfront, fancy hotels rise high, and the once-sleepy burbs of Mt Maunganui and Papamoa have woken up to new prosperity. This is about as Riviera as NZ gets. Online, www.downtowntauranga.co.nz is a commercial but useful resource.

Tauranga

0 — 200 m
0 — 0.1 miles

Tauranga

◎ Top Sights
1 Tauranga Art Gallery B3

◎ Sights
2 Brain Watkins House............................A4
3 Elms Mission House A1
4 Mission Cemetery B1
5 Monmouth Redoubt B2
6 Robbins Park B2

⊕ Activities, Courses & Tours
7 Dive Zone A4

⊟ Sleeping
8 City Suites..A2
9 Harbour City Motor Inn A3
10 Harbourside City Backpackers...........B3
11 Hotel on Devonport B4
12 Loft 109 ....B4
13 Roselands Motel A1
14 Trinity Wharf B1

⊗ Eating
15 City Markets B3
16 Collar & Thai B4
17 Elizabeth Cafe & Larder A4
18 Fresh Fish Markets B2
19 Harbourside B4
20 Mediterraneo Café...............................B4
21 Shima B3
22 Zeytin on the Strand...........................B3

⊖ Drinking & Nightlife
23 Brew..B3
24 Crown & Badger...................................B3
25 Phoenix...B3

⊕ Entertainment
Rialto Cinemas ....(see 16)

ROTORUA & THE BAY OF PLENTY TAURANGA

⊙ Sights

★ **Tauranga Art Gallery** GALLERY
(☏ 07-578 7933; www.artgallery.org.nz; cnr Wharf & Willow Sts; ⊙10am-4.30pm) **FREE** The Tauranga Art Gallery presents historic and contemporary art, and houses a permanent collection along with frequently changing local and visiting exhibitions. The building itself is a former bank, although you'd hardly know it – it's an altogether excellent space with no obvious compromise (cue applause). Touring the ground-floor and mezzanine galleries will take an hour or so.

Elms Mission House HISTORIC BUILDING
(www.theelms.org.nz; 15 Mission St; house adult/child $5/50c, gardens free; ⊙house 2-4pm Wed, Sat & Sun, gardens 9am-5pm daily) Built in 1847, Elms Mission House is the oldest building in the Bay of Plenty. Furnished in period style, it sits among other well-preserved mission buildings in leafy gardens. The spooky

Mission Cemetery (cnr Marsh St & Dive Cres; ⊙24hr) lies not far away – a shady tangle of trees and headstones.

Classic Flyers NZ MUSEUM
(☏ 07-572 4000; www.classicflyersnz.com; 8 Jean Batten Dr; adult/child/family $10/5/25; ⊙10am-4pm) Out near the airport, Classic Flyers NZ is an interesting aviation museum (biplanes, retired US Airforce jets, helicopters etc) with a buzzy on-site cafe.

Monmouth Redoubt ARCHAEOLOGICAL SITE, PARK
(Monmouth St; ⊙24hr) **FREE** Shaded by huge pohutukawa trees, spooky Monmouth Redoubt was a fortified site during the Maori Wars. Next door is **Robbins Park** (Cliff Rd), a verdant pocket of roses with sweeping views across to Mt Maunganui. At the foot of the

Redoubt on the end of the Strand is **Te Awa nui Waka**, a replica Maori canoe, on display in an open-sided building.

Minden Lookout
LOOKOUT

(Minden Rd) From Minden Lookout, about 10km west of Tauranga towards Katikati, there's a superb view back over the cranes in Tauranga Harbour and across the Bay of Plenty. To get there, take SH2 to Te Puna and turn off south on Minden Rd; the lookout is about 3km up the road.

Brain Watkins House
HISTORIC BUILDING

(☑ 07-578 1835; www.taurangahistorical.blogspot.co.nz; 233 Cameron Rd; adult/child/family $4/2/10; ☺ 2-4pm Sun) A demure Victorian villa stranded on a hill as the roads around it grew, Brain Watkins House (no, not Brian) was built in 1881 from kauri (wood) and remains one of Tauranga's best-preserved colonial homes.

Mills Reef Winery
WINERY

(☑ 07-576 8800; www.millsreef.co.nz; 143 Moffat Rd, Bethlehem; ☺ 10am-5pm) Stately Mills Reef, 7km from the town centre at Bethlehem, has tastings of its award-winning wines (dig the chardonnay) and a refined restaurant (read: great food but not much fun) that's open for lunch daily and dinner by reservation (mains $25 to $39).

Huria Marae
MARAE

(☑ 07-578 7838; www.huriamarae.co.nz; Te Kaponga St, Judea) FREE Huria Marae is on a nondescript suburban street, but has sensational carvings both inside and out. Call to organise permission to visit, or to book a cultural experience (large groups only).

🏃 Activities

The free *Tauranga City Walkways* pamphlet (from the i-SITE) details walks around Tauranga and Mt Maunganui. History buffs should pick up the free *Historic Tauranga* brochure and stroll around the town's cache of historic sites.

Adventure Bay of Plenty
KAYAKING, MOUNTAIN BIKING

(☑ 0800 238 267; www.adventurebop.co.nz; 2hr/half-day/full-day tours from $95/125/180) Offers an enticing array of adventure tours by kayak, mountain bike and horse. Half-day paddles around Mt Maunganui with a stop on Matakana Island cost $150/125 per adult/child. A two-to-three hour cycle around Tauranga costs $95.

Adrenalin Forest
EXTREME SPORTS

(☑ 07-929 8724; www.adrenalin-forest.co.nz; Upper Pyes Pa Rd, TECT All Terrain Park; adult/child $42/27; ☺ 10am-2.30pm daily, closed Mon & Tue Jun-Aug) About 26km from Tauranga en route to Rotorua is this heart-starter: a series of high-wires, flying foxes, platforms and rope bridges strung through a grove of tall conifers. There are six different routes of increasing difficulty to test your nerve.

Waimarino Adventure Park
KAYAKING, WATER SPORTS

(☑ 0800 456 996, 07-576 4233; www.waimarino.com; 36 Taniwha Pl; kayak tours from $65, kayak hire per hr/day $26/55, park day-pass adult/child $40/32; ☺ 10am-6pm Sep-Apr, 10am-5pm May-Aug) On the banks of the Wairoa River 8km west of town, Waimarino offers freedom kayak hire, self-guided kayak tours, sea kayaking trips and a magical Glowworm Tour ($120 per person) at McLaren Falls Park. The adventure park here has all kinds of watery distractions: a kayak slide, a diving board, a ropes course, water-walking zorbs, warm pools, and a human catapult called 'The Blob' – intense!

Kaimai Mamaku Forest Park
TRAMPING

(www.doc.govt.nz; SH29) FREE The backdrop to the Western Bay of Plenty is the rugged 70km-long Kaimai Mamaku Forest Park, 35km southwest of Tauranga, with tramps for the intrepid and huts (per person per night $5 to $15) and campsites ($6). For more info see DOC's pamphlet *Kaimai to Coast* ($2.50), or contact **Kaimai New Zealand Tours** (☑ 07-552 5257; www.kaimai-new-zealand-tours.com) to arrange a guided tramp.

Dolphin Blue
WILDLIFE TOUR

(☑ 027 666 8047; www.dolphinblue.co.nz; day trips adult/child $150/100; ☺ departs 8.30am) 🐬 Unhurried, small-group (15 people maximum) day trips across Tauranga Harbour and out onto the Bay of Plenty in pursuit of pods of dolphins. When you find them, you can jump in and splash around with them.

Dolphin Seafaris
WILDLIFE TOUR

(☑ 0800 326 8747, 07-577 0105; www.nzdolphin.com; half-day trip adult/child $140/95; ☺ departs Tauranga 8am, Mt Maunganui 8.15am) 🐬 Eco-attuned dolphin-spotting trips where you can get into the water and swim with the big fish (...sorry, mammals).

Blue Ocean Charters
FISHING

(☑ 0800 224 278, 07-544 3072; www.blueocean.co.nz; trips from $120) Fishing, diving and sightseeing trips (including one to Tuhua Island) on the TS *Ohorere,* MV *Te Kuia* and MV *Ratahi.*

Dive Zone
DIVING

(☑ 07-578 4050; www.divezone.co.nz; 213 Cameron Rd; trips/courses from $120/600; ⊘ 8am-6pm Mon-Fri, 7.30am-4pm Sat, 7.30am-2pm Sun) PADI-qualifying courses or trips to local wrecks and reefs, plus gear rental.

Elements Watersports
WATER SPORTS

(☑ 0800 486 729; www.elementsonline.co.nz; lessons from $20) If you're new to the sea and want to splash safely into the big blue, Elements Watersports runs sailing, windsurfing and jetskiing lessons, and has gear for hire.

Tauranga Tandem Skydiving
SKYDIVING

(☑ 07-574 8533; www.tandemskydive.co.nz; 2 Kittyhawk Way, Tauranga Airport; jumps 8000/10,000/12,000ft $285/325/375) Tauranga Tandem Skydiving offers jumps from three different heights, with views of Whakaari (White Island), Mt Ruapehu and across the Bay of Plenty on the way down.

☞ Tours

Tauranga Tasting Tours
GUIDED TOUR

(☑ 07-544 1383; www.tastingtours.co.nz; tours $130) Whips around a local brewery, Mills Reef and Morton Estate wineries, and back to town for cocktails.

No.8 Farm Tours
GUIDED TOUR

(☑ 07-579 3981; www.no8farmtours.co.nz; tours adult/child from $89/69) Half-day Tauranga tours, plus 4WD tours of a working NZ farm, featuring shearing, milking, sheep dogs, deer and morning tea.

Aerius Helicopters
SCENIC FLIGHTS

(☑ 0800 864 354; www.aerius.co.nz; flights from $65) Local flights and aerial excursions as far away as Lake Tarawera, Rotorua and Whakaari (White Island), departing Tauranga.

Gyrate
SCENIC FLIGHTS

(☑ 021 038 0760, 0800 3592 4976; www.gyrate.co.nz; flights from $135) Scenic flights around Tauranga/Mt Maunganui in a gyroplane (the jetski of the sky).

Shore Trips & Tours
GUIDED TOUR

(☑ 07-574 1779; www.shoretripsandtours.com; half-/full-day tours from $49/90) Trips around Tauranga's sights and enticements aimed at cruise-boat passengers finding their land legs. Longer tours to Rotorua also available.

✦✦ Festivals & Events

National Jazz Festival
MUSIC, FOOD & WINE

(www.jazz.org.nz) An Easter extravaganza of big blowers and scoobee-doobee-doo, with concerts and food and wine galore.

Tauranga Arts Festival
ARTS

(www.taurangafestival.co.nz) Kicking off on Labour weekend in October (in odd-numbered years), showcasing dance, comedy, plays and other things arty.

🛏 Sleeping

Harbourside City Backpackers
HOSTEL $

(☑ 07-579 4066; www.backpacktauranga.co.nz; 105 The Strand; dm/tw/d from $29/74/74; @ 🕸) Soak up the sea airs at this sociable hostel (a former hotel), deliciously handy to the Strand's bars and restaurants. Rooms are smallish but clean, and you'll spend more time on the awesome roof terrace anyway. There's no parking, but down the road is a public car park that empties out at the right time.

Loft 109
HOSTEL $

(☑ 07-579 5638; www.loft109.co.nz; 109 Devonport Rd, upstairs; dm/d/tr from $28/76/90; @ 🕸) This small, central hostel feels like somebody's flat, with an intimate kitchen-lounge and a cute little balcony over Devonport St. It's bright, with plenty of skylights and a gas fire for colder days. Super-relaxed without being lax about things like security or boozy badness.

Tauranga YHA
HOSTEL $

(☑ 07-578 5064, 0800 278 299; www.yha.co.nz; 171 Elizabeth St; dm from $29, d with/without bathroom $110/90; @ 🕸) 🌱 A well-kept, deceptively big YHA on the edge of town, with a large grassy backyard and a nearby mangrove swamp boardwalk to explore. Inviting dorms have individual lockers, and there's info available on local walking trails and a noticeboard for all things green.

Just the Ducks
Nuts Backpackers
HOSTEL $

(☑ 07-576 1366; www.justtheducksnuts.co.nz; 6 Vale St; dm from $27, with/without bathroom s $66/56, d $78/70; @ 🕸) Just out of the town centre, this friendly place has colourful rooms, a fulsome library, TVs strewn about and quirky touches like flowers planted in a bath-tub and duck-themed toilets – like a university share-house minus the parties. Free shuttles to/from the bus stop; self-contained flats also available.

Tauranga Tourist Park HOLIDAY PARK $
(☑ 07-578 3323; www.taurangatouristpark.co.nz; 9 Mayfair St; unpowered/powered sites from $30/35, cabins from $55; @ 🛜) The layout at this harbourside holiday park feels a bit tight (don't expect rolling acres), but it's well maintained, clean and tidy. Aim for a site down by the bay under the pohotukawa trees.

Roselands Motel MOTEL $$
(☑ 07-578 2294, 0800 363 093; www.roselands. co.nz; 21 Brown St; d/ste from $110/135; 🛜) Tarted up with splashes of orange paint and new linen, this sweet, old-style motel is in a quiet but central location. Expect spacious units (all with kitchenettes), friendly first-name-basis hosts and new TVs. Nice one.

Harbour City Motor Inn MOTEL $$
(☑ 07-571 1435, 0800 253 525; www.tauranga-harbourcity.co.nz; 50 Wharf St; d/1-bedroom from $150/170; 🛜) With a winning location right in the middle of town (and plenty of parking), this newish, lemon-yellow motor inn has all the mod cons. There are spa baths in each room, and friendly staff who can offer sound advice on your itinerary.

City Suites HOTEL $$
(☑ 07-577 1480; www.citysuites.co.nz; 32 Cameron Rd; r from $155; 🛜▨) The spacious rooms here (all with either terrace or balcony) have a rather regal feel, with king-sized beds and full kitchens. A swimming pool, free wi-fi and secure parking complete the list of essentials for wandering business bods.

Ambassador Motor Inn MOTEL $$
(☑ 0800 735 294, 07-578 5665; www.ambassador-motorinn.co.nz; 9 Fifteenth Ave; d/f from $110/175; 🛜▨) This tidy motel on the edge of town has noise-reducing glass for peaceful sleeps. Some rooms have spa baths; all have kitchen facilities. It's not overtly ambassadorial and a bit out of the way, but it's spotlessly clean and the new owners are keen to make a good impression.

Hotel on Devonport HOTEL $$$
(☑ 07-578 2668; www.hotelondevonport.net.nz; 72 Devonport Rd; d/ste from $165/205; @ 🛜) City-centre Devonport is top of the town, with bay-view rooms, noise-reducing glass, slick interiors and sassy staff, all of which appeal to business travellers and upmarket weekenders. Help yourself to the bowl of apples in the lobby.

Trinity Wharf HOTEL $$$
(☑ 07-577 8700, 0800 577 8700; www.trinitywharf. co.nz; 51 Dive Cres; d from $180; @ 🛜▨) This blocky three-storey number near the harbour bridge has a slick, contemporary lobby – all white tiles and spiky pot plants – leading to the upmarket in-house restaurant Halo (mains $15 to $36). Rooms are supersized and luxurious in tones *au naturel*. Amenities include an underutilised gym, infinity-edge swimming pool and free wi-fi. Very flashy.

✗ Eating

★**Grindz Café** CAFE $
(☑ 07-579 0017; www.facebook.com/pages/grindz-cafe/110512979024824; 50 First Ave; meals $5-15; ⊙ 7am-4pm Mon-Fri, 8am-3.30pm Sat, 8am-3pm Sun; 🛜 ✍) The undisputed highlight of wide-open First Ave is Grindz, a hip cafe with scattered footpath tables. Inside it's a roomy, split-level affair, with funky wallpaper, antiques and retro relics. Bagels, vegie stacks, muffins, cakes and salads are the order of the day, plus creative coffee (try 'The Trough' if you're sleepy: a four-shot soup bowl of caffeine heaven). Free wi-fi too.

Fresh Fish Markets FISH & CHIPS $
(☑ 07-578 1789; 1 Dive Cres; meals from $6; ⊙ 11am-8pm) A local legend serving up fresh fish and chips, with hexagonal outdoor tables on the water's edge and plenty of seagulls to keep you company.

Mediterraneo Café CAFE, MEDITERRANEAN $
(The Med; ☑ 07-577 0487; www.mediterraneocafe. co.nz; 62 Devonport Rd; mains $8-20; ⊙ 7am-4pm Mon-Fri, 7.30am-4pm Sat, 8am-4pm Sun; ✍) A hot spot reeling with regulars enjoying terrific coffee and scrumptious all-day breakfasts. Order from the blackboard or from the cabinet crammed with sandwiches, salads, flans and cakes. Lunchtime crowds can be frantic (but the chicken salad is worth it). Cute staff, and plenty of gluten-free and vegetarian options.

City Markets SELF CATERING $
(cnr Willow & Hamilton Sts; ⊙ 9am-5pm Mon-Fri, to noon Sat) For fresh fundamentals (fruit and veg, bread, eggs, milk), City Markets is a block back from the Strand.

Pak 'n Save SUPERMARKET $
(www.paknsave.co.nz; 476 Cameron Rd; ⊙ 8am-10pm) A short drive south of town.

Elizabeth Cafe & Larder MODERN NZ, BAR $$

(📞07-579 0950; www.elizabethcafe.co.nz; 247 Cameron Rd; mains breakfast & lunch $10-20, dinner $24-34; ⏰7am-4pm Mon & Tue, 7am-5pm Wed, 7am-9pm Thu & Fri, 8am-9pm Sat, 8am-4pm Sun) 'Eat, drink, enjoy' at Elizabeth, a hip new cafe-bar on the ground floor of a four-storey downtown office block. Predictably, many of the customers drift down from upstairs, but you don't need a suit to enjoy a knockout Moroccan lamb salad with a glass of Central Otago pinot gris. Interesting industrial aesthetics and Peroni on tap.

Zeytin on the Strand TURKISH $$

(📞07-579 0099; www.zeytin.co.nz; 83 The Strand; mains $20-30; ⏰11.30am-3pm & 4.30pm-late Tue-Sun; 🖋) Ask the locals to name their favourite restaurant, and odds-on they'll name Zeytin – a Turkish delight. Authentic Turkish fare, with something for everyone: kebabs, delicious homemade breads, dips, healthy salads, wood-fired pizza and a few exotic surprises.

Collar & Thai THAI $$

(📞07-577 6655; www.collarandthai.co.nz; Goddards Centre, 21 Devonport Rd; mains lunch $14-17, dinner $21-32; ⏰11.30am-2pm Mon-Sat, 5-10pm daily) No tie required at this upstairs eatery that artfully elaborates on Thai standards and uses plenty of fresh seafood. Perfect for a pre-movie meal (the Rialto Cinemas are right next door). Good-value lunch specials, too.

Shima JAPANESE, KOREAN $$

(📞07-571 1382; www.nzshima.co.nz; 15 Wharf St; mains $12-30; ⏰noon-3pm & 6pm-late) There are flashier Japanese joints in town, but Shima endures as a simple, unpretentious sushi and sashimi bar, hung with fans, umbrellas and lanterns. Bento boxes and set-price menus are great bang for your buck.

★Harbourside MODERN NZ $$$

(📞07-571 0520; www.harbourside.co.nz; Railway Bridge, The Strand; mains $26-38; ⏰11.30am-2.30pm & 5.30pm-late) In a marvellously atmospheric 100-year-old boathouse at the end of the Strand, Harbourside is the place for a romantic dinner, with lapping waves and the overhead railway bridge arching out over the harbour. The roast duck with Chinese cabbage, lime and chilli is hard to beat, or you can just swing by for a moody pre-dinner drink.

Somerset Cottage MODERN NZ $$$

(📞07-576 6889; www.somersetcottage.co.nz; 30 Bethlehem Rd, Bethlehem; mains $30-40; ⏰11.30am-2.30pm Wed-Fri, 6-9pm Mon-Sat) The most awarded restaurant in the Bay, Somerset Cottage is a simple-but-elegant venue for that special treat. The food is highly seasonal, made from the best NZ ingredients and impressively executed without being too fussy. Standout dishes include baked cheese soufflé, duck with coconut kumara and the famous liquorice ice cream.

🍷 Drinking & Entertainment

Brew CRAFT BEER, PUB

(www.brewpub.co.nz; 107 The Strand; ⏰4pm-late Mon-Thu, 11am-late Wed-Sun) The long concrete bar here has room for plenty of elbows, and plenty of glasses of Croucher's crafty seasonal ales, pilseners and stouts (pray the Ethiopian coffee stout is on tap). The vibe is social, with communal tables and plates of bar food designed to share ($8 to $28). And no TV! Winner.

Phoenix PUB

(www.thephoenixtauranga.co.nz; 67 The Strand; ⏰10.30am-late Mon-Fri, 8.30am-late Sat & Sun) Rising phoenix-like from the northern end of the Strand, this sprawling new gastropub pours fine Monteith's beers (once niche, now mainstream) and serves meaty pub meals (mains $20 to $34; try the pork ribs). Dressed-up drinkers; Red Hot Chilli Peppers on the stereo.

Crown & Badger PUB

(www.crownandbadger.co.nz; cnr The Strand & Wharf St; ⏰9am-late) A particularly convincing black-painted Brit boozer that does pukka pints of Tennent's and Guinness, and food along the lines of bangers-and-mash and BLTs (mains $17 to $29). Things get more energetic on weekends with live bands.

Rialto Cinemas CINEMA

(📞07-577 0445; www.rialtotauranga.co.nz; Goddards Centre, 21 Devonport Rd; tickets adult/child $18.50/12.50; ⏰opens 30min before screenings) Home to the Tauranga Film Society, the Rialto is the best spot in town to catch a flick: classic, offbeat, art-house and international. And you can sip a coffee or a glass of wine in the darkness.

ℹ Information

Paper Plus (17 Grey St; ⏰8.30am-5.30pm Mon-Fri, 9am-4pm Sat, 10am-3pm Sun) The local NZ Post branch.

Tauranga Hospital (☑07-579 8000; www.bopdhb.govt.nz; 375 Cameron Rd; ⊘24hr) A couple of kilometres south of town.

Tauranga i-SITE (☑07-578 8103; www.bayofplentynz.com; 8 Wharf St; ⊘8.30am-5.30pm, reduced winter hours; ☎) Local tourist information, bookings, InterCity bus tickets and DOC maps.

❶ Getting There & Away

AIR

Air New Zealand (☑07-577 7300; www.airnewzealand.co.nz; cnr Devonport Rd & Elizabeth St; ⊘9am-5pm Mon-Fri, 10am-1pm Sat) Has daily direct flights to Auckland, Wellington and Christchurch.

BUS

Twin City Express buses run twice daily Monday to Friday between Tauranga/Mt Maunganui and Rotorua via Te Puke ($11.60, 1½ hours).

InterCity tickets and timetables are available at the i-SITE. Destinations include the following:

DESTINATION	PRICE ($)	DURATION (HR)	FREQUENCY (DAILY)
Auckland	46	4	3
Hamilton	33	2	2
Rotorua	32	1½	2
Taupo	52	3	2
Wellington	55	9	1

Naked Bus offers substantial fare savings when you book in advance. Destinations include the following:

DESTINATION	PRICE ($)	DURATION (HR)	FREQUENCY (DAILY)
Auckland	16	3¼	3
Hamilton	10	3	2
Napier	35	5	2
Rotorua	10	1	3
Taupo	15	3	2
Wellington	23	9	1
Whakatane	18	3	1

Shuttle Bus

A couple of companies can pick you up at Auckland or Rotorua airports and bus you to Tauranga (though you'll pay upwards of $100 for the privilege).

Luxury Airport Shuttles (☑07-547 4444; www.luxuryairportshuttles.co.nz) Also shunts travellers between Tauranga Airport and Tauranga (from $10).

Apollo Connect Shuttles (☑07-218 0791; www.taurangashuttles.co.nz)

CAR

If you're heading to Hamilton on route K, the toll road costs $1.50 (pay at the toll booth).

❶ Getting Around

BICYCLE

Cycle Tauranga (☑0800 253 525, 07-571 1435; www.cycletauranga.co.nz; Harbour City Motor Inn, 50 Wharf St; per half-/full day $29/49) Has hybrid road-trail bikes for hire, including helmets, locks, saddle bags and maps. Tours also available.

BUS

Tauranga's bright yellow Bay Hopper buses run to most locations around the area, including Mt Maunganui ($3, 15 minutes) and Papamoa ($3, 30 minutes). There's a central stop on Wharf St; timetables available from the i-SITE.

CAR

Numerous car-rental agencies have offices in Tauranga, including **Rent-a-Dent** (☑0800 736 823, 07-578 1772; www.rentadent.co.nz; 19 Fifteenth Ave; ⊘8am-5pm Mon-Fri, 8am-noon Sat).

TAXI

A taxi from the centre of Tauranga to the airport or Mt Maunganui costs around $20. Call **Tauranga Mount Taxis** (☑07-578 6086; www.taurangataxis.co.nz).

Mt Maunganui

POP 30,400

Named after the hulking 232m hill that punctuates the sandy peninsula occupied by the township, up-tempo Mt Maunganui is often just called 'the Mount', or Mauao, which translates as 'caught by the light of day'. It's considered part of greater Tauranga, but really it's an enclave unto itself, with great cafes and restaurants, hip bars and fab beaches. Sun-seekers flock to the Mount in summer, supplied by an increasing number of 10-storey apartment towers studding the spit. Online, see www.mountmaunganui.org.nz for information.

❂ Sights & Activities

The Mount lays claim to being NZ's premier **surfing** city (they teach surfing at high school!). You can carve up the waves at **Mount Beach**, which has lovely beach

Mt Maunganui

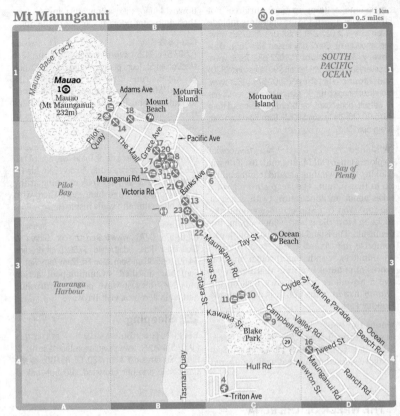

Mt Maunganui

◎ Top Sights
1 Mauao..A1

✦ Activities, Courses & Tours
2 Mount Hot Pools..................................A1
3 Mount Surfshop...................................B2
4 Rock House...C4

🛏 Sleeping
5 Beachside Holiday Park.....................B1
6 Belle Mer...C2
7 Mission Belle Motel............................B2
8 Mount Backpackers............................B2
9 Mt Maunganui B&B.............................C4
10 Pacific Coast Lodge &
    Backpackers......................................C3
11 Seagulls Guesthouse B&B.................C3
12 Westhaven Motel................................B2

✖ Eating
Drawing Room.............................(see 15)
13 Kwang Chow..B2
14 Mount Bistro..B2
15 Mount Mainstreet Farmers
    Market..B2
16 New World...D4
17 Providores Urban Food Store...........B2
18 Slowfish...B1
19 Thai Khan Koon...................................B3

◐ Drinking & Nightlife
20 Astrolabe..B2
21 Latitude 37...B2
22 Major Tom's..B3

✦ Entertainment
23 Bay City Cinemas................................B2

breaks and a 100m artificial surf reef not far offshore. Learn-to-surf operators include **Hibiscus** (☑ 027 279 9687, 07-575 3792; www.surfschool.co.nz; 2hr/2-day lesson $85/165), **Discovery Surf School** (☑ 027 632 7873; www.discoverysurf.co.nz; 2hr lesson $90, 4 lessons $320) and **Mount Surfshop** (☑ 07-575 9133; www.mountsurfshop.co.nz; 96 Maunganui Rd; rental per hr wetsuit/bodyboard/surfboard/paddleboard from $5/5/10/20, 2hr lesson $80; ⊙ 9am-5pm Mon-Sat, 10am-5pm Sun).

★ **Mauao**   MOUNTAIN, LOOKOUT
Explore Mauao (Mt Maunganui) itself on the walking trails winding around it and leading up to the summit. The steep **summit walk** takes about an hour return (with a rest at the top). You can also clamber around the rocks on **Moturiki Island**, which adjoins the peninsula. The island and the base of Mauao comprise the **Mauao Base Track** (3½km, 45 minutes), wandering through magical groves of pohutukawa trees that bloom between November and January. Pick up the *Mauao* map from the info desk at Beachside Holiday Park.

Mount Hot Pools   SWIMMING
(www.tcal.co.nz; 9 Adams Ave; adult/child/family $11/8/31; ⊙ 6am-10pm Mon-Sat, 8am-10pm Sun) If you've worked up a sweat walking up and down Mauao, take a long relaxing soak at these hotwater pools at the foot of the hill.

Canoe & Kayak   KAYAKING
(☑ 07-574 7415; www.canoeandkayak.co.nz; 3/5 MacDonald St; tours per person from $99) Canoe & Kayak runs 2½-hour kayaking trips around Mauao checking out seals and rock formations and hearing local legends, plus three-hour nocturnal glowworm paddles in nearby McLarens Falls Park.

Rock House   ROCK CLIMBING
(www.therockhouse.co.nz; 9 Triton Ave; adult/child $16.50/14.50, gear hire extra; ⊙ noon-9pm Tue-Fri, 10am-6pm Sat & Sun) Try rock climbing at the Rock House, a huge blue steel shed with huge blue climbing walls inside it.

Baywave   SWIMMING
(☑ 07-575 0276; www.tcal.co.nz; cnr Girven & Gloucester Rds; adult/child $7.50/5, hydroslide $4.60; ⊙ 5.30am-9pm Mon-Fri, 7am-7pm Sat & Sun) For unsalted swimming-pool action plus NZ's biggest wave pool, a hydroslide and aqua aerobics, visit Baywave.

🛏 Sleeping

Seagulls Guesthouse B&B   B&B, HOSTEL $
(☑ 07-574 2099; www.seagullsguesthouse.co.nz; 12 Hinau St; dm/s/d/f from $30/65/85/110; @ 🛜) Can't face another crowded, alcohol-soaked

---

THE WRECK OF THE RENA

On 5 October 2011, the 47,000-tonne cargo ship MV *Rena*, loaded with 1368 containers and 1900 tonnes of fuel oil, ran aground on Astrolabe Reef, 22km off the coast of Mt Maunganui. The ship had been attempting to enter Tauranga Harbour, NZ's busiest port, but inexplicably hit one of the most consistently charted obstacles in the way. Pitched acutely on the reef with a rupturing hull, the *Rena* started spilling oil into the sea and shedding containers from its deck. Over subsequent days, disbelieving locals watched as oil slicks, containers and dead fish and seabirds washed up on their glorious beaches.

The blame game began: the captain? The owners? The company that chartered the vessel? Thousands of volunteers pitched in to help with the clean-up. Salvors eventually managed to remove most of the oil from the ship, but on 8 January 2012 the *Rena* finally broke in two, spilling remnant oil and dozens more containers into the sea. The stern section subsequently slipped below the surface.

With the initial focus on preventing an oil spill, the elephant in the corner of the room – the *Rena* herself – seemed a problem too large. With refloating the ship no longer an option, debate raged on what to do: drag the bow section off the rocks too? A future dive site for the Bay of Plenty? At the time of writing the plan was to cut the bow section down to 1m below the water line, and remove the four-storey accommodation tower from the submerged stern.

The grounding has been an environmental and economic disaster, but long-term impacts are hard to gauge: local businesses suffered at the time but are back in full swing, and the beautiful beaches are clean again. See www.renaproject.co.nz for updates, or ask a local for their take on the situation (a sure-fire converstaion starter!).

hostel? On a quiet street not far from town, Seagulls is a gem: an immaculate, upmarket backpackers where the emphasis is on peaceful enjoyment of one's surrounds rather than wallowing in the excesses of youth (not that there's anything wrong with that). The best rooms have bathrooms and TVs. Free wi-fi.

Pacific Coast Lodge & Backpackers
HOSTEL $

(☏ 0800 666 622, 07-574 9601; www.pacificcoastlodge.co.nz; 432 Maunganui Rd; dm/d from $27/78; @ 🛜) Not far from the action, this efficiently run, sharp-looking hostel is sociable but not party-focused, with drinkers gently encouraged to migrate into town after 10pm. Purpose-built bunkrooms are spacious and adorned with beachy murals. Free bikes and surfboards.

Beachside Holiday Park
HOLIDAY PARK $

(☏ 07-575 4471; www.mountbeachside.co.nz; 1 Adams Ave; campsites from $35, on-site vans $60-90, cabins $80-130; @) With three different camping areas nooked into the foot of Mt Maunganui itself, this community-run park has spectacular camping with all the requisite facilities, plus it's handy to the Mount Hot Pools (discounts for campers) and a strip of good eateries. Reception is the local info centre.

Mount Backpackers
HOSTEL $

(☏ 07-575 0860; www.mountbackpackers.co.nz; 87 Maunganui Rd; dm/tw/tr from $25/80/90; @ 🛜) A tidy hostel on the main drag, bolstered by location – close to the beach and a mere stagger from the Mount's best restaurants and bars – plus extras like cheap surfboard and bike hire and discounted surf lessons.

Cosy Corner Holiday Park
HOLIDAY PARK $

(☏ 07-575 5899, 0800 684 654; www.cosycorner.co.nz; 40 Ocean Beach Rd; campsites from $40, cabins & flats $70-120; @ 🛜 🏊) This compact, spartan camping ground has a sociable feel, with barbecues, trampolines and a games room. Handy to the beach, too (access via a little path just across the road). New hot tub!

Mission Belle Motel
MOTEL $$

(☏ 0800 202 434, 07-575 2578; www.missionbellemotel.co.nz; cnr Victoria Rd & Pacific Ave; d/f from $130/190; 🛜) With a distinctly Tex-Mex exterior (like something out of an old Clint Eastwood movie), this family-run motel goes all modern inside, with especially good two-storey family rooms with large bathtubs, plus sheltered barbecue and courtyard areas.

Westhaven Motel
MOTEL $$

(☏ 07-575 4753; www.westhavenmotel.co.nz; 27a The Mall; units $100-210; 🛜) The 1969 architecture here is funky, but the new owners are modernising things room-by-room (get in now if you're a retro fan!). Full kitchens are perfect for self-caterers, and it's an easy walk to the shops and restaurants. The most affordable motel in miles.

Mt Maunganui B&B
B&B $$

(☏ 07-575 4013; www.mountbednbreakfast.co.nz; 463 Maunganui Rd; s/d incl cooked breakfast from $70/100; @ 🛜) This good-value five-room B&B on the main road into town offers a cosy guest lounge, basic shared kitchen, pool table, barbecue and cable TV. The two rooms at the front cop a bit of traffic noise, but the rest are fine. Good for groups.

Belle Mer
HOTEL, APARTMENTS $$$

(☏ 07-575 0011, 0800 100 235; www.bellemer.co.nz; 53 Marine Pde; apt $190-450; 🛜 🏊) A flashy beachside complex of one-, two- and three-bedroom apartments, some with sea-view balconies and others opening onto private courtyards (though you'll more likely head for the resort-style pool terrace). Rooms are tastefully decorated in warm tones with soft edges, and have everything you need for longer stays, with full kitchens and laundries.

🍴 Eating

Providores Urban Food Store
CAFE, DELICATESSEN $

(☏ 07-572 1300; 19a Pacific Ave; meals $5-22; ⊙ 7.30am-5pm, closed Mon & Tue Apr-Oct; 🍴) Mexican rugs and comfy couches set the mood here as your eyes peruse fresh-baked breads, buttery croissants, home-smoked meats and cheeses, organic jams and free-range eggs – perfect ingredients for a bang-up breakfast or a hamper-filling picnic on the beach. Superb.

Mount Mainstreet Farmers Market
MARKET $

(www.mountmaunganui.org.nz; Phoenix Car Park, Maunganui Rd; ⊙ 9am-1pm Sun) Roll up to the local farmers market for a Sunday morning fix-me-up: fresh fruit and vegies, coffee, pastries, honey, cheese, juices… Arts and crafts are banned!

New World
SUPERMARKET $

(www.newworld.co.nz; cnr Tweed St & Maunganui Rd; ⊙ 7am-9pm) A haven for self-caterers.

Slowfish
CAFE $$

(☑ 07-574 2949; www.slowfish.co.nz; Shop 5, Twin Towers, Marine Pde; mains $15-24; ⊙7am-4.30pm; ☑) There's no slacking off in the kitchen of this eco-aware cafe, which promotes the art of savouring fine, locally sourced food. It's a hit with the crowds: you'll have to crowbar yourself in the door or pounce on any available alfresco seat, but it's worth it for its free-range bacon and eggs, Greek salads and fish cakes with chilli jam.

Thai Khan Koon
THAI $$

(☑ 07-574 8500; www.thaikhankoon.co.nz; 277 Maunganui Rd; mains $15-19; ⊙11am-10pm Mon, Wed-Fri & Sun, 5-10pm Tue, 11am-late Sat) A couple of flapping Thai flags herald this low-key eatery on an unsexy part of the Mount's main street. But don't let the location, the faux orchids or shiny food photos put you off – the cooking here is the real deal. Try the *gaeng dang bhed* (red duck curry) or classic Thai fish cakes.

Kwang Chow
CHINESE $$

(☑ 07-575 5063; 241 Maunganui Rd; lunch/dinner $15/20; ⊙11.30am-10pm Tue-Sun) This all-you-can-eat Chinese place is a local favourite for a bargain bite that maintains tasty flavours rather than resorting to a bland melange. And great puddings. Cavernous interior with floorboards and refreshingly little gold/crimson/mirror festoonery.

★ Drawing Room
MODERN NZ, FRENCH $$$

(☑ 07-575 0096; www.thedrawingroom-nz.tumblr. com; 107 Maunganui Rd; mains $34; ⊙6pm-late Mon-Sat Apr-Oct, 3pm-late daily Nov-Mar) This outstanding new Frenchy food room fills a niche: upmarket but totally unpretentious, with a commitment to local produce and local art (the window mural changes monthly). Design-wise it's leather banquettes and timber floorboards; booze-wise it's NZ craft beers, single malts and an inspired selection of Kiwi and French wines. Order the pan-fried scallops, and leave room for a secret dessert!

Mount Bistro
MODERN NZ $$$

(☑ 07-575 3872; www.mountbistro.co.nz; 6 Adams Ave; mains $26-64; ⊙5.30-9pm Tue-Sun) The buttermilk-coloured Mount Bistro, an unpretentious fine-dining experience at the foot of Mauao, is onto a good thing: quality local meats (fish, lamb, beef, crayfish, chicken, duck) creatively worked into classic dishes (lamb shanks, seafood chowder) and served with élan. Makes for a classy night out.

☕ Drinking & Entertainment

★ Major Tom's
BAR, LIVE MUSIC

(www.majortomsbar.com; 297 Maunganui Rd; ⊙4-11pm Sun-Tue, 5-11pm Wed & Thu, 4pm-1am Fri & Sat) A funky little bar set back from the main drag in what looks like Major Tom's spaceship. Inside it's all kooky antiques, vintage couches, dangling inverted desk lamps and prints of Elvis, the *Mona Lisa* and (of course) David Bowie. Fabulous streetside terrace, cool tunes, free wi-fi and occasional live acts. Everybody sing: 'Planet Earth is blue, and there's nothing I can do...'

Astrolabe
PUB

(☑ 07-574 8155; www.astrolabe.co.nz; 82 Maunganui Rd; ⊙10am-1am) Run by Mac's brewery, Astrolabe conjures up a funky-retro 'bach' vibe, with floral carpet, bookshelves jammed with old novels, beach umbrellas, battered suitcases and vintage placemats. If all that doesn't float your holiday boat, a few pilseners and some blackened fish tacos just might (mains $15 to $25).

Latitude 37
BAR

(www.37.co.nz; 181 Maunganui Rd; ⊙4pm-1am Mon, noon-1am Tue-Sun; ☎) A slick, upmarket bar with stone-faced walls, fold-back windows and flaming torches out the front. A lot of folk come here to eat (mains $22 to $39... oh, the smoked bourbon mussels!), but it's also a beaut spot for a cold Heineken after a day in the surf.

Bay City Cinemas
CINEMA

(☑ 07-572 3311; www.baycitycinemas.co.nz; 249 Maunganui Rd; tickets adult/child $16/10; ⊙10am-late) Mainstream offerings.

ⓘ Information

The reception desk at Beachside Holiday Park doubles as an informal info centre for the Mount; open 8.30am to 7pm.

ⓘ Getting There & Around

BUS

InterCity and Naked Bus services visiting Tauranga also stop at Mt Maunganui, with fares similar to those to/from Tauranga. Buses stop on Salisbury Ave.

CAR

Mt Maunganui is across the harbour bridge from Tauranga, or accessible from the south via Te Maunga on SH2. For car hire, try **Rite Price Rentals** (☑ 07-575 2726, 0800 250 251; www.ritepricerentals.co.nz; 63 Totara St; ⊙8am-5pm).

Papamoa

POP 20,100

Papamoa is a burgeoning 'burb next to Mt Maunganui, separated now by just an empty paddock or two, destined for subdivision. With big new houses on pristine streets, parts of Papamoa have the air of a gated community, but the beach beyond the sheltering dunes is awesome – you can't blame folks for moving in.

Back a few kilometres from the beach, Blo-kart Heaven (07-572 4256; www.blokartheaven.co.nz; 176 Parton Rd; blokarting 1hr $50; 10am-4.30pm) is the place to attempt land-sailing around a custom-built speedway (blokarts are like seated windsurfers on wheels).

The sprawling Papamoa Beach Top 10 Holiday Resort (07-572 0816, 0800 232 243; www.papamoabeach.co.nz; 535 Papamoa Beach Rd; campsites from $40, villas & units $98-275; @) is a spotless, modern park, primed and priced beyond its caravan-park origins, with fab self-contained villas behind the dunes (*shhhh*, listen to the surf).

With its angular corrugated-iron exterior and tasteful caneware furnishings, Beach House Motel (07-572 1424, 0800 429 999; www.beachhousemotel.co.nz; 224 Papamoa Beach Rd; d from $130;) offers an immaculate, upmarket version of the Kiwi bach holiday, relaxed and close to the beach. There's a pool if the beach is too windy, and orange daisies poking up through rock gardens.

Bluebiyou (07-572 2099; www.bluebiyou. co.nz; 559 Papamoa Beach Rd; mains $15-38; noon-2.30pm & 5.30pm-late Wed & Thu, noon-late Fri & Sat, 10am-late Sun) is a casual, breezy restaurant riding high on the dunes, serving big brunches and seafood specialities. The prawn Benedict is a sure-fire Sunday morning start-me-up. Open seven days in summer.

Matakana Island

About 24km long and forming the seaward side of Tauranga Harbour, privately owned Matakana is laced with secluded white-sand surf beaches on its eastern shore (experienced surfers only). The community lifestyle here is laid-back and beachy, but the only way you can visit is on a kayak tour with Adventure Bay of Plenty (p294).

Katikati

POP 4060

'Katikat' to the locals, this busy little town was the only planned Ulster settlement in the world, and celebrates this history with a series of colourful murals. The Mural Town Information Centre (07-549 1658; www.katikati.org.nz; 36 Main Rd; 8am-5pm Mon-Fri, 9am-2pm Sat, 10am-2pm Sun;) sells a guide to the murals ($2.50), or you can take a small-group guided tour (07-549 2977; per person $5).

Sights & Activities

Katikati Heritage Museum   MUSEUM
(07-549 0651; www.katikatiheritagemuseum. co.nz; 3 Wharawhara Rd; adult/child $7.50/5; 9am-4pm) This rusty old museum traces local history with an engaging mix of Maori artefacts and Ulster history, some moa bones, old flat-tyre tractors and reputedly the largest bottle collection in the southern hemisphere.

Haiku Pathway   WALKWAY
(www.katikati.co.nz; 24hr) FREE Kicking off just near the information centre, the Haiku

---

OFF THE BEATEN TRACK

TUHUA (MAYOR ISLAND)

Commonly known as Mayor Island, this dormant volcano is 35km north of Tauranga. It's a privately owned island noted for its black, glasslike obsidian rock and birdlife, including a clutch of kiwi, introduced to the predator-free isle in 2006. Walking tracks cut through the overgrown crater valley, and the northwest corner is a marine reserve.

You need permission to visit from the island's *kaitiaki* (guardians), via the Tuhua Trust Board (07-577 0942). There's a $5 landing fee, and visitors must observe strict quarantine regulations. Accommodation is limited to basic camping/cabins ($10/30); bring your own food and water (no fridges). The landing fee is included in accommodation costs. Several boat-charter companies will take you to Tuhua, including Blue Ocean Charters (p295). Contact DOC (07-578 7677; taurangainfo@doc.govt.nz) in Tauranga for more info.

Pathway rambles along the Uretara River past boulders inscribed with haiku verses. A serene scene.

Katikati Bird Gardens
WILDLIFE RESERVE

(☑07-549 0912; www.birdgardens.co.nz; 263 Walker Rd E; adult/child/family $9.50/5/25; ☺10am-4.30pm) About 7km south of town, the 4-hectare Katikati Bird Gardens is aflap with native birdlife (ever seen a kawaupaka?). There's a cafe and gallery here, plus boutiquey cottage accommodation (double B&B $160).

Morton Estate
WINERY

(www.mortonestatewines.co.nz; 2389 SH2; ☺9.30am-5pm) The monastic-looking Morton Estate, one of NZ's bigger wineries, squats on SH2 8km south of Katikati. It's open for tastings and stock-ups: try the smooth-as-cream chardonnay.

🛏 Sleeping

Kaimai View Motel
MOTEL $$

(☑07-549 0398; www.kaimaiview.co.nz; 84 Main Rd; d from $120; 🛜🐾) Beyond a funky mural on the streetside wall, this jaunty, mod motel offers neat rooms (all named after NZ native trees) with CD player, kitchenette and, in larger rooms, spa. The namesake views extend over the back fence.

★ Warm Earth Cottage
CABIN, B&B $$$

(☑07-549 0962; www.warmearthcottage.co.nz; 202 Thompsons Track; d $220) Reignite your romance or simmer in simple pleasures at this rural idyll, 5km south of town then 2km west of SH2. Two pretty, electricity-less cottages sit by the swimmable Waitekohe River. Fire up the barbecue (generous barbecue packs $85), melt into a wood-fired outdoor bath, or chew through a book in the lovely guest lounge/library. Big DIY breakfasts are included in the price.

🍴 Eating

Ambria
MODERN NZ $$

(☑07-549 2272; www.ambria.co.nz; 5/62 Main Rd; mains lunch $15-19, dinner $24-36) Surprisingly atmospheric, Ambria is a hip bar-eatery in a nondescript shopping strip on the eastern side of town. Order a glass of Kiwi wine to wash over your pork belly stuffed with sage, apple and streaky bacon.

Talisman Hotel & Landing Restaurant
PUB $$

(☑07-549 2218; www.facebook.com/talisman-hotel; 7 Main Rd; mains $18-30; ☺11.30am-2.30pm & 5-9pm) The Talisman is the local boozer, with occasional live music (including 'Sing For Your Supper' nights – bring your guitar!) and the Landing Restaurant serving pubby standards: pizzas, steaks, lamb Wellington, pan-fried salmon and surf 'n' turf.

Te Puke
POP 7500

Welcome to the 'Kiwifruit Capital of the World', a busy town during the picking season when there's plenty of work around. The Te Puke Visitor Information Centre (☑07-573 9172; www.tepuke.co.nz; 130 Jellicoe St; ☺8am-5pm Mon-Fri, 9am-noon Sat; 🛜) is in the same building as the public library (staff will confirm that 'Puke' rhymes with cookie, not fluke).

For the low-down on all things kiwifruit, swing into Kiwi360 (☑0800 549 4360, 07-573 6340; www.kiwi360.com; 35 Young Rd, off SH2; admission free, tour adult/child/family $20/6/46; ☺9am-5pm) at the turn-off for Maketu. Sitting among orchards of nashi pears, citrus, avocados and (you guessed it) kiwifruit, this visitor centre peels off a range of attractions including a 35-minute 'kiwicart' orchard

---

HOT FUZZ: KIWIFRUIT

The humble kiwifruit earns NZ more than a billion dollars every year, and with the Bay of Plenty in the thick of the action, it's no wonder the locals are fond of them.

The fruit's origins are in China, where it was called the monkey peach (they were considered ripe when the monkeys munched them). As they migrated to NZ, they were renamed the Chinese gooseberry – they were a lot smaller then, but canny Kiwis engineered them to more generous sizes and began exporting them in the 1950s. The fruit was then sexily rebranded as the Zespri. Today the Zesprians grow two types of kiwifruit: the common fuzzy-covered green fruit, and the gold fruit with its smooth complexion. To learn more about the kiwifruit, visit Kiwi360 in Te Puke.

For visitors after a dollar or two, there's always kiwifruit-picking work around the area, most of it during harvest (May and June): don't expect to make much more than $14 an hour. Enquire at regional i-SITEs, or check online at www.picknz.co.nz.

tour, kiwifruit viewing tower (not much of a view) and a cafe serving kiwifruit delights.

After something sweeter? About 10km south of Te Puke in Paengaroa, **Comvita** (☑0800 493 782, 07-533 1987; www.experience-comvita.com; 23 Wilson Rd S, Paengaroa; admission free, guided tours adult/child/family $22.50/11/64; ⊙8.30am-5pm Mon-Fri, 9.30am-5pm Sat & Sun) FREE is home to NZ's most famous honey- and bee-derived health-care products. A big new visitor centre was being built when we visited: expect a cafe, shop and guided tours. Grab a pot of vitamin E cream with bee pollen and manuka honey on your way out.

Not far from Comvita, **Kaituna Jet** (☑0800 867 386; www.jetboating.co.nz; 316 SH33, Paengaroa; adult/child/family $104/49/277; ⊙9am-4pm) puts a few ripples on the surface of an otherwise tranquil stretch of the Kaituna River. Also nearby is **Briars Horse Trek** (☑07-533 2582; www.briarshorsetrek.co.nz; 540 SH33, Paengaroa; 1hr/2hr/4hr treks from $65/110/195), offering horse rides taking in the local forests and rivers.

Homestays and farmstays dapple the Te Puke area: ask the visitor centre for a list. For fruit-pickers and doyens of dorm-life there's basic hostel accommodation at **Hairy Berry** (☑07-573 8015; www.hairyberrynz.com; 2 No 1 Rd; dm/tw/d from $25/60/60; @🛜), a sociable, barn-like affair on the Whakatane side of town with a roomy communal space and small, tidy bedrooms.

Whakatane

POP 18,950

A true pohutukawa paradise, Whakatane (pronounced 'fokka-tar-nay') sits on a natural harbour at the mouth of the river of the same name. It's the hub of the Rangitaiki agricultural district, but there's much more to Whakatane than farming – blissful beaches, a sunny main-street vibe and volcanic Whakaari (White Island) for starters. And (despite Nelson's protestations) it's officially NZ's sunniest city.

◉ Sights

Te Manuka Tutahi Marae   MARAE
(☑07-308 4271; www.mataatua.com; 105 Muriwai Dr; ⊙9am-4pm Dec-Feb, reduced hours Mar-Nov) FREE The centrepiece of this recently opened Ngati Awa *marae* isn't new: **Mataatua Wharenui** (The House That Came Home) is a fantastically carved 1875

PADDLES & PIES: MAKETU

Take SH2 through Te Puke then turn left onto Maketu Rd, and you'll find yourself deposited at this seaside town which, although historic, has seen better days.

Maketu (population 1240) played a significant role in NZ's history as the landing site of *Te Arawa* canoe in 1340, commemorated with a somewhat underwhelming 1940 monument on the foreshore. Arguably, though, the town is more famous for **Maketu Pies** (☑07-533 2358; www.maketupies.co.nz; 6 Little Waihi Rd; ⊙9am-3.30pm Mon-Fri), baked fresh daily here and employing a good proportion of the population. You can buy a pie, hot from the oven, at the factory shopfront, or from the shop next door if you're here on a weekend (go for the legendary lamb and mint).

meeting house. In 1879 it was dismantled and shipped to Sydney, before spending 71 years in the Otago Museum from 1925. It was returned to the Ngati Awa in 1996. You can check out Mataatua Wharenui from the outside for free (behave respectfully), or book an excellent 90-minute cultural tour (adult/child $49/15).

★**Whakatane District Museum**   MUSEUM, GALLERY
(☑07-306 0509; www.whakatanemuseum.org.nz; Esplanade Mall, Kakahoroa Dr; admission by donation; ⊙9am-5pm Mon-Fri, 10am-2pm Sat & Sun) This impressive new museum-gallery in the library building has artfully presented displays on early Maori and European settlement in the area: Maori *taonga* (treasures) trace a lineage back to the *Mataatua* canoe. Other displays focus on Whakaari (White Island) and Motuhora (Whale Island). The gallery section presents a varied program of NZ and international exhibitions.

Wairere Falls   WATERFALL
(Toroa St) Tumbling down the cliffs behind the town, picture-perfect Te Wairere (Wairere Falls) occupies a deliciously damp nook, and once powered flax and flour mills and supplied Whakatane's drinking water. It's a gorgeous spot, and goes almost completely unheralded: in any other country there'd be a ticket booth, interpretive audiovisual displays and a hotdog van!

Whakatane

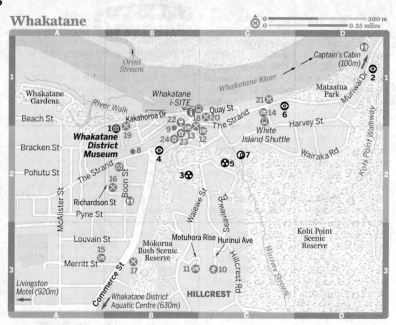

Whakatane

◎ Top Sights
1 Whakatane District Museum.................B2

◎ Sights
2 Muriwai's Cave.............................D1
3 Papaka Pa..................................B2
4 Pohaturoa..................................B2
5 Puketapu Pa................................C2
6 Te Manuka Tutahi Marae....................C1
7 Wairere Falls..............................C2

✦ Activities, Courses & Tours
8 Dive White Island.........................B2
9 Diveworks Dolphin & Seal
   Encounters...............................B2
10 Whakatane Observatory....................C3
   White Island Tours...................(see 14)

🛏 Sleeping
11 Motuhora Rise B&B........................B3
12 Tuscany Villas...........................C2

13 Whakatane Hotel..........................B2
14 White Island Rendezvous..................C1
15 Windsor Backpackers......................A3

🍴 Eating
16 Cafe Coco................................B2
17 Countdown................................B3
18 L'Epicerie...............................B1
19 Niko Niko................................B2
20 Roquette.................................C1
21 Wally's on the Wharf.....................C1

🍷 Drinking & Nightlife
   Craic................................(see 13)
   Detour...............................(see 22)
22 Office...................................B1

★ Entertainment
23 Boiler Room..............................B2
24 WhakaMax Movies..........................B2

Pohaturoa   LANDMARK, MONUMENT
(cnr The Strand & Commerce St) Beside a round-about on the Strand is Pohaturoa, a large *tapu* (sacred) rock outcrop, where baptism, death, war and *moko* (tattoo) rites were performed. The Treaty of Waitangi was signed here by Ngati Awa chiefs in 1840; there's a monument to the Ngati Awa chief Te Hurinui Apanui here too.

Muriwai's Cave   CAVE
(Muriwai Dr) The partially collapsed Te Ana o Muriwa (Muriwai's Cave) once extended 122m into the hillside and sheltered 60 people, including Muriwai, a famous seer

and aunt of Wairaka. Along with Wairere Falls and a rock in the harbour mouth, the cave was one of three landmarks Toroa was told to look for by his father Irakewa, when he arrived in the *Mataatua* canoe.

Te Papaka & Puketapu
ARCHAEOLOGICAL SITES, LOOKOUTS
On the clifftops behind the town are two ancient Ngati Awa *pa* sites – Te Papaka and Puketapu – both of which offer sensational (and very defendable) outlooks over Whakatane.

🏃 Activities

Feel like a stroll? The **Kohi Point Walkway** is highly recommended: a bushy four-hour, 5.5km track with panoramic clifftop views and a genuine 'gasp' moment when you set eyes on Otarawairere Bay. A short detour rewards you with amazing views from Toi's Pa (Kapua te rangi), reputedly the oldest *pa* site in NZ. You can also get to Toi's Pa by a partly unsealed access road off the Whakatane–Ohope road. From Ohope, you can catch the bus back to Whakatane if there aren't any more kilometres in your legs. Ask the i-SITE for a walk map.

A flatter option is the **River Walk** (two to three hours), following the Whakatane River past the Botanical Gardens, Muriwai's Cave and on to Wairaka's statue.

See p309 for info on boat and helicopter tours out to the explosive Whakaari (White Island) and p310 for trips to Motuhora (Whale Island).

Diveworks Dolphin & Seal Encounters
DIVING, WILDLIFE TOUR
(📞0800 354 7737, 07-308 2001; www.whale-islandtours.com; 96 The Strand; dolphin & seal swimming adult/child $160/130, diving incl gear from $215) This dive/ecotour company runs dolphin- and seal-swimming trips from Whakatane (cheaper if you're just watching from the boat), plus guided tours of Motuhora (Whale Island; adult child $120/85) and diving at Whakaari (White Island; two dives including gear $275). Fishing trips also available.

Whakatane Observatory
ASTRONOMY
(📞07-308 6495; www.whakatane.info/business/whakatane-astronomical-society; 22 Hurinui Ave; adult/child/family $15/5/35; ⊙7.30pm Tue & Fri) Up on a hilltop behind the town, Whakatane Observatory offers some plentiful Bay of Plenty star-spotting when the sky is clear.

Whakatane District Aquatic Centre
SWIMMING
(www.tlc.net.nz; 28 Short St; adult/child/family $4/2.20/11.50; ⊙6am-8pm Mon-Fri, 7am-6pm Sat & Sun) Indoor and outdoor pools, spa pools and a tubular yellow worm of a waterslide ($4.50).

Tui Glen Farm
HORSE RIDING
(📞027 232 5367, 07-323 6457; www.tuiglenfarm.com; Kawerau Loop Rd, Kawerau; 30min rides adult/child $35/25, 1hr ride $60/45) Close to Kawerau about 35km from Whakatane off SH30 to Rotorua, Tui Glen Farm offers horse treks through bush and farm for beginners and the adventurous. Basic dorm accommodation costs $35 per person; camping $10.

🛏 Sleeping

Whakatane Hotel
HOTEL $
(📞07-307 1670; www.whakatanehotel.co.nz; 79 The Strand; dm/s $25/40, d with/without bathroom from $75/55; 📶) This lovely old art-deco classic has 27 basic (but very decent) rooms upstairs in two wings. Clean shared bathrooms, high celings, communal kitchen... great value for money. Some rooms cop a bit of noise from the pub downstairs, but the owners try to shuffle people around to dodge the din.

Windsor Backpackers
HOSTEL $
(📞07-308 8040; www.windsorlodge-backpackers.co.nz; 10 Merritt St; dm/s/d from $27/48/66; @📶) Whakatane's best backpackers occupies a converted funeral parlour...so expect a restful sleep! Excellent rooms range from

---

WAKA LIKE A MAN

Whakatane's name originated some eight centuries ago, 200 years after the original Maori settlers arrived here. The warrior Toroa and his family sailed into the estuary in a huge ocean-going *waka* (canoe), the *Mataatua*. As the men went ashore to greet local leaders, the tide turned, and the *waka* – with all the women on board – drifted out to sea. Toroa's daughter, Wairaka, cried out *'E! Kia whakatane au i ahau!'* (Let me act as a man!) and, breaking the traditional *tapu* (taboo) on women steering a *waka*, she took up the paddle and brought the boat safely ashore. A whimsical **statue of Wairaka** stands proudly atop a rock in Whakatane's harbour in commemoration of her brave deed.

serviceable dorms to a couple of motel-standard doubles out the front. The communal kitchen, lounge and barbecue courtyard are spacious and tidy.

Awakeri Hot Springs   HOLIDAY PARK $
(📞07-304 9117; www.awakerisprings.co.nz; SH30; campsites $36, d cabins/flats/units $70/85/95; 🌐) About 16km from Whakatane on the road to Rotorua (SH30) you'll come to the immaculate Awakeri Hot Springs, an old-fashioned holiday park complete with (as the name suggests) hot springs (adult/child $7.50/5), picnic areas and a bed for every budget.

Captain's Cabin   APARTMENT $$
(📞07-308 5719; www.captainscabin.co.nz; 23 Muriwai Dr; d from $125, extra person $25) On the serene side of town with sparkling water views, this homely self-contained unit is perfect if you're hanging round for a few days (cheaper for two nights or more). A cosy living area cleverly combines bedroom, lounge, kitchen and dining, with a second smaller room and bijou bathroom – all sweetly decorated along nautical lines. Sleeps three.

White Island Rendezvous   HOTEL, B&B $$
(📞0800 733 529, 07-308 9500; www.whiteisland.co.nz; 15 The Strand E; d $100-160, apt from $200, B&B $190; 🌐) An immaculate 28-room complex run by the on-the-ball White Island Tour people (cheaper rates for tour-goers). Lots of balcony and deck space for inhaling the sea air, while interiors are decked out with timber floors for a nautical vibe. Deluxe rooms come with spas; disabled-access facilities available. The B&B next door includes cooked breakfast.

Tuscany Villas   MOTEL $$
(📞07-308 2244; www.tuscanyvillas.co.nz; 57 The Strand E; d $155-200; 🌐) This mod motel may be a long way from Florence, but still offers a few rays of Italian sunshine with interesting architecture, wrought-iron balconies and floral plantings wherever there's room. Rooms are luxurious and comfy, with super-king beds and spa pools.

Livingston Motel   MOTEL $$
(📞0800 770 777, 07-308 6400; www.livingston.co.nz; 42 Landing Rd; d/f $130/220; 🌐) It's a bit of a hike into town, but this spotless, ranch-style motel is the pick of the half-dozen dotted along the Landing. Expect spacious, well-kept units, comfy beds and large spas in executive suites.

Motuhora Rise B&B   B&B $$$
(📞07-307 0224; www.motuhorarise.com; 2 Motuhora Rise; s/d/tr incl breakfast $205/230/350; 🌐) At the top of the town in both senses (steep driveway!), this jaunty hilltop spot feels vaguely Rocky Mountains, and affords a distant glimpse of Motuhora (Whale Island). Expect a gourmet cheeseboard on arrival, along with other extras such as a home theatre, outdoor spa, and fishing rods and golf clubs. Kid-free zone.

🍴 Eating

Wally's on the Wharf   FISH & CHIPS $
(📞07-307 1100; www.whakatane.info/business/wallys-wharf; 2 The Strand; meals $6-19; ⏰11am-7pm) Wally knows a thing or two about fish and chips: hoki, snapper, flounder, john dory and tarakihi – done in the deep fry, on the grill or in terrific fish burgers. Whitebait fritters in season, and chips that score well on the crispometer. The reconstituted squid rings are a tad disappointing (but the seagulls don't seem to mind).

L'Epicerie   CAFE, FRENCH $
(📞07-308 5981; www.lepicerie.co.nz; 73 The Strand; mains $10-16; ⏰7.30am-3.30pm Mon-Fri, 8am-4pm Sat, 8.30am-2.30pm Sun) *Ooh-la-la!* This classic French cafe in downtown Whakatane is a real surprise, serving terrific omelettes, croissants, crêpes and *croque-monsieurs* at communal tables. Fabulous coffee and deli shelves crammed with preserves, breads, mustards and deliciously stinky French cheeses complete a very Franco scene.

Niko Niko   JAPANESE $
(https://foursquare.com/v/niko-niko-sushi/; 43 Kakahoroa Dr; sushi $2-3; ⏰9am-7pm) Quick-fire sushi joint tucked between the Strand and the waterfront. Order a couple of gorgeously presented chilli chicken rolls and hit the sunny outdoor tables.

Cafe Coco   CAFE $
(📞07-308 8337; www.whakatane.info/business/cafe-coco; 10 Richardson St; mains $8-19; ⏰7.30am-4.30pm Mon-Fri, 8.30am-2pm Sat) Coco is a hip, L-shaped corner spot serving bright, fresh cafe fare: bagels, panini, corn fritters, fresh juices, French toast, cakes, organic fair-trade coffee, eggs any which way...and the 'Crepe of the Week'. Very kid-friendly, too.

Countdown   SUPERMARKET $
(www.countdown.co.nz; 105 Commerce St; ⏰7am-10pm) Stock up on supplies.

Roquette
MODERN NZ, MEDITERRANEAN **$$$**

(📞07-307 0722; www.roquette-restaurant.co.nz; 23 Quay St; mains lunch $20-34, dinner $30-36; ⊙10am-late Mon-Sat) A modern waterside restaurant on the ground floor of one of the town's big new apartment building, ritzy Roquette serves up refreshing Mediterranean-influenced fare with lots of summery salads, risotto and fish dishes. Laid-back tunes, lots of glass and mosaics, good coffee and sexy staff to boot. Try the char-grilled lamb salad.

Drinking & Entertainment

Craic
IRISH PUB

(www.whakatanehotel.co.nz; Whakatane Hotel, 79 The Strand; ⊙11am-2am) The Craic is a busy locals' boozer of the Irish ilk, good for a pint or two, or a mug of hot chocolate if you're feeling sub-par. Fantastic streetside terrace for sunny afternoons, and solid pub grub (mains $13 to $22).

Office
BAR

(www.whakatane.info/business/office-bar-grill; 82 The Strand; ⊙11am-late) The sporty Office does what it does well: beer, big meals with chips and salad all over (mains $18 to $32), and live bands and/or DJs Thursday to Saturday nights. Next door is Detour (www.whakatane. info/business/detour-bar-lounge; 84 The Strand; ⊙noon-late), a classier lounge bar run by the same folks, serving tapas and cocktails to an over-25s crowd.

Boiler Room
CLUB, LIVE MUSIC

(www.whakatanehotel.co.nz; Whakatane Hotel, 79 The Strand; ⊙10pm-2.30am Fri & Sat) Whakatane's only club is next door to the Craic at the Whakatane Hotel – a cavernous, hedonistic space dotted with pool tables. DJs and live bands engage your ears and feet, often for free.

WhakaMax Movies
CINEMA

(📞07-308 7623; www.whakamax.co.nz; 99 The Strand; tickets adult/child $14/9; ⊙10am-late) Right in the middle of the Strand, WhakaMax screens new-release movies. Cheaper tickets before 4.30pm and on Tuesdays.

ℹ️ Information

Post Office (197 The Strand; ⊙8.30am-5pm Mon-Fri, 9am-noon Sat) Also has foreign exchange.

Whakatane Hospital (📞07-306 0999; www. bopdhb.govt.nz; cnr Stewart & Garaway Sts; ⊙24hr) Emergency medical treatment.

Whakatane i-SITE (📞0800 924 528, 07-306 2030; www.whakatane.com; cnr Quay St & Kakahoroa Dr; ⊙8am-5pm Mon-Fri, 10am-4pm Sat & Sun; 🛜) Free internet access (including 24-hour wi-fi on the terrace outside the building), tour bookings, accommodation and general DOC enquiries.

ℹ️ Getting There & Around

AIR

Air New Zealand (📞0800 737 000, 07-308 8397; www.airnewzealand.com) has daily flights linking Whakatane to Auckland.

BICYCLE

Explore the area on two wheels with a hybrid road/trail bike from **Barringtons Bike Hire** (📞0800 830 130, 07-308 4273; www.barringtonsmotorlodge.co.nz; 34 Landing Rd; bike hire per half-/full day $30/40, tandems $40/50).

BUS

InterCity buses stop outside the i-SITE and connect Whakatane with Rotorua ($20, 1½ hours, one daily), Tauranga ($30, eight hours, one daily via Rotorua) and Gisborne ($46, three hours, one daily via Opotiki), with onward connections.

Naked Bus destinations include the following:

DESTINATION	PRICE ($)	DURATION (HR)	FREQUENCY (DAILY)
Auckland	35	6	1
Gisborne	20	3¼	1
Hamilton	25	2½	1
Rotorua	19	1½	1
Tauranga	18	4	1
Wellington	65	10	1

Local Bay Hopper buses run to Ohope ($3, 45 minutes, six daily), Opotiki ($8.60, one hour, two daily Monday and Wednesday) and Tauranga ($13.70, two hours, one daily Monday to Saturday).

Shuttle Bus

White Island Shuttle (📞07-308 9588, 0800 733 529; www.whiteisland.co.nz; one way/return $60/35), run buy White Island Tours in Whakatane, drives the Rotorua–Whakatane route and can be used by nontour travellers.

Whakaari (White Island)

NZ's most active volcano (it last erupted in 2013) lies 49km off the Whakatane coast. The small island was originally formed by three separate volcanic cones of different

WORTH A TRIP

MOTUHORA (WHALE ISLAND)

Nine kilometres off Whakatane is Motuhora (Whale Island) – so-called because of its leviathan shape. This island is yet another volcano along the Taupo Volcanic Zone but is much less active, although there are hot springs along its shore. The summit is 353m high and the island has several historic sites, including an ancient *pa* (fortified village) site, a quarry and a camp.

Whale Island was originally home to a Maori settlement. In 1829 Maori massacred sailors from the trading vessel *Haweis* while it was anchored at Sulphur Bay. In 1867 the island passed into European ownership and remains privately owned, although since 1965 it has been a DOC-protected wildlife refuge for seabirds and shorebirds.

The island's protected status means landing is restricted, with tours running only from January to March. Operators include White Island Tours (p310), Diveworks Dolphin & Seal Encounters (p307) and KG Kayaks (p310).

ages. The two oldest have been eroded, while the younger cone has risen up between them. Mt Gisborne is the highest point on the island at 321m. Geologically, Whakaari is related to Motuhora (Whale Island) and Putauaki (Mt Edgecumbe), as all lie along Taupo Volcanic Zone.

The island is dramatic, with hot water hissing and steaming from vents over most of the crater floor. Temperatures of 600°C to 800°C have been recorded.

The island is privately owned so you can only visit it with a licensed tour operator. Fixed-wing air operators run flyover tours only, while boat and helicopter tours will usually include a walking tour around the island including a visit to the ruins of the sulphur-mining factory – an interesting story in itself. Most tours depart Whakatane; scenic flights are also possible ex-Tauranga and Rotorua.

☞ Tours

White Island Tours   BOAT TOUR
(☑ 0800 733 529, 07-308 9588; www.whiteisland.co.nz; 15 The Strand, Whakatane; 6hr tours adult/child $199/130; ⊘ departures btwn 7am & 12.30pm) The only official boat trip to Whakaari (on board the good ship *Pee Jay*), with dolphin-spotting en route and a two-hour tour of the island. Moutohora (Whale Island) tours adult/child $90/60.

White Island Flights   SCENIC FLIGHTS
(☑ 0800 944 834; www.whiteislandflights.co.nz; Whakatane Airport; flights per person $249) Fixed-wing scenic flights over Whakaari, with lots of photo opportunities. A Whakaari/Mt Tarawera combo flight costs $339.

Dive White Island   DIVING
(☑ 0800 348 394, 07-307 0714; www.divewhite.co.nz; 186 The Strand, Whakatane; snorkelling per person $225, 2hr dive with gear $395) Full-day snorkelling and diving trips with lunch and gear provided; underwater volcanic terrain and lots of fish to look at.

Frontier Helicopters   SCENIC FLIGHTS
(☑ 0800 804 354, 07-308 4188; www.vulcanheli.co.nz; Whakatane Airport; flights per person from $650) A two-hour trip to Whakaari (departing from Whakatane) that includes a one-hour guided walk on the volcano.

Ohope

POP 2760

Just 7km over the hill from Whakatane, Ohope has great beaches, perfect for lazing or surfing, and is backed by sleepy Ohiwa Harbour.

🏃 Activities

KG Kayaks   KAYAKING
(☑ 07-315 4005, 027 272 4073; www.kgkayaks.co.nz; tours $85-150, 2hr hire s/d $50/70) Explore Ohiwa Harbour with KG Kayaks, which offers freedom hire and 2½-hour guided tours ($85), plus four-hour kayak trips around Motuhora (Whale Island), which involves a boat trip initially ($150).

By Salt Spray Surf School   SURFING
(☑ 0211 491 972, 07-312 4909; www.facebook.com/bysaltspraysurfschool; 2hr lesson from $90) If you want to splash around in the Ohope Beach surf, get some lessons from Beaver at By Salt Spray Surf School, which provides all gear and offers discounts for groups.

🛏 Sleeping

Aquarius Motel
MOTEL $

(☑ 07-312 4550; www.aquariusmotorlodge.co.nz; 103 Harbour Rd; d $85-150; 🛜) For a quiet, affordable motel-style option, roll into Aquarius, a basic complex with various room configurations, all with kitchens and just 100m from the beach (you don't need a swimming pool).

Ohope Beach
Top 10 Holiday Park
HOLIDAY PARK $$

(☑ 07-312 4460, 0800 264 673; www.ohopebeach.co.nz; 367 Harbour Rd; unpowered/powered sites per person from $24/26, cabins/units/apts from $150/230/300; @ 🛜 ⊠) The Ohope Beach Top 10 Holiday Park is the very model of a modern holiday park, with a raft of family-friendly facilities: sports courts, minigolf, pool, plus some apartments peeking over the dunes at the Bay of Plenty. Busy as a woodpecker in summer (with prices to match).

🍴 Eating

Ohiwa Oyster Farm
SEAFOOD, FAST FOOD $

(☑ 07-312 4566; www.whakatane.info/business/ohiwa-oyster-farm; 111 Wainui Rd; meals $5-14; ⊙ 9am-8pm Nov-Feb, to 7pm Mar-Oct) Poised over a swampy back-reach of Ohiwa Harbour (serious oyster territory), this classic roadside fish shack is perfect for a fish-and-chip (and oyster) picnic.

Hui Bar & Grill
MODERN NZ $$

(☑ 07-312 5623; www.huibarandgrill.com; 19 Pohutukawa Ave; mains lunch $10-25, dinner $29-35; ⊙ 10am-late, closed Mon & Tue Jun-Aug) With polished concrete floors, white leather banquettes and fold-back windows, Hui is a ritzy new bar-grill making a splash in little Ohope's shopping strip. Try some pan-seared scallops with chorizo and watercress, or chipotle mussels with garlic and herbs. NZ wines; live music Friday nights and Sunday afternoons. Classy stuff.

Opotiki

POP 8440

The Opotiki area was settled from at least 1150, some 200 years before the larger 14th-century Maori migration. Maori traditions are well preserved here, with the work of master carvers lining the main street and the occasional facial *moko* passing by. The town acts as a gateway to the East Coast, and has excellent beaches – Ohiwa and Waiotahi – and an engaging museum.

👁 Sights & Activities

Pick up the *Historic Opotiki* brochure from the i-SITE (or download from www.opotikinz.com) for the low-down on the town's heritage buildings.

Opotiki Museum
MUSEUM

(www.opotikimuseum.org.nz; 123 Church St; adult/child/family $10/5/25; ⊙ 10am-4pm Mon-Fri, 10am-2pm Sat) Run by volunteers, Opotiki's excellent museum has interesting heritage displays including Maori *taonga*, militaria, re-created shopfronts (a barber, carpenter, printer...) and agricultural items including tractors and a horse-drawn wagon. Admission to the Shalfoon & Francis Museum is included in the ticket price.

Shalfoon & Francis Museum
MUSEUM

(www.opotikinz.com/archive/129271.html; 129 Church St; adult/child/family $10/5/25; ⊙ 10am-4pm Mon-Fri, 10am-2pm Sat) Opotiki's original general store has been born again, with shelves piled high with old grocery and hardware products. Handbags, sticky-tape dispensers, sets of scales, books – you name it, they had it. An amazing collection. Admission is included in your ticket to the main Opotiki Museum.

Hiona St Stephen's Church
CHURCH

(www.opotikinz.com/archive/129305.html; 128 Church St; ⊙ services 8am & 9.30am Sun, 10am Thu) White-weatherboard St Stephen's (1862) is an Anglican church with a perfectly proportioned timber-lined interior. Reverend Carl Volkner, known by the local Whakatohea tribe to have acted as a government spy, was murdered here in 1865. In 1992 the Governor-General granted Mokomoko, the man who hanged for the crime, a full pardon, which hangs in the lobby.

Hukutaia Domain
FOREST, ARCHAEOLOGICAL SITE

(☑ 07-315 3030; www.opotikinz.com/archive/129054.html; Woodlands Rd; ⊙ daylight hours) FREE Around 8km south of town is Hukutaia Domain, home to one of the finest collections of native plants in NZ. In the centre is Taketakerau, a 23m puriri tree estimated to be more than 2000 years old and a burial place for the distinguished dead of the Upokorehe *hapu* (subtribe) of Whakatohea. The remains have since been reinterred elsewhere.

Motu Trails
MOUNTAIN BIKING

(☑ 04-472 0030; www.motutrails.co.nz) One of the New Zealand Cycle Trail's 'Great Rides' (see p50), Motu Trails comprises three trails around Opotiki – the easy 19km Dunes Trail, intermediate 78km Motu Road Trail and advanced 44km Pakihi Track – parts of which combine to form the 91km Loop Trail. See the website for details. For bike hire and shuttle services see www.motucycletrails.com or www.hireandshuttle.co.nz.

Motu River Jet Boat Tours JETBOATING
(☑07-325 2735; www.motujet.co.nz; trips from adult/child $90/50) Runs as many as three 1½-hour trips on the Motu River (which runs through the Raukumara Ranges near Opotiki) every day through summer. Winter trips by arrangement.

Wet 'n' Wild RAFTING
(☑07-348 3191, 0800 462 7238; www.wetnwildrafting.co.nz; trips from $995) Offers 100km multi-day rafting and camping adventures on the Motu River (Grade III–IV rapids) near Opotiki.

☆ Festivals & Events

Opotiki Rodeo RODEO
(www.opotikirodeo.co.nz) Dust off your spurs and cowboy hat for the annual Opotiki Rodeo in December. Giddyup.

🛏 Sleeping

★Opotiki Beach House HOSTEL $
(☑07-315 5117; www.opotikibeachhouse.co.nz; 7 Appleton Rd; dm/s/d from $30/48/66; 🐾) A cruisy, shoe-free beachside pad with a sunny, hammock-hung deck, sea views and a *very* wide sandy backyard. Beyond the dorms and breezy lounge are decent doubles and a quirky caravan (sleeps two) for those who want a real taste of the Kiwi summer holiday. About 5km west of town; sleeps 14.

Central Oasis Backpackers HOSTEL $
(☑07-315 5165; www.centraloasisbackpackers.co.nz; 30 King St; dm/d from $22/54; 🐾) Inside a late-1800s kauri (timber) house, this central backpackers is run by a super-laid-back German dude a long way from home. It's a snug spot with spacious rooms, a crackling fire and a big front yard to hang out in. Max the dog patrols the front yard.

Capeview Cottage COTTAGE $$
(☑0800 227 384, 07-315 7877; www.capeview.co.nz; 167 Tablelands Rd; d $150, extra person $30; 🐾) Surrounded by chirruping birds and kiwifruit orchards, this serene, self-contained cottage has two bedrooms, a barbecue and a brilliant outdoor spa from which you can soak up some rather astonishing coastal views. Weekly rates available.

Eastland Pacific Motor Lodge MOTEL $$
(☑07-315 5524, 0800 103 003; www.eastlandpacific.co.nz; cnr Bridge & St John Sts; d from $110,1-/2-bedroom from $130/150; 🐾) Bright, clean Eastland is a well-kept motel with new carpets and TVs, spa baths as standard, and a wing of five new units out the back. The two-bedroom units are top value (extra person $30).

🍴 Eating

★Two Fish CAFE $
(102 Church St; snacks $5-10, mains $7-21; ⊙8am-4pm Mon-Fri, 8.30am-2pm Sat) Decent eating options are thin on the ground in Opotiki, so what a surprise to discover the best cafe this side of Tauranga! Serving up hefty homemade burgers, chowder, toasties, steak sandwiches, fab muffins and salads, plus a jumbo selection in the cabinet, Two Fish has happy staff, Cuban tunes and a retro-groovy interior and courtyard. And super coffee! Nice one.

New World SUPERMARKET $
(www.newworld.co.nz; 19 Bridge St; ⊙7am-9pm) Self-catering supplies.

☆ Entertainment

De Luxe Cinema CINEMA
(☑07-314 5344; www.odc.govt.nz/visiting/the-movies; 127 Church St; tickets adult/child $14/7; ⊙10am-late, reduced hours Jun-Aug) The beguiling old De Luxe shows recent movies and hosts the odd brass-band concert. Check the window for upcoming events, including the annual Silent Film Festival (www.silentfilmfest.org.nz) in September.

ℹ Information

DOC (☑07-315 1001; www.doc.govt.nz; 70 Bridge St; ⊙8am-noon Mon-Fri) In the same building as the i-SITE.
Opotiki i-SITE (☑07-315 3031; www.opotikinz.com; 70 Bridge St; ⊙9am-4.30pm Mon-Fri, 9am-1pm Sat & Sun; 🐾) The fancy new Opotiki i-SITE takes bookings for activities and transport and stocks the indispensable free East Coast booklet *Pacific Coast Highway*.

ℹ Getting There & Away

BUS
Travelling east from Opotiki there are two routes: SH2, crossing the spectacular Waioeka

Gorge, or SH35 around East Cape. The SH2 route offers some day walks in the Waioeka Gorge Scenic Reserve, with the gorge getting steeper and narrower as you travel inland, before the route crosses typically green, rolling hills, dotted with sheep, on the descent to Gisborne.

Buses pick up/drop off at the Hot Bread Shop on the corner of Bridge and St John Sts, though tickets and bookings are made through the i-SITE or **Travel Shop** (☏ 07-315 8881; www. travelshop.co.nz; 104 Church St; ⊗ 9am-4pm Mon-Fri). The Travel Shop also rents out bikes (per half-/full day $30/50).

InterCity has daily buses connecting Opotiki with Whakatane ($22, 45 minutes), Rotorua ($36, 2½ hours) and Auckland ($72, 7½ hours).

Heading south, daily buses connect Opotiki with Gisborne ($36, two hours).

Naked Bus runs daily services to destinations including the following:

DESTINATION	PRICE ($)	DURATION (HR)
Auckland	31	6
Gisborne	19	2½
Rotorua	23	2½
Tauranga	20	5
Wellington	45	11

The local Bay Hopper bus runs to Whakatane ($8.60, 1¼ hour, two daily Monday and Wednesday).

The East Coast

Includes ➡

East Cape 315

Pacific Coast
Highway 315

Gisborne 321

Te Urewera
National Park.............328

Hawke's Bay 330

Napier 331

Hastings, Havelock
North & Around 339

Cape Kidnappers.......343

Kaweka &
Ruahine Ranges 345

Best Outdoors

➡ Cape Kidnappers (p343)

➡ Cooks Cove Walkway
(p320)

➡ Hawke's Bay Trails (p331)

➡ Surfing in Gisborne (p324)

➡ Lake Waikaremoana Track
(p329)

Best Places to Stay

➡ Stranded in Paradise (p320)

➡ Clive Colonial Cottages
(p341)

➡ Millar Road (p341)

➡ Seaview Lodge B&B (p336)

Why Go?

New Zealand is known for its mix of wildly divergent landscapes, but on the East Coast it's the sociological contours that are most pronounced. From the earthy settlements of the East Cape to Havelock North's monied, wine-soaked streets, there's a full spectrum of NZ (New Zealand) life.

Maori culture is never more visible than on the East Coast. Exquisitely carved *marae* (meeting-house complexes) dot the landscape, and *te reo* and *tikanga* (the language and customs) are alive and well.

Intrepid types will have no trouble losing the tourist hordes – along the Pacific Coast Hwy (State Hwy 35; SH35), through rural back roads, on remote beaches, or in the mystical wilderness of Te Urewera National Park. And when the call of the wild gives way to caffeine withdrawal, you can get a quick fix in Gisborne and Napier. You'll also find plenty of wine here: the Hawke's Bay region is striped with vine-rows.

When to Go

➡ The East Coast basks in a warm, mainly dry climate. Summer temperatures around Napier and sunny Gisborne nudge 25°C, rarely dipping below 8°C in winter.

➡ The Hawke's Bay region basks in mild, dry, grape-growing conditions year-round, with an average annual rainfall of just 800mm. Harvest time is Autumn (March to May).

➡ In winter, heavy downpours sometimes wash out sections of the Pacific Coast Hwy around the East Cape: check road conditions at either end (Opotiki or Gisborne) before making the trip.

ℹ️ Getting There & Around

The region's only airports are in Gisborne and Napier. **Air New Zealand** (www.airnewzealand.co.nz) flies to both towns from Auckland and Wellington, and also to Napier from Christchurch. **Sunair Aviation** (www.sunair.co.nz) flies direct from Gisborne to Rotorua, Tauranga and Napier; and from Napier to Gisborne and Hamilton, with onward connections.

Regular **Intercity** (www.intercity.co.nz) and **Naked Bus** (www.nakedbus.com) services ply State Hwy 2 (SH2) and State Hwy 5 (SH5), connecting Gisborne, Opotiki, Wairoa, Napier and Hastings with all the main centres.

Transport is limited around East Cape and Te Urewera National Park. **Bay Hopper** (www.baybus.co.nz) runs between Opotiki and Potaka/Cape Runaway on Tuesdays and Thursdays ($15, two hours). **Cooks Passenger & Courier Services** (☑ 06-864 4711, 021 371 364) runs between Te Araroa and Gisborne ($50, 3½ hours) Monday to Saturday. Otherwise, bring your own wheels.

EAST CAPE

The slow-paced East Cape is a unique and special corner of NZ. It's a quiet place, where everyone seems to know everyone, their community ties built on rural enterprise and a shared passion for the ocean. Horseback riding, tractors on the beach, fresh fish for dinner – it's all part of daily life here.

Inland, the wild Raukumara Range forms the Cape's jagged spine. Near the edge of the sea, the 323km Pacific Coast Hwy (SH35) runs from Opotiki to Gisborne. Lonely shores lie strewn with driftwood, while picture-postcard sandy bays lure just a handful of visitors.

Pacific Coast Highway

The long and winding road around the North Island's easternmost point has long been a rite of road-trip passage for New Zealanders. And if you like scenic drives and don't mind attractions that are few and far between, you'll likely find the journey intrepid and captivating.

If you're short on time, head for Gisborne via SH2 from Opotiki – a 144km alternative via the Waioeka Gorge and the two- to three-hour walk leading off from the historic Tauranga Bridge. The route takes about 2½ hours to drive, although you could easily make a day of it.

Both routes are covered in the excellent *Pacific Coast Highway Guide,* available at Gisborne and Opotiki i-SITEs. Set off with a full petrol tank, and stock up on snacks and groceries – shops and petrol stations are in short supply. Sleeping and eating options are pretty spread out: we've listed them in the order you'll find them, heading east from Opotiki.

Opotiki to Te Kaha

The first leg offers hazy views across to Whakaari (White Island), a chain-smoking active volcano. The desolate beaches at **Torere**, **Hawai** and **Omaio** are steeply shelved and littered with flotsam. Check out the magnificent *whakairo* (carving) on the Torere school gateway. Hawai marks the boundary of the Whanau-a-Apanui tribe whose *rohe* (traditional land) extends to Cape Runaway.

About 42km east of Opotiki the road crosses the broad pebbly expanse of the **Motu River**, the first river in NZ to be designated as a protected wilderness area. Departing from the Motu bridge on the highway, Motu River Jet Boat Tours (p312) blats up the river all year round, weather permitting. **Wet 'n' Wild Rafting** (☑ 0800 462 7238; www.wetnwildrafting.co.nz; 2-5 days $995-1095) offers multiday excursions, with the longest taking

---

ESSENTIAL EAST COAST

Eat Delicious fresh produce from the Hastings Farmers Market (p339)

Drink Hawke's Bay chardonnay

Read Witi Ihimaera's 1987 novel *Whale Rider,* then watch the powerful 2002 movie adaptation

Listen to Uawa FM (88.5FM, 88.8FM, 99.3FM) in Tolaga Bay

Watch *Boy* (2010), Taika Waititi's record-breaking and hilarious film, shot at Waihau Bay

Go green Millton (p321) vineyard – organic, biodynamic, and delicious to boot

Online www.hawkesbaynz.com; www.gisbornenz.com; www.lonelyplanet.com/new-zealand/the-east-coast

Area code Opotiki east to Hicks Bay ☑ 07; rest of the region ☑ 06

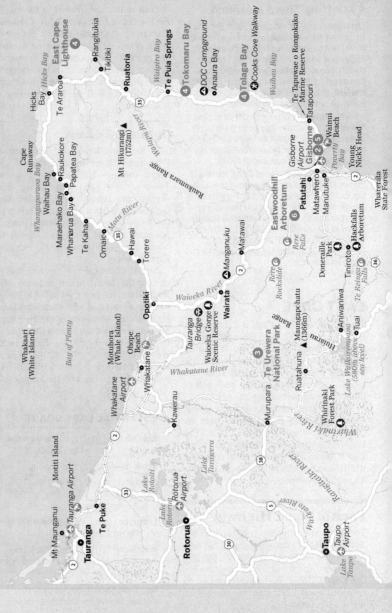

East Coast Highlights

1 Time-warping to the 1930s surrounded by art-deco delights in **Napier** (p332)

2 Sniffing and sipping your way around the wineries of **Hawke's Bay** (p342) or **Gisborne** (p321)

3 Losing yourself in the mighty forests and Maori culture of **Te Urewera National Park** (p328)

4 Counting off the landmarks as you cruise the coast: **Cape Kidnappers**, (p343), **Tolaga Bay**, (p320), **Tokomaru Bay** (p319) and the **East Cape Lighthouse** (p319)

5 Sliding a surfboard into the East Coast waves near **Gisborne** (p324)

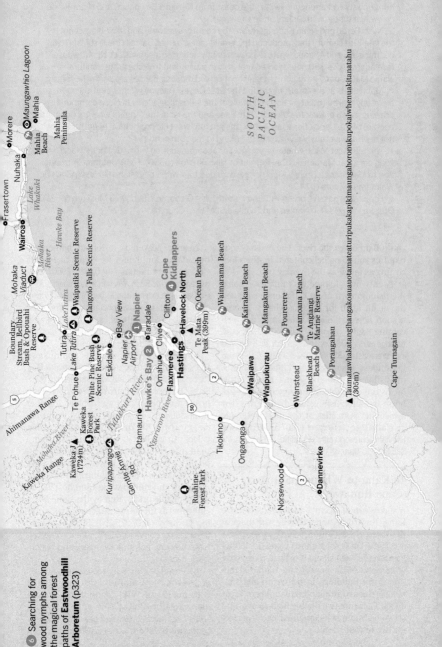

6 Searching for wood nymphs among the magical forest paths of **Eastwoodhill Arboretum** (p323)

MAORI NZ: THE EAST COAST

The main *iwi* (tribes) in the region are Te Whanau-a-Apanui (www.apanui.co.nz; west side of East Cape), Ngati Porou (www.ngatiporou.com; east side of East Cape), Ngati Kahungunu (www.kahungunu.iwi.nz; the coast from Hawke's Bay down) and Ngati Tuhoe (www.ngaituhoe.iwi.nz; inland in Te Urewera).

Ngati Porou and Ngati Kahungunu are the country's second- and third-biggest *iwi*. In the late 19th century they produced the great leaders James Carroll (the first Maori cabinet minister) and Apirana Ngata (who was briefly acting prime minister). Ngata, whose face adorns NZ's $50 note, worked tirelessly in parliament to orchestrate a cultural revival within Maoridom. The region's magnificent carved meeting houses are part of his legacy.

Maori life is at the forefront around the East Cape, in sleepy villages centred upon the many *marae* (meeting houses) that dot the landscape. Living in close communities, drawing much of their livelihoods off the sea and the land, the *tangata whenua* (local people) of the Cape offer a fascinating insight into what life might have been, had they not been so vigorously divested of their land in the 19th century.

You will meet Maori wherever you go. For accommodation with a distinctly Maori flavour, consider Maraehako Bay Retreat or Hikihiki's Inn (p330). For an intimate introduction to *Maoritanga* (things Maori), take a guided tour with Long Island Guides (p340) or Waimarama Tours (p340).

For a more passive brush with the culture, visit Gisborne's Tairawhiti Museum (p321), Otatara Pa (p334) in Napier, and Tikitiki's St Mary's Church.

you 100km down the river. The two-day tour requires you to be helicoptered in, therefore costing as much as the five-day trip.

Twenty-five kilometres further along, the fishing town of Te Kaha once sounded the death knell for passing whales. There's a shop here, a holiday park, and the welcoming B&B Tui Lodge (☑07-325 2922; www.tuilodge.co.nz; 200 Copenhagen Rd, Te Kaha; s/d incl breakfast $135/160; @). This five-room guesthouse sits on groomed 3-acre gardens, irresistible to tui and many other birds. Meals are available by arrangement, as are horse-trekking, fishing and diving trips. For a meal, try your luck at the mod waterside Te Kaha Beach Resort (☑07-325 2830; www.tekahabeachresort.com; 3 Hotel Rd, Te Kaha; mains $25-35; ◷3-9pm; ☎).

Te Kaha to Whangaparaoa (Cape Runaway)

A succession of sleepy bays extends from Te Kaha. Towards Whanarua Bay, the magical Waikawa B&B (☑07-325 2070; www.waikawa.net; 7541 SH35, Te Kaha; d/units from $110/130, extra person $35; @) sits in a private rocky cove with views of the sunset and White Island. The artful buildings blend weathered timber, corrugated iron and paua inlay to great effect. There are two double B&B rooms, and a two-bedroom self-contained bach, perfect for four to six people.

Nearby, heaven is a tub of homemade macadamia and honey ice cream at Pacific Coast Macadamias (☑07-325 2960; www.macanuts.co.nz; SH35, Whanarua Bay; snacks $3-9; ◷10am-3pm, extended hours Dec-Feb), with views along one of the most spectacular parts of the coast. Toasted sandwiches and nutty sweet treats make this a great lunch stop. Opening hours can be sketchy – call ahead.

Intertwined with ancient pohutukawa trees, the absolute seafront Maraehako Bay Retreat (☑07-325 2648; www.maraehako.co.nz; SH35, Maraehako Bay; dm/s/d $28/43/66; @) is a hostel that looks like it was cobbled together from flotsam and jetsam washed up in the craggy cove. It's rustic, but unique: what it lacks in crossed Ts and dotted Is it more than makes up for in *manaakitanga* (hospitality). Enjoy a spa under the stars ($5), free kayaks, as well as fishing charters, *marae* tours and guided walks (and no TV!), all at reasonable prices. Run by the same *hapu* (subtribe) as the retreat, Maraehako Camping Ground (☑07-325 2901; SH35, Maraehako Bay; sites per adult/child $12/8) offers clean toilets, showers, pohutukawa trees and beachfront nirvana.

At Papatea Bay stop to see the gateway of Hinemahuru Marae, intricately carved with images of WWI Maori Battalion soldiers. Nearby Christ Church Raukokore (1894) is a sweet beacon of belief on a lonely promontory. There are services at 11am on

Sundays, or the door is usually open at other times (look for the mouse on high).

Waihau Bay has a petrol pump at its western end, alongside the **Waihau Bay Lodge** ([📞]07-325 3805; www.thewaihaubaylodge.co.nz; Orete Point Rd, Waihau Bay; mains $25-35; ⊙4pm-late Sun-Wed, 2pm-late Thu-Sat), an old two-storey timber pub by the pier, serving hefty meals and with accommodation ranging from campsites ($15) to dorms ($35) and en suite units sleeping eight (double $185, extra person $25). There is also accommodation at **Oceanside Apartments** ([📞]07-325 3699; www.waihaubay.co.nz; 10932 SH35, Waihau Bay; d from $110; [@]), comprising two nicely kept motel units and a next-door bach (holiday home). Meals by arrangement.

Some 17km beyond Waihau Bay, **Whangaparaoa (Cape Runaway)**, where kumara was first introduced to NZ, can only be reached on foot.

Whangaparaoa (Cape Runaway) to East Cape

The road heads inland from Whangaparaoa, crossing into hilly Ngati Porou territory before hitting the coast at **Hicks Bay**, a real middle-of-nowhere settlement with a grand beach. Brilliant views distract from the barrack ambience at the 50-year-old **Hicks Bay Motel Lodge** ([📞]06-864 4880; www.hicksbaymotel.co.nz; 5198 SH35, Hicks Bay; dm $23, d $75-130, 2-bedroom units $165; [🛜][❄]), squatting high above the bay. The old-fashioned rooms are nothing flash, although the restaurant (mains $21 to $35, open for breakfast and dinner), shop, pool and glowworm grotto compensate.

Nearly 10km further is **Te Araroa**, a lone-dog village with two shops, a petrol station, takeaway and beautifully carved *marae*. The geology changes here from igneous outcrops to sandstone cliffs: the dense bush backdrop doesn't seem to mind which it grows on. More than 350 years old, 20m high and 40m wide, **Te-Waha-O-Rerekohu**, allegedly NZ's largest pohutukawa tree, stands in Te Araroa schoolyard. The progressive **East Cape Manuka Company** ([📞]06-864 4824; www.eastcapemanuka.co.nz; 4464 Te Araroa Rd, Te Araroa; ⊙8.30am-4.30pm daily Nov-Apr, Mon-Fri only May-Oct) is here too, selling soaps, oils, creams and honey made from potent East Cape manuka. It's a good stop for coffee, a cooked breakfast or a smoothie (meals and snacks $5 to $20). Check out the busy bees at work in the wall display. There's basic backpacker accommodation in a 135-year-old house at **Te Araroa Backpackers** ([📞]06-864 4896; www.teararoabackpackers.com; 57 Waione Rd, Te Araroa; dm from $25).

From Te Araroa, drive out to see the **East Cape Lighthouse**, the easterly tip of mainland NZ. It's 21km (30 minutes) east of town along a mainly unsealed road, with a 25-minute climb (750 steps!) to the lighthouse. Set your alarm and get up there for sunrise.

East Cape to Tokomaru Bay

Heading through farmland south of Te Araroa, the first town you come to is **Tikitiki**. If you haven't yet made it onto a *marae*, you'll get a fair idea of what you're missing out on by visiting the extraordinary **St Mary's Church** (1924). It's nothing special from the outside, but step inside for a sensory overload. There are woven *tukutuku* (flax panels) on the walls, geometrically patterned stained-glass windows, painted beams and amazing carvings – check out the little guys holding up the pulpit. A stained-glass crucifixion scene behind the pulpit depicts WWI Maori Battalion soldiers in attendance.

Amid the farming sprawl of **Rangitukia**, 8km down towards the coast from Tikitiki, **Eastender Horse Treks** ([📞]06-864 3033; www.eastenderhorsetreks.co.nz; 836 Rangitukia Rd, Rangitukia; 2/4hr treks $85/120) runs horse rides along the beach and can hook you up with bone-carving lessons (from $60). Note that the beach here is dicey for swimming.

FREEDOM TO CAMP

Gisborne District Council (GDC; [📞]0800 653 800; www.gdc.govt.nz/freedom-camping) is one of the few authorities to permit freedom camping (extremely cheap informal camping), but only at a handful of designated sites between Te Araroa and Gisborne from the end of September to early April. You can apply for a permit online for two, 10 or 28 consecutive nights at a cost of $10, $25 and $60 respectively. Freedom camping is a privilege, so please follow the requirements in the GDC *Freedom Camping* leaflet, available online or at visitor centres. Your own gas cooker, chemical toilet and water supply are obligatory.

LOCAL KNOWLEDGE

MURRAY BALL: THE BALLAD OF FOOTROT FLATS

Where the black Raukumara Ranges

Lie out east of everywhere,

The land's been stripped by sun and rain,

Until its bones are bare.

In this land of snarl-lipped razor backs

Of possums, deer and rats,

They talk a lot of working dogs

And the man from Footrot Flats.

Mt Hikurangi (1752m), jutting out of the Raukumara Range, is the highest non-volcanic peak on the North Island and the first spot on Earth to see the sun each day. According to local tradition it was the first piece of land dragged up when Maui snagged the North Island. The Ngati Porou version of the Maui story has his canoe and earthly remains resting here on their sacred mountain.

Continuing south, the road passes **Ruatoria** (shop, petrol and general desolation) and **Te Puia Springs** (ditto). Along this stretch a 14km loop road offers a rewarding detour to **Waipiro Bay**.

Eleven kilometres south of Te Puia is **Tokomaru Bay**, perhaps the most interesting spot on the entire route, with its broad beach framed by sweeping cliffs. The town has weathered hard times since the freezing works closed in the 1950s, but it still sports several attractions including good beginner surfing, swimming and **Te Puka Tavern** (06-864 5465; www.tepukatavern.co.nz; 135 Beach Rd, Tokomaru Bay; meals $10-27; 11am-late;). This well-run pub with cracker ocean views is a cornerstone of the community, keeping everyone fed and watered, and offering visitors a place to stay (units $140 to $180). You'll also find a supermarket, takeaway and post office here (...and a B&B in the former post office), plus some crumbling surprises at the far end of the bay. Up on the hill, 12-bed **Stranded in Paradise** (06-864-5870; www.bbh.co.nz; 21 Potae St; campsites per person $15, dm/s/d $28/45/66;) scores the awards for views, eco-loos and free wi-fi. There are two tricky loft rooms for sharing, a double downstairs and three wave-shaped cabins. Tenters have a panoramic knoll (astonishing views!) on which to pitch.

Tokomaru Bay to Gisborne

After a bucolic 22km of highway is the turn-off to **Anaura Bay**, 6km away. It's a definite 'wow' moment when it springs into view far below. Captain Cook arrived here in 1769 and commented on the 'profound peace' in which the people were living and their 'truly astonishing' cultivations. **Anaura Bay Walkway** is a two-hour, 3.5km ramble through steep bush and grassland, starting at the northern end of the bay. There's a standard Department of Conservation (DOC) **campsite** here (adult/child $6/3; fully self-contained campers only).

Campers are catered for best around these parts, although a few B&Bs come and go in the midst. Grassy **Anaura Bay Family Motor Camp** (06-862 6380; www.gisbornenz.com/accommodation/view/401; Anaura Bay Rd; sites per adult/child from $18/9;) is all about the location – right on the beachfront by the little stream where James Cook once stocked up with water. There's a decent kitchen, showers and toilets.

Back on the highway it's 14km south to **Tolaga Bay**, East Cape's largest community (population 765). There's an **information desk** (06-862 6826; uawafm@xtra.co.nz; 55 Cook St; 9am-5pm Mon-Fri) in the foyer of the local radio station (Uawa FM; 88.5FM). Just off the main street, **Tolaga Bay Cashmere Company** (06-862 6746; www.cashmere.co.nz; 31 Solander St; 10am-4pm Mon-Fri) inhabits the art-deco former council building. Watch the knitters knit, then perhaps purchase one of their delicate works: call to check they're open.

Tolaga is defined by its amazing **historic wharf**. Built in 1929 and commercially functional until 1968, it's the longest in the southern hemisphere (660m), and is caught somewhere between rusty decay and dedicated (expensive!) efforts to preserve it. Nearby is **Cooks Cove Walkway** (closed Aug-Oct), an easy 5.8km, 2½-hour loop through farmland and native bush to another cove where the captain landed. At the northern end of the beach is the **Tatarahake Cliffs Lookout**, a sharp 10-minute walk to an excellent vantage point.

Tolaga Bay Holiday Park (06-862 6716; www.tolagabayholidaypark.co.nz; 167 Wharf Rd, Tolaga Bay; sites from $16, cabins $40-100) is right next to the wharf. The stiff ocean breeze tousles Norfolk Island pines, and open lawns bask in the sunshine: it's a pretty special spot. Back in town, the 1930s faux-Tudor **To-**

laga Inn (☎06-862 6856; www.tolagainn.co.nz; 12 Cook St; dm/s/d $25/60/80) has basic but clean pub rooms upstairs, cheap bar meals downstairs ($6 to $10).

Around 16km north of Gisborne, the DOC-managed **Te Tapuwae o Rongokako Marine Reserve** is a 2450-hectare haven for many species of marine life including fur seals, dolphins and whales. Get out amongst it with **Dive Tatapouri** (☎06-868 5153; www.dive-tatapouri.com; 532 SH35, Tatapouri Beach), which offers dive trips, surf lessons, snorkel hire, a reef ecology tour and even shark-cage diving.

Gisborne

POP 34,800

'Gizzy' to her friends, Gisborne (pronounced Gis-born, not Gis-bun) is a pretty thing, squeezed between surf beaches and a sea of chardonnay, and proudly claims to be the first city on Earth to see the sun. It's a good place to put your feet up for a few days, hit the beach and sip some wine.

History

The Gisborne region has been settled for over 700 years. A pact between two migratory *waka* (canoe) skippers, Paoa of the *Horouta* and Kiwa of the *Takitimu*, led to the founding of Turanganui a Kiwa (now Gisborne). Kumara flourished in the fertile soil and the settlement blossomed.

In 1769 this was the first part of NZ sighted by Cook's expedition. Eager to replenish supplies and explore, they set ashore, much to the amazement of the locals. Setting an unfortunate benchmark for intercultural relations, the crew opened fire when the Maori men performed their traditional blood-curdling challenge, killing six of them.

The *Endeavour* set sail without provisions. Cook, perhaps in a fit of petulance, named the area Poverty Bay as 'it did not afford a single item we wanted'.

European settlement began in 1831 with whaling and farming, with missionaries following. In the 1860s battles between settlers and Maori erupted. Beginning in Taranaki, the Hauhau insurrection spread to the East Coast, culminating in the battle of Waerenga a Hika in 1865.

To discover Gisborne's historical spots, pick up the *Historic Walk* pamphlet from the i-SITE.

◉ Sights

★**Tairawhiti Museum** MUSEUM
(www.tairawhitimuseum.org.nz; Kelvin Rise, Stout St; adult/child $5/free, Mon free; ☉10am-4pm

---

GISBORNE WINERIES

With hot summers and fertile loam soils, the Waipaoa River valley to the northwest of Gisborne is one of New Zealand's foremost grape-growing areas. The region is traditionally famous for its chardonnay but is increasingly noted for gewürztraminer and pinot gris. See www.gisbornewine.co.nz for a cellar-door map. Opening hours scale back out of peak season. Five of the best:

Bushmere Estate (☎06-868 9317; www.bushmere.com; 166 Main Rd, Matawhero; ☉11am-5pm Wed-Sun) Great chardonnay, gewürztraminer, cafe lunches at the Bond Room (lunch mains $8 to $18, dinner Friday and Saturday only $16 to $28), and live music on summer Sundays.

Kirkpatrick Estate (☎06-862 7722; www.kew.co.nz; 569 Wharekopae Rd, Patutahi; ☉11am-4pm) Sustainable winery with lovely wines across the board, including a delicious malbec. Enjoy an antipasto platter in the sun.

Matawhero (☎06-867 6140; www.matawhero.co.nz; Riverpoint Rd, Matawhero; ☉11am-5pm Thu-Mon, daily Jan) Home of a particularly buttery chardy. Enjoy your picnic in bucolic splendour, accompanied by a flight of fine wines.

Millton (☎06-862 8680; www.millton.co.nz; 119 Papatu Rd, Manutuke; ☉by appointment Feb-Nov, 10am-5pm daily Dec & Jan) Sustainable, organic and biodynamic to boot. Bring a picnic and kick back surrounded by sturdy-trunked vines.

Gisborne Wine Centre (☎06-867 4085; www.gisbornewine.co.nz; Shed 3, 50 The Esplanade; ☉10am-5pm Sun-Wed, to 7pm Thu-Sat) Harbourside spot with a wide selection of the region's vino to sample (...the pervasive sea-scent may be hard to reconcile with the chardy on your palate).

Gisborne

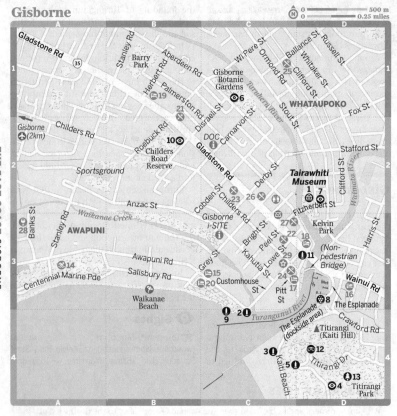

Gisborne

◉ Top Sights
1 Tairawhiti Museum D2

◉ Sights
2 Captain Cook Statue C4
3 Cook Monument C4
4 Cook Observatory D4
5 Cook's Plaza C4
6 Gisborne Botanic Gardens C1
7 Gisborne Farmers Market D2
8 Gisborne Wine Centre D3
9 Statue of Young Nick............................. C4
10 Sunshine Brewing Company B2
11 Te Tauihu Turanga Whakamana D3
12 Titirangi Lookout D4
13 Titirangi Park D4

✚ Activities, Courses & Tours
14 Olympic Pool A3

🛏 Sleeping
15 Captain Cook Motor Lodge C3
16 Gisborne YHA D3

17 Pacific Harbour Motor Inn..................... C3
18 Quality Hotel Emerald D3
19 Teal Motor Lodge B1
20 Waikanae Beach Top 10 Holiday
Park C3

⊗ Eating
Cafe 1874 .... (see 29)
21 Morrell's Artisan Bakery B1
22 Muirs Bookshop & Café C3
23 Pak N Save C2
24 USSCO Bar & Bistro C3
25 Villaggio C1
26 Yoko Sushi C2
27 Zest C3

⊜ Drinking & Nightlife
Rivers ....(see 18)
28 Smash Palace A3

❂ Entertainment
29 Dome Cinema C3
Poverty Bay Club .... (see 29)

Mon-Sat, 1.30-4pm Sun) The Tairawhiti Museum, with its new gallery extension, focuses on East Coast Maori and colonial history. It is Gisborne's arts hub, with rotating exhibits, and excellent historic photographic displays. There's also a maritime wing, with displays on *waka*, whaling and Cook's Poverty Bay, although these pale in comparison to the vintage surfboard collection.

There's a shop and tearoom-style cafe overlooking Kelvin Park, while outside is the reconstructed Wyllie Cottage (1872), Gisborne's oldest house.

Titirangi Park   PARK
High on Kaiti Hill overlooking the city, Titirangi was once a *pa* (fortified village). You can reach it by driving or walking up Queens Dr, or pick up the walking track at the Cook Monument. Near the summit is Titirangi Lookout and yet another Cook edifice, Cook's Plaza. Due to a cock-up of historic proportions, the Cook statue here looks nothing like Cap'n Jim. A plaque proclaims, 'Who was he? We have no idea!' Adjacent is a modest pohutukawa tree planted by Princess Di in 1983. Further on is the Cook Observatory (www.possumobservatory.co.nz/astrogas/cook_observatory01.htm; public viewing $5; ☉ viewing 8.30pm Tue), the world's eastern-most star-gazing facility.

Eastwoodhill Arboretum   GARDENS
(☑ 06-863 9003; www.eastwoodhill.org.nz; 2392 Wharekopae Rd, Ngatapa; adult/child/family $15/2/34; ☉ 9am-5pm) Arboreal nirvana, Eastwoodhill Arboretum is the largest collection of northern hemisphere trees and shrubs in the southern hemisphere. It's staggeringly beautiful, and you could easily lose a day wandering around the 25km of themed tracks in this pine-scented paradise. It's well signposted, 35km northwest of Gisborne. There's also accommodation (p325) here.

Gisborne Farmers Market   MARKET
(www.gisbornefarmersmarket.co.nz; cnr Stout & Fitzherbert Sts; ☉ 9.30am-12.30pm Sat) Stock up on fresh fruit, macadamia nuts (and macadamia nut paste!), smallgoods, honey, herbs, coffee, wine, bread, pastries, fish, cheese...all of it locally grown or procured.

Cook Monument   MONUMENT
At the foot of Titirangi Park is the spot where Cook first got NZ dirt on his boots. Little more than a patch of lawn with a grim obelisk, the scrappy site was also the landing point of the *Horouta waka*. Join the sweaty joggers on the steep track up Kaiti Hill, which starts near the monument.

Statue of Young Nick   MONUMENT
There's no let-up in Gisborne's *Endeavour* endeavours: in the riverside park is a dynamic statue of Nicholas Young, Cook's cabin boy, whose eagle eyes were the first to spot NZ (the white cliffs at Young Nick's Head). There's another Captain Cook statue nearby, erected on a globe etched with his roaming routes.

Gisborne Botanic Gardens   GARDENS
(www.gdc.govt.nz/botanical-gardens; Aberdeen Rd; ☉ 24hr) FREE The town gardens are sitting pretty beside the Taruheru River – a beaut spot for a picnic. Wiggle through the NZ native Bushland Walkway.

Te Tauihu Turanga Whakamana   MONUMENT
(The Canoe Prow; cnr Gladstone Rd & Customhouse St) Like a giant sundial, Te Tauihu Turanga Whakamana is a large modern sculpture in the shape of a *tauihu* (canoe prow) that celebrates early Maori explorers.

East Coast Museum
of Technology   MUSEUM
(ECMOT; www.ecmot.org.nz; SH2, Makaraka; adult/child $5/2; ☉ 10am-4pm Mon-Sat, 1-4pm Sun) Think analogue, rather than digital; old age rather than space age. About 5km west of the town centre, this improbable medley of farm equipment, fire engines and sundry appliances has found an appropriate home in a motley old milking barn and surrounding outhouses. Oh, the irony of the welcome sign...

Matawhero Church   CHURCH
(www.standrewsgis.org.nz/faith.html; Church Lane, off Saleyard Rd, Matawhero; ☉ 9am-5pm) Some 7km west of the centre in the suburb of Matawhero, this historic Presbyterian church is the only building in the village to have survived Te Kooti's 1868 raid. It's a sweet timber affair with a bell turret and lovingly tended gardens.

Sunshine Brewing Company   BREWERY
(☑ 06-867 7777; www.gisbornegold.co.nz; 109 Disraeli St; ☉ 9am-6pm Mon-Sat) FREE Sunshine Brewing Company, Gisborne's own natural brewery, offers four quality beers including the famous Gisborne Gold and its big brother Green. Free tours and tastings by arrangement.

TE KOOTI

Maori history is littered with mystics, prophets and warriors, one of whom is the legendary Te Kooti (rhymes with naughty, not booty).

In 1865 he fought with the government against the Hauhau (adherents of the Pai Marire faith, founded by another warrior-prophet) but was accused of being a spy and imprisoned on the Chatham Islands without trial.

While there, Te Kooti studied the Bible and claimed to receive visions from the archangel Michael. His charismatic preaching and 'miracles' – including producing flames from his hands (his captors claimed he used phosphorus from the head of matches) – helped win over the Pai Marire to his distinctly Maori take on Christianity.

In 1867 Te Kooti led an astounding escape from the Chathams, hijacking a supply ship and sailing to Poverty Bay with 200 followers. En route he threw a doubter overboard as a sacrifice. Upon their safe arrival, Te Kooti's disciples raised their right hands in homage to God rather than bowing submissively; *ringa tu* (upraised hand) became the name of his church.

Te Kooti requested a dialogue with the colonial government but was once again rebuffed, with magistrate Reginald Biggs demanding his immediate surrender. Unimpressed by Pakeha (European New Zealander) justice, Te Kooti commenced a particularly effective guerrilla campaign – starting by killing Biggs and around 50 others (including women and children, Maori and Pakeha) at Matawhero near Gisborne.

A four-year chase ensued. Eventually Te Kooti took refuge in the King Country, the Maori king's vast dominion where government troops feared to tread.

Proving the pointlessness of the government's approach to the whole affair, Te Kooti was officially pardoned in 1883. By this time his reputation as a prophet and healer had spread and his Ringatu Church was firmly established, and today claims more than 16,000 adherents.

🏃 Activities

Water Sports

Surfing is mainstream in Gisborne, with the teenage population looking appropriately shaggy. **Waikanae Beach** and **Roberts Road** are good for learners; experienced surfers get tubed south of town at the **Pipe**, or east at **Sponge Bay** and **Tuamotu Island**. Further east along SH35, **Wainui** and **Makorori** also have quality breaks. There's safe swimming between the flags at Waikanae and **Midway Beach**.

Surfing With Frank   SURFING
(📞 06-867 0823, 021 119 0971; www.surfingwithfrank.com; lessons $50-75) Surfing with Frank offers lessons at Wainui, as well as tours of the best East Coast and Taranaki breaks. Three-hour board and wetsuit hire $30.

Rere Rockslide   SWIMMING
(Wharekopae Rd; ⏰ daylight hours) **FREE** This natural phenomenon occurs in a section of the Rere River, 50km northwest of Gisborne along Wharekopae Rd. Grab a tyre tube or boogie board to cushion the bumps and slide down the 60m-long rocky run into the pool at the bottom. Three kilometres downriver, the **Rere Falls** send a 20m-wide curtain of water over a 5m drop; you can walk behind it if you don't mind getting wet.

Olympic Pool   SWIMMING
(Centennial Marine Pde, Midway Beach; adult/child $3.80/2.80; ⏰ 6am-8pm daily, from 8am Sat & Sun May-Aug) Gisborne's big pool is a tepid 50m indoor/outdoor affair with a wormlike waterslide.

Surfit Charters   DIVING
(📞 06-867 2970; www.surfit.co.nz; per person from $310) Awaken your sense of mortality with a shark-cage dive with Surfit Charters. Tamer fishing and snorkelling trips also available.

Walking

There are many kilometres of walks to tackle around Gisborne, starting with a gentle stroll along the river. The i-SITE can provide you with brochures for the *Historic Walk* and the *Walking Trails of Gisborne City*.

Winding its way through farmland and forest with commanding views, the **Te Kuri Walkway** (two hours, 5.6km, closed August to October) starts 4km north of town at the end of Shelley Rd.

☞ Tours

Gisborne Cycle Tour Company CYCLING
(☑ 06-927 7021; www.gisbornecycletours.co.nz;
half-/full-day tours from $100/200, freedom hire
per day from $50) Half-day to multiday guided
cycle tours around local sights and further
afield including wineries and Eastwoodhill
Aboretum. Cheaper rates for multiday freedom bike hire (maps and advice on tap).

⚘ Festivals & Events

Feast Gisborne FOOD, WINE
(www.feastgisborne.co.nz) On October's Labour
Day weekend, local winemakers and foodies
pool talents for Gisborne's food-and-wine
fest, held at a local vineyard. Top NZ musical
talent usually makes an appearance. Over-
18s only.

Rhythm & Vines MUSIC, WINE
(www.rhythmandvines.co.nz) A huge event on
the music calendar, R&V is a three-day festival leading up to New Year's Eve, featuring
big-time local and international bands and
DJs. Local accommodation feels the sqeeze.

🛏 Sleeping

Gisborne YHA HOSTEL $
(☑ 06-867 3269; www.yha.co.nz; 32 Harris St; dm/
s/d/f $30/50/66/108; @ 🛜) A short wander
across the river from town, this rambling
1925 charmer houses a well-kept hostel. The
rooms are large and comfy (even the 10-bed
dorm in the roof space), while outside the
deck and lawns entice conversations. Family en suite unit and surfboard and bike hire
also available.

**Waikanae Beach Top
10 Holiday Park** HOLIDAY PARK $
(☑ 06-867 5634, 0800 867 563; www.waikanae-
beachtop10.co.nz; 280 Grey St; sites from $22, cab-
ins & units $70-155; @ 🛜) Right by the beach
and an easy 10-minute walk to town, this
grassy holiday park offers good-value cabins and units, and grassy lanes for pitching
tents and parking vans. Some of the cheaper
cabins could use some TLC. Surfboards and
bikes for hire.

Teal Motor Lodge MOTEL $$
(☑ 06-868 4019, 0800 838 325; www.teal.co.nz;
479 Gladstone Rd; d $125-175, f $195-245; @ 🛜 🏊)
With super street appeal on the main drag
(500m into town), the vaguely alpine Teal
boasts a solid offering of tidy, family-friendly
units plus a saltwater swimming pool and im-
maculate lawns to run around on. Free wi-fi.

Eastwoodhill Arboretum LODGE $$
(☑ 06-863 9003; www.eastwoodhill.org.nz; 2392
Wharekopae Rd, Ngatapa; dm/tw/d incl garden admission $35/80/120) The bunks and private
rooms at Eastwoodhill Arboretum (p323)
are basic, but once you're here, endless
woody delights can fill your days and nights.
Meals available by arrangement, or you can
use the fully equipped kitchen (BYO food as
there aren't any shops nearby).

Pacific Harbour Motor Inn MOTEL $$
(☑ 06-867 8847; www.pacific-harbour.co.nz; 24
Reads Quay; d $125-195; @ 🛜) Overlooking the
harbour, this two-tier motel offers well-kept
units with kitchenettes and dinky little bal-
conies. A tad classier than your average mo-
tel (black leather couches!). The best rooms
face the river and get all-day sun.

Quality Hotel Emerald HOTEL $$
(☑ 06-868 8055; www.emeraldhotel.co.nz; 13 Glad-
stone Rd; r $140-280; @ 🛜 🏊) With allegedly
the largest hotel rooms in NZ, the contemporary Emerald revolves around its swimming-
pool area – a reasonable impersonation of
a foxy international. Surrounding it are 48
plush suites along epic corridors connecting
various wings (much nicer inside than out).
Free wi-fi; off-street parking.

Captain Cook Motor Lodge MOTEL $$
(☑ 0800 227 826; www.captaincook.co.nz; cnr Grey
St & Awapuni Rd; d from $125, 1-/2-bedroom units
from $145/165; 🛜) It's not the architecture
you're here for – 36 rooms strung along a
vast carpark – but the location, a quick dash
to the Waikanae Beach on the other side of
the adjacent holiday park.

Knapdale Eco Lodge LODGE $$$
(☑ 06-862 5444; www.knapdale.co.nz; 114 Snowsill
Rd, Waihirere; d incl breakfast from $398; @ 🛜) 🌿
Indulge yourself at this rural idyll, complete
with lake, farm animals and home-grown
produce. The mod lodge is filled with international artwork, its glassy frontage flowing
out to an expansive patio with brazier, barbecue and pizza oven. Five-course dinner by
arrangement ($85). To get here head 10km
northwest of Gisborne, via Back Ormond Rd.

🍴 Eating

Cafe 1874 CAFE $
(☑ 06-863 3165; www.1874.co.nz; 38 Childers Rd;
meals $7-22; ⊙ 7am-3pm Mon-Fri, 9am-2pm Sat; 🎨)
The creaky grandeur of the Poverty Bay gen-
tleman's club (1874) is reason enough to visit.
This cafe within it certainly adds impetus:

appealing counter food, all-day brunch, pizza, blackboard specials and reasonable prices. Love the big pew along the outside wall.

Zest CAFE $

(✓06-867 5787; www.zestcafe.co.nz; 22 Peel St; mains $8-16; ⊙6am-4pm Mon-Sat) Pop quiz: how many cafes are there in the Western world called 'Zest'? Plenty. But unoriginality aside, this is one of the East Coast's best, offering pizzas, pastas, big breakfasts, salads, wraps, waffles and smoothies. Again, nothing too original, but perfectly executed, affordable and superfresh. Hope the regular knitting group isn't taking up all the seats.

Muirs Bookshop & Café CAFE $

(www.muirsbookshop.co.nz; 62 Gladstone Rd; meals $8-13; ⊙9am-3.30pm Mon-Fri, to 3pm Sat) Situated above Muirs Bookshop, a beloved, age-old independent in a lovely heritage building, this simple cafe offers a small but sweet selection of counter food and excellent salads. Fans of fine espresso coffee and literature may need to be forcibly removed. Over-street balcony for balmy days.

Morrell's Artisan Bakery BAKERY $

(www.facebook.com/morrellsartisanbakery; 437 Gladstone Rd; items $4-9; ⊙7am-2pm Tue-Sat; ✓) Artisan bakers with killer pies, wholesome bread, delicious pastries and cookies, all made on site. Don't overlook the coconut and passionfruit custard slice.

Yoko Sushi SUSHI $

(✓06-868 6400; www.yokosushi.co.nz; 87 Grey St; sushi $5-12; ⊙8am-5pm Mon-Sat) If you're into sushi, Yoko will surely lure you in (even if your name's not John). Commendable sushi, along with the usual miso-lany of extras including beaut bento boxes.

Pak N Save SUPERMARKET $

(274 Gladstone Rd; ⊙7am-9pm) Fill up the trolley, and don't forget your Gisborne oranges.

Villaggio CAFE $$

(✓06-863 3895; villagio@threechefs.co.nz; 57 Ballance St; mains lunch $18-26, dinner $28-36; ⊙8am-4pm Sun-Wed, to late Thu-Sat) North of the river, push through the gate of this old art-deco house which has been stripped back to supersmart red, white and wood fundamentals. The menu offers fresh takes on classics (seafood chowder; fish and chips), plus colourful Med-style dishes (spaghetti with tomato, goat cheese and herbs; Moroccan vegetable tagine). Loiter in the garden over lunchtime wines.

★USSCO Bar & Bistro MODERN NZ $$$

(✓06-868 3246; www.ussco.co.nz; 16 Childers Rd; mains $30-42; ⊙4.30pm-late) Housed in the restored Union Steam Ship Company building (USSCO – get it?), this place is all class. Silky kitchen skills shine in a highly seasonal menu featuring the likes of soy-glazed pork belly with caramelized yams, parsnip puree and toasted nut salad. Devilishly good desserts, plus plenty of local wines and NZ craft beers. Generous portions, multicourse deals and live piano tunes.

🍷 Drinking & Entertainment

Smash Palace BAR

(✓06-867 7769; 24 Banks St; ⊙3pm-late Mon-Thu, 2pm-late Fri, noon-late Sat, 2-11pm Sun) Get juiced at the junkyard: an iconic drinking den in Gisborne's industrial wastelands, full to the gunwales with ephemera and its very own DC3 crash-landed in the beer garden. Occasional live music.

Rivers PUB

(cnr Gladstone Rd & Reads Quay; ⊙11am-late Mon-Sat, from noon Sun) This well-run, British-style pub does the business, offering steak-and-ale pie, proper pudding, big-screen telly and pool. It's also family friendly and cosy, with some choice artefacts adding a convincing veneer of history. Quiz nights Tuesdays.

Poverty Bay Club LIVE MUSIC, CINEMA

(✓06-863 2006; www.thepovertybayclub.co.nz; 38 Childers Rd; ⊙5pm-late Wed-Fri, 8pm-late Sat, 5.30pm-late Sun) Sharing this lovely old historic building with a cafe and art shop is Winston's Bar, where occasional live music and vintage board games transpire, as well as the bean-baggy Dome Cinema (✓08-324 3005; www.domecinema.co.nz; tickets $15; ⊙from 5.30pm Wed-Sun), which screens art-house flicks.

ℹ Information

DOC (Department of Conservation; ✓06-869 0460; www.doc.govt.nz; 63 Carnarvon St; ⊙8am-4.30pm Mon-Fri) Tourist information.

Gisborne Hospital (✓06-869 0500; www.tdh.org.nz; Ormond Rd; ⊙24hr)

Gisborne i-SITE (✓06-868 6139; www.gisbornenz.com; 209 Grey St; ⊙8.30am-5.30pm Mon-Fri, 9am-5pm Sat, 10am-4pm Sun; 🛜) Beside a doozy of a Canadian totem pole, this information centre has all and sundry, as well as a travel desk, internet access and toilets.

Police Station (✓06-869 0200; www.police.govt.nz; cnr Gladstone Rd & Customhouse St; ⊙24hr)

Post Office (www.nzpost.co.nz; 127 Gladstone Rd; ⊙8.30am-5pm Mon-Fri, 9am-noon Sat)

ℹ Getting There & Around

The i-SITE handles bookings for many local and national transport services.

AIR

Gisborne Airport (www.eastland.co.nz/ gisborne-airport; Aerodrome Rd) is 3km west of the city. Air New Zealand flies to/from Auckland and Wellington, with onward connections. Sunair Aviation flies direct from Gisborne to Rotorua, Tauranga and Napier.

BUS

InterCity buses depart daily from the i-SITE for Napier ($47, four hours) via Wairoa ($30, 1½ hours); and Auckland ($85, 10 hours) via Opotiki ($36, two hours) and Rotorua ($64, five hours).

Naked Bus daily destinations include Taupo ($24, 5½ hours) via Opotiki ($17, two hours) and Rotorua ($25, 4½ hours).

For courier services from Gisborne to Opotiki travelling via East Cape's scenic SH35, see p315.

CAR

Gisborne Airport Car Rental (☑1300 350 401; www.gisborneairportcarhire.co.nz) is an agent for seven car-hire companies including the big brands and local outfits.

TAXI

A city-to-airport taxi fare costs about $20.
Gisborne Taxis (☑06-867 2222)

Gisborne to Hawke's Bay

From Gisborne, heading south towards Napier you're confronted with a choice: follow SH2, which runs closer to the coast, or take SH36 inland via Tiniroto. Either way you'll end up in Wairoa.

The coastal route is a marginally better choice, being quicker and offering occasional views out to sea. However, SH36 (**Tiniroto Road**) is also a pleasant drive (or bike route) with several good stopping points along the way. **Doneraille Park**, 49km from Gisborne, is a peaceful bush reserve with a frigid river to jump into and freedom camping for self-contained vehicles (see p319). Tree lovers might like to check out **Hackfalls Arboretum** (☑06-863 7083; www. hackfalls.org.nz; 187 Berry Rd, Tiniroto; adult/child $10/free; ⊙9am-5pm), a 3km detour from the turn-off at the Tiniroto Tavern. The snow-white cascades of **Te Reinga Falls**, 12km further south, are well worth a stop.

WORTH A TRIP

MAHIA PENINSULA

The Mahia Peninsula's eroded hills, sandy beaches and vivid blue sea make it a mini-ringer of the Coromandel, without the tourist hordes and fancy subdivisions, and with the bonus of dramatic Dover-ish cliffs. It's an enduring holiday spot for East Coasters, who come largely for boaty, beachy stuff, and you can easily get in on the action if you have your own transport. A day or two could easily be spent visiting the scenic reserve and the bird-filled Maungawhio Lagoon, hanging out at the beach (Mahia Beach at sunset can be spectacular) or even playing a round of golf.

Mahia has several small settlements offering between them a couple of guesthouses, a campsite, a decent pub and a dairy. See www.voyagemahia. co.nz for peninsular info.

The busier SH2 route heads inland and soon enters the **Wharerata State Forest** (beware of logging trucks). Just out of the woods, 55km from Gisborne, **Morere Hot Springs** (☑06-837 8856; www.morerehotsprings. co.nz; SH2, Morere; adult/child $10/5; ⊙10am-5pm, extended hours Dec-Feb) burble up from a fault line in the **Morere Springs Scenic Reserve**. Have a dip, or tackle a bush walk (20 minutes to three hours) before taking the plunge. The main pool is near the entrance, or a five-minute walk through virgin rainforest leads to the Nikau Pools.

Also at Morere is the **Morere Tearooms & Camping Ground** (☑06-837 8792; www. morereaccommodation.co.nz; SH2, Morere; campsites from $17, d $60-90), where you can get a respectable toasted sandwich and avail yourself of lovely campsites and basic cabins alongside the babbling Tunanui Stream. Just over the stream is **Morere Hot Springs Lodge & Cabins** (☑06-837 8824; www.morerelodge.co.nz; SH2, Morere; d $80-120, extra adult/child $20/10), a farmy enclave with accommodation in a classic 1917 farmhouse and two cute self-contained cabins.

From Gisborne on SH2, keep an eye out for the brightly painted **Taane-nui-a-Rangi Marae** on the left. You can get a decent view from the road; don't enter unless invited.

SH2 continues south to Nuhaka at the northern end of Hawke Bay. From here it's west to Wairoa or east to the salty **Mahia**

Peninsula. Not far from the Nuhaka roundabout is **Kahungunu Marae** (www.visitwairoa.co.nz/pages/kahungunu_marae; cnr Ihaka & Mataira Sts). From the roadside, check out the carving at the house's apex: a standing warrior holding a *taiaha* (spear), less stylised than most traditional carving.

Te Urewera National Park

Shrouded in mist and mysticism, Te Urewera National Park is the North Island's largest, encompassing 2127 sq km of virgin forest cut with lakes and rivers. The highlight is Lake Waikaremoana (Sea of Rippling Waters), a deep crucible of water encircled by the Lake Waikaremoana Track, one of NZ's Great Walks. Rugged bluffs drop away to reedy inlets, the lake's mirror surface disturbed only by mountain zephyrs and the occasional waterbird taking to the skies.

The name Te Urewera still has the capacity to make Pakeha (white) New Zealanders feel slightly uneasy – and not just because it translates as 'The Burnt Penis'. There's something primal and untamed about this wild woodland, with its rich history of Maori resistance.

Lake Waikaremoana Track

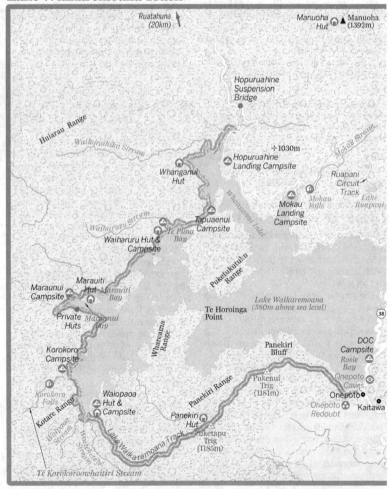

The local Tuhoe people – prosaically known as the 'Children of the Mist' – never signed the Treaty of Waitangi and fought with Rewi Maniapoto at Orakau during the Waikato Wars. The army of Te Kooti took refuge here during running battles with government troops. The claimant of Te Kooti's spiritual mantle, Rua Kenana, led a thriving community beneath the sacred mountain Maungapohatu (1366m) from 1905 until his politically motivated 1916 arrest. This effectively erased the last bastion of Maori independence in the country. Maungapohatu never recovered, and only a small settlement remains. Nearby, Ruatahuna's extraordi-nary Mataatua Marae celebrates Te Kooti's exploits.

Tuhoe remain proud of their identity and traditions, with around 40% still speaking *te reo* (the language) on a regular basis.

🏃 Activities

Lake Waikaremoana Track

This 46km, three- to four-day tramp scales the spectacular Panekiri Bluff (1180m), with open panoramas interspersed with fern groves and forest. The walk is rated as moderate with the only difficult section being the Panekiri ascent, and during summer it can get busy.

Although it's a year-round track, winter rain deters many people and makes conditions much more challenging. At this altitude (580m above sea level), temperatures can drop quickly, even in summer. Walkers should take portable stoves and fuel as there are no cooking facilities en route.

There are five **huts** (adult/child $32/free) and **campsites** (per night adult/child $14/free) spaced along the track, all of which must be prebooked through DOC, regardless of the season. Book at regional DOC offices, i-SITEs or online at www.greatwalks.co.nz.

If you have a car, it is safest to leave it at the Lake Waikaremoana Motor Camp or Big Bush Holiday Park then take a water taxi to the trailheads. Alternatively, you can take the fully catered, three-night guided tour offered by the enthusiastic and experienced **Walking Legends** (☏07-312 5297, 0800 925 569; www.walkinglegends.com; tours $1390).

Propel yourself onto the trail either clockwise from just outside **Onepoto** in the south or anticlockwise from **Hopuruahine Suspension Bridge** in the north.

Estimated walking times:

ROUTE	DURATION (HR)
Onepoto to Panekiri Hut	5
Panekiri Hut to Waiopaoa Hut	3-4
Waiopaoa Hut to Marauiti Hut	5
Marauiti Hut to Waiharuru Hut	2
Waiharuru Hut to Whanganui Hut	2½
Whanganui Hut to Hopuruahine Suspension Bridge	2

Other Walks

There are dozens of walks within the park's vast boundaries, most of which are outlined in DOC's *Lake Waikaremoana Walks* and *Recreation in Northern Te Urewera* pamphlets ($2.50). Plenty of short walks kick off

0 ————— 5 km
0 ————— 2.5 miles

Manuoha Track

Te Urewera National Park

Sandy Bay Hut

Lake Waikareiti (892m above sea level)

Day Shelter
Lake Waikareiti Track

Aniwaniwa Stream

+1061m

Papakorito Falls

Te Urewera National Park Visitor Centre

Lake Waikaremoana Motor Camp

Te Urewera National Park

Ngamoko Range

Ngamoko (1099m)

Lake Kaitawa
Big Bush Holiday Park

Tuai
Lake Whakamarino

Hikihiki's Inn

National Park Entrance

38

Wairoa (49km)

from the visitor centre and Lake Waikaremoana Motor Camp.

With its untouched islands, Lake Waikareiti is an enchanting place. Starting nearby the Te Urewera National Park Visitor Centre, it's an hour's walk to its shore. Once you're there you can explore it in a rowboat (keys from the visitor centre $20).

Accessed from the track to Lake Waikareiti, the more challenging Ruapani Circuit Track (six hours) passes through wetlands and dense virgin forest.

🛏 Sleeping & Eating

DOC has more than 30 huts and campsites within the park, most of which are very basic.

Lake Waikaremoana
Motor Camp HOLIDAY PARK $
(☑ 06-837 3826; www.holidayparks.co.nz; SH38, Lake Waikaremoana; sites per adult/child from $15/8, d cabins/units from $120/190) Right on the shore, this place has Swiss-looking chalets, fisher's cabins and campsites, most with watery views. The on-site shop is full of essentials (hot pies, chocolate, fishing flies...) and has a petrol pump.

Big Bush Holiday Park HOLIDAY PARK $
(☑ 06-837 3777, 0800 525 392; www.lakewaikaremoana.co.nz; SH38; sites/s/d from $15/30/60) About 4km from the Onepoto trailhead, Big Bush offers tent sites, trim cabins and backpacker rooms. Transfers to/from Wairoa, pick-ups/drop-offs around the lake, water taxis and storage also available.

Hikihiki's Inn B&B $$
(☑ 06-837 3701; www.hikihiki.co.nz; 9 Rotten Row, Tuai; s $80-120, d $160-240) In the sweet little settlement of Tuai, 6km from Onepoto, this little weatherboard gem serves as a B&B run by '100% Kiwi' hosts. Prices include continental breakfast; other meals at additional cost (24 hours notice required). Sleeps six.

ℹ Information

The DOC-run **Te Urewera National Park Visitor Centre** (☑ 06-837 3803; www.doc.govt.nz; Aniwaniwa; ⊙ 8am-4.45pm) has weather forecasts, accommodation information and hut or campsite passes for the Lake Waikaremoana Track.

ℹ Getting There & Around

Lake Waikaremoana is about an hour from Wairoa on SH38, which continues through to Rotorua. Around 95km of the entire 195km

Wairoa-to-Rotorua route is unsealed: it's a four-hour bone-rattling ride.

Big Bush Water Taxi (☑ 06-837 3777, 0800 525 392; www.lakewaikaremoana.co.nz) will ship you to either Onepoto or Hopuruahine trailhead ($50 return), with hut-to-hut pack transfers for the less gung-ho. It also runs shuttles to and from Wairoa ($50 one way).

HAWKE'S BAY

Hawke Bay, the name given to the body of water that stretches from the Mahia Peninsula to Cape Kidnappers, looks like it's been bitten out of the North Island's eastern flank. Add an apostrophe and an 's' and you've got a region that stretches south and inland to include fertile farmland, surf beaches, mountainous ranges and forests. With food, wine and architecture the prevailing obsessions, it's smugly comfortable but thoroughly appealing, and is best viewed through a rosé-tinted wineglass.

Wairoa to Napier

The small town of Wairoa (population 7900) is trying hard to shirk its rough-edged rep. Not scintillating enough to warrant an extended stay, the town has a couple of points of interest, including an exceptional (and exceptionally early-opening) pie shop called Oslers (☑ 06-838 8299; 116 Marine Pde; pies $3.50-4.50, meals $7-15; ⊙ 4.30am-4.30pm Mon-Fri, 6am-3pm Sat & Sun). Nonconsumable attractions include the plaque-studded River Walkway, the Wairoa Museum (☑ 06-838 3108; www.wairoamuseum.org.nz; 142 Marine Pde; ⊙ 10am-4pm Tue-Fri,to noon Sat) FREE inside an old bank, and a couple of motels if you're caught short. The Wairoa i-SITE (☑ 06-838 7440; www.visitwairoa.co.nz; cnr SH2 & Queen St; ⊙ 8am-5pm Mon-Fri, 10am-4pm Sat & Sun) is the spot for local info, including advice on Lake Waikaremoana.

The stretch of highway between Wairoa and Napier traipses through unphotogenic farmland and forestry blocks for much of its 117km. Most of it follows a railway line, currently only used for freight – you'll realise what a travesty this is when you pass under the Mohaka viaduct (1937), the highest rail viaduct in Australasia (97m).

Occupied by early Maori, Lake Tutira has walkways and a bird sanctuary. At Tutira village, just north of the lake, Pohokura Rd leads to the wonderful **Boundary Stream Scenic Reserve**, a major conservation area. Three loop tracks start from the road, ranging in length from 40 minutes to three hours. Also along this road you'll find the **Opouahi** and **Bellbird Bush Scenic Reserves**, which both offer rewarding walks. See www.doc.govt.nz for info on all of these reserves.

Off Waipatiki Rd, 34km outside Napier, Waipatiki Beach is a beaut spot boasting a low-key campsite and the 64-hectare **Waipatiki Scenic Reserve**. Further down the line, **White Pine Bush Scenic Reserve**, 29km from Napier on SH2, bristles with kahikatea and nikau palms. **Tangoio Falls Scenic Reserve**, 27km north of Napier, has Te Ana Falls, stands of wheki-ponga (tree ferns) and native orchids. Again, www.doc.govt.nz has the low-down on these reserves. Between White Pine and Tangoio Reserves the **Tangoio Walkway** (three hours return) follows Kareaara Stream.

The highway surfs the coast for the last 25km, with impressive views towards Napier. Hawke's Bay wine country starts in earnest at the mouth of the Esk River.

Napier

POP 57,240

The Napier of today – a charismatic, sunny, composed city with the air of an affluent English seaside resort – is the silver lining of the dark cloud that was the deadly 1931 earthquake. Rebuilt in the popular architectural styles of the time, the city retains a unique concentration of art-deco buildings. Don't expect the Chrysler Building – Napier is resolutely low-rise – but you will find intact 1930s facades and streetscapes, which can provoke a *Great Gatsby* swagger in the least romantic soul.

History

The area has been settled since around the 12th century and was known to Maori as Ahuriri. By the time James Cook eyeballed it in October 1769, Ngati Kahungunu was the dominant tribe, controlling the coast to Wellington.

In the 1830s whalers malingered around Ahuriri, establishing a trading base in 1839. By the 1850s the Crown had purchased – by often dubious means – 1.4 million acres of

---

CYCLE THE BAY

The 180km network of **Hawke's Bay Trails** (www.nzcycletrail.com/hawkes-bay-trails) – part of the national Nga Haerenga, New Zealand Cycle Trails project – offers cycling opportunities from short city scoots to hilly, single-track shenanagins. Dedicated cycle trails encircle Napier, Hastings and the coastline, with landscape, water and wine themes. Pick up the *Hawke's Bay Trails* brochure from the i-SITE or online.

Napier itself is very cycle friendly, particularly along Marine Pde where you'll find **Fishbike** (Map p334; ☑06-833 6979; www.fishbike.co.nz; 22 Marine Pde; bike hire per half-/full day $35/50, tandems $70/90; ☻9am-5pm) renting comfortable bikes – including tandems for those willing to risk divorce.

Mountain bikers head to **Eskdale Mountain Bike Park** (Map p332; ☑06-873 8793; www.hawkesbaymtb.co.nz; 3-week permit $10) for a whole lot of fun in the forest: see the website or call for directions. Hire mountain bikes from **Pedal Power** (Map p332; ☑06-844 9771; www.pedalpower.co.nz; 340 Gloucester St, Taradale; half-/full day from $30/60; ☻8am-5.30pm Mon-Fri, 9am-3pm Sat, 10am-3pm Sun), just out of the city centre in Taradale.

Given the conducive climate, terrain and multitudinous tracks, it's no surprise that numerous cycle companies pedal fully geared-up tours around the Bay, with winery visits near mandatory. Operators include the following:

Bike About Tours (☑06-845 4836; www.bikeabouttours.co.nz; tours half-/full day from $35/45)

Bike D'Vine (☑06-833 6697; www.bikedevine.com; tours adult/child from $35/15)

On Yer Bike Winery Tours (☑06-650 4627; www.onyerbikehb.co.nz; full day with/without lunch $60/50)

Takaro Trails (☑06-835 9030; www.takarotrails.co.nz; day rides from $40, 3-/5-day rides incl accommodation from $479/899)

Hawke's Bay

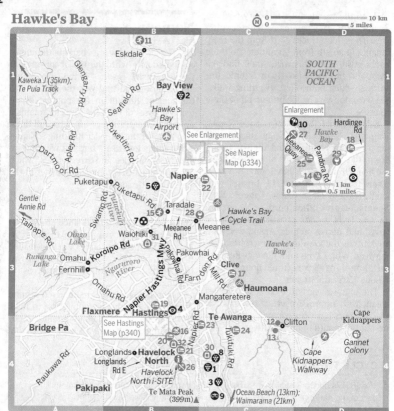

Hawke's Bay land, leaving Ngati Kahungunu with less than 4000 acres. The town of Napier was planned in 1854 and obsequiously named after the British general and colonial administrator Charles Napier.

At 10.46am on 3 February 1931, the city was levelled by a catastrophic earthquake (7.9 on the Richter scale). Fatalities in Napier and nearby Hastings numbered 258. Napier suddenly found itself 40 sq km larger, as the earthquake heaved sections of what was once a lagoon 2m above sea level (Napier's airport was once more 'port', less 'air'). A fevered rebuilding program ensued, constructing one of the world's most uniformly art-deco cities.

Sights

If you haven't got time for a guided or self-guided art-deco walking tour, just take to the streets – particularly Tennyson and Emerson. Remember to look up!

Deco Centre
TOURIST INFORMATION

(Map p334; www.artdeconapier.com; 7 Tennyson St; ☉9am-5pm) The relocated and revamped Deco Centre is the place to start your explorations. Its one-hour guided deco walk ($17) departs the i-SITE daily at 10am; the two-hour version ($20) leaves the Centre at 2pm daily. There's also a lovely little shop here, and brochures for the excellent self-guided *Art Deco Walk* ($7.50), *Art Deco Scenic Drive* ($5) and *Marewa Meander* ($3). You can also take a self-guided bike tour ($50, four hours), vintage car tour ($75, one hour), or kids' art-deco treasure hunt ($4).

★ Daily Telegraph Building
ARCHITECTURE

(Map p334; 49 Tennyson St) The Daily Telegraph is one of the stars of Napier's art-deco show, with superb zigzags, fountain shapes and ziggurat aesthetic. If the front doors are open, nip inside and ogle at the painstakingly restored foyer.

Hawke's Bay

◎ Sights
1 Black Barn Vineyards............................C4
2 Crab Farm Winery..................................B1
3 Craggy Range.......................................C4
4 Hastings Farmers Market....................B3
5 Mission Estate Winery.........................B2
6 National Tobacco Company
   Building..D2
7 Otatara Pa...B3
8 Te Mata Estate.....................................C4
9 Te Mata Peak Lookout.........................C4
10 Westshore Beach..................................C1

◉ Activities, Courses & Tours
11 Eskdale Mountain Bike Park................B1
12 Gannet Beach Adventures...................C4
13 Gannet Safaris......................................C4
14 Pandora Kayaks....................................D2
15 Pedal Power...B2
16 Splash Planet..B4

◎ Sleeping
17 Clive Colonial Cottages........................C3
18 Crown Hotel...D2
19 Eco Lodge Pakowhai.............................B3
20 Hastings Top 10 Holiday Park..............B4
21 Havelock North Motor Lodge...............B4

22 Kennedy Park Resort............................C2
23 Mangapapa Petit Hotel........................C4
24 Millar Road...C4
25 Rocks Motorlodge.................................D2

⊗ Eating
26 Bay Espresso...B4
   Deliciosa.......................................(see 21)
   Diva..(see 21)
   Pipi...(see 21)
27 Westshore Fish Café.............................C2

◎ Drinking & Nightlife
28 Filter Room..B2
29 Gintrap..D2
   Loading Ramp................................(see 21)
   Rose & Shamrock...........................(see 21)
   Thirsty Whale.................................(see 29)

◎ Entertainment
   Globe Theatrette...........................(see 18)

◎ Shopping
30 Arataki Honey..C4
31 Silky Oak Chocolate Company.............B3
   Strawberry Patch...........................(see 21)
32 Telegraph Hill..B4

★**MTG Hawke's Bay** MUSEUM, THEATRE (Museum Theatre Gallery; Map p334; ☎06-835 7781; www.mtghawkesbay.com; 1 Tennyson St; adult/child $15/free; ◎10am-6pm) The beating cultural heart of Napier is the newly renovated MTG. It's a gleaming-white museum-theatre-gallery space by the water, bringing together live performances, film screenings and regularly changing gallery and museum displays with touring and local exhibitions.

National Tobacco Company Building ARCHITECTURE (Map p332; cnr Bridge & Ossian Sts, Ahuriri) Around the shore at Ahuriri, the National Tobacco Company Building is arguably the region's deco masterpiece, combining art-deco forms with the natural motifs of art nouveau. Roses, raupo (bulrushes) and grapevines frame the elegantly curved entrance. During business hours, pull on the leaf-shaped brass door handles and enter the first two rooms.

Marine Parade STREET Napier's elegant seaside avenue is lined with huge Norfolk Island pines, and dotted with motels and charming timber villas. Along its length are parks, quirky **sunken gardens** (Map p334), a minigolf course, skate park, sound shell, swim centre and aquarium.

Near the north end of the parade is the **Tom Parker Fountain** (Map p334), best viewed at night when it's lavishly lit. Next to it is the **Pania of the Reef** (Map p334) sculpture, with her dubious boobs.

National Aquarium of New Zealand AQUARIUM (Map p334; www.nationalaquarium.co.nz; 546 Marine Pde; adult/child/family $20/10/54; ◎9am-5pm, feedings 10am & 2pm) Inside this modern complex with its stingray-inspired roof are piranhas, terrapins, eels, kiwi, tuatara and a whole lotta fish. Snorkellers can swim with sharks ($80), or sign up for a Little Penguin Close Encounter ($60).

Bluff Hill Lookout LOOKOUT (Map p334; Lighthouse Rd; ◎24hr) The convoluted route to the top of Bluff Hill (102m) goes up and down like an elevator on speed (best to drive), but rewards with expansive views across the port. Bring a picnic or some fish and chips.

Napier Urban Food Market MARKET (Map p334; www.hawkesbayfarmersmarket.co.nz; Lower Emerson St; ◎9am-1pm Sat) Score some superfresh local produce: fruit, veggies, bread, coffee, dairy products, honey wine...

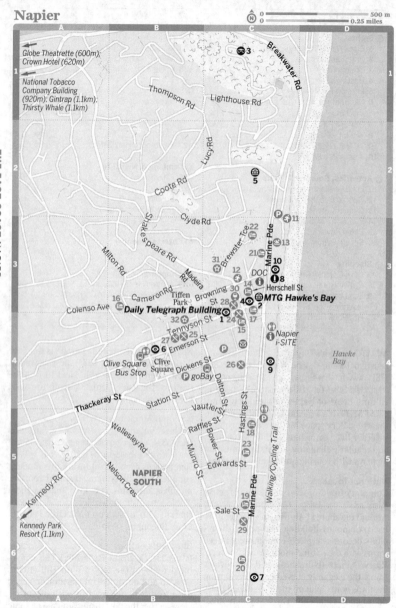

Globe Theatrette (600m);
Crown Hotel (620m)

National Tobacco
Company Building
(920m); Gintrap (1.1km);
Thirsty Whale (1.1km)

Kennedy Park
Resort (1.1km)

Napier Prison   HISTORIC BUILDING

(Map p334; ☏ 06-835 9933; www.napierprison.
com; 55 Coote Rd; adult/family $20/50; ⊘ 9am-
5pm) On the run from the law? Assuage
your guilt with a tour of the grim 1906 Napier Prison on the hill behind the town. It's
a self-guided audio set-up, available in 16
languages.

Otatara Pa   ARCHAEOLOGICAL SITE

(Map p332; www.doc.govt.nz; ⊘ 24hr) FREE
Wooden palisades, carved *pou* (memorial

Napier

◉ **Top Sights**
1 Daily Telegraph Building C3
2 MTG Hawke's Bay C3

◉ **Sights**
3 Bluff Hill Lookout C1
4 Deco Centre..C3
5 Napier Prison......................................C2
6 Napier Urban Food Market.................B4
7 National Aquarium of New
   Zealand...C6
8 Pania of the Reef C3
9 Sunken Gardens C4
10 Tom Parker Fountain C3

⊕ **Activities, Courses & Tours**
11 Fishbike...C3
12 New Zealand Wine Centre C3
13 Ocean Spa...C3

⊜ **Sleeping**
14 Archie's Bunker....................................C3
15 Criterion Art Deco
   Backpackers......................................C4
16 Green House on the Hill B3
17 Masonic Hotel C3
18 Napier YHA C5
19 Nautilus C5
20 Pebble Beach Motor Inn C6
21 Scenic Hotel Te Pania C3
   Sea Breeze B&B..........................(see 18)
22 Seaview Lodge B&B.............................C3
23 Stables Lodge Backpackers...............C5

⊗ **Eating**
24 Café Ujazi C4
25 Groove Kitchen Espresso B4
26 Kilim..C4
27 Kitchen Table B4
28 Mister D..C3
29 Restaurant Indonesia C6

◉ **Drinking & Nightlife**
   Emporium ....(see 17)
30 Guffle Bar..C3

⊛ **Entertainment**
31 Cabana Bar..C3
32 Napier Municipal Theatre B4

posts) and a carved gate help bring this *pa* site to life. An hour-long loop walk across grassy hills passes barely discernible archaeological remains but affords terrific views of the surrounding countryside. From the city head southwest on Taradale Rd and Gloucester St. Turn right into Springfield Rd just before the river.

🏃 Activities

Napier's pebbly beach isn't safe for swimming; locals head north of the city to Westshore (Map p332) or to the surf beaches south of Cape Kidnappers.

Pandora Kayaks KAYAKING
(Map p332; ☏06-835 0684; www.pandorakayaks. co.nz; 53 Pandora Rd; single/double kayaks per hour $15/22, bikes per day $40; ⊙9am-5pm) On the shore of Pandora Pond, these folks hire out kayaks, surfboards, windsurfers, standup paddle boards, small yachts and bikes. Windsurfing and sailing lessons available.

Ocean Spa SWIMMING
(Map p334; www.oceanspa.co.nz; 42 Marine Pde; adult/child $10.50/7.90, private pools 30min adult/ child $12.50/9.50; ⊙6am-9.45pm Mon-Sat, 8am-9.45pm Sun) A spiffy waterfront pool complex that features a lane pool, hot pools, a beauty spa and a gym.

New Zealand Wine Centre WINE TASTING
(Map p334; ☏06-835 5326; www.nzwinecentre. co.nz; 1 Shakespeare Rd; tastings 3/6 wines $16/29; ⊙10am-6pm daily, closed Sun Jun-Aug) No time for a full-blown Hawke's Bay winery tour? Swing by the NZ Wine Centre for a taste of region's best drops on 'Wine Tasting Adventures'.

Mountain Valley ADVENTURE SPORTS
(☏06-834 9756; www.mountainvalley.co.nz; 408 McVicar Rd, Te Pohue; horse treks/rafting/fishing per person from $30/60/250) Sixty kilometres north of Napier on SH5, Mountain Valley is a hub of outdoorsy action: horse trekking, white-water rafting, kayaking and fly fishing. There's also accommodation on site (sites/dorms/doubles from $12/22/70).

👉 Tours

See also p331 for bike-tour info.

Absolute de Tours BUS TOUR
(☏06-844 8699; www.absolutedetours.co.nz) Bus tours of the city, Marewa and Bluff Hill ($40) in conjunction with the Deco Centre, plus half-day tours of Napier and Hastings ($60).

Ferg's Fantastic Tours GUIDED TOUR, WINE
(☏0800 428 687; www.fergstours.co.nz; tours $40-120) Tours from two to seven hours, exploring Napier and surrounding areas: wineries, Te Mata Peak, lookouts and foodie stops.

Hawke's Bay Scenic Tours GUIDED TOUR
(☏06-844-5693; www.hbscenictours.co.nz; tours from $50) A grape-coloured bunch of tour

THE EAST COAST NAPIER

options including the 'Napier Whirlwind' and wineries.

Bay Tours & Charters
GUIDED TOUR, WINE

(☑ 06-845 2736; www.baytours.co.nz; tours from $40) Family-friendly tours, including a two-hour 'Napier Highlights' tour and a three-hour 'Best of the Bay' jaunt.

Packard Promenade
GUIDED TOUR

(☑ 06-835 0022; www.packardpromenades.co.nz; tours up to 4 people from $150) Offers deco and wine tours in a sassy 1939 Packard Six vintage car.

⭐ Festivals & Events

Art Deco Weekend
CULTURE

(www.artdeconapier.com) In the third week of February, Napier and Hastings cohost the sensational Art Deco Weekend. Around 200 events fill the week (dinners, picnics, dances, balls, bands, Gatsby-esque fancy dress), many of which are free. Bertie, Napier's art-deco ambassador, is omnipresent.

🛏 Sleeping

Napier YHA
HOSTEL $

(Map p334; ☑ 06-835 7039; www.yha.co.nz; 277 Marine Pde; dm/s/d from $26/45/69; @ 🛜) Napier's friendly YHA is housed in a lovely old timber beachfront villa with a seemingly endless ramble of rooms. There's a fabulous overhanging reading nook and a sunny rear courtyard. Staff can help with bookings and local info. A solid choice.

Criterion Art Deco Backpackers
HOSTEL $

(Map p334; ☑ 06-835 2059; www.criterionartdeco. co.nz; 48 Emerson St; dm/d/f from $26/85/120; @ 🛜) New owners are spending a lot of money sprucing up this 1st-floor, ruby-red downtown hostel – Napier's best Spanish Mission specimen – which has a beaut little balcony over Emerson St and an amazing old fireplace in the lounge area. A super-charming hostel on the way back up.

Kennedy Park Resort
HOLIDAY PARK $

(Map p332; ☑ 06-843 9126, 0800 457 275; www. kennedypark.co.nz; 1 Storkey St; sites from $46, cabins & units $61-227; @ 🛜 🏊) Less a camping ground and more an entire suburb of holidaymakers, this complex is top dog on the Napier camping scene. It's the closest camping ground to town (2.5km out, southwest of the centre) and has every facility imaginable, and a swath of cabin and unit configurations. And a karaoke machine!

Archie's Bunker
HOSTEL $

(Map p334; ☑ 0800 272 443, 06-833 7990; www. archiesbunker.co.nz; 14 Herschell St; dm/s/d from $25/35/62; @ 🛜) One street back from the foreshore, Archie's is a shipshape modern hostel filling an old office building. It's a quiet and secure arrangement with friendly owners and bike hire. A few rooms are windowless, but well ventilated. Massive DVD library for quiet nights in.

Stables Lodge Backpackers
HOSTEL $

(Map p334; ☑ 06-835 6242; www.stableslodge. co.nz; 370 Hastings St; dm/s/d from $25/55/69; 🛜) Formerly an actual stables, this is an atmospheric, affable place to get off your horse, with hippie vibes, a barbecue courtyard, murals, saddles festooned around the place and free wi-fi.

⭐ Seaview Lodge B&B
B&B $$

(Map p334; ☑ 06-835 0202; www.aseaviewlodge. co.nz; 5 Seaview Tce; s $130-140, d $170; 🛜) This grand Victorian villa (1890) is queen of all she surveys – which is most of the town and a fair bit of ocean. The elegant rooms have tasteful period elements and either bathroom or en suite. It's hard to resist a sunset tipple on the verandah, which opens off the relaxing guest lounge. Free wi-fi and off-street parking a bonus.

Pebble Beach Motor Inn
MOTEL $$

(Map p334; ☑ 0800 723 224, 06-835 7496; www. pebblebeach.co.nz; 445 Marine Pde; d/f from $145/165; 🛜) Unlike the majority of NZ motels, this one is owner-operated (they own the building, rather than lease it from a higher power) – so maintenence and service top the list of staff priorities. There are 25 immaculate rooms over three levels, all with kitchens, spas, balconies and ocean views. Full to capacity most nights.

Green House on the Hill
B&B $$

(Map p334; ☑ 06-835 4475; www.the-green-house. co.nz; 18b Milton Rd; s/d $110/135; 🛜) This meat-free '70s B&B is up a steep hill and rewards with leafy surrounds and magical city 'n' sea views. The guest floor has two bedrooms, one with an en suite and one with a private (but separate) bathroom. Home-baked goodies and fine herbal teas are likely to make an appearance. Great value. Free wi-fi, too.

Masonic Hotel
HOTEL $$

(Map p334; ☑ 06-835 8689; www.masonic.co.nz; cnr Tennyson St & Marine Pde; r $179-499; 🛜) The art-deco Masonic is arguably the heart of the old town, its accommodation, restaurants and bars taking up most of a city block. It's undergoing a gradual but much-needed refurb, and is shaping up nicely around its charming old bones. The cheaper 'original' rooms are unrefurbished, but still decent. Good online discounts and free wi-fi.

Rocks Motorlodge
MOTEL $$

(Map p332; ☑ 06-835 9626; www.therocksmotel. co.nz; 27 Meeanee Quay, Westshore; units $110-180; ☎) Just 80m from the beach, the Rocks has corrugated and mosaic stylings that have raised the bar on Westshore's motel row. Interiors are plush with colour splashes: some have spa baths, others clawfoot baths. Free internet, free gym, and a laundry for grubby road warriors.

Nautilus
HOTEL $$

(Map p334; ☑ 06-974 6550, 0508 628 845; www. nautilusnapier.co.nz; 387 Marine Pde; d/apt from $175/300; ☎) A newish, two-storey waterfront number with views from every room, kitchenettes, mod-deco decor, spa baths, private balconies and an in-house restaurant (not that you'll need it in Napier). Apartments sleep up to six.

Sea Breeze B&B
B&B $$

(Map p334; ☑ 06-835 8067; www.seabreezebnb. co.nz; 281 Marine Pde; s/d from $100/110; ☎) Inside this Victorian seafront earthquake survivor (1906) are three richly coloured themed rooms (Chinese, Indian and Turkish), decorated with a cornucopia of artefacts. A tad over-the-top perhaps, but there's free wi-fi and the price and location are right. Self-serve continental breakfast is included.

Scenic Hotel Te Pania
HOTEL $$$

(Map p334; ☑ 06-833 7733; www.scenichotels. co.nz; 45 Marine Pde; d/1-bedroom/2-bedroom from $185/255/400; @☎) Looking like a mini UN HQ by-the-sea, the refurbished, curvilicious, six-storey Te Pania has instant retro appeal. Rooms are far from retro, however, with designer linen, leather lounges and floor-to-ceiling windows that slide open for chestfuls of sea air.

Crown Hotel
HOTEL $$$

(Map p332; ☑ 06-833 8300; www.thecrownnapier.co.nz; cnr Bridge St & Hardinge Rd, Ahuriri; d/1-bedroom/apt from $189/199/400; @☎) The conversion of this 1932 pub into a ritzy apartment-style hotel must have broken a few fishermen's hearts. The new wing features muted tones, nice wallpaper and linen and super sea views. Bike hire available.

Eating

Groove Kitchen Espresso
CAFE $

(Map p334; www.groovekitchen.co.nz; 112 Tennyson St; meals $9-19; ☉8am-2pm Mon-Fri, 8.30am-2pm Sat & Sun; ☑) A sophisticated cafe squeezed into small, groovy space where the turntable spins and the kitchen cranks out A1 brunch along with trendsetting wraps, baps, salads and killer coffee. With a bit of luck you'll be around for one of the intermittent Thursday-night gigs.

Café Ujazi
CAFE $

(Map p334; www.facebook.com/ujazicafe; 28 Tennyson St; snacks $4-10, meals $9-19; ☉8am-5pm; ☑) The most bohemian of Napier's cafes, Ujazi folds back its windows and lets the alternative vibes spill out onto the pavement. It's a long-established, consistent performer offering blackboard meals and hearty counter food. Try the classic *rewana* special – a big breakfast on traditional Maori bread. Impressive tea menu.

Kitchen Table
CAFE $

(Map p334; www.pghb.co.nz/page/cafe; 138 Tennyson St; brunch $8-19; ☉breakfast & lunch; ☎) Sharing an airy gallery space with a local photography studio, this colourful and crafty cafe produces classic fare ('homemade loveliness'), traipsing from scones to goats' cheese salad. Plenty to inspire, both on the walls and on the menu. Love the tattoo-esque sign and kooky internal ephemera. Free wi-fi.

Westshore Fish Café
FISH & CHIPS $

(Map p332; ☑ 06-834 0227; 112 Charles St, Westshore; takeaway $7-12, meals $14-28; ☉5-8pm Tue & Wed, 11.30am-2pm & 5-8pm Thu-Sun) If you're the type who needs cutlery, sit-down meals are served in the dining room here. Otherwise, grab some takeaway fish and chips and attract gulls down at the beach.

Kilim
TURKISH $

(Map p334; ☑ 06-835 9100; 193 Hastings St; meals $10-17; ☉11am-9pm Sun-Thu, to 9.30pm Fri & Sat; ☑) An authentic Turkish cafe, adorned with suitably Ottoman cushions and wall hangings. The kebabby, felafelly, salady meals are fresh and tasty, but service can be a tad sluggish. Hair-straightening Turkish coffee.

★ Mister D
MODERN NZ $$

(Map p334; ☑ 06-835 5022; www.misterd.co.nz; 47 Tennyson St; mains lunch $15-29, dinner $25-29;

THE EAST COAST NAPIER

⏱ 7.30am-4pm Sun-Wed, to late Thu-Sun) This long, floorboardy room with its green-tiled bar is the pride of the Napier foodie scene. Hip and stylish but not unaffordable, with quick-fire service delivering the likes of pulled pork with white polenta or chunky corn fritters with bacon and maple syrup. Novelty of the Year award: donuts served with syringes full of chocolate, jam or custard (DIY injecting). Superpopular – bookings essential.

Restaurant Indonesia   INDONESIAN $$
(Map p334; ☑ 06-835 8303; www.restaurantindonesia.co.nz; 409 Marine Pde; mains $20-27; ⏱ 5.30-9pm; 🍴) Crammed with Indonesian curios, this intimate space oozes authenticity. Lip-smacking Indo-Dutch *rijsttafel* smorgasbords are the house speciality (14 dishes, $30 to $36) – a romantic option for those in the mood. Bookings advisable.

🍷 Drinking & Nightlife

⭐ Emporium   BAR
(Map p334; www.emporiumbar.co.nz; Masonic Hotel, cnr Tennyson St & Marine Pde; ⏱ 7am-late; 🛜) Napier's most civilised bar, Emporium, with it' marble-topped bar, fab art-deco details and old-fashioned relics strewn about, is supratmospheric. Brisk staff, creative cocktails, good coffee, NZ wines, bistro fare (plates $15 to $30) and prime location seal the deal.

Guffle Bar   BAR
(Map p334; www.guffle.co.nz; 29A Hastings St; ⏱ 4pm-late Tue-Fri, 6pm-late Sat) Cool tunes, stylin' drinks, genial pros behind the bar, and an on-display window seat: ingredients that lure Napier's nocturnal sophisticates through the doors.

Gintrap   PUB
(Map p332; www.gintrap.co.nz; 64 West Quay, Ahuriri; ⏱ 11am-late Mon-Fri, 9.30am-late Sat & Sun) The pick of the big rambling restaurant-bars out on the Ahuriri waterfront, where the city council is endeavouring to isolate noisy after-dark crowds. Seafood in the sunshine (mains $19 to $32).

Thirsty Whale   BAR
(Map p332; www.thethirstywhale.co.nz; 62 West Quay, Ahuriri; ⏱ 11am-late Mon-Fri, 9am-late Sat & Sun; 🛜) Does a whale drink? Or just filter krill? Either way, this big dockside bar is a sporty spot to join some fellow mammals for a brew or a bite (mains $14 to $34). Becomes a dance club on Friday and Saturday nights.

⭐ Entertainment

Napier Municipal Theatre   THEATRE
(Map p334; ☑ 06-835 1059; www.napiermunicipaltheatre.co.nz; 119 Tennyson St; ⏱ box office 9am-5pm Mon-Fri, to 12.30pm Sat) Not only the city's largest venue for the likes of rock concerts, dance and drama (1000 seats), but also one of the world's few working art-deco theatres. Worth going for the original foyer lighting alone! Box office on site.

Globe Theatrette   CINEMA
(Map p332; ☑ 06-833 6011; www.globenapier. co.nz; 15 Hardinge Rd, Ahuriri; tickets $16; ⏱ 1pm-late Wed-Sun, plus 6pm-late Tue Dec-Feb) A vision in purple, this boutique 45-seat cinema screens art-house flicks in a sumptuous cinema lounge with ready access to upmarket snacks and drinks.

Cabana Bar   LIVE MUSIC
(Map p334; ☑ 06-835 1102; www.cabana.net.nz; 11 Shakespeare Rd; ⏱ 6pm-late Wed-Sat) This legendary music venue of the '70s, '80s and '90s died in 1997, but thanks to some forward-thinking, toe-tapping folk, it's risen from the grave to save the day for Napier's gig lovers.

ⓘ Information

DOC (Department of Conservation; Map p334; ☑ 06-834 3111; www.doc.govt.co.nz; 59 Marine Pde; ⏱ 9am-4.15pm Mon-Fri) Maps, advice and passes.

Napier Health Centre (☑ 06-878 8109; www. hawkesbay.health.nz; 76 Wellesley Rd; ⏱ 24hr) Round-the-clock medical assistance.

Napier i-SITE (Map p334; ☑ 06-834 1911; www.napiernz.co.nz; 100 Marine Pde; ⏱ 9am-5pm, extended hours Dec-Feb; 🛜) Handy and helpful.

Napier Police Station (☑ 06-831 0700; www. police.govt.nz; 77 Station St; ⏱ 24hr)

Napier Post Office (Map p334; www.nzpost. co.nz; Shop 9-12 Ocean Boulevard, Dickens St; ⏱ 9am-5pm Mon-Fri, 9am-4pm Sat, 10am-2pm Sun)

ⓘ Getting There & Away

AIR

Hawke's Bay Airport (Map p332; www.hawkes-bay-airport.co.nz) is 8km north of the city.

Air New Zealand (☑ 06-833 5400; www. airnewzealand.co.nz; cnr Hastings & Station Sts; ⏱ 9am-5pm Mon-Fri, to noon Sat) runs direct flights to/from Auckland, Wellington and Christchurch. Sunair Aviation has direct weekday flights between Napier, Gisborne and Hamilton

BUS

InterCity buses can be booked online or at the i-SITE, and depart from the **Clive Square Bus Stop** (Map p334). Services run daily to Auckland ($82, 7½ hours) via Taupo ($33, two hours); Gisborne ($43, four hours) via Wairoa ($27, 2½ hours); and Wellington ($40, 5½ hours); plus four daily services to Hastings ($22, 30 minutes).

Naked Bus daily destinations include Wellington ($20, 5½ hours) via Palmerston North ($10, 2½ hours); and Auckland ($25, eight hours) via Taupo ($10, two hours).

❶ Getting Around

Most key sights in the city are reachable on foot, or you can speed things up by hiring a bicycle from Fishbike (p331).

BUS

goBay (Map p334; ☑ 06-878 9250; www.hbrc. govt.nz) local buses (fitted with bike racks!) run many times daily between Napier, Hastings and Havelock North. Napier to Hastings (adult/child $5.20/2.80) takes 30 minutes (express) or 55 minutes (all stops). Buses depart Dalton St Bus Stop.

CAR

See www.rentalcars.com for car-hire deals with companies at Hawke's Bay Airport, including the big brands and local outfits. **Rent-a-Dent** (☑ 0800 736 823, 06-834 0688; www. napiercarrentals.co.nz; Hawke's Bay Airport; ⊙ 8am-5pm Mon-Fri, to 1pm Sat) is also at the airport.

TAXI

A city-to-airport taxi costs around $22.
Hawke's Bay Combined Taxis (☑ 0800 627 437, 06-835 7777; www.hawkes-bay.blue-bubbletaxi.co.nz)
Super Shuttle (☑ 06-835 0055, 0800 748 885; www.supershuttle.co.nz; 1 way $20, extra person $5) Airport to Napier door-to-door.

Hastings, Havelock North & Around

POP 73,250

Positioned at the centre of the Hawke's Bay fruit bowl, busy Hastings is the commercial hub of the region, 20km south of Napier. A few kilometres of orchards still separate it from Havelock North, with its prosperous village atmosphere and the towering backdrop of Te Mata Peak.

◎ Sights & Activities

As with Napier, Hastings was similarly devastated by the 1931 earthquake and also boasts some fine art-deco and Spanish Mission buildings, built in the aftermath. Main-street highlights include the **Westerman's Building** (Map p340; cnr Russell & Heretaunga St E, Hastings), arguably the Bay's best example of the Spanish Mission style, although there are myriad architectural gems here. The i-SITE stocks the *Art Deco Hastings* brochure ($1), detailing two self-guided walks.

Te Mata Peak   PARK
(www.tematapark.co.nz) Rising melodramatically from the Heretaunga Plains 16km south of Havelock North, Te Mata Peak (399m) is part of the 98-hectare **Te Mata Trust Park**. The summit road passes sheep trails, rickety fences and vertigo-inducing stone escarpments, cowled in a bleak, lunar-meets-Scottish-Highland atmosphere. From the **lookout** (Map p332) on a clear day, views fall away to Hawke Bay, Mahia Peninsula and distant Mt Ruapehu.

The park's trails offer walks from 30 minutes to two hours: pick up the *Te Mata Trust Park* brochure from local i-SITEs.

Hastings City Art Gallery   GALLERY
(HCAG; Map p340; www.hastingscityartgallery. co.nz; 201 Eastbourne St E, Hastings; ⊙ 10am-4.30pm) FREE The city's gallery presents contemporary NZ and international art in a bright, purpose-built space. Expect some wacky stuff (much wackier than Hastings itself...).

Hastings Farmers Market   FARMERS MARKET
(Map p332; www.hawkesbayfarmersmarket.co.nz; Showgrounds, Kenilworth Rd; ⊙ 8.30am-12.30pm Sun) If you're around on Sunday, the Hastings market is mandatory. Bring an empty stomach, some cash and a roomy shopping bag.

Splash Planet   SWIMMING
(Map p332; ☑ 06-873 8033; www.splashplanet. co.nz; Grove Rd, Hastings; adult/child $26/18; ⊙ 10am-5.30pm Nov-Feb) A massive, watery wonderland with myriad pools, slides and aquatic distractions.

Airplay Paragliding   PARAGLIDING
(☑ 06-845 1977; www.airplay.co.nz; 1-day courses $220) Te Mata Peak is a paragliding hot spot, with updraughts aplenty. Airplay offers full-day beginners' courses if you're keen to take the drop.

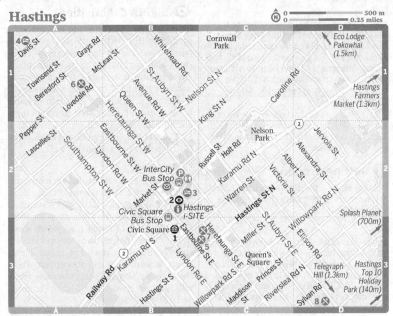

Hastings

◉ **Sights**
1 Hastings City Art Gallery B3
2 Westerman's Building B2

🛏 **Sleeping**
3 Rotten Apple...B2
4 Sleeping Giant.......................................A1

🍴 **Eating**
5 Opera Kitchen C3
6 Rush Munro's A1
7 Taste Cornucopia C3
8 Vidal...D3

👉 Tours

See p331 for two-wheeled tours around the area.

Long Island Guides   GUIDED TOUR
(☏06-874 7877; www.longislandtoursnz.com; half-day from $180) Customised tours across a wide range of interests including Maori culture, bush walks, kayaking, horse riding and, inevitably, food and wine.

Prinsy's Tours   WINE
(☏0800 004 237, 06-845 3703; www.prinsyexperience.co.nz; half-/full-day tours from $60/85) Affable half- or full-day wine jaunts, with

layman's-lingo explanations at four or five wineries.

Waimarama Tours   CULTURAL TOUR
(☏021 057 0935; www.waimaramaori.com; 2-4hr tours from $70) Maori-run tours of Te Mata Peak, with plenty of cultural insights en route.

Grape Escape   WINE
(☏0800 100 489; www.grapeescape.net.nz; tours from $70) Half-day winery tours, visiting four or five cellar doors, or six hours with a lunch stop ($90). Ask about beer tours if you're more of an ale hound.

🎊 Festivals & Events

Hastings Blossom Festival   CULTURE
(www.blossomfestival.co.nz) The Hastings Blossom Festival is a petalled spring fling, infamous for its 12-person 'riot' in 1960. The flowery insubordination happens in the second half of September: parades, arts, crafts and visiting artists.

🛏 Sleeping

Hastings Top 10 Holiday Park HOLIDAY PARK $
(Map p332; ☏06-878 6692; www.hastingstop10.co.nz; 610 Windsor Ave, Hastings; sites from $44, units $78-160, apt $300; @🛜🏊) Putting the 'park' back into holiday park, within its leafy

confines are sycamore hedges, a topiary 'welcome' sign, stream, ducks and accessible serenity. The pool and spa complex satisfies young and old. New tennis court.

Eco Lodge Pakowhai
HOSTEL $

(Map p332; ☑ 06-876 6997, 027 298 8910; www.ecolodge-pakowhai.co.nz; 1000 Pakowhai Rd; sites/dm/tw $20/25/60, d with/without bathroom $75/60; 🛜) ⏃ The same family have tilled this land since 1885, but the attitude here is very forward-thinking. The talkative owner cuts carbon with solar panels, rainwater-collection systems, worm farms, double-glazing...and is expert at finding farm work for travellers. Accommodation comprises neat new cabins or dorms in an old farmhouse. Good weekly rates; free wi-fi and laundry.

Rotten Apple
HOSTEL $

(Map p340; ☑ 06-878 4363; www.rottenapple.co.nz; 114 Heretaunga St E, Hastings; dm/s/d $26/50/70; @🛜) The central city, 1st-floor option and a fairly fruity affair, with orchard workers settled in paying weekly rates. There's a bit of deck, a decent kitchen and sociable vibes, and staff can help you find work (sorting the rotten apples from the good ones).

Sleeping Giant
HOSTEL $

(Map p340; ☑ 06-878 5393; www.hastingsbackpackers.co.nz; 109 Davis St, Hastings; dm/tw/d $20/50/60; @🛜) A messy-but-homey backpackers in a suburban house, a 10-minute walk to town. A posse of tanned, wiry agricultural workers ensures a sociable atmosphere in the fairly close communal confines. Pool table in the shed.

★Clive Colonial Cottages
RENTAL HOUSE $$

(Map p332; ☑ 06-870 1018; www.clivecolonialcottages.co.nz; 198 School Rd, Clive; d from $135; 🛜) A two-minute walk to the beach and almost equidistant from Hastings, Napier and Havelock, these three tasteful kitchen cottages encircle a courtyard garden on a 2-acre spread. Communal areas include barbecue, giant chess set and snooker room. Bikes on site; trail on doorstep.

Havelock North Motor Lodge
MOTEL $$

(Map p332; ☑ 06-877 8627; www.havelocknorthmotorlodge.co.nz; 7 Havelock Rd, Havelock North; units $135-195; 🛜) Smack-bang in the middle of Havelock North, this modern motel is a cut above the rest. Tidy one- and two-bedroom units feature spa baths, nice art and kitchenettes. Is the new Mexican joint across the street open yet?

Millar Road
RENTAL HOUSE $$$

(Map p332; ☑ 06-875 1977; www.millarroad.co.nz; 83 Millar Rd, Hastings; villas/houses from $400/650; 🛜⊠) Set in the Tuki Tuki Hills with vineyard and bay views, Millar Road is architecturally heaven-sent. Two plush villas (each sleep four) and a superstylish house (sleeps eight) are filled with NZ-made furniture and local artworks. Explore the 20-hectare grounds or look cool by the pool.

Mangapapa Petit Hotel
BOUTIQUE HOTEL $$$

(Map p332; ☑ 06-878 3234; www.mangapapa.co.nz; 466 Napier Rd, Havelock North; d incl breakfast $450-1500; @🛜⊠) A five-minute drive from Hastings, this heritage home (1885), surrounded by leafy gardens, a tennis court, swimming pool and short golf course, has been sympathetically adapted into a boutique hotel. Twelve suites offer period-style luxury; a restaurant and day spa up the indulgence stakes. 'Good afternoon Sir', says the dapper doorman.

✗ Eating

Taste Cornucopia
CAFE $

(Map p340; www.tastecornucopia.co.nz; 219 Heretaunga St E, Hastings; meals $7-22; ⊙ 7.30am-4pm Mon-Fri, 6.30pm-late Fri; ⏃) ⏃ An award-winning, high-ceilinged organic cafe in central Hastings, serving filling 'abundant' breakfasts, organic coffee, smoked-fish pies, curries, vegetarian lasagne and amazing 'marshmallows' that look like giant blobs of extruded toothpaste. Super NZ wine list, too. Tasty dinners Friday nights.

Bay Espresso
CAFE $

(Map p332; 19 Middle Rd, Havelock North; mains $10-19; ⊙ 7.30am-4pm Mon-Fri, 8am-4pm Sat & Sun) On Middle Rd in the middle of Havelock, this enduringly popular cafe is far from middling, serving up house-roasted organic coffee, handsome counter food and reasonable brunch. Blaring Freddie Mercury and blueberry pancakes – a winning combo.

Rush Munro's
ICE CREAM $

(Map p340; www.rushmunro.co.nz; 704 Heretaunga St W, Hastings; ice cream $3-8; ⊙ 11am-6pm Mon-Fri, to 7pm Sat & Sun, reduced winter hours) Rush Munro's is a Hastings icon, serving locally made ice cream since 1926. Try the maple walnut.

★Opera Kitchen
CAFE $$

(Map p340; www.operakitchen.co.nz; 312 Eastbourne St E, Hastings; mains $9-25; ⊙ 7.30am-4pm

Mon-Fri, 9am-3pm Sat & Sun; 🖉) Set your rudder right with some whiskey porridge with cream and giant oats at this mod, stylish cafe abutting Hawke's Bay Opera House. For a more practical start to the day, the farmers breakfast is also a winner. Heavenly baked goods, great coffee and snappy staff. Eat in, or outside in the suntrap courtyard.

Deliciosa　　　　　　　　　　TAPAS $$
(Map p332; 🖉 06-877 6031; www.deliciosa.co.nz; 21 Napier Rd, Havelock North; tapas $8-19; ⊘4pm-late Mon & Tue, 11am-late Wed-Sat) Great things come in small packages at this rosy little tapas bar, run by a displaced Seattleite. The kitchen delivers sassy, locally sourced edibles like pork belly with pomegranate jus and salt-and-pepper squid with orange and parsley, while the wine list roams from Spain to Italy and back. Terrific beer list, too.

Pipi　　　　　　　　　　PIZZERIA $$
(Map p332; 🖉 06-877 8993; www.pipicafe.co.nz; 16 Joll Rd, Havelock North; mains $16-28; ⊘4-10pm Tue-Sun) Shockingly pink with candy stripes and mismatched furniture, Pipi cheekily thumbs its nose at small-town conventionality. The food focus is on simple pasta dishes and Roman-style thin-crusted pizza. Pipi Bar is across the street if you're waiting for a table, and **Pipi Truck** randomly turns up around the Bay, taking the food to the streets (check Facebook for locations).

Diva　　　　　　　　　　MODERN NZ $$
(Map p332; 🖉 06-877 5149; www.divabar.co.nz; 10 Napier Rd, Havelock North; mains lunch $16-20, dinner $22-35; ⊘11.30am-2.30pm Tue-Fri, 5.30pm-late Tue-Sat) A sexy fusion of orange, black and chocolatey timber, Diva offers good-value lunches (from paua bugers to steaks) and bistro-style dinners featuring fresh seafood and seasonal specialities. Eat in the flashy dining room, at the groovy bar (small plates $5 to $17) or chatty pavement tables.

Vidal　　　　　　　　　　MODERN NZ $$$
(Map p340; 🖉 06-872 7440; www.vidal.co.nz; 913 St Aubyn St E, Hastings; mains lunch $25-29, dinner $28-36; ⊘11.30am-3pm & 6pm-late) There's nothing suburban about this winery restaurant on the backstreets of Hastings. The warm, wood-lined dining room is a worthy setting for such elegant food: order the annual signature dish (2013 market fish, 2014 venison), sip some syrah and feel your holiday come to fruition.

HAWKE'S BAY WINERIES

Once upon a time, this district was most famous for its orchards. Today it's vines that have top billing, with Hawke's Bay now NZ's second-largest wine-producing region. Expect excellent Bordeaux-style reds, syrah and chardonnay. Pick up the *Hawke's Bay Winery Guide* map from the i-SITE, or download it from www.winehawkesbay.co.nz. A few of our faves:

Black Barn Vineyards (Map p332; 🖉 06-877 7985; www.blackbarn.com; Black Barn Rd, Havelock North; ⊘9am-5pm Mon-Fri, 10am-5pm Sat & Sun) Hip, inventive winery with a bistro, gallery, Saturday farmers market (one of NZ's first) and an amphitheatre for concerts and movie screenings. Try the flagship chardonnay.

Crab Farm Winery (Map p332; 🖉 06-836 6678; www.crabfarmwinery.co.nz; 511 Main North Rd, Bay View; ⊘10am-5pm daily, 6pm-late Fri) Decent, reasonably priced wines and a great cafe with regular live troubadors and relaxed, rustic vibes. A good stop for lunch or a glass of rosé (or both).

Mission Estate (Map p332; 🖉 06-845 9354; www.missionestate.co.nz; 198 Church Rd, Taradale; ⊘9am-5pm Mon-Sat, 10am-4.30pm Sun) NZ's oldest winery (1851!). Follow the *looong* tree-lined drive up to the restaurant and cellar door, inside a magnificently restored seminary.

Te Mata Estate (Map p332; www.temata.co.nz; 349 Te Mata Rd, Havelock North; ⊘8.30am-5pm Mon-Fri, 10am-5pm Sat) 🖉 The legendary Coleraine red at this unpretentious, old-school, family-run winery is worth the trip alone.

Craggy Range (Map p332; 🖉 06-873 0141; www.craggyrange.com; 253 Waimarama Rd, Havelock North; ⊘10am-6pm, closed Mon & Tue Apr-Oct) Inside a cathedral-like 'wine barrel', the restaurant here, called Terroir, is one of the region's most consistent fine-dining experiences. Photogenic views of craggy Te Mata Peak.

☕ Drinking

Loading Ramp BAR
(Map p332; www.loadingramp.co.nz; 8 Treachers
Lane, Havelock North; ⊙3pm-late Tue-Sat) This
lofty timber space pulls a mixed crowd of
young 'uns and seasoned drinkers, here to
watch the All Blacks on the big screen, sip
Monteith's or chew tapas (or all three). Also
offers big pubby meals (mains $22 to $30).

Filter Room BREWERY
(Map p332; www.thefilterroom.co.nz; Awatoto Rd,
Meeanee; ⊙10am-5pm Sun-Thu, to 7pm Fri & Sat)
Surrounded by orchards, these folks proffer
impressive craft beers and ciders, brewed on
site, plus tasting trays and belly-filling food.

Rose & Shamrock PUB
(Map p332; www.roseandshamrock.co.nz; cnr Napier Rd & Porter Dr, Havelock North; ⊙10.30am-late)
A carpeted, dark-wood, Brit-style boozer
complete with 27 globe-trotting beers on tap
(*oooh*, Coopers Sparkling Ale from South
Australia!) and hearty pub grub (mains $14
to $26).

🛍 Shopping

The Hastings area appears to exist largely
for the satisfaction of our appetites, with a
plethora of boutique food producers.

Strawberry Patch FOOD
(Map p332; www.strawberrypatch.co.nz; 76 Havelock Rd, Havelock North; ⊙9am-5.30pm) Pick
your own berries in season (late November
through summer), or visit year-round for
fresh produce, picnic supplies, coffee and
real fruit ice cream ($4).

Arataki Honey FOOD
(Map p332; www.aratakihoneyhb.co.nz; 66 Arataki
Rd, Havelock North; ⊙9am-5pm) 🐝 Stock up
on buzzy by-products for your toast or your
skin at family-run Arataki. Hands-on displays outline the whole sticky cycle from
flower to jar. Free tastings.

Telegraph Hill FOOD
(Map p332; www.telegraphhill.co.nz; 1279 Howard
St, Hastings; ⊙9am-5pm Mon-Fri, plus 10am-3pm
Sat Oct-Mar) A passionate producer of olives,
oils and sundry Mediterranean-inspired
gourmet treats. Four-person picnic baskets
($40) available for on-site indulgence.

Silky Oak Chocolate Company FOOD
(Map p332; www.silkyoakchocs.co.nz; 1131 Links Rd,
Napier; ⊙9am-5pm Mon-Thu, 9am-4pm Fri, 10am-
4pm Sat & Sun) Watch the chocolatiers at work
while deliberating over mouthwatering truf-
fles and chocolate rugby balls. The museum
(adult/child $8/5) offers a cocoa-drenched
history and the odd ancient Mayan artefact.
There's a cafe here too.

ℹ Information

Hastings i-SITE (Map p340; ☑06-873 0080;
www.visithastings.co.nz; Westermans Bldg,
cnr Russell St & Heretaunga St E; ⊙9am-5pm
Mon-Fri, 9am-3pm Sat, 10am-2pm Sun; 🛜)
Internet access, free maps, trail brochures and
bookings.

Havelock North i-SITE (Map p332; ☑06-877
9600; www.havelocknorthnz.com; cnr Te Aute
& Middle Rds, Havelock North; ⊙10am-5pm
Mon-Fri, to 4pm Sat, to 3pm Sun; 🛜) Local info
in a cute little booth.

Hawke's Bay Hospital (☑06-878 8109; www.
hawkesbay.health.nz; Omahu Rd; ⊙24hr)

Police Station (☑06-873 0500; www.police.
govt.nz; 205 Railway Rd; ⊙24hr)

Post Office (Map p340; www.nzpost.co.nz;
100 Market St; ⊙8.30am-5pm Mon-Fri, 9am-
noon Sat)

ℹ Getting There & Away

Napier's Hawke's Bay Airport (p338) is a
20-minute drive away. **Air New Zealand** (☑06-
873 2200; www.airnewzealand.co.nz; 117 Heretaunga St W; ⊙9am-5pm Mon-Fri) has an office
in central Hastings.

Hastings' **InterCity Bus Stop** (Map p340)
is on Russell St. Book InterCity and Naked Bus
buses online or at the i-SITE.

ℹ Getting Around

goBay (☑06-878 9250; www.hbrc.govt.nz)
ocal buses (with bike racks) run between Hastings, Havelock North and Napier. Daily Hastings
to Napier buses (adult/child $5.20/2.80) take
30 minutes (express) or 55 minutes (all stops).
Hastings to Havelock North buses run Monday to
Saturday (adult/child $3.40/1.80, 35 minutes).
Buses depart Hastings' **Civic Square Bus Stop**
(Map p340).

Hastings Taxis (☑06-878 5055) is the local
cab service.

Cape Kidnappers

From mid-September to late April, Cape Kidnappers (named when local Maori tried to
kidnap Cook's Tahitian servant boy) erupts
with squawking gannets. These big birds
usually nest on remote islands but here they
settle for the mainland, completely unfazed
by human spectators.

The birds nest as soon as they arrive, and eggs take about six weeks to hatch, with chicks arriving in early November. In March the gannets start their migration; by May they're gone.

Early November to late February is the best time to visit. Take a tour or the walkway to the colony: it's about five hours return from the Clifton Reserve car park ($1) at the Clifton Motor Camp. En route are interesting cliff formations, rock pools, a sheltered picnic spot, and the gaggling gannets themselves. The walk is tide dependent: leave no earlier than three hours after high tide; start back no later than 1½ hours after low tide.

No regular buses go to Clifton, but the tour operators will transport you for an additional fee, or you could bike.

☞ Tours

Gannet Beach Adventures ECOTOUR
(Map p332; ☑06-8750 898, 0800 426 638; www.gannets.com; 475 Clifton Rd, Clifton; adult/child $42/24) Ride along the beach on a tractor-pulled trailer before wandering out on the Cape for 90 minutes. A good-fun, guided return trip over four hours, departing Clifton Reserve.

Gannet Safaris ECOTOUR
(Map p332; ☑06-875 0888, 0800 427 232; www.gannetsafaris.co.nz; 396 Clifton Rd, Te Awanga; adult/child $60/30) Overland 4WD trips across farmland into the gannet colony. Three-hour tours depart at 9.30am and 1.30pm. Pick-ups from Napier and Hastings cost extra.

Central Hawke's Bay

Grassy farmland stretches south from Hastings, dotted with the grand homesteads of Victorian pastoralists. It's an untouristed area (aka 'Lamb Country'), rich in history and deserted beaches. **Waipukurau** (aka 'Wai-puk'), the main town, isn't exactly thrilling but it's worth calling in to the extremely helpful **Central Hawke's Bay Information Centre** (☑06-858 6488; www.lambcountry.co.nz; Railway Esplanade; ⊙8.30am-4.30pm Mon-Fri, 10am-3pm Sat) in the old railway station.

◉ Sights & Activities

There are no fewer than six windswept beaches along the coast here: **Kairakau, Mangakuri, Pourerere, Aramoana, Blackhead**

and **Porangahau**. The first five are good for swimming, and between the lot they offer a range of sandy, salty activities including surfing, fishing and driftwoody, rock-pooly adventures. Between Aramoana and Blackhead Beach lies the DOC-managed **Te Angiangi Marine Reserve** – bring your snorkel.

It's a nondescript hill in the middle of nowhere, but the place with the world's longest name is good for a photo op. Believe it or not, **Taumatawhakatangihangakoauauotamateaturipukakapikimaungahoronukupokaiwhenuakitanatahu** is the abbreviated form of 'The Brow of a Hill Where Tamatea, the Man with the Big Knees, Who Slid, Climbed, and Swallowed Mountains, Known as Land Eater, Played his Flute to his Brother'. To get there, fuel-up in Waipukurau and drive 40km to the Mangaorapa junction on route 52. Turn left and go 4km towards Porangahau. At the intersection with the signposts, turn right and continue 4.3km to the sign.

Ongaonga, a historic village 16km west of Waipawa, has interesting Victorian and Edwardian buildings. Pick up a pamphlet for a self-guided walking tour from the info centre in Waipukurau.

The **Central Hawke's Bay Settlers Museum** (www.chbsettlersmuseum.co.nz; 23 High St, Waipawa; adult/child $2/free; ⊙10am-4pm) in **Waipawa** has pioneer artefacts, informative 'homestead' displays and a good specimen of a river *waka* (canoe).

🛏 Sleeping

Lochlea Backpacker Farmstay FARMSTAY, HOSTEL $
(☑06-855 4816; www.bbh.co.nz; 344 Lake Rd, Wanstead; dm/s/d/f from $26/37/56/137; ☜☒) Far removed from urban stress, this working sheep and cattle farm has breezy stands of trees on grazing slopes. Rooms are simple but the communal lounge is cosy. There's a pool, a tennis court and endless paddocks in which to act sheepish. Free pick-ups from Waipukurau Monday to Friday.

Gwavas Garden Homestead B&B $$
(☑06-856 5810; www.gwavasgarden.co.nz; 5740 SH50, Tikokino; d incl breakfast $160-180; ☜) Six kilometres from Tikokino, this grand 1890 Cornish homestead has enjoyed a faithful room-by-room renovation with floral wallpaper, period furnishings, portraits eyeballing you from the walls and heavy linens. Have breakfast on the veranda before a spot of lawn tennis or a wander through the bird-biased garden.

Eating

Paper Mulberry Café   CAFE $
(www.papermulberrycafe.co.nz; SH2, Pukehou; meals
$8-17; ⊘7am-4pm Wed-Mon) Halfway between
Waipukurau and Hastings, this retro cafe-
gallery in a 100-year-old, aquamarine-coloured
church serves excellent coffee, smoothies and
home-spun food (unbeatable fudge). Well
worth a stop for a chomp and a browse.

Misty River Café   CAFE $$
(☑06-857 8911; 12 High St, Waipawa; mains $10-20;
⊘9am-4pm Wed-Sun) A little bit of upmarket
vintage on the functional high street, this
jade-coloured cafe plates up lip-smacking
salads as well as corn fritters, pastas, nachos
and other faves. Drop-dead-gorgeous baking
(try the coconut and lime cake).

ⓘ Getting There & Away

InterCity and Naked Bus pass through Waipawa
and Waipukurau on their Wellington–Napier
routes.

Kaweka & Ruahine Ranges

The remote Kaweka and Ruahine ranges
separate Hawke's Bay from the Central
Plateau. These forested wildernesses offer
some of the North Island's best tramping.

See the DOC pamphlets *Kaweka Forest
Park & Puketitiri Reserves* and *Eastern
Ruahine Forest Park* for details of tracks
and huts (both available online at www.doc.
govt.nz).

An ancient 136km Maori track, now
know as the **Gentle Annie Road**, runs in-
land from Omahu near Hastings to Taihape,
via Otamauri and Kuripapango (where
there's a basic but charming DOC campsite,
adult/child $6/3). This isolated route takes
around three hours (or a couple of days by
bike).

Kaweka J, the highest point of the range
(1724m), can be reached by a three-to-five-
hour tramp from the end of Kaweka Rd;
from Napier take Puketitiri Rd then Whit-
tle Rd. The drive is worthwhile in itself;
it's partly unsealed and takes three hours
return.

Enjoy a soak in natural hot pools before
or after the three-hour walk on **Te Puia
Track**, which follows the picturesque **Mo-
haka River**. From Napier, take Puketitiri
Rd, then Pakautu Rd, then Makahu Rd to
the road-end **Mangatutu Hot Pools** (www.
doc.govt.nz). Parts of the road can be dicey –
bring a 4WD if you've got one.

The Mokaha can be rafted with **Mohaka
Rafting** (☑06-839 1808; www.mohakarafting.
com; from $95).

Wellington Region

Includes ➡

Wellington 348
Kapiti Coast...............369
Paekakariki................370
Waikanae & Around....371
The Wairarapa 372
Martinborough..........373
Cape Palliser 374
Greytown...................375
Masterton & Around . 376

Best Places to Eat

➡ Ortega Fish Shack (p363)

➡ Logan Brown (p363)

➡ Ombra (p363)

➡ Duke Carvell's (p363)

➡ Nikau Cafe (p362)

Best Places to Drink

➡ Goldings Free Dive (p364)

➡ Hawthorn Lounge (p365)

➡ Little Beer Quarter (p364)

➡ Havana (p365)

➡ Micro Wine Bar (p374)

Why Go?

If your New Zealand travels thus far have been all about the great outdoors and sleepy rural towns, Wellington will blow the cobwebs away. Art-house cinemas, funky boutiques, hip bars, theatres and lashings of restaurants – all can be found in the 'cultural capital'.

As the crossing point between the North and South Islands, travellers have long been passing through these parts. The likes of Te Papa and Zealandia now stop visitors in their tracks, and even a couple of days' pause will reveal myriad other attractions – a windswept and interesting harbour with a walkable waterfront, hillsides clad in pretty weatherboard houses, ample inner-city surprises and some of the freshest city air on the planet.

Less than an hour away to the north, the Kapiti Coast has a slower, beachy vibe, with Kapiti Island nature reserve a highlight. An hour away over the Rimutaka Range, the Wairarapa farm plains are dotted with quiet towns and famed wineries, hemmed in by a rugged, wild coastline.

When to Go?

➡ The capital has its fair share of blustery, cold, grey days, but such conditions prevail only part of the time. 'Windy Welly' breaks out into blue skies and T-shirt temperatures at least several days a year, when you'll hear folk exclaim 'You can't beat Wellington on a good day'.

➡ November to April are the warmer months, with average maximums hovering around 20°C. From May to August it's colder and wetter – daily temperatures lurk around 12°C.

➡ The Kapiti Coast and Wairarapa are a different story – they are both warmer, less windy, with more blue-sky days.

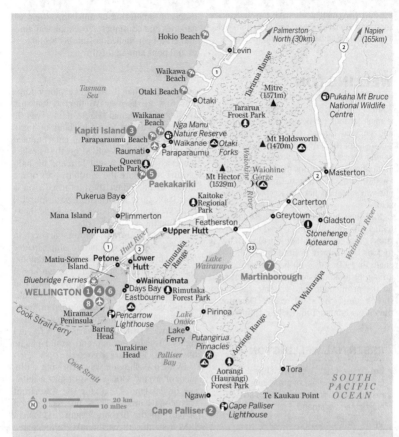

Wellington Region Highlights

1 Getting interactive at NZ's finest museum, Wellington's **Te Papa** (p354)

2 Scaling the lighthouse steps on wild and remote **Cape Palliser** (p374)

3 Meeting real live kiwi on a **Kapiti Island** (p370) night-time walk

4 Exploring the capital's creative side around **Cuba Street**

5 Rambling the dunes of **Queen Elizabeth Park** (p370) near beachy **Paekakariki**

6 Riding the ratchety **cable car** (p352) from Lambton Quay to the

leafy **Wellington Botanic Gardens** (p349)

7 Maintaining a straight line on your bicycle as you tour the picturesque **Martinborough wineries** (p373)

8 Discovering hidden shortcuts to surprising lookout points around **hilly Wellington** (p349) city

ℹ️ Getting There & Around

Wellington is a major transport hub, being the North Island port for the interisland ferries. Long-distance **KiwiRail Scenic Journeys** (☎ 04-495 0775, 0800 872 467; www.kiwirails-cenic.co.nz) trains run from Wellington to Auckland via Palmerston North. Wellington Airport is serviced by international and domestic airlines.

InterCity (☎ 04-385 0520; www.intercity. co.nz) is the main North Island bus company, travelling just about everywhere. Approaching Wellington city from the north, you'll pass through either the Kapiti Coast to the west via State Hwy1 (SH1), or the Wairarapa and Hutt Valley to the east via State Hwy2 (SH2).

Getting into and out of Wellington on regional trains and buses is a breeze. **Metlink** (☎ 0800

801 700; www.metlink.org.nz) is the one-stop shop for regional transport services, from Wellington to the Kapiti Coast and the Wairarapa.

WELLINGTON

POP 190,950 (CITY), 488,160 (REGION)

A small city with a big reputation, Wellington is most famous for being NZ's constitutional and cultural capital. It is *infamous* for its weather, particularly the gale-force winds wont to barrel through, wrecking umbrellas and obliterating hairdos. It also lies on a major fault line. And negotiating the inner-city one-way system is like the Krypton Factor on acid.

But don't be deterred, for these are mere trifles on Welly's multilayered, jam-packed stand of sweet treats. For starters it's lovely to look at, draped around bushy hillsides encircling a freshly whipped harbour. There are super lookouts on hilltops, golden sand on the promenade, and spectacular craggy shores along the south coast. Downtown, the city is compact and vibrant, buoyed by

ESSENTIAL WELLINGTON

Eat Yourself silly: Wellington has a gut-busting number of great cafes and restaurants; bring trousers with an elasticated waistband

Drink Coffee – espresso, AeroPress, Chemex, siphon, Swissgold, V60...you name it

Read Rousing words along Wellington's waterfront Writers Walk

Listen to Radio New Zealand National (101.3FM, www.radionz.co.nz) – programming for the people

Watch 'Wellington Airport Landings' on YouTube

Festival Sumner City (p356) – free fun in the sun, *in theory*

Go green Wairarapa's Pukaha Mt Bruce National Wildlife Centre is home to many species of native bird, as well as eels and tuatara

Online www.wellingtonnz.com, www.naturecoast.co.nz, www.wairarapanz.com; www.lonelyplanet.com/new-zealand/wellington

Area code ☑ 04

a decent smattering of museums, theatres, galleries and boutiques. A cocktail-, caffeine- and craft-beer-fuelled hospitality scene fizzes and pops among the throng.

History

Maori legend has it that the explorer Kupe was first to discover Wellington harbour. Wellington's original Maori name was Te Whanganui-a-Tara (great harbour of Tara), named after the son of a chief named Whatonga who had settled on the Hawke's Bay coast. Whatonga sent Tara and his half-brother to explore the southern part of the North Island. When they returned over a year later, their reports were so favourable that Whatonga's followers moved there, founding the Ngati Tara tribe.

The first European settlers arrived in the New Zealand Company's ship *Aurora* on 22 January 1840, not long after Colonel William Wakefield arrived to buy land from the Maori. However, Maori denied they had sold the land at Port Nicholson, or Poneke as they called it, as it was founded on hasty and illegal purchasing by the New Zealand Company. As in many parts of NZ, land rights struggles ensued, and would plague the country for years to come.

By 1850 Wellington was a thriving settlement of around 5500 people, despite a shortage of flat land. Originally the waterfront was along Lambton Quay, but reclamation of parts of the harbour began in 1852. In 1855 a significant earthquake raised many parts of Wellington, including the lower Hutt Valley and the land on which the modern Hutt Rd now runs.

In 1865 the seat of government was moved from Auckland to Wellington, although it took until the turn of the century for the city to really flourish. In the early 1900s the port prospered, while producer boards and banks sprung up in its surrounds. Other industries developed, pushing urban sprawl further afield into the Hutt Valley, Porirua, and the Kapiti Coast.

In modern times, the capital remains a stronghold of the public service, despite ongoing trims. It also boasts a good quotient of technology and creative industries.

◉ Sights

Museum of Wellington City & Sea MUSEUM (Map p350; www.museumswellington.org.nz; Queens Wharf; ☉10am-5pm) FREE For an imaginative, interactive experience of Welling-

MAORI NZ: WELLINGTON

In legend the mouth of Maui's Fish, and traditionally known as Te Whanganui-a-Tara, the Wellington area became known to Maori in the mid-19th century as 'Poneke' (a transliteration of Port Nicholas, its European name at the time).

The major *iwi* (tribes) of the region were Te Ati Awa and Ngati Toa. Ngati Toa was the *iwi* of Te Rauparaha, who composed the now famous 'Ka Mate' *haka*. Like most urban areas the city is now home to Maori from many *iwi*, sometimes collectively known as Ngati Poneke.

NZ's national museum, Te Papa (p354), presents excellent displays on Maori culture, traditional and modern, as well as a colourful *marae* (meeting house). In its gift store you can see excellent carving and other crafts, as you can in both Kura (p366) and Ora (p366) galleries nearby.

Kapiti Island Nature Tours (p370) offers an intimate insight into the Maori culture of the Wellington area, as does Kiwi Coastal Tours (p354).

ton's social and salty maritime history, swing into the Museum of Wellington. Highlights include a moving documentary about the tragedy of the *Wahine*, the interisland ferry that sank in the harbour entrance on a terrible, blustery day back in 1968, with a loss of 51 lives. Maori legends are also dramatically told using tiny hologram actors and special effects. The building itself is an old Bond Store dating from 1892.

★ **City Gallery**   GALLERY
(Map p358; www.citygallery.org.nz; Civic Sq, Wakefield St; charges may apply for major exhibits; ⊙10am-5pm) **FREE** Housed in the monumental old library in Civic Sq, Wellington's much-loved City Gallery does a cracking job of securing acclaimed contemporary international exhibitions, as well as unearthing and supporting those at the forefront of the NZ scene. A packed events calendar and excellent Nikau Cafe (p362) enhance the experience.

Academy Galleries   GALLERY
(Map p350; www.nzafa.com; 1 Queens Wharf; ⊙10am-5pm) **FREE** The showcase of the New Zealand Academy of Fine Arts, Academy Galleries presents frequently changing exhibitions by NZ artists.

New Zealand Portrait Gallery   GALLERY
(Map p350; www.nzportraitgallery.org.nz; Shed 11, Queens Wharf; ⊙10.30am-4.30pm) **FREE** Housed in the historic waterfront Shed 11, this gallery presents a diverse range of NZ portraiture from its own collection and frequently changing guest exhibitions.

Parliament House   CULTURAL BUILDING
(Map p350; www.parliament.nz; Bowen St; ⊙tours on the hour 10am-4pm) **FREE** The austere grey-and-cream Parliament House was completed in 1922. Free one-hour tours depart from the ground-floor foyer (arrive 15 minutes prior). Next door is the 1899 neo-Gothic Parliamentary Library building, as well as the modernist **Beehive** (Map p350), designed by British architect Sir Basil Spence and built between 1969 and 1980. Controversy surrounded its construction and – love it or loathe it – it's the architectural symbol of the country. Across the road are the **Government Buildings** (Map p350), the largest wooden building in the southern hemisphere, doing a pretty good impersonation of stone.

★ **Mt Victoria Lookout**   LOOKOUT
(Map p350) The city's most accessible viewpoint is on the top of 196m-high Mt Victoria, east of the city centre. You can take the Roseneath bus some of the way up, but the rite of passage is to sweat it out on the walk (ask a local for directions or just follow your nose). If you've got your own wheels, take Oriental Pde along the waterfront and then scoot up Carlton Gore Rd. If this whets your appetite, ask a local how to get to the wind turbine or Mt Kaukau – both higher, better, blinkin' marvellous.

★ **Wellington Botanic Gardens**   GARDENS
(Map p350) **FREE** The hilly, 25-hectare botanic gardens can be *almost* effortlessly visited via a cable-car ride (nice bit of planning, eh?), although there are several other entrances hidden in the hillsides. They boast a tract of original native forest along with varied collections including a beaut rose garden and international plant collections. Add in fountains, a cheerful playground, sculptures, duck pond, cafe, magical city views and much more, and you've got a grand outing indeed.

Greater Wellington

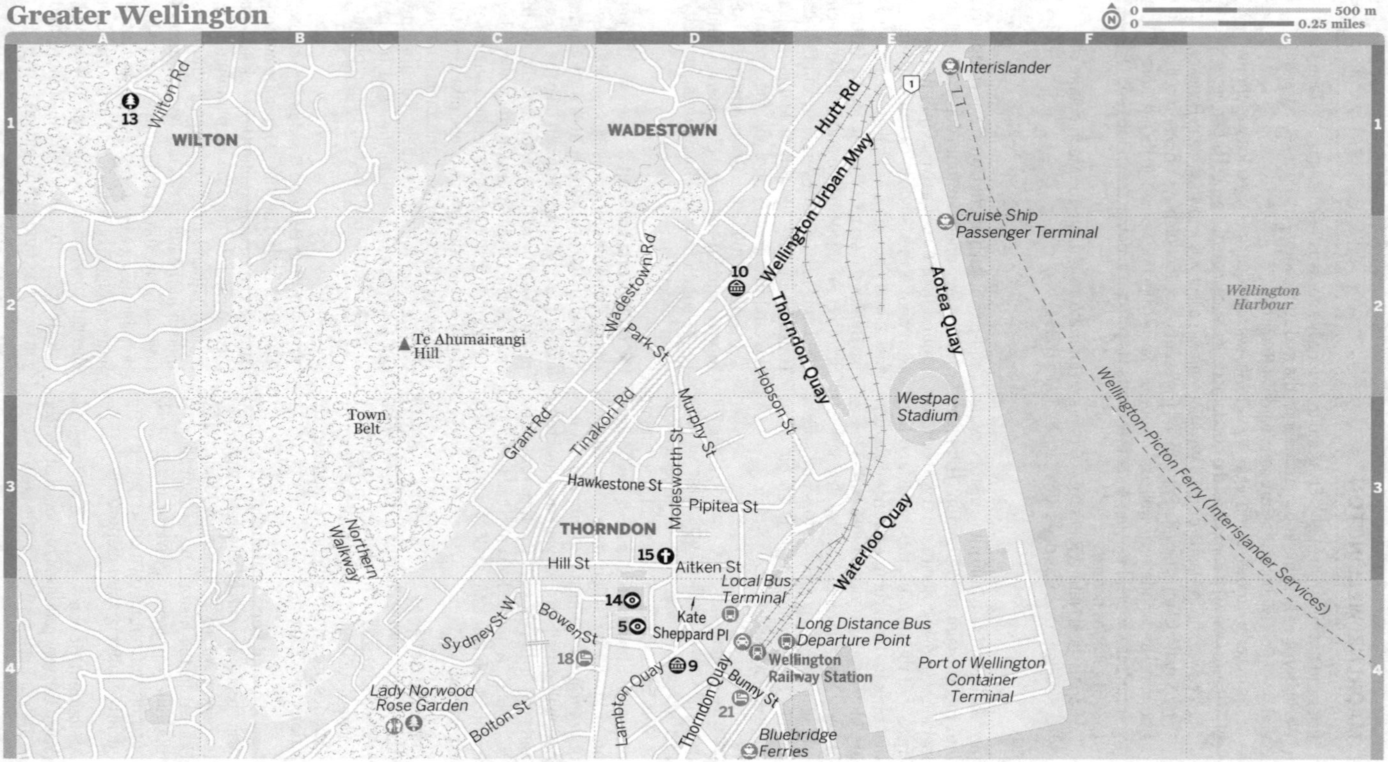

WILTON

13

Wilton Rd

WADESTOWN

Wadestown Rd

Park St

Hutt Rd

Wellington Urban Mwy

Thorndon Quay

Hobson St

10

▲ Te Ahumairangi Hill

Tinakori Rd

Grant Rd

Town Belt

Northern Walkway

Murphy St

Hawkestone St

Molesworth St

Pipitea St

THORNDON

Hill St

15

Aitken St

Local Bus Terminal

Kate

14

5

Sheppard Pl

9

Bowen St

18

Sydney St W

Bunny St

21

Thorndon Quay

Lambton Quay

Bolton St

Lady Norwood Rose Garden

Waterloo Quay

Aotea Quay

Westpac Stadium

Cruise Ship Passenger Terminal

Interislander

Wellington Harbour

Wellington-Picton Ferry (Interislander Services)

Long Distance Bus Departure Point

Wellington Railway Station

Bluebridge Ferries

Port of Wellington Container Terminal

N

500 m
0.25 miles

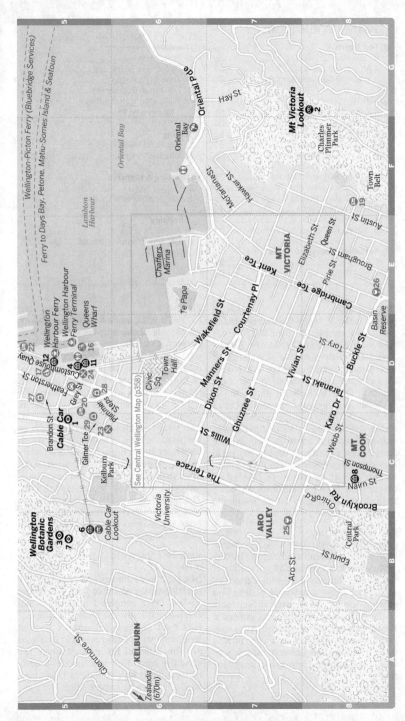

Greater Wellington

◎ Top Sights
1 Cable Car C5
2 Mt Victoria Lookout G8
3 Wellington Botanic Gardens B5

◎ Sights
4 Academy Galleries D5
5 Beehive D4
6 Cable Car Museum B5
7 Carter Observatory B5
8 Colonial Cottage Museum C8
9 Government Buildings D4
10 Katherine Mansfield Birthplace D2
11 Museum of Wellington City & Sea D5
12 New Zealand Portrait Gallery D5
13 Otari-Wilton's Bush A1
14 Parliament House D4
15 Wellington Cathedral of St Paul D3

◎ Activities, Courses & Tours
16 Ferg's Kayaks D5
17 Wild Winds D5

◎ Sleeping
18 Bolton Hotel C4
19 Booklovers B&B F8
20 CityLife Wellington D5
21 Downtown Backpackers D4
22 Wellington Waterfront
   Motorhome Park D5

◎ Eating
23 Boulcott Street Bistro C5
24 Charley Noble D5

◎ Drinking & Nightlife
25 Garage Project B7
26 Regional Wines & Spirits E8

◎ Shopping
27 Kirkcaldie & Stains D5
28 Old Bank Shopping Arcade D5
29 Vault C5

★ **Cable Car** CABLE CAR

(Map p350; www.wellingtoncablecar.co.nz; adult/child 1 way $4/1.50, return $7/2.50; ⊙ departs every 10min, 7am-10pm Mon-Fri, 8.30am-10pm Sat, 9am-9pm Sun) One of Wellington's most famous attractions is the little red cable car that clanks up the steep slope from Lambton Quay to Kelburn. At the top is the Wellington Botanic Gardens, the Carter Observatory (p352) and the small-but-nifty **Cable Car Museum** (Map p350; www.museumswellington.org.nz; admission free; ⊙ 10am-5pm), which evocatively depicts the cable car's story since it was built in 1902 to open up hilly Kelburn for settlement. Take the cable car back down the hill, or ramble down through the gardens (a 20- to 60-minute walk, depending on your wend).

Carter Observatory ASTRONOMY

(Map p350; ☎ 04-910 3140; www.carterobservatory.org; 40 Salamanca Rd; adult/child $18.50/8; ⊙ 10am-5pm, to 9.30pm Tue & Sat) At the top of the Botanic Gardens (p349), the Carter Observatory features a full-dome planetarium offering regular shows with virtual tours of the local skies; a multimedia display of Polynesian navigation, Maori cosmology and European explorers; and some of NZ's finest telescopes and astronomical artefacts. Check the website for evening stargazing times.

Zealandia WILDLIFE RESERVE

(☎ 04-920 9200; www.visitzealandia.com; Waiapu Rd; adult/child/family exhibition only $7.50/5/20, exhibition & valley $17.50/9/44; ⊙ 10am-5pm, last entry 4pm) ⚑ This groundbreaking ecosanctuary is tucked in the hills about 2km west of town (the Karori bus passes nearby, or see the Zealandia website for the free shuttle). Living wild within the fenced valley are more than 30 native bird species, including rare takahe, saddleback, hihi and kaka, as well as tuatara and little spotted kiwi. An excellent exhibition relays NZ's natural history and world-renowned conservation story. More than 30km of tracks can be explored independently, or on regular guided tours. The night tour provides an opportunity to spot nocturnal creatures including kiwi, frogs and glowworms (adult/child $75/36). Cafe and shop on site.

Katherine Mansfield Birthplace HISTORIC BUILDING

(Map p350; www.katherinemansfield.com; 25 Tinakori Rd, Thorndon; adult/child $8/2; ⊙ 10am-4pm Tue-Sun) Often compared to Chekhov and Maupassant, Katherine Mansfield is one of NZ's most distinguished authors, born in 1888, and dying of tuberculosis in 1923 aged 34. This Tinakori Rd house is where she spent five years of her childhood; it's a lovely heritage home with exhibitions in her honour, including a biographical film. Her short stories can be found in one volume, *The Collected Stories of Katherine Mansfield.*

Otari-Wilton's Bush
PARK

(Map p350; 160 Wilton Rd; ☉dawn-dusk) **FREE**
About 3km west of the city is Otari-Wilton's Bush, the only botanic gardens in NZ specialising in native flora. There are more than 1200 plant species here, including some of the city's oldest trees, as well as 11km of walking trails and delightful picnic areas. The Wilton bus from the city passes the gates.

Colonial Cottage Museum
MUSEUM

(Map p350; www.museumswellington.org.nz; 66 Nairn St, Mt Cook; adult/child $8/4; ☉noon-4pm Sat & Sun) Open daily during high summer, and weekends only the rest of the year, and just a five-minute amble from the top of Cuba St, Wellington's oldest cottage has been carefully restored (complete with an organic garden and chooks) to retell the stories of early settlers and life in their era. Check the website for current tour times, usually hourly.

Wellington Zoo
ZOO

(www.wellingtonzoo.com; 200 Daniell St; adult/child $20/10; ☉9.30am-5pm, last entry 4.15pm) ✐
Committed to conservation and research, with an active captive-breeding program, Wellington Zoo is home to a menagerie of native and exotic wildlife, including lions and tamarins. The nocturnal house has kiwi and tuatara. 'Close encounters' allow you to meet the big cats, red pandas, giraffes and those cute little meerkats (for a fee). The zoo is 4km south of the city; catch the Newtown bus.

Weta Cave
MUSEUM

(www.wetanz.com; cnr Camperdown Rd & Weka St, Miramar; ☉9am-5.30pm) **FREE** Film buffs will enjoy the Weta Cave, a fun, mind-boggling minimuseum of the Academy Award–winning company that brought *The Lord of the Rings, King Kong, The Adventures of Tintin* and *The Hobbit* to life. Learn how the company does it on the 45-minute 'Window into Workshop' guided tour (starting every half-hour, $20). The Weta Cave is 9km east of the city centre, a pleasant waterside bike ride or 20 minutes on the Miramar bus.

New Zealand Film Archive
CINEMA

(Map p358; 🎞film info line 04-499 3456; www.filmarchive.org.nz; cnr Taranaki & Ghuznee Sts; movies $8; ☉9am-5pm Mon-Fri, evening screenings 7pm Wed-Sat) **FREE** The Film Archive is a veritable vortex of NZ moving images, into which you could well get sucked for days on end. Its library holds more than 30,000 titles spanning feature films, documentaries, short films, home movies, newsreels, TV programs and advertisements. There are regular screenings in the cinema ($8), as well as a viewing library (free) where you can ferret out and watch films until you're square-eyed. Groovy on-site cafe.

Dowse Art Museum
GALLERY

(www.dowse.org.nz; 45 Laings Rd, Lower Hutt; ☉10am-5pm; 🛜) **FREE** Fifteen minutes' drive or via regular buses from downtown Wellington, the Dowse is worth visiting for its architecture alone. It's also a friendly, accessible art museum showcasing NZ art, craft and design, with a nice cafe to boot.

WELLINGTON IN ...

Two Days

To get a feel for the lie of the land, walk (or drive) up to the **Mt Victoria Lookout**, or ride the **cable car** up to the **Wellington Botanic Gardens**. After lunch on groovy **Cuba Street**, catch some Kiwi culture at **Te Papa** or the **Museum of Wellington City & Sea**. Top off the day by doing the rounds of the city's numerous craft-beer bars.

The next day, reconstitute with coffee and a plate of sage eggs at **Nikau** in the City Gallery, then head to **Zealandia** to meet the birds and learn about NZ conservation, or encounter some other bird-brains in a tour of **Parliament House**. Raid **Moore Wilson** for cheese and wine for a picnic supper in Waitangi Park, before heading back into the night lights for some live music, or a movie at the gloriously restored **Embassy Theatre**.

Four Days

Shake and bake the two-day itinerary, then decorate with the following: a seal-spotting safari along wild Cape Palliser, followed by a wine tasting or two around **Martinborough**. The next day, head to **Paekakariki** for an ocean swim and ice cream before wandering through the dunes of **Queen Elizabeth Park** next door.

DON'T MISS

TREASURES OF TE PAPA

★ Te Papa (Map p358; www.tepapa.govt.nz; 55 Cable St; ⊙10am-6pm Fri-Wed, to 9pm Thu) **FREE** is the city's 'must-see' attraction, and for reasons well beyond the fact that it's NZ's national museum. It's highly interactive, fun and full of surprises.

Aptly, 'Te Papa Tongarewa' loosely translates as 'treasure box'. The riches inside include an amazing collection of Maori artefacts and the museum's own colourful *marae* (meeting house); natural history and environment exhibitions; Pacific and NZ history galleries; Nga Toi/Arts Te Papa (the national art collection, see www.arts.tepapa.govt. nz), and hands-on 'discovery centres' for children. Expect impressive gallery spaces and plenty of high-tech twists. Big-name, temporary exhibitions incur an admission fee, although general admission is free.

You could spend a day exploring Te Papa's six floors but still not see it all. To cut to the chase, head to the information desk on level two and collect a map. For exhibition highlights and to get your bearings, the one-hour 'Introducing Te Papa' tour ($14) is a good idea; tours leave from the info desk at 10.15am, noon and 2pm daily in winter, more frequently in summer. Two cafes and two gift shops complete the Te Papa experience, one which could well take a couple of visits.

Petone Settlers Museum MUSEUM
(www.petonesettlers.org.nz; The Esplanade, Petone; ⊙10am-4pm Wed-Sun) **FREE** On the shell-strewn Petone foreshore, 10 minutes' drive from downtown Wellington or reachable by regular bus services, the art-deco Petone Settlers Museum recalls local migration and settlement in its charming *Tatou Tatou* exhibition.

🏃 Activities

Ferg's Kayaks KAYAKING
(Map p350; www.fergskayaks.co.nz; Shed 6, Queens Wharf; ⊙9am-8pm Mon-Fri, to 6pm Sat & Sun) Stretch your tendons with indoor rock climbing (adult/child $15/10), cruise the waterfront wearing in-line skates ($15 for two hours) or go for a paddle in a kayak or on a stand-up paddleboard (from $15 for one hour). There's also bike hire (one hour from $15) and guided kayaking trips.

Wild Winds WINDSURFING, PADDLEBOARDING
(Map p350; ☑04-473 3458; www.wildwinds.co.nz; 36 Customhouse Quay) With all this wind and water, Wellington was made for windsurfing, kiteboarding, and stand-up paddleboarding. Take on one or all three with Wild Winds; lessons start from $110 for two hours.

Makara Peak
Mountain Bike Park MOUNTAIN BIKING
(www.makarapeak.org; South Karori Rd, Karori; admission by donation) In the hills of Karori, 8km west of the city centre (on the Karori bus), this excellent 200-hectare park is laced with 60km of single-track ranging from be-

ginner to expert. The nearby **Mud Cycles** (☑04-476 4961; www.mudcycles.co.nz; 421 Karori Rd, Karori; half-day/full day/weekend bike hire from $30/45/75) has mountain bikes for hire, and runs guided tours for riders of all abilities. Wellington is a true MTB mecca – visit tracks.org.nz for the evidence.

👉 Tours

Walk Wellington WALKING TOUR
(www.walkwellington.org.nz; adult/child $20/10; ⊙tours 10am daily, plus 5.30pm Mon, Wed & Fri Nov-Mar) Informative and great-value two-hour walking tours focusing on the city and waterfront, departing the i-SITE. Book online, phone or just turn up.

Zest Food Tours GUIDED TOUR
(☑04-801 9198; www.zestfoodtours.co.nz; tours from $169) Runs three- to 5½-hour small-group foody tours; longer tours include lunch with matched wines at the legendary Logan Brown (p363).

Kiwi Coastal Tours 4WD TOURS
(☑0272 520 099; www.kiwicoastaltours.co.nz; 3/5hr tour $150/225) Excellent 4WD exploration of the rugged south coast in the company of a local Maori guide with plenty of stories to tell.

John's Hop On Hop Off BUS TOUR
(☑0274 535 880, 0800 246 877; www.hopon-hopoff.co.nz; per person $45) Flexible two-hour scenic loop of the city with 18 stops en route, starting at the i-SITE. Tickets are valid for 24 hours.

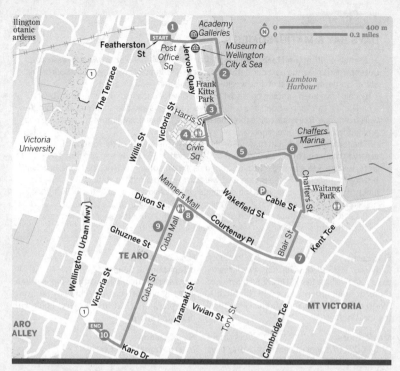

🏃 City Walk
City Sculpture

START POST OFFICE SQ
END KARO DR
LENGTH 3.5KM; TWO TO THREE HOURS

Begin at Post Office Sq, where Bill Culbert's ① **SkyBlues** noodles into the air, then cross Jervois Quay to pass between the New Zealand Academy of Fine Arts and Museum of Wellington City & Sea. At the Queens Wharf waterfront, turn south, past the big shed to the ② **Water Whirler**, the largely lifeless needle of experimental kineticist Len Lye that whirrs crazily into life on the hour several times a day.

Continue along the promenade or deviate through Frank Kitts Park, passing the graceful ③ **Albatross Fountain**. A short detour over the flotsam City to Sea Bridge, Civic Sq is surrounded by the i-SITE, library and City Gallery. Neil Dawson's ④ **Ferns** hangs in the air, attendant by a stand of nikau palms.

Back on the waterfront, continue past Te Raukura *whare waka* (canoe house) and ⑤ **Hikitia**, the world's oldest working crane

ship. Strip to your undies and jump off the diving platform, or perhaps just keep on trucking along wharf, past the bronze form of ⑥ **Solace in the Wind** leaning over the edge, alongside Katherine Mansfield's breezy contribution to the Wellington Writers Walk.

Cross the footbridge to Waitangi Park to eyeball some roller action, before heading south to Courtenay Pl via Chaffers St, and Blair St with its century-old warehouses.

On Courtenay Pl, check out the leggy form of the industrial ⑦ **Tripod**, before heading west. Cross Taranaki St to ⑧ **Te Aro Park** with its canoe prow and trip hazards.

Turn south when you hit Cuba St, heading up the pedestrian mall. Watch out for the sly, sloshy ⑨ **Bucket Fountain**.

Change down to granny gear and wander through doorways, all the way to the top of Cuba, into the remnant heritage precinct cut through by the controversial inner-city bypass. Bookend your sculpture walk with Regan Gentry's brilliant but ghostly ⑩ **Subject to Change**, and the Tonks' Well alongside.

WORTH A TRIP

DAYS BAY & MATIU/SOMES ISLAND

The small **Wellington Harbour Ferry** (Map p350; ☑ 04-499 1282; www.eastbywest.co.nz; Queens Wharf) plies the harbour between Queens Wharf and Days Bay in Eastbourne, via Matiu-Somes Island, and on fine weekends Petone and Seatoun as well.

Locals have been jumping on a boat to Days Bay for decades, where there's a beach, a park and a cafe, and a boatshed with kayaks, row boats and bikes for hire. A 10-minute walk from Days Bay leads to Eastbourne, a beachy township with more cafes, a cute pub and numerous other diversions.

The ferry also stops at at Matiu/Somes Island in the middle of the harbour. It's a reserved managed by the Department of Conservation (DOC), where you might see weta, tuatara, kakariki and little blue penguins, among other critters. The island is rich in history, having once been a prisoner-of-war camp and quarantine station. Take a picnic lunch, or even stay overnight in the campsite (adult/child $10/5) or in the DOC house; book online at www.doc.govt.nz or at Wellington's DOC visitor centre (p367).

It's a 20- to 30-minute chug across the harbour. There are 16 sailings on weekdays, eight on Saturday and Sunday (return fare adult/child $22/12).

Flat Earth CULTURAL TOUR
(☑ 04-472 9635, 0800 775 805; www.flatearth. co.nz; half- & full-day tours $175-385) An array of themed small-group tours (city highlights, Maori treasures, arts and Middle-earth filming locations).

Movie Tours GUIDED TOUR
(☑ 0274 193 077; www.adventuresafari.co.nz; tours from adult/child $45/30) Half- and full-day tours with more props, clips, and Middle-earth film locations than you can shake a staff at.

South Coast Shuttles GUIDED TOUR
(☑ 04-389 2161; www.southcoastshuttles.co.nz; 2½-hour tours $55; ☺ tours 10am & 1pm) Offers tailored tours as well as a scheduled daily two-hour city highlights tour including the south coast and Otari Wilton's Bush. Photographer's early-bird trip at 7am (two hours, $45).

Wellington Rover GUIDED TOUR
(☑ 04-471 0044, 0800 426 211; www.wellington-rover.co.nz; tours from adult/child $95/50) Half-to full-day tours of the city, seal colony and Hobbit habitat.

★⚡ Festivals & Events

Check at the Wellington i-SITE or visit www.wellingtonnz.com/events for listings; ticketed events can be found and booked via **Ticketek** (www.ticketek.co.nz) and **TicketDirect** (☑ 0800 224 224; www.ticketdirect.co.nz).

Summer City CULTURE
(www.wellington.govt.nz) A summertime event bonanza – many free and outdoors including the lovely 'Gardens Magic' concerts – from January to March.

New Zealand International Sevens SPORTS
(www.sevens.co.nz) The world's top seven-a-side rugby teams compete, but it's the crowd that plays up. Held in February; book with lightning speed.

New Zealand International Arts Festival CULTURE
(www.festival.co.nz) A month-long biennial (even years; around mid-February to mid-March) spectacular of theatre, dance, music, visual arts and literature. International acts aplenty.

Fringe NZ CULTURE
(www.fringe.org.nz) Three weeks across February and March of way-out-there experimental visual arts, music, dance and theatre.

New Zealand Comedy Festival COMEDY
(www.comedyfestival.co.nz) Three weeks of hysterics across April/May. World-famous-in-NZ comedians, and some truly world-famous ones, too.

Matariki CULTURE
(www.tepapa.govt.nz) Celebrating the Maori New Year (in June) with a free festival of dance, music and other events at Te Papa.

International Film Festival FILM
(www.nzff.co.nz) Two-week indie film fest screening the best of NZ and international cinema. Held over July/August.

Beervana BEER
(www.beervana.co.nz) A barrel-load of craft-beer aficionados roll into town for a weekend of supping and beard-stroking. In August.

Wellington on a Plate
FOOD

(www.wellingtononaplate.com) Lip-smacking program of gastronomic events, and bargains aplenty at restaurants around the city. Held in August.

World of WearableArt
FASHION

(www.worldofwearableart.com) A two-week run in September of the spectacular nightly extravaganza of amazing garments. Tickets are hot property.

Toast Martinborough
FOOD & DRINK

(www.toastmartinborough.co.nz) A day of hedonism around the Martinborough vineyards. Tickets = hot cakes. Held in November.

🛏 Sleeping

Wellington accommodation is generally more expensive than in regional areas. Standards are reasonably high, and there are plenty of options right in or within easy walking distance of the city centre. One hassle is the lack of parking, so it will pay to ask in advance about options if you have your own wheels.

Wellington's budget accommodation largely takes the form of multistorey hostel megaliths. There's no 'motel alley' in Wellington, but motels are scattered around the city fringe. Being the hub of government and business, self-contained apartments are popular, with bargains often available at weekends.

During the peak season (December to February), or during major events, book your bed well in advance.

Campsites are as rare as bad coffee in Wellington. Tenters should head to Wellington Top 10 Holiday Park (p359) in Seaview, or Paekakariki Holiday Park (p370). Motorhomers, however, can enjoy the super-convenient Wellington Waterfront Motorhome Park.

★ YHA Wellington City
HOSTEL $

(Map p358; ☑ 04-801 7280; www.yha.co.nz; cnr Cambridge Tce & Wakefield St; dm $29-36, d with/without bathroom $120/88; @🛜) 🏊 Wellington's best hostel wins points for fantastic communal areas including two big kitchens and dining areas, and separate rooms for games, reading and watching movies. Sustainable initiatives (recycling, composting and energy-efficient hot water) impress, and there's a comprehensive booking service at reception, along with espresso.

Nomads Capital
HOSTEL $

(Map p358; ☑ 0508 666 237, 04-978 7800; www.nomadscapital.com; 118 Wakefield St; dm $28-36, d $95-105; @🛜) Smack-bang in the middle of town, Nomads has good security, spick-and-span rooms, an on-site cafe-bar (free modest nightly meals and happy hour) and discounts for longer stays. Kitchen and lounge spaces are short on elbow room, but slick service, heritage features and location stop you dwelling on the negatives.

Trek Global
HOSTEL $

(Map p358; ☑ 0800 868 735, 04-471 3480; www.trekglobal.net; 9 O'Reilly Ave; dm $22-26, s $59, tw with/without bathroom $89/69; P@🛜) A highlight of this back-lane hostel is the funky and welcoming foyer hang-out and cosy TV lounge. The sleeping quarters and kitchens are squeezed into rabbit-warren corridors, but it's relatively quiet with clean rooms and laudable extras such as bike hire, parking ($20 per day), a women-only dorm with a suntrap terrace, and travel booking service.

WELLINGTON REGION WELLINGTON

WELLINGTON FOR CHILDREN

Let's cut to the chase: Welly's biggest hit for kids is Te Papa (p354), with the whole caboodle looking like it's curated by a team of five-year-old geniuses. It has interactive activities galore, more creepy, weird and wonderful things than you can shake a squid at, and heaps of special events for all ages. See the dedicated Kids page on the website for proof of Te Papa's prowess in this department.

Conveniently located either side of Te Papa are Frank Kitts Park and Waitangi Park, both with playgrounds and in close proximity to roller skates, ice cream and life-saving espresso for the grown-ups.

A ride up the cable car (p352) and a lap around the Wellington Botanic Gardens (p349) will get the wee ones pumped up, and when darkness descends head to the Carter Observatory (p352) to gaze at galaxies far, far away. On a more terrestrial bent, check out some crazy animals at the Wellington Zoo (p353) or Zealandia (p352).

Central Wellington

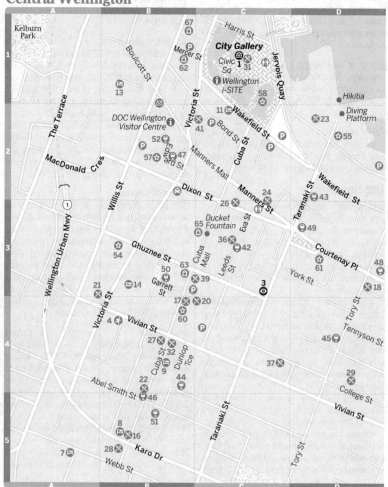

WELLINGTON REGION WELLINGTON

Downtown Backpackers HOSTEL **$**
(Map p350; 04-473 8482, 0800 225 725; www.
downtownbackpackers.co.nz; 1 Bunny St; dm $28-
31, s $68, d $85-95; @ 🛜) Housed in a historic
art-deco hotel at the railway end of town,
Downtown has tidy, bright rooms and plenty
of capacious, character-filled communal areas (be sure to check out the carved fireplace
in the bar). Budget meals in the cafe morning and night.

Cambridge Hotel HOSTEL **$**
(Map p358; 04-385 8829; www.cambridgehotel.
co.nz; 28 Cambridge Tce; dm $25-30, with/without
bathroom s $90/65, d $105/85; @ 🛜) Comfort-

able accommodation in a heritage hotel
with a ground-floor pub. En suite rooms
have Sky TV, phone and fridge (try for a
room at the back if you're a light sleeper).
The backpacker wing has a snug kitchen-
lounge, flash bathrooms and dorms with little natural light but sky-high ceilings. Bonus
$3 breakfast.

Wellington Waterfront
Motorhome Park MOTORHOME PARK **$**
(Map p350; www.wwmp.co.nz; 12 Waterloo Quay;
powered sites $50; 🛜) In reality it's simply
a waterfront car park, but it's nonetheless

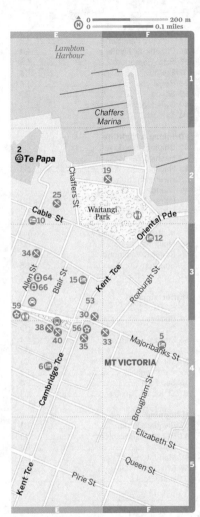

house is immaculate and inviting, and your friendly host will happily direct you to local sights.

Wellington Top 10 Holiday Park
HOLIDAY PARK **$**

(📞 0800 948 686, 04-568 5913; www.wellington-top10.co.nz; 95 Hutt Park Rd, Seaview; sites $45, cabins $60-100, motels $115-170; @ 🕾) This park, 13km northeast of Wellington, is convenient for the ferry. Family-friendly facilities include communal kitchens, games room, jumping pillow and a playground, but its industrial location detracts. Follow the signs off SH2 for Petone and Seaview, or take regular public transport.

Comfort & Quality Hotels
HOTEL **$$**

(Map p358; 📞 0800 873 553, 04-385 2156; www. hotelwellington.co.nz; 223 Cuba St; d $104-200; P @ 🕾 ⊠) In the heart of Cuba St, the CQ has two wings: the sympathetically renovated historic 'Trekkers' building with smaller, cheaper rooms (Comfort); and the snazzier high-rise 'Quality' which adjoins five fully self-contained apartments. Shared facilities include an in-house bar and restaurant (mains $14 to $35), and parking ($25 per day).

Booklovers B&B
B&B **$$**

(Map p350; 📞 04-384 2714; www.booklovers.co.nz; 123 Pirie St; s/d from $150/180; P @ 🕾) Author Jane Tolerton's gracious, book-filled B&B has three queen en suite guest rooms (one with an extra single bed). A bus service runs past the front gate to Courtenay Pl and the train station, and the city's 'green belt' begins right next door. Free wi-fi and parking.

Capital View Motor Inn
MOTEL **$$**

(Map p358; 📞 04-385 0515, 0800 438 505; www. capitalview.co.nz; 12 Thompson St; d $125-240; P 🕾) Many of the rooms in this well-maintained, multistorey building close to Cuba St do indeed enjoy capital views – especially the large, good-value penthouse (sleeps five). All are self-contained and spruce, and there's free parking.

Victoria Court
MOTEL **$$**

(Map p358; 📞 04-385 710, 0800 282 8502; www.victoriacourt.co.nz; 201 Victoria St; d $149-205; P 🕾) This central city option continues to deliver satisfaction in the inner city through its spacious studios and apartments with kitchenettes, quality joinery and soft furnishings, and recently refreshed bathrooms. There are two disabled-access units; larger units sleep up to six. Free on-site guest parking.

unbelievably convenient, offering overnight stays, and modest hourly rates for dayparking. Facilities comprise a sharp ablution block and power supply. Book online.

Moana Lodge
HOSTEL **$**

(📞 04-233 2010; www.moanalodge.co.nz; 49 Moana Rd, Plimmerton; dm $34, d with shared bathroom $86-96; @ 🕾) Just off SH1 and only a 30-minute train ride or drive from Wellington (25km), this exceptional waterfront backpackers offers sea views and relaxation within easy reach of the city. The lovely old

Central Wellington

◎ **Top Sights**
1 City Gallery C1
2 Te Papa E2

◎ **Sights**
3 New Zealand Film Archive...................C3

◆ **Activities, Courses & Tours**
4 On Yer Bike B4

🛏 **Sleeping**
5 Apollo Lodge....................................F4
6 Cambridge Hotel...............................E4
7 Capital View Motor Inn......................A5
8 City Cottages B5
9 Comfort & Quality Hotels B4
10 Museum Art Hotel E2
11 Nomads Capital C2
12 Ohtel..F3
13 Trek Global B1
14 Victoria Court...................................B3
15 YHA Wellington City E3

🍴 **Eating**
16 Arthur's B5
17 Aunty Mena's...................................B4
   Capitol ....(see 56)
18 Chow...D3
19 City Market F2
20 Duke Carvell's..................................C4
21 Farmers Market A3
22 Fidel's B4
23 Gelissimo Gelato D2
24 Great India C2
25 Harbourside Market E2
26 Little Penang C3
27 Logan Brown B4
28 Martha's Pantry B5
29 Moore Wilson Fresh...........................D4
30 Mt Vic Chippery................................E3
31 Nikau Cafe C1
32 Ombra B4
33 Ortega Fish Shack F4

34 Pandoro Panetteria............................E3
35 Phoenician Falafel.............................E4
36 Pizza Pomodoro C3
37 Prefab..C4
38 Regal E4
39 Scopa C3
40 Sweet Mother's Kitchen.....................E4
41 Tatsushi...C2

◐ **Drinking & Nightlife**
42 Goldings Free Dive C3
43 Hashigo Zake....................................D2
44 Havana...B4
45 Hawthorn Lounge..............................D4
46 Laundry..B5
   Library....................................(see 18)
47 Little Beer Quarter B2
48 Malthouse...D3
   Matterhorn ....(see 65)
49 Molly Malone's D3
50 Rogue & Vagabond B3
51 Southern Cross..................................B5
52 Vivo...B2

◎ **Entertainment**
53 BATS E3
54 Bodega...B3
55 Circa..D2
56 Embassy Theatre E4
57 Meow...B2
58 Michael Fowler Centre.......................C1
59 Paramount E3
60 San Fran B4
61 St James Theatre..............................D3

◎ **Shopping**
62 Bivouac Outdoor B1
63 Hunters & Collectors B3
64 Kura..E3
65 Mandatory..C3
66 Ora Design Gallery E3
67 Unity Books......................................B1

Apollo Lodge   MOTEL $$
(Map p358; ☑04-385 1849, 0800 361 645; www.
apollolodge.co.nz; 49 Majoribanks St; d $140-160,
q $190-240; P 🖥) Within staggering distance
of Courtenay Pl, Apollo Lodge is a loose
collation of 35 varied units (one and two
bedrooms), ranging from studios to family-
friendly units with full kitchen. Nearby
apartments available for longer-term stays.

City Cottages   RENTAL HOUSE $$
(Map p358; ☑021 073 9232; www.citybedand-
breakfast.co.nz; Tonks Gr; d/q $170/200) These
two tiny 1880 cottages sit among a precious
precinct of historic Cuba St buildings. Clever

conversion has transformed them into all-
mod-con, self-contained one-bedroom pads,
comfortable for two but sleeping up to four
thanks to a sofa bed. Stylish, convenient and
veerrrry Cuba. Road noise may be an issue.

CityLife Wellington   APARTMENT $$$
(Map p350; ☑04-922 2800, 0800 368 888; www.
heritagehotels.co.nz; 300 Lambton Quay; d from
$189; P @ 🖥) Luxurious serviced apart-
ments in the city centre, ranging from stu-
dios to three-bedroom arrangements, some
with full kitchen and in-room laundry fa-
cilities, and some with a harbour glimpse.
Weekend rates are great bang for your buck.

The vehicle entrance is from Gilmer Tce, off Boulcott St (parking $15.50 per day).

Ohtel
BOUTIQUE HOTEL $$$
(Map p358; ☑04-803 0600; www.ohtel.com; 66 Oriental Parade; d $295-425; ☎) Enjoy a slice of beautiful life at this bijou hotel on Oriental Pde. Individually decorated rooms and suites feature stylish furniture and contemporary artwork and ceramics, avidly collected by the architect-owner. Mix yourself a cocktail, then take a soak in the luxurious bathtubs.

Museum Art Hotel
HOTEL $$$
(Map p358; ☑04-802 8900, 0800 994 335; www.museumhotel.co.nz; 90 Cable St; r & apt Mon-Thu $209-399, Fri-Sun $189-349; @☎☀) Formerly known as 'Museum Hotel de Wheels' (to make way for Te Papa, it was rolled here from its original location 120m away), this art-filled hotel keeps the quirk-factor high. Bright-eyed staff, a very good restaurant with flamboyant decor, and groovy tunes piped into the lobby make a refreshing change from homogenised business hotels. Tasty weekend and weekly rates.

Bolton Hotel
HOTEL $$$
(Map p350; ☑04-472 9966, 0800 996 622; www.boltonhotel.co.nz; cnr Bolton & Mowbray Sts; d $189-359; @☎☀) ✈ Slick and well serviced, the lofty Bolton deserves its five stars. Room options are varied but share a common theme of muted tones, fine linens and colourful artwork. Most are spacious with full kitchen facilities and some enjoy park or city views. Warm your cockles in the heated pool, spa and sauna.

✖ Eating

Wellington offers exciting dining, with a bewildering array of options packed into the city centre (and plenty of fabulous options in the suburbs). Varied, contemporary cafes and upmarket restaurants are complemented by a broad range of budget options including oodles of noodle houses, with stiff competition keeping standards high and prices keen across the board.

Three excellent inner-city food markets run from dawn till around 2pm on Sundays – the seriously fruit-and-veg **Farmers Market** (Map p358; cnr Victoria & Vivian Sts), and the more varied **Harbourside Market** (Map p358; Wakefield St) next to Te Papa, where you'll also find artisan producers seducing foodies with their wares in the **City Market** (Map p358; Chaffers Dock Bldg, 1 Herd St; ☉8.30am-12.30pm Sun).

Moore Wilson Fresh
SUPERMARKET $
(Map p358; www.moorewilson.co.nz; cnr College & Tory Sts; ☉7.30am-6pm) A call-out to self-caterers: this positively swoon-inducing grocer is one of NZ's most committed supporters of independently produced and artisanal produce. If you want to sample the best of Wellington and NZ, here's your chance.

Gelissimo Gelato
ICE CREAM $
(Map p358; www.gelissimo.co.nz; 11 Cable St, Taranaki Wharf; gelato $4-8; ☉8am-5.30pm) The hottest thing in coldness is the gelato and sorbet made by Graham, who grew up in a fruiterer's shop and sure knows his apples (and raspberries, and chocolate...). Outpost along Oriental Bay.

Pandoro Panetteria
BAKERY $
(Map p358; www.pandoro.co.nz; 2 Allen St; items $3-8; ☉7am-5pm; ☑) This excellent Italian bakery serves inexpensive deliciousness (cakes, pastries and various savoury, bready, scrolly, rolly things) along with smooth coffee in sit-down surrounds. Another outlet at 14 Woodward St.

Little Penang
MALAYSIAN $
(Map p358; Oaks Complex, Dixon St; mains $8-13; ☉10.30am-8.30pm Mon-Sat) Among a troupe of great Malaysian places, teeny tiny Little Penang steals the show with its fresh-flavoured, often-fiery street food. Pick a yummy curry for your *nasi lemak,* traditionally accompanied with the eggy, nutty, saucy stuff, or go for the bargain eight-buck *nasi goreng.* Then go back for yummy curry puffs. Aim to avoid the lunchtime rush.

Aunty Mena's
VEGETARIAN $
(Map p358; 167 Cuba St; meals $10-19; ☉11.30am-9.30pm; ☑) The lightest and healthiest of Welly's noodle houses is Aunty Mena's, a cheery cafe cranking out tasty vegie/vegan Malaysian and Chinese dishes to a diverse clientele. Easy-clean, over-lit interior.

Phoenician Falafel
LEBANESE $
(Map p358; 10 Kent Tce; meals $8-16; ☉11.30am-9.30pm; ☑) Authentic falafel, shish and *shawarma* (kebab) served up by cheery Lebanese owners. The best kebabs in town, although its sister ship, Phoenician Cuisine at 245 Cuba St, comes a very close second.

★Mt Vic Chippery FISH & CHIPS $
(Map p358; www.mtvicchippery.co.nz; 5 Majoribanks St; meals $8-16; ⏲noon-9pm Wed-Sun, 4-9pm Mon & Tue) Flash fish and chips by numbers. 1. Choose your fish (at least three varieties). 2. Choose your coating (beer batter, panko crumb, tempura...). 3. Choose your chips (five varieties!). 4. Add aioli, coleslaw, salad or sauce, and a quality soft drink. 5. Chow down inside or take away. Burgers and battered sausages will placate the piscophobes.

Havana Coffee Works CAFE $
(www.havana.co.nz; 163 Tory St; snacks $4-7; ⏲8.30am-5pm Mon-Fri) Hitched on to the Havana headquarters and roastery, this fantastical 'First Class' coffee lounge offers a step back and forwards in time with its invented history and modern attitude towards quality service with speed. Nibbles are limited to the likes of scones and pies from the warmer.

Fidel's CAFE $
(Map p358; www.fidelscafe.com; 234 Cuba St; snacks $4-7, mains $10-24; ⏲7.30am-10pm; ☑) A Cuba St institution for caffeine-craving, alternative types. Eggs any-which-way, pizza and splendid salads are cranked out of the itsy kitchen, along with Welly's best milkshakes. Revolutionary memorabilia adorns the walls of the funky interior; decent outdoor areas too. A superbusy crew copes with the chaos admirably.

Martha's Pantry CAFE $
(Map p358; 276 Cuba St; snacks $4-9; ⏲9am-5pm Tue-Fri, 10am-5pm Sat & Sun) Run by the Ladies McLeod, whose roots lie in this neighbourhood, this tearoom commemorates their heritage in delicious style. Martha proffers finger sandwiches, delicate tarts, and tea in fine bone china, while across the road, **Arthur's** (Map p358; 272 Cuba St; mains $17-24; ⏲10am-late Wed-Sat) wears plaid and dishes up a manly fry-up, roasts and pork crackling snacks.

Sweet Mother's Kitchen AMERICAN $
(Map p358; www.sweetmotherskitchen.co.nz; 5 Courtenay Pl; mains $10-27; ⏲8am-10pm Sun-Thu, to late Fri & Sat; ☑) Perpetually brimming with cool cats, Sweet Mother's serves dubious but darn tasty takes on the Deep South, such as burritos, nachos, po' boys, jambalaya and key lime pie. It's cheap, cute, has craft beer and good sun.

Pizza Pomodoro PIZZA $$
(Map p358; ☎04-381 2929; www.pizzapomodoro.co.nz; 13 Leeds St; pizzas $13-24; ⏲noon-2pm Wed-Fri, 5-9pm Mon-Sat; ☑) Pomodoro's Massimo is so serious about his wood-fired pizza he's a member of the Associazione Verace Pizza Napoletana, founded to protect and promote real pizza. Take away or dine in the microspace, or eat Welly's best pizza at Goldings Free Dive (p364) with a cold beer in hand. Yes, please.

Prefab CAFE $$
(Map p358; www.pre-fab.co.nz; 14 Jessie St; breakfast $5-18, lunch $14-20; ⏲7am-4pm Mon-Fri, 8am-4pm Sat) A big, industrial-minimalist space houses the city's slickest espresso bar and roastery, owned by folks who started the capital's coffee ball rolling. Beautiful house-baked bread features on a menu of flavourful and well-executed offerings such as smoked fish, asparagus and poached egg for brekkie, or pork belly with rocket, apple and fennel salad for lunch. Sunny terrace.

★Nikau Cafe CAFE $$
(Map p358; www.nikaucafe.co.nz; City Gallery, Civic Sq; lunch $14-25; ⏲7am-4pm Mon-Fri, 8am-4pm Sat; ☑) An airy affair at the sophisticated end of the cafe scene, Nikau consistently dishes up some of the simplest but most delightful fare in town. Refreshing aperitifs, legendary kedgeree and sage eggs, divine sweets and sunny courtyard.

Tatsushi JAPANESE $$
(Map p358; 99 Victoria St; dishes $4-27; ⏲11.30am-2.30pm Tue-Sat, 6-10pm Wed-Sat) A compact, Zen-like space reassuringly dominated by an open kitchen from which authentic Japanese dishes emerge, such as superfresh sashimi, homemade *agedashi* tofu, *chazuke* soup, *sunomono* (dressed salad) and moreish Karaage chicken. Tatsushi is the real deal. Sushi and bento boxes to takeaway.

Chow FUSION $$
(Map p358; www.chow.co.nz; 45 Tory St; dishes $7-24; ⏲noon-midnight; ☑) Well-oiled Chow is a stylish pan-Asian restaurant-cum-bar, popular with folk with a penchant for zingy food in sociable surroundings, and creative cocktails. Daily deals, free wi-fi, and the fun Library bar (p365) through the back door.

Scopa ITALIAN $$
(Map p358; www.scopa.co.nz; cnr Cuba & Ghuznee Sts; mains $16-26; ⏲8am-late Mon-Fri, 9am-late Sat & Sun; ☑) Authentic pizza, pasta and gnocchi make dining at this modern *cucina* a pleasure. The *bianche* (white) pizzas make a refreshing change as do the *pizzaiolo* (pizzas of the week). Watch the groovy 'Cubans' from

a seat in the window. Lunchtime specials; sexy evenings complete with cocktails.

★Ombra
ITALIAN $$

(Map p358; www.ombra.co.nz; 199 Cuba St; snacks & small plates $4-18; ◎10am-late; ♪) This Venetian-style *bacaro* (taverna) dishes up mouth-watering Italian fare in a lively, warm atmosphere. Admire the on-trend distressed interior while sipping an aperitif then share tasty morsels like *arancino* (fried risotto ball), *pizzette* (minipizza) and meatballs. Round things off with a classic dessert such as tiramisu or saffron and honey pannacotta. *Delizioso!*

Capitol
MODERN NZ $$

(Map p358; www.capitolrestaurant.co.nz; cnr Kent Tce & Majoribanks St; mains $22-36; ◎noon-2.30pm & 5.30-9.30pm) This consistent culinary star serves simple, seasonal fare using premium local ingredients, carefully prepared with a nod to the classic Italian style. Try the parmesan-crusted lamb's liver. The dining room is a bit cramped and noisy, but elegant nonetheless, and who's going to gripe when presented with such fine cuisine? It's well worth a wait at the wee bar (no dinner bookings).

Great India
INDIAN $$

(Map p358; www.greatindia.co.nz; 141 Manners St; mains $15-32; ◎lunch & dinner; ♪) This is not your average curry house. While a tad more expensive than its competitors, this place consistently earns its moniker with distinctly flavoured curry and other high-quality specialities. Opt for the rice and bread selection if asked.

Regal
CHINESE $$

(Map p358; ☑04-384 6656; 7 Courtenay Pl; yum cha around $20) Yum cha is popular in Wellington, with many Chinese restaurants clustered around Courtenay Pl packing in the punters for their weekend ritual. The Regal pleases with speed, volume and quality, and excellence in the departments of prawn steamed dumplings, barbecue pork buns, Peking duck and coconut buns. Booking advised.

★Duke Carvell's
MEDITERRANEAN $$$

(Map p358; ☑04-385 2240; www.dukecarvell.co.nz; 6 Swan Lane; small plates $9-19, large plates $38-80; ◎noon-late Mon-Fri, 9am-late Sat & Sun) Join the handsome Duke for an indulgent culinary romp of the Mediterranean, swinging through shared plates such as house-made charcuterie, paella, chocolate mousse and noble cheeses. Heirloom artwork adorns the walls while low-cut chandeliers cast a sultry light on proceedings. Spectacular-value three-course lunch ($35 including a glass of wine).

★Ortega Fish Shack
SEAFOOD $$$

(Map p358; ☑04-382 9559; www.ortega.co.nz; 16 Marjoribanks St; mains $32-39; ◎5.30-10pm Tue-Sat) Fishing floats, salty portraits and Egyptian floor tiles set a colourful Mediterranean scene, a good hook on which to hang a seafood dinner. Fish comes many ways (roasted with Malaysian gravy, sashimi with lime dressing) while the afters head straight for France courtesy of orange crêpes and one of Welly's best cheeseboards. Excellent food in a relaxed yet upbeat environment.

Boulcott Street Bistro
BISTRO $$$

(Map p350; ☑04-499 4199; www.boulcottstreetbistro.co.nz; 99 Boulcott St; lunch mains $25-39, dinner mains $33-39; ◎noon-3pm & 6pm-late Mon-Fri, 5.30pm-late Sat & Sun) Savour classic bistro fare ministered by the inimitable Rex Morgan, within a precious heritage cottage secreted in high-rise surrounds. With no evening bookings, you may be forced to wait with a flute of fizz or glass of craft beer in the convivial bar. It'll be tough. Top-value two-course Sunday roasts ($45) and lunchtime specials ($20).

Charley Noble
MODERN NZ $$$

(Map p350; www.charleynoble.co.nz; Post Office Sq; starters & small plates $5-18, mains $22-40) Paul Hoather, chef-owner of the lauded and long-standing White House fine-dining restaurant, loosens up at this grand establishment in a newly renovated heritage building. Raw oysters and wood-fired meats follow fashion in ravishing style, but it's creative dishes such as pig's tail and pomegranate salad, and grilled octopus with crispy capers that really set this hot ticket alight.

★Logan Brown
MODERN NZ $$$

(Map p358; ☑04-801 5114; www.loganbrown.co.nz; 192 Cuba St; mains $45-51; ◎noon-2pm Mon-Sat, 5.30pm-late Mon-Sun; ☎) Routinely and deservedly touted as Wellington's best restaurant, Logan Brown oozes class without being pretentious or overly formal. Its 1920s banking chamber dining room is a stunner, as is the menu, which features such treats as Waikanae crab cakes and venison loin with goat's curd and cherry. The three-course bistro menu ($45) is an excellent and affordable way into Wellington's finest dining experience, although the epic wine list might force a blow-out. Bookings recommended.

Drinking & Nightlife

Wellingtonians love a late night, and it's common to see the masses heading into town at a time when normal folk would be boiling the kettle for cocoa. A lively music scene keeps things humming, along with respectable bar food, competitive cocktail concoctions, great NZ wines and tasty beer.

In fact the beer scene is where the action is, with Welly now a veritable whirlpool of crafty bars circled by a batch of local breweries. Put yourself in the pitcher at boho Aro's **Garage Project** (Map p350; www.garageproject.co.nz; 68 Aro Street; ☉noon-8pm Tue-Sat) microbrewery or fill a flagon at the bamboozling **Regional Wines & Spirits** (Map p350; www.regionalwines.co.nz; 15 Ellice St; ☉9am-10pm Mon-Sat, 11am-7.30pm Sun). See www.craftbeercapital.com for more propaganda.

The inner city is riddled with bars, with high concentrations around Courtenay Pl (short skirts, sexy shoes, and hair-raising hijinks); and Cuba/Victoria Sts (colourful and groovy with personality in spades). A short pub crawl can also be had along the waterfront.

Wellington's music scene predominates in pint-sized venues, most often in the corner of a bar. Big-gig listings can be found at www.undertheradar.co.nz and www.eventfinder.co.nz; look out for others as you walk the streets, or investigate venue websites and Facebook pages.

★ **Goldings Free Dive**　　　CRAFT BEER
(Map p358; www.goldingsfreedive.co.nz; 14 Leeds St; ☉noon-11pm; 🛜) Hidden down an up-swinging back alley near Cuba St, gloriously garish Goldings is a bijoux craft-beer bar with far too many merits to mention, although we'll single out ex-casino swivel chairs, a nice wine list, a ravishing Reuben sandwich plus pizza from Pomodoro, next door. Plastic fantastic gewgaws add colourful buckets of battiness.

Hashigo Zake　　　CRAFT BEER
(Map p358; www.hashigozake.co.nz; 25 Taranaki St; ☉noon-midnight; 🛜) This brick-walled bunker bar serves as the headquarters of a zealous importation business splicing a stimulating mix of big-flavoured international brewstars into a smartly selected NZ range. Ogling the oft-changing taps and brimming fridges is a wide range of hopheads, happy to stand elbow to elbow around the bar or squeeze into the acoustically sweet side-lounge on nano-gig nights (every Saturday at 10pm).

Malthouse　　　CRAFT BEER
(Map p358; www.themalthouse.co.nz; 48 Courtenay Pl; ☉3pm-late Mon & Tue, noon-1am Wed-Sun) At last count there were nearly 200 reasons to drink at this, the capital's original craft-beer bar – still boasting a high beer-geek quotient, and now housed in a low-key concrete box with leaners, comfy corner lounge, and popular alfresco area where you can watch the world go by. Check the blackboard for new brews, or ask savvy staff to serve something to suit your mood.

★ **Little Beer Quarter**　　　CRAFT BEER
(Map p358; www.littlebeerquarter.co.nz; 6 Edward St; 4pm-late Mon, noon-late Tue-Sat) Tucked away in a back lane, lovely LBQ is a lively bar handled with a lady's touch. It's warm, inviting, and soft in all the right places, but still packs a hop-headed punch with its well-curated taps and bottled selection. Good cocktails, wines and whiskies, too, plus tasty bar food along the lines of pizza and pork scratchings. Bargain specials Monday to Thursday.

Rogue & Vagabond　　　CRAFT BEER
(Map p358; www.rogueandvagabond.co.nz; 18 Garrett St) Right in the heart of Cuba fronting on to a precious pocket park, the Rogue is a lovably scruffy, colourful, kaleidoscopic craft-beer bar with heaps going on: 18 taps; voluminous, chewy-crust pizza ($15 to $22); regular, rockin' gigs; and sifting about on the patio or slouching around on the lawn.

Southern Cross　　　PUB
(Map p358; www.thecross.co.nz; 39 Abel Smith St; ☉8am-late) Welcoming to all – from frenetic five-year-olds to Nana with her knitting – the fun, easygoing Cross rambles around a series of colourful rooms, combining a respectable restaurant, lively bar, dance floor, pool table and the best garden bar in town. There's interesting beer on tap, food to suit all budgets, and regular events including bingo, gigs and quiz night.

Laundry　　　BAR
(Map p358; www.laundry.net.nz; 240 Cuba St; ☉10am-late Wed-Sun, 4pm-late Tue) Tumble into this junk-shop juke joint any time of the day or night for a tipple and a taco, and hang out with the hipsters in a wrinkle-free zone. Carousal is encouraged with regular gigs and deejays, lip-smacking libations and colourful, carnivalesque decor pasted up with a very rough brush. Trailer-trash backyard complete with a caravan.

Molly Malone's
IRISH PUB

(Map p358; www.mollymalones.co.nz; cnr Courtenay Pl & Taranaki St; ⊙11am-1am Sun-Thu, to 3am Fri & Sat) This highly polished Irish bar hosts live music nearly every night, and dishes up well-priced pub grub and a balcony overlooking the bustle. If the *craic* downstairs is too much for you, head up to the piano bar for a quiet dram.

Havana
BAR

(Map p358; www.havanabar.co.nz; 32 Wigan St; ⊙11.30am-late Mon-Fri, 3pm-late Sat) Go out of your way to find Havana, a mighty fine needle in Welly's hospitality haystack, hidden down a sidestreet and squeezed into two adjacent heritage cottages sharing a groovy backyard. Fortify yourself with tapas and top shelf, then chinwag, smoke or flirt, or all three, then break out your sexy legs in the microdisco.

Vivo
WINE BAR

(Map p358; www.vivowinebar.com; 19 Edward St; ⊙3pm-late Mon-Fri, 5pm-late Sat) If your idea of a good time is fine wine, tapas and conversation, head to Vivo. Match wines off an epic list with any of 30 delectable small plates, and relax in the brick-lined and timbered, cellarlike dining room. This is one of the city's real hidden gems – dark and twinkly, sensual and delicious.

Hawthorn Lounge
COCKTAIL BAR

(Map p358; www.hawthornlounge.co.nz; 82 Tory St; ⊙6pm-late Tue-Sat) This classy cocktail bar has a 1920s speakeasy feel, suited up in waistcoats and wide-brimmed fedoras. Sip a drink and play poker, or simply enjoy the behind-the-bar theatrics from the Hawthorn's serious mixologists twisting and turning classics into modern-day masterpieces. Kiss me, tease me, spoil me wines.

Library
BAR

(Map p358; www.thelibrary.co.nz; 53 Courtenay Pl; ⊙5pm-late) You'll find yourself in the right kind of bind at the book-filled Library, with its velveteen booths, board games and bestselling cocktails. An excellent all-round drink selection is complemented by a highly sharable menu of sweet and savoury treats including chocolate fondant and cheese. Live music on occasion.

Matterhorn
BAR

(Map p358; www.matterhorn.co.nz; 106 Cuba St; ⊙3pm-late) An early riser in Welly's 21st-century bar scene, the 'Horn still hovers around the top with its reputable food (tapas from mid-arvo, dinner daily, brunch weekends), snappy service and regular live music. The sultry, designerly style for which it is famous is now slightly faded and dated, but this matters little in the dimmed light of its bewitching hours.

☆ Entertainment

Wellington is home to a long-standing professional theatre, Circa, whose busy program is augmented by plenty of amateur companies and fringe performers, student shows and regular visiting tours. Peruse listings at www.eventfinder.co.nz. Many events are ticketed via Ticketek (www.ticketek.co.nz) box offices, located at St James Theatre (Map p358; 77 Courtenay Pl) and the Michael Fowler Centre (Map p358; 111 Wakefield St), as well as TicketDirect (www.ticketdirect.co.nz). Discount same-day tickets for some productions are often available at the i-SITE.

Wellywood has simply too many good indy cinemas to list, so here are a few inner-city picks. Movie times are listed in the daily *Dominion Post* and at www.flicks.co.nz.

Circa
THEATRE

(Map p358; ☑04-801 7992; www.circa.co.nz; 1 Taranaki St; ⊙Tue-Sun) Waterfront Circa

---

WELCOME TO WELLYWOOD

In recent years Wellington has stamped its place firmly on the world map as the home of NZ's dynamic film industry, earning itself the nickname 'Wellywood'. Acclaimed director Peter Jackson still calls Wellington home; the success of his *The Lord of the Rings* films and subsequent productions such as *King Kong*, *The Adventures of Tintin* and *The Hobbit* have made him a powerful Hollywood player, and have bolstered Wellington's reputation.

Canadian director James Cameron is now in on the action, with three *Avatar* sequels set to be shot in New Zealand. Cameron and his family are New Zealand residents, with landholding in rural Wairarapa.

Movie buffs can experience some local movie magic by visiting mini-museum the Weta Cave (p353), or one of many film locations around the region – a speciality of local guided-tour companies.

houses two auditoriums in which it shows everything from edgy new works to Christmas panto. Standby tickets available an hour before the show.

BATS
THEATRE

(🖉 04-802 4175; www.bats.co.nz; 1 Kent Tce) Wildly alternative but accessible BATS presents cutting-edge and experimental NZ theatre – varied, cheap and intimate – in its freshly revamped theatre.

Light House Cinema
CINEMA

(🖉 04-385-3337; www.lighthousecuba.co.nz; 29 Wigan St; adult/child $17.50/12.50) Tucked away near the top end of Cuba St, this small, stylish and modern cinema screens a wide range of mainstream, art-house and foreign films in three small theatres. High-quality snacks.

Embassy Theatre
CINEMA

(Map p358; 🖉 04-384 7657; www.eventcinemas. co.nz; 10 Kent Tce; adult/child from $18.50/13.50) Wellywood's cinema mothership is an art-deco darling, built in the 1920s. Today she screens mainly mainstream films with state-of-the-art sound and vision. Bars and cafe on site.

Paramount
CINEMA

(Map p358; 🖉 04-384 4080; www.paramount.co.nz; 25 Courtenay Pl; adult/child $15.90/10.50; ☺ noon-midnight) A lovely old complex screening largely art-house, documentary and foreign flicks.

Meow
LIVE MUSIC, BAR

(Map p358; www.welovemeow.co.nz; 9 Edward St; ☺ 4.30pm-late Mon, 10am-late Tue-Sun) Truly the cat's pyjamas, Meow goes out on a limb to host a diverse range of gigs and other performances, at the same time offering good-quality, inexpensive food at almost any time of day. There are treats for the sweet tooth, and a good selection of keenly priced craft beers. Mishmashed retro decor gives the place a speakeasy feel.

San Fran
LIVE MUSIC

(Map p358; www.sanfran.co.nz; 171 Cuba St; ☺ noon-late) This much-loved, midsized music venue is moving to a new beat, having boarded the craft-beer bandwagon and rockin' out smoky, meaty food along the way. Gigs still rule, dancing is de rigueur and the balcony still gets good afternoon sun.

Bodega
LIVE MUSIC

(Map p358; www.bodega.co.nz; 101 Ghuznee St; ☺ 4pm-late) A trailblazer of the city's modern live-music scene, the good-old Bodge' has demonstrated admirable endurance, hosting a regular and varied program of gigs – including frequent international acts – in a pleasant space with solid acoustics and a respectable dance floor.

 ## Shopping

Wellington supports a high number of independent shops including scores of design stores and clothing boutiques. There's still plenty that's Kiwi-made – despite cheap imports and online shopping – with retailers flying their home-grown flags with pride.

Unity Books
BOOKS

(Map p358; www.unitybooks.co.nz; 57 Willis St; ☺ 9am-6pm Mon-Fri, 10am-6pm Sat, 11am-2pm Sun) Setting the standard for every bookshop in the land. Dedicated NZ table piled high.

Vault
ARTS & CRAFTS

(Map p350; www.thevaultnz.com; 2 Plimmer Steps; ☺ 9.30am-5.30pm Mon-Thu, 9.30am-7pm Fri, 10am-5pm Sat, 11am-4.30pm Sun) Jewellery, clothing, bags, ceramics, cosmetics – a bonny store with lots of NZ-made, beautiful things.

Kura
ARTS & CRAFTS

(Map p358; www.kuragallery.co.nz; 19 Allen St; ☺ 10am-6pm Mon-Fri, 11am-4pm Sat & Sun) Contemporary indigenous art: painting, ceramics, jewellery and sculpture.

Ora Design Gallery
ARTS & CRAFTS

(Map p358; 23 Allen St; ☺ 9am-6pm Mon-Fri, 9am-5pm Sat, 10am-4pm Sun) Fresh, bold, bright contempoary art including sculpture, weaving and jewellery.

Mandatory
CLOTHING

(Map p358; www.mandatory.co.nz; 108 Cuba Mall; ☺ 10am-6pm Mon-Thu, 10am-7pm Fri, 10am-4.30pm Sat, noon-4pm Sun) Great service and sharp men's tailoring for the capital's cool cats.

Hunters & Collectors
VINTAGE

(Map p358; 134 Cuba St; ☺ 10am-6pm Mon-Sat, 11am-5pm Sun) Off-the-rack and vintage clothing (punk, skate and mod), plus shoes and accessories. Best-dressed window in NZ.

Bivouac Outdoor
OUTDOOR EQUIPMENT

(Map p358; www.bivouac.co.nz; 39 Mercer St; ☺ 9am-5.30pm Mon-Fri, 10am-5pm Sat & Sun) The best of several outdoor shops, staffed by people who know because they go.

Old Bank Shopping Arcade   SHOPPING CENTRE
(Map p350; www.oldbank.co.nz; cnr Lambton Quay
& Willis St; ⊙9am-6pm Mon-Fri, 10am-4pm Sat,
11am-3pm Sun) This dear old building is home
to indulgent boutiques, predominantly
clothing.

Kirkcaldie & Stains   DEPARTMENT STORE
(Map p350; 165-177 Lambton Quay; ⊙9am-5.30pm
Mon-Fri, 10am-5pm Sat & Sun) NZ's answer to
Bloomingdale's or Harrods, established in
1863. Bring your travel documents with you
for tax-free bargains.

ℹ Information

INTERNET ACCESS
Free wi-fi is available in most of the CBD (see
www.cbdfree.co.nz); the i-SITE also has internet
access.

MEDICAL SERVICES
**Wellington Accident & Urgent Medical
Centre** (✆04-384 4944; www.wamc.co.nz;
17 Adelaide Rd, Newtown; ⊙8am-11pm) No
appointment necessary; also home to the
after-hours pharmacy. It's close to the Basin
Reserve around the northern end of Adelaide Rd.
Wellington Hospital (✆04-385 5999; www.
ccdhb.org.nz; Riddiford St, Newtown; ⊙24hr)
One kilometre south of the city centre.

POST
Post Office (Map p358; 2 Manners St;
⊙8.30am-5.30pm Mon-Fri, 9am-3pm Sat) This
branch has the longest opening hours of all city
branches.

TOURIST INFORMATION
DOC Wellington Visitor Centre (Map p358;
✆04-384 7770; www.doc.govt.nz; 18 Manners
St; ⊙9.30am-5pm Mon-Fri, 10am-3.30pm Sat)
Bookings, passes and information for local and
national walks (including Great Walks), parks,
huts and camping.
Wellington i-SITE (Map p358; ✆04-802 4860;
www.wellingtonnz.com; Civic Sq, cnr Wakefield
& Victoria Sts; ⊙8.30am-5pm) Staff book
almost everything, and cheerfully distribute
Wellington's *Official Visitor Guide*, along with
other maps and helpful pamphlets. Internet
access and cafe.

USEFUL WEBSITES
Best of Wellington (www.bestofwellington.
co.nz) Entertaining, long-standing independent guidebook aimed at longer-staying
visitors.
Stuff (www.stuff.co.nz) Online news service
incorporating Wellington's newspaper, the
Dominion Post.

ℹ Getting There & Away

AIR
Wellington is an international gateway to NZ.
Wellington Airport (WLG; ✆04-385 5100;
www.wellingtonairport.co.nz; Stewart Duff Dr,
Rongotai; ⊙4am-1.30am) has touch-screen
information kiosks in the luggage hall. There's
also currency exchange, ATMs, car-rental desks,
shops and, of course, spectacular espresso. If
you're in transit or have an early flight, you can't
linger overnight inside the terminal.
Air New Zealand (✆0800 737 000; www.
airnewzealand.co.nz) Offers flights between
Wellington and most domestic centres, including Auckland, Nelson, Christchurch, Dunedin
and Queenstown. It also flies direct to Sydney,
Melbourne and Brisbane.
Jetstar (✆0800 800 995; www.jetstar.com)
Offers economical flights from Wellington
to Auckland and Christchurch, but takes no
prisoners when it comes to late check-in. It also
flies direct to Sydney and Melbourne.
Qantas (✆0800 808 767; www.qantas.com.
au) Flies direct between Wellington and Sydney
and Melbourne.
Soundsair (✆03-520 3080, 0800 505 005;
www.soundsair.com) Flies between Wellington
and Picton up to eight times daily (from $95),
Nelson (from $113) and Blenheim (from $95).

For human assistance, try the helpful folks at
Flight Centre (www.flightcentre.co.nz; cnr Willis
& Manners Sts; ⊙9am-5.30pm Mon-Fri, 10am-
4pm Sat).

BOAT
On a clear day, sailing into Wellington Harbour
or through the Marlborough Sounds is magical.
Cook Strait can cut up rough, but the big ferries
handle it well, and sport lounges, cafes, bars, information desks and cinemas but no pool tables.
There are two options for crossing the strait
between Wellington and Picton: Bluebridge and
the Interislander.

Booking online is the cheapest option, but folks
at the i-SITE and hotels will happily book for you.
Bluebridge is based at Waterloo Quay, opposite
the Wellington train station. The Interislander
terminal is about 2km northeast of the city centre; a shuttle bus ($2) runs to the Interislander
from platform 9 at Wellington train station (where
long-distance buses also depart). It also meets
arriving ferries, returning passengers to platform
9. There's also a taxi stand at the terminal.

Car-hire companies allow you to pick up/drop
off vehicles at ferry terminals. If you arrive outside business hours, arrangements can be made
to collect your vehicle from the terminal car park.
Bluebridge Ferries (Map p350; ✆04-471
6188, 0800 844 844; www.bluebridge.co.nz;

50 Waterloo Quay) Crossing takes 3½ hours; up to four sailings in each direction daily. Cars and campervans from $118; motorbikes $51; bicycles $10. Passenger fares from adult/child $51/26.

Interislander (Map p350; ☑ 0800 802 802, 04-498 3302; www.interislander.co.nz; Aotea Quay) Crossing takes three hours 10 minutes; up to five sailings in each direction daily. Cars are priced from $118; campervans (up to 5.5m) from $133; motorbikes from $56; bicycles $15. Passenger fares start from adult/child $55/28.

BUS

Wellington is a major bus-travel hub, with **Inter-City** (☑ 04-385 0520; www.intercity.co.nz) boasting the most extensive network. Services depart from platform 9 at the train station north to Auckland (11 hours) and all major towns in between and beyond such as Palmerston North (2¼ hours), Rotorua (7½ hours), and Napier (5½ hours). Buy tickets from the Intercity ticket window in the train station, or online for discounted fares.

Naked Bus (☑ 0900 625 33; www.nakedbus. com) runs north from Wellington to all major North Island destinations, including Palmerston North (2½ hours), Napier (five hours), Taupo (6½ hours) and Auckland (11½ hours), with myriad stops en route. Buses depart from opposite the Amora Hotel in Wakefield St, and collect more passengers at Bunny St opposite the railway station. Book online or at Wellington i-SITE; get in early for the cheapest fares.

TRAIN

Wellington train station has six **ticket windows** (☑ 0800 801 700; ◷ 6.30am-8pm Mon-Thu, to 1am Fri & Sat, to 7pm Sun), two selling tickets for **KiwiRail Scenic Journeys** (☑ 04-495 0775, 0800 872 467; www.kiwirailscenic.co.nz) trains, Interislander ferries and InterCity coaches; the other four ticketing local/regional **Tranz Metro** (☑ 0800 801 700; www.tranzmetro.co.nz) trains (Johnsonville, Melling, Hutt Valley, Kapiti and Wairarapa lines).

KiwiRail Scenic runs the just-hanging-in-there *Northern Explorer* service from Wellington to Auckland on Tuesday, Friday and Sunday, returning from Auckland on Monday, Thursday, and Saturday (from $99, 12 hours). KiwiRail also runs the *Capital Connection* commuter service from Palmerston North, leaving at 6.15am for Wellington, and returning to Palmerston North at 5.15pm.

❶ Getting Around

Metlink (☑ 0800 801 700; www.metlink.org. nz) is the one-stop shop for Wellington's regional bus, train and harbour ferry networks.

TO/FROM THE AIRPORT

Co-op Shuttles (☑ 04-387 8787; www.co-opshuttles.co.nz; 1/2 passengers $20/26) provides a door-to-door minibus service between the city and airport, 8km southeast of the city. It's cheaper if two or more passengers are travelling to the same destination. Shuttles meet all arriving flights.

The **Airport Flyer** (☑ 0800 801 700; www. airportflyer.co.nz) bus runs between the airport, Wellington and the Hutt Valley, with a fare to downtown Wellington costing around $9. Buses run from around 6am to 8pm.

A taxi between the city centre and airport costs around $30.

BICYCLE

If you're fit or keep to the flat, cycling is a viable option. City hirers include **On Yer Bike** (Map p358; ☑ 04-384 8480; www.onyerbikeavantiplus.co.nz; 181 Vivian St; half-day $20-30, full day $30-40, week $150) near Cuba St, and Ferg's Kayaks (p354) on the waterfront. Wellington's Regional Council shows great encouragement via the maps and suggestions on its **Journey Planner** (www.journeyplanner.org.nz).

BUS

Frequent and efficient bus services cover the whole Wellington region and run between approximately 6am and 11.30pm. Major bus terminals are at the Wellington train station, and on Courtenay Pl near the Cambridge Tce intersection. Pick up route maps and timetables from the i-SITE and convenience stores, or online from Metlink. Fares are determined by zones: a trip across the city centre (Zone 1) costs $2, and all the way north to Masterton (Zone 14) costs $18.

Metlink also runs the After Midnight bus service, departing from two convenient city stops (Courtenay Pl and Cuba St) between midnight and 4.30am Saturday and Sunday, following a number of routes to the outer suburbs. Fares range from $6.50 to $13.50, depending on how far away your bed is.

CAR

There are a lot of one-way streets in Wellington, and parking gets tight (and pricey) during the day. If you've got a car or a caravan, park on the outskirts and walk or take public transport into the city centre. Campervans can also park during the day at the Wellington Waterfront Motorhome Park and the open-air car park outside Te Papa.

Aside from the major international rental companies, Wellington has several operators that will negotiate cheap deals, especially for longer-term rentals of two weeks or more, but rates generally aren't as competitive as in Auckland. Rack rates range from around $40 to $80 per day; cars are usually a few years old and in pretty good condition. Operators include the following:

Jucy Rentals (☑ 0800 399 736, 04-380 6211; www.jucy.co.nz; 5 Ropa Lane, Miramar)

Apex Car Rental (☑ 0800 300 110, 04-385 2163; www.apexrentals.co.nz; 186 Victoria St)

Omega Rental Cars (📞0800 667 722, 04-472 8465; www.omegarentalcars.com; 77 Hutt Rd)

If you plan on exploring both North and South Islands, most companies suggest you leave your car in Wellington and pick up another one in Picton after crossing Cook Strait. This is a common (and more affordable) practice, and car-hire companies make it a painless exercise.

There are often cheap deals on car relocation from Wellington to Auckland, as most renters travel in the opposite direction. The catch is that you may only have 24 or 48 hours to make the journey.

TAXI

Packed ranks can be found on Courtenay Pl, at the corner of Dixon and Victoria Sts, on Featherston St and outside the railway station. Two of many operators:

Green Cabs (📞0508 447 336; www.green-cabs.co.nz)

Wellington Combined Taxis (📞04-384 4444; www.taxis.co.nz)

TRAIN

Tranz Metro (📞0800 801 700; www.tranzmetro.co.nz) operates four train routes running through Wellington's suburbs to regional destinations. Trains run frequently from around 6am to 11pm, departing Wellington train station. The routes: Johnsonville, via Ngaio and Khandallah; Kapiti, via Porirua, Plimmerton, Paekakariki and Paraparaumu; Melling, via Petone; the Hutt Valley via Waterloo to Upper Hut; and a Wairarapa service calling at Featherston, Carterton and Masterton. Timetables are available from convenience stores, the train station, Wellington i-SITE and online. Standard fares from Wellington to the ends of the five lines range from $5 to $18. A Day Rover ticket ($14) allows unlimited off-peak and weekend travel on all lines except Wairarapa.

KAPITI COAST

With wide, crowd-free beaches, the Kapiti Coast acts as a summer playground and suburban extension for Wellingtonians. The region takes its name from Kapiti Island, a wildlife sanctuary 5km offshore from Paraparaumu.

The mountainous Tararua Forest Park forms a dramatic backdrop along the length of the coastline and has some accessible day walks and longer tramps.

The Kapiti Coast makes an easy day trip from Wellington, but if you're after a few restful days there's enough of interest to keep you entertained.

🛈 Information

The Coast's official visitor centre is **Paraparaumu i-SITE** (📞04-298 8195; Coastlands Mall, Rimu Rd; ⏱9am-5pm Mon-Fri, 10am-2pm Sat & Sun), located within the Coastlands shopping centre, where you'll find all manner of other useful services such as banks, ATMs, post office and supermarkets.

🛈 Getting There & Around

AIR

The recently expanded **Kapiti Coast Airport** (PPQ; www.kapitiairport.co.nz; Toru Rd, Paraparaumu Beach) in Paraparaumu is a regular destination for **Air2there** (📞0800 777 000; www.air2there.com), with daily flights to Blenheim and Nelson, and **Air New Zealand** (📞0800 737 000; www.airnewzealand.co.nz), which flies direct to Auckland.

BUS

InterCity (📞04-385 0520; www.intercity.co.nz) stops at major Kapiti Coast towns on its services between Wellington (45 minutes) and northern destinations including Taupo (5½ hours) and Auckland (10 hours). Book online for best fares.

Naked Bus (📞0900 625 33; www.nakedbus.com) also stops at major Kapiti Coast towns on its daily services.

Metlink (📞0800 801 700; www.metlink.org.nz) runs local bus services around Paraparaumu, and up to Waikanae and Otaki, calling at highway and beach settlements.

CAR & MOTORCYCLE

Getting here from Wellington is a breeze by car: just follow SH1 for 30 minutes to Paekakariki, and around 45 to Paraparaumui. It's motorway most of the way.

TRAIN

Tranz Metro (p368) commuter trains between Wellington and the coast are easier and more frequent than buses. Services run from Wellington to Paraparaumu ($12, generally half-hourly off-peak between 6am and 11pm, with more services at peak times), stopping en route in Paekakariki ($10.50). Weekday off-peak fares (9am to 3pm) are up to $2 cheaper.

KiwiRail Scenic Journeys (📞04-495 0775, 0800 872 467; www.kiwirailscenic.co.nz) has long-distance *Northern Explorer* trains connecting Wellington and Auckland stopping at Paraparaumu, while the weekday-only, peak-hour *Capital Connection*, travelling to Wellington in the morning and back to Palmerston North in the evening, stops at Paraparaumu, Waikanae and Otaki.

Paekakariki

POP 1665

Paekakariki is an arty little seaside village stretched along a black-sand beach, serviced by a train station and passed by the highway to Wellington, 41km to the south.

◉ Sights & Activities

★**Queen Elizabeth Park**　　　PARK
(SH1; ⊘ gates 8am-8pm) FREE One of the last relatively unchanged areas of dune and wetland along this coast, this undulating 650-hectare beachside park offers swimming, walking, cycling and picnicking opportunities, as well as the Tramway Museum and Stables on the Park. There are three entrances: off Wellington Rd in Paekakariki, at MacKay's Crossing on SH1, and off the Esplanade in Raumati to the north.

Tramway Museum　　　MUSEUM
(www.wellingtontrams.org.nz; MacKay's Crossing entrance, Queen Elizabeth Park; admission by donation, all-day tram rides adult/child/family $10/5/24; ⊘ museum 10am-4.30pm daily, trams 11am-4.30pm Sat & Sun, daily 26 Dec-late Jan) A glimpse into historic Wellington by way of restored wooden trams and museum displays housed in a large garage, and on a 2km tram ride through Queen Elizabeth Park down to the beach. On-site ice-cream kiosk.

Stables on the Park　　　HORSE RIDING
(☎ 027 448 6764, 06-364 3336; www.stablesonthepark.co.nz; MacKay's Crossing entrance, Queen Elizabeth Park; 30-90min ride $50-100; ⊘ open most days in summer) Mandy and friends run guided rides on well-mannered horses. The 1½-hour trek will see you trot along the beach with views of Kapiti Island before heading inland on park tracks. Beginners are welcome.

🛏 Sleeping & Eating

Paekakariki Holiday Park　　HOLIDAY PARK $
(☎ 04-292 8292; www.paekakarikiholidaypark.co.nz; 180 Wellington Rd; sites per adult from $16, cabins & flats from $65; @ 🖥) This large, leafy park has rather tired and dated facilities, but is well located, 1.5km north of the township at the southern entrance to Queen Elizabeth Park.

Finn's　　　HOTEL, PUB $$
(☎ 04-292 8081; www.finnshotel.co.nz; 2 Beach Rd; d $135-150; 🖥) Finn's is the flashy beige suit of the low-key railway village, but redeems itself with spacious rooms, good-value meals (mains $17 to $29), craft beer on tap and an in-house 26-seat cinema. The hush glass keeps the highway at bay.

WORTH A TRIP

KAPITI ISLAND

Kapiti Island is the coastline's dominant feature, a 10km by 2km slice that since 1897 has been a protected reserve. Largely predator-free since 1998, it is home to a remarkable range and number of birds including many species that are now rare or extinct on the mainland.

The island is open to visitors, limited each day to 100 at Rangatira, where you can hike up to the 521m high point, Tuteremoana; and 60 visitors at the northern end, which has short, gentle walks to viewpoints and around a lagoon.

To visit the island, you must make your arrangements in advance with one of three licensed operators. Remember to reconfirm your arrangements on the morning of departure, as sailings are weather-dependent. All boats depart from Paraparaumu Beach, which can be reached by train. Services are provided by Kapiti Marine Charter (☎ 027 442 4850, 04-297 2585; www.kapitimarinecharter.co.nz; adult/child $95/55); Kapiti Tours (☎ 0800 527 484, 04-237 7965; www.ngatitoakapititours.co.nz; adult/child $105/65); and Kapiti Island Nature Tours (☎ 021 126 7525, 06-362 6606; www.kapitiislandnatetours.co.nz; boat transport adult/child $95/55), run by the Barrett and Clark whanau (family), who have a long-standing connection to the island. The latter offers day tours as well as a very special overnight stay (adult/child from $369/215), which includes an introduction to wildlife, history and Maori traditions, but also an after-dark walk in the bush to spot the cutest-ever bird, the rare little spotted kiwi. The price includes lodge accommodation in sole-occupancy rooms or bunk houses, with meals included.

More information can be found in the Department of Conservation (DOC) Kapiti Island Nature Reserve brochure or in person at the DOC Wellington Visitor Centre (p367).

Beach Road Deli
CAFE $

(5 Beach Rd; snacks $3-8, pizzas $13-22; ☺7am-8pm Wed-Sat, to 4.30pm Sun) Bijou deli and wood-fired pizzeria, stocked with home-baked bread and pastries, cheese, char-cuterie and assorted imported goodies. Heaven-sent for the highway traveller, pic-nicker, or those looking for a sausage to fry and a bun to put it in. Ace coffee.

Waikanae & Around

Heading north beyond Paekakariki, it's not long before it's time to slow down for an-other Kapiti Coast town. The first is **Para-paraumu** (population 17,190), the region's major commercial and residential hot spot. The town has two hubs: the main town on the highway, with shopping galore, and Para-paraumu Beach with its waterside park and walkway, decent swimming and other beachy attractions, including the stunning view out to Kapiti Island. The correct pronunciation is 'Pah-ra-pah-ra-oo-moo', meaning 'scraps from an oven', which is said to have originated when a Maori war party attacked the settle-ment and found only scraps of food remain-ing. It's a bit of a mouthful to pronounce; locals usually just corrupt it into 'Para-par-am'.

Around 15 minutes' drive (20km) north of Paraparamu is **Waikanae** (population 10,640), traditionally a retirees' favourite but in contemporary times a growing, go-ahead town encouraged by first-time-home-buyer flight from Wellington city. It's a pleasant and sunny seaside town, and a rewarding stop for some salt-tinged R&R.

◎ Sights & Activities

Nga Manu Nature Reserve WILDLIFE RESERVE
(www.ngamanu.co.nz; 281 Ngarara Rd; adult/child/family $15/6/35; ☺10am-5pm) Waikanae's main visitor attraction, Nga Manu Nature Reserve is a 15-hectare bird sanctuary dot-ted with picnic areas, bushwalks, aviaries and a nocturnal house with kiwi, owls and tuatara. The eels are fed at 2pm daily, and guided tours run on weekends at 2pm (Sun-day only in winter). To get here, turn sea-wards from SH1 onto Te Moana Rd and then right down Ngarara Rd and follow the signs.

Tuatara Brewery BREWERY
(www.tuatarabrewing.co.nz; 7 Sheffield St, Paraparau-mu; ☺11am-7pm Wed-Sun) Visit the oldest and most famous of Wellington's craft breweries at its industrial-estate premises where you can enjoy a tasting along with simple bar snacks (biersticks, pizza...) or preferably go on an en-lightening tour of the brewery with Mr McIn-ness, raconteur ($30, including tasting tray).

Southward Car Museum MUSEUM
(www.southwardcarmuseum.co.nz; Otaihanga Rd; adult/child $13/3; ☺9am-4.30pm) This museum has one of Australasia's largest collections of antique and unusual cars. Check out the DeLorean and the 1950 gangster Cadillac.

Waikanae Estuary Bird Tours ECOTOUR
(☎04-905 1001; www.kapitibirdtours.co.nz; 2hr tours $35) The Waikanae Estuary is a hot spot for birds, with around 60 species visit-ing during the year. You can expect to see around 20 on these personalised outings with a passionate guide, which end with a cup of tea and a freshly baked scone ($25 without refreshments).

Hemi Matenga Memorial Park WALKING
This 330-hectare native reserve overlooking Waikanae contains a large remnant of kohe-kohe forest. The reserve rises steeply from 150m to its highest point, Te Au (514m), a hike of around four hours. There are a couple of other tracks including the Kohekohe Walk, an easy 30-minute amble on a well-formed path. Access is off Reikorangi Rd, Waikanae.

⌂ Sleeping & Eating

Kapiti Gateway Motel MOTEL $$
(☎0800 429 360, 04-902 5876; www.kapitigateway.co.nz; 114 Main Rd, Waikanae; d $115-155; ☀�) Tidy, airy motel on the highway with solar-heated pool, great hospitality and excellent local ad-vice. Holiday hermits can make the most of the free wi-fi, kitchen facilities and Sky TV.

Long Beach CAFE $$
(www.longbeach.net.nz; 40 Tutere St, Waikanae; meals $16-30; ☺8.30am-10pm) Neighbourly, family-friendly Long Beach offers an extensive menu ranging from house-cured salmon and risotto through to pizza and fish and chips. With a large conservatory, it's bright and beachy, making it most suitable for socialising over a drink from an impeccable list. The Front Room cafe next door is also very good.

Ambience Café CAFE $$
(10 Seaview Rd, Paraparaumu; lunch $13-22; ☺8am-4pm Sun-Thu; ☑) A very 'Wellington' cafe, with both light and substantial meals made with relish, such as fish cakes, the BLT and colourful vegie options. Cake cabinet at full capacity, and great coffee (of course).

THE WAIRARAPA

The Wairarapa is the large tract of land east and northeast of Wellington, beyond the Tararua and Rimutaka Ranges. It is named after Wairarapa Moana – otherwise known as Lake Wairarapa and translating as 'sea of glistening waters'. This shallow 80-sq-km lake and the surrounding wetland is the focus of much-needed ecological restoration, redressing generations of sheep farming in its ambit. Fields of fluffy sheep still abound, as do vineyards and the associated hospitality which have turned the region into a decadent weekend retreat.

See www.wairarapanz.com for regional info, but also check out the Classic New Zealand Wine Trail (www.classicwinetrail. co.nz) – a useful tool for joining the dots throughout the Wairarapa and its neighbouring wine regions of Hawke's Bay and Marlborough.

Note that the telephone area code over here is ⌨06, not ⌨04 like most of the rest of the Wellington region.

❶ Getting There & Around

From Wellington, **Tranz Metro** (⌨0800 801 700; www.tranzmetro.co.nz) commuter trains run to Masterton ($17.50, five or six times daily on weekdays, two daily on weekends), calling at seven Wairarapa stations including Featherston and Carterton. For towns off the railway line, catch a Tranzit Coachlines bus (details available from **Metlink** (⌨0800 801 700; www.metlink. org.nz) Its services run to all major Wairarapa towns as well as north to Palmerston North.

WAIRARAPA WINE COUNTRY

Wairarapa's world-renowned wine industry was nearly crushed in infancy. The region's first vines were planted in 1883, but the prohibition movement in 1908 soon put a cap on that corker idea. It wasn't until the 1980s that winemaking was revived, after Martinborough's *terroir* (natural environment) was discovered to be similar to Burgundy in France. A few vineyards soon sprang up, but the number has now ballooned to around 40 regionwide. Martinborough is the undisputed hub of the action, but vineyards around Gladstone and Masterton are also on the up. Keep an eye out for the occasional olive groves with tasting rooms, nestled among the vines.

Martinborough plays host to Toast Martinborough (www.toastmartinborough.co.nz; tickets $70), held annually on the third Sunday in November. Enjoyable on many levels (standing up and quite possibly lying on the grass), this is a hugely popular wine, food and music event, and you'll have to be quick on the draw to get a ticket.

The Wairarapa Wines Harvest Festival (www.wairarapawines.co.nz; tickets $45) celebrates the beginning of the harvest with an extravaganza of wine, food and family fun. It's held at a remote riverbank setting 10 minutes from Carterton on a Saturday in mid-March.

Wairarapa's wineries thrive on visitors; around half of Martinborough's 25-odd wineries welcome visitors every day, with most of the rest open at the weekends. Well-oiled cellar doors swing wide open for tastings; some places feature a cafe or restaurant, while some will rustle up a picnic platter to be enjoyed in their gardens. The *Wairarapa Wine Trail Map* (available from the Martinborough i-SITE and many other locations) will aid your navigation. Read all about it at www.winesfrommartinborough.com.

A handy place to sample and purchase many wines, and get advice on local cellar doors is the Martinborough Wine Centre (www.martinboroughwinecentre.co.nz; 6 Kitchener St; ☺10am-5pm), which also sells local olive oils, books, clothing and art.

The best and most ecofriendly way to explore the Wairarapa's wines is by bicycle, as the flat landscape makes for puff-free cruising. You can also knock off quite a few on foot. Should you require transport, however, hop on the daily tasting tour run by Tranzit Tours (⌨06-370 6600, 0800 471 227; www.tranzittours.co.nz; tours from $150), which features four vineyard tastings, lunch and late-afternoon cheese and coffee.

Recommended Wineries

Ata Rangi (www.atarangi.co.nz; 14 Puruatanga Rd; ☺1-3pm Mon-Fri, noon-4pm Sat & Sun) One of the region's pioneering winemakers. Great drops across the board and cute cellar door.

Coney (⌨03-306 8345; www.coneywines.co.nz; Dry River Rd; ☺11am-4pm Fri-Sun) Fingers crossed that your tasting host will be the inimitable Tim Coney, an affable character who

Martinborough

POP 1470

The sweetest visitor spot in the Wairarapa, Martinborough is a pretty town with a leafy town square and some charming old buildings, surrounded by a patchwork of pasture and a pinstripe of grapevines. It is famed for its wineries, which draw in visitors to nose the pinot and polish it off with good food, and snooze it off at boutique accommodation. Beyond the wineries, you'll need your own vehicle, with most of this area's notable sights out on the coast and along its rural roads. As is often the case, getting there is half the fun: the Martinborough area is splendid for a scenic drive.

🛏 Sleeping

⭐ **Martinborough Top 10 Holiday Park**   HOLIDAY PARK $

(☏ 06-306 8946, 0800 780 909; www.martinboroughholidaypark.com; cnr Princess & Dublin Sts; sites per person from $18, cabins $65-139; @ 🖥) An appealing camping ground with grapevine views, just five minutes' walk to town. It has shady trees and the town pool over the back fence, making it a cooling oasis on sticky days. Cabins are basic but great value, freeing up your dollars for the cellar door. Bike hire available from $25 per day.

Claremont   MOTEL $$

(☏ 0800 809 162, 06-306 9162; www.theclaremont.co.nz; 38 Regent St; d $130-158, 4-person apt $280; 🖥) A classy accommodation enclave 15

makes a mighty syrah and may sing at random. Home to the excellent **Trio Cafe** (mains $23-26) too; bookings recommended.

Haythornthwaite (www.ht3wines.co.nz; 45 Omarere Rd; ⊙ 1-5pm) Sustainable, hands-on winemaking producing complex drops including cherrylike pinot noir and gorgeous gewürztraminer.

Margrain (www.margrainvineyard.co.nz; cnr Ponatahi & Huangarua Rds; ⊙ 11am-5pm Fri-Sun) High-quailty wines across a wide range can be tasted at this character-filled cellar door, with a casual on-site cafe overlooking the vines.

Palliser (www.palliser.co.nz; Kitchener St; ⊙ 10.30am-4pm) Wines so good, even the Queen has some stashed away in her cellar. Slick outfit.

Poppies (www.poppiesmartinborough.co.nz; 91 Puruatanga Rd; ⊙ 11am-4pm) Delectable hand-crafted wines served by the label's passionate winemaking and viticulturalist duo. Savour their wines alongside a well-matched platter at the stylishly simple cellar door.

Schubert (www.schubert.co.nz; 57 Cambridge Rd; ⊙ 11am-3pm) German imports who searched for and found the best spot in the world to produce their favourite wine: pinot noir. Compact cellar door large on personality with a fine range of wines including the unusual Tribianco, a blend of three white wine varieties.

Bicycle Rental

Bicycles are comfortable cruisers with saddle bags for your booty. Suffice to say, you ought to pay greater attention to your technique as the day wears on.

Christina Estate Vineyard (☏ 06-306 8920; christinaestate@xtra.co.nz; 28 Puruatanga Rd; full day bicycle/tandem $25/50; ⊙ 8.30am-6pm)

Green Jersey Cycle Tour Company (☏ 021 074 6640; www.greenjersey.co.nz; 3hr guided tour incl lunch $110)

March Hare (☏ 03-306 5010; www.march-hare.co.nz; 18 Kitchener St; full-day bike hire incl picnic lunch $65)

Martinborough Top 10 Holiday Park (☏ 06-306 8946, 0800 780 909; www.martinboroughholidaypark.com; cnr Princess & Dublin Sts; full day $35)

Martinborough Wine Centre (☏ 06-306 9040; www.martinboroughwinecentre.co.nz; 6 Kitchener St; half-/full day $25/35)

minutes' walk to the town centre, the Claremont has two-storey, self-contained units in great nick, modern studios with spa baths, and sparkling two-bedroom apartments, all at reasonable rates (even cheaper in winter and/or midweek). Private outlooks, attractive gardens, barbecue areas and bike hire.

Aylstone Retreat BOUTIQUE HOTEL $$$
(☑ 06-306 9505; www.aylstone.co.nz; 19 Huangarua Rd; d incl breakfast $230-260; 🛜) Set among the vines on the edge of the village, this elegant retreat is a winning spot for the romantically inclined. Six en suite rooms exude a lightly floral, French-provincial charm, and share a pretty posh reading room, while the whole shebang is surrounded by micromansion garden sporting lawns, boxed hedges and chichi furniture.

✖ Eating & Drinking

Café Medici CAFE $$
(www.cafemedici.co.nz; 9 Kitchener St; breakfast & lunch $13-23, dinner $24-32; ⊙ 8.30am-4pm, dinner from 6.30pm Thu-Sat) A perennial favourite among townsfolk and regular visitors, this airy cafe has Florentine flourishes and a sunny courtyard. Tasty, home-cooked food includes muffins and pies, lovely brunch dishes such as Spanish eggs, and Med-flavoured dinner options such as Moroccan lamb tagine. Great coffee, too.

★ Tirohana Estate MODERN NZ $$
(☑ 06-306 9933; www.tirohanaestate.com; 42 Puruatanga Rd; lunch mains $16-33, 3-course prix fixe dinner $59; ⊙ lunch noon-3pm, dinner 6pm-late Tue-Sun) A casual lunch over a glass or two will be much enjoyed on the terrace at this pretty vineyard, while evening dining in the elegant dining room is quite the occasion. The food, while 'comfort' in style (crumbed prawns, beef fillet and mash, bread-and-butter pudding), is amply proportioned, fresh and proficiently prepared. Impeccable service; dinner booking essential.

★ Micro Wine Bar WINE BAR
(www.microbar.co.nz; 14c Ohio St; ⊙ 3pm-late Thu-Mon) Moreish little Micro packs a punch with its excellent wine list (mostly local with some far-flung stars), notable craft-beer selection and yummy nibbles ranging from Asian dim sum to Mediterranean tapas. Catch the sun streetside, hole up in the romantic bar, or head to the sociable courtyard where an evening might slip very easily by.

Martinborough Hotel PUB
(www.themartinboroughhotel.com; Memorial Sq; ⊙ 8am-late) The historic Martinborough Hotel is home to the Settlers Bar, a friendly, well-run pub with a decent drinks list and both a bistro and bar menu (mains $18 to $32). Set yourself up in the sunshine on pavement tables or mingle inside with a mix of locals and out-of-towners.

☆ Entertainment

Circus CINEMA
(☑ movieline 06-306 9434; www.circus.net.nz; 34 Jellicoe St; adult/child $16/11; ⊙ 3pm-late Wed-Mon) Lucky old Martinborough sports its own art-house cinema, and a stylish one it is too. This modern, microsize complex has two comfy studio theatres and a cafe opening out on to a sunny, somewhat Zen garden. Reasonably priced food (mains $22 to $32) includes bar snacks, pizza, mains with plenty of seasonal veg, and gelato.

ℹ Information

Martinborough i-SITE (☑ 06-306 5010; www.wairarapanz.com; 18 Kitchener St; ⊙ 9am-5pm Mon-Fri, 10am-4pm Sat & Sun) This small office stocks wine-region maps, including one produced by the folks behind the useful site www.martinboroughnz.com.

Cape Palliser

The Wairarapa coast south of Martinborough around Palliser Bay and Cape Palliser is remote and sparsely populated, and a trip to its landmark lighthouse is a must-do if you can spare the time and have your own wheels. The drive to the Cape is just over an hour, but depending on stops you could take half- to a full day.

From Martinborough, the road wends through picturesque farmland before hitting the coast along Cape Palliser Road. This section of the drive is intensely scenic as it hugs the coast between the vast, wild ocean and black-sand beaches on the shoreside, and sheer cliffs on the other. Look for shadows of the South Island, visible on a clear day.

In these environs lies a significant wilderness area, Aorangi (Haurangi) Forest Park, which offers backcountry tramping, camping and a DOC cottage for rent. Detailed information is available from Martinborough i-SITE. Within the park are the Putangirua Pinnacles, accessed through the Putangirua Scenic Reserve where there is a DOC campsite and car park. Standing like giant organ pipes, these 'hoodoos' were formed by rain washing silt and sand away and exposing the underlying bedrock. It's an easy 1½-hour walk to the lookout, or take the 3½-hour loop track past hills and coastal viewpoints.

Heading south further along the coast is the wind-worn fishing village of Ngawi. The first things you'll notice here are the rusty bulldozers on the beach, used to drag fishing boats ashore. Note the grassy picnic spot next door. You won't find coffee here, but you will get a taste of salt.

Next stop is the malodorous seal colony, the North Island's largest breeding area for these fellers. Whatever you do in your quest for a photo, don't get between the seals and the sea. If you block their escape route they're likely to have a go at you!

Just beyond stands the Cape Palliser Lighthouse, where you can get a few puffs into the lungs on the 250-step climb to its foot. It's a beaut view from here, and a great place to linger if the wind isn't blowing your eyeballs into the back of your head.

On the way there or back, take the short detour to the crusty waterside settlement of Lake Ferry, overlooking Lake Onoke. The tastiest attraction here is the Lake Ferry Hotel (www.lakeferryhotel.co.nz; 1 Lake Ferry Rd; mains $12-28; ⊘ from 11am), happily trapped in a time warp with its formica tables and resident old-timers. Pull up a pew in the window and enjoy a good feed of fish and chips.

However, don't leave Lake Ferry without venturing beyond the pub to the grey, shingled dunes at the rivermouth where the water rushes and swirls while big black-backed gulls circle overhead. This is a classic coastal corner of NZ where nothing ever happens but there's plenty to see.

Martinborough i-SITE can help with accommodation options in the Lake Ferry and Cape Palliser area, which include campsites and holiday homes for rent.

Greytown

POP 2200

The most seductive of several small towns along SH2, Greytown has tarted itself up over recent years and is now home to a permanent population at critical mass, and waves of Wellington weekenders. It has plenty of accommodation, some decent food, three high-street pubs and some swanky shopping. Check out www.greytown.co.nz for more information.

⊙ Sights

Cobblestones Village Museum   MUSEUM
(www.cobblestonesmuseum.org.nz; 169 Main St; adult/child/family $5/2/10; ⊘10am-4.30pm) Greytown was the country's first planned inland town: intact Victorian architectural specimens line the main street. Sporting a spruce new information centre, this darling museum is an enclave of period buildings and various historic objects, dotted around pretty grounds inviting a lie-down on a picnic blanket.

Schoc Chocolates   CHOCOLATIERIE
(www.chocolatetherapy.com; 177 Main St) No picnic? No worries. Visit Schoc in its 1920s cottage beside Cobblestones Village Museum. Sublime flavours, worth every single penny of 12 bucks a tablet. Truffles, rocky road and peanut brittle, too. Free tastings.

Stonehenge Aotearoa   MONUMENT
(☑06-377 1600; www.stonehenge-aotearoa.co.nz; tours adult/child $16/13; ⊘10am-4pm Wed-Sun, tours 11am Sat & Sun & by appointment) About 10km from Greytown, this full-scale adaptation of the UK's Stonehenge is oriented for its southern-hemisphere location on a grassy knoll overlooking the Wairarapa Plain. Its mission: to bring the night sky to life, even in daylight. The pretour talk and audiovisual presentation are excellent, and the henge itself a pretty surreal sight. Self-guided 'Stone Trek' tours are also available for adult/child $8/4.

🍴 Sleeping & Eating

Greytown Campground   CAMPSITE $
(☑027 449 4980, 06-304 9387; www.greytown-campground.co.nz; Kuratawhiti St; sites per person $14, cabins $40) A basic camping option with equally basic facilities inluding two handkerchief-sized cabins, scenically spread through Soldiers Memorial Park, 500m from town.

Greytown Hotel   HOTEL $
(☑06-304 9138; www.greytownhotel.co.nz; 33 Main St; s/d with shared bathroom $50/80; ☎) A serious contender for 'oldest hotel in New Zealand', the Top Pub (as it's known) is looking tidy for her age. Upstairs rooms are small and basic but comfortable, with no-frills furnishings and shared bathrooms. Downstairs is a modern dining room, alongside an ol' faithful lounge-bar (meals $14 to $34) and popular garden-courtyard.

Oak Estate Motor Lodge
MOTEL **$$**

(☑0800 843 625, 06-304 8188; www.oakes-tate.co.nz; cnr Main St & Hospital Rd; r $125-190; 🕾) A stand of gracious roadside oaks and pretty gardens shield a smart complex of self-contained units: studios, one- and two-bedroom options.

French Baker
BAKERY **$**

(81 Main St; light meals $7-13; ⊗8am-3pm Mon-Fri, to 4pm Sat & Sun) Buttery croissants, tempting tarts and authentic breads – this artisan baking is le real McCoy. Grab and go from the cabinet, or tuck into a breakfast of muesli, toast or a bacon buttie washed down with espresso.

Saluté
TAPAS **$$**

(www.salute.net.nz; 83 Main St; tapas $8-17, pizzas $20; ⊗noon-late Wed-Sat, 10.30-3.30pm Sun; 🖉) Moroccan-flavoured Saluté will suit you down to the ground if you like saucy, succulent, crisp, charred and fried, along with lashings of olive oil and wedges of lemon. Food so colourful you'll forget you're in grey-town.

Masterton & Around

Masterton (population 20,100) is the Wairarapa's utilitarian hub, an unselfconscious town getting on with its business. Its main claim to immortality is the 50-year-old sheep-shearing competition, the international **Golden Shears** (www.goldenshears.co.nz), held annually in the first week of March.

Masterton spins the wool out a bit longer at the **Wool Shed** (www.thewoolshednz.com; Dixon St; adult/child/family $8/2/15; ⊗10am-4pm), a baaaa-loody marvellous little museum dedicated to NZ's sheep-shearing and wool-production industries. It's also a good place to get yourself a home-knit hat.

Next door is the region's foremost cultural institution, the small but rather splendid **Aratoi Wairarapa Museum of Art & History** (www.aratoi.co.nz; cnr Bruce & Dixon Sts; admission by donation; ⊗10am-4.30pm), which hosts an impressive program of exhibitions and events (and has a very nice shop!).

Opposite the Wool Shed and Aratoi is **Queen Elizabeth Park** (Dixon St), perfect for stretching your legs. Feed the ducks, dump someone on the see-saw, have a round of minigolf or practise your high catches on the cricket oval. Refuel with a magnificent meat pie, purchased from Masterton's notable

bakery, the **Ten O'Clock Cookie** (180 Queen St; ⊗7am-4.30pm Mon-Fri, 8am-2.30pm Sat).

If none of this is sounding particularly rock and roll, we've got news for you. Masterton has an absolutely ace music venue. **King Street Live** (www.kingstreetlive.co.nz; ⊗4pm late Thu-Sat, plus other event nights) lures a diverse range of performers to play in its properly outfitted and professionally run, acoustically excellent, groovalicious, complete-with-garden-bar music venue, co-owned by gentleman-player Warren Maxwell (of legendary Trinity Roots – play catch-up where you can).

There are a few interesting sights further afield, one of which is **Castlepoint**, on the coast 68km east of Masterton. It's a truly awesome, end-of-the-world place, with a reef, the lofty 162m-high Castle Rock, largely safe swimming and walking tracks. There's an easy (but sometimes ludicrously windy) 30-minute return walk across the reef to the lighthouse, where 70-plus shell species are fossilised in the cliffs. Another one-hour return walk runs to a huge limestone cave (take a torch), or take the 1½-hour return track from Deliverance Cove to Castle Rock. Keep well away from the lower reef when there are heavy seas. Ask the staff at Masterton i-SITE about accommodation here.

Thirty kilometres north of Masterton on SH2, **Pukaha Mt Bruce National Wildlife Centre** (www.pukaha.org.nz; aduld/child/family $20/6/50; ⊗9am-4.30pm) is not only one of NZ's most successful wildlife and captive breeding centres, it's also the most readily accessible bush experience off the highway. Get a good overview of the 1000-hectare wilderness on the scenic 1½-hour loop walk which affords good vantage points. The visitor centre has various exhibits including an interactive gallery, while alongside is a kiwi house with roaming adult birds, an incubation area and nursery. A series of aviaries allows viewing of other special native birds. The daily visitor program allows you to see tuatara being fed (11.30am), attend the eel-feeding (1.30pm) and watch the kaka circus (3pm). There are also guided walks, day time and at night (adult/child from $20/6). There's a cafe and shop on site.

The turn-off to the main eastern entrance of the **Tararua Forest Park** (www.doc.govt.nz) is just south of Masterton on SH2; follow Norfolk Rd about 15km to the gates. Mountain streams dart through virgin forest in this reserve, known as **Holdsworth**. A recreation area has swimming holes, picnic spots, campsites and a lodge. Heading into the hills, walks include short, easy family tramps, excellent one- or two-day tramps, and longer, challenging tramps for experienced bush-bods (west through to Otaki Forks). The resident caretaker has maps and hut accommodation info. Check weather and track updates before setting off, and be prepared to be baked, battered and buffeted by fickle conditions.

Further south is **Carterton**, another of the small rural towns that punctuates SH2. It boasts by far the best hanging flower baskets of the lot, and adds a raft of good secondhand shopping and some good cafes

to boot – don't pass through without stopping for a wander.

As you've had the stamina to read this far, it's only fair that we share with you one final tip. If you've got your own wheels, and you like a good garden bar, head to the **Gladstone Inn** (51 Gladstone Rd, Gladstone). Cheers!

ℹ Information

Masterton i-SITE (☑ 370 0900; www.wairara-panz.com; cnr Dixon & Bruce Sts; ⊘ 9am-5pm Mon-Fri, 10am-4pm Sat & Sun) Can sort you out with oodles of information including a copy of the *Wairarapa Visitor Guide*, advice on accommodation, and directions to the Gladstone Inn.

Marlborough & Nelson

Includes ➡

Picton	380
Queen Charlotte Track	386
Blenheim	390
Kaikoura	394
Nelson	400
Motueka	408
Abel Tasman National Park	412
Golden Bay	416
Kahurangi National Park	420
Nelson Lakes National Park	421

Best Places to Eat

➡ Rock Ferry (p392)

➡ Hopgood's (p405)

➡ Green Dolphin (p400)

➡ Sans Souci Inn (p418)

Best Places to Stay

➡ Te Mahia Bay Resort (p388)

➡ Watson's Way (p391)

➡ South Street Cottages (p405)

➡ Kerr Bay Campsite (p422)

Why Go

For many travellers, Marlborough and Nelson will be their introduction to what South Islanders refer to as the 'Mainland'. Having left windy Wellington, and made a white-knuckled crossing of Cook Strait, folk are often surprised to find the sun shining and the temperature up to 10 degrees warmer.

These top-of-the-south neighbours have much in common beyond an amenable climate: both boast renowned coastal holiday spots, particularly the Marlborough Sounds, Abel Tasman National Park and Kaikoura. There are two other national parks (Kahurangi and Nelson Lakes) amid more mountain ranges than you can poke a walking pole at.

And so it follows that these two regions have an abundance of produce, from game and seafood to summer fruits, but most famously the grapes that work their way into the wineglasses of the world's finest restaurants. Keep your penknife and picnic set at the ready.

When to Go

➡ The forecast is good: Marlborough and Nelson soak up some of New Zealand's sunniest weather, with January and February the warmest months when daytime temperatures average 22°C.

➡ July is the coldest, averaging 12°C. However, the top of the South sees some wonderful winter weather, with frosty mornings often giving way to sparklingly clear skies and T-shirt temperatures.

➡ The rumours are true: it *is* wetter and more windswept the closer you get to the West Coast.

➡ From around Christmas to mid-February, the top of the South teems with Kiwi holidaymakers, so plan ahead during this time and be prepared to jostle for position with a load of jandal-wearing families.

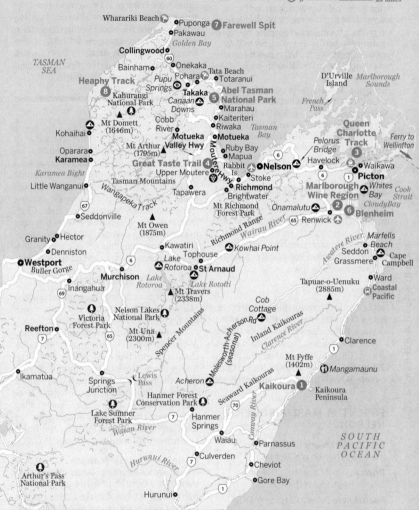

Marlborough & Nelson Highlights

① Getting up close to wildlife, including whales, seals, dolphins and albatross, in **Kaikoura** (p412)

② Nosing your way through the **Marlborough Wine Region** (p392)

③ Tramping or biking the **Queen Charlotte Track** (p386) in the Marlborough Sounds

④ Eating and drinking your way along Nelson's **Great Taste Trail** (p407)

⑤ Sea kayaking in postcard-perfect **Abel Tasman National Park** (p414)

⑥ Getting blown away at Blenheim's **Omaka Aviation Heritage Centre** (p390), one of New Zealand's best museums

⑦ Driving through a dunescape to **Farewell Spit** (p419), where there'll be gannets and godwits for company

⑧ Reaching the wild West Coast on foot, across Kahurangi National Park on the **Heaphy Track** (p420)

ⓘ Getting There & Around

Cook Strait can be crossed slowly and scenically on the ferries between Wellington and Picton, and swiftly on flights servicing key destinations.

InterCity is the major bus operator, but there are also local shuttles. From October to May, KiwiRail's *Coastal Pacific* train takes the scenic route from Picton to Christchurch, via Blenheim and Kaikoura.

Renting a car is easy, with a slew of car-hire offices in Picton and depots throughout the region.

Popular coastal areas such as the Marlborough Sounds and Abel Tasman National Park are best navigated on foot or by kayak, with water-taxi services readily available to join the dots.

MARLBOROUGH REGION

Picton is the gateway to the South Island and the launching point for Marlborough Sounds exploration. A cork's pop south of Picton is Blenheim and its world-famous wineries, and further south still is Kaikoura, the whale-watching town.

History

Long before Abel Tasman sheltered on the east coast of D'Urville Island in 1642 (more than 100 years before James Cook blew through in 1770), Maori knew the Marlborough area as Te Tau Ihu o Te Waka a Maui (the prow of Maui's canoe). It was Cook who named Queen Charlotte Sound; his reports made the area the best-known sheltered anchorage in the southern hemisphere. In 1827 French navigator Jules Dumont d'Urville discovered the narrow strait now known as French Pass. His officers named the island just to the north in his honour. In the same year a whaling station was established at Te Awaiti in Tory Channel, which brought about the first permanent European settlement in the district.

Picton

POP 2750

Half asleep in winter, but hyperactive in summer (with up to eight fully laden ferry arrivals per day), boaty Picton clusters around a deep gulch at the head of Queen Charlotte Sound. It's the main traveller port for the South Island, and the best base for tackling the Marlborough Sounds and Queen Charlotte Track. Over the last few years this little town has really bloomed, and offers visitors plenty of reason to linger even after the obvious attractions are knocked off the list.

◉ Sights & Activities

The majority of activity happens around the Marlborough Sounds, but landlubbers will still find plenty to occupy themselves.

The town has some very pleasant walks. A free i-SITE map details many of these, including an easy 1km track to Bob's Bay. The Snout Track (three hours return) continues along the ridge offering superb water views. Climbing a hill behind the town, the Tirohanga Track is a two-hour leg-stretching loop offering the best view in the house. For town explorations, hire bikes for the whole family from Wilderness Guides (p385).

Edwin Fox Maritime Museum MUSEUM
(www.edwinfoxsociety.co.nz; Dunbar Wharf; adult/child $10/4; ⊙ 9am-5pm) Purportedly the world's third-oldest wooden ship, the *Edwin Fox* was built in Calcutta and launched in 1853. During its career it carried troops to the Crimean War, convicts to Australia and immigrants to NZ. This museum has maritime exhibits, including the venerable old dear herself.

Eco World Aquarium WILDLIFE CENTRE
(www.ecoworldnz.co.nz; Dunbar Wharf; adult/child/family $22/10/55; ⊙ 10am-5.30pm Oct-Apr, 10am-4pm May-Sep) ⟋ The primary purpose of this centre is animal rehabilitation: all sorts of critters come here for fix-ups and rest-ups, and the odd bit of hanky panky! Special specimens include NZ's 'living dinosaur' – the tuatara –

ESSENTIAL MARLBOROUGH & NELSON

Eat Doris' bratwurst at the weekend markets in Nelson and Motueka

Drink A pint of Captain Cooker at Golden Bay's Mussel Inn (p417)

Read *How to Drink a Glass of Wine* by John Saker

Listen to The dawn chorus in Nelson Lakes National Park

Watch The tide roll in, and then watch it roll away again...

Festival Marlborough Wine Festival

Go Green On the Heaphy Track a hotbed of ecological wonderment

Online www.lovemarlborough.co.nz; www.nelsonnz.com; www.kaikoura.co.nz

Area code ☑ 03

as well as blue penguins, gecko and giant weta. Fish-feeding time (11am and 2pm) is a splashy spectacle. Sharing the ageing building is the **Picton Cinema** (☑ 03-573 6030; www.pictoncinemas.co.nz; Dunbar Wharf; adult/child $15/9), screening mainstream and edgy flicks.

Picton Museum   MUSEUM
(London Quay; adult/child $5/1; ⊙ 10am-4pm) If you dig local history – whaling, sailing and the 1964 Roller Skating Champs – this will float your boat. The photo displays are well worth a look, especially for five bucks.

🛏 Sleeping

Tombstone Backpackers   HOSTEL $
(☑ 03-573 7116, 0800 573 7116; www.tombstonebp.co.nz; 16 Gravesend Pl; dm $28-29, d with/without bathroom $85/78; @ 🛜) Rest in peace in smart dorms, double rooms or a self-contained apartment ($118). Also on offer is a spa overlooking the harbour, free breakfast, sunny reading room, pool table, free internet, ferry pick-up and drop-off... The list goes on.

Jugglers Rest   HOSTEL $
(☑ 03-573 5570; www.jugglersrest.com; 8 Canterbury St; campsites from $19, dm $32, d $70-75; ⊙ closed Jun-Sep; @ 🛜) 🖉 Jocular hosts keep all their balls up in the air at this well-run, ecofriendly, bunk-free backpackers. Peacefully located 10 minutes' walk from town or even less on a free bike. Cheery, private gardens are a good place to socialise with fellow travellers, especially during the occasional fire shows.

Sequoia Lodge Backpackers   HOSTEL $
(☑ 03-573 8399, 0800 222 257; www.sequoialodge.co.nz; 3a Nelson Sq; dm $26-29, d with/without bathroom $78/68; @ 🛜) A well-managed backpackers in a colourful, high-ceilinged Victorian house. It's a little out of the centre, but has bonuses including free wi-fi, hammocks, barbecues, a hot tub and nightly pudding. Complimentary breakfast May to October.

Buccaneer Lodge   LODGE $
(☑ 03-573 5002; www.buccaneerlodge.co.nz; 314 Waikawa Rd; s/d/tr $75/85/110; @ 🛜) The owners have spruced up this Waikawa Bay lodge to offer good en suite rooms, many with expansive views from the 1st-floor balcony. Courtesy town transfers, free bike hire and the pretty foreshore just five minutes' walk away.

Parklands Marina Holiday Park   HOLIDAY PARK $
(☑ 03-573 6343, 0800 111 104; www.parktostay.co.nz; 10 Beach Rd, Waikawa; campsites from $30, units

$55-95; @ 🛜 ⊞) Large, leafy campground with grassy sites, satisfactory cabins, plus ready access to boat-ilicious Waikawa Bay and Victoria Domain. It's a pleasant 3km walk/cycle to town. Courtesy transfers available.

Picton Top 10 Holiday Park   HOLIDAY PARK $
(☑ 03-573 7212, 0800 277 444; www.pictontop10.co.nz; 70 Waikawa Rd; campsites from $21, units $75-160; @ 🛜 ⊞) About 500m from town, this compact, well-kept place has plenty of lawn and picnic benches, plus crowd-pleasing facilities including playground, barbecue area and swimming pool.

Harbour View Motel   MOTEL $$
(☑ 03-573 6259, 0800 101 133; www.harbourviewpicton.co.nz; 30 Waikawa Rd; d $125-200; 🛜) The elevated position of this motel commands good views of Picton's mast-filled harbour from its tastefully decorated, self-contained studios with timber decks.

Bay Vista Waterfront Motel   MOTEL $$
(☑ 03-573 6733; www.bayvistapicton.co.nz; 303 Waikawa Rd, Waikawa; d $130-185; 🛜) This motel enjoys an enviable position on Waikawa foreshore, with views down Queen Charlotte Sound. All units have their own patio and share a big, lush lawn. Located 4km from Picton (courtesy transfer available by request).

Gables B&B   B&B $$
(☑ 03-573 6772; www.thegables.co.nz; 20 Waikawa Rd; s $100, d $140-170, units $155-200, all incl breakfast; @ 🛜) This historic B&B (once home to Picton's mayor) has three individually styled en suite rooms in the main house and two homely self-contained units out the back. Prices drop if you organise your own breakfast. Lovely hosts show good humour (ask about the Muffin Club).

Picton

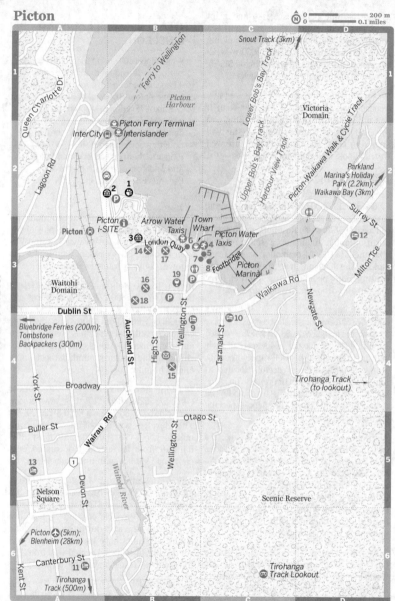

Whatamonga Homestay   HOMESTAY **$$**
(☑03-573 7192; www.whsl.co.nz; 425 Port Underwood Rd; d incl breakfast $175; @🖘) Follow Waikawa Rd, which becomes Port Underwood Rd, for 8km and you'll bump into this classy waterside option – two self-contained units with king-sized beds and balconies with magic views. Two other rooms under the main house (also with views) share a bathroom. Free kayaks, dinghies and fishing gear are available.

Picton

◎ Sights
1 Eco World Aquarium B2
2 Edwin Fox Maritime Museum..............B2
3 Picton Museum B3

⊕ Activities, Courses & Tours
4 Beachcomber Fun Cruises.................C3
5 Cougar Line C3
6 Dolphin Watch Nature Tours B3
7 Marlborough Sounds
 Adventure Company B3
8 Marlborough Travel...........................C3
 Wilderness Guides......................(see 6)

⊜ Sleeping
9 Gables B&B.......................................B4
10 Harbour View Motel..........................C4
11 Jugglers Rest....................................A6
12 Picton Top 10 Holiday Park D3
13 Sequoia Lodge Backpackers..............A5

⊗ Eating
14 Café Cortado B3
15 Fresh Choice Supermarket B4
16 Gusto B3
17 Le Café B3
18 Picton Village Bakkerij......................B3

⊖ Drinking & Nightlife
19 Seamus's B3

⊕ Entertainment
 Picton Cinema...............................(see 1)

✕ Eating & Drinking

Picton Village Bakkerij BAKERY **$**
(cnr Auckland & Dublin Sts; items $3-8; ⊙6am-4pm) Dutch owners bake trays of European goodies here, including interesting breads, filled rolls, cakes and custardy, tarty treats. An excellent stop before or after the ferry.

Gusto CAFE **$**
(33 High St; meals $14-20; ⊙7.30am-2.30pm; ⌨) This friendly and hard-working joint does beaut breakfasts including first-class salmon-scrambled egg and a 'Morning Glory' fry-up worth the calories. Lunch options include local mussels or a steak sandwich.

Fresh Choice Supermarket SUPERMARKET **$**
(Mariners Mall, 100 High St; ⊙7am-9pm) Pretty much the only choice, and fortunately a good one.

Le Café CAFE **$$**
(www.lecafepicton.co.nz; London Quay; lunch $12-24, dinner $20-34; ⊙7.30am-10.30pm; ⌨) A perennially popular spot for its quayside location, dependable food and Havana coffee. The likes of salami sandwiches and sweets are in the cabinet, while a good antipasto platter, generous pasta, local mussels, lamb and fish dishes feature à la carte. Laid-back atmosphere, craft beer and occasional live gigs make this a good evening hang-out.

Café Cortado CAFE **$$**
(www.cortado.co.nz; cnr High St & London Quay; mains $17-36; ⊙8am-late) A pleasant corner cafe and bar with sneaky views of the harbour through the foreshore's pohutukawa and palms. This consistent performer turns out fish dishes, good cheeseburgers and decent pizza.

Seamus's PUB
(25 Wellington St; meals $20-24; ⊙noon-1am) A snug drinking den, pouring a reliable Guinness and a good selection of whiskies. Mix this up with hearty food, regular live music and a sunny garden bar, and you've got the liveliest joint in town.

ⓘ Information

Picton i-SITE (☎03-520 3113; www.lovemarl-borough.co.nz; Foreshore; ⊙9am-5pm Mon-Fri, to 4pm Sat & Sun) All vital tourist guff including maps, Queen Charlotte Track information, lockers and transport bookings. Dedicated Department of Conservation (DOC) counter.

Picton Library (67 High St; ⊙8am-5pm Mon-Fri, 10am-1pm Sat; ☏) Free wi-fi.

Post Office (Mariners Mall, 72 High St)

ⓘ Getting There & Away

Make bookings for nationwide transport at Picton i-SITE.

AIR

Soundsair (☎03-520 3080, 0800 505 005; www.soundsair.co.nz) Flies daily between Picton and Wellington (adult/child from $95/85); a shuttle bus to/from the airstrip at Koromiko, 8km south, costs $7.

BOAT

There are two operators crossing Cook Strait between Picton and Wellington, and, although all ferries leave from more or less the same place, each has its own terminal. The main transport hub (with car-rental depots) is at the Inter-islander Terminal, which also has public showers, a cafe and internet facilities.

Bluebridge Ferries (☎0800 844 844, in Wellington 04-471 6188; www.bluebridge.co.nz; adult/child from $51/26; ☏) crossings takes 3½ hours, and the company runs up to four sailings in each direction daily. Cars and campervans from $118, motorbikes $51, bicycles $10. The sleeper service arrives in Picton at 6am.

Interislander (☑ 0800 802 802; www.inter-islander.co.nz; adult/child $55/28) Crossings take three hours 10 minutes; up to five sailings in each direction daily. Cars are priced from $118, campervans (up to 5.5m) from $133, motorbikes $56, bicycles $15.

BUS

Buses serving Picton depart from the Inter-islander terminal or nearby i-SITE.

InterCity (☑ 03-365 1113; www.intercity.co.nz) runs south to Christchurch (5½ hours) via Blenheim (30 minutes) and Kaikoura (2½ hours), with connections to Dunedin, Queenstown and Invercargill. Services also run to/from Nelson (2¼ hours), with connections to Motueka and the West Coast. At least one bus daily on each of these routes connects with a Wellington ferry service.

Smaller shuttle buses running from Picton to Christchurch include **Atomic Shuttles** (☑ 03-349 0697, 0508 108 359; www.atomictravel.

EXPLORING THE MARLBOROUGH SOUNDS

The Marlborough Sounds are a maze of peaks, bays, beaches and watery reaches, formed when the sea flooded deep river valleys after the last ice age. They are very convoluted: Pelorus Sound, for example, is 42km long but has 379km of shoreline.

Many spectacular locations can be reached by car. The wiggly 35km drive along Queen Charlotte Drive from Picton to Havelock is a great Sounds snapshot, but if you have a spare day, head out to French Pass (or even D'Urville Island) for some big-picture framing of the Outer Sounds. Roads are predominantly narrow and occasionally unsealed; allow plenty of driving time and keep your wits about you.

Sounds travel is invariably quicker by boat (for example, Punga Cove from Picton by car takes two to three hours, but just 45 minutes by boat). Fortunately, an armada of vessels offer scheduled and on-demand boat services, with the bulk operating out of Picton for the Queen Charlotte Sound, and some from Havelock for Kenepuru and Pelorus Sounds.

There are walking, kayaking and biking opportunities, but there's diving as well – notably the wreck of the *Mikhail Lermontov*, a Russian cruise ship that sank in Port Gore in 1986.

From Picton

Most of Picton's boat operators depart from the smart Town Wharf. They offer everything from direct lodge transfers to cruises taking in sites such as Ship Cove and Motuara Island bird sanctuary, to round-trip Queen Charlotte Track transport and pack transfers that allow trampers to walk without a heavy burden. Bikes and kayaks can also be transported.

Cougar Line (☑ 03-573 7925, 0800 504 090; www.cougarlinecruises.co.nz; Town Wharf; track round trip $105, full-day tour from $80) Queen Charlotte Track transport, plus various half- and full-day cruise/walk trips, including the rather special (and flexible) ecocruise to Motu-ara Island and a Ship Cove picnic.

Beachcomber Fun Cruises (☑ 03-573 6175, 0800 624 526; www.beachcombercruises.co.nz; Town Wharf; mail run $93, cruises from $35, track round trip $99) Two- to four-hour cruises, some with resort lunches. Cruise/walk, cruise/bike and Queen Charlotte Track options available.

Wilderness Guides (☑ 03-573 5432, 0800 266 266; www.wildernessguidesnz.com; Town Wharf; 1-day trip from $120, kayak/bike hire per day $60) Host of the popular and flexible one- to three-day 'multisport' trips (kayak/walk/cycle) plus many other guided and independent biking, hiking and kayaking tours including a remote Ship Cove paddle. A good range of bicycles also available for hire.

Marlborough Sounds Adventure Company (☑ 03-573 6078, 0800 283 283; www.marlboroughsounds.co.nz; Town Wharf; half- to 3-day packages $85-545) Bike-walk-kayak trips, with options to suit every inclination and duration. A top day option is the kayak and hike ($175). Gear rental (bikes, kayaks and camping equipment) also available.

Dolphin Watch Nature Tours (☑ 03-573 8040, 0800 945 354; www.naturetours.co.nz; Town Wharf; dolphin swimming/viewing $165/99, other tours from $75) Half-day 'swim with dolphins' and wildlife tours including trips to Motuara Island.

Myths & Legends Eco-Tours (☑ 03-573 6901; www.eco-tours.co.nz; half-/full-day cruises $200/250) A chance to get out on the water with a local Maori family – longtime locals,

co.nz), which can also be booked via **Naked Bus** (www.nakedbus.com).

TRAIN

KiwiRail Scenic (☎ 04-495 0775, 0800 872 467; www.kiwirailscenic.co.nz) Runs the *Coastal Pacific* service daily (October to May) each way between Picton and Christchurch via Blenheim and Kaikoura (and 22 tunnels and 175 bridges!), departing Christchurch at 7am, Picton at 1pm. Adult one-way Picton–Christchurch fares range

from $79 to $159. The service connects with the Interislander ferry.

ⓘ Getting Around

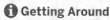

Shuttle services around town and beyond are offered by **Picton Shuttles** (☎ 027 696 5207). Cheap transport along the Queen Charlotte Drive between Picton and Havelock is offered by **Coleman Post** (☎ 027 255 8882; $15).

Renting a car in Picton is easy and competitively priced (as low as $35 per day), with

---

storytellers and environmentalists. There are six different trips to choose from, including bird-watching and visiting Ship Cove.

Marlborough Travel (☎ 03-577 9997, 0800 990 800; www.marlboroughtravel.co.nz; Town Wharf; adult/child $135/55; ☉ departs 1.30pm) Runs the 3½-hour 'Seafood Odyssea' cruise to a salmon farm, complete with salmon snack and sauvignon blanc.

Dive Boat Picton (☎ 03-573 7199, 0800 934 837; www.ninedives.co.nz; 6hr trip $195) Offers dive trips around the Sounds taking in marine reserves and various wrecks including the *Mikhail Lermontov*, plus diver training. Snorkelling and seal-swims also available.

Arrow Water Taxis (☎ 027 444 4689, 03-573 8229; www.arrowwatertaxis.co.nz; Town Wharf) Pretty much anywhere, on demand, for groups of four or more.

Picton Water Taxis (☎ 027 227 0284, 03-573 7853; www.pictonwatertaxis.co.nz) Water taxi and sightseeing trips around Queen Charlotte, on demand.

Float Plane (☎ 03-573 6866, 021 704 248; www.nz-scenic-flights.co.nz; Ferry Terminal; flights from $75) Offers Queen Charlotte Track and Sounds accommodation transfers, scenic flights, and flights and trips to Nelson, the Abel Tasman National Park and to the lower North Island.

From Anakiwa

Sea Kayak Adventures (☎ 03-574 2765, 0800 262 5492; www.nzseakayaking.com; cnr Queen Charlotte Dr & Anakiwa Rd; half-/two-day guided paddle $85/190) Guided and 'guided then go' kayaking with bike/hike options around Queen Charlotte, Kenepuru and Pelorus Sounds plus freedom kayak and mountain-bike rental (half-/full-day $40/60).

From Havelock

Pelorus Mail Boat (☎ 03-574 1088; www.mail-boat.co.nz; Jetty 1; adult/child $128/free; ☉ departs 9.30am Tue, Thu & Fri) Popular full-day boat cruise through the far reaches of Pelorus Sound on a genuine NZ Post delivery run. Bookings essential; BYO lunch. Picton and Blenheim pick-up and drop-off available.

Greenshell Mussel Cruise (☎ 0800 990 800, 03-577 9997; www.greenshellmusselcruise. co.nz; adult/child $115/39; ☉ departs 1.30pm) Three-hour cruise on a catamaran to mussel in on Kenepuru's aquaculture. Includes a tasting of steamed mussels and a glass of wine. Bookings essential.

Waterways Boating Safaris (☎ 03-574 1372; www.waterways.co.nz; 745 Keneperu Rd; half-/full-day $110/150) Be guided around Kenepuru Sound while piloting your own zippy boat. A unique and fun way to get out on the water, see the scenery and learn about the area's ecology and history. BYO lunch. Local pick-up and drop-offs.

Pelorus Sound Water Taxi (☎ 03-574 2151, 027 444 2852; www.pelorussoundwatertaxis. co.nz; Jetty 1a) Taxi and sightseeing trips from Havelock, around Pelorus, on demand.

Kenepuru Water Taxi (☎ 03-573 4344, 021 455 593; www.kenepuru.co.nz; 7170 Kenepuru Rd) Taxi and sightseeing trips around Kenepuru Sound, on demand.

numerous rental companies based at the Interislander ferry terminal and many others within a short walk. **Ace** (☐ 03-573 8939; www.acerentalcars.co.nz; Ferry Terminal), **Omega** (☐ 03-573 5580; www.omegarentalcars.com; 1 Lagoon Rd) and **Pegasus** (☐ 03-573 7733; www.carrentalspicton.co.nz; 1 Auckland St) are reliable local operators. Most agencies allow drop-offs in Christchurch; if you're planning to drive the North Island, most companies suggest you leave your car at Picton and pick up another one in Wellington after crossing Cook Strait.

Queen Charlotte Track

The hugely popular, meandering, 70km Queen Charlotte Track offers gorgeous coastal scenery on its way from historic Ship Cove to Anakiwa, passing through a mixture of privately owned land and DOC reserves. Access depends on the cooperation of local landowners; respect their property by utilising designated campsites and toilets, and carrying out your rubbish. Your purchase of the Track Pass ($15 to $18), available from operators in town and on the track, provides the co-op with the means to maintain and enhance the experience for all.

Queen Charlotte is a well-defined track, suitable for people of average fitness. Numerous boat and tour operators service the track, allowing you to walk the whole three-to five-day journey, or start and finish where you like, on foot or by kayak or bike. We're talking mountain biking here, and a whole lot of fun for fit, competent off-roaders. Part of the track is off-limits to cyclists from 1 December to the end of February, but there is still good riding to be had during this time.

Ship Cove is the usual (and recommended) starting point – mainly because it's easier to arrange a boat from Picton to Ship Cove than vice versa – but the track can be started from Anakiwa. There's a public phone at Anakiwa but not at Ship Cove.

Marlborough Sounds

Estimated walk times:

TRACK SECTION	DISTANCE (KM)	DURATION (HR)
Ship Cove to Resolution Bay	4.5	1½-2
Resolution Bay to head of Endeavour Inlet	10.5	2½-3
Endeavour Inlet to Camp Bay/Punga Cove	12	3-4
Camp Bay/Punga Cove to Torea Saddle/Portage	24	6-8
Torea Saddle/Portage to Te Mahia Saddle	7.5	3-4
Te Mahia Saddle to Anakiwa	12.5	3-4

🛏 Sleeping & Eating

The beauty of the Queen Charlotte Track is that there are plenty of great day-trip options, allowing you to base yourself in Picton. However, there is also plenty of accommodation, nicely spaced along the way, and boat operators will transport your luggage along the track for you.

At the self-sufficient end of the scale are six DOC campsites: **Schoolhouse Bay**, **Camp Bay**, **Bay of Many Coves**, **Black Rock**, **Cowshed Bay** and **Davies Bay**. All have toilets and a water supply but no cooking facilities. There's also a variety of resorts,

lodges, backpackers and guesthouses, of which our picks follow below, ordered from Ship Cove to Anakiwa. Unless you're camping, it pays to book your accommodation waaay in advance, especially in summer.

Numerous cafes are also dotted along the track, the majority of which will only be in full swing during high summer. Some – namely those at **Furneaux Lodge** (www.furneaux.co.nz), **Punga Cove Resort** (www.pungacove.co.nz; @ 🍴) and **Portage Resort Hotel** (www.peppers.co.nz/portage; 🛜 🍴) – are the in-house eateries of long-standing but not necessarily shipshape Sounds resorts. We recommend restricting your financial outlay to cold beer and bar snacks at these destinations.

A list of sleeping and eating options can be found in the official **Queen Charlotte Track Directory** (www.qctrack.co.nz).

Cnoc Na Lear   GUESTHOUSE **$$**
(📞03-579 8444; www.cnocnalear.co.nz; Endeavour Inlet; d/tr incl breakfast $195/255; 🛜) Sitting just above the track with bay views, this modern guesthouse offers plenty of home comforts including dinner and packed lunches by arrangement, as well as continental breakfast.

Mahana Lodge   LODGE **$$**
(📞03-579 8373; www.mahanalodge.co.nz; Endeavour Inlet; d $195; ⊙ closed Jun-Aug) 🍃 This beautiful property features a pretty waterside lawn and purpose-built lodge with four en suite doubles. Ecofriendly initiatives include bush regeneration, pest trapping and organic veggie patch. In fact, feel-good factors abound: free kayaks, home baking and a blooming conservatory where the evening meal is served (three courses $55).

Noeline's Homestay   HOMESTAY **$**
(📞03-579 8375; Endeavour Inlet; dm $35-40) Follow the pink arrows from Camp Bay to this relaxed homestay and be greeted by 70-something Noeline, 'the Universal Grandma', and her home-baked treats. It's a friendly arrangement with beds for five people, cooking facilities and great views.

Bay of Many Coves Resort   RESORT **$$$**
(📞03-579 9771, 0800 579 9771; www.bayofmanycoves.co.nz; Bay of Many Coves; 1-/2-/3-bedroom apt $640/845/995; 🛜 🍴) These plush and secluded apartments feature all mod cons and private balconies overlooking the water. As well as upmarket cuisine, there are various indulgences such as room service, massage, spa and hot tub.

Marlborough Sounds

🔵 Activities, Courses & Tours
1 Sea Kayak Adventures A4
2 Waterways Boating Safaris A4

🛏 Sleeping
3 Bay of Many Coves Campsite C3
4 Bay of Many Coves Resort C3
5 Black Rock Campsite C3
   Camp Bay Campsite .... (see 15)
6 Cnoc Na Lear C3
7 Davies Bay Campsite B4
8 Furneaux Lodge C2
9 Hopewell B3
10 Lochmara Lodge B3
   Mahana Lodge .... (see 15)
11 Mistletoe Bay B3
   Noeline's Homestay .... (see 15)
12 Nydia Bay DOC Campsite A3
13 Nydia Lodge A3
14 On the Track Lodge A3
15 Punga Cove Resort C3
16 Schoolhouse Bay Campsite D2
17 Smiths Farm Holiday Park A4
18 Whatamonga Homestay C4

DeBretts GUESTHOUSE **$**
(☑03-573 4522; www.stayportage.co.nz; s with/
without linen $50/45) The family-run duo of
DeBretts and **Treetops** (☑03-573 4404) offers a combined total of six bedrooms in two
homely backpackers on the hill behind Portage Resort. Torea Bay bag transfers included.

Lochmara Lodge RESORT **$$**
(☑03-573 4554; www.lochmaralodge.co.nz; Loch-
mara Bay; units $95-295; ☎) ⌖ This arty,
ecoretreat can be reached via the Queen
Charlotte Track or direct from Picton aboard
the lodge's water taxi ($55 return). There are
en suite doubles, units and chalets, all set in
lush surroundings, and a fully licensed cafe
and restaurant, plus a bathhouse where you
can indulge in a spa or massage.

Mistletoe Bay HOLIDAY PARK **$**
(☑03-573 4048; www.mistletoebay.co.nz; Mistle-
toe Bay; unpowered sites $32, dm/d $30/70, cabins
$140, linen $7.50; ☎) ⌖ Surrounded by bushy
hills, Mistletoe Bay offers attractive camp-
ing with no-frills facilities. There are eight
modern cabins sleeping up to six, plus a
bunkhouse. Environmental sustainability
abounds, as does the opportunity to jump
off the jetty, kayak in the bay or walk the
Queen Charlotte Track.

★**Te Mahia Bay Resort** RESORT **$$**
(☑03-573 4089; www.temahia.co.nz; d $148-248;
☎) This homely low-key resort is within cooee
of the Queen Charlotte Track in a picturesque bay on Kenepuru Sound. It has a range
of delightful rooms-with-a-view, our pick of
which is the great-value heritage units. The
on-site store has pre-cooked meals, pizza,
cakes, coffee and camping supplies (wine!),
plus there is kayak hire and massage.

Anakiwa Backpackers HOSTEL **$**
(☑03-574 1388; www.anakiwabackpackers.co.nz;
401 Anakiwa Rd; dm $35, d $85-105; ☎) At the
southern end of the track, this former
schoolhouse is a soothing spot to rest and
reflect. There are two doubles (one with en
suite), a three-bed dorm and a beachy self-
contained unit. Jocular owners will have you
jumping off the jetty for joy and imbibing espresso and ice cream (hallelujah) from their
little green caravan (open summer afternoons). Provisions available by arrangement
and free kayak hire.

Smiths Farm Holiday Park HOLIDAY PARK **$**
(☑03-574 2806, 0800 727 578; www.smithsfarm.
co.nz; 1419 Queen Charlotte Dr, Linkwater; campsites from $16, cabins $60-130, units $130; @☎)
⌖ Located on the aptly named Linkwater
flat between Queen Charlotte and Pelorus,
friendly Smiths makes a handy base camp
for the track and beyond. Well-kept cabins
and motel units face out onto the bushy
hillside, while livestock nibble around the
lush camping lawns. Short walks extend to a
waterfall and magical glow-worm dell.

ℹ Information

The best place to get track information and advice is Picton i-SITE (p383), which also handles
bookings for transport and accommodation. See
also the online **Queen Charlotte Track Directory** (www.qctrack.co.nz).

Kenepuru & Pelorus Sounds

Kenepuru and Pelorus Sounds, to the west of
Queen Charlotte Sound, are less populous and
therefore offer fewer traveller services, including transport. There's some cracking scenery,
however, and those with time to spare will be
well rewarded by their explorations.

Havelock is the hub of this area, the western bookend of the 35km Queen Charlotte
Drive (Picton being the eastern) and the
self-proclaimed 'Greenshell Mussel Capital
of the World'. While hardly the most rock-
and-roll of NZ towns, Havelock offers most
necessities, including accommodation, fuel
and food. As you get out into the Sounds be
prepared to encounter scant fuel and only
the occasional shop, which *may* have frozen
bread and out-of-date popsicles.

For finer detail, including a complete
list of visitor services, visit www.pelorusnz.
co.nz, which covers Havelock, Kenepuru
and Pelorus Sounds, and the extremities of
French Pass and D'Urville Island.

◉ Sights & Activities

If a stroll through the streets of Havelock
leaves you thinking that there *must* be more
to this area, you're right – and to get a taste
of it you need go no further than the Cul-
len Point Lookout, 10 minutes' drive from
Havelock along the Queen Charlotte Drive.
A short walk leads up and around a headland overlooking Havelock, the surrounding
valleys and Pelorus Sound. Look out for the
Havelock Map & Walkway Guide which details more walks in the area.

To venture out into the sounds themselves, see p385.

Nydia Track
WALKING

The Nydia Track (27km, 10 hours) starts at Kaiuma Bay and ends at Duncan Bay (or vice versa). Around halfway is beautiful Nydia Bay, where there's a DOC campsite (adult/child $6/1.50) and Nydia Lodge (☑03-520 3002; www.doc.govt.nz; dm $15, minimum charge $60), an unhosted 50-bed lodge. Also in Nydia Bay, On the Track Lodge (☑03-579 8411; www.nydiatrack.org.nz; dm $40, d $110-150) is a tranquil, ecofocused affair offering everything from packed lunches to evening meals and a hot tub. You'll need water and road transport to complete the journey; Havelock's Blue Moon Lodge runs a shuttle to Duncan Bay.

Pelorus Eco Adventures
KAYAKING

(☑03-574 2212, 0800 252 663; www.kayak-newzealand.com; Blue Moon Lodge, 48 Main Rd, Havelock; trips from $95) Float in an inflatable kayak on scenic Pelorus River, star of the barrel scene in *The Hobbit*. Wend your way down rapids, through crystal-clear pools and past native forest and waterfalls. No experience necessary; minimum two people.

🛏 Sleeping & Eating

There's plenty of accommodation along Kenepuru Rd, most of which is readily accessible off the Queen Charlotte Track. Other options in this area include some picturesque DOC campgrounds (most full to bursting in January), a few remote lodges and the very handy Smiths Farm (p388) holiday park at Linkwater, the crossroads for Queen Charlotte and Kenepuru, where you'll find a petrol station with snacks. Havelock has a couple of decent offerings.

Hopewell
LODGE $

(☑03-573 4341; www.hopewell.co.nz; 7204 Kenepuru Rd, Double Bay; dm from $40, d with/without bathroom from $135/100, 4-person cottage $240; @🖥) Beloved of travellers from near and far, remote Hopewell sits waterside surrounded by native bush. Savour the long, winding drive to get there, or take a water taxi from Te Mahia. Stay at least a couple of days, so you can chill out or enjoy the roll-call of activities: mountain biking, kayaking, sailing, fishing, eating gourmet pizza, soaking in the outdoor spa, and more.

Blue Moon Lodge
HOSTEL $

(☑03-574 2212; www.bluemoonhavelock.co.nz; 48 Main Rd, Havelock; dm $28, r with/without bath-room $96/76; @🖥) This pleasant and relaxed lodge has homely rooms in the main house (one with en suite), as well as cabins and a bunkhouse in the yard. Notable features include a sunny barbecue deck, inflatable kayak trips on the Pelorus River, and tramping track transport.

Havelock Garden Motel
MOTEL $$

(☑03-574 2387; www.gardenmotels.com; 71 Main Rd, Havelock; d $115-150; 🖥) Set in a large, graceful garden complete with dear old trees and a duck-filled creek, these 1960s units have been tastefully revamped to offer homely comforts. Local activities are happily booked for you.

ⓘ Getting There & Away

InterCity (☑03-365 1113; www.intercity.co.nz) Buses run daily from Picton to Havelock via Blenheim (one hour), and from Havelock to Nelson (1¼ hours). **Atomic Shuttles** (☑0508 108 359, 03-349 0697; www.atomictravel.co.nz) plies the same run. Cheap transport along the Queen Charlotte Drive between Picton and Havelock is offered by Coleman Post (p385). Buses depart mid-way down the high street, outside the restaurant with the mussels on the roof.

DON'T MISS

PELORUS BRIDGE

A pocket of deep, green forest tucked away among paddocks of bog-standard pasture, 18km west of Havelock, this scenic reserve contains one of the last stands of river-flat forest in Marlborough. It survived only because a town planned in 1865 didn't get off the ground by 1912, by which time obliterative logging made this little remnant look precious. Visitors can explore its many tracks, admire the historic bridge, take a dip in the limpid Pelorus River (alluring enough to star in Peter Jackson's *The Hobbit*), and partake in some home baking at the cafe. The fortunate few can stay overnight in DOC's small but perfectly formed Pelorus Bridge Campground (☑03-571 6019; www.doc.govt.nz; unpowered/powered sites per person $12/6), with its snazzy facilities building. Come sundown keep an eye out for long-tailed bats – the reserve is home to one of the last remaining populations in Marlborough.

Blenheim

POP 27,150

Blenheim is an agricultural town 29km south of Picton on the Wairau Plain between the Wither Hills and the Richmond Ranges. The town demonstrates little power as a visitor magnet; it is the attractions beyond the back fence that pull in the punters.

◎ Sights & Activities

Omaka Aviation Heritage Centre MUSEUM
(Map p391; www.omaka.org.nz; 79 Aerodrome Rd; adult/child/family $25/10/62; ☉10am-5pm) This captivating museum houses a splendid collection of original and replica Great War aircraft brought to life in a series of dioramas that depict dramatic wartime scenes, such as the death of the Red Baron. Memorabilia and photographic displays deepen the experience. The guided tour is an extra $5 extremely well spent. There's a cafe and shop on site, and next door is Omaka Classic Cars (Map p391; www.omakaclassiccars.co.nz; adult/child $10/ free; ☉10am-4pm), which houses more than 100 vehicles from the '50s to the '80s.

Marlborough Museum MUSEUM
(Map p391; www.marlboroughmuseum.org.nz; 26 Arthur Baker Pl, off New Renwick Rd; adult/child $10/5; ☉10am-4pm) Besides a replica township, vintage mechanicals and well-presented historical displays, there's the *Wine Exhibition*, for those looking to cap off their vineyard experiences.

Wither Hills Farm Park WALKING
In a town as flat as a pancake, this hilly 1100-hectare park provides welcome relief, offering a range of walks and mountain-bike trails with grand views across the Wairau Valley and out to Cloudy Bay. Pick up a map from the i-SITE or check the information panels at the many entrances including Redwood St and Taylor Pass Rd.

High Country Horse Treks HORSE RIDING
(☏03-577 9424; www.high-horse.co.nz; 961 Taylor Pass Rd; 1-3hr treks $50-120) These animal-mad folks run horse treks for all abilities from their base 11km southwest of town (call for directions).

✯ Festivals & Events

Marlborough Wine Festival FOOD & WINE
(www.wine-marlborough-festival.co.nz; tickets $55) Held in mid-February at Brancott Vineyard, this is an extravaganza of local wine, fine food and entertainment. Book accommodation well in advance.

🛏 Sleeping

🏠 Blenheim Town

Blenheim's budget beds fill with long-stay guests doing seasonal work; hostels will help find work and offer weekly rates. Midrange motels can be found on Middle Renwick Rd west of the town centre, and SH1 towards Christchurch.

Grapevine Backpackers HOSTEL $
(☏03-578 6062; www.thegrapevine.co.nz; 29 Park Tce; tent sites $18, dm $25, d $64-68, tr $81; @ ☎) Located inside an old maternity home 10 minutes' walk from the town centre, Grapevine has respectable rooms set aside for travellers. The kitchen is tight, but offset by free canoes and a peaceful barbecue deck by the Opawa River. Bike hire is $25 per day.

Koanui Lodge & Backpackers HOSTEL $
(☏03-578 7487; www.koanui.co.nz; 33 Main St; dm $26-30, d with/without bathroom $85/56; @ ☎) This well-worn hostel on the main road caters to both workers and casual visitors. Both the old villa and newer lodge wing are clean and tidy, but otherwise unremarkable.

Blenheim Top 10 Holiday Park HOLIDAY PARK $
(☏03-578 3667, 0800 268 666; www.blenheimtop10.co.nz; 78 Grove Rd; sites from $35, cabins $72-92, units & motels $100-145; @ ☎ ☀) Ten minutes' walk to town, this holiday park spreads out under and alongside the main road bridge over the Opawa River. Ask for the quietest spot available. Cabins and motel units are plain-Jane, set in a sea of asphalt. Fun-time diversions include a spa, pool, playground and bike hire ($20 per half-day).

171 on High MOTEL $$
(☏03-579 5098, 0800 587 856; www.171onhighmotel.co.nz; 171 High St; d $145-185; @ ☎) A welcoming option close to town, these tasteful, splash-o-colour studios and apartments are bright and breezy in the daytime, warm and shimmery in the evening. Expect a wide complement of facilities and 'extra mile' service.

Marlborough Wine Region

Marlborough Wine Region

⊙ Sights
1 Bladen Estate	A1
2 Brancott Estate Heritage Centre	B2
3 Cloudy Bay	C1
4 Forrest	B1
5 Framingham	A1
6 Gibson Bridge	B1
7 Huia	B1
8 Marlborough Museum	D2
9 Omaka Aviation Heritage Centre	C2
Omaka Classic Cars	(see 9)
10 Spy Valley Wines	A2
11 Te Whare Ra	A2
12 Wairau River	A1
13 Wither Hills	C2

⊜ Sleeping
14 Olde Mill House	B2
15 St Leonards	C2
16 Stonehaven	B1
17 Vintners Hotel	B1
18 Watson's Way Lodge	B1

⊗ Eating
19 Herzog Winery	B1
20 La Veranda	B1
21 Rock Ferry	C1
Wairau River	(see 12)
Wither Hills	(see 13)

MARLBOROUGH & NELSON BLENHEIM

🛏 Wine Region

★ Watson's Way Lodge
LODGE **$**

(Map p391; ☎03-572 8228; www.watsonsway-lodge.com; 56 High St, Renwick; dm $30, d $70-90; ⊗closed Aug-Sep; @🛜) This traveller-focused, purpose-built hostel has spick-and-span rooms, mainly twins and doubles, some with en suite. There are spacious leafy gardens dotted with fruit trees and hammocks, an outdoor claw-foot bath, bikes for hire (guest/public rate $18/28 per day) and local information aplenty.

Olde Mill House
B&B **$$**

(Map p391; ☎03-572 8458; www.oldemillhouse.co.nz; 9 Wilson St, Renwick; d $150; @🛜) On an elevated section in otherwise flat Renwick, this charming old house is a treat. Dyed-in-the-wool local hosts run a welcoming B&B, with stately decor, and homegrown fruit and homemade goodies for breakfast. Free bikes,

outdoor spa and gardens make this a tip-top choice in the heart of the wine country.

St Leonards
COTTAGES **$$**

(Map p391; ☎03-577 8328; www.stleonards.co.nz; 18 St Leonards Rd; d $120-350, extra adult $35; 🛜⚟) Tucked into the grounds of an 1886 homestead, these four rustic cottages offer privacy and a reason to stay put. Each is unique in its layout and perspective on the gardens and vines. Our pick is the Stables, with its lemon-grove view. Anyone for tennis?

Vintners Hotel
HOTEL **$$$**

(Map p391; ☎03-572 5094, 0800 684 190; www.mvh.co.nz; 190 Rapaura Rd; d $260-295; 🛜) Sixteen architecturally designed suites make the most of valley views and boast wet-room bathrooms and abstract art. The stylish reception building has a bar and restaurant opening out on to a cherry orchard and organic vegie garden.

MARLBOROUGH WINERIES

Marlborough is NZ's vinous colossus, producing around three quarters of the country's wine. At last count, there were 22,600 hectares of vines planted – that's approximately 26,500 rugby pitches! Sunny days and cool nights create the perfect conditions for cool-climate grapes: world-famous sauvignon blanc, top-notch pinot noir, and notable chardonnay, riesling, gewürztraminer, pinot gris and bubbly. Drifting between tasting rooms and dining among the vines is a quintessential South Island experience.

The majority of Marlborough's 148 wineries lie within the Wairau Valley around Blenheim and Renwick, with others blanketing the cooler Awatere Valley or creeping up the southern-side valleys of the Wairau.

A Taste of the Tastings

Around 35 wineries are open to the public. Our picks of the bunch provide a range of high-quality cellar door experiences, with most being open from around 10.30am till 4.30pm (some scale back operations in winter). Wineries may charge a small fee for tasting, normally refunded if you purchase a bottle. Pick up a copy of the *Marlborough Wine Trail* map from Blenheim i-SITE (p394), also available online at www.wine-marlborough.co.nz. If your time is limited, pop into **Wino's** (www.winos.co.nz; 49 Grove Rd) in Blenheim, a sterling one-stop shop for some of Marlborough's finer and less common drops.

Auntsfield Estate (www.auntsfield.co.nz; 270 Paynters Rd) Quality hand-crafted wines from this historic and picturesque vineyard at the foot of the hills. Tours by arrangement ($15).

Bladen Estate (Map p391; www.bladen.co.nz; 83 Conders Bend Rd) Bijou family winery that's big on charm.

Brancott Estate (Map p391; www.brancottestate.com; 180 Brancott Rd) Ubermodern cellar door and restaurant complex atop a hillock that overlooks one of the original sauvignon blanc vineyards.

Clos Henri (www.clos-henri.com; 639 SH63) French winemaking meets Marlborough terroir with *très bien* results. A beautifully restored local country church houses the cellar door.

Cloudy Bay (Map p391; www.cloudybay.co.nz; Jacksons Rd) Globally coveted sauvignon blanc, bubbly and pinot noir, and Jack's Raw Bar Summer Sundays for shucked oysters and clams. Decadent.

Forrest (Map p391; www.forrest.co.nz; 19 Blicks Rd) Doctor-owners produce and prescribe a range of fine vinous medicines, including some mood-altering riesling.

Framingham (Map p391; www.framingham.co.nz; 19 Conders Bend Rd) Consistent, quality wines including exceptional rieslings and stellar stickies.

Gibson Bridge (Map p391; www.gibsonbridge.co.nz; cnr Gee St & SH6) Peachy pinot gris, and a grandiose cellar door in a minuscule space.

Huia (Map p391; www.huia.net.nz; 22 Boyces Rd) Sustainable, small-scale winegrowing and the cutest yellow tasting room in town. Delectable dry-style gewürztraminer.

Saint Clair (www.saintclair.co.nz; 13 Selmes Rd; ⊙9am-5pm) Prepare to be blown away by the Pioneer Block and Reserve range sauvignon blanc and pinot noir. Cafe on site.

Spy Valley Wines (Map p391; www.spyvalleywine.co.nz; 37 Lake Timara Rd, Waihopai Valley) Stylish, edgy architecture at this espionage-themed winery, with great wines across the board. Memorable merchandise.

Te Whare Ra (Map p391; www.twrwines.co.nz; 56 Anglesea St, Renwick) Compact, hands-on winery creating gorgeous sauvignon blanc, riesling, gewürztraminer and pinot gris.

Wairau River (Map p391; www.wairauriverwines.com; 11 Rapaura Rd) Carbon-neutral family estate with some of Marlborough's oldest vines. Relaxing gardens and a fancy new cellar door.

Wither Hills (Map p391; www.witherhills.co.nz; 211 New Renwick Rd) 🌱 One of the region's flagship wineries and an architectural gem. Premium wines and enthralling winemaker-for-a-day tours ($45).

Yealands Estate (🖉 03-575 7618; www.yealandsestate.co.nz; cnr Seaview & Reserve Rds, Seddon) 🌱 Zero-carbon winemaking on a grand scale at this space-age winery near Seddon; tours by arrangement.

Best Wining & Dining

With wine there must be food, and here are our recommendations for dining among the vines. Opening hours are for summer, when bookings are recommended.

Wairau River (Map p391; 🖉 03-572 9800; www.wairauriverwines.com; cnr Rapaura Rd & SH6; mains $20-27; ⊙noon-3pm) 🌱 Modishly modified mudbrick bistro with wide verandah and beautiful gardens with plenty of shade. Order the mussel chowder or the double-baked blue-cheese soufflé. Relaxing and thoroughly enjoyable.

★ Rock Ferry (Map p391; 🖉 03-579 6431; www.rockferry.co.nz; 80 Hammerichs Rd; mains $22-26; ⊙11.30am-3pm) 🌱 Pleasant environment inside and out, with a slightly groovy edge. The compact summery menu – think tea-smoked salmon or organic open steak sandwich – is accompanied by wines from Marlborough and Otago.

Wither Hills (Map p391; 🖉 03-520 8284; www.witherhills.co.nz; 211 New Renwick Rd; mains $23-31, platters $36-56; ⊙11am-4pm) Simple, well-executed food in a stylish space. Pull up a beanbag on the Hockney-esque lawns and enjoy hot-smoked salmon, rib of beef or a platter, before climbing the ziggurat for impressive views across the Wairau.

Herzog Winery (Map p391; 🖉 03-572 8770; www.herzog.co.nz; 81 Jefferies Rd; mains $44-49, 5-course degustation menu with/without wine $197/125; ⊙restaurant from 7pm Wed-Sun, bistro 11am-10pm, reduced hours May-Oct) Refined dining in Herzog's opulent dining room. Beautifully prepared food and a remarkable wine list. Excellent-value bistro meals (mains $28 to $30) also available.

La Veranda (Map p391; 🖉 03-572 9177; www.laveranda.co.nz; 56 Vintage Lane; platters $19-23; ⊙11am-4.30pm Tue-Sun) Keenly priced platters of quality charcuterie, fromages and French desserts – the sort of lunch you should be eating at a vineyard. Eat outside or in Domaine George Michel's elegant restaurant.

Wine Tours

Wine tours are generally conducted in a minibus, last between four and seven hours, take in four to seven wineries and range in price from $65 to $95 (with a few grand tours up to around $200 for the day, including a winery lunch). The following are the grand crus:

Highlight Wine Tours (🖉 03-577-9046, 0800 494 638; www.highlightwinetours.co.nz) Visit a chocolate factory, too. Custom tours available.

Bubbly Grape (🖉 0800 228 2253, 027 672 2195; www.bubblygrape.co.nz) Three different tours including a gourmet lunch option.

Sounds Connection (🖉 0800 742 866, 03-573 8843; www.soundsconnection.co.nz) This operator partners up with Herzog for a wine-and-food-matched lunch.

Bike2Wine (🖉 0800 653 262, 03-572 8458; www.bike2wine.co.nz; 9 Wilson St, Renwick; standard/tandem per day $30/60, delivery or pick-up per bike $5-10) Your other option is to get around the grapes on two wheels. This operator offers self-guided, fully geared and supported tours.

MARLBOROUGH & NELSON MARLBOROUGH WINERIES

Stonehaven
B&B $$$

(Map p391; ☑ 03-572 9730; www.stonehavenhome-stay.co.nz; 414 Rapaura Rd; d incl breakfast $275-295; @🛜🗷) A stellar stone-and-timber B&B nestled among the picturesque vines, with two en suite guest rooms. Beds are piled high with pillows, breakfast is served in the summer house, and dinner is available by prior arrangement with rare wines from the cellar.

✖ Eating & Drinking

Hospitality can be pretty hit and miss in Blenny, with some of the best food found at the wineries.

Ritual Cafe
CAFE $

(10 Maxwell Rd; meals $7-18; ⊙7am-4pm Mon-Wed, to 10pm Thu-Sat) This hip joint, with its B-movie decor, booths and up-cycled furniture, is where Blenheim's cool cats come to purr over great coffee, all-day eggy brekkies and a counter-full of pastries and salads. Excellent smoothie hangover cures.

BV Gourmet
DELI, CAFE $

(www.bvgourmet.co.nz; 2a Park Tce; snacks $4-8; ⊙8am-5pm Mon-Fri, 9am-3pm Sat & Sun) Micro-sized cafe serving a compact range of pastries, salads, sweets and notable coffee. Picnickers will delight at the gluttonous selection of cheeses, meats and treats from NZ artisan producers and overseas.

Dodson Street
CRAFT BEER

(www.dodsonstreet.co.nz; 1 Dodson St) Pub and garden with a beer-hall ambience and suitably Teutonic menu (mains $17 to $27) featuring pork knuckle, wurst and schnitzel. Stars of the show are the 24 taps pouring quality craft beer including next-door neighbour Renaissance, the 2013 Brewer's Guild champion.

ⓘ Information

Blenheim i-SITE (Map p391; ☑ 03-577 8080, 0800 777 181; www.lovemarlborough.com; Railway Station; ⊙8.30am-5.30pm Mon-Fri, 9am-5pm Sat, 9am-4pm Sun) Information on Marlborough and beyond. Wine-trail maps and bookings for everything under the sun.

Post Office (cnr Scott & Main Sts)

Wairau Hospital (☑ 03-520 9999; www.nmdhb.govt.nz; Hospital Rd)

ⓘ Getting There & Around

AIR

Marlborough Airport (Map p391; www.marlboroughairport.co.nz) is 6km west of town on Middle Renwick Rd. **Air New Zealand** (☑ 0800 747 000;

www.airnewzealand.co.nz) has direct flights to/from Wellington, Auckland and Christchurch.
Soundsair (www.soundsair.co.nz) connects Blenheim with Wellington and Paraparaumu.

BICYCLE

Avantiplus (☑ 03-578 0433; www.bikemarlborough.co.nz; 61 Queen St; hire per half-/full day from $25/40) Rents bikes; longer hire and delivery by arrangement.

BUS

InterCity (☑ 03-365 1113; www.intercity.co.nz) buses run daily from the Blenheim i-SITE to Picton (30 minutes) and Nelson (1¾ hours). Buses also head down south to Christchurch (two daily) via Kaikoura. **Naked Bus** (www.nakedbus.com) tickets bargain seats on some of the same services, and on its own buses on major routes.

Shuttles (and tours) around Blenheim and the wider Marlborough region are offered by **Blenheim Shuttles** (☑ 03-577 5277, 0800 577 527; www.blenheimshuttles.co.nz).

TAXI

Four-wheeled rescue is offered by **Marlborough Taxis** (☑ 03-577 5511).

TRAIN

KiwiRail Scenic (☑ 04-495 0775, 0800 872 467; www.kiwirailscenic.co.nz) Runs the daily *Coastal Pacific* service, stopping at Blenheim en route to Picton (from $29; runs October to May) heading north, and Christchurch (from $79) via Kaikoura (from $49) heading south.

Kaikoura

POP 3550

Take SH1 132km southeast from Blenheim (or 183km north from Christchurch) and you'll encounter Kaikoura, a pretty peninsula town backed by the snowcapped Seaward Kaikoura Range. Few places in the world are home to such a variety of easily spottable wildlife: whales, dolphins, NZ fur seals, penguins, shearwaters, petrels and wandering albatross all live in the area or pass by.

Marine animals are abundant due to ocean-current and continental-shelf conditions: the seabed gradually slopes away from the land before plunging to more than 800m where the southerly current hits the continental shelf. This creates an upwelling of nutrients from the ocean floor into the feeding zone.

History

In Maori legend, Kaikoura Peninsula (Taumanu o Te Waka a Maui) was the seat where the demigod Maui placed his feet when he fished the North Island up from the depths. The area was heavily settled by Maori, with excavations showing that the area was a moa-hunter settlement about 800 to 1000 years ago. The name Kaikoura comes from 'Kai' (food) and 'koura' (crayfish).

James Cook sailed past the peninsula in 1770, but didn't land. His journal states that 57 Maori in four double-hulled canoes came towards the *Endeavour,* but 'would not be prevail'd upon to put along side'.

In 1828 Kaikoura's beachfront was the scene of a tremendous battle. A northern Ngati Toa war party, led by chief Te Rauparaha, bore down on Kaikoura, killing or capturing several hundred of the local Ngai Tahu tribe.

Europeans established a whaling station here in 1842, and the town remained a whaling centre until 1922 after which arming and fishing sustained the community. It was in the 1980s that wildlife tours began to transform the town into the tourist mecca it is today.

◎ Sights

Point Kean Seal Colony   WILDLIFE RESERVE
At the end of the peninsula seals laze around in the grass and on the rocks, lapping up all the attention. Give them a wide berth (10m), and never get between them and the sea – they will attack if they feel cornered and can move surprisingly fast.

Fyffe House   HISTORIC BUILDING
(www.fyffehouse.co.nz; 62 Avoca St; adult/child $10/free; ⊙10am-5.30pm daily Nov-Apr, to 4pm Thu-Mon May-Oct) Kaikoura's oldest surviving building, Fyffe House's whale-bone foundations were laid in 1844. Proudly positioned and fronted with a colourful garden, the little two-storey cottage offers a fascinating insight into the lives of colonial settlers. Interpretive displays are complemented by historic objects, while peeling wallpaper and the odd cobweb lend authenticity. Cute maritime-themed shop.

Kaikoura Museum   MUSEUM
(www.kaikoura.govt.nz; West End; adult/child $5/1; ⊙10am-4.30pm Mon-Fri, 2-4pm Sat & Sun) Housed in the new council building along with the library, this provincial museum displays historical photographs, Maori and colonial artefacts, a huge sperm-whale jaw and the fossilised remains of a plesiosaur.

Point Sheep Shearing Show   FARM
(www.pointsheepshearing.co.nz; Fyffe Quay; adult /child $10/5; ⊙shows 1.30pm & 4pm) The 30-minute Point Sheep Shearing Show at the Point B&B is fun and educational. You can feed a ram, and lambs between September and February. Classic NZ!

🏃 Activities

There's a safe swimming **beach** in front of the Esplanade, alongside which is a **pool** (adult/child $3/2; ⊙10am-5pm Nov-Mar) if you have a salt aversion.

Decent **surfing** can be found in the area, too, particularly at **Mangamaunu Beach** (15km north of town), where there's a 500m point break, which is fun in good conditions. Get the low-down, organise transport, learn to surf or hire gear from **Board Silly Surf Adventures** (☑0274 188 900, 0800 787 352; 134 Southbay Pde; 3hr lesson $75, board & suit from $45) based at South Bay. Gear hire and advice is also available from **R&R Sport** (www. rrsport.co.nz; 14 West End) and **Surf Kaikoura** (www.surfkaikoura.co.nz; 4 Beach Rd).

Kaikoura Peninsula Walkway   WALKING
A foray along this walkway is a must-do. Starting from the town, the three- to four-hour loop heads out to Point Kean, along the cliffs to South Bay, then back to town over the isthmus (or in reverse, of course). En route you'll see fur seals and red-billed seagull and shearwater colonies. Lookouts and interesting interpretive panels abound. Collect a map at the i-SITE or follow your nose.

Dive Kaikoura   DIVING
(☑03-319 6622, 0800 348 352; www.divekaikoura. co.nz; Yarmouth St; half-day $250) With its rocky formations and abundant marine life, the Kaikoura coast offers rewarding diving and snorkelling. Dive Kaikoura runs small-group trips and diver training.

Clarence River Rafting   RAFTING
(☑03-319 6993; www.clarenceriverrafting.co.nz; 3802 SH1, at Clarence Bridge; half-day trip adult/ child $120/80) Raft the bouncy Grade II rapids of the scenic Clarence River on a half-day trip (two hours on the water), or on longer journeys including a five-day trip with wilderness camping ($1350). Based on SH1, 40km north of Kaikoura near Clarence Bridge.

🧭 Tours

Wildlife tours are Kaikoura's speciality, particularly those involving whales (including sperm, pilot, killer, humpback and southern right), dolphins (Hector's, bottlenose and

MARLBOROUGH & NELSON KAIKOURA

Kaikoura

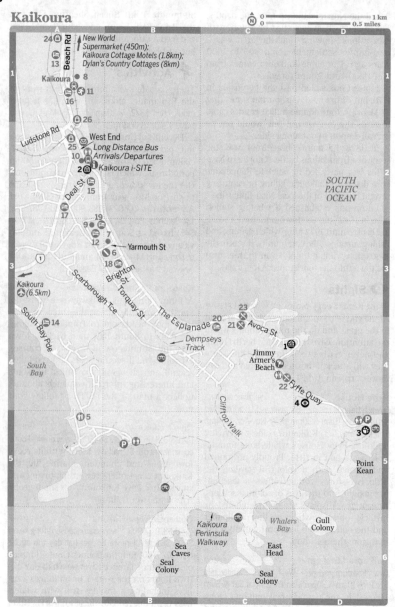

New World
Supermarket (450m);
Kaikoura Cottage Motels (1.8km);
Dylan's Country Cottages (8km)

Kaikoura

West End

Long Distance Bus
Arrivals/Departures

Kaikoura i-SITE

SOUTH
PACIFIC
OCEAN

Ludstone Rd

Deal St

Yarmouth St

Brighton St

Torquay St

Scarborough Tce

The Esplanade

Kaikoura
(6.5km)

South Bay Pde

South
Bay

Dempseys
Track

Avoca St

Jimmy
Armer's
Beach

Fyfe Quay

Cliftop Walk

Point
Kean

Kaikoura
Peninsula
Walkway

Whalers
Bay

Gull
Colony

Sea
Caves

East
Head

Seal
Colony

Seal
Colony

MARLBOROUGH & NELSON KAIKOURA

dusky) and NZ fur seals. There's also plenty of birdlife, including albatross and blue penguins. During summer, book your tour a few weeks ahead, and allow some leeway for lousy weather.

Whale-Watching

Your choices are boat, plane or helicopter. Aerial options are shorter and pricier, but allow you to see the whole whale, as opposed to just a tail, flipper or spout.

Kaikoura

◎ Sights
1 Fyffe House...C4
2 Kaikoura Museum..................................A2
3 Point Kean Seal Colony.......................D5
4 Point Sheep Shearing Show................D4

◔ Activities, Courses & Tours
Albatross Encounter ....(see 7)
5 Board Silly Surf Adventures.................A5
6 Dive Kaikoura B3
7 Dolphin Encounter.................................B3
8 Kaikoura Helicopters............................A1
9 Kaikoura Kayaks.....................................A3
10 Seal Swim Kaikoura...............................A2
11 Whale Watch Kaikoura..........................A1

◉ Sleeping
12 Albatross Backpacker Inn A3
13 Alpine Pacific Holiday Park...................A1

14 Bay Cottages...A4
15 Dolphin Lodge...A2
16 Kaikoura Top 10 Holiday Park A1
17 Nikau Lodge A2
18 Sails Motel...B3
19 Waves on the Esplanade A3
20 YHA Kaikoura Maui C4

◈ Eating
Cafe Encounter.............................. (see 7)
21 Green Dolphin C4
22 Kaikoura Seafood BBQ...........................C4
23 Pier Hotel...C4
Reserve Hutt .... (see 10)

◎ Shopping
24 Cods & Crayfish......................................A1
25 R&R Sport A2
26 Surf Kaikoura A1

Whale Watch Kaikoura ECOTOUR
(☏03-319 6767, 0800 655 121; www.whale-watch.co.nz; Railway Station; 3hr tour adult/child $145/60) ⚐ With knowledgeable guides and fascinating 'world of whales' on-board animation, Kaikoura's biggest operator heads out on boat trips (with admirable frequency) to introduce you to some of the big fellas. It'll refund 80% of your fare if no whales are sighted (success rate: 98%). If this trip is a must for you, allow a few days flexibility in case the weather turns to custard.

Kaikoura Helicopters SCENIC FLIGHTS
(☏03-319 6609; www.worldofwhales.co.nz; Railway Station; 15-60min flight from $100-490) Reliable whale-spotting flights (standard 30-minute tour $220 each for three or more people), plus jaunts around the peninsula, Mt Fyffe and peaks beyond.

Wings over Whales ECOTOUR
(☏0800 226 629, 03-319 6580; www.whales.co.nz; 30min flight adult/child $180/75) Light-plane flights departing from Kaikoura Airport, 7km south of town. Spotting success rate: 95%.

Dolphin- & Seal-Spotting

★ **Seal Swim Kaikoura** ECOTOUR
(☏03-319 6182, 0800 732 579; www.sealswimkaikoura.co.nz; 58 West End; tours $70-110, viewing adult/child $55/35; ⊙Oct-May) Take a (warmly wet-suited) swim with Kaikoura's healthy population of playful seals – including very cute pups – on two-hour guided snorkelling tours run by the Chambers family. Shore or boat options available.

Dolphin Encounter ECOTOUR
(☏0800 733 365, 03-319 6777; www.encounterkaikoura.co.nz; 96 Esplanade; swim adult/child $175/155, observation $90/45; ⊙tours 8.30am & 12.30pm year-round, plus 5.30am Nov-Apr) Here's your chance to rub shoulders with pods of dusky dolphins on three-hour tours. Limited numbers, so book in advance.

Kaikoura Kayaks KAYAKING
(☏03-319 7118, 0800 452 456; www.kaikourakayaks.co.nz; 19 Killarney St; 3hr tours adult/child $95/70; ⊙tours 8.30am, 12.30pm & 4.30pm Nov-Apr, 9am & 1pm May-Oct) Excellent guided sea-kayak tours to view fur seals and explore the peninsula's coastline. Family-friendly, kayak fishing and other on-demand trips available, plus freedom kayak and paddle-board hire.

Birdwatching

Albatross Encounter BIRDWATCHING
(☏03-319 6777, 0800 733 365; www.encounterkaikoura.co.nz; 96 Esplanade; adult/child $115/55; ⊙tours 9am & 1pm year-round, plus 6am Nov-Apr) Kaikoura is heaven for bird-nerds, who fly at the opportunity for a close encounter with pelagic species such as shearwaters, shags, mollymawks, petrels and the inimitable albatross.

Fishing

Fishing is a common obsession in Kaikoura, with local boaties angling for any excuse to go out for a little look-sea. It's a good opportunity to eat *kai koura* (eat crayfish). Trips start from around $60; the i-SITE (☏03-319 5641; www.kaikoura.co.nz; West End; ⊙9am-5pm Mon-Fri, to 4pm Sat & Sun, extended hours Dec-Mar) has a full list of operators.

MARLBOROUGH & NELSON KAIKOURA

Fishing at Kaikoura
FISHING

(☑03-319 3003; gerard.diedrichs@xtra.co.nz) Fishing, crayfishing, scenic tours and water-skiing, on the 6m *Sophie-Rose*.

Kaikoura Fishing Charters
FISHING

(☑03-319 6888; www.kaikourafishing.co.nz) Dangle a line from the 12m *Takapu*, then take your filleted, bagged catch home to eat.

Kaikoura Fishing Tours
FISHING

(☑0800 246 6597; www.kaikoura-fishing-tours. co.nz) Serious about scenery and seafood. Your catch is filleted ready for dinner.

Tramping & Cycling

For town riding, hire bicycles from R&R Sport (p395) and Surf Kaikoura (p395). While you're there, ask about the trail to the foot of Mt Fyffe.

Walks Kaikoura
WALKING

(☑027 473 2659, 027 437 2426; www.walkskaikoura.com; half-/full day from $75/145) Experienced local guides offer tailored walks around the area, from mountains to coast with heli options, plus cycle tours on quiet sealed roads and the newly developed riverside trail.

Kaikoura Coast Track
TRAMPING

(☑03-319 2715; www.kaikouratrack.co.nz; $230) This easy three-day, 37km, self-guided walk across private farmland combines coastal and alpine views. The price includes three nights' farm-cottage accommodation and pack transport; BYO sleeping bag and food. Starts 45km south of Kaikoura.

Kaikoura Wilderness Walks
TRAMPING

(☑03-319 6966, 0800 945 337; www.kaikourawilderness.co.nz; 1-/2-night package $1195/1595) ⌖ Two- or three-day guided walks through the privately owned Puhi Peaks Nature Reserve high in the Seaward Kaikoura Range. Package includes accommodation and sumptuous meals at the luxurious Shearwater Lodge.

Other Tours

Kaikoura Mountain Safaris
DRIVING TOUR

(☑03-319 6424, 021 869 643; www.kaikouramountainsafaris.co.nz; half-day tour adult/child $100/55, 1-day tour adult/child $165/100) Journey into the backcountry in a 4WD or Unimog – three different tours (departing from the i-SITE) take in alpine vistas, remote farms and the Clarence River valley.

Maori Tours Kaikoura
CULTURAL TOUR

(☑03-319 5567, 0800 866 267; www.maoritours. co.nz; 3½hr tour adult/child $134/74; ⊙tours 9am & 1.30pm) Fascinating half-day, small-group tours laced with Maori hospitality and local lore. Visit historic sites, hear legends and learn indigenous use of trees and plants. Advance bookings required.

🛏 Sleeping

Summer sees accommodation fill up, so book in advance or save your visit for the off-season when reduced rates are in the offing.

Albatross Backpacker Inn
HOSTEL $

(☑03-319 6090, 0800 222 247; www.albatross-kaikoura.co.nz; 1 Torquay St; dm $29-32, tw/d $69/74; @🕸) ⌖ This arty backpackers resides in three sweet buildings, one a former post office. It's colourful and close to the beach but sheltered from the breeze. As well as a laid-back lounge with musical instruments for jamming, there are decks and verandahs to chill out on.

Dolphin Lodge
HOSTEL $

(☑03-319 5842; www.dolphinlodge.co.nz; 15 Deal St; dm $28, d with/without bathroom $69/62; @🕸) This small home-away-from-home has green-thumbed owners who fuss over their lovely scented garden. Inside is a bit squeezed, but on dry days most of the action will be out on the fantastic deck, around the barbecue, or in the spa pool.

Alpine Pacific Holiday Park
HOLIDAY PARK $

(☑03-319 6275, 0800 692 322; www.alpine-pacific. co.nz; 69 Beach Rd; campsites from $46, cabins $78, units $130-195; @🕸🌊) This compact and proudly trimmed park copes well with its many visitors, and offers excellent facilities, including a shiny kitchen, resorty pool area and barbecue pavilion. Rows of cabins and units are slightly more stylish than average, and mountain views can be had from many angles.

Kaikoura Top 10 Holiday Park
HOLIDAY PARK $

(☑03-319 5362, 0800 363 638; www.kaikouratop10.co.nz; 34 Beach Rd; campsites $42-52, cabins $70-95, units $110-160; @🕸🌊) Hiding from the highway behind a massive hedge, this busy, well-maintained campground offers family-friendly facilities (heated pool, hot tub, trampoline) and cabins and units to the usual Top 10 standard.

YHA Kaikoura Maui
HOSTEL $

(☑03-319 5931, 0800 278 299; www.yha.co.nz; 270 Esplanade; dm $33, d $89-110, tr $102; @🕸) A 15-minute walk to town, this oceanside YHA boasts unobstructed views across the bay to the pine-lined esplanade and mighty peaks beyond. Many rooms enjoy similar views, as does the big-windowed dining room. Communal areas in this purpose-built (1962) hostel are tidy and functional, but a little rough around the edges.

★ **Dylan's Country Cottages** COTTAGES $$
(☑ 03-319 5473; www.lavenderfarm.co.nz; 268 Postmans Rd; d $195; ⊗ closed May-Aug; ☎) On the grounds of the delightful Kaikoura Lavender Farm, northwest of town, these two self-contained cottages make for an aromatic escape from the seaside fray. One has a private outdoor bath and a shower emerging from a tree; the other an indoor spa and handkerchief lawn. Homemade scones, preserves and free-range eggs for breakfast. Sweet, stylish and romantic.

Kaikoura Cottage Motels MOTEL $$
(☑ 03-319 5599, 0800 526 882; www.kaikoura-cottagemotels.co.nz; cnr Old Beach & Mill Rds; d $140-160; ☎) This enclave of eight modern tourist flats looks mighty fine, surrounded by attractive native plantings. Oriented for mountain views, the self-contained units sleep four between an open-plan studio-style living room and one private bedroom. Soothing sand-and-sky colour scheme and quality chattels.

Bay Cottages MOTEL $$
(☑ 03-319 5506; www.baycottages.co.nz; 29 South Bay Pde; cottages/motels $100/130; ☎) Here's a great-value option on South Bay, a few kilometres south of town: five tourist cottages with kitchenette and bathroom that sleep up to four, and two slick motel rooms with stainless-steel benches, a warm feel and clean lines. The cheery owner may even take you crayfishing in good weather.

Sails Motel MOTEL $$
(☑ 03-319 6145; www.sailsmotel.co.nz; 134 Esplanade; d $120-140, q $170; ☎) There are no sea views (nor sails) at this motel, so the cherubic owners have to impress with quality. Their four secluded, tastefully appointed self-contained units are down a driveway in a garden setting (private outdoor areas abound).

Nikau Lodge B&B $$$
(☑ 03-319 6973; www.nikaulodge.com; 53 Deal St; d $190-260; @☎) A waggly-tailed welcome awaits at this beautiful B&B high on the hill with grand-scale vistas. Five en suite rooms are plush and comfy, with additional satisfaction arriving in the form of cafe-quality breakfasts accompanied by fresh local coffee. Good humour, home baking, free wi-fi, complimentary drinks, a hot tub and blooming gardens: you may want to move in.

Waves on the Esplanade APARTMENTS $$$
(☑ 03-319 5890, 0800 319 589; www.kaikoura-apartments.co.nz; 78 Esplanade; apt $240-350; ☎) Can't do without the comforts of home? Here you go: spacious, luxury two-bedroom apartments with Sky TV, DVD player, two bathrooms, laundry facilities and full kitchen. Oh, and superb ocean views from the balcony. Rates are for up to four people.

🍴 Eating & Drinking

Kaikoura has a few swell cafes and restaurants, and many that plumb the depths.

Kaikoura Seafood BBQ SEAFOOD $
(Fyffe Quay; $5-9; ⊗ 10.30am-7pm) Conveniently located on the way to the Point Kean seal colony, this long-standing roadside barbecue is a great spot to sample local seafood, including crayfish and scallops, at an affordable price.

Reserve Hutt CAFE $
(72 West End; meals $10-20; ⊗ 9am-3pm) The best coffee in the town centre, roasted on site and espressed by dedicated baristas in Kaikoura's grooviest cafe. Puttin' out that rootsy retro-Kiwiana vibe we love so much, this is a neat place to linger over a couple of flatties and down a muffin, delicious ham croissant or the full eggy brunch.

CRAY CRAZY

Among all of Kaikoura's munificent marine life, the one species you just can't avoid is the crayfish, whose delicate flesh dominates local menus. Unfortunately (some say unnecessarily), it's pricey – at a restaurant, you'll (pardon the pun) shell out around $55 for half a cray or over $100 for the whole beast. You can also buy fresh, cooked or uncooked crays from **Cods & Crayfish** (81 Beach Rd; ⊗ 8am-6pm) and iconic **Nins Bin** (SH1; ⊗ 8am-6pm), a surf-side caravan 23km north of town. Upwards of $50 should get you a decent specimen. Alternatively, go out on a fishing tour, or simply head to the Kaikoura Seafood BBQ roadside stall near the peninsula seal colony where cooked crays can be gobbled in the sunshine, by the sea.

Cafe Encounter
CAFE $

(96 Esplanade; meals $8-23; ⊙7am-5pm; 🛜🍴) This cafe in the Encounter Kaikoura complex is more than just somewhere to wait for your trip. The cabinet houses respectable sandwiches, pastries and cakes, plus there's a tasteful range of daily specials such as pork schnitzel and fennel slaw. A sunny patio provides sea views.

New World Supermarket
SUPERMARKET $

(124-128 Beach Rd; ⊙7.30am-9pm) Ten minutes' walk from the town centre.

Pier Hotel
PUB $$

(📞03-319 5037; www.thepierhotel.co.nz; 1 Avoca St; lunch $15-23, dinner $27-38; ⊙11am-late) Situated in the town's primo seaside spot, with panoramic views, the historic Pier Hotel is a friendly and inviting place for a drink or a meal, whether outside or inside the character-filled public bar or dining rooms. Upstairs lodgings are worn and creaky, but good value (double room, including breakfast, from $90).

★ Green Dolphin
MODERN NZ $$$

(📞03-319 6666; www.greendolphinkaikoura.com; 12 Avoca St; mains $25-39; ⊙5-11pm) Kaikoura's consistent top-ender continues to dish up high-quality produce including seafood, beef, lamb and venison, as well as seasonal flavours such as fresh tomato soup. There are lovely homemade pasta dishes, too. The hefty drinks list demands attention, featuring exciting aperitifs, craft beer, interesting wines and more. Booking ahead is advisable, especially if you want to secure a table by the window and watch the daylight fade.

ⓘ Information

Kaikoura i-SITE (📞03-319 5641; www.kaikoura. co.nz; West End; ⊙9am-5pm Mon-Fri, to 4pm Sat & Sun, extended hours Dec-Mar) Helpful staff make tour, accommodation and transport bookings, and help with DOC-related matters.

Paperplus/Post Office (📞03-319 6808; 41 West End) Postal agent.

ⓘ Getting There & Away

BUS

Atomic Shuttles (📞0508 108 359, 03-349 0697; www.atomictravel.co.nz) Also services Kaikoura on its Christchurch to Picton run, which links with destinations as far afield as Nelson, Queenstown and Invercargill.

InterCity (📞03-365 1113; www.intercity.co.nz) Buses run between Kaikoura and Nelson (3½ hours), Picton (2¼ hours) and Christchurch

(2¾ hours). The bus stop is at the car park next to the i-SITE (tickets and info inside).

Naked Bus (📞0900 625 33; www.nakedbus. com) Tickets bargain seats on its own buses on major routes, and on other services dependent on capacity.

TRAIN

KiwiRail Scenic (📞0800 872 467; www. kiwirailscenic.co.nz) Runs the daily *Coastal Pacific* service, stopping at Kaikoura en route to Picton (from $59, 2¼ hours; runs October to May), and Christchurch (from $49, three hours). The northbound train departs Kaikoura at 9.54am; the southbound at 3.28pm.

ⓘ Getting Around

Kaikoura Shuttles (📞03-319 6166; www.kai-kourashuttles.co.nz) will run you around the local sights as well as to and from the airport.

NELSON REGION

The Nelson region is centred upon Tasman Bay but stretches north to Golden Bay and Farewell Spit, and south to Nelson Lakes. It's not hard to see why it's such a popular travel destination for both international and domestic traveller alike: not only does it boast three national parks (Kahurangi, Nelson Lakes and Abel Tasman), but it can also satisfy nearly every other whim, from food, wine and beer, art, craft and festivals, to that most precious of pastimes for which the region is well known: lazing about in the sunshine.

Nelson
POP 46,440

Dishing up a winning combination of great weather and beautiful surroundings, Nelson is hailed as one of NZ's most 'liveable' cities. In summer it fills up with visitors, who lap up its diverse offerings.

⊙ Sights

Nelson has an inordinate number of galleries, most of which are listed in the *Art & Crafts Nelson City* brochure (with walking-trail map) available from the i-SITE. A fruitful wander can be had by starting at the Fibre Spectrum (www.fibrespectrum.co.nz; 280 Trafalgar St), where you can pick up hand-woven woollens, before moving on to 'Lord of the Ring' jeweller Jens Hansen (www.jenshansen. com; 320 Trafalgar Sq), glassblower Flamedaisy (www.flamedaisy.com; 324 Trafalgar Sq), then around the corner to the home of Nelson pottery, South Street Gallery (www.nelsonpottery.co.nz; 10 Nile St W). More interesting local creations can be found at the Nelson Market (Montgomery Sq; ⊗ 8am-1pm Sat) on Saturday.

★ Christ Church Cathedral   CHURCH
(www.nelsoncathedral.org; Trafalgar Sq; ⊗ 8am-7pm Nov-Mar, to 5pm Apr-Oct) **FREE** The enduring symbol of Nelson, the art deco Christ Church Cathedral lords it over the city from the top of Trafalgar St. The best time to visit is during the 10am and 6pm Sunday services when you can hear the organist and choir on song.

Nelson Provincial Museum   MUSEUM
(www.nelsonmuseum.co.nz; cnr Hardy & Trafalgar Sts; adult/child $7/5; ⊗ 10am-5pm Mon-Fri, 10am-4.30pm Sat & Sun) This modern museum space is filled with cultural heritage and natural history exhibits which have a regional bias, as well as regular touring exhibitions (for which admission fees vary). It also features a great rooftop garden.

★ Suter Art Gallery   GALLERY
(www.thesuter.org.nz; 208 Bridge St; adult/child $3/50c, free Sat; ⊗ 10.30am-4.30pm) Adjacent to Queen's Gardens, Nelson's public art gallery presents changing exhibitions, floor talks, musical and theatrical performances, and films. The Suter undergoes a major renovation from August 2014, so check the website for the reopening date and details of relocated exhibits.

Founders Heritage Park   MUSEUM
(www.founderspark.co.nz; 87 Atawhai Dr; adult/child/family $7/5/15; ⊗ 10am-4.30pm) Two kilometres from the city centre, this park comprises a replica historic village with museum and gallery displays, and artisan products such as chocolate and clothing. It makes for a fascinating wander, which you can augment with a visit to the on-site Founders Brewery & Café (www.foundersbrewery.co.nz; meals $11-20; ⊗ 10am-6pm Sun-Thu, 10am-9pm Fri & Sat). With a sun-drenched hop garden and a range of freshly brewed beers arrayed on a $10 tasting tray, this is a lovely place for a leisurely meal or light snack. The beef burger is scrumptious!

Queens Gardens   GARDENS
(Bridge St) Immerse yourself in more than 120 years of botanical history in this ornamental garden, which commemorates the 50th jubilee of Queen Victoria's coronation. Great for a picnic or lawny lie-down.

Tahuna Beach   BEACH
Nelson's primo playground takes the form of an epic sandy beach (with lifeguards in summer), backed by a large grassy parkland with a playground, espresso cart, swimming pool, various other recreational facilities and an adjacent restaurant strip. Weekends can get veerrrrry busy around here!

🏃 Activities

Nelson offers plenty of opportunity to embrace the great outdoors.

Tramping & Cycling

There's plenty of walking and cycling to be enjoyed in and around the town, for which the i-SITE has maps. The classic walk from town is to the Centre of NZ atop the Botanical Reserve (Milton St), and if you enjoy that then ask about the Grampians. The Dun Mountain Trail network ranging over the hills to the south of the city centre has lots of interesting options for fit, keen mountain bikers, as does Codgers MTB Park. The new Great Taste Trail (p407) offers flat riding through the craft-beer- and wine-soaked countryside.

UBike   CYCLING
(✆ 0800 282 453; www.ubike.co.nz; Collingwood St Bridge; hire half-/full day $40/60) A short walk from the i-SITE, UBike hires city and mountain bikes from its riverside caravan. Trail maps and tips, plus espresso to get you going.

Gentle Cycling Company   CYCLING
(✆ 03-929 5652, 0800 932 453; www.gentlecycling.co.nz; 5/8hr tours $75/80) Self-guided cycle tours along the Great Taste Trail, with drop-ins (and tastings) at wineries, breweries, cafes and occasional galleries. Freedom bike hire (per day $45) and shuttles also available.

Biking Nelson   MOUNTAIN BIKING
(✆ 021 861 725, 0800 224 532; www.bikingnelson.co.nz; 3hr guided rides $115, bike hire half-/full day $45/65) Hit Nelson's mountain-bike trails with Dave and crew, who run entry-level to hard-core guided rides (all gear provided) and offer freedom rental and advice.

Bike Barn   CYCLING
(www.bikebarn.co.nz; 114 Hardy St; hire per day from $40) Bike hire in the central city, plus servicing and repairs.

Paragliding, Kitesurfing & Paddle Boarding

Nelson is a great place to get high or undry, with plenty of action in summer, particularly around the rather divine Tahuna Beach.

Central Nelson

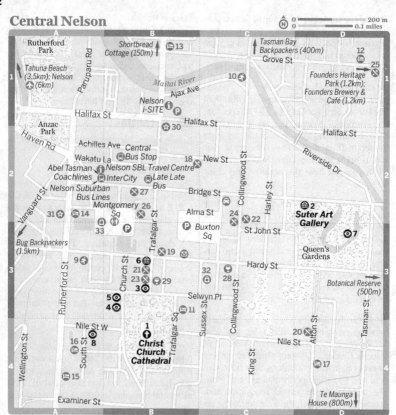

Tandem paragliding costs around $180, introductory kitesurfing starts at $150, and paddleboard hire is around $25 per hour.

Nelson Paragliding   PARAGLIDING
(☎03-544 1182; www.nelsonparagliding.co.nz)

Kitescool   KITESURFING, PADDLE BOARDING
(☎021 354 837; www.kitescool.co.nz)

Kite Surf Nelson   KITESURFING
(☎0800 548 363; www.kitesurfnelson.co.nz)

Supstar   PADDLE BOARDING
(☎021 0268 5552; www.supstarboards.co.nz)

Other Activities

★**Nelson Bonecarving**   CARVING
(☎03-546 4275; www.carvingbone.co.nz; 87 Green St, Tahunanui; full-day course $79) Admirers of Maori design will love Stephan's acclaimed bonecarving course. He'll supply materials, tools, instruction, encouragement and cups of tea (plus free pick-up/drop-off in town);

you supply inspiration and talent, and you'll emerge with your very own bone carving.

Happy Valley Adventures   ADVENTURE SPORTS
(☎03-545 0304, 0800 157 300; www.happyvalley-adventures.co.nz; 194 Cable Bay Rd; Skywire adult/child $85/55, quad-bike tours from $95, horse trek $75) Dangle 150m above the forest in the 'Skywire' (a chairlift/flying-fox hybrid), then soar through the air for its 1.65km length. If that ain't enough, take a quad-bike tour, or if it's too much, try a horse trek. Located 15-minute drive northeast of Nelson along SH6; on-site cafe.

Cable Bay Kayaks   KAYAKING
(☎03-545 0332, 0508 222 532; www.cablebaykayaks.co.nz; Cable Bay Rd; half-/full day guided trip $85/145) Fifteen minutes' drive from Nelson city, Nick and Jenny offer guided sea-kayaking trips exploring the local coastline where you'll likely meet local marine life (snorkelling gear on board) and may even enter a cave.

Central Nelson

◉ Top Sights
1 Christ Church Cathedral.......................B4
2 Suter Art Gallery....................................D2

◎ Sights
3 Fibre Spectrum......................................B3
4 Flamedaisy Glass Design......................B3
5 Jens Hansen...B3
6 Nelson Provincial Museum...................B3
7 Queens Gardens....................................D3
8 South Street Gallery.............................A4

◉ Activities, Courses & Tours
9 Bike Barn..A3
10 UBike..C1

◎ Sleeping
11 Accents on the Park..............................B3
12 Almond House..D1
13 Cedar Grove Motor Lodge.....................B1
14 Nelson YHA..A2
15 Palazzo Motor Lodge.............................A4
16 South Street Cottages...........................A4
17 Trampers Rest..D4

✕ Eating
18 DeVille..B2
19 Falafel Gourmet.....................................B3
20 Fish Stop..D4
21 Ford's..B3
22 Free House..C2
23 Hopgood's...B3
24 Indian Café...C2
25 Organic Greengrocer.............................D1
26 Penguino Ice Cream Café......................B2
    Stefano's..(see 30)
27 Swedish Bakery & Café.........................B2

◉ Drinking & Nightlife
28 Sprig & Fern...C3
29 Vic...B3

◉ Entertainment
30 State Cinemas..B2
31 Theatre Royal...A2

◎ Shopping
32 Nelson Farmers' Market........................C3
33 Nelson Market..A2

MARLBOROUGH & NELSON NELSON

☞ Tours

Bay Tours   GUIDED TOUR
(☏03-548 6486, 0800 229 868; www.baytoursnelson.co.nz; half-/full-day tours from $75/144) Nelson city, region, wine, beer, food and art tours. The full-day scenic tour includes a visit to Kaiteriteri and a cruise in Abel Tasman National Park.

Nelson Tours & Travel   GUIDED TOUR
(☏0272 375 007, 0800 222 373; www.nelsontoursandtravel.co.nz) CJ and crew run various small-group, flexible tours honing in on Nelson's edible, drinkable elements. The five-hour 'Best of Both Worlds' visits wineries and breweries ($95), or venture over to the Marlborough wineries on a day-long tour ($160).

✹ Festivals & Events

For current info on Nelson's active events program, visit www.itson.co.nz and www.nelsonfestivals.co.nz.

Nelson Jazz & Blues Festival   MUSIC
(www.nelsonjazzfest.co.nz) More than 50 scoobedoobop events over a week in January. Features local and international acts in halls and on street corners, regionwide.

Nelson Arts Festival   ARTS
(www.nelsonfestivals.co.nz) Over two weeks in October; events include a street carnival, exhibitions, cabaret, writers, theatre and music.

⛺ Sleeping

Accents on the Park   HOSTEL $
(☏03-548 4335, 0800 888 335; www.accentsonthepark.com; 335 Trafalgar Sq; campsites from $15, dm $20-28, d with/without bathroom from $92/60; @♠) This perfectly positioned hostel has a hotel feel with its professional staff, balconies, movie nights with free popcorn, free daily bread, wi-fi, soundproofed rooms, quality linen, fresh bathrooms and bikes for hire. On site, there's also **East St**, a groovy vegetarian cafe and bar.

Shortbread Cottage   HOSTEL $
(☏03-546 6681; www.shortbreadcottage.co.nz; 33 Trafalgar St; dm $26, s & d $58; @♠) This renovated 100-year-old villa has room for only a dozen or so beds but it's packed with charm and hospitality. It offers free internet, fresh-baked bread, and shortbread on arrival. It's also only a stone's throw from the town centre.

Tasman Bay Backpackers   HOSTEL $
(☏03-548 7950, 0800 222 572; www.tasmanbaybackpackers.co.nz; 10 Weka St; campsites from $18, dm $26-28, d $70-85; @♠) This well-designed, friendly hostel has airy communal spaces, hyper-coloured rooms, a sunny outdoor deck and a well-used hammock. Good freebies: wi-fi, bikes, breakfast during winter, and chocolate pudding and ice cream year-round.

Trampers Rest
HOSTEL $

(☑03-545 7477; 31 Alton St; dm/s/d $28/46/66; ☺closed Jun-Sep; @🖥) With just seven beds (no bunks), the tiny but much-loved Trampers is hard to beat for a homely environment. The enthusiastic owner is a keen tramper and cyclist, and provides comprehensive local information and free bikes. It has a small kitchen, a book exchange, and a piano for evening singalongs.

Bug Backpackers
HOSTEL $

(☑03-539 4227; www.thebug.co.nz; 226 Vanguard St; dm $25-28, d $66-100; @🖥) A well-kept hostel about 15 minutes' walk from town, occupying a converted villa, modern building next door and self-contained, well-priced unit sleeping up to five. The Bug emits *joie de vivre*, with an unashamedly bold colour scheme, quality beds, homely backyard and jovial owners. Free bikes, wi-fi and pick-ups/drop-offs.

Almond House
HOSTEL $

(☑03-545 6455; www.almondbackpackers.co.nz; 63 Grove St; dm/s/d $29/46/68; @🖥) Spread across a house and garden close to the city centre, four-bed dorms and double rooms at this hostel are decked out with colourful local art and quality linen, while the friendly vibe makes you feel like part of the family. Free internet and bikes.

Nelson YHA
HOSTEL $

(☑03-545 9988; www.yha.co.nz; 59 Rutherford St; dm/s/d from $33/66/87, d with bathroom $110; @🖥) A tidy, well-run, central hostel with high-quality communal areas including a soundproof TV room (including free DVDs), two well-organised kitchens and a sunny outdoor terrace. Excellent local knowledge for tours and activities, plus bookings.

Tahuna Beach Kiwi Holiday Park
HOLIDAY PARK $

(☑03-548 5159, 0800 500 501; www.tahunabeach.co.nz; 70 Beach Rd; sites/cabins/units from $18/55/100; @🖥) Close to Tahuna beach, 5km from the city, this mammoth park is home to thousands in high summer, which you'll either find hellish or bloody brilliant, depending on your mood. Off season, you'll have the minigolf mostly to yourself.

Te Maunga House
B&B $$

(☑03-548 8605; www.nelsoncityaccommodation.co.nz; 15 Dorothy Annie Way; s $90, d $125-140; ☺closed May-Sep; 🖥) Aptly named ('the mountain'), this grand old family home has exceptional views. Two doubles and a single, with their own bathrooms, are filled with characterful furniture and made up with good linens. Your hearty breakfast can be walked off up and down *that* hill. It's only a 10-minute climb (15 minutes in all, from town), but only the leggy ones will revel in it.

Palazzo Motor Lodge
MOTEL $$

(☑0800 472 5293, 03-545 81/1; www.palazzomotorlodge.co.nz; 159 Rutherford St; studios $130-225, apt $230-390; @🖥) Hosts with the most offer a cheerful welcome at this popular, modern, Italian-tinged motor lodge. The stylish studios and one- and two-room apartments feature enviable kitchens with decent cooking equipment, classy glassware and a dishwasher. The odd bit of dubious art is easily forgiven, particularly as Doris' sausage is available for breakfast.

Cedar Grove Motor Lodge
MOTEL $$

(☑0800 233 274, 03-545 1133; www.cedargrove.co.nz; cnr Trafalgar & Grove Sts; d $155-210; @🖥) A big old cedar landmarks this smart, mod-

---

THE WONDROUS WORLD OF WEARABLE ART

Nelson exudes creativity, so it's hardly surprising that NZ's most inspiring fashion show was born here. It began humbly in 1987 when creator Suzie Moncrieff held a local offbeat fashion show. The concept was to create a piece of art that could be worn and modelled. The idea caught on, and the World of WearableArt Awards Show became an annual event. Wood, papier mâché, paua shell, earplugs, soft-drink cans, ping-pong balls and more have been used to create garments; 'Bizarre Bra' entries are showstoppers.

The awards show has been transplanted to Wellington, but you can ogle entries at Nelson's **World of WearableArt & Classic Cars Museum** (WOW; www.wowcars.co.nz; 1 Cadillac Way; adult/child $22/8; ☺10am-5pm). High-tech galleries include a carousel mimicking a catwalk, and a glow-in-the-dark room.

More car than bra? Under the same roof are around 50 mint-condition classic cars and motorbikes. Exhibits change, but may include a 1959 pink Cadillac, a yellow 1950 Bullet Nose Studebaker convertible and a BMW bubble car. You can view another 70 vehicles in *The Classic Collection* next door ($8 extra). Cafe and art gallery on site.

ern block of spacious apartments just three minutes' walk to town. Its range of studios and doubles are plush and elegant, with full cooking facilities.

★**South Street Cottages**   RENTAL HOUSE $$$
(☑03-540 2769; www.cottageaccommodation.co.nz; South St; d from $230; 🐞) Stay on NZ's oldest preserved street in one of three elegant, two-bedroom self-contained cottages built in the 1860s. Each has all the comforts of home, including kitchen, laundry and courtyard garden; breakfast provisions supplied. There is a two-night minimum stay.

🍴 Eating

Nelson has a lively cafe scene as well as a varied array of restaurants. Self-caterers should steer resolutely towards the fruitful Nelson Market (p401) on Saturday and the farmers market (Morrison Sq, cnr Morrison & Hardy Sts ; ⊙11pm–4pm Wed) on Wednesday.

Falafel Gourmet   MIDDLE EASTERN $
(195 Hardy St; meals $8-18; ⊙9.30am-5.30pm Mon-Sat, to 8pm Fri; 🥗) A cranking joint dishing out the best kebabs for miles around. They're healthy, too!

Swedish Bakery & Café   BAKERY $
(www.theswedishbakery.co.nz; 54 Bridge St; snacks $2-8; ⊙8.30am-4pm Mon-Fri, 9am-2pm Sat) Delicious breads, pastries, cakes and small chocolate treats from the resident Scandinavian baker. Freshly filled rolls, bagels and croissants, too. Take your goodies away or eat in the bijou cafe.

Fish Stop   FISH & CHIPS $
(24 Alton St; fish & chips $5-9; ⊙11am-8pm) Five minutes' walk from the cathedral steps, this cracker chippy wraps up tasty fried treats with a smile. Small eat-in area.

Stefano's   PIZZERIA $
(91 Trafalgar St; pizzas $6-29; ⊙10am-late; 🥗) Located upstairs in the State Cinema complex, this Italian-run joint turns out some of NZ's best pizza. Thin, crispy and delicious, with some variations an absolute bargain. Wash it down with a beer and chase it with a creamy dessert.

Penguino Ice Cream Café   ICE CREAM $
(Montgomery Sq; ice creams $4-7; ⊙11am-5pm) Indulge yourself with superb gelato and sorbet, from vanilla and boysenberry to manuka honey and beyond. Next day, visit for a shake, fruit smoothie, sundae, or *stroopwafels*...

Organic Greengrocer   ORGANIC $
(www.organicgreengrocer.co.nz; cnr Tasman & Grove Sts; ⊙9am-5.30pm Mon-Fri, 10am-4pm Sat & Sun; 🥗) 🍃 Stocks foods for the sensitive, plus produce, organic tipples and natural bodycare. Food to go and coffee also on offer.

DeVille   CAFE $$
(22 New St; meals $11-20; ⊙9am-4pm Mon-Sat; 🥗) Most of DeVille's tables lie in its sweet walled courtyard, a hidden boho oasis in the inner city and the perfect place for a meal or morning tea. The food's good – from fresh baked goods to a chorizo-burrito brunch, caesar salad and sticky pork sandwich. Open late for live music Friday and Saturday in summer.

Indian Café   INDIAN $$
(☑03-548 4089; www.theindiancafe.com; 94 Collingwood St; mains $15-23; ⊙noon-2pm Mon-Fri, 5pm-late daily; 🥗) This saffron-coloured Edwardian villa houses an Indian restaurant that keeps the bhajis raised with impressive interpretations of Anglo-Indian standards, such as chicken tandoori, rogan josh and beef madras. Share the mixed platter to start, then mop up your mains with one of 10 different breads.

Ford's   MODERN NZ $$
(☑03-546 9400; www.fordsnelson.co.nz; 276 Trafalgar St; lunch $16-22; ⊙8am-late) Sunny pavement tables at the top of Trafalgar St make this a popular lunchtime spot, as does a menu of modern classics such as the excellent seafood chowder, steak sandwich and tuna niçoise. Make a short stop for coffee and a scone, or linger over dinner which leaps up a tenner or so.

★**Hopgood's**   MODERN NZ $$$
(☑03-545 7191; www.hopgoods.co.nz; 284 Trafalgar St; mains $34-38; ⊙5.30pm-late Mon-Sat, 11.30am-2pm Fri) Tongue-and-groove-lined Hopgood's is perfect for a romantic dinner or holiday treat. The food is decadent and skilfully prepared but unfussy, allowing quality local ingredients to shine. Try Asian crispy duck, or aged beef fillet with wild mushroom gratin. Desirable, predominantly Kiwi wine list. Bookings advisable.

🍷 Drinking & Nightlife

Nelson's got a bad (read: good) case of craftbeer fever, so if your budget allows it, hoppiness awaits. Cheaper thrills can be found at numerous establishments clustered on Bridge St towards the intersection with Collingwood.

IN PURSUIT OF HOPPINESS

The Nelson region lays claim to the title of craft-brewing capital of New Zealand. World-class hops have been grown here since the 1840s, and a dozen breweries are spread between Nelson and Golden Bay. One is McCashin's (www.mccashins.co.nz; 660 Main Rd, Stoke), a ground-breaker in the new era of craft brewing in NZ. Visit their historic cider factory for a tasting or tour.

Pick up a copy of the Nelson Craft Beer Trail map (available from the i-SITE and other outlets, and online at www.craftbrewingcapital.co.nz) and wind your way between brewers and pubs. Top picks for a tipple include the Free House Brewing Company, McCashins, the Moutere Inn (p408), Golden Bear (p408) and the Mussel Inn (p417).

Free House　　　　　　CRAFT BEER
(www.freehouse.co.nz; 95 Collingwood St) Come rejoice at this church of ales. Tastefully converted from its original, more reverent purpose, it's now home to an excellent, oft-changing selection of NZ craft beers. You can imbibe inside, out, or even in a yurt, where there's regular live music. Hallelujah.

Sprig & Fern　　　　　　CRAFT BEER
(www.sprigandfern.co.nz; 280 Hardy St) This outpost of Richmond's Sprig & Fern brewery offers 18 brews on tap, from lager through to doppelbock and berry cider. No pokies, no TV, just decent beer, occasional live music and a pleasant outdoor area. Pizzas can be ordered in. Look for a second Sprig at 143 Milton St, handy to Founders Park.

Vic　　　　　　　　　　　PUB
(www.vicbrewbar.co.nz; 281 Trafalgar St; ⊘ noon-late) A commendable example of a Mac's Brewbar, with trademark, quirky Kiwiana fit-out, including a knitted stag's head. Quaff a handle of ale, dine on honest pub grub (mains $12 to $33) and tap a toe to regular live music, including open-mike Mondays. Good afternoon sun and people-watching from streetside seating.

☆ Entertainment

Theatre Royal　　　　　　THEATRE
(www.theatreroyalnelson.co.nz; 78 Rutherford St) State-of-the-art theatre in a charmingly re-stored heritage building. This 'grand old lady of Nelson' (aged 136) boasts a full program of local and touring drama, dance and musical productions. Check the website for what's on and book online at www.ticketdirect.co.nz, or in person at the box office (⊘ 10am-4pm Mon-Fri, 10am-noon Sat). Encore!

State Cinemas　　　　　　CINEMA
(☑ 03-548 3885; www.statecinemas.co.nz; 91 Trafalgar St) This is the place to see mainstream, new-release flicks.

ℹ Information

Banks and ATMs pepper Trafalgar St.
After Hours & Duty Doctors (☑ 03-546 8881; 96 Waimea Rd; ⊘ 8am-10pm)
Nelson Hospital (☑ 03-546 1800; www.nmdhb.govt.nz; Waimea Rd)
Nelson i-SITE (☑ 03-548 2304; www.nelsonnz.com; cnr Trafalgar & Halifax Sts; ⊘ 8.30am-5pm Mon-Fri, 9am-4pm Sat & Sun) A slick centre complete with DOC information desk for the low-down on national parks and walks (including Abel Tasman and Heaphy tracks). Pick up a copy of the Nelson Tasman Visitor Guide.
Post Office (209 Hardy St)

ℹ Getting There & Away

AIR
Air New Zealand (☑ 0800 737 000; www.airnewzealand.co.nz) Direct flights to/from Wellington, Auckland, Christchurch and Palmerston North.

Soundsair (☑ 0800 505 005, 03-520 3080; www.soundsair.com) Flies daily between Nelson and Wellington.

BUS
Book Abel Tasman Coachlines, InterCity, KiwiRail Scenic and Interisland ferries at the **Nelson SBL Travel Centre** (☑ 03-548 1539; www.nelson-coachlines.co.nz; 27 Bridge St) or the i-SITE.

Abel Tasman Coachlines (☑ 03-548 0285; www.abeltasmantravel.co.nz) operates bus services to Motueka (one hour), Takaka (two hours), Kaiteriteri and Marahau (both two hours). These services also connect with Golden Bay Coachlines (p418) services for Takaka and around. Transport to/from the three national parks is provided by **Trek Express** (☑ 027 222 1872, 0800 128 735; www.trekexpress.co.nz).

Atomic Shuttles (☑ 03-349 0697; www.atomictravel.co.nz) runs from Nelson to Motueka (one hour), Picton (2¼ hours), Christchurch (7¾ hours) with a Greymouth connection, plus other southern destinations as far as Queenstown, Dunedin and Invercargill. Services can be booked at (and depart from) Nelson i-SITE.

InterCity (☑ 03-548 1538; www.intercity.co.nz; Bridge St, departs SLB Travel Centre) runs from Nelson to most key South Island destinations including Picton (two hours), Kaikoura (3½ hours), Christchurch (seven hours) and Greymouth (six hours).

ℹ Getting Around

TO/FROM THE AIRPORT

Nelson Airport is 6km southwest of town, near Tahunanui Beach. A taxi from there to town will cost around $25, or **Super Shuttle** (☑ 0800 748 885; www.supershuttle.co.nz) offers door-to-door service for $21 (additional passengers $17).

BICYCLE

Hire a bike from Stewarts Avanti Plus Nelson or UBike (p401).

BUS

Nelson Suburban Bus Lines (SBL; ☑ 03-548 3290; www.nelsoncoachlines.co.nz; 27 Bridge St) operates NBUS, the local service between Nelson and Richmond via Tahunanui and Bishopdale until about 7pm weekdays and 4.30pm on weekends. It also runs the **Late Late Bus** (☉ hourly 10pm-3am Fri & Sat) from Nelson to Richmond via Tahunanui, departing from the Westpac Bank on Trafalgar St. Maximum fare for these services is $4.

TAXI

Nelson City Taxis (☑ 03-548 8225)
Sun City Taxis (☑ 03-548 2666)

Nelson to Motueka

From Richmond, south of Nelson, there are two routes to Motueka: the busier, more populated coastal highway (SH60) and the inland Moutere Hwy, a pleasant alternative and a nice way of making a loop. Either way, this area is generously sprinkled with attrac-

tions, so allow enough time to pull off the road. The area can be explored by bicycle on the Great Taste Trail.

There are numerous **wineries** in this area; the *Nelson Wine Guide* pamphlet (www.wineart.co.nz) will help you find them.

Art and **craft galleries** are also in the vicinity. Find these in the *Nelson Art Guide* or *Nelson's Creative Pathways* pamphlets, both available from local i-SITEs, where you can also get information on accommodation around these parts.

SH60 via Mapua

Skirting around Waimea Inlet and along the Ruby Coast, this is the quickest route from Nelson to Motueka (around 45 minutes' drive), although there are various distractions to slow you down.

Just 10km from Richmond you'll hit **Waimea** (www.waimeaestates.co.nz; SH60; ☉ 10am-6pm) winery, where a diverse range of interesting wines is available to taste. The on-site **Cellar Door** (www.thecellardoor.net.nz; mains $16-29) is a stylish conservatory cafe with vine views and a tapas-style menu.

Masterpiece glass is blown at **Höglund Glass Art** (www.hoglundartglass.com; 52 Lansdowne Rd, Appleby; ☉ 10am-5pm), where you can watch Ola the master and his colleagues working the furnace.

Just up the road is the turn-off to **Rabbit Island**, a recreation reserve offering estuary views from many angles, sandy beaches and plenty of quiet pine forest. The bridge to the island closes at sunset; overnight stays are not allowed.

Seifried (www.seifried.co.nz; cnr SH60 & Redwood Rd; ☉ 10am-5pm) winery sits at the Rabbit Island turn-off. It's one of the region's biggest,

MARLBOROUGH & NELSON NELSON TO MOTUEKA

WORTH A TRIP

GREAT TASTE TRAIL

In a stroke of genius propelled by great weather and easy topography, Nelson has developed what is destined to be one of NZ's most popular cycle trails. Why? Because no other is so frequently punctuated by stops for food, wine, craft beer and art, as it passes through a range of landscapes from rolling countryside to estuary boardwalk.

The full 175km trail is due for completion in 2016, but there's plenty of track ready for riding now, including the 69km Coastal Route from Nelson to Kaiteriteri. This can be ridden over two days (there's plenty of accommodation along the way) or you can just bite off a little chunk such as a ride to lunch. A good taster would be the 14km section from Stoke (near Nelson city) to the wineries around Brightwater.

The cycle companies on p401 can help you with bike hire and advice; see also the trail site, **Great Taste Trail** (www.heartofbiking.org.nz).

and is home to a pleasant garden restaurant and the delicious Sweet Agnes riesling.

As you reach the end of the inlet, you can either continue along SH60 or detour along the original coast road, now named the Ruby Bay Scenic Route. Along it lies the settlement of Mapua at the mouth of the Waimea River, home to arty shops and eateries including the Smokehouse (www. smokehouse.co.nz; Mapua Wharf; fish & chips $8-12; ⊙11am-8pm), where you can get fish and chips to eat on the wharf in the company of seagulls, as well as delicious wood-smoked fish and pâté to go. There's also delightful indoor dining at Jellyfish (www.jellyfishmapua. co.nz; Mapua Wharf; lunch $13-20, dinner $25-35; ✐), where fishy dishes sit amid an inspiring menu of fusion cuisine.

In the same wharfside cluster you will undoubtedly sniff out the Golden Bear Brewing Company (www.goldenbearbrewing.com; Mapua Wharf; meals $10-20), a microbrewery with tons of stainless steel out back and a dozen or so brews out front. Authentic Mexican food will stop you from getting a sore head. Occasional live music, takeaway beers and tours.

A few kilometres before the scenic route rejoins SH60 is Jester House (www.jester-house.co.nz; 320 Aporo Rd, Tasman; meals $13-23; ⊙9am-5pm). It alone is a good reason to take this detour, as much for its tame eels as for the peaceful sculpture gardens that encourage you to linger over lunch. A short, simple menu puts a few twists into staples (wild pork burger, lavender shortbread), and there is local beer and wines. It's 8km to Mapua or Motueka.

Moutere Hwy

This road traverses gently rolling countryside, dotted with farms, orchards and lifestyle blocks. Visitor attractions are fewer and far between, but it's a scenic, bucolic drive nonetheless, particularly fruitful in high summer when the berry farms are on song. Local producers and artists are listed at www.moutereartisans.co.nz.

The turn-off to the Moutere is signposted at Appleby on SH60. Not far along is the turn-off to Old Coach Rd, from where you can follow the signs to Woollaston (www.woollaston.co.nz; School Rd, Upper Moutere; ⊙11am-4.30pm), a flash hilltop winery complete with tasting room and contemporary art gallery. The patio is a spectacular place to enjoy a platter for lunch.

Upper Moutere is the main settlement along this route. First settled by German immigrants and originally named Sarau, today it's a sleepy hamlet with a shop, cafe and allegedly NZ's oldest pub, the Moutere Inn (www. moutereinn.co.nz; 1406 Moutere Hwy; meals $12-30), complete with retro, workaday interior to match. This welcoming establishment serves honest meals (pizza, burgers and fish 'n' chips) and quality, predominantly local craft beer. Pull up a pew with a beer-tasting platter, sit outside on the sunny patio, or come along at night to hear regular live music.

Continuing along the Moutere Hwy, Neudorf Rd is well signposted, leading as it does to various delectables. Call into Neudorf Dairy (www.neudorfdairy.co.nz; 226 Neudorf Rd; 10am-5pm Wed-Sun) for award-winning handcrafted sheeps-milk cheeses and a picnic, or Neudorf (www.neudorf.co.nz; 138 Neudorf Rd; ⊙10am-5pm, closed weekends May-Oct) winery for gorgeous pinot noir and some of the country's finest chardonnay.

Motueka

POP 7600

Motueka (pronounced 'mott-oo-ecka', meaning 'Island of Weka') is a bustling agricultural hub, and a great base from which to explore the region. It has all the vital amenities, ample accommodation, cafes, roadside fruit stalls, and a clean and beautiful river offering swimming and fishing. Stock up here if you're en route to Golden Bay or the Abel Tasman and Kahurangi National Parks.

◉ Sights & Activities

While most of Mot's drawcards are out of town, there are a few attractions worth checking out, the buzziest of which is the active aerodrome, home to several air-raising activities. With a coffee cart on site, it's a good place to soak up some sun and views, and watch a few folks drop in.

While you might not realise it from the high street, Motueka is just a stone's throw from the sea. Eyeball the waters (with birds and saltwater baths) along the estuary walkway. Ask a local for directions or obtain a town map from the i-SITE.

To get a handle on the town, visit the i-SITE and collect the Motueka Art Walk pamphlet, detailing sculpture, murals and occasional peculiarities around town.

Motueka District Museum   MUSEUM
(140 High St; admission by donation; ⊙10am-4pm Mon-Fri Dec-Mar, 10am-3pm Tue-Fri Apr-Nov) An

interesting collection of regional artefacts, housed in a dear old school building.

Hop Federation
BREWERY

(☑ 03-528 0486; www.hopfederation.co.nz; 483 Main Rd, Riwaka) Pop in for tastings and take-aways (fill a flagon), or phone ahead to arrange a tour, at this teeny-weeny but terrific craft brewery 5km from Mot. Our pick of the ales is the hoppy, sessionable pale ale, ideal for a summer's day.

Skydive Abel Tasman
SKYDIVING

(☑ 03-528 4091, 0800 422 899; www.skydive. co.nz; Motueka Aerodrome, College St; jumps 13,000/16,500ft $299/399) Move over Taupo: we've jumped both and think Mot takes the cake (presumably so do the many sports jumpers who favour this drop zone, some of whom you may see rocketing in). DVDs and photos cost extra, but pick-up/drop-off from Motueka and Nelson are free.

Tasman Sky Adventures
SCENIC FLIGHTS

(☑ 027 229 9693, 0800 114 386; www.skyadventures.co.nz; Motueka Aerodrome, 60 College St; 30min flight $205) A rare opportunity to fly in a microlight. Keep your eyes open and blow your mind on a scenic flight above Abel Tasman National Park. Wow. And there's tandem hang gliding for the brave (15/30 minutes, 2500/5280ft $195/275).

U-fly Extreme
AEROBATICS

(☑ 03-528 8290, 0800 360 180; www.uflyextreme. co.nz; Motueka Aerodrome, College St; 15/20min $345/445) You handle the controls in an open-cockpit Pitts Special stunt biplane. No experience necessary, just a stomach for loop the loops and barrel rolls. Roger wilco!

🛏 Sleeping

Be warned: Mot's population doubles in summer. The i-SITE (p411) can help you squeeze in somewhere if you get stuck.

★Motueka Top 10 Holiday Park
HOLIDAY PARK $

(☑ 03-528 7189, 0800 668 835; www.motuekatop10.co.nz; 10 Fearon St; campsites from $40, cabins $55-130, units $99-350; @ 🕱 🕱) 🌱 A holiday park packed with plenty of grassy, green charm. Love those lofty kahikatea trees! Amenities are plentiful and shipshape including the family-friendly swimming pool and jumping pillow. Quality accommodation from tidy cabins through to a deluxe family unit sleeping up to 11. Local wine and bike tours by arrangement.

Eden's Edge Lodge
HOSTEL $

(☑ 03-528 4242; www.edensedge.co.nz; 137 Lodder Lane, Riwaka; campsites from $17, dm $28, d with/without bathroom $82/76; @ 🕱 🕱) Surrounded by orchards, 4km from Motueka, this purpose-built lodge comes pretty close

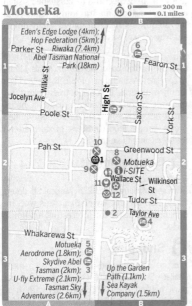

Motueka

0 —— 200 m
0 —— 0.1 miles

Motueka

🎯 Sights
1 Motueka District Museum.................B2

Activities, Courses & Tours
2 Wilsons Abel Tasman.........................B3

Sleeping
3 Avalon Manor Motel...........................A3
4 Equestrian Lodge Motel.....................B3
Hat Trick Lodge...........................(see 12)
5 Laughing Kiwi....................................A3
6 Motueka Top 10 Holiday Park............B1
7 Nautilus Lodge..................................B1

Eating
8 Motueka Sunday Market....................B2
9 Patisserie Royale...............................A2
10 Simply Indian...................................B2

Drinking & Nightlife
11 Sprig & Fern....................................B2

Entertainment
12 Gecko Theatre.................................B2

to backpacker heaven. Well-designed facilities include a gleaming kitchen and inviting communal areas. There's a rainwater pool in summer and bikes for hire, and it's all within walking distance of beer, ice cream and coffee.

Hat Trick Lodge
HOSTEL $

(03-528 5353; www.hattricklodge.co.nz; 25 Wallace St; dm $27, d with/without bathroom $70/62; @) A purpose-built lodge right in the middle of town. What it lacks in personality it makes up for in cleanliness, boasting ample off-street parking, a friendly tourist-oriented atmosphere and sunny balconies.

Laughing Kiwi
HOSTEL $

(03-528 9229; www.laughingkiwi.co.nz; 310 High St; dm $28, d with/without bathroom $74/66;) Compact, low-key YHA hostel with rooms spread between an old villa and a purpose-built backpacker lodge with a smart kitchen/lounge. The self-contained bach is a good option for groups (double $130).

Equestrian Lodge Motel
MOTEL $$

(03-528 9369, 0800 668 782; www.equestrianlodge.co.nz; Avalon Ct; d $120-156, q $165-220; @) No horses, no lodge, but no matter. This motel complex is close to town (off Tudor St), with expansive lawns, rose gardens, and a heated pool and spa. Rooms are plainly dressed but immaculate, and many have ovens. Cheerful owners will hook you up with local activities.

Nautilus Lodge
MOTEL $$

(03-528 4658, 0800 628 845; www.nautiluslodge.co.nz; 67 High St; d $162-225; @) A top-notch motel complex with 12 units decorated in neutral tones with low-profile furniture including European slatted beds. There are classy bathrooms and cooking facilities in all units, spa baths in some, Sky TV, and balconies and patios that collect afternoon sun.

Avalon Manor Motel
MOTEL $$

(03-528 8320, 0800 282 566; www.avalonmotels.co.nz; 314 High St; d $150-215;) Prominent L-shaped motel with spacious rooms, five minutes' walk from the town centre. All rooms have a contemporary vibe, with cooking facilities, while the sumptuous studios have king-size beds and large flat-screen TVs. There's also a guest barbecue, laundry and views of Mt Arthur.

Resurgence
LODGE, CHALETS $$$

(03-528 4664; www.resurgence.co.nz; Riwaka Valley Rd; d lodge from $625, chalets from $525; @) Choose a luxurious en suite lodge room or self-contained chalet at this magical green retreat 15 minutes' drive south of Abel Tasman National Park, and 30 minutes' walk from the picturesque source of the Riwaka River. Lodge rates include aperitifs and a four-course dinner, as well as breakfast; chalet rates are for B&B, with dinner an extra $100.

✕ Eating & Drinking

Patisserie Royale
BAKERY $

(152 High St; baked goods $2-8; 6am-4.30pm Mon-Sat, 6am-2pm Sun) The best of several Mot bakeries and worth every delectable calorie. Lots of French fancies and darn good pies.

Up the Garden Path
CAFE $$

(www.upthegardenpath.co.nz; 473 High St; meals $15-24; 9am-4pm;) Perfect for lunch or a coffee break, this licensed cafe-gallery kicks back in an 1890s house amid idyllic gardens. Unleash the kids in the playroom and linger over your blueberry pancakes, chicken burger, lamb souvlaki, pasta or lemon tart. Vegetarian, gluten- and dairy-free options available.

Simply Indian
INDIAN $$

(130 High St; mains $16-24; 11am-10pm Mon-Sat, 5-10pm Sun;) As the name suggests: no-nonsense curry in a no-frills setting. The food, however, is consistently good and relatively cheap. Expect the usual suspects such as tikka, tandoori, madras and vindaloo, and the ubiquitous naan prepared eight different ways. Takeaways available.

Sprig & Fern
CRAFT BEER

(www.sprigandfern.co.nz; Wallace St; meals $14-19; 2pm-late) A member of the Sprig & Fern family of taverns, this back-street tavern ups the ante among Motueka's drinking holes. Small but pleasant, it offers 20 hand-pulled brews, simple food (burgers, pizza, platters) and occasional live music.

☆ Entertainment

Gecko Theatre
CINEMA

(www.geckotheatre.co.nz; 23b Wallace St; tickets $9-13) Pull up an easy chair at this wee, independent theatre for interesting art-house flicks.

🔒 Shopping

Motueka Sunday Market
MARKET

(Wallace St; 8am-1pm) On Sunday the car park behind the i-SITE fills up with trestle tables for the Motueka Sunday Market:

produce, jewellery, buskers, arts, crafts and Doris' divine bratwurst.

ℹ️ Information

Motueka i-SITE (📞 03-528 6543; www.motuekaisite.co.nz; 20 Wallace St; ⊙ 8.30am-5pm Mon-Fri, 9am-4pm Sat & Sun) An excellent centre with helpful staff who handle bookings from Kaitaia to Bluff and provide local national-park expertise and necessaries.

Take Note/Post Office (207 High St) Bookshop moonlighting as a post office.

ℹ️ Getting There & Away

Bus services depart from Motueka i-SITE.

Abel Tasman Coachlines (📞 03-528 8850; www.abeltasmantravel.co.nz) Runs daily from Motueka to Nelson (one hour), Kaiteriteri (25 minutes) and Marahau (30 minutes). These services connect with Golden Bay Coachline services to Takaka (1¼ hours) and other Golden Bay destinations including Totaranui in Abel Tasman National Park, Collingwood, and on to the Heaphy Track trailhead. Note that from May to September all buses run less frequently.

Atomic Shuttles (📞 03-349 0697, 0508 108 359; www.atomictravel.co.nz) Run from Motueka to Nelson, connecting with further services via Christchurch over to Greymouth and down to Queenstown and Dunedin.

Motueka to Abel Tasman

Kaiteriteri

Known simply as 'Kaiteri', this seaside hamlet 13km from Motueka is the most popular resort town in the area. During the summer holidays its gorgeous, golden, safe-swimming beach feels more like Noumea than NZ, with more towels than sand. The beach is also a major departure point for Abel Tasman National Park transport, although Marahau is the main base. The village is also home to **Kaiteriteri Mountain Bike Park** (www.kaiteriterimtbpark.org.nz) with tracks to suit all levels of rider.

🛏️ Sleeping & Eating

Kaiteriteri Beach Motor Camp HOLIDAY PARK $
(📞 03-527 8010; www.kaiteriteribeach.co.nz; Sandy Bay Rd; campsites from $19, cabins $45-85; @ 🛜) A gargantuan park in pole position across from the beach. It's hugely popular, so book in advance. The on-site general store is very well stocked, as is the ice-cream hatch where a queue often forms.

Kaiteri Lodge LODGE $
(📞 03-527 8281; www.kaiterilodge.co.nz; Inlet Rd; dm $30-35, d $80-160; @ 🛜) Modern, purpose-built lodge with small, simple dorms and en suite doubles. The nautical decor adds some cheer to somewhat lazily maintained communal areas. The sociable on-site **Beached Whale** (dinner $18-28; ⊙ 4pm-late) bar serves wood-fired pizza, steak, and the like, while the host busts out a few tunes on his guitar. The Whale will be open when the big bus pulls in.

Torlesse Coastal Motels MOTELS $$
(📞 03-527 8063; www.torlessemotels.co.nz; 8 Kotare Pl, Little Kaiteriteri Beach; d $130-180, q & f $180-280; 🛜) Just 200m from Little Kaiteriteri Beach (around the corner from the main beach) is this congregation of roomy hillside units with pitched ceilings, full kitchens and laundries. Most have water views, and there's a barbecue deck and spa.

Bellbird Lodge B&B $$$
(📞 03-527 8555; www.bellbirdlodge.co.nz; Kaiteriteri-Sandy Bay Rd; d $275-350; @ 🛜) An up-market B&B 1.5km up the hill from Kaiteri Beach, offering two en suite rooms, bush and sea views, extensive gardens, spectacular breakfasts (featuring homemade muesli and fruit compote), and gracious hosts. Dinner by arrangement in winter, when local restaurant hours are irregular.

Shoreline RESTAURANT $$
(www.shorelinekaiteriteri.co.nz; cnr Inlet & Sandy Bay Rds; meals $15-24; ⊙ 8am-9pm, reduced hours Apr-Nov) A modern, beige cafe-bar-restaurant right on the beach. Punters chill out on the sunny deck, lingering over sandwiches, pizzas, burgers and other predictable fare, or pop in for coffee and cake. Erratic winter hours; burger booth out the back.

ℹ️ Getting There & Away

Kaiteriteri is serviced by Abel Tasman Coachlines (p415).

Marahau

POP 200

Further along the coast from Kaiteriteri and 18km north of Motueka, Marahau is the main gateway to Abel Tasman National Park. It's less of a town, more like a procession of holiday homes and tourist businesses.

If you're in an equine state of mind, **Pegasus Park** (📞 03-526 8050; www.pegasuspark.co.nz) and **Marahau Horse Treks** (📞 03-527 8425), both along Marahau–Sandy Bay

Rd, offer the chance to belt along the beach on a horse, your hair streaming behind you (children's pony rides $35, two-hour rides $90).

Sleeping & Eating

Barn
HOSTEL $

(☑03-527 8043; www.barn.co.nz; 14 Harvey Rd; unpowered/powered sites per person $14/16, dm $28, d $55-70; @🔊) This backpackers has hit its straps with comfortable new dorms, a fresh toilet block and grassy camping field added to a mix of micro-cabins, alfresco kitchens and barbecue areas. The barn itself is the hub – a communal kitchen and lounge area good for socialising, as is the central deck which has a fireplace. Activity bookings and secure parking available.

Kanuka Ridge
HOSTEL $

(☑03-527 8435; www.abeltasmanbackpackers.co.nz; Moss Rd, off Marahau-Sandy Bay Rd; dm $29, d & tw with/without bathroom $89/64; 🔊) Five minutes' drive from Marahau, this purpose-built cottage arrangement is ringed by forest, offering birdy, bushy surroundings for a bit of peace and quiet. Active hosts are willing and able to hook you up with activities inside and outside of the national park. Secure car parking available.

Ocean View Chalets
CHALET $$

(☑03-527 8232; www.accommodationabeltasman.co.nz; 305 Sandy Bay-Marahau Rd; d $145-235, q $290; 🔊) Positioned on a leafy hillside affording plenty of privacy, these cheerful, cypress-lined chalets are 300m from the Abel Tasman Track with views across Tasman Bay to Fisherman Island. All are self-contained; breakfast and packed lunches available.

Abel Tasman Marahau Lodge
MOTEL $$

(☑03-527 8250; www.abeltasmanmarahaulodge.co.nz; Sandy Bay-Marahau Rd; d $135-255; @🔊) ✈ Enjoy halcyon days in this arc of 12 lovely studios and self-contained units with cathedral ceilings, opening out on to landscaped gardens with lush lawns. There's also a fully equipped communal kitchen for self-caterers, plus spa and sauna. Cuckoos, tui and bellbirds squawk and warble in the bushy surrounds.

★ Fat Tui
BURGERS $

(cnr Marahau-Sandy Bay & Marahau Valley Rds; burgers $13-16; ⊘noon-8.30pm daily summer, Wed-Sun winter; ☑) Everyone's heard about this bird, based in a caravan that ain't rollin' anywhere fast. Thank goodness. Superlative burgers, such as the Cowpat (beef), the Ewe Beaut (lamb) and the Sparrow's Fart breakfast burger. Fish and chips, and coffee, too.

Park Cafe
CAFE $$

(www.parkcafe.co.nz; Harvey Rd; lunch $9-22, dinner $16-30; ⊘8am-late mid-Sep–May; ☑) Sitting at the Abel Tasman Track trailhead, this breezy cafe is perfectly placed for fuelling up or restoring the waistline. High-calorie options include the big breakfast, pizzas, burgers and cakes, but there are also seafood and salad options. Enjoy in the room with a view or in the sunny courtyard garden. Live music on occasion.

Hooked on Marahau
CAFE $$

(☑03-527 8576; Marahau-Sandy Bay Rd; lunch $15-19, dinner $24-29; ⊘hours vary) This popular place certainly reels them in, so reservations are advisable for dinner. The art-bedecked interior opens onto an outdoor terrace with distracting views. Lunch centres on salads, chowder and wraps, while the dinner menu boasts fresh fish of the day, green-lipped mussels and NZ lamb shanks.

🛈 Getting There & Away

Marahau is serviced by Abel Tasman Coachlines (p415).

Abel Tasman National Park

Coastal Abel Tasman National Park blankets the northern end of a range of marble and limestone hills that extend from Kahurangi National Park. Various tracks in the park include an inland route, although the coast track is what everyone is here for – it's NZ's most popular Great Walk.

Abel Tasman Coast Track

This is arguably NZ's most beautiful Great Walk – 51km of sparkling seas, golden sand, quintessential coastal forest, and hidden surprises such as Cleopatra's Pool. Such pulling power attracts nearly 30,000 overnight trampers and kayakers per year, who all stay at least one night in the park. A major attraction is the terrain: well cut, well graded and well marked. It's almost impossible to get lost and can be tramped in sneakers.

You will, however, probably get your feet wet, as this track features long stretches of beach and crazy tides. In fact the tidal differences in the park are among the greatest in

Abel Tasman National Park

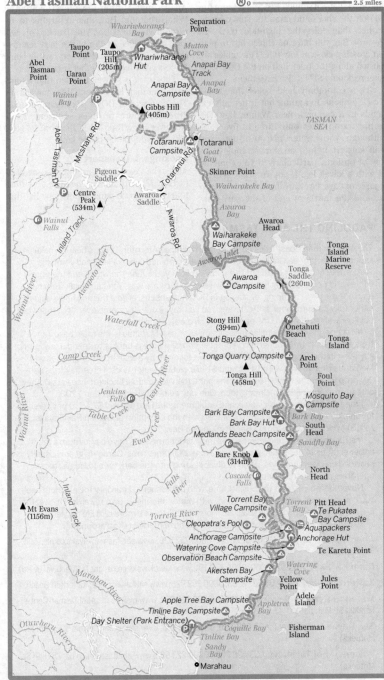

the country, up to a staggering 6m. At Torrent and Bark Bays, it's much easier and more fun to doff the shoes and cross the soggy sands, rather than take the high-tide track. At Awaroa Bay you have no choice but to plan on crossing close at low tide. Tide tables are posted along the track and on the DOC website; regional i-SITEs also have them.

It's a commonly held belief that Coast Track ends at Totaranui, but it actually extends to a car park near Wainui Bay. The entire tramp takes only three to five days, although with water taxi transport you can convert it into an almost endless array of options, particularly if you combine it with a kayak leg. If you can only spare a couple of days, a rewarding option is to loop around the northern end of the park, hiking the Coast Track from Totaranui, passing Anapai and Mutton Cove, overnighting at Whariwharangi Hut, then returning to Totaranui via the Gibbs Hill Track. This will give you a slice of the park's best features (beaches, seals, coastal scenery) while being far less crowded than other segments.

This track is so well trodden that a topographical map isn't essential for navigation. The map within DOC's *Abel Tasman Coast Track* brochure provides sufficient detail. However, NewTopo *Abel Tasman* 1:55,000 will give you the lay of the land.

Bookings & Transport

Along the Coast Track are four Great Walk huts ($32) with bunks, heating and flush toilets but no cooking facilities or lighting.

PADDLING THE ABEL TASMAN

The Abel Tasman Coast Track has long been trampers' territory, but its beauty makes it seductive spot for sea kayaking, which can be combined with walking and camping.

A variety of professional outfits are able to float you out on the water, and the possibilities and permutations for guided or freedom trips are vast. You can kayak from half a day to three days, camping, or staying in DOC huts, bachs, even a floating backpackers, either fully catered for or self-catering. You can kayak one day, camp overnight then walk back, or walk further into the park and catch a water taxi back.

Most operators offer similar trips at similar prices. Marahau is the main base, but trips also depart from Kaiteriteri. A popular choice if time is tight is to spend a few hours kayaking in the Tonga Island Marine Reserve, followed by a walk from Tonga Quarry to Medlands Beach. This will cost around $195 including water taxis. Three-day trips usually drop you at the northern end of the park, then you paddle back (or vice versa); they cost from around $620 including food. One-day guided trips are around $200.

Freedom rentals (double-kayak and equipment hire) are around $70/110 per person for one/two days; all depart from Marahau with the exception of Golden Bay Kayaks (p418), which is based at Tata Beach in Golden Bay.

Instruction is given to everyone, and most tour companies have a minimum age of either eight or 14 depending on the trip. None allow solo hires. Camping gear is usually provided on overnight trips; if you're disappearing into the park for a few days, most operators provide free car parking.

November to Easter is the busiest time, with December to February the absolute peak. You can, however, paddle all year round, with winter offering its own rewards. The weather is surprisingly amenable, the seals are more playful, there's more bird life and less haze.

Following are the main players in this competitive market (shop around):

Abel Tasman Kayaks (☑03-527 8022, 0800 732 529; www.abeltasmankayaks.co.nz; Main Rd, Marahau)

Kahu Kayaks (☑03-527 8300, 0800 300 101; www.kahukayaks.co.nz; cnr Marahau Valley Rd)

Kaiteriteri Kayaks (☑03-527 8383, 0800 252 925; www.seakayak.co.nz; Kaiteriteri Beach)

Marahau Sea Kayaks (☑03-527 8176, 0800 529 257; www.msk.co.nz; Abel Tasman Centre, Franklin St, Marahau)

Sea Kayak Company (☑03-528 7251, 0508 252 925; www.seakayaknz.co.nz; 506 High St, Motueka)

Wilsons Abel Tasman (☑03-528 2027, 0800 223 582; www.abeltasman.co.nz; 25 High St, Motueka)

There are also 19 designated Great Walk campsites ($14). As the Abel Tasman Track is a Great Walk, all huts and campsites must be booked in advance year-round, either online through Great Walks Bookings (0800 694 732; www.greatwalks.co.nz) or at DOC visitor centres, nationwide. Hut tickets and annual passes cannot be used on the track, and there is a two-night limit on staying in each hut or campsite, except for Totaranui campsite which has a one-night limit. Penalty fees apply to those who do not have a valid booking, and you may be required to leave the park.

Moored permanently in Anchorage Bay, Aquapackers (0800 430 744; www.aquapackers.co.nz; dm/d incl breakfast $75/195) is a converted 13m catamaran providing unusual but buoyant backpacker accommodation. Facilities are basic but decent; prices include bedding, dinner and breakfast. Bookings are essential. Totaranui Campsite (03-528 8083; www.doc.govt.nz; summer/winter $15/10) is an extremely popular facility with a whopping capacity (850 campers) and a splendid setting next to the beach backed by some of the best bush in the park. A staffed DOC office has interpretive displays, flush toilets, cold showers and a public phone.

The closest big town to Abel Tasman is Motueka, with nearby Marahau the southern gateway. Although Wainui is the official northern trailhead, it is more common to finish in Totaranui, either skipping the northernmost section or looping back to Totaranui over Gibbs Hill Track. All gateways are serviced between Abel Tasman Coachlines (03-548 0285; www.abeltasmantravel.co.nz) and Golden Bay Coachlines (03-525 8352; www.gbcoachlines.co.nz).

Once you hit the park, it is easy to get to/from any point on the track by water taxi, from Kaiteriteri or Marahau. Typical one-way prices from either: Anchorage and Torrent Bay ($33), Bark Bay ($38), Tonga ($40), Awaroa ($43) and Totaranui ($45). The following are key operators:

Abel Tasman Sea Shuttle   BOAT
(03-527 8688, 0800 732 748; www.abeltasmanseashuttles.co.nz; Kaiteriteri) Scheduled services with cruise/walk options. Also runs between Nelson and Kaiteriteri from 1 December to 31 March (adult/child return $40/20).

Abel Tasman Aqua Taxi   BOAT
(03-527 8083, 0800 278 282; www.aquataxi.co.nz; Marahau-Sandy Bay Rd, Marahau) Scheduled and on-demand services as well as boat/walk options.

Wilsons Abel Tasman   BOAT
(03-528 2027, 0800 223 582; www.abeltasman.co.nz; 265 High St, Motueka; pass adult/child $150/75) Offers an explorer pass for unlimited taxi travel on three days over a five-day period, plus backpacker specials and an array of tours.

Marahau Water Taxis   BOAT
(03-527 8176, 0800 808 018; Abel Tasman Centre, Franklin St, Marahau) Scheduled services plus boat/walk options.

Tours

Tour companies usually offer free Motueka pick-up/drop-off, with Nelson pick-up available at extra cost.

Abel Tasman Sailing Adventures   SAILING
(03-527 8375, 0800 467 245; www.sailingadventures.co.nz; Kaiteriteri; day trip $179) Scheduled and on-demand catamaran trips, with sail/walk/kayak combos available. The popular day trip includes lunch on Anchorage Beach.

Abel Tasman Tours & Guided Walks   GUIDED HIKE
(03-528 9602; www.abeltasmantours.co.nz; from $220) Small-group, day-long walking tours (minimum two people) that include packed lunch and water taxis.

Wilsons Abel Tasman   WALKING, KAYAKING
(03-528 2027, 0800 223 582; www.abeltasman.co.nz; 265 High St, Motueka; half-day cruise $78, cruise & walk $60-78, kayak & walk $80-195) Impressive array of cruises, walking, kayaking and combo tours, including a $35 backpacker day-walk and a barbecue cruise (great winter option). Luxurious beachfront lodges at Awaroa and Torrent Bay for guided-tour guests.

Abel Tasman Canyons   CANYONING
(03-528 9800, 0800 863 472; www.abeltasmancanyons.co.nz; full-day trip $250) Few Abel Tasman visitors explore the beautiful Torrent River. Here's your chance to journey down its staggeringly beautiful granite-lined canyon, via a fun-filled combination of swimming, sliding, abseiling and big leaps into jewel-like pools.

Golden Bay

Motueka to Takaka

From Motueka, SH60 takes a stomach-churning meander over Takaka Hill. On the way it passes dramatic lookouts over Tasman Bay and Abel Tasman National Park before swooping down towards Takaka and Collingwood. The best way to tackle this region is with your own wheels.

Takaka Hill (791m) butts in between Tasman Bay and Golden Bay. Just below the summit (literally) are the Ngarua Caves (SH60; adult/child $15/7; ☺ 45min tours hourly 10am-4pm Sep-May, open Sat & Sun only Jun-Aug), a rock-solid attraction karst in stone, where you can see myriad subterranean delights including moa bones. Access is restricted to tours – you can't go solo spelunking.

Also just before the summit is the turn-off to Canaan Downs Scenic Reserve, reached at the end of an 11km gravel road. This area stars in both the *Lord of the Rings* and *Hobbit* movies, but Harwood's Hole is the most famous feature here. It's one of the largest *tomo* (caves) in the country at 357m deep and 70m wide, with a 176m vertical drop. It's a 30-minute walk from the car park. Allow us to state the obvious: the cave is off-limits to all but the most experienced cavers. Mountain bikers with intermediate-level skills can venture along a couple of new loop tracks, or head all the way down to Takaka via the famous Rameka Track. There's a basic DOC Campsite (per person $6) here too.

Close to the zenith also lies the Takaka Hill Walkway, a three-hour loop walk through marble karst rock formations, native forest and farmland, and Harwood Lookout, affording fine views down the Takaka River Valley to Takaka and Golden Bay. For more walks on the sunny side of the hill, see DOC's brochure *Walks in Golden Bay*.

Takaka & Around

Boasting NZ's highest concentration of yoga pants, dreadlocks and alternative life-stylers, Takaka (population 1240) is nevertheless a largely down-to-earth town and the last 'big' centre before the road west ends at Farewell Spit. You'll find most things you need here, and a few things you don't, but we all have an unworn tie-dye tanktop in our wardrobe, don't we?

◉ Sights & Activities

Many of Takaka's sights can readily be reached via bicycle, with hire and maps available from the time-warped Quiet Revolution Cycle Shop (☑ 03-525 9555; www.quiet-revolution.co.nz; 11 Commercial St; bike hire per day $25-65) on the main street.

Te Waikoropupu Springs   SPRING

'Pupu Springs' are the largest freshwater springs in Australasia and reputedly the clearest in the world. About 14,000 litres of water per second surges from underground vents, creating 'dancing sands' and swirling curious plantlife throughout colourful pools, which are viewed from a network of tracks and are off-limits for swimming. From Takaka, head 4km northwest on SH60 and follow the signs inland for 3km from Waitapu Bridge.

Grove Scenic Reserve   LOOKOUT

Around 10 minutes' drive from Takaka (signposted down Clifton Rd) you will find this crazy limestone maze punctuated by gnarled old rata trees. The walkway takes around 10 minutes and passes an impressive lookout.

Rawhiti Cave   CAVE

(www.doc.govt.nz) The ultimate in geological eye candy around these parts are the phytokarst features of Rawhiti Cave, 15 minutes' drive from Takaka (reached via Motupipi, turning right into Glenview Rd, then left into Packard Rd and following the signs). The rugged two-hour-return walk (steep in places; dangerous in the wet) may well leave you speechless (although we managed 'monster', 'fangs', and even 'Sarlacc').

Golden Bay Museum & Gallery   MUSEUM

(Commercial St; admission by donation; ☺ 10am-4pm) This small museum's standout exhibits include a diorama depicting Abel Tasman's 1642 landing, and some dubious human taxidermy. Ask about the albatross. The adjoining gallery offers satisfying browsing of local and national knick-knackery and quite possibly the purchase of a quality souvenir. For additional arty ambling, look for the free *Artists in Golden Bay* and *Arts Trail* pamphlets.

Pupu Hydro Walkway   WALKING

This enjoyable two-hour circuit passes through beech forest, past engineering and gold-mining relics to the restored (and operational) Pupu Hydro Powerhouse, built in 1929. To get here, take the 4km gravel road signposted from Pupu Springs Rd.

Adventure Flights Golden Bay SCENIC FLIGHTS
(☑03-525 6167, 0800 150 338; www.adventure-flightsgoldenbay.co.nz; Takaka Airfield) Scenic and charter flights around Golden Bay and surrounds; from $40.

Golden Bay Air SCENIC FLIGHTS
(☑03-525 8725, 0800 588 885; www.goldenbayair.co.nz; Takaka Airfield) Scenic and charter flights around Golden Bay and surrounds; from $49.

🛏 Sleeping

Kiwiana HOSTEL $
(☑03-525 7676, 0800 805 494; www.kiwianabackpackers.co.nz; 73 Motupipi St; tent sites per person $18, dm/s/d $28/45/66; @ 🛜) Beyond the welcoming garden is a cute cottage where rooms are named after classic Kiwiana (the jandal, Buzzy Bee...). The garage has been converted into a convivial lounge, with wood-fired stove, table tennis, pool table, music, books and games; free bikes for guest use.

Annie's Nirvana Lodge HOSTEL $
(☑03-525 8766; www.nirvanalodge.co.nz; 25 Motupipi St; dm $28, d $60-66; @ 🛜) Tidy, homely YHA hostel: dorms in the main house, and four doubles at the bottom of the secluded courtyard garden, which is filled with timber furniture hewn by the friendly owner. Fluffy the cat is hanging in there and is a hirsute hit with guests.

Golden Bay Holiday Park HOLIDAY PARK $
(☑03-525 9742; www.goldenbayholidaypark.co.nz; Tukurua Rd; unpowered/powered sites $41/45, cabins d/tr $70/105; @ 🛜) Eighteen kilometres north of Takaka with an unpopulated beach right out front, this gem of a park has acres of grass, graceful shade trees and hedgerows, easily atoning for tight communal facilities. There are tidy, family-friendly cabins for budget travellers, and luxury beach houses sleeping up to four ($270 to $350).

Golden Bay Motel MOTEL $$
(☑03-525 9428, 0800 401 212; www.goldenbaymotel.co.nz; 132 Commercial St; d $100-145; 🛜) It's golden, alright: check out the paint job. Clean, spacious, self-contained units with decent older-style fixtures and decent older-style hosts. The rear patios overlook a lush green garden.

Adrift COTTAGES $$$
(☑03-525 8353; www.adrift.co.nz; Tukurua Rd; d $250-500; @ 🛜) 🌀 Adrift on a heavenly bed of beachside bliss is what you'll be in one of these five cottages dotted within beautifully landscaped grounds, right on the beach. Tuck into your breakfast hamper, then self-cater in the fully equipped kitchen, dine on the sunny deck, or soak in the spa bath.

✗ Eating & Drinking

Top Shop DAIRY $
(9 Willow St; snacks $2-9; ⊙6am-7pm Mon-Fri, 7.30am-6pm Sat & Sun) A dairy, tearoom and takeaway at the entrance to town with high-rating pies.

Fresh Choice SUPERMARKET $
(13 Willow St; ⊙8am-7pm) Stock up while you can.

Dangerous Kitchen CAFE $$
(46a Commercial St; meals $14-28; ⊙9am-late Mon-Sat; 🍴) 🌀 Dedicated to Frank Zappa ('In the kitchen of danger, you can feel like a stranger'), DK serves largely healthy, good-value fare such as felafel, pizza, spicy-bean burritos, fresh pasta, great baking and juices. Mellow and laid-back, with a sun-trap courtyard out back and people-watching out front.

⭐**Mussel Inn** PUB $$
(www.mussellinn.co.nz; 1259 SH60, Onekaka; all-day menu $5-18, dinner $23-30; ⊙11am-late, closed Jul-Aug) You will find one of NZ's most beloved brewery-taverns halfway between Takaka and Collingwood. The Mussel Inn is rustic NZ at its most genuine, complete with creaking timbers, a rambling beer garden with a brazier, live music, and hearty, home-made food. Sup a handle or two of 'Captain Cooker', a brown beer brewed naturally with manuka, or the delicious 'Bitter Ass'.

Brigand CAFE, BAR $$
(www.brigand.co.nz; 90 Commercial St; meals $16-35; ⊙11am-late Mon-Sat) Beyond the gates you'll find good food such as sandwiches, chowder and meaty mains served in a relaxed atmosphere. A garden bar and great baking feature, too. Equally important, the Brigand is a mainstay of the local entertainment scene with regular live music, and popular shake-a-leg open mike Thursdays.

Roots Bar BAR
(www.rootsbar.co.nz; 1 Commercial St; ⊙4.30pm-late Wed-Sun; 🛜) This popular dance-music-focused joint has decent beer on tap, a quality sound system, lively evenings, and a garden bar with the odd tree root and bedecked Bay resident lending colour.

Paul's Coffee Cart   CAFE
(Takaka Library car park; ⊙8am-1pm Mon-Sat) The dude with the tunes does the best brew in town from his cart tucked into the library car park.

☆ Entertainment

Village Theatre   CINEMA
(www.villagetheatre.org.nz; 32 Commercial St; adult/child $12.50/7) Demonstrating, yet again, provincial NZ's appetite for quality movies.

❶ Information

DOC Office (☑03-525 8026; www.doc.govt.nz; 62 Commercial St; ⊙1-3pm Mon-Fri) Information on Abel Tasman and Kahurangi National Parks, the Heaphy Track, Farewell Spit and Cobb Valley. Sells hut passes.

Golden Bay Visitor Centre (☑03-525 9136; www.goldenbaynz.co.nz; Willow St; ⊙10am-4pm Mon-Fri, to 2pm Sat & Sun) A friendly little centre with all the necessary information, including the indispensible official tourist map. Bookings and DOC passes.

❶ Getting There & Around

Golden Bay Air (☑0800 588 885, 03-525 8725; www.goldenbayair.co.nz) Flies at least once and up to four times daily between Wellington and Takaka.

Golden Bay Coachlines (☑03-525 8352; www.gbcoachlines.co.nz) Departs from Takaka on Golden Bay and runs through to Collingwood (25 minutes), the Heaphy Track (one hour), Totaranui (one hour), and over the hill to Motueka (1¼ hours) and Nelson (2¼ hours).

Pohara

POP 350

About 10km northeast of Takaka is pint-sized Pohara, a beachy village with a population that quadruples over summer. It has more flash holiday homes than other parts of Golden Bay, but an agreeable air persists nonetheless, aided by decent food and lodging, and a beach that at low tide is as big as Heathrow's runway. Look out for Golden Bay Blokarts (778 Abel Tasman Dr).

Pohara lies close to the northern gateway of Abel Tasman National Park. The largely unsealed road into the park passes Tarakohe Harbour (Pohara's working port), followed by Ligar Bay. It's worth climbing to the Abel Tasman lookout as you pass by.

The next settlement along is Tata Beach, where Golden Bay Kayaks (☑03-525 9095;

www.goldenbaykayaks.co.nz; half-day guided tours adult/child $85/35, freedom hire half-/full day $90/110) offers freedom rental of kayaks and stand-up paddle boards, as well as guided trips (including multiday) into Abel Tasman National Park.

Signposted from the Totaranui Rd at Wainui Bay is a leafy walk to the best cascade in the bay: Wainui Falls. It's a one-hour return trip, but you could easily take longer by dipping a toe or two in the river.

🛌 Sleeping & Eating

Pohara Beach Top 10 Holiday Park   HOLIDAY PARK $
(☑03-525 9500, 0800 764 272; www.poharabeach.com; 809 Abel Tasman Dr; campsites from $20, cabins & units $61-164; @ 🛜) Wow, what a big 'un! On a long grassy strip between the dunes and the main road, this place has a primo location – but in summer it can feel more like a suburb than the seaside. Beaut cabins abound. General store and takeaway on site.

Sans Souci Inn   LODGE, RESTAURANT $$
(☑03-525 8663; www.sanssouciinn.co.nz; 11 Richmond Rd; s/d $90/115, self-contained unit from $160, mains $32-35; ⊙closed Jul–mid-Sep; 🛜) 🍴 Sans Souci means 'no worries' in French, and this will be your mantra too after staying in one of the seven Mediterranean-flavoured, mud-brick rooms. Guests share a plant-filled, mosaic bathroom that has composting toilets, and an airy lounge and kitchen opening out onto the semi-tropical courtyard. Dinner in the on-site restaurant (bookings essential) is highly recommended; breakfast by request.

Ratanui   LODGE $$
(☑03-525 7998; www.ratanuilodge.com; 818 Abel Tasman Dr; d $155-269; @ 🛜 🏊) This boutique lodge is a contender for NZ's most romantic, with Victorian grandeur inside, and colourful cottage garden out the front. In addition to elegant rooms, there are myriad sensual stimulators such as swimming pool, massage service, cocktails and a candelabra-lit restaurant (open to the public; bookings required). Free bikes, too.

Penguin Café & Bar   PUB $$
(www.penguincafe.co.nz; 818 Abel Tasman Dr; lunch $13-22, dinner $20-33; ⊙10am-late Nov-Apr, 4pm-late Mon-Wed & 11am-late Thu-Sun May-Oct) A popular locals' hang-out, this well-run spot sports a large garden suited to sundowners and thirst-quenchers on sunny days. There's an open fire inside for the odd inclement

DON'T MISS

FAREWELL SPIT

Bleak, exposed and positively sci-fi, Farewell Spit is a wetland of international importance and a renowned bird sanctuary – the summer home of thousands of migratory waders, notably the godwit (which flies all the way from the Arctic tundra), Caspian terns and Australasian gannets. The 35km beach features colossal, crescent-shaped dunes, from where panoramic views extend across Golden Bay and a vast low-tide salt marsh. Walkers can explore the first 4km of the spit via a network of tracks (see DOC's *Farewell Spit* brochure), but beyond that point access is via tours, scheduled according to tide.

The human hub of the spit is the visitor centre-cum-cafe where there's plenty of parking. It's a convenient spot to write a postcard over a coffee, especially on an inclement day.

Farewell Spit Eco Tours (📞03-524 8257, 0800 808 257; www.farewellspit.com; Tasman St, Collingwood; tours $120-155) Operating for nearly 70 years, Paddy and his expert guides run tours ranging from two to 6½ hours, departing from Collingwood, taking in the spit, lighthouse, and up to 20 species of bird which may include gannets and godwits. Expect ripping yarns aplenty.

Farewell Spit Nature Experience (📞03-524 8992, 0800 250 500; www.farewellspit-tours.com; Pakawau; tours $120-145) This air-conditioned operator runs a four-hour tour departing from Farewell Spit Visitor Centre, and a six-hour option leaving from the Old School Cafe, Pakawau.

day. Chow down on belly-filling bar snacks, and look out for local seafood specials come dinner time.

🛈 Getting There & Away

Golden Bay Coachlines (📞03-525 8352; www.gbcoachlines.co.nz) Runs daily from Takaka to Pohara (15 minutes) on the way to Totaranui.

Collingwood & Around

Far-flung Collingwood (population 250) is the last town in this part of the country, and has a real end-of-the-line vibe. It's busy in summer, though for most people it's simply a launch pad for the Heaphy Track or trips to Farewell Spit.

The **Collingwood Museum** (Tasman St; admission by donation; ⊙10am-4pm) fills a tiny, unstaffed corridor with a quirky collection of saddlery, Maori artefacts, moa bones, shells and old typewriters, while the **Aorere Centre** next door houses multimedia presentations, including the works of the wonderful pioneer photographer, Fred Tyree.

No Collingwood visit would be complete without visiting **Rosy Glow** (54 Beach Rd; chocolates $3-5; ⊙10am-5pm Sat-Thu). Chocoholics: this is your cue. Don't miss it!

A foray to Farewell Spit is essential. From there, follow the signs to **Whariariki Beach** (6km unsealed road, then a 20-minute walk through Puponga Farm Park). It's a wild introduction to the West Coast, with mighty dune formations, looming rock islets just offshore and a seal colony at its eastern end. As inviting as a swim here may seem, be warned that there are strong undertows.

Befitting a frontier, this is the place to saddle up: head to **Cape Farewell Horse Treks** (📞03-524 8031; www.horsetreksnz.com; McGowan St, Puponga; ⊙treks from $75). Treks in this wind-blown country range from 1½ hours (to Pillar Point) to three hours (to Whariariki Beach), with longer (including overnight) trips by arrangement.

On the road to Whariariki Beach you'll pass Whariariki Beach Holiday Park (p420), a pretty, young campground with a pleasant communal building.

🛏 Sleeping & Eating

There's little in the way of refreshment round these parts, so keep some cheese and crackers up your sleeve.

★ **Innlet Backpackers & Cottages** HOSTEL $ (📞027 891 7728, 03-524 8040; www.theinnlet.co.nz; Collingwood-Puponga Rd, Pakawau; campsites from $23, dm/d $31/73, cabins from $83; @ 🖥) 🐾 This absolute charmer is 10km from Collingwood on the way to Farewell Spit. The main house has elegant backpacker rooms, and there are various campsites and self-contained options, including a cottage that sleeps six. Explore the local area on a bike or kayak, or venture out for a bushwalk on the property.

Somerset House HOSTEL **$**
(☏03-524 8624; www.backpackerscollingwood.
co.nz; 10 Gibbs Rd, Collingwood; dm/s/d incl
breakfast $30/46/72; ☺closed Jun-Sep; @☏) A
small, low-key hostel in a bright, historic
building on a hill with views from the deck.
Get tramping advice from the knowledgeable owners, who offer track transport, free
bikes and kayaks, and freshly baked bread
for breakfast.

Wharariki Beach Holiday Park HOLIDAY PARK **$**
(☏03-524 8507; www.whararikibeachholidaypark.
co.nz; campsites from $18, dm $25) Right next to
the Wharariki Beach track trailhead – perfectly located for those who want a sunset
walk – this simple campsite offers basic facilities in a pretty setting. There are horses
over the fence, and fowl rambling through
the grounds – avoid this place if peacock poo
is an issue for you.

Old School Cafe CAFE **$$**
(1115 Collingwood-Puponga Rd, Pakawau; mains
$14-31; ☺4pm-late Thu-Fri, 11am-late Sat & Sun)
These folks get an A for effort by provid-
ing honest food to an unpredictable flow of
passing trade. What it lacks in imagination
(steak, pizza and even a shrimp cocktail), it
more than makes up for with arty ambience,
a garden bar and a welcoming disposition.

❶ Getting There & Away

Golden Bay Coachlines (☏03-525 8352; www.
goldenbaycoachlines.co.nz) Runs twice daily
from Takaka to Collingwood (25 minutes).

Kahurangi National Park

Kahurangi – 'blue skies' in one of several
translations – is the second-largest of NZ's
national parks, and also one of its most
diverse. Its most eye-catching features are
geological, ranging from windswept beach-
es and sea cliffs, to earthquake-shattered
slopes and moraine-dammed lakes, and the
smooth, strange karst forms of the interior
tableland.

Around 85% of the 4520-sq-km park is
forested, with beech prevalent, along with
rimu and other podocarps. In all, more than
50% of all NZ's plant species can be found
in the park, including more than 80% of its
alpine plant species. Among the park's 60
birds species are great spotted kiwi, kea,
kaka and whio (blue duck). There are creepy
cave weta, weird beetles and a huge, leggy
spider, but there's also a majestic and an-
cient snail known as Powelliphanta – some-
thing of a (slow) flag bearer for the park's
animal kingdom. If you like a field trip filled
with plenty that's new and strange, Ka-
hurangi National Park will certainly satisfy.

The best-known walk in Kahurangi is the
Heaphy Track. The more challenging **Wan-
gapeka** and remote **Leslie-Karamea** are
less frequented, but these form just part of
a 650km network of tracks. Excellent full-
day and overnight walks can be had in the
Cobb Valley and **Mt Arthur/Tablelands**.
See www.doc.govt.nz for detailed informa-
tion on all Kahurangi tracks.

Heaphy Track

The Heaphy Track is one of the most popular
tracks in the country. A Great Walk in every
sense, it traverses diverse terrain – dense
native forest, the mystical Gouland Downs,
secluded river valleys, and beaches dusted in
salt-spray and fringed by nikau palms.

Although quite long, the Heaphy is well cut
and benched, making it easier than any other
extended tramp found in Kahurangi National
Park. That said, it may still be found arduous,
particularly in unfavourable weather.

By walking from east to west, most of the
climbing is done on the first day, and the
scenic beach walk is saved for the end, a fit-
ting and invigorating grand finale.

The track is open to mountain bikers
from May to September. Factoring in dis-
tance, remoteness and the possibility of bad
weather, this epic journey is only suited to
well-equipped cyclists with advanced riding
skills. A good port of call for more infor-
mation is the Quiet Revolution Cycle Shop
(p416) in Takaka.

A strong tramper could walk the Heaphy
in three days, but most people take four or
five days. For a detailed track description,
see DOC's *Heaphy Track* brochure. Estimat-
ed walking times:

ROUTE	DURATION (HR)
Brown Hut to Perry Saddle Hut	5
Perry Saddle Hut to Gouland Downs Hut	2
Gouland Downs Hut to Saxon Hut	1½
Saxon Hut to James Mackay Hut	3
James Mackay Hut to Lewis Hut	3½
Lewis Hut to Heaphy Hut	2½
Heaphy Hut to Kohaihai River	5

Bookings & Transport

Seven designated **Great Walk huts** ($32) lie along the track, which have bunks and a kitchen area, heating, flush toilets and washbasins with cold water. Most but not all have gas rings; a couple have lighting. There are also nine **Great Walk campsites** ($14), plus the beachside **Kohaihai Campsite** (www.doc.govt.nz; $6) at the West Coast trailhead. The two day shelters are just that; overnight stays are not permitted.

As the Heaphy is a Great Walk, all huts and campsites must be booked in advance year-round. Bookings can be made online through **Great Walks Bookings** (☑0800 694 732; www.greatwalks.co.nz) or at DOC visitor centres, nationwide. In person, the best spot for detailed Heaphy Track information and bookings is the DOC counter at the Nelson i-SITE (p406). Closer to the Golden Bay end of the track, hut tickets, bookings and other track information can be obtained from the DOC office (p418) or Visitor Centre (p418) in Takaka. See also www.heaphytrack.com, and DOC's *Heaphy Track* brochure.

The two road ends of the Heaphy Track are an almost unfathomable distance apart: 463km to be precise. From Takaka, you can get to the Heaphy Track (via Collingwood) with **Golden Bay Coachlines** (☑03-525 8352; www.gbcoachlines.co.nz; $33; ☺one hour. **Heaphy Bus** (☑0272 221 872, 0800 128 735; www.theheaphybus.co.nz) offers a round-trip shuttle service: drop off and pick up from Kohaihai ($110), and other on-demand local track transport. **Heaphy Track Help** (☑03-525 9576; www.heaphytrackhelp.co.nz) offers car relocations ($200 to $300, depending on the direction and time), food drops, shuttles and advice.

The Kohaihai trailhead is 15km from the small town of Karamea. **Karamea Express** (☑03-782 6757; info@karamea-express.co.nz) departs from the shelter at 1pm and 2pm for Karamea from October to the end of April ($15).

Flights between Karamea and Takaka are offered by **Adventure Flights Golden Bay** (☑03-525 6167, 0800 150 338; www.adventureflightsgoldenbay.co.nz; Takaka Airfield), from $185 per person (up to four people); **Golden Bay Air** (☑0800 588 885; www.goldenbayair.co.nz) from $169 per person; and **Helicopter Charter Karamea** (☑03-782 6111; www.karameahelicharter.co.nz), which will take up to three people for $750.

Tours

Bush & Beyond GUIDED HIKE
(☑03-528 9054; www.bushandbeyond.co.nz) Offers various tramping trips, ranging from Mt Arthur or Cobb Valley day walks ($220) through to a guided six-day Heaphy Track package ($1749).

Kahurangi Guided Walks GUIDED HIKE
(☑03-525 7177; www.kahurangiwalks.co.nz) Small-group adventures such as five-day Heaphy tramps ($1500) and various one-day trips, including Abel Tasman and the Cobb (from $170).

Nelson Lakes National Park

Nelson Lakes National Park surrounds two lakes – Rotoiti and Rotoroa – fringed by sweet-smelling beech forest with a backdrop of greywacke mountains. Located at the northern end of the Southern Alps, and with a dramatic glacier-carved landscape, it's an awe-inspiring place to get up on high.

Part of the park, east of Lake Rotoiti, is classed as a 'mainland island' where a conservation scheme aims to eradicate introduced pests (possums, stoats) and regenerate native flora and fauna. It offers excellent tramping, including short walks, lake scenery and one or two sandflies... The park is flush with bird life, and is famous for brown-trout fishing.

🏃 Activities

Many spectacular walks allow you to appreciate this rugged landscape, but before you tackle them, stop by the DOC Visitor Centre (p422) for maps, track/weather updates and to pay your hut or camping fees.

The five-hour **Mt Robert Circuit Track** starts south of St Arnaud and circumnavigates the mountain. The optional side trip along Robert Ridge offers staggering views into the heart of the national park. Alternatively, the **St Arnaud Range Track** (five hours return), on the east side of the lake, climbs steadily to the ridgeline adjacent to Parachute Rocks. Both tracks are strenuous, but reward with jaw-dropping vistas of glaciated valleys, arête peaks and Lake Rotoiti. Only attempt these tramps in fine weather. At other times they are both pointless (no views) and dangerous.

There are also plenty of shorter (and flatter) walks from Lake Rotoiti's Kerr Bay and the road end at Lake Rotoroa. These and the longer day tramps are described in DOC's *Walks in Nelson Lakes National Park* pamphlet ($2).

The fit and well-equipped can embark upon longer hikes such as the Lake Angelus Track. This magnificent two-to-three-day tramp follows Robert Ridge to Lake Angelus, where you can stay at the fine Angelus Hut (adult/child $20/10) for a night or two before returning to St Arnaud via one of three routes. Pick up or download DOC's *Angelus Hut Tracks & Routes* pamphlet ($2) for more details.

🛏 Sleeping & Eating

★ DOC Campsites   CAMPSITE $
(☑ 03-521 1806; www.doc.govt.nz) Near the Lake Rotoiti shore, the hugely popular Kerr Bay campsite has powered sites, toilets, hot showers, laundry and a kitchen shelter (unpowered/powered $10/15). Three kilometres from St Arnaud, the unpowered West Bay campsite ($6) has the bare necessities and is open in summer only. Bookings are essential over the Christmas and Easter holidays.

Travers-Sabine Lodge   HOSTEL $
(☑ 03-521 1887; www.nelsonlakes.co.nz; Main Rd; dm/d $26/62; @🖥) This modern hostel is a great base for outdoor adventure, being a short walk to Lake Rotoiti, inexpensive, clean and comfortable. It also has particularly cheerful technicolour linen in the dorms, doubles and a family room. The owners are experienced adventurers themselves, so tips come as standard; tramping equipment available for hire.

Nelson Lakes Motels   MOTEL $$
(☑ 03-521 1887; www.nelsonlakes.co.nz; Main Rd; d $120-130; @🖥) These log cabins and newer board-and-batten units offer all the creature comforts, including kitchenettes and Sky TV. Bigger units sleep up to six.

Alpine Lodge   LODGE $$
(☑ 03-521 1869; www.alpinelodge.co.nz; Main Rd; d $155-205; @🖥) Trying its darnedest to create an alpine atmosphere, this lodge has a range of accommodation, the pick of which are the split-level doubles with mezzanine bedroom, spa and pine timberwork aplenty. The adjacent backpacker lodge (dorm/double $29/69) is spartan but clean and warm, and hires mountain bikes. The in-house res-

taurant is snug, with mountain views and good food (meals $10 to $29). Long may the Sunday-night barbecue continue.

Tophouse Historic
Guesthouse   HISTORIC HOTEL $$
(☑ 03-521 1848, 0800 544 545; www.tophouse. co.nz; 68 Tophouse Rd; s/d incl breakfast $115/175) Nine kilometres from St Arnaud, this 1887 hotel retells fireside tales, tall and true. Refreshments inlude Devonshire teas, soup and sandwiches (lunch $10 to $18), and dinner by arrangement, plus there's NZ's smallest bar and a garden with mountain views. Bed and breakfast is offered in old-fashioned rooms within the hotel, and chalets out the back sleep up to four (doubles $110, per extra person $20).

St Arnaud Alpine
Village Store   SUPERMARKET, TAKEAWAY
(🕗 8am-6pm, takeaways 4.30-7.30pm Fri & Sat, daily Dec-Feb) The settlement's only general store sells groceries, petrol, beer and possum-wool socks. Mountain-bike hire per half-/full day is $20/40. It has tramping food, sandwiches and pies, with fish and chips cranking up on weekends and daily in peak season ($6 to $10).

ℹ Information

DOC Visitor Centre (☑ 03-521 1806; www. doc.govt.nz; View Rd; 🕗 8am-4.30pm, to 5pm in summer) Happily proffers park information (weather, activities) and hut passes, plus displays on park ecology and history.

ℹ Getting There & Around

Nelson Lakes Shuttles (☑ 03-521 1900, 021 490 095; www.nelsonlakesshuttles.co.nz) runs thrice-weekly scheduled services between Nelson and the national park from December to April (Monday, Wednesday and Friday; $45), and on-demand the rest of the year. It will also collect/drop off at Kawatiri Junction on SH63, to meet other bus services heading between Nelson and the West Coast, and offer services from St Arnaud through to Picton and Blenheim. Try also Trek Express (☑ 027 222 1872, 0800 128 735; www.trekexpress.co.nz), which regularly plies this route.

Rotoiti Water Taxis (☑ 021 702 278; www. rotoitiwatertaxis.co.nz) runs to/from Kerr Bay and West Bay to Lakehead Jetty ($100, up to four people). Kayaks, canoes and rowboats can also be hired from $40 per half-day; fishing trips and scenic lake cruises by arrangement.

The West Coast

Includes ➡

Reefton...................... 426

Westport & Around 428

Karamea & Around 431

The Great
Coast Road................ 433

Punakaiki & Paparoa
National Park............ 434

Greymouth................ 436

Hokitika...................... 440

Franz Josef Glacier 446

Fox Glacier 450

Haast Region 453

Haast.......................... 454

Haast Pass Highway .. 455

Best Short Walks

➡ Scotts Beach (p432)

➡ Charming Creek Walkway
(p431)

➡ Denniston Plateau (p428)

➡ Lake Matheson (p452)

Best Places to Stay

➡ Old Slaughterhouse (p431)

➡ Beaconstone Eco Lodge
(p433)

➡ Theatre Royal Hotel (p440)

➡ Okarito Campground
(p445)

Why Go?

Hemmed in by the wild Tasman Sea and the Southern Alps, the West Coast is like nowhere else in New Zealand.

The far extremities of the coast have a remote, end-of-the-road feel, from sleepy Karamea surrounded by farms butting up against Kahurangi National Park, to the southern end of State Hwy 6, gateway to New Zealand's World Heritage areas. In between is an alluring combination of wild coastline, rich wilderness, and history in spades.

Built on the wavering fortunes of gold, coal and timber, the stories of Coast settlers are hair-raising. A hardy and individual breed, they make up less than 1% of NZ's population, scattered around almost 9% of its land area.

Travellers tend to tick off the 'must see' sights of Punakaiki Rocks, and Franz Josef and Fox Glaciers. Deviate from the trail even a short way, however, and be awed by the spectacles that await you alone.

When to Go

➡ During summer the coast road gets relatively busy, particularly with campervan traffic.

➡ May to September can be warm and clear, with fewer crowds and cheaper accommodation.

➡ The West Coast has serious rainfall (around 5m annually) but still sees as much sunshine as Christchurch.

➡ That said, there's little point trying to dodge the drops on a visit to the Coast – just bring a raincoat and keep your fingers crossed.

➡ No matter what time of year, backcountry trampers should check conditions with local Department of Conservation (DOC) office staff. Rivers can prove seriously treacherous.

The West Coast Highlights

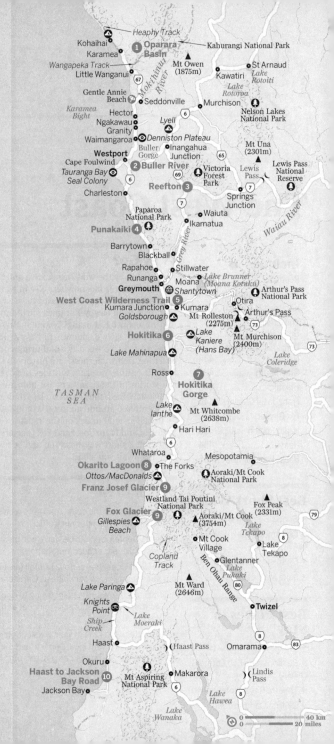

❶ Exploring the limestone forms and forest of the **Oparara Basin** (p432)

❷ Getting wet 'n' wild on the mighty **Buller River** (p425)

❸ Delving into the golden past around **Reefton** (p426)

❹ Marvelling at nature's beautiful fury at **Punakaiki's** (p434) Pancake Rocks

❺ Having a wheely good time on the **West Coast Wilderness Trail** (p439)

❻ Hunting out authentic local greenstone in the galleries of **Hokitika** (p440)

❼ Admiring the turquoise waters of **Hokitika Gorge** (p440)

❽ Kayaking through the bird-filled channels of **Okarito Lagoon** (p444)

❾ Flying high into the Southern Alps via **Franz Josef** (p446) and **Fox Glaciers** (p450)

❿ Reaching the end of the line on the scenic and historical highway from **Haast** to **Jackson Bay** (p454)

Kohaihai
Heaphy Track
Karamea
❶ **Oparara Basin**
Wangapeka Track — Kahurangi National Park
Little Wanganui
(67)
Mt Owen (1875m)
St Arnaud
Kawatiri
Lake Rotoiti
Gentle Annie Beach
Seddonville
Karamea Bight
Hector
Murchison
Lake Rotoroa
Ngakawau
(6)
Nelson Lakes National Park
Granity
Lyell
Waimangaroa
Denniston Plateau
Mt Una (2301m)
Buller Inangahua
Westport *Gorge* Junction
Cape Foulwind
(65)
Lewis Pass
Tauranga Bay ❷ **Buller River**
Victoria Forest Park
Lewis Pass National Reserve
Seal Colony
(69)
Lewis Pass
(6)
Reefton ❸
Charleston
(7)
Springs Junction
Paparoa National Park
Waiuta
Waiau River
Punakaiki ❹
Ikamatua
Barrytown
Blackball
Grey River
Rapahoe
Stillwater
Runanga
Moana
Lake Brunner
Arthur's Pass National Park
Greymouth Shantytown
(Moana Kotuku)
West Coast Wilderness Trail ❺
Otira
Kumara Junction Kumara
Arthur's Pass
Goldsborough
Mt Rolleston (2275m)
(73)
Hokitika ❻
Lake Kaniere (Hans Bay)
Mt Murchison (2400m)
Lake Coleridge
Lake Mahinapua
(73)
Ross
❼ **Hokitika Gorge**
TASMAN SEA
Lake Ianthe
Mt Whitcombe (2638m)
Hari Hari
Whataroa
(6)
Mesopotamia
Okarito Lagoon ❽ The Forks
Ottos/MacDonalds
Aoraki/Mt Cook National Park
Franz Josef Glacier ❾
Westland Tai Poutini National Park
Fox Peak (2331m)
Fox Glacier ❾
Aoraki/Mt Cook (3754m)
(79)
Gillespies Beach
Lake Tekapo
Mt Cook Village
Lake Tekapo
Copland Track
Glentanner
(8)
Lake Pukaki
Lake Paringa
Mt Ward (2646m)
(80)
Knights Point
Lake Moeraki
Twizel
Ship Creek
(8)
(83)
Haast
Omarama
(Haast Pass)
Okuru
Lindis Pass
Haast to Jackson Bay Road ❿
Mt Aspiring National Park
Makarora
Jackson Bay
(6)
Lake Hawea
(8)
Lake Wanaka

0 ——— 40 km
0 ——— 20 miles

ⓘ Getting There & Around

Air New Zealand (☑ 0800 737 000; www.airnz. co.nz) flies between Westport and Wellington, and Hokitika and Christchurch.

Coaches and shuttle transport – while not very frequent – are reliable, and reach pretty much everywhere you might like to go including Nelson, Christchurch and Queenstown. Major and extensive networks are operated by **Atomic Travel** (☑ 03-349 0697, 0508 108 359; www.atomic-travel.co.nz), **InterCity** (☑ 03-365 1113; www. intercity.co.nz) and **Naked Bus** (www.nakedbus. com), while **West Coast Shuttle** (☑ 03-768 0028, 0274 927 000; www.westcoastshuttle.co.nz) runs a daily service between Greymouth and Christchurch. Local shuttle operators go here and there.

The TranzAlpine (p436), one of the world's great train journeys, links Greymouth and Christchurch.

BULLER REGION

Coming from the east, Murchison is the gateway to the northern West Coast. From there, State Hwy 6 snakes through Buller Gorge, a journey that could easily take a day or two by the time you've taken a rafting or jetboating trip, explored Lyell, and stopped at other interesting sites along the way.

Your big decision is which way to head when you reach the forks at Inangahua. Continuing west along SH6 through the Lower Buller Gorge will lead you to Westport, the gateway to the far north. Head south from Inangahua on SH69 and you skip Punakaiki but reach Reefton, where you can either head west to the coast at Greymouth, or east over the Lewis Pass to Hanmer Springs. You can also cut directly through to the Lewis Pass via SH65, 10km west of Murchison.

Murchison & Buller Gorge

Murchison (population 490), 125km southwest of Nelson and 95km east of Westport, lies on the 'Four Rivers Plain'. In fact there aren't just four but multitudinous rivers, the mightiest being the Buller, which runs alongside the town. White-water sports and trout fishing are popular here, while the surrounding forested hills dish up adventure for the landlubbers.

⊙ Sights & Activities

Ask at the Murchison **visitor centre** (☑ 03-523 9350; www.nelsonnz.com; 47 Waller St; ⊙ 10am-6pm Oct-May, reduced hours Apr-Sep)

for a copy of the *Murchison District Map*, which features local walks, such as the Skyline, Six Mile and Johnson Creek tracks, plus mountain-bike rides. Staff can also hook you up with trout-fishing guides.

Murchison Museum MUSEUM
(60 Fairfax St; admission by donation; ⊙ 10am-4pm) This museum showcases all sorts of local memorabilia, the most interesting of which relate to the 1929 and 1968 earthquakes.

Wild Rivers Rafting RAFTING
(☑ 050 846 7238; www.wildriversrafting.co.nz; 2hr rafting adult/child $130/85) White-water rafting with Bruce and Marty on the particularly exciting Earthquake Rapids section of the beautiful Buller River (good luck with 'gunslinger' and the 'pop-up toaster'!).

Ultimate Descents RAFTING
(☑ 03-523 9899, 0800 748 377; www.rivers.co.nz; 38 Waller St; 2hr rafting $130, half-day kayaking $125) Offers white-water rafting and kayaking trips on the Buller, including half-day, gentler family excursions (adult/child $115/95). Helirafting trips by arrangement from their new base in Murchison.

Natural Flames Experience ECO TOUR
(☑ 0800 687 244; www.naturalflames.co.nz; adult/child $85/65) An enjoyable, informative half-day 4WD and bushwalking tour through

---

ESSENTIAL WEST COAST

Eat Whitebait, bought from an old-timer's back door at an honest price

Drink The only roast on the coast, Kawatiri Coffee

Read Eleanor Catton's 2013 Man Booker Prize–winning novel, *The Luminaries*, set around Hokitika

Listen to Karamea's laid-back community radio station on 107.5FM; you can even spin your own tunes

Watch *Denniston Incline* on YouTube, then imagine sitting in the wagon on the way down

Festival Go bush-food crazy at Hokitika's Wildfoods Festival (p442)

Go Green At West Coast Wildlife Centre (p446) – fluffy kiwi chicks! Too cute!

Online www.westcoastnz.com; www. buller.co.nz; www.glaciercountry.co.nz

Area code ☑ 03

remote valleys and beech forest to a hot spot amongst the trees and ferns, where natural gas seeping out of the ground has been burning since 1922. Boil a billy on the flames and cook pancakes before returning to civilisation.

Buller Gorge Swingbridge
BRIDGE

(☑0800 285 537; www.bullergorge.co.nz; SH6; bridge crossing adult/child $5/2; ⊗8am-7pm Dec-Apr, 9am-5pm May-Nov) About 14km west of Murchison is NZ's longest swingbridge (110m), across which lie short walks taking in the White Creek Faultline, epicentre of the 1929 earthquake. Coming back, ride the 160m Cometline Flying Fox, either seated (adult/child $30/15) or 'Supaman' ($45, or tandem adult/child $30/15).

Buller Canyon Jet
JETBOATING

(☑03-523 9883; www.bullercanyonjet.co.nz; SH6; adult/child $95/50; ⊗Sep-Apr) Launching from Buller Gorge Swingbridge is one of NZ's most scenic and best-value jetboat trips – 40 minutes of ripping through the beautiful Buller with a good-humoured captain.

🛏 Sleeping & Eating

Murchison has a few cafes, a couple of grocery stores, and a butchery curing notable bacon.

Kiwi Park Motels & Holiday Park
MOTEL, HOLIDAY PARK $

(☑03-523 9248, 0800 228 080; www.kiwipark. co.nz; 170 Fairfax St; unpowered/powered sites from $20/25, cabins $65-85, motels $140-225; @☎) This leafy park on the edge of town has plenty of accommodation options, from a campervan and tent area graced with mature trees, through to basic cabins, and roomy motels nestled amongst the blooms. Cheery hosts and a menagerie of friendly farm animals make this one happy family.

MAORI NZ: THE WEST COAST

For Maori, the river valleys and mountains of the West Coast were the traditional source of highly prized *pounamu* (greenstone), carved into tools, weapons and adornments. View the *pounamu* exhibit at Hokitika Museum (p440) to polish your knowledge of the precious rock before admiring the classy carvings created by the town's artists.

Lazy Cow
HOSTEL $

(☑03-523 9451; www.lazycow.co.nz; 37 Waller St; dm $30, d $74-90; @☎) It's easy to be a lazy cow here, with all the comforts of home including cosy bedrooms and a sunny backyard. Guests are welcomed with free muffins or cake, and there are freshly cooked evening meals available on evenings when the hosts aren't running their popular onsite Cow Shed (⊗6-9pm Thurs-Sat) restaurant.

Commercial Hotel
HOTEL $

(☑03-523 9696; www.commercialhotel.co.nz; cnr Waller & Fairfax Sts; s/d/tr $40/75/100; ⊗8am-8.30pm; @☎) This sunny corner pub with super street-appeal meets required standards in its dining room, and features a bar with a pool table, appealing outdoor tables, and solid pub grub (mains $14 to $29). Down the checkerboard-and-crimson hallway is a series of cheap but charming bedrooms sharing bathrooms and a cupboard-sized kitchen.

Murchison Lodge
B&B $$

(☑03-523 9196, 0800 523 9196; www.murchison-lodge.co.nz; 15 Grey St; s incl breakfast $150-210, d incl breakfast $175-235; ⊗closed May-Aug; ☎) ☞ Surrounded by native trees, this B&B is within a short walk of the Buller River; the owners' friendly dog will probably accompany you. Attractive timber features, quality artwork and charming hosts add to the comfortable feel. Home-reared bacon and eggs for breakfast, plus evening meals by arrangement.

ⓘ Information

There is no ATM in town; the postal agency is on Fairfax St.

The Murchison Visitor Centre (p425) has info on local activities and transport.

ⓘ Getting There & Away

Buses passing through Murchison between the West Coast and Nelson/Picton are **InterCity** (☑03-365 1113; www.intercity.co.nz) and **Naked Bus** (www.nakedbus.com), both of which stop at Beechwoods Cafe on Waller St, as does **Trek Express** (☑0272 221 872, 0800 128 735; www.trekexpress.co.nz), which runs frequently between Nelson and the Wangapeka/Heaphy Tracks during the peak tramping season.

Reefton

POP 1030

For generations, Reefton's claims to fame have been mining and its early adoption of the electricity grid and street lighting.

Hence the tagline, 'the city of light'. Today, however, it's a different story, one which starts – improbably – with the building of the world-class Roller Park, which attracts stunt-lovers from all corners of NZ. To quote a local, 'it's more than we deserve'. We disagree. If this many volunteers and sponsors are prepared to build such an edgy civic amenity in a town that still looks like the set of *Bonanza*, we suggest there's something a little bit special about this crazy little town.

◉ Sights & Activities

With loads of crusty old buildings situated within a 200-metre radius, Reefton is a fascinating town for a stroll. To find out who lived where and why, undertake the short **Heritage Walk** outlined in the *Historic Reefton* leaflet ($1), available from the i-SITE (p428), from where you can also collect the free *Reefton* leaflet detailing other short walks including the **Bottled Lightning Powerhouse Walk** (40 minutes).

Surrounding Reefton is the 2060-sq-km **Victoria Forest Park** (NZ's largest forest park), which sports diverse flora and fauna as well as hidden historic sites such as the old goldfields around Blacks Point. Starting (or ending) at Blacks Point, the enjoyable **Murray Creek Track** takes five hours round trip.

Other tramps in the Forest Park include the three-day **Kirwans** or two-day **Big River Track**, both of which can be traversed on a mountain bike. Pick up the free *Reefton Mountain Biking ('the best riding in history')* leaflet for more information; bikes can be hired from **Reefton Sports Centre** (☑ 03-732 8593; 56 Broadway; bike hire per day $30), where you can also inquire about the legendary trout fishing in the environs.

Blacks Point Museum MUSEUM
(Blacks Point, SH7; adult/child/family $5/3/12; ☉9am-noon & 1-4pm Wed-Fri & Sun, 1-4pm Sat Oct-Apr, plus school holidays during winter) Housed in an old church 2km east of Reefton on the Christchurch road, this museum is crammed with prospecting paraphernalia. Just up the driveway is the still-functional **Golden Fleece Battery** (adult/child $1/free; ☉1-4pm Wed & Sun Oct-Apr), used for crushing gold-flecked quartz. The Blacks Point walks also start from here.

Bearded Mining Company HISTORIC BUILDING
(Broadway; admission by donation; ☉9am-2pm) Looking like a ZZ Top tribute band, the fellas hangin' at this high-street mining hut are champing at the bit to rollick your socks off with tales tall and true. If you're lucky you'll get a cuppa from the billy.

Waiuta HISTORIC SITE
(www.waiuta.org.nz; off SH7) A once-burgeoning gold town abandoned in 1951 after the mineshaft collapsed, remote Waiuta is one of the West Coast's most famous ghost towns, complete with a big old rusty boiler, an overgrown swimming pool, stranded brick chimneys and the odd intact cottage, which face off against mother nature who has sent in the strangleweed. Spread over a square kilometre or so of plateau, surrounded by lowland forest and looking out towards the Southern Alps, Waiuta is a very satisfying place for an amble. To get to there, drive 23km south of Reefton on SH7 to the signposted turn-off from where it's another 17km, the last half of which is unsealed, winding and narrow in places. Ask at local i-SITEs for more information and maps.

☞ Tours

Reefton Gold Mine Tours CULTURAL TOUR
(☑ 027 442 4777, 03-732 8497; www.reeftongold. co.nz) Dig deeper into Reefton on a two-hour heritage tour ($25) taking in town highlights. The Gold Mine Tour (adult/child/family $55/30/120) visits the local mine, where you'll get views over the pit-edge and see plenty of huge machinery in action. Book at the i-SITE or the Broadway Tearooms.

🛏 Sleeping & Eating

It's slim pickings on the food front in Reefton, with self-catering or a night down the pub the safest bets.

Old Nurses Home GUESTHOUSE $
(☑ 03-732 8881; www.reeftonaccommodation. co.nz; 104 Shiel St; s/d $55/80; @ 🖥) This stately old building is warm and comfortable, with noteworthy communal areas including a pretty garden and patio. Bedrooms are clean and airy with comfy beds.

Reefton Motor Camp HOLIDAY PARK $
(☑ 03-732 8477; reeftonmotorcamp@xtra.co.nz; 1 Ross St; sites from $15, cabin d $45) On the Inangahua River and a minute's walk to Broadway, this older style camp sits beside a big green sports field and shady fir trees.

Lantern Court Motels MOTEL $$
(☑ 03-732 8574, 0800 526 837; www.lanterncourtmotel.co.nz; 63 Broadway; old units d $95-120, new units d $145-170; 🖥) This heritage hotel offers great

value, with self-catering options for everyone from singles to family groups, while the well-assimilated motel block next door offers all mod cons with a nod to classical styling.

Broadway Tearooms
BAKERY $

(31 Broadway; snacks $3-8, meals $10-20; ⊘5am-5pm) This joint gets by far the most day-time traffic, being a civilised place for a spot of lunch, and to pick up a fresh loaf or a packet of shortbread. Middle-of-the-road meals range from egg breakfasts to a whitebait lunch. Survey the high street from al fresco tables, or peruse the cute cruet set collection indoors.

Wilson's Hotel
PUB $$

(32 Broadway; mains $13-30; ⊘11am-11pm) A solid town pub pleasing all, from smokin' youth through to soup-slurping pensioners. Meat and three veg dominate the menu, but it's all hearty and homemade. Occasional bands and DJs raise the excitement level to somewhere under fever pitch.

ℹ Information

The **Reefton i-SITE** (☑03-732 8391; www.reefton.co.nz; 67 Broadway; ⊘9am-5pm Mon-Fri, 10am-3pm Sat & Sun) has helpful staff, and a compact re-creation of the Quartzopolis Mine (gold coin entry). There's internet at the library, which doubles as the postal agency.

ℹ Getting There & Away

East West Coaches (☑03-789 6251; www.east-westcoaches.co.nz) stops in Reefton every day except Saturday on the run between Westport (1¼ hours) and Christchurch (3¾ hours).

Westport & Around

POP 5600

The port of Westport made its fortune in coal mining, and coal still makes a considerable contribution to keeping the town stoked up. Beyond some respectable hospitality, the town contains little of prolonged interest, but makes a good base for exploring the fascinating coast north to Karamea, Oparara and the Heaphy Track.

◉ Sights & Activities

Westport is good for a stroll – the i-SITE can direct you to the Millenium Walkway and North Beach Reserve. The most thrilling adventure in the area is cave rafting with Norwest Adventures (p429), although mountain biking is gaining momentum as a popular pastime among local and visiting backcountry adventurers. The folk at Habitat Sports (p430) offer bike hire, maps and advice.

Coaltown Museum
MUSEUM

(www.coaltown.co.nz; 123 Palmerston St; adult/child $15/7; ⊘9am-5pm Mon-Fri, 10am-4pm Sat & Sun) Re-opened in 2013, the new-look Coaltown Museum retells the same old yarns of hard times, but this time with well-scripted display panels alongside an excellent selection of photographs, surrounding relics of local industries and general pioneer ephemera. The Denniston displays are a highlight.

Denniston Plateau
HISTORIC SITE

(www.doc.govt.nz) Nine kilometres inland and 600m above sea level, Denniston was once NZ's largest coal producer, with 1500 residents in 1911. By 1981 there were eight. Its claim to fame was the fantastically steep Denniston Incline, an engineering marvel enabling the cartage of coal wagons down a 45-degree hillside.

Denniston is fascinating, its ghostly remains brought to life with excellent interpretive displays. The *Denniston Rose Walking Tour* brochure ($2 from DOC and Westport Library; also available as an app) may lead keen readers to the local bookshop to buy Jenny Pattrick's evocative novels set in these parts. The Denniston Mine Experience (☑0800 881 880; www.denniston. co.nz; Denniston; 2hr tour adult/child $95/65) guided tours ride the 'gorge express' train into the historic Banbury mine for what is a slightly spooky but intriguing underground adventure.

The plateau can be reached via the Denniston Bridle Track (three hours up, two down), which follows sections of the Incline. Skilled mountain bikers should speak to the folks at Westport's Habitat Sports (p430) about maps and bike hire.

Cape Foulwind
Walkway & Seal Colony
WALKING, WILDLIFE

Poor old Abel Tasman. The first European to sight the Cape, in 1642, he named it Clyppygen Hoek (Rocky Point) but was eclipsed by James Cook in 1770 who clearly found it less than pleasing.

Today, on a good day, the Cape Foulwind Walkway (1½ hours return) makes for a wonderful amble. It traverses rolling hills between Lighthouse Rd at Omau in the north, and picturesque Tauranga Bay in the south, known for its surfing (and a cafe well worth visiting if it's open).

Towards the southern end is the seal colony where – depending on the season – up to 200 NZ fur seals dot the rocks below the coastal path. Further north the walkway passes a replica astrolabe (a navigational aid) and lighthouse. At Omau, at the walk's northern end, is the Star Tavern (p430), a good place for a pit-stop.

Cape Foulwind is well signposted from Westport, 13km to Omau and 16km to Tauranga Bay.

Old Ghost Road   TRAMPING, CYCLING
(www.oldghostroad.org.nz) One of the most ambitious of NZ's new cycle trails, the 80km Old Ghost Road follows a historic byway started in the 1870s but never completed when the gold rush petered out. Finally completed after an epic build, the spectacular track traverses native forests, tussock tops, river flats and valleys.

The southern end of the track is at Lyell, 50 minutes' drive (62km) east of Westport along the scenic Buller Gorge (SH6). The DOC campsite and day walks here have long been popular, with visitors drawn in by readily accessible historic sites including a graveyard secreted in the bush. The northern trailhead is at Seddonville (p431), 45 minutes' drive (50km) north of Westport off SH67, from where the track sidles along the steep-sided and utterly stunning Mokihinui River. Joining the two ends is a spectacular alpine section, with views from sunrise to sunset.

The track is dual use. Advanced mountain bikers can complete it in 2 to 3 days, while walkers are best to allow five. There are six huts along the way, all of which need to be booked in advance. The track can also be explored in day trips from either end, with both offering a satisfying adventure.

This track is brand-spanking new, and is only just bedding down, so check the website for the latest news, and visit Murchison and Westport i-SITEs for advice on transport and bookings.

Norwest Adventures   CAVING, RAILWAY
(03-788 8168, 0800 116 686; www.caverafting. com; SH6, Charleston) From its monolithic new base (with cafe) at Charleston, 26km south of Westport, this friendly bunch run 'Underworld' cave-rafting trips ($175, four hours) into the glow-worm-filled Nile River Caves. Glow without the flow (no rafting) is $110 per person. Tours begin with a fun rainforest railway ride, available separately (adult/child $20/15, 1½ hours). The Adventure Cav-

ing trip ($340, five hours) includes a 40m abseil into Te Tahi *tomo* (hole) with rock squeezes, waterfalls, prehistoric fossils and trippy cave formations.

🛏 Sleeping

Bazil's Hostel   HOSTEL $
(03-789 6410; www.bazils.com; 54 Russell St; dm $28, d without/with bathroom $68/90) Funky Bazil's is managed by sporty, well-travelled locals who run their own surf school (three-hour lesson $70; board and suit hire per day $30) and offer mountain-bike hire, free kayaks and hook-ups with other local activities. Bazil's thoughtfully corrals its tour-bus clientele into their own area, leaving indie travellers peace and quiet in the many mural-painted corners.

Trip Inn   HOSTEL $
(03-789 7367, 0800 737 773; www.tripinn. co.nz; 72 Queen Street; dm $27-29, d $74; @ 🛜) Westport's stately hostel option is a grand 150-year-old villa with mature gardens. There's a variety of tidy rooms within, plus more in an annexe, and voluminous communal areas.

Westport Holiday Park   HOLIDAY PARK $
(03-789 7043; www.westportholidaypark.co.nz; 31 Domett St; campsites from $34, d $98-145) What it lacks in landscaping it makes up for in consistent maintenance of its basic communal facilities and affordable A-frame 'chalets'. Fifteen minutes' walk to town; minigolf course out front.

Seal Colony Top
10 Holiday Park   HOLIDAY PARK $
(050 893 7876, 03-789 8002; www.top10westport.co.nz; 57 Marine Pde, Carters Beach; sites from $38, units $70-145; @ 🛜) Right on Carters Beach and conveniently located 4km from Westport and 12km to Tauranga Bay, this no-frills outfit offers a full range of facilities of a more-than-acceptable standard. A good option for tourers seeking a clean and peaceful stop-off, and perhaps even a swim.

Buller Court Motel   MOTEL $$
(03-789 7979; www.bullercourtmotel.co.nz; 253 Palmerston St; d $125-175, q $195-215; 🛜) One of many main-road options, this older-style complex is tastefully decorated and impresses with an away-from-the-road aspect and small but private grassy gardens.

Omau Settlers Lodge   LODGE $$
(03-789 5200; www.omausettlerslodge.co.nz; 1054 Cape Rd; r incl breakfast $135-155; 🛜) Close

to Cape Foulwind and across the road from the excellent Star Tavern, these contemporary and stylish units offer rest, relaxation and satisfying continental breakfasts. Rooms have kitchenettes, but a shared kitchen and dining room offers a chance to socialise. A hot tub surrounded by bush maximises the take-it-easy quotient.

Archer House B&B $$
(☑0800 789 877, 03-789 8778; www.archerhouse. co.nz; 75 Queen St; d incl breakfast $185-225; @ �}) This beautiful 1890 heritage home sleeps up to eight in three rooms with their own bathrooms, all sharing no fewer than three lounges, plus peaceful gardens. Lovely hosts, complimentary sherry and generous continental breakfast make this Westport's most refined accommodation option.

✗ Eating & Drinking

Westport has more than its fair share of pubs and other places to eat, with good odds on for decent espresso, and two big supermarkets for stocking up.

PR's Cafe CAFE $
(124 Palmerston St; meals $12-19; ⊙8am-4.30pm Mon-Fri, 8am-3pm Sat & Sun; �}) Low-key signage betrays the impressive effort by savvy PR's with its cabinet full of sharp sandwiches and pastries, and a counter groaning under the weight of amazing cakes (red velvet, Dutch apple) and cookies. An all-day menu delivers carefully composed, modern cafe meals such as salmon omelette with dill aioli, spanakopita, and seasonal specials.

Porto Bello BAR, RESTAURANT $$
(62 Palmerston St; meals $16-32; ⊙5pm-late) Roman columns and renaissance artwork give this place a classical feel, but the food has its roots firmly in the US of A. Craft beer on tap, $16.50 steak special, burgers with pickles, pizza and pork ribs keep the punters happy, as does occasional live music.

Star Tavern PUB
(6 Lighthouse Rd, Omau; meals $9-30) A motto of 'arrive as strangers, leave as friends' is backed up at this rural tavern handily positioned near Cape Foulwind. It dishes up generously proportioned grub in its old-fashioned dining room, a warm welcome, pool and a jukebox in its unprepossessing public bar, and relaxation in the garden. Proper hospitality, that's what this is.

ⓘ Information

The major banks are along Palmerston St. There's free wi-fi at the **Westport Library** (87 Palmerston St).

Buller Hospital (☑03-788 9030; Cobden St)

Department of Conservation Office (DOC; ☑03-788 8008; www.doc.govt.nz; 72 Russell St; ⊙8am-noon & 2-4.30pm Mon-Fri) DOC bookings and information can be gained from the i-SITE. For curly questions visit this field office.

Post Office (cnr Brougham & Palmerston Sts)

Westport i-SITE (☑03-789 6658; www.coaltown.co.nz; 123 Palmerston St; ⊙9am-5pm Mon-Fri, 10am-4pm Sat & Sun) Information on local tracks, walkways, tours, accommodation and transport. Self-help terminal for DOC information and hut/track bookings. See also www.westcoastnz.com.

ⓘ Getting There & Around

AIR
Air New Zealand (☑0800 737 000; www. airnewzealand.co.nz) has up to three flights per day to/from Wellington.

BUS
Westport is a stop on the daily Nelson to Fox Glacier runs of **InterCity** (☑03-365 1113; www. intercity.co.nz). Travel time to Nelson is 3½ hours, to Greymouth 2¼ hours, and to Franz Josef six hours. **Naked Bus** (www.nakedbus. com) runs the same route three times per week. Buses leave from the i-SITE.

East West Coaches (☑03-789 6251; www. eastwestcoaches.co.nz) operates a service through to Christchurch, via Reefton and the Lewis Pass, every day except Saturday, departing from the Caltex Petrol Station.

Karamea Express (☑03-782 6757; info@ karamea-express.co.nz) links Westport and Karamea (two hours) Monday to Friday May to September, plus Saturday from October to April, departing from the i-SITE.

Trek Express (☑0272 221 872, 0800 128 735; www.trekexpress.co.nz) passes through Westport on its frequent high-season tramper transport link between Nelson and the Wangapeka/Heaphy Tracks.

BICYCLE
Hire bikes and obtain advice from **Habitat Sports** (☑03-788 8002; www.habitatsports. co.nz; 234 Palmerston St; half-day bike hire $35; ⊙9am-5pm Mon-Fri, 9am-1pm Sat).

CAR
Hire some wheels at **Wesport Hire** (☑03-789 5038; wesporthire@xtra.co.nz; 294 Palmerston St).

TAXI

Buller Taxis (📞 03-789 6900) can take you to/from the airport (around $20).

Westport to Karamea

North along SH67, the road is pressed against the rocky shoreline by verdant hills. If you're driving all the way up to Karamea, fill your tank in Westport as it's 98km to the next petrol station.

The first town beyond Westport is **Waimangaroa**, with a shop worth a stop for a homemade pie and ice cream. Here you'll also find the turn-off to the Denniston Plateau (p428), which can be surveyed in as little as an hour.

Sleepy **Granity** is 30km north of Westport. Little happens here save the passing of flouro-vested mine workers heading up to **Stockton**, NZ's largest operational coal mine, which is located 8km inland.

The next coastal cluster is **Ngakawau**, shortly followed by **Hector** where stands a monument to Hector's dolphins, NZ's smallest, although you'll be lucky to see them unless your timing is impeccable.

Around 1km north of Hector is a rather special hostel nestled high on the hill amongst native bush, with epic views of the Tasman Sea. The **Old Slaughterhouse** (📞 027 529 7640, 03-782 8333; www.oldslaughterhouse.co.nz; dm $32-36, d $80; ⊙ sometimes closed Jun-Oct) 🌿, built mainly from recycled timbers, is dotted with great art and eclectic furniture, and has tranquil communal areas ideal for contemplation. The steep, 10-minute walk up the hill is well worth the effort and bolsters the off-the-grid charm.

In these parts you'll find the **Charming Creek Walkway**. One of the best day-walks on the Coast, this all-weather trail (six hours return) follows an old coal line through the Ngakawau River Gorge. Along its length are rusty relics galore, tunnels, a suspension bridge and waterfall, and lots of interesting plants and geological formations. Ask a local about transport if you don't want to walk it both ways.

You can start the walkway at Ngakawau, where you'll find the **Charming Creek B&B** (📞 03-782 8007; www.bullerbeachstay.co.nz; Ngakawau; d incl breakfast $139-169; 🛜). The rooms are indeed charming, and there's a driftwood-fired hot tub right by the sea where the self-contained 'Beach Nest' bach sleeps 3 to 4 ($95 to $135, minimum two-night stay). Ask

about the two-night walking package, which includes dinners and a picnic lunch.

The northern trailhead for the walkway is 10km beyond **Seddonville**, a small bush town on the Mokihinui River where **Seddonville Holiday Park** (📞 03-782 1314; 108 Gladstone St; campsites per person $10) offers respectable camping in the grounds of the old school. This small dot on the map is about to get slightly bigger, being the northern trailhead for the spectacular new Old Ghost Road (p429).

At the Mokihinui River mouth, 3km off the highway, is the not-so-gentle **Gentle Annie Beach**, and salty **Gentle Annie Coastal Enclave** (📞 0274 188 587, 03-782 1826; www.gentleannie.co.nz; De Malmanche Rd, Mokihinui; sites from $12, s/d/tr from $25/50/75, cabins $130; 🛜) where there are campsites, a lodge, a range of self-contained accommodation and the Cowshed Gallery & Cafe. There are also bush walks, a maze on a look-out point, and glow-worms nearby.

Between Mokihinui and Little Wanganui the road meanders over the thickly forested **Karamea Bluff**, affording expansive views of the Tasman Sea. It's worth stopping to do the **Lake Hanlon** walk (30 minutes return) on the Karamea side of the hill.

Karamea & Around

The relaxed town of Karamea (population 380) considers itself the West Coast's 'best kept secret', but those who've visited tend to boast about its merits far and wide. An end-of-the-road town it may well be, but it still has a bit of the 'hub' about it, servicing the end (or start) of the Heaphy and Wangapeka Tracks, and the magical Oparara Basin. With a friendly climate, and a take-it-easy mix of locals and chilled-out imports, the Karamea area is a great place to jump off the well-trodden tourist trail for a few lazy days.

🅞 Sights & Activities

Hats off to the Karamea community who have established the very pleasant **Karamea Estuary Walkway**, a long-as-you-like stroll bordering the estuary and Karemea River. It features plenty of birdlife and is best walked at sunset. Ask a local for directions, follow your nose, or pick up a leaflet from the Karamea Information & Resource Centre (p433). While you're there, pick up the free *Karamea* brochure, which details other walks, including **Big Rimu** (45 minutes return),

Flagstaff (one hour return) and the Zig Zag (one hour return).

Longer walks around Karamea include the Fenian Track (four hours return) leading to Cavern Creek Caves and Adams Flat, where there's a replica gold-miner's hut; and the first leg of the Wangapeka Track to Belltown Hut. The Wangapeka Track is a four-to-six-day backcountry trip suitable for experienced trampers only.

Other local activities include swimming, fishing, whitebaiting, kayaking and mountain biking. Your best bet for advice on these is to ask a local and use common sense – especially when it comes to the watery stuff. Flexible and friendly Karamea Outdoor Adventures (☑03-782 6181; www.karameaadventures.co.nz; Bridge St; guided kayak/riverbug trips from $60, kayak hire 2hr $30, bike hire 2hr $30) offers guided and freedom kayaking and riverbug trips on four West Coast rivers, plus mountain-bike hire, and advice on local excursions.

Heaphy Track

The West Coast road ends 14km from Karamea at Kohaihai, the western trailhead (and most commonly, the finish point) of the Heaphy Track, where there's also a DOC campsite (Department of Conservation; adult/child $6). A day walk or overnight stay can readily be had from here. Walk to Scotts Beach (1½ hours

return), or go as far as the fabulous new Heaphy Hut (huts/campsites $32/14) (five hours) and stay a night or two before returning.

This section can also be mountain-biked, as can the whole track (two to three days) from May to September; ask at Westport's Habitat Sports (p430) for bike hire and details.

Helicopter Charter Karamea (☑03-782 6111; www.karameahelicharter.co.nz; 79 Waverley St) can fly up to three people through to the northern trailhead in Golden Bay for $750; ask about other possible drop-off/pick-up points and bike transfers.

For detailed information on negotiating the Heaphy Track, see p420, or check out www.heaphytrack.com.

🛏 Sleeping & Eating

Cafes and restaurants are thin on the ground around these parts, so stock up at Karamea's Four Square and keep an eye out for 'open' signs.

Karamea Domain Camp CAMPSITE $
(☑03-782 6069; www.karamea.org.nz; Waverley St; sites 1/2 people unpowered $12/16, powered $13/18) In the middle of the (ahem) action, this very simple town camp lines up pitches along the edge of the sportsfield, with the cute old Plunket Rooms refashioned into communal facilities – simple kitchen and

---

DON'T MISS

OPARARA VALLEY

To quote a local: 'if this were anywhere else, there'd be hordes streaming in.' Too true. Lying within Kahurangi National Park, the Oparara Basin is a natural spectacle of the highest order – a hidden valley concealing wonders such as limestone arches and strange caves within a thick forest of massive, moss-laden trees that tower over an undergrowth of Dr Seuss-esque form in every imaginable hue of green. Excellent information panels can be perused at the main car park and picnic area.

The valley's signature sight is the 200m-long, 37m-high Oparara Arch, spanning the picturesque Oparara River – home to the super-cute, rare blue duck (whio) – which wends alongside the easy walkway (45 minutes return). The smaller but no less stunning Moria Gate Arch (43m long, 19m high) is reached via a simply divine forest loop walk (1½ hours) which also passes the Mirror Tarn.

Just a 10-minute walk from the second car park are the Crazy Paving & Box Canyon Caves. Take your torch to enter a world of weird subterranean shapes and rare, leggy spiders. Spiders, caves, darkness... sound like fun?

Beyond this point are the superb Honeycomb Hill Caves & Arch, accessible only by guided tours (3-/5-hour tours $95/150) run by the Karamea Information & Resource Centre. Ask about other guided tours of the area, and also about transport for the Oparara Valley Track, a rewarding five-hour independent walk through ancient forest, along the river, popping out at the Fenian Walk car park.

To drive to the valley from Karamea, travel 10km along the main road north and turn off at McCallum's Mill Rd where signposts will direct you a further 14km up and over into the valley along a road that is winding, gravel, rough in places and sometimes steep.

lounge, and adequate bathrooms and bunkrooms (per person $13).

Karama Holiday Park HOLIDAY PARK $
(☑03-782 6758; www.karamea.com; Maori Point Rd; sites d powered/unpowered $32/28, cabins $30-50, d $86-89; @ ⓢ) A simple, old-fashioned camp alongside the estuary in bush surrounds, 3km south of Karamea village. The classic weatherboard cabins are clean and well maintained.

Rongo Backpackers HOSTEL $
(☑03-782 6667; www.rongobackpackers.com; 130 Waverley St; sites from $20, dm $30-32, d $75; @ ⓢ) ◢ Part neo-hippie artists' haven and part organic vegie garden, this rainbow-coloured hostel even has its own community radio station (107.5 FM, www.karamearadio.com). Popular with long-term guests who often end up working within – either tending the garden or as de facto DJs. Every fourth night is free.

Karamea Farm Baches CABINS $
(☑03-782 6838; www.karameafarmbaches.com; 17 Wharf Rd; d/tr/q $95/120/145; @ ⓢ) ◢ Pushing reuse/recycle to the limit, these seven 1960s self-contained bachs are the real McCoy, right down to cobwebby corners and frayed bedspreads. If you dig organic gardening, friendly dogs and colourful hosts, this will win you over.

Karamea River Motels MOTEL $$
(☑03-782 6955; www.karameamotels.co.nz; 31 Bridge St; r $125-169; ⓢ) The smart rooms at this modern, rural motel range from studios to two-bedroom units. Features include long-range views, barbecues and lush gardens complete with lily pond.

Last Resort LODGE $$
(☑03-782 6617, 0800 505 042; www.lastresort.co.nz; 71 Waverley St; s $50, d $97-155, q $195; @ ⓢ) This iconic, rambling and rustic resort has had its ups and downs, but is currently riding a wave of friendly local hosts, accommodation upgrades and a general tidy up. Scope the joint with espresso or a beer in the cafe or bar (meals $9 to $25) or take the plunge into a range of rooms, from simple doubles to family suites hallmarked by extensive use of local timbers.

★**Karamea Village Hotel** PUB $$
(www.karameahotel.co.nz; cnr Waverley & Wharf Sts; meals $9-29; ⊘11am-11pm) Here lie simple pleasures and proper hospitality: a game of pool, a pint of ale, and a hot roast dinner followed by an old-fashioned pudding.

ℹ Information

Karamea Information & Resource Centre
(☑03-782 6652; www.karameainfo.co.nz; Market Cross; ⊘9am-5pm Mon-Fri, 10am-1pm Sat & Sun, shorter hours off-peak) This excellent, community-owned centre has the local low-down, internet access, maps and DOC hut tickets. It also doubles as the petrol station.

ℹ Getting There & Away

Karamea Express (☑03-782 6757; info@karamea-express.co.nz) links Karamea and Westport ($35, two hours, 7.40am Monday to Friday May to September, plus Saturdays from October to April). It also services Kohaihai twice daily during peak summer, and other times on demand. Wangapeka transport is also available.

Heaphy Bus (☑03-540 2042, 0800 128 735; www.theheaphybus.co.nz), based in Nelson, also runs between both ends of the Heaphy, as well as the Wangapeka.

Fly from Karamea to Takaka with **Helicopter Charter Karamea** (☑03-782 6111; www.karameahelicharter.co.nz; 79 Waverley St), **Golden Bay Air** (☑0800 588 885; www.goldenbayair.co.nz) or **Adventure Flights Golden Bay** (☑03-525 6167, 0800 150 338; www.adventureflightsgoldenbay.co.nz) for around $190 per person, then walk back on the Heaphy Track; contact the Information & Resource Centre for details.

Rongo Backpackers run track and town transport including services to Heaphy, Wangapeka, Oparara Basin and Westport on demand.

THE GREAT COAST ROAD

There are fine views all the way along this beautiful stretch of SH6, although its most famous attractions are the geologically fascinating Pancake Rocks at Punakaiki. Fill up in Westport if you're low on petrol and cash – there's no fuel until Runanga, 92km away, and the next ATM is in Greymouth.

Westport to Punakaiki

Set on 42 serene hectares, 17km south of Westport, the solar-powered, energy-efficient Beaconstone Eco Lodge (☑027 431 0491; www.beaconstoneecolodge.co.nz; Birds Ferry Rd; dm $28-31, d $70-74; ⊘Oct-May; ⓢ) ◢ is a bushy retreat with touches of Americana cool. Inside are cosy beds and a laid-back communal area, while beyond the doorstep are bush walks leading to peaceful river swimming holes. There's only room for 14, so booking is recommended.

Jack's Gasthof (☎03-789 6501; www.jacks-gasthof.co.nz; SH6; mains $12-28; ☺from 11am Oct-Apr) is 21km south of Westport on the Little Totara River, where Berliners Jack and Petra run their eternally popular pizzeria with adjacent bar improbably bejewelled with a disco ball. Avail yourself of campsites (from $6) and a basic room ($50) if you require a sleepover.

For a true taste of the region's gold mining past, swing into **Mitchell's Gully Gold Mine** (www.mitchellsgullygoldmine.co.nz; SH6; adult/child $10/free; ☺9am-5pm), 22km south of Westport, where you'll meet a pioneer's descendants and explore the family mine. There are interesting tales, relics, tunnels and railtracks, plus a giant waterwheel and the odd trap-door spider.

The next stop is **Charleston**, 26km south of Westport. It's hard to believe it now, but this place boomed during the 1860s gold rush, with 80 hotels, three breweries and hundreds of thirsty gold-diggers staking claims along the Nile River. There's not much left now except a motel, campground, a clutch of local houses and the brilliant Norwest Adventures (p429) with whom you can explore some utterly amazing hidden treasures.

From here to Punakaiki is a staggeringly beautiful panorama of lowland pakihi scrub and lush green forest alongside a series of bays dramatically sculpted by relentless ocean fury. Drive as slowly as the traffic behind you will allow.

Punakaiki & Paparoa National Park

Located midway between Westport and Greymouth is Punakaiki, a small settlement beside the rugged 380-sq-km Paparoa National Park. For most travellers it's a quick stop for coffee and a squiz at the Pancake Rocks, which is a shame because there's excellent tramping and other wild adventures, and plenty of accommodation.

◉ Sights

Paparoa National Park is blessed with high cliffs and empty beaches, a dramatic mountain range, crazy limestone river valleys, diverse flora, and a profusion of birdlife, including weka and the Westland petrel, a rare sea bird which nests only here.

Pancake Rocks   NATURAL FEATURE
Punakaiki is famous for its fantastic Pancake Rocks and blowholes. Through a layering

weathering process called stylobedding, the Dolomite Point limestone has formed into what looks like piles of thick pancakes. Aim for high tide (tide times are posted at the visitor information centre) when the sea surges into caverns and booms menacingly through blowholes. See it on a wild day and be reminded that Mother Nature really is the boss. An easy 15-minute walk loops from the highway out to the rocks and blowholes.

🏃 Activities

Tramps around Punakaiki include the **Truman Track** (30 minutes return) and the **Punakaiki–Porari Loop** (3½ hours), which goes up the spectacular limestone Pororari River gorge before popping over a hill and coming down the bouldery Punakaiki River to rejoin the highway.

Surefooted types can embark on the **Fox River Cave Walk** (three hours return), 12km north of Punakaiki and open to amateur explorers. BYO torch and sturdy shoes.

Other tramps in the national park are detailed in the DOC *Paparoa National Park* pamphlet ($1), and include the **Inland Pack Track** (two to three days), a route established by miners in 1866 to bypass difficult coastal terrain.

As many of Paparoa's inland walks are susceptible to river flooding it is vital that you obtain updates from the DOC visitor centre (p435) in Punakaiki before you depart.

Punakaiki Canoes   KAYAKING
(☎03-731 1870; www.riverkayaking.co.nz; SH6; canoe hire 2hr/full day $40/60, family rates available) This outfit rents canoes near the Pororari River bridge, for gentle, super-scenic paddling for all abilities.

Punakaiki Horse Treks   HORSE RIDING
(☎03-731 1839; www.pancake-rocks.co.nz; SH6; 3hr ride $160; ☺Nov-May) Punakaiki Horse Treks, based at Hydrangea Cottages, conducts equine outings in the Punakaiki Valley, with river crossings, finishing at the beach.

🛏 Sleeping & Eating

There's good news and bad news. The good news is that there's ample accommodation in Punakaiki. The bad news is that there's no grocery shop or petrol, and that the sole cafe may well fail to please. The tavern down the road, however, remains a consistently good performer. Keep it up, Team Pub!

★ **Punakaiki Beach Hostel** HOSTEL **$**
(📱03-731 1852; www.punakaikibeachhostel.co.nz; 4 Webb St; campsites per person $20, dm/s/d $28/54/75; @ 📶) A laid-back hostel with a sea-view verandah, just a short walk from Pancake Rocks. Co-operative owners have been-there-done-that and know exactly what you want: a clean hostel with good beds, great communal facilities, and staff who smile because they mean it. The cutesy, virtually-on-the-beach Sunset Cottage ($115) is well worth a splurge.

Punakaiki Beach Camp HOLIDAY PARK **$**
(📱03-731 1894; www.punakaikibeachcamp.co.nz; 5 Owen St; campsites per person powered/unpowered $20/17, d $48-92; 📶) With a backdrop of sheer cliffs, this salty, beachside park with good grass is studded with clean, old-style cabins and shipshape amenities. A classic Kiwi coastal campground.

Te Nikau Retreat HOSTEL **$**
(📱03-731 1111; www.tenikauretreat.co.nz; 19 Hartmount Pl; sites from $18, dm $28, d $75-90, cabins from $96; @ 📶) 🐾 Relax, restore and explore at this unconventional property consisting of numerous buildings nestled into their own rainforest nooks, just a short walk to the beach. There are rooms in the main building, several cute cabins, and the larger Nikau Lodge sleeping up to 9.

Hydrangea Cottages COTTAGES **$$**
(📱03-731 1839; www.pancake-rocks.co.nz; SH6; d $140-310; 📶) On a hillside overlooking the Tasman, these five standalone and mostly self-contained cottages (largest sleeping up to seven) are built from salvaged timber and river stones. It's a classy but relaxed enclave, with splashes of colourful mosaic and pretty cottage gardens. The owners also run the horse-trekking stables.

Punakaiki Tavern PUB **$$**
(www.punakaikitavern.co.nz; SH6; mains $19-33; ⊘8am-late; 📶) Whether it's breakfast, lunch or dinner, this pub does decent portions of honest food served in comfortable surrounds. Most nights the punters are a mix of local and international, so there's ample opportunity for conversation and friendly debate over the rules of pool.

❶ Information

The **Paparoa National Park visitor information centre and i-SITE** (📱03-731 1895; www.doc. govt.nz; SH6; ⊘9am-5pm Oct-Nov, to 6pm Dec-Mar, to 4.30pm Apr-Sep) has info on the park and track conditions, and handles bookings for attractions and accommodation including hut tickets.

An online directory of local activities and operators is maintained by **Punakaiki Promotions** (www.punakaiki.co.nz).

❶ Getting There & Away

InterCity (📱03-365 1113; www.intercity.co.nz) travels daily north to Westport (45 minutes), and south to Greymouth (45 minutes) and Fox Glacier (five hours). **Naked Bus** (www.nakedbus.com) runs to the same destinations three days a week. Both companies stop long enough for passengers to admire the Pancake Rocks.

Punakaiki to Greymouth

The highway from Punakaiki to Greymouth is flanked by white-capped waves and rocky bays on one side, and the steep, bushy Paparoa Ranges on the other.

At **Barrytown**, 17km south of Punakaiki, Steve and Robyn run **Barrytown Knifemaking** (📱03-731 1053, 0800 256 433; www.barrytownknifemaking.com; 2662 SH6, Barrytown; classes $150; ⊘closed Mon), where you can make your own knife – from hand-forging the blade to crafting a handle from native rimu timber. The day-long course features lunch, archery, axe-throwing and a stream of entertainingly bad jokes from Steve. Bookings essential, and transport from Punakaiki can be arranged.

With a rainforest backdrop and coastal views, **Ti Kouka House** (📱03-731 1460; www.tikoukahouse.co.nz; 2522 SH6, Barrytown; d incl breakfast $305; 📶) further amazes with its splendid architectural design, recycled building materials, and sculptural artwork both inside and out. It's an excellent B&B with three luxurious rooms.

Breakers (📱03-762 7743; www.breakers. co.nz; 1367 SH6, Nine Mile Creek; d incl breakfast $215-365; @ 📶), 14km north of Greymouth, is one of the best-kept secrets on the coast. Beautifully appointed en suite rooms overlook the sea, with fine surfing opportunities at hand for the intrepid. The hosts are sporty, friendly and have a nice dog.

Two kilometres south is **Rapahoe**, 12km shy of Greymouth. This tiny seaside settlement is the northern trailhead for the enjoyable Point Elizabeth Walkway (p436). Should you require refreshment before or after your walk, call in to the **Rapahoe Hotel** (1 Beach Rd; mains $12-29), a simple country pub offering warm hospitality and a good feed of fish and chips in a picturesque location.

GREYMOUTH REGION

Bookending NZ's most famous alpine pass and sitting more or less halfway along the West Coast highway, the Greymouth area provides easy access to the attractions north and south as well as offering a decent smattering of diversions within its boundaries.

Greymouth

POP 8900

Welcome to the 'Big Smoke', crouched at the mouth of the imaginatively named Grey River. The West Coast's largest town has gold in its veins, and today its fortunes still ebb and flow with the tide of mining, although dairy farming and tourism top up the coffers. The town is well geared for travellers, offering all the necessary services and the odd tourist attraction, the most famous of which is Shantytown.

◉ Sights & Activities

Shantytown MUSEUM
(www.shantytown.co.nz; Rutherglen Rd, Paroa; adult/child/family $31.50/15.50/74; ⊙8.30am-5pm) Eight kilometres south of Greymouth and 2km inland from SH6, Shantytown recreates a 1860s gold-mining town, complete with steam-train rides, post office, pub and Rosie's House of Ill Repute. There's also gold panning, a flying fox, sawmill, a gory hospital and 10-minute holographic movies in the Princess Theatre.

★ Left Bank Art Gallery GALLERY
(www.leftbankarts.org.nz; 1 Tainui St; admission by donation; ⊙10am-4pm daily) This 90-year-old former bank houses contemporary NZ jade carvings, prints, paintings, photographs and ceramics. The gallery also fosters and supports a wide society of West Coast artists.

History House Museum MUSEUM
(www.history-house.co.nz; 27 Gresson St; adult/child $6/2; ⊙10am-4pm Mon-Fri) This museum documents Greymouth's pre-1920 history with an impressive collection of photographs.

TranzAlpine TRAIN TOUR
(☑03-341 2588, 0800 872 467; www.kiwirailscenic.co.nz; adult/child one way from $99/69; ⊙departs Christchurch 8.15am, Greymouth 1.45pm) The TranzAlpine is one of the world's great train journeys, traversing the Southern Alps between Christchurch and Greymouth, from the Pacific Ocean to the Tasman Sea, passing through Arthur's Pass National Park. En route is a sequence of dramatic landscapes, from the flat, alluvial Canterbury Plains, through narrow alpine gorges, an 8.5km tunnel, beech-forested river valleys, and alongside a lake fringed with cabbage trees. The 4½-hour journey is unforgettable, even in bad weather (if it's raining on one coast, it's probably fine on the other).

Monteith's Brewing Co BREWERY
(☑03-768 4149; www.monteiths.co.nz; cnr Turumaha & Herbert Sts; ⊙10.30am-7.30pm) The original Monteith's brewhouse may simply be brand HQ for mainstream product largely brewed elsewhere, but it still delivers heritage in spades through its excellent-value tour (one hour, $20, includes generous samples; three to five tours per day). The flash tasting-room-cum-bar is now Greymouth's most exciting watering hole (tasty snacks $7 to $18) – shame it shuts up shop so early.

Floodwall Walk WALKING
Take a 10-minute riverside stroll along Mawhera Quay, or keep going for an hour or so, taking in the fishing harbour, breakwater and Blaketown Beach, which leads on to the West Coast Wilderness Trail (p439). Other local walks (most inclined towards mining heritage sites) are detailed in the free Greymouth map and brochure, available from the i-SITE (p438).

Point Elizabeth Walkway WALKING
Accessible from Dommett Esplanade in Cobden, 6km north of Greymouth, this enjoyable walkway (three hours return) skirts around a richly forested headland in the shadow of the Rapahoe Range to an ocean lookout, before continuing on to the northern trailhead at Rapahoe (12km from Greymouth) – small town, big beach, friendly local pub.

Kea Heritage Tours GUIDED TOUR
(☑0800 532 868; www.keatours.co.nz) Kea operates high-quality shuttle-bus tours with well-informed guides, and visits coast sites and those beyond. Short tours include the half-day Punakaiki Tour ($115), and the day-long Twin Glaciers ($295). Myriad other options include a multiday exploration of the Maori greenstone trails.

⊨ Sleeping

Global Village HOSTEL $
(☑03-768 7272; www.globalvillagebackpackers.co.nz; 42 Cowper St; sites per person $18, dm/d/tr/q $28/70/96/120; @☎) A collage of African and Asian art is infused with a passion-

Greymouth

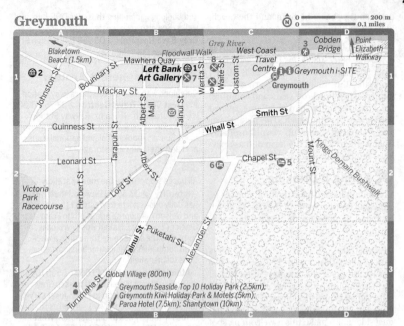

ate travellers' vibe here. Free kayaks – the Lake Karoro wetlands reserve is just metres away – and mountain bikes are on tap, and relaxation comes easy with a spa, sauna, barbecue and fire pit.

Noah's Ark Backpackers　　　HOSTEL $
(☑ 03-768 4868, 0800 662 472; www.noahs. co.nz; 16 Chapel St; sites per person $17, dm/s/d $27/54/68; @ 🛜) Originally a monastery, colourful Noah's has eccentric animal-themed rooms, a sunset-worthy balcony and quiet back garden with a spa pool. Mountain bikes and fishing rods are provided free of charge.

Ardwyn House　　　B&B $
(☑ 03-768 6107; ardwynhouse@hotmail.com; 48 Chapel St; s/d incl breakfast from $60/90; 🛜) This old-fashioned B&B nestles amid steep gardens on a quiet dead-end street. Mary, the well-travelled host, cooks a splendid breakfast.

**Greymouth Seaside
Top 10 Holiday Park**　　MOTEL, HOLIDAY PARK $
(☑ 03-768 6618, 0800 867 104; www.top10greymouth.co.nz; 2 Chesterfield St; sites $40-46, cabins $60-125, motel r $110-374; @ 🛜) Well positioned for sunset walks on the adjacent beach and 2.5km south of the town centre, this large park has various tent and camper-

Greymouth

◎ **Top Sights**
　1 Left Bank Art Gallery B1

◎ **Sights**
　2 History House Museum A1

◐ **Activities, Courses & Tours**
　3 Floodwall Walk D1
　4 Monteith's Brewing Co A3

◻ **Sleeping**
　5 Ardwyn House C2
　6 Noah's Ark Backpackers C2

◉ **Eating**
　7 Ali's Eating & Drinking B1
　8 DP:One Cafe C1
　9 Freddy's Cafe C1

van sites as well as accommodation ranging from simple cabins to deluxe seaview motels – arguably the flashest units in town. A shipshape stop for every budget.

**Greymouth Kiwi
Holiday Park & Motels**　MOTEL, HOLIDAY PARK $
(☑ 03-762 6768, 0800 101 222; www.southbeach. co.nz; 318 Main South Rd; sites $30-35, d $50-130; @ 🛜) This low-rise complex offers a range of cheap, no-frills accommodation, sandwiched

between the (busy) highway and the beach, 6km south of town.

Paroa Hotel HOTEL **$$**
(☑03-762 6860, 0800 762 6860; www.paroa. co.nz; 508 Main South Rd, Paroa; d $128-140; ☎) Opposite the Shantytown turn-off, this family-owned hotel (60 years and counting) has spacious units sharing a large lawned garden next to the beach. The notable bar and restaurant dishes up warm hospitality (mains $18 to $32) in the form of roast, pavlova, and beer, amid local clientele.

🍴 Eating & Drinking

Greymouth has a decent daytime cafe scene, but come evening some of the best food will be found at pubs on the town fringe and beyond.

DP:One Cafe CAFE **$**
(104 Mawhera Quay; meals $7-23; ☺8am-8pm Mon-Fri, 9am-5pm Sat & Sun; ☎) A stalwart of the Greymouth cafe scene, this hip joint serves great espresso, along with good-value grub. Groovy tunes, wi-fi, a relaxed vibe and quayside tables make this a welcoming spot to linger.

Freddy's Cafe CAFE **$**
(115 Mackay St; snacks $4-7, meals $8-18; ☺8am-5pm) Don't miss the doorway because upstairs the restrained-retro Freddy's beckons with good espresso, all-day hot meals (pancakes, seafood chowder, pasta) alongside an appealing selection of cabinet food. The likes of vegetarian quiche can be rounded off with several different chocolate options, including the venerable afghan biscuit.

Ali's Eating & Drinking CAFE **$$**
(9 Tainui St; mains $12-27; ☺8am-10pm Mon-Sat, to 3pm Sun) Painted in warm orange and adorned with local art, conservative but comfortable Ali's serves honest all-day food of global bent such as laksa, pasta, steak and whitebait, with lovely homemade desserts such as Knickerbocker Glory.

ℹ️ Information

Free town and regional maps are available at the i-SITE. Major banks huddle around Mackay and Tainui Sts. There's internet access at the i-SITE and **library** (18 Albert St; ☎).

Greymouth i-SITE (☑03-768 5101, 0800 473 966; www.greydistrict.co.nz; Railway Station, 164 Mackay St; ☺9am-5pm Mon-Fri, 9.30am-4pm Sat & Sun; ☎) The helpful crew at the railway station can assist with all manner of advice

and bookings, including those for DOC huts and walks. See also www.westcoastnz.com.

Grey Base Hospital (☑03-768 0499; High St)

Post Office (36 Tainui St)

ℹ️ Getting There & Around

Combined with the i-SITE in the railway station, the **West Coast Travel Centre** (☑03-768 7080; www.westcoasttravel.co.nz; Railway Station, 164 Mackay St; ☺9am-5pm Mon-Fri, 10am-4pm Sat & Sun; ☎) books local and national transport and offers luggage storage.

BUS

All buses stop outside the railway station.

InterCity (☑03-365 1113; www.intercity.co.nz) has daily buses north to Westport (two hours) and Nelson (six hours), and south to Franz Josef Glacier (3½ hours). **Naked Bus** (www.nakedbus. com) runs the same route three days a week. Both companies offer connections to destinations further afield.

Atomic Travel (☑03-349 0697, 0508 108 359; www.atomictravel.co.nz) passes Greymouth on its daily Nelson to Franz Josef service (and onward to Queenstown), as well as running across Arthur's Pass to Christchurch. **West Coast Shuttle** (☑03-768 0028, 0274 927 000; www.westcoastshuttle.co.nz) also runs a daily service between Greymouth and Christchurch.

CAR

Several car-hire company desks are located within the railway station. Local companies include **Alpine West** (☑03-768 4002, 0800 257 736; www.alpinerentals.co.nz; 11 Shelley St) and **NZ Rent-a-Car** (☑03-768 0379; www.nzrenta-car.co.nz; 170 Tainui St).

TAXI

Greymouth Taxis (☑03-768 7078)

Blackball

Around 25km upriver of Greymouth sits the ramshackle town of Blackball – established in 1866 to service gold diggers; coal mining kicked in between 1890 and 1964. The National Federation of Labour (a trade union) was conceived here, born from influential strikes in 1908 and 1931. This story is retold in historical displays on the main road.

Alongside you will find the hub of the town, **Formerly the Blackball Hilton** (☑03-732 4705, 0800 425 225; www.blackballhilton.co.nz; 26 Hart St; s/d with continental breakfast $55/110), where you can collect a copy of the helpful 'Historic Blackball' map. This official Historic Place has memorabilia galore, hot meals, cold beer, heaps of afternoon sun, and a host of rooms oozing the charm of yesteryear; it was named so after a certain global hotel chain got antsy when its name was appropriated.

Competing with the Hilton in the fame stakes is the **Blackball Salami Co** (www.blackballsalami.co.nz; 11 Hilton St; ⊙8am-4pm Mon-Fri, 9am-2pm Sat), manufacturer of tasty salami and sausages ranging from chorizo to black pudding.

Blackball's other claim to fame is as the southern end of the **Croesus Track**, a two-day historic goldfields route that clambers over a knob to reach Barrytown. Visit DOC's website for details.

Lake Brunner

Lying inland from Greymouth, **Lake Brunner** (www.golakebrunner.co.nz) can be reached via the SH7 turn-off at Stillwater, a journey of 39km. It can also be reached from the south via Kumara Junction.

One of many lakes in the area, Brunner is a tranquil spot for bushwalks, bird-spotting and various watersports including boating and fishing. Indeed, the local boast is that the lake and Arnold River are 'where the trout die of old age', which implies that the local fish are particularly clever or the fisherfolk are somewhat hopeless. Greymouth i-SITE can hook you up with a guide. Head to the marina to undertake one or all of several pretty short walks.

Moana is the main settlement, home to numerous accommodation options of which the best is **Lake Brunner Country Motel**

(☑03-738 0144; www.lakebrunnermotel.co.nz; 2014 Arnold Valley Rd; sites from $30, cabins $60-70, cottages d $135-145; ☎), 2km from the lake. It features cabins, cottages and campervan sites tucked into native plantings through park-like grounds, while tenters can enjoy the lush grassy camping field down the back. This is proper peace and quiet, unless you count birdsong and the bubbling of the spa pool.

Moana also has a couple of places to eat including a cafe opposite the station where the TranzAlpine train pulls in. There's also food at the petrol station, and the local pub, which is trending upward.

Kumara

POP 310

Thirty kilometres south of Greymouth, near the western end of Arthur's Pass (SH73), Kumara was yet another busy gold-rush town that ground to a halt, leaving behind a thin posse of flinty folk who have kept the town going to this day. And all to the greater good, for were it not for the Kumarians there would be no starting point for the **Coast to Coast** (www.coasttocoast.co.nz), NZ's most famous multisport race. Held each February, the strong, the brave and the totally knackered run-cycle-ride-kayak-bike a total of 243km all the way across the mountains to Christchurch, with top competitors dusting it off in just under 11 hours.

Having manned the starting gate with sterling hospitality for 30 years, this tiny town is well-oiled to cope with yet more sporty visitors, namely people cycling the

THE WEST COAST LAKE BRUNNER

WORTH A TRIP

A CYCLE ON THE WILD SIDE

Officially opened in 2013, the 120km **West Coast Wilderness Trail** (www.westcoastwildernesstrail.co.nz) is one of around two dozen new **NZ Cycle Trails** (www.nzcycletrail.com). Stretching from Greymouth to Hokitika (with plans to extend it further south to Ross), the gently graded track follows a mix of gold-rush trails, water races, logging tramways and historic railway lines, as well as forging new routes cross-country. Along the way it reveals outstanding landscapes of dense rainforest, glacial rivers, lakes and wetlands, with views all the way from the snow-capped mountains of the Southern Alps to the wild Tasman Sea.

The full shebang is a good four days of riding but, like many of the new cycle trails, it can easily be sliced up into sections of various lengths, catering to every ability and area of interest. The leg from Milltown to Kumara is shaping up as an excellent day ride, taking four to six hours and finishing at the resplendent Theatre Royal Hotel (p440).

Bike hire, transport and advice is available from the major setting-off points. In Hokitika, contact **Wilderness Trail Shuttle** (☑021 263 3299, 03-755 5042; www.wildernesstrailshuttle.co.nz) and in Greymouth try the folks at **West Coast Rail Trail** (☑03-768 6649, 0800 946 543; www.westcoastrailtrail.com).

West Coast Wilderness Trail (p439), which passes through the town. Anticipating their arrival is the show-stopping **Theatre Royal Hotel** (03-736 9277; www.theatreroyalhotel. co.nz; 81 Seddon St, SH73, Kumara; mains $22-42, d incl breakfast $135-290; 10am-late;), the fully restored highway stop that has kicked Kumara well and truly into the 21st century with its civilised bar, classy dining room, and sumptuous upstairs rooms styled after local personalities of old. The attention to detail in furnishings and heritage displays is simply wonderful. Stop in to enjoy some of the best food on the coast (fish and chips, local game, pizza and delicate cakes) or just pull in for a drink and a yarn with the locals.

Should you be to-ing or fro-ing over Arthur's Pass, consider staying at **Jacksons Retreat** (03-738 0474; www.jacksonsretreat. co.nz; Jacksons, SH73; sites from $35;) , 33km west of Arthur's Pass Village. Set upon 15 sloping acres with exceptional views over the Taramakau River, it offers stacks of excellent amenities for campervanner and tenter alike.

WESTLAND

The bottom third or so of the West Coast is known as Westland, a mix of farmland and rainforest backed by the Southern Alps, which pop straight up in a neck-cricking fashion. This region is most famous for its glaciers.

Hokitika

POP 3000

Popular with history buffs and the setting for numerous NZ novels – including the 2013 Man Booker Prize–winning *The Luminaries* by Eleanor Catton – Hokitika's riches come in many forms. Founded on gold, today the town is the stronghold of indigenous *pounamu* (greenstone), which jostles for attention amid many other arts and crafts, drawing rafts of visitors to the town's wide open streets.

Sights & Activities

Hokitika is a great base for walking and cycling. Download or collect a copy of DOC's brochure *Walks in the Hokitika Area* ($1), and visit **Hokitika Cycles & Sports World** (03-755 8662; www.hokitikasportsworld.co.nz; 33 Tancred St; bike hire per day $55) for cycle hire and advice on tracks including the West Coast Wilderness Trail (p439).

★ **Hokitika Museum**   MUSEUM
(www.hokitikamuseum.co.nz; 17 Hamilton St; adult/ child $5/2.50; 10am-5pm) Housed in the imposing Carnegie Building (1908), this is an exemplary provincial museum, with intelligently curated exhibitions presented in a clear, modern style. Highlights include the fascinating *Whitebait!* exhibition, and the *Pounamu* room – the ideal primer before you hit the galleries looking for greenstone treasures.

Sunset Point   LOOKOUT
(Gibson Quay) A spectacular vantage point at any time of day, this is – as the name suggests – the primo place to watch the light fade away. Surfers, seagulls, and fish and chips: *this* is New Zealand.

Hokitika Heritage Walk   WALK
Pick up the 50-cent leaflet from the i-SITE and wander the old wharf precinct. Another brochure details the **Hokitika Heritage Trail**, a 11km (two to three hour) loop taking in historic sites and interesting town views.

Glowworm Dell   NATURAL FEATURE
Just north of town, a short stroll from SH6 leads to a Glowworm Dell, an easy opportunity to enter the other-wordly home of NZ's native fungus gnat larvae (so not even a worm at all). An information panel at the entrance will further illuminate your way.

Lake Kaniere   LAKE
(www.doc.govt.nz) Lying at the heart of a 70-sq-km scenic reserve, beautiful Lake Kaniere is 8km long, 2km wide, 195m deep, and also quite cool, as you'll discover if you swim. You may, however, prefer simply to camp or picnic at **Hans Bay** (www.doc.govt. nz), or undertake one of numerous walks in the surrounds, ranging from the 15-minute Canoe Cove Walk to the seven-hour return gut-buster up Mt Tuhua. The historic **Kaniere Water Race Walkway** (3½ hours one way) forms part of the new West Coast Wilderness Trail.

Hokitika Gorge   GORGE
(www.doc.govt.nz) A picturesque 35km drive leads to Hokitika Gorge, a ravishing ravine with unbelievably turquoise waters coloured by glacial 'flour'. Point and shoot the scene from every angle via the short forest walkway and swingbridge. The gorge is well signposted from Stafford St (past the dairy factory). En route, you will pass **Kowhiti-**

Hokitika

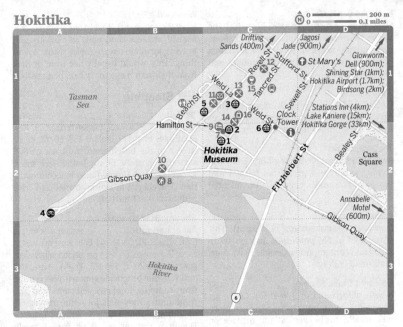

Hokitika

◎ Top Sights
1 Hokitika Museum C2

◎ Sights
2 Hokitika Craft Gallery C2
3 Hokitika Glass Studio C1
4 Sunset Point A2
5 Tectonic Jade C1
6 Waewae Pounamu C2

◎ Activities, Courses & Tours
7 Bonz 'N' Stonz C2
8 Hokitika Heritage Walk B2

◎ Sleeping
9 Teichelmann's B&B C2

◎ Eating
10 Dulcie's Takeaways B2
11 Fat Pipi Pizza C1
12 New World C1
13 Stumpers Cafe & Bar C1
14 Sweet Alice's Fudge
     Kitchen C1

◎ Drinking & Nightlife
15 West Coast Wine Bar C1

◎ Shopping
16 Hokitika Cycles & Sports
     World C1

THE WEST COAST HOKITIKA

rangi, the site of NZ's first mass-murder and a massive 12-day manhunt (immortalised in the 1982 classic film *Bad Blood*). A poignant roadside monument lines up the farmstead site through a stone shaft.

Galleries

Art and craft galleries are a strong spoke in Hoki's wheel, and you could easily spend a day spinning around the lot. There are plenty of opportunities to meet the artists, and in some studios you can watch them at work. Be aware that some galleries sell jade imported from Europe and Asia, as precious local *pounamu* (greenstone) is not surrendered lightly by the wilds.

Bonz 'N' Stonz   CARVING
(www.bonz-n-stonz.co.nz; 16 Hamilton St; full-day workshop $85-180) Design, carve and polish your own *pounamu*, bone or paua masterpiece, with tutelage from Steve. Prices vary with materials and design complexity. Bookings recommended.

Hokitika Craft Gallery
GALLERY

(www.hokitikacraftgallery.co.nz; 25 Tancred St) The town's best one-stop-shop, this co-op show-cases a wide range of local work including *pounamu*, jewellery, textiles, ceramics and woodwork.

Jagosi Jade
GALLERY

(☑ 03-755 6243; 246 Sewell St) Aden Hoglund carves traditional and modern Maori pieces from local stone; will make to order.

Tectonic Jade
GALLERY

(www.tectonicjade.com; 67 Revell St) This wel-coming gallery is a great spot to view and buy local *pounamu*, carved by the talented Rex Scott.

Waewae Pounamu
GALLERY

(www.waewaepounamu.co.nz; 39 Weld St) This stronghold of NZ *pounamu* displays tradi-tional and contemporary designs in its large, main-road gallery.

Hokitika Glass Studio
GALLERY

(www.hokitikaglass.co.nz; 9 Weld St) Glass art covering a continuum from garish to glori-ous; watch the blowers at the furnace on weekdays.

👉 Tours

Wilderness Wings
SCENIC FLIGHTS

(☑ 0800 755 8118; www.wildernesswings.co.nz; Hokitika Airport; flights from $285) Offers scenic flights over Hokitika, and further afield to Aoraki (Mt Cook) and the glaciers.

✹ Festivals & Events

Driftwood & Sand
ART

(www.driftwoodandsand.co.nz) During a week in January, flotsam and jetsam is fashioned into a surprising array of arty, crafty and daft sculpture on Hokitika beach.

Wildfoods Festival
FOOD

(www.wildfoods.co.nz) Held in early March, this festival attracts thousands of curious and brave gourmands who eat a whole lot of things they would usually flee from or flick from their hair. Legendary fun; book early.

🛏 Sleeping

⭐ Drifting Sands
HOSTEL $

(☑ 03-755 7654; www.driftingsands.co.nz; 197 Rev-ell St; sites from $16, dm/s/d $30/60/78; @ 🛜) Access to the beach from the back garden and this hostel's family-home feel make it our pick of Hoki's budget accommoda-tion. The cheery, fastidious owner and crisp bedlinens don't hurt either.

Shining Star Beachfront Accommodation
HOLIDAY PARK, MOTEL $

(☑ 03-755 8921, 0800 744 646; www.shiningstar. co.nz; 16 Richards Dr; sites per person unpowered/ powered $16/20, d $95-175; @ 🛜) Attractive and versatile beachside spot with everything from camping to classy self-contained sea-front units. Kids will love the menagerie, including pigs and alpacas straight from Dr Doolittle's appointment book. Parents might prefer the spa and sauna ($15 for two).

Birdsong
HOSTEL $

(☑ 03-755 7179; www.birdsong.co.nz; SH6; dm/s $30/60, d without/with bathroom $79/94; @ 🛜) Located 2.5km north of town, this bird-themed hostel has sea views and a homely atmosphere. Free bikes, handy beach access and hidden extras will entice you into ex-tending your stay.

Annabelle Motel
MOTEL $$

(☑ 050 854 9494, 03-755 8160; www.annabellemotel. co.nz; 214 Weld St; s $130, d $140-190; 🛜) Less than 1km from the Hoki clock tower, pretty An-

---

WHITEBAIT FEVER

On even the swiftest of visits to the Coast, you are sure to come across a little whitebait or two, whether being sold from Womble's back door, in a pattie sandwich, in museums, or in tales tall and true. These tiny, transparent fish are the young of some of NZ's pre-cious native fish, including inanga, kokopu, smelt and even eels. Strangely enough, they all look and taste the same.

Commanding up to $80 a kilo round these parts (and much more elsewhere), com-petition is tough to net the elusive fish. The season runs from August to November, when riverbanks and fishing stands are busy from Karamea to Haast.

The classic pattie recipe involves little more than an egg, and is accompanied by a wedge of lemon, although some would say that mint sauce is the best embellishment. The *Whitebait!* exhibition at Hokitika Museum (p440) will give you some idea as to what all the fuss is about.

nabelle is away from beach and town action but well located for peace and convenience. Tip-top units, decorated in green garden hues with plush furnishings, meet all middle-of-the-road modern standards.

Stations Inn MOTEL $$
(📞 03-755 5499; www.stationsinnhokitika.co.nz; Blue Spur Rd; d $170-300; 🐾) Five minutes' drive from town, high upon rolling hills that overlook the distant ocean, this modern motel complex has plush units featuring king-sized beds and spa bath. With a patio, pond and waterwheel out front, the ambient on-site restaurant (mains $30 to $45; open from 5pm Tuesday to Saturday) specialises in venison, beef and lamb, with petit fours and cheese for afters.

Teichelmann's B&B B&B $$$
(📞 03-755 8232; www.teichelmanns.co.nz; 20 Hamilton St; d $235-255; 🐾) Once home to surgeon, mountaineer and professional beard-cultivator Ebenezer Teichelmann, this is now a charming B&B. All rooms have their own bathrooms, including the more private Teichy's Cottage, in the garden oasis out back.

✖ Eating & Drinking

Dulcie's Takeaways FISH & CHIPS $
(cnr Gibson Quay & Wharf St; fish & chips $6-11; ⏲11am-9pm) Net yourself some excellent fush 'n' chups (try the turbot or blue cod), then scoff them straight from the paper at Sunset Point – a Hokitika highlight.

Sweet Alice's Fudge Kitchen SWEETS $
(27 Tancred St; ⏲10am-5pm) Treat yourself with a slice of Alice's all-natural, handmade fudge ($7), a real fruit ice cream, or a bag of boiled lollies – or maybe all three.

New World SUPERMARKET $
(116 Revell St; ⏲8am-8pm) If you're heading south, this is your last proper supermarket before Wanaka, 426km away!

★ Fat Pipi Pizza PIZZERIA $$
(89 Revell St; pizzas $20-30; ⏲noon-9pm Tue-Sun, 5-9pm Mon; 📶) Vegetarians, carnivores and everyone in between will be salivating for the pizza (including a whitebait version) made right before your eyes. Lovely cakes, honey buns and Benger juices, too. Best enjoyed in the garden bar.

Stumpers Cafe & Bar CAFE, BAR $$
(2 Weld St; lunch $10-22, dinner $18-36; ⏲7am-late) There's something for everyone here, at any time of the day. In the evening you'll find meaty mains, along with a whole host of locals meeting up for a pint and a game of pool.

West Coast Wine Bar WINE BAR
(108 Revell St; ⏲3-8pm Sun-Thu, 3pm-late Fri & Sat) Upping Hoki's sophistication factor, this weeny joint with a cute garden bar pours all sorts of deliciousness, and plates up a little nibble. Fine wines to go.

ℹ Information

Banks can be found on Weld and Revell Sts. There's free wi-fi at the **library** (20 Sewell St; ⏲9.30am-5.30pm Mon-Fri, 10am-1pm Sat).

Hokitika i-SITE (📞03-755 6166; www.hokitika.org; 36 Weld St; ⏲8.30am-6pm Mon-Fri, 9am-6pm Sat & Sun) One of NZ's best i-SITEs offers extensive bookings including all bus services. Also holds DOC info, although you'll need to book online or at DOC Visitor Centres further afield. See also www.westcoastnz.com.

Post Office (Revell St)

Westland Medical Centre (📞03-755 8180; 54a Sewell St; ⏲8.30am-10pm)

ℹ Getting There & Around

AIR

Hokitika Airport (www.hokitikaairport.co.nz; Airport Dr, off Tudor St) is 1.5km east of the centre of town. **Air New Zealand** (www.airnz.co.nz) has four flights daily to/from Christchurch.

BUS

InterCity (📞03-365 1113; www.intercity.co.nz) buses depart from Tancred St daily for Greymouth (45 minutes), Nelson (seven hours) and Franz Josef Glacier (two hours). **Naked Bus** (www.nakedbus.com) services the same destinations three times a week, with both companies offering connections to destinations further afield.

CAR

There are several car-hire branches at Hokitika Airport. **Hokitika Airport Car Rental** (📞0800 556 606; www.hokitikaairportcarhire.co.nz) offers online price comparisons, or enquire and book at the i-SITE.

TAXI

Hokitika Taxis (📞03-755 5075)

Hokitika to Westland Tai Poutini National Park

From Hokitika it's 140km south to Franz Josef Glacier. Most travellers fast forward without stopping, but there are some satisfying stopping points for the inclined. Intercity and Naked buses stop along this stretch of SH6.

Lake Mahinapua

On the highway eight kilometres south of Hokitika is the car park for the **Mahinapua Walkway** (two hours one way), a wonderful walk along an old logging tramway with relics and a diverse range of forest. (It's an even better bike ride.) Two kilometres further on is the entrance to **Lake Mahinapua Scenic Reserve**, with a picnic area, DOC campsite and several short walks.

Five kilometres further on is a signposted turn-off to the **West Coast Treetops Walkway** (☏ 050 887 3386, 03-755 5052; www.treetopsnz.com; 1128 Woodstock-Rimu Rd; aduld/child $38/15; ◷ 9am-5pm), a further 2km away. This steel walkway – 450 metres long and 20m off the ground – offers an unusual perspective on the rainforest canopy, featuring many old rimu and kamahi. The highlight is the 40m high tower, from which there are extensive views across Lake Mahinapua, the Southern Alps, and Tasman Sea. There's a cafe and souvenir shop in the information centre which also has a large sun-drenched patio.

Ross

Ross, 30km south of Hokitika, is where the unearthing of NZ's largest gold nugget (the 2.772kg 'Honourable Roddy') caused a kerfuffle in 1907. The **Ross Goldfields Heritage Centre** (www.ross.org.nz; 4 Aylmer St; ◷ 9am-4pm Dec-Mar, to 2pm Apr-Nov) displays a replica Roddy, along with a scale model ($2) of the town in its shiny years.

The **Water Race Walk** (one hour return) starts near the museum, passing old golddiggings, caves, tunnels and a cemetery. Try **gold panning** by hiring a pan from the information centre ($10) and head to Jones Creek to look for Roddy's great, great grandnuggets.

Established in 1866, the **Empire Hotel** (19 Aylmer St; meals $15-25) is one of the West Coast's hidden gems, the bar (and many of its patrons) testament to a bygone era. Breathe in the authenticity, along with a whiff of woodsmoke, over a pint and an honest meal.

Hari Hari

About 22km south of Lake Ianthe, Hari Hari is where swashbuckling Australian aviator Guy Menzies crash-landed his trusty biplane into a swamp after completing the first solo trans-Tasman flight from Sydney, in 1931. Read all about it and view a replica of his plane at a commemorative park at the southern end of town.

The **Hari Hari Coastal Walk** (www.doc.govt.nz) (2¾ hours) is a low-tide loop along the Poerua and Wanganui Rivers through bogs, estuaries and a swamp forest. The walk starts 20km from SH6, the last 8km unsealed; follow the signs from Wanganui Flats Rd. Tide times are posted at the Pukeko Tearooms, which serves decent food and coffee.

Should you need a sleepover, **Flaxbush Motels** (☏ 03-753 3116; www.flaxbushmotels.co.nz; SH6; d $65-120; ☎) has characterful cabins and units covering a wide range of budgets. It also has a friendly disposition towards birds (ducks and peacocks in particular), and a willingness to negotiate room rates for longer stays.

Whataroa

Near Whataroa, 35km south of Hari Hari, is the **Kotuku Sanctuary**, NZ's only nesting site for the kotuku (white heron), which roosts here between November and February. The only way to visit the nesting site is with **White Heron Sanctuary Tours** (☏ 03-753 4120, 0800 523 456; www.whiteherontours.co.nz; SH6, Whataroa; adult/child $120/55; ◷ 4 tours daily late Sep-Mar) on an enjoyable 2½-hour tour involving a gentle jetboat ride and short boardwalk to a viewing hide. Seeing the scores of birds perched in the bushes is a magical experience. A scenic rainforest tour without the herons is available year-round for the same price.

The tour people also run the **Sanctuary Tours Motel** (☏ 03-753 4120, 0800 523 456; www.whiteherontours.co.nz; SH6; cabins $65-75, d $110-135), with basic cabins with shared bathrooms ($10 extra for bedlinen), and enthusiastically painted motel units.

Glacier Country Scenic Flights (☏ 03-753 4096, 0800 423 463; www.glacieradventures.co.nz; SH6, Whataroa; flights $195-435) offers a range of scenic flights and helihikes, lifting off from Whataroa Valley. These guys give you more mountain-gawping for your buck than many of the operators flying from the glacier townships.

Okarito

Fifteen kilometres south of Whataroa is the turn-off to the Forks, branching west for 13km to the magical seaside hamlet of Okarito (population 30ish). It sits alongside **Okarito Lagoon**, the largest unmodified wetland in NZ and a superb place for spotting birds including rare kiwi and the majestic kotuku. Peaceful Okarito has no shops and limited visitor facilities, so stock up and book up before you arrive.

Sights & Activities

From a car park on the Strand you can begin the easy **Wetland Walk** (20 minutes), a longer walk to **Three Mile Lagoon** (2¾ hours return), and a jolly good puff up to **Okarito Trig** (1½ hours return), which rewards the effort with spectacular Southern Alps and Okarito Lagoon views (weather contingent).

Andris Apse Wilderness Gallery   GALLERY
(☑ 03-753 4241; www.andrisapse.com; 109 The Strand) Okarito is home to world-class landscape photographer Andris Apse. His precisely composed gallery showcases his beautiful works, printed on site and available to purchase, as are infinitely more affordable books. Ring ahead to check it's open, or look for the sandwich board at the end of the driveway.

Okarito Nature Tours   KAYAKING
(☑ 050 865 2748, 03-753 4014; www.okarito.co.nz; kayak half-/full day $60/70; ☎) Hires out kayaks for paddles into the lagoon and up into the luxuriant rainforest channels where all sorts of birds hang out. Guided tours are available (from $85), while overnight rentals ($85) allow experienced paddlers to explore further afield. There's excellent espresso and wi-fi in the welcoming office/lounge.

Okarito Boat Tours   WILDLIFE TOUR
(☑ 03-753 4223; www.okaritoboattours.co.nz) Okarito Boat Tours runs bird-spotting lagoon tours, the most fruitful of which is the 'early bird' (7.30am, 1½ hours, $70). Other worthy options include the one-hour sightseeing tour (2.30pm, $45), and the two-hour nature tours (9am and 11.30am, $85). Cheery, longtime Okaritians Paula and Swade can also fix you up with accommodation in the village.

Okarito Kiwi Tours   WILDLIFE TOUR
(☑ 03-753 4330; www.okaritokiwitours.co.nz; 3hr tours $75) Runs nightly expeditions to spot the rare bird (95% success rate) with an interesting education along the way. Numbers are limited to eight, so booking is recommended.

Sleeping

★**Okarito Campground**   CAMPSITE $
(off Russell St; sites adult/child $12.50/free) Okarito Campground is a breezy patch of community-managed greenery complete with kitchen and hot showers ($1). Gather driftwood from the beach for the fire-pit, or build your bonfire on the beach while the sun goes down. No reservations necessary.

Okarito Beach House   HOSTEL, LODGE $
(☑ 03-753 4080; www.okaritobeachhouse.com; The Strand; dm $28, d $60-100; ☎) The Okarito Beach House has a variety of accommodation. The weathered, self-contained 'Hutel' ($100) is worth every cent. The Summit Lodge has commanding views and the best dining-room table you've ever seen.

WESTLAND TAI POUTINI NATIONAL PARK

The biggest highlights of the Westland Tai Poutini National Park are the Franz Josef and Fox glaciers. Nowhere else at this latitude do glaciers come so close to the ocean. The glaciers' staggering development is largely due to the West Coast's ample rain; snow falling in the glaciers' broad accumulation zones fuses into clear ice at 20m depth, then surges down the steep valleys.

Some say Franz Josef is the superior ice experience, and, while it's visually more impressive, the walk to Fox is shorter, more interesting and often gets you closer to the ice. Both glacier faces are roped off to prevent people being caught in icefalls and river surges. The danger is very real – in 2009 two tourists were killed after being hit by falling ice when they ventured too close. The only way to get close to or on to the ice safely is on a guided tour.

Beyond the glaciers, the park's lower reaches harbour deserted Tasman Sea beaches, rising up through colour-splashed podocarp forests to NZ's highest peaks. Diverse and often unique ecosystems huddle next to each other in interdependent ecological sequence. Seals frolic in the surf as deer sneak through the forests. The resident endangered bird species include kakariki, kaka and rowi (the Okarito brown kiwi), as well as kea, the South Island's native parrot. Kea are inquisitive and endearing, but feeding them threatens their health.

Heavy tourist traffic often swamps the twin towns of Franz and Fox, 23km apart. Franz is the more action-packed of the two, while Fox has a more subdued alpine charm. From December to February, visitor numbers can get a little crazy in both, so consider travelling in the shoulder seasons: September/October and March/April.

Franz Josef Glacier

The early Maori knew Franz Josef as Ka Roimata o Hine Hukatere (Tears of the Avalanche Girl). Legend tells of a girl losing her lover who fell from the local peaks, and her flood of tears freezing into the glacier. The glacier was first explored by Europeans in 1865, with Austrian Julius Haast naming it after the Austrian emperor. The glacier car park is 5km from Franz Josef village; the primary viewpoint is a 40-minute walk from there.

◎ Sights & Activities

★ **West Coast Wildlife Centre**   WILDLIFE
(www.wildkiwi.co.nz; cnr Cron & Cowan Sts; day pass adult/child/family $30/18/80, with backstage pass $50/30/125; ☎) / This feel-good attraction ticks all the right boxes (exhibition, cafe, retail, wi-fi), then goes a whole lot further by actually breeding the rowi – the rarest kiwi in the world. The day pass is well worthwhile by the time you've viewed the conservation, glacier and heritage displays, and hung out with real, live kiwi in their ferny enclosure. The additional backstage pass into the incubating and chick-rearing area is a rare opportunity to learn how a species can be brought back from the brink of extinction, and a chance to go ga-ga over what may be the cutest babies on the planet.

Independent Walks

A rewarding alternative to driving to the glacier car park is the richly rainforested **Te Ara a Waiau Walkway/Cycleway**, starting from near the fire station at the south end of town. It's a one-hour walk (each way) or half that by bicycle (available for hire from Across Country Quad Bikes (p449) or the YHA (p449)).

Several glacier viewpoints are accessed from the car park, including **Sentinel Rock** (20 minutes return) and the **Ka Roimata o Hine Hukatere Walk** (1½ hours return), leading you to the terminal face (read the signs; respect the barriers).

GLACIERS FOR DUMMIES

During the last ice age (15,000 to 20,000 years ago) Westland's twin glaciers reached the sea. In the ensuing thaw they may have crawled back even further than their current positions, but in the 14th century a mini ice age caused them to advance to their greatest modern-era extent around 1750, and the terminal moraines from this time are still visible.

If you get rained in during your time in glacier country, here are a few glacier-geek conversation starters for the pub.

Ablation zone Where the glacier melts.

Accumulation zone Where the ice and snow collects.

Bergschrund A large *crevasse* in the ice near the glacier's starting point.

Blue ice As the accumulation zone (*névé*) snow is compressed by subsequent snowfalls, it becomes *firn* and then *blue ice*.

Calving The process of ice breaking away from the glacier terminal face.

Crevasse A crack in the glacial ice formed as it crosses obstacles while descending.

Firn Partly compressed snow en route to becoming *blue ice*.

Glacial flour Finely ground rock particles in the milky rivers flowing off glaciers.

Icefall When a glacier descends so steeply that the upper ice breaks into a jumble of ice blocks.

Kettle lake A lake formed by the melt of an area of isolated dead ice.

Moraine Walls of debris formed at the glacier's sides (*lateral moraine*) or end (*terminal moraine*).

Névé Snowfield area where *firn* is formed.

Seracs Ice pinnacles formed, like *crevasses*, by the glacier rolling over obstacles.

Terminal The final ice face at the bottom of the glacier.

Other longer walks include the **Douglas Walk** (one hour return), off the Glacier Access Rd, which passes moraine from the 1750 advance, and **Peter's Pool**, a small kettle lake. The **Terrace Track** (30 minutes return) is an easy amble over bushy terraces behind the village, with Waiho River views. Two good rainforest walks, **Tatare Tunnels** and **Callery Gorge Walk** (both around 1½ hours return), start from Cowan St.

The rougher **Roberts Point Track** (five hours return) heads off from the Douglas swing bridge (access via the Douglas Walk). The **Alex Knob Track** (eight hours return) runs from the Glacier Access Rd to the 1303m peak of Alex Knob. Look forward to three glacier lookouts and views to the coast (cloud cover permitting). Both Roberts Point and Alex Knob are suitable only for well-equipped and experienced trampers.

Check out the glacier in the morning or evening, before the cloud cover sets in or after it lifts. Expect fewer tour buses as well.

Pick up a copy of DOC's excellent *Glacier Region Walks* booklet ($2) which provides maps and illuminating background reading.

Guided Walks & Helihikes

Small group walks with experienced guides (boots, jackets and equipment supplied) are offered by **Franz Josef Glacier Guides** (☏03-752 0763, 0800 484 337; www.franzjosef-glacier.com; 6 Main Rd). Both standard tours require helicopter transfers to and from the ice: the 'Ice Explorer' ($325) is bookended by a four-minute flight, with around three hours on the ice; the easier 'Heli Hike' ($429) explores higher reaches of the glacier, requiring a 10-minute flight with around two hours on the ice. Taking around three hours, the 'Glacier Valley Walk' ($75) follows the Waiho River up to the moraine, offering a chance to get beyond the public barriers for close up views of the ice. All trips are $10–30 cheaper for children.

Aerial Sightseeing

Forget sandflies and mozzies. The buzzing you're hearing is a swarm of aircraft in the skies around the glaciers and just beyond in the realm of Aoraki/Mt Cook. A common heliflight ($200–230) is 20 minutes long, and goes to the head of Franz Glacier with a snow landing up top. A 'twin glacier' flight – taking in Fox as well as Franz in around 30 minutes – costs in the region of $300, with a full-monty 40-minute trip (swooping around Aoraki/Mt Cook) from $400. Fares for chil-

dren under 15 are between 60% and 70% of the adult price. Shop around: most operators are situated on the main road in Franz Josef.

Air Safaris   SCENIC FLIGHTS
(☏03-752 0716, 0800 723 274; www.airsafaris. co.nz) Franz' only fixed-wing flyer offers a 30-minute 'twin glacier' ($250) and 50-minute 'grand traverse' ($340).

Fox & Franz Josef Heliservices   SCENIC FLIGHTS
(☏03-752 0793, 0800 800 793; www.scenic-flights. co.nz)

Glacier Helicopters   SCENIC FLIGHTS
(☏03-752 0755, 0800 800 732; www.glacierheli-copters.co.nz)

Helicopter Line   SCENIC FLIGHTS
(☏03-752 0767, 0800 807 767; www.helicopter. co.nz)

Mountain Helicopters   SCENIC FLIGHTS
(☏03-752 0046, 0800 369 432; www.mountain-helicopters.co.nz)

Other Activities

Glacier Country Kayaks   KAYAKING
(☏03-752 0230, 0800 423 262; www.glacierkay-aks.com; 46 Cron St; 3hr kayak $105, 4hr kayak & walk $145) Take a guided kayak trip on Lake Mapourika (7km north of Franz), with fascinating commentary, birdlife, mountain views, a serene channel detour, and an additional bushwalk on offer. Go in the morning for better conditions. Ask about family trips, freedom rental and stand-up paddle-board hire.

Glacier Hot Pools   HOT POOLS
(www.glacierhotpools.co.nz; 63 Cron St; adult/child $25/18; ☉1-9pm) Skilfully embedded into pretty rainforest greenery on the edge of town, this stylish outdoor hot-pool complex is perfect après-hike or on a rainy day. Communal pools, private ones ($42.50 per 45 minutes) and massage also available.

Skydive Franz   SKYDIVING
(☏03-752 0714, 0800 458 677; www.skydivefranz. co.nz; Main Rd) Claiming NZ's highest jump (18,000ft, 80 seconds freefall, $559), this company also offers 15,000ft for $419, and 12,000ft for $319. With Aoraki/Mt Cook in your sights, this could be the most scenic jump you ever do.

Eco-Rafting   RAFTING
(☏03-755 4254, 0508 669 675; www.ecorafting. co.nz; family trip adult/child $135/110, 7hr trip

Franz Josef Glacier & Village

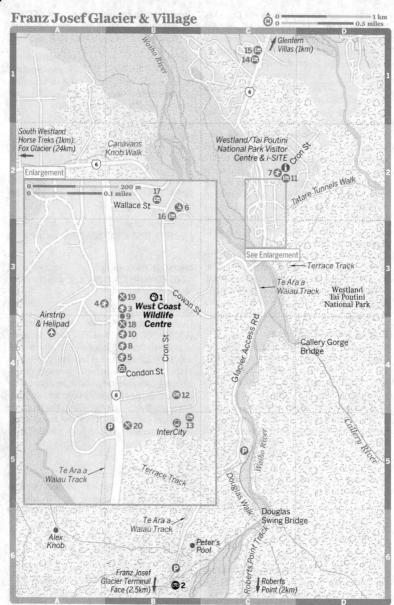

$450) Rafting adventures throughout the coast, from gentle, family trips to the seven hour 'Grand Canyon' trip on the Whataroa River with its towering granite walls. Includes a 15-minute helicopter ride.

South Westland Horse Treks HORSE RIDING
(☎ 03-752 0223, 0800 187 357; www.horsetreknz. com; Waiho Flats Rd; 2hr trek $99) Located 5km west of town, this trekking company runs one- to six-hour equine excursions across farmland and remote beaches.

Franz Josef Glacier & Village

◎ **Top Sights**
1 West Coast Wildlife Centre................... B3

◎ **Sights**
2 Sentinel Rock B6

◆ **Activities, Courses & Tours**
  Across Country Quad Bikes...........(see 3)
3 Air Safaris B3
4 Fox & Franz Josef Heliservices.............. A3
5 Franz Josef Glacier Guides.................... B4
6 Glacier Country Kayaks B2
  Glacier Helicopters........................(see 3)
7 Glacier Hot Pools C2
8 Helicopter Line....................................... B4
9 Mountain Helicopters............................ B4

10 Skydive Franz..B4

◎ **Sleeping**
11 58 on Cron..C2
12 Chateau Franz B4
13 Franz Josef Glacier YHA........................B5
14 Franz Josef Top 10 Holiday Park........... C1
15 Holly Homestead................................... C1
16 Rainforest Retreat.................................B2
17 Te Waonui Forest Retreat.....................B2

◎ **Eating**
18 Four Square B4
19 Landing Bar & Restaurant.....................B3
20 Picnics..B5

Glacier Valley Eco Tours   GUIDED TOUR
(☑ 03-752 0699, 0800 999 739; www.glaciervalley.
co.nz) Offers leisurely three- to eight-hour walking tours around local sights ($70 to $160), packed with local knowledge. Glacier shuttle service ($12.50 return).

Across Country Quad Bikes   QUAD BIKING
(☑ 03-752 0123, 0800 234 288; www.acrosscountry-quadbikes.co.nz; Air Safaris Bldg, SH6) Four-wheeled outings, rockin' and rollin' through the rainforest (two hours, rider/passenger $160/70). Mountain-bike hire available (half-/full day $25/40).

🛏 Sleeping

Franz Josef Glacier YHA   HOSTEL $
(☑ 03-752 0754; www.yha.co.nz; 2-4 Cron St; dm $23-30, s $57, d $85-110; @ ☎) This tidy hostel has warm, spacious communal areas, family rooms, free sauna, on-site bike hire and a booking desk for transport and activities. It has 130 beds, but you'll still need to book ahead.

**Franz Josef Top 10
Holiday Park**   HOLIDAY PARK $
(☑ 03-752 073, 0800 467 8975; www.franz-joseftop10.co.nz; 2902 Franz Josef Hwy; campsites $40-45, d $65-165; @ ☎) This spacious holiday park, 1.5km from the township, has ship-shape facilities and more sleeping options than you can shake a stick at. Tenters are well catered for with sunny, free-draining grassy sites away from the road, looking out over farmy paddocks.

Chateau Franz   HOSTEL $
(☑ 03-752 073, 0800 728 3728; www.sircedrics.
co.nz; 8 Cron St; dm $23-33, d $50-110; @ ☎)

This ramshackle enclave of dorms and motelesque units offers a decent bolthole, with respectable beds and enticing extras such as a spa pool, free soup and unlimited internet. Worn but welcoming communal areas include a sunny patio, two kitchens, and den with a wood burner.

Rainforest Retreat   HOSTEL, HOLIDAY PARK $$
(☑ 03-752 0220, 0800 873 346; www.rainforestretreat.co.nz; 46 Cron St; sites $39, dm $28-32, d $85-220; @ ☎) This capacious enterprise packs plenty of options into its forested grounds, the pick of which are the 'huts', 'houses' and 'lodges' nestled in the bush. Campervans enjoy similar privacy but lose out on high-use communal facilities, as do backpackers who may well arrive on a large tour bus. The on-site Monsoon Bar has a low top shelf, lively atmosphere and decent meals ($22 to $32).

58 on Cron   MOTEL $$
(☑ 03-752 0627, 0800 662 766; www.58oncron.
co.nz; 58 Cron St; d $175-245; ☎) Lacking imagination in both name and decor, these motel units nevertheless impress with their comfort, cleanliness, mod cons and considerate attitude to guests.

★**Glenfern Villas**   APARTMENT $$$
(☑ 03-752 005, 0800 453 6334; www.glenfern.
co.nz; SH6; d $230-289; ☎) A handy 3km out of the tourist hubbub, these delightful one- and two-bedroom villas sit amid groomed grounds with private decks surveying mountain scenery. Top-notch beds, full kitchens, bike hire and family-friendly facilities strongly suggest 'holiday', not 'stop-off'.

Holly Homestead
B&B $$$

(☑03-752 0299; www.hollyhomestead.co.nz; SH6; d $265-430; @ 🖥) Guests are welcomed with fresh home baking at this wisteria-draped 1926 B&B. Choose from three characterful en suite rooms or a suite, all of which share a deck perfect for that sundowner. Children over 12 welcome.

Te Waonui Forest Retreat
HOTEL $$$

(☑03-752 0555, 0800 696 963; www.tewaonui. co.nz; 3 Wallace St; s/d from $579/699; @ 🖥) 🖋 Franz' top-end hotel appears earthy and unflashy, with the inside following suit in natural, textured tones brightened by bold, zippy carpet. It offers a classy package of porter service, degustation dinners (included, along with breakfast, in the price) and a snazzy bar, along with luxurious rooms in which you'll sleep like a log. All have a deck facing into the forest.

✖ Eating

Expect to have numerous dining choices, but be prepared that they might not set your culinary world on fire; some menus haven't changed since the last ice age.

Picnics
BAKERY $

(SH6; snacks $3-7; ⊙8am-5pm) Follow the bright pink sandwich boards to this cracking little bakery. Heaps of good-value ready-to-scoff goods, including epic pasties suitable for bagging for a picnic lunch, or heating up later at dinner time. Other enticements include fresh bread and 'donut Saturday'.

Landing Bar & Restaurant
PUB $$

(www.thelandingbar.co.nz; SH6; mains $20-40; ⊙7.30am-late; 🖥) This busy but well-run pub offers an inordinately huge menu of crowd-pleasing food such as burgers, steaks and pizza. The patio – complete with sunshine and gas heaters – is a good place to warm up after a day on the ice.

Four Square
SUPERMARKET

(SH6; ⊙7.45am-9.30pm) Mr Four Square comes to the party, big time.

❶ Information

Wi-fi is available at most accommodation providers and several eating joints. There's an ATM on the main street, and the postal agency is located at **Glacier Motors** (SH6).

Franz Josef Health Centre (☑03-752 0700, 0800 7943 2584; 97 Cron St; ⊙9am-4pm Mon-Fri) South Westland's main medical centre.

Westland/Tai Poutini National Park Visitor Centre & i-SITE
(☑03-752 0796; www.doc. govt.nz; Cron St; ⊙8.30am-6pm summer, 8.30am-5pm winter) Regional DOC office with good exhibits, weather information and track updates; the i-SITE desk books major nationwide transport except the Interislander. See also www.glaciercountry.co.nz.

❶ Getting There & Around

The bus stop is opposite the Four Square supermarket.

InterCity (☑03-365 1113; www.intercity. co.nz) has daily buses south to Fox Glacier (35 minutes) and Queenstown (eight hours); and north to Nelson (10 hours). Some services can also be booked via Atomic Travel (p425). Book at the DOC Visitor Centre or YHA. **Naked Bus** (www.nakedbus.com) services the same routes three times a week. Both provide connections to destinations further afield.

Glacier Valley Shuttle (☑03-752 0699, 0800 999 739; www.glaciervalley.co.nz) runs scheduled shuttle services to the glacier car park (return trip $12.50).

Fox Glacier

Fox is smaller and quieter than Franz Josef, with a farmy feel and more open aspect. Beautiful Lake Matheson is a highlight, as are the historic sites and the beach itself down at Gillespies Beach.

◉ Sights & Activities
Glacier Valley Walks

It's 1.5km from Fox Village to the glacier turn-off, and a further 2km to the car park, which you can reach under your own steam via Te Weheka Walkway/Cycleway, a pleasant rainforest trail starting just south of the Bella Vista motel. It's just over an hour each way to walk, or 30 minutes to cycle (leave your bikes at the car park – you can't cycle on the glacier walkways). Hire bikes from Westhaven (p452).

From the car park, the terminal face is 30 to 40 minutes' walk. How close you can get to it depends on conditions. Obey all signs: this place is dangerously dynamic.

Short walks near the glacier include the Moraine Walk (over a major 18th-century advance) and Minnehaha Walk. The River Walk extends to the Chalet Lookout Track (1½ hours return) leading to a glacier lookout. The fully accessible River Walk Lookout Track (20 minutes return) starts from the Glacier View Road car park and allows

Fox Glacier & Village

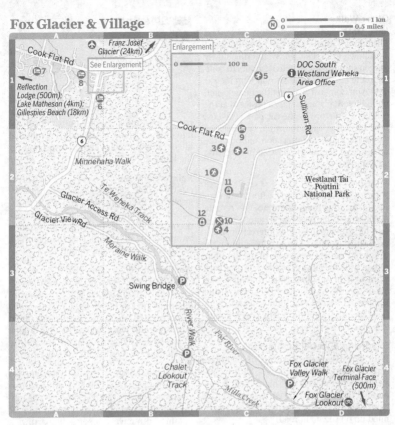

people of all abilities the chance to view the glacier.

Pick up a copy of DOC's excellent *Glacier Region Walks* booklet ($2) which provides maps and illuminating background reading.

Fox Glacier Guiding   GUIDED WALK
(☑ 03-751 0825, 0800 111 600; www.foxguides. co.nz; 44 Main Rd) Guided walks (equipment provided) are organised by Fox Glacier Guiding. Half-day walks cost $132/105 per adult/child; full-day walks are $185. Helihikes cost $399/369 per adult/child, while a day-long introductory ice-climbing course costs $320 per adult. Note that age restrictions vary depending on the trip. There are also easygoing two-hour interpretive walks to the glacier (adult/child $49/35). Longer guided helihike adventures are also available.

Fox Glacier & Village

⊙ Activities, Courses & Tours
	Fox & Franz Josef Heliservices	....(see 1)
1	Fox Glacier Guiding	C2
2	Glacier Helicopters	C2
3	Helicopter Line	C2
4	Mountain Helicopters	C3
5	Skydive Fox Glacier	C1

⊜ Sleeping
6	Fox Glacier Lodge	A1
7	Fox Glacier Top 10 Holiday Park	A1
8	Rainforest Motel	A1
9	Westhaven	C2

⊗ Eating
10	Last Kitchen	C2

⊕ Shopping
11	Fox Glacier General Store	C2
12	Fox Glacier Motors	C2

Other Walks

Lake Matheson
LAKE

The famous 'mirror lake' can be found about 5km down Cook Flat Rd. Wandering slowly (as you should), it will take 1½ hours to complete the circuit. At the far end – on a clear day – you may, just *may,* get the money shot, but failing that you can buy a postcard at the excellent gift store by the car park. The best time to visit is early morning, or when the sun is low in the late afternoon, although the presence of the Matheson Cafe means that any time is a good time.

Gillespies Beach
BEACH

Follow Cook Flat Rd for its full 21km (unsealed for the final 12km) to the remote black-sand Gillespies Beach, site of an old mining settlement. Various interesting walks can be had from here, from a five-minute zip to the old miners' cemetery, to the 3½-hour return walk to Galway Beach where seals are wont to haul out. Don't disturb their lazing about. On the way there or back, stop at the signposted **Peak View Picnic Area** to spin the dial and determine exactly which mountain you're looking at.

Skydiving & Aerial Sightseeing

With Fox Glacier's backdrop of Southern Alps, rainforest and ocean, it's hard to imagine a better place to get high. Costs at Fox parallel those at Franz Josef, as does healthy competition, which sees all heli-operators lined up on the main road.

Skydive Fox Glacier
SKYDIVING

(☑ 03-751 0080, 0800 751 0080; www.skydivefox. co.nz; Fox Glacier Airfield, SH6) Eye-popping scenery abounds on leaps from 16,000ft ($399) or 12,000ft ($299). The airfield is conveniently located three minutes' walk from the centre of town.

Fox & Franz
Josef Heliservices
SCENIC FLIGHTS

(☑ 03-751 0866, 0800 800 793; www.scenic-flights. co.nz)

Glacier Helicopters
SCENIC FLIGHTS

(☑ 03-751 0803, 0800 800 732; www.glacierheli-copters.co.nz; SH6)

Helicopter Line
SCENIC FLIGHTS

(☑ 03-752 0767, 0800 807 767; www.helicopter. co.nz; SH6)

Mountain Helicopters
SCENIC FLIGHTS

(☑ 03-751 0045, 0800 369 423; www.mountainhe-licopters.co.nz)

🛏 Sleeping

★Fox Glacier Top 10
Holiday Park
HOLIDAY PARK $

(☑ 03-751 0821, 0800 154 366; www.fghp.co.nz; Kerrs Rd; sites per person from $20, s/d $70, cabins & units $70-215; @ 🛜) This park has options to suit all budgets, from well-draining tent sites and gravel campervan sites, to lodge rooms and upscale motel units. Shipshape amenities include a splendid communal kitchen/dining room, and a playground for the kids.

Rainforest Motel
MOTEL $$

(☑ 03-751 0140, 0800 724 636; www.rainforest-motel.co.nz; 15 Cook Flat Rd; d $115-145; 🛜) Rustic log cabins on the outside with neutral decor on the inside. Epic lawns for running around on or simply enjoying the mountain views. A tidy, good-value option.

Westhaven
MOTEL $$

(☑ 03-751 0084, 0800 369 452; www.thewest-haven.co.nz; SH6; d $145-185; @ 🛜) These architecturally precise suites are a classy combo of corrugated steel and local stone amid burnt-red and ivory walls. The deluxe king rooms have spa baths, and there are bikes to hire for the energetic (half-/full day $20/40).

Fox Glacier Lodge
B&B, MOTEL $$$

(☑ 03-751 0888, 0800 369 800; www.foxglacier-lodge.com; 41 Sullivan Rd; d $195-225; 🛜) Beautiful timber adorns the exterior and interior of this attractive property, imparting a mountain chalet vibe. Similarly woody self-contained mezzanine units with spa baths and gas fires are also available.

Reflection Lodge
B&B $$$

(☑ 03-751 0707; www.reflectionlodge.co.nz; 141 Cook Flat Rd; d $210; 🛜) The gregarious hosts of this ski-lodge-style B&B go the extra mile to make your stay a memorable one. Blooming gardens complete with Monet-like pond and alpine views seal the deal.

🍴 Eating & Drinking

Fox would be a total stodge-fest were it not for a duo of notably good cafes.

Last Kitchen
CAFE $$

(cnr Sullivan Rd & SH6; lunch $10-20, dinner $22-32; ⊙ noon-late) Making the most of its sunny corner location with outside tables, the Last Kitchen is a relatively elegant option offering contemporary à la carte cafe fare such as halloumi salad, five-spice pork belly and genuinely gourmet burgers. It lacks extensive counter food, but will satisfy for coffee and cake, and fine wine and nibbles.

★**Matheson Cafe**　　　　MODERN NZ **$$**
(☑ 03-751 0878; www.lakematheson.com; Lake Matheson Rd; breakfast & lunch $9-20, dinner $17-33; ⊙ 8am-late Nov-Mar, 8am-4pm Apr-Oct) Near the shores of Lake Matheson, this cafe does everything right: sharp architecture that maximises inspiring mountain views, strong coffee, craft beers and upmarket fare ranging from smoked salmon breakfast bagels, to slow-cooked lamb followed by berry crumble. Next door is the ReflectioNZ Gallery stocking quality, primarily NZ-made art and souvenirs.

ℹ Information

Activity operators and accommodation providers are well-oiled at providing information on local services (and usually a booking service), but you can also find online info courtesy of the **Fox Glacier Tourism Promotions Group** (www. foxglaciertourism.co.nz) and at www.glaciercountry.co.nz. There's an ATM at **Fox Glacier General Store** (⊙ 8am-8pm), the last one until Wanaka-headed south. **Fox Glacier Motors** (SH6) is your last chance for fuel before Haast, 120km away.

DOC South Westland Weheka Area Office (☑ 03-751 0807; SH6; ⊙ 10am-2pm Mon-Fri) This is no longer a general visitor-information centre, but has the usual DOC information, hut tickets and weather/track updates.

Fox Glacier Guiding (☑ 03-751 0825, 0800 111 600; www.foxguides.co.nz; SH6) Books Inter-city and Atomic buses, and provides postal and currency-exchange services.

Fox Glacier Health Centre (☑ 03-751 0836, 0800 7943 2584; SH6) Clinic opening hours are displayed at the centre, or ring the 0800 number for assistance from the Franz Clinic.

ℹ Getting There & Around

Most buses stop outside the Fox Glacier Guiding building.

InterCity (☑ 03-365 1113; www.intercity. co.nz) runs two buses a day north to Franz Josef (40 minutes), the morning bus continuing to Nelson (11 hours). Daily southbound services run to Queenstown (7½ hours). Some services can also be booked via Atomic Travel (p425).

Naked Bus (www.nakedbus.com) runs three times a week north along the coast all the way through to Nelson, and south to Queenstown.

Fox Glacier Shuttles (☑ 0800 369 287), staffed by the inimitable Murray, will drive you around the area from Franz Josef to the Copland Valley, and including Lake Matheson, Gillespies Beach and the glaciers. Look for him parked up opposite Fox Glacier Motors.

SOUTH TO HAAST

From Fox Glacier it's a 120km (two-hour) drive to Haast, along a scenic stretch of highway chopped through lowland forest and occasional pasture, with views inland to sheer-sided valleys and intermittent but grand views seaward.

About 26km south of Fox Glacier, along SH6, is the Copland Valley trailhead, the western end of the Copland Track. It's a six-to-seven-hour tramp to legendary Welcome Flat where thermal springs bubble just metres from the door of DOC's Welcome Flat Hut (adult/child $15/7.50). Unsurprisingly, the hut and its adjacent campsite are extremely popular, with a warden in attendance, so both must be booked in advance either online or in person at DOC visitor centres.

Lake Moeraki, 31km north of Haast, is a rippling fishing lake. At its southern end is one of NZ's best ecolodges, Wilderness Lodge Lake Moeraki (☑ 03-750 0881; www. wildernesslodge.co.nz; SH6; d incl breakfast & dinner $700-1000; ☎) ✎. SIn a verdant setting on the edge of a river channel, it offers comfortable rooms and four-course dinners, but the real delight here are the outdoor activities, such as kayak trips and coastal walks, guided by people with conservation in their blood.

About 5km south of Lake Moeraki is the much-photographed Knights Point, where the Haast road was eventually opened in 1965. Stop here if humanly possible.

Ship Creek, 15km north of Haast, is a terrific place to stretch the legs, boasting two fascinating walks with interesting interpretive panels: the Dune Lake Walk (30 minutes return), which is all sand dunes and stunted forest, leading to a surprising view, and the unsurprisingly swampy Kahikatea Swamp Forest Walk (20 minutes return).

If you haven't had your fill of whitebait yet, call into the Curly Tree Whitebait Company (⊙ 10am-5pm), 10km north of Haast at the Waita River bridge. Exemplary whitebait patties for $8, plus bait to go at the market price.

HAAST REGION

The Haast region is a major wilderness area. The area's kahikatea and rata forests, wetlands, sand dunes, seal and penguin colonies, birdlife and sweeping beaches ensured its inclusion in the Southwest New Zealand (Te Wahipounamu) World Heritage Area.

Haast

Some 120km south of Fox Glacier, Haast crouches around the mouth of the wide Haast River in three distinct pockets: Haast Junction, Haast Village and Haast Beach. As well as being a handy stop for filling the tank and tummy, it's also the gateway to some spectacular scenery which can be explored in various ways, down to the end of the line at Jackson Bay. Pick up or download a copy of DOC's brochure *Walks and Activities in the Haast Area* ($2) to survey the options.

If you're heading north, check your fuel gauge as Haast petrol station is the last one before Fox Glacier.

🛏 Sleeping

Haast Beach Holiday Park   HOLIDAY PARK $
(☎ 03-750 0860, 0800 843 226; www.haastpark. com; 1348 Jackson Bay Rd, Haast Beach; sites from $34, dm $25, d $45-110) Well worth the 14km drive south of Haast Junction, this old dear dishes up just enough charm, with its clean and tidy facilities that range from basic cabins to self-contained units, and a pleasant campers' block with comfortable lounge and views from the deck. The Hapuka Estuary Walk is across the road, and it's a 20-minute walk to an epic beach.

Haast River Top 10   HOLIDAY PARK $
(☎ 03-750 0020, 0800 624 847; www.haasttop10. co.nz; SH6, Haast Village; sites unpowered/powered $38/42, d $110-155; @ 🛜) This highwayside

WORTH A TRIP

JACKSON BAY ROAD

From Haast Junction, the road most travelled is SH6, upwards or across. But there is another option, and that is south... to the end of the line.

The road to Jackson Bay is quiet and intensely scenic. Towered over by Southern Alps, the farms on the flat and the settlements dotted between them stand testament to some of the hardiest souls who ever attempted settlement in NZ. Up until the 1950s, the only way to reach Haast overland was via bush tracks from Hokitika and Wanaka. Supplies came by a coastal shipping service that called every couple of months or so.

Besides the ghosts and former glories, which make an appearance here and there, there's plenty to warrant a foray down to Jackson Bay.

Near Okuru is the Hapuka Estuary Walk (20 minutes return), a winding boardwalk that loops through a sleepy wildlife sanctuary with good interpretation panels en route.

Five kilometres further south (19km south of Haast Junction) is where you'll find the base for Waiatoto River Safaris (☎ 03-750 0780, 0800 538 723; www.riversafaris.co.nz; Jackson Bay Rd; adult/child $199/139; ⊘ trips 10am, 1pm & 4pm), which offers a hair-tousling two-hour jetboat trip upriver into the mountains, then down to the sea, with plenty of natural- and human-history stories along the way.

The road continues west to Arawhata Bridge, where a turn-off leads to the Ellery Creek Walkway, 3.5km away. This pleasant amble through mossy beech forest (1½ hours return) leads to Ellery Lake, where a picnic bench encourages lunch with perhaps a skinny dip for afters.

It's less than an hour's drive from Haast town to the fishing hamlet of Jackson Bay, the only natural harbour on the West Coast. Migrants arrived here in 1875 under a doomed settlement scheme, their farming and timber-milling aspirations mercilessly shattered by never-ending rain and the lack of a wharf, not built until 1938. Those families who stayed turned their hands to largely subsistence living.

With good timing you will arrive when the Cray Pot (☎ 03-750 0035; fish & chips $17-29; ⊘ noon-4pm) is open. This place is just as much about the dining room (a caravan) and location (looking out over the bay) as it is about the honest seafood, including a good feed of fish and chips, crayfish, chowder or whitebait. Ask a local to confirm current opening times.

Walk off your fries on the Wharekai Te Kou Walk (40 minutes return) to Ocean Beach, a tiny bay that hosts pounding waves and some interesting rock formations, or the longer (three to four hour) Smoothwater Bay Track, nearby.

holiday park has a hangar for its amenities block, a bit of a style winner save for the lack of a door. (Waiter, there's a sandfly in my soup.) Motel units are light, spacious and enjoy great views when the weather's kind.

Haast Lodge
LODGE **$**

(☑ 03-750 0703, 0800 500 703; www.haastlodge. com; Marks Rd, Haast Village; sites from $16, dm $25, d/tw $55-65, units d $98-130; @ 🛜) Covering all accommodation bases, Haast Lodge offers clean, well-maintained facilities which include a pleasant communal area for lodge-users and campervanners, and tidy motel units at the Aspiring Court next door.

Collyer House
B&B **$$**

(☑ 03-750 0022; www.collyerhouse.co.nz; Cuttance Rd, Okuru; d $180-250; @ 🛜) This gem of a B&B has thick bathrobes, quality linen, beach views and a sparkling host who cooks a terrific breakfast. This all adds up to make Collyer House a comfortable, upmarket choice. Follow the signs off SH6 for 12km down Jackson Bay Rd.

✖ Eating & Drinking

Okoto Espresso
CAFE **$**

(Haast Village; snacks $2-10) Look out for the rusty hut being towed by the orange Landrover. Where you find it you'll encounter excellent coffee, smoothies and whitebait fritters.

Haast Foodcentre
SUPERMARKET **$**

(Pauareka Rd) This small supermarket stocks sufficient provisions for meal-making, along with fried takeaways and coffee.

Hard Antler
PUB **$$**

(Marks Rd, Haast Village; dinner $20-30; ⊙ dining 11am-9pm) This display of deer antlers is enough to give you the horn. So is the general ambience of this big, bold pub. Plain, meaty food on offer.

ℹ Information

The **DOC Haast Visitor Information Centre** (☑ 03-750 0809; www.doc.govt.nz; cnr SH6 & Jackson Bay Rd; ⊙ 9am-6pm Nov-Mar, to 4.30pm Apr-Oct) has town and backcountry information and has a landline for DIY accommodation and activity bookings. The all-too-brief Haast landscape film *Edge of Wilderness* (adult/child $3/free) screens in the theatrette.

General regional information and visitor services listings can be found on the online directory administered by **Haast Promotions** (www.haastnz.com).

ℹ Getting There & Away

InterCity (☑ 03-365 1113; www.intercity.co.nz) buses stop at the visitor information centre on their daily runs between the West Coast and Queenstown. **Naked Bus** (www.nakedbus.com) also passes through three times a week.

Haast Pass Highway

Early Maori travelled this route between Central Otago and the West Coast in their quest for *pounamu*, naming it Tioripatea, meaning 'Clear Path'. The first party of Europeans to make the crossing may well have been led by the German geologist Julius von Haast, in 1863 – hence the name of the pass, river and township – but evidence suggests that Scottish prospector Charles Cameron may have pipped Haast at the post. It was clearly no mean feat, for such is the terrain that the Haast Pass Highway wasn't opened until 1965.

Heading inland from Haast towards Wanaka (145km, 2½ hours), the highway (SH6) snakes alongside the Haast River, crossing the boundary into Mt Aspiring National Park shortly after you hit fourth gear. The further you go, the narrower the river valley becomes, until the road clambers around sheer-sided valley walls streaked with waterfalls and scarred by rock slips. Princely sums are involved in keeping this highway clear, and even so it sets plenty of traps for unwary drivers.

Stop to admire the scenery, availing yourself of the many signposted lookouts and short walkways such as **Fantail** and **Thunder Creek** falls. These are detailed in DOC's booklet *Walks along the Haast Highway* ($2), but sufficient detail is provided at the trailheads.

The highway tops out at the 563m pass mark, shortly after which you will reach food and fuel at Makarora. Oh, hello Otago!

Christchurch & Canterbury

Includes ➡

Christchurch 457
Lyttelton 477
Banks Peninsula 478
Hanmer Springs 485
Waipara Valley 489
Selwyn District 490
Methven 492
Geraldine 495
Timaru 496
Lake Tekapo 500
Aoraki/Mt Cook
National Park 502

Best Places to Eat

➡ Pegasus Bay (p489)

➡ Cornershop Bistro (p473)

➡ C1 Espresso (p471)

➡ Saggio di Vino (p472)

➡ Addington Coffee Co-op (p472)

Best Places to Stay

➡ Double Dutch (p483)

➡ Maison de la Mer (p483)

➡ Chalet Boutique Motel (p501)

➡ Halfmoon Cottage (p483)

Why Go?

Nowhere in New Zealand is changing and developing as fast as post-earthquake Christchurch, and visiting the country's second-largest city as it's being rebuilt and reborn is both interesting and inspiring.

A short drive from Christchurch's dynamic re-emergence, Banks Peninsula conceals hidden bays and beaches – a backdrop for wildlife cruises with a sunset return to the attractions of Akaroa. To the north are the vineyards of the Waipara Valley and the family-holiday ambience of Hanmer Springs. Westwards, the well-ordered farms of the Canterbury Plains morph quickly into the dramatic wilderness of the Southern Alps.

Canterbury's summertime attractions include tramping along the braided rivers and alpine valleys around Arthur's Pass and mountain biking around the turquoise lakes of the Mackenzie Country. During winter, the attention switches to the skifields. Throughout the seasons, Aoraki/Mt Cook, the country's tallest peak, stands sentinel over this diverse region.

When to Go

➡ Canterbury is one of NZ's driest regions, as moisture-laden westerlies from the Tasman Sea dump their rainfall on the West Coast before hitting the eastern South Island. Visit from January to March for hot and settled summer weather and plenty of opportunities to get active amid the region's spectacular landscapes.

➡ It's also festival time in Christchurch with January's World Buskers Festival and the Ellerslie International Flower Show in March.

➡ Hit the winter slopes from July to October at Mt Hutt or on Canterbury's smaller club ski fields.

ℹ Getting There & Around

AIR

Christchurch's international airport is the South Island's main hub. Air New Zealand flies here from 15 domestic destinations, while Jetstar has flights from Auckland, Wellington and Queenstown. Air New Zealand also flies between Timaru and Wellington.

BUS

Christchurch is the hub for coaches and shuttles heading up the coast as far as Picton, down the coast to Dunedin (and on to Te Anau), through the Alps to Greymouth and across country to Queenstown.

TRAIN

The *TranzAlpine* service connects Christchurch and Greymouth, and the *Coastal Pacific* chugs north to Picton, with ferry connections across Cook Strait to the North Island.

CHRISTCHURCH

POP 342,000

Welcome to a vibrant city in transition, coping creatively with the aftermath of NZ's second-worst natural disaster. Traditionally the most English of NZ cities, Christchurch's heritage heart was all but hollowed out following the 2010 and 2011 earthquakes that left 186 people dead.

Punts still glide gently down the Avon River, and the Botanic Gardens and Hagley Park remain some of NZ's finest public spaces. But in the empty lots and abandoned buildings left in the wake of the earthquakes, interesting art projects have sprung up, and clever, creative people are slowly starting to make things happen. Each new opening and restoration is greeted with enthusiasm by a grateful public, frustrated by the pace of the rebuild and eager to see what shape their future city will take.

If you're worried that your interest in post-earthquake Christchurch may seem in poor taste, don't be. Locals are genuinely keen to welcome sensitive visitors back to their city – and despite the heartache, they're the first to acknowledge how fascinating it all is.

History

The first people to live in what is now Christchurch were moa hunters, who arrived around 1250. Immediately prior to colonisation, the Ngai Tahu tribe had a small seasonal village on the banks of the Avon called Otautahi.

When British settlers arrived in 1880 it was an ordered Church of England project; the passengers on the 'First Four Ships' were dubbed by the British press 'the Canterbury Pilgrims'. Christchurch was meant to be a model of class-structured England in the South Pacific, not just another scruffy colonial outpost. Churches were built rather than pubs, the fertile farming land was deliberately placed in the hands of the gentry, and wool made the elite of Christchurch wealthy.

In 1856 Christchurch officially became NZ's first city, and a very English one at that. Town planning and architecture assumed a close affinity with the 'Mother Country' and English-style gardens were planted, earning it the nickname, the 'Garden City'. To this day, Christchurch in spring is a glorious place to be.

⊙ Sights

◉ City Centre

★ **Botanic Gardens** GARDENS
(Map p464; www.ccc.govt.nz; Rolleston Ave; ⊘7am-8.30pm Oct-Mar, to 6.30pm Apr-Sep) **FREE**
Strolling through these blissful 30 riverside hectares of arboreal and floral splendour is a

---

ESSENTIAL CANTERBURY

Eat Salmon spawned in the shadow of NZ's tallest mountains

Drink NZ's best craft beer at Pomeroy's Old Brewery Inn (p473)

Read *Old Bucky & Me,* a poignant account of the 2011 earthquake by Christchurch journalist Jane Bowron

Listen to Scribe's *The Crusader* (2003), still the best shout-out to the region, with a name that references Canterbury's Super Rugby team

Watch *Heavenly Creatures,* Sir Peter Jackson's best film not involving hobbits, set in Christchurch

Go green At the ecofriendly Okuti Garden (p483) on Banks Peninsula

Online www.christchurchnz.com, www.mtcooknz.com

Area code ☑ 03

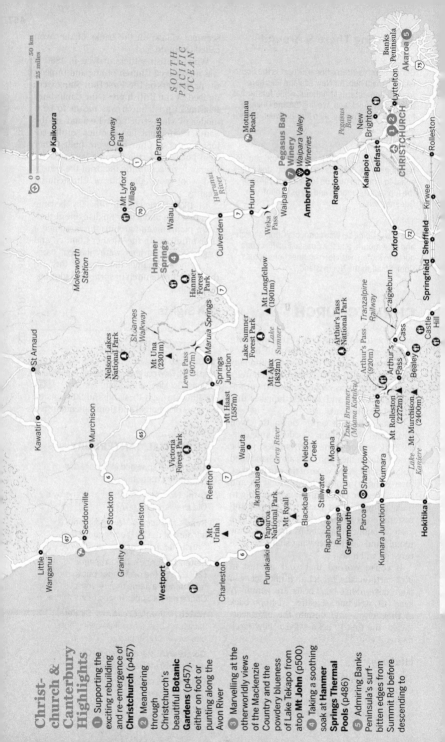

Christchurch & Canterbury Highlights

1 Supporting the exciting rebuilding and re-emergence of **Christchurch** (p457)

2 Meandering through Christchurch's beautiful **Botanic Gardens** (p457), either on foot or punting along the Avon River

3 Marvelling at the otherworldly views of the Mackenzie Country and the powdery blueness of Lake Tekapo from atop **Mt John** (p500)

4 Taking a soothing soak at **Hanmer Springs Thermal Pools** (p486)

5 Admiring Banks Peninsula's surf-bitten edges from Summit Rd before descending to

7 **Pegasus Bay Winery** Waipara Valley Wineries

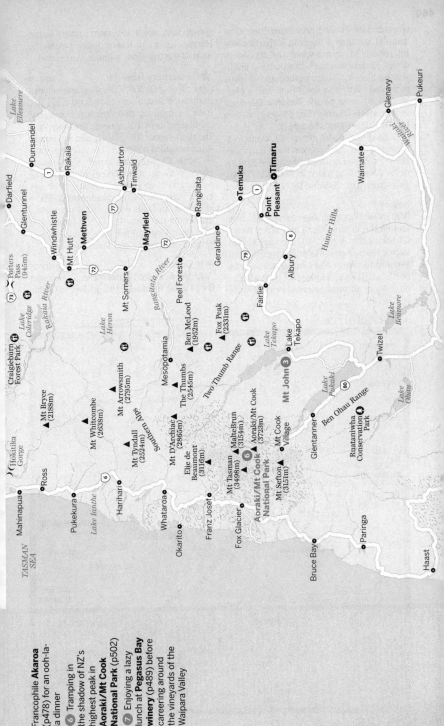

Francophile **Akaroa**
(p478) for an ooh-la-la dinner

6 Tramping in
the shadow of NZ's
highest peak in
**Aoraki/Mt Cook
National Park** (p502)

7 Enjoying a lazy
lunch at **Pegasus Bay
winery** (p489) before
careering around
the vineyards of the
Waipara Valley

consummate Christchurch experience. Gorgeous at any time of the year, it's particularly impressive in spring when the rhododendrons, azaleas and daffodil woodland are in riotous bloom. There are thematic gardens to explore, lawns to sprawl on, and a playground adjacent to the **Botanic Gardens Information Centre** (Map p464; ⊙9am-4pm Mon-Fri, 10.15am-4pm Sat & Sun).

Guided walks ($10) depart at 1.30pm (mid-September to April) from the Canterbury Museum, or you can tour around the gardens in the **Caterpillar train** (☑0800 88 22 23; www.gardentours.co.nz; adult/child $18/9; ⊙11am-3pm).

Hagley Park
PARK

(Map p464; Riccarton Ave) Wrapping itself around the Botanic Gardens, Hagley Park is Christchurch's biggest green space, stretching for 165 hectares. Riccarton Ave splits it in two and the Avon River snakes through the north half. It's a great place to stroll, whether on a foggy autumn morning or on a warm spring day, when the cherry trees lining Harper Ave are in flower. Joggers make the most of the tree-lined avenues, year-round.

★ Canterbury Museum
MUSEUM

(Map p464; ☑03-366 5000; www.canterburymuseum.com; Rolleston Ave; ⊙9am-5pm) **FREE** Yes, there's a mummy and dinosaur bones, but the highlights of this museum are more local and more recent. The Maori galleries contain some beautiful *pounamu* (greenstone) pieces, while Christchurch Street is an atmospheric walk through the colonial past. The reproduction of Fred & Myrtle's gloriously kitsch Paua Shell House embraces Kiwiana at its best, and kids will enjoy the interactive displays in the Discovery Centre (admission $2). Hour-long guided tours commence at 3.30pm on Tuesday and Thursday.

Arts Centre
HISTORIC BUILDINGS

(Map p464; www.artscentre.org.nz; 2 Worcester Blvd) Dating from 1877, this enclave of Gothic

Christchurch

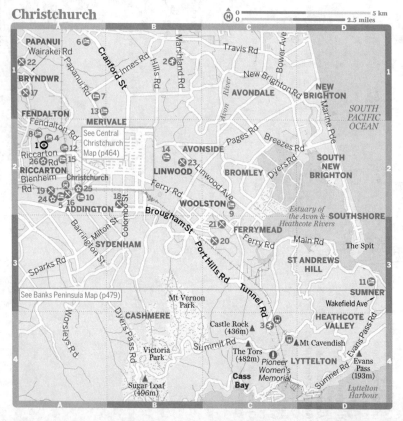

Revival buildings was originally Canterbury College, the forerunner of Canterbury University. The college's most famous alumnus was the father of nuclear physics Lord Ernest Rutherford, the NZ physicist who first split the atom in 1917 (that's him on the $100 bill).

You'll have to be content to admire the architecture from the street, as the complex was badly damaged in the earthquakes. Some parts are scheduled to reopen at the end of 2015, but the whole restoration is expected to take 10 years.

Quake City MUSEUM
(Map p464; www.quakecity.co.nz; 99 Cashel St; adult/child $10/free; ⊙10am-6pm) One of the new must-sees of Christchurch, this little museum tells the story of the earthquakes through photography, video footage and various artefacts, including bits fallen off the Cathedral and the statue of the 'founder of Canterbury' John Robert Godley that toppled from its perch in the square. Most affecting of all is the film featuring locals telling their own stories from that fateful day.

★**Cathedral Square** SQUARE
(Map p464) Christchurch's historic hub sits at the heart of the grid of streets that delineate the devastated city centre. At its centre (at the time of writing, at least) is what remains of ChristChurch Cathedral. Built in 1881, this much-loved icon of the city has become emblematic of the battle between those who seek to preserve what remains of Christchurch's heritage, the fiscal pragmatists, and those ideologically inclined to things new.

The February 2011 earthquake brought down the Gothic church's 63m-high spire, leaving only the bottom half of the tower. Subsequent earthquakes in June 2011 and December 2011 destroyed the cathedral's prized stained-glass rose window. Despite the nave remaining largely intact, the deconstruction and demolition of the cathedral was announced in March 2012 by the Anglican Diocese. Heritage advocates launched court proceedings to prevent the demolition, and at the time of writing, cases were still pending.

Other heritage buildings around Cathedral Sq were also badly damaged, but one modern landmark left unscathed is the 18m-high metal sculpture *Chalice,* designed by Neil Dawson. It was erected in 2001 to commemorate the new millennium.

Gap Filler OUTDOORS
(www.gapfiller.org.nz) With so much empty space around the city, this organisation is doing its best to fill it with interesting things. Installations range from whimsical bits of art, to moving memorials to earthquake victims,

Christchurch

◉ **Sights**
1 Riccarton House & Bush......................A2

⊕ **Activities, Courses & Tours**
2 Bone Dude...B1
3 Gondola..C4

🛏 **Sleeping**
4 Anselm House...A2
5 Arena Motel...A2
6 Christchurch Top 10...............................A1
7 Elm Tree House.......................................A1
8 Fendalton House.....................................A2
9 Haka Lodge..C2
10 Jailhouse...A2
11 Le Petit Hotel...D3
12 Lorenzo Motor Inn.................................A2
13 Merivale Manor.......................................A1
14 Old Countryhouse..................................B2
15 Roma on Riccarton................................A2
   Sumner Bay Motel.........................(see 11)

⊗ **Eating**
16 Addington Coffee Co-op.......................A2
   Bamboozle..(see 11)
17 Bodhi Tree..A1

18 Burgers & Beers Inc...............................B2
   Christchurch Farmers'
   Market...(see 4)
   Cornershop Bistro.........................(see 11)
19 Edesia..A2
20 Gustav's...C3
21 Holy Smoke...C3
22 Kinji...A1
   Mosaic by Simo...............................(see 16)
23 Under the Red Verandah.......................B2

⊕ **Drinking & Nightlife**
   The Brewery.....................................(see 20)
   Volstead Trading Company.........(see 15)

⊕ **Entertainment**
24 AMI Stadium...A2
   Court Theatre.................................(see 16)
25 Dux Live...A2
   Hollywood Cinema.........................(see 11)
26 Hoyts Riccarton.....................................A2

🛍 **Shopping**
   Sunday Artisan Market..................(see 4)
   The Tannery.....................................(see 20)
   Westfield Riccarton.......................(see 26)

CHRISTCHURCH IN...

Two Days

After breakfast at **C1 Espresso**, take some time to walk around the ruined and regenerating city centre, visit **Quake City** and wander through **Cathedral Square**. Make your way to the **Arts Centre** and put together your own informal lunch at **Canterbury Cheesemongers**. After lunch, visit the excellent **Canterbury Museum** and take a walk through the lovely **Botanic Gardens**. That evening, explore the Victoria St dining and drinking strip.

Start day two at the **Addington Coffee Co-op** and then head up to the gondola for the views and a walk at the top. Continue on to Lyttelton for lunch before returning to the city for a punt on the **Avon River**. Head out to Sumner for a late-afternoon swim or a stroll, then stop for dinner and catch a flick at the **Hollywood Cinema**.

Four Days

Follow the two-day itinerary, then head to Akaroa to explore its wildlife-rich harbour, and Banks Peninsula's beautiful outer bays. On day four, visit **Orana Wildlife Park** and then finish the day at the **Tannery** in Woolston.

---

to a minigolf course scattered around different abandoned lots. There are pianos to play, books to read and giant chess pieces to manoeuvre. One of the larger projects is the **Pallet Pavilion** (Map p464; www.palletpavilion. com; cnr Kimore & Durham Sts; 🐦), a large cafe-bar–performance space demarcated by blue-painted storage pallets.

Things are changing constantly, so check out the Gap Map on the website, or simply wander the streets and see what you can find.

Transitional Cathedral   CHURCH
(Map p464; www.christchurchcathedral.co.nz; 234 Hereford St; suggested donation $5; ⊙9am-5pm) Universally known as the Cardboard Cathedral due to the 98 cardboard tubes used in its construction, this interesting structure serves as both the city's temporary Anglican cathedral and as a concert venue. Designed by Japanese 'disaster architect' Shigeru Ban, the entire building was built in 11 months.

⊙ Suburbs

Riccarton House & Bush   GARDENS, FOREST
(Map p460; www.riccartonhouse.co.nz; 16 Kahu Rd, Riccarton) FREE Historic Riccarton House (1856) has been closed to the public since the earthquakes but hundreds still head to the pretty grounds for the Saturday Farmers Market (p473) and Sunday Artisan Market (p475). Just behind the main house, cute little **Deans Cottage** is the oldest building on the Canterbury Plains, dating from 1843.

Even more venerable is the small patch of predator-free bush behind the cottage.

Enclosed by a vermin-proof fence, this is the last stand of kahikatea floodplain forest in Canterbury. Kahikatea is NZ's tallest native tree, growing to heights of 60m; the tallest trees here are a mere 30m and around 300 to 600 years old. A short loop track heads through the heart of the forest.

International Antarctic Centre   EDUCATION CENTRE
(📞0508 736 4846; www.iceberg.co.nz; 38 Orchard Rd, Christchurch Airport; adult/child $39/19; ⊙9am-5.30pm) Part of a huge complex built for the administration of the NZ, US and Italian Antarctic programs, this centre gives visitors the opportunity to see penguins and learn about the icy continent. Attractions include the Antarctic Storm chamber, where you can get a taste of -18°C wind chill.

The 'Xtreme Pass' (adult/child $59/29) includes the '4D theatre' (a 3D film with moving seats and a water spray) and rides on a Hägglund all-terrain amphibious Antarctic vehicle. An optional extra is the Penguin Backstage Pass (adult/child $25/15), which takes visitors behind the scenes of the Penguin Encounter.

A free shuttle departs from outside the Canterbury Museum on the hour from 10am to 4pm, and from the Antarctic Centre on the half-hour.

Orana Wildlife Park   ZOO
(www.oranawildlifepark.co.nz; McLeans Island Rd, McLeans Island; adult/child $28/9; ⊙10am-5pm) Orana describes itself as an 'open range zoo' and you'll know what they mean if you opt

to jump in the cage for the lion encounter (an additional $35). There's an excellent, walk-through native-bird aviary, a nocturnal kiwi house, and a reptile exhibit featuring tuatara. Most of the 80-hectare grounds are devoted to Africana, including rhinos, giraffes, zebras, lemurs and cheetahs.

Willowbank Wildlife Reserve ZOO
(www.willowbank.co.nz; 60 Hussey Rd, Northwood; adult/child $28/11; ⊙9.30am-7pm Oct-Apr, to 5pm May-Sep) ✐ About 10km north of the central city, Willowbank focuses on native NZ critters (including kiwis), heritage farmyard animals and hands-on enclosures with wal-labies, deer and lemurs. There's also a re-created Maori village. In the evening this is the setting for the **Ko Tane** (www.kotane.co.nz; adult/child $135/68; ⊙5.30pm) cultural experience, which includes a traditional Maori welcome, cultural performance and *hangi* (earth oven) meal.

🏃 Activities

Boating

Antigua Boat Sheds BOATING, KAYAKING
(Map p464; ☑03-366 6768; www.boatsheds. co.nz; 2 Cambridge Tce; ⊙7am-5pm) Dating from 1882, the photogenic green-and-white

---

THE CANTERBURY EARTHQUAKES

Christchurch's seismic nightmare began at 4.35am on 4 September 2010. Centred 40km west of the city, a 40-second, 7.1-magnitude earthquake jolted Cantabrians from their sleep, and caused widespread damage to older buildings in the central city. Close to the quake's epicentre in rural Darfield, huge gashes erupted amid grassy pastures and the South Island's main railway line was bent and buckled. Because the tremor struck in the early hours of the morning when most people were home in bed, there were no fatalities, and many Christchurch residents felt that the city had dodged a bullet.

Fast forward to 12.51pm on 22 February 2011, when central Christchurch was busy with shoppers and workers enjoying their lunch break. This time the 6.3-magnitude quake was much closer, centred just 10km southeast of the city and only 5km deep. The tremor was significantly more extreme, and many locals report being flung violently and almost vertically into the air. The peak ground acceleration exceeded 1.8, almost twice the acceleration of gravity.

When the dust settled after 24 traumatic seconds, NZ's second-largest city had changed forever. The towering spire of the iconic ChristChurch Cathedral lay in ruins; walls and verandahs had cascaded down on shopping strips; and two multistorey buildings had pancaked. Of the 185 deaths (across 20 nationalities), 115 occurred in the six-storey Canterbury TV building, where many international students at a language school were killed. Elsewhere, the historic port town of Lyttelton was badly damaged; roads and bridges were crumpled; and residential suburbs in the east were inundated as a process of rapid liquefaction saw tonnes of oozy silt rise from the ground.

In the months that followed literally hundreds of aftershocks rattled the city's traumatised residents (and claimed one more life), but the resilience and bravery of Cantabrians quickly became evident. From the region's rural heartland, the 'Farmy Army' descended on the city, armed with shovels and food hampers. Social media mobilised 10,000 students, and the Student Volunteer Army became a vital force for residential clean-ups in the city's beleaguered eastern suburbs. Heartfelt aid and support arrived from across NZ, and seven other nations sent specialised urban-search-and-rescue teams.

The impact of the events of a warm summer's day in early 2011 will take longer than a generation to resolve. Entire streets and neighbourhoods in the eastern suburbs have had to be abandoned, and Christchurch's heritage architecture is irrevocably damaged. Three years after the quake, families in some parts of the city were still living in substandard accommodation, waiting for insurance claims to be settled. Around 80% of the buildings within the city centre's famed four avenues have been or are due to be demolished, and at the time of writing the empty blocks are an eerie sight, leaving much of the city centre looking like a giant car park.

Plans for the next 20 years of the city's rebuild include a compact, low-rise city centre, large green spaces, and parks and cycleways along the Avon River. It's estimated that the total rebuild and repair bill could reach $40 billion.

Central Christchurch

Papanui Rd→
40

Bealey Ave
20

Carlton Mill Rd

Avon River

Harper Ave

Park Tce

13
38

Dublin St

Dorset St

Victoria St

39

Montreal St

19

35

43
42

North Hagley
Park

Lake
Albert

6

Lake
Victoria

P

Park Tce
26

Cranmer
Sq

Chester St W

Armagh St

5

DOC

Christ's College

Rolleston Ave

24

Gloucester St

1

Botanic
Gardens

Canterbury
Museum 2

11

Christchurch
i-SITE

4

17

31
33

Montreal St

12

Worcester Blvd

Cambridge Tce

Hereford St

Riccarton Ave

Cashel St

Christchurch
Hospital

10

Bridge of
Remembrance

Cambridge Tce

Oxford Tce

Avon River

32

South
Hagley
Park

St Asaph St

Hagley Ave

Stewart St

Antigua St

Montreal St

Durham St S

←Lincoln Rd

Moorhouse Ave
37

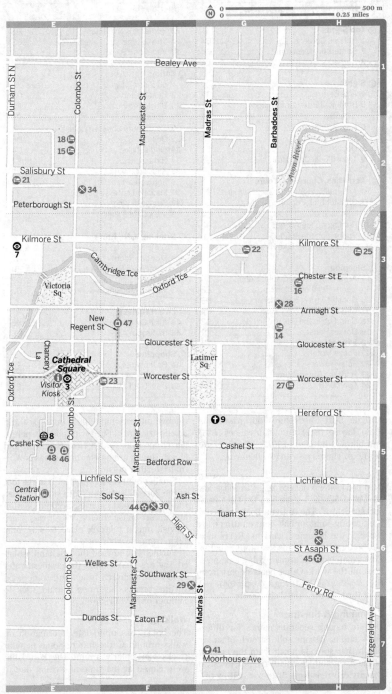

Central Christchurch

◎ **Top Sights**
1 Botanic Gardens.................................B4
2 Canterbury Museum...........................C4
3 Cathedral Square...............................E4

◎ **Sights**
4 Arts Centre.......................................C4
5 Botanic Gardens Information
     Centre...B3
6 Hagley Park......................................B3
7 Pallet Pavilion..................................E3
8 Quake City......................................E5
9 Transitional Cathedral......................G5

◉ **Activities, Courses & Tours**
10 Antigua Boat Sheds..........................C5
11 Christchurch Personal Guiding
     Service..C4
12 Punting on the Avon.........................D4
     Punting on the Avon....................(see 10)
13 Vintage Peddler Bike Hire Co.............C1

◉ **Sleeping**
14 Around the World Backpackers...........G4
15 CentrePoint on Colombo.....................E2
16 Chester Street Backpackers...............H3
17 Classic Villa.....................................C4
18 Colombo in the City..........................E2
19 Dorset House....................................C1
20 Eliza's Manor....................................D1
21 Focus Motel......................................E2
22 Foley Towers.....................................G3
23 Heritage Christchurch........................F4
24 Orari B&B...D4

25 Pomeroy's on Kilmore........................H3
26 The George.......................................C3
27 Vagabond Backpackers........................G4

◉ **Eating**
     50 Bistro....................................(see 26)
28 Beat Street......................................G3
29 Black Betty......................................F6
30 C1 Espresso.....................................F6
31 Canterbury Cheesemongers................D4
32 Dose..D6
33 Fiddlesticks......................................D4
34 Himalayas...E2
35 King of Snake...................................C2
36 Lotus Heart......................................H6
37 Luciano Espresso Bar.........................B7
38 Saggio di Vino..................................C1
39 Vic's Cafe & Bake.............................D1

◉ **Drinking & Nightlife**
40 Carlton...C1
41 Monday Room....................................G7
     Pomeroy's Old Brewery Inn.........(see 25)
42 Revival...D2
43 Tequila Mockingbird...........................D2

◉ **Entertainment**
44 Alice Cinematheque...........................F6
45 darkroom..H6

◉ **Shopping**
46 Ballantynes......................................E5
47 New Regent St..................................F4
48 Re:START Mall...................................E5

Antigua Boat Sheds hires out row boats ($35), kayaks ($12), Canadian canoes ($35) and bikes (adult/child $10/5); all prices are per hour. There's also an excellent cafe.

Punting on the Avon   BOATING
(Map p464; www.punting.co.nz; 2 Cambridge Tce; adult/child $25/12; ⊙9am-6pm Oct-Mar, 10am-4pm Apr-Sep) ✐ The Antigua Boat Sheds are the starting point for half-hour punting trips through the botanical gardens. Relax in a flat-bottomed boat while a strapping lad in Edwardian clobber, armed with a long pole, does all the work. Other boats depart from the Worcester St bridge (Map p464) and punt through the ruined city centre.

Swimming & Surfing

Despite having separate names for different sections, it's one solid stretch of sandy beach that spreads north from the estuary of the Avon and Heathcliff rivers. Closest to the city centre is New Brighton, with a dis-

tinctive pier reaching 300m out to sea and a pedestrian mall lined with phoenix palms. On either side, South New Brighton and North Beach are quieter options, as is Waimairi, further north.

Smaller but prettier Sumner is at the foot of the Port Hills, on the south side of the estuary. With good eateries, accommodation and an art-house cinema, it's an easy place to visit and a relaxing place to stay, only 12km from the city centre.

Further east around the headland, isolated Taylors Mistake has the cleanest water of any Christchurch beach and some good surfing breaks. Beginners should stick to Sumner or New Brighton.

Walking

The i-SITE has up-to-date information on walks around Christchurch. Some popular tracks, particularly around the Port Hills, were closed at the time of writing due to rock falls and instability following the earthquakes, so it's vital to check the current situation before setting off (search www.ccc.govt.nz with the keywords 'Port Hills').

For great views of the city, take the walkway from the Sign of the Takahe on Dyers Pass Rd. The various 'Sign of the...' places in this area were originally roadhouses built during the Depression as rest stops. This walk leads up to the Sign of the Kiwi through Victoria Park and then along Summit Rd to Scotts Reserve, with several lookout points along the way.

You can walk to Lyttelton on the Bridle Path (1½ hours), which starts at Heathcote Valley (take bus 28). The Godley Head Walkway (two hours return) begins at Taylors Mistake, crossing and recrossing Summit Rd, and offers beautiful views on a clear day.

Cycling

Christchurch has more cyclists than any other NZ city, due to its flatness and over 330km of on- and off-road cycleways. These are detailed on the city council's website (www.ccc.govt.nz), which also has updates on the current status of mountain-bike tracks through the Port Hills.

The 49km Little River Railtrail (www.littleriverrailtrail.co.nz) links the Christchurch suburb of Hornby to the Banks Peninsula hamlet of Little River. A couple of small sections traverse roads without cycle lanes, although this is only temporary. Join the trail 20km from Little River at Motukarara for the best of the ride.

City Cycle Hire   BICYCLE RENTAL
(☑03-377 5952; www.cyclehire-tours.co.nz; bike half-/full day $25/35, mountain bike half-/full day $30/45) Offers door-to-door delivery of on- and off-road city bikes and touring bikes. They'll also meet you with a bike at the top of the gondola if you fancy a 16km descent ($70 including gondola ride; 1½ hours).

Natural High   BICYCLE RENTAL
(☑03-982 2966; www.naturalhigh.co.nz; 690a Harewood Rd, Harewood; per day/week from $50/175) Rents touring and mountain bikes, and can assist with guided and self-guided bicycle touring through Canterbury and the South Island.

Vintage Peddler Bike Hire Co   BICYCLE RENTAL
(Map p464; ☑03-365 6530; www.thevintagepeddler.co.nz; 16 Bealey Ave; per hour/day $15/30) Take to two retro wheels on these funky vintage bicycles. Helmets, locks and local knowledge are all supplied.

Other Activities

Gondola   CABLE CAR
(Map p460; www.gondola.co.nz; 10 Bridle Path Rd; return adult/child $25/12; ☺10am-5pm) Take a ride to the top of Mt Cavendish (500m) on this 945m cable car for wonderful views over the city, Lyttelton, Banks Peninsula and the Canterbury Plains. At the top there's a cafe and the child-focused *Time Tunnel* ride through historical scenes. You can also walk to Cavendish Bluff Lookout (30 minutes return) or the Pioneer Women's Memorial (one hour return).

Tram   TRAM
(☑03-377 4790; www.tram.co.nz; adult/child $10/free) Prior to the earthquakes, historic trams operated on a 2.5km inner-city loop. Limited services resumed in late 2013, heading between New Regent St and Canterbury Museum (35 minutes), but the route will expand as the rebuild continues.

Bone Dude   COURSE
(Map p460; ☑03-385 4509; www.thebonedude.co.nz; 153 Marshland Rd, Shirley; from $60; ☺1-4pm Mon-Fri, 10am-1pm Sat) Creative types should consider booking a session with the Bone Dude, who'll show you how to carve your own bone pendant (allow three hours). Sessions are limited to eight participants, so book ahead.

Garden City Helicopters   SCENIC FLIGHT
(☑03-358 4360; www.helicopters.net.nz; 20min $199) Flights above the city and Lyttelton let you observe the impact of the earthquake and the rebuilding efforts.

ⓘ WELCOME ABOARD COMBOS

Welcome Aboard (☑03-365 8282; www.welcomeaboard.co.nz) is the company that runs the punting, tram, gondola and Botanic Garden caterpillar tours, as well as Thrillseekers Adventures in Hanmer Springs. A baffling array of combo tickets is available which will save you some money if you're considering doing more than one activity. It also operates the six-hour Grand Tour (adult/child $119/69), which includes all four Christchurch-based activities and a stop in Sumner.

Tours

Discovery Tours BUS TOUR
(☑ 0800 372 879; www.discoverytravel.co.nz; tours from $130) Excursions to Akaroa, Aoraki/Mt Cook, Hanmer Springs, Kaikoura and the Waipara Valley wine region. The Arthur's Pass tour (adult/child $355/178) packs the *TranzAlpine* train, jetboating and a farm tour into one action-packed day.

Hassle Free Tours BUS TOUR
(☑ 03-385 5775; www.hasslefree.co.nz) Explore Christchurch on an open-top double-decker bus (adult/child $29/15). Regional options include a 4WD alpine safari, jetboating on the Waimakariri River, and visiting the location of Edoras from the *Lord of the Rings* trilogy.

Red Bus Rebuild Tour BUS TOUR
(☑ 0800 500 929; www.redbus.co.nz; adult/child $29/15) Commentaries focus on the past, present and future of earthquake-damaged sites in the city centre. Tours take 90 minutes and include video footage of the former streetscape.

Christchurch Sightseeing Tours BUS TOUR
(☑ 0508 669 660; www.christchurchtours.co.nz; tours from $75) City tours, plus further-afield detours to Akaroa, Hanmer Springs and the Waipara wine region.

Christchurch Bike Tours CYCLING
(☑ 0800 733 257; www.chchbiketours.co.nz; 2/4hr $50/160) Informative, two-hour tours loop around the city daily, heading to the Farmers Market on Saturday mornings. Also available is a four-hour gourmet food tour ending with a three-course lunch. Tours leave from the Antigua Boat Sheds.

Christchurch Segway Tours CYCLING
(☑ 027 542 1887; www.urbanwheels.co.nz; per person $190) Two-hour two-wheeled guided tours through the city centre, Hagley Park and Riccarton.

Hiking Guys TOUR
(☑ 09-281 4481; www.hikingguys.co.nz; adult/child $445/223) Day trips incorporating the *TranzAlpine* train and tramping around Arthur's Pass. Multiday trips also available.

Christchurch Personal Guiding Service WALKING TOUR
(Map p464; ☑ 03-383 2495; Rolleston Ave; tours $15; ☺1pm daily) Nonprofit organisation offering informative two-hour city walks. Buy tickets and join tours at the i-SITE or at the red-and-black kiosk nearby.

South Pacific Motorcycle Tours DRIVING TOUR
(☑ 03-312 0066; www.motorbiketours.co.nz) Jump on a hog for a fully guided or self-guided multiday road trip.

Festivals & Events

Check www.bethere.co.nz for a comprehensive listing of festivals and events.

Garden City SummerTimes MUSIC
(www.summertimes.co.nz) Say g'day to summer at a huge array of outdoor events between December and March.

World Buskers Festival PERFORMING ARTS
(www.worldbuskersfestival.com) National and international talent entertain passers-by for 10 days in mid-January. Check the website for locations – and don't forget to put money in the hat.

Festival of Flowers FLORAL
(www.festivalofflowers.co.nz) A blooming spectacle around Christchurch's heritage gardens for three weeks in February.

Ellerslie Flower Show FLORAL
(www.ellerslieflowershow.co.nz) Hagley Park comes alive in late February/early March with NZ's biggest flower show.

Christchurch Arts Festival PERFORMING ARTS
(www.artsfestival.co.nz) Midwinter arts extravaganza over a month from mid-August, celebrating music, theatre and dance.

Festa ARCHITECTURE
(www.festa.org.nz) The spotlight is shone on Christchurch's post-earthquake 'transitional architecture' over Labour Weekend in October.

NZ Cup & Show Week HORSE RACING
(www.nzcupandshow.co.nz) Includes the NZ Cup horse race, fashion shows, fireworks and the centrepiece A&P Show, where the country comes to town. Held over a week in November.

Sleeping

City Centre

Chester Street Backpackers HOSTEL $
(Map p464; ☑ 03-377 1897; www.chesterst.co.nz; 148 Chester St E; dm/tw/d $32/68/70; @ ⊛) This relaxed wooden villa is painted in bright colours and has a large library in the sunny front room. The friendly house cat is a regular guest at hostel barbecues. It's popular; book ahead.

Dorset House
HOSTEL $

(Map p464; ☎03-366 8268; www.dorsethouse.
co.nz; 1 Dorset St; dm/s $39/90, d $105-110;
P @ 🖤 🛜) 🍃 Built in 1871, this wooden villa
has a sunny deck, a large regal lounge with
a log fire, a pool table, and beds instead of
bunks. It's a short stroll to Hagley Park.

Around the World Backpackers
HOSTEL $

(Map p464; ☎03-365 4363; www.aroundtheworld.
co.nz; 314 Barbadoes St; dm $30, d $76-80; P @ 🛜)
We love AtW's friendly vibe, Kiwiana decor
and sunny back garden (complete with hammocks and a barbecue). Ask about the 'Love
Shack' if you're visiting with the closest of
travelling companions.

Foley Towers
HOSTEL $

(Map p464; ☎03-366 9720; www.backpack.co.nz/
foley.html; 208 Kilmore St; dm $30-33, d with/
without bathroom $78/72; P @ 🛜) Sheltered
by well-established trees, Foley Towers provides well-maintained rooms encircling quiet garden-trimmed courtyards. Dorms sleep
six in three sets of bunks, or there are share
rooms containing three single beds.

Vagabond Backpackers
HOSTEL $

(Map p464; ☎03-379 9677; www.vagabondhostel.
co.nz; 232 Worcester St; dm $26-30, s $53, d $60-
70; P @ 🛜) This old place is reminiscent of a
big shared house. There's an appealing garden, and the grungy ambience is matched
with prices that are cheaper than most.

★ Pomeroy's on Kilmore
B&B $$

(Map p464; ☎03-374 3532; www.pomeroysonkil-
more.co.nz; 282 Kilmore St; r $145-195; P 🛜) Even
if this cute wooden cottage wasn't the sister
and neighbour of Christchurch's best craft-
beer pub, it would still be one of our favour-
ites. Three of the five elegantly furnished
rooms open on to a sunny garden and rates
include a self-serve continental breakfast.

Focus Motel
MOTEL $$

(Map p464; ☎03-943 0800; www.focusmotel.com;
344 Durham St N; r $150-200; P 🛜) Sleek and
centrally located, this friendly motel offers
studio and one-bedroom units with big-
screen TVs, iPod docks, kitchenettes and
super-modern decor. There's a guest barbecue and laundry, and pillowtop chocolates
sweeten the deal.

CentrePoint on Colombo
MOTEL $$

(Map p464; ☎03-377 0859; www.centrepointonco-
lombo.co.nz; 859 Colombo St; r/apt from $165/190;
P 🛜) The friendly Kiwi-Japanese manage-
ment have imbued this centrally located mo-
tel with style and comfort. Little extras like
stereos, blackout curtains and spa baths (in
the deluxe rooms) take it to the next level.

Colombo in the City
MOTEL $$

(Map p464; ☎03-366 8775; www.motelcolombo.
co.nz; 863 Colombo St; d $170-190, apt $190-290;
P @ 🛜) Colombo's attractive units are
equipped with Sky TV, CD players, double-
glazed windows and spa baths. Options range
from studios to two-bedroom apartments.

Heritage Christchurch
HOTEL $$$

(Map p464; ☎03-983 4800; www.heritagehotels.
co.nz; 28-30 Cathedral Sq; ste $235-440; 🛜) 🍃
Standing grandly on Cathedral Sq while all
around is in ruins, the 1909 Old Govern-
ment Building owes its survival to a thorough
strengthening when it was converted to a
hotel in the 1990s. After a three-year post-
earthquake restoration its spacious suites are
more elegant than ever. All have full kitchens.

Orari B&B
B&B $$$

(Map p464; ☎03-365 6569; www.orari.co.nz; 42
Gloucester St; s $175-235, d $195-255; P 🛜) Orari
is an 1893 home that has been simply updated with light-filled, pastel-toned rooms and
inviting guest areas, as well as a lovely front

CHRISTCHURCH FOR CHILDREN

There's no shortage of kid-friendly sights and activities in Christchurch. If family fun is a
priority, consider planning your travels around NZ's biggest children's festival, **KidsFest**
(www.kidsfest.org.nz). It's held every July and is chock-full of shows, workshops and parties. The annual World Buskers Festival (p468) is also bound to be a hit.

For picnics and open-air frolicking, visit the Botanic Gardens (p457); there's a playground
beside the cafe, and little kids will love riding on the Caterpillar train. Extend your nature-
based experience with a wildlife encounter at Orana Wildlife Park (p462) or the Willowbank
Wildlife Reserve (p463), or get them burning off energy in a rowboat or kayak from the Antigua Boatsheds (p466). Fun can be stealthily combined with education at the International
Antarctic Centre (p462) and the Discovery Centre at Canterbury Museum (p460).

If the weather's good, hit the beaches at Sumner or New Brighton.

garden. A neighbouring block, constructed in a sympathetic style, contains five three-bedroom apartments.

The George
HOTEL $$$

(Map p464; ☑ 03-379 4560; www.thegeorge.com; 50 Park Tce; r $295-315, ste $472-630; P @ 🛜) ⚓ The George has 53 handsomely decorated rooms within a 1970s-looking building on the fringe of Hagley Park. Discreet staff attend to every whim, and ritzy features include huge TVs, luxury toiletries and glossy magazines.

Classic Villa
B&B $$$

(Map p464; ☑ 03-377 7905; www.theclassicvilla. co.nz; 17 Worcester Blvd; s $179, d $289-389, ste $489; P 🛜) ⚓ Pretty in pink, this 1899 house is one of Christchurch's most elegant accommodation options. Rooms are trimmed with antiques and Turkish rugs, and the Mediterranean-style breakfast is a shared social occasion.

Eliza's Manor
HOTEL $$$

(Map p464; ☑ 03-366 8584; www.elizas.co.nz; 82 Bealey Ave; r $235-345; P 🛜) ⚓ An infestation of teddy bears has done little to dint the heritage appeal of this large 1861 mansion. Wisteria curls around weatherboards, while inside the rooms are spacious and frilly.

Merivale

Merivale Manor
MOTEL $$

(Map p460; ☑ 03-355 7731; www.merivalemanor. co.nz; 122 Papanui Rd; d $145-180; P 🛜) A gracious 19th-century Victorian mansion is the hub of this elegant motel, with units both in the main house and in the more typically motel-style blocks lining the drive. Accommodation ranges from studios to two-bedroom apartments.

Elm Tree House
B&B $$$

(Map p460; ☑ 03-355 9731; www.elmtreehouse. co.nz; 236 Papanui Rd; r/ste $265/295; P 🛜) Built in the 1920s, elegant Elm Tree House has six stylish rooms and suites, a dining area leading to sunny rose gardens, and a spacious, wood-lined guests' lounge with a working Wurlitzer jukebox.

Fendalton

Anselm House
B&B $$

(Map p460; ☑ 03-343 4260; www.anselmhouse. co.nz; 34 Kahu Rd; s $190; P 🛜) When we visited, post-earthquake repairs were continuing on this architecturally interesting home, but

guests were still able to stay in the blissful 'river room', gazing over the gurgling Avon. Hopefully the 'rococo room' will be back up-and-running during the lifetime of this book.

Fendalton House
B&B $$

(Map p460; ☑ 03-343 1661; www.fendaltonhouse. co.nz; 28a Kotare St; r $165; P 🛜) There's only one guest room available at this friendly, homestay-style B&B amid the pleasant streets of leafy Fendalton. Rates include a cooked breakfast and free wi-fi.

Riccarton

Lorenzo Motor Inn
MOTEL $$

(Map p460; ☑ 03-348 8074; www.lorenzomotor-lodge.co.nz; 36 Riccarton Rd; units $159-239; P 🛜) There's a Mediterranean vibe to this trim two-storey motel – the best of many on the busy Riccarton Rd strip. Units range from studio to two-bedroom apartments and some have spa baths and little balconies.

Roma on Riccarton
MOTEL $$

(Map p460; ☑ 03-341 2100; www.romaonriccar-ton.com; 38 Riccarton Rd; d $158-230; P 🛜) It may be the mirror image of neighbouring Lorenzo, but they're completely separate businesses. Like its twin, the units are all thoroughly modern, ranging from studios to two-bedroom apartments.

Addington

Jailhouse
HOSTEL $

(Map p460; ☑ 03-982 7777; www.jail.co.nz; 338 Lincoln Rd; dm $32-35, tw/d $89/92; @ 🛜) From 1874 to 1999 this was Addington Prison; it's now one of Christchurch's most appealing and friendly hostels. Private rooms are a bit on the small side – they don't call them cells for nothing.

Arena Motel
MOTEL $$

(Map p460; ☑ 03-338 4579; www.arenamotel.co.nz; 30 Whiteleigh Ave; d $135-185; P 🛜) Within walking distance of the railway station and the increasingly hip Addington strip, the Arena has tidy modern units with kitchenettes, ranging in size from studios to two-bedroom apartments.

Sumner

Le Petit Hotel
HOTEL $$

(Map p460; ☑ 03-326 6675; www.lepetithotel.co.nz; 16 Marriner St; d $155; P @ 🛜) Relaxed coffee-and-croissant breakfasts, friendly owners and the close proximity to Sumner beach and some of Christchurch's best restaurants make this a definite '*oui*' from us. Get in early and request an upstairs room with a view.

Sumner Bay Motel
MOTEL $$

(Map p460; ☑03-326 5969; www.sumnermotel.co.nz; 26 Marriner St; d $159-185; P) The studio, one- and two-bedroom units at this striking, contemporary complex all have either balconies or courtyards, plus quality furnishings and Sky TV. Two-bedroom units contain full kitchens; the rest have kitchenettes.

🏠 Other Suburbs

Haka Lodge
HOSTEL $

(Map p460; ☑03-980 4252; www.hakalodge.com; 518 Linwood Ave, Woolston; dm/d/apt $32/79/170; ☎) Sprawled across three floors of a modern suburban house, Haka Lodge is one of Christchurch's newest hostels. Rooms are spotless and colourful, and end-of-day treats include a comfy lounge and bird-filled garden.

Old Countryhouse
HOSTEL $

(Map p460; ☑03-381 5504; www.oldcountryhouse-nz.com; 437 Gloucester St, Linwood; dm $35-37, d with/without bathroom $102/92; P@☎) Spread between three separate villas, 1km east of Latimer Sq, this chilled-out hostel has handmade wooden furniture, a reading lounge and a lovely garden filled with native ferns. A spa pool and sauna heat things up.

Christchurch Top 10
HOLIDAY PARK $

(Map p460; ☑03-352 9176; www.christchurchtop10.co.nz; 39 Meadow St, Papanui; sites $39-50, unit with/without bathroom from $94/76; P@☎🏊) It could do with some freshening up, but this is the best of Christchurch's holiday parks. Accommodation ranges from sites to simple cabins and motel units, and there's an indoor pool, games rooms and a playground for the kids.

Airport Gateway
MOTEL $$

(☑03-358 7093; www.airportgateway.co.nz; 45 Roydvale Ave, Burnside; d $155-195; P@☎) Handy for those early flights, this large motel has a variety of rooms with good facilities. A 24-hour airport transfer is available at no extra charge. The newer block is very comfortable and good value.

🍴 Eating

Following the February 2011 earthquake, many restaurants were forced to abandon their damaged buildings and move to the suburbs. As a result you'll find some real treats lurking in unlikely blocks of neighbourhood shops. Key dining precincts are Victoria St (to the northwest of the City Centre), Addington, Riccarton, Merivale and the beachside suburb of Sumner.

🍽 City Centre

★ C1 Espresso
CAFE $

(Map p464; www.c1espresso.co.nz; 185 High St; mains $10-19; ⊙7am-10pm; ☎) 🍴 Resurrected from the rubble, C1 has reopened better than ever in a grand former post office that somehow escaped the cataclysm. Recycled materials fill the interior (Victorian oak panelling, bulbous 1970s light fixtures) and tables spill onto a little square. The food, coffee and service are excellent too.

Black Betty
CAFE $

(Map p464; www.blackbetty.co.nz; 163 Madras St; mains $10-20; ⊙8am-4pm; ☎) Infused with aromas from Switch Espresso's roasting operation, Black Betty's industrial-chic warehouse is a popular destination for students from nearby CPIT. Attractions include all-day breakfasts, excellent counter food and the best of NZ wine and craft beers.

Vic's Cafe & Bake
CAFE $

(Map p464; www.vics.co.nz; 132 Victoria St; mains $11-18; ⊙7.30am-4.30pm) Pop in for a robust breakfast on the big shared tables or linger over lunch on the front terrace. Otherwise grab baked goodies and still-warm artisan bread for a DIY riverside picnic.

Canterbury Cheesemongers
DELI $

(Map p464; www.cheesemongers.co.nz; rear, 301 Montreal St; sandwiches $5-8; ⊙9am-5pm Tue-Sat) Pop in to buy artisan cheeses, or craft your own sandwich by combining freshly baked sourdough bread and ciabatta with a whole cheese shop of dairy goodies. Coffee and juices complete a good-value lunch.

Beat Street
CAFE $

(Map p464; 324 Barbadoes St; mains $10-19; ⊙7am-5pm Sun-Tue, to 10pm Wed-Sat; ✍) Welcome to the grungy hub of Christchurch cafe-cool. Free range this and organic that combine with terrific eggy breakfasts, gourmet pies and robust coffee. Look out for open mic music and poetry nights.

Dose
CAFE, JAPANESE $

(Map p464; www.cafedose.co.nz; 77 Tuam St; mains $7-19; ⊙7.30am-4pm Mon & Tue, to late Wed-Sat)

Excellent coffee and superior counter food combine here with toasted bagels and what may just be Christchurch's best eggs Benedict. In the evenings Dose morphs into an *izakaya* bar with tasty grilled skewers and ice-cold Japanese beer.

King of Snake
ASIAN $$
(Map p464; ☑ 03-365 7363; www.kingofsnake. co.nz; 145 Victoria St; mains $24-37; ☺ 11am-3.30pm Mon-Fri, 5.30-10pm daily) Dark wood, gold tiles and purple skull-patterned wallpaper fill this so-hip-right-now restaurant and cocktail bar with just the right amount of sinister opulence. The adventurous menu gainfully plunders the cuisines of Asia – from India to Korea – to delicious, if pricey, effect.

Fiddlesticks
RESTAURANT, BAR $$
(Map p464; ☑ 03-365 0533; www.fiddlesticksbar. co.nz; 48 Worcester Blvd; mains $20-40; ☺ 9am-late) Sidle into slick Fiddlesticks and seat yourself in either the more formal dining room or in the glassed-in patio attached to the curvy cocktail bar. Food ranges from soups and beautifully presented salads to fancy meat pies and Angus steaks.

Lotus Heart
VEGETARIAN $$
(Map p464; www.thelotusheart.co.nz; 363 St Asaph St; mains $13-22; ☺ 7.30am-3pm Tue-Sun & 5-9pm Fri & Sat; ☑) ✔ Run by students of Sri Chimnoy, this vegetarian eatery serves curry, pizza, wraps, freshly squeezed organic juices and filled pita pockets. Organic, vegan and gluten-free options abound, and there's an interesting gift shop onsite.

50 Bistro
EUROPEAN $$
(Map p464; ☑ 03-371 0250; www.thegeorge.com; 50 Park Tce; breakfast $17-22, lunch $20-24, dinner $20-37; ☺ 6.30am-late; ☑) The more casual restaurant at the George is a bustling affair, serving savvy local twists on classic bistro flavours. Try the Nifty 50 lunch menu – $29 for soup and a main dish.

Himalayas
INDIAN $$
(Map p464; ☑ 03-377 8935; www.himalayas.co.nz; 830a Colombo St; lunch $9-14, dinner $18-24; ☺ 11.30am-2pm Tue-Fri & 5pm-late Tue-Sun; ☑) Himalayas' stylish dining room showcases lots of subcontinental favourites, including vegetarian options like the creamy *dal makhani* (black lentils cooked with aromatic spices). The *kadhai* chicken is studded with chilli, ginger and coriander – perfect with a cold beer.

★ Saggio di Vino
EUROPEAN $$$
(Map p464; ☑ 03-379 4006; www.saggiodivino. co.nz; 179 Victoria St; mains $35-42; ☺ 5-10pm) Despite the Italian name, the menu has a heavy French accent at this elegant restaurant, which is quite possibly Christchurch's best. Expect delicious takes on terrine, duck *confit* and Café de Paris steak, and a well-laden cheese trolley to finish you off.

Addington

★ Addington Coffee Co-op
CAFE $
(Map p460; www.addingtoncoffee.org.nz; 297 Lincoln Rd; mains $6-19; ☺ 7.30am-4pm Mon-Fri, 9am-4pm Sat & Sun; ☏☑) One of Christchurch's biggest and most bustling cafes is also one of its best. A compact stall selling organic cotton T-shirts jostles for attention with delicious cakes, gourmet pies and the legendary house breakfasts. An onsite laundromat completes the deal for busy travellers.

Luciano Espresso Bar
CAFE $
(Map p464; www.facebook.com/LucianoEspresso; 76 Moorhouse Ave; mains $10-21; ☺ 7am-4.30pm) 'Christchurch's best coffee' is the claim, and we're not about to argue. Order from the interesting selections on the menu or peruse the drool-inducing items on the counter. Slick decor distracts from the incessant traffic outside.

Mosaic by Simo
MOROCCAN $
(Map p460; www.simos.co.nz; 300 Lincoln Rd; tapas & mains $8-19; ☺ 9am-9pm Mon-Sat) This deli-cafe is popular for its takeaway *bocadillos* (grilled wraps filled with a huge selection of Middle Eastern and African-inspired fillings, sauces and toppings). Other tasty offerings include sauteed calamari, spicy *merguez* sausages and tagines.

Edesia
EUROPEAN $$$
(Map p460; ☑ 03-943 2144; www.edesia.co.nz; 12 Show Pl; lunch $25-29, dinner $38-43; ☺ 11.30am-3pm Mon-Wed, 8.30am-3pm Thu & Fri, 8.30am-1pm Sat, 5.30-10pm daily) Ignore the office-park location; Edesia's version of fine dining is worth seeking out. The dinner menu includes innovative spins on local venison and lamb, while lunch includes pasta and salads. After work it morphs into a cosy bar for local desk jockeys.

Woolston

Gustav's
RESTAURANT, BAR $$
(Map p460; ☑ 03-389 5544; www.gustavs.co.nz; The Tannery, Garlands Rd, Woolston; tapas $10-14,

mains $28-33; ⊙11am-late) Hexagonal oak tables and vintage wallpaper add a touch of Edwardian class, while live jazz and the clatter of diners sharing dishes creates a convivial hubbub. Local meat and seafood features prominently, although the flavours are international.

Holy Smoke
CAFE, DELI **$$**

(Map p460; www.holysmoke.co.nz; 650 Ferry Rd, Woolston; mains $12-19; ⊙7am-4.30pm Tue-Sat) Here's your chance to get acquainted with the unique character of *manuka* (NZ tea tree). At this friendly deli-cafe it's used to smoke everything from bacon to salmon, which then make their way into cooked breakfasts and counter food.

Sumner

★Cornershop Bistro
FRENCH **$$**

(Map p460; ✐03-326 6720; www.cornershopbistro. co.nz; 32 Nayland St, Sumner; lunch $17-21, dinner $27-35; ⊙10am-3pm Fri-Sun, 5.30-10pm Wed-Sun) Classic dishes such as *coq au vin* are expertly executed at this superior French-style bistro which never forgets it's in a relaxed beachside suburb. Spend longer than you planned to linger over brunch.

Bamboozle
ASIAN **$$**

(Map p460; ✐03-326 7878; www.facebook.com/ bamboozlerestaurant; 6 Wakefield St; mains $18-29; ⊙5-10pm Tue-Sat) Asian fusion is the name of the game at stylish Bamboozle, where talented chefs conjure up innovative spins on traditional dishes. Leave room for one of Christchurch's best crème brûlées.

Other Suburbs

Christchurch Farmers' Market
MARKET **$**

(Map p460; www.christchurchfarmersmarket.co.nz; 16 Kahu Rd, Riccarton; ⊙9am-noon Sat) Held in the pretty grounds of Riccarton House, this excellent farmers market offers a tasty array of organic fruit and vegies, South Island cheeses and salmon, local craft beer and ethnic treats.

Kinji
JAPANESE **$$**

(Map p460; ✐03-359 4697; www.kinjirestaurant. com; 279b Greers Rd, Bishopdale; mains $16-18; ⊙5.30-10pm Mon-Sat) The destruction of its central city premises sparked a move to a tucked-away suburban site for this acclaimed Japanese restaurant. Fortunately its loyal clientele has followed, making bookings essential. Tuck into the likes of sashi-

mi and ginger squid but save room for the green-tea tiramisu, a surprising highlight.

Under the Red Verandah
CAFE **$$**

(Map p460; www.utrv.co.nz; cnr Tancred & Worcester Sts, Linwood; mains $10-20; ⊙7.30am-4pm;) A post-earthquake change of premises has done nothing to dint UTRV's popularity with Christchurch foodie types. Take a seat under said verandah and tuck into baked goodies, oaty pancakes and corn fritters.

Bodhi Tree
BURMESE **$$**

(Map p460; ✐03-377 6808; www.bodhitree. co.nz; 399 Ilam Rd, Bryndwr; dishes $13-18; ⊙6-10pm Tue-Sat; ✐) Bodhi Tree has been wowing locals with the subtle flavours of Burmese cuisine for more than a decade. The starter-sized dishes feature exceptionally fresh ingredients and are designed to be shared. Standouts include *le pet thoke* (pickled tea-leaf salad) and *ciandi thoke* (grilled eggplant).

Burgers & Beers Inc
BURGERS **$$**

(Map p460; www.burgersandbeersinc.co.nz; 355 Colombo St, Sydenham; burgers $13-18; ⊙11am-late) Quirkily named gourmet burgers – try the Woolly Sahara Sand Hopper (Moroccan-spiced lamb with lemon yoghurt) or the Shagged Stag (venison with tamarillo and plum chutney) – and an ever-changing selection of Kiwi craft beers give you reason to head south.

🍷 Drinking & Nightlife

City Centre

Pomeroy's Old Brewery Inn
PUB

(Map p464; www.pomspub.co.nz; 292 Kilmore St; ⊙3-11pm Tue-Thu, noon-11pm Fri-Sun) Welcoming Pomeroy's is the city's hoppy hub for fans of NZ's rapidly expanding craft-beer scene. A wide range of guest taps showcase brews from around the country. There's regular live music, and the attached Victoria's Kitchen does great pub food (mains $22 to $26).

Carlton
BAR

(Map p464; www.carltonbar.co.nz; 1 Papanui Rd, Merivale; ⊙11am-midnight Sun-Wed, to 2am Thu-Sat) The rebuilt Carlton's ultramodern look includes old planning maps plastered to the walls and visual references to the shipping containers out of which it operated when the historic Carlton pub collapsed. The upstairs deck is a prime spot on a sunny afternoon.

Revival
BAR

(Map p464; www.revivalbar.co.nz; 94 Victoria St; ◷4-9pm Mon & Tue, to midnight Wed, to 3am Thu-Sun) ⏍ Revival is the hippest of Christchurch's container bars, with regular DJs and a funky lounge area dotted with a quirky collection of automotive rear ends and vintage steamer trunks.

Tequila Mockingbird
BAR, RESTAURANT

(Map p464; www.tequilamockingbird.co.nz; 98 Victoria St; shared plates $8-24; ◷11.30am-late Mon-Fri, 5pm-late Sat & Sun) If the awesome name's not enough to lure you through the door of this upmarket Latin bar-restaurant, then perhaps the Caribbean-inflected cocktails, nifty decor and late-night DJs will. The food's excellent too.

Monday Room
WINE BAR

(Map p464; www.themondayroom.co.nz; 367 Moorhouse Ave; ◷8am-late Mon-Fri, 10am-late Sat & Sun) Part cafe, part restaurant and part wine bar, the versatile Monday Room is the kind of place to hang out at any time. Occupying a restored heritage building, the funky interior is a background for interesting brunch and lunch options; later in the day, tapas, craft beers, cocktails and live musicians take centre stage.

Suburbs

★ The Brewery
BREWERY

(Map p460; www.casselsbrewery.co.nz; 3 Garlands Rd, Woolston; ◷7am-late) An essential destination for beer-loving travellers, the Cassels & Sons brewery crafts its beer using a wood-fired brew kettle, resulting in big, bold beers. Tasting trays are available for the curious and the indecisive, live bands perform most nights, and the food – including wood-fired pizzas – is top-notch, too.

Volstead Trading Company
BAR

(Map p460; www.volstead.co.nz; 55 Riccarton Rd, Riccarton; ◷4-11pm Mon-Sat) Comfy old sofas from your last student flat combine with quirky murals and interesting craft beers in this very cool shabby-chic bar. If you're peckish, dig into popcorn, nachos and toasted sandwiches.

☆ Entertainment

For live music and club listings, see www.christchurchmusic.org.nz or www.mukuna.co.nz. Also look out for the *Groove Guide* magazine in cafes.

Court Theatre
THEATRE

(Map p460; ☑03-963 0870; www.courttheatre.org.nz; Bernard St, Addington) Christchurch's original Court Theatre was an integral part of the city's Arts Centre but was forced to relocate to this warehouse after the earthquakes. The new premises are much more spacious; it's a great venue to see popular international plays and works by NZ playwrights.

Dux Live
LIVE MUSIC

(Map p460; www.duxlive.co.nz; 363 Lincoln Rd, Addington) One of the kingpins of the live-music scene, this intimate 250-capacity space has gigs most nights.

darkroom
LIVE MUSIC

(Map p464; www.facebook.com/darkroom.nz; 336 St Asaph St; ◷5pm-late Wed-Sun) A hip combination of live-music venue and bar, darkroom has lots of Kiwi beers and great cocktails. Live gigs are frequent – and frequently free.

AMI Stadium
STADIUM

(Rugby League Park; Map p460; www.crfu.co.nz; 95 Jack Hinton Dr, Addington) Following the destruction of AMI Stadium at Lancaster Park, the traditional home of rugby union and cricket in Christchurch, the Canterbury Rugby Union have shifted its home games to Rugby League Park (confusingly now also known as AMI Stadium due to sponsorship rights). The Crusaders play here from late February to July in the Super Rugby tournament, while from July to September, Canterbury plays in NZ's domestic rugby championship.

Alice Cinematheque
CINEMA

(Map p464; ☑03-365 0615; www.aliceinvideoland.co.nz; 209 Tuam St; adult/child $16/12) There are only 38 seats at this Egyptian-themed art-house cinema, attached to the excellent Alice in Videoland specialty video and DVD store.

Hollywood Cinema
CINEMA

(Map p460; www.hollywoodcinema.co.nz; 28 Marriner St; adult/child $16/10) Mainly art-house and foreign-language flicks in the seaside suburb of Sumner.

Hoyts Riccarton
CINEMA

(Map p460; www.hoyts.co.nz; Westfield Riccarton, Riccarton Rd; adult/child $16.50/11.50) Hollywood blockbusters screen at Christchurch's most central multiplex.

🛍 Shopping

🛍 City Centre

Re:START Mall   MALL
(Map p464; www.restart.org.nz; Cashel Mall; ☺10am-5pm; 🐾) This colourful labyrinth of shops based in shipping containers was the first retail activity in the Christchurch CBD after the earthquakes. With a couple of decent cafes and a good selection of stores, it's a pleasant place to stroll. Note that Re:START is only intended to be temporary, so it may disappear at any time.

Ballantynes   DEPARTMENT STORE
(Map p464; www.ballantynes.com; cnr Colombo & Cashel Sts; ☺9am-5pm) A venerable Christchurch department store selling men's and women's fashions, cosmetics, travel goods and specialty NZ gifts. Fashionistas should check out the Contemporary Lounge upstairs.

New Regent St   MALL
(Map p464; www.newregentstreet.co.nz) A forerunner to the modern mall, this pretty little stretch of pastel Spanish Mission–style shops was described as NZ's most beautiful street when it was completed in 1932. Fully restored post-earthquake, it's once again a pleasant place to stroll and peruse the tiny galleries, gift shops and cafes.

🛍 Suburbs

★ The Tannery   SHOPPING CENTRE
(Map p460; www.thetannery.co.nz; 3 Garlands Rd, Woolston; ☺10am-5.30pm Mon-Sat, to 4pm Sun) In a city mourning the loss of its heritage, this post-earthquake conversion of a Victorian tannery couldn't be more welcome. The 19th-century industrial buildings have been zhooshed up with period-style tiles, wrought iron and stained glass, and filled with boutique stores selling everything from books to fashion to surfboards. Bored partners of frenzied shoppers can slink off for a drink in The Brewery or Gustav's (p472). Alice in Videoland is planning to open two cinemas here.

Westfield Riccarton   MALL
(Map p460; www.westfield.co.nz; Riccarton Rd, Riccarton; ☺9am-6pm Sat-Wed, to 9pm Thu & Fri) Since the earthquakes, shopping in Christchurch has largely been focused on the city's suburban malls. The most convenient for visitors is this megamall, west of the city centre. As well as a huge selection of fashion, homeware and entertainment outlets, there's a cinema multiplex, a supermarket and 22 food outlets.

Sunday Artisan Market   MARKET
(Map p460; 16 Kahu Rd, Riccarton; ☺11am-2pm Sun) Held in the leafy grounds of Riccarton House, this small market combines local arts-and-crafts vendors with gourmet food stalls and live music.

ℹ Information

MEDIA

Cityscape (www.cityscape-christchurch.co.nz) Quarterly entertainment and events magazine available in inner-city cafes and retailers. Check the website for updates on new openings around town.

The Press (www.stuff.co.nz/the-press/) Christchurch's newspaper, published Monday to Saturday. Friday's edition has entertainment listings.

MEDICAL SERVICES

24 Hour Surgery (☑03-365 7777; www.24hoursurgery.co.nz; cnr Bealey Ave & Colombo St) No appointment necessary.

Christchurch Hospital (☑03-364 0640, emergency dept 03-364 0270; www.cdhb.govt. nz; 2 Riccarton Ave) Has a 24-hour emergency department.

Urgent Pharmacy (☑03-366 4439; cnr Bealey Ave & Colombo St; ☺6-11pm Mon-Fri, 9am-11pm Sat & Sun) Located beside the 24 Hour Surgery.

TOURIST INFORMATION

Airport i-SITE (☑03-353 7774; www.christchurchnz.com; ☺7.30am-7pm)

Christchurch i-SITE (Map p464; ☑03-379 9629; www.christchurchnz.com; Botanic Gardens, Rolleston Ave; ☺8.30am-5pm, extended in summer)

DOC (Department of Conservation; Map p464; ☑03-379 4082; www.doc.govt.nz; Botanic Gardens Information Centre, Armagh St; ☺9am-4pm Mon-Fri, 10.15am-4pm Sat & Sun) Information on South Island national parks and walks.

Visitor Kiosk (Map p464; Cathedral Sq; ☺9.30am-5pm)

USEFUL WEBSITES

CERA (www.cera.govt.nz) The Canterbury Earthquake Recovery Authority has the lowdown on rebuild plans and status updates.

Christchurch & Canterbury Tourism (www.christchurchnz.com) Official tourism website for the city and region.

Christchurch City Council (www.christchurch.org.nz) The city council's official website.

Neat Places (www.neatplaces.co.nz) A local blogger's authoritative view of the best of Christchurch's shopping, eating and drinking.

ⓘ Getting There & Away

AIR

Christchurch Airport (CHC; ☏ 03-358 5029; www.christchurchairport.co.nz; Durey Rd) is the South Island's main international gateway (see the transport chapter for international flights). The newly modernised and expanded airport has excellent facilities, including baggage storage, hire-car counters, ATMs, foreign-exchange offices and an i-SITE visitor information centre.

The following are the domestic airlines flying from Christchurch and the destinations that they serve:

Air New Zealand (☏ 0800 737 000; www.air-newzealand.co.nz) Air New Zealand–operated flights head to/from Auckland, Wellington, Dunedin and Queenstown. Code-share flights with smaller regional airlines head to/from Blenheim, Hamilton, Hokitika, Invercargill, Napier, Nelson, New Plymouth, Palmerston North, Paraparaumu, Rotorua and Tauranga.

Jetstar (☏ 0800 800 995; www.jetstar. com) Flies to/from Auckland, Wellington and Queenstown.

BUS

The following services stop outside the Canterbury Museum on Rolleston St, unless otherwise stated. Enquire at the i-SITE about seasonal ski shuttles.

Akaroa French Connection (☏ 0800 800 575; www.akaroabus.co.nz; one way/return $25/45) Daily service to Akaroa.

Akaroa Shuttle (☏ 0800 500 929; www. akaroashuttle.co.nz; one way/return $35/50) Heads to Akaroa daily, increasing to twice daily from November to April.

Atomic Shuttles (☏ 03-349 0697; www. atomictravel.co.nz) Destinations include Picton ($35, 5¼ hours), Greymouth ($45, 3¾ hours), Timaru ($25, 2½ hours), Dunedin ($30 to $35, 5¾ hours) and Queenstown ($50, seven hours).

Budget Buses & Shuttles (☏ 03-615 5119; www.budgetshuttles.co.nz; ☉ Mon-Sat) Offers a door-to-door shuttle to Geraldine ($57) and Timaru ($47), along with cheaper scheduled runs (from $27).

Hanmer Connection (☏ 0800 242 663; www. hanmerconnection.co.nz; one way/return $30/50) Daily bus to/from Hanmer Springs via Amberley and Waipara.

InterCity (☏ 03-365 1113; www.intercity.co.nz) The most reliable of the coach services, with the most extensive network. The main bus stop is on Armagh St, between New Regent and Manchester Sts. Coaches head to Picton (from $26, 5¼ hours), Timaru (from $28, 2½ hours), Dunedin (from $40, six hours) and Queenstown (from $55, eight to 11 hours) twice daily; and to Te Anau (from $61, 10¾ hours) daily.

Knightrider (☏ 03-342 8055; www.knightrider. co.nz) Has a bus departing from 118 Bealey Ave most evenings, heading to Timaru ($38, three hours), Oamaru ($43, four hours), Moeraki ($47, five hours) and Dunedin ($50, six hours).

Naked Bus (www.nakedbus.com; prices vary; ☏) Destinations include Picton (4½ to 5¾ hours), Kaikoura (1½ hours), Dunedin (six hours), Wanaka (7½ hours) and Queenstown (eight hours).

West Coast Shuttle (☏ 03-768 0028; www. westcoastshuttle.co.nz) Buses stop outside Central Station on Tuam St, heading to/from Springfield ($30, 1¼ hours), Arthur's Pass ($40, 2¾ hours) and Greymouth ($53, four hours).

TRAIN

Christchurch railway station (☏ 03-341 2588; www.kiwirailscenic.co.nz; Troup Dr, Addington; ☉ ticket office 6.30am-3pm) is the terminus for two highly scenic train journeys. At the time of writing there was a free shuttle from city-centre accommodation to the station, although this may not continue; enquire at the i-SITE or ask your accommodation provider.

The *Coastal Pacific* runs daily from October to April departing from Christchurch at 7am and arriving at Picton at 12.13pm ($79 to $159). Other stops include Waipara ($59, 56 minutes), Kaikoura ($49 to $69, three hours) and Blenheim ($79 to $159, 4¾ hours). It then departs Picton at 1pm, returning to Christchurch at 6.21pm.

The *TranzAlpine* is widely considered one of the best train journeys in the world. It operates year-round with a daily train between Christchurch and Greymouth ($99 to $198, 4½ hours) via Springfield ($89, one hour), Arthur's Pass ($89, 2½ hours) and Lake Brunner ($99 to $198, 3½ hours).

ⓘ Getting Around

TO/FROM THE AIRPORT

Christchurch Airport is only 10km from the city centre but a **taxi** between the two can cost a hefty $45 to $65. Alternatively, the airport is well served by **public buses** (www.metroinfo. co.nz). Bus 3 heads through Riccarton (25 minutes) to the central bus station (35 minutes) and on to Sumner (70 minutes). Bus 29 heads through Fendalton (10 minutes) to the bus station (30 minutes). Both services cost $8 and run every half-hour from roughly 7am to 11pm.

Shuttle services include the following:

Steve's Shuttle (☑0800 101 021; www.steve-shuttle.co.nz; city centre fare $18, plus $5 per additional passenger; ☺3am-6pm)

Super Shuttle (☑0800 748 885; www.super-shuttle.co.nz; city centre fare $19, plus $5 for additional passengers; ☺24hr)

CAR & MOTORCYCLE
Hire

Most major car- and campervan-rental companies have offices in Christchurch, as do numerous smaller local companies. Operators with national networks often want cars to be returned from Christchurch to Auckland because most renters travel in the opposite direction, so you may find a cheaper price on a northbound route.

Local options include the following:

Ace Rental Cars (☑03-360 3270; www.ace-rentalcars.co.nz; 20 Abros Pl, Burnside)

First Choice (☑03-358 6132; www.firstchoice.co.nz; Christchurch Airport)

New Zealand Motorcycle Rentals & Tours (☑09-486 2472; www.nzbike.com; 22 Lowther St, Sockburn) Also leads guided motorbike tours.

Omega Rental Cars (☑03-377 4558; www.omegarentalcars.com; 252 Lichfield St)

Pegasus Rental Cars (☑03-358 5890; www.rentalcars.co.nz; 578 Wairakei Rd, Burnside)

Purchase

Scour hostel notice boards and check out **Backpackers Car Market** (☑03-377 3177; www.backpackercarschristchurch.co.nz; 33 Battersea St; ☺9.30am-5pm), **Turners Auctions** (☑03-343 9850; www.turners.co.nz; 1 Detroit Pl; ☺8am-6pm Mon-Fri, 10am-4pm Sat & Sun), www.trademe.co.nz and www.autotrader.co.nz.

PUBLIC TRANSPORT

Christchurch's **Metro** (☑03-366 8855; www.metroinfo.co.nz) bus network is inexpensive and efficient. Most buses run from **Central Station** (Map p464; 46-50 Lichfield St). Get timetables from the i-SITE or the station's information kiosk. Tickets (adult/child $3.50/1.80) can be purchased on board and include one free transfer within two hours. Metrocards allow unlimited two-hour/full-day travel for $2.50/5, but the cards cost $10 and must be loaded up with a minimum of $10 additional credit.

TAXI

Blue Star (☑03-379 9799; www.bluestartaxis.org.nz)

First Direct (☑0800 505 555; www.firstdirect.net.nz)

Gold Band (☑0800 379 5795; www.goldband-taxis.co.nz)

AROUND CHRISTCHURCH

Lyttelton

POP 2860

Southeast of Christchurch are the prominent Port Hills, which slope down to the city's port on Lyttelton Harbour. Christchurch's first European settlers landed here in 1850 to embark on their historic trek over the hills. Nowadays a 2km road tunnel makes the journey considerably quicker.

Lyttelton was badly damaged during the 2010 and 2011 earthquakes, and many of the town's heritage buildings along London St were subsequently demolished. However Lyttelton has re-emerged as one of Christchurch's most interesting communities. The town's artsy, independent and bohemian vibe is stronger than ever, and it's once again a hub for good bars, cafes and restaurants. It's well worth catching the bus from Christchurch and getting immersed in the local scene, especially on a Saturday morning when the market's buzzing.

From Lyttelton, **Black Cat** (☑03-384 0621; www.blackcat.co.nz; B Jetty, Lyttelton Wharf) provide ferries to sheltered Quail Island (adult/child return $25/13, October to April only), as well as to sleepy Diamond Harbour (adult/child one way $6.20/3.10).

✖ Eating

Lyttelton Farmers' Market   MARKET $

(www.lyttelton.net.nz; London St; ☺10am-1pm Sat) Every Saturday morning, food stalls take the place of cars on Lyttelton's main street. As well as being a great place to stock up on produce, there's always plenty of baked goods and hot food to snack on. Head around the corner to the primary school for the concurrent antiques market.

Samo Lyttelton   CAFE $

(www.samo.co.nz; 3 Canterbury St; mains $9-19; ☺8am-3.30pm) Following the destruction of local institution Lyttelton Coffee Company, some of the former staff set up this ramshackle cafe in a garage around the corner. It may possibly disappear when LCC is back on its feet in London St, but until then, this is Lyttelton's best cafe.

Freemans   ITALIAN, BAR $$

(☑03-328 7517; www.freemansdiningroom.co.nz; 47 London St; breakfast $15-18, lunch $22-25, dinner

$22-37; ◎ 3pm-late Mon-Fri, 10am-late Sat & Sun) Freemans does fresh pasta, top-notch pizzas and brews from Christchurch's Three Boys brewery. Grab a spot on the deck for great harbour views, and take in Sunday afternoon jazz concerts from 3pm.

Fisherman's Wharf SEAFOOD **$$**
(www.fishermanswharf.net.nz; 39 Norwich Quay; mains $14-29; ◎ 11.30am-8pm Fri-Sun) Part alfresco bar and part gourmet fish-and-chippie, Fisherman's Wharf is a top spot for a cold beer and tasty seafood. Try the fish of the day – prepared any of four ways – and watch the goings on at the rugged working port.

🍷 Drinking & Nightlife

Wunderbar BAR
(www.wunderbar.co.nz; 19 London St, enter from rear car park; ◎ 5pm-2am Mon-Fri, 1pm-3am Sat & Sun) Wunderbar is a top spot to see NZ's more interesting acts, from raucous rock to late-night/early-morning dub. The kooky decor alone is worth a trip to Lyttelton.

Porthole BAR
(www.portholebar.co.nz; cnr Canterbury & London Sts; ◎ 11am-1am; 🛜) Porthole is yet another funky reinvention of the humble shipping container. Local wines and Kiwi craft beers are served in the buzzy interior, while laidback Lyttelton folk chill on the alfresco deck. There's live music most nights.

ℹ️ Information

Lyttelton Visitor Information Centre (☑ 03-328 9093; www.lytteltonharbour.info; 20 Oxford St; ◎ 10am-4pm)

ℹ️ Getting There & Away

Buses 28 and 535 run from Christchurch to Lyttelton (adult/child $3.50/1.80, 25 minutes). At the time of writing, the Summit Rd to Christchurch and the road to Sumner were closed.

Governors Bay

POP 870
From Lyttelton, the harbour road wends west for a scenic 9km to pretty Governors Bay, where there are a couple of good spots for lunch. If you continue on you'll reach Banks Peninsula via a winding route that's longer but more scenic than SH75.

🛏️ Sleeping & Eating

Governors Bay Hotel PUB **$$**
(☑ 03-329 9433; www.governorsbayhotel.co.nz; 52 Main Rd; d $110-160, mains $18-33; ◎ 11am-late; 🛜) Dating from 1870, this is one of NZ's oldest still-operating pubs. You couldn't want for a more inviting deck to knock back an afternoon tipple on, and the food is excellent too, covering all of the classic pub-grub bases. Upstairs is accommodation in chicly renovated rooms with shared bathrooms.

She Chocolat CAFE **$$**
(☑ 03-329 9825; www.shechocolat.com; 79 Main Rd; mains $13-20; ◎ 10am-4pm) These New Age chocoholics conjure up excellent food and terrific views. Chocolate has embedded itself deeply into the menu, infiltrating porridge, kumara cakes and rice-paper rolls, plus there's a range of truffles to enjoy with your coffee.

Banks Peninsula

POP 3050
Gorgeous Banks Peninsula (Horomaka) was formed by two giant volcanic eruptions about eight million years ago. Harbours and bays radiate out from the peninsula's centre, giving it an unusual cogwheel shape. The historic town of Akaroa, 80km from Christchurch, is a highlight, as is the absurdly beautiful drive along Summit Rd around the edge of one of the original craters. It's also worth exploring the little bays that dot the peninsula's perimeter.

The waters around Banks Peninsula are home to the smallest and one of the rarest dolphin species, the Hector's dolphin, found only in NZ waters. A range of tours depart from Akaroa to spot these and other critters, including white-flippered penguins, orcas and seals.

Akaroa ('Long Harbour' in Maori) was the site of the country's first French settlement and descendants of the original French pioneers still reside here. It's a charming town that strives to re-create the feel of a French provincial village, down to the names of its streets and houses. Generally it's a sleepy place but the peace is periodically shattered by hordes descending from gargantuan cruise ships. The ships used to dock in Lyttelton Harbour but since the earthquakes Akaroa has been a popular substitute. Even when Lyttelton's back on its feet, the ships will be reluctant to leave.

Banks Peninsula

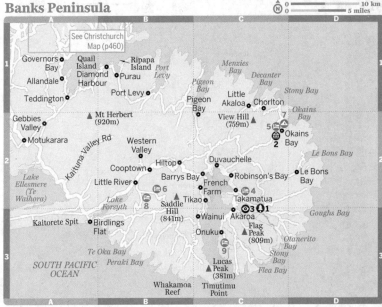

History

James Cook sighted the peninsula in 1770. Thinking it was an island, he named it after the naturalist Sir Joseph Banks.

In 1831, Onawe *pa* (fortified village) was attacked by the Ngati Toa chief Te Rauparaha and in the massacres that followed, the local Ngai Tahu population was dramatically reduced. Seven years later, whaling captain Jean Langlois negotiated the purchase of Banks Peninsula from the survivors and returned to France to form a trading company. With French government backing, 63 settlers headed for the peninsula in 1840, but only days before they arrived, panicked British officials sent their own warship to raise the flag at Akaroa, claiming British sovereignty under the Treaty of Waitangi. Had the settlers arrived two years earlier, the entire South Island could have become a French colony, and NZ's future might have been quite different.

The French did settle at Akaroa, but in 1849 their land claim was sold to the New Zealand Company, and in 1850 a large group of British settlers arrived. The heavily forested land was cleared and soon farming became the peninsula's main industry.

Banks Peninsula

⊙ Sights
1 Hinewai Reserve C3
2 Okains Bay Maori & Colonial
   Museum C2
3 Tree Crop Farm C3

⊜ Sleeping
4 Coombe Farm C2
5 Double Dutch C2
6 Little River Campground B2
7 Okains Bay Camping Ground C2
8 Okuti Garden B2
9 Onuku Farm Hostel C3

⊙ Sights

◉ Akaroa

★ Giant's House GARDEN
(Map p480; www.thegiantshouse.co.nz; 68 Rue Balguerie; adult/child $20/10; ⊙noon-5pm Jan-Apr, 2-4pm May-Dec) An ongoing labour of love from local artist Josie Martin, this playful and whimsical combination of sculpture and mosaics cascades down a hillside garden above Akaroa. Echoes of Gaudí and Miró can be found in the intricate collages of mirrors,

Akaroa

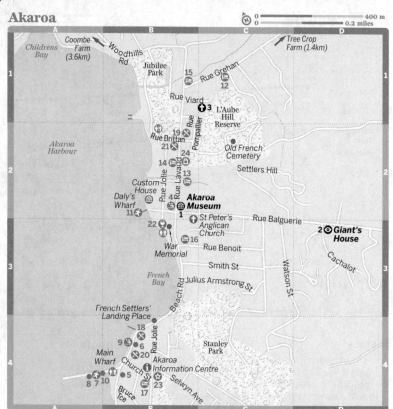

tiles and broken china, and there are many surprising nooks and crannies to discover. Martin also exhibits her paintings and sculpture in the lovely 1880 house, the former residence of Akaroa's first bank manager.

★ Akaroa Museum   MUSEUM

(Map p480; www.akaroamuseum.org.nz; cnr Rues Lavaud & Balguerie; adult/child $4/1; ⊙10.30am-4.30pm) This interesting museum is spread over several historic buildings, including the old courthouse; the tiny 1858 Custom House by Daly's Wharf; and one of NZ's oldest houses, Langlois-Eteveneaux. It has interesting displays on the peninsula's once-significant Maori population, a courtroom diorama and a 20-minute audiovisual display on peninsular history.

St Patrick's Catholic Church   CHURCH

(Map p480; www.akaroacatholicparish.co.nz; 29 Rue Lavaud; ⊙8am-8pm) Akaroa's cute frilly-edged Catholic church was built in 1865, replacing an earlier one which had blown down in a storm. The richly coloured stained glass was imported from Stuttgart.

Tree Crop Farm   GARDEN

(Map p479; ☑03-304 7158; www.treecropfarm. com; Rue Grehan; admission $5; ⊙10am-4pm in good weather only; ☎) This quirky private wilderness garden (based loosely on Renoir's) has rambling, overgrown tracks and sheepskin-covered couches on a ramshackle verandah. Rustic, romantic accommodation (double $200 to $250) is available in 'Bohemian love shacks', each with its own outdoor wood-heated bath.

⊙ Other Areas

Okains Bay Maori & Colonial Museum   MUSEUM

(Map p479; www.okainsbaymuseum.co.nz; 1146 Okains Bay Rd; adult/child $10/2; ⊙10am-5pm) Northeast of Akaroa, this collection of Maori

Akaroa

⊙ **Top Sights**
1 Akaroa Museum......................................B2
2 Giant's House...D3

⊙ **Sights**
3 St Patrick's Catholic Church.................C1

⊕ **Activities, Courses & Tours**
4 Akaroa Adventure Centre.....................B2
5 Akaroa Cooking School.........................B4
6 Akaroa Dolphins....................................B4
7 Akaroa Sailing Cruises..........................A4
8 Black Cat Cruises...................................A4
9 Captain Hector's Sea Kayaks...............B4
10 Coast Up Close......................................B4
11 Fox II Sailing..B2

⊜ **Sleeping**
12 Beaufort House......................................C1
13 Bon Accord..B2

14 Chez la Mer...B2
15 La Rochelle...B1
16 Maison de la Mer...................................B3
17 Tresori Motor Lodge..............................B4

⊗ **Eating**
18 Akaroa Fish & Chips..............................B4
    Bully Hayes.....................................(see 18)
19 Little Bistro...B2
20 Trading Rooms......................................B4
21 Vangionis...B2

⊝ **Drinking & Nightlife**
22 Harbar..B3

⊕ **Entertainment**
23 Akaroa Cinema & Café..........................B4

⊜ **Shopping**
24 Artisans' Gallery....................................B2

CHRISTCHURCH & CANTERBURY BANKS PENINSULA

and European pioneer artefacts includes a reproduction meeting house, a sacred 15th-century god stick and a war canoe.

Hinewai Reserve FOREST
(Map p479; Long Bay Rd) ✔ Get a glimpse of what the peninsula once looked like in this privately owned 10.5-sq-km nature reserve, which has been replanted with native forest. Pick up a brochure from the visitor centre outlining the 15km of walking tracks.

🏃 Activities

The information centre can provide information and booklets on walks around the peninsula, including the three-hour **Akaroa Historic Area Walk**, taking in the old wooden buildings and churches that give Akaroa its character. Audioguides for go-it-alone walking tours are also available ($10).

Banks Peninsula Track WALKING
(☑06-304 7612; www.bankstrack.co.nz; 2-day/4-day from $150/230; ☺Oct-Apr) This privately owned and maintained 35km four-day walk traverses farmland and forest along the dramatic coast east of Akaroa. Fees include transport from Akaroa and hut accommodation. The two-day option covers the same ground at twice the pace.

Fox II Sailing SAILING
(Map p480; ☑0800 369 7245; www.akaroafoxsail. co.nz; Daly's Wharf; adult/child $75/30; ☺departs 10.30am & 1.30pm Jan-May) Enjoy the scenery, observe the marine wildlife, learn about the

history and try your hand at sailing on NZ's oldest gaff-rigged ketch.

Akaroa Sailing Cruises SAILING
(Map p480; ☑0800 724 528; www.aclasssailing. co.nz; Main Wharf; adult/child $75/38) Set sail for a 2½-hour hands-on cruise on a gorgeous 1946 A-Class yacht.

Akaroa Guided Sea Kayaking Safari KAYAKING
(☑021 156 4591; www.akaroakayaks.com; 3hr/half-day $125/159) Paddle out at 7.30am on a three-hour guided Sunrise Nature Safari, or if early starts aren't your thing, try the 11.30am Bays & Nature Paddle. The half-day Try Sea Kayaking Experience is a more challenging option.

Akaroa Adventure Centre KAYAKING, CYCLING
(Map p480; ☑03-304 8709; 74a Rue Lavaud; ☺9am-6pm) Rents out sea kayaks (per hour/day $20/60), bikes (per hour $15), fishing rods (per day $10) and surfboards (per day $28).

Captain Hector's Sea Kayaks KAYAKING, CANOEING
(Map p480; ☑03-304 7866; Beach Rd) Rents kayaks (per day $45), canoes (per hour $20) paddleboats (per hour $30) and waterbikes (per hour $35).

🎣 Courses

Akaroa Cooking School COOKING COURSE
(Map p480; ☑021 166 3737; www.akaroacooking. co.nz; 81 Beach Rd; per person $210) Options include popular 'Gourmet in a Day' sessions

(10am to 4pm) and occasional specialised barbecue classes. All sessions end with consuming your self-prepared feast, accompanied by local wines. Check the website for the school's occasional forays into specific ethnic cuisines, including Thai, French and Italian.

⌲ Tours

Pohatu Plunge
TOUR

(☑ 03-304 8552; www.pohatu.co.nz) Runs evening tours to a white-flippered penguin colony (adult/child $70/55); they're best during the August to January breeding season, but possible throughout the year. Sea kayaking and 4WD nature tours are also available (both adult/child $90/65), with the option of staying overnight in a secluded cottage.

Akaroa Farm Tours
TOUR

(☑ 03-304 8511; www.akaroafarmtours.com; adult/child $80/50) Tours depart from the information centre and head to a hillcountry farm near Paua Bay for sheering demonstrations, sheepdog shenanigans, garden strolls and homemade scones; allow 2½ hours.

Akaroa Dolphins
BOAT TOUR

(Map p480; ☑ 03-304 7866; www.akaroadolphins.co.nz; 65 Beach Rd; adult/child $74/35; ⊙ 12.45pm year-round, plus 10.15am & 3.15pm Oct-Apr) Two-hour wildlife cruises with a complimentary drink and home baking. Say hi to Murphy – wildlife-spotting dog extraordinaire – for us. He even stars in his own children's picture book, available at the Akaroa Dolphins office.

Black Cat Cruises
BOAT TOUR

(Map p480; ☑ 03-304 7641; www.blackcat.co.nz; Main Wharf; nature cruise $72/30, dolphin swim $145/120) As well as a two-hour nature cruise, Black Cat offers a three-hour 'swimming with dolphins' experience. Wet suits and snorkelling gear are provided, plus hot showers back on dry land. Observers can tag along (adult/child $75/35) but only 12 people can swim per trip, so book ahead. Cruises have a 98% success rate in seeing dolphins, and an 81% success rate in actually swimming with them (there's a $50 refund if there's no swim).

Coast Up Close
BOAT TOUR

(Map p480; ☑ 0800 126 278; www.coastupclose.co.nz; Main Wharf; adult/child from $70/25; ⊙ departs 10.15am & 1.45pm) Scenic boat trips with an emphasis on wildlife watching. Fishing trips can be arranged.

Tuatara Tours
WALKING TOUR

(☑ 03-962 3280; www.tuataratours.co.nz; per person $1575; ⊙ Nov-Apr) You'll only need to carry your daypack on the guided **Akaroa Walk**, a leisurely 46km, three-day stroll from Christchurch to Akaroa via Diamond Harbour. The rate includes good accommodation and lots of gourmet food.

Eastern Bays Scenic Mail Run
DRIVING TOUR

(☑ 03-304 8526; tour $70; ⊙ 9am Mon-Fri) Travel along with the posties to visit isolated communities and bays on this 120km, five-hour delivery service. The minibus departs from the visitor information centre; bookings are essential as there are only eight seats available.

✦✦ Festivals & Events

French Fest
FOOD & WINE

(www.frenchfest.co.nz) This Gallic-inspired get-together has an emphasis on food, wine, music and art. Don't miss (or stand on) *Le Race D'Escargots*, where sleek, highly trained snails negotiate a compact course. There's also a French Waiters' Race. It's held in October in odd-numbered years.

🛏 Sleeping

⌂ Akaroa

Chez la Mer
HOSTEL $

(Map p480; ☑ 03-304 7024; www.chezlamer.co.nz; 50 Rue Lavaud; dm $28-31, r with/without bathroom $83/73; ☎) Pretty in pink, this friendly back-packers has well-kept rooms and a shaded garden, complete with fish ponds, hammocks, barbecue and outdoor seating. It's a TV-free zone but free bikes and fishing rods are available.

Bon Accord
HOSTEL $

(Map p480; ☑ 03-304 7782; www.bon-accord.co.nz; 57 Rue Lavaud; dm/s/d from $27/63/69; ☎) This colourful but somewhat shabby backpackers spills over two neighbouring houses in the centre of town. Relax on the deck or in the two cosy lounges, or dive into the herb-filled garden to release your inner French chef.

La Rochelle
MOTEL $$

(Map p480; www.larochellemotel.co.nz; 1 Rue Grehan; d $140; ☎) Tidy, central and reasonably priced, La Rochelle has a range of compact motel units, each of which opens onto a little semi-private terrace or balcony. Opt for a bigger bedroom and smaller bathroom or vice versa.

Tresori Motor Lodge
MOTEL **$$**

(Map p480; ☑ 03-304 7500; www.tresori.co.nz; cnr Rue Jolie & Church St; d $155-205; @ 🐾) Units are clean and smart at this modern 12-unit motel. They all have kitchenettes, but given that they're so close to Akaroa's waterfront cafe and restaurant strip, you needn't worry about using them.

★Maison de la Mer
B&B **$$$**

(Map p480; ☑ 03-304 8907; www.maisondelamer. co.nz; 1 Rue Benoit; r $475-550; 🐾) If it were in France we'd call this lovely wooden house belle époque, but given it's in Akaroa let's stick with Edwardian. Either way, this luxury B&B is *magnifique*. The two rooms in the main house have a discreetly French feel, while the spacious boathouse is nautically themed. All have sublime views.

Beaufort House
B&B **$$$**

(Map p480; ☑ 03-304 7517; www.beauforthouse. co.nz; 42 Rue Grehan; r $350) Tucked away along a quiet street and behind gorgeous gardens, this lovely 1898 house has been converted into a luxurious B&B. The only one of the four rooms without an en suite compensates with a large private bathroom with a clawfoot tub just across the hall.

Okains Bay

★Double Dutch
HOSTEL **$**

(Map p479; ☑ 03-304 7229; www.doubledutch. co.nz; 32 Chorlton Rd; dm/s $30/60, d with/without bathroom $80/74; @ 🐾) Posh enough to be a B&B but budget-friendly, this relaxed hostel is perched in farmland on a secluded river estuary. There's a general store (and a beach) just a short walk away, but it's best to bring your own ingredients for the flash kitchen.

Okains Bay Camping Ground
CAMPSITE **$**

(Map p479; ☑ 03-304 8789; www.okainsbay-camp.co.nz; 1162 Okains Bay Rd; sites adult/child $12/6) This basic campsite sits on a pine-tree-peppered ground right by the beach. Facilities are limited to kitchens, toilets and coin-operated hot showers. Pay your fees at the house at the camping ground's entrance.

Little River

Okuti Garden
ECO-STAY **$**

(Map p479; ☑ 03-325 1913; www.okuti.co.nz; 216 Okuti Valley Rd; per adult/child $40/20; @ 🐾) Part eco-aware homestay, part WWOOFer's haven, this is an all-round funky and friendly place to stay. Options include sleeping in a teepee, Mongolian yurt, house truck, earth-brick cottage or farmhouse. Vegetarian breakfasts ($20) are available and there's a generous supply of fresh herbs to kickstart your creativity in the shared kitchen.

Little River Campground
HOLIDAY PARK **$**

(Map p479; ☑ 03-325 1014; www.littlerivercamp-ground.co.nz; 287 Okuti Valley Rd; sites from $17, cabins $40-110) Accommodation in this sprawling family campground ranges from grassy tent sites through to rustic Kiwiana cabins. Added benefits for the kids include campfires, a mud slide and a natural swimming hole in the river.

Other Areas

★Halfmoon Cottage
HOSTEL **$**

(☑ 03-304 5050; www.halfmoon.co.nz; SH75; dm/s/d $30/53/78; ⊘ often closed Jun-Sep; 🐾) This pretty cottage at Barrys Bay (12km from Akaroa) is a blissful place to spend a few days lazing on the big verandahs or in the hammocks dotting the gardens. The rooms are warmly decorated, and the local environs can be explored by bicycle or kayak. The hostel was for sale when we visited, so make sure you call ahead.

Onuku Farm Hostel
HOSTEL **$**

(Map p479; ☑ 03-304 7066; www.onuku.co.nz; Hamiltons Rd, Onuku; sites from $15, dm/d from $28/66; ⊘ Oct-Apr; @ 🐾) Set on a working sheep farm 6km south of Akaroa, this blissfully isolated backpackers has a grassy camping area and simple, tidy rooms in a farmhouse. For more privacy and breathtaking sea views, opt for one of the two rooms in newly built Tonga Hut ($80). The owners also run swimming-with-dolphins tours ($100) and kayaking trips ($50).

Coombe Farm
B&B **$$**

(Map p479; ☑ 03-304 7239; www.coombefarm. co.nz; 18 Old Le Bons Track, Takamatua Valley; d $160-180; 🐾) Choose between staying in the private and romantic Shepherd's Hut – complete with an outdoor bath – or in the historic farm house, now lovingly restored and dotted with interesting contemporary art and Asian antiques. After breakfast you can negotiate the farm's private forest and stream walkway.

✖ Eating & Drinking

Barrys Bay Cheese
CHEESE FACTORY **$**

(☑ 03-304 5809; www.barrysbaycheese.co.nz; Christchurch-Akaroa Rd; cheese $7-11; ⊘ 9am-5pm)

Situated close to where the main road hits Akaroa Harbour (12km from Akaroa), this enticing cheesery handcrafts and sells fine cheddar, maasdam and gouda. Crackers and chutney are available for a spontaneous seaside snack.

Akaroa Fish & Chips
FISH & CHIPS $

(Map p480; 59 Beach Rd; mains $6-19; ◎11am-8pm) Order takeaways and sit by the ocean, or grab a table and tuck into blue cod, scallops, oysters and other assorted deep-fried goodness. Either way, keep a close eye on the local posse of eager cats and seagulls.

Vangionis
ITALIAN $$

(Map p480; ✆03-304 7714; www.vangionis.co.nz; 40f Rue Lavaud; tapas $7-19, mains $25-39; ◎5-10pm Wed-Sun) Thin-crust pizzas, tapas, pasta and Canterbury beers and wines all feature at this Tuscan-style trattoria. Try to secure a table in the lovely olive tree and lavender-lined courtyard. Takeaway pizzas are also available.

Bully Hayes
CAFE $$

(Map p480; www.bullyhayes.co.nz; 57 Beach Rd; breakfast $16-22, lunch $19-26, dinner $24-42; ◎8am-9pm; 🕸) Named after a well-travelled American buccaneer, Bully Hayes is Akaroa's best breakfast option. The afternoon sun draws the lunchtime crowd to the sheltered courtyard for burgers and fresh seafood, and keeps them lingering over Monteith's beers and local wines through the afternoon.

★ Little Bistro
FRENCH $$$

(Map p480; ✆03-304 7314; www.thelittlebistro. co.nz; 33 Rue Lavaud; mains $28-40; ◎5pm-late Tue-Sat) *Très petite, très chic* and very tasty. Look forward to classic bistro style given a proud Kiwi spin with local seafood, South Island wines and Canterbury craft beers. The menu changes seasonally, but usually includes favourites such as crusted lamb or Akaroa salmon terrine.

Trading Rooms
FRENCH $$$

(Map p480; ✆03-304 7656; www.thetradingrooms. co.nz; 71 Beach Rd; lunch $18-29, dinner $32-38; ◎10am-3pm Thu-Mon, 5-10pm Fri-Mon) Akaroa's most upmarket restaurant occupies its most impressive waterside shopfront. Grab a seat at one of the little marble-topped tables and tuck into the likes of snails, mussels, terrine, French onion soup and cassoulet. At lunch the Gallic guard drops a little, with burgers and Spanish tortillas creeping onto the menu.

Harbar
BAR, CAFE

(Map p480; www.harbar.co.nz; 83 Rue Jolie; ◎10am-9.30pm) A perfect waterfront location combines with rustic outdoor seating to produce Akaroa's best place for a sundowner drink. Tuck into pizza or fish and chips.

☆ Entertainment

Akaroa Cinema & Café
CINEMA

(Map p480; ✆03-304 7678; www.cinecafe.co.nz; cnr Rue Jolie & Selwyn Ave; adult/child $15/13; 🕸) Grab some wine at the attached cafe and settle in to watch an art-house, classic or foreign flick.

🛍 Shopping

Artisans' Gallery
ARTS & CRAFTS

(Map p480; 45 Rue Lavaud; ◎11am-4pm) The output of local artisans working in fabrics, glass, ceramics and wood is showcased in this cute little shop.

ℹ Information

Akaroa Information Centre (Map p480; ✆03-304 8600; www.akaroa.com; 120 Rue Jolie; ◎9am-5pm) Tours, activities, accommodation and postal services.

ℹ Getting There & Away

Akaroa French Connection (✆0800 800 575; www.akaroabus.co.nz; one way/return $25/45) Daily shuttle service to/from Christchurch.

Akaroa Shuttle (✆0800 500 929; www. akaroashuttle.co.nz; one way/return $35/50) Heads to/from Christchurch daily, increasing to twice daily from November to April.

NORTH CANTERBURY

Heading south from Kaikoura, SH1 crosses the Hundalee Hills and heads into Hurunui District, an area known for its wine and the thermal resort of Hanmer Springs. It's also the start of the Canterbury Plains, a vast, flat, richly agricultural area partitioned by distinctive braided rivers. The region is bounded to the west by the Southern Alps. If you're crossing into Canterbury from either Westport or Nelson, the most direct route cuts through the Alps on the beautiful Lewis Pass Rd (SH7).

Lewis Pass

The northernmost of the three main mountain passes connecting the West Coast to the east, 907m-high Lewis Pass is not as steep

MAORI NZ: CANTERBURY

Only 14% of Maori live on the South Island but of those, half of them live in Canterbury. The first major tribe to become established here were Waitaha, who were subsequently conquered and assimilated into the Ngati Mamoe tribe in the 16th century. In the following century, they in turn were conquered and subsumed by Ngai Tahu (www.ngaitahu. iwi.nz), a tribe that has its origins in the East Coast of the North Island.

In 1848 most of Canterbury was sold to the crown under an agreement which stipulated that an area of 10 acres per person would be reserved for the tribe; less than half of that actually was. With so little land left to them, Ngai Tahu were no longer able to be self-sufficient and suffered great financial hardship. It wasn't until 1997 that this injustice was addressed, with the tribe receiving an apology from the crown and a settlement valued at $170 million. Part of the deal was the official inclusion of the Maori name for the most spiritually significant part of the tribe's ancestral land: Aoraki/Mt Cook.

Today, Ngai Tahu is considered to be one of Maoridom's great success stories, with a reputation for good financial management, sound cultural advice and a portfolio including property, forestry, fisheries and many high-profile tourism operations.

There are many ways to engage in Maori culture in Canterbury. Artefacts can be seen at Canterbury Museum (p460), Akaroa Museum (p480), Okains Bay Maori & Colonial Museum (p480) and South Canterbury Museum (p498). Willowbank Wildlife Reserve (p463) has a replica Maori village and an evening cultural show. Further south in Timaru, the Te Ana Maori Rock Art Centre (p497) has interactive displays and arranges tours to see centuries-old work in situ.

as the others (Arthur's and Haast) and the forest isn't as dense either. Mainly it's comprised of beech (red and silver) and kowhai trees growing along river terraces.

The area has some interesting tramps, passing through beech forest with a backdrop of snowcapped mountains, lakes, and alpine tarns and rivers. Popular tracks include the St James Walkway (66km; three to five days) and the paths through Lake Sumner Forest Park; see the Department of Conservation (DOC) pamphlet *Lake Sumner & Lewis Pass* ($2). Subalpine conditions apply, so make sure you sign the intentions books at the huts.

Maruia Springs (☏03-523 8840; www. maruiasprings.co.nz; SH7; d $179-199; ⊙pools 8am-7.30pm; @🖥) is a small, Japanese-style hot-spring resort on the banks of the Maruia River, 7km west of Lewis Pass, with elegant minimalist accommodation, a cafe-bar and a Japanese restaurant (breakfast and dinner only). In the thermal pools (adult/child $20/9, free for guests), water with black mineral flakes of 'hot spring flowers' is pumped into a gender-segregated traditional Japanese bathhouse and outdoor rock pools. It's a magical setting during a winter snowfall, but mind the sandflies in summer. Massages (30/60 minutes $48/90) and private spa houses (45 minutes $26) are available.

From Lewis Pass the highway wiggles east for 62km before reaching the turn-off to Hanmer Springs.

Hanmer Springs

POP 843

Ringed by sculpted mountains, Hanmer Springs is the main thermal resort on the South Island. It's a pleasantly low-key spot to indulge yourself, whether soaking in hot pools, dining out or being pampered in the spa complex. In case that all sounds too soporific, fear not; there are plenty of family-friendly activities on offer, including a few to get the adrenaline pumping.

◉ Sights & Activities

Wai Ariki Farm Park   FARM, ZOO
(☏03-315 7772; www.waiariki-farmpark.co.nz; 108 Rippingale Rd; adult/child $12/6; ⊙10am-4pm Tue-Sun, daily during school holidays) With more animals than Dr Dolittle's Facebook page, Wai Ariki is a great spot for kids. Llamas, Tibetan yaks, deer, rabbits, guinea pigs and goats all feature, and many of the critters can be hand-fed; horse treks for the young ones are also available (from $50). For mum and dad there's a licensed cafe and craft gallery.

★ **Hanmer Springs Thermal Pools** SPA
(☑03-315 0000; www.hanmersprings.co.nz; 42 Amuri Ave; adult/child $20/10, locker $2; ◷10am-9pm) 🏊 Maori legend has it that these springs formed as a result of embers from Mt Ngauruhoe in the North Island falling from the sky. The main pool complex consists of a series of large pools of various temperatures, along with smaller landscaped rock pools, a fresh-water 25m lap pool with a whirlpool attached, private thermal pools ($30 per 30 minutes) and a cafe. Kids of all ages will love the water-slides and speedy superbowl ride ($10).

The adjacent **Spa** (☑0800 873 529, 03-315 0029; www.hanmerspa.co.nz; ◷10am-7pm) has massage and beauty treatments from $75. Entry to the pools is discounted to $12 if you partake of the spa's facilities.

Hanmer Forest Park WALKING
Walkers and mountain bikers will find plenty of room to move within the 130 sq km expanse of forest abutting the town. The easy Woodland Walk starts 1km up Jollies Pass Rd and goes through Douglas fir, poplar and redwood stands. It joins the Majuba Walk, which leads to Conical Hill Lookout and then heads back towards town (1½ hours). The i-SITE stocks a *Forest Park Walks* booklet and a mountain-bike trail map (both $3).

Thrillseekers Adventures ADVENTURE SPORTS
(☑03-315 7046; www.thrillseekers.co.nz; Hanmer Springs Rd) Bungy off a 35m-high bridge ($169), jetboat the Waiau Gorge (adult/child $115/60), white-water raft (Grade II to III) down the Waiau River (adult/child $149/79) or get dirty on a quad-bike (adult/child $149/99). The Thrillseekers Adventure centre is next to the bridge near the turn-off from SH7 but there's a **booking office** (☑03-315 7346; www.thrillseekers.co.nz; Conical Hill Rd; ◷9am-5pm) in town (which also has free internet terminals).

Hanmer Springs Adventure Centre ADVENTURE SPORTS
(☑03-315 7233; www.hanmeradventure.co.nz; 20 Conical Hill Rd; ◷8.30am-5pm) Offers quad-biking (from $129), mountain-bike shuttles to the top of Jack's Pass ($115), clay-shooting ($35) and archery ($35). It also books local tours and rents mountain bikes (per hour/day from $19/45), fishing rods (per day $29) and ski/snowboard gear.

Hanmer Springs Ski Area SKIING
(☑027 434 1806; www.skihanmer.co.nz; day pass adult/child $60/30) Only 17km from town via an unsealed road, this small complex has runs to suit all levels of ability. The Adventure Centre provides shuttles during the season.

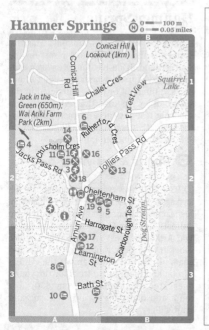

Hanmer Springs ⬥N 0━━━100 m / 0━━━0.05 miles

Hanmer Springs

🟠 Activities, Courses & Tours
1 Hanmer Springs Adventure
   Centre..A2
2 Hanmer Springs Thermal Pools A2
3 Thrillseekers Adventures.....................A2

🟢 Sleeping
4 Chalets Motel A2
5 Cheltenham House................................B2
6 Hanmer Backpackers............................A1
7 Hanmer Springs Top 10 ....A3
8 Kakapo Lodge A3
9 Rosie's A2
10 Scenic Views...A3
11 St James A2
12 Tussock Peak Motor Lodge.................A3

❌ Eating
13 Chantellini's...B2
14 Coriander's A2
15 Hanmer Springs Bakery A2
16 Malabar A2
17 No. 31 ....A3
18 Powerhouse Cafe.................................A2

🟠 Drinking & Nightlife
19 Monteith's Brewery Bar A2

MOLESWORTH STATION

Filling up 180 mountainous sq km between Hanmer Springs and Blenheim, Molesworth Station is NZ's largest farm, with the country's largest cattle herd (up to 10,000). It's also an area of national ecological significance and the entire farm is now administered by **DOC** (Department of Conservation; ☑ 03-572 9100; www.doc.govt.nz).

Visits are usually only possible when the Acheron Rd through the station is open from November to early April (weather permitting; check with DOC or at the Hanmer Springs i-SITE). The 207km drive from Hanmer Springs north to Blenheim on this narrow, un-sealed backcountry road takes around six hours; note that the gates are only open from 7am to 7pm, and overnight camping (adult/child $6/3) is permitted in certain areas (no open fires allowed). Pick up DOC's *Molesworth Station* brochure from the i-SITE or download it from their website.

Molesworth Heritage Tours (☑ 03-315 7401; www.molesworth.co.nz; tours $198-750; ☑ Oct-May) leads 4WD coach trips to the station from Hanmer Springs. Day tours include a picnic lunch, but there's also a five-hour 'no frills' option. From the Blenheim side, **Molesworth Tours** (☑ 03-572 8025; www.molesworthtours.co.nz) offers one- to four-day all-inclusive heritage and 4WD trips ($190 to $1835), as well as four-day fully supported (and catered) mountain-bike adventures ($1450).

Mt Lyford Alpine Resort SKIING
(☑ 03-315 6178, snow-phone 03-366 1220; www.mtlyford.co.nz; day pass $70/35) This skifield is 60km from Hanmer, off the Inland Rd to Kaikoura.

🛏 Sleeping

Hanmer Backpackers HOSTEL $
(☑ 03-315 7196; www.hanmerbackpackers.co.nz; 41 Conical Hill Rd; sites from $16, dm $28, with/without bathroom s $71/61, d $74/64; 🛜) The town's original backpackers is a cosy, wood-lined haven with friendly, well-travelled Dutch/Japanese hosts. Well-maintained shared social areas and free fruit, coffee and (occasionally) home-baking all add further big ticks.

Rosie's B&B $
(☑ 03-315 7095; www.rosiesbandbhanmer.co.nz; 9 Cheltenham St; tw $85-95, d with/without bathroom $130/95) Rosie has left the building but the hospitality continues at this homely hostel-like B&B. Most rooms share bathrooms. Rates include a continental breakfast and scrummy toasted croissants.

Jack in the Green HOSTEL $
(☑ 03-315 5111; www.jackinthegreen.co.nz; 3 Devon St; site/dm $20/29, d with/without bathroom $86/70; @🛜) This charming old converted home is a 10-minute walk from the centre. Large rooms (no bunks), relaxing gardens and a lovely lounge area are the main drawcards. For extra privacy, book a garden 'chalet' with an en suite.

Kakapo Lodge HOSTEL $
(☑ 03-315 7472; www.kakapolodge.co.nz; 14 Amuri Ave; dm $28, d with/without bathroom $90/66; @🛜) The YHA-affiliated Kakapo has a roomy kitchen and lounge, chill-busting underfloor heating and a 1st-floor deck. Bunk-free dorms (some with bathrooms) are joined by a motel-style unit ($100) with its own TV and cooking facilities.

Hanmer Springs Top 10 HOLIDAY PARK $
(☑ 03-315 7113; www.hanmerspringstop10.co.nz; Bath St; sites $36-46, unit with/without bathroom from $95/78; @🛜) This family-friendly park is just a few minutes' walk from the pools. Kids will love the playground and the trampoline. Take your pick from basic cabins (BYO everything) to two-bedroom motel units with everything supplied.

★**Woodbank Park Cottages** COTTAGES $$
(☑ 03-315 5075; www.woodbankcottages.co.nz; 381 Woodbank Rd; d $200) These two matching cottages in a woodland setting are around 10 minutes' drive from Hanmer, but feel a million miles away. Decor is crisp and modern, bathrooms and kitchens are well appointed and wooden decks come equipped with gas barbecues and rural views.

Chalets Motel MOTEL $$
(☑ 03-315 7097; www.chaletsmotel.co.nz; 56 Jacks Pass Rd; d $135-180; 🛜) Soak up the mountain views from these tidy, reasonably priced, free-standing wooden chalets, set on the slopes behind the town centre. All have full kitchens and the more expensive units have spa baths.

Tussock Peak Motor Lodge   MOTEL $$

(📞03-315 5191; www.tussockpeak.co.nz; 2 Leamington St; d $150-165; 🛜) Modern, spotless and central, Tussock Peak has colourful decor and friendly service that's a cut above other motels on Hanmer's main drag. Units come in studio, one- and two-bedroom incarnations, and some have spa baths and balconies.

Scenic Views   MOTEL $$

(📞03-315 7419; www.hanmerscenicviews.co.nz; 2 Amuri Ave; d $140-220; 🛜) An attractive timber-and-stone complex with modern studios (one with an outdoor spa pool) and two- and three-bedroom apartments. Mountain views come as standard.

Cheltenham House   B&B $$$

(📞03-315 7545; www.cheltenham.co.nz; 13 Cheltenham St; r $235-280; 🛜) This large 1930s house has room to fit a billiard table and grand piano, as well as four art-filled suites in the main house and two in cosy garden cottages. Cooked gourmet breakfasts are delivered to the rooms and wine is served in the evening.

St James   APARTMENTS $$$

(📞03-315 5225; www.thestjames.co.nz; 20 Chisholm Cres; apt $190-365; 🛜) Luxuriate in a schmick modern apartment with all the mod cons, including an iPod dock and a kitchen with the latest Fisher & Paykel appliances. Sizes range from studios to two-bedroom apartments.

🍴 Eating & Drinking

Hanmer Springs Bakery   BAKERY $

(16 Conical Hill Rd; ⏰6am-4pm) In peak season, queues stretch out the door for this humble bakery's meat pies and salmon bagels.

Malabar   ASIAN $$

(📞03-315 7745; www.malabar.co.nz; 5 Conical Hill Rd; lunch $10-22, dinner $28-33; ⏰5-10pm Sun-Fri, 11.30am-10pm Sat) This elegant eatery presents Asian cuisine from Beijing to Bangalore, although the emphasis is more on the Indian. All dishes are designed to be shared. A limited takeaway menu of Indian, Chinese and Thai favourites is also available.

Powerhouse Cafe   CAFE $$

(📞03-315 5252; www.powerhousecafe.co.nz; 8 Jacks Pass Rd; brunch $15-23, dinner $36; ⏰7.30am-3pm daily, 6-10pm Sat; 🛜) Power up with a huge High Country breakfast or a Highland Fling caramelised whisky-sodden porridge. Return for a burger, laksa or curry platter for lunch, and pop back again on Saturday evening when it morphs into a bistro.

Coriander's   INDIAN $$

(📞03-315 7616; www.corianders.co.nz; Chisholm Cres; mains $14-22; ⏰11.30am-2pm Mon-Fri, 5-10pm daily; 🍴) Spice up your life at this brightly painted North Indian restaurant. It's a beef-free zone, but there are plenty of tasty lamb, chicken and seafood dishes to choose from, and a particularly good vegetarian selection.

⭐Chantellini's   FRENCH $$$

(📞03-315 7667; www.chantellinis.com; 11 Jollies Pass Rd; mains $36-39; ⏰6-10pm Mon-Sat) Tucked away behind the main street, this quiet oasis offers a winning combination of classic French cooking, generous portions and charming service. Chandeliers and black drapes create an elegant ambience.

No. 31   MODERN NZ $$$

(📞03-315 7031; 31 Amuri Ave; mains $32-39; ⏰5.30-11pm Tue-Sun) It's complicated, sophisticated modern fare that's on offer in this pretty wooden cottage, but unlike many of its ilk, the serves here are quite substantial. The upmarket ambience befits the prices; the paper napkins don't.

Monteith's Brewery Bar   PUB

(www.mbbh.co.nz; 47 Amuri Ave; ⏰9am-11pm) The best pub in town features lots of different Monteith's beers and tasty tucker from cooked breakfasts ($12 to $17), to bar snacks ($10 to $17) to full meals ($23 to $35). Live musicians kick off from 4pm Sundays.

ℹ Information

Hurunui i-SITE (📞03-315 0000; www.visithanmersprings.co.nz; 42 Amuri Ave; ⏰10am-5pm) Books transport, accommodation and activities.

ℹ Getting There & Away

The **main bus stop** is near the corner of Amuri Ave and Jacks Pass Rd.

Hanmer Connection (📞0800 242 663; www.hanmerconnection.co.nz; one way/return $30/50) Daily bus to/from Christchurch via Waipara and Amberley.

Hanmer Tours & Shuttle (📞03-315 7418; www.hanmertours.co.nz) Runs shuttles to/from Waipara ($20), Amberley ($20), Christchurch city centre ($30) and Christchurch Airport ($40).

Waipara Valley

Conveniently stretched along SH1 near the Hanmer Springs turn-off, this resolutely rural area makes for a tasty pitstop en route to Christchurch. The valley's warm dry summers followed by cool autumn nights have proved a winning formula for growing grapes, olives, hazelnuts and lavender. Since vines were planted in 1982, it has swiftly built its reputation as a producer of riesling, chardonnay and pinot noir, and the valley's wineries now produce over 250,000 cases annually.

To explore the valley's bounty fully, pick up a copy of the Waipara Valley Map (or download it from www.waiparawine.co.nz) or visit www.foodandwinetrail.co.nz. Otherwise, you'll spot several of the big players from the highway. The area's two main towns are tiny Waipara and slightly larger Amberley, although the latter is just outside the main wine-growing area.

The annual **Waipara Wine & Food Festival** (www.waiparawineandfood.co.nz) is held in March.

🛏 Sleeping

Waipara Sleepers HOSTEL $

(📞03-314 6003; www.waiparasleepers.co.nz; 12 Glenmark Dr, Waipara; sites from $20, dm $25, s $35-45, d $55-65; @ 🎧) Train tragics will appreciate this unusual hostel, where you can bunk down in converted carriages and cook your own meals in the 'station house'. The facilities are fairly basic and you'll need to bring your own sleeping bag for the dorm room.

🍴 Eating & Drinking

Pukeko Junction CAFE, DELI $

(www.pukekojunction.co.nz; 458 Ashworths Rd (SH1); mains $10-19; ⊗9am-4.30pm) One of the most popular roadside pitstops, this cafe-cum-giftstore in Leithfield (south of Amberley) serves delicious baked goods including gourmet sausage rolls and lamb shank pies. As well as arts and crafts, the store stocks a good selection of local wine.

Nor'wester CAFE $$

(www.norwestercafe.co.nz; 95 Carters Rd (SH1); breakfast $9-21, lunch $18-26, dinner $20-39; ⊗9am-late) Bluster into this old wooden villa on the main street of Amberley for great coffee, yummy muffins and a whole variety of

cooked meals, ranging from pizza and pasta to bistro-style meals in the evening.

Brew Moon CAFE, BREWERY $$

(www.brewmooncafe.co.nz; 150 Ashworths Rd (SH1); mains $16-28; ⊗10am-late) Just south of Amberley on SH1, Brew Moon crafts six different beers along with seasonal brews; sample four of them for $16. The menu stretches from cooked breakfast to gourmet pizza, pasta and daily fish specials.

Waipara Hills WINERY, CAFE $$

(www.waiparahillswines.co.nz; 780 Glasnevin Rd (SH1); mains $23-27; ⊗tastings 10am-5pm, restaurant 10am-3pm) Hard to miss in an impressive edifice immediately south of Waipara, this winery produces an excellent Gewürztraminer, as well as the more common valley varietals. The cafe serves leisurely lunches on the terrace, and in summer the winery hosts occasional big-name concerts (see www.adayonthegreen.com.au).

Waipara Springs WINERY, CAFE $$

(www.waiparasprings.co.nz; SH1; mains $20-27; ⊗11am-5pm; 🎧) Slightly north of Waipara township, this is one of the valley's oldest vineyards. The attached cafe serves platters and bistro-style lunches.

★**Pegasus Bay** RESTAURANT, WINERY $$$

(📞03-314 6869; www.pegasusbay.com; Stockgrove Rd; mains $38-45; ⊗restaurant noon-4pm, tastings 10am-5pm) It's fitting that Waipara Valley's premier winery should have the loveliest setting and one of Canterbury's best restaurants. Beautiful gardens set the scene but it's the contemporary NZ menu that steals the show, taking advantage of superb local produce and recommending wines to match.

ⓘ Getting There & Away

The *Coastal Pacific* train from Christchurch to Picton stops at Waipara. Wine tours are available from several Christchurch-based companies.

Hanmer Connection (📞0800 242 663; www.hanmerconnection.co.nz) Heads to Hanmer Springs ($20, 50 minutes) and Christchurch ($20, 1¼ hours).

Hanmer Tours & Shuttle (📞03-315 7418; www.hanmertours.co.nz) Runs shuttles to/from Hanmer Springs ($20), Christchurch city centre ($15) and Christchurch Airport ($25).

InterCity (📞03-365 1113; www.intercity.co.nz) Coaches head to/from Picton (from $24, 4½ hours), Blenheim (from $22, four hours), Kaikoura (from $13, 1¾ hours) and Christchurch (from $10, one hour) twice daily.

CENTRAL CANTERBURY

While the dead-flat agricultural heartland of the Canterbury Plains blankets the majority of the region, there's plenty of interest for travellers in the west, where the Southern Alps soar to snowy peaks. Here you'll find Canterbury's best ski fields and some brilliant wilderness walks.

Unusually for NZ, the most scenic routes avoid the coast, and most items of interest can be accessed from one of two spectacular roads: the Great Alpine Highway (SH73), which barrels from Christchurch across the plains and into the mountains, and the Inland Scenic Route (SH72), which skirts the dividing line between the two.

Selwyn District

Named after NZ's first Anglican bishop, this largely rural district has swallowed an English map book and regurgitated place names such as Lincoln, Darfield and Sheffield to punctuate this green and pleasant land. Yet any illusions of Albion are quickly dispelled by the looming presence of the snow-capped Southern Alps, providing a rugged retort to 'England's mountains green'.

Selwyn's numerous ski fields may not be the country's most glamorous but they provide plenty of thrills for rampant ski bunnies. Porters (p48) is the main commercial field, but club fields include Mt Olympus (p48), Mt Cheeseman (p48), Broken River (p48), Craigieburn Valley (p48) and Temple Basin (p48).

The highly scenic Great Alpine Highway pierces the heart of the district on its journey between Christchurch and the West Coast. Before it leaves the Canterbury Plains, it passes through the little settlement of Springfield (population 219), which is distinguished by two notable monuments. One honours Rewi Alley (1897–1987), a local lad who became a great hero of the Chinese Communist Party, and surely the only party member to be offered a knighthood (he declined, naturally, but accepted companionship of the Queen's Service Order); for more about his fascinating life, stop to read the information panels.

The other monument is a giant pink-iced doughnut, originally erected to promote *The Simpsons Movie* but now a permanent feature – one can only imagine what Alley would make of it.

Heading west from Springfield, the landscape starts expanding until the highway is hidden within the mountainous folds of the Torlesse and Craigieburn Ranges. Just when you think it couldn't get more spectacular, views open up across the braided Waimakariri River.

Arthur's Pass village (www.arthurspass. com; population 62) is 4km from the pass of the same name. At 900m, it's NZ's highest-altitude settlement and a handy base for tramps, climbs and skiing. To say that it rains a lot up here is an understatement.

Maori used this pass to cross the Southern Alps long before its 'discovery' by Arthur Dobson in 1864. The Westland gold rush created the need for a dependable crossing over the Alps from Christchurch, and the coach road was completed within a year. Later, the coal and timber trade demanded a railway, duly completed in 1923.

⦿ Sights & Activities

Castle Hill LANDMARK
The jagged limestone outcrops of Castle Hill loom above the highway, roughly 33km from Springfield, looking surprisingly reminiscent of an ancient ruin. Unsurprisingly, this area is a favourite of rock climbers and boulderers. Scenes from *The Chronicles of Narnia* were filmed in the area.

Cave Stream Scenic Reserve CAVE
(www.doc.govt.nz) Near Broken River Bridge, 2km past Castle Hill, it's well worth stopping to take a look at the large circular outlet of this 594m-long cave, even if you're not planning to explore its depths. If a one-hour walk in waist-deep cold water through the pitch-black cave sounds appealing, take all the necessary precautions (check the water level and take a helmet, at least one light source per person, spare batteries etc); for details, pick up DOC's *Cave Stream Scenic Reserve* pamphlet. It's recommended that you walk up the outlet end and exit via the fixed ladder beside the 3m waterfall at the inlet.

Craigieburn Forest Park FOREST
(www.doc.govt.nz) Beech forest covers the lower slopes and valleys of this mountainous area, giving way to tussock and alpine scrub on the peaks. You may spot some South Island edelweiss, karearea (NZ falcons) and kea (native parrots). The Craigieburn Range has several peaks over 2000m and is one of NZ's best skiing areas, with slopes that suit advanced skiers. Ski fields include Mt

Cheeseman, Broken River and Craigieburn Valley. The DOC website lists numerous day walks (pick up a copy of the *Craigieburn Forest Park Day Walks* pamphlet), longer tramps and mountain-bike tracks to suit intermediate to advanced riders.

Arthur's Pass National Park   NATIONAL PARK
(www.doc.govt.nz) In 1923 this vast (1143 sq km) alpine wilderness became the South Island's first national park. Day tramps offer endless views of snowcapped peaks, many of them over 2000m; the highest is Mt Murchison (2400m). DOC's *Discover Arthur's Pass* booklet details dozens of walks as well as backcountry huts and camping areas. The newest track is the **Arthur's Pass Walkway**, a safe and reasonably easy track from the village to the Dobson Memorial at the summit of the pass (2½ hours return).

Other options include the **Devils Punchbowl walking track** (one hour return) to a 131m waterfall, and the steep walk to beautiful views at **Temple Basin ski field** (three hours return). The **Bealey Spur track** (four to five hours return) offers expansive views of the Waimakariri River valley and surrounding mountains. The pleasant **Dobson Nature Walk** (30 minutes return) is best from November to February when the alpine flowers are blooming.

Fit trampers might like to tackle the **Avalanche Peak track** (eight hours return). Longer tramps with superb alpine backdrops include the **Goat Pass track** (two days) and the longer and more difficult **Harman Pass** and **Harpers Pass tracks**. These tracks require previous tramping experience as flooding can make the rivers dangerous and the weather is extremely changeable; ask DOC first. For specific information on weather conditions see www.softrock.co.nz.

Rubicon Horse Treks   HORSE RIDING
(✆03-318 8886; www.rubiconvalley.co.nz; 534 Rubicon Rd) Operating from a sheep farm 6km from Springfield, Rubicon offers hour-long farm treks ($50), two-hour river, valley or sunset rides ($85), and six-hour mountain trail rides ($250).

🛏 Sleeping

🏠 Springfield to Bealey

Smylies Accommodation   HOSTEL $
(✆03-318 4740; www.smylies.co.nz; 5653 West Coast Rd, Springfield; dm/s/d $30/50/70; @🕾)

✎ This welcoming YHA-associated hostel has a large communal kitchen and a vast book and DVD library. There's also a handful of self-contained motel units ($85 to $160) and a three-bedroom cottage ($220). In winter, packages including ski-equipment rental and ski-field transport are on offer.

Flock Hill Lodge   MOTEL, HOSTEL $$
(✆03-318 8196; www.flockhill.co.nz; Great Alpine Hwy, Craigieburn Valley; dm/d $31/155; @🕾) In a tranquil spot close to Craigieburn Forest Park and Lake Pearson, this high-country sheep station has a cosy bar-restaurant, comfortable two-bedroom motel units and large cottages with kitchenettes. Unfussy backpackers can stay in rustic shearers' quarters.

Wilderness Lodge   LODGE $$$
(✆03-318 9246; www.wildernesslodge.co.nz; Cora Lynn Rd, Bealey; s $450-699 d $700-1160; 🕾) For an absolute middle-of-nowhere atmosphere, this alpine lodge hidden within a beech forest on a 24-sq-km sheep station takes some beating. The standalone studios with private spa baths feel even more remote. Rates include breakfast, dinner and guided activities, but even then they seem inflated.

🏠 Arthur's Pass

Camping is possible near the basic **public shelter** (adult/child $6/3) opposite DOC, where there's running water, a sink, tables and toilets. You can also camp for free at **Klondyke Corner**, 8km south of Arthur's Pass, where perks are limited to a toilet and stream water for boiling.

Mountain House YHA   HOSTEL $
(✆03-318 9258; www.trampers.co.nz; 83 Main Rd; sites $22, dm $27-31, s/d/unit $74/86/145; @🕾) Straddling the highway in the centre of the village, this excellent complex includes a well-kept hostel, two upmarket motel units and two three-bedroom cottages with log fires ($340). Campers will need to take their chances with the kleptomaniacal keas.

Arthur's Pass Village B&B   B&B $$
(✆021 394 776; www.arthurspass.org.nz; 72 School Tce; d $100; 🕾) ✎ This former railway cottage is now a cosy B&B, complete with an open fire, free-range bacon and eggs and homebaked bread for breakfast, and the company and conversation of the interesting owners. Home-cooked dinners are also available ($35). The two guest bedrooms share a bathroom.

Arthur's Pass Alpine Motel MOTEL $$
(☑03-318 9233; www.apam.co.nz; 52 Main Rd; d $125-145; 🐾) On the southern approach to the village, this older-style motel has simple units, some with gas fires. If you're snowed in there's a good DVD library and satellite TV.

✖ Eating

Famous Sheffield Pie Shop BAKERY $
(www.sheffieldpieshop.co.nz; 51 Great Alpine Hwy, Sheffield; pies $4-5; ⊙7.30am-4pm) This road-side bakery in the quiet Canterbury Plains hamlet of Sheffield turns out some of the region's best meat pies. There are more than 20 different varieties on offer, along with filled rolls, sweet things and surprisingly good coffee.

Arthur's Pass Store & Cafe CAFE $
(85 Main Rd, Arthur's Pass; mains $5-15; ⊙8am-5pm; 🐾) Sells sandwiches, burgers, pies and breakfasts, alongside petrol and basic groceries.

Wobbly Kea CAFE, BAR $$
(www.wobblykea.co.nz; 108 Main Rd, Arthur's Pass; breakfast $10-17, mains $23-25; ⊙9am-8pm) Breakfast at the Wobbly Kea is a local tradition designed to set you up for the most active of days. At night, this friendly cafe-bar serves steak, curry, pasta and pizza. Take-away pizza ($29) is also available.

❶ Information

DOC Arthur's Pass Visitor Centre (☑03-318 9211; www.doc.govt.nz; 80 Main Rd; ⊙8.30am-4.30pm) Has displays on the park, including a short video on the history of Arthur's Pass. Staff also provide information and advice on suitable tramps and on the park's changeable weather. You can purchase route guides and detailed topographical maps, and hire locator beacons (highly recommended). Computers are provided for you to log your tramping intentions on the AdventureSmart website (www.adventuresmart.org.nz).

❶ Getting There & Away

BUS

Atomic Shuttles (☑03-349 0697; www.atomictravel.co.nz) From Arthur's Pass a bus heads to/from Christchurch ($35, 2½ hours), Springfield ($35, one hour), Lake Brunner ($30, 50 minutes) and Greymouth ($35, 1¼ hours).

West Coast Shuttle (☑03-768 0028; www.westcoastshuttle.co.nz) Buses stopping at Arthur's Pass head to/from Christchurch ($40, 2¾ hours), Springfield ($30, one hour) and Greymouth ($30, 1¾ hours).

CAR

Make sure you check your petrol before you leave Springfield (or Hokitika or Greymouth if you're travelling in the other direction). There's a pump at Arthur's Pass Store but it's expensive and only operates from 8am until 5pm.

TRAIN

TranzAlpine (☑0800 872 467; www.kiwirail-scenic.co.nz; all fares $89) One train in each direction stops in Arthur's Pass, heading to/from Springfield (1½ hours) and Christchurch (2½ hours), or Lake Brunner (one hour) and Greymouth (two hours).

Methven

POP 1330

Methven is busiest in winter, when it fills up with snow bunnies heading to nearby Mt Hutt. At other times tumbleweeds don't quite blow down the main street – much to the disappointment of the wannabe gunslingers arriving for the raucous October rodeo. Over summer it's a low-key and affordable base for hikers, bikers and fisher-folk.

Dominating the town centre, two giant historic pubs glower at each other across the main street. Despite the rivalry between the Blue Pub and the Brown Pub (it's actually beige, but don't tell them that), they're surprisingly similar.

🏃 Activities

Ask at the i-SITE about walking trails, horse riding, mountain biking, fishing, clay-shooting, archery, golfing, scenic helicopter flights and jetboating through the nearby Rakaia Gorge.

Methven Heliski SKIING
(☑03-302 8108; www.methvenheli.co.nz; Main St; 5-run day trips $975; ⊙Jul-Sep) Trips include guide service, safety equipment and lunch.

Black Diamond Safaris SKIING
(☑027 450 8283; www.blackdiamondsafaris.co.nz; ⊙May-Oct) Provides access to uncrowded club ski fields by 4WD. Prices start at $100 for 4WD transport and safety equipment only, while $275 includes a lift pass, guiding and lunch.

Aoraki Balloon Safaris BALLOONING
(☑03-302 8172; www.nzballooning.com; flights $385) Early morning combos of snowcapped peaks and a breakfast with bubbly.

Skydiving NZ
SKYDIVING

(☑03-302 9143; www.skydivingnz.com; Pudding Hill Airfield) Offers tandem jumps from 12,000ft ($335) and 15,000ft ($440).

Big Al's Snow Sports
EQUIPMENT RENTAL

(☑03-302 8003; www.bigals.co.nz; The Square, Main St; mountain bikes per hr/day from $15/45) In winter the focus is ski and snowboard gear, while in summer Big Al turns his attention to mountain biking. Ask for a map of Mt Hutt Bike Park (near the bottom of Mt Hutt Skifield Access Rd) which has 26 tracks ranging from kid-friendly to extreme.

🛏 Sleeping

Some accommodation is closed in summer, but the following are open year-round. During the ski season, it pays to book well ahead, especially for budget accommodation. We've listed summer prices; expect them to rise in winter.

Alpenhorn Chalet
HOSTEL $

(☑03-302 8779; www.alpenhorn.co.nz; 44 Allen St; dm $30, d $65-85; @🛜) This small, inviting home has a conservatory housing an indoor garden and a spa pool. A log fire, free internet and complimentary espresso coffee seal the deal. Bedrooms are spacious and brightly coloured, with lots of warm, natural wood. Some of the doubles have en-suite bathrooms.

Redwood Lodge
HOSTEL $

(☑03-302 8964; www.redwoodlodge.co.nz; 3 Wayne Pl; s $50-60, d $90; @🛜) Despite being a BBH member there are no dorms at this charming family-friendly hostel. En-suite doubles have their own TVs, and there's a large shared lounge and kitchen. Bigger rooms can be reconfigured to accommodate families.

Big Tree Lodge
HOSTEL $

(☑03-302 9575; www.bigtreelodge.co.nz; 25 South Belt; dm $35-40, r $75, apt $120-160; @🛜) Once a vicarage, this relaxed hostel has bunk-free dorms and wood-trimmed bathrooms. Tucked just behind is Little Tree Studio, a self-contained unit sleeping up to four people.

Snow Denn Lodge
HOSTEL $

(☑03-302 8999; www.methvenaccommodation. co.nz; cnr McMillan & Bank Sts; dm $25, d with/without bathroom $80/70; @🛜) Spread over two identical large wooden buildings, this modern YHA-associated lodge has appealing dining and living areas, including large kitchens. Prices include breakfast and equipment hire (bikes, golf clubs, fishing gear etc). A bit more attention to scrubbing the bathrooms would lift it up the list.

Whitestone Cottages
RENTAL HOUSES $$$

(☑021 179 0257; www.whitestonecottages.co.nz; 3016 Methven Hwy; house $210-350) For those mid-holiday moments when you just want to spread out, cook a meal, do your laundry and have your own space, these four large free-standing houses on the edge of town are just the ticket. Each sleeps six in two en-suite bedrooms.

🍴 Eating & Drinking

Aqua
JAPANESE $

(112 Main St; mains $11-17; ⊙5-9pm Jan-Oct) Dive into this tiny relaxed restaurant where kimono-clad waitresses serve *yakisoba* (fried noodles), *ramen* (noodle soup) and *izakaya*-style dishes (small plates to share over drinks) to grateful guests. Top it off with sesame or green-tea ice cream.

Cafe 131
CAFE $

(131 Main St; meals $10-20; ⊙7.30am-5pm; 🛜) Polished timber and leadlight windows lend warmth and style to this smart eatery. The menu extends to all-day breakfasts, good-value platters, soup, pasta and sandwiches, but beer and wine takes over later in the day. It's also the town's de facto internet cafe.

Cafe Primo
CAFE $

(38 McMillan St; meals $7-18; ⊙7.30am-4pm) Sandwiched in and around the souvenir

---

DON'T MISS

MT HUTT SKI AREA

Canterbury's premier ski field, Mt Hutt (p48) has the largest skiable area of any of NZ's commercial fields (365 hectares), with its longest run stretching for 2km. Half of the terrain is suitable for intermediate skiers, with a quarter each for beginners and advanced. Usually the season runs from mid-June to mid-October.

The skifield is only 26km from Methven but in wintry conditions the drive takes about 40 minutes; allow two hours from Christchurch. **Methven Travel** (☑03-302 8106, 0800 684 888; www.methventravel.co.nz) runs mountain buses in season ($20).

teaspoons and Buzzy Bee bookends of this secondhand shop are tasty cakes, panini and legendary bacon and egg sandwiches. You'll also unearth Methven's best coffee.

Blue Pub PUB
(www.thebluepub.co.nz; Barkers Rd; mains $20-35; 🛜) Drink at the bar crafted from a huge slab of native timber, or tuck into robust meals in the quieter cafe. Afterwards, challenge the locals to a game of pool or watch the rugby on the big screen.

☆ Entertainment

Cinema Paradiso CINEMA
(☑ 03-302 1957; www.cinemaparadiso.co.nz; Main St; adult/child $15/10) Quirky cinema with an arthouse skew.

ⓘ Information

Medical Centre (☑ 03-302 8105; The Square, Main St; ⊘ 8.30am-5.30pm)

Methven i-SITE (☑ 03-302 8955; www.amazingspace.co.nz; 160 Main St; ⊘ 7.30am-6pm Jul-Sep, 9am-5pm Mon-Fri, 10am-3pm Sat & Sun Oct-Jun; 🛜) The information centre is housed in the Heritage Centre, which also includes a cafe, art gallery (free) and the hands-on *NZ Alpine & Agriculture Encounter* (adult/child $18/10).

ⓘ Getting There & Around

Methven Travel (☑ 03-302 8106; www.methventravel.co.nz) Runs shuttles between Methven and Christchurch Airport ($42) three to four times a week, increasing to three times daily in the ski season.

Mt Somers

The small settlement of Mt Somers sits on the edge of the Southern Alps, beneath the mountain of the same name. The biggest drawcard to the area is the **Mt Somers track** (30km), a one- to two-day hike circling the mountain, linking the popular picnic spots of Sharplin Falls and Woolshed Creek. Trail highlights include volcanic formations, Maori rock drawings, deep river canyons and botanical diversity. The route is subject to sudden weather changes, so precautions should be taken.

There are two DOC huts on the track: Pinnacles Hut and Woolshed Creek Hut (adult/child $15/7.50). Hut tickets and information are available at the **Mt Somers General Store** (61 Pattons Rd; ⊘ 8am-6pm).

🛏 Sleeping & Eating

Mt Somers Holiday Park HOLIDAY PARK $
(☑ 03-303 9719; www.mountsomers.co.nz; Hoods Rd; sites $18-32, cabin with/without bathroom $80/55) This small, friendly and well-maintained park offers both powered and unpowered sites. Ensuite cabins are fully made up, but you'll need to bring your own linen (or hire it) for the standard cabins.

Stronechrubie CHALETS, RESTAURANT $$
(☑ 03-303 9814; www.stronechrubie.co.nz; cnr Hoods Rd & SH72; d $120-160, mains $33-38; ⊘ restaurant 6.30-9pm Wed-Sat; 🛜) Comfortable chalets ranging in size from studio to two-bedroom are scattered across bird-filled gardens at this oddly named lodge. The intimate restaurant showcases local produce such as beef, lamb, venison and duck.

SOUTH CANTERBURY

After crossing the Rangitata River into South Canterbury, SH1 and the Inland Scenic Route (SH72) narrow to within 8km of each other at the quaint town of Geraldine. Here you can choose to take the busy coastal highway through the port city of Timaru (and on to Oamaru and Dunedin), or continue inland on SH79 into the Mackenzie Country, the expansive high ground from which NZ's tallest peaks rise above powder blue lakes. Most travellers pick the latter.

The Mackenzie Basin is a wild, tussock-strewn bowl at the foot of the Southern Alps, carved out by ancient glaciers. It takes its name from the legendary James 'Jock' McKenzie, who ran his stolen flocks in this then-uninhabited region in the 1840s. When he was finally caught, other settlers realised the potential for grazing in this seemingly inhospitable land and followed in his footsteps.

Director Sir Peter Jackson made the most of this rugged and untamed landscape while filming the *Lord of the Rings* films.

Peel Forest

Tucked away between the foothills of the Southern Alps and the Rangitata River (well signposted from SH72), the Peel Forest is among NZ's most important remnants of indigenous podocarp (conifer) forest. Many of the totara, kahikatea and matai trees here are hundreds of years old and are home to an abundance of bird life including riflemen, kereru (wood pigeons), bellbirds, fantails and grey warblers. One example of totara on the Big Tree Walk (30 minutes return) is 31m tall, has a circumference of 9m and is over 1000 years old. There are also trails to Emily Falls (1½ hours return), Rata Falls (two hours return) and Acland Falls (one hour return); pick up the *Peel Forest Park* brochure ($2) from Peel Forest Store.

A road from nearby Mt Peel sheep station leads to Mesopotamia, the run of English writer Samuel Butler in the 1860s. His experiences here partly inspired his famous satire *Erewhon* ('nowhere' backwards, almost).

◎ Sights & Activities

St Stephen's Church CHURCH
Sitting in a pretty glade right next to the general store, this gorgeous little Anglican church (1885) has a warm wooden interior and some interesting stained glass. Look for St Francis of Assisi surrounded by NZ flora and fauna (get the kids to play spot-the-tuatara).

Peel Forest Horse Trekking HORSE RIDING
(☑ 03-696 3703; www.peelforesthorsetrekking.co.nz; 1hr/2hr/half-day/full day $55/110/220/380) Ride through lush forest on short stints or multiday treks ($982 to $1623, minimum four people). Accommodation packages are available in conjunction with Peel Forest Lodge.

Rangitata Rafts RAFTING
(☑ 0800 251 251; www.rafts.co.nz; Rangitata Gorge Rd; ⊙ Sep-May) Head out for an exhilarating three-hour trip through Grade V rapids in the Rangitata Gorge ($208, minimum age 15), or start further down the Rangitata River for a gentler two-hour journey through Grade II rapids ($165, minimum age six).

Hidden Valleys RAFTING
(☑ 03-696 3560; www.hiddenvalleys.co.nz; ⊙ Sep-May) They may be based in Peel Forest but this crew doesn't limit itself to rafting the Rangitata. Multiday expeditions head to the Waimakariri, Waiau, Landsborough, Grey and Waiatoto Rivers, peaking with a five-day trip down the Clarence (near Kaikoura). Short, child-friendly trips on the Rangitata River are also available (adult/child $200/180).

⊨ Sleeping & Eating

DOC Camping Ground CAMPSITE $
(☑ 03-696 3567; www.peelforest.co.nz; sites per adult/child $18/8.50, cabins $50-80) Beside the Rangitata River, about 3km beyond the Peel Forest Store, this excellent campground is equipped with basic two- to four-berth cabins (bring your own sleeping bag), hot showers and a kitchen. Check in at the store.

Peel Forest Lodge LODGE $$$
(☑ 03-696 3703; www.peelforestlodge.co.nz; d $350, additional people $40; ☎) Would-be Davy Crocketts with champagne tastes will love this beautiful log cabin hidden in the forest. There are four rooms sleeping eight people, but they only take one booking at a time, so you and your posse will have the place to yourselves. It's fully self-contained, but meals can be arranged.

Peel Forest Store CAFE, SELF-CATERING $$
(☑ 03-696 3567; www.peelforest.co.nz; lunch $13-15, dinner $24-30; ⊙ 9am-5.30pm Sun-Thu, to 8.30pm Fri & Sat) Your one-stop-shop for groceries, takeaway food and internet access also runs the camping ground and the attached cafe-bar. Cooked meals include burgers, pizza and steaks.

Geraldine
POP 2420

Consummately Canterbury in its dedication to English-style gardening, pretty Geraldine has a village vibe and an active arts scene. In spring, duck behind the war memorial on Talbot St to the River Garden Walk, where green-fingered locals have gone completely bonkers planting azaleas and rhododendrons.

◎ Sights

Vintage Car & Machinery Museum MUSEUM
(178 Talbot St; adult/child $10/free; ⊙ 9.30am-4pm daily Oct-May, 10am-4pm Sat & Sun Jun-Sep) You don't have to be a rev-head to enjoy this vintage car collection. The oldest is a 1907 De Dion-Bouton but the most impressive is a gleaming, fully restored 1926 Bentley. There's also a purpose-built Daimler used for the 1954 royal tour, plus some very nice Jags, 1970s muscle cars and all sorts of farm machinery.

1066 - A Medieval Mosaic GALLERY
(www.1066.co.nz; 10 Wilson St; ⊙ 10am-4pm) **FREE** One can only marvel at the obsessive-compulsion behind this 42m re-creation of the Bayeux Tapestry, painted onto a backdrop made from two-million steel bits sourced from discarded industrial knitting machine parts. Just as impressive are the bespoke mathematical puzzles and games for sale. And if you're feeling chilly, the world's biggest woollen jersey is also on display.

Geraldine Historical Museum
MUSEUM

(5 Cox St; ☉10am-3pm Mon-Sat, 12.30-3pm Sun) **FREE** Occupying the photogenic Town Board Office building (1885), this cute little museum tells the town's story with an eclectic mix of exhibits including old photos, a wedding dress and a pump organ (which you're welcome to play).

🏃 Activities

Big Rock Canyons
CANYONING

(☑03-693 8904; www.bigrockcanyons.co.nz; ☉Nov-Apr) Offers slippy, slidey day-long adventures in the Kaumira Canyon ($260), as well as five others of varying degrees of difficulty.

Skydiving Kiwis
SKYDIVING

(☑0800 359 549; www.skydivingkiwis.com; 1 Brodie Rd) Kiwis aren't so great at flying but we expect they're quite good at plummeting. Strap yourself to the human version for a 6000ft ($235), 9000ft ($285) or 12,000ft ($335) leap. Flights depart from Rangitata Island Airport, 21km east of Geraldine.

🛏 Sleeping

Rawhiti House
HOSTEL $

(☑03-693 8252; www.rawhitibackpackers.co.nz; 27 Hewlings St; dm/s/d $32/50/72; @🖿) On a hillside on the edge of town, this former maternity hospital is now a sunny and spacious hostel with good communal areas, comfortable rooms and sparkling bathrooms. Bikes are available to borrow.

Geraldine Kiwi Holiday Park
HOLIDAY PARK $

(☑03-693 8147; www.geraldineholidaypark.co.nz; 39 Hislop St; sites $33-36, units with/without bathroom from $80/50; @🖿) 🖋 This top-notch holiday park is set amid well-established trees across the road from a grassy park. Besides budget cabins and motel units, there's a TV room and playground.

Scenic Route Motor Lodge
MOTEL $$

(☑03-693 1700; www.motelscenicroute.co.nz; 28 Waihi Tce; d $135-140; 🖿) There's a vague heritage feel to this stone-and-timber motel, but the modern units have double-glazing, flatscreen TVs and broadband internet. Larger studios have spa baths.

🍴 Eating

Four Peaks Plaza at the corner of Talbot and Cox Sts has a bakery, deli, cafes and the Talbot Forest cheese shop. Every Saturday during summer the town kicks into organic action with a **farmers market** (☉9am-12.30pm).

Verde
CAFE $

(45 Talbot St; mains $11-18; ☉9am-4pm) Down the lane beside the old post office and enveloped in beautiful gardens, this excellent cafe is easily the best of Geraldine's eateries. It's just a shame that it's not open for dinner.

Coco
SWEETS, CAFE $

(www.coco-geraldine.co.nz; 10 Talbot St; truffles $2; ☉10am-5pm) For a quality sugar rush, visit Coco for handmade choccies, designer teas, coffee, hot chocolate and cake.

☆ Entertainment

Geraldine Cinema
CINEMA

(☑03-693 8118; www.facebook.com/GeraldineCinema; Talbot St; adult/child $10/8) Snuggle in to watch a Hollywood favourite or an art-house surprise. There's also occasional live music, usually with a folk, blues or country spin.

ℹ Information

Geraldine Visitor Centre (☑03-693 1006; www.southcanterbury.org.nz; cnr Talbot & Cox Sts; ☉10am-3pm)

ℹ Getting There & Away

Atomic Shuttles (☑03-349 0697; www.atomictravel.co.nz) Daily buses to/from Christchurch ($30, two hours), Lake Tekapo (from $21, 1¼ hours), Twizel ($25, two hours), Cromwell ($35, 4¼ hours) and Queenstown ($35, five hours).

Budget Buses & Shuttles (☑03-615 5119; www.budgetshuttles.co.nz; ☉Mon-Sat) Offers a door-to-door shuttle to Christchurch ($57), along with a cheaper scheduled run ($47).

InterCity (☑03-365 1113; www.intercity.co.nz) Daily coaches head to/from Christchurch (from $32, 2¼ hours), Lake Tekapo (from $21, 1¼ hours), Mt Cook Village (from $38, three hours), Cromwell (from $40, 4¾ hours) and Queenstown (from $42, 5¾ hours).

Timaru

POP 26,900

The port city of Timaru is a handy stopping-off point halfway between Christchurch and Dunedin. Many travellers prefer to kick on 85km further south to the smaller, more charming Oamaru, but Timaru has a few worthy attractions of its own. The town's name comes from the Maori name Te Maru, meaning 'The Place of Shelter'. No permanent settlement existed here until 1839, when the Weller brothers set up a whaling station. The *Caroline*, a sailing ship that transported whale oil, gave the picturesque bay its name.

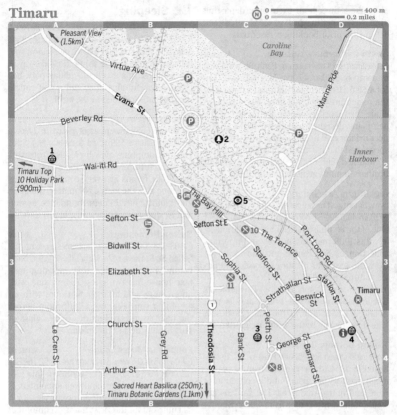

◎ Sights

Caroline Bay Park   PARK, BEACH

(Marine Pde) Ranging from a formal Edwardian-style park below the cliffs of the Bay Hill, to a large lawn, to an extensive dune system and then the beach, Caroline Bay is Timaru's favourite locale. The formal section includes a soundshell, a war memorial and the 1000 romantic blooms, arbours and water features of the **Trevor Griffiths Rose Garden** `FREE`. Hector's dolphins are regular visitors to the bay and you may be lucky enough to spot a seal, sea lion or a penguin on the beach; if you do, keep your distance.

Te Ana Maori Rock Art Centre   MUSEUM

(☏03-687 7372; www.teana.co.nz; 2 George St; adult/child admission $20/10, tour $125/50; ⏰10am-3pm) Passionate Ngai Tahu guides bring this innovative multimedia exhibition about Maori rock paintings to life. You can

Timaru

◎ Sights
1 Aigantighe Art Gallery	A2
2 Caroline Bay Park	C2
3 South Canterbury Museum	C4
4 Te Ana Maori Rock Art Centre	D4
5 Trevor Griffiths Rose Garden	C2

🛏 Sleeping
6 Panorama Motor Lodge	B2
7 Sefton Homestay	B3

🍴 Eating
8 Arthur St Café	C4
9 Fusion	B2
10 Ginger & Garlic	C3
11 Zest	C3

🍷 Drinking & Nightlife
Speight's Ale House	(see 4)

also take a three-hour excursion (departing 2pm, November to April) to see isolated rock art in situ; prior booking is essential.

South Canterbury Museum
MUSEUM

(www.timaru.govt.nz/museum; Perth St; admission by donation; ◷10am-4.30pm Tue-Fri, 1.30-4.30pm Sat & Sun) Historical and natural artefacts of the region are displayed here. Highlights include the Maori section and a replica of the aeroplane designed and flown by local pioneer aviator and inventor Richard Pearse. It's speculated that his mildly successful attempts at manned flight came before the Wright brothers' famous achievement in 1903.

Aigantighe Art Gallery
GALLERY

(www.timaru.govt.nz/art-gallery; 49 Wai-iti Rd; ◷10am-4pm Tue-Fri, noon-4pm Sat & Sun) FREE One of the South Island's largest public galleries, this 1908 mansion houses an important collection of NZ, Pacific and European art from the past four centuries. Local luminaries featured include Frances Hodgkins, Colin McCahon and Ralph Hotere. The gallery's Gaelic name means 'at home' and is pronounced 'egg-and-tie'. If the gallery's closed, take time to explore the sculpture garden.

Timaru Botanic Gardens
GARDENS

(cnr King & Queen Sts; ◷8am-dusk) FREE Established in 1864, these gardens feature ponds, a conservatory, an aviary and a collection of roses and native tree ferns. The gardens are south of the centre; enter from Queen St.

Sacred Heart Basilica
CHURCH

(7 Craigie Ave, Parkside) Roman Catholic with a definite emphasis on the Roman, this beautiful neoclassical church (1911) impresses with multiple domes, Ionian columns and richly coloured stained glass. Its architect, Francis Petre, also designed the large basilicas in Christchurch (now in ruins) and Oamaru. Inside, there's an art nouveau feel to the plasterwork, which includes intertwined floral and sacred heart motifs. There are no set opening hours; try the side door.

✹ Festivals & Events

Timaru Festival of Roses
CULTURAL

(www.festivalofroses.co.nz) Three days of public and private garden displays in late November.

Christmas Carnival
MUSIC

(www.carolinebay.org.nz) Held from 26 December to mid-January at Caroline Bay, this fun festival (inaugurated in 1912) includes concerts, events and carnival rides.

🛏 Sleeping

Timaru Top 10 Holiday Park
HOLIDAY PARK $

(☎03-684 7690; www.timaruholidaypark.co.nz; 154a Selwyn St, West End; sites $38-42, unit with/without bathroom from $92/62; @ ☎) ✈ Tucked away in the suburbs, this excellent holiday park has clean, colourful amenities and a golf course nearby that's included in the tariff.

Pleasant View
B&B $$

(☎03-686 6651; www.pleasantview.co.nz; 2 Moore St, Waimataitai; s $99-115, d $129-145; ☎) Spot Hector's dolphins over breakfast from this modern clifftop house overlooking Caroline Bay. Both rooms are very comfortable, but only one gets the views. No matter, the large guest lounge has them in abundance, as well as a Nespresso machine and a mammoth TV.

Sefton Homestay
B&B $$

(☎03-688 0017; www.seftonhomestay.co.nz; 32 Sefton St, Seaview; r/ste $125/135; ☎) Set back behind a pretty garden, this imposing heritage house has two guest rooms: one with an en suite, and a larger bedroom with an adjoining sunroom and a bathroom across the hall. Swap travel stories over a glass of port in the guest sitting room.

Panorama Motor Lodge
MOTEL $$

(☎03-688 0097; www.panorama.net.nz; 52 The Bay Hill; units from $135; ☎) The rooms in this hilltop motel are modern and well appointed. If you're given a choice of an ocean view or a spa unit, opt for the view; there's a communal spa pool and sauna in the complex anyway.

🍴 Eating & Drinking

Arthur St Café
CAFE $

(8 Arthur St; mains $9-19; ◷7am-5.30pm Mon-Fri, 9am-3pm Sat) Excellent coffee and cruisy Kiwi dub is always a good way to ease into the day. Decked out with retro furniture, Timaru's funkiest eatery offers quiches, bagels and locally famous breakfasts. There's also occasional live music with an alternative and folkie spin.

Zest
PIZZERIA, CAFE $$

(☎03-688 8313; www.zestrestaurant.co.nz; 4a Elizabeth St; lunch $15-20, dinner $19-29; ◷10am-10pm) Neapolitans might sniff at the non-traditional toppings, but the Greek and Hawaiian pizzas served in this converted church hall have plenty of fans. The menu is rounded out with a crowd-pleasing line-up of curry, pasta, schnitzel, steak and salad.

Fusion CAFE, RESTAURANT **$$**
(☑03-688 8550; www.restaurantfusion.co.nz; 64 The Bay Hill; breakfast $15-18, lunch $17-22, dinner $24-31; ☺10am-10pm) The modish red and black decor sets the scene for a menu that channels both Mediterranean and Asian flavours. Between meals it's a good spot for coffee and cake, complete with views of Caroline Bay.

Ginger & Garlic MODERN NZ **$$$**
(☑03-688 3981; www.gingerandgarlic.co.nz; 335 Stafford St; mains $26-39; ☺4-10pm) Timaru's most sophisticated cuisine is showcased at this long-running local favourite. Asian, Middle Eastern and European flavours are paired with quality local produce on the adventurous menu.

Speight's Ale House PUB
(www.timarualehouse.co.nz; 2 George St; ☺11.30am-late; 🛜) Hands down the best of Timaru's pubs, this brewery showcase serves hearty pub meals – burgers, steak and seafood – and the full range of Speight's beers on tap. It's worth a visit just to see the inside of the 1870s Landing Service Building.

❶ Information

Timaru Visitor Centre (☑03-687 9997; www.southcanterbury.org.nz; 2 George St; ☺10am-3pm)

❶ Getting There & Away

AIR

Air New Zealand (☑0800 737 000; www.airnewzealand.co.nz) Subsidiary airline Eagle Airways flies between Wellington and Timaru's Richard Pearse Airport (TIU; Falvey Rd, Levels) two to four times daily.

BUS

Atomic Shuttles (☑03-349 0697; www.atomictravel.co.nz) Stops by the visitor centre, en route to Christchurch ($25, 2½ hours), Oamaru ($20, 1¼ hours) and Dunedin ($25, 2¾ hours).

Budget Buses & Shuttles (☑03-615 5119; www.budgetshuttles.co.nz; ☺Mon-Sat) Offers a door-to-door shuttle to Christchurch ($47), along with scheduled runs ($27).

InterCity (☑03-365 1113; www.intercity.co.nz) Stops outside the train station, with buses to Christchurch (from $28, 2½ hours, two daily), Oamaru (from $14, one hour, two daily), Dunedin (from $32, three hours, two daily), Gore (from $47, six hours, daily) and Te Anau (from $51, eight hours, daily).

Knightrider (☑03-342 8055; www.knightrider.co.nz) Has a bus most nights to/from Christ-

urch ($38, three hours), Oamaru ($28, 1¼ hours), Moeraki ($39, 2¼ hours) and Dunedin ($44, 3¼ hours).

Fairlie
POP 693

Leafy Fairlie is often described as 'the gateway to the Mackenzie'. To the west the landscape changes as the road ascends Burkes Pass to the open spaces of the Mackenzie Country. It's a good place to stop for lunch.

⦿ Sights & Activities

The information centre can provide information on nearby mountain biking tracks. The main ski resort, Mt Dobson (p47), lies in a 3km-wide treeless basin 26km northwest of Fairlie. There's also a club skifield 29km northwest at Fox Peak (p48) in the Two Thumb Range.

Fairlie Heritage Museum MUSEUM
(www.fairlieheritagemuseum.co.nz; 49 Mt Cook Rd; adult/child $5/free; ☺9.30am-4.30pm) Farm machinery, model airplanes and horse-drawn wagons fill this mildly interesting local heritage museum, and there's an old cottage to explore, decked out as if its last owner had just popped out for a bottle of milk. There's a little cafe attached too.

🛏 Sleeping & Eating

Pinewood Motels MOTEL **$$**
(☑03-685 8599; www.pinewoodmotels.co.nz; 25-27 Mt Cook Rd; d $105-125; 🛜) Pine ceilings add a rustic touch to these comfortable, good-value units, decked out with flat-screen TVs. Two-bedroom family units have full kitchens, while the studios have kitchenettes.

Eat Deli & Bar CAFE **$$**
(www.eatdeliandbar.co.nz; 76 Main St; mains $10-20; ☺8am-4pm Tue-Sun) Family-friendly, with a kids' play area, Eat also drags in grown-ups with its excellent coffee and counter food, often with a subtle Asian spin. There's also beer, wine and complimentary internet access.

❶ Information

Fairlie Heartland Resource & Information Centre (☑03-685 8496; www.fairlienz.com; 67 Main St; ☺10am-4pm Mon-Fri)

❶ Getting There & Away

Atomic Shuttles (☑03-349 0697; www.atomictravel.co.nz) Daily buses to/from Christchurch

($30, 2½ hours), Geraldine ($20, 35 minutes), Lake Tekapo ($20, 40 minutes), Cromwell ($35, 3¾ hours) and Queenstown ($35, 4½ hours).

InterCity (✆03-365 1113; www.intercity.co.nz) Daily coaches head to/from Christchurch (from $34, 3¼ hours), Lake Tekapo (from $13, 35 minutes), Mt Cook (from $30, 2½ hours), Cromwell (from $39, four hours) and Queenstown (from $40, five hours).

Lake Tekapo

POP 369

At the southern end of its namesake lake, this little town has unobstructed views across turquoise water to a backdrop of rolling hills and snowcapped mountains. It's a popular stop for tour groups, with buses bound for Mt Cook and Queenstown allowing passengers to pop out for a quick ice cream, coffee and photo opportunity.

Rather than rushing on, it's worth staying to experience the region's glorious night sky from atop nearby Mt John. In 2012 the Aoraki Mackenzie area was declared an International Dark Sky Reserve, one of only five in the world.

◉ Sights & Activities

When the Mackenzie Basin was scoured out by glaciers, Mt John (1029m) remained as an island of tough bedrock in the centre of a vast river of ice. A road leads to the summit, or you can walk via a circuit track (2½ hours return). To extend it to an all-day walk, continue on to Alexandrina and McGregor Lakes. Other walks are detailed in free maps available around town.

Mountain bikes (per hour/half-day $10/25) and kayaks (per hour $25) can be hired at the

BLUE CRUSH

The blazing turquoise colour of Lake Tekapo, a characteristic it shares with others nearby such as Lake Pukaki, is due to sediment in the water. Known as 'rock flour', it was created when the lake's basin was gouged out by a stony-bottomed glacier moving across the land's surface, with the rock-on-rock action grinding out fine particles that ended up being suspended in the glacial melt water. This sediment gives the water a milky quality and refracts the sunlight beaming down, hence the brilliant colour.

Lake Tekapo YHA. In winter, Lake Tekapo is a base for downhill skiing at Mt Dobson (p47) or Roundhill (p48), and cross-country skiing on the Two Thumb Range.

Church of the Good Shepherd CHURCH
(⊘9am-5pm) The prime disgorging point for tour buses, this interdenominational lakeside church was built of stone and oak in 1935. A picture window behind the altar gives churchgoers a distractingly divine view of lake and mountain majesty; needless to say, it's a firm favourite for weddings. Come early in the morning or late afternoon to avoid the peace-shattering hordes.

Nearby is a statue of a collie, a tribute to the sheepdogs that helped develop the Mackenzie Country.

Tekapo Springs SPA, TUBING
(✆03-680 6550; www.tekaposprings.co.nz; 6 Lakeside Dr; adult/child hot pools $20/15, fun park per activity $20/15, combo $52/36; ⊘10am-9pm) Work your way up the hill from the 36°C pool, to the 38°C pool and finally to the 40°C pool, where you can soak in the thermal waters surrounded by native trees, gazing out at the lake. To truly beat the winter chills, there's a steam room and sauna ($8 extra), and if you need extra pampering, there's a day spa (massage from $55).

But that's only half the story. Attached to the complex is a fun park which in winter offers ice-skating and snow-tubing, while in summer there's the world's largest inflatable slide and slippery-slope tubing.

Mackenzie Alpine Horse Trekking HORSE RIDING
(✆0800 628 269; www.maht.co.nz; 1hr/day/overnight $60/280/350) Organises high-country equine explorations, including overnight camping trips.

☞ Tours

Earth & Sky TOUR
(✆03-680 6960; www.earthandsky.co.nz; SH8) Thanks to its pollution-free skies and its distance from any major towns, Lake Tekapo is one of the finest spots on the planet to view the heavens. Nightly stargazing tours head up to University of Canterbury's observatory on Mt John (adult/child $135/80). Day tours of the facility are given on demand in winter, but in summer there's usually a guide available at the observatory from around midday to 3pm (adult/child $20/10).

For those on a tighter budget or with small children in tow (the minimum age for Mt John tours is eight), there are hour-long night tours to the smaller Cowan Observatory (adult/child $80/50).

Air Safaris   SCENIC FLIGHTS
(☑03-680 6880; www.airsafaris.co.nz; SH8) ✈
Unless you're a serious mountaineer with time to kill, you won't get better views of Aoraki/Mt Cook and its glaciers than those offered on the 'Grand Traverse' flights (adult/child $340/220). A similar flight goes from Glentanner Park, but with higher prices (adult/child $375/265).

Tekapo Helicopters   SCENIC FLIGHTS
(☑03-680 6229; www.tekapohelicopters.co.nz; SH8) Has five options, from a 20-minute flight ($195) to an hour-long trip taking in Aoraki/Mt Cook and Fox and Franz Josef Glaciers ($500). All flights include an alpine landing and views of Aoraki/Mt Cook.

Cruise Tekapo   BOAT TOUR
(☑027 479 7675; www.cruisetekapo.co.nz) ✈
Lake cruises (from 25 minutes to two hours long) and fishing expeditions.

🛏 Sleeping

Tailor-Made-Tekapo Backpackers   HOSTEL $
(☑03-680 6700; www.tailor-made-backpackers.co.nz; 9-11 Aorangi Cres; dm $29-31, s $62, d with/without bathroom $84/74; @ 🖥) Favouring beds rather than bunks, this sociable hostel is spread over several well-tended houses on a peaceful street. There's also a barbecue-equipped garden complete with well-established trees and a children's playground. The hostel was on the market when we last visited, so call ahead.

Lake Tekapo YHA   HOSTEL $
(☑03-680 6857; www.yha.co.nz; 3 Simpson Lane; dm $36-39, d $98; @ 🖥) ✈ There are only three private rooms, the dorms are a little crammed and it's relatively pricey for a hostel but, wow, look at those views! Snuggle around the open fire in winter, or chill out by the lake in summer.

★**Chalet Boutique Motel**   APARTMENTS $$
(☑03-680 6774; www.thechalet.co.nz; 14 Pioneer Dr; units $185-295; 🖥) The 'boutique motel' tag doesn't do this superb lakeside complex justice. It might just about cover the four comfortable units in the main house, but doesn't come close to describing the modern two-bedroom house (with attached studio

LAKE PUKAKI LOOKOUT

Continuing on SH8 from Lake Tekapo, after 39km the even larger Lake Pukaki comes into view. There's a reason why every tourist bus pulls up at the lookout, about 8km further along. On a clear day it offers a picture-perfect view over the weirdly blue lake to Aoraki/Mt Cook and its surrounding peaks.

Beside the lookout, the **Lake Pukaki Information Centre** (www.mtcook-alpinesalmon.com; SH8; ⊙8.30am-6pm) is actually an outpost of Mt Cook Alpine Salmon, the highest salmon farm on the planet. The actual farm operates in a hydroelectric canal system on the eastern edge of the lake. It's currently not open for visitors, so drop into the information centre and grab some sashimi ($10) or stock up for a fishy dinner.

apartment) next door, or the wonderfully private 'Henkel hut' next to that.

Peppers Bluewater Resort   RESORT $$
(☑03-360 1063; www.peppers.co.nz; SH8; d $111-226, apt $256-466; 🖥) Sprawling around rocky ponds and tussocky gardens, this large resort offers a variety of smart, contemporary accommodation, ranging from poky hotel rooms to spacious three-bedroom apartments and everything in between.

Lake Tekapo Lodge   B&B $$$
(www.laketekapolodge.co.nz; 24 Aorangi Cres; r $300-450; 🖥) It's time to get kooky at this fabulously idiosyncratic but totally luxurious B&B, filled to the brim with contemporary Kiwi art. The rooms aren't overly large but the extremely comfortable beds and ooh-la-la lake views more than compensate.

Glacier Rock Bed & Breakfast   B&B $$$
(☑03-680 6669; www.glacierrock.co.nz; 35 Lochinver Ave; d $210-250; @ 🖥) ✈ One of the couple who own this striking home was also its architect – and that's his art in the gallery downstairs. The two guest rooms are spacious, warm and airy, and breakfast is served in a sunny room with huge picture windows.

🍴 Eating

★**Astro Café**   CAFE $
(Mt John Observatory, Godley Peaks Rd; mains $6-11; ⊙10am-5pm) This glass-walled pavilion atop Mt John has spectacular 360-degree views

across the entire Mackenzie Basin – quite possibly one of the planet's best locations for a cafe. Tuck into bagels with local Aoraki salmon, or fresh ham-off-the-bone sandwiches; the coffee and cake are good too.

Kohan JAPANESE $$
(www.kohannz.com; SH8; mains $11-19, bento box $25-35) Kohan serves some of the South Island's best Japanese food, and the lake views do their best to distract from the style-devoid cafeteria ambience. With a salmon farm just up the road, you can be sure the sashimi is ultrafresh. Leave room for the handmade green-tea ice cream.

Run 77 CAFE $$
(www.run77laketekapo.co.nz; SH8; mains $11-22; ☺7.30am-4pm; ☎) Relax on chunky wooden furniture and enjoy sandwiches, burgers and pies made from local salmon, and beef, lamb and venison from the owner's high-country spread (the *real* Run 77). Soups, salads and anitipasto platters tick both the healthy and tasty boxes.

Mackenzie's Bar & Grill PUB $$
(SH8; lunch $15-20, dinner $22-34; ☺11.30am-late Mon-Fri, 10am-late Sat & Sun) Serving up interesting spins on steak, chicken and seafood, everything at Mackenzie's comes with a side order of stellar lake and mountain views. Robust dishes like lamb shanks and Aoraki salmon are the perfect answer to an active day's adventuring.

ⓘ Information

Tekapo Springs Sales & Information Centre
(☎03-680 6579; SH8; ☺10am-6pm) Since the i-SITE closed, the folks from Tekapo Springs have filled the gap, dispensing brochures and advice. The only bookings they take are for their own complex though.

ⓘ Getting There & Away

Atomic Shuttles (☎03-349 0697; www.atomic-travel.co.nz) Daily buses to/from Christchurch ($30, 3¼ hours), Geraldine ($20, 1¼ hours), Twizel ($20, 40 minutes), Cromwell ($30, three hours) and Queenstown ($30, 3¾ hours).

Cook Connection (☎0800 266 526; www.cookconnect.co.nz) Shuttle service to Mt Cook ($35, 1½ hours).

InterCity (☎03-365 1113; www.intercity.co.nz) Daily coaches head to/from Christchurch (from $36, 3¾ hours), Geraldine (from $21, 1¼ hours), Mt Cook (from $30, 1½ hours), Cromwell (from $36, 2¾ hours) and Queenstown (from $36, 4¾ hours).

Aoraki/Mt Cook National Park

The spectacular 700-sq-km Aoraki/Mt Cook National Park, along with Fiordland, Aspiring and Westland National Parks, is part of the Southwest New Zealand (Te Wahipounamu) World Heritage Area, which extends from Westland's Cook River down to Fiordland. Fenced in by the Southern Alps and the Two Thumb, Liebig and Ben Ohau Ranges, more than one-third of the park has a blanket of permanent snow and glacial ice.

Of the 23 NZ mountains over 3000m, 19 are in this park. The highest is mighty Aoraki/Mt Cook – at 3724m it's the tallest peak in Australasia. Known to Maori as Aoraki (Cloud Piercer), after an ancestral deity in Maori mythology, the mountain was given its English name in 1851, in honour of explorer James Cook.

This region has always been the focus of climbing in NZ. On 2 March 1882 William Spotswood Green and two Swiss alpinists failed to reach the summit of Cook after an epic 62-hour ascent. But two years later a trio of local climbers – Tom Fyfe, George Graham and Jack Clarke – were spurred into action by the news that two well-known European alpinists were coming to attempt Cook, and set off to climb it before the visitors. On Christmas Day 1894 they ascended the Hooker Glacier and north ridge, a brilliant climb in those days, and stood on the summit.

In 1913 Australian climber Freda du Faur became the first woman to reach the summit. In 1948 Edmund Hillary's party climbed the south ridge; Hillary went on to become the first to reach the summit of Mt Everest. Since then, most of the daunting face routes have been climbed.

Among the region's many great peaks are Sefton, Tasman, Silberhorn, Malte Brun, La Perouse, Hicks, De la Beche, Douglas and the Minarets. Many can be ascended from Westland National Park, and there are climbers' huts on both sides of the divide.

Aoraki/Mt Cook is a wonderful sight, assuming there's no cloud in the way. Most visitors arrive on tour buses, stop at the Hermitage hotel for photos, and then zoom off back down SH80. Hang around to soak up this awesome peak and the surrounding landscape and to try the excellent short walks. On the trails, look for the thar, a Himalayan goat; the chamois, smaller and of lighter build than the thar, and originally hailing from Europe; and red deer, also European. Summertime brings into bloom the Mt Cook lily, a large mountain buttercup, and mountain daisies, gentians and edelweiss.

⊙ Sights

DOC Aoraki/Mt Cook Visitor Centre INTERPRETATION CENTRE
(📞 03-435 1186; www.doc.govt.nz; 1 Larch Grove; ⊗ 8.30am-4.30pm) FREE As well as being the font of all knowledge about tramping routes and weather conditions, DOC's visitor centre has excellent displays on local flora, fauna and history, as well as videos and a sunken garden showcasing a historic mountain hut. Most activities can be booked here.

Sir Edmund Hillary Alpine Centre MUSEUM
(www.hermitage.co.nz; The Hermitage; adult/child $20/10; ⊗ 7am-8.30pm Oct-Mar, 8am-7pm Apr-Sep) This multimedia museum opened just three weeks before the January 2008 death of the man widely regarded as the greatest New Zealander of all time. Sir Ed's commentary tracks were recorded only a few months before he died. As well as memorabilia and displays about mountaineering, there's a domed digital planetarium (showing four different digital presentations) and a cinema (screening four documentaries, including the *Mt Cook Magic* 3D movie and a fascinating 75-minute film about Sir Ed's conquest of Mt Everest).

Tasman Glacier GLACIER
At 27km long and up to 3km wide, the Tasman is the largest of NZ's glaciers, but it's melting fast, losing hundreds of metres from its length each year. It is also melting from the top down, shrinking around 150m in depth since it was first surveyed in 1891. In its lower section the melts have exposed rocks, stones and boulders, which form a solid unsightly mass on top of the ice. Despite this considerable melt, at its thickest point the ice is still estimated to be over 600m deep.

Tasman Lake, at the foot of the glacier, only started to form in the early 1970s and now stretches to 7km. The ongoing effects of climate change are expected to extend it to 16km within the next 20 years. The lake is covered by a maze of huge icebergs which are continuously being sheared off the glacier's terminal face. On 22 February 2011 the Christchurch earthquake caused a 1.3km long, 300m high, 30-million-tonne chunk of ice to break off, causing 3.5m waves to roll into the tourist boats on the lake at the time (no one was injured).

In the glacier's last major advance (17,000 years ago), the glacier crept south far enough to carve out Lake Pukaki. A later advance did not reach out to the valley sides, so there's a gap between the outer valley walls and the lateral moraines of this later advance. The unsealed Tasman Valley Rd, which branches off Mt Cook Rd 800m south of the village, travels through this gap. From the Blue Lakes shelter, 8km along the road, the **Tasman Glacier View Track** (40 minutes return) leads to a viewpoint on the moraine wall, passing the Blue Lakes on the way.

🏃 Activities

Hiking & Climbing

Various easy walks from the Hermitage area are outlined in brochures available from DOC. Longer walks are only recommended for those with mountaineering experience, as conditions at higher altitudes are severe and the tracks dangerous. If you intend staying at any of the park's huts, it's essential to register your intentions at the DOC visitor centre and pay the hut fee. Intentions cards are also recommended for longer day walks.

For the experienced, there's unlimited scope for climbing, but regardless of your skills, take every precaution – more than 200 people have died in climbing accidents here. The bleak *In Memoriam* book in the visitor information centre begins with the first death on Aoraki/Mt Cook in 1907, and since then more than 70 climbers have died on the peak.

Highly changeable weather is typical here: Aoraki/Mt Cook is only 44km from the coast and weather conditions rolling in from the Tasman Sea can mean sudden storms. Unless you're experienced in such conditions, don't climb anywhere without a guide.

Check with the park rangers before attempting any climb and always heed their advice. Fill out a climbers-intentions card before starting out – so rangers can check on you if you're overdue coming out – and sign out again when you return. The visitor centre also hires locator beacons (per three days/week $30/40).

Walkers can use the **public shelter** (⊗ 8am-7pm Oct-Apr, to 5pm May-Sep) in the village, which has running water, toilets and coin-operated showers. Note that this shelter cannot be used for overnight stays.

Hooker Valley Track HIKING
Perhaps the best of the day walks, this track (three hours return from the village) heads up the Hooker Valley and crosses three

Aoraki/Mt Cook National Park

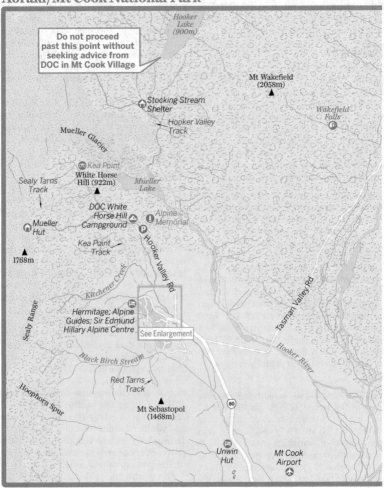

swing bridges to the Stocking Stream and the terminus of the Hooker Glacier. After the second swing bridge, Aoraki/Mt Cook totally dominates the valley, and you'll often see icebergs floating in Hooker Lake.

Kea Point Track   HIKING

The trail to Kea Point (two hours return from the village) is lined with native plants and ends at a platform with excellent views of Aoraki/Mt Cook, the Hooker Valley and the ice faces of Mt Sefton and the Footstool. Despite the name, you're no more likely to see a kea here than in other parts of the park.

Sealy Tarns Track   HIKING

The walk to Sealy Tarns (three to four hours return) branches off the Kea Point Track and continues up the ridge to Mueller Hut (dorm $36), a comfortable 28-bunk hut with gas, cooking facilities and longdrop toilets.

Alpine Recreation   HIKING, CLIMBING

(☏ 03-680 6736, 0800 006 096; www.alpinerecreation.com) Based in Lake Tekapo, Alpine Recreation organises high-altitude guided treks, as well as mountaineering courses and ski touring. Also on offer are guided ascents of Aoraki/Mt Cook, Mt Tasman and other peaks.

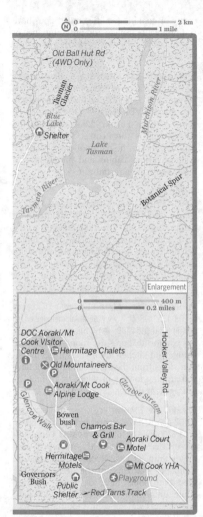

Snow Sports

Alpine Guides
SNOW SPORTS

(☑ 03-435 1834; www.alpineguides.co.nz) Ski-touring, heliskiing, guided climbs and mountaineering courses. Its store in the Hermitage sells travel clothing, outdoor and mountaineering gear, and rents ice axes, crampons, daypacks and sleeping bags.

Southern Alps Guiding
SNOW SPORTS

(☑ 03-435 1890; www.mtcook.com; Old Mountaineers, 3 Larch Grove Rd) From June to October heliskiers can head up Tasman Glacier for a 10km to 12km downhill run ($830 to $870).

Private guiding is also available, as well as three- to four-hour helihiking trips on Tasman Glacier year-round ($450).

Other Activities

Glentanner Horse Trekking
HORSE RIDING

(☑ 03-435 1855; www.glentanner.co.nz; 1/2/3hr ride $70/90/150; ⊗ Nov-Apr) Leads guided treks on a high-country sheep station with options suited to all levels of experience.

Glacier Sea-Kayaking
KAYAKING

(☑ 03-435 1890; www.mtcook.com; per person $145; ⊗ Oct-Apr) Guided trips head out on the terminal lake of the Tasman or the Mueller Glacier. There are usually icebergs to negotiate, but if this is your prime reason for taking the trip, it pays to check in advance whether there actually are any. Because of the danger of ice carving from the ends of the glaciers, you can only admire them and the larger icebergs from a distance. Expect to spend about an hour on the water; book at the Old Mountaineers Cafe.

Big Sky
STARGAZING

(☑ 0800 686 800; www.hermitage.co.nz; adult/child $60/30, planetarium only $24/12) NZ's southern sky is introduced by a 45-minute presentation in the Alpine Centre's digital planetarium, before participants venture outside to study the real deal with telescopes, binoculars and an astronomy guide. If the weather's not cooperating, the experience is confined to the planetarium.

☞ Tours

Tasman Valley 4WD & Argo Tours
TOUR

(☑ 0800 686 800; www.mountcooktours.co.nz; adult/child $75/38) Offers a 90-minute Argo (8WD all-terrain vehicle) tour checking out the Tasman Glacier and its terminal lake. Expect plenty of alpine flora and an interesting commentary along the way. Book online or at the Hermitage hotel activities desk.

Glacier Explorers
BOAT TOUR

(☑ 03-435 1641; www.glacierexplorers.com; adult/child $145/70) Head out on the terminal lake of the Tasman Glacier onboard a custom-built MAC boat and get up close and personal with 300-year-old icebergs. Book at the activities desk at the Hermitage.

Helicopter Line
SCENIC FLIGHTS

(☑ 03-435 1801; www.helicopter.co.nz) From Glentanner Park, the Helicopter Line offers 20-minute Alpine Vista flights ($230), an exhilarating 35-minute flight over the Ben

DON'T MISS

ALPS 2 OCEAN CYCLE TRAIL

Hoping to give the Otago Central Rail Trail a ride for its money, this new mountain-biking route stretches from Mt Cook Village to Oamaru, via Twizel, Lake Ohau Lodge, Omarama, Otematata, Kurow and Duntroon. While there are some quite long sections on SH83, about 40% of the trail is offroad. It's mainly downhill too, descending 780m over its 300km course.

The route is split into eight sections which can be tackled individually or consecutively as a four- to six-day ride. The official start involves an expensive helicopter trip over the Tasman River, so you might like to pick up the trail later at the southern end of Lake Pukaki.

See www.alps2ocean.com for more.

Ohau Range ($345) and a 40-minute Mountains High flight over the Tasman Glacier and alongside Aoraki/Mt Cook ($425). All feature snow landings.

Mount Cook Ski Planes SCENIC FLIGHTS
(☑03-430 8034; www.mtcookskiplanes. com) Based at Mt Cook Airport, offering 40-minute (adult/child $405/295) and 55-minute (adult/child $530/405) flights, both with snow landings. Flightseeing without a landing is a cheaper option; try the 25-minute Mini Tasman trip (adult/child $275/255) or 45-minute Alpine Wonderland (adult/child $370/275).

🛏 Sleeping

Accommodation is more expensive in Mt Cook Village than in Twizel, but the thrill of waking up so close to the mountains is worth the additional expense.

Mt Cook YHA HOSTEL $
(☑03-435 1820; www.yha.co.nz; 4 Bowen Dr; dm $37, d $118; @🛜) 🅟 Handsomely decked out in pine, this excellent hostel has a free sauna, drying room, log fires and DVDs. Rooms are clean and warm, although some are a tight squeeze (particularly the twin bunk rooms).

DOC White Horse Hill Campground CAMPSITE $
(☑03-435 1186; Hooker Valley Rd; site per adult/ child $10/5) Located 2km up the Hooker Valley from Aoraki/Mt Cook village, this self-registration campsite doesn't have electricity or cooking facilities but it does have running water, toilets and an abundance of blissful views. It's also perfectly positioned for tackling various walking tracks.

Glentanner Park Centre HOLIDAY PARK $
(☑03-435 1855; www.glentanner.co.nz; Mt Cook Rd; sites $19-22, dm $29, unit with/without bathroom from $160/80; @🛜) 🅟 On the northern shore of Lake Pukaki, 22km south of the village, this is the nearest fully equipped campground to the national park. Facilities include various cabins and motel units, a bunk room and a restaurant.

Unwin Hut HOSTEL $
(☑03-435 1100; www.alpineclub.org.nz; Mt Cook Rd; dm adult/child $30/15; 🛜) About 3.5km before the village, this lodge belongs to the New Zealand Alpine Club (NZAC). Members get preference, but beds are usually available for climbing groupies. There are basic bunks (bring your own linen), and a big common room with a fireplace and kitchen.

Aoraki/Mt Cook Alpine Lodge LODGE $$
(☑03-435 1860; www.aorakialpinelodge.co.nz; Bowen Dr; d $164-189; @) This modern lodge has comfortable en-suite rooms and a huge lounge and kitchen area. The superb mountain views from the barbecue area will have you arguing for the privilege of grilling the sausages for dinner.

Aoraki Court Motel MOTEL $$$
(☑03-435 1111; www.aorakicourt.co.nz; 26 Bowen Dr; d $205-295) While it wouldn't command these prices elsewhere, this clump of new motel units is very good indeed. Feature wallpaper sharpens up the decor, and the tiled bathrooms have designery touches. Some units have spa baths but all have kitchenettes and gee-golly mountain views.

Hermitage HOTEL $$$
(☑03-435 1809; www.hermitage.co.nz; Terrace Rd; r $239-599; @🛜) Completely dominating Mt Cook Village, this famous hotel offers fantastic mountain views. While the corridors in some of the older wings can seem a little hospital-like, all of the rooms have been renovated to a high standard. As well as the hotel, the Hermitage offers motel rooms and well-equipped A-frame chalets.

🍴 Eating & Drinking

Old Mountaineers CAFE, BAR $$
(www.mtcook.com; Bowen Dr; breakfast $10-15, lunch $15-26, dinner $18-35; ⊙10am-9pm daily Nov-Apr,

Tue-Sun May & Jul-Oct; 🛜) 🥤 A good-value alternative to the eateries at the Hermitage, this large eatery provides mountain views through picture windows or from outside tables in summer. As well as cooked breakfasts, it delivers top-notch burgers, pizza, pasta and salad. Linger to study the old black-and-white pics and mountaineering memorabilia.

Panorama MODERN NZ $$$
(📞0800 686 800, 03-435 1809; www.hermitage. co.nz; Terrace Rd; mains $34-40; ⊗6-10pm) The Hermitage's signature restaurant is by far the best of the hotel's dining options, which include a buffet restaurant and a lacklustre cafe. The sophisticated fare is well matched to wonderful views and interesting mid-20th-century architecture.

Chamois Bar & Grill PUB
(www.mountcookbackpackers.co.nz; Bowen Dr; ⊗4pm-late) Upstairs in Mt Cook Backpacker Lodge, in the heart of the village, this large bar offers pub grub, a pool table, a big-screen TV and the occasional live gig.

ℹ Information

The DOC visitor centre (p503) is the best source of local information. The nearest ATM and supermarket are in Twizel.

ℹ Getting There & Away

The village's small airport only serves aerial sightseeing companies. Some of these may be willing to combine transport to the West Coast (ie Franz Josef) with a scenic flight, but flights are heavily dependent on weather.

If you're driving, fill up at Lake Tekapo or Twizel. There is petrol at Mt Cook, but it's expensive and involves summoning an attendant from the Hermitage (for a fee).

Cook Connection (📞0800 266 526; www.cook-connect.co.nz) Shuttle services to Lake Tekapo ($35, 1½ hours) and Twizel ($25, one hour).

InterCity (📞03-365 1113; www.intercity.co.nz) Daily coaches head to/from Christchurch (from $67, 5¼ hours), Geraldine (from $38, three hours), Lake Tekapo, (from $30, 1½ hours), Cromwell (from $59, 2¾ hours) and Queenstown (from $64, four hours). They stop at the YHA and the Hermitage, both of which handle bookings.

Twizel

POP 1140

It wasn't long ago that New Zealanders maligned Twizel. The forest-ringed town just south of Lake Pukaki was built in 1968 to serv-

ice construction of the nearby hydroelectric power station, and was due to be abandoned in 1984 when the project was completed. Now Twizel's residents are having the last laugh as new lakeside subdivisions have been built to take advantage of the area's relaxed lakes-and-mountains lifestyle. Accommodation, eateries, petrol and groceries are all better value in Twizel than Mt Cook Village.

◉ Sights & Activities

Nearby Lake Ruataniwha is popular for rowing, boating and windsurfing. Fishing in local rivers, canals and lakes is also big business; ask at the information centre about local guides.

Kaki Visitor Hide WILDLIFE RESERVE
(📞03-435 3124; adult/child $20/10; ⊗9.30am & 4.30pm late Oct-Apr) The rare kaki (black stilt) is found only in NZ, and a breeding program is aiming to increase the population at the Ahuriri Conservation Park. It's possible to get a close-up look at these elusive birds by booking a one-hour guided tour through the information centre. Tours depart from the centre, but you'll need your own transport.

☞ Tours

OneRing Tours TOUR
(📞0800 213 868; www.lordoftheringstour.com) How often do you get the opportunity to charge around like a mad thing weilding replica *LOTR* gear? Not often enough! Tours head onto the sheep station used for the location of the Battle of the Pelennor Fields and include lots of information about the filming. Choose between a two-hour version (adult/child $84/45), a truncated one-hour option (adult/child $64/35) and an adults-only twilight tour, enjoying beer, wine and nibbles as the sun sets over Gondor ($115).

Helicopter Line SCENIC FLIGHTS
(📞03-435 0370; www.helicopter.co.nz; Pukaki Airport, Harry Wigley Dr) Flight options include the hour-long Aoraki/Mt Cook Discovery ($640), the 45-minute Southern Alps Experience ($520), the 35-minute Alpine Scenic Flight ($345) and the 25-minute Alpine Express ($265). All but the shortest guarantee snow landings.

⊨ Sleeping

Twizel Holiday Park HOLIDAY PARK $
(📞03-435 0507; www.twizelholidaypark.co.nz; 122 Mackenzie Dr; sites from $34, dm $30, units $95-215; 🛜) Offers green, flower-filled grounds

OFF THE BEATEN TRACK

RUATANIWHA CONSERVATION PARK

Taking in a large chunk of the space between Lake Pukaki and Lake Ohau, this 368 sq km protected area includes the Ben Ohau Range and various valleys and beech forests. The numerous walks in this vast expanse are detailed in DOC's *Ruataniwha Conservation Park* pamphlet (available online). There are also five good mountain-bike tracks.

DOC huts and camping areas are scattered throughout the park, but for a more comfortable stay, try **Lake Ohau Lodge** (☑ 03-438 9885; www.ohau.co.nz; Lake Ohau Rd; s $101-180, d $107-205) 🥾, idyllically sited on the western shore of the rower-friendly lake. Accommodation includes everything from budget rooms with shared facilities, to upmarket rooms with decks and mountain views. The lodge is the wintertime service centre for the Ohau Ski Field (p47). In summer it's a quieter retreat. DB&B packages are available.

and accommodation in a refurbished maternity hospital. There are a few en-suite cabins, a bunkroom and room for tents and campervans. The modern, self-contained cottages are particularly good value.

★**Omahau Downs** B&B $$
(☑ 03-435 0199; www.omahau.co.nz; SH8; s/d $115/135, cottage $125-225; ⊘ closed Jun-Aug; 🕸) This farmstead, 2km north of Twizel, has two cosy, self-contained cottages (one sleeping up to six), and a lodge with sparkling, modern rooms and a deck looking out at the Ben Ohau Range. An essential experience is a moonlit, wood-fired outdoor bath ($20).

Mountain Chalets MOTEL, HOSTEL $$
(☑ 03-435 0785; www.mountainchalets.co.nz; Wairepo Rd; dm $28, d $110-130; 🕸) Wooden ceilings add a rustic quality to these cosy, well-equipped, self-contained A-frame chalets, available as studio, one- and two-bedroom units. There's also a small, laid-back lodge that's perfect for backpackers.

Heartland Lodge B&B $$$
(☑ 03-435 0008; www.heartland-lodge.co.nz; 19 North West Arch; apt $160, s $230-260, d $270-300; 🕸) Built on the leafy outskirts of town, this large modern house has a surfeit of space, translating to a large wraparound living area downstairs and spacious guest rooms above. Prices include cooked breakfasts, unless you're staying in 'the retreat', a separate apartment with its own kitchenette.

🍴 Eating & Drinking

★**Shawty's** CAFE, BAR $$
(☑ 03-435 3155; www.shawtys.co.nz; 4 Market Pl; brunch $12-20, dinner $29-34; ⊘ 8.30am-3pm Mon & Tue, 8.30am-late Wed-Sun Apr-Oct, to late daily Nov-Mar; 🕸) Cool beats and craft beers create a mood that's surprisingly sophisticated for Twizel. Big breakfasts and gourmet pizzas ($14 to $18) are a good way to start and end an active day amid the surrounding alpine vistas. The adjacent Grappa Lounge has DJs and live music in summer.

Poppies Cafe CAFE $$
(☑ 03-435 0848; www.poppiescafe.com; 1 Benmore Pl; brunch $10-20, dinner $23-35; ⊘ 10am-3pm & 5.30-9pm; 🕸) Lunch showcases the likes of gourmet pies, burgers and pasta, while dinner features more substantial fare; excellent pizzas ($20 to $24) occupy a tasty middle ground. It's located on the outskirts of town near the Mackenzie Country Inn.

Jasmine Thai Café THAI $$
(1 Market Pl; lunch $12, dinner $18-22; ⊘ noon-2pm Tue-Sat & 5-9pm daily) The zesty and zingy flavours of your favourite Southeast Asian beach holiday have travelled well to get this far inland. Alcohol is BYO, so grab a few cold beers from the Four Square supermarket to ease Jasmine's authentic Thai heat.

ℹ Information

Twizel Information Centre (☑ 03-435 3124; Market Pl; ⊘ 8.30am-5pm Mon-Fri, 11am-2pm Sat & Sun)

ℹ Getting There & Away

Atomic Shuttles (☑ 03-349 0697; www.atomic-travel.co.nz) Daily buses to/from Christchurch ($35, 3¾ hours), Geraldine ($25, two hours), Lake Tekapo ($20, 40 minutes), Cromwell ($30, 2¼ hours) and Queenstown ($30, 3¼ hours).

Cook Connection (☑ 0800 266 526; www.cookconnect.co.nz) Shuttle services to Mt Cook Village ($25, one hour).

InterCity (☑ 03-365 1113; www.intercity.co.nz) Daily coaches head to/from Christchurch (from $40, 5¼ hours), Lake Tekapo (from $13, 50 minutes), Mt Cook Village (from $32, one hour), Cromwell (from $29, two hours) and Queenstown (from $35, three hours).

Dunedin & Otago

Includes ➡

Omarama	511
Waitaki Valley	512
Oamaru	513
Dunedin	520
Otago Peninsula	531
Naseby	535
Lauder, Omakau & Ophir	536
Alexandra	537
Clyde	538
Cromwell & Around	539

Best Places to Eat

➡ Riverstone Kitchen (p518)

➡ Fleur's Place (p519)

➡ The Shed at Northburn Station (p540)

➡ Pitches Store (p536)

➡ Otago Farmers' Market (p526)

Best Places to Stay

➡ Burn Cottage Retreat (p540)

➡ Pitches Store (p536)

➡ Dunstan House (p539)

➡ Pen-y-bryn Lodge (p517)

Why Go?

Otago has attractions both urban and rural, ranging from quirky towns to world-class wineries and some of the country's most accessible wildlife. Its historic heart is Dunedin, home to a vibrant student culture and arts scene. From the town's stately Edwardian train station, catch the famous Taieri Gorge Railway inland, and continue on two wheels along the craggily scenic Otago Central Rail Trail.

Those seeking colonial New Zealand can soak up the frontier atmosphere of gold-rush towns such as Clyde, St Bathans, Naseby and cute-as-a-button Ophir. For wildlife, head to the Otago Peninsula, where penguins, albatross, sea lions and seals are easily sighted. Seaside Oamaru has a wonderful historic precinct, resident penguin colonies and a quirky devotion to Steampunk culture.

Unhurried and overflowing with picturesque scenery, Otago is generous to explorers who are after a more leisurely style of holiday.

When to Go

➡ February and March have settled, sunny weather (usually...), and the juicy appeal of fresh apricots, peaches and cherries.

➡ At Easter, hook yourself a Southern Man at the Middlemarch Singles Ball, or drown your sorrows at the Clyde Wine & Food Festival.

➡ Take to two wheels on the Otago Central Rail Trail during the quieter months of May and December.

➡ In November watch the pros battle it out on the Highlands Motorsport Park, then ride graciously into the past on a penny farthing bicycle at Oamaru's Victorian Heritage Celebrations.

N	0	50 km
	0	25 miles

Timaru

Lake Wanaka
Lake Hawea
Lindis Pass
Omarama
Lake Benmore
Lake Aviemore
Otematata
Lake Waitaki
Kurow
Takiroa Maori Rock Art Site
Duntroon
Waitaki Valley
Waitaki River
Glenavy
Waitaki
Ngapara
Hilderthorpe

Wanaka
Dunstan Range
Hawkdun Range
St Bathans
Tarras
Mt Pisa
Bendigo
Lake Dunstan
Becks
Naseby
Elephant Rocks
Oamaru

Cardrona
Cromwell
Lauder
Omakau
Ophir
Wedderburn
Ranfurly
Dansevs Pass
Kakanui
Queenstown
Bannockburn
Clyde Dam
Chatto Creek
Waipiata
Kokonga
Waianakarua
All Day Bay
Clyde
Alexandra
Hyde
Macraes Flat
Moeraki
Nevis River
Otago Central Rail Trail
Dunback
Shag Point
Lake Roxburgh
Rock & Pillar Range
Palmerston
Roxburgh
Clutha River
Middlemarch
Raes Junction
Lake Mahinerangi
Pukerangi
Taieri Gorge Railway
Seacliff
Waitati
Lawrence
Outram
Port Chalmers
Otago Peninsula
Tapanui
Beaumont Forest
Mosgiel
Portobello
Dunedin
Gore
Manuka Gorge Scenic Reserve
Waihola
St Clair Beach
Mataura
Clinton
Milton
Edendale
Balclutha
Kaitangata
Invercargill (24km)
The Catlins

SOUTH PACIFIC OCEAN

Mataura River

Dunedin & Otago Highlights

1 Experiencing a heritage past, and a possible Steampunk future, in kooky **Oamaru** (p511)

2 Peering at penguins, admiring albatross and staring at seals on **Otago Peninsula** (p531)

3 Exploring New Zealand's southern heritage in quaint backcountry villages such as **Ophir** (p536) and **Naseby** (p535)

4 Taste-testing some of the planet's best pinot noir in the wineries scattered around **Cromwell** (p539)

5 Sampling local beers and listening out for local bands in the bars and cafes of **Dunedin** (p520)

6 Cycling through lonely vistas of brown and gold along the **Otago Central Rail Trail** (p534)

7 Winding through gorges, alongside canyons and across tall viaducts on the snaking **Taieri Gorge Railway** (p524)

ℹ Getting There & Around

Air New Zealand (☑ 0800 737 000; www.airnewzealand.co.nz) flies from Dunedin to Christchurch, Wellington and Auckland, and **Jetstar** (☑ 0800 800 995; www.jetstar.com) flies to Auckland. The only train services are heritage trips from Dunedin to Middlemarch and Dunedin to Palmerston. The main bus routes follow SH1 or SH8.

WAITAKI DISTRICT

The broad, braided Waitaki River provides a clear dividing line between Otago and Canterbury to the region's north. The Waitaki Valley is a direct but less-travelled route from the Southern Alps to the sea, featuring freaky limestone formations, Maori rock paintings and ancient fossils. The area is also one of NZ's newest winemaking regions, and a major component of the new Alps 2 Ocean Cycle Trail (p506) that links Aoraki/Mt Cook National Park to Oamaru on the coast. The district's main town, Oamaru, is a place of penguins and glorious heritage architecture.

Omarama

POP 267

At the head of the Waitaki Valley, Omarama is surrounded by mountain ranges and fabulous landscapes. Busy times in this sleepy place include the rodeo (28 December) and the sheepdog trials (March).

◉ Sights & Activities

Clay Cliffs Paritea   LANDMARK
This bizarre moonscape is the result of two million years of erosion on layers of silt and gravel that were exposed along the active Ostler fault line. The cliffs are on private land; before setting out, pay the $5 vehicle admission fee at Omarama Hot Tubs. To get to the area, head north from town for 4km on SH8, turn left onto Quailburn Rd, and then turn left after 4km onto unsealed Henburn Rd.

Wrinkly Rams   FARM
(☑ 03-438 9751; www.thewrinklyrams.co.nz; 24 Omarama Ave; adult/child $20/10) A regular stop for tour buses, Wrinkly Rams stages 30-minute shearing and sheepdog shows, including lamb-feeding in season. Phone ahead to tag along with a tour group, or book your own one-off show. Attached is one of Omarama's better **cafes** (mains $7-25; ⊙ 7am-4.30pm; 🛜).

Omarama Hot Tubs   SPA
(☑ 03-438 9703; www.hottubsomarama.co.nz; 29 Omarama Ave; per 1-/2-/3-/4-person tub $45/80/105/120, pod 75/140/180/200; ⊙ 11am-late) If your legs are weary after mountain biking or hiking, or you just want to cosy up with your significant other, these private, wood-fired hot tubs could be just the ticket. The concept is Japanese, but with the surrounding mountain ranges, the lakeside setting and a pristine night sky, you could only be on the South Island of NZ.

Choose between a 90-minute soak in a tub (each has its own dressing room) or a two-hour session in a 'wellness pod', which includes a sauna. The chemical-free glacier and snow-melt water is changed after each booking, and the used water is recycled for irrigation. Therapeutic massages (30/60 minutes $60/100) and beauty treatments are also available.

Glide Omarama   GLIDING
(☑ 03-438 9555; www.glideomarama.com) The area's westerlies and warm summer thermals allow for world-class gliding over the hills and spectacular Southern Alps, and a national gliding meet is held here in December or January. This crew offers lessons and scenic flights ranging from 30 minutes ($325) to three hours ($640).

DUNEDIN & OTAGO OMARAMA

ESSENTIAL OTAGO

Eat Cheese from Oamaru's Whitestone factory

Drink Central Otago pinot noir

Read *Owls Do Cry* by Oamaru's Janet Frame

Listen to *Tally Ho! Flying Nun's Greatest Bits,* a 2011 compilation marking the 30th anniversary of Dunedin's iconic record label

Watch *In My Father's Den* (2004), set in Central Otago

Festival Oamaru's Victorian Heritage Celebrations in late November

Go green Tiptoe down to Otago Peninsula beaches in search of yellow-eyed penguins

Online www.dunedinnz.com, www.centralotagonz.com

Area code ☑ 03

🛏 Sleeping & Eating

Buscot Station FARMSTAY, HOSTEL **$**
(☑ 027 222 1754; SH8; site/dm/s/d $10/25/43/61)
For a completely different and uniquely Kiwi experience, grab a room in the homely farmhouse attached to a huge sheep and cattle station, or a bed in the large dormitory out the back. Look for it on SH8, 10km north of Omarama.

Omarama Top 10 HOLIDAY PARK **$**
(☑ 03-438 9875; www.omaramatop10.co.nz; SH8; sites $34-39, unit with/without bathroom $110/55; @🛜) This streamside holiday park is a peaceful green space to camp in. Standard cabins are compact, but larger en suite and self-contained motel units are available.

Ladybird Hill WINERY **$$**
(www.ladybirdhill.co.nz; 1 Pinot Noir Ct; mains $6-32; ⊙10am-4pm Thu-Sun Aug-Jun) Sure, you can do it the easy way and simply order a leisurely lunch from the menu. Or you can grab a rod, catch a salmon from the well-stocked ponds and wait until it's prepared, smoked and served to your table ($37, which feeds two to three adults). Other attractions include a kids' playground and walking tracks through the hillside vineyard.

ℹ Information

Omarama Hot Tubs doubles as the information office, and can assist with accommodation and transport information. See www.discoveromarama.co.nz for more information.

MAORI NZ: OTAGO

The early Maori history of Otago echoes that of Canterbury (p485), with Ngai Tahu the dominant tribe at the time the British arrived. One of the first parcels of land that Ngai Tahu sold was called the Otago block, a 1618-sq-km parcel of land which changed hands in 1844 for £2400. The name Otago reflects the Ngai Tahu pronunciation of Otakou, a small village on the far reaches of the Otago Peninsula, where there's still a *marae* (Maori meeting place).

Dunedin's Otago Museum (p523) has the finest Maori exhibition in the South Island, including an ornately carved *waka taua* (war canoe) and finely crafted *pounamu* (greenstone). Maori rock art can still be seen in situ in the Waitaki Valley.

ℹ Getting There & Away

InterCity (☑ 03-471 7143; www.intercity.co.nz) Daily coaches head to/from Christchurch (from $42, 5¾ hours), Mt Cook Village (from $32, 1¼ hours), Twizel (from $13, 19 minutes), Cromwell (from $23, 1½ hours) and Queenstown (from $32, 2½ hours).

Atomic Shuttles (☑ 03-349 0697; www.atomictravel.co.nz) Services stop in Omarama for a break before continuing on to Christchurch ($35, four hours), Lake Tekapo ($20, one hour), Twizel ($20, 20 minutes), Cromwell ($25, 1½ hours) and Queenstown ($30, 2¼ hours).

Waitaki Valley

Wine, waterskiing and salmon-fishing are just some of the treats on offer along this little-travelled route. Coming from Omarama, SH83 passes an array of arrestingly blue lakes, each abutted by a hydroelectric power station. For a scenic detour along the north bank, leave the highway at Otematata and cross over the huge Benmore Dam, then cross over Aviemore Dam to rejoin the highway.

A succession of sleepy little heartland towns line the highway, peppered with rustic heritage bank buildings and pubs. One of the most appealing is tiny lost-in-time **Kurow** (population 302), the home town of World Cup–winning All Blacks captain Richie McCaw. From almost-as-cute **Duntroon** (population 90), adventurous (and appropriately insured) drivers can take the unsealed road over Danseys Pass to Naseby.

Although they've got a long way to go to attain the global reputation that their colleagues on the other side of the mountains in Central Otago enjoy, a few winemaking pioneers in Waitaki Valley are making wine that international experts are taking notice of.

◎ Sights

👁 Kurow

Kurow Heritage & Information Centre MUSEUM
(☑ 03-436 0950; www.kurow.org.nz; SH83; ⊙9.30am-4pm Mon-Fri) While Richie McCaw might get all the attention these days, Kurow's other famous son was Arnold Nordmeyer (1901–1989), a Labour Party leader who was one of the key architects of NZ's welfare and public-health system. His memory is honoured in this interesting community museum, which jokingly refers to itself as the National Museum of Social Security.

Vintner's Drop WINERY
(☎03-436 0545; www.ostlerwine.co.nz; 45 Bledisloe St; ☺noon-5pm Thu-Sun Nov-Mar) Housed in Kurow's old post office, Vintner's Drop acts as a tasting room for Ostler Vineyards. It also sells wine from seven other small local producers.

Pasquale Kurow Winery WINERY
(☎03-436 0443; www.pasquale.co.nz; 5292 Kurow-Duntroon Rd; ☺10am-4pm Nov-Mar) The valley's most impressive winery, Pasquale produces killer pinot noir, pinot gris and riesling, as well as less common varietals such as gerwürtztraminer, arneis and viognier. Drop in for a wine-tasting session ($10, refundable upon purchase) and a winery platter ($38), including smoked Aoraki salmon and local Whitestone cheese.

◉ Duntroon & Around

Takiroa Maori
Rock Painting Site ARCHAEOLOGICAL SITE
FREE Hidden within the honeycomb cliffs lining the highway, this well-signposted site, 3km west of Duntroon, features centuries-old drawings of mystical creatures, animals and even a sailing ship.

Vanished World Centre MUSEUM
(www.vanishedworld.co.nz; 7 Campbell St; adult/child $7.50/free; ☺10.30am-4.30pm Fri-Mon) Perhaps there wouldn't be quite so many bad dolphin tattoos and dancing-penguin films if more people stopped in Duntroon to check out this small but interesting volunteer-run centre. Once you see the 25-million-year-old fossils of shark-toothed dolphins and giant penguins, they suddenly don't seem so cute.

Pick up a copy of the *Vanished World Trail* map outlining 20 different interesting geological locations around the Waitaki Valley and North Otago coast.

Maerewhenua Maori
Rock Painting Site ARCHAEOLOGICAL SITE
(Livingstone-Duntroon Rd) **FREE** Sheltered by an impressive limestone overhang, this site contains charcoal-and-ochre paintings dating to before the arrival of Europeans in NZ. Head east from Duntroon and take the first right after crossing the Maerewhenua River; the site is on the left after about 400m.

Elephant Rocks FILM LOCATION
Sculpted by wind, rain and rivers, the huge limestone boulders of this bizarre landscape were utilised as Aslan's Camp in the NZ-filmed *Narnia* series (2005). They're located on farmland about 5.5km south of the highway; follow the signs after crossing the Maerewhenua River.

Oamaru
POP 12,900
Nothing moves very fast in Oamaru. Tourists saunter, locals linger and penguins waddle. Even oft-celebrated heritage modes of transport – penny farthings and steam trains – reflect an unhurried pace. Most travellers come here for the penguins, but hang around and you'll sense the wellspring of eccentricity bubbling under the surface. Put simply, this is New Zealand's coolest town.

Down by the water, a neighbourhood of once-neglected Victorian buildings now swarms with oddballs, antiquarians and bohemians of all stripes, who run offbeat galleries, fascinating shops, hip venues and even an 'urban winery'. Most visible are the Steampunks, their aesthetic boldly celebrating the past and the future with an ethos of 'tomorrow as it used to be'. What Oamaru used to be was rich and ambitious. In its 1880s heyday, Oamaru was about the same size as Los Angeles was at the time. Refrigerated meat-shipping had its origins nearby and the town became wealthy enough to build the imposing buildings that grace Thames St today. However, the town overreached itself and spent the end of the 19th century teetering on the verge of bankruptcy.

Economic decline in the 20th century meant that there wasn't the impetus to swing the wrecking ball with the same reckless abandon that wiped out much of the built heritage of NZ's main centres. It's only in recent decades that canny creative types have cottoned on to the uniqueness of Oamaru's surviving Victorian streetscapes and have started to unlock this otherwise unremarkable town's potential for extreme kookiness.

◎ Sights

★**Blue Penguin Colony** WILDLIFE
(☎03-433 1195; www.penguins.co.nz; Waterfront Rd; ☺10am-sunset) 🐧 In an old limestone quarry near the waterfront, you can see the little tykes from the Oamaru little penguin colony surfing in and wading ashore. The penguins arrive in clumps just before dark (around 5.30pm in midwinter and 9.30pm midsummer), and it takes them about an

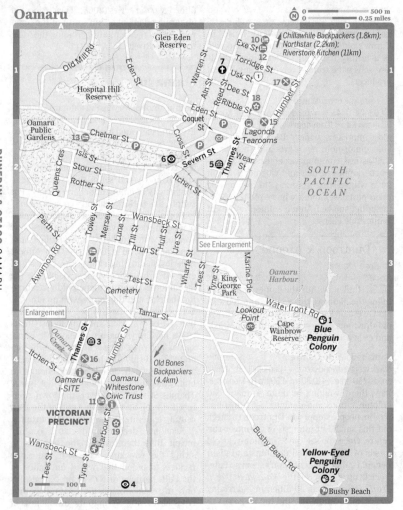

hour to all come ashore. Stands are set up on either side of the waddle route. General admission (adult/child $28/14) will give you a good view of the action but the premium stand ($40/20), accessed by a boardwalk through the nesting area, will get you closer.

You'll see the most penguins (up to 180) in November and December. From March to August there may be only 50 to 70 birds. Nightly viewing times are posted at the i-SITE (p519). Use of cameras is prohibited and you're advised to dress warmly.

To understand the centre's conservation work and its success in increasing the pen-guin population, take the daytime, behind-the-scenes tour (self-guided adult/child $10/5 or guided $16/8); packages that combine night viewing and the daytime tour are available.

Do not under any circumstances wander around the rocks beside the sea here at night looking for penguins. It's damaging to their environment and spoils studies into the human effects on the birds.

★ Yellow-Eyed Penguin Colony   WILDLIFE
(Bushy Beach Rd) FREE Larger and much rarer than their little blue cousins, yellow-eyed

Oamaru

◎ **Top Sights**
1 Blue Penguin Colony D4
2 Yellow-Eyed Penguin Colony D5

◎ **Sights**
3 Forrester Gallery A4
4 Friendly Bay Playground B5
5 North Otago Museum C2
6 Oamaru Public Gardens B2
7 St Patrick's Basilica C1
Steampunk HQ ....(see 9)

◎ **Activities, Courses & Tours**
8 Oamaru Cycle Works A5
9 Oamaru Steam & Rail A4

◎ **Sleeping**
10 AAA Thames Court Motel C1
11 Criterion Hotel A4

12 Highfield Mews C1
13 Oamaru Top 10 .... A2
14 Pen-y-bryn Lodge A3

◎ **Eating**
Harbour St Bakery ....(see 11)
15 Midori C2
16 Steam A4
17 Whitestone C1

◎ **Drinking & Nightlife**
Birdlands ....(see 11)
Criterion Hotel ....(see 11)
Fat Sally's ....(see 5)

◎ **Entertainment**
18 Limelight Cinema C1
19 Penguin Club B5

penguins waddle ashore at Bushy Beach in the late afternoon to feed their young. Despite their Maori name, hoiho, meaning 'noisy shouter,' they're extremely shy; if they see or hear you they'll head back into the water and the chicks will go hungry.

In order to protect these endangered birds, the beach is closed to people at 3pm, but there are hides set up on the cliffs (you'll need binoculars for a decent view). The best time to see them is two hours before sunset.

★ **Victorian Precinct** NEIGHBOURHOOD
Consisting of only a couple of blocks centred on Harbour and Tyne Sts, this atmospheric enclave has some of NZ's best-preserved Victorian commercial buildings. Descend on a dark and foggy night and it's downright Dickensian. It's also ground zero for all that is hip, cool and freaky in Oamaru, and one of the most fun places to window-shop in the entire South Island. Wander around during the day and you'll discover antiquarian bookshops, antique stores, galleries, vintage clothing shops, kooky gift stores, artist studios and craft bookbinders. At night there are some great little bars, and you might even see a penguin swaggering along the street – we did!

The precinct is at its liveliest on Sundays when the excellent Oamaru farmers market is in full swing and tourists on penny farthings wobble up and down Harbour St. Note that some shops and attractions are closed on Mondays.

Steampunk HQ GALLERY
(www.steampunkoamaru.co.nz; 1 Itchen St; adult/child $10/2; ⊙10am-4pm) Discover an alternative past – or maybe a quirky version of the future – in this fascinating art project celebrating Steampunk culture. Ancient machines wheeze and splutter, and the industrial detritus of the last century or so is repurposed and reimagined to creepy effect. Bring a coin to fire up the sparking, space-age locomotive out the front.

Friendly Bay Playground PLAYGROUND
(Wansbeck St) Steampunk for kiddies: this awesome playground includes swings suspended from a giant penny farthing, a slippery pole accessed from an armoured elephant, and a giant hamster wheel.

Thames St STREET
Oamaru's main drag owes its expansive girth to the need to accommodate the minimum turning circle of a bullock cart. Oamaru's grand pretensions reached their peak in a series of gorgeous buildings constructed from the milky local limestone (known as Oamaru stone or whitestone), with their forms reflecting the fashion of the times; there's a particular emphasis on the neoclassical.

Impressive examples include the Forrester Gallery (at No 9, built 1883), the ANZ Bank (No 11, 1871), the Waitaki District Council building (No 20, 1883), the North Otago Museum (No 60, 1882), the Courthouse (No 88, 1883) and the Opera House

(No 92, 1907). For more information, pick up the *Historic Oamaru* pamphlet from the i-SITE (p519).

Forrester Gallery GALLERY
(www.forrestergallery.com; 9 Thames St; ⊙10.30am-4.30pm) FREE Housed in a temple-like former bank building, the Forrester Gallery has an excellent collection of regional and NZ art. It's a good place to see works by Colin McCahon, one of NZ's most significant modern artists.

North Otago Museum MUSEUM
(www.northotagomuseum.co.nz; 60 Thames St; ⊙10.30am-4.30pm Mon-Fri, 1-4.30pm Sat & Sun) FREE Behind its classical facade, the North Otago Museum has exhibits on Maori and Pakeha (European New Zealander) history, writer Janet Frame, architecture and geology.

Oamaru Public Gardens GARDENS
(Severn St; ⊙dawn-dusk) FREE Opened in 1876, these beautiful gardens are a lovely place to chill out on a hot day, with expansive lawns, waterways, bridges and a children's playground.

St Patrick's Basilica CHURCH
(64 Reed St) If you've ever fantasised about being transported back to ancient Rome, stroll through the Corinthian columns and into this gorgeous Catholic church. Renowned architect Francis Petre went for the full time warp with this one, right down to a coffered ceiling and a cupola above the altar.

 Activities

Oamaru Steam & Rail TRAIN RIDE
(www.oamaru-steam.org.nz; adult/child/family 1 way $5/2/12, return $8/3/20; ⊙11am-4pm Sun) On Sundays, take a half-hour ride on a vintage steam train from the Victorian Precinct to the waterfront.

Oamaru Cycle Works CYCLING
(✆027 439 5331; 4 Wansbeck St; lesson & ride $20) For a thoroughly Victorian-era thrill, take a vertiginous ride on a penny farthing along Harbour St. Ask David the owner about his intrepid penny-farthing trek up the entire length of New Zealand. He also rents out 1940s-style bikes (half-/full day $20/45). Opening hours vary; call for times.

BEST PLACES TO SEE...

Yellow-Eyed Penguins

One of the world's rarest penguins, the endangered hoiho (yellow-eyed penguin) is found along the Otago coast. It's estimated that of the roughly 4000 penguins that remain, about a quarter of these nest on deserted beaches in the southeast of the South Island.

The encroachment of humans on their habitat is one of the main causes of the penguins' decline, and the penguins have been badly distressed by tourists using flash photography or traipsing through the nesting grounds; under no circumstances should you approach one. Even loud voices can disturb them. For this reason, the best way to see one in the wild is through an organised tour onto private land, such as through Nature's Wonders (p531) or Penguin Place (p532) on the Otago Peninsula, or from the cliffs at Bushy Beach (p514) near Oamaru.

Little Penguins

Nowhere near as rare as their yellow-eyed cousins, little penguins sometimes pop up in the oddest places (window-shopping in Oamaru's Victorian Precinct, for instance). Also known as blue penguins, little blue penguins, korora (in Maori) and fairy penguins (in Australia), these little cuties can spend days out at sea before returning to their colony just before dusk in batches known as rafts.

Although you might chance upon one at night in Oamaru or on the Otago Peninsula, the best places to see them arrive en masse are at Oamaru's Blue Penguin Colony (p513) or at the Royal Albatross Centre (p531) on the Otago Peninsula.

Sea Lions

Sea lions are most easily seen on a tour, but are regularly present at Sandfly Bay, Allans Beach and Victory Beach on the Otago Peninsula. They are predominantly bachelor males vacationing from Campbell Island or the Auckland Islands. Give them plenty of space, as these powerful beasts can really motor over the first 20m.

Vertical Ventures
CYCLING, ROCK CLIMBING

(☑03-434 5010; www.verticalventures.co.nz) Rent a mountain bike (from $40 per day), or join guided mountain-biking trips, including the Alps 2 Ocean Cycle Trail (seven days including transport, food and accommodation $2700) and helibiking day trips (from $415). The 'vertical' part comes in the form of rock climbing (from $140 per person).

🖝 Tours

Penguins Crossing
WILDLIFE TOUR

(☑03-437 0753; www.travelheadfirst.com; adult/ child $55/20) Door-to-door tour taking in the blue and yellow-eyed colonies. Price includes standard admission to the blue-penguin colony.

✯✯ Festivals & Events

Oamaru Wine & Food Festival
WINE, FOOD

(www.oamaruwineandfoodfest.co.nz) Showcasing North Otago's food and wine scene. On the third Sunday in February.

Victorian Heritage Celebrations
CULTURE

(www.vhc.co.nz) Five days of costumed hijinks, culminating in a grand fete. In mid-November.

🛏 Sleeping

★ Old Bones Backpackers
HOSTEL $

(☑03-434 8115; www.oldbones.co.nz; Beach Rd; r $90, campervan per person $20; @ 🛜) About 5km south of Oamaru on the coast road, this top-notch dorm-free hostel has spacious rooms off a sunny, central space. Relax in this isolated setting listening to the surf crashing over the road.

Chillawhile Backpackers
HOSTEL $

(☑03-437 0168; www.chillawhile.co.nz; 1 Frome St; dm $26-30, s/d $55/70; @ 🛜) Unleash your creative spirit at this funky and colourful hostel in a two-storey Victorian residence. Guests are encouraged to draw and paint, or create sweet soul music on the hostel's varied instruments.

Waitaki Waters
HOLIDAY PARK $

(☑03-431 3880; www.campingoamaru.co.nz; 305 Kaik Rd; sites/cabins from $14/50) The enthusiastic young owner sees that the bathrooms and kitchens are sparkling and the hedges manicured at this simple campground, 3km off SH1, 20km north of Oamaru. Cabins are simple but well maintained; bring your own bedding.

Oamaru Top 10
HOLIDAY PARK $

(☑03-434 7666; www.oamarutop10.co.nz; 30 Chelmer St; sites $40-44, units with/without bathroom from $105/65; @ 🛜) Grassy and well maintained, this Top 10 has trees out the back and the public gardens next door. Standard cabins are basic, but the other units (with varying levels of self-contained comfort) are much nicer.

Highfield Mews
MOTEL $$

(☑03-434 3437; www.highfieldmews.co.nz; 244 Thames St; d $140-170; @ 🛜) 🍴 Motels have come a long away from the gloomy concrete-block constructions of the 1960s and '70s, as this new-build attests. The units are basically smart apartments, with kitchens, desks, stereos, tiled bathrooms and outdoor furniture.

Criterion Hotel
HOTEL $$

(☑03-434 6247; www.criterionhotel.co.nz; 3 Tyne St; s $60, d with/without bathroom $120/90; 🛜) Period rooms at this lovingly restored 1877 hotel are smallish, but the guest lounge is large and the beds are new. Rates include a help-yourself continental breakfast. Downstairs there's the distraction of a great corner pub.

AAA Thames Court Motel
MOTEL $$

(☑03-434 6963; www.aaathamescourt.co.nz; 252 Thames St; d $120-150; 🛜) 🍴 A good option for families, this older motel has been given a biege-over (the colour of our times) and the renovated units are comfortable and well priced. For an extra $5 it's worth trading up from a studio to a much larger one-bedroom unit.

★ Pen-y-bryn Lodge
B&B $$$

(☑03-434 7939; www.penybryn.co.nz; 41 Towey St; r $550-625) Well-travelled foodie owners have thoroughly revitalised this beautiful 1889 residence. Predinner drinks are served in the antiques-studded drawing room, and you can opt for rates (from $850) which include a four-course dinner in the fabulous dining room.

✗ Eating

Steam
CAFE $

(www.facebook.com/steamoamaru; 7 Thames St; mains $4-7; ⊗8am-5pm Mon-Fri, 8.30am-2pm Sat & Sun) Steam specialises in coffees and fruit juices, and is a good spot to stock up on freshly ground Java for your own travels. Settle in for breakfast, or partake of a freshly baked muffin.

DON'T MISS

RIVERSTONE

It's well worth taking the 14km trip from Oamaru to this idiosyncratic complex, hidden along the unassuming short stretch of SH1 between the braided mouth of the Waitaki River and the SH83 turn-off.

First and foremost it's the home of **Riverstone Kitchen** (☎ 03-431 3505; www.riverstonekitchen.co.nz; 1431 SH1, Hilderthorpe; brunch & lunch $14-29, dinner $29-32; ⊗ 9am-5pm Thu-Mon, 6pm-late Thu-Sun; ☑), a sophisticated cafe/restaurant that outshines any in Oamaru itself. Leather couches and polished-concrete floors set the scene for a menu that's modern without being overworked. Much of the produce is from the extensive on-site kitchen gardens (take a look, they're impressive), topped up with locally sourced duck, venison, pork, chicken and beef. It's a smashing brunch option, with excellent coffee and legendary truffled scrambled eggs.

Next door, behind a set of fake heritage shopfronts, **Riverstone Country** (⊗ 9am-5pm) is literally packed to the rafters with gifts, crafts, homewares, garden ornaments and Christmas decorations. Outside, George the belligerent cockatoo rules over an aviary stocked with canaries, lorikeets and guinea pigs.

If this all points to an eccentric mind at the helm, take a look at the moated castle being constructed at the rear of the complex. Once the finishing touches are added to the six towers, moat and drawbridge, that's where the owners will reside.

Whitestone
DELI, CAFE $

(www.whitestonecheese.co.nz; 3 Torridge St; ⊗ 9am-5pm) The home of award-winning artisan cheeses, Whitestone is a local culinary institution, and the little factory-door cafe is a fine place to challenge one's arteries. Food is limited to the likes of cheese scones, cheese-only platters ($5) and large platters with crackers and quince paste ($18).

Harbour St Bakery
BAKERY $

(4 Harbour St; pies $5; ⊗ 10am-4pm Tue-Sun) Selling both European-style bread and Kiwi meat pies, this Dutch bakery covers its bases well. Grab an outdoor seat and watch Oamaru's heritage street life scroll past like an old-time movie.

Northstar
MODERN NZ $$

(☎ 03-437 1190; www.northstarmotel.co.nz; 495a Thames Hwy; lunch $17-20, dinner $26-31; ⊗ noon-3pm & 6-9pm) Surprisingly upmarket for a restaurant attached to a SH1 motel, Northstar is the first choice for Oamaruvians with something to celebrate. Expect robust bistro fare with a touch of contemporary flair.

Midori
JAPANESE $$

(☎ 03-434 9045; www.facebook.com/MidoriJapaneseSushiBarAndRestaurant; 1 Ribble St; sushi $8-11, mains $12-18; ⊗ 10.30am-8.30pm Mon-Sat, noon-8.30pm Sun) Housed in a heritage stone building, Midori's sashimi and sushi makes the most of fresh local seafood. Other carefully prepared dishes include salmon on rice and teriyaki blue cod.

🍷 Drinking & Nightlife

Criterion Hotel
PUB

(www.criterionhotel.co.nz; 3 Tyne St; ⊗ 11.30am-late Tue-Sun) The most Victorian of the Victorian Precinct's watering holes, this corner beauty has a good beer selection and plenty of local wines. There's usually live music on Fridays.

Birdlands
WINE BAR

(www.birdlands-wine.com; 3 Harbour St; ⊗ 8pm-late Thu, 1pm-late Fri-Sun) Oamaru's hippest spot: not only does Birdlands serve excellent wine, it's made here too, from grapes grown in the Waitaki. Also on offer are craft beers, other local wine, Whitestone cheese boards and live music most weekends.

Fat Sally's
PUB

(☎ 03-434 8368; www.facebook.com/fatsallys; 84 Thames St; ⊗ 11.30am-late Tue-Sun) The fat lady is popular with locals, especially early in the evening when they're often tucking into a substantial pub meal. Come along on a Wednesday night for the rollicking pub quiz.

☆ Entertainment

Penguin Club
LIVE MUSIC

(www.thepenguinclub.co.nz; Emulsion Lane, off Harbour St; admission varies) Tucked down an atmospheric alley off a 19th-century street, the Penguin's unusual location matches its acts: everything from touring Kiwi bands to punky/grungy/rocky/country locals. The last Friday of the month is open-stage jam night.

Limelight Cinema CINEMA
(☑03-434 1070; www.limelightcinema.co.nz; 239 Thames St; adult/child $15/10) Cheaper on Tuesdays.

ℹ Information

Oamaru i-SITE (☑03-434 1656; www.visit-oamaru.co.nz; 1 Thames St; ◷10am-4pm; 🖥) Mountains of information including details on local walking trips and wildlife, plus daily penguin-viewing times are posted here. There's also bike hire (per day $40) and an interesting 10-minute DVD on the history of the town.

Oamaru Whitestone Civic Trust (☑03-434 5385; www.historicoamaru.co.nz; 2 Harbour St; ◷10am-4pm) Vintage B&W photos of Oamaru's heritage, maps, information and walking tours of the historic precinct.

ℹ Getting There & Away

Most buses and shuttles depart from the **Lagonda Tearooms** (191 Thames St; ◷9am-4.30pm). Both the tearooms and the i-SITE take bookings.

InterCity (☑03-471 7143; www.intercity.co.nz) Two daily coaches to/from Christchurch (from $21, 4¼ hours), Timaru (from $14, one hour), Moeraki (from $11, 30 minutes) and Dunedin (from $14, 40 minutes), and one to Te Anau (from $29, 6½ hours).

Atomic Shuttles (☑03-349 0697; www.atomictravel.co.nz) Daily buses to/from Christchurch ($30, 3¾ hours), Timaru ($20, 1¼ hours) and Dunedin ($20, 1¾ hours).

Coast Line Tours (☑03-434 7744; www.coastline-tours.co.nz) Shuttles to/from Dunedin ($30) with a detour to Dunedin airport possible.

Knightrider (www.knightrider.co.nz) Has a bus most nights to/from Christchurch ($43, four hours), Christchurch airport ($48, 3¾ hours), Timaru ($28, 1¼ hours), Moeraki ($25, one hour) and Dunedin ($33, two hours).

Naked Bus (☑0900 625 33; www.nakedbus.com; prices vary) Daily buses head to/from Christchurch (3¾ hours), Timaru (1¼ hours), Moeraki (35 minutes) and Dunedin (1¾ hours).

Moeraki

The name Moeraki means 'sleepy sky', which should give you some clue as to the pace of life in this little fishing village. You might be surprised to learn that this was one of the first European settlements in NZ, with a whaling station established here in 1836. Since then, Moeraki has nurtured the creation of several national treasures, from Frances Hodgkins' paintings to Keri Hulme's *The Bone People*, and Fleur Sullivan's cooking.

Apart from Fleur's eponymous restaurant, the main attraction is the collection of large spherical boulders scattered along a beautiful stretch of beach like a kid's giant discarded marbles. The famed **Moeraki Boulders** (Te Kaihinaki) lie just off SH1, a kilometre north of the Moeraki turn-off. Try to time your visit with low tide.

It's a pleasant 45-minute walk along the beach from the village to the boulders. Head in the other direction on the Kaiks Wildlife Trail and you'll reach a cute old wooden lighthouse. You might even spot yellow-eyed penguins and fur seals (be sure to keep your distance).

🛏 Sleeping & Eating

Olive Grove Lodge & Holiday Park HOSTEL $
(☑03-439 5830; www.olivebranch.co.nz; SH1, Waianakarua; sites/dm $12/31, d with/without bathroom $85/75) 🖉 Nestled in a loop of the Waianakarua River, 12km north of the Moeraki turn-off, this organic farm offers both bucolic camping sites and a colourful lodge with a sunny communal lounge. Kids will love the playground and highland cattle; parents will love the spa, eco lifestyle, organic vegies and peaceful vibe.

Moeraki Village Holiday Park HOLIDAY PARK $
(☑03-439 4759; www.moerakivillageholidaypark.co.nz; 114 Haven St; sites $32, unit with/without bathroom $100/60; @🖥) Occupying a small field above the road into town, this complex offers powered sites, basic cabins (bring your own linen) and fully equipped motel units.

Moeraki Beach Motel MOTEL $$
(☑03-439 4862; www.moerakibeachmotels.co.nz; cnr Beach & Haven Sts; d from $105) The four split-level units at this motel aren't about to win any design awards, but they are spacious. Each has a full kitchen and a balcony.

★Fleur's Place SEAFOOD $$$
(☑03-439 4480; www.fleursplace.com; Old Jetty, 169 Haven St; mains $32-42; ◷9.30am-late Wed-Sun) There's a rumble-tumble look about it, but this timber hut houses one of the South Island's best seafood restaurants. Head for the upstairs deck and tuck into fresh chowder, tender muttonbird and other ocean bounty. Bookings are strongly recommended.

ℹ Getting There & Away

All of the buses on the Oamaru–Dunedin run stop on SH1 by the Moeraki turn-off. From here it's a 2km walk into the centre of the village.

DUNEDIN

POP 121,000

Two words immediately spring to mind when Kiwis think of their seventh-largest city: 'Scotland' and 'students'. The 'Edinburgh of the South' is immensely proud of its Scottish heritage, never missing an opportunity to break out the haggis and bagpipes on civic occasions.

In fact, the very name Dunedin is derived from the Scottish Gaelic name for Edinburgh: Dùn Èideann. The first permanent European settlers, two shiploads of pious, hard-working Scots, arrived at Port Chalmers in 1848, and included the nephew of Scotland's favourite son, Robbie Burns. A statue of the poet dominates the Octagon, the city's civic heart, and the city even has its own tartan.

If there were a tenuous link between the Scottish and the students that dominate Dunedin in term time, it would probably be whisky. The country's oldest university provides plenty of student energy to sustain the local bars, and in the 1980s it even spawned its own internationally influential indie music scene, with Flying Nun Records and the 'Dunedin sound'.

Dunedin is an easy place in which to while away a few days. Weatherboard houses ranging from stately to ramshackle pepper its hilly suburbs, and bluestone Victorian buildings punctuate the compact city centre. It's a great base for exploring the wildlife-rich Otago Peninsula, which officially lies within the city limits.

◉ Sights

★ **Toitu Otago Settlers Museum** MUSEUM
(Map p522; www.toituosm.com; 31 Queens Gardens; ⊙10am-4pm Fri-Wed, to 8pm Thu; ☜) FREE
Storytelling is the focus of this excellent interactive museum. The engrossing Maori section is followed by a large gallery where floor-to-ceiling portraits of Victorian-era

Dunedin & the Otago Peninsula

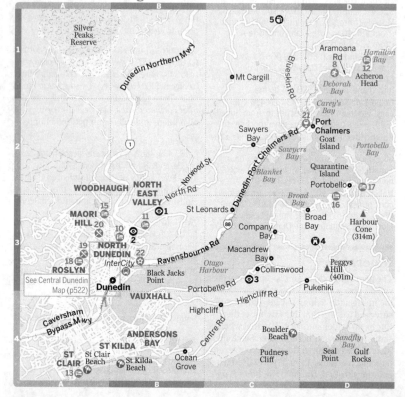

settlers stare out from behind their whiskers and lace; click on the terminal to learn more about the individuals that catch your eye. Other displays include a re-created passenger-ship cabin, an awesome car collection and a room devoted to the underground stars of Flying Nun Records.

★ **Railway Station** HISTORIC BUILDING
(Map p522; Anzac Ave) Featuring mosaic-tile floors and glorious stained-glass windows, Dunedin's striking bluestone railway station (built between 1903 and 1906) claims to be NZ's most-photographed building. Head upstairs for the **NZ Sports Hall of Fame** (Map p522; www.nzhalloffame.co.nz; Dunedin Railway Station; adult/child $5/2; ☉10am-4pm), a small museum devoted to the nation's obsession, and the **Art Station** (Map p522; www.otagoartsociety.co.nz; ☉10am-4pm), the local Art Society's gallery and shop.

Dunedin Public Art Gallery GALLERY
(Map p522; www.dunedin.art.museum; 30 The Octagon; ☉10am-5pm; 🛜) FREE Explore NZ's art scene at this expansive and airy gallery. Only a fraction of the collection is displayed at any given time, with most of the space given over to often-edgy temporary shows.

Speight's Brewery BREWERY
(Map p522; 📞03-477 7697; www.speights.co.nz; 200 Rattray St; adult/child $25/10; ☉noon, 2pm, 4pm & 6pm Jun-Sep, plus 5pm & 7pm Oct-May) Speight's has been churning out beer on this site since the late 1800s. The 90-minute tour offers samples of six different brews, and there's an option to combine a tour with a

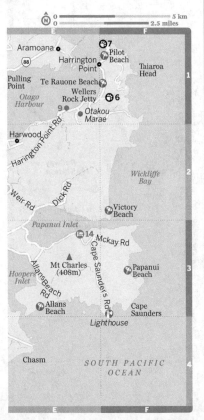

Dunedin & the Otago Peninsula

◎ Sights
1 Baldwin St	B3
2 Dunedin Botanic Garden	B3
3 Glenfalloch Woodland Garden	C3
4 Larnach Castle	D3
Nature's Wonders Naturally	(see 7)
5 Orokonui Ecosanctuary	C1
6 Penguin Place	F1
7 Royal Albatross Centre & Fort Taiaroa	F1

⊕ Activities, Courses & Tours
8 Hare Hill	D1
9 Monarch Wildlife Cruises & Tours	E1
St Clair Hot Salt Water Pool	(see 13)

⊜ Sleeping
10 858 George St	B3
11 Arden Street House	B3
12 Billy Brown's	D1
13 Hotel St Clair	A4
14 Kaimata Retreat	E3
Larnach Castle Lodge	(see 4)
15 Leith Valley Touring Park	A3
Majestic Mansions	(see 13)
16 McFarmers Backpackers	D3
Penguin Place Lodge	(see 6)
17 Portobello Motel	D2
18 Roslyn Apartments	A3

✖ Eating
1908 Cafe	(see 17)
19 Luna	A3
20 No 7 Balmac	A3
Portobello Hotel & Bistro	(see 17)
Starfish	(see 13)

◎ Drinking & Nightlife
21 Chick's Hotel	D2

✦ Entertainment
22 Forsyth Barr Stadium	B3

Central Dunedin

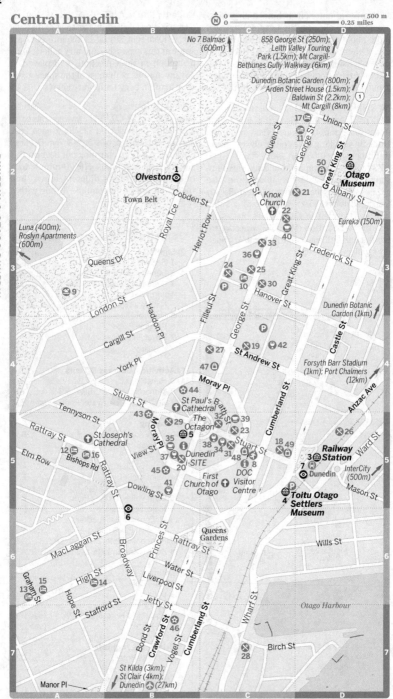

N
0 ____ 500 m
0 ____ 0.25 miles

No 7 Balmac (600m)

858 George St (250m);
Leith Valley Touring
Park (1.5km); Mt Cargill-
Bethunes Gully Walkway (6km)

Dunedin Botanic Garden (800m);
Arden Street House (1.5km);
Baldwin St (2.2km);
Mt Cargill (8km)

Queen St

George St

Union St

17
11

50

2
Otago
Museum

Great King St

Albany St

Olveston 1

Town Belt

Cobden St

Royal Tce

Heriot Row

Pitt St

Knox
Church

21

Eureka (150m)

Luna (400m);
Roslyn Apartments
(600m)

Queens Dr

22

40

33

36

9

London St

Haddon Pl

Filleul St

24

25

10

30

George St

Hanover St

Great King St

Frederick St

3

Dunedin Botanic
Garden (1km)

Castle St

Cargill St

York Pl

27

19

42

St Andrew St

Forsyth Barr Stadium
(1km); Port Chalmers
(12km)

47

Moray Pl

44

Cumberland St

Anzac Ave

4

Stuart St

Tennyson St

43

29

St Paul's
Cathedral

The
Octagon

32

39

Bath St

23

Moray Pl

26

Ward St

Rattray St

St Joseph's
Cathedral

35

5

38

34

31

48

Stuart St

18
49

Railway
Station

3

Elm Row

12
16

Bishops Rd

View St

i

Dunedin
i-SITE

20

37

45

41

First
Church of
Otago

DOC
Visitor
Centre

8

7
Dunedin

InterCity
(500m)

Mason St

5

Rattray St

Dowling St

6

MacLaggan St

Broadway

Princes St

Queens
Gardens

Rattray St

Water St

Toitu Otago
Settlers
Museum

4

Wills St

6

Graham St

13

15

High St

14

Hope St

Stafford St

Liverpool St

Jetty St

Otago Harbour

Bond St

Crawford St

46

Vogel St

Cumberland St

Wharf St

Birch St

28

7

St Kilda (3km);
St Clair (4km);
Dunedin (27km)

Manor Pl

Central Dunedin

◎ Top Sights
1 Olveston B2
2 Otago Museum D2
3 Railway Station D5
4 Toitu Otago Settlers Museum C5

◎ Sights
Art Station ....(see 3)
5 Dunedin Public Art Gallery B5
New Zealand Sports Hall of Fame .(see 3)
6 Speight's Brewery B6
7 Taieri Gorge Railway D5

✪ Activities, Courses & Tours
8 Cycle World C5
9 Moana Pool A3

▣ Sleeping
10 315 Euro C3
11 Bluestone on George D2
12 Brothers Boutique Hotel A5
13 Chalet Backpackers A6
14 Dunedin Palms Motel A6
15 Fletcher Lodge A6
16 Hogwartz A5
17 Kiwi's Nest D1

✖ Eating
18 Best Cafe C5
19 Circadian Rhythm C4
20 Etrusco at the Savoy B5
21 Everyday Gourmet D2
22 Governor's C2
23 Izakaya Yuki C5
24 Miga C3
25 Modaks Espresso C3
Nova Cafe ....(see 5)

26 Otago Farmers Market D5
27 Paasha C4
28 Plato C7
Saigon Van ....(see 19)
29 Scotia B5
30 The Good Oil C3
31 Two Chefs Bistro C5
32 Velvet Burger C5
33 Velvet Burger C3

☕ Drinking & Nightlife
34 Albar C5
Carousel ....(see 34)
Di Lusso ....(see 31)
35 Mazagran Espresso Bar B5
36 Mou Very C3
37 Pequeno B5
38 Pop C5
Speight's Ale House ....(see 6)
39 Strictly Coffee Company C5
Stuart St Mac's Brewbar ....(see 38)
40 The Fix C3
41 Tonic B5
42 Urban Factory C4

✦ Entertainment
43 Fortune Theatre B5
44 Metro Cinema B4
45 Rialto Cinemas B5
46 Sammy's B7

▢ Shopping
47 Bivouac Outdoor C4
48 Gallery De Novo C5
49 Stuart St Potters Cooperative C5
50 University Book Shop D2

DUNEDIN & OTAGO DUNEDIN

meal at the neighbouring Ale House (lunch/dinner $55/61).

★ **Olveston**　　　　　　　　　　HOUSE
(Map p522; ☑ 03-477 3320; www.olveston.co.nz; 42 Royal Tce; adult/child $19/9.50; ⊙ tours 9.45am, 10.45am, noon, 1.30pm, 2.45pm & 4pm) Although it's a youngster by European standards, this spectacular 1906 mansion provides a wonderful window into Dunedin's past. Until 1966 it was the family home of the wealthy Theomin family, notable patrons of the arts who were heavily involved with endowing the Public Art Gallery.

This artistic bent is evident in Olveston's grand interiors, which include works by Charles Goldie and Frances Hodgkins (a family friend). A particular passion was Japanese art, and the home is liberally peppered with exquisite examples. The family

was Jewish, and the grand dining table is set up as if for Shabbat dinner.

Entry is via fascinating guided tours; it pays to book ahead. There's also a pretty little garden to explore.

★ **Otago Museum**　　　　　　　MUSEUM
(Map p522; www.otagomuseum.govt.nz; 419 Great King St; admission by donation; ⊙ 10am-5pm) The centrepiece of this august institution is *Southern Land, Southern People,* showcasing Otago's cultural and physical past and present, from geology and dinosaurs to the modern day. The *Tangata Whenua* Maori gallery houses an impressive *waka taua* (war canoe), wonderfully worn old carvings, and some lovely *pounamu* (greenstone) weapons, tools and jewellery.

Other major galleries include *Pacific Cultures, People of the World* (including the requisite mummy), *Nature, Maritime* and

TAIERI GORGE RAILWAY

With narrow tunnels, deep gorges, winding tracks, rugged canyons and more than a dozen stone and wrought-iron viaduct crossings (up to 50m high), the scenic **Taieri Gorge Railway** (Map p522; ☑ 03-477 4449; www.taieri.co.nz; departs Dunedin Railway Station, Anzac Ave; ☉ office 8.30am-5pm Mon-Fri, to 3pm Sat-Sun) consistently rates highly with visitors.

The four-hour return trip aboard 1920s heritage coaches travels to Pukerangi (one way/return $59/89), 58km away. Some trains carry on to Middlemarch (one way/return $71/107) – which is particularly handy for those cycling the Otago Central Rail Trail – or you can opt for a train-coach trip to Queenstown (one way $139).

the *Animal Attic*. The hands-on *Discovery World* (adult/child $10/5) is mainly aimed at kids, although the tropical forest, filled with colourful live butterflies, is an all-ages treat.

Check the timing of the daily guided tours ($12) and free gallery talks on the website.

Dunedin Botanic Garden
GARDENS

(Map p520; www.dunedinbotanicgarden.co.nz; cnr Great King St & Opoho Rd; ☉ dawn-dusk) FREE
Dating from 1863, these 22 peaceful, grassy and shady hectares include rose gardens, rare natives, a four-hectare rhododendron dell, glasshouses, a playground and a cafe. Kids love tootling about on the Community Express 'train' (adult/child $3/1).

Baldwin St
STREET

(Map p520) The world's steepest residential street (or so says the *Guinness Book of World Records*), Baldwin St has a gradient of 1 in 2.86 (19°). From the city centre, head 2km north up Great King St to where the road branches sharp left to Timaru. Get in the right-hand lane and continue straight ahead. This becomes North Rd, and Baldwin St is on the right after 1km.

🏃 Activities

Swimming & Surfing

St Clair and St Kilda are both popular swimming beaches (though you need to watch for rips at St Clair). Both have consistently good left-hand breaks, and you'll also find good surfing at Blackhead further south, and at Aramoana on Otago Harbour's North Shore.

Moana Pool
SWIMMING

(Map p522; 60 Littlebourne Rd, Roslyn; adult/child $6/3; ☉ 6am-10pm Mon-Fri, 7am-7pm Sat & Sun) This indoor pool complex has waterslides, wave machines, a spa and a gym.

St Clair Hot Salt Water Pool
SWIMMING

(Map p520; Esplanade, St Clair; adult/child $5.70/2.60; ☉ 7am-7pm Oct-Mar) This heated outdoor pool sits on the western headland of St Clair Beach.

Esplanade Surf School
SURFING

(☑ 0800 484 141; www.espsurfschool.co.nz; 1½hr group lessons $60, private instruction $120) Operating from a van parked at St Clair Beach in summer (call at other times), this experienced crew provides equipment and lessons.

Walking & Cycling

The **Otago Tramping and Mountaineering Club** (www.otmc.co.nz) organises weekend day and overnight tramps, often to the Silver Peaks Reserve north of Dunedin. Nonmembers are welcome, but must contact trip leaders beforehand.

Tunnel Beach Walkway
WALKING

(Tunnel Beach Rd, Blackhead) This short but extremely steep track (15 minutes down, 30 back up) accesses a dramatic stretch of coast where the wild Pacific has carved sea stacks, arches and unusual formations out of the limestone. It takes its name from a hand-hewn stone tunnel at the bottom of the track, which civic father John Cargill had built to give his family access to secluded beachside picnics. Strong currents make swimming here dangerous.

The track is 7km southwest of central Dunedin. Head south on Princes St and continue as it crosses under the motorway and then a railway bridge. Turn right at the next traffic lights onto Hillside Rd and follow it until the end, then make a quick left then right onto Easther Cres. Stay on this road for 3.5km (it changes name several times) and then look for Tunnel Beach Rd on the left.

Mt Cargill-Bethunes Gully Walkway
WALKING

Yes, it's possible to drive up 676m Mt Cargill, but that's not the point. The track (3½ hours return) starts from Norwood St, which is accessed from North Rd. From Mt Cargill, a trail continues to the 10-million-year-old, lava-formed Organ Pipes and, after another half hour, to Mt Cargill Rd on the other side of the mountain.

Cycle World · BICYCLE RENTAL
(Map p522; ☑03-477 7473; www.cycleworld.co.nz; 67 Lower Stuart St; per day $40; ⊙8.30am-6pm Mon-Fri, 10am-3pm Sat & Sun) Rents out bikes, performs repairs and has mountain-biking information.

🏃 Tours

Tasty Tours · TOUR
(☑03-453 1455; www.tastytours.co.nz; adult/child from $99/59) Tuck into local seafood, cheese, chocolate and beer on specialised foodie tours.

Back to Nature Tours · BUS TOUR
(☑0800 286 000; www.backtonaturetours.co.nz) 🏆 The full-day Royal Peninsula tour (adult/child $189/125) heads to points of interest around Dunedin before hitting the Otago Peninsula. Stops include Larnach Castle's gardens (castle entry is extra), a pub lunch, Penguin Place and the Royal Albatross Centre. There's also a half-day option which visits various bays and beaches (adult/child $79/55) and another tackling the Lovers Leap and Chasm tracks (adult/child $89/55). Tours depart from Port Chalmers, Dunedin i-SITE and centrally located accommodation.

First City Tours · BUS TOUR
(adult/child $25/15; ⊙ buses depart the i-SITE 9am, 10.30am, 1pm & 2.30pm) Double-decker bus tours loop around the city, stopping at the Otago Museum, Speight's, Botanic Gardens and Baldwin St.

Walk Dunedin · WALKING TOUR
(☑03-434 3300; www.toituosm.com; 2hr walk $30; ⊙10am) History-themed strolls around the city organised by the Settlers Museum. They depart from the i-SITE.

🛏 Sleeping

🛏 City Centre

Hogwartz · HOSTEL $
(Map p522; ☑03-474 1487; www.hogwartz.co.nz; 277 Rattray St; dm $29, s $60, d with/without bathroom from $80/64, apt $110-165; @☏) The Catholic bishop's residence from 1872 to 1999, this beautiful building is now a fascinating warren of comfortable and sunny rooms, many with harbour views. The old coach house and stables have recently been converted into swankier en suite rooms and apartments.

Chalet Backpackers · HOSTEL $
(Map p522; ☑03-479 2075; www.chaletbackpackers.co.nz; 296 High St; dm/s/d $29/43/66; @☏) The kitchen of this rambling old building is big, sunny and festooned with flowers, and there's also a compact garden, pool table, piano and rumours of a ghost. There are no en suite rooms but some have handbasins.

315 Euro · MOTEL $$
(Map p522; ☑03-477 9929; www.eurodunedin.co.nz; 315 George St; d $160-200; ℗☏) This sleek complex is accessed by an unlikely-looking alley off Dunedin's main retail strip. Choose from modern studios or larger one-bedroom apartments with full kitchens. Double glazing keeps George St's irresistible buzz at bay.

Dunedin Palms Motel · MOTEL $$
(Map p522; ☑03-477 8293; www.dunedinpalmsmotel.co.nz; 185-195 High St; units $155-250; ℗☏) A mercifully short stroll up from the city centre, the Palms has smartly renovated studio, one- and two-bedroom units arrayed around a central car park.

Fletcher Lodge · B&B $$$
(Map p522; ☑03-477 5552; www.fletcherlodge.co.nz; 276 High St; s $295-500, d $335-595, apt $650-775; ℗@☏) 🏆 Originally home to one of NZ's wealthiest industrialists, this gorgeous red-brick mansion is just minutes from the city, but the secluded gardens feel wonderfully remote. Rooms are elegantly trimmed with antique furniture and ornate plaster ceilings.

Brothers Boutique Hotel · HOTEL $$$
(Map p522; ☑03-477 0043; www.brothershotel.co.nz; 295 Rattray St; d $170-395; ℗☏) Rooms in this 1920s Christian Brothers residence have been refurbished beyond any monk's dreams, while still retaining many unique features. The chapel room ($320) includes the original arched stained-glass windows. There are great views from the rooftop units.

🛏 North Dunedin

Kiwi's Nest · HOSTEL $
(Map p522; ☑03-471 9540; www.kiwisnest.co.nz; 597 George St; dm $28, s with/without bathroom $60/45, d $80/70, apt $95; @☏) This wonderfully homely two-storey house has a range of tidy centrally heated rooms, some with en suites, fridges and kettles. Plus it's a flat walk to the Octagon – something few Dunedin hostels can boast.

858 George St
MOTEL **$$**

(Map p520; ☑03-474 0903; www.858george-streetmotel.co.nz; 858 George St; units $135-280; ⓟ⏏) ✎ Cleverly designed to blend harmoniously with the neighbourhood's two-storey Victorian houses, this top-quality motel complex has units ranging in size from studios to two bedrooms. Each has a terrace or small balcony.

Bluestone on George
APARTMENTS **$$$**

(Map p522; ☑03-477 9201; www.bluestonedunedin.co.nz; 571 George St; apt $190-235; ⓟ⏏) If you're expecting an imposing old bluestone building, think again: this four-storey block couldn't be more contemporary. The elegant studio units are decked out in muted tones, with kitchenettes, laundry facilities and tiny balconies.

St Clair

Majestic Mansions
APARTMENTS **$$**

(Map p520; ☑03-456 5000; www.st-clair.co.nz; 15 Bedford St; apt $139-210; ⓟ⏏) One street back from St Clair beach, this venerable 1920s apartment block has been thoroughly renovated, keeping the layout of the original little flats but sprucing them up with feature wallpaper and smart furnishings.

Hotel St Clair
HOTEL **$$$**

(Map p520; ☑03-456 0555; www.hotelstclair.com; 24 Esplanade; r $205-255, ste $370; ⓟ⏏) Soak up St Clair's surfy vibe from the balcony of your chic room in this contemporary medium-rise hotel. All but the cheapest have ocean views, and the beach is only metres from the front door.

Other Suburbs

Leith Valley Touring Park
HOLIDAY PARK **$**

(Map p520; ☑03-467 9936; www.leithvalleytouringpark.co.nz; 103 Malvern St, Woodhaugh; sites $38, units with/without bathroom from $92/49; ⓟ⏏) ✎ This holiday park is surrounded by native bush studded with walks, glow-worm caves and a small creek. Self-contained modern motel units are spacious, and tourist flats are smaller but have a more rustic feel (linen required).

Roslyn Apartments
APARTMENTS **$$**

(Map p520; ☑03-477 6777; www.roslynapartments.co.nz; 23 City Rd, Roslyn; 1-/2-bedroom apt $195/330; ⓟ⏏) Modern decor and brilliant city and harbour views are on tap at these apartments, just a short walk from Roslyn's eating strip. Leather furniture and designer kitchens add a touch of class.

Arden Street House
B&B **$$**

(Map p520; ☑03-473 8860; www.ardenstreethouse.co.nz; 36 Arden St, North East Valley; s $75, d with/without bathroom $130/120; ⓟ⏏) With crazy artworks, an organic garden, charming hosts and a porthole in the bathroom, this 1930s hilltop house makes a wonderfully eccentric base. To get here from the city, drive up North Rd, turn right into Glendining Ave and then left into Arden St.

✗ Eating

Inexpensive Asian restaurants are clustered along George St; most do takeaways. Uphill from the Octagon, Roslyn has good restaurants and cafes, and the beachy ambience of St Clair is great for a lazy brunch.

✗ City Centre

★Otago Farmers Market
MARKET **$**

(Map p522; www.otagofarmersmarket.org.nz; Dunedin Railway Station; ⊙8am-12.30pm Sat) This thriving market is all local, all edible (or drinkable) and mostly organic. Grab felafels or espresso to sustain you while you browse, and stock up on fresh meats, seafood, vegies and cheese for your journey. Also pick up some locally brewed Green Man organic beer. Sorted.

The Good Oil
CAFE **$**

(Map p522; 314 George St; mains $9-17; ⊙7.30am-4pm) This sleek little cafe is Dunedin's top spot for coffee and cake. If you're still waking up, kick-start the day with imaginative brunches such as kumara hash with hot smoked salmon.

Circadian Rhythm
VEGAN, VEGETARIAN **$**

(Map p522; www.circadianrhythm.co.nz; 72 St Andrew St; mains $9-13; ⊙11am-9pm Mon-Sat; ✔) Specialising in organic curries, felafels and stir-fries, this meat-free cafe is also a music venue, with jazz on Friday nights from 5.30pm. Dunedin's Emerson's and Green Man beers are both available, so you don't have to be *too* healthy.

Best Cafe
FISH & CHIPS **$**

(Map p522; www.facebook.com/bestcafedunedin; 30 Stuart St; takeaways $6-10, mains $10-23; ⊙11am-2.30pm & 5-8pm Mon-Sat) Serving up fish and chips since 1932, this local stalwart has its winning formula down pat, complete with vinyl tablecloths, hand-cut chips and curls of butter on white bread. If there are a few of you, try the 'Old School' platter ($43).

Velvet Burger
BURGERS $

(Map p522; www.velvetburger.co.nz; 150 Stuart St; mains $9-16; ⊙11.30am-late) Well positioned for the postbeer crowd, Velvet Burger's gourmet offerings are an excellent alcohol sop, especially the mammoth Goneburger (beef, chicken *and* bacon). There's another VB (Map p522) at 375 George St (same hours).

Modaks Espresso
CAFE, BAR $

(Map p522; 337-339 George St; mains $9-16; ⊙7.30am-4pm; 🖉) This funky little place with brick walls, mismatched Formica tables and couches for slouching is popular with students and those who appreciate chilled-out reggae while they nurse a pot of tea. Plump toasted bagels warm the insides in winter.

Saigon Van
VIETNAMESE $

(Map p522; 66 St Andrew St; mains $9-19; ⊙11.30am-2pm & 5-9pm Tue-Sun) The decor looks high-end Asian, but the food is definitely budget-friendly. Try the combination spring rolls and a bottle of Vietnamese beer to re-create lazy nights in Saigon. The bean-sprout-laden *pho* (noodle soup) and salads are also good.

Etrusco at the Savoy
ITALIAN $$

(Map p522; 🖉03-477 3737; www.etrusco.co.nz; 8a Moray Pl; mains $17-21; ⊙5.30pm-late) NZ has very few dining rooms to match the Edwardian elegance of the Savoy, with its moulded ceilings, stained-glass crests, brass chandeliers, green Ionian columns and fabulously over-the-top lamps. Pizza and pasta might seem like an odd fit, but Etrusco's deliciously rustic dishes absolutely hold their own.

Nova Cafe
CAFE $$

(Map p522; 🖉03-479 0808; www.novadunedin.co.nz; 29 The Octagon; breakfast $15-18, lunch $18-24, dinner $18-34; ⊙7am-11pm Mon-Fri, 8.30am-10pm Sat & Sun) Not surprisingly, this extension of the art gallery has a stylish look about it. Start the day with the interesting breakfast selections, dabble in some Asian flavours for lunch, then finish the day with bistro-style grills and a glass of wine.

Miga
KOREAN $$

(Map p522; 🖉03-477 4770; www.migadunedin.co.nz; 4 Hanover St; mains $16-39; ⊙11am-2pm & 5-10pm Mon-Sat) Settle into a booth at this attractive brick-lined eatery, and order claypot rice or noodle dishes from the extensive menu. Otherwise go for broke and cook a Korean barbecue right at your table.

Scotia
MODERN SCOTTISH $$

(Map p522; 🖉03-477 7704; www.scotiadunedin.co.nz; 199 Stuart St; mains $18-32; ⊙4pm-late Tue-Sun) Occupying a cosy heritage townhouse, Scotia toasts all things Scottish with a wall full of single-malt whisky and hearty fare such as smoked salmon and Otago hare. The two Scottish Robbies – Burns and Coltrane – look down approvingly on a menu that also includes haggis and whisky-laced pâté.

Paasha
TURKISH $$

(Map p522; www.paasha.co.nz; 32 St Andrew St; lunch $12-20, dinner $21-34) Authentic Turkish kebabs, dips and salads are faithfully created at this long-running Dunedin favourite. It's a top place for takeaways, and most nights the spacious and warm interior is filled with groups drinking Efes beer and sharing heaving platters of tasty Ottoman goodness.

Izakaya Yuki
JAPANESE, BAR $$

(Map p522; 29 Bath St; dishes $5-10; ⊙noon-2pm Mon-Fri, 5pm-2.30am daily; 🖥🖉) Cute and cosy, with a huge array of small dishes on which to graze, Yuki is a lovely spot for supper or a relaxed, drawn-out Japanese meal. Make a night of it with sake or Asahi beer, sushi and sashimi, and multiple plates of *kushiyaki* (grilled skewers).

JUST GIVE ME THE COFFEE & NO ONE WILL GET HURT

Dunedin has some excellent coffee bars in which you can refuel and recharge.

Fix (Map p522; 15 Frederick St; ⊙Mon-Sat) Wage slaves queue at the pavement window every morning, while students and others with time on their hands relax in the courtyard. Fix doesn't serve food, but you can bring along your own.

Mazagran Espresso Bar (Map p522; 36 Moray Pl; ⊙8am-6pm Mon-Fri, 10am-2pm Sat) The godfather of Dunedin's coffee scene, this compact wood-and-brick coffee house is the source of the magic bean for many of the city's restaurants and cafes.

Strictly Coffee (Map p522; www.strictlycoffee.co.nz; 23 Bath St; ⊙7.30am-4pm Mon-Fri) Stylish retro coffee bar hidden down grungy Bath St. Different rooms provide varying views and artworks to enjoy while you sip and sup.

Plato
MODERN NZ $$$

(Map p522; ☑ 03-477 4235; www.platocafe.co.nz; 2 Birch St; brunch $16-22, dinner $32-33; ⊗ 11am-2pm Sun, 6pm-late daily) The kooky decor (including collections of toys and beer tankards) gives little indication of the seriously good food on offer at this relaxed eatery by the harbour. Seafood features prominently in a menu full of international flavours.

Two Chefs Bistro
FRENCH $$$

(Map p522; www.twochefsbistro.com; 121 Stuart St; mains $34-37; ⊗ noon-3pm Fri, 6-10pm daily) French bistro dishes flirt with Asian and North African flavours on the plate, while high ceilings and dark wood conjure up a romantic ambience. The service is the opposite of French stereotypes: delightful but not always efficient. Save room for dessert.

North Dunedin

Everyday Gourmet
CAFE, DELI $

(Map p522; www.everydaygourmet.net.nz; 466 George St; mains $7-16; ⊗ 8am-5pm) Apart from cooked breakfasts, most of the goodies beckon from the counter of this excellent bakery-style cafe and deli. It's light, bright and extremely popular, with a good selection of magazines and newspapers.

Governor's
CAFE $$

(Map p522; 438 George St; mains $10-19; ⊗ 7am-4pm) Popular with students, Governor's does a nice line in early-morning pancakes and other light meals. If you're feeling a little off the pace after the previous night, a strong coffee and a mixed grill are just what the doctor ordered.

Other Suburbs

No 7 Balmac
CAFE $$

(Map p520; ☑ 03-464 0064; www.no7balmac.co.nz; 7 Balmacewen Rd, Maori Hill; brunch $15-25, dinner $28-37; ⊗ 7am-late Mon-Fri, 8.30am-late Sat, 8.30am-5pm Sun) We wouldn't recommend walking to this sophisticated cafe at the top of Maori Hill; luckily it's well worth the price of a cab. The fancy fare stretches to the likes of venison pie and dry-aged beef. If you're on a diet, avoid eye contact with the sweets cabinet.

Starfish
CAFE, BAR $$

(Map p520; ☑ 03-455 5940; www.starfishcafe.co.nz; 7/240 Forbury Rd, St Clair; brunch $14-20, dinner $20-30; ⊗ 7am-5pm Sun-Tue, to late Wed-Sat) Starfish is the coolest creature in the growing restaurant scene at St Clair Beach.

Pop out on a weekday to score an outside table, and tuck into gourmet pizza and wine. Dinner is a more sophisticated beast.

Luna
MODERN NZ $$$

(Map p520; ☑ 03-477 2227; www.lunaroslyn.co.nz; 314 Highgate, Roslyn; lunch $14-25, dinner $34-37; ⊗ noon-late) Make the trek to Roslyn for an inventive menu and outstanding harbour views in this glass-encased hilltop pavilion; ask for a window seat when you book. A more relaxed option is a drink in the classy bar, accompanied by selections from the 'Luna Bites' menu.

☕ Drinking & Nightlife

Mou Very
BAR

(Map p522; www.facebook.com/MouVeryBar; 357 George St; ⊗ 7am-12.30pm) Welcome to one of the world's smallest bars – it's only 1.8m wide, but is still big enough to host regular DJs, live bands and poetry readings. There are just six bar stools, so patrons spill out into an adjacent laneway. By day, it's a handy caffeine-refuelling spot.

Albar
BAR

(Map p522; 135 Stuart St; ⊗ 11am-late) This former butcher is now a bohemian little bar attracting maybe the widest age range in Dunedin. Most punters are drawn by the many single-malt whiskies, interesting tap beers and cheap-as-chips bar snacks ($6 to $9).

Di Lusso
COCKTAIL BAR

(Map p522; www.dilusso.co.nz; 117 Stuart St; ⊗ 4pm-3am Mon-Sat) Upmarket and designery with wood panelling, chandeliers and a backlit drinks display, Di Lusso serves seriously good cocktails. DJs play from Thursday to Saturday.

Carousel
COCKTAIL BAR

(Map p522; www.carouselbar.co.nz; upstairs 141 Stuart St; ⊗ 5pm-late Tue-Sat) Tartan wallpaper, a roof deck and great cocktails leave the dressed-up clientele looking pleased to be seen somewhere so deadly cool. DJs spin deep house until late on the weekends, and there's live jazz on Friday evenings.

Stuart St Mac's Brewbar
BAR

(Map p522; www.stuartst.co.nz; 12 The Octagon; ⊗ 10am-late) Nelson's Mac's brewery is making a strike deep into Speights' territory in the form of this funky bar right on the Octagon. It's the sunniest spot for an afternoon drink, and after the sun sets there's often live music.

Speight's Ale House
PUB
(Map p522; www.thealehouse.co.nz; 200 Rattray St; ☺11.30am-late) Busy even in the nonuniversity months, the Ale House is a favourite of strapping young lads in their cleanest dirty shirts. It's a good spot to watch the rugby on TV and to try the full range of Speight's beers.

Pequeno
COCKTAIL BAR
(Map p522; www.pequeno.co.nz; behind 12 Moray Pl; ☺5pm-late Mon-Fri, 7pm-late Sat & Sun) Down the alleyway opposite the Rialto cinema, Pequeno attracts a sophisticated crowd with leather couches, a cosy fireplace and an excellent wine and tapas menu. Music is generally laid-back and there's live jazz on Fridays.

Tonic
BAR
(Map p522; www.tonicbar.co.nz; 138 Princes St; ☺4pm-late Tue-Fri, 6pm-late Sat) Limited-release Kiwi craft beers, single-malt whiskies and good cocktails appeal to a different crowd than Dunedin's numerous student pubs. Antipasto plates, cheeseboards and pizza are good reasons to stay for another drink.

Urban Factory
CLUB
(Map p522; www.urbanfactory.co.nz; 101 Great King St; ☺10pm-3am) The hippest of NZ's touring bands, regular DJ sessions and carefully crafted cocktails.

Pop
CLUB
(Map p522; downstairs, 14 The Octagon; ☺10pm-late Wed-Sat) Pop serves Dunedin's best martinis and prides itself on seriously good DJs playing funk and house.

☆ Entertainment

Metro Cinema
CINEMA
(Map p522; ☎03-471 9635; www.metrocinema.co.nz; Moray Pl; adult/student $13/12) Within the town hall, Metro shows art-house and foreign flicks.

Rialto Cinemas
CINEMA
(Map p522; ☎03-474 2200; www.rialto.co.nz; 11 Moray Pl; adult/child $16/10) Blockbusters and art-house flicks. Rates often cheaper on Tuesdays.

Fortune Theatre
THEATRE
(Map p522; ☎03-477 8323; www.fortunetheatre.co.nz; 231 Stuart St) The world's southernmost professional theatre company has been staging dramas, comedies, pantomimes, classics and contemporary NZ productions for almost 40 years. Shows are performed – watched over by the obligatory theatre ghost – in a Gothic-style old Wesleyan church.

Sammy's
LIVE MUSIC
(Map p522; 65 Crawford St) Dunedin's premier live-music venue draws an eclectic mix of genres from noisy-as-hell punk to chilled reggae and gritty dubstep. It's the venue of choice for visiting Kiwi bands and up-and-coming international acts.

Forsyth Barr Stadium
STADIUM
(Map p520; www.forsythbarrstadium.co.nz; 130 Anzac Ave) Constructed for the 2011 Rugby World Cup, this is the only major stadium in NZ with a fully covered roof. It's the home ground for the Highlanders Super 15 rugby team (www.thehighlanders.co.nz) and the Otago rugby team (www.orfu.co.nz).

🛍 Shopping

George St is Dunedin's main shopping strip.

Gallery De Novo
ARTS & CRAFTS
(Map p522; www.gallerydenovo.co.nz; 91 Stuart St; ☺9.30am-5.30pm Mon-Fri, 10am-3pm Sat & Sun) This interesting, contemporary fine-art gallery is worth a look, whether you're likely to invest in a substantial piece of Kiwi art or not.

Stuart St Potters Cooperative
ARTS & CRAFTS
(Map p522; 14 Stuart St; ☺10am-5pm Mon-Fri, 9am-3pm Sat) Locally designed and made pottery and ceramic art.

Bivouac Outdoor
OUTDOOR EQUIPMENT
(Map p522; www.bivouac.co.nz; 171 George St; ☺9am-5.30pm Mon-Fri, 10am-4pm Sat & Sun) Clothing, footwear and rugged gear.

University Book Shop
BOOKS
(Map p522; www.unibooks.co.nz; 378 Great King St; ☺8.30am-5.30pm Mon-Fri, 11am-3pm Sat & Sun) Dunedin's best bookshop, with lots of Maori, Pacific and NZ titles.

ℹ Information

MEDICAL SERVICES

Dunedin Hospital (☎03-474 0999, emergency department 0800 611 116; www.southerndhb.govt.nz; 201 Great King St)

Urgent Doctors & Accident Centre (☎03-479 2900; www.dunedinurgentdoctors.com; 95 Hanover St; ☺8am-11.30pm) There's also a late-night pharmacy next door.

TOURIST INFORMATION

DOC Visitor Centre (Department of Conservation; Map p522; ☎03-477 0677; www.doc.govt.nz; 1st fl, 77 Stuart St; ☺8.30am-5pm Mon-Fri) Information and maps on regional walking tracks, Great Walks bookings and hut tickets.

Dunedin i-SITE (Map p522; ☑ 03-474 3300; www.isitedunedin.co.nz; 26 Princes St; ⊙ 8.30am-5pm)

❶ Getting There & Away

AIR

For information on international flights, see p662. Domestic options include the following:

Air New Zealand (☑ 0800 737 000; www.airnewzealand.co.nz) Flies to/from Auckland, Wellington and Christchurch.

Jetstar (☑ 0800 800 995; www.jetstar.com) Flies to/from Auckland.

BUS

Buses and shuttles leave from the Dunedin Railway Station, except where we've noted otherwise.

InterCity (Map p520; ☑ 03-471 7143; www.intercity.co.nz; 7 Halsey St) Coaches to/from Christchurch (from $40, six hours) and Oamaru (from $14, 40 minutes) twice daily, and Cromwell (from $20, 3¼ hours), Queenstown (from $22, 4¼ hours) and Te Anau (from $37, 4½ hours) daily.

Alpine Connexions (☑ 03-443 9120; www.alpineconnexions.co.nz) Shuttles head to/from Alexandra ($40), Clyde ($40), Cromwell ($45), Queenstown ($45) and Wanaka ($45), as well as key stops on the Otago Central Rail Trail.

Atomic Shuttles (☑ 03-349 0697; www.atomictravel.co.nz) To/from Christchurch (from $30, 5¾ hours), Oamaru ($20, 1¾ hours), Cromwell ($30, 3¾ hours), Wanaka ($35, 4½ hours) and Invercargill ($37, 3¼ hours).

Catch-a-Bus (☑ 03-449-2024; www.catcha-bus.co.nz) Door-to-door shuttle between Dunedin and Cromwell stopping at Otago Central Rail Trail towns along the way. Bikes can be transported.

Coast Line Tours (☑ 03-434 7744; www.coastline-tours.co.nz) Shuttles to Oamaru ($30) depart from the Octagon; detours to Dunedin airport and Moeraki can be arranged.

Knightrider (☑ 03-342 8055; www.knightrider.co.nz) Has a bus most nights to/from Christchurch ($50, six hours), Christchurch Airport ($55, 5½ hours), Timaru ($44, 3¼ hours), Moeraki ($33, 1¼ hours) and Oamaru ($33, two hours).

TRAIN

Two interesting train journeys start at Dunedin's railway station (p521): the Taieri Gorge Railway (p524) and the **Seasider** (www.seasider.co.nz; 1-way/return $59/89). The latter journeys up the coast to Palmerston and back.

❶ Getting Around

TO & FROM THE AIRPORT

Dunedin Airport (DUD; ☑ 03-486 2879; www.flydunedin.com; Airport Rd, Momona) is 27km southwest of the city. A standard taxi ride between the city and the airport costs $80 to $90. There is no public bus service. For door-to-door shuttles, try **Kiwi Shuttles** (☑ 03-487 9790; www.kiwishuttles.co.nz; per 1/2/3/4 passengers $20/36/48/60) or **Super Shuttle** (☑ 0800 748 885; www.supershuttle.co.nz; per 1/2/3/4 passengers $25/35/45/55).

BUS

Dunedin's **GoBus** (☑ 03-474 0287; www.orc.govt.nz; adult fare $2-6.70) network extends across the city. It's particularly handy for getting to St Clair, St Kilda, Port Chalmers and as far afield as Portobello on the Otago Peninsula. Buses run regularly during the week, but services are greatly reduced (or nonexistent) on weekends and holidays.

CAR

The big rental companies all have offices in Dunedin, and inexpensive local outfits include **Get Away** (☑ 03-489 7614; www.getawaycarhire.co.nz) and **Driven Rentals** (☑ 03-453 6576; www.drivenrentals.co.nz).

TAXI

Dunedin Taxis (☑ 03-477 7777; www.dunedin-taxis.co.nz)

Otago Taxis (☑ 03-477 3333)

AROUND DUNEDIN

Port Chalmers & Around

POP 1370

Little Port Chalmers is only 13km out of Dunedin but it feels a world away. Somewhere between working class and bohemian, Port Chalmers has a history as a port town but has increasingly attracted Dunedin's arty types. Dunedin's best rock-and-roll pub, **Chick's Hotel** (Map p520; 2 Mount St; ⊙ 4pm-1am Wed-Sun) is an essential after-dark destination, and daytime attractions include a few raffish cafes, design stores and galleries.

◉ Sights & Activities

Traditional rock climbing (nonbolted) is popular at Long Beach and the cliffs at Mihiwaka, both accessed via Blueskin Rd north of Port Chalmers.

Orokonui Ecosanctuary WILDLIFE RESERVE

(Map p520; ☑ 03-482 1755; www.orokonui.org.nz; 600 Blueskin Rd; adult/child $16/8; ☺ 9.30am-4.30pm) This 307-hectare predator-free nature reserve encloses cloud forest on the mountainous ridge above Port Chalmers and stretches to the estuary on the opposite side. Its mission is to provide a mainland refuge for species usually exiled to offshore islands for their own protection. Rare bird species include kiwi, saddlebacks, takahe and kaka, while reptiles include tuatara and Otago skinks.

Visiting options include self-guided tours, hour-long guided tours (adult/child $30/15; departing daily at 11am and 1.30pm) and two-hour guided tours (adult/child $45/22; departing daily at 11pm). You'll need to book ahead for the two-hour twilight tours (adult/child $69/39). It's a well-signposted 6km drive from the main road into Port Chalmers.

Hare Hill HORSE RIDING

(Map p520; ☑ 03-472 8496; www.horseriding-dunedin.co.nz; 207 Aramoana Rd; treks $80-160) Horse treks include thrilling beach rides and farm treks.

🛏 Sleeping

Billy Brown's HOSTEL

(Map p520; ☑ 03-472 8323; www.billybrowns.co.nz; 423 Aramoana Rd, Hamilton Bay; dm/d $30/75) On a farm 5km further along the road from Port Chalmers, this hostel has magnificent views across the harbour to the peninsula. There's a lovely rustic shared lounge with cosy wood-burner, and plenty of retro vinyl to spin. If you're not comfortable with big dogs, look elsewhere.

❶ Getting There & Away

On weekdays, 15 buses travel between Dunedin's Cumberland St and Port Chalmers, with two additional services on Friday nights (adult/child $4.70/2.70). On Saturdays this reduces to 11, and on Sundays to three.

Otago Peninsula

POP 4220

The Otago Peninsula has the South Island's most accessible diversity of wildlife. Albatross, penguins, fur seals and sea lions are some of the highlights, as well as rugged countryside, wild walks, beaches and interesting historical sites. Despite a host of tours exploring the peninsula, the area maintains its quiet rural air. Call into the Dunedin i-SITE (p530) for brochures and maps, or visit www.otago-peninsula.co.nz.

👁 Sights

Royal Albatross Centre
& Fort Taiaroa WILDLIFE RESERVE

(Map p520; ☑ 03-478 0499; www.albatross.org.nz; Taiaroa Head; ☺ 11.30am-dusk) Taiaroa Head, at the peninsula's northern tip, has the world's only mainland royal albatross colony, along with a late-19th-century military fort. The fort was built in 1885 in response to a perceived threat of a Russian invasion. Its Armstrong Disappearing Gun was designed to be loaded and aimed underground, then popped up like the world's slowest jack-in-the-box to be fired.

Albatross are present throughout the year, but the best time to see them is from December to February, when one parent is constantly guarding the young while the other delivers food throughout the day. Sightings are most common in the afternoon when the winds pick up; calm days don't see much bird action. The main glassed-in observation area is closed during the breeding season, from mid-September to late November. From late November to December the birds are nestbound so it's difficult to see their magnificent wingspan.

The only public access to the area is by guided tour. The hour-long Classic tour (adult/child $39/19) focuses on the albatross, or there's a 30-minute Fort tour (adult/child $19/9); the two can be combined on the Unique tour ($49/24).

Little penguins swim ashore at Pilots Beach (just below the car park) around dusk to head to their nests in the dunes. For their protection, the beach is closed to the public every evening, but viewing is possible from a specially constructed wooden platform (adult/child $20/10). Depending on the time of year, 50 to 500 penguins might waddle past.

Nature's Wonders Naturally WILDLIFE RESERVE

(Map p520; ☑ 03-478 1150; www.natureswonders.co.nz; Taiaroa Head; adult/child $55/45; ☺ tours from 10.15am) What makes the improbably beautiful beaches of this coastal sheep farm different from other important wildlife habitats is that (apart from pest eradication and the like) they're left completely alone. No tagging or weighing is carried out, and many of the multiple private beaches haven't suffered a human footprint in years.

The result is that yellow-eyed penguins can often be spotted (through binoculars) at any time of the day, and NZ fur seals laze around rocky swimming holes, blissfully unphased by tour groups passing by. Depending on the time of year, you might also see whales and little penguin chicks.

The tour is conducted in 'go-anywhere' Argos vehicles by enthusiastic guides, at least some of which double as true-blue Kiwi farmers. If you don't believe it, ask about the sheep-shed experience (price on application).

Penguin Place   WILDLIFE RESERVE
(Map p520; ☑03-478 0286; www.penguinplace. co.nz; 45 Pakihau Rd; adult/child $49/15) Situated on private farmland, this reserve protects nesting sites of the yellow-eyed penguin. Ninety-minute tours focus on penguin conservation and close-up viewing from a system of hides. Between October and March, tours run regularly from 10.15am to 90 minutes before sunset. Between April and September they run from 3.15pm to 4.45pm. Bookings are recommended.

Larnach Castle   CASTLE
(Map p520; ☑03-476 1616; www.larnachcastle. co.nz; 145 Camp Rd; castle & grounds adult/child $28/10, grounds only $13/4; ⊙9am-7pm Oct-Mar, to 5pm Apr-Sep) 🅿 Standing proudly on top of a hill, this gorgeous Gothic Revival mansion was built in 1871 by Dunedin banker, merchant and Member of Parliament William Larnach, to impress his wife, who descended from French nobility. It didn't bring him much happiness, however. After his first two wives died and his third was rumoured to be having an affair with his son, Larnach shot himself in a committee room in Parliament in 1898. His son later followed suit.

The mansion is filled with intricate woodwork and exquisite antique furnishings, and the crenelated tower offers expansive views of the peninsula. A self-guided tour brochure is provided with admission, or you can buy an iPhone tour app which peoples the rooms with costumed actors ($5). After lording it about in the mansion, take a stroll through the pretty gardens or settle in for the 3pm high tea in the ballroom cafe.

Glenfalloch Woodland Garden   GARDENS
(Map p520; www.glenfalloch.co.nz; 430 Portobello Rd; adult/child $5/free; ⊙9.30am-dusk) Expect spectacular harbour views at this 12-hectare garden, filled with flowers, walking tracks and swaying mature trees, including a 1000-year-old matai. The Portobello bus stops out the front.

Activities

The peninsula's coastal and farmland walkways offer blissful views and the chance of spotting some wildlife; pick up or download the *DOC Walks Around Dunedin* brochure. A popular walking destination is beautiful **Sandfly Bay**, reached from Seal Point Rd (moderate, one hour return). From the end of Sandymount Rd, you can follow a trail to the impressive **Chasm** (20 minutes). Note that the Lovers Leap track and the Chasm track at Sandymount are closed from August to October for lambing.

Wild Earth Adventures   KAYAKING
(☑03-489 1951; www.wildearth.co.nz; trips from $115) Offers trips in double sea kayaks, with wildlife often sighted en route. Trips take between three hours and a full day, with pickups from the Octagon in Dunedin.

Tours

Elm Wildlife Tours   TOUR
(☑03-454 4121; www.elmwildlifetours.co.nz; trips from $105) 🅿 Well-regarded, small-group, wildlife-focused tours, with options to add the Royal Albatross Centre or a Monarch Cruise. Pick-up and drop-off from Dunedin is included.

Monarch Wildlife Cruises & Tours BOAT TOUR
(Map p520; ☑03-477 4276; www.wildlife.co.nz) 🅿 One-hour boat trips from Wellers Rock (adult/child $49/22), and half- ($89/32) and full-day ($235/118) tours from Dunedin. You may spot sea lions, penguins, albatross and seals.

Sleeping

McFarmers Backpackers   HOSTEL $
(Map p520; ☑03-478 0389; www.otago-peninsula. co.nz; 774 Portobello Rd; s $53, d & tw $66-76, cottages $120-150) On a working sheep farm with harbour views, this rustic timber lodge and self-contained cottage are steeped in character and feel instantly like home. The Portobello bus goes past the gate.

Penguin Place Lodge   HOSTEL $
(Map p520; ☑03-478 0286; www.penguinplace. co.nz; 45 Pakihau Rd; adult/child $30/12) Atop a quiet hill surrounded by farmland, this lodge has a good shared kitchen, a bright lounge, and basic double and twin rooms. There are views across the farm and harbour, and you're next-door neighbours with the penguins. Linen costs $5 extra.

Portobello Motel
MOTEL $$

(Map p520; ☎ 03-478 0155; www.portobellomotels.com; 10 Harington Point Rd; d $145-160; ☎) These sunny modern, self-contained units are just off the main road in Portobello. Studio units have small decks overlooking the bay. Spacious one- and two-bedroom units are also available, but lack the views.

Larnach Castle Lodge
LODGE $$

(Map p520; ☎ 03-476 1616; www.larnachcastle.co.nz; 145 Camp Rd; r stable/lodge/estate $155/280/420; @ ☎) ✍ Larnach Castle's back-garden lodge has 12 individually, whimsically decorated rooms. Less frivolous are the atmospheric rooms in the 140-year-old stables. A few hundred metres from the castle, Camp Estate country house has luxury suites worthy of a romantic splurge. Rates for each option include breakfast and castle entry, and dinner in the castle can be arranged.

Kaimata Retreat
LODGE $$$

(Map p520; ☎ 03-456 3443; www.kaimatanz.com; 297 Cape Saunders Rd; bach/r/lodge $160/525/1500; @ ☎) ✍ This luxury ecolodge has three rooms overlooking a gloriously isolated inlet on the eastern edge of the peninsula. Tours can be arranged, and a chef is available in summer for evening meals. For a cheaper option with similar views, book Betty's Bach, a retro self-contained holiday house nearby.

✖ Eating

1908 Cafe
RESTAURANT $$

(Map p520; ☎ 03-478 0801; www.1908cafe.co.nz; 7 Harington Point Rd; lunch $13-24, dinner $31-34; ☺ 11.30am-2pm Wed-Sun, 6-10pm daily) Salmon, venison and steak are joined by fresh fish and blackboard specials at this casual, friendly restaurant. At lunch they're replaced by cafe fare, such as soup and toasted sandwiches. The venerable interiors are cheerfully embellished with local art.

Portobello Hotel & Bistro
PUB $$

(Map p520; www.portobellohotelandbistro.co.nz; 2 Harington Point Rd; lunch $13-19, dinner $24-29; ☺ 11.30am-late) Refreshing thirsty travellers since 1874, the Portobello pub is still a popular pit stop. Grab a table in the sun and tuck into seafood chowder, a burger, a felafel wrap or a steak.

ⓘ Getting There & Around

On weekdays, 13 buses travel between Dunedin's Cumberland St and Portobello Village (adult/child $5.80/3.40). On Saturdays this reduces to 10, and on Sundays to four. Once on the peninsula, it's tough to get around without your own transport. Most tours will pick you up from your Dunedin accommodation.

There's no petrol on the peninsula.

CENTRAL OTAGO

Rolling hills that turn from green to gold in the relentless summer sun provide a backdrop to a succession of tiny, charming goldrush towns where rugged, laconic 'Southern Man' types can be seen propping up the bar in lost-in-time pubs. As well as being one of the country's top wine regions, there are fantastic opportunities for those on two wheels, whether mountain biking along old gold-mining trails or traversing the district on the Otago Central Rail Trail.

Middlemarch & Around

POP 156

With the Rock & Pillar Range as an impressive backdrop, the small town of **Middlemarch** (www.middlemarch.co.nz) is the terminus of the Taieri Gorge Railway, and also one end of the Otago Central Rail Trail. It's famous in NZ for the Middlemarch Singles Ball (held across Easter in odd-numbered years), where southern men gather to entice city gals to the country life.

✦ Activities

Catering to riders on the Otago Central Rail Trail year-round, both of the following businesses have large depots on Middlemarch's main street and provide bike rental and logistical support, including shuttles, bag transfers and an accommodation booking service. They also have depots in Clyde, at the other end of the trail.

Cycle Surgery
BICYCLE RENTAL

(☎ 03-464 3630; www.cyclesurgery.co.nz; Swansea St; rental per day $35; ☺ depot mid-Sep–mid-May)

Trail Journeys
BICYCLE RENTAL

(☎ 03-464 3213; www.trailjourneys.co.nz; Swansea St; rental per day $40; ☺ depot Sep-Apr)

⛏ Sleeping & Eating

Otago Central Hotel
HOTEL $$

(☎ 03-444 4800; www.hydehotel.co.nz; SH87, Hyde; with/without bathroom s $100/80, d $170/130; ☎) Most of the tidy rooms in this cool old hotel, 27km along the trail from Middlemarch,

OTAGO CENTRAL RAIL TRAIL

Stretching from Dunedin to Clyde, the Central Otago rail branch linked small, inland goldfield towns with the big city from the early 20th century through to the 1990s. After the 150km stretch from Middlemarch to Clyde was permanently closed, the rails were ripped up and the trail resurfaced. The result is a year-round mainly gravel trail that takes bikers, walkers and horseback riders along a historic route containing old rail bridges, viaducts and tunnels.

With excellent trailside facilities (toilets, shelters and information), few hills, gob-smacking scenery and profound remoteness, the trail attracts well over 25,000 visitors annually. March is the busiest time, when there are so many city slickers on the track that you might have to wait 30 minutes at cafes en route for a panini. Consider September for a quieter ride.

The trail can be followed in either direction. The entire trail takes approximately four to five days to complete by bike (or a week on foot), but you can obviously choose to do as short or long a stretch as suits your plans. There are also easy detours to towns such as Naseby and St Bathans.

Mountain bikes can be rented in Dunedin, Middlemarch, Alexandra and Clyde. Any of the area's i-SITEs can provide detailed information. See www.otagocentralrailtrail.co.nz and www.otagorailtrail.co.nz for track information, recommended timings, accommodation options and tour companies.

Due to the popularity of the trail, a whole raft of sleeping and eating options have sprung up in remote locales en route, although some stops are still poorly served.

have private bathrooms but only some are en suite. It's no longer a working pub and the licensed cafe on the sunny terrace shuts at 4pm, leaving the set dinner the only meal option for many miles around.

Kissing Gate Cafe CAFE $
(2 Swansea St; mains $7-18; ☺ 8.30am-4pm) Sit out under the fruit trees in the pretty garden of this cute little wooden cottage and tuck into a cooked breakfast, meatloaf, frittata or some home baking. Nana-chic at its best.

Quench CAFE, BAR $$
(☎ 03-464 3070; 31 Snow Ave; brunch $6-16, dinner $21-29; ☺ 8am-9pm Sun-Thu, to 11.30pm Fri & Sat Sep-Apr, to 4pm May-Aug) Opposite the railway station, Quench lives up to its name with cooked breakfasts, pies and the Rail Burger (recommended if you're beginning the Rail Trail), and ice-cold Speight's on tap (*definitely* recommended if you've just finished the trail).

❶ Getting There & Away

The scenic **Taieri Gorge Railway** (☎ 03-477 4449; www.taieri.co.nz; ☺ Sun May-Sep,Fri & Sun Oct-Apr) has only limited runs between Dunedin and Middlemarch; most services end at Pukerangi Station, 20km away. Both of the main cycle companies offer shuttles to Dunedin, Pukerangi and the Rail Trail towns.

Ranfurly & Around

POP 663

After a series of fires in the 1930s, Ranfurly was rebuilt in the architectural style of the day, and a few attractive art deco buildings still line its sleepy main drag. The teensy town is trying hard to cash in on this meagre legacy, calling itself the 'South Island's art deco capital' and holding an annual **Art Deco Festival** (www.ranfurlyartdeco.co.nz) on the last weekend of February. There's even an Art Deco Museum in the admittedly fabulous Centennial Milk Bar building on the main street.

For a self-guided tour, grab a copy of the *Rural Art Deco – Ranfurly Walk* brochure from the **Ranfurly i-SITE** (☎ 03-444 1005; www.centralotagonz.com; 3 Charlemont St; ☺ 9am-5pm; ☎) in the old train station. While you're there, check out the local history and Sports Hall of Fame displays.

To explore the rugged terrain made famous by noted local landscape artist Grahame Sydney, contact **Maniototo 4WD Safaris** (☎ 03-444 9703; www.maniototo4wdsafaris.co.nz; half-/full day $130/190).

There are a couple of cafes in town and an old pub which serves meals and rents rooms.

🛏 Sleeping

Peter's Farm Lodge   LODGE **$**
(☑03-444 9811; www.petersfarm.co.nz; 113 Tregonning Rd, Waipiata; per person $55) Set on a sheep farm 13km south of Ranfurly, this rustic 1882 farmhouse offers comfy beds, hearty barbecue dinners ($25) and free pick-ups from the rail trail. Kayaks, fishing rods and gold pans are all available, so it's worth staying a couple of nights. Further beds are available in neighbouring Tregonnings Cottage (1882).

Hawkdun Lodge   MOTEL **$$**
(☑03-444 9750; www.hawkdunlodge.co.nz; 1 Bute St; s/d from $125/175; 🛜) *∂* This smart new boutique motel is the best option in the town centre by far. Each unit has a kitchenette with a microwave, but travelling chefs can flex their skills in the guest kitchen and on the barbecue. Rates include a continental breakfast.

Kokonga Lodge   B&B **$$$**
(☑03-444 9774; www.kokongalodge.co.nz; 33 Kokonga-Waipiata Rd; r $285; @🛜) *∂* Just off SH87 between Ranfurly and Hyde, this upmarket rural property offers six contemporary en suite rooms, one of which housed Sir Peter Jackson when he was filming *The Hobbit* in the area. The Rail Trail passes nearby.

❶ Getting There & Away

Trail Journey's **Catch-a-Bus** (☑03-449 2024; www.catchabus.co.nz) shuttle passes through Ranfurly on its way between Cromwell and Dunedin.

Naseby

POP 120

Cute as a button, surrounded by forest and dotted with 19th-century stone buildings, Naseby is the kind of small town where life moves slowly. That the town is pleasantly obsessed with the fairly insignificant world of NZ curling indicates there's not much else going on. It's that lazy small-town vibe, along with good mountain-biking and walking trails through the surrounding forest, that make Naseby an interesting place to stay for a couple of days.

🏃 Activities

Maniototo Curling International   CURLING
(☑03-444 9878; www.curling.co.nz; 1057 Channel Rd; per 1½hr adult/family $30/80; ☺10am-5pm) All year round you can shimmy after curl-

ing stones at the indoor ice rink; tuition is available. In winter there's also an outdoor ice rink to skate around.

Naseby Ice Luge   SNOW SPORTS
(☑03-444 9270; www.lugenz.com; 1057 Channel Rd; adult/child $30/25; ☺Jun-Aug) Hurtle 360m down a hillside on a wooden sled. Bookings are recommended.

🛏 Sleeping & Eating

Royal Hotel   PUB **$**
(☑03-444 9990; www.naseby.co.nz; 1 Earne St; dm $40, r with/without bathroom $100/70; 🛜) The better of the town's historic pubs, the 1863 Royal Hotel sports the royal coat of arms and what just might be NZ's most rustic garden bar. Rooms are simple but spotless, and the meals are good too (mains $25 to $30).

Naseby Lodge   APARTMENTS **$$**
(☑03-444 8222; www.nasebylodge.co.nz; cnr Derwent & Oughter Sts; 1-/2-bedroom apt $170/260; 🛜) Constructed of environmentally friendly straw-bale walls sheathed in rustic corrugated iron, these free-standing modern apartments are smart and spacious, with fully equipped kitchens and underfloor heating in the bathrooms. There's also a good restaurant on site.

Old Doctor's Residence   B&B **$$$**
(☑03-444 9775; www.olddoctorsresidence.co.nz; 58 Derwent St; r/ste $275/325; 🛜) *∂* Old doctors take note: this is how to reside! Sitting behind a pretty garden, this gorgeous 1870s house offers two luxurious guest rooms and a lounge where wine and nibbles are served of an evening. The suite has a sitting room and an en suite bathroom (with a fabulous make-up desk). The smaller room's bathroom is accessed from the corridor.

Black Forest Café   CAFE **$**
(☑03-444 9820; 7 Derwent St; mains $10-17; ☺9am-4pm) Fresh baking and good coffee feature at this cafe. Inside, stone walls, bright colours and warm polished wood create a pleasant ambience. The wide-ranging menu includes bagels, panini and creamy smoothies made from Central Otago fruit.

❶ Information

Ernslaw One Forestry Office (☑03-444 9995; www.ernslaw.co.nz/naseby-recreational-area/; 34 Derwent St) Administers the 500-hectare recreation reserve within the privately owned

Naseby Forest. Call in for maps of walking tracks and mountain bike trails.

Naseby Information & Crafts (✑03-444 9961; Derwent St; ◷11am-2pm Sun, Mon & Fri, to 4pm Sat)

❶ Getting There & Away

The Ranfurly–Naseby Rd leaves SH85 4km north of Ranfurly. There's no public transport and cyclists should factor in a 12km detour from the Rail Trail. From Naseby, you can wind your way on unsealed roads northeast through spectacular scenery to Danseys Pass and through to Duntroon in the Waitaki Valley.

St Bathans

A worthwhile 17km detour north from SH85 heads into the foothills of the imposing Dunstan Mountains and on to diminutive St Bathans. This once-thriving gold-mining town of 2000 people is now home to only half a dozen permanent residents living amid a cluster of cutesy 19th-century buildings.

The Blue Lake is an accidental attraction: a large hollow filled with amazingly blue water that has run off abandoned gold workings. Walk along the sculpted cliffs to the lookout for a better view of the alien landscape (one hour return).

The Vulcan Hotel (✑03-447 3629; stbathans.vulcanhotel@xtra.co.nz; Loop Rd; r per person $60) is an atmospheric (and famously haunted) spot to drink, eat or stay in. Considering St Bathans' tiny population, you'll find the bar here pretty busy on a Friday night as thirsty shearers from around the valley descend en masse. Further accommodation is available at the nearby St Bathans Jail & Constable's Cottage (✑0800 555 016; www.stbathansnz.co.nz; $145-340).

Lauder, Omakau & Ophir

Separated by 8km of SH85, tiny Lauder and larger Omakau (population 250) are good stops if you're in need of a feed and a bed. However, the area's real gem is adorable Ophir (population 50), 2km from Omakau across the Manuherikia River.

Gold was discovered here in 1863 and the town swiftly formed, adopting the name of the biblical place where King Solomon sourced his gold. By 1875, the population hit over 1000 but when the gold disappeared, so did the people. Ophir's fate was sealed when

the railway bypassed it in 1904, leaving its main street trapped in time.

The most photogenic of its many heritage buildings is the still-functioning 1886 post office (www.historic.org.nz; Swindon St; ◷9am-noon Mon-Fri). At the far end of the town, the sealed road ends at the 1870s wooden-planked Dan O'Connell Bridge, a bumpy but scenic crossing which continues via a gravel road to SH85.

Ophir lays claim to the country's largest range of temperatures: from −21.6°C to 35°C (Alexandra, just up the road, once recorded a temperature of 38°C).

🛏 Sleeping & Eating

Muddy Creek Cutting B&B $$
(✑03-447 3682; www.muddycreekcutting.co.nz; SH85, Lauder; per person $80) Art fills the walls of this charmingly restored 1930s mudbrick farmhouse, with five bedrooms that share two bathrooms. Dinners with a local, organic spin are also available ($55 per person).

Omakau Commercial Hotel PUB $$
(✑03-447 3715; www.omakauhotel.co.nz; 1 Harvey St, Omakau; s with/without bathroom from $79/55, d from 109/105; 🕾) There's an old-fashioned ambience to this venerable pub, where good-value rooms, excellent food and local company are all on tap. The bedrooms don't have televisions or kettles, but these are available in the guest lounge downstairs.

Chatto Creek Tavern HOTEL $$
(✑03-447 3710; www.chattocreektavern.co.nz; 1544 SH85, Chatto Creek; dm/s/d without bathroom $50/90/120) Dating from 1886, this attractive stone hotel sits right beside the Rail Trail and highway, 10km southwest of Omakau. Pop in for a whitebait fritter (in season) or steak sandwich, or rest your weary calf muscles in a dorm bed or double room. Rates include breakfast.

★Pitches Store B&B, RESTAURANT $$$
(✑03-447 3240; www.pitches-store.co.nz; 45 Swindon St, Ophir; r $250, brunch $9-19, dinner $33-35; ◷restaurant 10am-late daily Nov-May, 11am-late Fri-Mon Jun-Oct) Formerly a general store and butcher, this heritage building has been sensitively transformed into six elegant guest rooms and a humdinger of a restaurant. Exposed-stone walls may speak of the past but the menu is stridently contemporary.

Stationside Cafe CAFE $
(Lauder-Matakanui Rd, Lauder; mains $8-18; ◷7am-5pm Oct-Apr) Home baking and coun-

try cooking are showcased at this great little trailside place. Options include healthy salads, sandwiches, soups and pasta.

Muddy Creek Cafe
CAFE $

(2 Harvey St, Omakau; mains $8-16; ⊗8.30am-7pm Mon-Sat, 10am-7pm Sun) Take a break from the Rail Trail at this friendly spot festooned with old radios. Cafe treats include all-day breakfasts, pasta, pies and ice cream, or you can grab a burger or fish and chips from the takeaway counter.

Alexandra

POP 4800

Unless you've come especially for the Easter Bunny Hunt or September's NZ Merino Shearing Championships, the main reason to visit unassuming Alexandra is mountain biking. It's the biggest Rail Trail settlement by far, offering more eating and sleeping options than the rest of the one-horse (or fewer) towns on the route. It's also the start of the brand-new Roxburgh Gorge Trail.

Alex, as it's known to the locals, marks the southeastern corner of the acclaimed Central Otago wine region. Of the dozen wineries in the immediate vicinity, only a handful are open for tastings. These are detailed on the *Central Otago Wine Map,* available from the i-SITE (p538).

◉ Sights & Activities

Walkers and mountain bikers will love the old gold trails weaving through the hills; collect maps from the i-SITE. The Alexandra–Clyde 150th Anniversary Walk (12.8km, three hours one way) is a riverside trail that's fairly flat with ample resting spots and shade.

Central Stories
MUSEUM

(www.centralstories.com; 21 Centennial Ave; admission by donation; ⊗10am-4pm) Central Otago's history of gold-mining, winemaking, orcharding and sheep farming is covered in this excellent regional museum which shares a building with the i-SITE.

Roxburgh Gorge Trail
MOUNTAIN BIKING

(www.roxburghgorge.co.nz) Opened to considerable fanfare in 2013, this well-constructed cycling and walking track was intended to connect Alexandra to Roxburgh Dam. As access through some of the farmland in the middle section wasn't successfully negotiated, riding the 'full trail' requires pre-arranging a 13km ferry trip ($95) through

the local information centres. Once you add on the noncompulsory track-maintenance fee ($25), it makes it a very expensive trail indeed. An alternative is to make a return trip from each end: Alexandra–Doctors Point (20km return) or Roxburgh Dam–Shingle Peak (22km return). Note, parts of the trail are rated Grade III and are not recommended for those under 15 years.

From Roxburgh Dam you can continue on the Clutha Gold Trail (www.cluthagold.co.nz), an easier 73km track which follows the Clutha through Roxburgh to Beaumont and then heads to Lawrence. The same maintenance fee covers both tracks.

Altitude Bikes
BICYCLE RENTAL

(☑03-448 8917; www.altitudeadventures.co.nz; 88 Centennial Ave; per day from $25) Rents bikes and organises logistics for riders on the Otago Central, Clutha Gold and Roxburgh Gorge trails.

Clutha River Cruises
BOAT TOUR

(☑03-449 3173; www.clutharivercruises.co.nz; adult/child $90/45; ⊗11am & 2pm Oct-May) Explore the scenery and history of the region on a 2½-hour boat trip; book at the i-SITE.

🛏 Sleeping

Marj's Place
HOSTEL $

(☑03-448 7098; www.marjsplace.co.nz; 5 Theyers St; dm $25-30, s/d $40/70; @ 🤶) The standard varies widely between the three neighbouring houses that comprise Marj's sprawling 'place'. The 'homestay' has private rooms, a Finnish sauna and a spa bath. It's much nicer, not to mention cleaner, than the 'backpackers', which is let mainly to seasonal workers.

Quail Rock
B&B $$

(☑03-448 7224; www.quailrock.co.nz; 5 Fairway Dr; s/d from $100/150) Perched high above town, this very comfortable B&B offers equal servings of privacy and mountain views. Homemade preserves give breakfast a unique touch, and dinners are also available. And yes, quail are often seen scratching around the rocks in the garden.

🍴 Eating

Tin Goose Cafe
CAFE $

(www.thetingoosecafe.com; 22 Centennial Ave; $8-16; ⊗6am-5pm) Start the day with a cooked breakfast and then return for home-style baking and superior counter food, including interesting salads.

WORTH A TRIP

ROXBURGH

Heading south from Alexandra, SH8 winds along rugged, rock-strewn hills above the Clutha River as it passes Central Otago's famous orchards. In season, roadside fruit stalls sell just-picked stone fruit, cherries and berries. En route are a scattering of small towns, many dating from gold-rush days.

Thirteen kilometres south of Alexandra, **Speargrass Inn** (☑03-449 2192; www.speargrassinn.co.nz; 1300 Fruitlands-Roxburgh Rd (SH8), Fruitlands; d $180; 🐾) has three units in attractive gardens. The original 1869 building houses a charming **cafe** (lunch $18-21, dinner $20-31; ⊙9am-4pm Mon & Thu, 9am-7pm Fri-Sun). It's a good place to stop for coffee and cake, and stock up on tasty homemade preserves and chutneys.

Further south, the Clutha broadens into **Lake Roxburgh**, with a large hydroelectric power station at its terminus, before rushing past Roxburgh itself (population 522). Call into the friendly **Visitor Information Centre** (☑03-446 8920; www.centralotagonz.com; 120 Scotland St; ⊙9am-5pm daily Nov-Mar, Mon-Fri Apr-Oct) for information on mountain biking, water sports and seasonal fruit-picking work in the surrounding apple and stone-fruit orchards.

Another source of fruit-picking contacts is **Villa Rose Backpackers** (☑03-446 8761; www.villarose.co.nz; 79 Scotland St; dm $30, d with/without bathroom $105/80; 🐾). This lovely old bungalow has spacious dorm rooms, comfortable self-contained units and a huge modern kitchen.

Before you leave Roxburgh, drop into **Jimmy's Pies** (☑03-444-8596; 143 Scotland St; pies $4-6; ⊙7.30am-5pm Mon-Fri), renowned across the South Island since 1959. If you're at a loss as to which meaty pastry to choose, try the apricot chicken – you're in orchard country after all.

Continuing south from Roxburgh, the road passes through Lawrence and the Manuka Gorge Scenic Reserve, a scenic route through wooded hills and gullies. SH8 joins SH1 near Milton.

Red Brick   EUROPEAN $$$
(☑03-448 9174; www.redbrickrestaurant.co.nz; off Limerick St; dinner $32-33; ⊙4.30pm-late Tue-Sun) Housed in what was Alexandra's first bakery, Red Brick is positioned beside a shoppers' car park, the last place you'd expect to find such sophisticated Modern European cooking. Most ingredients and wines are locally sourced.

ℹ Information

Alexandra i-SITE (☑03-448 9515; www.centralotagonz.com; 21 Centennial Ave; ⊙9am-5pm; 🐾) Pick up a free map of this very spread-out town.

ℹ Getting There & Away

InterCity (☑03-471 7143; www.intercity.co.nz) A daily coach heads to/from Dunedin (from $21, three hours), Roxburgh (from $14, 34 minutes), Clyde (from $15, nine minutes), Cromwell (from $18, 24 minutes) and Queenstown (from $22, 1½ hours).

Atomic Shuttles (☑03-349 0697; www.atomictravel.co.nz) A daily bus heads to/from Dunedin ($30, 2¼ hours), Roxburgh ($15, 30 minutes), Cromwell ($15, 50 minutes) and Wanaka ($20, 1¾ hours).

Alpine Connexions (☑03-443 9120; www.alpineconnexions.co.nz) Shuttles head to/from Dunedin ($40), Clyde ($15), Cromwell ($24), Queenstown ($35) and Wanaka ($35), as well as key stops on the Otago Central Rail Trail.

Clyde

POP 1020

Much more charming than his buddy Alex, 8km down the road, Clyde looks more like a 19th-century gold-rush film set than a real town. Set on the banks of the emerald-green Clutha River, Clyde (www.clyde.co.nz) retains a friendly, small-town feel, even when holidaymakers arrive in numbers over summer. It's also one end of the Otago Central Rail Trail (see p534).

⊙ Sights & Activities

Clyde Historical Museums   MUSEUM
(5 Blyth St; admission by donation; ⊙2-4pm Tue-Sun Sep-Apr) The main building showcases Maori and Victorian exhibits and provides information about the Clyde Dam. Larger

exhibits (machinery, horse-drawn carts etc) are housed in the Herb Factory complex at 12 Fraser St.

Trail Journeys
BICYCLE RENTAL

(📞 03-449 2150; www.trailjourneys.co.nz; 16 Springvale Rd; ⊙ tours Sep-Apr) 🚲 Right by the Rail Trailhead, Trail Journeys rents bikes (from $40 per day) and arranges cycling tours, baggage transfers and shuttles. It also has a depot in Middlemarch.

🎎 Festivals & Events

Clyde Wine & Food Festival
WINE, FOOD

(www.promotedunstan.org.nz) Showcases the region's produce and wines on Easter Sunday.

🛏 Sleeping

Clyde gets crammed with Rail Trailers in February and March, so book in advance.

Post Master's House
B&B $

(📞 03-449 2488; www.postofficecafeclyde.co.nz; 4 Blyth St; d with/without bathroom $125/95) Antique furnishings are dotted around the large and lovely rooms in this pretty stone cottage. Two of the three rooms share an en suite bathroom; the third has its own.

⭐ Dunstan House
B&B $$

(📞 03-449 2295; www.dunstanhouse.co.nz; 29 Sunderland St; s $95, d with/without bathroom from $160/120; ⊙ Oct-Apr; 🛜) This restored late-Victorian balconied inn has lovely bar and lounge areas, and rooms decorated in period style. The less expensive rooms share bathrooms but are just as comfortable and atmospheric.

Oliver's
B&B $$$

(📞 03-449 2600; www.oliverscentralotago.co.nz; Holloway Rd; d $205-345; 🛜) 🚲 Oliver's fills an 1860s merchant's house and stone stables with luxurious rooms decked out with old maps, heritage furniture and claw-foot baths. Most rooms open onto a secluded garden courtyard.

🍴 Eating

Bank Cafe
CAFE $

(www.bankcafe.co.nz; 31 Sunderland St; $9-15; ⊙ 9am-4pm) Grab a table inside or out and tuck into cakes, slices, waffles and delicious burgers. The robust takeaway sandwiches are perfect for lunch on two wheels.

Post Office Café & Bar
CAFE $$

(www.postofficecafeclyde.co.nz; 2 Blyth St; mains $15-32; ⊙ 10am-9pm) Clyde's 1899 post office houses a popular restaurant famous for its garden tables and hearty food. There are loads of nooks and crannies conducive to newspaper perusing.

🛍 Shopping

Central Gourmet Galleria
FOOD

(www.centralone.co.nz; 27 Sunderland St; ⊙ 10am-5pm daily Aug-May, Tue-Sat Jun & Jul) Stocks a selection of award-winning local wines, many of which you won't find anywhere else. There are also plenty of Central Otago foodie treats such as jams and chutneys.

ℹ️ Getting There & Away

InterCity (📞 03-471 7143; www.intercity.co.nz) A daily coach heads to/from Dunedin (from $19, 3¼ hours), Roxburgh (from $12, 44 minutes), Alexandra (from $15, nine minutes), Cromwell (from $10, 14 minutes) and Queenstown (from $13, 1½ hours).

Alpine Connexions (📞 03-443 9120; www.alpineconnexions.co.nz) Shuttles head to/from Dunedin ($40), Alexandra ($15), Cromwell ($24), Queenstown ($35) and Wanaka ($35), as well as key stops on the Otago Central Rail Trail.

Cromwell & Around

POP 4150

Cromwell has a charming lakeside historic precinct, a great weekly farmers market and perhaps the South Island's most over-the-top 'big thing' – a selection of giant fruit by the highway.

It's also at the very heart of the prestigious Central Otago wine region (www.cowa.org.nz), known for its extraordinarily good pinot noir and, to a lesser extent, riesling, pinot gris and chardonnay. The Cromwell Basin – which stretches from Bannockburn, 5km southwest of Cromwell, to north of Lake Dunstan – accounts for over 70% of Central Otago's total wine production. Pick up the *Central Otago Wine Map* for details of upwards of three dozen local wineries.

⊙ Sights & Activities

Old Cromwell Town
HISTORIC BUILDING

(www.oldcromwell.co.nz) When the Clyde Dam was completed in 1992, it flooded the original Cromwell village including the town centre, 280 homes, six farms and 17 orchards. Many historic buildings were disassembled before the flooding and have since been rebuilt in a pedestrianised precinct beside Lake Dunstan. While some have been set up as period pieces (stables and the like), others house some good cafes, galleries and interesting shops. In summer there's an excellent weekly **farmers market** (⊙9am-1pm Sun Nov-Feb) and monthly **craft market** (10am-2pm every 3rd Sun Nov-Feb).

Highlands Motorsport Park MOTOR SPORTS
(⌨03-445 4052; www.highlands.co.nz; cnr SH6 & Sandflat Rd; ⊙10am-5pm) Transformed from a paddock into a topnotch 4km racing circuit in just 18 months, this revheads' paradise hosted its first major event in 2013 – the inaugural three-day Highlands 101, now scheduled to take place every November.

Outside of the big events, budding speed freaks can start out on the go-karts ($35 per 10 minutes) before taking a 200km/h ride in the Highlands Taxi ($75 for two people), completing three laps of the circuit as a passenger in a Porsche GT3 ($295), or having a go at the wheel of a Suzuki Swift GT3 ($295).

If you'd prefer a less racy experience, the **National Motorsport Museum** (adult/child $20/8) showcases racing cars and displays about Kiwi racing legends such as Bruce McLaren, Possum Bourne, Emma Gilmour and Scott Dixon. Plus there's free minigolf.

Goldfields Jet JETBOATING
(⌨03-445 1038; www.goldfieldsjet.co.nz; adult/child $95/49) Zip through the Kawarau Gorge on a 40-minute jetboat ride.

☞ Tours

Central Otago Motorcycle Hire TOUR
(⌨03-445 4487; www.comotorcyclehire.co.nz; 271 Bannockburn Rd; per day from $185) The sinuous and hilly roads of Central Otago are perfect for negotiating on two wheels. This crew hires bikes and advises on improbably scenic routes. They also offer guided Gravel 'n' Gold trail-bike tours (from $195) and extended road tours (from $575).

Bannockburn Historic Goldfields Tours WALKING TOUR
(⌨03-445 1559; www.bannockburngold.co.nz; per person $15-29) Informative tours exploring Bannockburn's gold-mining heritage.

⌂ Sleeping

Cromwell Top 10 HOLIDAY PARK $
(⌨03-445 0164; www.cromwellholidaypark.co.nz; 1 Alpha St; sites $40-42, units with/without bathroom $105/75; @ 🐾) The size of a small European

nation and packed with cabins and self-contained units of various descriptions, all set in tree-lined grounds.

⭐**Burn Cottage Retreat** RENTAL HOUSE $$
(⌨03-445 3050; www.burncottageretreat. co.nz; 168 Burn Cottage Rd; d $195-200; 🐾) Set amongst walnut trees and gardens 3km northwest of Cromwell, Burn Cottage has three luxury self-contained cottages with classy decor, spacious kitchens and modern bathrooms. Bed-and-breakfast accommodation is available in the main house.

Carrick Lodge MOTEL $$
(⌨03-445 4519; www.carricklodge.co.nz; 10 Barry Ave; d $135-160; @ 🐾) One of Cromwell's more stylish motels, Carrick's spacious, modern units are just a short stroll from the main shopping complex. Executive units have spa baths and views over the golf course.

✕ Eating & Drinking

Grain & Seed Café CAFE $
(Melmore Tce; meals $10-14; ⊙9am-4pm) Set in a beautiful stone building that was once Jolly's Grain Store, this cute cafe serves up big, delicious, inexpensive meals. Grab an outside table beside the lake.

⭐**The Shed at Northburn Station** MODERN NZ $$
(⌨03-445 1743; www.northburn.co.nz; 45 Northburn Station Rd; mains $25; ⊙10.30am-4.30pm) Outside tables take advantage of lake and mountain views at this acclaimed winery restaurant, 5km from Cromwell on the eastern side of Lake Dunstan. The seasonal menu consists of only a handful of dishes, done exceptionally well.

Armando's Kitchen CAFE $$
(71 Melmore Tce; breakfast $10-17, lunch $17-22; ⊙9.30am-4pm daily Dec-Mar, Tue-Sun Apr-Nov) Old Cromwell Town is best enjoyed from the heritage verandah of Armando's Kitchen, with an espresso or gourmet ice cream in hand. The homemade pasta, pizza, pies and cakes are all excellent.

Mt Difficulty MODERN NZ $$$
(⌨03-445 3445; www.mtdifficulty.co.nz; 73 Felton Rd, Bannockburn; platters $19-28, mains $35-36; ⊙tastings 10.30am-4.30pm, restaurant noon-4pm) As well as making our favourite pinot noir, Mt Difficulty is a lovely spot for a leisurely lunch looking down over the valley. Desserts are particularly decadent.

ⓘ Information

Cromwell i-SITE (☏ 03-445 0212; www.
centralotagonz.com; 47 The Mall; ⊗ 9am-5pm)
Stocks the *Walk Cromwell* brochure, covering local mountain-bike and walking trails,
including the nearby gold-rush ghost town of
Bendigo.

ⓘ Getting There & Away

InterCity (☏ 03-471 7143; www.intercity.co.nz)
There are four daily coaches to Queenstown
(from $10, one hour), and one to Fox Glacier
(from $44, 6½ hours), Christchurch (from $40,
4¾ hours), Alexandra (from $18, 24 minutes)
and Dunedin (from $20, 3¼ hours).

Alpine Connexions (☏ 03-443 9120; www.
alpinecoachlines.co.nz) Scheduled shuttles to/
from Clyde ($24, 20 minutes), Alexandra ($24,
35 minutes), Queenstown ($25, one hour) and
Wanaka ($25, 45 minutes).

Atomic Shuttles (☏ 03-349 0697; www.
atomictravel.co.nz) Daily buses head to/from
Queenstown ($15, 50 minutes), Alexandra ($15,
50 minutes), Roxburgh ($25, 1¼ hours), Dun-
edin ($30, 3¾ hours) and Christchurch ($40,
5¼ hours).

Catch-a-Bus (☏ 03-449 2024; www.catcha-
bus.co.nz) Bike-friendly shuttles to Clyde (20
minutes), Alexandra (30 minutes), Ranfurly (1¾
hours), Middlemarch (2¾ hours) and Dunedin
(3¾ hours).

Naked Bus (www.nakedbus.com; prices vary)
Buses head to/from Queenstown, Wanaka,
Twizel, Tekapo and Christchurch.

Queenstown & Wanaka

Includes ➡

Queenstown 543
Glenorchy & Around...561
Arrowtown 565
Wanaka 569
Cardrona 577
Lake Hawea 577
Makarora 578

Best Places to Eat

➡ Francesca's Italian Kitchen (p575)

➡ La Rumbla (p568)

➡ Bistro Gentil (p575)

➡ Botswana Butchery (p558)

➡ Fergbaker (p557)

Best Places to Stay

➡ Riversong (p574)

➡ The Dairy (p556)

➡ Altamont Lodge (p573)

➡ Arrowtown Lodge (p567)

➡ Wanaka Bakpaka (p573)

Why Go?

With a cinematic background of mountains and lakes, and a 'what can we think of next?' array of adventure activities, it's little wonder Queenstown tops the itineraries of many travellers.

Slow down slightly in Wanaka – Queenstown's less flashy cousin – which also has good restaurants, bars and outdoor adventures on tap. With Mt Aspiring National Park nearby, you're only a short drive from true New Zealand wilderness.

Slow down even more in Glenorchy, an improbably scenic reminder of what Queenstown and Wanaka were like before the adventure groupies moved in. Negotiate the Greenstone and Routeburn Tracks for extended outdoor thrills, or kayak the upper reaches of Lake Wakatipu.

Across in historic Arrowtown, consider the town's gold-mining past over a chilled wine or dinner in a cosy bistro. The following day there'll be plenty more opportunities to dive back into Queenstown's action-packed whirlwind.

When to Go

➡ The fine and settled summer weather from January to March is the perfect backdrop to Queenstown's active menu of adventure sports and outdoor exploration. March also brings the Gibbston Wine & Food Festival to Queenstown Gardens.

➡ Easter sees an inundation of mountain bikers for the Queenstown Bike Festival.

➡ In late June the Queenstown Winter Festival celebrates the coming of the ski season. From June to August, the slopes surrounding Queenstown and Wanaka are flush with an international crew of ski and snowboard fans.

➡ Spring thaws herald Wanaka Fest in October.

❶ Getting There & Around

Domestic flights head to Queenstown from Auckland, Wellington and Christchurch; for international services, see the Transport chapter. Queenstown is also the main bus hub, with services radiating out to the West Coast (via Wanaka and Haast Pass), Christchurch, Dunedin (via Central Otago), Invercargill and Te Anau. Wanaka also has services to Christchurch and Dunedin.

QUEENSTOWN

POP 12,500

Surrounded by the soaring indigo heights of the Remarkables and framed by the meandering coves of Lake Wakatipu, it's little wonder that Queenstown is a show-off. Noone's ever visited and said, 'I'm bored'. Looking like a small town, but displaying the energy of a small city, Queenstown wears its 'Global Adventure Capital' badge proudly, and most visitors take the time to do crazy things they've never done before.

A new Queenstown is also emerging, with a cosmopolitan restaurant and arts scene, excellent vineyards and five international-standard golf courses. Go ahead and jump off a bridge or out of a plane, but take time to slow down and experience Queenstown without the adrenaline. At the very least, find a lakeside bench at dusk and immerse yourself in one of NZ's most beautiful views.

Queenstown is well used to visitors with international accents, so expect great tourist facilities but also big crowds, especially in summer and winter. Autumn (March to May) and spring (October to November) are slightly quieter, but Queenstown is a true year-round destination.

The town's restaurants and bars are regularly packed with a mainly young crowd that really know how to holiday. If you're a more private soul, drop in to see what all the fuss is about, but then get out and about by exploring the sublime wilderness further up the lake at Glenorchy.

History

The region was deserted when the first Pakeha (white person) arrived in the mid-1850s, although there is evidence of previous Maori settlement. Sheep farmers came first, but after two shearers discovered gold on the banks of the Shotover River in 1862, a deluge of prospectors followed.

Queenstown & Wanaka Highlights

❶ Doing things you've only dreamed about in **Queenstown** (p545), the adrenaline-rush capital of NZ

❷ Soaking up the sophisticated small-town vibe and sublime lake views of **Wanaka** (p569)

❸ Relaxing and dining in **Arrowtown** (p565) after a day's mountain biking and gold panning

❹ Walking the peaceful **Routeburn Track** (p562), arguably the best of NZ's Great Walks.

❺ Exploring the upper reaches of Lake Wakatipu from sleepy **Glenorchy** (p561) by horseback, kayak or jetboat

❻ Restraining the urge to yodel as you stroll through the sublime Matukituki Valley on the **Rob Roy Glacier Track** (p572)

❼ Partying the night away among a multitude of accents on a **Queenstown bar-hop** (p559)

Queenstown Region

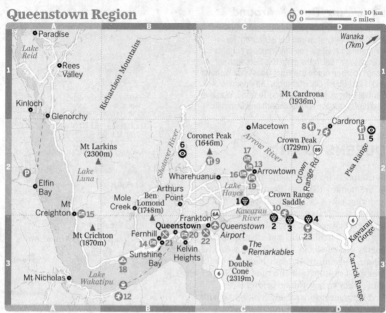

Queenstown Region

◎ Sights
1 Amisfield Winery & Bistro	C2
2 Chard Farm	C3
3 Gibbston Valley Wines	C3
4 Peregrine	D3
5 Pisa Conservation Area	D2
6 Skippers Canyon	B2

✪ Activities, Courses & Tours
7 Backcountry Saddle Expeditions	D2
8 Cardrona Alpine Resort	D2
9 Coronet Peak	C2
Eforea: Spa at Hilton	(see 22)
10 Kawarau Bridge Bungy	C2
11 Snow Farm New Zealand	D2
Spa at Millbrook	(see 16)
12 Walter Peak Farm	B3

⊨ Sleeping
13 Arrowfield Apartments	C2
14 Evergreen Lodge	B3
15 Little Paradise Lodge	A2
16 Millbrook	C2
17 The Arrow	C2
18 Twelve Mile Delta	B3
19 Viking Lodge	C2
20 Villa del Lago	B3

⊗ Eating
21 VKnow	B3
22 Wakatipu Grill	C3

◉ Drinking & Nightlife
23 Gibbston Tavern	D3

Within a year Queenstown was a mining town with streets, permanent buildings and a population of several thousand. It was declared 'fit for a queen' by the NZ government, hence Queenstown was born. Lake Wakatipu was the principal means of transport, and at the height of the boom there were four paddle steamers and 30 other craft plying the waters.

By 1900 the gold had petered out and the population was a mere 190. It wasn't until the 1950s that Queenstown became a popular holiday destination.

◉ Sights

Lake Wakatipu LAKE

Shaped like a perfect cartoon thunderbolt, this gorgeous lake has a 212km shoreline and reaches a depth of 379m (the average depth is over 320m). Five rivers flow into it but only one (the Kawarau) flows out, making it prone to sometimes quite dramatic floods.

If the water looks clean, that's because it is. Scientists have rated it as 99.9% pure – making it the second-purest lake water in the world. In fact, you're better off dipping your glass in the lake than buying bottled water. It's also very cold. That beach by Marine Pde may look tempting on a scorching day, but trust us – you won't want to splash about in water that hovers around 10°C year-round. Because cold water increases the risk of drowning, local bylaws require the wearing of life jackets in all boats under 6m, including kayaks, on all of the district's lakes.

Maori tradition sees the lake's shape as the burnt outline of the evil giant Matau sleeping with his knees drawn up. Local lad Matakauri set fire to the bed of bracken on which the giant slept in order to rescue his beloved Manata, a chief's daughter who was kidnapped by the giant. The fat from Matau's body created a fire so intense that it burnt a hole deep into the ground.

★ **Queenstown Gardens** PARK
(Map p548; Park St) Set on its own little tongue of land framing Queenstown Bay, this pretty park was laid out by those garden-loving Victorians as a place to promenade. The clothes may have changed (they've certainly shrunk), but people still flock to this leafy peninsula to stroll, picnic and laze about. Less genteel types head straight for the frisbee golf course (p550).

Other highlights of the park include an ice-skating rink, skateboard park, lawn-bowling club, tennis courts, mature exotic trees (including large sequoias and some fab monkey puzzles by the rotunda) and a rose garden. There's also a memorial to Captain Robert Scott (1868–1912), leader of the doomed South Pole expedition, which includes an engraving of his moving final message.

St Peter's Anglican Church CHURCH
(Map p552; www.stpeters.co.nz; 2 Church St) This pretty wood-beamed stone building (1932) has an impressive organ and colourful stained glass. Take a look at the eagle-shaped cedar lectern, carved and donated in 1874 by Ah Tong, a Chinese immigrant.

Underwater World VIEWPOINT
(Map p552; www.kjet.co.nz; main jetty; adult/child $5/3; ⊙8.30am-5pm) Six giant windows showcase life under the lake in this reverse aquarium (the people are behind glass). Large brown trout abound, and look out for freshwater eels and scaup (diving ducks), which cruise right past the windows – especially when the coin-operated food-release box is triggered.

Kiwi Birdlife Park BIRD SANCTUARY
(Map p552; www.kiwibird.co.nz; Brecon St; adult/child $42/21; ⊙9am-5pm, shows 11am & 3pm) These 5 acres are home to 10,000 native plants, tuatara and scores of birds, including kiwi, kea, moreporks, parakeets and extremely rare black stilts. Stroll around the aviaries, watch the conservation show, and tiptoe quietly into the darkened kiwi houses.

★ **Skyline Gondola** CABLE CAR
(Map p548; www.skyline.co.nz; Brecon St; adult/child return $27/16) Hop aboard for fantastic views. At the top there's the inevitable cafe, restaurant, souvenir shop and observation deck, as well as the Queenstown Bike Park (p549) and Skyline Luge (p550). At night there are Maori culture shows from Kiwi Haka (p560) and stargazing tours (including gondola adult/child $79/39).

Walking trails include a loop track through the Douglas firs (30 minutes return). The energetic (or frugal) can forgo the gondola and hike to the top on the Tiki Trail (p546).

 Activities

A baffling array of activities is offered by a baffling number of shops in the town centre. It's even more confusing due to the fact that some shops change their name from winter to summer, some run multiple activities from the same shop, and some activities

---

ESSENTIAL QUEENSTOWN & WANAKA

Eat A leisurely lunch at a vineyard restaurant

Drink One of the surprising seasonal brews by Wanaka Beerworks' (p569)

Read *Walking the Routeburn Track* by Philip Holden for a wander through the history, flora and fauna of this tramp

Listen to The silence as you kayak blissfully around Glenorchy and Kinloch

Watch *Top of the Lake*, the Jane Campion–directed TV series set around the top of Wakatipu

Online www.queenstownnz.co.nz; www.lakewanaka.co.nz

Area code ☎ 03

MAORI NZ: QUEENSTOWN & WANAKA

The same transition from moa-hunter to Waitaha, to Ngati Mamoe to Ngai Tahu rule took place here as in other parts of the South Island. Lake Wakatipu is shrouded in legend, and sites to its north were highly valued sources of greenstone.

The Ngai Tahu *iwi* (tribe) owns Shotover Jet (p547) and Dart River Jet Safaris (p563), the latter of which involves a cultural component. Other cultural insights are offered by Kiwi Haka (p560), who perform nightly atop the gondola, and Million Dollar Cruise's Maori culture trips (p550).

are branded differently but are actually the same thing. Several places call themselves information centres, but only the i-SITE (p560) is the true, independent, official information centre.

If you're planning on tackling several activities, various combination tickets are available, including those offered by Queenstown Combos (☑ 03-442 7318; www.combos.co.nz).

Tramping & Climbing

Pick up the *Wakatipu Walks* brochure ($5) from the Department of Conservation (DOC) for local tramping tracks ranging from easy one-hour strolls to tough eight-hour slogs.

Queenstown Hill Walkway HIKING
(Map p548) The strenuous trek up 900m Queenstown Hill takes two to three hours return. Access is from Belfast Tce.

Ben Lomond Track HIKING
(Map p548) The track to the summit of Ben Lomond (1748m, six to eight hours return) is a steep tramp requiring a high-level of fitness and shouldn't be underestimated. Snow and ice can make it even more difficult; in winter check at DOC or the i-SITE before setting out. It starts by following the Tiki Trail from Lomond Ave.

Tiki Trail WALKING
(Map p548) The hour-long walk up to the top of the gondola is not particularly scenic, but the views at the top are excellent. You can access the track from either Brecon St or Lomond Ave.

Guided Nature Walks WALKING
(☑ 03-442 7126; www.nzwalks.com; adult/child from $105/65) Excellent walks in the Queenstown area, including a *Walk & Wine* option and snowshoeing in winter.

Ultimate Hikes HIKING
(Map p552; ☑ 03-450 1940; www.ultimatehikes.co.nz; 9 Duke St; ☺ 8am-6pm Nov-Apr) ✎ Offers day walks on the Routeburn Track (adult/child $169/85) and the Milford Track (adult/child $295/95) from Queenstown. Or you can do the multiday tracks in their entirety, staying in Ultimate Hikes' own staffed lodges rather than DOC huts, where hot meals and en suite bathrooms await (Routeburn/Milford from $1225/1930).

Climbing Queenstown ROCK CLIMBING
(☑ 03-450 2119; www.climbingqueenstown.com; from $149) Rock climbing, via ferrata (climbing with fixed metal rungs, rails, pegs and cables) and alpine trekking led by qualified guides.

Bungy & Swings

AJ Hackett Bungy BUNGY JUMPING
(Map p552; ☑ 03-450 1300; www.bungy.co.nz; The Station, cnr Camp & Shotover Sts) The bungy originators now operate bungy from three sites in the Queenstown area, with giant swings available at two of them. It all started at the historic 1880 Kawarau Bridge (Map p544; adult/child $180/130), 23km from Queenstown (transport included). In 1988 it became the world's first commercial bungy site, offering a 43m leap over the river.

The closest to Queenstown are the Ledge Bungy (Map p548; adult/child $180/130) and Ledge Swing (Map p548; adult/child $150/100) at the top of the Skyline Gondola; the leap is only 47m, but it's 400m above town. In winter you can even leap into the dark.

Last but most pant-wetting is the Nevis Bungy (per person $260) – the highest bungy in Australasia. 4WD buses will transport you from the Kawarau Bridge site onto private farmland where you can jump from a specially constructed pod, 134m above the Nevis River. The Nevis Swing (solo/tandem $320/180) starts 160m above the river and cuts a 300-degree arc across the canyon on a rope longer than a rugby field – yes, it's the world's biggest swing.

Shotover Canyon Swing EXTREME SPORTS
(Map p552; ☑ 03-442 6990; www.canyonswing.co.nz; booking office 35 Shotover St; per person

$215, additional swings $35) *Be released loads of different ways – backwards, in a chair, upside down. From there it's a 60m free fall and a wild swing across the canyon at 150km/h.

White-Water Rafting & Sledging

Queenstown Rafting RAFTING
(Map p552; ☑ 03-442 9792; www.rafting.co.nz; 35 Shotover St; rafting/helirafting $199/285) *Rafts year-round on the choppy Shotover River (Grade III to V) and calmer Kawarau River (Grade II to III). Trips take four to five hours with two to three hours on the water. Helirafting trips are an exciting alternative. Participants must be at least 13 years old and weigh more than 40kg. If you book through other rafting companies such as Extreme Green (☑ 03-442 8517; www.nzraft.com; rafting/helirafting $195/279) and Challenge (☑ 0800 423 836, 03-442 7318; www.raft.co.nz; rafting/helirafting $195/279), you'll end up on the same trips.

Family Adventures RAFTING
(☑ 03-442 8836; www.familyadventures.co.nz; adult/child $179/120) Gentler (Grade I to II) trips on the Shotover suitable for children three years and older. Operates in summer only.

Serious Fun EXTREME SPORTS
(☑ 03-442 5262; www.riversurfing.co.nz; per person $195) The only company to surf the infamous Chinese Dogleg section of the Kawarau River, on what's basically a glorified boogie board.

Frogz EXTREME SPORTS
(☑ 03-441 2318; www.frogz.co.nz; per person $195) Steer buoyant sleds on the rapids and whirlpools of the Kawarau River.

Jetboating

Skippers Canyon Jet JETBOATING
(☑ 03-442 9434; www.skipperscanyonjet.co.nz; Skippers Rd; adult/child $129/79) *Incorporates a 30-minute blast through the narrow gorges of the remote Skippers Canyon (Map p544), on the upper reaches of the Shotover River. The three-hour return trips (picking up from Queenstown accommodation) also cover the region's gold-mining history.

Shotover Jet JETBOATING
(☑ 03-442 8570; www.shotoverjet.com; Gorge Rd, Arthurs Point; adult/child $129/69) *Half-hour trips through the rocky Shotover Canyons, with lots of thrilling 360-degree spins.

K Jet JETBOATING
(Map p552; ☑ 03-409 0000; www.kjet.co.nz; adult/child $119/69) One-hour trips on the Kawarau and Lower Shotover Rivers, leaving from the main jetty.

Skydiving, Gliding & Parasailing

NZone SKYDIVING
(Map p552; ☑ 03-442 5867; www.nzone.biz; 35 Shotover St; 9000-15,000ft jumps $269-439) *Jump out of a perfectly good airplane – with a tandem skydiving expert.

G Force Paragliding PARAGLIDING
(Map p548; ☑ 03-441 8581; www.nzgforce.com; per person $199) Tandem paragliding from the

QUEENSTOWN & WANAKA QUEENSTOWN

QUEENSTOWN IN...

Two Days

Start your day at **Vudu Cafe & Larder** before either hitting the slopes or heading to Shotover St to book your adrenaline-charged activities. Ride the **Skyline Gondola** to get the lay of the land and have a go on the **luge**. Head out on the **Skippers Canyon Jet** and then wind down with a walk through **Queenstown Gardens** to capture dramatic views of the **Remarkables** at dusk. Have a sunset drink at **Pub on Wharf** before dinner at **Botswana Butchery** and an evening of bar-hopping.

The next day fuel up at **Fergbaker** before devoting the morning to snowboarding, bungy jumping, skydiving or white-water rafting. Spend the afternoon on two wheels, either at the **Queenstown Bike Park** or touring around the **Gibbston** wineries. Have dinner at **Public** before hitting the bars.

Four Days

Follow the two-day itinerary, then head to **Arrowtown** to wander the **Chinese settlement** and browse the shops. The following day, drive along the shores of Lake Wakatipu to tiny **Glenorchy**. Have lunch at the **Glenorchy Cafe** and then drive to the trailhead of the **Routeburn Track** for a short tramp.

Queenstown

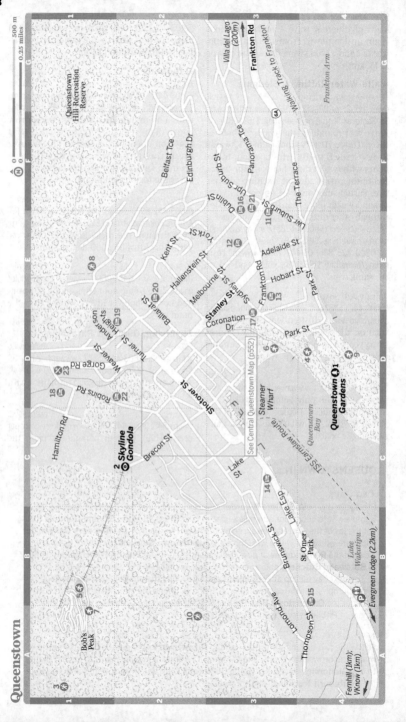

QUEENSTOWN & WANAKA QUEENSTOWN

Queenstown Hill Recreation Reserve

Bob's Peak

Lake Wakatipu

Queenstown Bay

Frankton Arm

Villa del Lago (200m)

Walking Track to Frankton

Frankton Rd

Evergreen Lodge (2.2km)

Fernhill (1km);
VKnow (1km)

See Central Queenstown Map (p552)

TSS Earnslaw Route

Queenstown Route

Steamer Wharf

**Queenstown ()1
Gardens**

**2 Skyline ()
Gondola**

0 500 m
0 0.25 miles

Queenstown

⊙ **Top Sights**
1 Queenstown Gardens D4
2 Skyline Gondola C2

⊙ **Activities, Courses & Tours**
3 Ben Lomond Track A1
4 Frisbee Golf D4
5 G Force Paragliding B1
  Ledge Bungy .... (see 5)
  Ledge Swing .... (see 5)
6 Playground D3
7 Queenstown Bike
  Park A1
8 Queenstown Hill
  Walkway E1
9 Queenstown Ice Arena D4
  Skyline Luge .... (see 5)
10 Tiki Trail A2
  Ziptrek Ecotours .... (see 5)

⊜ **Sleeping**
11 Alexis Queenstown E3
12 Amity Lodge E3
13 Black Sheep Lodge E3
14 Bumbles C3
15 Butterfli Lodge B4
16 Chalet Queenstown B&B F3
17 Coronation Lodge D3
18 Creeksyde Top 10 .... D1
19 Hippo Lodge D2
20 Historic Stone House E2
21 Queenstown Motel Apartments F3
22 Queenstown Park D2

⊗ **Eating**
23 Mediterranean Market D1

⊙ **Entertainment**
  Kiwi Haka .... (see 5)

top of the gondola or from Coronet Peak (9am departures are $20 cheaper).

Coronet Peak Tandem
PARAGLIDING, HANG GLIDING
(☑ 0800 467 325; www.tandemparagliding.com; from $189) Offering spectacular take-offs from Coronet Peak, with free pick-ups from Queenstown accommodation.

Skytrek
PARAGLIDING, HANG GLIDING
(☑ 0800 759 873; www.skytrek.co.nz; from $190) Soar on tandem flights from Coronet Peak; transfers included.

Queenstown Paraflights
PARASAILING
(Map p552; ☑ 0800 225 520; www.paraflights. co.nz; solo/tandem per person $159/129) Float 200m above the lake as you're pulled behind a boat. Departs from the main pier.

Elevation Paragliding School
PARAGLIDING
(☑ 0800 359 444; www.elevation.co.nz; instruction from $240) Learn the paragliding ropes and graduate to four solo flights.

Mountain Biking

With the opening of the Queenstown Bike Park, the region is now firmly established as an international focus for the sport. If you're in town for a while, consider joining the Queenstown Mountain Bike Club (www. queenstownmtb.co.nz).

The Queenstown Trail – more than 100km in total – links five scenic smaller trails showcasing Queenstown, Arrowtown, Gibbston, Lake Wakatipu and Lake Hayes. The trail is suitable for cyclists of all levels

Queenstown Bike Park
MOUNTAIN BIKING
(Map p548; ☑ 03-441 0101; www.queenstown-bikepark.co.nz; Skyline; half-/full day $60/85; ⊙10am-6pm Sep-Nov, Mar & Apr, to 8pm Dec-Feb) Thirteen different trails – from easy (green) to extreme (double black) – traverse Bob's Peak high above the lake. Once you've descended on two wheels, simply jump on the gondola and do it all over again. The best trail for novice riders is the 6km-long Hammy's Track, which is studded with lake views and picnic spots. BYO bike.

Vertigo Bikes
MOUNTAIN BIKING
(Map p552; ☑ 03-442 8378; www.vertigobikes. co.nz; 4 Brecon St; rental half-/full day from $39/59) If you're serious about getting into mountain biking QT-style, Vertigo is an essential first stop. Options include skills training clinics (from $149), guided sessions in the Queenstown Bike Park ($159), downhill rides into Skippers Canyon (two runs $159) and Remarkables helibiking ($399).

Fat Tyre Adventures
MOUNTAIN BIKING
(☑ 0800 328 897; www.fat-tyre.co.nz; tours from $229) Tours cater to different abilities, with day tours, multiday tours, helibiking and singletrack riding. Bike hire and trail snacks are included.

Outside Sports
BICYCLE RENTAL
(Map p552; ☑ 03-441 0074; www.outsidesports. co.nz; 36-38 Shotover St) One-stop shop for bike rentals and trail information. It also sells outdoor gear and rent skis and snowboards in winter.

QUEENSTOWN ON A BUDGET

Play Frisbee golf for free in Queenstown Gardens then hit the hiking trails, or hire a bike for the many tracks in the area. Fuel up at Fergbaker and Fergburger (p557), or head to the Mediterranean Market (p557) for lakeside picnic supplies.

Queenstown Bike Hire   BICYCLE RENTAL
(Map p552; ☑ 03-442 6039; 28 Church St; ☺ 9am-dark) Best for tandems (per hour $30) and lakefront bike rides (per hour/day $14/38). It also hires kayaks, scooters, cars and snow chains.

Skiing & Snowboarding

Queenstowners have two excellent ski fields to choose between in the Remarkables (p47) and Coronet Peak (p47), and when they fancy a change of scenery, there's always Cardrona and Treble Cone (p47) near Wanaka. Coronet Peak is the only field to offer night skiing, which is an experience not to be missed.

The ski season generally lasts from around June to September. Tune into 99.2FM from 6.45am to 9am to hear snow reports. In winter the shops are full of ski gear for purchase and hire; Outside Sports (p549) is a reliable option.

Even outside of the main season, heli-skiing is an option for cashed-up serious skiers; try Over The Top Helicopters (p551), **Harris Mountains Heli-Ski** (☑ 03-442 6722; www.heliski.co.nz; from $825), or **Southern Lakes Heliski** (☑ 03-442 6222; www.heliski.nz.com; from $820).

Other Activities

It would be impractical to list absolutely every activity on offer in Queenstown. If you're interested in golf, minigolf, sailing or diving, enquire at the i-SITE.

Skyline Luge   LUGE
(Map p548; ☑ 03-441 0101; www.skyline.co.nz; Skyline; 1/2/3/5 rides incl gondola $36/39/45/50; ☺ 10am-dusk) Ride the gondola to the top, then hop on a three-wheeled cart to ride the 800m track. Nail the 'scenic' run once and you're allowed on the advanced track with its banked corners and tunnel.

Queenstown Ice Arena   ICE SKATING
(Map p548; ☑ 03-441 8000; www.queenstownicearena.co.nz; 29 Park St; entry incl skate hire $15; ☺ 10am-5pm Sun-Thu, to 9.30pm Fri & Sat Apr-Oct) Slip-slide around the rink or watch a game of ice hockey.

Ziptrek Ecotours   ZIPLINE
(Map p548; ☑ 03-441 2102; www.ziptrek.com; Skyline) ✈ Incorporating a series of ziplines (flying foxes), this harness-clad thrill ride takes you from treetop to treetop high above Queenstown. Ingenious design and eco-friendly values are a bonus. Choose from the two-hour four-line 'Moa' tour (adult/child $129/79) or the gnarlier three-hour six-line 'Kea' option ($179/129).

Canyoning.co.nz   CANYONING
(☑ 03-441 3003; www.canyoning.co.nz) Half-day trips in the nearby 12-Mile Delta Canyons ($185) or the remote Routeburn Valley ($250).

XD Dark Ride   GAMING
(Map p552; ☑ 03-441 8080; 1/7 Earl St; session $30; ☺ 11am-late) Shoot up zombies or Wild West outlaws in the equivalent of a bi-screen multiplayer computer game, with 3D vision, surround sound and multisensory seats. Great fun for a rainy day.

Stu Dever Fishing Charters   FISHING
(☑ 027 433 3052; www.fishing-queenstown.co.nz; 2hr adult/child $120/60) Salmon and trout fishing from the 34ft launch *Chinook*.

Frisbee Golf   FRISBEE
(Map p548; www.queenstowndiscgolf.co.nz; Queenstown Gardens) FREE A series of 18 tree-mounted chain baskets set among the trees; local sports stores sell frisbees and scorecards.

☞ Tours

Lake Cruises

TSS Earnslaw   BOAT TOUR
(Map p552; ☑ 0800 656 501; www.realjourneys.co.nz; Steamer Wharf, Beach St; tours from $55) The stately, steam-powered TSS *Earnslaw* celebrated a centenary of continuous service in 2012. Once the lake's major means of transport, now its ever-present cloud of black soot seems a little incongruous in such a pristine setting. Climb aboard for the standard 1½-hour Lake Wakatipu tour (adult/child $55/22) or take a 3½-hour excursion to the high-country **Walter Peak Farm** (Map p544; adult/child $68/20) for sheep-shearing demonstrations and sheep-dog performances (adult/child $75/22).

Million Dollar Cruise   BOAT TOUR
(Map p552; ☑ 03-442 9770; www.milliondollarcruise.co.nz; ☺ tours 11am, 2pm & 4pm) Good-value,

informative 90-minute cruises heading up the Frankton end of the lake, past the multi-million-dollar real estate of Kelvin Heights ($25). It also offers Maori Culture cruises with commentary by Ngai Tahu guides ($55).

Scenic Flights

Air Milford   SCENIC FLIGHTS
(☑ 03-442 2351; www.airmilford.co.nz) Options include a Milford Sound flyover (adult/child $420/255), a fly-cruise-fly combo ($499/300), and longer flights to Doubtful Sound and Aoraki/Mt Cook.

Glenorchy Air   SCENIC FLIGHTS
(☑ 03-442 2207; www.glenorchy.net.nz) Scenic trips from Queenstown or Glenorchy include a Milford Sound fly-cruise-fly option (adult/child $445/275) and an Aoraki/Mt Cook flyover (adult/child $625/350).

Over the Top Helicopters   HELICOPTER
(☑ 03-442 2233; www.flynz.co.nz; trips from $265) Around Queenstown and beyond.

Sunrise Balloons   BALLOONING
(☑ 03-442 0781; www.ballooningnz.com; adult/child $445/295) One-hour sunrise rides including a champagne breakfast.

Winery Tours

Most tours include wineries in the Gibbston and Cromwell Basin subregions.

Appellation Central Wine Tours   WINE TASTING
(☑ 03-442 0246; www.appellationcentral.co.nz; $175-225) Tours include platter lunches at a winery restaurant.

Queenstown Wine Trail   WINE TASTING
(☑ 03-441 3990; www.queenstownwinetrail.co.nz) Choose from a five-hour tour with tastings at four wineries ($139) or a shorter Summer Sampler tour with lunch included ($160).

Cycle de Vine   CYCLING
(☑ 0800 328 897; www.cycledevine.co.nz; adult/child $155/95; ⊙ Oct-May) Cruise on a retro

---

GIBBSTON WINERIES & WALKS

Gung-ho visitors to Queenstown might be happiest dangling off a giant rubber band, but as they're plunging towards the Kawarau River, they might not realise they're in the heart of Gibbston, one of Central Otago's main wine subregions, accounting for around 20% of plantings.

Almost opposite the Kawarau Bridge, a precipitous 2km gravel road leads to **Chard Farm** (Map p544; ☑ 03-442 6110; www.chardfarm.co.nz; Chard Rd; ⊙ 11am-5pm), the most picturesque of the Gibbston wineries. A further 800m along the Gibbston Hwy (SH6) is **Gibbston Valley Wines** (Map p544; www.gibbstonvalleynz.com; tastings $5-12; ⊙ 10am-5pm), a large complex with a 'cheesery' and a restaurant. Tours of the impressive wine cave leave on the hour from 10am to 4pm ($15 including tastings).

A further 3km along SH6, **Peregrine** (Map p544; ☑ 03-442 4000; www.peregrinewines.co.nz; ⊙ 10am-5pm) is one of Gibbston's top wineries, producing excellent sauvignon blanc, pinot gris, riesling and, of course, pinot noir. Also impressive is the winery's architecture – a bunkerlike building with a roof reminiscent of a falcon's wing in flight.

Although it's just outside Gibbston (and most of its grapes are grown near Cromwell), the best of all the wineries in the Queenstown region is **Amisfield** (Map p544; ☑ 03-442 0556; www.amisfield.co.nz; 10 Lake Hayes Rd; dishes $18-34; ⊙ tasting 10am-6pm, restaurant 11am-3pm & 5.30-8pm), by the shores of Lake Hayes. When you select your five wines for tasting ($8, refundable on purchase), make sure you try some of its internationally acclaimed pinot noir. The highly regarded bistro serves dishes designed to be shared with a few friends on the sunny deck. In the evenings the 'Trust the Chef' menu comes into play (per person $60), where Amisfield's canny chefs magic up tasty diversions based on whatever is in season.

The **Gibbston River Trail** is a scenic walking and mountain-biking track that follows the Kawarau River from the Kawarau Bridge to Peregrine winery (one to two hours, 5km). From Peregrine, walkers (but not cyclists) can continue on the **Wentworth Bridge Loop** (one hour, 2.7km), which crosses over old mining works on timber and steel bridges.

While you're in the area, be sure to call into the impossibly rustic **Gibbston Tavern** (Map p544; www.gibbstontavern.co.nz; 8 Coal Pit Rd), just off the highway past Peregrine. Ask to try the tavern's own Moonshine Wines, as you won't find them anywhere else.

Ask at the Queenstown i-SITE or DOC centre for maps and information about touring.

Central Queenstown

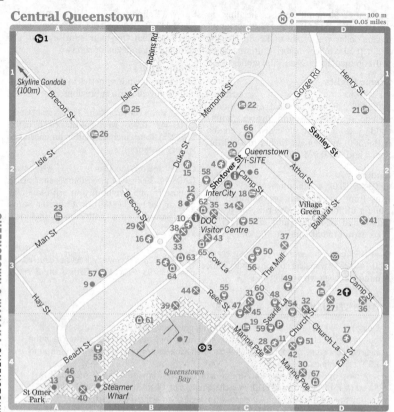

QUEENSTOWN & WANAKA QUEENSTOWN

bicycle around Gibbston. Tours include three different wineries and a picnic lunch beside the meandering Kawarau River.

Milford Sound

Day trips from Queenstown to Milford Sound via Te Anau take 12 to 13 hours, including a two-hour cruise on the sound. Bus-cruise-flight options are also available, as is pick-up from the Routeburn Track finish line. To save on travel time and cost, consider visiting Milford from Te Anau (p581).

BBQ Bus   TOUR
(☎03-442 1045; www.milford.net.nz; adult/child $195/100) Smaller groups (up to 22 people) and a barbecue lunch.

Real Journeys   TOUR
(Map p552; ☎0800 656 501; www.realjourneys. co.nz; Steamer Wharf, Beach St; adult/child from $178/89) Day or overnight tours to Milford and Doubtful Sounds.

Kiwi Discovery   TOUR
(Map p552; ☎03-442 8794; www.kiwidiscovery. com; 37 Camp St) 🍃 Milford Sound trips, ski packages and trailhead transport.

Quad & 4WD Tours

Off Road Adventures   DRIVING TOUR
(Map p552; ☎03-442 7858; www.offroad.co.nz; 61a Shotover St) Exciting off-road 4WD (from $109), quad-bike (from $199) and dirt-bike ($269) tours.

Nomad Safaris   DRIVING TOUR
(Map p552; ☎03-442 6699; www.nomadsafaris. co.nz; 37 Shotover St; adult/child from $169/85) Take in stunning scenery and hard-to-get-to backcountry vistas around Skippers Canyon and Macetown, or head on a 'Safari of the Scenes' through Middle-earth locations around Glenorchy and the Wakatipu Basin. You can also quad-bike through a sheep station on Queenstown Hill ($245).

Central Queenstown

◎ Sights
1 Kiwi Birdlife Park......................A1
2 St Peter's Anglican Church................D3
3 Underwater World.....................C4

✦ Activities, Courses & Tours
4 AJ Hackett Bungy.....................C2
5 Hush Spa.............................B3
K Jet..............................(see 3)
6 Kiwi Discovery.......................C2
7 Million Dollar Cruise.................B4
8 Nomad Safaris........................B2
NZone............................(see 12)
9 Off Road Adventures..................A3
10 Outside Sports.......................B3
11 Queenstown Bike Hire.................C4
Queenstown Paraflights.............(see 3)
12 Queenstown Rafting...................B2
13 Real Journeys........................A4
Shotover Canyon Swing...........(see 12)
14 TSS Earnslaw.........................A4
15 Ultimate Hikes.......................B2
16 Vertigo Bikes........................B3
17 XD Dark Ride.........................D4

⌂ Sleeping
18 Adventure Queenstown.................C2
19 Eichardt's Private Hotel.............C4
20 Goodstays............................C2
21 Haka Lodge...........................D1
22 Last Resort..........................C1
23 Lomond Lodge.........................A2
24 Nomads...............................D3
25 Southern Laughter....................B1
26 The Dairy............................A2

✕ Eating
27 @Thai................................D3
28 Aggy's Shack.........................C4
29 Bella Cucina.........................B3
30 Botswana Butchery....................D4
31 Captain's Restaurant.................C3
32 Devil Burger.........................D3
Eichardt's Bar....................(see 19)
Fergbaker.........................(see 33)
33 Fergburger...........................B3
34 Fishbone.............................C2
35 Habebe's.............................C2
36 Halo.................................D3
37 Kappa................................C3
38 Lick.................................B3
39 Patagonia............................B3
40 Public Kitchen & Bar.................A4
41 Rata.................................D3
42 Sasso................................C4
43 Vudu Cafe............................C3
44 Vudu Cafe & Larder...................B3
45 Winnie's.............................C3

◷ Drinking & Nightlife
46 Atlas Beer Cafe......................A4
47 Ballarat Trading Company.............C3
48 Bardeaux.............................C3
49 Barmuda..............................C3
50 Debajo...............................C3
51 Monty's..............................D4
52 New Zealand Wine Experience..........C3
53 Pub on Wharf.........................A4
54 Searle Lane..........................C3
55 Surreal..............................C3
56 Tardis Bar...........................C3
57 The Find.............................A3
58 World Bar............................C2
59 Zephyr...............................C4

★ Entertainment
60 Reading Cinemas......................C3

ⓐ Shopping
61 Arts & Crafts Market.................B4
62 Fetch................................C2
63 Kapa.................................B3
64 Kathmandu............................B3
65 Small Planet Outlet Store............C3
66 Small Planet Sports..................C2
67 Vesta................................D4

Queenstown Heritage Tours TOUR
(☎03-409 0949; www.queenstown-heritage.co.nz; adult/child $160/80) ✎ Skippers Canyon is reached by a narrow, winding road built by gold panners in the 1800s. This scenic but hair-raising 4WD route runs from Arthurs Point towards Coronet Peak and then above the Shotover River, passing gold-rush sights. Wine tours are also available.

Other Tours
Segway on Q TOUR
(☎03-442 8687; www.segwayonq.com) Explore the town and Queenstown Gardens on a two-hour spin (adult/child $119/109), or cruise for an hour around Queenstown Bay (adult/child $85/75).

Art Adventures GUIDED TOUR
(☎0800 582 878; www.artadventures.co.nz) Provides studio and gallery tours ($200) or the opportunity to work with professional tutors on your own masterpiece ($310).

🎪 Festivals & Events
Gibbston Wine & Food Festival FOOD, WINE
(www.gibbstonwineandfood.co.nz) Gibbston comes to Queenstown Gardens for the day in mid-March.

QUEENSTOWN FOR CHILDREN

While Queenstown is brimming with activities, some of them have age restrictions that may exclude the youngest in your group. Nevertheless, you shouldn't have any trouble keeping the littlies busy.

All-age attractions include Kiwi Birdlife Park (p545), lake cruises on the TSS *Earnslaw* (p550) and 4WD tours of narrow, snaking Skippers Canyon (p547). Queenstown Gardens (p545) has a good beachside playground (Map p548) near the entrance on Marine Pde. Also in the park, Queenstown Ice Arena (p550) is great for a rainy day, and there's Frisbee Golf (p550). The Skyline Gondola (p545) offers a slow-moving activity from dizzying heights. Small children can also ride the luge (p550) with an adult but need to be greater than 110cm in height and six years old to go it alone.

For a high that will make sugar rushes seem passé, a surprising number of activities cater to little daredevils. Children as young as two can take a tandem ride with Queenstown Paraflights (p549), provided the smallest harness fits them. Family Adventures (p547) runs gentler rafting trips suitable for anyone over three. Five-year-olds can take a wilder ride on the Shotover Jet (p547) and six-year-olds can tackle the ziplines with Ziptrek Ecotours (p550). Fearless 10-year-olds can bungy or swing at any of AJ Hackett's jumps (p546), except the Nevis Bungy (minimum age 13).

Several places in town hire out tandem bicycles and child-sized mountain bikes. Queenstown Bike Hire (p550) also rents foot scooters and baby buggies, plus toboggans in winter.

For more ideas and information – including details of local babysitters – see the i-SITE (p560) or www.kidzgo.co.nz.

Queenstown Bike Festival SPORTS
(www.queenstownbikefestival.co.nz) Ten days of two-wheeled action at Easter.

Queenstown Winter Festival SPORTS
(www.winterfestival.co.nz) Ten days of wacky ski and snowboard activities, live music, comedy, fireworks, a community carnival, parade, ball and plenty of frigid frivolity in late June.

Gay Ski Week SPORT, GAY
(www.gayskiweekqt.com) The South Island's biggest and most fun gay and lesbian event in late August/early September.

🛏 Sleeping

Queenstown has endless accommodation options, but midpriced rooms are hard to come by. The hostels, however, are extremely competitive, offering ever-more extras to win custom – they're worth considering even if it's not usually your thing. Places book out and prices rocket during the peak summer (December to February) and ski (June to September) seasons; book well in advance.

Goodstays (Map p552; 🗹 03-442 7518; www.goodstays.co.nz; 1st fl, 19 Camp St) has a huge variety of holiday homes and apartments on its website, with prices ranging from around $150 to $2000 per night; a minimum stay of three nights applies.

Nearby **DOC campsites** (adult/child $6/3) include **Twelve Mile Delta** (Map p544), 11km out of town towards Glenorchy, and Skippers, near Coronet Peak.

🛏 Central Queenstown

Adventure Queenstown HOSTEL $
(Map p552; 🗹 03-409 0862; www.aqhostel.co.nz; 36 Camp St; dm $29-35, d/tr $120/135; @ 🛜) Run by experienced travellers (as evidenced by the photos on display), this central hostel has spotless dorms, a modern kitchen and envy-inducing balconies. Free stuff includes unlimited internet, international calling to 30 countries, bicycles and frisbees. Private rooms have en suite bathrooms (as do some of the dorms), iPod docks and Blueray players.

Haka Lodge HOSTEL $
(Map p552; 🗹 03-442 4970; www.hakalodge.com; 6 Henry St; dm $29-31, r $79; 🅿 🛜) Slap your thighs and kick up your heels, this *haka* is well worth participating in. In response to traveller research, the brightly painted dorms have custom-built bunks including large lockable storage chests, privacy curtains, personal lights and electrical sockets.

Butterfli Lodge HOSTEL $
(Map p548; 🗹 03-442 6367; www.butterfli.co.nz; 62 Thompson St; dm/s/d $30/66/69; 🅿 🛜)

This pretty little hostel sits on a quiet hillside west of the town centre, ruled over by Jimmy the cat. There are no bunks but no en suite bathrooms either. You won't believe the views from the deck.

Nomads
HOSTEL **$**

(Map p552; 03-441 3922; www.nomadshostels.com; 5 Church St; dm $28-37, r $110-135; @ 🛜) With a prime location near Queenstown's nightlife, this massive hostel has facilities galore including its own minicinema, en suite rooms, massive kitchens and an on-site travel agency. It even sweetens the deal with free breakfast and dinner.

Creeksyde Top 10
HOLIDAY PARK **$**

(Map p548; 03-442 9447; www.camp.co.nz; 54 Robins Rd; campsites $49-52, d $77, units with/without bathroom $128/89; P @ 🛜) In a garden setting, this pretty spot has accommodation ranging from basic tent sites to self-contained motel units. Quirky touches include oddball sculptures and an ablutions block disguised as a medieval oast house.

Hippo Lodge
HOSTEL **$**

(Map p548; 03-442 5785; www.hippolodge.co.nz; 4 Anderson Heights; campsites $20, dm $29-30, s $42, d with/without bathroom from $90/70; P @ 🛜) Homely and slightly shabby, this relaxed hostel has a student-flat vibe, although it's a lot cleaner than that implies. The views come with a correspondingly high number of stairs.

Bumbles
HOSTEL **$**

(Map p548; 03-442 6298; www.bumblesbackpackers.co.nz; cnr Lake Esplanade & Brunswick St; campsites/dm/r $20/30/65; P @ 🛜) Enjoying a prime lakeside location, this popular wee hive has colourful decor and a supremely laid-back vibe. The 10 beds are split between one private room and one dorm, and there's limited space for tents and campervans.

Black Sheep Lodge
HOSTEL **$**

(Map p548; 03-442 7289; www.blacksheepbackpackers.co.nz; 13 Frankton Rd; dm $29, d $75-85; P @ 🛜) This place keeps younger social types happy with a spa pool, frisbees and a truckload of DVDs. There are also plenty of private nooks and crannies for escaping with your favourite book. Rooms share bathrooms.

Last Resort
HOSTEL **$**

(Map p552; 03-442 4320; www.tlrqtn.com; 6 Memorial St; dm $30; @ 🛜) Supercentral, this smaller hostel is reached across a tiny brick-and-timber bridge traversing a bubbling brook in the backyard. The setting is lovely but the facilities could do with an upgrade.

Southern Laughter
HOSTEL **$**

(Map p552; 03-441 8828; www.sircedrics.co.nz; 4 Isle St; dm $26-29, r with/without bathroom $80/70; P 🛜) Lame jokes cover the walls of this sprawling old-school hostel. The rooms are fine but the bathrooms are a little shabby. Free veggie soup and a spa pool are added benefits.

Amity Lodge
MOTEL **$$**

(Map p548; 03-442 7288; www.amitylodge.co.nz; 7 Melbourne St; units from $170; P 🛜) In a quiet street around a five-minute walk up from the town centre, this angular white block

---

REMEMBER, YOU'RE ON HOLIDAY...

Here's our pick of the best experiences to slow down, recharge, and remind your body that there's more to the travelling life than scaring yourself silly.

➡ Onsen Hot Pools (p568) has private Japanese-style hot tubs with mountain views. Book ahead and one will be warmed up for you.

➡ To reboot your system after a few days of skiing, biking and jetboating, ease into in-room massage and spa treatments with the **Mobile Massage Company** (0800 426 161; www.queenstownmassage.co.nz; 1hr from $115; 🕘 9am-9pm).

➡ Slow down even more by checking into **Hush Spa** (Map p552; 03-442 9656; www.hushspa.co.nz; 1st fl, 32 Rees St; 30/60min massage from $70/125; 🕘 9am-9pm Tue-Fri, to 7pm Sat) for a massage, hot-rock therapy or a pedicure.

➡ For truly world-class spa treatments, make the short trek to Millbrook near Arrowtown, where the **Spa at Millbrook** (Map p544; 03-441 7017; www.millbrook.co.nz; Malaghans Rd; treatments from $230) has been rated one of the world's best.

➡ Catch a water taxi across the lake to **Eforea: Spa at Hilton** (Map p544; 03-450 9416; www.queenstownhilton.com; Hilton Queenstown, Peninsula Rd; treatments from $120).

has renovated one- and two-bedroom units and friendly owners. The triple glazing is more about keeping out the cold than noise.

Coronation Lodge
LODGE $$

(Map p548; ☑ 03-442 0860; www.coronationlodge. co.nz; 10 Coronation Dr; d $165-185; P 🛜) Right beside Queenstown Gardens, this tidy block has basement parking, plush bed linen, wooden floors and Turkish rugs. Larger rooms have kitchenettes.

Alexis Queenstown
MOTEL $$

(Map p548; ☑ 03-409 0052; www.alexisqueens-town.co.nz; 69 Frankton Rd; unit from $155; P 🛜) This modern hillside motel is an easy 10-minute walk from town along the lakefront. The pleasant self-contained units have thoughtful extras such as stereos and robes, along with beaut lake views.

Queenstown Motel Apartments
MOTEL $$

(Map p548; ☑ 03-442 6095; www.qma.co.nz; 62 Frankton Rd; unit from $125; P @ 🛜) This well-run spot has a mixture of newer units with smart decor, and older, cheaper 1970s-style units. There's a handy on-site laundry, and the lake and mountain views are uniformly great – even from the cheaper accommodation.

Lomond Lodge
LODGE $$

(Map p552; ☑ 03-442 8235; www.lomondlodge. com; 33 Man St; d $145-169; P @ 🛜) A makeover has modernised Lomond Lodge's cosy decor. Share your on-the-road stories with fellow travellers around the garden barbecue. Larger family apartments ($299 for up to four people) are also available.

⭐ The Dairy
BOUTIQUE HOTEL $$$

(Map p552; ☑ 03-442 5164; www.thedairy.co.nz; 10 Isle St; s $435-465, d $465-495; P @ 🛜) 🚩 Once a corner store, the Dairy is now a luxury B&B with 13 rooms packed with classy touches like designer bed linen, silk cushions and luxurious mohair rugs. Rates include cooked breakfasts and freshly baked afternoon teas.

Eichardt's Private Hotel
BOUTIQUE HOTEL $$$

(Map p552; ☑ 03-441 0450; www.eichardtshotel. co.nz; 1-3 Marine Pde; apt $1250-1900, r $1700-1950; P 🛜) Dating from 1867, this restored hotel enjoys an absolute lakefront location. Each of the five giant suites has a fireplace, king-sized bed, heated floor, lake-sized bath tub and lake views. Four nearby apartments are equally luxurious.

Queenstown Park
BOUTIQUE HOTEL $$$

(Map p548; ☑ 03-441 8441; www.queenstown-parkhotel.co.nz; 21 Robins Rd; r $295-395; P 🛜) 🚩 White curtains billow over beds decked out in luxurious linen at this very chic 16-room hotel. The 'Remarkables rooms' have balconies facing over a park to the mountain range (there aren't any lake views). The gondola-facing rooms are smaller but have courtyards; all have kitchenettes.

Historic Stone House
APARTMENTS $$$

(Map p548; ☑ 03-442 9812; www.historicstone-house.co.nz; 47 Hallenstein St; apt from $225; P 🛜) Formerly the mayor's digs, this lovely stone building (1874) has been converted into a three-bedroom apartment, with an additional one-bedroom unit in a wooden extension and another in an elevated building behind it. Inside, modern kitchens and bathrooms meld with antique furniture, while outside there are established gardens and a spa pool.

Chalet Queenstown B&B
B&B $$$

(Map p548; ☑ 03-442 7117; www.chaletqueens-town.co.nz; 1 Dublin St; s/d $195/245; P 🛜) The seven perfectly appointed rooms at this stylish B&B are decked out with flat-screen TVs, interesting original artworks and quality bed linen. All have balconies with views; get in early and request one looking over the lake.

🛏 Surrounds

Shotover Top 10 Holiday Park
HOLIDAY PARK $

(☑ 03-442 9306; www.shotoverholidaypark.co.nz; 70 Arthurs Point Rd, Arthurs Point; campsites $38, units with/without bathroom from $100/65; P @ 🛜) 🚩 High above the Shotover River, this family-friendly park with brand-new motel units is 10 minutes' drive from the hustle and bustle of Queenstown. Fall out of your campervan straight onto the famous Shotover Jet.

Little Paradise Lodge
LODGE $$

(Map p544; ☑ 03-442 6196; www.littleparadise. co.nz; Glenorchy-Queenstown Rd, Mt Creighton; dm $45, r with/without bathroom $140/120) Wonderfully eclectic, this slice of arty paradise is the singular vision of the Swiss/Filipina owners. Each rustic room features wooden floors, quirky artwork and handmade furniture. Outside the fun continues with a back-to-nature swimming hole and well-crafted walkways through beautiful gardens.

Asure Queenstown
Gateway Apartments
MOTEL **$$**

(⌨03-442 3599; www.gateway.net.nz; 1066 Frankton Rd, Frankton; apt from $155; P🐾) On the highway near the airport (and hence cheaper than its equivalents in the town proper), this motel complex has modern two-bedroom split-level apartments with private courtyards. Request a rear unit for a quieter stay.

Villa del Lago
APARTMENTS **$$$**

(Map p544; ⌨03-442 5727; www.villadellago.co.nz; 249 Frankton Rd, Queenstown East; apt from $260; P🐾) 🍴 Clinging to the cliffs between the highway and the lake, these spacious apartments have lake-facing terraces and all the mod cons including a full kitchen, laundry and gas fire. The water taxi stops at the private jetty.

Evergreen Lodge
B&B **$$$**

(Map p544; ⌨03-442 6636; www.evergreenlodge. co.nz; 28 Evergreen Pl, Sunshine Bay; r $695; P@🐾) Tucked away above Sunshine Bay, this luxurious American-run B&B offers bigger-than-Texas rooms in a supremely private location with unfettered lake and mountain views. Add complimentary beer and wine, and a sauna and gym, and you've got a very relaxing escape from Queenstown's bustle.

✖ Eating

Central Queenstown

★ Fergburger
BURGERS **$**

(Map p552; www.fergburger.com; 42 Shotover St; burgers $10-19; ◷8.30am-5am) Queenstown's famous Fergburger has now become a tourist attraction in itself, forcing many locals to look elsewhere for their big-as-your-head gourmet-burger fix. We think the original is still worth the wait. Queue nicely please.

★ Fergbaker
BAKERY **$**

(Map p552; 42 Shotover St; items $6-9; ◷6.30am-4.30am) Fergburger's sweeter sister bakes all manner of tempting treats – and although most things look tasty with 3am beer goggles on, these withstand the daylight test admirably. Goodies include meat pies, filled rolls, danish pastries and banoffee tarts.

Patagonia
SWEETS, CAFE **$**

(Map p552; www.patagoniachocolates.co.nz; 50 Beach St; mains $10-18; ◷9am-8pm; 🐾) Delicious hot chocolate, homemade choccies, and Queenstown's best ice cream – what more do you want? How about a lakefront location and free wi-fi? Start the day with a 'chocolate croissant breakfast' and finish it with warm *churros* (Spanish doughnuts).

Devil Burger
BURGERS **$**

(Map p552; www.devilburger.com; 5-11 Church St; mains $10-19; ◷10.30am-midnight Sun & Mon, to 4am Tue-Sat) Look out Ferg – you've got competition in the Queenstown burger wars. This diabolical new kid on the block also does tasty wraps. Try the hangover-busting 'Walk of Shame' wrap, stuffed with what's basically a full cooked breakfast.

Lick
ICE CREAM **$**

(Map p552; 40 Shotover St; mains $8-13; ◷10am-10pm) Summer? Tuck into gourmet ice cream in flavours like toffee apple or macadamia nut. Winter? How about hearty concoctions such as soup and fresh pasta.

Aggy's Shack
FISH & CHIPS **$**

(Map p552; cnr Marine Pde & Church St; $9-20; ◷11am-10pm) Head to this simple lakeside gazebo for fish and chips, including juicy blue cod, and the opportunity to try a few Maori flavours like smoked eel, kina (sea urchin) and titi (muttonbird).

Habebe's
MIDDLE EASTERN **$**

(Map p552; www.habebes.co.nz; Plaza Arcade, 30 Shotover St; meals $8-17; ◷8am-5.30pm; 🍴) Middle Eastern–inspired salads and wraps. Soups and yummy pies (try the chicken, kumara and mushroom one) break the mould.

Mediterranean Market
DELI **$**

(Map p548; www.mediterranean.co.nz; 53 Robins Rd; ◷8am-6.30pm Mon-Sat, 10am-6pm Sun) Fill up a basket for a lakeside picnic from this fantastic deli and bakery.

Public Kitchen & Bar
MODERN NZ **$$**

(Map p552; ⌨03-442 5969; www.publickitchen. co.nz; Steamer Wharf, Beach St; dishes $15-45; ◷noon-11pm) The trend towards informal, shared dining has come to Queenstown in the form of this excellent waterfront eatery. Grab a posse and order a selection of plates of varying sizes from the menu; the meaty dishes, in particular, are excellent.

Vudu Cafe & Larder
CAFE **$$**

(Map p552; www.vudu.co.nz; 16 Rees St; mains $13-19; ◷7.30am-6pm) Excellent home-style baking combines with great coffee and tasty cooked breakfasts at this cosmopolitan cafe. Admire the huge photo of a much less-populated Queenstown from an inside table, or head through to the rear garden for lake and mountain views. There's another branch (Map p552; 23 Beach St) around the corner.

Eichardt's Bar
TAPAS $$

(Map p552; www.eichardtshotel.co.nz; 1-3 Marine Pde; breakfast $16-18, lunch $24-26, tapas $7-10; ⊙7.30am-10pm) Elegant without being stuffy, this small bar attached to Eichardt's Private Hotel is a wonderful refuge from the buzz of the streets. Foodwise, tapas is the main focus – and although the selection isn't particularly Spanish, it is particularly delicious.

Sasso
ITALIAN $$

(Map p552; ☑03-409 0994; www.sasso.co.nz; 14-16 Church St; mains $25-36; ⊙4-10pm) Whether you're snuggled by one of the fireplaces inside the stone cottage (1882) or you've landed a table under the summer stars on the front terrace, this upmarket Italian eatery isn't short on atmosphere. Thankfully the food's excellent too.

Captain's Restaurant
EUROPEAN $$

(Map p552; ☑03-441 1633; www.captains.co.nz; 11 The Mall; brunch $14-27, dinner $28-50; ⊙9am-late) Exposed stone walls add atmosphere inside, but the people-watching opportunities of the street tables can't be beaten on a sunny day. The menu morphs from cafe-style dishes to heartier bistro classics as the day progresses.

Winnie's
PIZZERIA, BAR $$

(Map p552; www.winnies.co.nz; L1, 7 The Mall; mains $16-28; ⊙noon-late; 🖘) Part-bar and part-restaurant, Winnie's always seems busy. Pizzas with a Thai, Mexican or Moroccan accent and massive burgers, pasta and steaks soak up the alcohol and keep energy levels high. On balmy nights the whole roof opens up and the party continues until the wee smalls.

Bella Cucina
ITALIAN $$

(Map p552; ☑03-442 6762; www.bellacucina.co.nz; 6 Brecon St; mains $26-36; ⊙5-10pm) Settle into one of Queenstown's cosiest and most romantic dining rooms and tuck into beautifully simple food done just right. Fresh pasta and risotto are highlights, while the rustic woodfired pizza is perfect for sharing.

Halo
CAFE $$

(Map p552; ☑03-441 1411; www.haloforbiddenbite. co.nz; Camp St; brunch $11-19, dinner $23-29; ⊙7am-5pm Mon & Tue, to 9pm Wed-Sun) This stylish, sunny place effortlessly blurs the line between breakfast, lunch and dinner. The breakfast burrito will set you up for a day's adventuring. There's plenty of outdoor seating.

Kappa
JAPANESE $$

(Map p552; L1, 36a The Mall; lunch $11-14, dinner $17-28; ⊙noon-10pm) Queenstown's best Japanese eatery is also its most casual. Fresh tuna and salmon feature in good-value lunchtime bento boxes. Later on, linger longer with excellent tempura and Japanese beer and sake. In summer watch the passing parade from the upstairs deck.

@Thai
THAI $$

(Map p552; www.atthai.co.nz; L1, 8 Church St; lunch $15, dinner $17-28; ⊙noon-10pm Wed-Mon) Head up the semihidden set of stairs for *pad Thai* worth writing home about, and *hor-mok* seafood red curry that will blow your mind. Takeaways are also available.

★ Botswana Butchery
MODERN NZ $$$

(Map p552; ☑03-442 6994; www.botswanabutchery.co.nz; 17 Marine Pde; mains $34-45; ⊙noon-11pm) Lake views and schmick interiors set the scene for a scintillating menu that's predominantly but not exclusively meaty, and a wine list of telephone-directory dimensions. The $15 Express Lunch is a great deal.

Rata
MODERN NZ $$$

(Map p552; ☑03-442 9393; www.ratadining.co.nz; 43 Ballarat St; mains $37-38; ⊙noon-11pm) After gaining Michelin stars for restaurants in London, New York and LA, chef-owner Josh Emett has brought his exceptional but surprisingly unflashy cooking back home in the form of this upmarket but informal back-lane eatery. Native bush sets the scene for a short menu showcasing the best seasonal NZ produce.

Fishbone
SEAFOOD $$$

(Map p552; ☑03-442 6768; www.fishbonequeenstown.co.nz; 7 Beach St; mains $29-38; ⊙5-10pm) Queenstown's more than a few miles inland, but that doesn't prevent Fishbone from sourcing the best NZ seafood. Everything from scallops to snapper is treated with a light and inventive touch.

✖ Surrounds

VKnow
MODERN NZ $$

(Map p544; ☑03-442 5444; www.vknow.co.nz; 155 Fernhill Rd, Fernhill; pizzas $19-30, mains $26-36; ⊙4pm-late) We agree, the name is dumb. But don't let that put you off this extremely friendly, casual restaurant – the kind that everyone wishes was tucked away in their neighbourhood. The menu showcases local venison, blue cod and Canterbury lamb.

Wakatipu Grill
EUROPEAN $$$

(Map p544; ☑03-450 9400; www.queenstown-hilton.com; Hilton Queenstown, Peninsula Rd, Kelvin Heights; mains $34-52; ⊘4pm-late Wed-Sun) The Hilton sprawls along the lakeside by the Kawarau River outlet, and part of the fun of visiting its signature restaurant is the 8km water-taxi ride. The grill menu stretches to Fred Flintstone–sized Angus T-bones but would-be Wilmas can opt for freshly shucked oysters, pasta or French-influenced fish, lamb and duck dishes.

Gantley's
FRENCH $$$

(☑03-442 8999; www.gantleys.co.nz; 172 Arthurs Point Rd, Arthurs Point; mains $37-44; ⊘6-10pm) Gantley's French-influenced menu and highly regarded wine list justify the 7km journey from Queenstown. The atmospheric dining experience is showcased in a stone-and-timber building, built in 1863 as a wayside inn. If you feel like splurging, try the six-course *degustation* ($90).

🍷 Drinking & Nightlife

Drinking is almost a competitive sport in Queenstown, and there's a good range of options for after-dark carousing. Live music and clubbing are a nightly affair, and even on Monday and Tuesday nights you should have no problem finding a bar open until 4am.

A couple of outfits run organised pub crawls, where a wristband buys you a riotous night of discounted drinks, giveaways and games along the way; look for the ads in hostels and bars around town.

Ballarat Trading Company
PUB

(Map p552; www.ballarat.co.nz; 7-9 The Mall; ⊘11am-late) Stuffed bears, rampant wall-mounted ducks and a re-created colonial general store – there's really no competition for the title of Queenstown's most eclectic decor. Beyond the grab bag of infuences, Ballarat is quite a traditional spot, with gleaming beer taps, sports on TV, occasional lapses into 1980s music and robust meals.

Zephyr
BAR

(Map p552; 1 Searle Lane; ⊘8pm-4am) Queenstown's coolest indie rock bar is located – as all such places should be – in a grungy basement off a back lane.

Pub on Wharf
PUB

(Map p552; www.pubonwharf.co.nz; 88 Beach St; ⊘10am-late; 🛜) Ubercool interior design combines with handsome woodwork and lighting fit for a hipster hideaway. Fake sheep heads reinforce that you're still in NZ, and Mac's beers on tap, scrummy nibbles and a decent wine list make this a great place to settle in for the evening. There's live music nightly.

Monty's
PUB

(Map p552; www.montysbar.co.nz; 12 Church St) On warm summer days, the patio at this Monteith's Brewery 'concept bar' is prime real estate. Bands crank up from Thursday to Sunday night.

New Zealand Wine Experience
WINE BAR

(Map p552; ☑03-409 2226; www.winetastes.com; 14 Beach St; ⊘10.30am-10pm) Here's something different: load up cash on a smart card and then help yourself to tasting pours or glasses of over 90 NZ wines dispensed through an automated gas-closure system. There's also a whisky corner, and cheese platters are available.

Bardeaux
WINE BAR

(Map p552; Eureka Arcade, Searle Lane; ⊘4pm-4am) This small, low-key, cavelike wine bar is all class. Under a low ceiling are plush leather armchairs and a fireplace made from Central Otago schist. The wine list is extraordinary, with the price of several bottles reaching four digits.

Atlas Beer Cafe
BAR

(Map p552; www.atlasbeercafe.com; Steamer Wharf, Beach St; ⊘10am-2am) Perched at the end of Steamer Wharf, this pint-sized bar specialises in beers from Dunedin's Emerson's Brewery and regular guest beers from further afield. The small but tasty food menu includes tapas.

Searle Lane
BAR

(Map p552; www.searlelane.co.nz; 15 Church St; ⊘11am-late) Pool tables, lunch specials and shared rotisserie chickens make this a top spot for getting to know any new arrivals at your hostel. Free-flowing beer and well-mixed cocktails will help things along.

Barmuda
COCKTAIL BAR

(Map p552; Searle Lane; ⊘3pm-late) A huge open fire makes Barmuda's walled-in courtyard an inviting space, even in cooler weather.

Surreal
BAR

(Map p552; www.surrealbar.co.nz; 7 Rees St; ⊘noon-late; 🛜) The big attraction at this otherwise average bar is the roof terrace – a wonderfully hidden-away spot for an alfresco drink. Later in the evening DJ-inspired goings-on kick off and the dance floor comes to life. Tuesday is open-mic night.

Debajo
CLUB

(Map p552; www.facebook.com/Debajoqueenstown; Cow Lane; ⊙10pm-4am) The perennial end-of-night boogie spot – house and big beat gets the dance floor heaving till closing time.

Tardis Bar
BAR

(Map p552; www.tardisbar.com; Skyline Arcade, 20 Cow Lane) A good dance bar with regular DJs playing hip-hop, drum 'n' bass and dub. Like Dr Who's phone booth, it's surprisingly roomy inside.

World Bar
BAR

(Map p552; www.theworldbar.co.nz; 27 Shotover St; ⊙4pm-late) Before it was destroyed by fire in 2013, the World Bar was Queenstown's legendary party hub. At the time of writing, ambitious rebuilding plans were well underway and we're hoping it will reopen before this book hits the shelves. If not, the same crew is running The Find (Map p552; 53 Shotover St) as a pop-up gap-filler, just down the road.

☆ Entertainment

Pick up the *Source* (www.facebook.com/SourceNZ), a free monthly flyer with a gig guide and events listings.

Kiwi Haka
TRADITIONAL DANCE

(Map p548; ☑03-441 0101; www.skyline.co.nz; Skyline; adult/child excl gondola $39/26) For a traditional Maori cultural experience, head to the top of the gondola. There are three 30-minute shows nightly; bookings are essential.

Reading Cinemas
CINEMA

(Map p552; ☑03-442 9990; www.readingcinemas.co.nz; 11 The Mall; adult/child $17/11) Discounts on Tuesdays.

🛍 Shopping

★ Vesta
ARTS & CRAFTS

(Map p552; www.vestadesign.co.nz; 19 Marine Pde; ⊙10.30am-5.30pm) Showcasing really cool NZ-made art and craft, Vesta is full of interesting prints, paintings, glass art and gifts. It's housed in Williams Cottage (1864), Queenstown's oldest home. It's worth visiting just to check out the 1930s wallpaper and 1920s garden.

Kapa
ARTS & CRAFTS

(Map p552; www.kapa.co.nz; 29 Rees St; ⊙10am-8pm) Quirky and eclectic NZ design infused with a healthy dose of contemporary Maori culture.

Fetch
CLOTHING

(Map p552; www.fetchnz.com; 34 Shotover St; ⊙10am-6pm) Grab a uniquely Kiwi hand-screened T-shirt or create your own design as a wearable souvenir of the time you bungied, mountain-biked and ziplined to adventure-sports nirvana.

Kathmandu
OUTDOOR EQUIPMENT

(Map p552; www.kathmandu.co.nz; 88 Beach St; ⊙10am-6pm) A well-known and good-quality NZ-founded chain selling tents, sleeping bags, rugged backpacks, active footwear and stylish adventure clothing.

Small Planet Sports
OUTDOOR EQUIPMENT

(Map p552; www.smallplanetsports.com; 17 Shotover St; ⊙9am-7pm Oct-May, 8am-9pm Jun-Sep) New and used outdoor equipment. There's also a cheaper outlet store (Map p552; 23 Beach St) in town.

Arts & Crafts Market
MARKET

(Map p552; www.marketplace.net.nz; Earnslaw Park; ⊙9.30am-3.30pm Sat) Locally crafted gifts and souvenirs, on the lakefront beside Steamer Wharf.

ℹ Information

DOC Visitor Centre (Department of Conservation; Map p552; ☑03-442 7935; www.doc.govt.nz; 38 Shotover St; ⊙8.30am-5pm) Backcountry Hut Passes and weather and track updates; on the mezzanine floor above Outside Sports. Head here to pick up confirmed bookings for the Routeburn Track.

Queenstown i-SITE (Map p552; ☑03-442 4100; www.queenstown-vacation.com; cnr Shotover & Camp Sts; ⊙8.30am-7pm) Friendly and informative (but perpetually frantic), the staff can help with bookings and information on Queenstown, Gibbston, Arrowtown and Glenorchy.

ℹ Getting There & Away

AIR

For information on international flights, see the Transport chapter. Both **Air New Zealand** (☑0800 737 000; www.airnewzealand.co.nz) and **Jetstar** (☑0800 800 995; www.jetstar.com) fly to Queenstown from Auckland, Wellington and Christchurch.

BUS

Most buses and shuttles stop on Athol St or opposite the i-SITE; check when you book.

Alpine Connexions (☑03-443 9120; www.alpinecoachlines.co.nz) Shuttles head to/from Cardrona ($35), Wanaka ($35), Cromwell ($25), Alexandra ($35) and Dunedin ($45), as well as key stops on the Otago Central Rail Trail.

Atomic Shuttles (☏03-349 0697; www. atomictravel.co.nz) Daily bus to Cromwell ($15, 50 minutes), Omarama ($30, 2¼ hours), Twizel ($30, 3¼ hours), Lake Tekapo ($30, 3¾ hours) and Christchurch ($50, seven hours).

Connect Wanaka (www.connectabus.com) Heads to/from Wanaka twice daily ($35, 1½ hours).

InterCity (Map p552; ☏03-442 4922; www. intercity.co.nz) Daily coaches to/from Wanaka (from $17, 1½ hours), Franz Josef (from $62, eight hours), Dunedin (from $22, 4¼ hours) and Invercargill ($48, three hours), and twice daily to Christchurch (from $55, eight to 11 hours).

Naked Bus (www.nakedbus.com) Two buses to Wanaka (1¼ hours) daily; one to Cromwell (one hour), Franz Josef (six hours) and Christchurch (nine hours); and less frequent services to Te Anau (2¾ hours). Prices vary.

TRAMPERS' & SKIERS' TRANSPORT

Kiwi Discovery (p552) also offers mountain and trailhead transport.

Info & Track Centre (☏03-442 9708; www. infotrack.co.nz; 37 Shotover St; ⏱7.30am–8pm) During the Great Walks season, this agency provides transfers to the trailheads for the Routeburn, Greenstone and Caples, and Rees-Dart Tracks.

NZSki Snowline Express (www.nzski.com; return $15) During the ski season shuttles depart from outside the Snow Centre on Duke St every 20 minutes from 8am until 11.30am, heading to both Coronet Peak and the Remarkables. Buses return as they fill up, from 1.30pm onwards. They also leave on the hour from 4pm to 7pm for night skiing at Coronet Peak, returning on the half hour from 5.30pm to 9.30pm.

Trackhopper (☏021-187 7732; www.trackhopper.co.nz; from $230, plus fuel costs) Offers a handy car-relocation service from either end of the Routeburn, Greenstone and Caples and Rees-Dart Tracks.

ⓘ Getting Around

TO/FROM THE AIRPORT

Queenstown Airport (ZQN; Map p544; ☏03-450 9031; www.queenstownairport.co.nz; Sir Henry Wrigley Dr, Frankton) is 7km east of the town centre.

Connnectabus (☏03-441 4471; www.connectabus.com) route 11 runs to to the airport from Camp St every 15 minutes from 6.50am to 11pm (adult/child $8/5). There are also services to Arrowtown and Wanaka.

Super Shuttle (☏0800 748 885; www.supershuttle.co.nz; fare $16) picks up and drops off in Queenstown.

Queenstown Taxis (☏03-450 3000; www.queenstown.bluebubbletaxi.co.nz) and **Green**

Cabs (☏0508 447 336; www.greencabs.co.nz) charge around $35.

PUBLIC TRANSPORT

Connnectabus (☏03-441 4471; www.connectabus.com) has various colour-coded routes, reaching as far as Sunshine Bay, Fernhill, Arthurs Point, Frankton and Arrowtown. A day pass (adult/child $20/12) allows travel on the entire network. Pick up a route map and timetable from the i-SITE. Buses leave from Camp St.

AROUND QUEENSTOWN

Glenorchy & Around

POP 360

Set in achingly beautiful surroundings, postage-stamp-sized Glenorchy is the perfect low-key antidote to Queenstown. An expanding range of adventure operators will get you active on the lake and in nearby mountain valleys by kayak, horse or jetboat, and if you prefer to strike out on two legs, the mountainous region at the northern end of Lake Wakatipu is the setting for some of the South Island's finest tramps.

Those with sturdy wheels can explore the superb valleys north of Glenorchy. **Paradise** lies 15km northwest of town, just before the start of the Dart Track (p562). Keep your expectations low: Paradise is just a paddock, but the gravel road there runs through beautiful farmland fringed by majestic mountains. You might recognise it from *The Lord of the Rings (LOTR)* movies as the approach to both Isengard and Lothlorien.

🏃 Activities

Almost all organised activities offer shuttles to and from Queenstown for a small surcharge. Other activities on offer include farm tours, fly-fishing, guided photography tours and cookery classes; enquire at the Queenstown i-SITE (p560).

Tramping

DOC's *Head of Lake Wakatipu* and *Wakatipu Walks* brochures (both $5) detail day walks taking in the Routeburn Valley, Lake Sylvan, Dart River and Lake Rere. Two of the best short tracks are the **Routeburn Nature Walk** (one hour), at the start of the Routeburn Track, and the **Lake Sylvan tramp** (one hour 40 minutes).

Before setting out on any of the longer tramps, call into DOC in Queenstown (p560) or **Te Anau** (📋 03-249 7924; www.doc.govt.nz; cnr Lakefront Dr & Te Anau-Manapouri Rd; ⊘8.30am-4.30pm, to 6pm 9 Dec-16 Mar) for the latest track conditions and to purchase detailed maps. Another good resource is Lonely Planet's *Tramping in New Zealand*.

For track snacks or meals, stock up on groceries in Queenstown. Track transport is at a premium during the summer Great Walks season (late October to March); try to book in advance. Many of the local accommodation providers offer trailhead transport; see p561 for services from Queenstown.

★**Routeburn Track** HIKING
(www.doc.govt.nz; huts/campsites Nov-Apr $54/18, May-Oct $15/5) Passing through a huge variety of landscapes with fantastic views, the 32km-long, two- to four-day Routeburn Track is one of the most popular rainforest/subalpine tracks in NZ. It's one of NZ's nine designated 'Great Walks', and many trampers rate it as the very best.

Increased pressure on the track has necessitated the introduction of an online booking system in the Great Walks season, which covers all huts and campsites on the route. You'll then need to call into the DOC Visitor Centre in either Queenstown or Te Anau to collect actual tickets, either the day before or on the day of departure. Outside of the season, bookings aren't required but you'll still need to visit one of the DOC centres to purchase your hut and campsite tickets.

The Routeburn track remains open in winter. However, to traverse the alpine section after the snow falls is not recommended for casual hikers, as winter mountaineering skills are required. There are 32 avalanche paths across the section between Routeburn Falls hut and Howden hut, and the avalanche risk continues through to spring. Always check conditions with DOC.

The track can be started from either end. Many people travelling from Queenstown try to reach the **Divide** in time to catch the bus to Milford and connect with a cruise on the sound. En route, you'll take in breathtaking views from **Harris Saddle** and the top of nearby **Conical Hill**, from where you can see waves breaking at Martins Bay. From **Key Summit**, there are panoramic views of the Hollyford Valley and the Eglinton and Greenstone River Valleys.

There are car parks at both ends of the track, but they're unattended, so don't leave any valuables in your car.

ROUTE	ESTIMATED WALKING TIME (HR)
Routeburn Shelter to Flats Hut	1½-2½
Flats Hut to Falls Hut	1-1½
Falls Hut to Mackenzie Hut	4½-6
Mackenzie Hut to Howden Hut	3-4
Howden Hut to the Divide	1-1½

Greenstone & Caples Tracks HIKING
(huts adult/child $15/5) Following meandering rivers through peaceful valleys, these tracks form a loop that many trampers stretch out into a moderate four- or five-day tramp. Basic huts en route are Mid Caples, Upper Caples, McKellar and Greenstone; Backcountry Hut Passes must be purchased in advance.

Both tracks meet up with the Routeburn Track; you can either follow its tail end to the Divide or (if you've prebooked) pursue it back towards Glenorchy. From McKellar Hut you can tramp two or three hours to Howden Hut on the Routeburn Track, which is an hour from the Divide.

Access to the Greenstone and Caples Tracks is from Greenstone Wharf; nearby you'll find unattended parking.

ROUTE	ESTIMATED WALKING TIME (HR)
Greenstone Wharf to Mid Caples Hut	2-3
Mid Caples Hut to Upper Caples Hut	2-3
Upper Caples Hut to McKellar Hut	5-8
McKellar Hut to Greenstone Hut	5-7
Greenstone Hut to Greenstone Wharf	3-5

Rees-Dart Track HIKING
(huts/campsites $15/5) This is a difficult, demanding four- to five-day circular route from the head of Lake Wakatipu, taking you through valleys and over an alpine pass, with the possibility of a side trip to the Dart Glacier if you're suitably equipped and experienced. Access by vehicle is possible as far as Muddy Creek on the Rees side, from where it's six hours to Shelter Rock Hut.

Most people go up the Rees track first and come back down the Dart. Backcountry Hut Passes must be purchased in advance for the

Routeburn, Greenstone & Caples Tracks

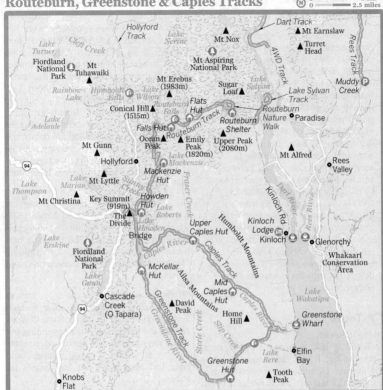

three basic DOC huts (Shelter Rock, Daleys Flat and Dart).

ROUTE	ESTIMATED WALKING TIME (HR)
Muddy Creek to Shelter Rock Hut	6-8
Shelter Rock Hut to Dart Hut	4-6
Dart Hut to Daleys Flat Hut	5-7
Daleys Flat Hut to Paradise	6-8

Horse Riding

Dart Stables HORSE RIDING
(☑03-442 5688; www.dartstables.com; Coll St) Options include a two-hour 'River Wild' ride ($135) and a 1½-hour 'Ride of the Rings' trip ($175) for Hobbity types. If you're really keen, consider the overnight two-day trek with a sleepover in Paradise ($705).

High Country Horses HORSE RIDING
(☑03-442 9915; www.high-country-horses.co.nz; Priory Rd) Offers many choices, ranging from an hour-long 'Rees River Ride' ($80) to overnight and multiday treks.

Other Activities

Dart River Jet Safaris JETBOATING
(☑03-442 9992; www.dartriver.co.nz; adult/child $219/119; ⏱departs 9am & 1pm) Journeys into the heart of the Dart River wilderness, including a short walk through the beech forest and a 4WD trip. The round trip from Glenorchy takes three hours. You can also combine a jet-boat ride with a river descent in an inflatable three-seater 'funyak' (adult/child $319/219). Prices include Queenstown pick-ups.

Skydive Paradise SKYDIVING
(☑03-442 8333; www.skydiveparadise.co.nz; Glenorchy airport; 12,000-15,000ft jump $335-409) Tandem skydiving above some of the planet's most spectacular scenery.

LOCAL KNOWLEDGE

THE REES VALLEY

Acclaimed NZ film-maker Jane Campion, whose 2013 TV series *Top of the Lake* was filmed in the region, reflects on her connection to the Rees Valley.

'As many times a year as I can, I travel to a holiday hut up the Rees Valley, at the top end of Lake Wakatipu. I love the lake, the majesty of the surrounding mountains, the good weather in the basin, the walks, the rivers, the end-of-the-world feeling and the laconic people who live nearby. Everyone who has visited me up here is infected by the ready magic of the landscape and the sensation of worldly troubles dissolving. Lake Sylvan is one of many good bush walks in the area – a fairly short walk for this scale of landscape, but the intimacy of being inside the bush immediately gives you a sense of delight. Recently the lake has been high and is phenomenal to swim in.'

☞ Tours

Ultimate Hikes
WALKING TOUR
(☑ 03-450 1940; www.ultimatehikes.co.nz; ⊙ Nov–mid-Apr) If you fancy comfort while adventuring, Ultimate Hikes offers a three-day guided tramp on the Routeburn (from $1225); a six-day Grand Traverse, combining walks on the Routeburn and Greenstone Tracks (from $1660); and the Classic, an eight-day tour combining the Routeburn and Milford Tracks (from $3155). All trips include meals and accommodation in Ultimate's own comfortable huts. It also offers a one-day Routeburn Encounter ($169).

Glenorchy Base
WALKING TOUR
(☑ 03-409 0960; www.glenorchybase.co.nz; half-/full day from $350/420) Specialises in guided walks around the Glenorchy area. Highlights include bird-watching around Lake Sylvan and a Routeburn Track day walk.

Private Discovery Tours
DRIVING TOUR
(☑ 03-442 2299; www.rdtours.co.nz) Half-day 4WD tours head through a high-country sheep station in a remote valley between Mts Earnslaw and Alfred (adult/child $185/92). Full-day tours include LOTR sites around Paradise (adult/child $295/150). Prices include pick-up from Queenstown.

🛏 Sleeping & Eating

Kinloch Lodge
LODGE, CAFE $
(☑ 03-442 4900; www.kinlochlodge.co.nz; Kinloch Rd; dm $35, d with/without bathroom from $140/85; @ 🕾) 🖉 Across Lake Wakatipu from Glenorchy (26km by road; five minutes by boat), this wonderfully remote 1868 lodge rents mountain bikes, offers guided kayaking and provides transfers to tramping trailheads. The Heritage Rooms are small but stylish, with shared bathrooms. Rooms in the YHA-associated hostel are comfy and colourful, and there's a post-tramp hot tub. The excellent cafe-bar is open for lunch year-round and for à la carte dinners in summer and set dinners in winter.

DOC Kinloch Campsite
CAMPSITE $
(www.doc.govt.nz; Kinloch Rd; adult/child $6/3) Right by the lake and Kinloch Lodge, this standard DOC campsite has toilets, a barbecue and pure lake water for drinking. Head to the lodge for hot showers ($6) and meals.

Mt Earnslaw Motels
MOTEL $$
(☑ 03-442 6993; mtearnslaw@xtra.co.nz; 89 Oban St, Glenorchy; r $120; 🕾) Springtime flowers enliven the gardens of this unassuming but tidy seven-room motel. The well-priced units have comfy recliners, small kitchens and large beds, but won't win any awards for style.

Glenorchy Lake House
B&B $$$
(☑ 03-442 7084; www.glenorchylakehouse.co.nz; Mull St, Glenorchy; r $325-380; 🕾) After a day's tramping, recharge in the spa pool of this lakefront B&B. Other little luxuries include Egyptian cotton sheets, flat-screen TVs and nice toiletries. Transfers to the Routeburn and Greenstone Tracks are available.

Glenorchy Cafe
CAFE $$
(Mull St, Glenorchy; mains $10-20, pizzas $25; ⊙ 9am-5pm Sun-Wed, to 9pm Thu-Sat Jan-Apr, 10am-5pm Sun-Fri, to 9pm Sat May-Dec) Grab a sunny table out the back of this cute little cottage and tuck into cooked breakfasts, sandwiches and soup. Head inside at night to partake in pizza and beer underneath the oddball light fixtures.

Glenorchy Hotel
PUB $$
(☑ 03-442 9902; www.glenorchy-nz.co.nz; Mull St, Glenorchy; mains $15-29) The rooms are crappy but the front garden of the local pub isn't a bad spot for a beer or filling meal.

ℹ Information

There is a petrol station in Glenorchy, but fill up with cheaper fuel before you leave Queenstown. There's an ATM at the Glenorchy Hotel.

Glenorchy Information Centre & Store
(☑ 03-409 2049; www.glenorchy-nz.co.nz; Mull St, Glenorchy; ⊙ 9am-6pm) Attached to the Glenorchy Hotel, this little shop is a good source of updated weather and track information. Fishing rods and mountain bikes can be hired. Ask about trail maps for walking or mountain biking in the nearby Whakaari Conservation Area.

ℹ Getting There & Away

Glenorchy lies at the head of Lake Wakatipu, a scenic 40-minute (46km) drive northwest from Queenstown. With sweeping vistas and gem-coloured waters, the sealed road is wonderfully scenic but its constant hills are a killer for cyclists. There are no bus services; see p561 for details of trampers' shuttles

---

Arrowtown

POP 2450

Beloved by day trippers from Queenstown, exceedingly quaint Arrowtown sprang up in the 1860s following the discovery of gold in the Arrow River. Today pretty, tree-lined avenues retain more than 60 of their original goldrush buildings, but the only gold flaunted these days are the credit cards being waved in the expanding array of fashionable shops.

Instead of joining the bonanza of daytime tourists, take advantage of improved public transport to stay in the town and use it as a base for exploring Queenstown and the wider region. That way you can enjoy Arrowtown's history, charm and excellent restaurants when the tour buses have decamped back to Queenstown

⊙ Sights

Chinese Settlement   HISTORIC SITE
(Buckingham St; ⊙ 24hr) **FREE** Arrowtown has NZ's best example of a gold-era Chinese settlement. Interpretive signs explain the lives of Chinese diggers during and after the gold rush (the last resident died in 1932), while restored huts and shops make the story more tangible. Subjected to significant racism, the Chinese often had little choice but to rework old tailings rather than seek new claims.

Lake District Museum & Gallery   MUSEUM
(www.museumqueenstown.com; 49 Buckingham St; adult/child $8/2; ⊙ 8.30am-5pm) Exhibits cover the gold-rush era and the early days of Chi-

nese settlement around Arrowtown. Younger travellers will enjoy the Museum Fun Pack ($5), which includes activity sheets, museum treasure hunts, greenstone and a few flecks of gold. You can also rent pans here to try your luck panning for gold on the Arrow River ($5); you're more likely to find some traces if you head away from the town centre.

St Patrick's Catholic Church   CHURCH
(www.stjosephsqueenstown.co.nz; 7 Hertford St) Apart from the impressive Star of David–shaped rose window, this 1874 stone church wouldn't be worth noting if it weren't for its connection to Australia's only Catholic saint. Acclaimed educator St Mary of the Cross, aka Mary McKillop (1842–1909), founded a convent in the tiny 1870s miners cottage next door. There are interesting displays on the saint in the church and in the restored cottage. Try the doors; they're often unlocked.

🏃 Activities

The information centre stocks a *Cycling & Walking Trail* brochure ($1) outlining some excellent tracks in the area. One particularly good new cycling route is the Arrow River Bridges Track (12km) from Arrowtown to the Kawarau Bridge, which traverses various new suspension bridges and a tunnel cut under the highway.

Arrowtown Bike Hire   MOUNTAIN BIKING
(☑ 0800 224 473; www.arrowtownbikehire.co.nz; 59 Buckingham St; half-/full-day rental $35/49)

> **OFF THE BEATEN TRACK**
>
> ## MACETOWN
>
> Fourteen kilometres north of Arrowtown lies Macetown, a gold-rush ghost town reached via a rugged, flood-prone road (the original miners' wagon track), which crosses the Arrow River more than 25 times. Don't even think about taking the rental car here – instead trips are made from Queenstown and Arrowtown by 4WD vehicle, with gold panning included. Operators include Nomad Safaris (p552) and Southern Explorer (p567), or you can join a mountain-bike trip there with Arrowtown Bike Hire (p565).
>
> You can also hike there from Arrowtown (16km, 7½ hours return), but it's particularly tricky in winter and spring; check with the information centre about conditions before heading out.

Arrowtown

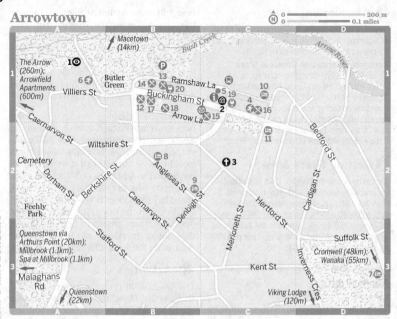

Arrowtown

◎ Sights
1 Chinese Settlement	A1
2 Lake District Museum & Gallery	C1
3 St Patrick's Catholic Church	C2

✚ Activities, Courses & Tours
4 Arrowtown Bike Hire	C1
5 Arrowtown Legends Tour	C1
6 Dudley's Cottage	A1
Queenstown Bike Tours	(see 6)
Southern Explorer	(see 4)

⌂ Sleeping
7 Arrowtown Born Of Gold	D3
8 Arrowtown Lodge	B2
9 Old Villa	B2
10 Poplar Lodge	C1
11 Shades of Arrowtown	C2

✷ Eating
12 Arrowtown Bakery	B1
13 Bonjour	B1
14 Cook's Store & Deli	B1
15 La Rumbla	C1
16 Provisions	C1
17 Saffron	B1
18 Stables	B1

◉ Drinking & Nightlife
Blue Door	(see 17)
19 Fork & Tap	C1
20 New Orleans Hotel	B1

✪ Entertainment
Dorothy Browns	(see 17)

Get active on two wheels on the many new mountain-biking trails around Arrowtown, or join a Mountain Bike Mania tour ($199, October to April) combining 4WD and mountain-biking action and exploring the former gold-rush village of Macetown. Multiday rentals are also available.

Queenstown Bike Tours MOUNTAIN BIKING
(☏ 03-442 0339; www.queenstownbiketours.co.nz; Dudley's Cottage, 4 Buckingham St) Rents bikes

(adult/child $59/29) and gets you started on various self-guided adventures, including wine tours. On the 'Gold Rush Run' ($85) you're given a gold-panning lesson and equipment, and sent out along the Arrow River to claim your own lucky stake.

Dudley's Cottage GOLD PANNING
(www.facebook.com/dudleyscottage; 4 Buckingham St; ☾ 9am-5pm) Call into this historic cottage for a gold-panning lesson ($10) or to have a

go panning a trough filled with water and a bucket of gravel from the river ($15). Otherwise, rent a pan and shovel ($6) or sluice box ($25) and head out on your own.

☞ Tours

Arrowtown Legends Tour BUS TOUR
(☏ 0800 405 066; www.connectabus.com; Ramshaw Lane; tours $20; ⊙ tours 10am, 11am, 1pm, 2pm, 3pm & 4pm) Arrowtown is tiny but this double-decker bus (an ex-London Routemaster) manages a 30-minute loop, complete with an interesting commentary.

Southern Explorer DRIVING TOUR
(☏ 03-441 1144; www.southernexplorer.co.nz; 59 Buckingham St; day tours $65-160) Runs 4WD day tours exploring the improbably scenic landscapes and old mining history around Arrowtown, Skippers Canyon and Glenorchy. Options include overnight camping in Skippers Canyon or Macetown.

🛏 Sleeping

Poplar Lodge HOSTEL $
(☏ 03-442 1466; www.poplarlodge.co.nz; 4 Merioneth St; dm/s/apt $30/62/120, d with/without bathroom $99/70; 🐾) Budget accommodation options are limited in A-town, but this converted house is an excellent choice. The hostel has a quiet, homely feel, with rooms that are pleasantly sleep conducive. There's also a self-contained unit in the neighbouring cottage.

Arrowtown Born Of Gold HOLIDAY PARK $
(☏ 03-442 1876; www.arrowtownholidaypark.co.nz; 12 Centennial Ave; campsites $36, units $120-160; @🐾) Close to the centre, this unexceptional holiday park offers a lane of en suite cabins trimmed with roses and a newish amenities block with coin-operated showers.

★ Arrowtown Lodge B&B $$
(☏ 03-442 1101; www.arrowtownlodge.co.nz; 7 Anglesea St; d $160; 🐾) From the outside, the guest rooms look like heritage cottages, but inside they're cosy and modern, with en-suite bathrooms. Each has a private entrance from the pretty gardens. A continental breakfast is provided.

Old Villa B&B $$
(☏ 03-442 1682; www.arrowtownoldvilla.co.nz; 13 Anglesea St; s $110, d $140-160; 🐾) Freshly baked bread and homemade preserves welcome visitors to this heritage-style villa with a garden just made for summer barbe-

cues. The two en suite double rooms come trimmed with fresh flowers. One of the rooms has an additional single bed.

Shades of Arrowtown MOTEL $$
(☏ 03-442 1613; www.shadesofarrowtown.co.nz; cnr Buckingham & Merioneth Sts; d $110-155; 🐾) Tall shady trees and a garden setting give these stylish bungalow-style cottages a relaxed air. The two-storey family unit (from $180) is good value if you're travelling with the whole clan.

Viking Lodge MOTEL $$
(Map p544; ☏ 03-442 1765; www.vikinglodge.co.nz; 21 Inverness Cres; units $145-193; 🐾🏊) These older A-frame units have a family-friendly stamp. If the kids still have energy after a day's travelling, wear them out even more in the swimming pool or on the playground.

The Arrow BOUTIQUE HOTEL $$$
(Map p544; ☏ 03-409 8600; www.thearrow.co.nz; 63 Manse Rd; d from $395; 🐾) Five understated but luxurious suites feature at this modern property on the outskirts of Arrowtown. Accommodation is chic and contemporary with huge picture windows showcasing the surrounding countryside. Breakfast is included.

Arrowfield Apartments APARTMENTS $$$
(Map p544; ☏ 03-442 0012; www.arrowfield.co.nz; 115 Essex Ave, Butel Park; apt $250-475; 🐾) Lining a quiet crescent in a new development on the edge of town, these 3 spacious townhouses all have internal garages, full kitchens, gas fires and three bedrooms. Doors can be locked off for a smaller, cheaper rental.

Millbrook RESORT $$$
(Map p544; ☏ 03-441 7000; www.millbrook.co.nz; Malaghans Rd; d from $245; @🐾🏊) 🍽 Just outside Arrowtown, this enormous resort is a town unto itself. Cosy private villas have every luxury and there's a top-class golf course right at your front door. At the end of the day, take your pick from four restaurants, or relax at the spa (p555).

🍴 Eating

Arrowtown Bakery BAKERY, CAFE $
(Buckingham St; mains $6-15; ⊙ 8am-4pm) Equal parts bakery and cafe, this little eatery serves a wide selection of gourmet savoury pies ($5.50), including exotic flavours such as venison and Thai chicken. Or you can just settle in for coffee and a slice.

Provisions
CAFE $

(www.provisions.co.nz; 65 Buckingham St; mains $9-19; ⊙8.30am-5pm) One of Arrowtown's oldest cottages is now a cute cafe surrounded by fragrant gardens. Pop in for breakfast or a coffee and don't leave town without trying one of its deservedly famous sticky buns. Staff bake everything on site, including bread and bagels.

Cook's Store & Deli
DELI, CAFE $

(www.cooksdeli.co.nz; 21 Ramshaw Lane; mains $9-12; ⊙8.30am-5pm) Attached to a wine store, this little deli-cafe is a good place to pick up picnic fixings including local cheeses, bagels and artisan breads.

★ La Rumbla
TAPAS $$

(☑03-442 0509; www.larumbla.co.nz; 54 Buckingham St; tapas $9-18; ⊙4pm-midnight Tue-Thu, 2pm-2am Fri & Sat, 4-11pm Sun) Tucked behind the post office, this little gem does a brilliant job of bringing the bold flavours and late-dining habits of Spain to sleepy little Arrowtown. Local produce is showcased in tasty bites such as lamb meatballs and Southland suede croquettes.

Bonjour
FRENCH $$

(☑03-409 8946; www.bonjour-arrowtown.com; 25 Ramshaw Lane; breakfast $7-19, lunch $11-19, dinner $25-31; ⊙8.30am-3pm Sun-Wed, to 10pm Thu-Sat) Come for breakfast and tuck into coffee and croissants, or one of the 18 different crepes and galettes that are served throughout the day. Come back for dinner to treat yourself to cheese fondue or classic bistro-style dishes.

QUEENSTOWN & WANAKA ON RAINY DAYS

Book in for a Japanese-style spa experience at Onsen Hot Pools (☑03-442 5707; www.onsen.co.nz; 160 Arthurs Point Rd, Arthurs Point; tub for 2 $80; ⊙11am-10pm) in Queenstown, or catch a bus across to Arrowtown for a movie at the quirky Dorothy Browns cinema. If you're holed up in Wanaka, Cinema Paradiso (p576) or Ruby's (p576) are equally cool. Other all-weather attractions in Wanaka include Puzzling World (p569), and the excellent Wanaka Transport & Toy Museum (p569) or Warbirds & Wheels (p569). If you're visiting from April to October, go ice skating at the Queenstown Ice Arena (p550).

Stables
CAFE $$

(☑03-442 1818; www.stablesrestaurant.co.nz; 28 Buckingham St; lunch $16-19, dinner $32-38; ⊙11am-3pm & 5-9pm; 🐾) With courtyard tables adjoining a grassy square, Stables is a good spot for an alfresco lunch. Later at night, step inside the 1860s stone building for a more intimate dining experience which leans heavily on the char grill.

Saffron
MODERN NZ $$$

(☑03-442 0131; www.saffronrestaurant.co.nz; 18 Buckingham St; lunch $23-29, dinner $37-40; ⊙noon-3pm & 6pm-late) Saffron serves grown-up food in a formal and sophisticated setting. The ever-changing trio of curries effortlessly traverses Asia, while other dishes jet to Europe and back. Fans can purchase *The Taste of Central Otago* cookbook, showcasing the restaurant's best recipes.

🍷 Drinking & Nightlife

Blue Door
BAR

(www.saffronrestaurant.co.nz; 18 Buckingham St; ⊙5pm-late) Hidden away behind a tricky-to-find blue door, this cool little bar has a formidable wine list and enough rustic ambience to keep you entertained for the evening. Low ceilings, an open fire and abundant candles create an intimate quaffing location.

Fork & Tap
PUB

(www.theforkandtap.co.nz; 51 Buckingham St; ⊙11am-11pm) Craft beers, great food and a sunny, kid-friendly back garden make this the pick of Arrowtown's pubs. Built in 1865 as a bank, it now hosts Irish bands on Wednesdays and other acts on Sundays in summer.

New Orleans Hotel
PUB

(www.neworleanshotel.co.nz; 27 Buckingham St; ⊙8am-11pm; 🐾) Dating from 1866, this gold-rush pub still has the right amount of rough edge to provide a juxtaposition to Arrowtown's relentless quaintness. The gnarled prospectors have long been replaced with (mainly) young local men shooting pool, watching sport on TV and knocking back a beer on the back deck.

☆ Entertainment

Dorothy Browns
CINEMA

(☑03-442 1964; www.dorothybrowns.com; Ballarat Arcade, Buckingham St; adult/child $19/10) This is what a cinema should be like: comfortable seating with the option to cuddle with your neighbour. Fine wine and cheeseboards are available to accompany the mostly art-house films. Every screening in the main theatre has an intermission – the perfect opportunity to tuck into a tub of gourmet ice cream.

ℹ Information

Arrowtown Visitor Information Centre (📋03-442 1824; www.arrowtown.com; 49 Buckingham St; ☺8.30am-5pm) Shares premises with the Lake District Museum & Gallery.

ℹ Getting There & Away

Connectabus (📋03-441 4471; www.connectabus.com) runs regular services (7.45am to 11pm) on its No 10 route from Frankton to Arrowtown. From Queenstown, you'll need to catch a No 11 bus to the corner of Frankton and Kawarau Rds, and change there. The only direct service is the double-decker bus heading out on the first Arrowtown Legends Tour (p567) of the day, which departs Queenstown at 9.30am ($8).

WANAKA

POP 6480

Which is better, Queenstown or Wanaka? That's the perennial question around these parts and one which doesn't have an easy answer. It's hard to say which is more beautiful – both have blissful lake and mountain settings. Ditto, the jury's out as to which offers better skiing and tramping opportunities.

The main difference is in size, scale and buzz. Unlike its amped-up sibling across the Crown Range, Wanaka retains a laid-back, small-town feel. It's definitely not a sleepy hamlet anymore though, and new restaurants and bars are adding a veneer of sophistication. And while it doesn't have quite the same range of adrenaline-inducing activities on offer, Wanaka is no slacker on the outdoor-adventure front. Importantly, it's also cheaper.

◉ Sights

Puzzling World   AMUSEMENT PARK
(www.puzzlingworld.com; 188 Wanaka Luggate Hwy/SH84; adult/child $18/12; ☺8.30am-5.30pm) A 3D Great Maze and lots of fascinating brain-bending visual illusions to keep people of all ages bemused, bothered and bewildered. It's en route to Cromwell, 2km from town.

National Transport & Toy Museum MUSEUM
(www.wanakatransportandtoymuseum.com; 851 Wanaka Luggate Hwy/SH6; adult/child $15/5; ☺8.30am-5pm) Small armies of Smurfs, Star Wars figurines and Barbie dolls share billing with dozens of classic cars and a mysteriously

acquired MiG jet fighter in this vast collection, which fills four giant hangers near the airport. There are around 30,000 items in total, including plenty of toys you're bound to remember from rainy childhood afternoons.

Wanaka Beerworks   BREWERY
(www.wanakabeerworks.co.nz; SH6; tours & tasting $10; ☺tastings 11am-4pm, tours 2pm Thu-Tue) Somewhat incongruously attached to the toy museum, this small brewery's two main beers (Cardrona Gold lager and Brewski pilsner) are complemented by seasonal brews. Dave the owner is a real-deal Belgian brewing supremo.

Warbirds & Wheels   MUSEUM
(www.warbirdsandwheels.com; Wanaka Airport, 11 Lloyd Dunn Av; adult/child $20/5; ☺9am-5pm) Dedicated to NZ combat pilots, the aircraft they flew and the sacrifices they made, this museum features Hawker Hurricanes, a de Havilland Vampire and lots of shiny, beautifully restored classic cars. Grab a bite to eat and fire up the jukebox in the retro diner.

Rippon   WINERY
(www.rippon.co.nz; 246 Mt Aspiring Rd; ☺noon-4.30pm Jul-Apr) Along with just about the best view of any NZ winery, Rippon has great wine too. To save fights as to who's going to be the designated driver, take a 2km stroll along the lakeside and look out for the track up the hill from the end of Sargood Dr.

🏃 Activities

Wanaka is the gateway to Mt Aspiring National Park and to the Treble Cone (p47), Cardrona (p577), Harris Mountains and Pisa Range Ski Areas.

Tramping

For walks close to town, including various lakeside walks, pick up the DOC brochure *Wanaka Outdoor Pursuits* ($3.50). The short climb to the top of **Mt Iron** (527m, 1½ hours return) reveals panoramic views.

To the north of Wanaka, the usually unpeopled **Minaret Burn Track** (six to seven hours) in the Mt Alta Conservation Area is suitable for walking and mountain biking. After about two to three hours, a track heads down to **Colquhouns Beach**, a great swimming spot.

Aspiring Guides   MOUNTAINEERING, SKIING
(📋03-443 9422; www.aspiringguides.com; L1, 99 Ardmore St) With over 20 years of alpine experience, this crew offers a multitude of options, including guided wilderness hiking (from three to eight days); mountaineering

Wanaka

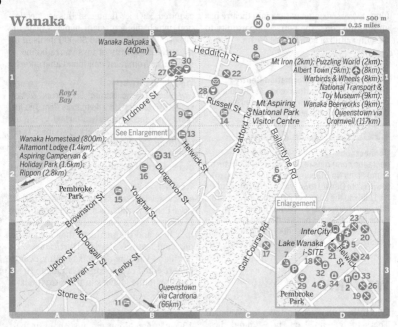

Wanaka

🔵 Activities, Courses & Tours
1 Aspiring Guides.............................D3
2 Cardrona Alpine Resort Booking
   Office..D3
3 Lakeland Adventures.......................D3
4 Outside Sports...............................D3
5 Thunderbikes................................D3
6 Wanaka Golf Club..........................C2
7 Wanaka Kayaks.............................C3

🛏 Sleeping
8 Archway Motels............................C1
9 Asure Brookvale...........................B1
10 Criffel Peak View..........................C1
11 Harpers.....................................B3
12 Lakeside....................................B1
13 Matterhorn South.........................B2
14 Mountain View Backpackers............C1
15 Wanaka View Motel.......................B2
16 YHA Wanaka Purple Cow................B2

🍴 Eating
17 Bistro Gentil...............................C3
18 Boaboa Food Company...................D3
19 Federal Diner..............................D3
20 Francesca's Italian Kitchen.............D3
21 Kai Whakapai..............................D3
22 Red Star....................................C1
23 Relishes Cafe..............................D3
24 Ritual..D3
25 Soulfood....................................B1
26 Spice Room................................D3
27 The Landing................................B1
   Yohei...................................(see 4)

🍷 Drinking & Nightlife
28 Barluga & Woody's........................C1
29 Gin & Raspberry...........................D3
   Lalaland.................................(see 1)
30 Opium.......................................B1

🎬 Entertainment
31 Cinema Paradiso...........................B2

🛍 Shopping
32 Chop Shop..................................D3
33 Gallery Thirty Three......................D3
34 MT Outdoors...............................D3
   Picture Lounge.........................(see 4)

and ice-climbing courses; guided ascents of Mt Aspiring, Aoraki/Mt Cook and Mt Tasman; and off-piste skiing (one- to five-day backcountry expeditions).

**Alpinism
& Ski Wanaka** MOUNTAINEERING, SKIING
(☏ 03-442 6593; www.alpinismski.co.nz; from $135)
Guided day walks and overnight tramps, and

more full-on mountain assaults, courses and ski touring.

Adventure Consultants
MOUNTAINEERING

(☑ 03-443 8711; www.adventureconsultants.com; 5 days from $4100) Offers two-days excursions on Brewster Glacier ($890) and three-day trips in Gillespies Pass ($1250) in Mt Aspiring National Park, as well as longer treks, ascents (Mts Aspiring, Tutoko, Tasman and Aoraki/Mt Cook) and mountaineering courses.

Rock Climbing

Excellent rock climbing can be found at Hospital Flat – 25km from Wanaka towards Mt Aspiring National Park.

Basecamp Wanaka
ROCK CLIMBING

(☑ 03-443 1110; www.basecampwanaka.co.nz; 50 Cardrona Valley Rd; adult/child $20/17; ☺ noon-8pm Mon-Fri, 10am-6pm Sat & Sun) Before you hit the mountains, learn the ropes on climbing walls.

Wanaka Rock Climbing
ROCK CLIMBING

(☑ 03-443 6411; www.wanakarock.co.nz) Introductory rock-climbing course (half-/full day $140/210), a half-day abseiling intro ($140), and bouldering and multipitch climbs for the experienced.

Mountain Biking

Hundreds of kilometres of tracks and trails in the region are open to mountain bikers. Pick up the DOC brochure *Wanaka Outdoor Pursuits* ($3.50), describing mountain-bike rides ranging from 2km to 24km, including the Deans Bank Loop Track (12km).

One particularly scenic new route is the Newcastle Track (12km), which follows the raging blue waters of the Clutha River from the Albert Town Bridge to Red Bridge. You can make it a 30km loop by joining the Upper Clutha River Track at Luggate.

Thunderbikes
BICYCLE RENTAL

(☑ 03-443 2558; www.thunderbikes.co.nz; 16 Helwick St; ☺ 9am-5pm) Hires bikes (half-/full day from $20/35) and carries out repairs. It is located inside the Board House, which also rents ski and snowboard gear in season, and sells outdoorsy clothes.

Outside Sports
BICYCLE RENTAL

(www.outsidesports.co.nz; Spencer House Mall, 23 Dunmore St; ☺ 9am-6pm) Rents (half/-full day from $35/55), repairs and sells bikes, along with snow-sports equipment and clothing.

Other Activities

Deep Canyon
CANYONING

(☑ 03-443 7922; www.deepcanyon.co.nz; canyoning from $220; ☺ Oct-Apr) Loads of climbing, walking and waterfall-abseiling through confined, wild gorges.

Skydive Lake Wanaka
SKY DIVING

(☑ 03-443 7207; www.skydivewanaka.com; sky diving from $329) Jump from 12,000ft or go the whole hog with a 15,000ft leap and 60 seconds of freefall.

Wanaka River Journeys
JETBOATING, WALKING

(☑ 03-443 4416; www.wanakariverjourneys.co.nz; adult/child $229/119) 🌱 Combination bush walk (50 minutes) and jetboat ride in the gorgeous Matukituki Valley.

Wanaka Kayaks
KAYAKING

(☑ 0800 926 925; www.wanakakayaks.co.nz; from per hour $12; ☺ 9am-6pm Dec-Mar) Rents kayaks ($14 per hour), stand-up paddle boards ($18 per hour), and catamarans ($60 per hour), and offers guided paddle-powered tours of the lake (half/full day $75/149). It's on the lakefront, opposite 163 Ardmore St.

Wanaka Paragliding
PARAGLIDING

(☑ 0800 359 754; www.wanakaparagliding.co.nz; tandem $199) Count on around 20 minutes soaring on the summer thermals around Treble Cone.

Hatch
FISHING

(☑ 03-443 8446; www.hatchfishing.co.nz; 2 adults half-/full day $490/750) Lakes Wanaka and Hawea and the surrounding rivers have excellent trout fishing. Hatch offers guided fly-fishing, with the option of accessing remote spots by helicopter or jetboat.

Pioneer Rafting
RAFTING

(☑ 03-443 1246; www.ecoraft.co.nz; half-day adult/child $145/85, full day $195/105) Raft on the high-volume Clutha, with Grade II to III rapids, gold panning and bird-watching.

Wanaka Golf Club
GOLF

(☑ 03-443 7888; www.wanakagolf.co.nz; Ballantyne Rd; green fees $60) A spectacular 18-hole course.

⛵ Tours

Scenic Flights

U-Fly
SCENIC FLIGHTS

(☑ 03-445 4005; www.u-flywanaka.co.nz; flights from $199) Scratch 'flying a plane' off the bucket list on a scenic flight over Mt Aspiring National Park. Don't fret, there are dual

DON'T MISS

MT ASPIRING NATIONAL PARK

Verdant valleys, alpine meadows, unspoiled rivers, more than 100 glaciers and sheer mountains make **Mt Aspiring National Park** (www.doc.govt.nz) an outdoor enthusiast's paradise. Protected as a national park in 1964, and later included in the Southwest New Zealand (Te Wahipounamu) World Heritage Area, the park now blankets 3555 sq km along the Southern Alps, from the Haast River in the north to its border with Fiordland National Park in the south. Lording it over all is colossal Mt Aspiring (Tititea; 3033m), the highest peak outside the Aoraki/Mt Cook area.

While the southern end of Mt Aspiring National Park near Glenorchy includes better known tramps such as the Routeburn (p562), Greenstone and Caples (p562) and Rees-Dart (p562) Tracks, there are plenty of blissful short walks and more demanding multiday tramps in the Matukituki Valley, close to Wanaka; see the Department of Conservation (DOC) brochure *Matukituki Valley Tracks* ($2).

The dramatic **Rob Roy Glacier Track** (two to four hours return) takes in glaciers, waterfalls and a swing bridge. It's a moderate walk, but some parts are quite steep. The **West Matukituki Valley Track** goes on to Aspiring Hut (four to five hours return; peak/off-peak $25/20 per night), a scenic walk over mostly grassy flats. For overnight or multiday tramps offering great views of Mt Aspiring, continue up the valley to Liverpool Hut (at an elevation of 1000m; $15 per night) and French Ridge Hut (at 1465m; $20 per night).

Many of these tramps are prone to snow and avalanches and can be treacherous. It is extremely important to consult DOC in Wanaka (p578) and to purchase hut tickets before heading off. You should also register your intentions on www.adventuresmart.org.nz.

Tracks are reached from Raspberry Creek at the end of Mt Aspiring Rd, 50km from Wanaka. The road is unsealed for 30km and involves nine ford crossings; it's usually fine in a 2WD, except in very wet conditions (check at DOC).

controls ready to take over at a moment's notice – they're not completely insane.

Classic Flights SCENIC FLIGHTS
(☎ 03-443 4043; www.classicflights.co.nz; flights from $249) ✈ Runs sightseeing flights in a vintage Tiger Moth or Waco biplane. 'Biggles' goggles and flowing silk scarf provided.

Wanaka Helicopters HELICOPTER
(☎ 03-443 1085; www.wanakahelicopters.co.nz) Options range from 15-minute tasters ($95) to two-hour-plus trips to Milford Sound ($995).

Aspiring Helicopters HELICOPTER
(☎ 03-443 7152; www.aspiringhelicopters.co.nz) Take a 20-minute flight ($170) or a 2½-hour trip to Milford Sound ($1250); in-between options include Mt Aspiring.

Alpine Helicopters HELICOPTER
(☎ 03-443 4000; www.alpineheli.co.nz) Options range from a 20-minute flight ($185) to the four-hour Fiordland Heli Traverse ($7500 for up to six).

Wanaka Flightseeing SCENIC FLIGHTS
(☎ 03-443 8787; www.flightseeing.co.nz) Spectacular flyovers of Mt Aspiring ($240), Aoraki/Mt Cook ($435) and Milford Sound ($490).

Other Tours

Adventure Wanaka CRUISE, FISHING
(☎ 03-443 6665; www.adventurewanaka.com) Offers lake cruises and fishing trips in an 8m launch.

Lakeland Adventures CRUISE, KAYAKING
(☎ 03-443 7495; www.lakelandadventures.co.nz; Log Cabin, 100 Ardmore St) Has two-hour trips to Stevensons Island (adult/child $95/55) and a three-hour trip to Mou Waho island (adult/child $165/55); both include guided nature walks and morning or afternoon tea. Otherwise you can hire a kayak ($15 per hour) and paddle your way to Ruby Island.

Also offers one-hour jetboat trips across the lake (adult/child $109/55) and water taxis to the start of the Minaret Burn track ($75).

Eco Wanaka Adventures HIKING, CRUISE
(☎ 03-443 2869; www.ecowanaka.co.nz; half-/full day from $105/170) ✈ Guided tours include a full-day trek to the Rob Roy glacier ($250), a four-hour cruise and walk on Mou Waho island, and a full-day cruise-4WD combo ($390).

Wanaka Bike Tours MOUNTAIN BIKING
(☎ 0800 862 453; www.wanakabiketours.co.nz; tours from $99) Guided trips including heli-biking options.

Ridgeline Adventures
DRIVING TOUR

(📞 0800 234 000; www.ridgelinenz.com; tours from $140) Explore the wilderness surrounding Wanaka on a 4WD nature safari.

Funny French Cars
DRIVING TOUR

(📞 027 386 6932; www.funnyfrenchcars.co.nz) Ride in a classic Citroen around Central Otago wineries (per person $165), up into the hills for a picnic lunch (per person $150), or tour the highlights of Wanaka (per car per hour $80).

⭐ Festivals & Events

Warbirds over Wanaka
AIRSHOW

(📞 03-443 8619, 0800 496 920; www.warbirds-overwanaka.com; Wanaka Airport; 3-day adult/child $190/45) Held every second Easter (even-numbered years), this incredibly popular international airshow attracts upwards of 50,000 people. Tickets for the first day only cost $65/15 per adult/child, the second and third days are $90/15 each.

Rippon Festival
MUSIC

(www.ripponfestival.co.nz) Held every second year in early February (even-numbered years) at the lakeside Rippon Vineyard. Big-name Kiwi acts headline with a variety of styles represented, including R&B, reggae, rock, pop and punk.

Wanaka Fest
CARNIVAL

(www.wanakafest.co.nz) This four-day event in mid-October has the feel of a small-town fair. Street parades, live music, wacky competitions and fine regional produce get the locals saying g'day to the warmth of spring.

🛏 Sleeping

In summer, and especially around New Year, prices and demand increase considerably. During winter, the town receives an influx of international snowboarders.

📍 Wanaka

★ Altamont Lodge
LODGE $

(📞 03-443 8864; www.altamontlodge.co.nz; 121 Mt Aspiring Rd; s/d without bathrooms $49/79; 🛜) At the quiet end of town, Altamont has tidy little rooms which share bathrooms and a spacious, well-equipped kitchen. Natural wood gives it a ski-lodge ambience, while the spa pool and roaring fire in the lounge will warm you up postslopes.

★ Wanaka Bakpaka
HOSTEL $

(📞 03-443 7837; www.wanakabakpaka.co.nz; 117 Lakeside Rd; dm $28-29, d with/without bathroom $90/70; @🛜) An energetic husband-and-wife team run this friendly hostel above the lake with just about the best views in town. Amenities are top shelf and the onto-it staff consistently offer a red-carpet welcome to weary travellers. It's worth considering paying a bit extra for the en suite double with the gorgeous views.

YHA Wanaka Purple Cow
HOSTEL $

(📞 03-443 1880; www.yha.co.nz; 94 Brownston St; dm $31-34, d with/without bathroom from $95/81; @🛜) 🍃 In the top echelons of NZ YHAs, the Purple Cow offers a range of shared and private rooms, including some with en suites in a newer building out the back. Best of all is the large lounge, with commanding lake and mountain views, and a wood stove.

Aspiring Campervan & Holiday Park
HOLIDAY PARK $

(📞 03-443 7766; www.campervanpark.co.nz; Studholme Rd; campsites $20-25, s/d $25/60, units with/without bathroom from $75/65; @ 🛜) Grassy sites for tents and campervans, lots of trees, and pretty views add up to a relaxing spot. Facilities include a barbecue area with gas heaters, and free wi-fi, spa pool and sauna. Older-style motel units have all been renovated, and the newest budget cabins are warm and cosy with wooden floors.

Matterhorn South
HOSTEL $

(📞 03-443 1119; www.matterhornsouth.co.nz; 56 Brownston St; dm $28-35, d with/without bathroom from $115/80; @🛜) Split between two buildings – the 'lodge' and the slightly rougher-around-the-edges 'backpackers' – this friendly spot has clean, good-value dorms and private rooms. Each has its own kitchen and lounge, and the garden is a great place to relax after a day's adventuring.

Mountain View Backpackers
HOSTEL $

(📞 03-443 9010; www.wanakabackpackers.co.nz; 7 Russell St; dm $27-29, d $68; 🅿@🛜) This colourfully renovated and characterful house features a manicured lawn and warm, comfortable rooms. Fire up the barbecue after a busy day's exploring. Handy features include a drying room and off-street parking.

Criffel Peak View
B&B $$

(📞 03-443 5511; www.criffelpeakview.co.nz; 98 Hedditch St; s $130, d $160-165, apt $270) Situated in a quiet cul-de-sac, this excellent B&B has three rooms sharing a large lounge with a log fire and a sunny wisteria-draped deck. The charming hostesses live in a separate house behind, which has a self-contained two-bedroom apartment attached.

Harpers
B&B $$

(☏ 03-443 8894; www.harpers.co.nz; 95 McDougall St; tw/d $140/160) The garden (with pond and waterfall no less...) is a labour of love for the retiree owners at this quiet, homely B&B. Legendary breakfasts are served on a sunny deck with expansive views. You'd be wise to factor a leisurely second cup of breakfast coffee into your day's plans.

Wanaka View Motel
MOTEL $$

(☏ 03-443 7480; www.wanakaviewmotel.co.nz; 122 Brownston St; units $120-195; ☎) The refurbished Wanaka View has five apartments with Sky TV, spa baths, full kitchens and lake views; the largest has three bedrooms. There's also a comfortable studio unit tucked around the back, which is cheaper but doesn't have a kitchen or view.

Archway Motels
MOTEL $$

(☏ 03-443 7698; www.archwaymotels.co.nz; 64 Hedditch St; units from $120; ☎) This older motel with clean and spacious units and chalets is a short uphill walk from the town centre. Friendly and helpful owners, new flat-screen TVs, and cedar hot tubs with mountain views make Archway great value in a sometimes-expensive town. Check online for good off-peak discounts.

Asure Brookvale
MOTEL $$

(☏ 03-443 8333; www.brookvale.co.nz; 35 Brownston St; d $150-180; ☎☒) At this older-style motel with studio and family units, the patios open onto a grassy lawn edged by a gently flowing creek. There's also a barbecue, hot tub and swimming pool.

Lakeside
APARTMENTS $$$

(☏ 03-443 0188; www.lakesidewanaka.co.nz; 7 Lakeside Rd; apt $295-795; ☎☒) 🖋 Luxuriate in a modern apartment in a prime position overlooking the lake, right by the town centre. All have three bedrooms but can be rented with only one or two bedrooms open. The swimming pool is a rariety in these parts and an appealing alternative to the frigid lake on a sweltering day.

Wanaka Homestead
LODGE $$$

(☏ 03-443 5022; www.wanakahomestead.co.nz; 1 Homestead Close; d $269, cottages $399-499; @☎) 🖋 Wooden interiors, oriental rugs and local artwork punctuate this boutique lodge, which has won awards for its eco-friendly approach. Despite the focus on green good deeds, it's still luxurious, with underfloor heating and an under-the-stars hot tub. Choose from rooms in the main lodge or in self-contained cottages.

🏨 Albert Town

★ Riversong
B&B $$

(☏ 03-443 8567; www.riversongwanaka.co.nz; 5 Wicklow Tce; d $160-190; ☎) Across from the Clutha River in nearby Albert Town, Riversong has two guest bedrooms in a lovely weatherboard house. The well-travelled owner has a fabulous nonfiction library. If you can tear yourself away from the books, there's excellent trout fishing just metres away.

Wanaka Alpine Lodge
B&B, APARTMENTS $$$

(☏ 03-443 5355; www.wanakaalpinelodge.co.nz; 114 Albert Town-Lake Hawea Rd; r $259-289, apt $390; ☎) Guests in the four spacious, modern bedrooms are pampered with home baking, an evening glass of wine and a cedar hot tub. It's slightly out of town, but the young owners will lend you a mountain bike to get around on and even chauffeur you in for dinner.

🍴 Eating

Boaboa Food Company
FAST FOOD $

(www.facebook.com/boaboafc; 137 Ardmore St; mains $10-18; ⊘10am-9pm) Fancy burgers (spiced pulled pork, high-country salmon, porterhouse steak) are the mainstay of this white-tiled takeway bar, but it also does fish and chips and fried chicken. There are only a handful of high tables, but the lakefront beckons.

Kai Whakapai
CAFE, BAR $

(cnr Helwick & Ardmore Sts; brunch $7-18, dinner $17-22; ⊘7am-11pm) An absolute Wanaka institution, Kai (the Maori word for food) is the place to be for a liquid sundowner accompanied by a massive sandwich or pizza. Locally brewed Wanaka Beerworks beers are on tap and there are Central Otago wines as well.

Red Star
BURGERS $

(26 Ardmore St; burgers $10-17; ⊘11.30am-11pm; 🖋) Red Star spoils diners with a menu featuring inventive ingredients and 22 different burgers. Everybody is catered for – even vegetarians, who get a show-stopping three choices.

Soulfood
ORGANIC, CAFE $

(www.soulfoodwanaka.co.nz; 74 Ardmore St; mains $10-15; ⊘8am-6pm Mon-Fri, to 4pm Sat & Sun; 🖋)

It's not soul food in the African American sense; rather this little organics store offers a healthy range of id-affirming soups, pizza, pasta and muffins. Not everything's strictly vegetarian, with wild venison and free-range bacon breaking the spell. Juices and smoothies are suitably virtuous, but coffee's limited to the plunger variety.

Yohei
SUSHI $

(Spencer House Mall, 23 Dunmore St; mains $12-15; ☺8am-5.30pm; 🛜🅿) Tucked away in a shopping arcade, this funky Japanese-inspired eatery does interesting local spins on sushi (how about venison?), and superlative juices and smoothies. There's also a good range of vego options and free wi-fi with any $4 purchase.

★Francesca's Italian Kitchen
ITALIAN $$

(📞03-443 5599; www.fransitalian.co.nz; 93 Ardmore St; mains $20-25; ☺noon-3pm & 5.30pm-late) Ebulliently expat Francesca has brought the big flavours and easy conviviality of an authentic Italian family trattoria to Wanaka in the form of this stylish and perennially busy eatery. Even simple things like pizza, pasta and polenta chips are exceptional. She also runs a pizza cart from the New World car park.

Florence's Foodstore & Cafe
CAFE $$

(www.florencesfoodstore.co.nz; 71 Cardrona Valley Rd; mains $16; ☺8.30am-4pm) Wood, corrugated iron and jute-cladding create a rustic feel for this edge-of-town gourmet providore. Call in for the region's prettiest salmon Benedict, as well as French-style pastries and delicious ham-and-cheese baguettes.

Relishes Cafe
CAFE $$

(📞03-443 7538; www.relishescafe.co.nz; 99 Ardmore St; brunch $11-20, dinner $31-35; ☺7am-10pm) A cafe by day with good breakfast and lunch options, this place transforms itself at night into a sophisticated restaurant with a good wine list. Try the free-range pork belly or Aoraki salmon, and toast the lakefront setting with a glass of Central Otago's finest.

Spice Room
INDIAN $$

(📞03-443 1133; www.spiceroom.co.nz; 43 Helwick St; mains $21-25; ☺5.30-10pm; 🅿) The combination of an authentic curry, crispy garlic naan and cold beer is a great way to recharge after a day's snowboarding or tramping. Beyond the spot-on renditions of all your subcontinental favourites, the Spice Room springs a few surprises, with starters including a zingy scallops masala salad.

Ritual
CAFE $$

(18 Helwick St; mains $10-20; ☺9am-5pm) A classic 21st-century Kiwi cafe, Ritual is smart but not too trendy, gay-friendly but family-friendly too, and filled to the gills with delicious food. The counter positively groans under the weight of tasty salads, slices and scones.

Federal Diner
CAFE $$

(www.federaldiner.co.nz; 47 Helwick St; mains $9-21; ☺7am-4pm; 🛜) Tucked away in a back lane, this cosmopolitan cafe delivers robust breakfasts, excellent coffee and chunky gourmet sandwiches. Try the 'Roaster Coaster' with slow-roasted pork shoulder and apple sauce on ciabatta. Service is sometimes chaotic.

★Bistro Gentil
FRENCH $$$

(📞03-443 2299; www.bistrogentil.co.nz; 76a Golf Course Rd; mains $30-42; ☺11.30am-2pm Sat & Sun, 5-9pm Wed-Sun, extended Dec-Feb) Lake views, fabulous NZ art, oodles of wines by the glass and delicious modern French cuisine – Gentil ticks plenty of boxes for a memorable night out. On a balmy night, request an outside table.

The Landing
MODERN NZ $$$

(📞03-443 5099; www.thelandinglakewanaka.co.nz; L1, 80 Ardmore St; mains $29-39; ☺5-10pm) Local beef, lamb and salmon is served in innovative ways in this upmarket upstairs restaurant at the apex of the main streets. The beautifully presented dishes do well to compete with the spectacular lake views.

🍷 Drinking & Nightlife

Barluga & Woody's
BAR

(Post Office Lane, 33 Ardmore St; ☺4pm-2.30am) The tucked-away Post Office Lane complex is Wanaka's coolest drinking destination – despite the lack of lake views. Sharing both a courtyard and owners, these neighbouring bars operate more or less in tandem, especially when there's a DJ event on. Barluga's leather armchairs and retro wallpaper bring to mind a refined gentlemen's club. Wicked cocktails and killer back-to-back beats soon smash that illusion. Woody's plays the role of the younger brother, with pool tables and indie sounds.

Lalaland
COCKTAIL BAR

(www.lalalandwanaka.co.nz; L1, 99 Ardmore St; ☺3pm-2am) Keep a watchful eye on the lake or sink into a comfy chair at this little, low-lit, completely over-the-top cocktail palace/bordello. The young barmeister-owner truly knows his stuff, concocting elixirs to suit every mood. Entry is via the rear stairs.

Gin & Raspberry
COCKTAIL BAR

(www.ginandraspberry.co.nz; L1, 155 Ardmore St; ⊙4pm-late) If you're in the swing for bling, this lush bar offers gilded mirrors, sparkling chandeliers, a piano and a central fireplace. Classic movies provide a backdrop to classic cocktails (including seven different martinis), and the occasional live band fires things up.

Opium
CLUB

(L1, 68 Ardmore St; ⊙9pm-late Wed-Sun) An Asian-themed club with DJs and occasional live music. It's popular in winter with the snowboarder crowd, but in summer the lakefront bars are busier.

☆ Entertainment

Cinema Paradiso
CINEMA

(☑03-443 1505; www.paradiso.net.nz; 72 Brownston St; adult/child $15/9) Stretch out on a comfy couch or in an old Morris Minor at this Wanaka institution, screening the best of Hollywood and art-house flicks. At intermission the smell of freshly baked cookies wafts through the theatre, although the homemade ice cream is just as alluring.

Ruby's
CINEMA

(☑03-443 6901; www.rubyscinema.co.nz; 50 Cardrona Valley Rd; adult/child $19/13) Channelling a lush New York or Shanghai vibe, this hip-art-house-cinema-meets-chic-cocktail-bar is a real surprise in outdoorsy Wanaka. Luxuriate in the huge cinema seats, or chill out in the red-velvet lounge with craft beers, classic cocktails and sophisticated bar snacks. You'll find Ruby's concealed within the Basecamp Wanaka building on the outskirts of town.

🔒 Shopping

Picture Lounge
PHOTOGRAPHY

(www.thepicturelounge.co.nz; Spencer House Mall, 23 Dunmore St) Showcases large-format art shots, mainly of local landscapes.

Chop Shop
CLOTHING

(www.chop.co.nz; Pembroke Mall) The best coffee in town and a natty range of locally designed beanies and cool T-shirts for the discerning snowboarder.

Gallery Thirty Three
ARTS & CRAFTS

(www.gallery33.co.nz; 33 Helwick St; ⊙10am-5pm) Pottery, glass and jewellery from local artists.

MT Outdoors
OUTDOOR EQUIPMENT

(www.mtoutdoors.co.nz; 17 Dunmore St; ⊙9am-6pm) Rents and sells rock-climbing, mountaineering, camping and tramping gear.

ⓘ Information

Lake Wanaka i-SITE (☑03-443 1233; www.lakewanaka.co.nz; 103 Ardmore St; ⊙8.30am-5.30pm) Extremely helpful but always busy.

Mt Aspiring National Park Visitor Centre (DOC; ☑03-443 7660; www.doc.govt.nz; Ardmore St; ⊙8.30am-5pm daily Nov-Apr, Mon-Sat May-Oct) In an A-framed building on the edge of the town centre, this Department of Conservation centre takes hut bookings and offers advice on tracks and conditions. There's a small display on Wanaka geology, flora and fauna.

Wanaka Medical Centre (☑03-443 7811; www.wanakamedical.co.nz; 23 Cardrona Valley Rd; ⊙8am-6pm Mon-Fri, 9am-noon & 4-6pm Sat & Sun) Patches up adventure-sports mishaps.

ⓘ Getting There & Away

Alpine Connexions (☑03-443 9120; www.alpinecoachlines.co.nz) Links Wanaka with Queenstown, Cromwell, Alexandra, Dunedin and the Rail Trail towns of Central Otago. It also has shuttles to Wanaka Airport, the Mt Aspiring trailheads and Lake Hawea in summer, and Cardrona and Treble Cone in winter.

Atomic Shuttles (☑03-349 0697; www.atomictravel.co.nz) Daily bus to/from Dunedin ($35, 4½ hours) via Cromwell ($15, 50 minutes), Alexandra ($20, 1¾ hours) and Roxburgh ($30, 2¼ hours).

Connectabus (☑0800 405 066; www.connectabus.com; 1-way/return $35/65) Handy twice-daily service linking Wanaka with Queenstown airport (1¼ hours) and Queenstown (1½ hours). Free pick-up from most accommodation.

InterCity (☑03-442 4922; www.intercity.co.nz) Coaches depart from outside the Log Cabin on the lakefront, with daily services to Cromwell (from $10, 44 minutes), Queenstown (from $17, 1½ hours), Lake Hawea (from $10, 24 minutes), Makarora (from $12, 1¾ hours) and Franz Josef (from $43, 6½ hours).

Naked Bus (www.nakedbus.com) Services to Queenstown, Cromwell, Franz Josef, Lake Tekapo and Christchurch. Prices vary.

ⓘ Getting Around

Adventure Rentals (☑03-443 6050; www.adventurerentals.co.nz; 20 Ardmore St) Hires cars and 4WDs.

Yello (☑03-443 5555; www.yello.co.nz) Taxis and shuttles.

AROUND WANAKA

Cardrona

The cute hamlet of Cardrona reached its zenith in the 1870s at the height of the gold rush, when its population numbered over a thousand. Now it's a sleepy little place which wakes up with a jolt for the ski season.

With views of foothills and countless snowy peaks, the Crown Range Road from Cardrona to Queenstown is one of the South Island's most scenic drives. At 1076m, it's the highest sealed road in NZ. It passes through tall, swaying tussock grass in the Pisa Conservation Area (Map p544), which has several short walking trails. There are some great places to stop and drink in the view, particularly at the Queenstown end of the road before you start the switchback down towards Arrowtown. However, the road is narrow and winding, and needs to be tackled with care in poor weather. In winter it's sometimes closed after heavy snows, and you'll often need snow chains for your wheels.

🏃 Activities

Cardrona Alpine Resort   SKIING
(Map p544; ☑ 03-443 7341; www.cardrona.com; off Cardrona Valley Rd; day pass adult/child $99/51; ⊙ 9am-4pm Jul-Sep) Well-organised and professional, this 345-hectare ski field offers runs to suit all abilities (25% beginners, 50% intermediate, 25% advanced) at elevations ranging from 1670m to 1860m. In season it operates a booking office (☑ 03-443 7411; 18 Dunmore St) in Wanaka where you can buy ski passes and book Yello shuttles (return adult/child $35/28).

Snow Farm New Zealand   SKIING
(Map p45; ☑ 03-443 7542; www.snowfarmnz. com; off Cardrona Valley Rd; day pass adult/child $40/20) In winter this is home to fantastic cross-country skiing, snowshoeing, sledding and dog-sled tours, with over 40km of groomed trails. Lessons and ski hire are available.

Backcountry Saddle Expeditions   HORSE RIDING
(Map p544; ☑ 03-443 8151; www.backcountrysaddles.co.nz; Crown Range Rd; adult/child $85/65) Runs horse treks through the Cardrona Valley on Appaloosa horses.

🛏 Sleeping & Eating

Cardrona Hotel   PUB $$
(☑ 03-443 8153; www.cardronahotel.co.nz; Crown Range Rd; d $185; ⊙ bar 10am-2am) Après-ski, this iconic hotel really comes into its own. This classic southern pub first opened its doors in 1863, and today you'll find a good restaurant (mains $20 to $32) and a great garden bar. The lovingly restored rooms have snug, country-style furnishings and patios opening onto the garden (expect some noise on summer nights).

❶ Getting There & Away

Ski shuttles are offered by **Alpine Connexions** (☑ 03-443 9120; www.alpinecoachlines.co.nz), **Yello** (☑ 03-443 5555; www.yello.co.nz) and Ridgeline Adventures (p573) in Wanaka, and Kiwi Discovery (p552) in Queenstown.

Lake Hawea

POP 2180

The small town of Lake Hawea, 15km north of Wanaka, sits near the dam at the southern end of its 141-sq-km namesake. Separated from Lake Wanaka by a narrow isthmus called the Neck, blue-grey Lake Hawea is 35km long and 410m deep, and home to trout and landlocked salmon. The lake was raised 20m in 1958 to facilitate the power stations downriver.

🛏 Sleeping & Eating

Lake Hawea Holiday Park   HOLIDAY PARK $
(☑ 03-443 1767; www.haweaholidaypark.co.nz; SH6; campsites $16-34, units with/without bathroom $130/60; @ 🤶) On the lakeshore, this spacious and peaceful old-fashioned holiday park is a favourite of fishing and boating enthusiasts. Units range from a block of basic cabins with brightly painted doors to motel units and cottages.

Lake Hawea Hotel   HOTEL $$
(☑ 03-443 1224; www.lakehawea.co.nz; 1 Capell Ave; dm/d $30/180, lunch $11-27, dinner $19-32; 🤶) It's looking a little shabby from the outside, but the rooms have been refurbished and have unbeatable views across the lake. The complex includes a large bar and restaurant with equally stellar vistas.

❶ Getting There & Away

InterCity (☑ 03-442 4922; www.intercity. co.nz) Coaches stop at the dam (SH6) daily, heading to/from Queenstown (from $20, two hours), Cromwell (from $14, 1¼ hours), Wanaka (from $10, 24 minutes), Makarora (from $10, 1¼ hours) and Franz Josef (from $40, six hours).

Makarora

POP 40

Remote Makarora is the last frontier before you cross Haast Pass and enter the wild West Coast – and it certainly feels that way. Aside from the tour buses passing through, it feels wonderfully remote.

🏃 Activities

Tramping

Short tramps in this secluded area include the Bridal Track (1½ hours one way, 3.5km), from the top of Haast Pass to Davis Flat, and the Blue Pools Walk (30 minutes return), where you may see huge rainbow and brown trout.

Longer tramps go through magnificent countryside but shouldn't be undertaken lightly. Changeable alpine and river conditions mean you must be well prepared; consult with DOC before heading off. Its *Tramping in the Makarora Region* brochure ($2) is a worthwhile investment.

Gillespie Pass HIKING

The three-day Gillespie Pass loop tramp goes via the Young, Siberia and Wilkin Valleys. This is a high pass with avalanche danger in winter and spring. With a jetboat ride down the Wilkin to complete it, this rates as one of NZ's most memorable tramps.

Wilkin Valley Track HIKING

The Wilkin Valley Track heads off from Kerin Forks Hut – at the top of the Wilkin River – and on to Top Forks Hut and the picturesque Lakes Diana, Lucidus and Castalia (one hour, 1½ hours and three to four hours respectively from Top Forks Hut). Jetboats go to Kerin Forks, and a service goes across the Young River mouth when the Makarora floods. Another option is to use the High River Route from the Blue Pools (7km and two hours). Enquire at Wilkin River Jets or DOC.

Other Activities

Siberia Experience ADVENTURE TOUR

(☏03-443 4385; www.siberiaexperience.co.nz; adult/child $310/287) 🏃 This thrill-seeking extravaganza combines a 25-minute scenic small-plane flight, a three-hour bush walk through a remote mountain valley and a half-hour jetboat trip down the Wilkin and Makarora Rivers in Mt Aspiring National Park. It's possible to arrange transfers from Wanaka.

Wilkin River Jets JETBOATING

(☏03-443 8351; www.wilkinriverjets.co.nz) A superb 50km, one-hour jetboating trip (adult/child $110/57) into Mt Aspiring National Park, following the Makarora and Wilkin Rivers. It's cheaper than Queenstown options, and it can be combined with a helicopter ride.

Southern Alps Air SCENIC FLIGHTS

(☏0800 345 666, 03-443 4385; www.southernalpsair.co.nz) 🏃 Trip to Aoraki/Mt Cook and the glaciers (adult/child $435/275), Milford Sound flyovers ($405/255) and Milford flycruise combos ($490/305).

ℹ Information

DOC Visitor Centre (☏03-443 8365; www.doc.govt.nz; SH6; ⊙8am-5pm daily Dec-Mar, Mon-Fri Nov & Apr) Call in to check conditions and routes before undertaking any wilderness tramps. The nearest DOC camping grounds (adult/child $6/3) are on SH6 at Cameron Flat, 10km north of Makarora, and at Boundary Creek, 18km south of Makarora on the shores of Lake Wanaka.

Makarora Tourist Centre (☏03-443 8372; www.makarora.co.nz; 5944 Haast Pass-Makarora Rd/SH6; ⊙8am-8pm) A large complex incorporating a cafe, bar, shop, information centre, camping ground, bunk house and self-contained units.

ℹ Getting There & Away

InterCity (☏03-442 4922; www.intercity.co.nz) Daily coaches to/from Queenstown (from $24, 3½ hours), Cromwell (from $19, 2½ hours), Wanaka (from $12, 1¾ hours), Lake Hawea (from $10, 1¼ hours) and Franz Josef (from $36, 4¾ hours).

Fiordland & Southland

Includes ➡

Te Anau 581

Milford Sound/
Piopiotahi 590

Manapouri 591

Doubtful Sound 592

Invercargill..................595

The Catlins 599

Stewart Island/
Rakiura 603

Best Places to Eat

➡ Redcliff Cafe (p584)

➡ Miles Better Pies (p584)

➡ Yesteryears Museum Cafe (p594)

➡ The Batch (p597)

➡ South Sea Hotel (p609)

Best Places to Stay

➡ Milford Sound Lodge (p591)

➡ A boat on Doubtful Sound (p593)

➡ Victoria Railway Hotel (p597)

➡ Newhaven Holiday Park (p603)

➡ Jo & Andy's B&B (p608)

Why Go?

Welcome to scenery that travellers dream of and cameras fail to do justice.

To the west is Fiordland National Park, with jagged misty peaks, glistening lakes, and a remote and pristine stillness. Enter this beautiful isolation via the world-famous Milford Track, just one of many trails that meander through densely forested, glacier-sculptured valleys confined by mighty mountain ranges. Fiordland is also home to Milford and Doubtful Sounds, where verdant cliffs soar almost vertically from deep, indigo waters. Both fiords are relatively easy to reach and explore by road, boat or kayak.

In Southland's east, a sharp turn off the beaten track leads through the peaceful Catlins, where waterfalls cascade through lush forest and diverse wildlife congregates around a rugged, beautiful coastline.

And then there's the end of the line – Stewart Island/Rakiura, an isolated isle home to friendly seafarers and a flock of beautiful rare birds including New Zealand's beloved icon, the kiwi.

When to Go

➡ Visit from December to April for the best chance of settled weather amid Fiordland's notoriously fickle climate (although chances are, you'll still see rain!).

➡ Late October to late April is the Great Walks season for the Milford, Kepler, Routeburn and Rakiura Tracks, so you'll need to book in advance if you want to hike these popular tracks.

➡ Stewart Island/Rakiura's changeable weather can bring four seasons in one day, at any time of year, although the temperature is milder than you'd expect, with winter averaging around 10°C and summer 16.5°C.

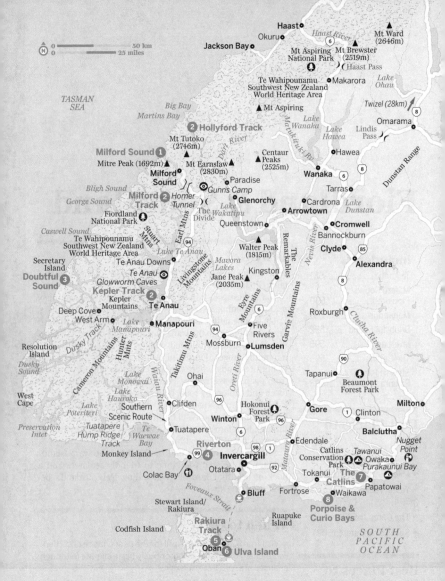

Fiordland & Southland Highlights

1 Sea kayaking, dwarfed by the steep cliffs of **Milford Sound** (p590)

2 Hiking through a World Heritage wilderness on the **Kepler** (p585), **Milford** (p586) or **Hollyford Tracks** (p588)

3 Soaking up sunset and sunrise on a **Doubtful Sound overnight cruise** (p593)

4 Discovering Southland's colourful history at Riverton's excellent **Te Hikoi museum** (p594)

5 Savouring the solitude on the **Rakiura Track** (p607), NZ's southernmost Great Walk

6 Immersing yourself in the bird-filled paradise on **Ulva Island** (p605)

7 Exploring side roads, forest waterfalls and lonely southern beaches in the peaceful, windswept **Catlins** (p599)

8 Spotting rare wildlife such as Hector's dolphins and yellow-eyed penguins at **Porpoise and Curio Bays** (p600)

ⓘ Getting There & Around

Air New Zealand (☏ 0800 737 000; www.airnz.
co.nz) connects Invercargill with Christchurch,
while **Stewart Island Flights** (☏ 03-218 9129;
www.stewartislandflights.com) connects Invercargill with Oban, as do ferry services run by
Stewart Island Experience (p610).

Major bus operators running between Te Anau
and Invercargill (connecting to Queenstown or
Dunedin) are **InterCity** (☏ 03-471 7143; www.
intercity.co.nz) and **Naked Bus** (www.nakedbus.
com), although this route is also serviced by
Tracknet (☏ 0800 483 262; www.tracknet.
net). **Atomic Shuttles** (☏ 03-349 0697, 0508
108 359; www.atomictravel.co.nz) runs between
Dunedin and Invercargill via Gore. The Southern
Scenic Route is plied by **Bottom Bus** (☏ 03-477
9083; www.travelheadfirst.com).

FIORDLAND

Formidable Fiordland is NZ's largest and
most impenetrable wilderness, a jagged,
mountainous, densely forested landmass
ribbed with deeply recessed sounds (which
are technically fiords) reaching inland like
crooked fingers from the Tasman Sea.

Fiordland National Park forms part of
the Te Wahipounamu Southwest New Zealand World Heritage Area, a combination
of four national parks in the southwest
corner of NZ. Te Wahipounamu (the Place
of Greenstone) covers 26,000 sq km and is
recognised internationally for its cultural
significance to Ngai Tahu, as well as for the
area's unique fauna and wildlife. The other
three parks are Aoraki/Mt Cook, Westland
Tai Poutini, and Mt Aspiring.

It is walkers who can delve the deepest
into this remote and magical area, not only
on the famous, multiday Milford, Kepler
and Hollyford Tracks, but even on short day
walks, easily accessible off the highway.

Te Anau

POP 1910

Peaceful, lakeside Te Anau township is the
main gateway to Fiordland National Park
tramps and the ever-popular Milford Sound,
as well as a pleasant place to while away a
few days.

To the east are the pastoral areas of central Southland, while west across Lake Te
Anau lie the rugged mountains of Fiordland.
The lake, NZ's second-largest, was gouged
out by a huge glacier and has several arms
that extend into the mountainous, forested
western shore. Its deepest point is 417m,
about twice the depth of Loch Ness.

◉ Sights & Activities

Te Anau is primarily a gateway to the great
wilderness of Te Wahipounamu, which
boasts such crowd-pullers as Milford Sound.
However, there's plenty to keep you occupied around the town itself, as well as out on
the water and in the air.

Te Anau Glowworm Caves   CAVE
Once present only in Maori legends, these
impressive caves were rediscovered in 1948.
Accessible only by boat, the 200m-long system of caves is a magical place with sculpted
rocks, waterfalls small and large, whirlpools
and a glittering glowworm grotto in its inner reaches. **Real Journeys** (☏ 0800 656 501;
www.realjourneys.co.nz) runs 2¼-hour guided
tours ($75/22 per adult/child), reaching the
heart of the caves by a walkway and a short
underground boat ride.

DOC Te Anau Wildlife Centre WILDLIFE CENTRE
(Te Anau-Manapouri Rd; admission by donation;
☺dawn-dusk) Here's a chance to see native
bird species difficult to spot in the wild, including the precious icon of Fiordland, the
extremely rare takahe.

ESSENTIAL FIORDLAND & SOUTHLAND

Eat Fish and chips – these southerners
maintain very high standards

Drink Craft beers brewed by Invercargill Brewery

Read *The Land of Doing Without* by
Julia Bradshaw, or *Pioneers of Martin's
Bay* by Alice Mackenzie – true Hollyford
tales

Listen to The roar of waterfalls on the
road to Milford Sound

Watch *Ata Whenua*, an eye-popping
aerial advertisement for the region,
screened at Fiordland Cinema in Te Anau

Go green Visit bird-filled Ulva Island,
for a glimpse into how NZ was and
could be again

Online www.fiordland.org.nz, www.
southlandnz.com, www.southernscenic-
route.co.nz, www.stewartisland.co.nz

Area code ☏ 03

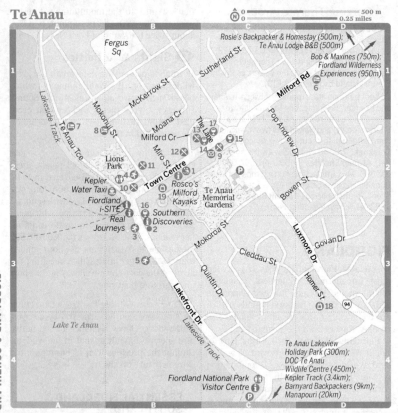

Te Anau

Activities, Courses & Tours
1 Rosco's Milford Kayaks	B2
2 Southern Discoveries	B3
3 Southern Lakes Helicopters	B3
4 Te Anau Bike Hire	B2
5 Wings & Water Te Anau	B3

Sleeping
6 Keiko's Cottages B&B	D1
7 Te Anau Top 10 Holiday Park	A2
8 Te Anau YHA Hostel	A2

Eating
Fresh Choice Supermarket	(see 13)
9 Mainly Seafood	C2
10 Miles Better Pies	B2
11 Redcliff Cafe	B2
12 Ristorante Pizzeria Da Toni	B2
13 Sandfly Cafe	B2

Drinking & Nightlife
14 Black Dog Bar	C2
15 Fat Duck	C2
16 Moose	B2
17 Ranch Bar & Grill	C2

Entertainment
Fiordland Cinema	(see 13)

Shopping
18 Bev's Tramping Gear Hire	D3
19 Outside Sports	B2

Southern Lakes Helicopters SCENIC FLIGHTS (☎ 03-249 7167; www.southernlakeshelicopters. co.nz; Lakefront Dr) Flights over Te Anau for 25 minutes ($195), longer trips over Doubtful, Dusky and Milford Sounds (from $540), and a chopper/walk/boat option on the Kepler Track ($185).

Wings & Water Te Anau SCENIC FLIGHTS
(☑03-249 7405; www.wingsandwater.co.nz; Lakefront Dr) Ten-minute local flights (adult/child $95/55), and longer flights over the Kepler Track and Doubtful and Milford Sounds (from $225).

Luxmore Jet JETBOATING
(☑0800 253 826; www.luxmorejet.com; adult/child $99/49) One-hour trips on the Upper Waiau River (aka the River Anduin).

Short Walks & Bike Rides

Te Anau's Lakeside Track makes for a delightful stroll in either direction – north to the marina and around to the Upukerora River (around an hour return), or south past the National Park Visitor Centre and on to the control gates and start of the Kepler Track (50 minutes). Hire bikes and obtain cycle-track maps from Outside Sports (p584) or Te Anau Bike Hire (7 Mokonui St; mountain bikes per hour/day from $12/30; ⊙ from 10am Sep-Apr).

Day tramps in the national park are readily accessible from Te Anau. Kepler Water Taxi (☑03-249 8364; stevsaunders@xtra.co.nz; 1-way/return $25/50) will scoot you over to Brod Bay from where you can walk to Mt Luxmore (seven to eight hours) or back along the Lakeside Track to Te Anau (two to three hours). During summer, Trips & Tramps (☑0800 305 807, 03-249 7081; www.tripsandtramps.com; ⊙Oct-Apr) offers small-group, guided hikes on the Kepler and Routeburn, amongst other tracks. Real Journeys (p593) runs guided day hikes (adult/child $195/127, November to mid-April) along an 11km stretch of the Milford Track. A number of day walks can also be completed by linking with regular bus services run by Tracknet (☑0800 483 262; www.tracknet.net).

For self-guided adventures, pick up DOC's *Fiordland National Park Day Walks* brochure ($2) from Te Anau i-SITE or Fiordland National Park Visitor Centre or download it at www.doc.govt.nz.

🛏 Sleeping

Accommodation can get booked out in the peak season (December to February). Book early if possible.

Bob & Maxines HOSTEL $
(☑03-249 7429; bob.anderson@woosh.co.nz; 20 Paton Pl, off Oraka St; dm $33, d $86-100; 🛜) Only 2.5km out of town, off the Te Anau–Milford Hwy, this relaxed and modern hostel gets rave reviews for the big mountain vistas from the communal lounge. Warm up beside the woodburner, cook up a storm in the well-equipped kitchen, or just chill out. Free bikes and wi-fi.

Rosie's Backpacker & Homestay HOSTEL $
(☑03-249 8431; www.rosiesbackpackers.co.nz; 23 Tom Plato Dr; dm/d $33/78; ⊙closed Jun-Jul; @🛜) You're immediately made to feel part of the family in this smart and intimate homestay, a short walk north of the town centre.

Te Anau YHA Hostel HOSTEL $
(☑03-249 7847; www.yha.co.nz; 29 Mokonui St; dm $27-32, d $84-92; @🛜) This centrally located, modern hostel has great facilities and comfortable, colourful rooms. Play volleyball in the grassy backyard, crank up the barbecue or get cosy by the fire in the lounge.

Barnyard Backpackers HOSTEL $
(☑03-249 8006; www.barnyardbackpackers.com; 80 Mt York Rd, off SH95; dm $29-31, d $76; @) On a deer farm 8km south of town, this rustic communal building and its collection of bunk-free, en suite log cabins sit on a view-laden hillside. The main lodge is great for playing pool or sitting around the toasty fireplace.

Te Anau Lakeview Holiday Park HOLIDAY PARK $
(☑03-249 7457, 0800 483 262; www.teanauholidaypark.co.nz; 77 Manapouri-Te Anau Hwy; sites per person from $17, dm/s $28/36, units $70-260; @🛜) This 22-acre, grassy lakeside holiday park has plenty of room to pitch your tent or park your van. It also has a wide range of accommodation from basic dorms and singles through to tidy cabins and motels, and rather swanky Marakura Apartments with enviable lake and mountain views. Friendly staff will hook you up with local activities and transport.

Te Anau Top 10 Holiday Park HOLIDAY PARK $
(☑03-249 7462, 0800 249 746; www.teanautop10.co.nz; 128 Te Anau Tce; sites per person from $20, units $75-166; @🛜) Near the town and lake with private sites, a playground, spa bath, bike hire, a barbecue area and modern kitchen facilities. Well-priced cabins and units run from basic to fancy.

Keiko's Cottages B&B B&B $$
(☑03-249 9248; www.keikos.co.nz; 228 Milford Rd; d $165-195; ⊙closed Jun-Aug; 🛜) The private, self-contained cottages here are lovely, and surrounded by Japanese-style gardens. A Japanese breakfast in the morning and a bamboo-bordered hot tub in the evening are worthy extras.

Te Anau Lodge B&B
B&B $$$

(☑ 03-249 7477; www.teanaulodge.com; 52 Howden St; d $240-350; @ �) The former 1930s-built Sisters of Mercy Convent, relocated to a grand location just north of town, is a heavenly accommodation option. Sip your complimentary wine in a chesterfield in front of the fire, retire to your spa before collapsing on a king-size bed, then awaken to a fresh, delicious breakfast in the old chapel.

✗ Eating

★ Miles Better Pies
PIES $

(cnr Town Centre & Mokonui St; pies $5-7) The bumper selection includes venison, lamb and mint, and fruit pies. There are a few pavement tables, but sitting beside the lake is nicer.

Mainly Seafood
FISH & CHIPS $

(www.mainlyseafood.co.nz; 106 Town Centre; fish & chips $7-11, burgers $8-14; ⊙ 10am-8.30pm) Commendable fish and chips, and burgers with homemade patties – yippee! Massage chair ($2) for if the queue stresses you out.

Fresh Choice Supermarket
SUPERMARKET $

(5 Milford Cres; ⊙ 7am-9pm) A decent-sized supermarket right in the middle of town.

Sandfly Cafe
CAFE $$

(9 The Lane; breakfast & lunch $7-18; ⊙ 7am-4.30pm; ⓢ) Clocking the most local votes for the town's best espresso, simple but satisfying Sandfly is a top spot to enjoy an all-day breakfast, soup, pie or sweet treat, while listening to cruisy music or sunning yourself on the lawn.

Ristorante Pizzeria Da Toni
ITALIAN $$

(☑ 03-249 4305; 1 Milford Cres; pizzas $23-25, mains $20-29; ⊙ 4-10pm Mon-Fri, noon-10pm Sat & Sun; ✐) This rather utilitarian space is *bella*fied by red gingham tablecloths, the odd splash of Roman and Venetian art and excellent, authentic Italian fare. Wood-fired pizzas with simple, high-quality toppings and homemade pastas are the stars of the show, supported by fine $10 desserts, thoughtful service and a baroque soundtrack.

★ Redcliff Cafe
RESTAURANT $$$

(www.theredcliff.co.nz; 12 Mokonui St; mains $31-39; ⊙ 4-10pm) Housed in a replica old settler's cottage, relaxed Redcliff offers generous fine dining in a convivial atmosphere backed by sharp service. The predominantly locally sourced food is truly terrific: try the wild venison or hare. Kick off or wind it up with a drink in the rustic front bar, which often hosts live music.

♚ Drinking & Entertainment

Fat Duck
BART

(124 Town Centre; ⊙ 8.30am-late; ⓢ) This corner bar with alfresco seating is a sound choice for a pint or two of Mac's. Marginally trendy gastropub style is reflected in fair modern fare (breakfast $13 to $20, dinner $22 to $39).

Ranch Bar & Grill
PUB

(www.theranchbar.co.nz; 111 Town Centre) Popular with locals for its generous pub meals, head here for a quality Sunday roast dinner ($15) and daily happy hour from 8pm to 9pm.

Moose
PUB

(www.themoose.co.nz; 84 Lakefront Dr) Head to this waterfront bar for late-afternoon beer and bar snacks on the patio. Plain all-day meals range from $20 to $35.

Fiordland Cinema
CINEMA

(☑ 03-249 8812; www.fiordlandcinema.co.nz; 7 The Lane; ⓢ) In between back-to-back showings of the excellent *Ata Whenua* (adult/child $10/5), essentially a 32-minute advertisement for Fiordland scenery, Fiordland Cinema serves as the local movie house. The adjacent Black Dog Bar is the town's most sophisticated watering hole.

🔒 Shopping

Bev's Tramping Gear Hire
OUTDOOR EQUIPMENT

(☑ 03-249 7389; www.bevs-hire.co.nz; 16 Homer St; ⊙ 9am-noon & 5.30-7pm, closed Sun mornings) Lovely Bev walks the talk, hires tramping and camping equipment, and sells Back Country dehydrated meals. From May to October, only open by prior arrangement.

Outside Sports
OUTDOOR EQUIPMENT

(www.outsidesports.co.nz; 38 Town Centre; ⊙ 9am-5pm) Tramping and camping equipment for sale, or hire, plus bike rental (half-/full day $30/50).

ⓘ Information

Fiordland i-SITE (☑ 03-249 8900; www.fiordland.org.nz; 85 Lakefront Dr; ⊙ 8.30am-5.30pm) Activity, accommodation and transport bookings.

Fiordland Medical Centre (☑ 03-249 7007; 25 Luxmore Dr; ⊙ 8am-5.30pm Mon-Fri, to noon Sat)

Fiordland National Park Visitor Centre (DOC; ☑ 03-249 0200; www.doc.govt.nz; cnr Lakefront Dr & Te Anau-Manapouri Rd; ⊙ 8.30am-4.30pm) Can assist with Great Walks bookings, general hut tickets and information, with the bonus of a natural-history display and a shop stocking essential topographical maps for backcountry trips.

Post Office (100 Town Centre; ⊘8.30am-5.30pm Mon-Fri, 9.30am-5pm Sat) In bookshop.

Real Journeys (☎0800 656 501; www.real-journeys.co.nz; Lakefront Dr; ⊘9am-5pm) Booking office for local tours and activities.

Rosco's Milford Kayaks (☎0800 476 726; www.roscosmilfordkayaks.com; 72 Town Centre; ⊘9am-5pm) Booking office for active pursuits.

Southern Discoveries (☎0800 264 536; www.southerndiscoveries.co.nz; Lakefront Dr; ⊘9am-5pm) Booking office for local tours and activities.

🛈 Getting There & Away

InterCity (☎03-471 7143; www.intercity.co.nz) has daily bus services between Te Anau and Queenstown (2½ hours), Invercargill (2½ hours) and Dunedin (4¾ hours). Buses depart outside Kiwi Country on Miro St.

Bottom Bus (☎03-477 9083; www.travel-headfirst.com) is a hop-on, hop-off bus service linking Te Anau to Queenstown, Invercargill and Milford Sound (1½ hours). **Naked Bus** (www.nakedbus.com) links Te Anau with Queenstown, Invercargill and Milford Sound.

Te Anau-based **Tracknet** (☎0800 483 262; www.tracknet.net) runs regular services north to Queenstown and south to Invercargill, as well as servicing tramping trailheads and Milford Sound.

Around Te Anau

Te Anau is the gateway to two Great Walks – the Kepler and Milford – and the less visited but equally worthy Hollyford. Detailed information can be found in Lonely Planet's *Hiking & Tramping New Zealand* guide, and from the helpful folk at the Fiordland National Park Visitor Centre, where you can also register your intentions via the Adventuresmart website (www.adventuresmart.org.nz).

Kepler Track

Opened in 1988 to relieve pressure on the Milford and Routeburn, the Kepler is one of NZ's best-planned tracks and now one of its most popular: a moderately strenuous 60km

Kepler Track

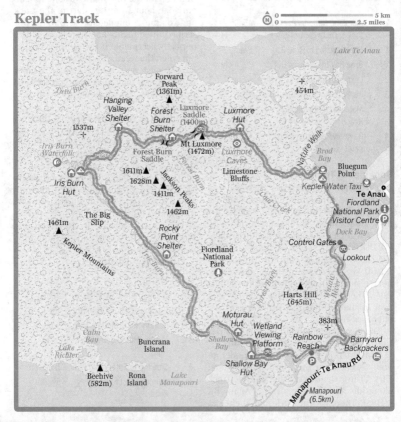

loop beginning and ending at the Waiau River control gates at southern end of Lake Te Anau. It features an all-day tramp across the mountaintops taking in incredible panoramas of the lake, the Jackson Peaks and the Kepler Mountains. Along the way it traverses rocky ridges, tussock lands and peaceful beech forest.

The route can be covered in four days, staying in the three huts, although it is possible to reduce the tramp to three days by continuing past Moturau Hut and leaving the track at Rainbow Reach swing bridge. However, spending a night at Moturau Hut on the shore of Lake Manapouri is an ideal way to end this tramp. The track can also be walked in either direction, although the most popular is Luxmore–Iris Burn–Moturau.

The alpine sections require a good level of fitness and may be closed in winter, although this is a heavily weather-dependent track at any time of year.

Estimated walking times:

DAY	ROUTE	TIME
1	Fiordland National Park Visitor Centre to control gates	45min
1	Control gates to Brod Bay	1½hr
1	Brod Bay to Luxmore Hut	3½-4½hr
2	Luxmore Hut to Iris Burn Hut	5-6hr
3	Iris Burn Hut to Moturau Hut	5-6hr
4	Moturau Hut to Rainbow Reach	1½-2hr
4	Rainbow Reach to control gates	2½-3½hr

Bookings & Transport

The Kepler is a Great Walk. Between late October and mid-April you must obtain a Great Walk pass (hut per night $54) for the huts. Passes must be obtained in advance, and it will pay to book early, either online via DOC's Great Walks Bookings (☑0800 694 732; www.greatwalks.co.nz) or in person at a DOC visitor centre. In the off-season the huts revert to backcountry Serviced huts ($15). There are campsites at Brod Bay and near Iris Burn Hut (Great Walks season $15, out of season free).

The recommended map for this tramp is 1:60,000 Parkmap 335-09 (Kepler Track).

Conveniently, the track begins under an hour's walk from the Fiordland National Park Visitor Centre, via the lakeside track alongside the Manapouri–Te Anau Rd (SH95). There's a car park and shelter at the control gates. Tracknet (☑0800 483 262; www.tracknet.net) runs shuttles to the trailhead ($6) and offers secure parking.

Kepler Water Taxi (☑03-249 8364; stevsaunders@xtra.co.nz) offers early-morning boat services across Lake Te Anau to Brod Bay ($25), slicing 1½ hours off the first day's tramp.

Milford Track

The best-known track in NZ and routinely touted as 'the finest walk in the world', the Milford is an absolute stunner, complete with rainforest, deep glaciated valleys, a glorious alpine pass surrounded by towering peaks, and powerful waterfalls including the legendary Sutherland Falls, one of the loftiest in the world. All these account for its popularity: more than 14,000 trampers complete the 54km-long track each year.

During the Great Walks season, the track can only be walked in one direction, starting from Glade Wharf. You must stay at Clinton Hut the first night, despite it being only one hour from the start of the track, and you must complete the trip in the prescribed three nights and four days. This is perfectly acceptable if the weather is kind, but when the weather turns sour you'll still have to push on across the alpine Mackinnon Pass and may miss some rather spectacular views. It's all down to the luck of the draw.

During the Great Walk season, the track is also frequented by guided tramping parties, which stay at cosy, carpeted lodges with hot showers and proper food. If that sounds appealing, contact Ultimate Hikes (☑03-450 1940, 0800 659 255; www.ultimatehikes.co.nz; 5-day tramp $1930-2095), the only operator permitted to run guided tramps of the Milford.

The track is covered by NewTopo map Milford Track 1:55,000, and 1:70,000 Parkmap 335-01 (Milford Track).

Estimated walking times:

DAY	ROUTE	TIME
1	Glade Wharf to Glade House	20min
1	Glade House to Clinton Hut	1hr
2	Clinton Hut to Mintaro Hut	5-6hr
3	Mintaro Hut to Dumpling Hut	6-7hr
3	Side trip to Sutherland Falls	1½hr return
4	Dumpling Hut to Sandfly Point	5½-6hr

Milford Track

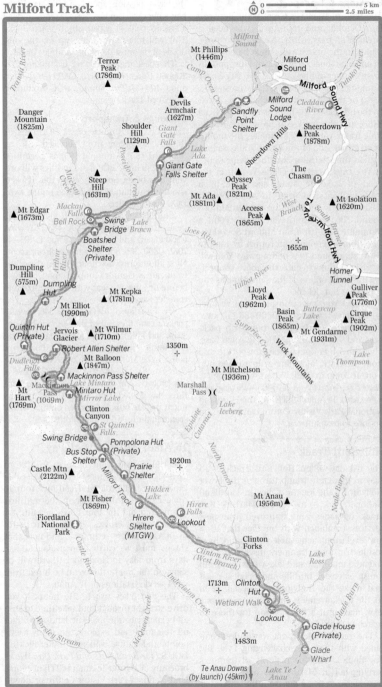

Transit River

Terror Peak (1786m) ▲

Danger Mountain (1825m) ▲

Mt Phillips (1446m) ▲

Camp Oven Creek

Milford Sound

Milford

Milford Sound

Devils Armchair (1627m) ▲

Shoulder Hill (1129m) ▲

Giant Gate Falls

Sandfly Point Shelter

Milford Sound Lodge

Cleddau River

Milford Sound Hwy

Sheerdown Peak (1878m) ▲

Sheerdown Hills

Lake Ada

Giant Gate Falls Shelter

Steep Hill (1631m) ▲

Poseidon Creek

Mackay Creek

Mt Edgar (1673m) ▲

Mackay Falls
Bell Rock

Swing Bridge

Boatshed Shelter (Private)

Lake Brown

Lake Ada

Mt Ada (1881m) ▲

Odyssey Peak (1821m) ▲

Access Peak (1865m) ▲

North Branch

West Branch

The Chasm P

Te Anau–milford Hwy

Mt Isolation (1620m) ▲

Joes River

1655m +

South Branch

Homer Tunnel

Gulliver Peak (1776m) ▲

Cirque Peak (1902m) ▲

Dumpling Hill (575m) ▲

Dumpling Hut

Arthur River

Mt Kepka (1781m) ▲

Mt Elliot (1990m) ▲

Talbot River

Lloyd Peak (1962m) ▲

Basin Peak (1865m) ▲

Mt Gendarme (1931m) ▲

Buttercup Lake

Lake Thompson

Quintin Hut (Private)

Jervois Glacier

Mt Wilmur (1710m) ▲

Robert Allen Shelter

Dudleigh Falls

Mt Balloon (1847m) ▲

Surprise Creek

1350m +

Wick Mountains

Mackinnon Pass Shelter

Mt Hart (1769m) ▲

Mackinnon Pass (1069m)

Lake Mintaro

Mintaro Hut

Mirror Lake

Mt Mitchelson (1936m) ▲

Marshall Pass) (

Lake Iceberg

Clinton Canyon

St Quintin Falls

Swing Bridge

Bus Stop Shelter

Pompolona Hut (Private)

Prairie Shelter

Epidote Cataract

North Branch

Castle Mtn (2122m) ▲

Milford Track

1920m +

Mt Fisher (1869m) ▲

Hidden Lake

Hirere Falls

Mt Anau (1956m) ▲

Neale Burn

Fiordland National Park

Hirere Shelter (MTGW)

Lookout

Clinton Forks

Castle River

Clinton River (West Branch)

Lake Ross

Worsley Stream

McQueen Creek

Indecision Creek

1713m +

Clinton Hut

Wetland Walk

Clinton River

Glade Burn

Lookout

Glade House (Private)

Glade Wharf

1483m +

Te Anau Downs (by launch) (45km) ↓

Lake Te Anau

FIORDLAND & SOUTHLAND

Bookings & Transport

The Milford Track is a Great Walk. Between late October and mid-April, you need a Great Walk pass ($162) to cover your three nights in the huts. Passes must be obtained in advance (book early to avoid disappointment), either online via DOC's Great Walks Bookings (☑0800 694 732; www.greatwalks. co.nz) or in person at a DOC visitor centre. In the off-season the huts revert to Serviced ($15), and the track can be walked in any time frame you like. This makes the month or so either side of the Great Walks season a great time to tramp, weather dependent.

The track starts at Glade Wharf, at the head of Lake Te Anau, accessible by a 1½-hour boat trip from Te Anau Downs, 29km from Te Anau on the road to Milford Sound. The track finishes at Sandfly Point, a 15-minute boat trip from Milford Sound village from where you can return by road to Te Anau, around two hours away. You will be given options to book the above connecting transport online, at the same time as you book your hut tickets.

To book your own transport, your best bet is to contact Tracknet (☑0800 483 262; www. tracknet.net), which offers round-trip packages and secure parking at its Te Anau base. There are other options for transport to and from the track, including a float-plane hop from Te Anau to Glade Wharf with Wings & Water Te Anau (☑03-249 7405; www.wingsandwater.co.nz). Te Anau i-SITE and the Fiordland National Park Visitor Centre can advise on options to best suit you.

Hollyford Track

The five-day, 58km Hollyford Track is an easy to moderate tramp through the lower Hollyford – the longest valley in Fiordland National Park – to remote Martin's Bay. Track upgrades and improved transport services, combined with the fact that it's a low-level tramp achievable year-round, have resulted in more trampers discovering the splendid mountain and lake vistas, beautiful forest, extensive birdlife and magical coast that make the Hollyford so special. Even so, the track averages only 4000 trampers a year, making it a good option for those in search of solitude.

The track is basically one way (unless combined with the super-challenging Pyke–Big Bay Route), with the majority of trampers turning tail at Martins Bay and retracing their steps, or flying out from the airstrip at the bay. If possible, spend an extra day in the bay, where you can view a seal colony and get a sneaky peak at a penguin, if you're lucky. This will more than make up for the misdeeds of the most demonic sandflies in NZ.

The best maps for this tramp are NZ-Topo50 *CB09 (Hollyford), CA09 (Alabaster)* and *CA08 (Milford Sound)*. DOC produces a Hollyford Track brochure.

Bookings & Transport

Trampers have the use of six DOC huts on the track, ranging from Serviced ($15) to Standard ($5). Camping ($5) is permitted next to the huts, although sandflies will prevent this being remotely enjoyable. Tickets should be obtained in advance online from DOC visitor centres.

Shuttles services for the Hollyford trailhead are Tracknet (☑0800 483 262; www. tracknet.net) and Trips & Tramps (☑03-249 7081, 0800 305 807; www.tripsandtramps.com). Nine kilometres (two hours' walk) shy of the trailhead is Gunn's Camp, a good bolthole before or after the feat with car storage and transfers available.

Fly Fiordland (☑0800 359 346; www.fly-fiordland.com) flies out of the Martins Bay airstrip, and Milford Sound for $160 per person (minimum two people), while jetboat trips along Lake McKerrow are offered by Hollyford Track (☑03-442 3000, 0800 832 226; www. hollyfordtrack.com), which also runs excellent three-day guided trips on the Hollyford staying at private huts/lodges and ending with a scenic flight to Milford Sound ($1895).

Te Anau–Milford Highway

The 119km road from Te Anau to Milford (SH94) offers the most easily accessible experience of Fiordland. Head out from Te Anau early (8am) or later in the morning (11am) to avoid the tour buses heading for midday sound cruises. Fill up with petrol in Te Anau before setting off, and note that chains must be carried on avalanche-risk days from May to November (there will be signs on the road); these can be hired from most service stations in Te Anau.

The trip takes two to 2½ hours if you drive straight through, but take time to stop and experience the majestic landscape. Pull off the road and explore the many viewpoints and nature walks en route. Pick up DOC'S *Fiordland National Park Day Walks* brochure ($2) from Te Anau i-SITE or Fiordland National Park Visitor Centre or download it at www.doc.govt.nz. The brochure also details the 10 basic DOC campsites ($6 per person) along the highway. All are scenic but also popular with sandflies.

The first part of the road meanders through rolling farmland atop the lateral moraine of the glacier that once gouged out Lake Te Anau. At the 29km mark the road passes Te Anau Downs, where an easy 45-minute return walk leads through forest to Lake Mistletoe, a small glacier-formed lake.

The road then heads into the Eglinton Valley, at first pocketed with sheepy pasture, then reaching deeper wilderness immersion as it crosses the boundary into Fiordland National Park. The knobby peaks, thick beech forest, lupin-lined river banks and grassy meadows are a grand sight indeed.

Just past the Mackay Creek campsite (at 51km) are great views to Pyramid Peak (2295m) and Ngatimamoe Peak (2164m) ahead. The boardwalk at Mirror Lakes (at 58km) takes you through beech forest and wetlands, and on a calm day the lakes reflect the mountains across the valley.

At 63km is Knob's Flat (☎03-249 9122; www.knobsflat.co.nz; sites per person $15, d $130-150), which has six self-contained units catering to trampers and anglers but perfect for those who appreciate the simple things in life such a cosy room with a view. And boy, do these units have views. Unpowered sites cater to those who want back-to-nature camping with the relative luxuries of hot showers and a kitchen with a fridge and gas cookers.

At the 77km mark is Cascade Creek and Lake Gunn. This area was known to Maori as O Tapara, and a stopover for parties heading to Anita Bay in search of *pounamu* (greenstone). The Lake Gunn Nature Walk (45 minutes return) loops through tall red beech forest ringing with bird calls, with side trails leading to quiet lakeside beaches.

At 84km the vegetation changes as you pass across the Divide, the lowest east–west pass in the Southern Alps. The roadside shelter here is used by trampers either finishing or starting the Routeburn, Greenstone or Caples Tracks, with bus services pulling in and out with regularity. From here you can embark on a marvellous two-hour return walk along the the start of the Routeburn, climbing up through beech forest to the alpine tussockland of Key Summit. On a good day the views of the Humboldt and Darran mountains are sure to knock your socks off, and the nature walk around the boggy tops and stunted beech is a great excuse to linger.

From the Divide, the road falls into the beech forest of the Hollyford Valley (stop at Pop's View for a great outlook) and there's a worthwhile detour off SH94 down the Lower Hollyford to Gunn's Camp, 8km along the unsealed road leading to the Hollyford Track, a further 9km away, where you will also find the track to Humboldt Falls (30 minutes return).

Also known as Hollyford Camp, Gunn's Camp (www.gunnscamp.org.nz; Lower Hollyford Valley Rd; camping per person $15, dm $25, cabins $65, bed linen extra $5) is a stronghold of colourful pioneer legends – of ridiculously difficult road-building, and of Davey Gunn, the hard-core bushman who drove stock then guided tourists through the valley for 25 years before falling off his horse and drowning in 1950. This 1930s public-works camp has a small shop and museum (adult/child $2/free), as well as original cabins with coal/wood-fired stoves, one newer bunkroom and a similarly modern communal kitchen-lounge. Payment is by cash or credit cards only, and the electricity generator gets switched off at 10pm.

Back on the main road to Milford, the road climbs through the cascade-tastic valley to the Homer Tunnel, 101km from Te Anau and framed by a spectacular, high-walled, ice-carved amphitheatre. Begun as a relief project in the 1930s and finally opened to motor traffic in 1954, the tunnel is one way, with the world's most alpine set of traffic lights to direct traffic. Dark, magnificently rough-hewn and dripping with water, the 1270m-long tunnel emerges at the other end at the head of the spectacular Cleddau Valley. Any spare 'wows' might pop out about now. Kea (alpine parrots) hang around the tunnel looking for food from tourists, but don't feed them as it's bad for their health.

About 10km before Milford, the wheelchair- and pram-friendly Chasm Walk (20 minutes return) is well worth a stop. The forest-cloaked Cleddau River plunges through eroded boulders in a narrow chasm, creating deep falls and a natural rock bridge. From here, watch for glimpses of Mt Tutoko (2746m), Fiordland's highest peak, above the beech forest just before Milford.

Milford Sound/Piopiotahi

POP 114

The first sight of Milford Sound is stunning. Sheer rocky cliffs rise out of still, dark waters, and forests clinging to the slopes sometimes relinquish their hold, causing a 'tree avalanche' into the waters. The spectacular, photogenic 1692m-high Mitre Peak rises dead ahead.

Milford Sound receives about half a million visitors each year, many of them crammed into the peak months (January and February). Some 14,000 arrive by foot, via the Milford Track which ends at the sound. Many more drive from Te Anau, but most arrive via the multitude of bus tours. But don't worry: out on the water all this humanity seems tiny compared to nature's vastness.

⊙ Sights & Activities

The clue is in the name: Milford Sound is all about the water, and the landforms that envelop it. It's enough to make you go misty-eyed, as an average annual rainfall of 7m fuels innumerable cascading waterfalls. The unique ocean environment – caused by freshwater sitting atop warmer seawater – replicates deep-ocean conditions, encouraging the activity of marine life such as dolphins, seals and penguins. Getting out on the water is a must.

One of the best perspectives you can get of Milford Sound is from a kayak, dwarfed by the cliffs. Two operators can get you out on the water, both of which have booking offices in Te Anau.

Rosco's Milford Kayaks KAYAKING
(☑ 0800 476 726, 03-249 8500; www.roscosmilfordkayaks.com; 72 Town Centre, Te Anau; trips $99-255) Guided, tandem-kayak trips including the 'Morning Glory' ($189), a challenging paddle the full length of the fiord to Anita Bay, and the easier 'Stirling Sunriser' ($189), which ventures beneath the 151m-high Stirling Falls. Among many other options are trips 'your grandmother could do', and kayak-walk combos on the Milford Track.

Fiordland Wilderness Experiences KAYAKING
(☑ 03-249-7700, 0800 200 434; www.seakayakfiordland.co.nz; Sandy Brown Rd, Te Anau; per person $145; ⊙ Sep-Apr) Offers guided six-hour trips on Milford Sound, with four to five hours on the water.

Descend Scubadiving DIVING
(☑ 0800 337 2363; www.divemilfordsound.co.nz; ex Te Anau/Milford $349/299) Offering a chance to see marine life unique to the Fiordland marine reserve (including a multitude of corals), Descend runs day trips with four hours' cruising on Milford Sound (7m alloy cat), with two dives along the way. Transport, equipment, lunch, hot drinks and snack supplied.

☞ Tours

A cruise on Milford Sound is Fiordland's most accessible experience, as evident from the slew of cruise companies located in the flash **cruise terminal** (⊙ 8am-5.15pm Oct-Apr, 9am-4.15pm May-Sep), a 10-minute walk from the cafe and car park.

Each cruise company claims to be quieter, smaller, bigger, cheaper, or in some way preferable to the rest. What really makes a difference is the timing of the cruise. Most bus tours aim for 1pm sailings so if you avoid that time of day there'll be less people on the boat (and on the road). With some companies you get a better price on cruises outside rush hour, too.

If you're particularly keen on wildlife, ask whether there'll be a nature guide on board. It's wise to book ahead regardless. You generally need to arrive 20 minutes before departure. Most companies offer coach transfers from Te Anau for an additional cost. Day trips from Queenstown make for a very long 13-hour day.

All the cruises visit the mouth of the sound, just 15km from the wharf, poking their prow into the choppy waves of the Tasman Sea. The shorter cruises visit less of the en route 'highlights', which include Bowen Falls, Mitre Peak, Anita Bay and Stirling Falls.

Only visitable on boat trips run by Milford Sound Cruises and Mitre Peak Cruises, **Milford Discovery Centre** (adult/child $36/18; ⊙ 9am-3.45pm) is a five-storey, largely submerged Deep Underwater Observatory offering a chance to view deep-water corals, tube anemones and bottom-dwelling sea perch.

Real Journeys BOAT TOUR
(☑ 0800 656 501, 03-249 7416; www.realjourneys.co.nz; adult/child from $70/22) Milford's biggest operator runs various trips including the popular 1¾-hour scenic cruise (adult $70 to $93, child $22). The nature cruise (2½ hours, adult $85 to $95, child $22) hones in on wildlife with a specialist nature guide providing commentary. Overnight cruises are also available, on which you can kayak

and take nature tours in tender crafts en route. Such trips depart from the Milford terminal around 4.30pm and return around 9.30am the following day. The *Milford Wanderer,* modelled on an old trading scow, accommodates 36 passengers in two- and four-bunk cabins (with shared bathrooms) and costs adult/child twin-share $335/168, or quad-share $278/139. The *Milford Mariner* sleeps 60 in more-upmarket, en suite, generally twin-share cabins (adult $284 to $405, child $142 to $203). Cheaper prices apply April through September; coach transport from Te Anau is extra.

Go Orange
BOAT TOUR

(☑ 03-249 8585, 0800 246 672; www.goorange. co.nz; adult $49-70, child $15) Real Journeys' low-cost two-hour cruises (leaving 9am, 12.30pm, 3.30pm) go along the full length of the sound with the bonus of a complimentary snack.

Jucy Cruize
BOAT TOUR

(☑ 0800 500 121; www.jucycruize.co.nz; adult/ child from $50/15) Offers 1½-hour trips on a 200-seater boat.

Mitre Peak Cruises
BOAT TOUR

(☑ 0800 744 633; www.mitrepeak.com; adult/child from $70/17) Two-hour cruises in smallish boats (maximum capacity 75). The 4.30pm cruise is good because many larger boats are heading back at this time.

Southern Discoveries
BOAT TOUR

(☑ 0800 264 536; www.southerndiscoveries.co.nz; adult/child from $70/16) A range of trips exploring Milford Sound, all lasting around two hours. The 2¼-hour wildlife cruise operates on a smaller (75-person) boat.

🛌 Sleeping & Eating

★ Milford Sound Lodge
LODGE $

(☑ 03-249 8071; www.milfordlodge.com; SH94; sites from $20, dm $33; @ 🛜) Alongside the Cleddau River, 1.5km from the Milford hub, this simple but comfortable lodge has a down-to-earth, active vibe. Travellers and trampers commune in the lounge or onsite Pio Pio Cafe (meals $7 to $22), which provides meals, wine and espresso. Very comfortable chalets ($195 to $295) enjoy an absolute riverside location. Booking ahead is strongly recommended.

Blue Duck Café & Bar
CAFE $$

(lunch $6-18, dinner $16-27; ⊙ cafe 8.30am-4.30pm, bar 4pm-late) Catering to a captive audience, this unpredictable cafe serves pies, sandwiches and suchlike during the day, then turns the tables for evenings of pizza and beer in the bar. You'll find the Blue Duck on the edge of the main Milford car park; activity booking office on site.

❶ Getting There & Away

BUS

InterCity (☑ 03-471 7143; www.intercity.co.nz) runs daily bus services to Milford Sound from Te Anau (three hours) and Queenstown (six hours) on to which you can add a cruise when you book. **Naked Bus** (www.nakedbus.com) also runs from Te Anau to the sound.

Te Anau–based **Tracknet** (☑ 0800 483 262; www.tracknet.net) provides regular Milford Sound services, with connections south from Invercargill, and north from Queenstown. **Fiordland Tours** (☑ 021 537 704, 0800 247 249; www.fiordlandtours.co.nz) runs small-group day tours and transport taking in Milford (with cruise) as well as the Hollyford.

All these buses pass the Divide and the start/ end of the Routeburn, Greenstone and Caples Tracks.

CAR

Fill up with petrol in Te Anau before setting off. Chains must be carried on avalanche-risk days from May to November (there will be signs on the road), and can be hired from service stations in Te Anau.

Manapouri
POP 230

Manapouri is the jumping-off point for cruises to Doubtful Sound, with most visitors heading straight to the boat harbour for the ferry to West Arm. This leaves the town sleepy and somewhat underrated, for not only is Lake Manapouri one of NZ's most beautiful, with a backdrop rivalling Te Anau, there are ample interesting things to do and local people to do them with.

In 1969 Manapouri was the site of NZ's first major environmental campaign. The original plan for the West Arm hydroelectric power station, built to supply electricity for the aluminium smelter near Invercargill, required raising the level of the lake by 30m. A petition gathered a staggering 265,000 signatures (17% of voting-age New Zealanders at the time) and the issue contributed to the downfall of the government at the following election. The win proved big for environmentalists, for not only was the power station built without the lake levels being changed, it also spawned more nationwide environmental action through the '70s and '80s.

Activities

By crossing the Waiau River at Pearl Harbour you can embark on day walks as detailed in DOC's *Fiordland National Park Day Walks* brochure. The classic outing is the Circle Track (three hours return) which can be extended to Hope Arm (five to six hours return). You can cross the river aboard a hired row boat or water taxi from Adventure Manapouri (☑ 03-249 8070; www.adventuremanapouri.co.nz; row boat hire per day $30, Waiau River water taxi return $15), which can also be contacted via Manapouri Stores.

Running between the northern entrance to Manapouri township and Pearl Harbour, the one-hour Frasers Beach walk offers picnic and swimming spots as well as fantastic views across the lake.

The Kepler Track is accessible from the northern end of Lake Manapouri at Rainbow Reach, 10km north of town.

Manapouri is also a staging point for the remote Dusky Track, a highly challenging 84km tramp taking eight to 10 days. For more information contact DOC or Lake Hauroko Tours (☑ 03-226 6681; www.duskytrack.co.nz).

Kayaking offers a wonderful perspective on the grandeur of Manapouri's surrounds. Adventure Kayak & Cruise (☑ 03-249 6626, 0800 324 966; www.fiordlandadventure.co.nz; 33 Waiau St) rents kayaks from $50 per person per day from October to April (minimum group size two; VHF radios provided free of charge). It also offers kayaking trips on Doubtful Sound from $245 per person.

🛏 Sleeping & Eating

Freestone Backpackers HOSTEL $
(☑ 03-249 6893; www.freestone.co.nz; 270 Hillside-Manapouri Rd; dm $22-33, d $66-86; 🛜) 🐾 These rustic cabins nestle on a hillside about 3km east of town, each with a small kitchen, potbelly stove and verandah. Bathrooms are communal. A converted family home offers another eight beds for singles, doubles and twins, with communal facilities including a full kitchen. Ask about boat cruises.

Possum Lodge HOLIDAY PARK $
(☑ 03-249 6623; www.possumlodge.co.nz; 13 Murrell Ave; sites 2 people $35, dm $20, units $56-106; 🛜) An attractive wee holiday park nestled into forest by the lake, this property has enviable campervan sites, very basic cabins, old-style motels and a fully equipped kitchen.

Manapouri Motels & Holiday Park HOLIDAY PARK $
(☑ 03-249 6624; www.manapourimotels.co.nz; 86 Cathedral Dr; sites from $16, units $58-130; @ 🛜) This eccentric but ultimately charming old-style camping ground features inexpensive cabins from mock–Swiss Alpine to sweet little weatherboard, quiet campsites, and a homely amenities block. But wait, there's more...including a fleet of old Morris Minors and a collection of vintage pinball machines.

Manapouri Stores CAFE $
(29 Waiau St; ⊙7am-7pm) Serves traditional tea-room food and espresso, stocks basic groceries, and can hook you up with row boats.

Lakeview Café & Bar PUB $$
(68 Cathedral Dr; pizzas $18-20, mains $18-34; ⊙11am-10pm; 🛜) Serves substantial meals with a generous side order of lake views from the front lawn. The adjacent public bar dishes up a dash of local history on the walls and in person.

ℹ Getting There & Away

Tracknet (☑ 0800 483 262; www.tracknet.net) runs between Te Anau and Manapouri twice daily from October to May, and on demand at other times of the year; these services connect with Queenstown and Invercargill.

Doubtful Sound

Magnificent Doubtful Sound is a wilderness area of fractured and gouged mountains, dense forest, and thundering waterfalls. One of NZ's largest sounds (three times the length and 10 times the area of Milford), Doubtful is technically a fiord (being carved by glaciers, rather than rivers). It is also much, *much* less visited. If you have the time and the money, it's an essential experience.

Until relatively recently, only the most intrepid tramper or sailor ever explored Doubtful Sound. Even Captain Cook only observed it from off the coast in 1770, because he was 'doubtful' whether the winds in the sound would be sufficient to blow the ship back out to sea. The sound became more accessible when the road over Wilmot Pass opened in 1959 to facilitate construction of the West Arm power station.

Getting to Doubtful Sound involves boarding a boat at Pearl Harbour in Manapouri for a one-hour trip to West Arm power station, followed by a 22km (40-minute) drive over Wilmot Pass to Deep Cove (permanent population: two) where you hop aboard a boat for your cruise on the sound. Manapouri is the easiest place to base yourself, although Te Anau and Queenstown pick-ups are readily organised through the cruise-boat operators.

☞ Tours

Your major considerations here are overnight (infinitely preferable) or day trip, and size of boat. Other considerations are whether you want to tour the power station. Overnight cruises include meals plus the option of fishing and kayaking. Note that the only Manapouri-based company specialising in kayak tours on Doubtful is Adventure Kayak & Cruise (☎0800 324 966; www.fiordlandadventure.co.nz; day trips $245; overnight kayaking & camping $385; ☺Oct-Apr).

Fiordland Cruises　　　　BOAT TOUR
(☎0800 368 283; www.fiordlandcruises.co.nz; s/d $600/1200) Overnight cruise on the *Southern Secret* (maximum 12 passengers); cabins are en suite doubles.

Deep Cove Charters　　　　BOAT TOUR
(☎0800 249 682; www.deepcovecharters.co.nz; s bunk $500, tw/d cabin $1100/1200) Overnight cruises on board the *Seafinn* (maximum 12 passengers).

Real Journeys　　　　BOAT TOUR
(☎0800 656 501; www.realjourneys.co.nz) The day-long 'wilderness cruise' (adult $245 to $265, child $65) includes a three-hour journey aboard a modern catamaran with a specialist nature guide. The overnight cruise, which runs from September to May, is aboard the *Fiordland Navigator,* which sleeps 70 in en suite cabins: twin-share (adult $417 to $595, child $209 to $298), and quad-share (adult $263 to $375, child $132 to $188). Some trips include a visit to Manapouri underground power station.

Go Orange　　　　BOAT TOUR
(☎0800 246 672; www.goorange.co.nz; adult $199-225, child $99-112.50) This is Real Journeys' low-cost trip, run on a 45-passenger vessel. The day-long cruise includes a power station visit and a three-hour cruise along the length of the sound.

Fiordland Expeditions　　　　BOAT TOUR
(☎0508 888 656; www.fiordlandexpeditions.co.nz; from $450) Overnight cruise on the *Tutoko II* (maximum 14 passengers).

Fiordland Wilderness Experiences KAYAKING
(☎0800 200 434; www.seakayakfiordland.co.nz; Sandy Brown Rd, Te Anau; per person $399-2750; ☺Oct-Apr) Two- to five-day kayaking and camping trips around Doubtful Sound, and six-day kayaking trips in remote Dusky Sound. Accommodation is on the expedition vessel *Breaksea Girl* and includes all meals and transfers.

SOUTHLAND

New Zealand's 'deep south' is a starkly contrasting mix of raw coastlines, untouched wilderness and great swaths of farmland. Laid-back and lightly populated, it's a region where getting off the beaten path goes with the territory.

Southern Scenic Route

The quiet Southern Scenic Route begins in Queenstown and heads south via Te Anau to Manapouri, Tuatapere, Riverton and Invercargill. From Invercargill it continues north through the Catlins to Dunedin. See www.southernscenicroute.co.nz or pick up the free *Southern Scenic Route* map to join all the dots. Public transport along this route is nonexistent except for the Catlins coast section serviced by Bottom Bus.

Tuatapere & Around

From Manapouri the road follows the Waiau River south between the scoured Takitimu and forested Hunter Mountains. Near Clifden is the elegant Clifden Suspension Bridge, built in 1899 and one of the longest bridges in the South Island. Information panels, a picnic table and toilets encourage a pit stop.

Just south of the suspension bridge is the turn-off to Lake Hauroko, the deepest lake in NZ and surrounded by dark, brooding, steeply forested slopes. The Dusky Track also ends (or begins) here. The 32km-drive from the highway is mostly unsealed; Tuatapere-based Lake Hauroko Tours (☎03-226 6681; www.duskytrack.co.nz; tours incl lunch $120; ☺Nov-Apr) offers day trips with a lake cruise.

Formerly a timber-milling town, sleepy Tuatapere (population 555) is now largely a farming centre. Those early woodcutters were very efficient, so only a remnant of a once-large tract of native podocarp (conifer) forest remains.

Wilderness, however, is not far away. Tuatapere is the base for the Hump Ridge Track, conceived and built by the local community, and opened in 2001. The three-day, 58km track makes relatively easy work of a tramp across craggy heights. Rich in natural and cultural history – from spectacular coastal and alpine scenery to the intriguing relics of a historic timber town – there's birdlife aplenty, and the chance to see Hector's dolphins on the lonely windswept coast on the way back to the start point. En route the path crosses a number of towering historic wooden viaducts, including NZ's highest.

To hike the track you need to book through the Tuatapere Humpridge Track Information Centre (☑ 0800 486 774, 03-226 6739; www.humpridgetrack.co.nz; 31 Orawia Rd; ⊙ 9.30am-5pm, limited hours in winter). Packages include transport to the trailhead (at Rarakau, 19km from Tuatapere) and comfortable lodge accommodation. The tramp is possible year-round and operates in three seasonal bands, priced accordingly (from $175), with guided tramps also available. Advance bookings are essential.

The Humpridge information centre also houses general regionwide tourist information. If you're interested in taking a spin on NZ's steepest river, ask about the two local jetboat operators – W-Jet (☑ 0800 376 174; www.wjet.co.nz; from $225) and Humpridge Jet (☑ 0800 270 556; www.wildernessjet.co.nz; from $210). Sharing the building is the Bushman's Museum (admission by donation), featuring relics and photographic records of the area's timber-milling past.

Tuatapere has a couple of excellent foody stops. Do not, we repeat, *do not* go past Yesteryears Museum Cafe (3a Orawia Rd; light meals $5-10; ⊙ 7.30am-5.30pm) – unless of course it's closed, which would be dreadful because you'd miss a chance to put some Johnny Cash on the stereogram, buy homemade jam, drink a Deep South ice-cream milkshake and nibble one of Aunt Daisy's sugar buns while perusing the displays of domestic jumble from a bygone era.

Lucky old Tuatapere has another great cafe at Last Light Lodge (☑ 03-226 6667; www.lastlightlodge.com; 2 Clifden Hwy; sites from $14, dm $30, s/d $55/70; @ ⊛), a capacious accommodation complex offering cabins, dorms and grassy campsites. The lodge owner is a chef of considerable skill, serving up coffee and fine cake, and sophisticiated meals featuring lots of home-grown goodness from the on-site gardens. The new deck and garden make dining (and drinking great craft beer) here a real treat in fine weather.

On SH99, around 10km south of Tuatapere, stop at the spectacular lookout at McCracken's Rest. Cast your eye down the arcing sweep of Te Waewae Bay – where Hector's dolphins and southern right whales are occasionally sighted – to the snowy peaks of Fiordland.

Just past Urepuki is the turn-off for Monkey Island, a grassy islet just metres off shore and accessible at low tide. The beach is a great spot at sunset.

Colac Bay is a popular holiday place and a good surfing spot. Southerlies provide the best swells here, but it's pretty consistent year-round and never crowded. Colac Bay Tavern & Holiday Park (☑ 03-234 8399; www.colacbaytavern.co.nz; 15 Colac Bay Rd; meals $15-27, sites from $13, cabins s/d $33/62; ⊛) is a welcoming spot for a meal of wood-fired pizza or fish and chips, with the convenience of a decent camping ground with basic rooms out the back.

For more information on Tuatapere and the Western Southland area, see www.westernsouthland.co.nz.

Riverton & Around

POP 1430

Quiet little Riverton, only 38km short of Invercargill, is worth a lunch stop and, if nearAntarctic swimming takes your fancy, the Riverton Rocks area and Taramea Bay are good for a dip. Across from the beach you will find the Beach House (126 Rocks Hwy; mains $16-35; ⊙ 10am-10pm; ⊛), a stylish, comfortable cafe famous for seafood, especially its creamy chowder. On a sunny summer's day the outside tables are a must. The other 90% of the time, retire inside to admire the view through the window.

Riverton really does rock, but its fascinating geological make-up is only part of the story, as you will discover at Te Hikoi Southern Journey (☑ 03-234 8260; www.tehikoi.co.nz; adult/child $6/free; ⊙ 10am-5pm Oct-Apr, to 4pm May-Sep). This cracker little museum relates local stories in clever and inspiring ways. Oh, that all small-town museums could be this good! Inside you will also find the Riverton Visitor Information Centre, which can assist with maps and heritage trails, as well accommodation.

Just along the road in an insanely turquoise building that has been various forms of eatery since 1891, Mrs Clark's Café (108 Palmerston St; meals $12-25; ☺7am-4pm; 🛜) serves thoroughly contemporary and delicious daytime food (beaut baking!) alongside ace espresso and craft beer.

The South Coast Environment Centre (www.sces.org.nz; 154 Palmerston St) has a good range of organic groceries and is the local WWOOF agent.

Invercargill

POP 49,900

This flat and somewhat featureless town tends to inspire ambivalence in its visitors, yet it satisfies all key requirements as a pit stop between the Catlins, Stewart Island/ Rakiura and Fiordland. Moreover, it sports some handsome buildings, a notable craft brewery, a decent dining scene, a few arty bits and pleasant open spaces.

⊙ Sights & Activities

The streets of Invercargill boast a slew of historic buildings and other features which can be discovered with the *Invercargill Heritage Trail* brochure. The *Short Walks* brochure details various walks in and around the town, including several around Sandy Point butting out on to the Oreti River. Oreti Beach, 10km to the southwest of town, is a nice spot for a walk or swim.

Southland Museum & Art Gallery   GALLERY
(www.southlandmuseum.com; Queens Park, 108 Gala St; admission by donation; ☺9am-5pm Mon-Fri, 10am-5pm Sat & Sun) Invercargill's cultural hub has permanent displays on Southland's natural and human history, recounting plenty of fascinating tales around maritime exploits in particular. Be sure to view 'Beyond the Roaring Forties' if you're headed to Stewart Island/Rakiura. The art-gallery area hosts exhibitions from contemporary local arts spliced with occasional international shows.

The museum's rock stars are undoubtedly the tuatara, NZ's unique lizardlike reptiles, unchanged for 220 million years. If the slow-moving, 100-years-old-and-counting patriarch Henry is any example, they're not planning to do much for the next 220 million years either. Feeding time is 4pm on Fridays; outside opening hours they can be viewed through windows at the rear of the pyramid.

If you're a fan of motorcyclist Burt Munro's speedy achievements as captured in *The World's Fastest Indian* (2005), make a beeline for the museum's short but sweet display then follow up with a visit to E Hayes & Sons (www.ehayes.co.nz; 168 Dee St) hardware store where you can see his famous motorbike in the flesh. Further evidence of Southland's petrolheadism will manifest in the next few years in the world's finest truck museum. We kid you not – we've eyeballed the exhibits already.

Anderson Park Art Gallery   GALLERY
(McIvor Rd; admission by donation; ☺ gallery 10am-5pm, gardens 8am-dusk) In a 1925 Georgian-style manor, this excellent gallery contains works from many NZ artists. The landscaped gardens are studded with trees and trails, and include a children's playground and *wharepuni* (sleeping house). The gallery is 7km north of the city centre; follow North Rd then turn right into McIvor Rd.

Invercargill Brewery   BREWERY
(www.invercargillbrewery.co.nz; 72 Leet St; ☺10am-6pm) NZ's great southern brewery has 20 taps for flagon-fills plus a bottled section of its own brews and guests'. Pop in for a tasting, or the 45-minute daily tour at 1pm ($15). Our favourites are the crisp Biman Pilsner and the chocolatey Pitch Black stout.

Queens Park   PARK
Wander around the half-wild, half-tamed Queens Park – a whopping 81 hectares of trees, plant collections, playing fields, ponds, children's playground and even a Wonderland castle.

🛏 Sleeping

Many places will store luggage for guests heading to Stewart Island/Rakiura. Motels cluster along Hwy 1 East (Tay St) and Hwy 6 North (North Rd).

Southern Comfort Backpackers   HOSTEL $
(☏ 03-218 3838; coupers@xtra.co.nz; 30 Thomson St; dm $28, s $58-66, d $68-74; @ 🛜) This large, lovely old house offers a well-equipped kitchen and TV-free lounge (hooray!) as well as colourful rooms including spacious doubles. Pick herbs from the peaceful gardens: you'd hardly know you were five minutes' walk from town. Cash only.

Invercargill

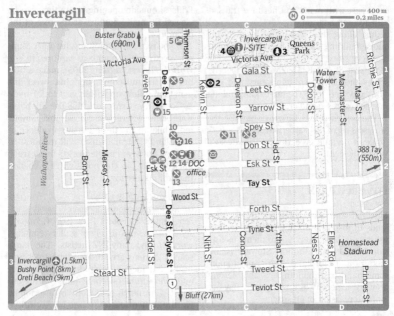

0 _____ 400 m
0 _____ 0.2 miles

Invercargill

◎ Sights
1 E Hayes & Sons	B1
2 Invercargill Brewery	C1
3 Queens Park	C1
4 Southland Museum & Art Gallery	C1

🛏 Sleeping
5 Southern Comfort Backpackers	B1
6 Tuatara Backpackers	B2
7 Victoria Railway Hotel	B2

🍴 Eating
8 Batch	C2

9 Colonial Bakery	B1
10 Rocks	B2
11 Seriously Good Chocolate Company	C2
12 Three Bean Café	B2
13 Turkish Kebabs	B2

🍷 Drinking & Nightlife
14 Kiln	B2
15 Louie's	B1

✴ Entertainment
16 Tillermans Music Lounge	B2

Tuatara Backpackers HOSTEL **$**
(☎ 03-214 0954; www.tuataralodge.co.nz; 30-32 Dee St; dm $25-29, d $69-80; @ 🖥) The town's largest hostel has heaps of basic rooms stacked three floors high in a central city building. If natural light is big on your hit list, ask for a room without the gloom. The ground-floor cafe doubles as a traveller hub, and the Bluff bus for Stewart Island/Rakiura stops just outside.

Invercargill Kiwi Holiday Park HOLIDAY PARK **$**
(☎ 03-235 8031, 0800 234 600; www.invercargill-kiwihp.co.nz; 352 Lorneville-Dacre Rd; sites per person $19, units d $60-120; @ 🖥) 🐾 Plenty of person-

ality is packed into this well-set-out holiday park surrounded by farmland. Homely units feature lovingly preserved and enhanced retro style, while the new 'Barn' communal camping facilities block is one of the nicest we've seen. Rural relaxation, grassy sites, a playground and friendly animals – what a charmer. Around 10km north of Invercargill centre, east of the Lorneville roundabout.

Invercargill Top 10
Holiday Park HOLIDAY PARK **$**
(☎ 03-218 9032, 0800 486 873; www.invercargill-top10.co.nz; 77 McIvor Rd; sites from $20, units $78-150; @ 🖥) A particularly attractive option for

motel- and cabin-dwellers, this leafy park 6.5km north of town also has pleasant sites and smart communal facilities.

Bushy Point Fernbirds HOMESTAY $$

(☑ 03-213 1302; www.fernbirds.co.nz; 197 Grant Rd, Otatara; s/d incl breakfast $140/150; @ 🐾) 🐾 Two friendly corgis are among the hosts at this eco-aware homestay set on the edge of 4.5 hectares of private forest reserve and wetlands. Fernbirds is very popular with birding types, so booking ahead is essential. It's five minutes' drive from central Invercargill, and rates include a guided walk in the reserve.

★ Victoria Railway Hotel HISTORIC HOTEL $$

(☑ 0800 777 557, 03-218 1281; www.hotelinvercargill.com; cnr Leven & Esk Sts; d $145-195; @ 🐾) For a hit of 19th-century heritage, the plush and individually styled en suite rooms and swanky guests' areas in this grand old refurbished hotel fit the bill. Partake of breakfast or dinner in the elegant dining room, or a locally brewed ale in the cosy house bar. Singles and twins should inquire about bargain rooms.

388 Tay MOTEL $$

(☑ 03-217 3881, 0508 388 829; www.388taymotel.co.nz; 388 Tay St; d $125-160; 🐾) Modern and spacious units and a friendly welcome are standard at this well-run spot that's a standout along Invercargill's Tay St motel alley.

✖ Eating

Seriously Good Chocolate Company CAFE $

(147 Spey St; ⊘ 8am-5pm Mon-Fri, 9am-2pm Sat) This sweet little cafe specialises in artisan chocolates (around $2.50 each), which can be nibbled alongside espresso, or spirited away in lovely gift boxes. Our seriously good recommendation is the ginger. And the hard caramel. And the rocky road...

Turkish Kebabs TURKISH $

(29 Esk St; kebabs from $10; ⊘ 10am-10pm; ☑) Generously proportioned felafel, meaty kebabs and mixed plates are served up in a pleasant dining space or available to take away. Other ethnic take-out joints lie nearby.

Colonial Bakery BAKERY $

(25a Gala St; snacks $2-8; ⊘ 7.30am-5pm Tue-Fri, to 3pm Sat & Sun) Euro goods such as baguettes, croissants and seedy Swiss-style breads nudge their way into a line of Kiwi classics such as fruit buns, meat pies and the ridiculous cheese roll.

Three Bean Café CAFE $

(73 Dee St; meals $11-20; ⊘ 7am-4pm Mon-Fri, 8am-2.30pm Sat) This main-street cafe prides itself on good coffee then matches the promise with carefully prepared snacks such as savoury pies and delightful lemon cake, and more substantial meals such as soup, salad and burgers. Helpful staff get our thumbs up, too.

★ Batch CAFE $$

(173 Spey St; meals $10-20; ⊘ 7am-4pm) Large shared tables, a relaxed beachy ambience, and top-notch coffee and smoothies add up to the cafe regularly being voted Southland's best. Delicious counter food includes bagels and brownies, and a smallish wine and beer list partners healthy lunch options. Open for platters on Friday nights, until 7.30pm.

Rocks CAFE $$

(☑ 03-218 7597; www.shop5rocks.com; Courtville Pl, 101 Dee St; lunch $12-25, dinner $21-37; ⊘ 10am-2pm & 5pm-late Tue-Sat) Tucked away in a shopping arcade, this stylish candlelit bar with exposed brick and burgundy walls boasts fine dining at reasonable prices. Lunch highlights include belly pork open sandwiches, pastas and salads, while stars of the extended evening menu are venison in blueberry sauce and the Sicilian fish bowl.

Buster Crabb RESTAURANT $$

(www.bustercrabb.co.nz; 326 Dee St; lunch mains $16-27, dinner mains $24-39; ⊘ 10.30am-late) Inexplicably named after a British navy frogman who went missing in 1956, Buster Crabb, housed in a spacious heritage villa, is one of Invercargill's best dining experiences. Local workers crowd in for lunchtime salads, roasts, burgers and platters; come evenings the char grill gets fired up for meaty mains like rib-eye wrapped in bacon.

🍷 Drinking & Entertainment

Kiln BART

(www.thekiln.co.nz; 7 Don St; mains $30-35; ⊘ 11am-late) Invercargill's best gastropub is also its most stylish, with trendy wallpaper and muted lighting from oversized lampshades. Food worth the wait comes in epic portions and runs a well-honed gamut from mussels and caesar salad, to fish and chips or a joint of meat to share between friends. Thursday $15 steak and live music Friday.

GORE

Around 66km northeast of Invercargill, Gore is the proud 'home of country music' in NZ, with the annual **Gold Guitar Week** (www.goldguitars.co.nz) in late May and early June ensuring the town's accommodation is booked out for at least 10 days per year. For the other 355 days, good reasons to stop include a notable art gallery, a neat little museum and the chance to view vintage aeroplanes.

Sharing the same building, the **Hokonui Moonshine Museum** (www.hokonuiwhiskey.com; admission $5; ⊘ 8.30am-5pm Mon-Fri, 9.30am-4pm Sat, 1-4pm Sun) and **Gore Historical Museum** (admission by donation) combine to celebrate Gore's proud history of fishing, farming and illegal distilleries. Admission to the Moonshine Museum includes a wee dram of the local liquid gold.

The outstanding **Eastern Southland Gallery** (☎ 03-208 9907; www.esgallery.co.nz; 14 Hokonui Dr; admission by donation; ⊘ 10am-4.30pm Mon-Fri, 1-4pm Sat & Sun) – aka the 'Goreggenheim' – in Gore's century-old former public library houses a hefty collection of NZ art including a large Ralph Hotere collection. The amazing John Money Collection combines indigenous folk art from West Africa and Australia with works by iconic New Zealand artist Rita Angus.

Croydon Aircraft Company (www.croydonaircraft.com; 1558 Waimea Hwy, SH94; admission $10; ⊘ 9.30am-4.30pm Mon-Fri, 11am-3pm Sat & Sun), 16km along SH94 towards Queenstown, restores vintage aircraft. Inside a viewing hangar (admission $10) several gems can be seen including a rare Dragonfly. Flights are also offered in a 1930s Tiger Moth biplane ($95/220 for 10/30 minutes). The adjacent **Moth** (www.themoth.co.nz; 1558 Waimea Hwy, SH94; lunch $12-26, dinner $27-45) is a bright and breezy place for a meal.

See www.gorenz.com for more on Gore.

Louie's　　　　　　　　　　　　　　BAR
(142 Dee St; mains $20-30; ⊘ 11.30am-late Tue-Sat) This cosy downtown bar is an enjoyable place to while away an evening, snuggled into a sofa or nook or fireside. Soak up fine beer, wine and spirits with tapas-style food ($13 to $17) or tuck into a main course ($30 to $32). Expect chilled-out music; occasional live gigs.

Tillermans Music Lounge　　　LIVE MUSIC
(16 Don St; ⊘ open on gig nights) The saviour of Southland's live-music fans, Mr Tillerman's venue hosts everything from thrash to flash, with a battered old dance floor to show for it. Visit the fun downstairs Vinyl Bar, which is open more regularly, to find out what's coming up and put in your request for Roxy Music.

❶ Information

DOC office (☎ 03-211 2400; www.doc.govt.nz; 7th fl, 33 Don St; ⊘ 8.30am-4.30pm Mon-Fri) Call in for DOC-related information and maps only if the i-SITE fails you or if you can't get to a DOC visitor centre.

Invercargill i-SITE (☎ 03-211 0895; www.invercargillnz.com; Queens Park, 108 Gala St; ⊘ 8am-5pm Mon-Fri, to 4pm Sat & Sun) Sharing the Southland Museum & Art Gallery building, the i-SITE can help with all general enquiries including DOC tracks, and is a godsend if you're stuck for Stewart Island/Rakiura or Catlins accommodation options .

Post office (51 Don St; ⊘ 8.30am-5.30pm Mon-Fri, 9am-1pm Sat)

❶ Getting There & Away

AIR

Air New Zealand flights link Invercargill to Christchurch (one hour) and onward, several times a day.

BUS

Buses leave from the Invercargill i-SITE, where you can also book your tickets. Travel time to Dunedin is four hours, Te Anau three hours, Queenstown four hours, and Christchurch 10 hours.

Atomic Shuttles (☎ 03-349 0697, 0508 108 359; www.atomictravel.co.nz) To Dunedin and Christchurch via Gore.

InterCity (☎ 03-471 7143; www.intercity.co.nz) To Te Anau and Queenstown, and Dunedin and Christchurch via Gore.

Naked Bus (www.nakedbus.com) To Queenstown, and Dunedin and Christchurch via Gore.

Tracknet (☎ 0800 483 262; www.tracknet.net) To Te Anau and Queenstown.

ⓘ Getting Around

Invercargill Airport (☏ 03-218 6367; www.invercargillairport.co.nz; 106 Airport Ave) is 3km west of central Invercargill. The door-to-door **Airport Shuttle** (☏ 03-214 3434) costs $5 to $10 from the city centre to the airport; more for residential pick-up. By taxi it's around $22; try **Blue Star Taxis** (☏ 03-217 7777).

Bluff

POP 1791

Bluff is Invercargill's port, 27km south of the city. It's also home to NZ's only aluminum smelter, but the main reason folk come here is to catch the ferry to Stewart Island/Rakiura or to pose for photos beside the **Stirling Point signpost**, which signifies that you've reached the furthest southern reaches of NZ. Sorry to disappoint you, but you haven't, for despite the oft-quoted phrase 'from Cape Reinga to Bluff' and the fact that SH1 terminates at Stirling Point, the South Island's southernmost point is Slope Point in the Catlins, with Stewart Island/Rakiura and remote dots of rock lying even further south. But let's not let the facts get in the way of a good story...

Salty tales abound round these parts, as evident in the small **Bluff Maritime Museum** (☏ 03-212 7534; 241 Foreshore Rd; adult/child $2/free; ⊙10am-4.30pm Mon-Fri, 1-5pm Sat & Sun), complete with century-old oyster boat and steam engine. It also houses interesting displays on Bluff history. The *Bluff Heritage Trail* brochure will guide you around local points of interest.

Oysters are Bluff's most famous export, celebrated during the **Bluff Oyster & Food Festival** (www.bluffoysterfest.co.nz) held annually around May. Buy fresh oysters in season from late March to late August from **Fowlers Oysters** (Ocean Beach Rd; ⊙9am-5pm Mar-Aug) on the way into town on the left.

Near the Four Square supermarket, **Stella's** (64 Gore St; ⊙7am-3pm) is your best bet for a coffee before braving the ferry crossing to Stewart Island/Rakiura. The muttonbird pie might prove a questionable decision.

For more information see www.bluff.co.nz.

The Catlins

The most direct route between Invercargill and Dunedin is via SH1. The pastoral scenery is pretty, but not as spectacular as the SH92 route via the Catlins coast. The Catlins is an enchanting region, combining lush farmland, native forests, usual coastal landmarks and empty beaches, bushwalks and wildlife-spotting opportunities. On a clear summer's day it is a beauty to behold. In the face of an Antarctic southerly it's an entirely different kettle of fish. Good luck.

Public transport is limited to the **Bottom Bus** (☏ 03-477 9083; www.travelheadfirst.com), which travels swiftly through from Dunedin three days a week. By far the best way to explore the area is with your own wheels. It's a slow-going route, with plenty of winding bits, narrows, gravel sections and optional detours, but this is *all* about the journey, rather than the destination. Allow a few days if at all possible, and make sure you have on hand the *Southern Scenic Route* brochure and the purple *Catlins* brochure and map, which detail every dot. The yellow heritage-trail pamphlet is also worth hunting down.

Flora & Fauna

The Catlins is a wonderful place for independent wildlife-watching. Fur seals and sea lions laze along the coast, while in spring migratory southern right whales are occasionally spotted. Dolphins are also frequent visitors.

Unlike much of Southland, tall kahikatea, totara and rimu forests still exist in the Catlins. Prolific birdlife includes the wonderfully noisy tui, and you'll also see kereru (NZ pigeons). Among many other birds are the endangered yellow-eyed penguin and the rare mohua (yellowhead).

🏃 Activities

Catlins Wildlife Trackers   WILDLIFE TOUR
(☏ 03-415 8613, 0800 228 5467; www.catlins-eco-tours.co.nz) ⚑ Based near Papatowai and running since 1990, Catlins Wildlife Trackers offers customised guided walks and tours with a focus on ecology. If you want to see the beloved mohua, penguins, sea lions or other wildlife, Mary and Fergus will track them down for you. Their fully guided three-night/two-day package costs $800, including all food, accommodation and transport.

Catlins River-Wisp Loop Track   TRAMPING
(www.doc.govt.nz) Opened in 2013, this 24km loop comprises two 12km sections: the low-level, well-formed Catlins River Walk (five to six hours), and the Wisp Walk (four to five hours), a higher-altitude tramp with a side trip to Rocky Knoll boasting great views and subalpine vegetation. The routes can be

The Catlins

Map: The Catlins. 0—20 km / 0—10 miles. Gore (25km), Balclutha (12km), Clutha River (Matau Branch), Edendale, Invercargill (32km), Maclennan River, Catlins River, Purekireki, Chutha River (Koau Branch), Kaka Point, Catlins Conservation Park, Mokoreta River, Mt Pye (720m)▲, River-Wisp Loop Track, Owaka Valley, Nugget Point Lighthouse, Forest Range, Waikawa River, Tahakopa River, Tawanui, Owaka, Roaring Bay, Maclennan Range, Matai Falls, Pounawea, Cannibal Bay, Quarry Hills, Purakaunui Falls, Surat Bay, McLean Falls, Lake Wilkie, Papatowai, Jack's Bay & Blowhole, Tokanui, Purakaunui Bay, Fortrose, Niagara, Long Point, Tahakopa Bay, Haldane, Waikawa, Cathedral Caves, Tautuku Bay, Otara, Chaslands Mistake, SOUTH PACIFIC OCEAN, Waipapa Point Lighthouse, Slope Point, Curio Bay/Porpoise Bay, Mataura River

walked in either direction as one long day, divided over two days, or split into shorter sections accessed via various entry/exit points. The main access is via Catlins Valley Road, south of Owaka.

Catlins Surf School   SURFING
(☑ 03-246 8552; www.catlins-surf.co.nz) Located in Porpoise Bay, the Catlins Surf School runs 90-minute surfing lessons for $50. The occasional group of dolphin spectators is free of charge. If you're already confident on the waves, hire a board and wetsuit (very necessary) for three hours ($40). Owner Nick also offers tuition in stand-up paddleboarding (two hours, $75).

Catlins Horse Riding   HORSE RIDING
(☑ 027 269 2904, 03-415 8368; www.catlinshorse-riding.co.nz; 41 Newhaven Rd, Owaka; 1/2/3hr rides $60/100/150) Explore the idiosyncratic coastline and landscapes on four legs with Catlins Horse Riding. Learners treks and the full gallop available.

ℹ️ Information

The i-SITEs in Invercargill and Balclutha have lots of Catlins information. On the road, you'll pass two information centres: the small Catlins Info Centre in Owaka or even smaller **Waikawa Information Centre** (☑ 03-246 8464; waikawamuseum@ hyper.net.nz; Main Rd; ☉10am-5pm). Online, see www.catlins.org.nz and www.catlins-nz.com.

The Catlins has no banks and limited options for eating out and grocery shopping. There's an ATM at the Four Square supermarket in Owaka, and petrol stations (hours can be irregular) in Fortrose, Papatowai and Owaka.

Invercargill to Papatowai

Heading east and south from Invercargill, SH92 enters the Catlins region at Fortrose. Take the turn-off here towards Waipapa Point and use the coastal route via Haldane, Waikawa and Niagara (where you rejoin SH92).

The Waipapa Point lighthouse dates from 1884, three years after the wreck of SS *Tararua*. Information panels recount the terrible tale, in which 131 people lost their lives. Tiptoe through the sea lions to survey the beach.

Follow the signs to Slope Point, the South Island's true southerly point. A 20-minute walk across farmland leads to a signpost designating this landmark in underwhelming fashion. The views more than make up for it, not only of the ocean but of the chunky rocks tumbling down to meet it. The track is closed in September and October for lambing.

Further east at Curio Bay, fossilised Jurassic-age trees are visible for four hours either side of low tide. Yellow-eyed penguins waddle ashore here an hour or so before sunset. Do the right thing and keep your distance. Backing on to Curio is Porpoise Bay, a popular travellers' stop with numerous accommodation options. Blue penguins nest in the dunes and in summer Hector's dolphins come here to rear their young. Whales are occasional visitors, and fur seals and sea lions may also be seen. There's safe swimming on the beach, and an excellent surf school.

The next civilised stop is Waikawa, which has a small museum, information centre, some accommodation and a takeaway. Keep on trucking to McLean Falls. The car park is 4km off the highway, with the falls themselves a 40-minute return walk through tree ferns and rimu.

Cutting back 150m into cliffs, the huge, arched Cathedral Caves (www.cathedralcaves. co.nz; adult/child $5/1) are only accessible for two hours either side of low tide (tide timetables are posted on the website, at the highway turn-off and at visitor facilities). From SH92 it's 2km to the car park, then a ferny 15-minute walk down to the beach – rather stunning in itself – and a further five minutes to the caves.

Around 6km further east, an easy forest walk leads to the dark peaty waters of Lake Wilkie (20 minutes return). Bellbirds may ring. Another 1km further along the highway, a short gravel road leads to sweeping Tautuku Bay, which can also be viewed from on high at the Florence Hill Lookout just before the descent into Papatowai.

The must-see in Papatowai is the Lost Gypsy Gallery (☑03-415 8908; SH92; ◷10am-5pm Thu-Tue, closed May-Sept; ☎). Fashioned from remaindered bits and bobs, artist Blair Sommerville's intricately crafted automata are wonderfully irreverent. The bamboozling collection in the bus (free entry) is a teaser for the carnival of creations through the gate ($5 entry, children under 12 not allowed). The buzz, bong and bright lights of the organ are bound to tickle your ribs. Espresso caravan and wi-fi on site.

Papatowai has a couple of short walks, a picnic spot at the mouth of the Tahakopa River, a handful of accommodation options and a general store selling petrol.

🛏 Sleeping

SLOPE POINT

Slope Point Backpackers   HOSTEL $
(☑03-246 8420; www.slopepoint.co.nz; 164 Slope Point Rd; sites per person from $12, dm $22-27, d $47, unit $87; @☎) This rural property has modern dorms and rooms, along with a great-value self-contained unit. There are grassy tent pitches and gravel sites for campervans, and the owners' children are always keen to show off the working farm. Board games, puzzles and loads of magazines take the place of TV.

CURIO BAY

Curio Bay Holiday Park   HOLIDAY PARK $
(☑03-246 8897; valwhyte@hotmail.com; 601 Curio Bay Rd; sites unpowered/powered 2 people $20/30) Tucked into an outcrop between Curio and Porpoise Bays, within easy walking distance to both, this camp offers private campsites hidden in a sea of tall flax. It's a truly beautiful place to camp, despite seriously ancient amenities. Long-promised upgrades are apparently in the pipeline. Guided nature walks are available.

Lazy Dolphin Lodge   HOSTEL $
(☑03-246 8579; www.lazydolphinlodge.co.nz; 529 Curio Bay Rd; dm/d/tw $35/76/76; @☎) This perfect hybrid of seaside holiday home and hostel is looking totally swell. Light and airy bedrooms sport cheerful linen, and there are two kitchens and lounges. The upstairs area is king for its deck overlooking Porpoise Bay.

Curio Bay Boutique Studios   APARTMENTS $$
(☑03-246 8797; www.curiobay.co.nz; 501 Curio Bay Rd; d $160-200) Three plush units are on offer here – one apartment attached to the hosts' house, and two similar down the road. All are self-contained, decorated in rustic, beachy style, with big windows and sun-drenched decks right next to the beach. A larger cottage is good for groups. Lovely options offering a touch of romance.

Catlins Beach Cottages   RENTAL HOUSE $$
(☑03-246 8552; www.catlins-surf.co.nz; houses $110-190) A range of self-contained cottages and houses around Curio Bay can be rented through Catlins Surf School. One-night rentals are fine, and it's a good option for travelling families or groups of up to six.

WAIKAWA

Penguin Paradise Holiday Lodge   HOSTEL $
(☑03-246 8552; www.catlins-surf.co.nz; 612 Niagara-Waikawa Rd; dm/d/tw $28/60/60) Laid-back backpackers in a heritage cottage in Waikawa village near the estuary. Special deals combine one night's accommodation and a 90-minute surf lesson ($75).

Waikava Harbourview   RENTAL HOUSE $$
(☑03-246 8866; www.southcatlins.co.nz; 14 Larne St; d $130-170) Waikava Harbourview is a four-bedroom house that's a good option for families or a group; up to 10 people can be accommodated. Opened in 2009, the newer one- and two-bedroom Harakeke and Toi Tois units are also good value.

MCLEAN FALLS

Catlins Kiwi Holiday Park HOLIDAY PARK **$**
(☑ 03-415 8338; www.catlinsnz.com; SH92; sites
from $20, cabins s/d $50/74, units $135-195; @ ☎)
Formerly known as McLean Falls Holi-
day Park, this modern holiday park offers
personality-packed accommodation ranging from cute cabins to smart family motels.
Tenters get the more ambient of the camping
options; all share good communal amenities.
Hop along to the on-site Whistling Frog Cafe
for some of the Catlins' best food.

PAPATOWAI

Hilltop LODGE **$**
(☑ 03-415 8028; www.hilltopcatlins.co.nz; 77 Tahakopa Valley Rd; dm $34, d $85-100) High on a hill
1.5km out of town, with native forest at the
back door and surrounded by a sheep farm,
these two shipshape cottages command
spectacular views of the Tahakopa Valley
and coast. Rent by the room or the whole
house; the en suite double is the pick of a
very nice bunch.

Catlins Mohua Park COTTAGES **$$**
(☑ 03-415 8613, 0800 228 5467; www.catlinsmohua-
park.co.nz; 744 Catlins Valley Rd; d $120-200) 🌿
Situated on the edge of a peaceful 14-hectare
nature reserve (7km off the highway), these
four luxurious self-contained cottages are the
perfect base for exploration, although with
such interesting mixed forest and birdlife on
the doorstep, you may well just want to sit
still for a bit. The owners have other accom-
modation options available at Papatowai.

 Eating

You'll find roadside takeaways in Waikawa
and Papatowai. The Papatoawi general store
has a limited range of groceries.

Whistling Frog Café & Bar CAFE **$$**
(☑ 03-415 8338; www.whistlingfrogcafe.com; SH92;
McLeans Falls; mains $20-32; ☺ 8.30am-9pm; ☎)
🌿 Colourful and fun, the Frog has a serious
approach to food and drink, offering craft
beer on tap (happy hour 4.30pm to 6pm)
and a refreshingly cosmopolitan menu.
We're talking a seriously rich steak-and-ale
pie with gourmet fries and a side salad with
blueberry dressing and candied nuts. Or
duck salad with blue cheese and rocket. Rib-
bit! Located at the Catlins Kiwi Holiday Park.

Niagara Falls Café CAFE **$$**
(www.niagarafallscafe.co.nz; 256 Niagara-Waikawa
Rd, Niagara; lunch mains $13-27, dinner $23-35;

☺ 8am-10pm; ☎ 🍴) Located in an old school-
house, this is a friendly spot to linger over
coffee and a scone, or tuck into homemade
meals from breakfast through dinner. Tasty
lamb burgers are sandwiched into freshly
baked bread, and there's blue cod and chow-
der as well as plenty of vegetarian options.
Bask in the grassy garden with a local craft
beer or fine wine.

Papatowai to Balclutha

From Papatowai, follow the highway north
to Matai Falls (a 30-minute return walk)
on the Maclennan River, then head south-
east on the signposted road to the tiered
Purakaunui Falls (20 minutes return). Both
falls are reached via cool, dark forest walks
through totara and tree fern.

Continue along the gravel road from
Purakaunui Falls to the 55m-deep Jack's
Blowhole. In the middle of a paddock 200m
from the sea but connected by a subterrane-
an cavern, this huge cauldron was named af-
ter Chief Tuhawaiki, nicknamed Bloody Jack
for his cussin'. It's a fairly brisk 30-minute
walk each way.

Owaka is the Catlins' main town (popula-
tion a hefty 303), bolstered by the Catlins
Info Centre & Owaka Museum (adult/child
$5/free; ☺ 9.30am-1pm & 1.30-4.30pm Mon-Fri,
10am-4pm Sat & Sun), which houses displays
on local history. The Catlins' reputation
as a shipwreck coast is explained in video
presentations. A petrol station, Four Square
supermarket with an ATM, and several run-
of-the-mill places to eat make Owaka a use-
ful spot for stocking up before moving on.

Pounawea, 4km east, is a beautiful ham-
let on the edge of the Catlins River Estuary.
Just across the inlet is Surat Bay, notable
for the sea lions that lie around the beach
between here and Cannibal Bay, an hour's
beach walk away.

Heading north from Owaka, detour off
SH92 to Nugget Point and walk out to the
lighthouse. This is the king of the Catlins
viewpoints, made all the more interesting
by the wave-thrashed cliffs, toothy nug-
gets, seals and sea lions lolling about below.
There's also plenty of birdlife, such as soar-
ing shearwaters and spoonbills huddling in
the lea of the breeze.

Just shy of the Nugget Point car park is
the car park for Roaring Bay, where a well-
placed hide allows you to see yellow-eyed
penguins coming ashore (best two hours be-
fore sunset). Obey all signs: as you can see,

this is a pretty precarious existence. If you don't have your own transport, nightly twilight tours ([phone] 0800 525 278; www.catlins.co.nz; per person $30) are run by the folks at Nugget View & Kaka Point Motels.

From Nugget Point the road loops back through the little township of Kaka Point, which has a surfy swimming beach, several accommodation options and a waterfront pub. The road continues north from here to Balclutha.

🛏 Sleeping & Eating

You won't starve along this stretch, as there are numerous food stops dotted along the highway. However, an investment in cheese and crackers may save you being smothered in chips.

OWAKA & PURAKAUNUI

DOC Camping Grounds   CAMPSITE $
(www.doc.govt.nz; adult/child $6/3) There are DOC camping grounds at Purakaunui Bay and inland at Tawanui.

POUNAWEA

Pounawea Motor Camp   HOLIDAY PARK $
([phone] 03-415 8483; www.catlins-nz.com/pounawea-motor-camp; Park Lane; sites from $30, units $50-80; [wifi]) Right on the estuary and next to a precious remant of native forest, this small park is best suited to tenters and campervanners who share a dated kitchen and smart bathrooms with the dwellers of some musty cabins. Tall trees and birdsong are the key features here.

Pounaewa Grove Motel   MOTEL $$
([phone] 03-415 8339; www.pounaweagrove.co.nz; 5 Ocean Grove; d $130; [wifi]) If you're looking for modern units with big, comfy beds, plush textiles, flat-screen TVs and sharp bathrooms, this four-unit studio complex will tick all the boxes. If you're looking for room to swing a cat, it will need to be a small one.

SURAT BAY

⭐ **Newhaven Holiday Park**   HOLIDAY PARK $
([phone] 03-415 8834; www.newhavenholiday.com; Newhaven Rd; sites unpowered/powered $32/35, units $66-120; [wifi]) Sitting on the estuary edge at the gateway to the Surat Bay beach walk, this delightful little holiday park has nice sites with good communal facilities, along with cheerful cabins and three self-contained flats. Play with the giant chess set or lounge around on the lawn.

NUGGET & KAKA POINTS

Kaka Point Camping Ground   HOLIDAY PARK $
([phone] 03-412 8801; www.kakapointcamping.co.nz; 39 Tarata St; cabins s/d $30/56; [wifi]) Cabins are basic but functional, and there are grassy hedged areas for campers. Bushwalks delve into the surrounding forest, and it's a short, though steep, stroll downhill to the beach and village.

Nugget Lodge   LODGE $$
([phone] 03-412 8783; www.nuggetlodge.co.nz; Nugget Rd; d $175; [wifi]) Sitting on a seaside knoll on the road south to the lighthouse are two modern bach-style self-contained units – one with balcony, one with private garden. It's worth including the lodge's huge continental breakfast ($12.50 per person) with freshly baked bread and homemade muesli. If you're lucky you might spy a couple of resident sea lions lolling on the beach below you.

Nugget View & Kaka Point Motels MOTEL $$
([phone] 0800 525 278; www.catlins.co.nz; 11 Rata St; d $95-200; [wifi]) A veritable minivillage of motel options ranging from good-value older units through to more modern ones with spa baths. All except one have a sea-view verandah. The friendly owners also operate day tours of the Catlins, and twilight tours ($30 per person) to view Nugget Point and the penguin colony at Roaring Bay.

Point Café & Bar   PUB $$
(58 Esplanade; meals $13-30) Prop yourself at the driftwood bar for a cool beer, play pool or grab a window seat for a sea view. Takeaways and ice creams are available at the attached store – $10 will get you burger and a scoop of hokeypokey ice cream.

Stewart Island/Rakiura

Travellers who undertake the short jaunt to Stewart Island/Rakiura will be rewarded with a warm welcome from both the local kiwi and the local Kiwis. NZ's 'third' island is a good place to spy the country's shy, feathered icon in the wild, and the close-knit community of Stewart Islanders (population 381) are relaxed hosts. If you're staying on the island for just a few days, don't be too surprised if most people quickly know who you are and where you came from – especially if you mix and mingle over a beer at

Stewart Island (North)

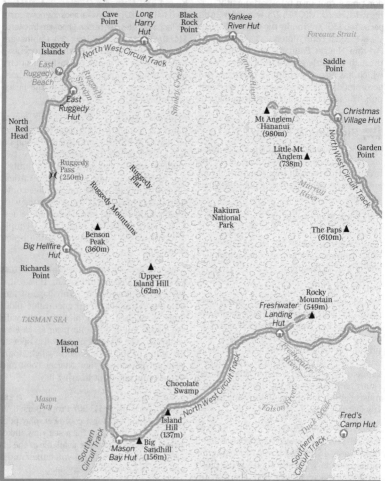

Ruggedy Islands
Cave Point
Long Harry Hut
Black Rock Point
Yankee River Hut
Foveaux Strait

North West Circuit Track

East Ruggedy Beach
Saddle Point

Ruggedy Stream

Smoky Creek

Yankee River

East Ruggedy Hut

North Red Head

Mt Anglem/ Hananui (980m)
Christmas Village Hut

North West Circuit Track

Ruggedy Pass (250m)

Ruggedy Flat

Little Mt Anglem (738m)
Garden Point

Ruggedy Mountains

Murray River

Rakiura National Park

The Paps (610m)

Benson Peak (360m)

Big Hellfire Hut

Richards Point

Upper Island Hill (62m)

Rocky Mountain (549m)

TASMAN SEA

Freshwater Landing Hut

Freshwater River

Mason Head

North West Circuit Track

Chocolate Swamp

Toison River

Mason Bay

Island Hill (137m)

Southern Circuit Track

Duck Creek

Fred's Camp Hut

Southern Circuit Track

Mason Bay Hut
Big Sandhill (156m)

NZ's southernmost pub, in the main settlement of Oban.

The island offers up plenty of active adventure including kayaking, and tramping the Great Walk or other tramps in Rakiura National Park which makes up 85% of the land area. As well as beautiful coastal and inland scenery, a major impetus for such excursions is birdlife. Stewart Island/Rakiura is a bird sanctuary of international repute, and even the most amateur of spotters will likely be distracted by the constant – and utterly glorious – squawking, singing and flitting of feathery flocks.

History

Stewart Island's Maori name is Rakiura (Glowing Skies), and you only need to catch a glimpse of a spectacular blood-red sunset or the aurora australis to see why. According to myth, NZ was hauled up from the ocean by Maui, who said, 'Let us go out of sight of land, far out in the open sea, and when we have quite lost sight of land, then let the anchor be dropped'. The North Island was the fish that Maui caught, the South Island his canoe and Rakiura was the anchor – Te Punga o te Waka o Maui.

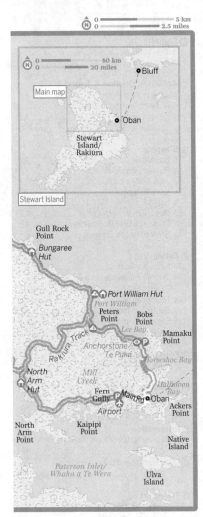

In June 1864 Stewart and the adjacent islets were bought from local Maori for £6000. Early industries were sealing, timber-milling, fish-curing and shipbuilding, with a short-lived gold rush towards the end of the 19th century. Today the island's economy is dependent on tourism and fishing.

Flora & Fauna

With an absence of mustelids (ferrets, stoats and weasels) and large areas of intact forest, Stewart Island/Rakiura has one of the largest and most diverse bird populations of anywhere in NZ. Even in the streets of Oban the air resonates with birds such as tui, bellbirds and kaka, which share their island home with weka, kakariki, fernbirds, robins and Rakiura tokoeka/kiwi. There are also plenty of shore- and seabirds including dotterels, shags, mollymawks, prions, petrels and albatross, as well as the sooty shearwater which is seen in large numbers during breeding season. Ask locals about the evening parade of penguins on a small beach near the wharf; and *please* – don't feed the birds. It's bad for them.

Exotic animals include two species of deer, the red and the Virginia (whitetail), introduced in the early 20th century, as were brush-tailed possums, which are now numerous throughout the island and destructive to the native bush. Stewart Island/Rakiura also has NZ fur seals, NZ sea lions, elephant seals and occasionally leopard seals that visit the beaches and rocky shores.

Beech, the tree that dominates much of NZ, is absent from Stewart Island/Rakiura. The predominant lowland bush is podocarp forest, with exceptionally tall rimu, miro, totara and kamahi forming the canopy. Because of mild winters, frequent rainfall and porous soil, most of the island is a lush forest, thick with vines and carpeted in deep green ferns and mosses.

◉ Sights

★ Ulva Island   ISLAND
A tiny paradise covering only 250 hectares, Ulva Island/Te Wharawhara is a great place to see lots of birds. Established as a bird sanctuary in 1922, it remains one of Stewart Island/Rakiura's wildest corners – 'a rare taste of how NZ once was and perhaps could be again', according to DOC. The island was declared rat free in 1997 and three years later

There is evidence that parts of Rakiura were occupied by moa hunters as early as the 13th century. The titi (muttonbird or sooty shearwater) on adjacent islands were an important seasonal food source for the southern Maori.

The first European visitor was Captain Cook. Sailing around the eastern, southern and western coasts in 1770 he mistook it for the bottom end of the South Island and promptly named it South Cape. In 1809 the sealing vessel *Pegasus* circumnavigated Rakiura and named it after its first officer, William Stewart.

Oban

Oban

⊙ Sights
1 Presbyterian Church...........................B1
2 Rakiura Museum.................................B2

Activities, Courses & Tours
3 Observation Rock..............................A3
4 Ruggedy Range Wilderness
   Experience...A2
Stewart Island Experience.........(see 22)

Sleeping
5 Bay Motel...A2
6 Bunkers Backpackers.........................A2
7 Jo & Andy's B&B.................................A2
8 Kaka Retreat......................................A1
9 Latt 47...B3
10 Observation Rock Lodge....................A3
11 Stewart Island Backpackers..............A2
12 Stewart Island Lodge.........................B3

⊗ Eating
13 Bird on a Pear....................................B1
14 Church Hill Restaurant &
    Oyster Bar...B1
15 Four Square......................................B1
16 South Sea Hotel................................B2
17 Stewart Island Smoked
    Salmon..A1

Entertainment
18 Bunkhouse Theatre............................A2

Shopping
19 Fernery..A2
20 Glowing Sky.......................................B2

Information
21 Rakiura National Park Visitor
    Centre...A2
Stewart Island Experience Red
   Shed...(see 22)

Transport
22 Stewart Island Experience.................B1

was chosen as the site to release endangered South Island saddlebacks. Today the air is alive with birdsong, which can be appreciated on walking tracks in the island's northwest as detailed in *Ulva: Self-Guided Tour* ($2), available from the DOC visitor centre. Many paths intersect amid beautiful stands of rimu, miro, totara and rata. Any water-taxi company will run you to the island from Golden Bay wharf, with scheduled services run by **Ulva Island Ferry** (📞03-219 1013; return adult/child $20/10; ⊙departs 9am, noon & 4pm; returns noon, 4pm & 6pm). To get the most out of Ulva Island, go on a tour with Ulva's Guided Walks (p607).

Rakiura Museum MUSEUM
(Ayr St; adult/child $2/50c; ⊙10am-1.30pm Mon-Sat, noon-2pm Sun) Historic photographs are stars of this small museum focused on local natural and human history, and featuring Maori artifacts, whaling gear and household items.

Presbyterian Church CHURCH
(Kamahi Rd) This wooden church has perched on a knoll overlooking the bay since 1904. One local wagers that shipwrights had a hand in its building: 'some of the joints are a pleasure to behold.'

🏃 Activities

Rakiura National Park protects 85% of the island, making it a mecca for trampers and bird-watchers. There are plenty of tracks on which to explore the wilderness, ranging from short, easy trails readily accessible on foot from Oban, to the epic North West Circuit, one of NZ's most legendary backcountry tramps.

Numerous operators offer guided tours: walking, driving, boating and by air, most focusing on wildlife with history slotted in. Independent walkers have plenty to choose from; visit Rakiura National Park Visitor Centre for details on local tramps, long and short, and huts along the way. The trails in DOC's *Stewart Island/Rakiura Short Walks* pamphlet ($2) would keep you busy for several days, and a bit less if you hire a bike from the Red Shed to fast-track the road sections. Longer tramps can also be shortened and indeed enhanced via an air hop with Rakiura Helicopters ([J]03-219 1155; www.rakiurahelicopters.co.nz), or Stewart Island Flights (p610), which works with Rakiura Charters to offer the fulfilling day-long or overnight Coast to Coast cross-island hike. Both air operators offer scenic flights.

If you haven't ever sea-fished, or just fancy it, this is the place, for NZ boasts no better fishers. Oh, and the answer to the question of swimming is definitely yes: yes, it is possible, and yes, you will probably freeze your nuts off.

Day Walks

Observation Rock WALKING
This short but quite sharp 15-minute climb reaches the Observation Rock lookout where there are panoramic views of Paterson Inlet, Mount Anglem and Mount Rakeahua. The trail is clearly marked from the end of Leonard Rd, off Ayr St.

Ackers Point WALKING
This three-hour return walk features an amble around the bay to a bushy track passing the historic Stone House (built 1835) at Harrald Bay before reaching Ackers Point Lighthouse where there are wide views of Foveaux Strait and the chance to see blue penguins and a colony of titi.

Overnight Tramps

Rakiura Track TRAMPING
(www.doc.govt.nz) One of NZ's nine Great Walks, the 39km, three-day Rakiura Track is a peaceful and leisurely loop which sidles around beautiful beaches before climbing over a 250m-high forested ridge and traversing the sheltered shores of Paterson Inlet/ Whaka a Te Wera. It passes sites of historical interest and introduces many of the common sea- and forest birds of the island.

Rakiura Track is actually only 32km long, but adding in the road sections at either end bumps it up to 39km, conveniently forming a circuit from Oban. It's a well-defined circuit requiring a moderate level of fitness, suitable for tramping year-round. Being a Great Walk, it has been gravelled to eliminate most of the mud for which the island is infamous.

There are two Great Walk huts ($22) en route, which need to be booked in advance, either via Great Walks Bookings ([J]0800 694 732; www.greatwalks.co.nz) or in person at the national park visitor centre. There is a limit of two consecutive nights in any one hut. Camping ($6) is permitted at the Standard campsites near the huts, and also at Maori Beach.

North West Circuit Track TRAMPING
(www.doc.govt.nz) The North West Circuit Track is Stewart Island/Rakiura's legendary tramp, a demanding coastal epic around a remote and natural coastline featuring isolated beaches, sand dunes, birds galore and miles of mud. It's 125km and takes 10 to 12 days, although there are several options for shortening it involving boats and planes.

The track begins and ends in Oban. There are well-spaced huts along the way, all of which are Standard ($5) except for two Great Walk Huts ($22) which must be booked in advance. A North West Circuit Pass ($35) provides for a night in each of the backcountry huts. Detailed information and essential topographical maps are available from DOC; and do register your intentions at the Adventuresmart website (www.adventuresmart. org.nz) as this is no easy walk in the park.

Tours

Ulva's Guided Walks WALKING TOUR
([J]03-219 1216; www.ulva.co.nz) Focused firmly on birding and guided by expert naturalists, these excellent half-day tours ($125; transport included) explore Ulva Island. Book at the Fernery. If you're a mad-keen twitcher, look for the Birding Bonanza trip ($400) on Ulva's website.

Stewart Island Experience GUIDED TOUR
([J]03-219 0056, 0800 000 511; www.stewartisland-experience.co.nz; [clock]12 Elgin Tce) Runs 2½-hour Paterson Inlet cruises (adult/child $90/22) via Ulva Island; 1½-hour minibus tours of Oban and the surrounding bays ($45/25); and 2½-hour marine-life nature cruises with semisubmersible viewing ($90/45).

Bravo Adventure Cruises BIRDWATCHING
([J]03-219 1144; www.kiwispotting.co.nz) Departing around sunset, Bravo runs small-group kiwi-spotting tours ($140) on a scenic reserve reached by a 30-minute boat trip and involving gentle walking through forest and on a beach.

SPOTTING A KIWI: A BRUSH WITH THE GODS

Stewart Island/Rakiura is one of the few places on earth where you can spot a kiwi in the wild. Considered the king of the forest by Maori, the bird has been around for 70 million years and is related to the now-extinct moa. Brown feathers camouflage the kiwi against its bush surroundings and a nocturnal lifestyle means spying a kiwi in the wild is a challenge. This is compounded by Stewart Island/Rakiura's fickle weather, with tours sometimes cancelled – allow a few nights on the island if you're desperate for a sighting.

As big as a barnyard chicken and estimated to number around 20,000 birds, the Stewart Island/Rakiura brown kiwi (*Apteryx australis lawryi*, also known as the tokoeka) is larger in size, longer in the beak and thicker in the legs than its northern cousins. They are also the only kiwi active during daylight hours, and birds may be seen around sunrise and sunset foraging for food in grassed areas and on beaches where they mine sandhoppers under washed-up kelp. If you spot one, keep silent, and stay still and well away. The birds' poor eyesight and single-mindedness in searching for food will often lead them to bump right into you.

Rakiura Charters BOAT TOUR, FISHING
(☑0800 725 487, 03-219 1487; www.rakiuracharters.co.nz; adult/child from $100/70) The most popular outing on the *Rakiura Suzy* is the half-day fishing cruise which stops in at the historic Whalers' Base. Trips can be tailored to suit timing and interests, such as wildlife-spotting and hiking.

Leask Bay Fishing Charters FISHING
(☑027 828 1147, 03-219 1391; www.leaskbaycharters.co.nz; per person $80, min 2 people) Go handlining with Andy on his family heirloom, the 110-year-old *Rawhiti*. Eat your catch for lunch on the morning trip; take it away for dinner on the afternoon trip.

Lo Loma Fishing Charters FISHING
(☑027 393 8362, 03-219 1141) Join Squizzy Squires on the *Lo Loma* for a fun handlining fishing trip.

Phil's Sea Kayak KAYAKING
(☑03-219 1444, 027 444 2323; trips from $79) Stewart Island/Rakiura's only kayaking guide, Phil runs trips on Paterson Inlet tailored for all abilities which include Ulva Island and sandy beaches, with sightings of wildlife along the way. Watch for good weather and give him a bell.

Ruggedy Range Wilderness Experience BIRDWATCHING
(☑0274 784 433, 03-219 1066; www.ruggedyrange.com; Main Rd) Nature-guide Furhana runs small-group guided walks including half- and full-day trips to Ulva Island ($120/185), and overnight trips to see kiwi in the wild ($525).

🛌 Sleeping

Finding accommodation can be difficult, especially in the low season when many places shut down. Booking ahead is highly recommended. The island has many holiday homes, which are often good value and offer the benefit of self-catering, which is especially handy if you do a spot of fishing (although many impose a two-night minimum stay or charge a surcharge for one night). Invercargill i-SITE and the Stewart Island Experience Red Shed can help you book such rentals. See also www.stewartisland.co.nz.

⭐ **Jo & Andy's B&B** B&B $
(☑03-219 1230; jariksem@clear.net.nz; cnr Morris St & Main Rd; s $60, d & tw $90; @🕾) A great option for budget travellers, this cosy blue home squeezes in twin, double and single rooms. A big breakfast of muesli, fruit and homemade bread prepares you for the most active of days. Jo and Andy are splendid company and there's hundreds of books if the weather packs up.

Bunkers Backpackers HOSTEL $
(☑03-219 1160; www.bunkersbackpackers.co.nz; 13 Argyle St; dm/d $32/76; ⊗ closed mid-Apr–mid-Oct; @🕾) A converted wooden villa houses Stewart Island/Rakiura's most promising hostel option, which is somewhat squeezed but offers the benefits of a sunny garden and inner village location.

Stewart Island Backpackers HOSTEL $
(☑03-219 1114; www.stewartislandbackpackers.com; cnr Dundee & Ayr Sts; sites $20, dm/d $35/70; 🕾) The island's biggest backpackers has an

adequate offering of rooms with up to four beds in a dorm, many of which face onto a courtyard. Somewhat shabby on last inspection, the communal lounge and kitchen are adequate and there's a barbecue area which traps some decent sun. There are terraced, grassy tents sites behind the lodge.

Stewart Island Lodge   LODGE $$
(☑ 03-219 0085; www.stewartislandlodge.co.nz; Nichol Rd; d incl breakfast $195; @ ☎) On a hill overlooking the bay, five minutes' walk to town, this grand lodge has six comfortable en suite rooms. Shared facilities include a sunny balcony, lounge and dining patio for partaking of the continental breakfast or your own meals prepared in the guest kitchen. As it's owned by Stewart Island Experience, enquire about island tours and transport.

Latt 47   RENTAL HOUSE $$
(☑ 03-219 1330; john.barry@clear.net.nz; 12a Excelsior Rd; d $180) This modern hillside house sleeps up to four. Debbie can also hook you up with other suitable Stewart Island/Rakiura accommodation.

Bay Motel   MOTEL $$
(☑ 03-219 1119; www.baymotel.co.nz; 9 Dundee St; d $175-200; ☎) Modern, comfortable units with lots of light and views over the harbour. Some rooms have spa baths, all have kitchens and two are wheelchair-accessible. When you've exhausted the island's bustling after-dark scene, Sky TV's on hand for on-tap entertainment.

Kaka Retreat   MOTEL $$$
(☑ 03-219 1252; www.kakaretreat.co.nz; 7 Miro Cres; d $230-256; @ ☎) These studio units are among the island's best, with plush interiors, flash bathrooms and private verandahs, although kitchen facilities are scant. Two older-style but smart fully self-contained units offer good value for up to six people.

Port of Call B&B   B&B, RENTAL HOUSE $$$
(☑ 0272 244 4722, 03-219 1394; www.portofcall. co.nz; Leask Bay Rd; s/d incl breakfast $320/385) Take in ocean views, relax before an open fire, or explore an isolated beach. Port of Call is 2km southwest of Oban, near Acker's Point. Two cosy self-contained options are available – The Bach, near the B&B ($250), and Hunter Cottage ($190) in Oban. All have a two-night minimum stay, and guided walks and water-taxi trips can also be arranged.

Observation Rock Lodge   LODGE $$$
(☑ 027 444 1802, 03-219 1444; www.observation-rocklodge.co.nz; 7 Leonard St; d standard/deluxe package $395/780; ☎) Secluded in bird-filled bush with views south to Golden Bay, Annett and Phil's delightful lodge has two stylish, luxurious rooms with private decks and shared lounge. Guided activites, sauna, hot tub and Annett's gourmet meals are inclusive in the deluxe package (breakfast and dinner) or by arrangement as additions to the standard B&B rate.

🍴 Eating

Bird on a Pear   CAFE $
(meals $10-18; ⊙ 7am-3.30pm) Upstairs on the wharf with Halfmoon Bay views, the Bird is a bright and breezy spot to enjoy a cooked breakfast, lunch or coffee and fresh home baking.

Four Square   SUPERMARKET $
(Elgin Tce; ⊙ 7.30am-7pm) Beyond a good selection of the usual groceries, this shop stocks sandwiches, blue cod and a few surprises besides.

Stewart Island Smoked Salmon   FISH $
(www.siss.co.nz; Miro Cres) If you're a fan of freshly smoked salmon, pop up to the smokehouse to see if anyone's in. This sweet, hot-smoked fish is a tasty treat for a picnic or pasta.

★ South Sea Hotel   PUB $$
(www.stewart-island.co.nz; 26 Elgin Tce; mains $16-30; ⊙ 7am-9pm; ☎) Welcome to one of NZ's classic pubs, complete with stellar cod and chips, beer by the quart, civilised cafe ambience in the dining room, and plenty of friendly banter in the public bar. Great at any time of day (or night), but try to wash up for the Sunday-night quiz – an unforgettable, fun slice of island life hosted by Quizmistress Vicki. Basic rooms available (double $90 to $115) and studio motels out back ($165).

Church Hill Restaurant
& Oyster Bar   CAFE, BAR $$$
(☑ 03-219 1123; www.churchill.co.nz; 36 Kamahi Rd; lunch $14-28, dinner $36-48; ⊙ lunch noon-2.30pm, dinner from 5.30pm) During summer this heritage villa's sunny deck provides hilltop views, and in cooler months you can get cosy inside beside the open fire. Big on local seafood, highlights include oysters and smoked salmon, prepared in refined modern style, followed by excellent desserts such as fig and pear sticky pudding. Dinner bookings advisable.

☆ Entertainment

Bunkhouse Theatre CINEMA
(☑027 867 9381; Main Rd; $10; ☺screenings 2pm
& 4pm) Oban's comfy little theatre screens
the quirky, cute 40-minute film *A Local's
Tail*, which provides an entertaining overview of Stewart Island/Rakiura history and
culture. Jaffas and DIY popcorn.

🛍 Shopping

Fernery ART & CRAFTS
(www.thefernerynz.com; Main Rd; ☺10.30am-
5pm, reduced hours in winter) A delightful store
stocking local art, craft, cards and books.

Glowing Sky CLOTHING
(www.glowingsky.co.nz; Elgin Tce; ☺10am-5pm)
Hand-printed T-shirts with Maori designs
and NZ-made merino clothing.

ℹ Information

Stewart Island/Rakiura has no banks. There's an
ATM in the Four Square which has a mind of its
own; credit cards are accepted for most activities. Wi-fi is available at the South Sea Hotel and
most accommodation. Mobile phone service is
limited to Telecom (027) numbers.

The best place for information on the mainland
is Invercargill i-SITE. Online, see www.stewarti-
sland.co.nz.

Post office (Elgin Tce; ☺8am-6pm Mon-Fri,
9am-5pm Sat & Sun) At Stewart Island Flights.

Rakiura National Park Visitor Centre (☑03-
219 0008; www.doc.govt.nz; Main Rd; ☺8am-
5pm Jan-Mar, reduced hours Apr-Dec) Stop
in to obtain information on short walks and
overnight tramps, as well as hut bookings and
passes, topographical maps, books, and a few
tramping essentials such as insect repellent
and wool socks. Information displays introduce
Stewart Island/Rakiura's flora and fauna, while
a video library provides entertainment and
education (a good rainy day Plan B). Register
your intentions here via Adventuresmart.

Stewart Island Experience Red Shed
(☑03-219 0056, 0800 000 511; www.
stewartislandexperience.co.nz; 12 Elgin Tce;
☺7.30am-6.30pm) Conveniently located next
to the wharf, the helpful crew at the Red Shed
can hook you up with nearly everything on and
around the island including accommodation,

guided tours, boat trips, bikes, scooters and
rental cars.

Stewart Island Health Centre (☑03-219
1098; Argyle St; ☺10am-12.30pm) Has 24-hour
on-call service.

ℹ Getting There & Away

AIR

Stewart Island Flights (☑03-218 9129; www.
stewartislandflights.com; Elgin Tce; adult/child 1
way $117.50/75, return $203/118) Flies between
the island and Invercargill three times daily, with
good standby and over-60s discounts.

BOAT

Stewart Island Experience (☑0800 000
511, 03-212 7660; www.stewartislandexperi-
ence.co.nz; Main Wharf) The passenger-only
ferry runs between Bluff and Oban (adult/
child $75/38 one way) up to four times daily
(reduced in winter). Book a few days ahead
in summer. The crossing takes one hour and
can be a rough ride. The company also runs a
shuttle between Bluff and Invercargill (adult/
child $24/12) with pick-ups and drop-offs in
Invercargill at the i-SITE, Tuatara Backpackers
and Invercargill Airport. Cars and campervans
can be stored in a secure car park at Bluff for
an additional cost.

A shuttle also runs between Bluff and Queenstown (adult/child $73/36), and Bluff and Te
Anau (adult/child $73/36) with pick-up and
drop-off at the Real Journeys offices.

ℹ Getting Around

Water taxis offer pick-ups and drop-offs to
remote parts of the island – a handy service
for trampers. The taxis also service Ulva Island
(return $25).

Aihe Eco Charters & Water Taxi (☑03-219
1066; www.aihe.co.nz)

Rakiura Water Taxi (☑027 354 9991, 0800
725 487; www.rakiurawatertaxi.co.nz)

Stewart Island Water Taxi & Eco Guiding
(☑03-219 1394, 0800 469 283; www.stewart-
islandwatertaxi.co.nz)

Rakiura Helicopters can also provide remote
access.

Rent a scooter (per half-/full day from
$60/70) or a car (per half-/full day from
$65/95) from Stewart Island Experience.

Understand New Zealand

NEW ZEALAND TODAY 612

Recovery from the Christchurch earthquake, sporting successes and musical mastery...time to take a Kiwi temperature check.

HISTORY 614

James Belich treads a NZ timeline, from Maori origins to Pakeha arrivals and recent ructions.

ENVIRONMENT 624

Vaughan Yarwood gives the low-down on the land, flora and fauna, national parks and environmental issues.

MAORI CULTURE 631

John Huria writes about NZ's first people: history, religion, legends, traditions and the arts (and, of course, the *haka*).

THE KIWI PSYCHE 638

Global psychiatry: lie down on this couch, NZ, and tell us all about yourself.

ARTS & MUSIC 643

The best Kiwi books, movies, TV, music and visual arts...this little nation punches well above its artistic weight.

New Zealand Today

New Zealand has had a bad run on the disaster front in recent years, between devastating earthquakes and a mining tragedy, not to mention the usual storms, droughts, drownings, sinkings and suchlike that make headline news. The global financial crisis hasn't helped either, with money troubles well and truly trickling down to ground level. Despite this, a typically plucky New Zealand public turns to the sporting arena – and increasingly the arts – to put a smile on its dial.

Best on Film

The Hobbit trilogy (Sir Peter Jackson; 2012–14)
Lord of the Rings trilogy (Sir Peter Jackson; 2001–03)
The Piano (Jane Campion; 1993)
Whale Rider (Niki Caro; 2002)
Once Were Warriors (Lee Tamahori; 1994)

Best in Print

The Luminaries (Eleanor Catton; 2013)
Mister Pip (Lloyd Jones; 2007)
Live Bodies (Maurice Gee; 1998)
The 10pm Question (Kate de Goldi; 2009)
The Collected Stories of Katherine Mansfield (2007)

Etiquette

Rugby Try to feign some enthusiasm!
Possums Don't express any affection for the tree-munching possum.
Australanders Be sure never to mistake a New Zealander for an Australian.
Dinnertime In Maori culture, sitting on a table is bad manners.

Shaky Isles

New Zealand has had it tough over the last few years. It may be a long way away from just about everywhere, but it is not immune to the vagaries of the global economy. In September 2010, just as the country was edging out of its worst recession in 30 years, a magnitude 7.1 earthquake struck near Christchurch, the nation's second-largest city. The damage was extensive but miraculously no lives were lost, partly because the earthquake occurred in the early hours of the morning when people were in their beds.

Then, in the early afternoon of 22 February 2011, a magnitude 6.3 earthquake struck Christchurch. This time, 185 people lost their lives. Numerous buildings, already weakened by the September 2010 quake and its aftershocks, were damaged beyond repair and had to be demolished completely.

The city's rebuild has been slow; the city centre didn't re-open fully until mid-2013. Cantabrians, however, have displayed admirable resilience and innovation, helping Christchurch to re-emerge as one of NZ's most exciting cities. Fringe suburbs have been reinvigorated, such as Woolston ('Coolston') and Addington, while a cardboard (yes cardboard!) cathedral has been brought into the fold. The city was named by Lonely Planet as one of the world's top 10 cities in *Best in Travel 2013*.

Christchurch isn't the only place to be awarded such a plaudit, with the South Island's West Coast named one of the world's must-visit regions in *Best in Travel 2014*. This is a timely boost for a region still reeling in the aftermath of one of NZ's worst disasters – the loss of 29 men in the Pike River coalmine explosions in November 2010. This widely felt tragedy further pushed the bounds of the country's emotional and economic resilience.

The nation's nerves were jangled yet again in July and August 2013 as a swarm of moderate earthquakes struck the top of the South Island. Widely felt in the capital, they served as a seismic reminder that New Zealanders do indeed live on the shaky isles.

Reasons to be Cheerful

Christchurch's recovery and rebuild is still a major preoccupation, producing good news and bad stories in equal measure. On one hand it is testing relationships between the citizens and government agencies, as tough decisions are made about fix-ups and payouts. On the other, Christchurch's recovery reinforces Kiwis' perceptions of themselves as 'battlers' with strong communities and civic pride.

New Zealanders have little difficulty in finding something to feel proud about. While the All Blacks remain a foundation – not only for their sporting achievements but as figureheads for 'brand NZ' – the depth of Kiwi talent ranges far beyond the rugby pitch. Following the All Blacks' success at the 2011 Rugby World Cup, this featherweight country punched well above its weight at the 2012 London Olympics. Claiming six gold medals, Team NZ gave traditional rival and sporting giant Australia a run for its money as it only managed to win one more. Other Kiwi sporting stars making their mark around the globe include young golfing sensation Lydia Koh, NBA rookie Steve Adams, IndyCar speedster Scott Dixon, and Valerie Adams: the greatest female shot-putter the world has ever seen.

While Sir Peter Jackson holds his position as a heavyweight in cinema with his blockbusting adaptations of *The Hobbit,* another major player has thrown his hat into the ring. Canadian director James Cameron has set up a rural home base near Wellington, and will create the *Avatar* sequels in the capital, bringing substantial investment and cementing NZ's reputation as a world-class film-making destination.

Pop pundits are also taking note of new Kiwi stars, with Grammy Award–winning Lorde (she of *Pure Heroine*, one of *Rolling Stone*'s albums of 2013) and Kimbra (of Goyte's 2012 smash-hit *Somebody That I Used to Know*) making huge impressions. Pages are also being turned on the international literary scene, as evidenced by Cantabrian Eleanor Catton. Her voluminous historical novel *The Luminaries* claimed one of the world's most coveted publishing accolades, the Man Booker Prize, in 2013, only the second New Zealander to do so.

POPULATION: **4.5 MILLION**

AREA: **268,680 SQ KM**

GDP GROWTH: **1.4%**

INFLATION: **1.4%**

UNEMPLOYMENT: **6.2%**

if New Zealand were 100 people

69 would be European
14 would be Māori
9 would be Asian
7 would be Pacific Islanders
1 would be Other

where they live

(% of New Zealanders)

63 North Island
20 South Island
10 Australia
5 Rest of the World
2 Travelling

population per sq km

NEW ZEALAND   AUSTRALIA   USA

👤 ≈ 3 people

History

by James Belich

New Zealand's history is not long, but it is fast. In less than a thousand years these islands have produced two new peoples: the Polynesian Maori and European New Zealanders. The latter are often known by their Maori name, 'Pakeha' (though not all like the term). NZ shares some of its history with the rest of Polynesia, and with other European settler societies, but has unique features as well. It is the similarities that make the differences so interesting, and vice versa.

Making Maori

One of New Zealand's foremost modern historians, James Belich has written a number of books on NZ history and hosted the TV documentary series *The New Zealand Wars*.

Despite persistent myths, there is no doubt that the first settlers of NZ were the Polynesian forebears of today's Maori. Beyond that, there are a lot of question marks. Exactly where in east Polynesia did they come from – the Cook Islands, Tahiti, the Marquesas? When did they arrive? Did the first settlers come in one group or several? Some evidence, such as the diverse DNA of the Polynesian rats that accompanied the first settlers, suggests multiple founding voyages. On the other hand, only rats and dogs brought by the founders have survived, not the more valuable pigs and chickens. The survival of these cherished animals would have had high priority, and their failure to be successfully introduced suggests fewer voyages.

NZ seems small compared with Australia, but it is bigger than Britain, and very much bigger than other Polynesian islands. Its regions vary wildly in environment and climate. Prime sites for first settlement were warm coastal gardens for the food plants brought from Polynesia – kumara (sweet potato), gourd, yam and taro – sources of workable stone for knives and adzes; and areas with abundant big game. NZ has no native land mammals apart from a few species of bat, but 'big game' is no exaggeration: the islands were home to a dozen species of moa (a large flightless bird), the largest of which weighed up to 240kg, about twice the size of an ostrich. There were also other species of flightless birds and large sea mammals such as fur seals, all unaccustomed to being hunted. For people from small Pacific islands, this was like hitting the jackpot.

TIMELINE	AD 1000–1200	1642	1769
	Possible date of the arrival of Maori in NZ. Solid archaeological evidence points to about AD 1200, but much earlier dates have been suggested for the first human impact on the environment.	First European contact: Abel Tasman arrives on an expedition from the Dutch East Indies (Indonesia) to find the 'Great South Land'. His party leaves without landing, after a sea skirmish with Maori.	European contact recommences with visits by James Cook and Jean de Surville. Despite some violence, both manage to communicate with Maori. This time NZ's link with the outside world proves permanent.

The first settlers spread far and fast, from the top of the North Island to the bottom of the South Island within the first 100 years. High-protein diets are likely to have boosted population growth.

By about 1400, however, with the big-game supply dwindling, Maori economics turned from big game to small game – forest birds and rats – and from hunting to gardening and fishing. A good living could still be made, but it required detailed local knowledge, steady effort and complex communal organisation, hence the rise of the Maori tribes. Competition for resources increased, conflict did likewise, and this led to the building of increasingly sophisticated fortifications, known as *pa*. Vestiges of *pa* earthworks can still be seen around the country (on the hilltops of Auckland, for example).

The Maori had no metals and no written language (and no alcoholic drinks or drugs). But their culture and spiritual life was rich and distinctive. Between Rangi-nui (sky father) and Papa-tu-a-nuku (earth mother) were various gods of land, forest and sea, joined by deified ancestors over time. The mischievous demigod Maui was particularly important. In legend, he vanquished the sun and fished up the North Island before meeting his death between the thighs of the goddess Hine-nui-te-po in an attempt to conquer the human mortality embodied in her. Maori traditional performance art, the group singing and dancing known as *kapa haka*, has real power, even for modern audiences. Visual art, notably woodcarving, is something special – 'like nothing but itself', in the words of 18th-century explorer-scientist Joseph Banks.

Rumours of late survivals of the giant moa bird abound, but none have been authenticated. So if you see a moa in your travels, photograph it – you have just made the greatest zoological discovery of the last 100 years.

Enter Europe

NZ became an official British colony in 1840, but the first authenticated contact between Maori and the outside world took place almost two centuries earlier in 1642, in Golden Bay at the top of the South Island. Two Dutch ships sailed from Indonesia, to search for southern land and anything valuable it might contain. The commander, Abel Tasman, was instructed to pretend to any natives he might meet 'that you are by no means eager for precious metals, so as to leave them ignorant of the value of the same'.

When Tasman's ships anchored in the bay, local Maori came out in their canoes to make the traditional challenge: friends or foes? Misunderstanding this, the Dutch challenged back, by blowing trumpets. When a boat was lowered to take a party between the two ships, it was attacked. Four crewmen were killed. Tasman sailed away and did not come back; nor did any other European for 127 years. But the Dutch did leave a name: 'Nieuw Zeeland' or 'New Sealand'.

Contact between Maori and Europeans was renewed in 1769, when English and French explorers arrived, under James Cook and Jean de

Abel Tasman named NZ 'Statenland', assuming it was connected to Staten Island near Argentina. It was subsequently named after the province of Zeeland in Tasman's Holland.

➡ Captain Cook statue

1772	1790s	1818–36
Marion du Fresne's French expedition arrives; it stays for some weeks at the Bay of Islands. Relations with Maori start well, but a breach of Maori *tapu* (sacred law) leads to violence.	Whaling ships and sealing gangs arrive in the country. Relations are established with Maori, with Europeans depending on the contact for essentials such as food, water and protection.	Intertribal Maori 'Musket Wars' take place: tribes acquire muskets and win bloody victories against tribes without them. The wars taper off in 1836, probably due to the equal distribution of weapons.

THE MORIORI & THEIR MYTH
....

One of NZ's most persistent legends is that Maori found mainland NZ already occupied by a more peaceful and racially distinct Melanesian people, known as the Moriori, whom they exterminated. This myth has been regularly debunked by scholars since the 1920s, but somehow hangs on.

To complicate matters, there were real 'Moriori', and Maori did treat them badly. The real Moriori were the people of the Chatham Islands, a windswept group about 900km east of the mainland. They were, however, fully Polynesian, and descended from Maori – 'Moriori' was their version of the same word. Mainland Maori arrived in the Chathams in 1835, as a spin-off of the Musket Wars, killing some Moriori and enslaving the rest. But they did not exterminate them. The mainland Moriori remain a myth.

Surville. Relations were more sympathetic, and exploration continued, motivated by science, profit and great power rivalry. Cook made two more visits between 1773 and 1777, and there were further French expeditions.

Unofficial visits, by whaling ships in the north and sealing gangs in the south, began in the 1790s. The first mission station was founded in 1814, in the Bay of Islands, and was followed by dozens of others: Anglican, Methodist and Catholic. Trade in flax and timber generated small European–Maori settlements by the 1820s. Surprisingly, the most numerous category of European visitor was probably American. New England whaling ships favoured the Bay of Islands for rest and recreation; 271 called there between 1833 and 1839 alone. To whalers, 'rest and recreation' meant sex and drink. Their favourite haunt, the little town of Kororareka (now Russell), was known to the missionaries as 'the hellhole of the Pacific'. New England visitors today might well have distant relatives among the local Maori.

One or two dozen bloody clashes dot the history of Maori–European contact before 1840 but, given the number of visits, inter-racial conflict was modest. Europeans needed Maori protection, food and labour, and Maori came to need European articles, especially muskets. Whaling stations and mission stations were linked to local Maori groups by intermarriage, which helped keep the peace. Most warfare was between Maori and Maori: the terrible intertribal 'Musket Wars' of 1818–36. Because Northland had the majority of early contact with Europe, its Ngapuhi tribe acquired muskets first. Under their great general Hongi Hika, Ngapuhi then raided south, winning bloody victories against tribes without muskets. Once they acquired muskets, these tribes saw off Ngapuhi, but also raided further south in their turn. The domino effect

For a thorough overview of NZ history from Gondwanaland to today, visit www. history-nz.org.

1837	1840	1844	1858
Possums are introduced to NZ from Australia. Brilliant.	Starting at Waitangi in the Bay of Islands on 6 February, around 500 chiefs countrywide sign the Treaty of Waitangi to 'settle' sovereignty once and for all. NZ becomes a nominal British colony.	Young Ngapuhi chief Hone Heke challenges British sovereignty, first by cutting down the British flag at Kororareka (now Russell), then by sacking the town itself. The ensuing Northland war continues till 1846.	The Waikato chief Te Wherowhero is installed as the first Maori King.

continued to the far south of the South Island in 1836. The missionaries claimed that the Musket Wars then tapered off through their influence, but the restoration of the balance of power through the equal distribution of muskets was probably more important.

Europe brought such things as pigs (at last) and potatoes, which benefited Maori, while muskets and diseases had the opposite effect. The negative effects have been exaggerated, however. Europeans expected peoples like the Maori to simply fade away at contact, and some early estimates of Maori population were overly high – up to one million. Current estimates are between 85,000 and 110,000 for 1769. The Musket Wars killed perhaps 20,000, and new diseases did considerable damage too (although NZ had the natural quarantine of distance: infected Europeans usually recovered or died during the long voyage, and smallpox, for example, which devastated native Americans, did not make it here). By 1840 the Maori had been reduced to about 70,000, a decline of at least 20%. Maori bent under the weight of European contact, but they certainly did not break.

> The Ministry for Culture & Heritage's history website (www.nzhistory.net.nz) is an excellent source of info on NZ history.

Making Pakeha

By 1840, Maori tribes described local Europeans as 'their Pakeha', and valued the profit and prestige they brought. Maori wanted more of both, and concluded that accepting nominal British authority was the way to get them. At the same time, the British government was overcoming its reluctance to undertake potentially expensive intervention in NZ. It too was influenced by profit and prestige, but also by humanitarian considerations. It believed, wrongly but sincerely, that Maori could not handle the increasing scale of unofficial European contact. In 1840 the two peoples struck a deal, symbolised by the treaty first signed at Waitangi on 6 February that year. The Treaty of Waitangi now has a standing not dissimilar to that of the Constitution in the US, but is even more contested. The original problem was a discrepancy between British and Maori understandings of it. The English version promised Maori full equality as British subjects in return for complete rights of government. The Maori version also promised that Maori would retain their chieftainship, which implied local rights of government. The problem was not great at first, because the Maori version applied outside the small European settlements. But as those settlements grew, conflict brewed.

> Similarities in language between Maori and Tahitian indicate close contact in historical times. Maori is about as similar to Tahitian as Spanish is to French, despite the 4294km separating these island groups.

In 1840 there were only about 2000 Europeans in NZ, with the shanty town of Kororareka as the capital and biggest settlement. By 1850 six new settlements had been formed with 22,000 settlers between them. About half of these had arrived under the auspices of the New Zealand Company and its associates. The company was the brainchild of Edward

1860–69	1861	1863–64	1868–72
First and Second Taranaki wars, starting with the controversial swindling of Maori land by the government at Waitara, and continuing with outrage over the confiscation of more land as a result.	Gold discovered in Otago by Gabriel Read, an Australian prospector. As a result, the population of Otago climbs from less than 13,000 to over 30,000 in six months.	Waikato Land War. Up to 5000 Maori resist an invasion mounted by 20,000 imperial, colonial and 'friendly' Maori troops. Despite surprising successes, Maori are defeated and much land is confiscated.	East Coast war. Te Kooti, having led an escape from his prison on the Chatham Islands, leads a holy guerrilla war in the Urewera region. He finally retreats to establish the Ringatu Church.

CAPTAIN JAMES COOK

If aliens ever visit earth, they may wonder what to make of the countless obelisks, faded plaques and graffiti-covered statues of a stiff, wigged figure gazing out to sea from Alaska to Australia, from NZ to North Yorkshire, from Siberia to the South Pacific. James Cook (1728–79) explored more of the Earth's surface than anyone in history, and it's impossible to travel the Pacific without encountering the captain's image and his controversial legacy in the lands he opened to the West.

For a man who travelled so widely, and rose to such fame, Cook came from an extremely pinched and provincial background. The son of a day labourer in rural Yorkshire, he was born in a mud cottage, had little schooling, and seemed destined for farm work – and for his family's grave plot in a village churchyard. Instead, Cook went to sea as a teenager, worked his way up from coal-ship servant to naval officer, and attracted notice for his exceptional charts of Canada. But Cook remained a little-known second lieutenant until, in 1768, the Royal Navy chose him to command a daring voyage to the South Seas.

In a converted coal ship called *Endeavour*, Cook sailed to Tahiti, and then became the first European to land at NZ and the east coast of Australia. Though the ship almost sank after striking the Great Barrier Reef, and 40% of the crew died from disease and accidents, the *Endeavour* limped home in 1771. On a return voyage (1772–75), Cook became the first navigator to pierce the Antarctic Circle and circled the globe near its southernmost latitude, demolishing the ancient myth that a vast, populous and fertile continent surrounded the South Pole. Cook also criss-crossed the Pacific from Easter Island to Melanesia, charting dozens of islands between. Though Maori killed and cooked 10 sailors, the captain remained strikingly sympathetic to islanders. 'Notwithstanding they are cannibals,' he wrote, 'they are naturally of a good disposition.'

On Cook's final voyage (1776–79), in search of a northwest passage between the Atlantic and Pacific, he became the first European to visit Hawaii, and coasted America from Oregon to Alaska. Forced back by Arctic pack ice, Cook returned to Hawaii, where he was killed during a skirmish with islanders who had initially greeted him as a Polynesian god. In a single decade of discovery, Cook had filled in the map of the Pacific and, as one French navigator put it, 'left his successors with little to do but admire his exploits'.

But Cook's travels also spurred colonisation of the Pacific, and within a few decades of his death, missionaries, whalers, traders and settlers began transforming (and often devastating) island cultures. As a result, many indigenous people now revile Cook as an imperialist villain who introduced disease, dispossession and other ills to the Pacific (hence the frequent vandalising of Cook monuments). However, as islanders revive traditional crafts and practices, from tattooing to *tapa* (traditional barkcloth), they have turned to the art and writing of Cook and his men as a resource for cultural renewal. For good and ill, a Yorkshire farm boy remains the single most significant figure in the shaping of the modern Pacific.

Tony Horwitz is a Pulitzer-winning reporter and nonfiction author.
In researching Blue Latitudes *(or* Into the Blue*), Tony travelled the Pacific – 'boldly going where Captain Cook has gone before'.*

1886–87	1893
Tuwharetoa tribe gifts the mountains of Ruapehu, Ngauruhoe and Tongariro to the government to establish only the world's fourth national park.	NZ becomes the first country in the world to grant the vote to women, following a campaign led by Kate Sheppard, who petitioned the government for years.

RAIMUND LINKE / GETTY IMAGES ©

➡ Mt Tongariro, Tongariro National Park (p262)

Gibbon Wakefield, who also influenced the settlement of South Australia. Wakefield hoped to short-circuit the barbarous frontier phase of settlement with 'instant civilisation', but his success was limited. From the 1850s his settlers, who included a high proportion of upper-middle-class gentlefolk, were swamped by succeeding waves of immigrants that continued to wash in until the 1880s. These people were part of the great British and Irish diaspora that also populated Australia and much of North America, but the NZ mix was distinctive. Lowland Scots settlers were more prominent in NZ than elsewhere, for example, with the possible exception of parts of Canada. NZ's Irish, even the Catholics, tended to come from the north of Ireland. NZ's English tended to come from the counties close to London. Small groups of Germans, Scandinavians and Chinese made their way in, though the last faced increasing racial prejudice from the 1880s, when the Pakeha population reached half a million.

Much of the mass immigration from the 1850s to the 1870s was assisted by the provincial and central governments, which also mounted large-scale public works schemes, especially in the 1870s under Julius Vogel. In 1876 Vogel abolished the provinces on the grounds that they were hampering his development efforts. The last imperial governor with substantial power was the talented but Machiavellian George Grey, who ended his second governorship in 1868. Thereafter, the governors (governors-general from 1917) were largely just nominal heads of state; the head of government, the premier or prime minister, had more power. The central government, originally weaker than the provincial governments, the imperial governor and the Maori tribes, eventually exceeded the power of all three.

The Maori tribes did not go down without a fight, however. Indeed, their resistance was one of the most formidable ever mounted against European expansion, comparable to that of the Sioux and Seminole in the US. The first clash took place in 1843 in the Wairau Valley, now a wine-growing district. A posse of settlers set out to enforce the myth of British control, but encountered the reality of Maori control. Twenty-two settlers were killed, including Wakefield's brother, Arthur, along with about six Maori. In 1845 more serious fighting broke out in the Bay of Islands, when Hone Heke sacked a British settlement. Heke and his ally Kawiti baffled three British punitive expeditions, using a modern variant of the traditional *pa* fortification. Vestiges of these innovative earthworks can still be seen at Ruapekapeka (south of Kawakawa). Governor Grey claimed victory in the north, but few were convinced at the time. Grey had more success in the south, where he arrested the formidable Ngati Toa chief Te Rauparaha, who until then wielded great influence on both sides of Cook Strait. Pakeha were able to swamp the few Maori living in the South Island, but the fighting of the 1840s confirmed that the North

'I believe we were all glad to leave New Zealand. It is not a pleasant place. Amongst the natives there is absent that charming simplicity...and the greater part of the English are the very refuse of society.' Charles Darwin, referring to Kororareka (Russell), in 1860.

'Kaore e mau te rongo – ake, ake!' (Peace never shall be made – never, never!) War chief Rewi Maniapoto in response to government troops at the battle of Orakau, 1864.

1901	1908	1914–18	1931
New Zealand politely declines the invitation to join the new Commonwealth of Australia, but thanks for asking.	NZ physicist Ernest Rutherford is awarded the Nobel Prize in chemistry for 'splitting the atom', investigating the disintegration of elements and the chemistry of radioactive substances.	NZ's contribution to WWI is staggering for a country of just over one million people: about 100,000 NZ men serve overseas. Some 60,000 become casualties, mostly on the Western Front in France.	Napier earthquake kills 131 people.

LAND WARS

Five separate major conflicts made up what are now collectively known as the New Zealand Wars (also referred to as the Land Wars or Maori Wars). Starting in Northland and moving throughout the North Island, the wars had many complex causes, but *whenua* (land) was the one common factor. In all five wars, Maori fought both for and against the government, on whose side stood the Imperial British Army, Australians and NZ's own Armed Constabulary. Land confiscations imposed on the Maori as punishment for involvement in these wars are still the source of conflict today, with the government struggling to finance compensation for what are now acknowledged to have been illegal seizures.

Northland war (1844–46) 'Hone Heke's War' began with the famous chopping of the flagpole at Kororareka (now Russell) and 'ended' at Ruapekapeka (south of Kawakawa). In many ways, this was almost a civil war between rival Ngapuhi factions, with the government taking one side against the other.

First Taranaki war (1860–61) Starting in Waitara, the first Taranaki war inflamed the passions of Maori across the North Island.

Waikato war (1863–64) The largest of the five wars. Predominantly involving the Kingitanga (King Movement; p183), the Waikato war was caused in part by what the government saw as a challenge to sovereignty. However, it was land, again, that was the real reason for friction. Following defeats such as Rangiriri, the Waikato people were pushed entirely from their own lands, south into what became known as the King Country.

Second Taranaki war (1865–69) Caused by Maori resistance to land confiscations stemming from the first Taranaki war, this was perhaps the war in which the Maori came closest to victory, under the brilliant, one-eyed prophet-general Titokowaru. However, once he lost the respect of his warriors (probably through an indiscretion with the wife of one of his warriors), the war too was lost.

East Coast war (1868–72) Te Kooti's holy guerrilla war. For more on Te Kooti, see p324.

Errol Hunt

Island at that time comprised a European fringe around an independent Maori heartland.

In the 1850s settler population and aspirations grew, and fighting broke out again in 1860. The wars burned on sporadically until 1872 over much of the North Island. In the early years a Maori nationalist organisation, the Kingitanga (King Movement), was the backbone of resistance. In later years some remarkable prophet-generals, notably Titokowaru and Te Kooti, took over. Most wars were small-scale, but the Waikato war of 1863–64 was not. This conflict, fought at the same time as the American Civil War, involved armoured steamships, ultramodern heavy artillery, telegraph and 10 proud British regular regiments. Despite the odds,

1935–49	1936	1939–45	1948
First Labour government in power, under Michael Savage. This government creates NZ's pioneering version of the welfare state, and also takes some independent initiatives in foreign policy.	NZ aviatrix Jean Batten becomes the first aviator to fly solo from Britain to NZ.	NZ troops back Britain and the Allied war effort during WWII; from 1942 a hundred thousand or so Americans arrive to protect NZ from the Japanese.	Maurice Scheslinger invents the Buzzy Bee, NZ's most famous children's toy.

the Maori won several battles, such as that at Gate Pa, near Tauranga, in 1864. But in the end they were ground down by European numbers and resources. Maori political, though not cultural, independence ebbed away in the last decades of the 19th century. It finally expired when police invaded its last sanctuary, the Urewera Mountains, in 1916.

Welfare & Warfare

From the 1850s to the 1880s, despite conflict with Maori, the Pakeha economy boomed on the back of wool exports, gold rushes and massive overseas borrowing for development. The crash came in the 1880s, when NZ experienced its Long Depression. In 1890 the Liberals came to power, and stayed there until 1912, helped by a recovering economy. The Liberals were NZ's first organised political party, and the first of several governments to give NZ a reputation as 'the world's social laboratory'. NZ became the first country in the world to give women the vote in 1893, and introduced old-age pensions in 1898. The Liberals also introduced a long-lasting system of industrial arbitration, but this was not enough to prevent bitter industrial unrest in 1912–13. This happened under the conservative 'Reform' government, which had replaced the Liberals in 1912. Reform remained in power until 1928, and later transformed itself into the National Party. Renewed depression struck in 1929, and the NZ experience of it was as grim as any. The derelict little farmhouses still seen in rural areas often date from this era.

In 1935 a second reforming government took office: the first Labour government, led by Michael Joseph Savage, easily NZ's favourite Australian. For a time the Labour government was considered the most socialist government outside Soviet Russia. But, when the chips were down in Europe in 1939, Labour had little hesitation in backing Britain.

NZ had also backed Britain in the Boer War (1899–1902) and WWI (1914–18), with dramatic losses in WWI in particular. You can count the cost in almost any little NZ town. A central square or park will contain a memorial lined with names – more for WWI than WWII. Even in WWII, however, NZ did its share of fighting: a hundred thousand or so New Zealanders fought in Europe and the Middle East. NZ, a peaceful-seeming country, has spent much of its history at war. In the 19th century it fought at home; in the 20th, overseas.

Better Britons?

British visitors have long found NZ hauntingly familiar. This is not simply a matter of the British and Irish origin of most Pakeha. It also stems from the tightening of NZ links with Britain from 1882, when refrigerated cargoes of food were first shipped to London. By the 1930s, giant

Maurice Shadbolt's *Season of the Jew* (1987) is a semifictionalised story of bloody campaigns led by warrior Te Kooti against the British in Poverty Bay in the 1860s. Te Kooti and his followers compared themselves to the Israelites who were cast out of Egypt. To find out more about the New Zealand Wars, visit www.newzealandwars.co.nz.

The Waitangi Treaty Grounds, where the Treaty of Waitangi was first signed in 1840, is now a tourist attraction for Kiwis and non-Kiwis alike. Each year on 6 February, Waitangi hosts treaty commemorations and protests.

1953	1973	1974	1981
New Zealander Edmund Hillary, with Tenzing Norgay, 'knocks the bastard off'; the pair become the first men to reach the summit of Mt Everest.	Fledgling Kiwi prog-rockers Split Enz enter a TV talent quest...finishing second to last.	Pacific Island migrants who have outstayed visas are subjected to Dawn Raids (crackdowns by immigration police) under Robert Muldoon and the National government. These raids continue till the early 1980s.	Springbok rugby tour divides the nation. Many New Zealanders show a strong anti-apartheid stance by protesting the games. Other Kiwis feel that sport and politics should not mix, and support the South African tour going ahead.

ships carried frozen meat, cheese and butter, as well as wool, on regular voyages taking about five weeks one way. The NZ economy adapted to the feeding of London, and cultural links were also enhanced. NZ children studied British history and literature, not their own. NZ's leading scientists and writers, such as Ernest Rutherford and Katherine Mansfield, gravitated to Britain. This tight relationship has been described as 'recolonial', but it is a mistake to see NZ as an exploited colony. Average living standards in NZ were normally better than in Britain, as were the welfare and lower-level education systems. New Zealanders had access to British markets and culture, and they contributed their share to the latter as equals. The list of 'British' writers, academics, scientists, military leaders, publishers and the like who were actually New Zealanders is long. Indeed, New Zealanders, especially in war and sport, sometimes saw themselves as a superior version of the British – the Better Britons of the south. The NZ–London relationship was rather like that of the American Midwest and New York.

'Recolonial' NZ prided itself, with some justice, on its affluence, equality and social harmony. But it was also conformist, even puritanical. Until the 1950s it was technically illegal for farmers to allow their cattle to mate in fields fronting public roads, for moral reasons. The 1953 American movie, *The Wild One,* was banned until 1977. Sunday newspapers were illegal until 1969, and full Sunday trading was not allowed until 1989. Licensed restaurants hardly existed in 1960, nor did supermarkets or TV. Notoriously, from 1917 to 1967, pubs were obliged to shut at 6pm. Yet the puritanical society of Better Britons was never the whole story. Opposition to Sunday trading stemmed, not so much from belief in the sanctity of the Sabbath, but from the belief that workers should have weekends too. Six o'clock closing was a standing joke in rural areas, notably the marvellously idiosyncratic region of the South Island's West Coast. There was always something of a Kiwi counterculture, even before imported countercultures took root from the 1960s.

There were also developments in cultural nationalism, beginning in the 1930s but really flowering from the 1970s. Writers, artists and filmmakers were by no means the only people who 'came out' in that era.

Coming In, Coming Out

The 'recolonial' system was shaken several times after 1935, but managed to survive until 1973, when Mother England ran off and joined the Franco–German commune now known as the EU. NZ was beginning to develop alternative markets to Britain, and alternative exports to wool, meat and dairy products. Wide-bodied jet aircraft were allowing the world and NZ to visit each other on an increasing scale. NZ had only 36,000 tourists in 1960, compared with more than two million a

---

Wellington-born Nancy Wake (code named 'The White Mouse') led a guerrilla attack against the Nazis with a 7000-strong army. She had the multiple honours of being the Gestapo's most-wanted person and being the most decorated Allied service-woman of WWII.

The Six o'clock Swill referred to the frantic after-work drinking at pubs when men tried to drink as much as possible from 5.05pm until strict closing time at 6pm.

1985

Rainbow Warrior sunk in Auckland by French government agents to prevent the Greenpeace protest ship from making its intended voyage to Moruroa, where the French government is conducting a nuclear-testing program.

1992

Government begins reparations for land confiscated in the Land Wars, and confirms Maori fishing rights in the 'Sealord deal'. Major settlements of historical confiscation follow.

1995

Peter Blake and Russell Coutts win the Americas Cup for NZ, sailing *Black Magic;* red socks become a matter of national pride.

PAUL KAY/GETTY IMAGES ©

→ *Rainbow Warrior* memorial

year now. Women were beginning to penetrate first the upper reaches of the workforce and then the political sphere. Gay people came out of the closet, despite vigorous efforts by moral conservatives to push them back in. University-educated youths were becoming more numerous and more assertive.

From 1945, Maori experienced both a population explosion and massive urbanisation. In 1936, Maori were 17% urban and 83% rural. Fifty years later, these proportions had reversed. The immigration gates, which until 1960 were pretty much labelled 'whites only', widened, first to allow in Pacific Islanders for their labour, and then to allow in (east) Asians for their money. These transitions would have generated major socioeconomic change whatever happened in politics. But most New Zealanders associate the country's recent 'Big Shift' with the politics of 1984.

In 1984, NZ's third great reforming government was elected – the fourth Labour government, led nominally by David Lange and in fact by Roger Douglas, the minister of finance. This government adopted an antinuclear foreign policy, delighting the left, and a more-market economic policy, delighting the right. NZ's numerous economic controls were dismantled with breakneck speed. Middle NZ was uneasy about the antinuclear policy, which threatened NZ's ANZUS alliance with Australia and the US. But in 1985 French spies sank the antinuclear protest ship *Rainbow Warrior* in Auckland Harbour, killing one crewman. The lukewarm American condemnation of the French act brought middle NZ in behind the antinuclear policy, which became associated with national independence. Other New Zealanders were uneasy about the more-market economic policy, but failed to come up with a convincing alternative. Revelling in their new freedom, NZ investors engaged in a frenzy of speculation, and suffered even more than the rest of the world from the economic crash of 1987.

The early 21st century is an interesting time for NZ. Like NZ food and wine, film and literature are flowering as never before, and the new ethnic mix is creating something very special in popular music. There are continuities, however – the pub, the sportsground, the quarter-acre section, the bush, the beach and the bach (holiday home) – and they too are part of the reason people like to come here. Realising that NZ has a great culture, and an intriguing history, as well as a great natural environment, will double the bang for your buck.

NZ's staunch antinuclear stance earned it the nickname 'The Mouse that Roared'.

Scottish influence can still be felt in NZ, particularly in the south of the South Island. NZ has more Scottish pipe bands per capita than Scotland itself.

2004	2010	2011	2013
Maori TV begins broadcasting – for the first time, a channel committed to NZ content and the revitalisation of Maori language and culture hits the small screen.	A cave-in at Pike River coalmine on the South Island's West Coast kills 29 miners.	A severe earthquake strikes Christchurch, killing 185 people and badly damaging the central business district. NZ hosts (and wins!) the Rugby World Cup.	New Zealand becomes one of 15 countries in the world to legally recognise same-sex marriage.

Environment

by Vaughan Yarwood

New Zealand is a young country – its present shape is less than 10,000 years old. Having broken away from the supercontinent of Gondwanaland (which included Africa, Australia, Antarctica and South America) in a stately geological dance some 85 million years ago, it endured continual uplift and erosion, buckling and tearing, and the slow fall and rise of the sea, as ice ages came and went.

Vaughan Yarwood is a historian and travel writer who is widely published in New Zealand and internationally. His most recent book is *The History Makers: Adventures in New Zealand Biography*.

The Land

Straddling the boundary of two great colliding slabs of the earth's crust – the Pacific plate and the Indian/Australian plate – to this day NZ remains the plaything of nature's strongest forces.

The result is one of the most varied and spectacular landscapes in the world, ranging from snow-dusted mountains and drowned glacial valleys to rainforests, dunelands and an otherworldly volcanic plateau. It is a diversity of landforms you would expect to find across an entire continent rather than a small archipelago in the South Pacific.

Evidence of NZ's tumultuous past is everywhere. The South Island's mountainous spine – the 650km-long ranges of the Southern Alps – is a product of the clash of the two plates; the result of a process of rapid lifting that, if anything, is accelerating. Despite NZ's highest peak, Aoraki/Mt Cook, losing 10m from its summit overnight in a 1991 landslide, the Alps are on an express elevator that, without erosion and landslides, would see them 10 times their present height within a few million years.

On the North Island, the most impressive changes have been wrought by volcanoes. Auckland is built on an isthmus peppered by scoria cones, on many of which you can still see the earthworks of *pa* (fortified villages) built by early Maori. The city's biggest and most recent volcano, 600-year-old Rangitoto Island, is just a short ferry ride from the downtown wharves. Some 300km further south, the classically shaped cone of snowcapped Mt Taranaki/Egmont overlooks tranquil dairy pastures.

But the real volcanic heartland runs through the centre of the North Island, from the restless bulk of Mt Ruapehu in Tongariro National Park, northeast through the Rotorua lake district out to NZ's most active volcano, White Island, in the Bay of Plenty. Called the Taupo Volcanic Zone, this great 250km-long rift valley – part of a volcano chain known as the 'Pacific Ring of Fire' – has been the seat of massive eruptions that have left their mark on the country physically and culturally.

Most spectacular were the eruptions from the volcano that created Lake Taupo. Considered the world's most productive volcano in terms of the amount of material ejected, Taupo last erupted 1800 years ago in a display that was the most violent anywhere on the planet within the past 5000 years.

You can experience the aftermath of volcanic destruction on a smaller scale at Te Wairoa (the Buried Village), near Rotorua on the shores of Lake Tarawera. Here, partly excavated and open to the public, lie the remains of a 19th-century Maori village overwhelmed when nearby Mt Tarawera erupted without warning. The famous Pink and White Terraces (one of several claimants to the popular title 'eighth wonder of the world') were destroyed overnight by the same upheaval.

But when nature sweeps the board clean with one hand she often rebuilds with the other: Waimangu Valley, born of all that geothermal violence, is the place to go to experience the hot earth up close and personal amid geysers, silica pans, bubbling mud pools and the world's biggest hot spring; or you can wander around Rotorua's Whakarewarewa Thermal Village, where descendants of Maori displaced by the eruption live in the middle of steaming vents and prepare food for visitors in boiling pools.

A second by-product of movement along the tectonic plate boundary is seismic activity – earthquakes. Not for nothing has NZ been called 'the Shaky Isles'. Most quakes only rattle the glassware, but one was indirectly

ENVIRONMENTAL ISSUES IN NEW ZEALAND

Employing images of untouched landscapes, Tourism New Zealand's 100% Pure marketing campaign has been critically acclaimed, and is the envy of tourism organisations worldwide. Such portrayals of a pristine environment have, however, been repeatedly rumbled in recent years as environmentalists – and the media – place NZ's 'clean green' credentials under the microscope. Mining, offshore oil and gas exploration, pollution, biodiversity loss, conservation funding cuts, and questionable urban planning – there have been endless hooks for bad-news stories, and numerous reasons to protest.

A 2013 university study found that New Zealanders rate water quality as the country's most serious environmental issue. Their concern is well founded, with one-third of NZ's 425 lakes, rivers and beaches deemed unsafe for swimming; research from diverse quarters confirms that the health of NZ's waterways is in serious decline. The primary culprit is 'dirty dairying' – cow effluent leaching into freshwater ecosystems, carrying with it high levels of nitrates, as well as bacteria and parasites such as E. coli and giardia.

The dairy industry is NZ's biggest export earner, and it continues to boom with more land being converted, despite clear evidence of its detrimental effects, which include the generation of half of NZ's greenhouse gas emissions. Parliamentary Commissioner for the Environment, Jan Wright, has referred to the matter as a 'classic economy versus environment dilemma'. NZ's dominant dairy cooperative – Fonterra – has expressed a commitment to upping its game to ensure farm management practices 'preserve New Zealand's clean green image'; some farmers are indeed cleaning up their act.

There are many other threats to water and land ecosystems, including proliferation of invasive weeds and pests, with biodiversity loss continuing in parallel. The worst offenders are possums, stoats and rats, which chomp through swathes of forest and kill wildlife, particularly birds. Controversy rages at the Department of Conservation's use of 1080 poison (sodium fluoroacetate) to control these pests, despite it being sanctioned by prominent environmental groups such as Forest & Bird and the Parliamentary Commissioner for the Environment. Vehement opposition to 1080 is expressed by such diverse camps as hunters and animal-rights activists, who cite detriments such as by-kill, and the poison's transmittal into waterways.

This is just one of DOC's increasing range of duties, which includes processing applications for mining within the conservation estate. Public feeling runs high on this issue, too, as demonstrated by recent ructions over opencast coalmining on the West Coast's Denniston Plateau. DOC has increasingly found itself in the thick of it; at the same time as budget cuts and major internal restructuring have left it appearing thinner on the ground.

Meanwhile, NZ's principle legislation governing the NZ environment – the 1991 Resource Management Act – is undergoing controversial reforms suspected of opening the door to further exploitation of the environment. NGOs and community groups – evervigilant and already making major contributions to the welfare of NZ's environment – will find plenty to keep them occupied in the years to come.

Sarah Bennett & Lee Slater

responsible for creating an internationally celebrated tourist attraction: in 1931, an earthquake measuring 7.9 on the Richter scale levelled the Hawke's Bay city of Napier, causing huge damage and loss of life. Napier was rebuilt almost entirely in the then-fashionable art-deco architectural style, and walking its streets today you can relive its brash exuberance in what has become a mecca for lovers of art deco.

However, the North Island doesn't have a monopoly on earthquakes. In September 2010 Christchurch was rocked by a magnitude 7.1 earthquake. Less than six months later, in February 2011, a magnitude 6.3 quake destroyed much of the city's historic heart and claimed 185 lives, making it the country's second-deadliest natural disaster. NZ's second city continues to be jostled by aftershocks as it builds anew.

The South Island can also see some evidence of volcanism – if the remains of the old volcanoes of Banks Peninsula weren't there to repel the sea, the vast Canterbury Plains, built from alpine sediment washed down the rivers from the Alps, would have eroded long ago.

But in the south it is the Southern Alps themselves that dominate, dictating settlement patterns, throwing down engineering challenges and offering outstanding recreational opportunities. The island's mountainous backbone also helps shape the weather, as it stands in the path of the prevailing westerly winds which roll in, moisture-laden, from the Tasman Sea. As a result, bush-clad lower slopes of the western Southern Alps are among the wettest places on earth, with an annual precipitation of some 15,000mm. Having lost its moisture, the wind then blows dry across the eastern plains towards the Pacific coast.

The North Island has a more even rainfall and is spared the temperature extremes of the South, which can plunge when a wind blows in from Antarctica. The important thing to remember, especially if you are tramping at high altitude, is that NZ has a maritime climate. This means weather can change with lightning speed, catching out the unprepared.

Flora & Fauna

NZ may be relatively young, geologically speaking, but its plants and animals go back a long way. The tuatara, for instance, an ancient reptile unique to these islands, is a Gondwanaland survivor closely related to the dinosaurs, while many of the distinctive flightless birds here (ratites) have distant African and South American cousins.

Due to its long isolation, the country is a veritable warehouse of unique and varied plants, most of which are found nowhere else. And with separation of the landmass occurring before mammals appeared on the scene, birds and insects have evolved in spectacular ways to fill the gaps.

The now-extinct flightless moa, the largest of which grew to 3.5m tall and weighed over 200kg, browsed open grasslands much as cattle do today (skeletons can be seen at Auckland Museum), while the smaller kiwi still ekes out a nocturnal living rummaging among forest leaf litter for insects and worms, much as small mammals do elsewhere. One of the country's most ferocious-looking insects, the mouse-sized giant weta, meanwhile, has taken on a scavenging role elsewhere filled by rodents.

As one of the last places on Earth to be colonised by humans, NZ was for millennia a safe laboratory for such risky evolutionary strategies, but with the arrival of Maori and, soon after, Europeans, things went downhill fast.

Many endemic creatures, including moa and the huia, an exquisite songbird, were driven to extinction, and the vast forests were cleared for their timber and to make way for agriculture. Destruction of habitat and the introduction of exotic animals and plants have taken a terrible environmental toll and New Zealanders are now fighting a rearguard battle to save what remains.

NZ is one of the most spectacular places in the world to see geysers. Rotorua's short-lived Waimangu geyser, formed after the Mt Tarawera eruption, was once the world's largest, often gushing to a dizzying height of 400m.

Nature Guide to the New Zealand Forest, by J Dawson and R Lucas, is a beautifully photographed foray into the world of NZ's forests. These lush treasure houses are home to ancient species dating from the time of the dinosaurs.

Birds & Animals

The first Polynesian settlers found little in the way of land mammals – just two species of bat – but forests, plains and coasts alive with birds. Largely lacking the bright plumage found elsewhere, NZ's birds – like its endemic plants – have an understated beauty that does not shout for attention.

Among the most musical is the bellbird, common in both native and exotic forests everywhere except Northland, though like many birds it is more likely to be heard than seen. Its call is a series of liquid bell notes, most often sounded at dawn or dusk.

The tui, another nectar eater and the country's most beautiful songbird, is a great mimic, with an inventive repertoire that includes clicks, grunts and chuckles. Notable for the white throat feathers that stand out against its dark plumage, the tui often feeds on flax flowers in suburban gardens but is most at home in densely tangled forest ('bush' to New Zealanders).

Fantails are commonly encountered on forest trails, swooping and jinking to catch insects stirred up by passing hikers, while pukeko, elegant swamp hens with blue plumage and bright-red beaks, are readily seen along wetland margins and even on the sides of roads nearby – be warned, they have little road sense.

If you spend any time in the South Island high country, you are likely to come up against the fearless and inquisitive kea – an uncharacteristically drab green parrot with bright-red underwings. Kea are common in the car parks of the Fox and Franz Josef Glaciers, where they hang out for food scraps or tear rubber from car windscreens.

Then there is the takahe, a rare flightless bird thought extinct until a small colony was discovered in 1948, and the equally flightless kiwi, NZ's national emblem and the nickname for New Zealanders themselves. The kiwi has a round body covered in coarse feathers, strong legs and a long, distinctive bill with nostrils at the tip for sniffing out food. It is not easy to find them in the wild, but they can be seen in simulated environments. One of the best is the Otorohanga Kiwi House, which also has native falcons, moreporks (owls) and weka.

The sustainability icon ✔ in this book marks places that demonstrate a commitment to sustainability. Travellers seeking other sustainable tourism operators should look for operators accredited with Qualmark Green (www.qualmark.co.nz) or listed at Organic Explorer (www.organicexplorer.co.nz).

KIWI SPOTTING

A threatened species, the kiwi is also nocturnal and difficult to see in the wild, although you can do this in Trounson Kauri Park in Northland, Okarito on the West Coast and on Stewart Island. They can, however, be observed in many artificially dark 'kiwi houses':

➡ Auckland Zoo (p71)
➡ Kiwi North, Maunu (p127)
➡ Rainbow Springs Rotorua (p289)
➡ Otorohanga Kiwi House & Native Bird Park (p184)
➡ National Aquarium of New Zealand, Napier (p333)
➡ Nga Manu Nature Reserve, Waikanae (p371)
➡ Pukaha Mount Bruce National Wildlife Centre, near Masterton (p376)
➡ Wellington Zoo (p353)
➡ West Coast Wildlife Centre, Franz Josef (p446)
➡ Orana Wildlife Park, Christchurch (p462)
➡ Willowbank Wildlife Reserve, Christchurch (p463)
➡ Kiwi Birdlife Park, Queenstown (p545)

To get a feel for what the bush used to be like, take a trip to Tiritiri Matangi Island. This regenerating island is an open sanctuary and one of the country's most successful exercises in community-assisted conservation.

Bird-watching

The flightless kiwi is the species most sought after by bird-watchers. Sightings of the Stewart Island subspecies are common at all times of the year. Elsewhere, wild sightings of this increasingly rare nocturnal species are difficult, apart from in enclosures. Other birds that twitchers like to sight are the royal albatross, white heron, Fiordland crested penguin, yellow-eyed penguin, Australasian gannet and wrybill.

On the Coromandel Peninsula, the Firth of Thames (particularly Miranda) is a haven for migrating birds, while the Wharekawa Wildlife Refuge at Opoutere Beach is a breeding ground of the endangered NZ dotterel. There's also a very accessible Australasian gannet colony at Muriwai, west of Auckland, and one in Hawke's Bay. There are popular trips to observe pelagic birds out of Kaikoura, and royal-albatross viewing on the Otago Peninsula.

Marine Mammal–Watching

Kaikoura, on the northeast coast of the South Island, is NZ's nexus of marine mammal–watching. The main attraction here is whale-watching, but this is dependent on weather conditions, so don't expect to just be able to rock up and head straight out on a boat for a dream encounter. The sperm whale, the largest toothed whale, is pretty much a year-round resident, and depending on the season you may also see migrating humpback whales, pilot whales, blue whales and southern right whales. Other mammals – including fur seals and dusky dolphins – are seen year-round.

Kaikoura is also an outstanding place to swim with dolphins. Pods of up to 500 playful, dusky dolphins can be seen on any given day. Dolphin swimming is common elsewhere in NZ, with the animals gathering off the North Island near Whakatane, Paihia, Tauranga and in the Hauraki Gulf, and off Akaroa on the South Island's Banks Peninsula. Seal swimming is possible in Kaikoura and in the Abel Tasman National Park.

Trees

No visitor to NZ (particularly Australians!) will go for long without hearing about the damage done to the bush by that bad-mannered Australian import, the brush-tailed possum. The long list of mammal pests introduced to NZ, whether accidentally or for a variety of misguided reasons, includes deer, rabbits, stoats, pigs and goats. But by far the most destructive is the possum, 70 million of which now chew through millions of tonnes of foliage a year despite the best efforts of the Department of Conservation (DOC) to control them.

B Heather and H Robertson's *Field Guide to the Birds of New Zealand* is a comprehensive guide for bird-watchers and a model of helpfulness for anyone even casually interested in the country's remarkable bird life. Another good guide is *Birds of New Zealand: Locality Guide* by Stuart Chambers.

TOWERING KAURI

When Chaucer was born this was a sturdy young tree. When Shakespeare was born it was 300 years old. It predates most of the great cathedrals of Europe. Its trunk is sky-rocket straight and sky-rocket bulky, limbless for half its height. Ferns sprout from its crevices. Its crown is an asymmetric mess, like an inverted root system. I lean against it, give it a slap. It's like slapping a building. This is a tree out of Tolkien. It's a kauri.

Joe Bennett, author of A Land of Two Halves, *referring to the McKinney kauri in Northland*

National Parks & Forest Parks

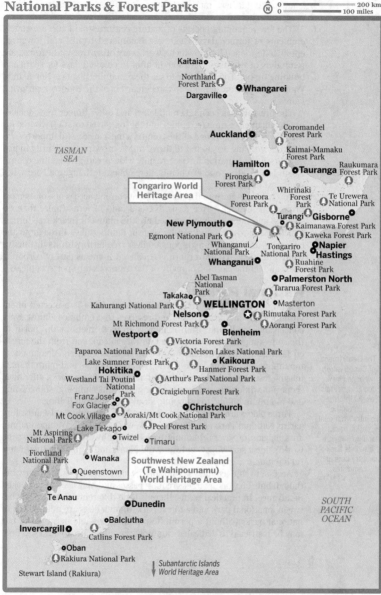

Among favoured possum food are NZ's most colourful trees: the kowhai, a small-leaved tree growing to 11m, which in spring has drooping clusters of bright-yellow flowers (NZ's national flower); the pohutukawa, a beautiful coastal tree of the northern North Island which bursts into vivid red flower in December, earning the nickname 'Christmas tree'; and a similar crimson-flowered tree, the rata. Rata species are found on both islands; the northern rata starts life as a climber on a host tree (that it eventually chokes).

The few remaining pockets of mature centuries-old kauri are stately emblems of former days. Their vast hammered trunks and towering, epiphyte-festooned limbs, which dwarf every other tree in the forest, are reminders of why they were sought after in colonial days for spars and building timber. The best place to see the remaining giants is Northland's Waipoua Kauri Forest, home to three-quarters of the country's surviving kauri.

The pressure has been taken off kauri and other timber trees, including the distinctive rimu (red pine) and the long-lived totara (favoured for Maori war canoes), by one of the country's most successful imports – *Pinus radiata*. Pine was found to thrive in NZ, growing to maturity in just 35 years, and plantation forests are now widespread through the central North Island – the southern hemisphere's biggest, Kaingaroa Forest, lies southeast of Rotorua.

You won't get far into the bush without coming across one of its most prominent features – tree ferns. NZ is a land of ferns (more than 80 species) and most easily recognised are the mamaku (black tree fern) – which grows to 20m and can be seen in damp gullies throughout the country – and the 10m-high ponga (silver tree fern) with its distinctive white underside. The silver fern is equally at home as part of corporate logos and on the clothing of many of the country's top sportspeople.

National Parks

A third of the country – more than 50,000 sq km – is protected in environmentally important parks and reserves that embrace almost every conceivable landscape: from mangrove-fringed inlets in the north to the snow-topped volcanoes of the Central Plateau, and from the forested fastness of the Ureweras in the east to the Southern Alps' majestic mountains, glaciers and fiords. The 14 national parks and more than 25 marine reserves and parks, along with numerous forest parks, offer huge scope for wilderness experiences, ranging from climbing, snow skiing and mountain biking, to tramping, kayaking and trout fishing.

Three places are World Heritage areas: NZ's Subantarctic Islands, Tongariro National Park and Southwest New Zealand (Te Wahipounamu), an amalgam of several national parks in southwest NZ that boast the world's finest surviving Gondwanaland plants and animals in their natural habitats.

Access to the country's wild places is relatively straightforward, though huts on walking tracks require passes and may need to be booked in advance. In practical terms, there is little difference for travellers between a national park and a forest park, though dogs are not allowed in national parks without a permit. Camping is possible in all parks, but may be restricted to dedicated camping grounds – check with DOC first.

The Department of Conservation website (www.doc.govt.nz) has useful information on the country's national parks, tracks and walkways. It also lists backcountry huts and campsites.

Maori Culture

by John Huria

'Maori' once just meant 'common' or 'everyday', but now it means...let's just begin by saying that there is a lot of 'then' and a lot of 'now' in the Maori world. Sometimes the cultural present follows on from the past quite seamlessly; sometimes things have changed hugely; sometimes we just want to look to the future.

Maori today are a diverse people. Some are engaged with traditional cultural networks and pursuits; others are occupied with adapting tradition and placing it into a dialogue with globalising culture. The Maori concept of *whanaungatanga* – family relationships – is important to the culture. And families spread out from the *whanau* (extended family) to the *hapu* (subtribe) and *iwi* (tribe) and even, in a sense, beyond the human world and into the natural and spiritual worlds.

Maori are New Zealand's *tangata whenua* (people of the land), and the Maori relationship with the land has developed over hundreds of years of occupation. Once a predominantly rural people, many Maori now live in urban centres, away from their traditional home base. But it's still common practice in formal settings to introduce oneself by referring to home: an ancestral mountain, river, sea or lake, or an ancestor. There's no place like home, but it's good to be away as well.

If you're looking for a Maori experience in NZ you'll find it – in performance, in conversation, in an art gallery, on a tour...

John Huria (Ngai Tahu, Muaupoko) has an editorial, research and writing background with a focus on Maori writing and culture. He was senior editor for Maori publishing company Huia (NZ) and now runs an editorial and publishing services company, Ahi Text Solutions Ltd (www.ahitextsolutions.co.nz).

Maori Then

Some three millennia ago people began moving eastward into the Pacific, sailing against the prevailing winds and currents (hard to go out, easier to return safely). Some stopped at Tonga and Samoa, and others settled the small central East Polynesian tropical islands.

The Maori colonisation of Aotearoa began from an original homeland known to Maori as Hawaiki. Skilled navigators and sailors travelled across the Pacific, using many navigational tools – currents, winds, stars, birds and wave patterns – to guide their large, double-hulled ocean-going craft to a new land. The first of many was the great navigator Kupe, who arrived, the story goes, chasing an octopus named Muturangi. But the distinction of giving NZ its well-known Maori name – Aotearoa – goes to his wife, Kuramarotini, who cried out, '*He ao, he ao tea, he ao tea roa!*' (A cloud, a white cloud, a long white cloud!).

Kupe and his crew journeyed around the land, and many places around Cook Strait (between the North and South Islands) and the Hokianga in Northland still bear the names that they gave them and the marks of his passage. Kupe returned to Hawaiki, leaving from (and naming) Northland's Hokianga. He gave other seafarers valuable navigational information. And then the great *waka* (ocean-going craft) began to arrive.

The *waka* that the first settlers arrived on, and their landing places, are immortalised in tribal histories. Well-known *waka* include *Takitimu,*

Kupe's passage is marked around NZ: he left his sails (Nga Ra o Kupe) near Cape Palliser as triangular landforms; he named the two islands in Wellington Harbour Matiu and Makoro after his daughters; his blood stains the red rocks of Wellington's south coast.

HOW THE WORLD BEGAN

In the Maori story of creation, first there was the void, then the night, then Rangi-nui (sky father) and Papa-tu-a-nuku (earth mother) came into being, embracing with their children nurtured between them. But nurturing became something else. Their children were stifled in the darkness of their embrace. Unable to stretch out to their full dimensions and struggling to see clearly in the darkness, their children tried to separate them. Tawhiri-matea, the god of winds, raged against them; Tu-mata-uenga, the god of war, assaulted them. Each god child in turn tried to separate them, but still Rangi and Papa pressed against each other. And then Tane-mahuta, god of the great forests and of humanity, placed his feet against his father and his back against his mother and slowly, inexorably, began to move them apart. Then came the world of light, of demigods and humanity.

In this world of light Maui, the demigod ancestor, was cast out to sea at birth and was found floating in his mother's topknot. He was a shape-shifter, becoming a pigeon or a dog or an eel if it suited his purposes. He stole fire from the gods. Using his grandmother's jawbone, he bashed the sun so that it could only limp slowly across the sky, so that people would have enough time during the day to get things done (if only he would do it again!). Using the South Island as a canoe, he used the jawbone as a hook to fish up Te Ika a Maui (the fish of Maui) – the North Island. And, finally, he met his end trying to defeat death itself. The goddess of death, Hine-nui-te-po, had obsidian teeth in her vagina (obsidian is a volcanic glass that takes a razor edge when chipped). Maui attempted to reverse birth (and hence defeat death) by crawling into her birth canal to reach her heart as she slept. A small bird – a fantail – laughed at the absurd sight. Hine-nui-te-po awoke, and crushed Maui between her thighs. Death one, humanity nil.

Kurahaupo, Te Arawa, Mataatua, Tainui, Aotea and *Tokomaru*. There are many others. Maori trace their genealogies back to those who arrived on the *waka* (and further back as well).

What would it have been like making the transition from small tropical islands to a much larger, cooler land mass? Goodbye breadfruit, coconuts, paper mulberry; hello moa, fernroot, flax – and immense space (relatively speaking). NZ has over 15,000km of coastline. Rarotonga, by way of contrast, has a little over 30km. There was land, lots of it, and a flora and fauna that had developed more or less separately from the rest of the world for 80 million years. There was an untouched, massive fishery. There were great seaside mammalian convenience stores – seals and sea lions – as well as a fabulous array of birds.

Arriving for the first time in NZ, two crew members of *Tainui* saw the red flowers of the pohutukawa tree, and they cast away their prized red feather ornaments, thinking that there were plenty to be had on shore.

The early settlers went on the move, pulled by love, by trade opportunities and greater resources; pushed by disputes and threats to security. When they settled, Maori established *mana whenua* (regional authority), whether by military campaigns, or by the peaceful methods of intermarriage and diplomacy. Looking over tribal history it's possible to see the many alliances, absorptions and extinctions that went on.

Histories were carried by the voice, in stories, songs and chants. Great stress was placed on accurate learning – after all, in an oral culture where people are the libraries, the past is always a generation or two away from oblivion.

Maori lived in *kainga* (small villages) which often had associated gardens. Housing was quite cosy by modern standards – often it was hard to stand upright while inside. From time to time people would leave their home base and go to harvest seasonal foods. When peaceful life was interrupted by conflict, the people would withdraw to *pa* (fortified dwelling places).

And then Europeans began to arrive.

Maori Today

Today's culture is marked by new developments in the arts, business, sport and politics. Many historical grievances still stand, but some *iwi* (Ngai Tahu and Tainui, for example) have settled historical grievances and are major forces in the NZ economy. Maori have also addressed the decline in Maori language use by establishing *kohanga reo, kura kaupapa Maori* and *wananga* (Maori-medium preschools, schools and universities). There is now a generation of people who speak Maori as a first language. There is a network of Maori radio stations, and Maori TV is attracting a committed viewership. A recently revived Maori event is becoming more and more prominent – Matariki, or Maori New Year. The constellation Matariki is also known as the Pleiades. It begins to rise above the horizon in late May or early June and its appearance traditionally signals a time for learning, planning and preparing as well as singing, dancing and celebrating. Watch out for talks and lectures, concerts, dinners and even formal balls.

The best way to learn about the relationship between the land and the *tangata whenua* (people of the land) is to get out there and start talking with Maori.

Religion

Christian churches and denominations are important in the Maori world: televangelists, mainstream churches for regular and occasional worship, and two major Maori churches (Ringatu and Ratana) – we've got it all.

But in the (non–Judaeo Christian) beginning there were the *atua Maori,* the Maori gods, and for many Maori the gods are a vital and relevant force still. It is common to greet the earth mother and sky father when speaking formally at a *marae* (meeting-house complex). The gods are represented in art and carving, sung of in *waiata* (songs), invoked through *karakia* (prayer and incantation) when a meeting house is opened, when a *waka* is launched, even (more simply) when a meal is served. They are spoken of on the *marae* and in wider Maori contexts. The traditional Maori creation story is well known and widely celebrated.

The Arts

There are many collections of Maori *taonga* (treasures) around the country. Some of the largest and most comprehensive are at Wellington's Te Papa Museum and the Auckland Museum. Canterbury Museum in Christchurch also has a good collection, and Hokitika Museum has an exhibition showing the story of *pounamu* (nephrite jade, or greenstone).

You can check out a map that shows *iwi* distribution and a good list of *iwi* websites on Wikipedia (www.en.wikipedia.org/wiki/list_of_iwi)

You can stay up to date with what is happening in the Maori arts by reading *Mana* magazine (available from most newsagents), listening to *iwi* stations (www.irirangi.net) or weekly podcasts from Radio New Zealand (www.radionz.co.nz). Maori TV also has regular features on the Maori arts – check out www.maoritelevision.com.

Maori TV went to air in 2004, an emotional time for many Maori who could at last see their culture, their concerns and their language in a mass medium. Over 90% of content is NZ made, and programs are in both Maori and English: they're subtitled and accessible to everyone. If you want to really get a feel for the rhythm and meter of spoken Maori from the comfort of your own chair, switch to Te Reo, a Maori-language-only channel.

Ta Moko

Ta moko is the Maori art of tattoo, traditionally worn by men on their faces, thighs and buttocks, and by women on their chins and lips. *Moko* were permanent grooves tapped into the skin using pigment (made from burnt caterpillar or kauri gum soot), and bone chisels: fine, sharp combs for broad work, and straight blades for detailed work. Museums in the major centres – Auckland, Wellington and Christchurch – all display traditional implements for *ta moko.*

See Ngahuia Te Awekotuku's book *Mau Moko: The World of Maori Tattoo* (2007) for the big picture, with powerful, beautiful images and an incisive commentary.

The modern tattooist's gun is common now, but bone chisels are coming back into use for Maori who want to reconnect with tradition. Since the general renaissance in Maori culture in the 1960s, many artists have taken up *ta moko* and now many Maori wear *moko* with quiet pride and humility.

Can visitors get involved, or even get some work done? The term *ki-rituhi* (skin inscriptions) has arisen to describe Maori-motif–inspired modern tattoos that non-Maori can wear.

Carving

For information on Maori arts today, check out Toi Maori at www. maoriart.org.nz.

Traditional Maori carving, with its intricate detailing and curved lines, can transport the viewer. It's quite amazing to consider that it was done with stone tools, themselves painstakingly made, until the advent of iron (nails suddenly became very popular).

Some major traditional forms are *waka* (canoes), *pataka* (storage buildings) and *wharenui* (meeting houses). You can see sublime examples of traditional carving at Te Papa in Wellington, and at the following:

Auckland Museum (p68) Maori Court.

Hell's Gate (p289) Carver in action every day; near Rotorua.

Otago Museum (p523) Nice old *waka* and *whare runanga* (meeting house) carvings; Dunedin.

Putiki Church (p231) Interior covered in carvings and *tukutuku* (wall panels); Wanganui.

Taupo Museum (p249) Carved meeting house.

Te Manawa (p240) Museum with a Maori focus; Palmerston North.

Waikato Museum (p169) Beautifully carved *waka taua* (war canoe); Hamilton.

Wairakei Terraces (p251) Carved meeting house; Taupo.

Waitangi Treaty Grounds (p142) *Whare runanga* and *waka taua*.

Whakarewarewa Thermal Village (p276) The 'living village' – carving, other arts, meeting house and performance; Rotorua.

Whanganui Regional Museum (p231) Wonderful carved *waka;* Wanganui.

The apex of carving today is the *whare whakairo* (carved meeting house). A commissioning group relates its history and ancestral stories to a carver, who then draws (sometimes quite loosely) on traditional motifs to interpret or embody the stories and ancestors in wood or composite fibreboard.

Rongomaraeroa Marae, by artist Cliff Whiting, at Te Papa in Wellington is a colourful example of a contemporary re-imagining of a traditional art form. The biggest change in carving (as with most traditional arts) has been in the use of new mediums and tools. Rangi Kipa uses a synthetic polymer called Corian to make his *hei tiki* (carved, stylised human figure worn around the neck; also called a *tiki*) the same stuff that is used to make kitchen benchtops. You can check out his gallery at www.rangikipa.com.

Weaving

Weaving was an essential art that provided clothing, nets and cordage, footwear for rough country travel, mats to cover earthen floors, and *kete* (bags) to carry stuff in. Many woven items are beautiful as well as practical. Some were major works – *korowai* (cloaks) could take years to finish. Woven predominantly with flax and bird feathers, they are worn now on ceremonial occasions, a stunning sight.

Working with natural materials for the greater good of the people involved getting things right by maintaining the supply of raw material and ensuring that it worked as it was meant to. Protocols were necessary, and women were dedicated to weaving under the aegis of the gods. Today, tradition is greatly respected, but not all traditions are necessarily followed.

Flax was (and still is) the preferred medium for weaving. To get a strong fibre from flax leaves, weavers scraped away the leaves' flesh with a mussel shell, then pounded until it was soft, dyed it, then dried it. But contemporary weavers are using everything in their work: raffia, copper wire, rubber – even polar fleece and garden hoses!

The best place to experience weaving is to contact one of the many weavers running workshops. By learning the art, you'll appreciate the examples of weaving in museums even more. And if you want your own? Woven *kete* and backpacks have become fashion accessories and are on sale in most cities. Weaving is also found in dealer art galleries around the country.

Haka

Experiencing *haka* can get the adrenaline flowing, as it did for one Pakeha observer in 1929 who thought of dark Satanic mills: 'They looked like fiends from hell wound up by machinery'. *Haka* can be awe-inspiring; they can also be uplifting. The *haka* is not only a war dance – it is used to welcome visitors, honour achievement, express identity or to put forth very strong opinions.

Haka involve chanted words, vigorous body movements, and *pukana* (when performers distort their faces, eyes bulging with the whites showing, perhaps with tongue extended).

The well-known *haka* 'Ka Mate', performed by the All Blacks before rugby test matches, is credited to the cunning fighting chief Te Rauparaha. It celebrates his escape from death. Chased by enemies, he hid himself in a food pit. After they had left, a friendly chief named Te Whareangi (the 'hairy man' referred to in the *haka*), let him out; he climbed out into the sunshine and performed 'Ka Mate'.

You can experience *haka* at various cultural performances including at Mitai Maori Village (p287), Tamaki Maori Village (p287), Te Puia (p275) and Whakarewarewa Thermal Village (p276) in Rotorua; **Ko Tane** (☏03-359 6226; www.kotane.co.nz; 60 Hussey Rd, Willowbank Wildlife Reserve; dancing, tour & dinner package adult/child $110/54; ☉5.30pm Mon & Thu-Sat) at Willowbank in Christchurch; Maori Tours (p398) in Kaikoura; and Myths & Legends Eco-tours (p385) in Picton.

But the best displays of *haka* are at the national Te Matatini National Kapa Haka Festival (p645), when NZ's top groups compete. It is held every two years, with the festival in February 2015 to take place in Christchurch.

Contemporary Visual Art

A distinctive feature of Maori visual art is the tension between traditional Maori ideas and modern artistic mediums and trends. Shane Cotton produced a series of works that conversed with 19th-century painted meeting houses, which themselves departed from Maori carved houses. Kelcy Taratoa uses toys, superheroes and pop urban imagery alongside weaving and carving design.

Of course not all Maori artists use Maori motifs. Ralph Hotere is a major NZ artist who 'happens to be Maori' (his words), and his career-long exploration of black speaks more to modernism than the traditional *marae* context.

Contemporary Maori art is by no means only about painting. Many other artists use installations as the preferred medium – look out for work by Jacqueline Fraser and Peter Robinson.

There are some great permanent exhibitions of Maori visual arts in the major centres. Both the Auckland and Christchurch Art Galleries hold strong collections, as does Wellington's Te Papa.

MAORI CULTURE MAORI TODAY

Maori legends are all around you as you tour NZ: Maui's *waka* became today's Southern Alps; a *taniwha* (supernatural creature) formed Lake Waikaremoana in its death throes; and a rejected Mt Taranaki walked into exile from the central North Island mountain group, carving the Whanganui River.

Contemporary Theatre

The 1970s saw the emergence of many Maori playwrights and plays, and theatre is a strong area of Maori arts today. Maori theatre drew heavily on the traditions of the *marae*. Instead of dimming the lights and immediately beginning the performance, many Maori theatre groups began with a stylised *powhiri* (traditional Maori welcome into a *marae*), had space for the audience to respond to the play, and ended with a *karakia* or a farewell.

VISITING MARAE

As you travel around NZ, you will see many *marae* (meeting-house complexes). Often *marae* are owned by a descent group. They are also owned by urban Maori groups, schools, universities and church groups, and they should only be visited by arrangement with the owners. Some *marae* that may be visited include: Huria Marae (p294) in Tauranga; Koriniti Marae (p236) on the Whanganui River Rd; Te Manuka Tutahi Marae (p305) in Whakatane; and the marae at Te Papa (p354) museum in Wellington.

Marae complexes include a *wharenui* (meeting house), which often embodies an ancestor. Its ridge is the backbone, the rafters are ribs, and it shelters the descendants. There is a clear space in front of the *wharenui* (ie the *marae atea*). Sometimes there are other buildings: a *wharekai* (dining hall); a toilet and shower block; perhaps even classrooms, play equipment and the like.

Hui (gatherings) are held at *marae*. Issues are discussed, classes conducted, milestones celebrated and the dead farewelled. *Te reo* Maori (the Maori language) is prominent, sometimes exclusively so.

Visitors sleep in the meeting house if a *hui* goes on for longer than a day. Mattresses are placed on the floor, someone may bring a guitar, and stories and jokes always go down well as the evening stretches out...

The Powhiri

If you visit a *marae* as part of an organised group, you'll be welcomed in a *powhiri*. The more common ones are outlined here.

There may be a *wero* (challenge). Using *taiaha* (quarter-staff) moves a warrior will approach the visitors and place a baton on the ground for a visitor to pick up.

There is a *karanga* (ceremonial call). A woman from the host group calls to the visitors and a woman from the visitors responds. Their long, high, falling calls begin to overlap and interweave and the visiting group walks on to the *marae atea*. It is then time for *whaikorero* (speechmaking). The hosts welcome the visitors, the visitors respond. Speeches are capped off by a *waiata* (song), and the visitors' speaker places a *koha* (gift, usually an envelope of cash) on the *marae*. The hosts then invite the visitors to *hariru* (shake hands) and *hongi*. Visitors and hosts are now united and will share light refreshments or a meal.

The Hongi

Press forehead and nose together firmly, shake hands, and perhaps offer a greeting such as '*Kia ora*' or '*Tena koe*'. Some prefer one press (for two or three seconds, or longer), others prefer two shorter (press, release, press). Men and women sometimes kiss on one cheek. Some people mistakenly think the *hongi* is a pressing of noses only (awkward to aim!) or the rubbing of noses (even more awkward).

Tapu

Tapu (spiritual restrictions) and *mana* (power and prestige) are taken seriously in the Maori world. Sit on chairs or seating provided (never on tables), and walk around people, not over them. The *powhiri* is *tapu*, and mixing food and *tapu* is right up there on the offence-o-meter. Do eat and drink when invited to do so by your hosts. You needn't worry about starvation: an important Maori value is *manaakitanga* (kindness).

Depending on area, the *powhiri* has gender roles: women *karanga* (call), men *whaikorero* (orate); women lead the way on to the *marae*, men sit on the *paepae* (the speakers' bench at the front). In a modern context, the debate around these roles continues.

Taki Rua is an independent producer of Maori work for both children and adults and has been in existence for over 25 years. As well as staging its shows in the major centres, it tours most of its work – check out its website (www.takirua.co.nz) for the current offerings. Maori drama is also often showcased at the professional theatres in the main centres as well as the biennial New Zealand Festival. Hone Kouka and Briar Grace-Smith (both have published playscripts available) have toured their works around NZ and to festivals in the UK.

Contemporary Dance

Contemporary Maori dance often takes its inspiration from *kapa haka* (cultural dance) and traditional Maori imagery. The exploration of pre-European life also provides inspiration. For example, a Maori choreographer, Moss Patterson, used *kokowai* (a body-adorning paste made from reddish clay and shark oil) as the basis of his most recent piece of the same name.

NZ's leading specifically Maori dance company is the **Atamira Dance Collective** (www.atamiradance.co.nz), which has been producing critically acclaimed, beautiful and challenging work since 2000. If that sounds too earnest, another choreographer to watch out for is Mika Torotoro, who happily blends *kapa haka*, drag, opera, ballet and disco into his work. You can check out clips of his work at www.mika.co.nz.

Maori Film-Making

Although there had already been successful Maori documentaries (*Patu!* and the *Tangata Whenua* series are brilliant, and available from some urban video stores), it wasn't until 1987 that NZ had its first fiction feature-length movie by a Maori director with Barry Barclay's *Ngati*. Mereta Mita was the first Maori woman to direct a fiction feature, with *Mauri* (1988). Both Mita and Barclay had highly political aims and ways of working, which involved a lengthy preproduction phase, during which they would consult with and seek direction from their *kaumatua* (elders). Films with significant Maori participation or control include the harrowing *Once Were Warriors* and the uplifting *Whale Rider*. Oscar-shortlisted Taika Waititi, of Te Whanau-a-Apanui descent, wrote and directed *Eagle vs Shark* and *Boy*.

The **New Zealand Film Archive** (www.filmarchive.org.nz) is a great place to experience Maori film, with most showings being either free or relatively inexpensive. It has offices in Auckland and Wellington.

Maori Writing

There are many novels and collections of short stories by Maori writers, and personal taste will govern your choices. How about approaching Maori writing regionally? Read Patricia Grace *(Potiki, Cousins, Dogside Story, Tu)* around Wellington, and maybe Witi Ihimaera *(Pounamu, Pounamu, The Matriarch, Bulibasha, The Whale Rider)* on the North Island's East Coast. Keri Hulme *(The Bone People, Stonefish)* and the South Island go together like a mass of whitebait bound in a frying pan by a single egg (ie very well). Read Alan Duff *(Once Were Warriors)* anywhere, but only if you want to be saddened, even shocked. Definitely take James George *(Hummingbird, Ocean Roads)* with you to Auckland's West Coast beaches and Northland's Ninety Mile Beach. Paula Morris *(Queen of Beauty, Hibiscus Coast, Trendy but Casual)* and Kelly Ana Morey *(Bloom, Grace Is Gone)* – hmm, Auckland and beyond? If poetry appeals you can't go past the giant of Maori poetry in English, the late, lamented Hone Tuwhare *(Deep River Talk: Collected Poems)*. Famously sounding like he's at church and in the pub at the same time, you *can* take him anywhere.

The first NZ hip-hop song to become a hit was Dalvanius Prime's *Poi E*, which was sung entirely in Maori by the Patea Maori Club. It was the highest-selling single of 1984 in NZ, outselling all international artists.

Music plays an important role in traditional and contemporary Maori culture.

Read Hirini Moko Mead's *Tikanga Maori*, Pat and Hiwi Tauroa's *Visiting a Marae*, and Anne Salmond's *Hui* for detailed information on Maori customs.

The Kiwi Psyche

New Zealand is like that little guy at school when they're picking rugby teams – quietly waiting to be noticed, desperately wanting to be liked. Then, when he does get the nod, his sheer determination to prove himself propels him to score a completely unexpected try. When his teammates come to congratulate him he stares at the ground and mumbles, 'It was nothing, ay'.

What Makes Kiwis Tick?

Ironically, the person responsible for the nuclear age was a New Zealander. In 1917 Ernest Rutherford was the first to split the nucleus of an atom. His face appears on the $100 note.

While NZ is a proud little nation, Kiwis traditionally don't have time for show-offs. Jingoistic flag-waving is generally frowned upon. People who make an impression on the international stage are respected and admired, but flashy tall poppies have traditionally had their heads lopped off. This is perhaps a legacy of NZ's early egalitarian ideals – the ones that sought to avoid the worst injustices of the 'mother country' (Britain) by breaking up large landholdings and enthusiastically adopting a 'cradle to grave' welfare state. 'Just because someone's got a bigger car than me, or bigger guns, doesn't make them better' is the general Kiwi attitude.

NZ has rarely let its size get in the way of making a point on the international stage. A founding member of the League of Nations (the precursor to the UN), it ruffled feathers between the world wars by failing to blindly follow Britain's position. It was in the 1980s, however, that things got really interesting.

A Turbulent Decade

Modern Kiwi culture pivots on the 1980s. Firstly, the unquestioned primacy of rugby union as a source of social cohesion (which rivalled the country's commitment to the two world wars as a foundation of nation-building) was stripped away when tens of thousands of New Zealanders took to the streets to protest a tour by the South African rugby side in 1981. The protesters held that the politics of apartheid not only had a place in sport, they trumped it. The country was starkly divided; there were riots in paradise. The scar is still strong enough that most New Zealanders over the age of 40 will recognise the simple phrase 'the tour' as referring to those events.

'...a sordid act of international state-backed terrorism...' – Prime Minister David Lange, describing the bombing of the *Rainbow Warrior* (1986)

The tour protests both harnessed and nourished a political and cultural renaissance among Maori that had already been rolling for a decade. Three years later that renaissance found its mark when a reforming Labour government gave statutory teeth to the Waitangi Tribunal, an agency that has since guided a process of land return, compensation for past wrongs and interpretation of the Treaty of Waitangi (the 1840 pact between Maori and the Crown) as a living document.

At the same time antinuclear protests that had been rumbling for years gained momentum, with mass blockades of visiting US naval ships. In 1984 Prime Minister David Lange barred nuclear-powered or armed ships from entering NZ waters. The mouse had roared. As a result the US threw NZ out of ANZUS, the country's main strategic military alliance, which also included Australia, declaring NZ 'a friend but not an ally'.

However, it was an event in the following year that completely changed the way NZ related to the world, when French government agents launched an attack in Auckland Harbour, sinking Greenpeace's antinuclear flagship *Rainbow Warrior* and killing one of its crew. Being bombed by a country that NZ had fought two world wars with – and the muted or nonexistent condemnation by other allies – left an indelible mark. It strengthened NZ's resolve to follow its own conscience in foreign policy and in 1987 NZ became a nuclear-free zone.

From the Boer to Vietnam Wars, NZ had blithely trotted off at the behest of the UK or US. Not anymore, as was demonstrated by its lack of involvement in the invasion of Iraq. That's not to say that the country shirks its international obligations: NZ troops continue to be deployed in peacekeeping capacities throughout the world.

If that wasn't enough upheaval for one decade, 1986 saw another bitter battle split the community – this time over the decriminalisation of homosexuality. The debate was particularly rancorous, but the law that previously incarcerated consenting gay adults was repealed, paving the way for the generally accepting society that NZ is today. In 1999 Georgina Beyer, an openly transsexual former prostitute, would win a once safe rural seat off a conservative incumbent, and in 2013 NZ legalised same-sex marriage.

Yet while the 1980s saw the country jump to the left on social issues, simultaneous economic reforms were an extreme step to the right (to paraphrase one-time Hamiltonian Richard O'Brien's song 'The Time Warp'). The public sector was slashed, any state assets that weren't bolted to the floor were sold off, regulation was removed from many sectors, trade barriers dismantled and the power of the unions greatly diminished.

For many, Sir Edmund Hillary, the first person to climb Mt Everest, was the consummate New Zealander: humble, practical and concerned for social justice. A public outpouring of grief followed his death in 2008.

THE KIWI PSYCHE A TURBULENT DECADE

'SO, WHAT DO YOU THINK OF NEW ZEALAND?'

That, by tradition, is the question that visitors are asked within an hour of disembarking in NZ. Sometimes they might be granted an entire day's research before being asked to pronounce, but asked they are. The question – composed equally of great pride and creeping doubt – is symbolic of the national consciousness.

When George Bernard Shaw visited for four weeks in 1934, he was deluged with what-do-you-think-of questions from newspaper reporters the length of the country. Although he never saw fit to write a word about NZ, his answers to those newspaper questions were collected and reprinted as *What I Saw in New Zealand: The Newspaper Utterances of George Bernard Shaw in New Zealand*. Yes, people really were that keen for vindication.

Other visitors were more willing to pronounce in print, including the British Liberal MP David Goldblatt, who wrote an intriguing and prescient little book called *Democracy at Ease: A New Zealand Profile*. Goldblatt found New Zealanders a blithe people: kind, prosperous and fond of machines.

For the bon vivant Goldblatt, the attitude towards food and drink was all too telling. He found only 'the plain fare and even plainer fetch and carry of the normal feeding machine of this country' and shops catering 'in the same pedestrian fashion for a people never fastidious – the same again is the order of the day'.

Thus, a people with access to some of the best fresh ingredients on earth tended to boil everything to death. A nation strewn almost its entire length with excellent microclimates for viticulture produced only fortified plonk. Material comfort was valued, but was a plain thing indeed.

It took New Zealanders a quarter of a century more to shuck 'the same dull sandwiches', and embrace a national awareness – and, as Goldblatt correctly anticipated, it took 'hazards and misfortunes' to spur the 'divine discontent' for change.

But when it did happen, it really happened.

Russell Brown is a journalist and manager of the popular Public Address blog site (www.publicaddress.net).

A SPORTING CHANCE

The arena where Kiwis have most sated their desperation for recognition on the world stage is in sport. In 2012 NZ was ranked the most successful sporting nation per capita in the world (in 2013 it slipped to third, behind Slovenia and Norway). NZ are the current world champions in Rugby Union, holding both the men's and women's world cup.

For most of the 20th century, NZ's All Blacks dominated international rugby union, with one squad even dubbed 'The Invincibles'. Taking over this pastime of the British upper class did wonders for national identity and the game is now interwoven with NZ's history and culture. The 2011 Rugby World Cup victory did much to raise spirits after a year of tragedy and economic gloom.

For all rugby's influence on the culture, don't go to a game expecting to be caught up in an orgy of noise and cheering. Rugby crowds at Auckland's Eden Park are as restrained as their teams are cavalier, but they get noisier as you head south. In contrast, a home game for the NZ Warriors rugby league team at Auckland's Mt Smart Stadium is a thrilling spectacle, especially when the Polynesian drummers kick in.

Despite the everyman appeal of rugby union in NZ (unlike in the UK), rugby league retains the status of the working-class sport and support is strongest in Auckland's Maori, Polynesian and other immigrant communities.

Netball is the leading sport for women and the one in which the national team, the Silver Ferns, perpetually vies for world supremacy with the Australians – one or other of the countries has taken the world championship at every contest (except for a three-way tie in 1979).

In 2010 the All Whites, NZ's national soccer (football) squad, competed in the FIFA World Cup for the second time ever, emerging with the totally unanticipated distinction of being the only unbeaten team in the competition. They didn't win any games either, but most Kiwis were overjoyed to have seen their first ever world cup goals and three draws. Sadly, they failed to qualify for the 2014 tournament.

Other sports in which NZ punches above its weight include sailing, rowing, canoeing, equestrian, cycling and triathlon. The most Olympic medals NZ has won have been in athletics, particularly in track and field events. Cricket is the established summer team sport, although not one in which the Kiwis are currently setting the world alight.

If you truly want to discover the good, the bad and the ugly of the national psyche, the sporting field isn't a bad place to start.

There was broad agreement that the old economy had to be restructured, but the reforms carried a heavy price. The old social guarantees were no longer as sure. Today, New Zealanders work long hours for lower wages than their Australian cousins would ever tolerate. Compared with other Organisation for Economic Co-operation and Development (OECD) nations, NZ family incomes are low, child poverty rates are high and the gap between rich and poor is widening.

Yet there is a dynamism about NZ that was rare in the 'golden weather' years before the reforms. NZ farmers take on the world without the massive subsidies of yore, and Wellington's inner city – once virtually closed after dark by oppressive licensing laws – now thrives with great bars and restaurants.

As with the economic reforms, the 'Treaty process' of redress and reconciliation with Maori makes some New Zealanders uneasy, more in their uncertainty about its extent than that it has happened at all. The Maori population sat somewhere between 85,000 and 110,000 at the time of first European contact 200 years ago. Disease and warfare subsequently decimated the population, but a high birth rate now sees about 15% of New Zealanders (599,000 people) identify as Maori, and that proportion is likely to grow.

Until 2010, NZ was rated second in the Global Peace Index behind Iceland. In 2011 it dropped to third place behind Denmark – something to do with all those *haka* (war dances) performed during the Rugby World Cup, perhaps?

The implication of the Treaty is one of partnership between Maori and the British Crown, together forging a bicultural nation. After decades of attempted cultural assimilation it's now accepted in most quarters that the indigenous culture has a special and separate status within the country's ethnic mix. For example, Maori is an official language and there is a separate electoral roll granting Maori guaranteed parliamentary seats.

Yet room has had to be found for the many New Zealanders of neither British nor Maori heritage. In each new wave of immigration there has been a tendency to demonise before gradually accepting and celebrating what the new cultures have to offer. This happened with the Chinese in the mid-19th century, Croatians at the beginning of the 20th, Pacific Islanders in the 1970s and, most recently, the Chinese again in the 1990s. That said, NZ society is more integrated and accepting than most. People of all races are represented in all levels of society and race isn't an obstacle to achievement.

For the younger generation, for whom the 1980s are prehistory, political apathy is the norm. In the 2011 general election only 75% of the population turned out to vote; for the under 30s this drops to less than 64%.

People born in other countries make up 25.2% of NZ residents. Of these, the main places of origin are England (21.5%), China (8.9%), India (6.7%), Australia (6.3%), South Africa (5.4%), Fiji (5.3%) and Samoa (5.1%).

THE KIWI PSYCHE A LONG WAY FROM BRITAIN

A Long Way from Britain

Most Kiwis (except perhaps the farmers) probably wish it rained a little less and they got paid a little more, but it sometimes takes a few years travelling on their 'Big OE' (Overseas Experience – a traditional rite of passage) before they realise how good they've got it. In a 2014 study of the quality of life in the world's major cities, Auckland was rated third and Wellington 12th.

Despite all the change, key elements of the NZ identity are an unbroken thread, and fortune is still a matter of economics rather than class. If you are served well in a restaurant or shop, it will be out of politeness or pride in the job, rather than servility.

In country areas and on bush walks don't be surprised if you're given a cheery greeting from passers-by, especially in the South Island. In a legacy of the British past, politeness is generally regarded as one of the highest virtues. A 'please' and 'thank you' will get you a long way. The three great exceptions to this rule are: a) on the road, where genteel Dr Jekylls become raging Mr Hydes, especially if you have the misfortune of needing to change lanes in Auckland; b) if you don't speak English very well; and c) if you are Australian.

The latter two traits are the product of insularity and a smallness of world view that tends to disappear among Kiwis who have travelled (and luckily many do). The NZ–Australian rivalry is taken much more seriously on this side of the Tasman Sea. Although it's very unlikely that Kiwis

NZ is defined as a state in the Australian constitution. At the time of Australia's federation into one country it was hoped that NZ would join. On this side of the Tasman that idea proved as unpopular then as it does now.

IT'S A WOMAN'S WORLD

NZ is justifiably proud of being the first country in the world to give women the vote (in 1893). Kate Sheppard, the hero of the women's suffrage movement, even features on the country's $10 bill. Despite that early achievement, the real role for women in public life was modest for many years. That can hardly be said now. Since 1997 the country has had two female prime ministers and for a time in 2000 every key constitutional position was held by a woman, including the prime minister, attorney general, chief justice, governor general and head of state – although New Zealanders can't take credit for choosing Betty Windsor for the latter role. At the same time a Maori queen headed the Kingitanga (King Movement) and a woman led NZ's biggest listed corporation. Things have slipped since and only two of those roles are held by women – and, yes, one of those is filled by Queen Elizabeth II.

will be rude outright, visiting Aussies must get pretty sick of the constant ribbing, much of it surprisingly ill-humoured. It's a sad truth that while most Australians would cheer on a NZ sports team if they were playing anyone other than their own, the opposite is true in NZ.

Number-Eight Wire

You might on your travels hear the phrase 'number-eight wire' and wonder what on earth it means. It's a catchphrase New Zealanders still repeat to themselves to encapsulate a national myth: that NZ's isolation and its pioneer stock created a culture in which ingenuity allowed problems to be solved and tools to be built from scratch. A NZ farmer, it was said, could solve pretty much any problem with a piece of number-eight wire (the gauge used for fencing on farms).

No matter where you are in NZ, you're never more than 128km from the sea.

It's actually largely true – NZ farms are full of NZ inventions. One reason big offshore film and TV producers bring their projects here – apart from the low wages and huge variety of locations – is that they like the can-do attitude and ability to work to a goal of NZ technical crews. Many more New Zealanders have worked as managers, roadies or chefs for famous recording artists (everyone from Led Zeppelin and U2 to Madonna) than have enjoyed the spotlight themselves. Which just goes to show that New Zealanders operate best at the intersection of practicality and creativity, with an endearing (and sometimes infuriating) humility to boot.

Arts & Music

It took a hundred years for post-colonial New Zealand to develop its own distinctive artistic identity. In the first half of the 20th century it was writers and visual artists who led the charge. By the 1970s NZ pub rockers had conquered Australia, while in the 1980s, indie music obsessives the world over hooked into Dunedin's weird and wonderful alternative scene. However, it took the success of the film industry in the 1990s to catapult the nation's creativity into the global consciousness.

Literature

In 2013 New Zealanders rejoiced to hear that 28-year-old Eleanor Catton had become only the second NZ writer to ever win the Man Booker Prize, arguably the world's most prestigious award for literature. Lloyd Jones had come close in 2007 when his novel *Mister Pip* was shortlisted, but it had been a long wait between drinks since Keri Hulme took the prize in 1985. Interestingly, both Catton's epic historical novel *The Luminaries* and Hulme's haunting *The Bone People* were set on the numinous West Coast of the South Island – both books capturing something of the raw and mysterious essence of the landscape.

Catton and Hulme continue in a proud line of NZ women writers, starting in the early 20th century with Katherine Mansfield. Mansfield's work began a Kiwi tradition in short fiction, and for years the standard was carried by novelist Janet Frame, whose dramatic life was depicted in Jane Campion's film of her autobiography, *An Angel at My Table*. Frame's novel *The Carpathians* won the Commonwealth Writers' Prize in 1989.

Less recognised internationally, Maurice Gee has gained the nation's annual top fiction gong six times, most recently with *Blindsight* (2005). His much-loved children's novel *Under the Mountain* (1979) was made into a seminal NZ TV series in 1981 and then a major motion picture in 2009. In 2004 the adaptation of another of his novels, *In My Father's Den* (1972), won major awards at international film festivals and is one of the country's highest-grossing films.

Maurice is an auspicious name for NZ writers, with the late Maurice Shadbolt achieving much acclaim for his many novels, particularly those set during the NZ Wars. Try *Season of the Jew* (1987) or *The House of Strife* (1993).

MAORI VOICES IN PRINT

Some of the most interesting and enjoyable NZ fiction voices belong to Maori writers, with Booker winner Keri Hulme leading the way. Witi Ihimaera's novels give a wonderful insight into small-town Maori life on the East Coast – especially *Bulibasha* (1994) and *The Whale Rider* (1987), which was made into an acclaimed film. Patricia Grace's work is similarly filled with exquisitely told stories of rural *marae*-centred life: try *Mutuwhenua* (1978), *Potiki* (1986), *Dogside Story* (2001) or *Tu* (2004).

Cinema & TV

If you first got interested in NZ by watching it on the silver screen, you're in good company. Sir Peter Jackson's NZ-made *The Hobbit* and *The Lord of the Rings* trilogies were the best thing to happen to NZ tourism since Captain Cook.

Yet NZ cinema is hardly ever easygoing. In his BBC-funded documentary, *Cinema of Unease,* NZ actor Sam Neill described the country's film industry as 'uniquely strange and dark', producing bleak, haunted work. One need only watch Lee Tamahori's harrowing *Once Were Warriors* (1994) to see what he means.

The *Listener*'s film critic, Philip Matthews, makes a slightly more upbeat observation: 'Between (Niki Caro's) *Whale Rider,* (Christine Jeffs') *Rain* and *Lord of the Rings,* you can extract the qualities that our best films possess. Beyond slick technical accomplishment, all share a kind of land-mysticism, an innately supernatural sensibility'.

You could add to this list Jane Campion's *The Piano* (1993), Brad McGann's *In My Father's Den* (2004) and Jackson's *Heavenly Creatures* (1994) – all of which use magically lush scenery to couch disturbing violence. It's a land-mysticism constantly bordering on the creepy.

Even when Kiwis do humour it's as resolutely black as their rugby jerseys; check out Jackson's early splatter-fests and Taika Waititi's *Boy* (2010). Exporting NZ comedy hasn't been easy, yet the HBO-produced TV musical parody *Flight of the Conchords* – featuring a mumbling, bumbling Kiwi folk-singing duo trying to get a break in New York – has found surprising international success.

It's the Polynesian giggle-factor that seems likeliest to break down the bleak house of NZ cinema, with feel-good-through-and-through *Sione's Wedding* (2006) netting the second-biggest local takings of any NZ film.

New Zealanders have gone from never seeing themselves in international cinema to having whole cloned armies of Temuera Morrisons invading the universe in *Star Wars*. Familiar faces such as Cliff Curtis and Karl Urban seem to constantly pop up playing Mexican or Russian gangsters in action movies. Many of them got their start in long-running soap opera *Shortland St* (7pm weekdays, TV2).

Visual Arts

The NZ 'can do' attitude extends to the visual arts. If you're visiting a local's home don't be surprised to find one of the owner's paintings on the wall or one of their mate's sculptures in the back garden, pieced together out of bits of shell, driftwood and a length of the magical 'number-eight wire'.

Other than 2003's winner *Return of the King, The Piano* is the only NZ movie to be nominated for a Best Picture Oscar. Jane Campion was the first Kiwi nominated as Best Director and Peter Jackson the first to win it.

The only Kiwi actors to have won an Oscar are Anna Paquin (for *The Piano*) and Russell Crowe (for *Gladiator*). Paquin was born in Canada but moved to NZ when she was four, while Crowe moved from NZ to Australia at the same age.

MIDDLE-EARTH TOURISM

If you are one of those travellers inspired to come down under by the scenery of the *Lord of the Rings (LOTR)* movies, you won't be disappointed. Peter Jackson's decision to film in NZ wasn't mere patriotism. Nowhere else on earth will you find such wildly varied, unspoiled landscapes – not to mention poorly paid actors.

You will doubtless recognise some places from the films. For example, Hobbiton (near Matamata), Mt Doom (instantly recognisable as towering Ngauruhoe) and the Misty Mountains (the South Island's Southern Alps). The visitor information centres in Wellington, Twizel or Queenstown should be able to direct you to local *LOTR* sites of interest. If you're serious about finding the exact spots where scenes were filmed, buy a copy of Ian Brodie's nerdtastic *The Lord of the Rings: Location Guidebook,* which includes instructions, and even GPS coordinates, for finding all the important places.

This is symptomatic of a flourishing local art and crafts scene cultivated by lively tertiary courses churning out traditional carvers and weavers, jewellery-makers, multimedia boffins, and moulders of metal and glass. The larger cities have excellent dealer galleries representing interesting local artists working across all media.

Not all the best galleries are in Auckland or Wellington. The energetic Govett-Brewster Art Gallery (p216) – home to the legacy of sculptor and film-maker Len Lye – is worth a visit to New Plymouth in itself, and Gore's Eastern Southland Gallery (p598) has an important and growing collection.

Traditional Maori art has a distinctive visual style with well-developed motifs that have been embraced by NZ artists of every race. In the painting medium, these include the cool modernism of the work of Gordon Walters and the more controversial pop-art approach of Dick Frizzell's *Tiki* series. Likewise, Pacific Island themes are common, particularly in Auckland. An example is the work of Niuean-born Auckland-raised John Pule.

It should not be surprising that in a nation so defined by its natural environment, landscape painting constituted the first post-European body of art. John Gully and Petrus van der Velden were among those to arrive and paint memorable (if sometimes overdramatised) depictions of the land.

A little later, Charles Frederick Goldie painted a series of compelling, realist portraits of Maori, who were feared to be a dying race. Debate over the political propriety of Goldie's work raged for years, but its value is widely accepted now: not least because Maori themselves generally acknowledge and value them as ancestral representations.

From the 1930s NZ art took a more modern direction and produced some of the country's most celebrated artists including Rita Angus, Toss Woollaston and Colin McCahon. McCahon is widely regarded to have been the country's most important artist. His paintings might seem inscrutable, even forbidding, but even where McCahon lurched into Catholic mysticism or quoted screeds from the Bible, his spirituality was rooted in geography. His bleak, brooding landscapes evoke the sheer power of NZ's terrain.

Music
by Gareth Shute

NZ music began with the *waiata* (singing) developed by Maori following their arrival in the country. The main musical instruments were wind instruments made of bone or wood, the most well known of which is the *nguru* (also known as the 'nose flute'), while percussion was provided by chest- and thigh-slapping. These days, the liveliest place to see Maori music being performed is at *kapa haka* competitions in which groups compete with their own routines of traditional song and dance: track down the **Te Matatini National Kapa Haka Festival** (www.tematatini.co.nz) which happens in March in odd-numbered years at different venues (Christchurch in 2015). In a similar vein, Auckland's Pasifika Festival (p77) represents each of the Pacific Islands. It's a great place to see both traditional and modern forms of Polynesian music: modern hip-hop, throbbing Cook Island drums, or island-style guitar, ukulele and slide guitar.

Gareth Shute wrote this music section. He is the author of four books, including *Hip Hop Music in Aotearoa* and *NZ Rock 1987–2007*. He is also a musician and has toured the UK, Europe and Australia as a member of the Ruby Suns and the Brunettes. He now plays in indie soul group the Cosbys.

Classical & Opera

Early European immigrants brought their own styles of music and gave birth to local variants during the early 1900s. In the 1950s Douglas Lilburn became one of the first internationally recognised NZ classical composers. More recently the country has produced a number of

THE BROTHERS FINN

There are certain tunes that all Kiwis can sing along to, given a beer and the opportunity. A surprising proportion of these were written by Tim and Neil Finn, many of which have been international hits.

Tim Finn first came to prominence in the 1970s group Split Enz. When the original guitarist quit, Neil flew over to join the band in the UK, despite being only 15 at the time. Split Enz amassed a solid following in Australia, NZ and Canada before disbanding in 1985.

Neil then formed Crowded House with two Australian musicians (Paul Hester and Nick Seymour) and one of their early singles, 'Don't Dream It's Over', hit number two on the US charts. Tim later did a brief spell in the band, during which the brothers wrote 'Weather with You' – a song that reached number seven on the UK charts, pushing their album *Woodface* to gold sales. The original line-up of Crowded House played their final show in 1996 in front of 100,000 people on the steps of the Sydney Opera House (though Finn and Seymour reformed the group in 2007 and continue to tour and record occasionally). Tim and Neil have both released a number of solo albums, as well as releasing material together as the Finn Brothers.

More recently, Neil has also remained busy, organising a set of shows and releases under the name Seven Worlds Collide – a collaboration with well-known overseas musicians including Jeff Tweedy (Wilco), Johnny Marr (The Smiths) and members of Radiohead. His latest band is the Pajama Club, a collaboration with wife Sharon and Auckland musicians Sean Donnelly and Alana Skyring.

Neil's son Liam also has a burgeoning solo career, touring the US with Eddie Vedder and the Black Keys and appearing on the *Late Show with David Letterman*. Both Tim and Neil were born in the small town of Te Awamutu: the local museum has a collection documenting their work.

world-renowned musicians in this field, including opera singer Dame Kiri Te Kanawa, million-selling pop diva Hayley Westenra, composer John Psathas (who created music for the 2004 Olympic Games) and composer-percussionist Gareth Farr (who also performs in drag under the name Lilith).

Rock

New Zealand also has a strong rock scene, its most acclaimed exports being the revered indie label Flying Nun and the music of the Finn Brothers.

In 1981 Flying Nun was started by Christchurch record store owner Roger Shepherd. Many of the early groups came from Dunedin, where local musicians took the DIY attitude of punk but used it to produce a lo-fi indie-pop that received rave reviews from the likes of *NME* in the UK and *Rolling Stone* in the US. *Billboard* even claimed in 1989: 'There doesn't seem to be anything on Flying Nun Records that is less than excellent.'

Many of the musicians from the Flying Nun scene still perform live to this day, including David Kilgour (from the Clean) and Shayne Carter (from the Straitjacket Fits, and subsequently Dimmer and the Adults). the Bats are still releasing albums, and Martin Phillipps' band the Chills released a live album in 2013.

For indie rock fans, a great source of local info is www.cheeseontoast.co.nz, which lists gigs and has band interviews and photos. For more on local hip-hop, pop and rock, check out www.thecorner.co.nz and the long-running www.muzic.net.nz.

Reggae, Hip-Hop & Dance

The genres of music that have been adopted most enthusiastically by Maori and Polynesian New Zealanders have been reggae (in the 1970s) and hip-hop (in the 1980s), which has led to distinct local forms. In Wellington, a thriving jazz scene took on a reggae influence to create a host of groups that blended dub, roots and funky jazz – most notably Fat Freddy's Drop. The national public holiday, Waitangi Day, on 6 February, also happens to fall on the birthday of Bob Marley and annual reggae concerts are held on this day in Auckland and Wellington.

The local hip-hop scene has its heart in the suburbs of South Auckland, which have a high concentration of Maori and Pacific Island residents. This area is home to one of New Zealand's foremost hip-hop labels, Dawn Raid, which takes its name from the infamous early-morning house raids of the 1970s that police performed on Pacific Islanders suspected of outstaying their visas. Dawn Raid's most successful artist is Savage, who sold a million copies of his single 'Swing' after it was featured in the movie *Knocked Up*. Within New Zealand, the most well-known hip-hop acts are Scribe, Che Fu and Smashproof (whose song 'Brother' held number one on the NZ singles charts longer than any other local act).

Dance music gained a foothold in Christchurch in the 1990s, spawning dub/electronica outfit Salmonella Dub and its offshoot act, Tiki Taane. Drum 'n' bass remains popular locally and has spawned internationally renowned acts such as Concord Dawn and Shapeshifter.

An up-to-date list of gigs in the main centres is listed at www.rip-itup.co.nz. Tickets for most events can be bought at www.ticketek.co.nz, www.ticketmaster.co.nz, or, for smaller gigs, www.undertheradar.co.nz.

New Music

Since 2000, the NZ music scene has developed new vitality after the government convinced commercial radio stations to adopt a voluntary quota of 20% local music. This enabled commercially oriented musicians to develop solid careers. Rock groups such as Shihad, the Feelers and Op-shop have thrived in this environment, as have a set of soulful female solo artists (who all happen to have Maori heritage): Bic Runga, Anika Moa and Brooke Fraser (daughter of All Black Bernie Fraser). NZ also produced two internationally acclaimed garage rock acts over this time: the Datsuns and the D4.

Current Kiwis garnering international recognition include the incredibly gifted songstress Kimbra (who sang on Gotye's global smash 'Somebody That I Used To Know'); indie anthem alt-rockers the Naked & Famous; multitalented singer-songwriter Ladyhawke; the arty Lawrence Arabia; and the semi-psychedelic Unknown Mortal Orchestra. Aaradhna is a much-touted R&B singer currently making a splash with her album *Trebel & Reverb*, which won 'Album of the Year' at the 2013 New Zealand Music Awards.

A wide range of cultural events are listed on www.eventfinder.co.nz. This is a good place to find out about concerts, classical music recitals and *kapa haka* performances. For more specific information on the NZ classical music scene, see www.sounz.org.nz.

Venues

In Auckland the main rock venues are the Kings Arms Tavern (p91) and Cassette Nine (p90), though two joint venues in St Kevins Arcade (off Karangahape Rd) are also popular – the Wine Cellar & Whammy Bar (p91). Ding Dong Lounge (p90) and Portland Public House (p92) are also worth a look. Wellington is rife with live-music venues – mostly around Cuba St – from Meow (p366) to Bodega (p366).

GOOD LORDE!

Of course, the big news in Kiwi music recently has been the success of Lorde, a singer-songwriter from Devonport on Auckland's North Shore. Known less regally to her friends as Ella Yelich-O'Connor, 16-year-old Lorde cracked the number-one spot on the US Billboard charts in 2013 with her magical, schoolyard-chant-evoking hit 'Royals' – the first NZ solo artist to top the American charts. 'Royals' then went on to win the 'Song of the Year' Grammy in 2014. Her debut album *Pure Heroine* has spawned a string of hits and is selling millions of copies worldwide. Not bad for 16!

Unfortunately the music scene in Christchurch was crippled by the earthquakes in late 2010 and early 2011. In the interim, a number of temporary spaces have opened up as gig venues; a full list of events can be found at www.christchurchmusic.org.nz.

Further south, many local bands tour through Queenstown during the ski season, and the spirit of the Flying Nun scene is kept alive at **Chicks Hotel** (2 Mount St) in Port Chalmers (near Dunedin).

Festivals

A number of festivals happen over summer, including new year's celebration **Rhythm & Vines** (www.rhythmandvines.co.nz) in Gisborne. The touring international alt-rock fest **Big Day Out** (www.bigdayout.com) seemed destined for the scrapheap but was relaunched in Auckland in 2014. Also recommended is the underground festival held early each year by **A Low Hum** (www.alowhum.com). World music fans flock to the local version of **WOMAD** (World of Music Arts & Dance; www.womad.co.nz) in New Plymouth, which features both local and overseas acts.

The TV show *Popstars* originated in New Zealand, though the resulting group, True Bliss, was short-lived. The series concept was then picked up in Australia, the UK and the US, inspiring the *Idol* series.

Survival Guide

DIRECTORY A–Z... 650

Accommodation........ 650

Children............... 652

Climate................ 653

Customs Regulations ... 653

Discount Cards......... 653

Electricity 654

Embassies &
Consulates 654

Food & Drink........... 654

Gay & Lesbian
Travellers.............. 654

Health................. 655

Insurance.............. 656

Internet Access......... 656

Legal Matters 656

Maps.................. 657

Money................. 657

Opening Hours 657

Post................... 658

Public Holidays......... 658

Safe Travel............. 658

Telephone 658

Time.................. 659

Toilets................ 659

Tourist Information 659

Travellers with
Disabilities............. 660

Visas.................. 660

Volunteering 661

Women Travellers........661

Work..................661

TRANSPORT.......662

GETTING THERE
& AWAY 662

Entering the Country.... 662

Air..................... 662

Sea 663

GETTING AROUND.......663

Air..................... 663

Bicycle 664

Boat 665

Bus 665

Car & Motorcycle....... 666

Hitching &
Ride-Sharing........... 668

Local Transport......... 668

Train 669

Directory A–Z

Accommodation

Across New Zealand you can bed down in historic guesthouses, facility-laden hotels, uniform motel units, beautifully situated campsites, and hostels that range in character from clean-living to tirelessly party-prone.

If you're travelling during peak tourist seasons, book your bed well in advance. Accommodation is most in demand (and at its priciest) during the summer holidays from Christmas to late January, at Easter, and during winter in snowy resort towns like Queenstown.

Visitor information centres provide reams of local accommodation information, often in the form of folders detailing facilities and up-to-date prices; many can also make bookings on your behalf.

For online listings, check out the websites of the **Automobile Association** (AA; ☑0800 500 444; www.aa.co.nz) and **Jasons** (www.jasons.com).

B&Bs

Bed and breakfast (B&B) accommodation in NZ pops up in the middle of cities, in rural hamlets and on stretches of isolated coastline, ranging from suburban bungalows to stately manors.

Breakfast may be 'continental' (cereal, toast and tea or coffee), 'hearty continental' (add yoghurt, fruit, home-baked bread or muffins), or a stomach-loading cooked meal (eggs, bacon, sausages...). Some B&B hosts may also cook dinner for guests and advertise dinner, bed and breakfast (DB&B) packages.

B&B tariffs are typically in the $120 to $180 bracket (per double), though some places charge upwards of $300 per double. Some hosts cheekily charge hefty prices for what is, in essence, a bedroom in their home. Off-street parking is often a bonus in the big cities.

Bed & Breakfast Book (www.bnb.co.nz)

Bed & Breakfast Directory (www.bed-and-breakfast. co.nz)

Camping & Holiday Parks

Campers and campervan drivers alike converge upon NZ's hugely popular 'holiday parks', slumbering peacefully in powered and unpowered sites, cheap bunk rooms (dorm rooms), cabins and self-contained units (often called motels or tourist flats). Well-equipped communal kitchens, dining areas, and games and TV rooms often feature. In cities, holiday parks are usually a fair way from the action, but in smaller towns they can be impressively central or near lakes, beaches, rivers and forests.

The nightly cost of camping in a holiday park is usually between $15 and $20 per adult, with children charged half-price; powered sites are a couple of dollars more. Cabin/unit accommodation normally ranges from $70 to $120 per double. Unless noted otherwise, the prices we've listed for campsites, campervan sites, huts and cabins are for two people.

SLEEPING PRICE RANGES

The following price indicators used throughout this book refer to a double room with bathroom during high season:

$ less than $100

$$ $100–200

$$$ more than $200

Price ranges generally increase by 20% to 25% in Auckland, Wellington and Christchurch. Here you can still find budget accommodation at up to $100 per double, but midrange stretches from $100 to $240, with top-end rooms more than $240.

DOC CAMPSITES & FREEDOM CAMPING

A fantastic option for those in campervans is the 250-plus vehicle-accessible 'Conservation Campsites' run by the **Department of Conservation** (DOC; www.doc.govt. nz), with fees ranging from free (basic toilets and fresh water) to $15 per adult (flush toilets and showers). DOC publishes free brochures with detailed descriptions and instructions to find every campsite (even GPS coordinates). Pick up copies from DOC offices before you hit the road, or visit the website.

DOC also looks after hundreds of 'Backcountry Huts' and 'Backcountry Campsites' which can only be reached on foot. See the website for details. 'Great Walk' huts and campsites are also managed by DOC: see p40 for info.

NZ is so photogenic, it's tempting to just pull off the road at a gorgeous viewpoint and camp the night. But never just assume it's OK to camp somewhere: always ask a local or check with the local i-SITE, DOC office or commercial campground. If you are freedom camping, treat the area with respect. Note that if your chosen campsite doesn't have toilet facilities and neither does your campervan, it's illegal for you to sleep there (your campervan must also have an on-board grey-water storage stytem). Legislation allows for $200 instant fines for camping in prohibited areas, or improper disposal of waste (in cases where dumping waste could damage the environment, fees are up to $10,000). See www.camping. org.nz for more freedom-camping tips.

Farmstays

Farmstays open the door to the agricultural side of NZ life, with visitors encouraged to get some dirt beneath their fingernails at orchards and dairy, sheep and cattle farms. Costs can vary widely, with B&Bs

WWOOFING

If you don't mind getting your hands dirty, an economical way of travelling around NZ involves doing some voluntary work as a member of the international **Willing Workers on Organic Farms** (WWOOF; ☎03-544 9890; www.wwoof.co.nz) scheme. Down on the farm, in exchange for a hard day's work, owners provide food, accommodation and some hands-on organic farming experience. Contact farm owners a week or two beforehand to arrange your stay, as you would for a hotel or hostel – don't turn up unannounced!

A one-year online membership costs $40; an online membership and a farm-listing book, which is mailed to you, costs an extra $10 plus postage. You should have a Working Holiday Visa when you visit NZ, as the immigration department considers WWOOFers to be working.

generally ranging from $80 to $120. Some farms have separate cottages where you can fix your own food, while others offer low-cost, shared, backpacker-style accommodation.

Farm Helpers in NZ (FHINZ; www.fhinz.co.nz) produces a booklet ($25) that lists around 350 NZ farms providing lodging in exchange for four to six hours' work per day. **Rural Holidays NZ** (www.ruralholidays. co.nz) lists farmstays and homestays throughout the country on its website.

Hostels

NZ is packed with backpacker hostels, both independent and part of large chains, ranging from small, homestay-style affairs with a handful of beds to refurbished hotels and towering modern structures in the big cities. Hostel bed prices listed throughout this book are nonmember rates, usually between $25 and $35 per night.

HOSTEL ORGANISATIONS

Budget Backpacker Hostels (BBH; www.bbh. co.nz) NZ's biggest hostel group with around 275 hostels. Membership costs $45 for 12 months and entitles you to stay at member hostels at rates listed in the annual (free) BBH Backpacker Accommodation booklet. Nonmembers pay an extra $3 per night. Pick up a membership card from any member hostel or order one online for $50; see the website for details.

YHA New Zealand (Youth Hostels Association; www.yha. co.nz) More than 25 hostels in prime South Island locations. The YHA is part of the **Hostelling International** (HI; www.hihostels.com) network, so if you're already a HI member in your own country, membership entitles you to use NZ hostels. If you don't already have a home membership, you can join at major NZ YHA hostels or online for $42, valid for 12 months. Nonmembers pay an extra $3 per night.

Base Backpackers (www. stayatbase.com) Chain with

BOOK YOUR STAY ONLINE

For more accommodation reviews by Lonely Planet authors, check out http://lonelyplanet.com/new-zealand/hotels. You'll find independent reviews, as well as recommendations on the best places to stay. Best of all, you can book online.

seven hostels around NZ: Bay of Islands, Auckland, Rotorua, Taupo, Wellington, Wanaka and Queenstown, plus affiliates in Nelson and Dunedin (...and a Christchurch hostel closed for post-quake repairs) . Expect clean dorms, girls-only areas and party opportunities aplenty. Offers a 10-night 'Base Jumping' accommodation card for $239, bookable online.

VIP Backpackers (www.vipbackpackers.com) International organisation affiliated with around 20 NZ hostels (not BBH or YHA), mainly in the cities and tourist hot spots. For around $61 (including postage) you'll receive a 12-month membership entitling you to a $1 discount off nightly accommodation. Join online or at VIP hostels.

Nomads Backpackers (www.nomadsworld.com) Seven franchises in NZ: Auckland, Rotorua, Taupo, Waitomo, Wellington, Abel Tasman National Park and Queenstown. Membership costs $49 for 12 months and, like VIP, offers $1 off the cost of nightly accommodation. Join at participating hostels or online.

Pubs, Hotels & Motels

➡ The least expensive form of NZ hotel accommodation is the humble pub. NZ's old pubs are often full of character (and characters), although some are grotty, ramshackle places that are best avoided. Check if there's a band playing the night you're staying – you could be in for a sleepless night. In the cheapest pubs, singles/doubles might cost as little as $30/60 (with a shared bathroom down the hall), though $50/80 is more common.

➡ At the top end of the hotel scale are five-star international chains, resort complexes and architecturally splendorous boutique hotels, all of which charge a hefty premium for their mod cons, snappy service and/or historic opulence. We quote 'rack rates' (official advertised rates) for such places, but discounts and special deals often apply.

➡ NZ's towns have a glut of nondescript, low-rise motels and 'motor lodges', charging between $80 and $180 for double rooms. These tend to be squat structures skulking by highways on the edges of towns. Most are modernish (though decor is often mired in the early 2000s) and have similar facilities, namely tea- and coffee-making equipment, fridge, and TV – prices vary with standard.

Rental Accommodation

The basic Kiwi holiday home is called a 'bach' (short for 'bachelor', as they were historically used by single men as hunting and fishing hideouts); in Otago and Southland they're known as 'cribs'. These are simple self-contained cottages that can be rented in rural and coastal areas, often in isolated locations. Prices are typically $80 to $150 per night, which isn't bad for a whole house or self-contained bungalow. For more upmarket holiday houses, expect to pay anything from $150 to $400 per double.

➡ www.holidayhomes.co.nz

➡ www.bookabach.co.nz

➡ www.holidayhouses.co.nz

➡ www.nzapartments.co.nz

Children

NZ is a terrific place to travel with kids: safe and affordable, with loads of playgrounds, kid-centric activities, a moderate climate and chilli-free cuisine. For helpful general tips, see Lonely Planet's *Travel with Children*. Handy online resources for kids' activities and travel info include:

➡ www.kidzgo.co.nz

➡ www.kidspot.co.nz

➡ www.kidsnewzealand.com

➡ www.kidsfriendlynz.com

Practicalities

➡ Many motels and holiday parks have playgrounds, games and DVDs, and, occasionally, fenced swimming pools and trampolines. Cots and highchairs aren't always available at budget and midrange accommodation, but top-end hotels supply them and often provide child-minding services. Many B&Bs promote themselves

---

PRACTICALITIES

News Leaf through Auckland's *New Zealand Herald*, Wellington's *Dominion Post* or Christchurch's *The Press* newspapers. Online see www.nzherald.co.nz or www.stuff.co.nz.

TV Watch one of the national government-owned TV stations (TV One, TV2, TVNZ 6, Maori TV and the 100% Maori-language Te Reo) or the subscriber-only Sky TV (www.skytv.co.nz).

Radio Tune in to Radio National for current affairs and Concert FM for classical and jazz (see www.radionz.co.nz for frequencies). Kiwi FM (www.kiwifm.co.nz) showcases NZ music; Radio Hauraki (www.hauraki.co.nz) cranks out the rock.

DVDs Kiwi DVDs are encoded for Region 4, which includes Mexico, South America, Central America, Australia, the Pacific and the Caribbean.

Weights & Measures NZ uses the metric system.

Climate

Auckland

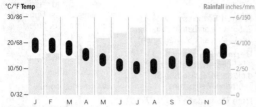

°C/°F **Temp**   **Rainfall** inches/mm

Christchurch

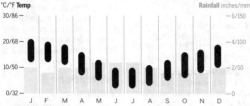

°C/°F **Temp**   **Rainfall** inches/mm

Queenstown

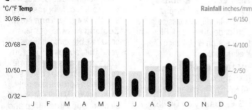

°C/°F **Temp**   **Rainfall** inches/mm

as kid-free, and hostels tend to focus on the backpacker demographic, but there are plenty of hostels (including YHA) that do allow kids.

➡ For specialised childcare, try www.rockmybaby.co.nz, or look under 'babysitters' and 'child care centres' in the *Yellow Pages* directory.

➡ Check that your car-hire company can supply the right-sized seat for your child, and that the seat will be properly fitted. Some companies legally require you to fit car seats yourself.

➡ Most Kiwis are relaxed about public breastfeeding. Alternatively, cities and major towns have public rooms where parents can go to feed a baby or change a nappy (diaper); check with the local visitor information centre, or ask a local.

➡ Kids' and family rates are often available for accommodation, tours, attraction entry fees, and air, bus and train transport, with discounts of as much as 50% off the adult rate. Note that the definition of 'child' can vary from under 12 to under 18 years; toddlers (under four years old) usually get free admission and transport.

➡ There are plenty of family-friendly restaurants in NZ with highchairs and kids' menus. Pubs often serve kids' meals and most cafes and restaurants (with the exception of upmarket eateries) can handle the idea of child-sized portions.

➡ NZ's medical services and facilities are world-class, with goods like formula and disposable nappies widely available.

Customs Regulations

For the low-down on what you can and can't bring into NZ, see the **New Zealand Customs Service** (www.customs.govt.nz) website. Per-person duty-free allowances:

➡ 1125mL of spirits or liqueur

➡ 4.5L of wine or beer

➡ 200 cigarettes (or 50 cigars or 250g of tobacco)

➡ dutiable goods up to the value of $700

It's a good idea to declare any unusual medicines. Tramping gear (boots, tents etc) will be checked and may need to be cleaned before being allowed in. You must declare any plant or animal products (including anything made of wood), and food of any kind. Weapons and firearms are either prohibited or require a permit and safety testing.

Discount Cards

➡ The internationally recognised **International Student Identity Card** is produced by the **International Student Travel Confederation** (ISTC; www.istc.org), and issued to full-time students aged 12 and over. It provides discounts on accommodation, transport and admission to attractions. The ISTC also produces the **International Youth Travel Card**, available to folks under 30 who are not full-time students, with equivalent benefits to the ISIC. Also similar is the **International Teacher Identity Card**, available to teaching professionals. All three cards (NZ$30 each) are available online at www.isiccard.co.nz, or from student travel companies like STA Travel.

➡ The **New Zealand Card** (www.newzealandcard.com) is a $35 discount pass that'll score you between

5% and 50% off a range of accommodation, tours, sights and activities.

➡ Travellers over 60 with some form of identification (eg an official seniors card) are often eligible for concession prices.

Electricity

To plug yourself into the electricity supply (230V AC, 50Hz), use a three-pin adaptor (the same as in Australia; different to British three-pin adaptors).

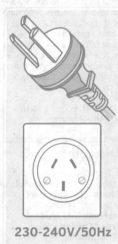

230-240V/50Hz

Embassies & Consulates

Most principal diplomatic representations to NZ are in Wellington, with a few in Auckland.

Australian High Commission (☑04-473 6411; www. australia.org.nz; 72-76 Hobson St, Thorndon, Wellington)

Canadian High Commission (☑04-473 9577; Lvl 11, 125 The Terrace, Wellington)

Chinese Embassy (☑04-474 9631; www.chinaembassy. org.nz; 2-6 Glenmore St, Kelburn, Wellington)

Fijian High Commission (☑04-473 5401; www.fiji.org. nz; 31 Pipitea St, Thorndon, Wellington)

French Embassy (☑04-384 2555; www.ambafrance-nz.org; 34-42 Manners St, Wellington)

German Embassy (☑04-473 6063; www.wellington. diplo.de; 90-92 Hobson St, Thorndon, Wellington)

Irish Consulate (☑09-977 2252; www.ireland.co.nz; Lvl 3, Tower 1, 205 Queen St, Auckland)

Israeli Embassy (☑04-439 9500; http://embassies.gov.il/ wellington; Lvl 13, Bayleys Bldg, 36 Brandon St, Wellington)

Japanese Embassy (☑04-473 1540; www.nz.emb-japan. go.jp; Lvl 18, The Majestic Centre, 100 Willis St, Wellington)

Netherlands Embassy (☑04-471 6390; http:// newzealand.nlembassy.org; Lvl 10, Cooperative Bank Bldg, cnr Featherston & Ballance Sts, Wellington)

UK High Commission (☑04-924 2888; www.gov.uk; 44 Hill St, Thorndon, Wellington)

US Embassy (☑04-462 6000; http://newzealand. usembassy.gov; 29 Fitzherbert Tce, Thorndon, Wellington)

Food & Drink

New Zealand's restaurants and cafes are adept at throwing together traditional staples (lamb, beef, venison, green-lipped mussels) with Asian, European and pan-Pacific flair. Eateries themselves range from fish-and-chip shops and pub bistros to retro-styled cafes, restaurant-bars with full à la carte service and crisp-linen fine dining rooms. Tipping is not mandatory, but feel free if you've had a happy culinary experience (about 10% of the bill). For online listings:

➡ www.dineout.co.nz

➡ www.menus.co.nz

On the liquid front, NZ wine is world class (especially sauvignon blanc and pinot noir), and you'll be hard-pressed to find a NZ town of any size without decent espresso. NZ microbrewed beers have also become mainstream.

Vegetarians & Vegans

Most large urban centres have at least one dedicated vegetarian cafe or restaurant: see the **Vegetarians New Zealand** (www.vegetarians. co.nz) website for listings. Beyond this, almost all restaurants and cafes offer some vegetarian menu choices (although sometimes only one or two). Many eateries also provide gluten-free and vegan options. Always check that stocks and sauces are vegetarian, too.

In this book, the vegetarian icon ☑ in Eating listings indicates a good vegetarian selection.

Gay & Lesbian Travellers

The gay and lesbian tourism industry in NZ isn't as high-profile as it is in neighbouring

EATING PRICE RANGES

Listings within this book are in order of author preference within their respective budget ranges. The following price indicators used throughout refer to the average price of a main course:

$ less than $15

$$ $15–32

$$$ more than $32

Australia, but homosexual communities are prominent in Auckland and Wellington, with myriad support organisations across both islands. NZ has progressive laws protecting the rights of gays and lesbians: same-sex marriage was legalised here in 2013. Generally speaking, Kiwis are fairly relaxed and accepting about homosexuality, but that's not to say that homophobia doesn't exist.

Resources

There are loads of websites dedicated to gay and lesbian travel in NZ. **Gay Tourism New Zealand** (www.gaytourismnewzealand.com) is a good starting point, with links to various sites. Other worthwhile queer websites include the following:

➡ www.gaynz.com
➡ www.gaynz.net.nz
➡ www.lesbian.net.nz
➡ www.gaystay.co.nz

Check out the nationwide magazine *express* (www.gayexpress.co.nz) every second Wednesday for the latest happenings, reviews and listings on the NZ gay scene.

Festivals & Events

Big Gay Out (www.biggayout.co.nz) Free festival (food, drink, entertainment) held every February in Auckland.

Out Takes (www.outtakes.org.nz) G&L film festival staged in Auckland and Wellington in May/June.

Gay Ski Week (www.gayskiweekqt.com) Annual Queenstown snow-fest in August/September.

Health

New Zealand is one of the healthiest countries in the world in which to travel. Diseases such as malaria and typhoid are unheard of, and the absence of poisonous snakes or other dangerous

TO MARKET, TO MARKET

There are more than 50 farmers markets held around NZ. Most happen on weekends and are upbeat local affairs, where visitors can meet local producers and find fresh regional produce. Mobile coffee is usually present, and tastings are offered by enterprising and innovative stall holders. Bring a carry bag, and get there early for the best stuff! Check out www.farmersmarkets.org.nz for market locations, dates and times.

animals makes outdoor adventures here less risky than in neighbouring Australia.

Before You Go
MEDICATIONS

Bring medications in their original, clearly labelled containers. A signed and dated letter from your physician describing your medical conditions and medications (including generic names) and any requisite syringes or needles, is also wise.

VACCINATIONS

NZ has no vaccination requirements for any traveller, but the World Health Organization recommends that all travellers should be covered for diphtheria, tetanus, measles, mumps, rubella, chickenpox and polio, as well as hepatitis B, regardless of their destination. Ask your doctor for an *International Certificate of Vaccination* (or 'the yellow booklet'), which will list all the vaccinations you've received.

HEALTH INSURANCE

Health insurance is essential for all travellers. While health care in NZ is of a high standard and not overly expensive by international standards, considerable costs can be built up and repatriation can be pricey.

If your current health insurance doesn't cover you for medical expenses incurred overseas, consider extra insurance – see www.lonelyplanet.com/travel-insurance for more informa-

tion. Find out in advance if your insurance plan will make payments directly to providers or reimburse you later for overseas health expenditures.

In New Zealand
AVAILABILITY & COST OF HEALTH CARE

NZ's public hospitals offer a high standard of care (free for residents). All travellers are covered for medical care resulting from accidents that occur while in NZ (eg motor-vehicle accidents, adventure-activity accidents) by the **Accident Compensation Corporation** (ACC; www.acc.co.nz). Costs incurred due to treatment of a medical illness that occurs while in NZ will only be covered by travel insurance. For more details, see www.moh.govt.nz and www.acc.co.nz.

The 24-hour, free-call **Healthline** (☑0800 611 116; www.health.govt.nz) offers health advice throughout NZ.

PHARMACEUTICALS

Over-the-counter medications are widely available in NZ through private chemists. These include painkillers, antihistamines and skin-care products. Some medications, such as antibiotics and the contraceptive pill, are only available via a prescription obtained from a general practitioner. If you take regular medications, bring an adequate supply and details of the generic name, as brand names differ country-to-country.

INFECTIOUS DISEASES

The giardia parasite is widespread in NZ waterways: drinking untreated water from streams and lakes is not recommended. Using water filters and boiling or treating water with iodine are effective ways of preventing the disease. Symptoms consist of intermittent diarrhoea, abdominal bloating and wind. Effective treatment is available (tinidazole or metronidazole).

ENVIRONMENTAL HAZARDS

➡ Hypothermia is a significant risk, especially during winter and year-round at altitude. Mountain ranges and/or strong winds produce a high chill factor, which can cause hypothermia even in moderate temperatures. Early signs include the inability to perform fine movements (such as doing up buttons), shivering and a bad case of the 'umbles' (fumbles, mumbles, grumbles, stumbles). To treat, minimise heat loss: remove wet clothing, add dry clothes with wind- and waterproof layers, and consume water and carbohydrates to allow shivering to build the internal temperature. In severe hypothermia, shivering actually stops; this is a medical emergency requiring rapid evacuation in addition to the above measures.

➡ NZ has exceptional surf beaches. The power of the surf can fluctuate as a result of the varying slope of the seabed at many beaches. Check with local surf-lifesaving organisations before entering the surf and be aware of your own limitations and expertise.

Insurance

➡ A watertight travel insurance policy covering theft, loss and medical problems is essential. Some policies specifically exclude designated 'dangerous activities' such as scuba diving, bungy jumping, white-water rafting, skiing and even tramping. If you plan on doing any of these things (a distinct possibility in NZ!), make sure your policy covers you fully.

➡ It's worth mentioning that under NZ law, you cannot sue for personal injury (other than exemplary damages). Instead, the country's **Accident Compensation Corporation** (ACC; www.acc.co.nz) administers an accident compensation scheme that provides accident insurance for NZ residents and visitors to the country, regardless of fault. This scheme, however, does not negate the necessity for your own comprehensive travel-insurance policy, as it doesn't cover you for such things as income loss, treatment at home or ongoing illness.

➡ Consider a policy that pays doctors or hospitals directly, rather than you paying on the spot and claiming later. If you have to claim later, keep all documentation. Some policies ask you to call (reverse charges) to a centre in your home country where an immediate assessment of your problem is made. Check that the policy covers ambulances and emergency medical evacuations by air.

➡ Worldwide travel insurance is available at www.lonelyplanet.com/travel-insurance. You can buy, extend and claim online anytime – even if you're already on the road.

Internet Access

Wi-Fi & Internet Service Providers

➡ You'll be able to find wi-fi access around the country, from hotel rooms to pub beer gardens to hostel dorms. Usually you have to be a guest or customer to log-on; you'll be issued with an access code. Sometimes it's free, sometimes there's a charge.

➡ The country's main telecommunications company is **Telecom New Zealand** (www.telecom.co.nz), which has wireless hotspots around the country where you can purchase prepaid access cards. Alternatively, purchase a prepaid number from the login page at any wireless hotspot using your credit card. See Telecom's website for hotspot listings.

➡ If you've brought your palmtop or laptop, consider buying a prepaid USB modem (aka a 'dongle') with a local SIM card: both Telecom and **Vodafone** (www.vodafone.co.nz) sell these from around $100. If you want to get connected via a local internet service provider (ISP), options include the following:

Clearnet (☑0508 888 800; www.clearnet.co.nz)

Earthlight (☑03-479 0303; www.earthlight.co.nz)

Slingshot (☑0800 892 000; www.slingshot.co.nz)

Internet Cafes

There are fewer internet cafes around these days than there were five years ago (thanks to the advent of mobile devices and wi-fi) but you'll still find them in most sizable towns. Access at cafes ranges from $4 to $6 per hour.

Most youth hostels have both computers for internet access and wi-fi, as do many hotels and caravan parks. Many public libraries have internet access, including wi-fi, but generally it's provided for research, not for travellers to check Facebook.

Legal Matters

➡ Marijuana is widely indulged in but illegal: anyone caught carrying this or other illicit drugs will have the book thrown at them.

→ Drink-driving is a serious offence and remains a significant problem in NZ. The legal blood alcohol limit is 0.08% for drivers over 20, and zero for those under 20.

→ If you are arrested, it's your right to consult a lawyer before any formal questioning begins.

Maps

The **Automobile Association** (AA; ☎0800 500 444; www.aa.co.nz/travel) produces excellent city, town, regional, island and highway maps, available from its local offices. It also produces a detailed *New Zealand Road Atlas*. Other reliable countrywide atlases, available from visitor information centres and bookshops, are published by Hema, KiwiMaps and Wises.

Land Information New Zealand (LINZ; www.linz.govt.nz) publishes several map series, including street, country and holiday maps, national park and forest park maps, and topographical trampers' maps. Scan the larger bookshops, or try the nearest DOC office or visitor information centre for topo maps.

Online, log onto **AA Maps** (www.aamaps.co.nz) or **Yellow Maps** (www.maps.yellowpages.co.nz) to pinpoint exact NZ addresses.

Money

ATMs & Eftpos

Branches of the country's major banks across both islands have ATMs, but you won't find them everywhere (eg not in small towns).

Many NZ businesses use electronic funds transfer at point of sale (Eftpos), allowing you to use your bank card (credit or debit) to make direct purchases and often withdraw cash as well. Eftpos is available practically everywhere: just like an ATM, you'll need a personal identification number (PIN).

Bank Accounts

We've heard mixed reports on the subject of travellers opening bank accounts in NZ, and bank websites are vague. Some sources say opening an account is as simple as flashing a few pieces of ID; other sources say banks won't allow visitors to open an account unless the application is accompanied by proof of employment. Either way, do your homework before you arrive and be prepared to shop around to get the best deal.

Credit & Debit Cards

CREDIT CARDS

Credit cards such as Visa and MasterCard are widely accepted for everything from a hostel bed to a bungy jump, and are pretty much essential for car hire. They can also be used for over-the-counter cash advances at banks and from ATMs, but be aware that such transactions incur charges. Diners Club and American Express cards are not as widely accepted.

DEBIT CARDS

Debit cards enable you to draw money directly from your home bank account using ATMs, banks or Eftpos facilities. Any card connected to the international banking network (Cirrus, Maestro, Visa Plus and Eurocard) should work with your PIN. Fees will vary depending on your home bank; ask before you leave. Alternatively, companies such as Travelex offer debit cards with set withdrawal fees and a balance you can top-up from your personal bank account while on the road.

Currency

NZ's currency is the NZ dollar, comprising 100 cents. There are 10c, 20c, 50c, $1 and $2 coins, and $5, $10, $20, $50 and $100 notes. Prices are often still marked in single cents and then rounded to the nearest 10c when you hand over your money.

Moneychangers

Changing foreign currency or travellers cheques is usually no problem at NZ banks or at licensed moneychangers (eg Travelex) in the major cities. Moneychangers can be found in all major tourist areas, cities and airports.

Taxes & Refunds

The Goods and Services Tax (GST) is a flat 15% tax on all domestic goods and services. Prices in this book include GST. There's no GST refund available when you leave NZ.

Travellers Cheques

Amex, Travelex and other international brands of travellers cheques are a bit old-fashioned these days, but they're easily exchanged at banks and moneychangers. Present your passport for identification when cashing them; shop around for the best rates.

Opening Hours

Note that most attractions close on Christmas Day and Good Friday.

Shops & businesses 9am to 5.30pm Monday to Friday, and 9am to 12.30pm or 5pm Saturday. Late-night shopping (until 9pm) in larger cities on Thursday and/or Friday nights. Sunday trading in most big towns and cities.

Supermarkets 8am to 7pm, often 9pm or later in cities.

Banks 9.30am to 4.30pm Monday to Friday; some city branches also open Saturday mornings.

Post offices 8.30am to 5pm Monday to Friday; larger branches also 9.30am to 1pm Saturday. Postal desks in newsagencies open later.

Restaurants noon to 2.30pm and 6.30pm to 9pm, often until 11pm Fridays and Saturdays.

Cafes 7am to 4pm or 5pm.

Pubs Noon until late; food from noon to 2pm and from 6pm to 8pm.

Post

The services offered by **New Zealand Post** (☎0800 501 501; www.nzpost.co.nz) are reliable and reasonably inexpensive. See the website for current info on national and international zones and rates, plus post office locations.

Public Holidays

NZ's main public holidays:

New Year 1 and 2 January

Waitangi Day 6 February

Easter Good Friday and Easter Monday; March/April

Anzac Day 25 April

Queen's Birthday First Monday in June

Labour Day Fourth Monday in October

Christmas Day 25 December

Boxing Day 26 December

In addition, each NZ province has its own anniversary-day holiday. The dates vary: when they fall on Friday to Sunday, they're usually observed the following Monday; if they fall on Tuesday to Thursday, they're held on the preceding Monday. Provincial anniversary holidays:

Southland 17 January

Wellington 22 January

Auckland 29 January

Northland 29 January

Nelson 1 February

Otago 23 March

Taranaki 31 March

South Canterbury 25 September

Hawke's Bay 1 November

Marlborough 1 November

Chatham Islands 30 November

Westland 1 December

Canterbury 16 December

School Holidays

The Christmas holiday season, from mid-December to late January, is part of the summer school vacation: expect transport and accommodation to book-out in advance, and queues at tourist attractions. There are three shorter school-holiday periods during the year: from mid- to late April, early to mid-July, and mid-September to early October. For exact dates see the **Ministry of Education** (www.minedu.govt.nz) website.

Safe Travel

Although it's no more dangerous than other developed countries, violent crime does happen in NZ, so it's worth taking sensible precautions on the streets at night or if staying in remote areas. Gang culture permeates some parts of the country; give any black-jacketed, insignia-wearing groups a wide berth.

Theft from cars is a problem around NZ – travellers are viewed as easy marks. Avoid leaving valuables in vehicles, no matter where they're parked; you're tempting fate at tourist parking areas and trailhead car parks.

GOVERNMENT TRAVEL ADVICE

The following government websites offer travel advisories and information on current hot spots:

Australian Department of Foreign Affairs (www.smarttraveller.gov.au)

British Foreign & Commonwealth Office (www.gov.uk/fco)

Foreign Affairs, Trade & Development Canada (www.international.gc.ca)

US Department of State (www.travel.state.gov)

Don't underestimate the dangers posed by NZ's unpredictable, ever-changing climate, especially in high-altitude areas. Hypothermia is a real risk.

NZ has been spared the venomous creatures found in neighbouring Australia (spiders, snakes, jellyfish…). Sharks patrol NZ waters, but rarely nibble on humans. Much greater ocean hazards are rips and undertows, which can quickly drag swimmers out to sea: heed local warnings.

Kiwi roads are often made hazardous by speeding locals, wide-cornering campervans and traffic-ignorant sheep. Set yourself a reasonable itinerary and keep your eyes on the road. Cyclists take care: motorists can't always overtake easily on skinny roads.

In the annoyances category, NZ's sandflies are a royal pain (the intense itching can last for months). Lather yourself with insect repellent in coastal areas, even if you're only sitting on the edge of a beach for a minute or two.

Telephone

Telecom New Zealand (www.telecom.co.nz) The key domestic player, with a stake in the local mobile (cell) market.

Vodafone (www.vodafone.co.nz) Mobile-network option.

2 Degrees (www.2degreesmobile.co.nz) Mobile-network option.

Mobile Phones

Mobile phone numbers are preceded by the prefix ☎021, ☎022, ☎025 or ☎027. Mobile phone coverage is good in cities and towns and most parts of the North Island, but can be patchy away from urban centres on the South Island.

If you want to bring your own phone and use a prepaid service with a local SIM card, Vodafone is a practical option. Any Vodafone shop (found in most major towns) will set you up with a SIM card and phone number (about $40); top-ups can be purchased at newsagencies, post offices and petrol stations practically anywhere.

Alternatively, if you don't bring your own phone from home, you can rent one from **Vodafone Rental** (www.vodarent.co.nz) from $5 per day (for which you'll also need a local SIM card), with pick-up and drop-off outlets at NZ's major airports. We've also had some positive feedback on **Phone Hire New Zealand** (www.phonehirenz.com) which hires out mobile phones, SIM cards, modems and GPS systems.

Local Calls

Local calls from private phones are free! Local calls from payphones cost $1 for the first 15 minutes, and $0.20 per minute thereafter, though coin-operated payphones are scarce (and if you do find one, chances are the coin slot will be gummed up); you'll generally need a phonecard. Calls to mobile phones attract higher rates.

International Calls

Payphones allow international calls, but the cost and international dialling code for calls varies by provider. International calls are relatively inexpensive and subject to specials that reduce the rates even more, so it's worth shopping around – consult the *Yellow Pages* for providers.

To make international calls from NZ, you need to dial the international access code ☑00, then the country code and the area code (without the initial ☑0). So for a London number, you'd dial ☑00-44-20, then the number.

If dialling NZ from overseas, the country code is ☑64, followed by the appropriate area code minus the initial ☑0.

Long Distance Calls & Area Codes

NZ uses regional two-digit area codes for long-distance calls, which can be made from any payphone. If you're making a local call (ie to someone else in the same

town), you don't need to dial the area code. But if you're dialling within a region (even if it's to a nearby town with the same area code), you do have to dial the area code.

Information & Toll-Free Calls

Numbers starting with ☑0900 are usually recorded information services, charging upwards of $1 per minute (more from mobiles); these numbers cannot be dialled from payphones.

Toll-free numbers in NZ have the prefix ☑0800 or ☑0508 and can be called free of charge from anywhere in the country, though they may not be accessible from certain areas or from mobile phones. Telephone numbers beginning with ☑0508, ☑0800 or ☑0900 cannot be dialled from outside NZ.

Phonecards

NZ has a wide range of phonecards available, which can be bought at hostels, newsagencies and post offices for a fixed-dollar value (usually $5, $10, $20 and $50). These can be used with any public or private phone by dialling a toll-free access number and then the PIN on the card. Shop around – rates vary from company to company.

Time

NZ is 12 hours ahead of GMT/UTC and two hours ahead of Australian Eastern Standard Time. The Chathams are 45 minutes ahead of NZ's main islands.

In summer, NZ observes daylight-saving time, where clocks are wound forward by one hour on the last Sunday in September; clocks are wound back on the first Sunday of the following April.

Toilets

Toilets in NZ are sit-down Western style. Public toilets are plentiful, and are usually

fairly clean with working locks and plenty of toilet paper.

See www.toiletmap.co.nz for public toilet locations around the country.

Tourist Information

Tourism New Zealand

The website for the official national tourism body, **Tourism New Zealand** (www.newzealand.com), is the best place for pretrip research. Emblazoned with the hugely successful 100% Pure New Zealand branding, the site has information in several languages, including German and Japanese, and also lists Tourism New Zealand contact offices overseas (Australia, UK, USA etc).

Local Tourist Offices

Almost every Kiwi city or town seems to have a visitor information centre. The bigger centres stand united within the outstanding **i-SITE** (www.newzealand.com/travel/i-sites) network – around 80 info centres affiliated with Tourism New Zealand. i-SITEs have trained staff, information on local activities and attractions, and free brochures and maps. Staff can also book activities, transport and accommodation.

Bear in mind that some information centres only promote accommodation and tour operators who are paying members of the local tourist association, and that sometimes staff aren't supposed to recommend one activity or accommodation provider over another.

There's also a network of **Department of Conservation** (DOC; www.doc.govt.nz) visitor centres to help you plan activities and make bookings. DOC visitor centres – in national parks, regional centres and major cities – usually also have displays on local lore, flora, fauna and biodiversity.

Travellers with Disabilities

Kiwi accommodation generally caters fairly well for travellers with disabilities, with a significant number of hostels, hotels, motels and B&Bs equipped with wheelchair-accessible rooms. Many tourist attractions similarly provide wheelchair access, with wheelchairs often available.

Tour operators with accessible vehicles operate from most major centres. Key cities are also serviced by 'kneeling' buses (buses that hydraulically stoop down to kerb level to allow easy access), and taxi companies offer wheelchair-accessible vans. Large car-hire firms (Avis, Hertz etc) provide cars with hand controls at no extra charge (advance notice required).

Activities

Want to tackle a wilderness pathway? Pick up a copy of Accessible Walks by Anna and Andrew Jameson ($30 including postage), with first-hand descriptions of 100-plus South Island walks. It's available online at www.accessiblewalks.co.nz.

If cold-weather activity is more your thing, see the Disabled Snowsports NZ (www.disabledsnowsports.org.nz) website.

Resources

Weka (www.weka.net.nz) Good general information, with categories including Transport and Travel.

Royal New Zealand Foundation of the Blind (www.rnzfb.org.nz)

National Foundation for the Deaf (www.nfd.org.nz)

Mobility Parking (www.mobilityparking.org.nz) Info on mobility parking permits and online applications.

Visas

Visa application forms are available from NZ diplomatic missions overseas, travel agents and Immigration New Zealand (☑09-914 4100, 0508 558 855; www.immigration.govt.nz). Immigration New Zealand has over a dozen offices overseas; consult the website.

Visitor Visa

Australian citizens don't need a visa to visit NZ and can stay indefinitely (provided they have no criminal convictions). UK citizens don't need a visa either and can stay in the country for up to six months.

Citizens of another 56 countries that have visa-waiver agreements with NZ don't need a visa for stays of up to three months, provided they have an onward ticket and sufficient funds to support their stay. Nations in this group include Canada, France, Germany, Ireland, Japan, the Netherlands, South Africa and the USA.

Citizens of other countries must obtain a visa before entering NZ. Visas come with three months' standard validity and cost NZ$130 if processed in Australia or certain South Pacific countries (eg Samoa, Fiji), or around NZ$165 if processed elsewhere in the world.

A visitor's visa can be extended for stays of up to nine months within one 18-month period, or to a maximum of 12 months in the country. Applications are assessed on a case-by-case basis; you may need to provide proof of adequate funds to sustain you during your visit (NZ$1000 per month) plus an onward ticket establishing your intent to leave. Apply for extensions at any Immigration New Zealand office.

Work Visa & Working Holiday Scheme

WORK VISA

It's illegal for foreign nationals to work in NZ on a visitor visa, except for Australians who can legally gain work without a visa or permit. If you're visiting NZ to find work, or you already have an employment offer, you'll need to apply for a work visa, which translates into a work permit once you arrive and is valid for up to three years. You can apply for a work permit after you're in NZ, but its validity will be backdated to when you entered the country. The fee for a work visa fluctuates between NZ$230 and NZ$360, depending on where and how it's processed (paper or online) and the type of application.

WORKING HOLIDAY SCHEME

Eligible travellers who are only interested in short-term employment to supplement their travels can take part in one of NZ's working holiday schemes (WHS). Under these schemes citizens aged 18 to 30 years from 40 countries – including Canada, France, Germany, Ireland, Japan, Malaysia, the Netherlands, Scandinavian countries, the UK and the USA – can apply for a visa. For most nationalities the visa is valid for 12 months. It's only issued to those seeking a genuine working holiday, not permanent work, so you're not supposed to work for one employer for more than three months.

Most WHS-eligible nationals must apply for this visa from within their own country; residents of some countries can apply online. Applicants must have an onward ticket, a passport valid for at least three months from the date they will leave NZ and evidence of at least NZ$4200 in accessible funds. The application fee is NZ$165 regardless of where you apply, and isn't refunded if your application is declined.

The rules vary for different nationalities, so make sure you read up on the specifics of your country's agreement with NZ at www.immigration.govt.nz/migrant/stream/work/workingholiday.

Volunteering

NZ presents a swathe of active, outdoorsy volunteer opportunities for travellers to get some dirt under their fingernails and participate in conservation programs. Programs include anything from tree-planting and weed removal to track construction, habitat conservation and fencing. Ask about local opportunities at any regional i-SITE visitor information centre, or check out www. conservationvolunteers. org.nz and www.doc.govt. nz/getting-involved, both of which allow you to browse for opportunities by region. Another resource is www.helpx. net, which lists volunteering opportunities on farms where you can work in exchange for accommodation.

Women Travellers

NZ is generally a very safe place for women travellers, although the usual sensible precautions apply: avoid walking alone late at night and never hitchhike alone. If you're out on the town, always keep enough money aside for a taxi back to your accommodation. Lone women should also be wary of staying in basic pub accommodation unless it looks safe and well managed. Sexual harassment is not a widely reported problem in NZ, but of course it does happen.

See www.womentravel. co.nz for more information.

Work

If you arrive in NZ on a visitor visa, you're not allowed to work for pay. If you're caught breaching this visa condition, you could be booted back to where you came from.

If you have been approved for a WHS visa, look into the possibilities for temporary employment. There's plenty of casual work around, mainly in agriculture (fruit picking,

farming, wineries), hospitality (bar work, waiting tables) or at ski resorts. Office-based work can be found in IT, banking, finance and telemarketing. Register with a local office-work agency to get started.

Seasonal fruit picking, pruning and harvesting is prime short-term work for visitors. More than 30,000 hectares of apples, kiwifruit and other fruit and veg are harvested from December to May. Rates are around $12 to $17 an hour (not much) for physically taxing toil, working in the dirt under the hot sun – turnover of workers is high. You're usually paid by how much you pick (per bin, bucket or kilogram): if you stick with it for a while, you'll get faster and fitter and can actually make some reasonable cash. Prime North Island picking locations include the Bay of Islands (Kerikeri and Paihia), rural Auckland, Tauranga and the Bay of Plenty, Gisborne and Hawke's Bay (Napier and Hastings); on the South Island try Nelson (Tapawera and Golden Bay), Marlborough (around Blenheim) and Central Otago (Alexandra and Roxburgh).

Winter work at ski resorts and their service towns includes bartending, waiting, cleaning, ski-tow operation and, if you're properly qualified, ski or snowboard instructing.

Resources

Backpacker publications, hostel managers and other travellers are the best sources of info on local work possibilities. **Base Backpackers** (www.stayatbase.com/work) runs an employment service via its website, while the Notice Boards page on **Budget Backpacker Hostels** (BBH; www.bbh.co.nz) lists job vacancies in BBH hostels and a few other possibilities.

Kiwi Careers (www.careers. govt.nz) lists professional opportunities in various fields (agriculture, creative, health, teaching, volunteer work and recruitment), while **Seek**

(www.seek.co.nz) is one of the biggest job-search networks, with thousands of jobs listed.

Check ski-resort websites for work opportunities in the snow; in the fruit-picking/ horticultural realm, try the following websites:

➡ www.seasonalwork.co.nz
➡ www.seasonaljobs.co.nz
➡ www.picknz.co.nz
➡ www.pickingjobs.com

Income Tax

Death and taxes – no escape! For most travellers, Kiwi dollars earned in NZ will be subject to income tax, deducted from payments by employers – a process called Pay As You Earn (PAYE). Standard NZ income tax rates are 12.2% for annual salaries up to $14,000, then 19.2% up to $48,000, 31.7% up to $70,000, then 34.7% for higher incomes. A NZ Accident Compensation Corporation (ACC) scheme levy (around 2%) will also be deducted from your pay packet. Note that these rates tend to change slightly year-to-year.

If you visit NZ and work for a short time (eg on a working-holiday scheme), you may qualify for a tax refund when you leave. Complete a *Refund Application – People Leaving New Zealand IR50* form and submit it with your tax return, along with proof of departure (eg air-ticket copies) to the **Inland Revenue Department** (www.ird.govt.nz). For more info, see the IRD website, or contact the **Inland Revenue Non-Resident Centre** (☏03-951 2020; nonres@ird.govt.nz; Private Bag 1932, Dunedin 9054).

IRD Number

Travellers undertaking paid work in NZ must obtain an IRD (Inland Revenue Department) number. Download the *IRD Number Application – Individual IR595* form from the **Inland Revenue Department** (www.ird.govt. nz) website. IRD numbers normally take eight to 10 working days to be issued.

Transport

GETTING THERE & AWAY

New Zealand is a long way from almost everywhere – most travellers jet in from afar. Flights, cars and tours can be booked online at lonelyplanet.com/bookings.

Entering the Country

Disembarkation in New Zealand is generally a straightforward affair, with only the usual customs declarations and the luggage carousel scramble to endure. Under the Orwellian title of 'Advance Passenger Screening', documents that used to be checked after you touched down in NZ (passport, visa etc) are now checked before you board your flight – make sure all your documentation is in order so that your check-in is stress-free.

Passport

There are no restrictions when it comes to foreign citizens entering NZ. If you have a current passport and visa (or don't require one; see p660), you should be fine.

Air

There are a number of competing airlines that service NZ if you're flying in from Asia, Europe or North America, though ultimately you'll still pay a lot for a flight unless you jet in from Australia. NZ's abundance of year-round activities means that airports are busy most of the time: if you want to fly at a particularly popular time of year (eg over the Christmas period), book well in advance.

The high season for flights into NZ is during summer (December to February), with slightly less of a premium on fares over the shoulder months (October/November and March/April). The low season generally tallies with the winter months (June to August), though this is still a busy time for airlines ferrying ski bunnies and powder hounds.

Airports & Airlines
INTERNATIONAL AIRPORTS

A number of NZ airports handle international flights, with Auckland receiving most traffic:

Auckland International Airport (Map p64; ☎09-275 0789; www.aucklandairport.co.nz; Ray Emery Dr, Mangere)

Christchurch International Airport (☎03-358 5029; www.christchurchairport.co.nz; 30 Durey Rd)

Dunedin International Airport (DUD; ☎03-486 2879; www.dnairport.co.nz; 25 Miller Rd, Momona)

CLIMATE CHANGE & TRAVEL

Every form of transport that relies on carbon-based fuel generates CO_2, the main cause of human-induced climate change. Modern travel is dependent on aeroplanes, which might use less fuel per kilometre per person than most cars but travel much greater distances. The altitude at which aircraft emit gases (including CO_2) and particles also contributes to their climate change impact. Many websites offer 'carbon calculators' that allow people to estimate the carbon emissions generated by their journey and, for those who wish to do so, to offset the impact of the greenhouse gases emitted with contributions to portfolios of climate-friendly initiatives throughout the world. Lonely Planet offsets the carbon footprint of all staff and author travel.

Hamilton International Airport (☑07-848 9027; www.hamiltonairport.co.nz; Airport Rd)

Queenstown Airport (☑03-450 9031; www.queenstownairport.co.nz; Sir Henry Wrigley Dr)

Rotorua International Airport (☑07-345 8800; www.rotorua-airport.co.nz; SH30)

Wellington Airport (☑04-385 5100; www.wellingtonairport.co.nz; Stewart Duff Dr, Rongotai)

AIRLINES FLYING TO & FROM NEW ZEALAND

New Zealand's own international carrier is **Air New Zealand** (www.airnewzealand.co.nz), which flies to runways across Europe, North America, eastern Asia and the Pacific, and has an extensive network across NZ.

Winging-in from Australia, **Virgin Australia** (www.virginaustralia.com), **Qantas** (www.qantas.com.au), **Jetstar** (www.jetstar.com) and Air New Zealand are the key players. Air New Zealand also flies in from North America, but you can head south with **Air Canada** (www.aircanada.com) and **American Airlines** (www.aa.com), too.

From Europe, the options are a little broader, with **British Airways** (www.britishairways.com), **Lufthansa** (www.lufthansa.com) and **Virgin Atlantic** (www.virginatlantic.com) entering the fray, and plenty of others stopping in NZ on broader round-the-world routes.

From Asia and the Pacifc there are myriad options, with direct flights from China, Japan, Singapore, Malaysia, Thailand and many Pacific island nations.

Sea

It's possible (though by no means easy or safe) to make your way between NZ and Australia, and some smaller Pacific islands, by hitching

rides or crewing on yachts. Try asking around at harbours, marinas, and yacht and sailing clubs. Popular yachting harbours in NZ include the Bay of Islands and Whangarei (both in Northland), Auckland and Wellington. March and April are the best months to look for boats heading to Australia. From Fiji, October to November is a peak departure season to beat the cyclones that soon follow in that neck of the woods.

If you're looking for something with a slower pace, plenty of passenger cruise liners stop in NZ on the South Pacific legs of their respective schedules: try **P&O Cruises** (www.pocruises.com.au) for starters.

Alternatively, a berth on a cargo ship or freighter to/from New Zealand is a quirky way to go: check out websites such as www.freightercruises.com and www.freighterexpeditions.com.au for more info.

GETTING AROUND

Air

Those who have limited time to get between NZ's attractions can make the most of a widespread (and very reliable and safe) network of intra- and inter-island flights.

DEPARTURE TAX

An international departure tax of NZ$25 applies when leaving three of NZ's smaller international airports: Hamilton, Rotorua and the sporadically international Palmerston North. At all other airports the tax has been replaced with a NZ$12.50 Passenger Service Charge (PSC), which is included in your ticket price. At Hamilton, Rotorua and Palmerston North, departure tax must be paid separately at the airport before you board your flight (via credit card or cash). For kids under 12 it's NZ$10, and free for kids under two.

Airlines in New Zealand

The country's major domestic carrier, Air New Zealand, has an aerial network covering most of the country, often operating under the Air New Zealand Link moniker on less popular routes. Australia-based Jetstar also flies between main urban areas. Between them, these two airlines carry the vast majority of domestic passengers in NZ. Beyond this, several small-scale regional operators provide essential transport services to outlying islands such as Great Barrier Island in the Hauraki Gulf, to Stewart Island and the Chathams. Operators include the following:

Air Chathams (www.airchathams.co.nz) Services to the remote Chatham Islands from Wellington, Christchurch and Auckland.

Air Fiordland (www.airfiordland.com) Services around Milford Sound, Te Anau and Queenstown.

Air New Zealand (www.airnewzealand.co.nz) Offers flights between 30-plus domestic destinations, plus myriad overseas destinations.

Air West Coast (www.airwestcoast.co.nz) Operates charter/scenic flights ex-Greymouth, winging over the west coast glaciers and Aoraki/Mt Cook, and stopping in Milford Sound, Queenstown and Christchurch.

Air2there.com (www.air2there.com) Connects

destinations across Cook Strait, including Paraparaumu, Wellington, Nelson and Blenheim.

FlyMySky (www.flymysky. co.nz) At least three flights daily from Auckland to Great Barrier Island.

Golden Bay Air (www. goldenbayair.co.nz) Flies regularly between Wellington, Nelson and Takaka in Golden Bay. Also connects to Karamea for Heaphy Track trampers.

Great Barrier Airlines (www.greatbarrierairlines.co.nz) Plies the skies over Great Barrier Island, Auckland, Tauranga and Whangarei.

Jetstar (www.jetstar.com) Joins the dots between key tourism centres: Auckland, Wellington, Christchurch, Dunedin and Queenstown (and flies Queenstown to Melbourne and Sydney; Christchurch to Melbourne, Sydney and the Gold Coast; and Auckland to Melbourne, Adelaide, the Gold Coast and Cairns).

Salt Air (www.saltair.co.nz) Charter flights from Auckland to the Bay of Islands.

Soundsair (www.soundsair. co.nz) Numerous flights each day between Picton and Wellington, plus flights from Wellington to Blenheim, Nelson and Whanganui.

Stewart Island Flights (www.stewartislandflights.com) Flies between Invercargill and Stewart Island.

Sunair (www.sunair.co.nz) Flies to Whitianga from Auckland, Great Barrier Island and Tauranga, plus numerous other North Island connections between Hamilton, Napier, Rotorua, Gisborne and New Plymouth.

Air Passes

With discounting being the norm these days, and a number of budget airlines now serving the trans-Tasman route as well as the Pacific islands, the value of air passes isn't as red-hot as in the past.

Available exclusively to travellers from the USA or Canada who have bought

an Air New Zealand fare to NZ from the USA or Canada, Australia or the Pacific Islands, Air New Zealand offers the good-value **New Zealand Explorer Pass**. The pass lets you fly between up to 27 destinations in New Zealand, Australia and the South Pacific islands (including Norfolk Island, Tonga, Vanuatu, Tahiti, Fiji, Niue and the Cook Islands). Fares are broken down into four discounted, distance-based zones: zone one flights start at US$79 (eg Auckland to Christchurch); zone two from US$109 (eg Auckland to Queenstown); zone three from US$214 (eg Wellington to Sydney); and zone four from US$295 (eg Tahiti to Auckland). You can buy the pass before you travel, or after you arrive in NZ.

Star Alliance (www. staralliance.com) offers the sector-based **South Pacific Airpass**, valid for selected journeys within NZ, and between NZ, Australia and several Pacific islands, including Fiji, New Caledonia, Tonga, the Cook Islands and Samoa. Passes are available to nonresidents of these countries, must be issued outside NZ in conjunction with Star Alliance international tickets, and are valid for three months. A typical Sydney–Christchurch–Wellington–Auckland–Nadi pass cost NZ$1050 at the time of research.

Bicycle

Touring cyclists proliferate in NZ, particularly over summer. The country is clean, green and relatively uncrowded, and has lots of cheap accommodation (including camping) and abundant fresh water. The roads are generally in good nick, and the climate is generally not too hot or cold. Road traffic is the biggest danger: trucks overtaking too close to cyclists are a particular threat. Bikes and cycling gear

are readily available to rent or buy in the main centres, as are bicycle repair shops.

By law all cyclists must wear an approved safety helmet (or risk a fine); it's also vital to have good reflective safety clothing. Cyclists who use public transport will find that major bus lines and trains only take bicycles on a 'space available' basis and charge up to $10. Some of the smaller shuttle bus companies, on the other hand, make sure they have storage space for bikes, which they carry for a surcharge.

If importing your own bike or transporting it by plane within NZ, check with the relevant airline for costs and the degree of dismantling and packing required.

See www.nzta.govt.nz/traffic/ways/bike for more bike safety and legal tips, and p50 for info on Nga Haerenga, New Zealand Cycle Trail – a network of 22 'Great Rides' across NZ.

Hire

Rates offered by most outfits for renting road or mountain bikes range from $10 to $20 per hour and $30 to $50 per day. Longer-term rentals may be available by negotiation. You can often hire bikes from your accommodation (hostels, campgrounds etc), or rent more reputable machines from bike shops in the larger towns.

Buying a Bike

Bicycles can be readily bought in NZ's larger cities, but prices for newer models are high. For a decent hybrid bike or rigid mountain bike you'll pay anywhere from $800 to $1800, though you can get a cheap one for around $500 (but you still then need to buy panniers, helmet, lock etc, and the cost quickly climbs). Other options include the post-Christmas sales and midyear stocktakes, when newish cycles can be heavily discounted.

Boat

NZ may be an island nation but there's virtually no long-distance water transport around the country. Obvious exceptions include the boat services between Auckland and various islands in the Hauraki Gulf, the inter-island ferries that chug across Cook Strait between Wellington and Picton, and the passenger ferry that negotiates Foveaux Strait between Bluff and the town of Oban on Stewart Island.

If you're cashed-up, consider the cruise liners that chug around the NZ coastline as part of broader South Pacific itineraries: **P&O Cruises** (www.pocruises.com.au) is a major player.

Bus

Bus travel in NZ is relatively easy and well organised, with services transporting you to the far reaches of both islands (including the start/end of various walking tracks), but it can be expensive, tedious and time-consuming.

NZ's dominant bus company is **InterCity** (www.intercity.co.nz), which can drive you to just about anywhere on the North and South Islands. InterCity also has a South Island sightseeing arm called **Newmans Coach Lines** (☏09-583 5780; www.newmanscoach.co.nz), travelling between Queenstown, Christchurch and the West Coast glaciers. **Naked Bus** (www.nakedbus.com) has similar routes and remains the main competition. Both bus lines offer fares as low as $1(!).

Seat Classes & Smoking

There are no allocated economy or luxury classes on NZ buses (very democratic), and smoking on the bus is a definite no-no.

Reservations

Over summer, school holidays and public holidays, book well in advance on popular routes (a week or two if possible). At other times a day or two ahead is usually fine. The best prices are generally available online, booked a few weeks in advance.

Bus Passes

If you're covering a lot of ground, both **InterCity** (www.intercity.co.nz) and **Naked Bus** (www.nakedbus.com) offer bus passes that can be cheaper than paying as you go, but they do of course lock you into using their respective networks. InterCity also offers a 10% discount for YHA, ISIC, Nomands, BBH or VIP card holders, and passes are generally valid for 12 months.

NATIONWIDE PASSES

Flexipass A hop-on/hop-off InterCity pass, allowing travel to pretty much anywhere in NZ, in any direction, including the Interislander ferry accross Cook Strait. The pass is purchased in blocks of travel time: minimum 15 hours ($119), maximum 60 hours ($449). The average cost of each block becomes cheaper the more hours you buy. You can top up the pass if you need more time.

Flexitrips An InterCity bus-pass system whereby you purchase a specific number of bus trips (eg Auckland to Tauranga would count as one trip) in blocks of five, with or without the Cook Strait ferry trip included. Five/15/30 trips including the ferry cost $210/383/550 (subtract $54 if you don't need the ferry).

Aotearoa Adventurer, **Kiwi Explorer**, **Kia Ora New Zealand** and **Tiki Tour New Zealand** Hop-on/hop-off, fixed-itinerary nationwide passes offered by InterCity. These passes link up tourist hot spots and range in price from $645 to $1219. See www.travelpass.co.nz for details.

Naked Passport (www.nakedpassport.com) A Naked Bus pass that allows you to buy trips in blocks of five, which you can add to any time, and book each trip as needed. Five/15/30 trips cost $151/318/491. An unlimited pass costs $597 – great value if you're travelling NZ for many moons.

NORTH ISLAND PASSES

InterCity also offers 13 hop-on/hop-off, fixed-itinerary North Island bus passes, ranging from short $43 runs between Rotorua and Taupo, to $249 trips from Auckland to Wellington via the big sights in between. See www.travelpass.co.nz for details.

SOUTH ISLAND PASSES

On the South Island, InterCity offers 11 hop-on/hop-off, fixed-itinerary passes, ranging from $43 trips between Christchurch and Kaikoura, to $583 loops around the whole island. See www.travelpass.co.nz for details.

Shuttle Buses

As well as InterCity and Naked Bus, regional shuttle buses fill in the gaps between the smaller towns. Operators include the following (not a finite list), offering regular scheduled services and/or charter tours:

Abel Tasman Travel (www.abeltasmantravel.co.nz) Traverses the roads between Nelson, Motueka, Golden Bay, and Kahurangi and Abel Tasman National Parks.

Alpine Scenic Tours (www.alpinescenictours.co.nz) Runs tours around Taupo and into Tongariro National Park, plus the ski fields around Mt Ruapehu and Mt Tongariro.

Atomic Shuttles (www.atomictravel.co.nz) Has services throughout the South Island, including to Christchurch, Dunedin, Invercargill, Picton, Nelson, Greymouth/Hokitika, Te Anau and Queenstown/Wanaka.

Cook Connection (www.cookconnect.co.nz) Triangulates between Mt Cook, Twizel and Lake Tekapo.

East West Coaches (www.eastwestcoaches.co.nz) Offers a service between Christchurch and Westport via Reefton.

Hanmer Connection (www.atsnz.com) Twice-daily services between Hanmer Springs and Christchurch.

Go Kiwi Shuttles (www.go-kiwi.co.nz) Links Auckland with Whitianga on the Coromandel Peninsula daily, with extensions to Rotorua in summer.

Knightrider (www.knightrider.co.nz) Runs a nocturnal service from Christchurch to Dunedin return. David Hasselhoff nowhere to be seen....

Topline Tours (www.toplinetours.co.nz) Connects Te Anau and Queenstown.

Tracknet (www.tracknet.net) Daily track transport (Milford, Routeburn, Hollyford, Kepler etc) between Queenstown, Te Anau, Milford Sound, Invercargill, Fiordland and the West Coast.

Trek Express (☑027 222 1872, 0800 128 735; www.trekexpress.co.nz) 4WD shuttle services to all tramping tracks in the top half of the South Island.

Waitomo Wanderer (www.travelheadfirst.com) Does a loop from Rotorua or Taupo to Waitomo.

West Coast Shuttle (www.westcoastshuttle.co.nz) Daily bus from Greymouth to Christchurch and back.

Backpacker Buses

If you feel like clocking up some kilometres with like-minded fellow travellers, the following operators run fixed-itinerary bus tours, nationwide or on the North or South Island. Accommodation and hop-on/hop-off flexibility are often included.

Adventure Tours New Zealand (www.adventure-tours.com.au)

Bottom Bus (☑03-477 9083; www.travelheadfirst.com)

Flying Kiwi (www.flyingkiwi.com)

Kiwi Experience (www.kiwiexperience.com)

Haka Tours (www.hakatours.com)

Stray Travel (www.straytravel.com)

Car & Motorcycle

The best way to explore NZ in depth is to have your own wheels. It's easy to hire cars and campervans at good rates. Alternatively, if you're in NZ for a few months, you might consider buying your own vehicle.

Automobile Association

NZ's **Automobile Association** (AA; ☑0800 500 444; www.aa.co.nz/travel) provides emergency breakdown services, maps and accommodation guides (from holiday parks to motels and B&Bs).

Members of overseas automobile associations should bring their membership cards – many of these bodies have reciprocal agreements with the AA.

Drivers Licences

International visitors to NZ can use their home country drivers licence – if your licence isn't in English, it's a good idea to carry a certified translation with you. Alternatively, use an International Driving Permit (IDP), which will usually be issued on the spot (valid for 12 months) by your home country's automobile association.

Fuel

Fuel (petrol, aka gasoline) is available from service stations across NZ: unless you're cruising around in something from the '70s, you'll be filling up with 'unleaded' or LPG (gas). LPG is not always stocked by rural suppliers; if you're on gas, it's safer to have dual-fuel capability. Aside from remote locations like Milford Sound and Mt Cook, petrol prices don't vary much from place to place: per-litre costs at the time of research were around $2.40.

Hire

CAMPERVAN

Check your rear-view mirror on any far-flung NZ road and you'll probably see a shiny white campervan (aka mobile home, motor home, RV) packed with liberated travellers, mountain bikes and portable barbecues cruising along behind you.

Most towns of any size have a campground or holiday park with powered sites (where you can plug your vehicle in) for around $35 per night. There are also 250-plus vehicle-accessible **Department of Conservation** (DOC; www.doc.govt.nz) campsites around NZ, ranging in price from free to $15 per adult: check the website for info.

You can hire campervans from dozens of companies. Prices vary with season, vehicle size and length of rental.

A small van for two people typically has a minikitchen and fold-out dining table, the latter transforming into a double bed when dinner is done and dusted. Larger 'superior' two-berth vans include shower and toilet. Four- to six-berth campervans are the size of trucks (and similarly sluggish) and, besides the extra space, usually contain a toilet and shower.

Over summer, rates offered by the main rental firms for two-/four-/six-berth vans start at around $160/200/290 per day for a month-long rental, dropping to as low as $45/60/90 per day during winter.

Major operators include the following:

Apollo (☑0800 113 131, 09-889 2976; www.apollocamper.co.nz)

Britz (☑0800 831 900, 09-255 3910; www.britz.co.nz) Also does 'Britz Bikes' (add a mountain or city bike from $13 per day).

Kea (☑0800 520 052, 09-448 8800)

Maui (☑0800 651 080, 09-255 3910; www.maui.co.nz)

United Campervans
(☑0800 759 919, 09-275 9919;
www.unitedcampervans.co.nz)

Wilderness Motorhomes
(☑09-255 5300; www.wilder-
ness.co.nz)

BACKPACKER VAN RENTALS

Budget players in the
campervan industry offer
slick deals and funky (often
gregariously spray-painted:
Jimi Hendrix, *Where The
Wild Things Are*, Sly Stone
etc), well-kitted-out vehicles
for backpackers. Rates are
competitive (from $35/50
per day for a two-/four-berth
van May to September; from
$100/150 per day December
to February). Operators include the following:

Backpacker Sleeper Vans
(☑0800 321 939, 03-359 4731;
www.sleepervans.co.nz)

Escape Campervans
(☑0800 216 171; www.escape-
rentals.co.nz)

Hippie Camper (☑0800 113
131; www.hippiecamper.co.nz)

Jucy (☑0800 399 736, 09-
374 4360; www.jucy.co.nz)

**Mighty Cars & Camp-
ers** (☑0800 422 267; www.
mightycampers.co.nz)

Spaceships (☑0800 772
237, 09-526 2130; www.space-
shipsrentals.co.nz)

Wicked Campers (☑0800
246 870, 09-634 2994; www.
wickedcampers.co.nz)

CAR

Competition between car-
rental companies in NZ is
torrid, particularly in the big
cities and Picton. Remember
that if you want to travel
far, you need unlimited kilometres. Some (but not all)
companies require drivers to
be at least 21 years old – ask
around.

Most car-hire firms sug-
gest (or insist) that you don't
take their vehicles between
islands on the Cook Strait
ferries. Instead, you leave
your car at either Wellington
or Picton terminal and pick
up another car once you've

crossed the strait. This saves
you paying to transport a
vehicle on the ferries, and is a
pain-free exercise.

INTERNATIONAL RENTAL COMPANIES

The big multinational companies have offices in most
major cities, towns and airports. Firms sometimes offer
one-way rentals (eg collect
a car in Auckland, leave it in
Wellington), but there are
often restrictions and fees.
On the other hand, an operator in Christchurch may
need to get a vehicle back
to Auckland and will offer an
amazing one-way car relocation deal (sometimes free!).

The major companies
offer a choice of either unlimited kilometres, or 100km
(or so) per day free, plus so
many cents per subsequent
kilometre. Daily rates in
main cities typically start
at around $40 per day for a
compact, late-model, Japanese car, and around $75 for
medium-sized cars (including GST, unlimited kilometres
and insurance).

Avis (☑0800 655 111, 09-526
2847; www.avis.co.nz)

Budget (☑0800 283 438, 09-
529 7784; www.budget.co.nz)

Europcar (☑0800 800 115;
www.europcar.co.nz)

Hertz (☑0800 654 321, 03-
358 6789; www.hertz.co.nz)

Thrifty (☑0800 737 070, 03-
359 2721; www.thrifty.co.nz)

LOCAL RENTAL COMPANIES

Local rental firms dapple
the *Yellow Pages*. These are
almost always cheaper than
the big boys – sometimes
half the price – but the cheap
rates may come with seri-
ous restrictions: vehicles are
often older, and with less
formality sometimes comes
a less protective legal struc-
ture for renters.

Rentals from local firms
start at around $30 per day
for the smallest option. It's
obviously cheaper if you rent
for a week or more, and there

are often low-season and
weekend discounts.

Affordable, independent
operators with national networks include the following:

a2b Car Rentals (☑0800
545 000; www.a2b-carrentals.
co.nz)

Ace Rental Cars (☑0800
502 277, 09-303 3112; www.
acerentalcars.co.nz)

Apex Rentals (☑0800 939
597, 03-379 6897; www.apex-
rentals.co.nz)

Go Rentals (☑0800 467
368, 09-525 7321; www.goren-
tals.co.nz)

Omega Rental Cars
(☑0800 525 210, 09-377 5573;
www.omegarentalcars.com)

Pegasus Rental Cars
(☑0800 803 580, 03-548
2852; www.rentalcars.co.nz)

Transfercar (☑09-630 7533;
www.transfercar.co.nz) One-way
relocation specialists.

MOTORCYCLE

Born to be wild? NZ has great
terrain for motorcycle touring, despite the fickle weather in some regions. Most of
the country's motorcycle-
hire shops are in Auckland
and Christchurch, where you
can hire anything from a little
50cc moped (aka nifty-fifty)
to a throbbing 750cc touring motorcycle and beyond.
Recommended operators
(who also run guided tours)
with rates from $80 to $345
per day:

**New Zealand Motorcycle
Rentals & Tours** (☑09-486
2472; www.nzbike.com)

**Te Waipounamu Motor-
cycle Tours** (☑03-377 3211;
www.motorcycle-hire.co.nz)

Insurance

Rather than risk paying out
wads of cash if you have an
accident, you can take out
your own comprehensive insurance policy, or (the usual
option) pay an additional fee
per day to the rental company to reduce your excess.
This brings the amount you
must pay in the event of an

accident down from around $1500 or $2000 to around $200 or $300. Smaller operators offering cheap rates often have a compulsory insurance excess, taken as a credit-card bond, of around $900.

Most insurance agreements won't cover the cost of damage to glass (including the windscreen) or tyres, and insurance coverage is often invalidated on beaches and certain rough (4WD) unsealed roads – read the fine print.

See p656 for info on NZ's **Accident Compensation Corporation** (ACC; www.acc.co.nz) insurance scheme (fault-free personal injury insurance).

Purchase

Buying a car then selling it at the end of your travels can be one of the cheapest and best ways to see NZ. Auckland is the easiest place to buy a car, followed by Christchurch: scour the hostel noticeboards. **Turners Auctions** (www.turners.co.nz) is NZ's biggest car-auction operator, with 11 locations.

LEGALITIES

Make sure your prospective vehicle has a Warrant of Fitness (WoF) and registration valid for a reasonable period: see the **Land Transport New Zealand** (www.landtransport.govt.nz) website for details.

Buyers should also take out third-party insurance, covering the cost of repairs to another vehicle in an accident that is your fault: try the **Automobile Association** (AA; ☎0800 500 444; www.aa.co.nz/travel). NZ's no-fault Accident Compensation Corporation scheme covers personal injury, but make sure you have travel insurance, too.

If you're considering buying a car and want someone to check it out for you, various car-inspection companies inspect cars for around $150; find them at car auc-

tions, or they will come to you. Try **Vehicle Inspection New Zealand** (VINZ; ☎0800 468 469, 09-573 3230; www.vinz.co.nz) or the AA.

Before you buy it's wise to confirm ownership of the vehicle, and find out if there's anything dodgy about the car (eg stolen, or outstanding debts). The AA's **LemonCheck** (☎0800 536 662, 09-420 3090; www.lemoncheck.co.nz) offers this service ('Pry before you buy' – ha-ha...).

BUY-BACK DEALS

You can avoid the hassle of buying/selling a vehicle privately by entering into a buy-back arrangement with a dealer. Predictably, dealers often find sneaky ways of knocking down the return-sale price, which may be 50% less than what you paid, so hiring or buying and selling a vehicle yourself (if you have the time) is usually a better bet.

Road Hazards

Kiwi traffic is usually pretty light, but it's easy to get stuck behind a slow-moving truck or campervan – pack plenty of patience. There are also lots of slow wiggly roads, one-way bridges and plenty of gravel (unsealed) roads, all of which require a more cautious driving approach. And watch out for sheep!

To check road conditions call ☎0800 444 449 or see www.nzta.govt.nz/traffic/current-conditions.

Road Rules

Kiwis drive on the left-hand side of the road; cars are right-hand drive. Give way to the right at intersections.

At single-lane bridges (of which there are a surprisingly large number), a smaller red arrow pointing in your direction of travel means that *you* give way.

Speed limits on the open road are generally 100km/h; in built-up areas the limit is usually 50km/h. Speed

cameras and radars are used extensively.

All vehicle occupants must wear a seatbelt or risk a fine. Small children must be belted into approved safety seats.

Always carry your licence when driving. Drink-driving is a serious offence and remains a significant problem in NZ, despite widespread campaigns and severe penalties. The legal blood alcohol limit is 0.08% for drivers over 20, and 0% (zero!) for those under 20.

Hitching & Ride-Sharing

NZ is no longer immune from the perils of solo hitching (especially for women). Those who decide to hitch are taking a small but potentially serious risk. Hitching is never entirely safe, and we don't recommend it. That said, it's not unusual to see hitchhikers along country roads.

Alternatively, check hostel noticeboards for ride-share opportunities, or have a look online at www.carpoolnz.org or www.nationalcarshare.co.nz.

Local Transport

Bus, Train & Tram

NZ's larger cities have extensive bus services but, with a few honourable exceptions, they are mainly daytime, weekday operations; weekend services can be infrequent or nonexistent. Negotiating inner-city Auckland is made easier by the Link and free City Circuit buses; Hamilton also has a free city-centre loop bus; Christchurch has a free city-shuttle service and the historic tramway (now open again after the earthquake). Most main cities have late-night buses for boozy Friday and Saturday nights.

The only cities with decent train services are Auckland and Wellington, with four and five suburban routes respectively.

Taxi

The main cities have plenty of taxis and even small towns may have a local service.

Train

NZ train travel is about the journey, not about getting anywhere in a hurry.
KiwiRail Scenic Journeys (☎0800 872 467, 04-495 0775; www.kiwirailscenic. co.nz) operates four routes, listed following; reservations can be made through KiwiRail Scenic Journeys

directly, or at most train stations (notably not at Palmerston North or Hamilton), travel agents and visitor information centres:

Capital Connection Weekday commuter service between Palmerston North and Wellington.

Coastal Pacific Between Christchurch and Picton.

Northern Explorer Between Auckland and Wellington.

TranzAlpine Over the Southern Alps between Christchurch and Greymouth.

Train Passes

A KiwiRail Scenic Journeys **Scenic Journey Rail Pass**

(www.kiwirailscenic.co.nz/ scenic-rail-pass) allows unlimited travel on all of its rail services, including passage on the Wellington–Picton Interislander ferry. There are two types of pass, both requiring you to book your seats a minimum of 24 hours before you want to travel:

Fixed Pass Limited duration fares for one/two/three weeks, costing $599/699/799 per adult (a little bit less for kids).

Freedom Pass Affords you travel on a certain number of days over a 12-month period; a three-/ seven-/nine-day pass costs $417/903/1161.

Language

New Zealand has three official languages: English, Maori and NZ sign language. Although English is what you'll usually hear, Maori has been making a comeback. You can use English to speak to anyone in New Zealand, but there are some occasions when knowing a small amount of Maori is useful, such as when visiting a *marae*, where often only Maori is spoken. Some knowledge of Maori will also help you interpret the many Maori place names you'll come across.

KIWI ENGLISH

Like the people of other English-speaking countries in the world, New Zealanders have their own, unique way of speaking the language. The flattening of vowels is the most distinctive feature of Kiwi pronunciation. For example, in Kiwi English, 'fish and chips' sounds more like 'fush and chups'. On the North Island sentences often have 'eh!' attached to the end. In the far south a rolled 'r' is common, which is a holdover from that region's Scottish heritage – it's especially noticeable in Southland.

MAORI

The Maori have a vividly chronicled history, recorded in songs and chants that dramatically recall the migration to New Zealand from Polynesia as well as other important events. Early missionaries were the first to record the language in a written form using only 15 letters of the English alphabet.

Maori is closely related to other Polynesian languages such as Hawaiian, Tahitian and Cook Islands Maori. In fact, New Zealand Maori and Hawaiian are quite similar, even though more than 7000km separates Honolulu and Auckland.

The Maori language was never dead – it was always used in Maori ceremonies – but over time familiarity with it was definitely on the decline. Fortunately, recent years have seen a revival of interest in it, and this forms an integral part of the renaissance of *Maoritanga* (Maori culture). Many Maori people who had heard the language spoken on the *marae* for years but had not used it in their day-to-day lives, are now studying it and speaking it fluently. Maori is taught in schools throughout New Zealand, some TV programs and news reports are broadcast in it, and many English place names are being renamed in Maori. Even government departments have been given Maori names: for example, the Inland Revenue Department is also known as Te Tari Taake (the last word is actually *take*, which means 'levy', but the department has chosen to stress the long 'a' by spelling it 'aa').

In many places, Maori have come together to provide instruction in their language and culture to young children; the idea is for them to grow up speaking both Maori and English, and to develop a familiarity with Maori tradition. It's a matter of some pride to have fluency in the language. On some *marae* only Maori can be spoken.

Pronunciation

Maori is a fluid, poetic language and surprisingly easy to pronounce once you remember to split each word (some can be amazingly long) into separate syllables. Each syllable ends in a vowel. There are no 'silent' letters.

Most consonants in Maori – *h*, *k*, *m*, *n*, *p*, *t* and *w* – are pronounced much the same

WANT MORE?

For in-depth language information and handy phrases, check out Lonely Planet's *South Pacific Phrasebook*. You'll find it at **shop.lonelyplanet.com**, or you can buy Lonely Planet's iPhone phrasebooks at the Apple App Store.

as in English. The Maori r is a flapped sound (not rolled) with the tongue near the front of the mouth. It's closer to the English 'l' in pronunciation.

The *ng* is pronounced as in the English words 'singing' or 'running', and can be used at the beginning of words as well as at the end. To practise, just say 'ing' over and over, then isolate the 'ng' part of it.

The letters *wh*, when occuring together, are generally pronounced as a soft English 'f'. This pronunciation is used in many place names in New Zealand, such as Whakatane, Whangaroa and Whakapapa (all pronounced as if they begin with a soft 'f'). There is some local variation: in the region around the Whanganui River, for example, *wh* is pronounced as in the English word 'when'.

The correct pronunciation of the vowels is very important. The examples below are a rough guideline – it helps to listen carefully to someone who speaks the language well. Each vowel has a long and a short sound, with long vowels often denoted by a line over the letter or a double vowel. We have not indicated long and short vowel forms in this book.

Vowels

a	as in 'large', with no 'r' sound
e	as in 'get'
i	as in 'marine'
o	as in 'pork'
u	as the 'oo' in 'moon'

Vowel Combinations

ae, ai	as the 'y' in 'sky'
ao, au	as the 'ow' in 'how'
ea	as in 'bear'
ei	as in 'vein'
eo	as 'eh-oh'
eu	as 'eh-oo'
ia	as in the name 'Ian'
ie	as the 'ye' in 'yet'
io	as the 'ye o' in 'ye old'
iu	as the 'ue' in 'cue'
oa	as in 'roar'
oe	as in 'toe'
oi	as in 'toil'
ou	as the 'ow' in 'how'
ua	as the 'ewe' in 'fewer'

Greetings & Small Talk

Maori greetings are becoming increasingly popular – don't be surprised if you're greeted with *Kia ora*.

Welcome!	*Haere mai!*
Hello./Good luck./ Good health.	*Kia ora.*
Hello. (to one person)	*Tena koe.*
Hello. (to two people)	*Tena korua.*
Hello. (to three or more people)	*Tena koutou.*
Goodbye. (to person staying)	*E noho ra.*
Goodbye. (to person leaving)	*Haere ra.*
How are you? (to one person)	*Kei te pehea koe?*
How are you? (to two people)	*Kei te pehea korua?*
How are you? (to three or more people)	*Kei te pehea koutou?*
Very well, thanks./ That's fine.	*Kei te pai.*

Maori Geographical Terms

The following words form part of many Maori place names in New Zealand, and help you understand the meaning of these place names. For example: Waikaremoana is the Sea *(moana)* of Rippling *(kare)* Waters *(wai)*, and Rotorua means the Second *(rua)* Lake *(roto)*.

a – of
ana – cave
ara – way, path or road
awa – river or valley
heke – descend
hiku – end; tail
hine – girl; daughter
ika – fish
iti – small
kahurangi – treasured possession; special greenstone
kai – food
kainga – village
kaka – parrot
kare – rippling
kati – shut or close
koura – crayfish
makariri – cold
manga – stream or tributary
manu – bird
maunga – mountain
moana – sea or lake
moko – tattoo
motu – island
mutu – finished; ended; over
nga – the (plural)

noa – ordinary; not *tapu*
nui – big or great
nuku – distance
o – of, place of...
one – beach, sand or mud
pa – fortified village
papa – large blue-grey mudstone
pipi – common edible bivalve
pohatu – stone
poto – short
pouri – sad; dark; gloomy
puke – hill
puna – spring; hole; fountain
rangi – sky; heavens
raro – north
rei – cherished possession
roa – long
roto – lake
rua – hole in the ground; two
runga – above
tahuna – beach; sandbank
tane – man
tangata – people
tapu – sacred, forbidden or taboo
tata – close to; dash against; twin islands
tawaha – entrance or opening
tawahi – the other side (of a river or lake)
te – the (singular)
tonga – south
ure – male genitals
uru – west

waha – broken
wahine – woman
wai – water
waingaro – lost; waters that disappear in certain seasons
waka – canoe
wera – burnt or warm; floating
wero – challenge
whaka... – to act as ...
whanau – family
whanga – harbour, bay or inlet
whare – house
whenua – land or country
whiti – east

Here are some more place names composed of words in the list:

Aramoana – Sea *(moana)* Path *(ara)*
Awaroa – Long *(roa)* River *(awa)*
Kaitangata – Eat *(kai)* People *(tangata)*
Maunganui – Great *(nui)* Mountain *(maunga)*
Opouri – Place of *(o)* Sadness *(pouri)*
Te Araroa – The *(te)* Long *(roa)* Path *(ara)*
Te Puke – The *(te)* Hill *(puke)*
Urewera – Burnt *(wera)* Penis *(ure)*
Waimakariri – Cold *(makariri)* Water *(wai)*
Wainui – Great *(nui)* Waters *(wai)*
Whakatane – To Act *(whaka)* as a Man *(tane)*
Whangarei – Cherished *(rei)* Harbour *(whanga)*

GLOSSARY

Following is a list of abbreviations, 'Kiwi English', Maori and slang terms used in this book and which you may hear in New Zealand.

All Blacks – NZ's revered national rugby union team
ANZAC – Australia and New Zealand Army Corps
Aoraki – *Maori* name for Mt Cook, meaning 'Cloud Piercer'
Aotearoa – *Maori* name for NZ, most often translated as 'Land of the Long White Cloud'
aroha – love

B&B – 'bed and breakfast' accommodation
bach – holiday home (pronounced 'batch'); see also crib
black-water rafting – rafting or tubing underground in a cave

boozer – public bar
bro – literally 'brother'; usually meaning mate
BYO – 'bring your own' (usually applies to alcohol at a restaurant or cafe)

choice/chur – fantastic; great
crib – the name for a bach in Otago and Southland

DB&B – 'dinner, bed and breakfast' accommodation
DOC – Department of Conservation (or Te Papa Atawhai); government department that administers national parks, tracks and huts

eh? – roughly translates as 'don't you agree?'

farmstay – accommodation on a Kiwi farm
football – rugby, either union or league; occasionally soccer

Great Walks – set of nine popular tramping tracks within NZ
greenstone – jade; *pounamu*
gumboots – rubber boots or Wellingtons; originated from diggers on the gum-fields

haka – any dance, but usually a war dance
hangi – oven whereby food is steamed in baskets over embers in a hole; a *Maori* feast
hapu – subtribe or smaller tribal grouping
Hawaiki – original homeland of the *Maori*

hei tiki – carved, stylised human figure worn around the neck; also called a *tiki*

homestay – accommodation in a family house

hongi – *Maori* greeting; the pressing of foreheads and noses, and sharing of life breath

hui – gathering; meeting

i-SITE – information centre

iwi – large tribal grouping with common lineage back to the original migration from *Hawaiki*; people; tribe

jandals – contraction of 'Japanese sandals'; flip-flops; thongs; usually rubber footwear

jersey – jumper, usually woollen; the shirt worn by rugby players

kauri – native pine

kia ora – hello

Kiwi – New Zealander; an adjective to mean anything relating to NZ

kiwi – flightless, nocturnal brown bird with a long beak

Kiwiana – things uniquely connected to NZ life and culture, especially from bygone years

kiwifruit – small, succulent fruit with fuzzy brown skin and juicy green flesh; aka Chinese gooseberry or zespri

kumara – Polynesian sweet potato, a *Maori* staple food

Kupe – early Polynesian navigator from *Hawaiki*, credited with the discovery of the islands that are now NZ

mana – spiritual quality of a person or object; authority or prestige

Maori – indigenous people of NZ

Maoritanga – things *Maori*, ie *Maori* culture

marae – sacred ground in front of the *Maori* meeting house; more commonly used to refer to the entire complex of buildings

Maui – figure in *Maori* (Polynesian) mythology

mauri – life force/principle

moa – large, extinct flightless bird

moko – tattoo; usually refers to facial tattoos

nga – the (plural); see also *te*

ngai/ngati – literally, 'the people of' or 'the descendants of'; tribe (pronounced 'kai' on the South Island)

NZ – universal term for New Zealand; pronounced 'en zed'

pa – fortified *Maori* village, usually on a hilltop

Pacific Rim – modern NZ cuisine; local produce cooked with imported styles

Pakeha – *Maori* for a white or European person

Pasifika – Pacific Island culture

paua – abalone; iridescent paua shell is often used in jewellery

pavlova – meringue cake topped with cream and kiwifruit

PI – Pacific Islander

poi – ball of woven flax

pounamu – *Maori* name for *greenstone*

powhiri – traditional *Maori* welcome onto a marae

rip – dangerously strong current running away from the shore at a beach

Roaring Forties – the ocean between 40° and 50° south, known for very strong winds

silver fern – symbol worn by the *All Blacks* and other national sportsfolk on their jerseys; the national netball team is called the Silver Ferns

sweet, sweet as – all-purpose term like choice; fantastic, great

tapu – strong force in *Maori* life, with numerous meanings; in its simplest form it means sacred, forbidden, taboo

te – the (singular); see also *nga*

te reo – literally 'the language'; the *Maori* language

tiki – short for *hei tiki*

tiki tour – scenic tour

tramp – bushwalk; trek; hike

tuatara – prehistoric reptile dating back to the age of dinosaurs

tui – native parson bird

wahine – woman

wai – water

wairua – spirit

Waitangi – short way of referring to the Treaty of Waitangi

waka – canoe

Warriors – NZ's popular rugby league club, affiliated with Australia's NRL

Wellywood – Wellington, because of its thriving film industry

zorbing – rolling down a hill inside an inflatable plastic ball

Behind the Scenes

SEND US YOUR FEEDBACK

We love to hear from travellers – your comments keep us on our toes and help make our books better. Our well-travelled team reads every word on what you loved or loathed about this book. Although we cannot reply individually to postal submissions, we always guarantee that your feedback goes straight to the appropriate authors, in time for the next edition. Each person who sends us information is thanked in the next edition – the most useful submissions are rewarded with a selection of digital PDF chapters.

Visit **lonelyplanet.com/contact** to submit your updates and suggestions or to ask for help. Our award-winning website also features inspirational travel stories, news and discussions.

Note: We may edit, reproduce and incorporate your comments in Lonely Planet products such as guidebooks, websites and digital products, so let us know if you don't want your comments reproduced or your name acknowledged. For a copy of our privacy policy visit lonelyplanet.com/privacy.

OUR READERS

Many thanks to the travellers who used the last edition and wrote to us with helpful hints, useful advice and interesting anecdotes:

Amanda Howard, Anke Zylmann, Annamaria Armijo, Annamarie Critchard, Assi Paula, Belen Oton, Cat Mongeon, Catherine Waters, Cerina Triglavcanin, Craig Grant, Dan Simpson, Daniel James Romero, David Lacy, Erin Crampton, Eva Havas, George Ekel, Greg Rogos, Harvey Singer, Helen Bonser, Jaap Voogd, Julia Münchbach, Karen Warren, Kath Gardiner, Katherine Shea, Kathleen Robbins, Michael Hume, Mick Garton, Miriam Smith, Nico Bryant-Stevens, Nina Wensing, Penelope Clute, Peter Ellis, Rod Leschasin, Rosana Zeni, Sally Moyes, Sandra Scott-Harrison, Stefan Wehmeier, Tony Burkitt, Wiremu Fitzgerald, Xavier Alcober, Yann Meyer, Zach Johnston

AUTHOR THANKS

Charles Rawlings-Way

Thanks to the many generous, knowledgeable and quietly self-assured Kiwis I met on the road, especially the staff at the Palmerston North, Hastings and New Plymouth i-SITEs who flew through my questions with the greatest of ease. Huge thanks to Errol Hunt for signing me up (again), and the in-house Lonely Planet staff who schmoozed this book through production. Humongous gratitude to my tireless, witty and professional co-authors – Sarah, Peter, Brett and Lee – who infused this book with humour and local low-down. Most of all, thank you Meg, Ione and Remy for holding the fort while I was away.

Brett Atkinson

Thanks to all of the i-SITE, DOC and information centre staff who patiently answered all my questions. Cheers to the clever craft brewers of New Zealand for sustenance on the road, and to Carol for support on occasional forays to offshore islands. Thanks to my fellow authors, the most professional and wittiest bunch one could aspire to work with, and huge thanks and friendship to the mighty Errol Hunt.

Sarah Bennett & Lee Slater

Thanks to everyone who helped us on the road, including RTO and visitor information centre staff, tourism operators and travellers. Special thanks to DOC staff, especially Penny McIntosh and Katrina Henderson. Big ups to everyone in-house at Lonely Planet, and to our fellow authors – Brett, Charles and Peter. Thanks also to Sarah Ewing. To all who provided a park for our camper, a fridge for the flagon, and even a feed of *kaimoana* on occasion: *arohanui, e hoa ma.*

Peter Dragicevich

I owe a great debt of thanks to Hamish Blennerhassett, Harry and Ngaio Tyler, and all the Tyler cousins for their help and companionship during the research of this book. But above all, I'd like to thank Errol Hunt – editor extraordinaire, all-round great guy, originator of the 'four more years' chant at the 2011 Rugby World Cup final, and the person most responsible for making this one of Lonely Planet's most successful titles over many successive editions.

ACKNOWLEDGMENTS

Climate Map Data (CRMS and Discover titles) Climate map data adapted from Peel MC, Finlayson BL & McMahon TA (2007) 'Updated World Map of the Köppen-Geiger Climate Classification', *Hydrology and Earth System Sciences*, 11, 1633–44.

Cover photograph: Hot-air balloon near Methven, David Wall/Getty

THIS BOOK

This 17th edition of Lonely Planet's New Zealand guidebook was researched and written by Charles Rawlings-Way, Brett Atkinson, Sarah Bennett, Peter Dragiceveich and Lee Slater. They also wrote the previous edition. This guidebook was commissioned in Lonely Planet's Melbourne office, and produced by the following:

Commissioning Editor Errol Hunt

Coordinating Editor Andrea Dobbin

Product Editor Elin Berglund

Senior Cartographer Diana Von Holdt

Book Designer Wendy Wright

Senior Editor Claire Naylor

Assisting Editors Rosie Nicholson, Katie O'Connell, Charlotte Orr, Monique Perrin, Gabrielle Stefanos

Assisting Cartographers Corey Hutchison, Valentina Kremenchutskaya

Cover Researcher Naomi Parker

Thanks to Sasha Baskett, Ryan Evans, Larissa Frost, Genesys India, Jouve India, Elizabeth Jones, Catherine Naghten, Karyn Noble, Martine Power, Dianne Schallmeiner, Angela Tinson, Glenn van der Knijff, Tasmin Waby

Index

A

Abel Tasman National Park 14, 412-15, **413**, **15**
accommodation 650-2, *see also individual locations*
activities, *see individual activities*
Adams Flat 432
Ahipara 154-6
air travel 662-3, 663-4
Akaroa 19, 478-84, **480**, **19**
Alexandra 537-8
All Blacks 613, 640
Anaura Bay 320
Anchor Bay 118
animals 626-30, *see also individual animals*
Anzac Bay 209
Aoraki/Mt Cook National Park 502, **504**, **42**
aquariums
  Eco World Aquarium 380
  Kelly Tarlton's Sealife Aquarium 69
  National Aquarium of New Zealand 333
Arahaki Lagoon 289
Aramoana Hill 235
area codes 21, 659
Aroha Island 145-6
Arrowtown 565-9, **566**
art galleries, *see museums & galleries*
Arthur's Pass village 490
arts 643-8, *see also individual arts*
Atene 235
Auckland 9, 62-97, **64**, **66-7**, **70**, **78**, **81**, **84**, **86**, **9**
  accommodation 79-82
  activities 72-4
  children, travel with 76
  drinking & nightlife 90-2

Map Pages **000**
Photo Pages **000**

  entertainment 92-3
  festivals & events 76-7, 79
  food 82-9
  history 62
  information 94
  itineraries 63
  music 91
  shopping 93-4
  sights 62-5, 68-72
  tours 74, 76
  travel to/from 94-6
  travel within 96-7
  walking tours 75
Auckland Harbour 9
Auckland region 55, 60-120, **61**
  accommodation 60
  climate 60
  food 60
  highlights 61
  travel seasons 60
Awakino 190

B

B&Bs 650
Banks Peninsula 19, 478-84, **479**
Barrytown 435
bathrooms 659
Bay of Islands 10, 55, 134-48, **135**, **11**
  accommodation 121
  climate 121
  food 121
  highlights 122
  travel seasons 121
Bay of Plenty 56, 292-313, **274**
Baylys Beach 161
beaches 26
  Auckland 74
  Baylys Beach 161
  Cathedral Cove 205, **24**
  Gentle Annie Beach 431
  Gillespies Beach 452
  Great Exhibition Bay 153

  Hahei Beach 205
  Hawkes Bay 344
  Hot Water Beach 206-7
  Kai Iwi Beach 231
  Mangawhai 124
  Matakana 119
  New Chum's Beach 201
  Ngarunui Beach 176
  Orewa 115
  Shipwreck Bay 155
  Tahuna Beach 401
  Tawharanui Regional Park 118
  Waiheke Island 98
beer 25, *see also breweries*
bellbirds 627
bicycle travel, *see cycling*
bird parks, *see also zoos & wildlife centres*
  Katikati Bird Gardens 304
  Kiwi Birdlife Park 545
  Native Bird Recovery Centre 127
  Otorohanga Kiwi House & Native Bird Park 184
  Royal Albatross Centre 531
  Wingspan National Bird of Prey Centre 289
birds 626-30, *see also individual birds*
birdwatching 628
  Kaikoura 397
  Miranda 194
  Okarito 445
  Stewart Island/Rakiura 607, 608
  Thames 195
Blackball 438-9
Blenheim 390-4
Blue Lake 536
blue penguins 513-14, 516, 517
Bluff 599
boat travel 663, 665, *see also canoeing & kayaking*

Bob's Bay 380
books 612, *see also literature*
Bream Bay 125-6
Bream Head 131
breweries 22
  Dunedin 521, 523
  Gisborne 323
  Greymouth 436
  Invercargill 595
  Leigh 120
  Mapua 408
  Motueka 409
  Nelson 406
  New Plymouth 219
  Palmerston North 241
  Paraparaumu 371
  Wanaka 569
  Whenuakite 205
budget 21
Buller Gorge 425-6
Buller region 425-33
bungy jumping 49
  Auckland 73
  Hamner Springs 486
  Queenstown 546
  Rotorua 279
  Taupo 254
bus travel 665-6, 668
business hours 21, 657

C

Cable Bay 150
Cambridge 179-80
camping 650-1
Campion, Jane 564, 644
Cannibal Bay 602
canoeing & kayaking 54
  Abel Tasman National Park 414, 415
  Ahipara 155
  Aoraki/Mt Cook National Park 505
  Auckland 73
  Banks Peninsula 481
  Bay of Islands 134

Cambridge 179
Christchurch 463, 466-7
Coromandel Town 198
Doubtful Sound 593
Franz Josef Glacier 447
Goat Island Marine
  Reserve 120
Hahei 206
Horeke 157
Kaikoura 397
Kawhia 183
Manapouri 592
Marlborough Sounds
  384
Milford Sound 590
Mt Maunganui 300
Napier 335
National Park Village 268
Nelson 402
New Plymouth 220
Ohakune 270
Ohope 310
Okarito 445
Otago Peninsula 532
Pelorus River 389
Puhoi 116
Punakaiki 434
Raglan 174
Rotorua 280-1
Stewart Island/Rakiura
  608
Tata Beach 418
Taupo 253
Tauranga 294
Tauranga Bay 149
Urupukapuka Island 145
Waiheke Island 101
Wanaka 571, 572
Wellington 354
Whangamata 208-9
Whanganui National Park
  236-7
Whangarei 128
Canterbury 57, 456-508,
  458-9
accommodation 456
climate 456
food 456
highlights 458-9
travel seasons 456
canyoning
Abel Tasman National
  Park 415
Geraldine 496
Queenstown 550
Thames 196
Waitakere Ranges 111
Wanaka 571
Cape Kidnappers 343-4

Cape Maria van Diemen
  152
Cape Palliser 374-5
Cape Reinga 152-4
Capital Connection 669
car travel 666-8
Cardrona 577
Carterton 377
Cascade Creek 589
Castlepoint 501
cathedrals, see churches &
  cathedrals
Catlins 599-603, **600**
Catton, Eleanor 613, 643
caves
Abbey Caves 127
Aranui Cave 186
Cathedral Caves 601
Cavern Creek Caves 432
Cave Stream Scenic
  Reserve 490
Crazy Paving & Box
  Canyon Caves 432
Glowworm Cave 186
Harwood's Hole 416
Honeycomb Hill Caves &
  Arch 432
Kawiti Glowworm Caves
  137
Muriwai's Cave 306-7
Ngarua Caves 416
Rawhiti Cave 416
Ruakuri Cave 186
Ruatapu Cave 253
Te Anau Glowworm
  Caves 581
Waitomo Caves 13,
  185-9, **185**, 13
caving 49-50
cell phones 20, 658-9
Central Plateau 56, 262-72,
  247
accommodation 246
climate 246
food 246
highlights 247
travel seasons 246
Charleston 429, 434
children, travel with 652-3
Auckland 76
Christchurch 469
Queenstown 554
Wellington 357
Christchurch 57, 457,
  460-77, **460**, **464-5**
accommodation 468-71
activities 463, 466-7
children, travel with 469
drinking & nightlife
  473-4

earthquakes 463, 612
entertainment 474
festivals & events 468
food 471-3
history 457, 463
information 475-6
itineraries 462
shopping 475
sights 457, 460-3
tours 468
travel to/from 476
travel within 476-8
churches & cathedrals
Christ Church 138-9
Christ Church Cathedral
  401
Holy Trinity Cathedral 69
St Patrick's Cathedral 63
Taranaki Cathedral 217
Transitional Cathedral
  22, 462
cinema, see films
Cleddau Valley 589
climate 20, 653, see
  also individual regions
Clyde 538-9
Coastal Pacific 669
Colac Bay 594
Collingwood 419-20
Colville 200
consulates 654
Cook, Captain James 618
Coopers Beach 150
Copland Valley 453
Coroglen 205
Coromandel 55, 192-212,
  164, **193**, 2
accommdation 163
climate 163
highlights 164
travel seasons 163
Coromandel Town 197-200
costs 21
crayfish 399
credit cards 657
Croatian immigrants 155
Cromwell 539-41
Crowded House 646
culture 643-8
Curio Bay 600
curling 535
currency 20
customs regulations 653
cycling 664, see also
  mountain biking
Ahipara 155
Alps 2 Ocean Cycle
  Trail 506
Banks Peninsula 481

Cambridge 179
Christchurch 467
Clyde 539
Dunedin 525
Gisborne 325
Great Lake Trail 251
Great Lake Walkway 251
Great Taste Trail 407
Hauraki Rail Trail 194
Hawke's Bay 331
Kaikoura 398
Makahana 119
Marlborough Sounds
  384
Middlemarch 533
Nelson 401
New Plymouth 220
Nga Haerenga, New
  Zealand Cycle Trail 50,
  179, 238
Oamaru 516-17
Pou Herenga Tai Twin
  Coast Cycle Trail 134
Takaka 416
Te Anau 583
Te Ara a Waiau Walkway/
  Cycleway 446
Te Weheka Walkway/
  Cycleway 450
Thames 196
Timber Trail 191
Tongariro River Trail 259
Waiheke Island 101
Waihi 210
Wairarapa 373
West Coast Wilderness
  Trail 22, 439
Whitianga 203

D
dance 637
dangers, see safety
Dargaville 161-2
Days Bay 356
Denniston Plateau 428
Dickey's Flat 211
disabilities, travellers
  with 660
diving 54
Auckland 73
Bay of Islands 134
Gisborne 324
Great Barrier Island 106
Hahei 206
Kaikoura 395
Karikari Peninsula 152
Leigh 119-20
Milford Sound 590
Poor Knights Islands 132

diving continued
  Tairua 207
  Tauranga 295
  Te Tapuwae o Rongokako
    Marine Reserve 321
  Whakatane 307
  Whitianga 202
dolphins 136, 294, 307,
  384, 397, 594, 599,
  628, **20**
Dome Forest 117
Doubtful Sound 592-3
Doubtless Bay 150-1
drinking & nightlife 25,
  see also individual
  locations
drinks, see beer, wine
driving, see car travel
driving licenses 666
Dunedin 58, 520-30, **522**
  accommodation 525-6
  activities 524-5
  drinking & nightlife
    528-9
  entertainment 529
  food 526-8
  information 529-30
  shopping 529
  sights 520-1, 523-4
  travel to/from 530
  travel within 530
Duntroon 512-13
D'Urville Island 384, 388
DVDs 652

E
earthquakes 463, 612-13
East Cape 315-30
East Coast 56, 314-45,
  316-17
  accommodation 314
  climate 314
  food 314
  highlights 316-17
  travel seasons 314
East Coast war 620
economy 638-41
electricity 654
embassies 654
emergencies 21
environment 624-30
environmental issues 625
etiquette 612
events, see festivals &
  events

exchange rates 21
extreme sports 23, 49-54,
  see also individual
  sports

F
Fairlie 499-500
fantails 627
Farewell Spit 419
farmstays 651
festivals & events 27-30,
  648, see also individual
  locations
  Art Deco Weekend 27-8,
    336
  Auckland International
    Boat Show 30, 77
  Auckland International
    Cultural Festival 77
  Auckland Pride Festival
    76-7
  Bluff Oyster & Food
    Festival 28-9, 599
  Festival of Lights 27, 220
  Fringe NZ 27, 356
  Gay Ski Week 554, 655
  Marlborough Wine &
    Food Festival 27, 390
  Matariki 29, 356
  National Jazz Festival
    28, 295
  Nelson Arts Festival
    30, 403
  New Zealand Festival 27
  New Zealand Inter-
    national Comedy
    Festival 29, 77
  New Zealand Inter-
    national Film Festival
    29, 77
  New Zealand Inter-
    national Sevens
    28, 356
  Out Takes 77, 655
  Pasifika Festival 28, 77
  Pohutukawa Festival 30
  Queenstown Winter
    Festival 29, 554
  Rhythm & Vines 30,
    325, 648
  Russell Birdman 29, 137
  Splore 28, 77
  Taranaki International
    Arts Festival 29, 220
  Te Matatini National
    Kapa Haka Festival
    28, 645
  Toast Martinborough 30,
    357, 372
  Waitangi Day 27, 137
  Wanganui Festival of
    Glass 30, 231

Wellington Sevens
  28, 356
Wildfoods Festival 28,
  442
WOMAD 28, 220, 648
World Buskers Festival
  27, 468
World of WearableArt
  30, 357
film locations 22, 181, 190
films 612, 644
  Maori films 637
Finn, Neil 646
Finn, Tim 646
Fiordland 58, 581-93, **580**
  accommodation 579
  climate 579
  food 579
  highlights 580
  travel seasons 579
fishing
  Gisborne 324
  Great Barrier Island 106
  Kaikoura 397-8
  Napier 335
  Queenstown 550
  Rotorua 282
  Stewart Island/Rakiura
    608
  Taupo 254-5
  Tauranga 295
  Turangi 259
  Wanaka 571, 572
Fletcher Bay 201
Flight of the Conchords
  644
Flying Nun 646
food 25, 654, see also
  individual locations
football, see rugby, soccer
Forgotten World Highway
  226
Fort Taiaroa 531
fortified villages 117
Fortrose 600
Fox Glacier 13, 450-3, **451**
Foxton 244
Frame, Janet 643
Franz Josef Glacier 13, 446-
  50, **448**, **12**
French Pass 384, 388
Fringe NZ 27, 356
Frying Pan Lake 292

G
galleries, see museums &
  galleries
gannets 114
Gap Filler 22

gay & lesbian travellers
  654-5, 554
  Auckland 76-7, 90
Gee, Maurice 643
Gemstone Bay 205
geography 624-6
Geraldine 495-6
Giant's House 479-80
Gisborne 321-7
glaciers 446
Gladstone 377
Glenorchy 561-5
Glowworm Dell 440
Golden Bay 416-20
Goldmine Experience 195
golf
  Rotorua 282
  Taupo 255
  Wanaka 571
Gore 598
Governors Bay 478
Granity 431
Great Barrier Island 106-10,
  108
Great Coast Road 433-5
Great Walks 38-9, see also
  tramping, walks
  Abel Tasman Coast Track
    38, 412, 414-16
  Heaphy Track 16, 38,
    420-1, 432, **16**
  Kepler Track 38, 585-6,
    592, **585**
  Lake Waikaremoana
    Track 38, 329, **328-9**
  Milford Track 38, 586,
    588, **587**, **42**
  Rakiura Track 38, 607
  Routeburn Track 38,
    562, **563**
  Tongariro Northern
    Circuit 38, 263
  Whanganui Journey 38,
    236-7
Greymouth 436-8, **437**
Greymouth region 436-40
Greytown 375-6

H
Haast 454-5
Haast Pass Highway 455
Haast region 453-5
Hackfalls Arboretum 327
Hahei 205-6
haka 635
Hamilton 167-72, **168**
hang gliding 50, 549
Hanmer Springs 485-8, **486**
Hari Hari 444

Hastings 339-43, **340**
Hauraki Gulf 9, 97-110, **8-9**
Havelock 388
Havelock North 339-43
Hawai 315
Hawera 229
Hawke's Bay 330-45, **332**
health 655-6
Heaphy Track 16, 38, 420-1, 432, **16**
Hector 431
Hector's dolphins 431, 497, 594, **20**
Helena Bay 133
heliskiing 47
Hells Gate 289
Hicks Bay 319
hiking, see Great Walks, tramping, walks
Hiruharama 235
historic sites 23
history 614-23
hitching 668
Hobbit, The 190, 644
Hokianga 156-9
Hokitika 440-3, **441**
Hokitika Gorge 440
Holdsworth 376-7
holiday parks 650-1
holidays 658
Hollyford Valley 589
Homer Tunnel 589
Hone Heke 139
Hope Arm 592
Horeke 157
horse riding 50
  Ahipara 155
  Aoraki/Mt Cook National Park 505
  Bay of Islands 135
  Baylys Beach 161
  Blenheim 390
  Cardrona 577
  Catlins 600
  Collingwood 419
  Franz Josef Glacier 448
  Glenorchy 563
  Lake Tekapo 500
  Manawatu Gorge 245
  Marahau 411-12
  Napier 335
  Ohakune 270
  Paekakariki 370
  Paengaroa 305
  Pakiri 120
  Peel Forest 495
  Port Chalmers 531
  Punakaiki 434

Rangitukia 319
River Valley 272
Rotorua 282
Springfield 491
Taupo 254
Waireinga (Bridal Veil Falls) 177
Whakatane 307
Whitianga 203
hostels 651-2
Hot Water Beach 206-7
hot-air ballooning
  Auckland 74
  Hamilton 169
hotels 652
huia 626
Hukutaia Domain 311
Hulme, Keri 643

I
ice skating 550
immigration 660, 662
Inferno Crater Lake 292
Inglewood 225-6
insurance
  car 667-8
  health 655
  travel 656
internet access 656
internet resources 21
Invercargill 595-9, **596**
itineraries 31-5

J
Jackson Bay 454
Jackson Bay Road 454
Jackson, Peter 613, 644
jetboating 52
  Auckland 74
  Bay of Islands 136
  Buller Gorge 426
  Cambridge 179
  Cromwell 540
  Glenorchy 563
  Hamner Springs 486
  Humpridge 594
  Makahan 118-19
  Makarora 578
  Opotiki 312
  Palmerston North 241
  Queenstown 547
  Rotorua 279-80
  Taumarunui 192
  Taupo 254
  Te Anau 583
  Wanaka 571
  Whanganui National Park 237

jet-skiing
  Bay of Islands 134
  Tauranga 295

K
Kai Iwi Lakes 160-1
Kaikoura 11, 394-400, **11**
Kaitaia 154
Kaiteriteri 411
Kaka Point 603
Kapiti Coast 369-71
Kapiti Island 370
Karamea 431-3
Karamea Bluff 431
Karangahake Gorge 211-12
Karekare 111-12
Karikari Peninsula 151-2
Katikati 303-4
kauri 628, 630
Kawakawa 137
Kawau Island 105-6
Kaweka J 345
Kaweka Ranges 345
Kawhia 183-4
kayaking, see canoeing & kayaking
kea 627
Kenepuru 388-9
Kennedy Bay 201
Kerikeri 145-8, **146**
Key Summit 589
King Country 182-92, **166**
Kingitanga 183
Kiritehere 189
kiteboarding 52, 54
  Karikari Peninsula 152
  Makahan 118-19
  Nelson 402
  Ocean Beach 176
  Wellington 354
kiwifruits 304
kiwis 608, 627
Knights Point 453
Kohaihai 432
Kohukohu 156-7
Koriniti 235
Kotuku Sanctuary 444
Kuaotunu 201
Kumara 439-40
Kumara Box 161
Kumeu 113-14
Kurow 512-13

L
Lake Brunner 439
Lake Ferry 375
Lake Gunn 589

Lake Hanlon 431
Lake Hauroko 593
Lake Hawea 577-8
Lake Kaniere 440
Lake Karapiro 179
Lake Mahinapua 444
Lake Matheson 452
Lake Mistletoe 589
Lake Moeraki 453
Lake Pukaki 501
Lake Rotorua 278
Lake Roxburgh 538
Lake Tarawera 291-2
Lake Taupo region 248-62, **247**
  accommodation 246
  climate 246
  food 246
  highlights 247
  travel seasons 246
Lake Tekapo 500-2, **5**
Lake Tutira 330-1
Lake Waikareiti 330
Lake Wakatipu 544-5, **19**
Lake Wilkie 601
languages 20, 670-3
Larnach Castle 532
Lauder 536-7
legal matters 656-7
Leigh 119-20
lesbian travellers, see gay & lesbian travellers
Levin 244
Lewis Pass 484-5
Ligar Bay 418
literature 612, 613, 643
  Maori writing 637, 643
Lord of the Rings, The 22, 180, 644
Lorde 62, 613, 647
luge 550
Luminaries, The 613
Lyell 429
Lyttelton 477-8

M
Macetown 565
Mackay Creek 589
Mahia Peninsula 327, 327-8
Maitai Bay 151
Makarora 578
Maketu 305
Makorori 324
Manapouri 591-2
Manawatu Gorge 244-5
Mangapurua Trig 238
Mangawhai 124-5
Mangonui 150

Maniaroa Marae 190
Manu Bay 176, **53**
Maori people 15, 23-4,
    631-7, **15**
  arts 633-7, 249, 287, 634
  history 307, 310, 324,
    614-15, 616-17, 619-21,
    623, 631-3
  language 670-2
  literature 643
  politics 640-1
  regional highlights 77,
    126, 167, 217, 249, 278,
    318, 349, 381, 426,
    485, 512, 546
  religion 633
maps 657
Mapua 407-8
marae 636
  East Coast 327-8
  Hokianga 156
  King Country 183
  Papatea Bay 318
  Tauranga 294
  Whakatane 305
Marahau 411-12
markets 25-6, 655
Marlborough region 57,
    380-400, **379**, **391**
  accommodation 378
  climate 378
  food 378
  highlights 379
  travel seasons 378
Marlborough Sounds
    384-5, **386**
Marlborough Wine & Food
    Festival 27, 390
Marokopa 189
Martinborough 373-4
Masterton 376
Matakana 118-19
Matakana Island 303
Matakohe 162
Matamata 180-1
Matapouri 132
Matauri Bay 148-9
Matheson Bay 119
Matiu/Somes Island 356
Mauao 300
measures 652
medical services 655
Methven 492-4
Middlemarch 533-4
Milford Sound 18, 590-1, **18**

Map Pages **000**
Photo Pages **000**

Mill Bay 150
Miranda 194
Mirror Lakes 589
Mitimiti 156
moa 626
Moana 439
mobile phones 20, 658-9
Moeatoa 189
Moeraki 519
Moeraki Boulders 519
Mohaka River 345
Mokai Gravity Canyon 272
Mokau 190, 219
Molesworth Station 487
money 20, 21, 653-4, 657
Monkey Island 594
Moriori people 616
motels 652
motorcycle travel 666-8
motorsports 540
Motu River 315
Motuara Island 384
Motueka 408-11, **409**
Motuhora (Whale Island)
    310
Motuihe Island 98
Motuora Island 105
Moturiki Island 300
Motutapu Island 97-8
Motuti 156
mountain biking 50-1, *see
    also* cycling
  Arrowtown 565-6
  Clutha Gold Trail 537
  Fairlie 499
  Franz Josef Glacier 449
  Great Barrier Island 106
  Hamner Springs 486
  Helensville 114
  Kaiteriteri 411
  Mt Te Aroha 182
  National Park Village 268
  Nelson 401
  Ohakune 269, 270
  Old Ghost Road 429
  Opotiki 311-12
  Otago Central Rail Trail
    534, **17**
  Owhango 192
  Queenstown 549-50
  Redwoods Whakare-
    warewa Forest 291
  Rotorua 280
  Roxburgh Gorge Trail
    537
  Tauranga 294
  Wanaka 571, 572
  Wellington 354
  Whangamata 208-9

Whanganui National
    Park 238
Whirinaki Forest Park 289
mountaineering 51
  Mt Taranaki 224
  Wanaka 569-71
Moutere 408
movie locations 22, 181,
    190
movies, *see* films
Mt Eden 65
Mt Hikurangi 320
Mt Humphries 238
Mt Iron 569
Mt John 500
Mt Karioi 177
Mt Manaia 131
Mt Maunganui 298-302,
    299
Mt Pirongia 177
Mt Pureora 191
Mt Somers 494
Mt Taranaki (Egmont
    National Park) 223-5, **2**
Mt Titiraupenga 191
Mt Tutoko 589
Murchison 425-6
Muriwai Beach 114
museums & galleries
  1066 – A Medieval
    Mosaic 495
  Aigantighe Art Gallery
    498
  Akaroa Museum 480
  Anderson Park Art
    Gallery 595
  Andris Apse Wilderness
    Gallery 445
  Aratoi Wairarapa
    Museum of Art &
    History 376
  ArtsPost 169
  Bluff Maritime Museum
    599
  Bohemian Museum
    116
  Buried Village 291
  Butler Point Whaling
    Museum 150
  Central Hawke's Bay
    Settlers Museum 344
  Central Stories 537
  Chronicle Glass Studio
    231
  Clapham's Clocks 127
  Classic Flyers NZ 293
  Classics Museum 169
  Coaltown Museum
    22, 428
  Cobblestones Village
    Museum 375

Colonial Cottage
    Museum 353
Coromandel Mining &
    Historic Museum 198
Dowse Art Museum 353
East Coast Museum of
    Technology 323
Eastern Southland
    Gallery 598
Edwin Fox Maritime
    Museum 380
Fairlie Heritage Museum
    499
Forrester Gallery 516
Fun Ho! National Toy
    Museum 226
Govett-Brewster Art
    Gallery 216-17
Hokonui Moonshine
    Museum 598
Jagosi Jade 442
Katikati Heritage
    Museum 303
Kawhia Regional
    Museum & Gallery 183
KD's Elvis Presley
    Museum 229
Kiwi North 127
Lake District Museum &
    Gallery 565
Left Bank Art Gallery
    436
Lopdell House Gallery
    110
Lost Gypsy Gallery 601
McCahon House 110
Mercury Bay Museum
    202
MOTAT (Museum of
    Transport & Techno-
    logy) 71
MTG Hawke's Bay 22,
    333
Museum of Wellington
    City & Sea 348-9
National Army Museum
    272
National Transport & Toy
    Museum 569
Nelson Provincial
    Museum 401
New Zealand Portrait
    Gallery 349
New Zealand Rugby
    Museum 240
Nga Toi/Arts Te Papa 22
North Otago Museum
    516
Okains Bay Maori &
    Colonial Museum
    480-1
Old Library Arts Centre
    127

Old School Arts Centre 173
Omaka Aviation Heritage Centre 390
Opotiki Museum 311
Otago Museum 523-4
Percy Thomson Gallery 226
Petone Settlers Museum 354
Puke Ariki 216
Quake City 22, 461
Real Tart Gallery 217
Rewa's Village 145
Sarjeant Gallery 231
School of Mines & Mineralogical Museum 195
Shalfoon & Francis Museum 311
Shantytown 436
Sir Edmund Hillary Alpine Centre 503
South Canterbury Museum 498
South Street Gallery 401
Southland Museum & Art Gallery 595
Southward Car Museum 371
Steampunk HQ 515
Suter Art Gallery 401
Tainui Historical Society Museum 190
Tairawhiti Museum 321, 323
Taranaki Aviation, Transport & Technology Museum 219
Taranaki Pioneer Village 226
Tawhiti Museum 229
Te Ana Maori Rock Art Centre 497-8
Te Manawa 240
Te Papa 354
Toitu Otago Settlers Museum 520-1
Tramway Museum 370
Vanished World Centre 513
Victoria Battery Tramway & Museum 211
Vintage Car & Machinery Museum 495
Volcanic Activity Centre 250
Voyager – New Zealand Maritime Museum 65
Waewae Pounamu 442

Waiheke Museum & Historic Village 99
Waihi Arts Centre & Museum 210
Wallace Arts Centre 72
Warbirds & Wheels 569
Warkworth & District Museum 118
Weta Cave 353
Whakatane District Museum 22, 305
Whanganui Regional Museum 230-1
Whanganui Riverboat Centre 231
World of WearableArt & Classic Cars Museum 404
music 91, 613, 645-8
MV *Rena* 300

N
Napier 331-9, **334**
Naseby 535-6
National Park Village 267-9
national parks & reserves 630, **629**, see also parks & reserves
Nelson 400-7, **402**
Nelson region 57, 400-22, **379**
   accommodation 378
   climate 378
   food 378
   highlights 379
   travel seasons 378
netball 640
New Plymouth 216-23, **218**
New Zealand International Sevens 28, 356
newspapers 652
Ngakawau 431
Ngaruawahia 167
Ngarunui Beach 176
Ngarupupu Point 189
Nga-Tapuwae-o-te-Mangai 153
Ngawi 375
Ngunguru 132
Ninety Mile Beach 152-4
Northern Explorer 669
Northland 55, 121-62, **122-3**
   accommodation 121
   climate 121
   food 121
   highlights 122
   travel seasons 121
Northland War 139, 620
Nugget Point 602

O
Oakura 227-8
Oamaru 513-19, **514**
Oban **606**
Ocean Beach 176
Ohakune 269-72
Ohinemutu 278
Okarito 444-5
Okarito Lagoon 444-5
Omahuta Forest 148
Omaio 315
Omakau 536-7
Omapere 158-9
Omarama 511-12
Ongaonga 344
Opapake Pa 188
Oparara Basin 432
Oparara Valley 432
opening hours 21, 657
Ophir 536-7
Opito 202
Opononi 158-9
Opotiki 311-13
Opoutere 208
Opua Forest 143
Opunake 228-9
Orakau 179
Orakei Korako 253
Orewa 115-16
Oriuwaka Ecological Area 289
Orokawa Bay 209
Otago 17, 58, 509-41, **510**
   accommodation 509
   climate 509
   food 509
   highlights 510
   travel seasons 509
Otago Peninsula 16, 531-3, **520-1, 16**
Otorohanga 184-5
Owaka 602
Owhango 192

P
pa 117
Paaku 207
Pacific Coast Highway 315-21
Pacific Islanders 93
paddleboarding
   Bay of Islands 135
   Makahana 118-19
   Nelson 402
   Wellington 354
   Whangamata 209
Paekakariki 370-1
Paeroa 212

Paihia 141-5, **142**
painting 644-5
Pakiri 120
Palmerston North 240-4, **241**
Papamoa 303
Papatea Bay 318
Papatowai 601
Paradise 561
paragliding 50, 54
   Nelson 402
   Queenstown 547, 549
   Te Mata Peak 339
   Wanaka 571
Paraparaumu 371
parasailing 52, 54
   Bay of Islands 134
   Queenstown 549
   Taupo 254
Parihaka 227
Parituto 217
parks & reserves
   Abel Tasman National Park 14, 412-15, **413, 15**
   AH Reed Memorial Kauri Park 127
   Albert Park 63
   Aoraki/Mt Cook National Park 502, **504, 42**
   Aorangi (Haurangi) Forest Park 374-5
   Arthur's Pass National Park 491
   Bellbird Bush Scenic Reserve 331
   Boundary Stream Scenic Reserve 331
   Brooklands Park 217
   Canaan Downs Scenic Reserve 416
   Caroline Bay Park 497
   Connells Bay 99
   Coromandel Forest Park 198
   Craigieburn Forest Park 490-1
   Dead Dog Bay 99
   Doneraille Park 327
   Eastwoodhill Arboretum 323
   Goat Island Marine Reserve 120
   Gumdiggers Park 153
   Hagley Park 460
   Hanmer Forest Park 486
   Hauraki Gulf Maritime Park 97-110
   Hemi Matenga Memorial Park 371

parks & reserves *continued*
Hinewai Reserve 481
Kahurangi National Park 420-1, 432, **16**
Kuirau Park 278
Lake Mahinapua Scenic Reserve 444
Lake Sumner Forest Park 485
Long Bay Regional Park 115
Mahurangi Regional Park 117
Mangapohue Natural Bridge Scenic Reserve 189
Mimiwhangata Coastal Park 133
Monmouth Redoubt 293-4
Mt Aspiring National Park 572
Mt Taranaki (Egmont National Park) 223-5
Nelson Lakes National Park 421-2
Nga Manu Nature Reserve 371
Ngaiotonga Scenic Reserve 133
North Beach Reserve 428
One Tree Hill 71-2
Opouahi Scenic Reserve 331
Otari-Wilton's Bush 353
Paparoa National Park 434-5
Parry Kauri Park 118
Piripiri Caves Scenic Reserve 189
Pirongia Forest Park 177
Puerora Forest Park 191
Pukeiti 217-18
Pukekura Park 216
Queen Elizabeth Park 370, 376
Queens Park 595
Rangikapiti Pa Historic Reserve 150
Redwoods Whakare-warewa Forest 289, 291
Riccarton Bush 462
Robbins Park 293-4
Rotokura Ecological Reserve 271
Ruakuri Scenic Reserve 188

Ruapekapeka Pa Historic Reserve 139
Ruataniwha Conservation Park 508
Scandrett Regional Park 117
Shakespear Regional Park 115
Sugar Loaf Islands Marine Park 217
Tangoio Falls Scenic Reserve 331
Tararua Forest Park 376-7
Tawharanui Regional Park 118
Te Angiangi Marine Reserve 344
Te Mata Peak 339
Te Paki Recreation Reserve 152-3
Te Tapuwae o Rongokako Marine Reserve 321
Te Urewera National Park 328-30
Titirangi Park 323
Tongariro National Park 14, 262-6, **264**, **14**, **34**
Tree Crop Farm 480
Trounson Kauri Park 160
Victoria Forest Park 427
Wai Ariki Farm Park 485
Waipatiki Scenic Reserve 331
Wairere Boulders Nature Park 157
Wenderholm Regional Park 116
Western Springs 71
Westland Tai Poutini National Park 445-53
Whanganui National Park 235, **236**
Whangaruru North Head Scenic Reserve 133
Whirinaki Forest Park 289
White Pine Bush Scenic Reserve 331
Willowbank Wildlife Reserve 463
Wither Hills Farm Park 390
Parua Bay 131
passports 660, 662
Pataua 131
Peach Cove 131
Peel Forest 494-5
Pelorus Bridge 389
Pelorus Sounds 388-9
penguins 513-14, 514-15, 516, 517, 532, 599

phonecards 659
Piano, The 644
Picton 380-6, **382**
Piha 112-13
Piopiotahi 590-1
Pipiriki 235-6
Pisa Conservation Area 577
planning, *see also individual regions*
budgeting 21
calendar of events 27-30
internet resources 21
itineraries 31-5
New Zealand basics 20-1
New Zealand's regions 55-8
repeat visitors 22
travel seasons 20, 27-30
plants 626-30
Pohara 418-19
politics 638-41
Poor Knights Islands 131-3
population 613
Porpoise Bay 600
Port Chalmers 530-1
Port Charles 201
postal services 658
Pounawea 602
Pouto Point 162
public holidays 658
pubs 652
Puhoi 116-17
Pukearuhe 219
Puketapu 307
Puketi Forest 148
Puketui Valley 208
Punakaiki 434-5
Pungarehu 228
Putangirua Pinnacles 374-5

Q
quad biking 155, 157
Queen Charlotte Drive 384
Queenstown 18, 58, 543-61 **544**, **548**, **552**, **18**
accommodation 554-7
activities 545-50
children, travel with 554
drinking & nightlife 559-60
entertainment 560
festivals & events 553-4
food 557-9
history 543-4
information 560
itineraries 547
shopping 560
sights 544-5

tours 550-61
travel to/from 560-1
travel within 561
Queenstown region 543-69, **543**
accommodation 542
climate 542
food 542
highlights 543
travel seasons 542

R
Rabbit Island 407
radio 652
rafting, *see* white-water rafting
Raglan 173-6, **173**
Rainbow Springs 288
Rainbow Warrior 149
Rainbow's End 72
Rakiura 603-10, **604**, **606**
Ranana 235
Ranfurly 534-5
Rangatira 370
Rangiaowhia 178-9
Rangipo Desert 272
Rangiputa 151-2
Rangiriri 166-7
Rangitoto Island 97-8
Rangitukia 319
Rapahoe 435
Rawene 157-8
Rawhiti 133
Reefton 426-8
Rees Valley 564
religion 633
responsible travel 41
Riverstone 518
Riverton 594-5
Riverton Rocks 594
Roaring Bay 602
rock climbing 51
Hamilton 169
Mt Maunganui 300
Queenstown 546
Raglan 174
Rotorua 279
Wanaka 571
Wharepapa South 179
Ross 444
Rotoroa Island 105
Rotorua 13, 56, 275-88, **276**, **12**
accommodation 283-5
activities 278-82
drinking & nightlife 286-7
entertainment 286-7

food 285-6
history 275
information 287-8
itineraries 280
shopping 287
tours 282-3
travel to/from 288
travel within 288
Roxburgh 538
Ruahina Ranges 345
Ruatoria 320
Ruby Bay Scenic Route 408
rugby 14, 613, 640, **14**
Russell 138-41, **138**
Russell Road 133

S

safety 658
hiking 37, 263
hitching 668
road 668
sailing
Abel Tasman National Park 415
Auckland 72-3
Banks Peninsula 481
Bay of Islands 134, 135-6
Coromandel Town 198
Napier 335
Taupo 253
Tauranga 295
Whitianga 203
Sanctuary Mountain Maungatautari 178
sandboarding 158
Sandy Bay 132, 152
scuba diving, see diving
seals & sea lions 375, 385, 395, 397, 428-9, 516, 599
Seddonville 429, 431
Selwyn 490-2
senior travellers 654
Shadbolt, Maurice 643
Shannon 244
Sheepworld 118
Ship Cove 384
Ship Creek 453
skiing & snowboarding 26, 44-8
Aoraki/Mt Cook National Park 505
Awakino 48
Broken River 48
Cardrona 47, 577
Cheeseman 48
Coronet Peak 47, **17**, **46**
Craigieburn Valley 48

Fox Peak 48
Hanmer Springs 48, 486-7
HeliPark New Zealand 48
Manganui 47, 224
Methven 492
Mt Dobson 47
Mt Hutt 48, 493
Mt Lyford 48
Mt Olympus 48
Orewa 115
Porters 48
Queenstown 550
Rainbow 48
Remarkables, the 47
Roundhill 48
Selwyn 490
Snow Farm New Zealand 47
Taupo 254
Temple Basin 48
Tongariro National Park 265-6
Treble Cone 47, **46**
Turoa 45, 47
Wanaka 569-71
Whakapapa 45, 47
skydiving 51
Auckland 73
Fox Glacier 452
Franz Josef Glacier 447
Geraldine 496
Glenorchy 563
Methven 493
Motueka 409
Queenstown 547
Rotorua 279
Taupo 254
Tauranga 295
Wanaka 571
Whangarei 128
Smugglers Bay 131
snorkelling
Gisborne 324
Goat Island Marine Reserve 120
Hahei 206
Leigh 119-20
Marlborough Sounds 385
Tairua 207
Te Angiangi Marine Reserve 344
Whangamata 208-9
snowboarding, see skiing & snowboarding
soccer 640
Southern Scenic Route 593-5

Southland 58, 593-610, **580**
accommodation 579
climate 579
food 579
highlights 580
travel seasons 579
Spirits Bay 152
Sponge Bay 324
sports 640, see also individual sports
Springfield 490
St Bathans 536
Stardome Observatory 72
Stewart Island/Rakiura 603-10, **604**, **606**, **24**
Stingray Bay 205
Stockton 431
Stony Bay 201
Stratford 226
Surat Bay 602
Surf Highway 45 227-9
surfing 52
Ahipara 155
Auckland 74
Catlins 600
Dunedin 524
Gisborne 324
Great Barrier Island 106
Kaikoura 395
Kumara Patch 228
Manu Bay 176, **53**
Mt Maunganui 298, 300
Napier 335
New Plymouth 219
Ngarunui Beach 176
Oakura 227
Ohope 310
Opunake 228
Poor Knights Islands 132
Raglan 174
Stent Rd 228
Taupo Bay 150
Whale Bay 176
Whangamata 208-9
Surville Cliffs 152

T

ta moko 633-4
Taieri Gorge Railway 524
Taihape 272
Taipa 150
Tairua 207-8
takahe 627
Takaka 416-18
Takaka Hill 416
Tapotupotu Bay 152
Tapu 197

Tarakohe Harbour 418
Taramea Bay 594
Taranaki 56, 213-45, **214-15**
accommodation 213
climate 213
highlights 214
travel seasons 213
Taranaki wars 620
Tararua Wind Farm 245
Tasman, Abel 615-16
Tasman Glacier 503
Tasman Lake 503
tattoos 633-4
Taumarunui 191-2
Taumata Trig 238
Taumatawhakatangihanga-koauauotamateaturipu-kakapikimaungahoro-nukupokaiwhenuaki-tanatahu 344
Taupiri 171
Taupo 56, 248-58, **250**, **252**
accommodation 256-7
activities 251-5
drinking & nightlife 258
entertainment 258
festivals & events 256
food 257-8
history 248-9
information 258
sights 249-51
tours 255
travel to/from 258
travel within 258
Tauranga 292-8, **293**
Tauranga Bay 148-9
Tautuku Bay 601
Tawarau Forest 189
taxis 669
Te Anau 581-5, **582**
Te Anau Downs 589
Te Anau-Milford Highway 588-93
Te Apiti Wind Farm 245
Te Araroa 319
Te Aroha 181-2
Te Awamutu 177-8
Te Hana Te Ao Marama 117
Te Haruhi Bay 115
Te Henga (Bethells Beach) 113
Te Kaha 318
Te Kooti 324
Te Kuiti 189-90
Te Papa 354
Te Papaka 307
Te Puia 275-6

Te Puia Springs 320
Te Puke 304-5
Te Puru 197
Te Waewae Bay 594
Te Waikoropupu Springs 416
telephone services 20, 658-9
Te-Waha-O-Rerekohu 319
Thames 194-7, **195**
Three Mile Lagoon 445
Tikitiki 319
Timaru 496-9, **497**
time 20, 659
Tiritiri Matangi Island 105
Titirangi 110-11
toilets 659
Tokomaru Bay 320
Tolaga Bay 320
Tongariro National Park 14, 262-6, **264**, 14, 34
Torere 315
Toto Gorge 177
tourist information 659
train travel 19, 668, 669
tram travel 668
tramping 24-5, 36-43, see also Great Walks, walks
  guided walks 43
  huts & campsites 40-3
  internet resources 37
  maps 37
TranzAlpine Railway 19, 669, 19
travel to/from New Zealand 662-3
travel within New Zealand 663-9
Treaty of Waitangi 141, 142-3
trees 628-30
trekking, see Great Walks, tramping, walks
trout 260
Tryphena 106
Tuamotu Island 324
Tuatapere 593-4
Tuhua (Mayor Island) 303
Turangi 259-62, **259**
Tutukaka 132
TV 644, 652
Twizel 507-8

U
Ulva Island 605-6
Urenui 219

Urquharts Bay 131
Urupukapuka Island 145

V
vacations 658
visas 20, 660
volcanoes
  Auckland 73
  Maunganui Bluff 160
  Motuhora (Whale Island) 310
  Mt Eden 65
  Mt Ngauruhoe 262, **34**
  Mt Ruapehu 262
  Mt Taranaki (Egmont National Park) 223-5
  Mt Tongariro 262
  Mt Victoria 70-1
  One Tree Hill 71-2
  Rangitoto 73, 97-8
  Whakaari (White Island) 309-10
volunteering 661

W
Waihau Bay 319
Waiheke Island 98-104, **100**
Waihi 209-11
Waikanae 371
Waikato 55, 165-82, **164**
  accommodation 163
  climate 163
  highlights 164
  travel seasons 163
Waikato River 169
Waikato war 620
Waikawa 601
Waikawau 189
Waikawau Bay 201
Waimamaku 159
Waimangaroa 431
Waimangu Volcanic Valley 292
Wainui 324
Wainui Bay 418
Waioeka Gorge 315
Wai-O-Tapu Thermal Wonderland 292
Waiotemarama 159
Waiouru 272
Waipara Valley 489
Waipawa 344
Waipiro Bay 320
Waipoua Forest 159-60
Waipu 125-6
Waipukurau 344
Wairakei **250**

Wairarapa, the 372-7
Wairoa 330
Waitakere Ranges 111, **34**
Waitaki Valley 512-13
Waitangi 141-5
Waitangi Treaty Grounds 142-3
Waitomo Caves 13, 185-9, **185**, 13
Waiwera 116
wakeboarding 118-19
walks, see also individual locations, Great Walks, tramping
  Aoraki/Mt Cook National Park 503-4
  Aotea Track 40
  Auckland 74
  Banks Peninsula Track 40, 481
  Cambridge 179
  Cape Reinga Coastal Walkway 40, 152
  Caples Track 562, **563**
  Charming Creek Walkway 431
  Christchurch 466-7
  Copland Track 453
  Coromandel Coastal Walkway 198, 201
  Coromandel Forest Park 198
  Croesus Track 439
  Doubtless Bay 150
  Dunedin 524-5
  Fox Glacier 450-2
  Franz Josef Glacier 446-7
  Gentle Annie Road 345
  Gibbston 551
  Gisborne 324
  Glenorchy 561-3
  Great Barrier Island 106-7
  Greenstone Track 562, **563**
  Hari Hari 444
  Hemi Matenga Memorial Park 371
  Hillary Trail 111
  Hollyford Track 40, 588
  Hump Ridge Track 594
  Kaikoura Coast Track 40, 398
  Karamea 431-2
  Karangahake Gorge 211
  Makarora 578
  Manapouri 592
  Mangawhai 124
  Marlborough Sounds 384

Mt Aspiring National Park 572
Mt Holdsworth–Jumbo Circuit 40
Mt Maunganui 300
Mt Somers 494
Mt Taranaki (Egmont National Park) 224
Mt Te Aroha 182
Mueller Hut Route 40, 504
Nelson Lakes National Park 421-2
New Plymouth 219
North West Circuit Track 607
Nydia Track 389
Ohakune 269
Oparara Valley 432
Pelorus Track 40
Picton 380
Pouakai Circuit 40, 224
Puerora Forest Park 191
Puketi Forest 148
Puketui Valley 198
Punakaiki & Paparoa National Park 434
Queen Charlotte Track 40, 386-7
Queenstown 546
Rameka Track 416
Rangitoto Island Summit 40
Rees-Dart Track 40, 562-3
Rob Roy Glacier Track 572
Rotorua 281-2
St James Walkway 40, 485
Stewart Island/Rakiura 607
Taupo 251-2
Tauranga 294
Tawarau Forest 189
Te Araroa 40
Te Urewera National Park 329-30
Tongariro Alpine Crossing 14, 40, 264-5, 14
Tongariro River Trail 259
Trounson Kauri Park 160
Tuatapere Hump Ridge Track 40
Turangi 259
Waiheke Island 101
Waitakere Ranges 111
Waitomo Caves 188
Westport 428-9
Whangamata 208-9

Whangamumu Scenic
Reserve 133
Whanganui National Park
237-8
Whangarei 128
Whangarei Heads 131
Whangaroa Harbour
149-50
Whirinaki Forest Park
289
Wanaka 58, 569-76, **570**
Wanaka region **543**
accommodation 542
climate 542
food 542
highlights 543
travel seasons 542
Wanganui, *see* Whanganui
Warkworth 117-18
waterfalls
Aratiatia Rapids 249-50
Fantail Falls 455
Haruru Falls 143
Huka Falls 249
Humboldt Falls 589
Marokopa Falls 189
Matai Falls 602
McLean Falls 601
Okere Falls 281
Owharoa Falls 211
Purakaunui Falls 602
Tarawera Falls 281
Te Reinga Falls 327
Te Wairoa Falls 291
Thunder Creek Falls 455
Waiau Falls 202
Wainui Falls 418
Waireinga (Bridal Veil
Falls) 177
Wairere Falls 181, 305
Whangarei Falls 127
weather 20, 653, *see
also individual regions*
websites 21
weights 652
Wellington 10, 348-69,
350-1, 358-9, 10
activities 354
children, travel with 357
drinking & nightlife
364-5

entertainment 365-6
festivals & events 356-7
food 361-3
history 348
information 367
itineraries 353
shopping 366-7
sights 348-9, 352-4
tours 354, 356
travel to/from 367-8
travel within 368-9
walking tours 355
Wellington region 57,
346-77, **347**
climate 346
drinking & nightlife 346
food 346
highlights 347
travel seasons 346
Wellington Sevens 28, 356
West Coast 57, 423,
423-55, **424**
accommodation 423
climate 423
highlights 424
travel seasons 423
Westland 440-5
Westport 428-31
Whakaari (White Island)
309-10
Whakapapa Village 266-7
Whakatane 305-9, **306**
Whale Bay 132, 176
whales 628
whale-watching 396-7
Whananaki 132
Whanarua Bay 318
Whangamata 208-9
Whangamomona 226
Whangamumu Harbour 133
Whanganui 229-35, **230**
Whanganui River Road 235
Whangaparapara 106
Whangapoua 201
Whangarei 126-31, **128-9**
Whangarei District 124-33
Whangarei Heads 131
Whangaroa Harbour
149-50
Whareorino Forest 189

Wharepapa South 179
Wharerata State Forest 327
Whataroa 444
Whatuwhiwhi 151
Whenuakite 205
White Cliffs 219
whitebait 442
white-water rafting 54
Buller Gorge 425
Franz Josef Glacier 447-8
Hamner Springs 486
Kaikoura 395
Motu River 315, 318
Napier 335
Ohakune 270
Opotiki 312
Peel Forest 495
Queenstown 547
River Valley 272
Rotorua 280-1
Taupo 253
Turangi 259-60
Wanaka 571
Whitianga 202-5, **203**
wildlife reserves, *see* zoos
& wildlife reserves
Willing Workers on Organic
Farms 651
Wilsons Bay 197
windsurfing
Napier 335
Ocean Beach 176
Tauranga 295
Wellington 354
wine 25, *see also* wineries
wineries 25
Auckland 95
Gibbston 551
Gisborne 321
Hawke's Bay 342
Kaitaia 154
Karangahake Gorge
211-12
Karikari Peninsula 152
Katikati 304
Kumeu 113-14
Kurow 513
Marlborough region
392-3, **391**, 26
Napier 335

Neudorf 408
Seifried 407-8
Tauranga 294
Waiheke Island 98-9
Waimea 407
Waipara Valley 489
Wairarapa 372-3
Wanaka 569
Woollaston 408
women in New Zealand 641
women travellers 661
work 661
World Buskers Festival
27, 468
World of WearableArt
30, 357
WWOOF 651

Y

yellow-eyed penguins
514-15, 516, 517, 532,
599

Z

ziplining
Queenstown 550
Rotorua 22, 278-9
Waiheke Island 101
zoos & wildlife reserves,
see also bird parks
Auckland Zoo 71
DOC Te Anau Wildlife
Centre 581
Hamilton Zoo 169
Kingdom of Zion 127-8
Nature's Wonders
Naturally 531-2
Orana Wildlife Park
462-3
Orokonui
Ecosanctuary 531
Paradise Valley Springs
289
Point Kean Seal Colony
395
Pukaha Mt Bruce
National Wildlife
Centre 376
Wellington Zoo 353
Wharekawa Wildlife
Refuge 208
Zealandia 352

Map Legend

Sights

- Beach
- Bird Sanctuary
- Buddhist
- Castle/Palace
- Christian
- Confucian
- Hindu
- Islamic
- Jain
- Jewish
- Monument
- Museum/Gallery/Historic Building
- Ruin
- Sento Hot Baths/Onsen
- Shinto
- Sikh
- Taoist
- Winery/Vineyard
- Zoo/Wildlife Sanctuary
- Other Sight

Activities, Courses & Tours

- Bodysurfing
- Diving
- Canoeing/Kayaking
- Course/Tour
- Skiing
- Snorkelling
- Surfing
- Swimming/Pool
- Walking
- Windsurfing
- Other Activity

Sleeping

- Sleeping
- Camping

Eating

- Eating

Drinking & Nightlife

- Drinking & Nightlife
- Cafe

Entertainment

- Entertainment

Shopping

- Shopping

Information

- Bank
- Embassy/Consulate
- Hospital/Medical
- Internet
- Police
- Post Office
- Telephone
- Toilet
- Tourist Information
- Other Information

Geographic

- Beach
- Hut/Shelter
- Lighthouse
- Lookout
- Mountain/Volcano
- Oasis
- Park
- Pass
- Picnic Area
- Waterfall

Population

- Capital (National)
- Capital (State/Province)
- City/Large Town
- Town/Village

Transport

- Airport
- Border crossing
- Bus
- Cable car/Funicular
- Cycling
- Ferry
- Metro station
- Monorail
- Parking
- Petrol station
- Subway station
- Taxi
- Train station/Railway
- Tram
- Underground station
- Other Transport

Note: Not all symbols displayed above appear on the maps in this book

Routes

- Tollway
- Freeway
- Primary
- Secondary
- Tertiary
- Lane
- Unsealed road
- Road under construction
- Plaza/Mall
- Steps
- Tunnel
- Pedestrian overpass
- Walking Tour
- Walking Tour detour
- Path/Walking Trail

Boundaries

- International
- State/Province
- Disputed
- Regional/Suburb
- Marine Park
- Cliff
- Wall

Hydrography

- River, Creek
- Intermittent River
- Canal
- Water
- Dry/Salt/Intermittent Lake
- Reef

Areas

- Airport/Runway
- Beach/Desert
- Cemetery (Christian)
- Cemetery (Other)
- Glacier
- Mudflat
- Park/Forest
- Sight (Building)
- Sportsground
- Swamp/Mangrove